Rick [barcode: D0444966] ®

GREAT
BRITAIN

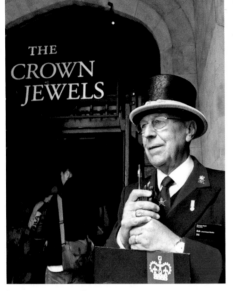

THE
CROWN
JEWELS

CONTENTS

▶ Great Britain 5
  Great Britain's
    Top Destinations 13
  Planning Your Trip 21
  Travel Smart 31

ENGLAND 34

▶ London 37
▶ Windsor & Cambridge . . . 205
▶ Bath 242
▶ Glastonbury & Wells 284
▶ Avebury, Stonehenge
  & Salisbury 304
▶ The Cotswolds 336
  Chipping Campden 348
  Stow-on-the-Wold 365
  Moreton-in-Marsh 386
▶ Stratford-upon-Avon 396
▶ Ironbridge Gorge 423
▶ Liverpool 436
▶ The Lake District 471
  Keswick 479
  Ullswater Lake Area 502
  South Lake District 504
▶ York 512
▶ Durham &
  Northeast England 563

WALES 602

▶ North Wales 609
  Conwy 614
  Caernarfon 639
  Snowdonia National Park . . . 646
  Northeast Wales 658

▶ South Wales 666
  Cardiff 667
  The Wye Valley 690

SCOTLAND 698

▶ Edinburgh 707
▶ Glasgow 819
▶ Stirling & Nearby 868
▶ St. Andrews 891
▶ Oban & the
  Inner Hebrides 913
▶ Glencoe & Fort William . . . 951
▶ Inverness & Loch Ness . . . 970
▶ Britain: Past & Present . . . 1001
▶ Practicalities 1026
  Tourist Information 1026
  Travel Tips 1027
  Money 1028
  Sightseeing 1034
  Sleeping 1039
  Eating 1050
  Staying Connected 1060
  Transportation 1065
  Resources from Rick Steves . . . 1081
▶ Appendix 1083
  Holidays & Festivals 1083
  Books & Films 1085
  Conversions & Climate 1094
  Packing Checklist 1097
  British-Yankee Vocabulary . . 1098
▶ Index 1102
▶ Map Index 1130

Welcome to Rick Steves' Europe

Travel is intensified living—maximum thrills per minute and one of the last great sources of legal adventure. Travel is freedom. It's recess, and we need it.

I discovered a passion for European travel as a teen and have been sharing it ever since—through my tours, public television and radio shows, and travel guidebooks. Over the years, I've taught millions of travelers how to best enjoy Europe's blockbuster sights—and experience "Back Door" discoveries that most tourists miss.

This book offers you a balanced mix of Great Britain's biggies (such as Big Ben and Stonehenge) and more intimate locales (ancient Roman lookouts and misty Scottish isles). It's selective: Rather than listing dozens of hikes in the Lake District, I recommend only the best ones. And it's in-depth: My self-guided museum tours and city walks provide insight into the country's vibrant history and today's living, breathing culture.

I advocate traveling simply and smartly. Take advantage of my money- and time-saving tips on sightseeing, transportation, and more. Try local, characteristic alternatives to expensive hotels and restaurants. In many ways, spending more money only builds a thicker wall between you and what you traveled so far to see.

We visit Great Britain to experience it—to become temporary locals. Thoughtful travel engages us with the world, as we learn to appreciate other cultures and new ways to measure quality of life.

Judging by the positive feedback I receive from readers, this book will help you enjoy a fun, affordable, and rewarding vacation—whether it's your first trip or your tenth.

Have a brilliant holiday! Happy travels!

Rick Steves

GREAT BRITAIN

What's so great about Britain? Plenty. You can watch a world-class Shakespeare play, do The Beatles blitz in Liverpool, and walk along a windswept hill in the footsteps of Wordsworth. Climb cobblestone streets as you wander Edinburgh's Royal Mile, or take a ferry to a remote isle. Ponder a moody glen, lonesome stone circle, or ruined abbey. Try getting your tongue around a few Welsh words, relax in a bath in Bath, and enjoy evensong at Westminster Abbey. Stroll through a cute-as-can-be Cotswold town, try to spot an underwater monster in Loch Ness, and sail along the Thames past Big Ben. Great Britain has it all.

Regardless of the revolution we had 230-some years ago, many American travelers feel that they "go home" to Great Britain. This popular tourist destination retains a strange influence and power over us.

The isle of Great Britain is small (about the size of Idaho)—600 miles long and 300 miles at its widest point. Its highest mountain (Scotland's Ben Nevis) is 4,406 feet, a foothill by our standards. The population is a fifth that of the US. But at its peak in the mid-1800s, Great Britain owned one-fifth of the world and accounted for over half of the planet's industrial output. Today, though its landholdings have greatly diminished, its impact remains huge.

Great Britain is a major global player, with a rich heritage, lively present, and momentous future. Whether its

In Britain, the people are down-to-earth, and the scenery is charming and iconic.

impending departure from the European Union ("Brexit") speeds up or slows down its progress, the result is sure to be interesting.

It's easy to think that "Britain" and "England" are one and the same. But actually, three unique countries make up Great Britain: England, Wales, and Scotland. (Add Northern Ireland and it's called the United Kingdom—but you'll need a different guidebook.) Let's take a quick tour through Great Britain's three nations.

ENGLAND

England is a cultural, linguistic touchstone for the almost one billion humans who speak English. It's the core of the United Kingdom: home to four out of five UK citizens, the seat of government, the economic powerhouse, and the center of higher learning.

South England, which includes London, has always had more people and more money than the north. Blessed with rolling hills, wide plains, and the River Thames, this region for centuries was rich with farms and its waterways flowed with trade. Then and now, high culture flourished in London, today a thriving metropolis of eight million people.

Britain's Pub Hub

In Britain, a pub is a home away from home. Spend some time in one and you'll have your finger on the pulse of the community. These cozy hangouts are extended living rooms, where locals and travelers alike can eat, drink, get out of the rain, watch a sporting event, and meet people.

Britain's pubs are also national treasures, with great cultural value and rich histories, not to mention good beer and grub. Crawling between classic pubs is more than a tipsy night out—it's bona fide sight-seeing. Each offers a glimpse—and a taste—of traditional British culture.

The odd names of pubs can go back hundreds of years. Because many medieval pub-goers were illiterate, pubs were simply named for the picture hanging outside (e.g., The Crooked Stick, The Queen's Arms—meaning her coat of arms).

The Golden Age for pub build-ing was in the late Victorian era (c. 1880–1905). In this class-conscious time, pubs were divided into sec-tions by screens (now mostly gone), allowing the wealthy to drink in a more refined setting. Pubs were re-ally "public houses," featuring nooks (snugs) for groups and clubs to meet, friends and lovers to rendez-vous, and families to get out of the house at night.

Fancy, late-Victorian pubs often come with heavy embossed wall-paper ceilings, decorative tile work, finely etched glass, ornate carved stillions (the big central hutch for storing bottles and glass), and even urinals equipped with a place to set your glass. Today, as more and more banks move out of lavish, high-rent old buildings, they're being refitted as pubs with elegant bars and free-standing stillions. ▶▶▶

Pubs are neighborhood hang-outs with personality, quaint names, and cozy or even elegant settings.

▶▶▶ Pubs often serve traditional dishes, such as "bangers and mash" (sausages and mashed potatoes) and roast beef with Yorkshire pudding, but you're just as likely to find pasta, curried dishes, and quiche.

And, of course, there's the number-one reason people have always flocked to pubs: beer. The British take great pride in their brews. Many Brits think that drinking beer cold and carbonated, as Americans do, ruins the taste. Most pubs will have lagers (cold, refreshing, American-style beer), ales (amber-colored, cellar-temperature beer), bitters (hop-flavored ale, perhaps the most typical British beer), and stouts (dark and somewhat bitter, like Guinness). At pubs, long-handled pulls are used to pull the traditional, rich-flavored "real ales" up from the cellar. These are the connoisseur's favorites: fermented naturally, varying from sweet to bitter, often with a hoppy or nutty flavor. Short-handled pulls mean colder, fizzier, mass-produced, and less interesting keg beers.

Pubs offer hearty food (such as bangers and mash), various ales and beer, and friendly service.

Like in days past, people go to a pub to be social. If that's your aim, stick by the bar (rather than a table) and people will assume you're in the mood to talk. Go pubbing in the evening for a lively time. No matter what time of day, a visit to a historic pub is an enriching experience. ▪

Known today for its beautiful landscapes, hilly North England tends to have poor soil, so the traditional economy was based on livestock (grazing cows and sheep). In the 19th century, however, as the north became a center of coal mining and iron production, its heartland was dotted with belching smokestacks. But now its working-class cities and ports (such as Liverpool) are experiencing a comeback, buoyed by tourism, vibrant arts scenes, and higher employment.

England's economy can stand alongside those of many much larger nations. It boasts high-tech industries (software, chemicals, aviation), international banking, textile manufacturing, and significant beef exports. England is an urban, industrial, and post-industrial colossus, yet its farms, villages, and people are down-to-earth.

For the tourist, England offers a little of everything we associate with Britain: castles, cathedrals, and ruined abbeys; chatty locals nursing beers in village pubs; mysterious prehistoric stone circles and Roman ruins; tea, scones, and clotted cream; hikes across unspoiled, sheep-speckled hillsides; and drivers who cheerfully wave from the "wrong" side of the road. And then there's London, a world in itself, with famous cathedrals (St. Paul's), museums (British Museum), and royalty (Buckingham Palace). London rivals New York as the best scene for live theater, and England entertains millions of people with its movies and music.

Bustling London offers nonstop entertainment, while England's countryside provides a tranquil retreat.

For a thousand years, England has been the cultural heart of Britain. Parliamentary democracy, science (Isaac Newton), technology (Michael Faraday), and education (Cambridge and Oxford) were nurtured here. In literature, England has few peers in any language, producing great legends (King Arthur, *Beowulf*, and *The Lord of the Rings*), poetry (by Chaucer, Wordsworth, and Byron), novels (by Dickens, Austen, and J. K. Rowling), and plays (by Shakespeare).

You can trace the evolution of England's long, illustrious history as you travel. Prehistoric peoples built the mysterious stone circles of Stonehenge and Avebury. Then came the Romans, who built Hadrian's Wall and the baths at Bath. Viking invaders left their mark in York, and the Normans built the Tower of London. As England Christianized, the grand cathedrals of Salisbury, Wells, and Durham arose. Next came the castles and palaces of the English monarchs (Windsor) and the Shakespeare sights from the era of Elizabeth I (Stratford-upon-Avon). Then tiny England became a maritime empire (the *Cutty Sark* at Greenwich) and the world's first industrial power (Ironbridge Gorge). England's Romantic poets were inspired by the unspoiled nature and villages of the Lake District and the Cotswolds. In the 20th century, gritty Liverpool gave the world The Beatles. Today London is on the cutting edge of 21st-century trends.

WALES

Humble, charming Wales is traditional and beautiful—it seems trapped in a time warp. At first, you'll feel you're still in England, but soon you'll awaken to the crusty yet poetic vitality of this small country. Don't ask for an "English breakfast" at your B&B—they'll politely remind you that it's a "Welsh breakfast," made with Welsh ingredients.

For the tourist, Wales is a land of stout castles (Conwy, Caernarfon, and more), salty harbors, chummy community choirs, slate-roofed villages, and a landscape of mountains, moors, and lush green fields dotted with sheep. Snowdonia National Park is a hiker's paradise, with steep but manageable mountain trails, cute-as-a-hobbit villages (Beddgelert and Betws-y-Coed), and scenery more striking than most anything in England. Fascinating slate-mine museums (such

Wales builds its towns with native stone (Beddgelert, left) and boasts Europe's longest town name, with 58 letters, nicknamed Llanfair PG.

as at Blaenau Ffestiniog), handy home-base towns (Conwy and Caernarfon), and enticing offbeat attractions round out Wales' appeal.

Culturally, Wales is "a land of poets and singers"—or so says the national anthem. From the myths of Merlin and King Arthur to the 20th-century poetry of Dylan Thomas, Wales has a long literary tradition. In music, the country nourishes its traditional Celtic folk music (especially the harp).

You'll enjoy hearing the locals speak Welsh with one another (before effortlessly switching to English for you). Their tongue-twisting, fun-to-listen-to language, with its mix of harsh and melodic tones, transports listeners to another time and place.

SCOTLAND

Rugged, feisty, and spirited Scotland is the home of kilts, bagpipes, golf, shortbread, haggis, and whisky—to wash down the haggis.

Scotland consists of two parts: the Lowlands (flatter, southern, and urban) and the Highlands (rugged, northern, and remote). The Lowlands star the Scottish capital of Edinburgh, with its bustling Royal Mile and stirring hilltop castle. The underrated city of Glasgow has a friendly, down-

to-earth appeal and youthful vibe, while St. Andrews has world-famous golf courses and sandy beaches.

To commune with the traditional Scottish soul, head for the Highlands' hills, lochs (lakes), castles, and whisky distilleries (where sampling is encouraged). The Highlands are bisected by the engineering marvel of the Caledonian Canal, which includes the famous Loch Ness (wave hi to Nessie). Hardy souls set sail from Oban for nearby islands.

While the Scots are known for their telltale burr and some unique words (aye, just listen for a wee blether), they're also trying to keep alive their own Celtic tongue: Gaelic (pronounced "gallic"). Few Scots speak Gaelic in everyday life, but legislation protects it, and it's beginning to appear on road signs. That's just one small sign of the famously independent Scottish spirit. Since the days of William "Braveheart" Wallace, the Scots have chafed under English rule. Thanks to the recent trend of "devolution," Scotland has become increasingly autonomous and has its own parliament.

Whether you're going to Scotland, Wales, England, or (my choice) all three, you'll have a grand adventure—and a great experience—in Great Britain. Cheerio!

Great Britain's Top Destinations

There's so much to see in Great Britain and so little time. This overview breaks Britain's top destinations into must-see sights (to help first-time travelers plan their trip) and worth-it sights (for those with extra time or special interests). I've also suggested a minimum number of days to allow per destination.

MUST-SEE DESTINATIONS

These top cities give you an excellent, diverse sampler of the best of Great Britain.

▲▲▲London (allow 3-4 days)
London has world-class museums, bustling markets, and cutting-edge architecture sharing the turf with the Tower of London and St. Paul's Cathedral. Enjoy London's cuisine scene, parks, grand squares, and palaces. Live theater takes center stage at night.

▲▲▲Bath (2 days)
Bath is a genteel Georgian showcase city, built around an ancient Roman bath. Its glorious abbey, harmonious architecture, engaging walking tours, and small-town feel make it a good candidate for your first stop in Britain. Fun day trips include Glastonbury, Wells, Stonehenge, and more.

▲▲▲York (1-2 days)
The walled medieval town has a grand Gothic cathedral (with a divine evensong) and fine museums (Viking, Victorian, and railway). Classy restaurants hide out in the atmospheric old center, with its "snickelway" passages and colorful Shambles shopping lane.

▲▲▲Edinburgh (2 days)
The proud, endlessly entertaining Scottish capital has an imposing castle, attractions-studded Royal Mile, and excellent museums. You'll see all the clichés (ghost tours, whisky tastings, haggis, bagpipes, and kilts) and enjoy exuberant nightlife, especially during the city's famous festivals in August, featuring theater, music, and dance.

London's Millennium Bridge leading to St. Paul's; Bath's ancient Roman Baths museum and riverside setting; a street festival in Edinburgh

WORTH-IT DESTINATIONS

You can weave any of these destinations—rated ▲ or ▲▲—into your itinerary. It's easy to add some destinations based on proximity (if you're going to the Cotswolds, Stratford-upon-Avon is next door), but some out-of-the-way places (such as Hadrian's Wall or Inverness) can also merit the journey, depending on your time and interests.

ENGLAND

▲▲Windsor and Cambridge (1-2 days)
Good day trips from London include Windsor, starring the Queen's impressive home-sweet-castle. Cambridge, one of England's best university towns, features the stunning King's College Chapel and Wren Library.

▲▲Glastonbury and Wells (1 day)
Little Glastonbury has a mystical, New Age vibe, with its Holy Grail and King Arthur lore. The enjoyable town of Wells has an ingeniously fortified cathedral. Both towns are easy to visit from Bath.

▲▲Avebury, Stonehenge, and Salisbury (1 day)
For spine-tingling stone circles, see famed Stonehenge (worth ▲▲▲ on its own) and the smaller, less touristy Avebury. Nearby is Salisbury and its striking cathedral.

▲▲The Cotswolds (1-2 days)
These quaint villages—the cozy market town of Chipping Campden, popular Stow-on-the-Wold, and the handy transit hub of Moreton-in-Marsh—are scattered over a hilly countryside, which can be fun to explore on foot, by bike, or by car.

Cambridge's King's College Chapel; Glastonbury's ruined abbey; a Cotswolds pub stop; Changing of the Guard at Windsor

▲Stratford-upon-Avon (half-day to 1 day)
Shakespeare's pretty hometown, featuring residences that belonged to the bard and his loved ones, is the top venue for performances of his plays.

▲Ironbridge Gorge (half-day to 1 day)
Boasting the planet's first iron bridge, this unassuming village was the birthplace of the Industrial Revolution, with sights and museums that tell the world-changing story.

▲Liverpool (half-day to 1 day)
The rejuvenated port city is The Beatles' hometown, with a host of related sights (including the homes of John and Paul), museums, and pub-and-club nightlife.

▲▲The Lake District (2 days)
This peaceful region, dotted with lakes, hills, and sheep, is known for its enjoyable hikes, time-passed valleys, and William Wordsworth and Beatrix Potter sights.

▲Durham and Northeast England (1-2 days)
The youthful workaday town has a magnificent cathedral, plus (nearby) an open-air museum, the Roman remains of Hadrian's Wall, Holy Island, and Bamburgh Castle.

WALES

▲▲North Wales (1-2 days)
The scenically rugged land features castle towns (Conwy, Caernarfon, and Beaumaris), the natural beauty of Snowdonia National Park, tourable slate mines (Blaenau Ffestiniog),

colorful Welsh villages (Beddgelert and Llangollen), and charming locals who speak a tongue-twisting old language.

▲▲South Wales (1-2 days)
The revitalized Welsh capital of Cardiff, poetic Tintern Abbey, castle towns (Caerphilly and Chepstow), and an open-air museum of Welsh culture offer an easy, rewarding look at Wales from Bath or the Cotswolds.

SCOTLAND

▲▲Glasgow (1-2 days)
The best sight of Scotland's underrated, cultural "second city" may be its chatty, welcoming locals, with its nightlife a close second. The city is a hotbed of Art Nouveau architecture, thanks to native son Charles Rennie Mackintosh.

▲Stirling and Nearby (half-day to 1 day)
Stirling, one of Scotland's top castles (home of the Stuart kings), overlooks a historic plain, with great sights nearby—from sculptures of giant horse heads to a Ferris wheel for boats to the time-warp village of Culross.

▲▲St. Andrews (1 day)
Famous for golf, this is the only town in Britain where tee time is more prized than tea time. St. Andrews also boasts Scotland's top university and has a long sandy beach, both of which contribute to the town's youthful vibe.

Boats moored in the Lake District (opposite); Caernarfon Castle in North Wales; Cardiff in South Wales

▲▲Oban and the Inner Hebrides (1-2 days)

The port town of Oban, with an easy-to-visit distillery, is a handy anchor for boat trips to the isles of the Inner Hebrides: rugged Mull, spiritual Iona, and remote Staffa's puffin colony and striking basalt columns.

▲Glencoe and Fort William (half-day to 1 day)

The village of Glencoe is near the stirring "Weeping Glen," where government Redcoats killed the clansmen who sheltered them. Today the region offers lush Highland scenery and fine hikes, plus the transit-hub town of Fort William.

▲▲Inverness and Loch Ness (half-day to 1 day)

The pleasant, regional capital is a launchpad for day trips to Highland sights, including Culloden Battlefield (Scotland's Alamo) and monster-spotting at the famous Loch Ness.

Touring Glasgow's museums; golfing at St. Andrews; visiting the idyllic isle of Iona

Planning Your Trip

To plan your trip, you'll need to design your itinerary—choosing where and when to go, how you'll travel, and how many days to spend at each destination. For my best general advice on sightseeing, accommodations, restaurants, and more, see the Practicalities chapter.

DESIGNING AN ITINERARY

As you read this book and learn your options...

Choose your top destinations.

My recommended itinerary (see the sidebar on the next page) gives you an idea of how much you can reasonably see in three weeks, but you can adapt it to fit your own interests and time frame.

If you enjoy big cities, you could easily spend a week in London (top-notch museums, food, street life, and entertainment); Edinburgh and Glasgow are also engaging and lively. For a slower pace of life, settle in any of Britain's many appealing towns, such as York or Bath. If villages beckon, linger in the Cotswolds, where time has all but stopped.

Nature lovers get wonderfully lost in the Lake District, Wales, and the Scottish Highlands. Sailors depart from Oban for islands beyond.

Literary fans make a pilgrimage to Stratford-upon-Avon (Shakespeare), Bath (Austen), and the Lake District (Wordsworth and Potter). Beatles fans from here, there, and everywhere head to Liverpool.

Britain's Best Three-Week Trip by Car

While this three-week itinerary is designed for car travel, it can also be done, with modifications, by public transportation (see page 25).

Day	Plan	Sleep in
1	Arrive in London, connect to Bath (by train or bus)	Bath
2	Sightsee Bath	Bath
3	Pick up car, visit Avebury, Wells, Glastonbury, or Stonehenge	Bath
4	South Wales, Cardiff, Tintern	Chipping Campden
5	Explore the Cotswolds, Blenheim	Chipping Campden
6	Stratford	Ironbridge Gorge
7	Ironbridge Gorge to North Wales	Conwy
8	Highlights of North Wales	Conwy
9	Liverpool	Liverpool
10	South Lake District	Keswick area
11	North Lake District	Keswick area
12	Drive up west coast of Scotland	Oban
13	Explore the Highlands, Loch Ness	Edinburgh
14	Edinburgh	Edinburgh
15	Edinburgh	Edinburgh
16	Hadrian's Wall, Beamish Museum, Durham's cathedral and evensong	Durham
17	Drive to York, turn in car	York
18	York	York
19	Early train to London	London
20	London	London
21	London	London
22	Whew!	

History buffs choose their era: prehistoric (Stonehenge), ancient Roman (Bath and Hadrian's Wall), medieval (York), Industrial Revolution (Ironbridge Gorge), royal (Tower of London, Windsor Castle, Edinburgh Castle), and many more. If you've ever wanted to storm a castle before afternoon tea, you're in the right place.

Decide when to go.

May through September is peak season, with longer days, the best weather, a busy schedule of tourist fun—and big

crowds (especially in cities). Early spring and fall still offer decent weather and smaller crowds. Winter travelers encounter fewer tourists and soft room prices (except in London), but sightseeing hours are shorter and the weather is reliably bad. In the countryside, some attractions open only on weekends or close entirely (Nov-Feb). While rural charm falls with the leaves, city sightseeing is fine in winter.

For weather specifics, see the climate chart in the appendix.

Expect a mix of sun and clouds, whether at Scotland's gigantic Kelpies or England's top-of-the-world Lake District.

Connect the dots.

Link your destinations into a logical route. Determine which cities you'll fly into and out of. Begin your search for transatlantic flights at Kayak.com.

Decide if you'll travel by car or public transportation, or a combination. A car is helpful for exploring the Cotswolds, Ironbridge Gorge, the Lake District, or Scottish Highlands (where public transportation can be sparse), but is useless in big cities (park it). Some travelers rent a car on site for a day or two, and use public transportation for the rest.

Trains are faster and more expensive than buses (which don't run as often on Sundays). Minibus tours can cover regional sights efficiently for travelers without wheels.

To determine approximate travel times between destinations, study the driving map in the Practicalities chapter or check Google Maps; visit NationalRail.co.uk for train schedules.

If traveling beyond Great Britain, consider taking the Eurostar train (for instance, London to Paris) or a budget flight; check Skyscanner.com for flights within Europe.

Write out a day-by-day itinerary.

Figure out how many destinations you can comfortably fit in. Don't overdo it—few travelers wish they'd hurried more. Allow enough days per stop (see estimates in "Great Britain's Top Destinations," earlier). Minimize one-night stands, especially consecutive ones. It can be worth taking a late-afternoon drive or train ride to settle into a town for two

Britain's Best Three-Week Trip by Public Transportation

For three weeks without a car, cut back on the sights with the most frustrating public transportation (parts of Wales, Ironbridge Gorge, and the Scottish Highlands). Lacing together the cities by train is slick (though some journeys in this itinerary involve transfers—usually just one). Buses, slower and cheaper, can get you where the trains don't go (but service is scarce on Sundays).

Day	Plan	Sleep in
1	Arrive in London, connect to Bath (by train or bus)	Bath
2	Sightsee Bath	Bath
3	Stonehenge and Avebury by minibus day tour	Bath
4	To Cotswolds by train to Moreton-in-Marsh (2.5 hours), then bus to Chipping Campden (0.5 hour)	Chipping Campden (or Moreton-in-Marsh)
5	Cotswolds, or day-trip to Stratford (1.5 hours by bus), or Blenheim (1 hour by train-plus-bus)	Chipping Campden (or Moreton-in-Marsh)
6	To North Wales by train (5-6 scenic hours)	Conwy
7	See highlights of North Wales on a leisurely train and bus loop	Conwy
8	To Liverpool by train (2 hours)	Liverpool
9	To Lake District by train to Penrith, then bus to Keswick (about 3 hours)	Keswick
10	Explore Lake District on foot and/or by bus or boat	Keswick
11	To Oban, Scotland, by train (5-6 scenic hours)	Oban
12	Boat tour of islands of Mull, Iona, and possibly Staffa	Oban
13	To Glasgow by train or bus (3 hours)	Glasgow
14	More Glasgow, then to Edinburgh by train (1 hour)	Edinburgh
15	Edinburgh	Edinburgh
16	Edinburgh	Edinburgh
17	To York by train (2.5 hours)	York
18	York	York
19	Early train to London (2 hours)	London
20	London	London
21	London	London
22	Whew!	

consecutive nights—and gain a full day for sightseeing. Include sufficient time for transportation; whether you travel by car or public transit, it'll take you a half-day to get between most destinations.

Staying in a home base (like London or Bath) and making day trips can be more time-efficient than changing locations and hotels.

Take sight closures into account. Avoid visiting a town on the one day a week its must-see sights are closed. Check if any holidays or festivals fall during your trip—these attract crowds and can close sights (for the latest, visit Britain's tourist website, www.visitbritain.com).

Give yourself some slack. Every trip, and every traveler, needs downtime for doing laundry, picnic shopping, people-watching, and so on. Pace yourself. Assume you will return.

Cosmopolitan London celebrates cultural festivals. Make time for people-watching.

Trip Costs Per Person

Run a reality check on your dream trip. You'll have major transportation costs in addition to daily expenses.

Flight: A round-trip flight from the US to London costs about $900-1,500, depending on where you fly from and when.

Public Transportation: For a three-week trip, allow $725 for second-class trains and bus travel, and $30 for the London Tube. A BritRail pass is a good value; buy it before you go. In some cases, a short flight can be cheaper than taking the train.

Car Rental: Allow roughly $250 per week, not including tolls, gas, parking, and insurance.

AVERAGE DAILY EXPENSES PER PERSON

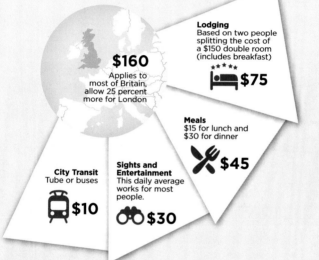

$160
Applies to most of Britain, allow 25 percent more for London

Lodging
Based on two people splitting the cost of a $150 double room (includes breakfast)
$75

Meals
$15 for lunch and $30 for dinner
$45

City Transit
Tube or buses
$10

Sights and Entertainment
This daily average works for most people.
$30

Budget Tips

To cut your daily expenses, take advantage of the deals you'll find throughout Great Britain and mentioned in this book.

City transit passes (for multiple rides or all-day usage) decrease your cost per ride. For example, it's smart to get an Oyster card in London, valid on the Tube and buses.

Avid sightseers buy combo-tickets or passes that cover multiple museums. If a town doesn't offer deals, visit only the sights you most want to see, and seek out free sights and experiences (people-watching counts).

Some businesses—especially hotels and walking-tour companies—offer discounts ▶▶▶

Rick Steves Great Britain

▶▶▶ to my readers (look for the RS% symbol in the hotel listings in this book).

Reserve your rooms directly with the hotel. Some hotels offer a discount if you pay in cash and/or stay three or more nights (check online or ask). Rooms can cost less outside of peak season. And even seniors can sleep cheap in hostels (most have private rooms) for about $30 per person. Or check Airbnb-type sites for deals.

It's no hardship to eat cheap in Britain. You can get tasty, inexpensive meals at pubs, cafeterias, chain restaurants, ethnic eateries, and fish-and-chips joints. Some upscale restaurants offer early-bird dinner specials. Most grocery stores sell ready-made sandwiches; cultivate the art of picnicking in atmospheric settings.

When you splurge, choose an experience you'll always remember, such as an elegant afternoon tea or a splashy London musical. Minimize souvenir shopping; focus instead on collecting wonderful memories. ◼

Eating Indian food is "going local" in Britain. Save money when you can, but splurge on experiences, like a play in London.

BEFORE YOU GO

You'll have a smoother trip if you tackle a few things ahead of time. For more information on these topics, see the Practicalities chapter (and RickSteves.com for helpful travel tips and talks).

Make sure your travel documents are valid. If your passport is due to expire within six months of your ticketed date of return, you need to renew it. Allow up to six weeks to renew or get a passport (www.travel.state.gov).

Arrange your transportation. Book your international flights. Figure out your transportation options. It's worth thinking about buying train tickets online in advance, getting a rail pass, renting a car, or booking cheap European flights. (You can wing it once you're there, but it may cost more.)

Book rooms well in advance, especially if your trip falls during peak season or any major holidays or festivals.

Make reservations or buy tickets in advance for must-see plays, special tours, or sights. If there's a show you're set on seeing, purchase tickets before you go. At Stonehenge, you'll need reservations to go inside the circle. To tour the interior of the Lennon and McCartney homes in Liverpool, reserve ahead.

Edinburgh is crowded in August during festival time; book ahead for theater, dance, and the Military Tattoo. You can also book online for Edinburgh Castle. To golf at St. Andrews' famous Old Course, you must apply in the year prior to when you want to play. In London, you can save time in line by buying Fast Track tickets for some sights.

Consider travel insurance. Compare the cost of the insurance to the cost of your potential loss. Check whether your existing insurance (health, homeowners, or renters) covers you and your possessions overseas.

Call your bank. Alert your bank that you'll be using your debit and credit cards in Europe. Ask about transaction fees, and get the PIN number for your credit card. You don't need to bring pounds for your trip; you can withdraw currency from cash machines in Europe.

Use your smartphone smartly. Sign up for an international service plan, or rely on Wi-Fi. Download any apps you'll want on the road, such as maps, transit schedules, and Rick Steves Audio Europe (see sidebar).

Rip up this book! Turn chapters into mini guidebooks: Break the book's spine and use a utility knife to slice apart chapters, keeping gummy edges intact. Reinforce the chapter spines with clear wide tape; use a heavy-duty stapler; or make or buy a cheap cover (see RickSteves.com), swapping out chapters as you travel.

Pack light. You'll walk with your luggage more than you think. I travel for weeks with a single carry-on bag and a daypack. Use the packing checklist in the appendix as a guide.

Rick's Free Video Clips and Audio Tours

Travel smarter with these free, fun resources:

Rick Steves Classroom Europe, a powerful tool for teachers, is also useful for travelers. This video library contains over 400 short clips excerpted from my public television series. Enjoy these videos as you sort through options for your trip and to better understand what you'll see in Europe. Check it out at Classroom.RickSteves.com (just enter a topic in the search bar to find everything I've filmed on a subject).

Rick Steves Audio Europe, a free app, makes it easy to download my audio tours and listen to them offline as you travel. For this book (look for the 🎧), these audio tours cover

sights and neighborhoods in London and Edinburgh. The app also offers insightful interviews from my public radio show with experts from Europe and around the globe. Find it in your app store or at RickSteves.com/AudioEurope.

Travel Smart

If you have a positive attitude, equip yourself with good information (this book), and expect to travel smart, you will.

Read—and reread—this book. To have an "A" trip, be an "A" student. Note opening hours of sights, closed days, crowd-beating tips, and whether reservations are required or advisable. Check the latest at RickSteves.com/update.

Be your own tour guide. As you travel, get up-to-date info on sights, reserve tickets and tours, reconfirm hotels and travel arrangements, and check transit connections. Visit local tourist information offices. Upon arrival in a new town, lay the groundwork for a smooth departure; confirm the train, bus, or road you'll take when you leave.

Outsmart thieves. Pickpockets abound in crowded places where tourists congregate. Treat commotions as smokescreens for theft. Keep your cash, credit cards, and passport secure in a money belt tucked under your clothes; carry only a day's spending money in your front pocket. Don't set valuable items down on counters or café tabletops, where they can be quickly stolen or easily forgotten.

Minimize potential loss. Keep expensive gear to a minimum. Bring photocopies or take photos of important documents (passport and cards) to aid in replacement if they're lost or stolen. Back up photos and files frequently.

Guard your time and energy. Taking a taxi can be a good value if you're too tired to tackle the Tube or wait for a bus. To avoid long lines, follow my crowd-beating tips, such as making advance reservations, or sightseeing early or late.

Be flexible. Even if you have a well-planned itinerary,

expect changes, strikes, closures, sore feet, bad weather, and so on. Your Plan B could turn out to be even better.

Connect with the culture. Interacting with locals carbonates your experience. Enjoy the friendliness of the British people. Ask questions; most locals are happy to point you in their idea of the right direction. Set up your own quest for the friendliest pub, favorite castle, best London show, or silliest name for a sweet treat. When an opportunity pops up, make it a habit to say "yes."

Great Britain...here you come!

ENGLAND

ENGLAND

England (pop. 55 million) is a hilly country about the size of Louisiana (50,350 square miles) that occupies the southern two-thirds of the isle of Britain (with 80 percent of its population). Scotland is to the north and the English Channel to the south, with the North Sea to the east and Wales (and the Irish Sea) to the west. England's highest mountain (Scafell Pike in the Lake District) is 3,206 feet, a foothill by American standards. Fed by ocean air, the climate is mild, with a chance of cloudy, rainy weather almost any day of the year.

England has an economy that can stand alongside many much larger nations. It boasts high-tech industries (software, chemicals, aviation), international banking, and textile manufacturing, and is a major exporter of beef. While farms and villages remain, England is now an urban, industrial, and post-industrial colossus.

England traditionally has been very class-conscious, with the land-wealthy aristocracy, the middle-class tradesmen, and the lower-class farmers and factory workers. While social stratification has diminished somewhat with the new global economy, regional differences remain strong. Locals can often identify where someone is from by their dialect or local accent—Geordie, Cockney, or Queen's English.

England is set apart from its fellow UK countries (Scotland, Wales, and Northern Ireland) by its ethnic makeup. Traditionally, those countries had Celtic roots, while the English mixed in Saxon

and Norman blood. In the 20th century, England welcomed many Scots, Welsh, and Irish as low-wage workers. More recently, it's become home to immigrants from former colonies of its worldwide empire—particularly from India, Pakistan, Bangladesh, the Caribbean, and Africa—and to workers from poorer Eastern European countries. These days it's not a given that every "English" person speaks English. Nearly one in three citizens does not profess the Christian faith. As the world becomes more interconnected, it's possible for many immigrants to physically inhabit the country while remaining closely linked to their home culture—rather than truly assimilating into England.

This is the current English paradox. England—the birthplace and center of the extended worldwide family of English speakers—is losing its traditional Englishness. Where Scotland, Wales, and Northern Ireland have cultural movements to preserve their local languages and customs, England does not. Politically, there is no

"English" party in the UK Parliament; England must depend on the decisions of the UK government at large. Except for the occasional display of an English flag (the red St. George's cross on a white background) at a football (soccer) match, many English people don't really think of themselves as "English"—more as "Brits," a part of the wider UK.

Today, England races forward as a leading global player. Whether the UK's impending departure from the European Union (Brexit) speeds up or slows down England's progress, the result is sure to be interesting (for more on Brexit, see page 1015). With its rich heritage, lively present, and momentous future, England is a culturally diverse land in transition. Catch it while you can.

LONDON

London is more than 600 square miles of urban jungle—a world in itself and a barrage on all the senses. On my first visit, I felt extremely small. The city's museums and landmarks are just the beginning. It's the L.A., D.C., and N.Y.C. of Britain—a living, breathing, thriving organism...a coral reef of humanity.

London has changed dramatically in recent years, and many visitors are surprised to find how "un-English" it is. ESL (English as a second language) seems like the city's first language, as native Brits are now a minority in major parts of the city that once symbolized white imperialism. London is a city of eight million separate dreams, inhabiting a place that tolerates and encourages them. Arabs have nearly bought out the area north of Hyde Park. Chinese takeouts outnumber fish-and-chips shops. Eastern Europeans pull pints in British pubs, and Italians express your espresso. Many hotels are run by people with foreign accents (who hire English chambermaids), while outlying suburbs are home to huge communities of Indians and Pakistanis.

The city, which has long attracted tourists, seems perpetually at your service, with an impressive slate of sights, entertainment, and eateries, all linked by a great transit system. With just a few days here, you'll get no more than a quick splash in this teeming human tidal pool. But with a good orientation, you'll find London manageable and fun. You'll get a sampling of the city's top sights, history, and cultural entertainment, and a good look at its ever-changing human face.

Blow through the city on the open deck of a double-decker orientation tour bus, and take a pinch-me-I'm-in-London walk through the West End. Ogle the crown jewels at the Tower of Lon-

LONDON

don, gaze up at mighty Big Ben, and see the Houses of Parliament in action. Cruise the Thames River, and take a spin on the London Eye. Hobnob with poets' tombstones in Westminster Abbey, and visit with Leonardo, Botticelli, and Rembrandt in the National Gallery. Enjoy Shakespeare in a replica of the Globe theater and marvel at a glitzy, fun musical at a modern-day theater. Whisper across the dome of St. Paul's Cathedral, then rummage through our civilization's attic at the British Museum. And sip your tea with pinky raised and clotted cream dribbling down your scone.

PLANNING YOUR TIME

The sights of London alone could easily fill a trip to England. It's a great one-week get-away. But on a three-week tour of England, I'd give London three busy days. You won't be able to see everything, so don't try. You'll keep coming back to London. After dozens of visits myself, I still enjoy a healthy list of excuses to return. If you're flying in to one of London's airports, consider starting your trip in Bath and making London your English fi-nale. Especially if you hope to enjoy a play or concert, a night or two of jet lag is bad news.

Here's a suggested three-day schedule:

Day 1

Use my Westminster Walk to link the following sights:

9:00	Be in line at Westminster Abbey (opens at 9:30, closed Sun), to tour the place with fewer crowds.
11:00	Visit the Churchill War Rooms.
13:00	Eat lunch at the Churchill War Rooms café or nearby, or grab a later lunch near Trafalgar Square.
15:00	Visit the National Gallery and any nearby sights that interest you (National Portrait Gallery or St. Martin-in-the-Fields Church)
Evening	Dinner and a play in the West End.

Day 2

8:30	Take a double-decker hop-on, hop-off London sightseeing bus tour (from Victoria Station or Green Park).
10:00	Hop off at Trafalgar Square and walk briskly to Buckingham Palace to secure a spot to watch the Changing of the Guard.

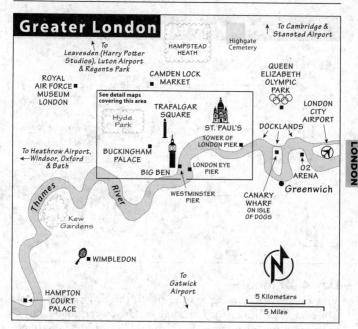

11:00   Buckingham Palace (guards usually change May-July daily at 11:00, Aug-April Sun-Mon, Wed, and Fri—confirm online).

14:00   After lunch, tour the British Museum.

16:00   Tour the British Library.

Evening   Choose from a play, concert, or walking tour, or do some shopping at one of London's elegant department stores (Harrod's, Liberty, and Fortnum & Mason are open until 20:00 or 21:00 except on Sun).

Day 3

9:00   Tower of London (crown jewels first, then Beefeater tour and White Tower; note that the Tower opens at 10:00 Sun-Mon).

12:00   Grab a picnic, catch a boat at Tower Pier, and have lunch on the Thames while cruising to Blackfriars Pier.

13:00   Tour St. Paul's Cathedral and climb its dome for views (cathedral closed Sun except for worship).

15:00   Walk across Millennium Bridge to the South Bank to visit the Tate Modern, Shakespeare's Globe, or other sights.

Evening   Catch a play at Shakespeare's Globe, or see the other suggestions under Days 1 and 2.

LONDON

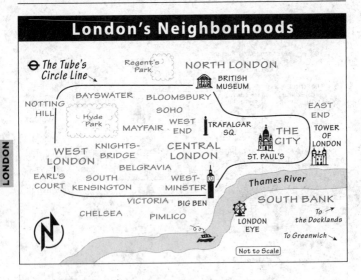

London's Neighborhoods

⊖ *The Tube's Circle Line*

Regent's Park

NORTH LONDON

BRITISH MUSEUM

BAYSWATER BLOOMSBURY

NOTTING HILL

Hyde Park

SOHO

WEST END

TRAFALGAR SQ.

MAYFAIR

EAST END

THE CITY

TOWER OF LONDON

WEST LONDON KNIGHTS-BRIDGE

CENTRAL LONDON

ST. PAUL'S

EARL'S COURT SOUTH KENSINGTON

BELGRAVIA

WEST-MINSTER

Thames River

VICTORIA BIG BEN

CHELSEA PIMLICO

SOUTH BANK

LONDON EYE

To the Docklands

To Greenwich →

Not to Scale

Day 4 (or more)

Visit London's remaining top-tier sights: the Victoria and Albert Museum, Tate Britain, or London Eye. Or you can choose one of the city's many other museums (Natural History Museum, Imperial War Museum, Museum of London, etc.); take a day trip, cruising to Kew Gardens or Greenwich; or hit a street market.

Orientation to London

To grasp London more comfortably, see it as the old town in the city center without the modern, congested sprawl. (Even from that perspective, it's still huge.)

The Thames River (pron. "tems") runs roughly west to east through the city, with most sights on the North Bank. Mentally, maybe even physically, trim down your map to include only the area between the Tower of London (to the east), Hyde Park (west), Regent's Park (north), and the South Bank (south). This is roughly the area bordered by the Tube's Circle Line. This four-mile stretch between the Tower and Hyde Park (about a 1.5-hour walk) looks like a milk bottle on its side (see map above), and holds 80 percent of the sights mentioned in this chapter.

The sprawling city becomes much more manageable if you think of it as a collection of neighborhoods.

Central London: This area contains Westminster and what Londoners call the West End. The Westminster district includes Big Ben, Parliament, Westminster Abbey, and Buckingham Palace—the grand government buildings from which Britain is ruled. Trafalgar Square, London's gathering place, has many major museums. The West End is the center of London's cultural life, with bustling squares: Piccadilly Circus and Leicester Square host cinemas, tourist traps, and nighttime glitz. Soho and Covent Garden are thriving people zones with theaters, restaurants, pubs, and boutiques. And Regent and Oxford streets are the city's main shopping zones.

North London: Neighborhoods in this part of town—including Bloomsbury, Fitzrovia, and Marylebone—contain such major sights as the British Museum and the overhyped Madame Tussauds Waxworks. Nearby, along busy Euston Road, is the British Library, plus a trio of train stations (one of them, St. Pancras International, is linked to Paris by the Eurostar "Chunnel" train).

The City: Today's modern financial district, called simply "The City," was a walled town in Roman times. Gleaming skyscrapers are interspersed with historical landmarks such as St. Paul's Cathedral, legal sights (Old Bailey), and the Museum of London. The Tower of London and Tower Bridge lie at The City's eastern border.

East London: Just east of The City is the East End—the former stomping ground of Cockney ragamuffins and Jack the Ripper, and now an increasingly gentrified neighborhood of hipsters, "popup" shops, and an emerging food scene.

The South Bank: The South Bank of the Thames River offers major sights (Tate Modern, Shakespeare's Globe, London Eye, Imperial War Museum) linked by a riverside walkway. Within this area, Southwark (SUTH-uck) stretches from the Tate Modern to London Bridge. Pedestrian bridges connect the South Bank with The City and Trafalgar Square.

West London: This huge area contains neighborhoods such as Mayfair, Belgravia, Pimlico, Chelsea, South Kensington, and Notting Hill. It's home to London's wealthy and has many trendy shops and enticing restaurants. Here you'll find a range of museums (Victoria and Albert Museum, Tate Britain, and more), my top hotel recommendations, lively Victoria Station, and the vast green expanses of Hyde Park and Kensington Gardens.

Outside the Center: The Docklands, London's version of Manhattan, is farther east than the East End. Historic Greenwich is southeast of London and across the Thames. Kew Gardens and Hampton Court Palace are southwest of London. To the north of London is the Warner Bros. Studio Tour for Harry Potter fans.

TOURIST INFORMATION

It's amazing how hard it can be to find unbiased sightseeing information and advice in London. You'll see "Tourist Information" offices advertised everywhere, but most are private agencies that make a big profit selling tours and advance sightseeing and/or theater tickets; others are run by Transport for London (TFL) and are primarily focused on providing public-transit advice.

The City of London Information Centre, on the street just below St. Paul's Cathedral, is the only publicly funded—and impartial—"real" TI (Mon-Sat 9:30-17:30, Sun 10:00-16:00; Tube: St. Paul's, tel. 020/7332-1456, www.visitthecity.co.uk).

While officially a service of The City (London's financial district), this office also provides information about the rest of London. It sells Oyster cards, London Passes, and advance "Fast Track" sightseeing tickets (all described later). It also stocks various free publications: *London Planner* (a monthly that lists all the sights, events, and hours), walking-tour brochures, the biweekly *Official London Theatre Guide,* a free Tube and bus map, the *Guide to River Thames Boat Services,* and brochures describing self-guided themed walks in The City (including Dickens, modern architecture, Shakespeare, film locations, and walks for kids).

The TI gives out a free map of The City and sells several city-wide maps; ask if they have a free map with coupons for discounts on sights. Skip their theater box office; you're better off booking direct.

Visit London, which serves the greater London area, doesn't have an office you can visit in person—but does have an information-packed website (www.visitlondon.com).

Fast Track Tickets: To skip the ticket-buying queues at certain London sights, you can buy Fast Track tickets (sometimes called "priority pass" tickets) in advance—and they're typically cheaper than tickets sold right at the sight. These are particularly smart for the Tower of London (a voucher you exchange for a ticket at the Tower's group-ticket window), The Shard, and Madame Tussauds Waxworks, all of which get very busy in high season. They're available through various sales outlets (including the City of London TI, souvenir stands, and faux TIs scattered throughout touristy areas).

London Pass: This pass, which covers many big sights and lets you skip some lines, is expensive but potentially worth the investment for extremely busy sightseers who will be using it on consecutive days. Among the many sights it includes are the Tower of London, Westminster Abbey, Churchill War Rooms, and Windsor Castle, as well as many temporary exhibits and audioguides at otherwise "free" biggies. Think through your sightseeing plans, study their website to see what's covered, and do the math before you buy. Note: Adding an Oyster card to your order is a needless complication; it's easier to buy them on arrival (£75/1 day, £99/2 days, £125/3 days, £169/6 days, £199/10 days; days are calendar days rather than 24-hour periods; comes with 180-page guidebook, also sold at major train stations and airports, tel. 020/7293-0972, www.londonpass.com).

ARRIVAL IN LONDON

For more information on getting to or from London, see "London Connections" at the end of this chapter.

By Train: London has nine major train stations, all connected by the Tube (subway). All have ATMs, and many of the larger stations also have shops, fast food, exchange offices, and luggage storage. From any station, you can ride the Tube or taxi to your hotel.

By Bus: The main intercity bus station is Victoria Coach Station, one block southwest of Victoria train/Tube station.

By Plane: London has six airports. Most tourists arrive at Heathrow or Gatwick airport, although flights from elsewhere in Europe may land at Stansted, Luton, Southend, or London City airport.

HELPFUL HINTS

Theft Alert: Wear a money belt and keep your wallet in your front pocket. The Artful Dodger is alive and well in London. Be on guard, particularly on public transportation and in places crowded with tourists, who, considered naive and rich, are targeted. The Changing of the Guard scene is a favorite for thieves. More than 7,500 purses are stolen annually at Covent Garden alone.

Pedestrian Safety: Cars drive on the left side of the road—which can be as confusing for foreign pedestrians as for foreign drivers. Before crossing a street, I always look right, look left, then look right again just to be sure. While Londoners are champion jaywalkers, you shouldn't try it; jaywalking is treacherous when you're disoriented about which direction traffic is coming from.

Medical Problems: Local hospitals have good-quality 24-hour emergency care centers, where any tourist who needs help can be seen by a doctor. Your hotel has details. St. Thomas' Hospital, immediately across the river from Big Ben, has a fine reputation.

Sunday Sightseeing: On Sundays, the Houses of Parliament, City Hall, and Old Bailey are closed and the neighborhood called The City is dead. Westminster Abbey and St. Paul's are open for worship but closed to sightseers (the Diamond Jubilee Galleries at the Abbey is closed). Most big stores open late (11:30) and close early (18:00). Most street markets flourish but Portobello Road and Borough markets are closed. Many theaters are quiet, as most actors take today off—Shakespeare's Globe is an exception.

"Free" Museums: Many of London's great museums don't charge admission—though they do suggest a donation (typically £5).

Advance Tickets: Buying tickets online in advance is always smart if you don't mind sticking to a schedule. You'll generally save a few pounds per sight and can skip the ticket-buying line once you arrive—though you may need to wait in a security line or pick up your ticket at the sight.

You must book ahead for The Making of Harry Potter: Warner Bros. Studio Tour. For summer, weekends, and holiday periods, consider booking ahead (or risk wasting time in long lines) for the following London sights: Westminster Abbey, the Houses of Parliament, the Churchill War Rooms, St. Paul's Cathedral, the Tower of London, and the London Eye.

Getting Your Bearings: London is well signed, with thoughtfully designed, pedestrian-focused maps all over town—especially handy when exiting Tube stations. In this sprawling city—where predictable grid-planned streets are relatively rare—it's also smart to use a good map. For suggestions, see page 1034.

Festivals: For one week in February and another in September, fashionistas descend on the city for **London Fashion Week** (www.londonfashionweek.co.uk). The famous **Chelsea Flower Show** blossoms in late May (book ahead for this popular event at www.rhs.org.uk/chelsea). During the annual **Trooping the Colour** in June, there are military bands and pageantry, and the Queen's birthday parade (www.qbp.army.mod.uk). Tennis fans pack the stands at the **Wimbledon Tennis Championship** in late June to early July (www.wimbledon.com), and partygoers head for the **Notting Hill Carnival** in late August.

Traveling in Winter: London dazzles year-round, so consider visiting in winter, when airfares and hotel rates are generally cheaper and there are fewer tourists. For ideas on what to do, see the "Winter Activities in London" article at www.ricksteves.com/winteracts.

Useful Apps: Mapway's free **Tube Map London Underground** and **Bus Times London** (www.mapway.com) apps show the easiest way to connect Tube stations and provide bus stops and route information. When you are online, the apps provide live updates about delays, closures, and time estimates for your journey. The handy **Citymapper** app for London covers every mode of public transit in the city. And **Time Out London**'s free app has reviews and listings for theater, museums, and movies. See page 1034 for mapping app suggestions.

Bookstores: Located between Covent Garden and Leicester Square, the very good **Stanfords Travel Bookstore** stocks a huge selection of guidebooks (including current editions of my titles), travel-related novels, maps, and gear (Mon-Sat 9:00-20:00, Sun 11:30-18:00, 7 Mercer Walk, Tube: Leicester Square, tel. 020/7836-1321, www.stanfords.co.uk).

Two impressive **Waterstones** bookstores have the biggest collection of travel guides in town: on Piccadilly (Mon-Sat 9:00-22:00, Sun 12:00-18:30, café, great views from top-floor bar, 203 Piccadilly, tel. 0843-290-8549) and on Trafalgar Square (Mon-Sat 9:00-21:00, Sun 12:00-18:00, Costa Café on second floor, tel. 020/7839-4411).

Daunts Books, in a church-like Edwardian building, is a North London staple known for arranging books by geography, regardless of subject or author (Mon-Sat 9:00-19:30, Sun 11:00-18:00, 83 Marylebone High Street, Tube: Baker Street, tel. 020/7724-2295, www.dauntbooks.co.uk).

Foyles' flagship store is a world of books (and literary events), between Soho and Covent Garden (Mon-Sat 9:00-21:00, Sun 11:30-18:00, 107 Charing Cross Road, tel. 020/7437-5660, www.foyles.co.uk).

Baggage Storage: Train stations have left-luggage counters, where each bag is scanned (just like at the airport); expect up to 45-minute waits (£12.50/24 hours per item, most stations open daily 7:00-23:00). You can also store bags at the airports (similar rates and hours, www.left-baggage.co.uk).

GETTING AROUND LONDON

To travel smart in a city this size, you must get comfortable with public transportation. London's excellent taxis, buses, and subway (Tube) system can take you anywhere you need to go—a blessing for travelers' precious vacation time, not to mention their feet. And, as the streets become ever more congested, the key is to master the Tube.

For more information about public transit (bus and Tube), the best source is the helpful *Welcome to London* brochure, which includes both a Tube map and a handy schematic map of the best bus routes (available free at TIs, museums, and hotels).

For specific directions on how to get from point A to point B on London's transit, detailed transit maps, updated prices, and general information, check www.tfl.gov.uk or call the info line at 0343-222-1234.

Tickets and Cards

London's is one of the most expensive public transit systems in the world, so for most tourists, the Oyster Card transit pass is better than individual tickets. Here's the lowdown.

The transit system has nine zones, but almost all tourist sights

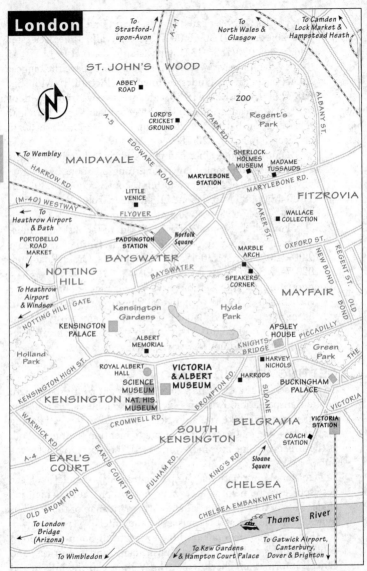

are within Zones 1 and 2, so those are the prices I've listed. For more information, visit www.tfl.gov.uk/tickets.

Individual Tickets: Paper tickets for the Tube are ridiculously expensive (£5 per Tube ride). At every Tube station, tickets are sold at easy-to-use self-service machines (hit "Adult Single" and enter your destination). Tickets are valid only on the day of purchase. But unless you're literally taking only one Tube ride your entire visit, you'll save money (and time) by buying an Oyster card.

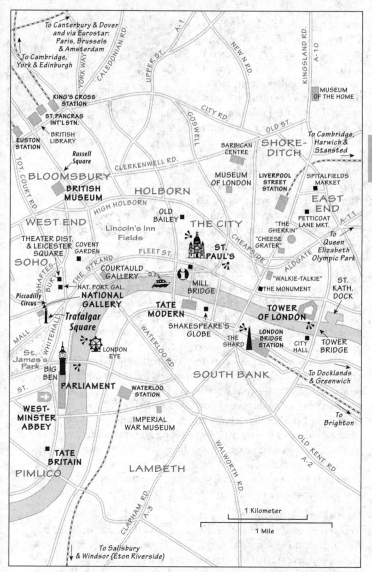

Oyster Card: A pay-as-you-go Oyster card allows you to ride the Tube, buses, Docklands Light Railway (DLR), and Overground (mostly suburban trains) for about half the rate of individual tickets. To use the card, simply touch it against the yellow card reader at the turnstile or entrance. It flashes green and the fare is automatically deducted. (You must also tap your card again to "touch out" as you exit the Tube, but not buses.)

Buy the card at any Tube station ticket machine, or look for nearby shops displaying the Oyster logo, where you can purchase a card or add credit without the wait. You'll pay a refundable £5 deposit up front, then load it with as much credit as you'll need. One ride between Zones 1 and 2 during peak time costs £2.90; off peak is a little cheaper (£2.40/ride). The system

comes with an automatic price cap that guarantees you'll never pay more than £7 in one day for rides within Zones 1 and 2. If you think you'll take two or more rides in a day, £7 of credit will cover you, but it's smart to add a little more if you expect to travel outside the city center. If you're staying six or more days, consider adding a 7-Day Travelcard to your Oyster card (details below). For a three-day visit, I get an Oyster card with £20 of credit, for a total of £25.

Note that Oyster cards are not shareable among companions taking the same ride; all travelers need their own. If your balance gets low, simply add credit—or "top up"—at a ticket machine or shop. You can always see how much credit remains on your card (along with a list of where you've traveled) by touching it to the pad at any ticket machine.

You'll see advertisements for "contactless payment" using a credit card or mobile device, but that service is intended for residents, not travelers—your best bet is an Oyster card.

Remember to turn in your Oyster card after your last ride (you'll get back the £5 deposit and unused balance up to £10) at a ticket window or by selecting "Pay as you go refund" on any ticket machine that gives change. This will deactivate your card. For balances of more than £10, you must go to a ticket window for your refund. If you don't deactivate your card, the credit never expires—you can use it again on a future trip.

Passes and Discounts
7-Day Travelcard: Various Tube passes and deals are available but the only option of note is the 7-Day Travelcard. This is the best choice if you're staying six or more days and plan to use public transit a lot (£35.10 for Zones 1-2; £64.20 for Zones 1-6). For most travelers, the Zone 1-2 pass works best. Heathrow Airport is in Zone 6, but there's no need to buy the Zones 1-6 version if that's the only ride outside the city center you plan to take—instead you can pay a small supplement to cover the difference. You can add the 7-Day Travelcard to your Oyster card, or purchase the paper version at any National Rail train station.

Families: A paying adult can take up to four kids (ages 10 and under) for free on the Tube, Docklands Light Railway (DLR), Overground, and buses. Kids ages 11-15 get a discount. Explore other child and student discounts at www.tfl.gov.uk/tickets—or ask a Tube station employee.

River Cruises: A Travelcard gives you a 33 percent discount on most Thames cruises (described later under "Tours in London: By Cruise Boat"). The Oyster card gives you roughly a 10 percent discount on Thames Clippers (including the Tate Boat museum ferry).

By Tube

London's subway system is called the Tube or Underground (but never "subway," which, in Britain, refers to a pedestrian underpass).

The Tube is one of this planet's great people-movers and usually the fastest long-distance transport in town (runs Mon-Sat about 5:00-24:00, Sun about 7:00-23:00; Central, Jubilee, Northern, Piccadilly, and Victoria lines also run Fri-Sat 24 hours). Two other commuter rail lines are tied into the network and use the same tickets: the Docklands Light Railway (called DLR) and the Overground. The new Crossrail system will eventually cut through central London connecting Heathrow with Paddington, Bond, and Liverpool Street Tube stations on the Elizabeth line before continuing to the city's outlying eastern neighborhoods.

Get your bearings by studying a map of the system, free at any station, or download a transit app (described earlier). Each line has a name (such as Circle, Northern, or Bakerloo) and two directions (indicated by the end-of-the-line stops). Find the line that will take you to your destination, and figure out roughly which direction (north, south, east, or west) you'll need to go to get there.

At the Tube station, there are two ways to pass through the turnstile. With an Oyster card, touch it flat against the turnstile's yellow card reader, both when you enter and exit the station. With a paper ticket or paper Travelcard, feed it into the turnstile, reclaim it, and hang on to it—you'll need it later.

Find your train by following signs to your line and the (general) direction it's headed (such as

Central Line: Eastbound). Since some tracks are shared by several lines, double-check before boarding: Make sure your destination is one of the stops listed on the sign at the platform. Also, check the electronic signboards that announce which train is next, and make sure the destination (the end-of-the-line stop) is the direction you want. Some trains, particularly on the Circle and District lines, split off for other directions, but each train has its final destination marked above its windshield and on the side of the cars.

Trains run about every 3-10 minutes. (The Victoria line brags that it's the most frequent anywhere, with trains coming every 100 seconds at peak time.) A general rule of thumb is that it takes 30 minutes to travel six Tube stops (including walking time within stations), or roughly 5 minutes per stop.

When you leave the system, "touch out" with your Oyster card at the electronic reader on the turnstile, or feed your paper ticket into the turnstile (it will eat your now-expired ticket). With a paper Travelcard, it will spit out your still-valid card. Check maps and signs for the most convenient exit.

The system can be fraught with construction delays and breakdowns. Pay attention to signs and announcements explaining necessary detours. Rush hours (8:00-10:00 and 16:00-19:00) can be packed and sweaty. If one train is stuffed—and another is coming in three minutes—it may be worth a wait to avoid the sardine routine. Also, the cars closer to the middle of the train are generally more crowded, so if you anticipate crowds, stand closer to the ends of the platform. I've often scored a seat on an otherwise packed train using this simple strategy. (But note that at a few shorter stations, the doors of the cars at the very start and end of the train can't open—listen for announcements and move closer to the middle of the platform if necessary.)

For help, check out the "Plan a Journey" feature at www.tfl.gov.uk.

Tube Etiquette and Tips

- When your train arrives, stand off to the side and let riders exit before you board.
- When the car is jam-packed, avoid using the hinged seats near the doors of some trains—they take up valuable standing space.
- If you're blocking the door when the train stops, step out of the car and off to the side, let others off, then get back on.
- Talk softly in the cars. Listen to how quietly Londoners communicate and follow their lead.
- On escalators, stand on the right and pass on the left. But note that in some passageways or stairways, you might be directed

to walk on the left (the direction Brits go when behind the wheel).
- Discreet eating and drinking are fine; drinking alcohol and smoking are banned.
- Be zipped up to thwart thieves.
- Carefully check exit options before surfacing to street level. Signs point clearly to nearby sights—you'll save lots of walking by choosing the right exit.

By Bus

If you figure out the bus system, you'll swing like Tarzan through the urban jungle of London (see sidebar for a list of handy routes).

O		
Oakwood ⊖	N91	ⓞ ⓧ
Old Coulsdon	N68	Aldwych
Old Ford	N8	Oxford Circus
Old Kent Road Canal Bridge	53, N381	ⓠ
	453	ⓐ ⓠ
	N21	ⓖ
Old Street ⊖ ≋	243	Aldwych
Orpington ≋	N47	ⓖ
Oxford Circus ⊖	Any bus	ⓙ
	N18	ⓖ

P		
Paddington ⊖ ≋	23, N15	ⓝ ⓞ ⓕ
Palmers Green ≋	N29	ⓖ
Park Langley	N3	ⓐ ⓝ
Peckham	12	ⓐ ⓟ
	N89, N343	ⓖ
	N136	ⓐ ⓝ
	N381	ⓠ
Penge Pawleyne Arms	176	ⓠ
	N3	ⓐ ⓝ
Petts Wood ≋	N47	ⓖ
Pimlico Grosvenor Road	24	ⓐ ⓝ
Plaistow Greengate	N15	ⓞ ⓕ
Plumstead ≋	53	ⓠ
Plumstead Common	53	ⓠ
Ponders End	N279	ⓖ

Get in the habit of hopping buses for quick little straight shots, even just to get to a Tube stop. However, during bump-and-grind rush hours (8:00-10:00 and 16:00-19:00), you'll usually go faster by Tube.

You can't buy single-trip tickets for buses, and you can't use cash to pay when boarding. Instead, you must have an Oyster card, a paper Travelcard, or a one-day Bus & Tram Pass (£5, can buy on day of travel only—not beforehand, from ticket machine in any Tube station). If you're using your Oyster card, any bus ride in downtown London costs £1.50 (capped at £4.50/day).

The first step in mastering London's bus system is learning how to decipher the bus-stop signs. The accompanying photo shows a typical sign listing the buses (the N91, N68, etc.) that come by here and their destinations (Oakwood, Old Coulsdon, etc.). In the first column, find your destination on the list—e.g., to Paddington (Tube and rail station). In the next column, find a bus that goes there—the #23 (routes marked "N" are night-only). In the final column, a letter within a circle (e.g., "H") tells you exactly which nearby bus stop to use. Find your stop on the accompanying bus-stop map, then make your way to that stop—you'll know it's yours because it will have the same letter on its pole.

Handy Bus Routes

The best views are upstairs on a double-decker. Check the bus stop closest to your hotel—it might be convenient to your sightseeing plans. Here are some of the most useful routes:

Route #9: High Street Kensington to Knightsbridge (Harrods) to Hyde Park Corner to Trafalgar Square to Aldwych (Somerset House).

Route #11: Victoria Coach Station to Victoria Station (train) to Westminster Abbey to Trafalgar Square to Covent Garden to St. Paul's and Liverpool Street Station and the East End.

Route #15: Trafalgar Square to St. Paul's to Tower of London (occasionally with heritage "Routemaster" old-style double-decker buses).

Routes #23 and #159: Paddington Station (#159 begins at Marble Arch) to Oxford Circus to Piccadilly Circus to Trafalgar Square; from there, #23 heads east to St. Paul's and Liverpool Street Station, while #159 heads to Westminster and the Imperial War Museum. In addition, several buses (including #6, #12, and #139) also make the corridor run between Marble Arch, Oxford

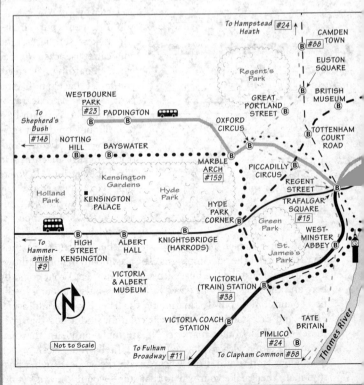

Circus, Piccadilly Circus, and Trafalgar Square.

Route #24: Pimlico to Victoria Station to Westminster Abbey to Trafalgar Square to Euston Square, then all the way north to Camden Town (Camden Lock Market) and Hampstead Heath.

Route #38: Victoria Station to Hyde Park Corner to Piccadilly Circus to British Museum.

Route #88: Tate Britain to Westminster Abbey to Trafalgar Square to Piccadilly Circus to Oxford Circus to Great Portland Street Station (Regent's Park), then north to Camden Town.

Route #148: Westminster Abbey to Victoria Station to Notting Hill and Bayswater (by way of the east end of Hyde Park and Marble Arch).

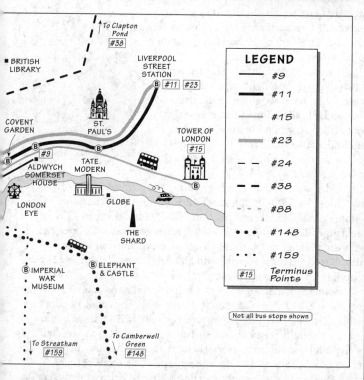

When your bus approaches, it's wise to hold your arm out to let the driver know you want on. Hop on and confirm your destination with the driver (often friendly and helpful).

As you board, touch your Oyster card to the card reader, or show your paper Travelcard or Bus & Tram Pass to the driver. Unlike on the Tube, there's no need to show or tap your card when you hop off. On the older heritage "Routemaster" buses without card readers (used on the #15 route on summer weekends), you simply take a seat, and the conductor comes around to check cards and passes.

To alert the driver that you want to get off, press one of the red buttons (on the poles between the seats) before your stop.

By Taxi

London is the best taxi town in Europe. Big, black, carefully regulated cabs are everywhere—there are about 25,000 of them.

I've never met a crabby cabbie in London. They love to talk, and they know every nook and cranny in town. I ride in a taxi each day just to get my London questions answered. Drivers must pass a rigorous test on "The Knowledge" of London geography to earn their license.

If a cab's top light is on, just wave it down. Drivers flash lights when they see you wave. They have a tight turning radius, so you can hail cabs going in either direction. If waving doesn't work, ask someone where you can find a taxi stand. Telephoning a cab will get you one in a few minutes, but costs a little more (tel. 0871-871-8710).

Rides start at £3. The regular tariff #1 covers most of the day (Mon-Fri 5:00-20:00), tariff #2 is during "unsociable hours" (Mon-Fri 20:00-22:00 and Sat-Sun 5:00-22:00), and tariff #3 is for nighttime (22:00-5:00) and holidays. Rates go up about 20 percent with each higher tariff. Extra charges are explained in writing on the cab wall. All cabs accept credit and debit cards. Tip a cabbie by rounding up (maximum 10 percent).

Connecting downtown sights is quick and easy, and will cost you about £8-12 (for example, St. Paul's to the Tower of London, or between the two Tate museums). For a short ride, three adults in a cab generally travel at close to Tube prices—and groups of four or five adults should taxi everywhere. All cabs can carry five passengers, and some take six, for the same cost as a single traveler.

Don't worry about meter cheating. Licensed British cab meters come with a sealed computer chip and clock that ensures you'll get the correct tariff. The only way a cabbie can cheat you is by taking a needlessly long route. Don't, however, take a cab in bad traffic—especially to a destination efficiently served by the Tube.

If you overdrink and ride in a taxi, be warned: Taxis charge up to £60 for "soiling" (a.k.a., pub puke).

By Uber

Uber faces legal challenges in London and may not be operating when you visit. If Uber is running, it can be much cheaper than a taxi and is a handy alternative if there's a long line for a taxi or if no cabs are available. Uber drivers generally don't know the city as well as regular cabbies, and they don't have the access to some fast lanes that taxis do. Still, if you like using Uber, it can work great here.

By Car

If you have a car, stow it—you don't want to drive in London. An £11.50 **congestion charge** is levied on any private car entering the city center during peak hours (Mon-Fri 7:00-18:00, no charge Sat-Sun and holidays). You can pay the fee either online or by phone (www.cclondon.com, from within the UK call 0343/222-2222, from outside the UK call 011-44-20/7649-9122, phones answered Mon-Fri 8:00-22:00, Sat 9:00-15:00, be ready to give the vehicle registration number and country of registration). There are painfully stiff penalties for late payments.

By Boat

It's easy to connect downtown London sights between Westminster and the Tower of London by boat (see page 61).

By Bike

London operates a citywide bike-rental program similar to ones in other major European cities, and new bike lanes are still cropping up around town. Still, London isn't (yet) ideal for biking. Its network of designated bike lanes is far from complete, and the city's many one-way streets (not to mention the need to bike on the "wrong" side) can make biking here a bit more  challenging. If you're accustomed to urban biking, it can be a good option for connecting your sightseeing stops, but if you're just up for a joyride, stick to London's large parks.

Santander Cycles, intended for quick point-to-point trips, are fairly easy to rent and a giddy joy to use. These cruisers have big, cushy seats, a bag rack with elastic straps, and three gears. Approximately 750 bike-rental stations are scattered throughout the city. To rent a bike, you'll pay an access fee (£2/day). The first 30 minutes are free; if you keep the bike for longer, you'll be charged £2 for every additional 30-minute period. Maps showing docking stations are available at major Tube stations, at www.tfl.gov.uk, and via the free app.

Helmets are not provided, so ride carefully. Stay to the far-left side of the road and watch closely at intersections for *left*-turning cars. Be aware that in most parks (including Hyde Park/Kensington Gardens) only certain paths are designated for bike use—you can't ride just anywhere. Maps posted at park entrances identify bike paths, and non-bike paths are generally clearly marked.

Some bike tour companies also rent bikes (for details, see their listings later in this chapter).

Tours in London

∩ To sightsee on your own, download my free Rick Steves Audio Europe app with **audio tours** that illuminate some of London's top sights and neighborhoods, including my Westminster Walk, Historic London: The City Walk, and tours of the British Museum, British Library, and St. Paul's Cathedral (see sidebar on page 30 for details).

BY HOP-ON, HOP-OFF DOUBLE-DECKER BUS

London is full of hop-on, hop-off bus companies competing for your tourist pound. I've focused on the two companies I like the most: **Original** and **Big Bus.** Both offer essentially the same tours of the city's sightseeing highlights—an experience rated ▲▲▲.

These once-over-lightly bus tours drive by all the famous sights, providing a stress-free way to get your bearings and see the biggies: Piccadilly Circus, Trafalgar Square, Big Ben, St. Paul's, the Tower of London, Marble Arch, Victoria Station, and elsewhere. With a good guide, decent traffic, and nice weather, I'd sit back and enjoy the entire tour. (If traffic is bad or you don't like your guide, you can hop off and try the next departure.)

Each company offers at least one route with live (English-only) guides, and a second (sometimes slightly different route) with recorded, dial-a-language narration. In addition to the overview tours, both Original and Big Bus include the Thames River boat trip by City Cruises (between Westminster and the Tower of London) and several walking tours. Employees for both companies will

Combining a London Bus Tour and the Changing of the Guard

For a grand and efficient intro to London, consider catching an 8:30 departure of a hop-on, hop-off overview bus tour, riding most of the loop (which takes just over 1.5 hours, depending on traffic). Hop off just before 10:00 at Trafalgar Square (Cockspur Street, stop "S") and walk briskly to Buckingham Palace to find a spot to watch the Changing of the Guard ceremony at 11:00.

try hard to sell you tickets and Fast Track admissions to various sights in London. Review your sightseeing plan carefully in advance so you can take advantage of offers that will save you time or money, but skip the rest.

Pick up a map from any flier rack or from one of the countless salespeople, and study the color-coded system. Sunday morning—when traffic is light and many museums are closed—is a fine time for a tour. Traffic is at its peak around lunch and during the evening rush hour (around 17:00).

Buses run daily about every 10-15 minutes in summer and every 10-20 minutes in winter, starting at about 8:30. The last full loop usually leaves Victoria Station at around 20:00 in summer, and 17:00 in winter.

You can buy tickets online in advance, from drivers, or from staff at street kiosks (credit cards accepted at kiosks at major stops such as Victoria Station; the standard tickets are typically valid 24 hours in summer, 48 hours in winter).

Original London Sightseeing Bus Tour

They offer two versions of their basic highlights loop, both marked with a yellow triangle (confirm version with the driver before boarding): **The Original Tour** (T1, live guide) and the **City Sightseeing Tour** (T2, same route but with recorded narration and a kids' soundtrack option). Other routes include the orange-triangle **British Museum Tour** (T5, connecting the museum and King's Cross neighborhoods with central London), and the blue-triangle **Royal Borough Tour** (T4, high-end shopping and regal hangouts). All routes are covered by the same ticket (£32, RS%—£6 discount with this book, limit four discounts per book, they'll rip off the corner of this page—raise bloody hell if the staff or driver won't honor this discount; www.theoriginaltour.com).

Big Bus London Tours

For £37 (cheaper online), you get the same basic overview tours: Red buses come with a live guide, while the blue route has a recorded narration and a one-hour longer path that goes around Hyde Park. These pricier Big Bus tours tend to have more departures—meaning shorter waits for those hopping on and off (tel. 020/7808-6753, www.bigbustours.com).

BY BUS OR CAR

London by Night Sightseeing Tour

Various companies offer a 1- to 2-hour circuit, but after hours, with no extras (e.g., walks, river cruises), at a lower price. While the narration can be lame, the views at twilight are grand—though note that it stays light until late on summer nights, and London just doesn't do floodlighting as well as, say, Paris. **Golden Tours** buses depart at 19:00 and 20:00 from their offices on Buckingham Palace Road (£28, tel. 020/7630-2028; www.goldentours.com). **See London By Night** buses offer live English guides and daily departures from Green Park (next to the Ritz Hotel) at 19:30, 20:00, 20:30, 21:15, 21:45, and 22:15; Oct-March at 19:30 and 21:20 only (£28.50, tel. 020/7183-4744, www.seelondonbynight.com). For a memorable and economical evening, munch a scenic picnic dinner on the top deck. (There are plenty of takeaway options near the various stops.)

Driver-Guides

These guides have cars or a minibus (particularly helpful for travelers with limited mobility), and also do walking-only tours: **Janine Barton** (£390/half-day, £575/day, day tours outside of London start at £625 depending on the distance, registered Blue Badge guide, tel. 020/7402-4600, www.seeitinstyle.synthasite.com, jbsiis@aol.com); **Mike Dickson** (£345/half-day, £535/day, overnights also possible, registered Blue Badge guide; mobile 07769/905-811, michael.dickson5@btinternet.com); and **David Stubbs** (£375 for 1-3 people, £395 for 4-6 people, £415 for 7-8, also does tours to the Cotswolds, Stonehenge, Stratford, Windsor Castle, and Bath; mobile 07775-888-534, www.londoncountrytours.co.uk, info@londoncountrytours.co.uk).

ON FOOT

Top-notch local guides lead (sometimes big) groups on walking tours—worth ▲▲—through specific slices of London's past. Look for brochures at TIs or ask at hotels. *Time Out*, the weekly entertainment guide, lists some, but not all, scheduled walks. Check with the various tour companies by phone or online to get their full picture.

To take a walking tour, simply show up at the announced location and pay the guide. Then enjoy two chatty hours of Dickens,

Harry Potter, the Plague, Shakespeare, street art, The Beatles, Jack the Ripper, or whatever is on the agenda.

London Walks

Just perusing this leading company's fascinating lineup opens me up to dimensions of London I never considered, and inspires me to stay longer. Their extensive daily schedule is online, as well as in a white *London Walks* brochure (most reliably found in the Café in the Crypt, below Trafalgar Square's St. Martin-in-the-Fields Church). Their two-hour walks are led by top-quality professional guides ranging from archaeologists to actors (£12, cash only, walks offered year-round, private tours available, tel. 020/7624-3978, www.walks.com).

London Walks also offers day trips into the countryside, a good option for those with limited time (£20 plus £15-70 for transportation and admission costs, cash only: Stonehenge/Salisbury, Oxford/Cotswolds, Cambridge, Bath, and so on). These are economical in part because everyone gets group discounts for transportation and admissions.

Sandemans New London "Free Royal London Tour"

This company offers tours covering the basic London sights in a youthful, light, and irreverent way that can be both entertaining and fun, but it's misleading to call them "free," as tips are expected. Given that London Walks offers daily tours at a reasonable price, taking this "free" tour makes no sense to me (daily at 10:00, 11:00, and 13:00; meet at Covent Garden Piazza by the Apple Store, Tube: Covent Garden). Sandemans also offers guided tours for a charge, including a Pub Crawl (£10, nightly at 19:30, meet at Brewmaster, 37 Cranbourn Street, Tube: Leicester Square, www.neweuropetours.eu).

Beatles Walks

Fans of the still-Fab Four can take one of three Beatles walks (London Walks has two that run 5 days/week; for more on Beatles sights, see page 107).

Jack the Ripper Walks

Each walking-tour company seems to make most of its money with "haunted" and Jack the Ripper tours. While almost no hint of the dark and scary London of Jack the Ripper's time survives, guides do a good job of spinning the story.

Two reliably good two-hour tours start every night at the Tower Hill Tube station exit. **London Walks** leaves nightly at 19:30, plus Saturdays at 15:00 (£12, pay at the start, tel. 020/7624-3978, www.jacktheripperwalk.com). **Ripping Yarns,** which leaves nightly at 18:30, is guided by off-duty Yeoman Warders—the Tower of London "Beefeaters" (£8, pay at end, mobile 07813-559-

301, www.jack-the-ripper-tours.com). After taking both, I found the London Walks tour more entertaining, informative, and with a better route (along quieter, once hooker-friendly lanes, with less traffic), starting at Tower Hill and ending at Liverpool Street Station. Groups can be huge for both, and one group can be nearly on top of another, but there's always room—just show up.

Private Walks with Local Guides

Standard rates for London's registered Blue Badge guides are about £165-200 for four hours and £270 or more for nine hours (tel. 020/7611-2545, www.guidelondon.org.uk or www.britainsbestguides.org). I know and like these fine local guides: **Sean Kelleher,** an engaging storyteller who knows his history (tel. 020/8673-1624, mobile 07764-612-770, sean@seanlondonguide.com); **Britt Lonsdale,** who's great with families (£265/half-day, £365/day, tel. 020/7386-9907, mobile 07813-278-077, brittl@btinternet.com); **Joel Reid,** an imaginative guide who breathes life into the major sights but also loves sharing off-the-beaten-track London (mobile 07887-955-720, joelyreid@gmail.com); and two others who work in London when they're not on the road leading my Britain tours: **Tom Hooper** (mobile 07986-048-047, tomh1@btinternet.com) and **Gillian Chadwick** (£300/day, mobile 07889-976-598, gillychad@hotmail.co.uk). If you have a particular interest, London Walks (see earlier) can book one for your exact focus (£215/half-day).

BY BIKE

Many of London's best sights can be laced together with a pleasant pedal through its parks.

London Bicycle Tour Company

Three tours leave from their base next to the Imperial War Museum, south of the Thames (all are £27). Sunday is the best, as there is less car traffic; optional helmets are included. The following tour times are for peak season (April-Oct); times are different for off-season, when you need to book ahead (**Classic Tour**—daily at 10:30, 8 miles, 3 hours, includes Westminster, Buckingham Palace, Covent Garden, and St. Paul's; **Love London Tour**—daily at 14:30, 8 miles, 3 hours, includes Westminster, Buckingham Palace, Hyde Park, Soho, and Covent Garden; **Old Town Tour**—Sat-Sun at 14:00, 9 miles, 3.5 hours, includes south side of the river to Tower Bridge, the East End, The City, and St. Paul's). They also rent bikes (£3.50/hour, £20/day; office open daily 9:30-18:00, shorter hours Nov-March, 74 Kennington Road, tel. 020/7928-6838, www.londonbicycle.com).

Fat Tire Bike Tours

These bike tours cover the highlights of downtown London, on two different itineraries (RS%—£2 discount with this book): **Royal London** (£26, daily at 11:00 in peak season, also at 15:30 in summer, 7 miles, 4 hours, meet at Queensway Tube station; includes Parliament, Buckingham Palace, Hyde Park, and Trafalgar Square) and **River Thames** (£48, nearly daily in summer at 10:30, 4.5 hours, reservations required, meet just outside Southwark Tube Station; includes London Eye, St. Paul's, Tower of London, and London Bridge). Their guiding style is light, mixing history with humor (must reserve ahead for kids' bikes, off-season tours also available, mobile 078-8233-8779, www.fattiretours.com/london). They also offer a range of walking tours that include a fish-and-chips dinner, a beer-tasting pub tour, and theater packages.

BY CRUISE BOAT

London offers many made-for-tourist cruises, most on slow-moving, open-top boats accompanied by entertaining commentary (an

experience worth ▲▲). Several companies offer essentially the same trip. Generally speaking, you can either do a **short city-center cruise** by riding a boat 30 minutes from Westminster Pier to Tower Pier (particularly handy if you're interested in visiting the Tower of London anyway), or take a **longer cruise** that includes a peek at the East End, riding from Westminster all the way to Greenwich (save time by taking the Tube back).

Each company runs cruises daily, about twice hourly, from morning until dark; many reduce frequency off-season. Boats come and go from various docks in the city center. The most popular places to embark are Westminster Pier (at the base of Westminster Bridge across the street from Big Ben) and London Eye Pier (also known as Waterloo Pier, across the river).

A one-way trip within the city center costs about £11; going all the way to Greenwich costs about £3 more. Most companies charge around £4 more for a round-trip ticket. Others sell hop-on, hop-off day tickets (around £19). But I'd rather savor a one-way cruise, then zip home by Tube.

You can buy tickets at kiosks on the docks; always ask about discounts (they vary by company). With a Travelcard, you get a 33 percent discount off most cruises; the Oyster card can often be used as payment but nets you a discount only on Thames Clippers.

Thames Boat Piers

Thames boats (both tour and commuter boats) stop at these piers in the town center and beyond. While Westminster Pier is the most popular, it's not the only dock in town. Consider all the options (listed from west to east, as the Thames flows—see the color maps in the back of this book).

Millbank Pier (North Bank): At the Tate Britain museum, used primarily by the Tate Boat ferry service (express connection to Tate Modern at Bankside Pier).

Westminster Pier (North Bank): Near the base of Big Ben, offers round-trip sightseeing cruises and lots of departures in both directions (though the Thames Clippers boats don't stop here). Nearby sights include Parliament and Westminster Abbey.

London Eye Pier (a.k.a. **Waterloo Pier,** South Bank): At the base of the London Eye; good, less-crowded alternative to Westminster, with many of the same cruise options (Waterloo Station is nearby).

Embankment Pier (North Bank): Near Covent Garden, Trafalgar Square, and Cleopatra's Needle (the obelisk on the Thames). This pier is used mostly for special boat trips, such as some RIB (rigid inflatable boats) and lunch and dinner cruises.

Festival Pier (South Bank): Next to the Royal Festival Hall, just downstream from the London Eye.

Blackfriars Pier (North Bank): In The City, not far from St. Paul's.

Bankside Pier (South Bank): Directly in front of the Tate Modern and Shakespeare's Globe.

London Bridge Pier (a.k.a. **London Bridge City Pier,** South Bank): Near the HMS *Belfast.*

Tower Pier (North Bank): At the Tower of London, at the east edge of The City and near the East End.

St. Katharine's Pier (North Bank): Just downstream from the Tower of London.

Canary Wharf Pier (North Bank): At the Docklands, London's new "downtown."

Greenwich, Kew Gardens, and **Hampton Court Piers:** These outer London piers may also come in handy.

You can purchase drinks and overpriced snacks on board. Budget travelers can pack a picnic for the cruise.

The three dominant companies are **City Cruises** (handy 45-minute cruise from Westminster Pier to Tower Pier; www.citycruises.com), **Thames River Services** (fewer stops, classic boats, friendlier and more old-fashioned feel; www.thamesriverservices.co.uk), and **Circular Cruise** (full cruise takes about an hour, operated by Crown River Services, www.circularcruise.london). I'd skip the **London Eye**'s River Cruise from London Eye Pier, as it's more expensive and shorter. The speedy **Thames Clippers** (described later) are designed more for no-nonsense transport than lazy sightseeing.

To compare all of your options in one spot, head to Westminster Pier, which has a row of kiosks for all of the big outfits.

Cruising Downstream, to Greenwich: Both **City Cruises** and **Thames River Services** head from Westminster Pier to Greenwich. The cruises are usually narrated by the captain, with most commentary given on the way to Greenwich. The companies' prices are the same, though their itineraries are slightly different (Thames River Services makes only one stop en route and takes an hour, while City Cruises makes two stops and adds about 15 minutes). The **Thames Clippers** boats, described below, are cheaper and faster (about 20-55 minutes to Greenwich), but have no commentary and no up-top seating.

Cruising Upstream, to Kew Gardens and Hampton Court Palace: Thames River Boats leave for Kew Gardens from Westminster Pier (£15 one-way, £22 round-trip, discounts with Travelcard, 2-4/day depending on season, 1.5 hours, boats sail April-Oct, about half the trip is narrated, www.thamesriverboats.co.uk). Most boats continue on to Hampton Court Palace for an additional £4 (and another 1.5 hours).

Commuting by Clipper

The sleek, 220-seat catamarans used by **Thames Clippers** are designed for commuters rather than sightseers. Think of the boats as express buses on the river—they zip through London every 20-30 minutes, stopping at most of the major docks en route. They're fast: roughly 20-30 minutes from Embankment to Tower, 10 more minutes to Docklands/Canary Wharf, and 15 more minutes to Greenwich. The boats are less pleasant for joyriding than the cruises described earlier, with no commentary and no open deck up top (the only outside access is on a crowded deck at the exhaust-choked back of the boat, where you're jostling for space to take photos). Any one-way ride in Central London (roughly London Eye to Tower Pier) costs £8.60; a one-way ride to East London (Canary Wharf and Greenwich) is £10, and a River Roamer all-day ticket costs £19.80 (discounts online and with Travelcard and Oyster card, www.thamesclippers.com).

Thames Clippers also offers two express trips. The **Tate Boat** ferry service, which directly connects the Tate Britain (Millbank Pier) and the Tate Modern (Bankside Pier), is made for art lovers (£8.60 one-way, covered by River Roamer day ticket; buy ticket at kiosks or self-service machines before boarding or use Oyster Card;

London at a Glance

▲▲▲**Westminster Abbey** Britain's finest church and the site of royal coronations and burials since 1066. **Hours:** Abbey—Mon-Fri 9:30-16:30, Wed until 19:00, Sat 9:00-16:00 (Sept-April until 14:00); Diamond Jubilee Galleries—Mon-Fri 10:00-16:00, Sat 9:30-15:30; closed Sun except for worship. See page 68.

▲▲▲**Churchill War Rooms** Underground WWII headquarters of Churchill's war effort. **Hours:** Daily 9:30-18:00, July-Aug until 19:00. See page 77.

▲▲▲**National Gallery** Remarkable collection of European paintings (1250-1900), including Leonardo, Botticelli, Velázquez, Rembrandt, Turner, Van Gogh, and the Impressionists. **Hours:** Daily 10:00-18:00, Fri until 21:00. See page 83.

▲▲▲**British Museum** The world's greatest collection of artifacts of Western civilization, including the Rosetta Stone and the Parthenon's Elgin Marbles. **Hours:** Daily 10:00-17:30, Fri until 20:30 (select galleries only). See page 96.

▲▲▲**British Library** Fascinating collection of important literary treasures of the Western world. **Hours:** Mon-Thu 9:30-20:00, Fri until 18:00, Sat until 17:00, Sun 11:00-17:00. See page 103.

▲▲▲**St. Paul's Cathedral** The main cathedral of the Anglican Church, designed by Christopher Wren, with a climbable dome and daily evensong services. **Hours:** Mon-Sat 8:30-16:30, closed Sun except for worship. See page 108.

▲▲▲**Tower of London** Historic castle, palace, and prison housing the crown jewels and a witty band of Beefeaters. **Hours:** Tue-Sat 9:00-17:30, Sun-Mon from 10:00; Nov-Feb closes one hour earlier. See page 115.

▲▲▲**Victoria and Albert Museum** The best collection of decorative arts anywhere. **Hours:** Daily 10:00-17:45, Fri until 22:00 (select galleries only). See page 136.

▲▲**Houses of Parliament** Famous for Big Ben and occupied by the Houses of Lords and Commons. **Hours:** When Parliament is in session, generally open Oct-late July Mon-Thu, closed Fri-Sun and during recess late July-Sept. Guided tours offered year-round on Sat and most weekdays during recess. See page 73.

▲▲**Trafalgar Square** The heart of London, where Westminster, The City, and the West End meet. See page 81.

▲▲**National Portrait Gallery** A *Who's Who* of British history, featuring portraits of this nation's most important historical figures. **Hours:** Daily 10:00-18:00, Fri until 21:00. See page 87.

▲▲Covent Garden Vibrant people-watching zone with shops, cafés, street musicians, and an iron-and-glass arcade that once hosted a produce market. See page 89.

▲▲Changing of the Guard at Buckingham Palace Hour-long spectacle at Britain's royal residence. **Hours:** May-July daily at 11:00, Aug-April Sun-Mon, Wed, and Fri. See page 93.

▲▲London Eye Enormous observation wheel, dominating—and offering commanding views over—London's skyline. **Hours:** Daily 10:00-20:30 or later, Sept-May 11:00-18:00. See page 123.

▲▲Imperial War Museum Exhibits examining military conflicts from the early 20th century to today. **Hours:** Daily 10:00-18:00. See page 124.

▲▲Tate Modern Works by Monet, Matisse, Dalí, Picasso, and Warhol displayed in a converted powerhouse complex. **Hours:** Daily 10:00-18:00, Fri-Sat until 22:00. See page 126.

▲▲Shakespeare's Globe Timbered, thatched-roof reconstruction of the Bard's original "wooden O." **Hours:** Theater complex, museum, and actor-led tours generally daily 9:00-17:30; April-Oct generally morning theater tours only. Plays are also staged here. See page 127.

▲▲Tate Britain Collection of British painting from the 16th century through modern times, including works by Blake, the Pre-Raphaelites, and Turner. **Hours:** Daily 10:00-18:00. See page 130.

▲▲Natural History Museum A Darwinian delight, packed with stuffed creatures, engaging exhibits, and enthralled kids. **Hours:** Daily 10:00-18:00. See page 140.

▲▲Greenwich Historic borough just east of the city center, with *Cutty Sark* tea clipper, Royal Observatory, and a pleasant market. **Hours:** Most sights open daily 10:00-17:00. See page 141.

▲▲Kew Gardens Greenhouses, an arboretum, and many gardens hosting diverse plants from around the world. **Hours:** Mon-Thu 10:00-19:00, Fri-Sun until 20:00, closes earlier Sept-March. See page 145.

▲▲Hampton Court Palace The opulent digs of Henry VIII. **Hours:** Daily 10:00-18:00, Nov-March until 16:30. See page 146.

for frequency and times, see www.tate.org.uk/visit/tate-boat). The **O2 Express** runs only on nights when there are events at the O2 arena (departs from London Eye Pier, can sell out in advance).

Westminster Walk

Just about every visitor to London strolls along historic White-hall from Big Ben to Trafalgar Square. This self-guided walk gives meaning to that touristy ramble (most of the sights you'll see are described in more detail later). Under London's modern traffic and big-city bustle lie 2,000 fascinating years of history. You'll get a whirlwind tour as well as a practical orientation to London. ∩ You can download a free, extended audio version of this walk; see page 30.

Start halfway across ❶ **Westminster Bridge** for that "Wow, I'm really in London!" feeling. Get a close-up view of the **Houses of Parliament** and **Big Ben** (floodlit at night). Downstream you'll see the **London Eye,** the city's giant Ferris wheel. Down the stairs to Westminster Pier are boats to the Tower of London and Greenwich (downstream) or Kew Gardens (upstream).

En route to Parliament Square, you'll pass a ❷ **statue of Boadicea,** the Celtic queen who unsuccessfully resisted Roman invaders in AD 60. Julius Caesar was the first Roman general to cross the Channel, but even he was weirded out by the island's strange inhabitants, who worshipped trees, sacrificed virgins, and went to war painted blue. Later, Romans subdued and civilized them, building roads and making this spot on the Thames—"Londinium"—a major urban center.

You'll find four red phone booths lining the north side of ❸ **Parliament Square** along Great George Street—great for a phone-box-and-Big-Ben photo op.

Wave hello to Winston Churchill and Nelson Mandela in Parliament Square. To Churchill's right is the historic **Westminster Abbey,** with its two stubby, elegant towers. The white building (flying the Union Jack) at the far end of the square houses Britain's **Supreme Court.**

Head north up Parliament Street, which turns into ❹ **Whitehall,** and walk toward Trafalgar Square. You'll see the thought-provoking ❺ **Cenotaph** in the middle of the boulevard, reminding passersby of the many Brits who died in the last century's world wars. To visit the **Churchill War Rooms,** take a left before the Cenotaph, on King Charles Street.

Continuing on Whitehall, stop at the barricaded and guarded ❻ **#10 Downing Street** to see the British "White House," the traditional home of the prime minister since the position was created in the early 18th century. Break the bobby's boredom and ask him

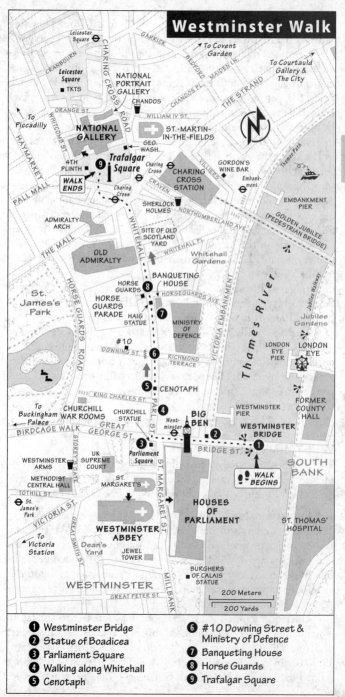

Westminster Walk

❶ Westminster Bridge
❷ Statue of Boadicea
❸ Parliament Square
❹ Walking along Whitehall
❺ Cenotaph

❻ #10 Downing Street & Ministry of Defence
❼ Banqueting House
❽ Horse Guards
❾ Trafalgar Square

a question. The huge building across Whitehall from Downing Street is the **Ministry of Defence** (MOD), the "British Pentagon."

Nearing Trafalgar Square, look for the 17th-century ❼ **Banqueting House** across the street, which is just about all that remains of what was once the biggest palace in Europe—Whitehall Palace. If you visit, you can enjoy its ceiling paintings by Peter Paul Rubens, and the exquisite hall itself. Also take a look at the ❽ **Horse Guards** behind the gated fence. For 200 years, soldiers in cavalry uniforms have guarded this arched entrance that leads to Buckingham Palace. These elite troops constitute the Queen's personal bodyguard.

The column topped by Lord Nelson marks ❾ **Trafalgar Square,** London's central meeting point. The stately domed building on the far side of the square is the **National Gallery,** which is filled with the national collection of European paintings, and has a classy café in the Sainsbury Wing. To the right of the National Gallery is the 1722 **St. Martin-in-the-Fields Church** and its Café in the Crypt.

To get to Piccadilly from Trafalgar Square, walk up Cockspur Street to Haymarket, then take a short left on Coventry Street to colorful **Piccadilly Circus** (see map on page 90).

Near Piccadilly, you'll find several theaters. **Leicester Square** (with its half-price TKTS booth for plays—see page 154) thrives just a few blocks away. Walk through trendy **Soho** (north of Shaftesbury Avenue) for its fun pubs. From Piccadilly or Oxford Circus, you can take a taxi, bus, or the Tube home.

Sights in Central London

WESTMINSTER

These sights are listed in roughly geographical order from Westminster Abbey to Trafalgar Square, and are linked in my self-guided Westminster Walk (above) and my free 🎧 audio tour.

▲▲▲Westminster Abbey

The greatest church in the English-speaking world, Westminster Abbey is where England's kings and queens have been crowned and buried since 1066. Like a stony refugee camp huddled outside St. Peter's Pearly Gates, Westminster Abbey has many stories to tell. To experience the church more vividly, take a live tour, or attend evensong or an organ concert.

Cost and Hours: £23, £5 more for timed-entry ticket to worthwhile Queen's Diamond Jubilee Galleries, family ticket available, cheaper online; Abbey—Mon-Fri 9:30-16:30, Wed until 19:00 (main church only), Sat 9:00-16:00 (Sept-April until 14:00), guided tours available; Queen's Galleries—Mon-Fri 10:00-16:00,

Sat 9:30-15:30; cloister—Mon-Sat 8:00-18:00; closed Sun to sightseers but open for services; last entry one hour before closing; Tube: Westminster or St. James's Park, tel. 020/7222-5152, www.westminster-abbey.org.

Timed-Entry Tickets: Avoid long ticket-buying lines (especially in summer) by buying a timed-entry ticket on the Abbey's website (don't buy tickets from copycat websites; use the official ".org" site). If you choose to add the Queen's Galleries, book that entry about an hour after you'll start your Abbey visit.

When to Go: It's most crowded every day at midmorning and all day Saturdays and Mondays. Visit early, during lunch, or late to avoid tourist hordes. Weekdays after 14:30 are less congested; come late and stay for the 17:00 evensong.

Church Services and Music: Mon-Fri at 7:30 (prayer), 8:00 and 12:30 (communion), 17:00 evensong (on Wed it's spoken, not sung); Sat at 8:00 (communion), 9:00 (prayer), 15:00 (evensong; May-Aug it's at 17:00); Sun services generally come with more music: at 8:00 (communion), 10:00 (sung Matins), 11:15 (sung Eucharist), 15:00 (evensong), 18:30 (evening service). Services are free to anyone, though visitors who haven't paid church admission aren't allowed to linger afterward. Free organ recitals are usually held Sun at 17:45 (30 minutes). Things can change, so get the latest info for your particular day from posted signs or the Abbey's website.

Tours: The included audioguide is excellent. Vergers (docents) give informative 90-minute guided tours (£5, schedule posted outside and inside entry, up to 6/day in summer, 2-4/day in winter).

⊙ Self-Guided Tour: You'll have no choice but to follow the steady flow of tourists through the church, along the route laid out for the audioguide. Here are the Abbey's top stops.

• *Walk straight through the north transept. Follow the crowd flow to the right, passing through a number of...*

❶ Memorials: Westminster Abbey has become a place where the nation comes to remember its own. You'll pass by statues on tombs, stained glass on walls, and plaques in the floor, all honoring illustrious Brits, both famous and not so famous.

• *Now enter the spacious nave and take it all in.*

❷ Nave: Look down the long and narrow center aisle of the church. Lined with the praying hands of the Gothic arches, glowing with light from the stained glass, this is more than a museum. With saints in stained glass, heroes in carved stone, and the bodies

LONDON

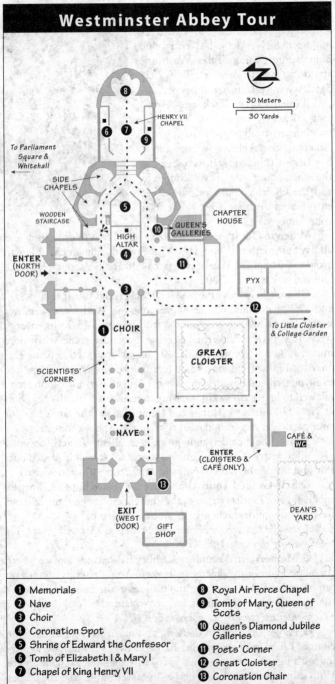

Westminster Abbey Tour

30 Meters
30 Yards

HENRY VII CHAPEL

To Parliament Square & Whitehall

SIDE CHAPELS

WOODEN STAIRCASE

CHAPTER HOUSE

QUEEN'S GALLERIES

HIGH ALTAR

ENTER (NORTH DOOR)

PYX

CHOIR

SCIENTISTS' CORNER

GREAT CLOISTER

To Little Cloister & College Garden

NAVE

ENTER (CLOISTERS & CAFÉ ONLY)

CAFÉ & WC

DEAN'S YARD

EXIT (WEST DOOR)

GIFT SHOP

1. Memorials
2. Nave
3. Choir
4. Coronation Spot
5. Shrine of Edward the Confessor
6. Tomb of Elizabeth I & Mary I
7. Chapel of King Henry VII
8. Royal Air Force Chapel
9. Tomb of Mary, Queen of Scots
10. Queen's Diamond Jubilee Galleries
11. Poets' Corner
12. Great Cloister
13. Coronation Chair

of England's greatest citizens under the floor stones, Westminster Abbey is the religious heart of England.

The king who built the Abbey was Edward the Confessor. Find him in the stained glass windows on the left side of the nave (as you face the altar). He's in the third bay from the end (marked *S. Edwardus rex...*), dressed in white and blue, with his crown, scepter, and ring. The Abbey's 10-story nave is the tallest in England. The sleek chandeliers, 10 feet tall, look small in comparison (16 were given to the Abbey by the Guinness family).

On the floor near the west entrance of the Abbey is the flower-lined Grave of the Unknown Warrior, one ordinary WWI soldier buried in soil from France with lettering made from melted-down weapons from that war. Take time to contemplate the 800,000 men from the British Empire who gave their lives. Their memory is so revered that, when Kate Middleton walked up the aisle on her wedding day, by tradition she had to step around the tomb.

• *Now walk straight up the nave toward the altar. This is the same route every future monarch walks on the way to being crowned. Midway up the nave, you pass through the colorful screen of an enclosure known as the...*

❸ **Choir:** These elaborately carved wood and gilded seats are where monks once chanted their services in the "quire"—as it's known in British churchspeak. Today, it's where the Abbey's boys choir sings the evensong. Up ahead, the "high" (main) altar—which usually has a cross and candlesticks atop it—sits on the platform up the five stairs.

❹ **Coronation Spot:** The area immediately before the high altar is where every English coronation since 1066 has taken place. Royalty are also given funerals here, and it's where most of the last century's royal weddings have taken place, including the unions of Queen Elizabeth II and Prince Philip (1947) and Prince William and Kate Middleton (2011).

• *Now veer left and follow the crowd. Pause at the wooden staircase on your right. This is the royal tomb that started it all.*

❺ **Shrine of Edward the Confessor:** Step back and peek over the dark coffin of Edward I to see the tippy-top of the green-and-gold wedding-cake tomb of King Edward the Confessor—the man who built Westminster Abbey. It was finished just in time to bury Edward and to crown his foreign successor, William the Conqueror, in 1066. After Edward's death, people prayed at his tomb, and, after getting good results, he was made a saint. His personal renown began the tradition of burying royalty in this church. Edward's tall, central tomb (which unfortunately lost some of its luster when Henry VIII melted down the gold coffin case) is surrounded by the tombs of eight other kings and queens.

• *At the top of the stone staircase, veer left into the private burial chapel of Queen Elizabeth I.*

❻ Tomb of Queens Elizabeth I and Mary I: Although only one effigy is on the tomb (Elizabeth's), there are actually two queens buried beneath it, both daughters of Henry VIII (by different mothers). Bloody Mary—meek, pious, sickly, and Catholic—enforced Catholicism during her short reign (1553-1558) by burning "heretics" at the stake.

Elizabeth—strong, clever, and Protestant—steered England on an Anglican course. She holds a royal orb symbolizing that she's queen of the whole globe. When 26-year-old Elizabeth was crowned in the Abbey, her right to rule was questioned (especially by her Catholic subjects) because she was considered the bastard seed of Henry VIII's unsanctioned marriage to Anne Boleyn. But Elizabeth's long reign (1559-1603) was one of the greatest in English history, a time when England ruled the seas and Shakespeare explored human emotions. When she died, thousands turned out for her funeral in the Abbey. Elizabeth's face on the tomb, modeled after her death mask, is considered a very accurate take on this hook-nosed, imperious "Virgin Queen" (she never married).

• *Continue into the ornate, flag-draped room up a few more stairs (directly behind the main altar).*

❼ Chapel of King Henry VII (the Lady Chapel): The light from the stained-glass windows; the colorful banners overhead; and the elaborate tracery in stone, wood, and glass give this room the festive air of a medieval tournament. The prestigious Knights of the Bath meet here, under the magnificent ceiling studded with gold pendants. The ceiling—of carved stone, not plaster (1519)—is the finest English Perpendicular Gothic and fan vaulting you'll see (unless you're going to King's College Chapel in Cambridge). The ceiling was sculpted on the floor in pieces, then jigsaw-puzzled into place. It capped the Gothic period and signaled the vitality of the coming Renaissance.

• *Go to the far end of the chapel and stand at the banister in front of the modern set of stained-glass windows.*

❽ Royal Air Force Chapel: Saints in robes and halos mingle with pilots in parachutes and bomber jackets. This tribute to WWII flyers is for those who earned their angel wings in the Battle of Britain (July-Oct 1940). A bit of bomb damage has been preserved—the little glassed-over hole in the wall below the windows in the lower left-hand corner.

• *Exit the Chapel of Henry VII. Turn left into a side chapel with the tomb (the central one of three in the chapel).*

❾ Tomb of Mary, Queen of Scots: The beautiful, French-educated queen (1542-1587) was held under house arrest for 19 years by Queen Elizabeth I, who considered her a threat to her sovereignty. Elizabeth got wind of an assassination plot, suspected Mary was behind it, and had her first cousin (once removed) beheaded. When Elizabeth died childless, Mary's son—James VI, King of Scots—also became King James I of England and Ireland. James buried his mum here (with her head sewn back on) in the Abbey's most sumptuous tomb.

• *Exit Mary's chapel. Continue on, until you emerge in the south transept. Look for the doorway that leads to a stairway and elevator to the...*

❿ Queen's Diamond Jubilee Galleries: In 2018, the Abbey opened a space that had been closed off for 700 years—an internal gallery 70 feet above the main floor known as the triforium. This balcony—with stunning views over the nave—now houses a small museum of interesting objects related to the Abbey's construction, the monarchs who worshipped here, royal coronations, and more from its 1,000-year history. (Because of limited space, a timed-entry ticket is required.)

• *After touring the Queen's Galleries, return to the main floor. You're in...*

⓫ Poets' Corner: England's greatest artistic contributions are in the written word. Many writers (including Chaucer, Lewis Carroll, T. S. Eliot, and Charles Dickens) are honored with plaques and monuments; relatively few are actually buried here. Shakespeare is commemorated by a fine statue that stands near the end of the transept, overlooking the others.

• *Exit the church (temporarily) at the south door, which leads to the...*

⓬ Great Cloister: You're entering the inner sanctum of the Abbey's monastery. The buildings that adjoin the church housed the monks. Cloistered courtyards like this gave them a place to stroll in peace while meditating on God's creations.

• *Go back into the church for the last stop.*

⓭ Coronation Chair: A gold-painted oak chair waits here under a regal canopy for the next coronation. For every English coronation since 1308 (except two), it's been moved to its spot before the high altar to receive the royal buttocks. The chair's legs rest on lions, England's symbol.

▲▲Houses of Parliament (Palace of Westminster)

This Neo-Gothic icon of London, the site of the royal residence from 1042 to 1547, is now the meeting place of the legislative branch of government. Like the US Capitol in Washington, DC, the complex is open to visitors. You can view parliamentary sessions

LONDON

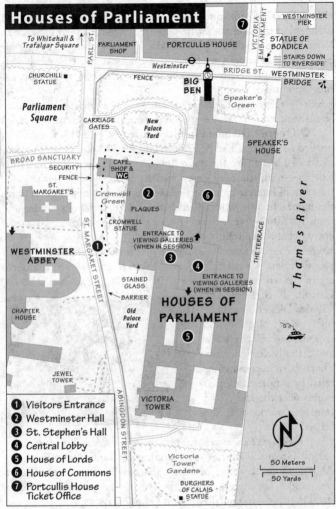

Houses of Parliament

1 Visitors Entrance
2 Westminster Hall
3 St. Stephen's Hall
4 Central Lobby
5 House of Lords
6 House of Commons
7 Portcullis House Ticket Office

in either the bickering House of Commons or the sleepy House of Lords. Or you can simply wander on your own (through a few closely monitored rooms) to appreciate the historic building itself.

The Palace of Westminster has been the center of political power in England for nearly a thousand years. In 1834, a horrendous fire gutted the Palace. It was rebuilt in a retro, Neo-Gothic style that recalled England's medieval Christian roots—pointed arches, stained-glass windows, spires, and saint-like statues. At the same time, Britain was also retooling its government. Democracy was on the rise, the queen became a constitutional monarch, and Parliament emerged as the nation's ruling body. The Palace

of Westminster became a symbol—a kind of cathedral—of democracy. A visit here offers a chance to tour a piece of living history and see the British government in action.

Cost and Hours: Free when Parliament is in session, otherwise must visit with a paid tour (see next); nonticketed entry generally Oct-late July, House of Commons—Mon 14:30-22:30, Tue-Wed 11:30-19:30, Thu 9:30-17:30; House of Lords—Mon-Tue 14:30-22:00, Wed 15:00-22:00, Thu 11:00-19:30; last entry depends on debates; exact day-by-day schedule at www.parliament.uk.

Tours: Audioguide-£19.50, guided tour-£26.50, tours available Sat year-round 9:00-16:30 and most weekdays during recess (late July-Sept), 1.5 hours. Confirm the tour schedule and book ahead at www.parliament.uk or by calling 020/7219-4114. The ticket office also sells tour tickets, but there's no guarantee same-day spaces will be available (ticket office open Mon-Fri 10:00-16:00, Sat 9:00-16:30, closed Sun, in Portcullis House next to Westminster Tube Station, entrance on Victoria Embankment). For either a guided tour or an audioguide, arrive at the visitors entrance on Cromwell Green 20 minutes before your tour time to clear security.

Choosing a House: The House of Lords meets in a more ornate room, and the wait time is shorter (likely less than 30 minutes). The House of Commons is where major policy is made, but the room is sparse, and wait times are longer (30-60 minutes or more).

Crowd-Beating Tips: For the public galleries, lines tend to be longest at the start of each session, particularly on Wednesdays; for the shortest wait, show up later in the afternoon (but don't push it, as things sometimes close down early).

❷ Self-Guided Tour: Enter midway along the west side of the building (across the street from Westminster Abbey), where a tourist ramp leads to the ❶ **visitors entrance.** Line up for the airport-style security check. You'll be given a visitor badge. If you have questions, the attendants are helpful.

• *First, take in the cavernous...*

❷ **Westminster Hall:** This vast hall—covering 16,000 square feet—survived the 1834 fire, and is one of the oldest and most important buildings in England. England's vaunt-

ed legal system was invented in this hall, as this was the major court of the land for 700 years. King Charles I was tried and sentenced to death here. Guy Fawkes was condemned for plotting to blow up the Halls of Parliament in 1605.

• *Continue up the stairs, and enter...*

❸ St. Stephen's Hall: This long, beautifully lit room was the original House of Commons. Members of Parliament (MPs) sat in church pews on either side of the hall—the ruling faction on one side, the opposition on the other. The room's murals depict major events in English history.

• *Continue into the...*

❹ Central Lobby: This ornate, octagonal, high-vaulted room is often called the "heart of British government," because it sits midway between the House of Commons (to the left) and the House of Lords (right). Video monitors list the schedule of meetings and events going on in this 1,100-room governmental hive. This is the best place to admire the Palace's interior decoration—carved wood, chandeliers, statues, and floor tiles. The room's decor trumpets the enlightenment of the British governing system. The colorful mosaics over the four doors represent the countries of the United Kingdom.

• *This lobby marks the end of the public space where you can wander freely. From here, you'll visit the House of Lords or the House of Commons. If either house is in session, you'll go through a series of narrow halls and staircases to reach the upper viewing galleries.*

❺ House of Lords: When you're called, you'll walk to the Lords Chamber by way of the long Peers' Corridor—referring to the House's 800 unelected members, called "Peers." Paintings on the corridor walls depict the antiauthoritarian spirit brewing under the reign of Charles I. When you reach the House of Lords Chamber, you'll watch the proceedings from the upper-level visitors gallery. Debate may occur among the few Lords who show up at any given time, but these days, their role is largely advisory—they have no real power to pass laws on their own.

The Lords Chamber is church-like and impressive, with stained glass and intricately carved walls. At the far end is the Queen's gilded throne, where she sits once a year to give a speech to open Parliament. In front of the throne sits the woolsack—a cushion stuffed with wool. Here the Lord Speaker presides, with a ceremonial mace behind the backrest. To the Lord Speaker's right are the members of the ruling party (a.k.a. "government") and to his left are the members of the opposition (the Labour Party). Unaffiliated Crossbenchers sit in between.

❻ House of Commons: The Commons Chamber may be much less grandiose than the Lords', but this is where the sausage gets made. The House of Commons is as powerful as the Lords, prime minister, and Queen combined. Of today's 650-plus MPs, only 450 can sit—the rest have to stand at the ends. As in the House of Lords, the ruling party sits on the right of the Speaker, opposition sits on the left.

Keep an eye out for two red lines on the floor, which must not be crossed when debating the other side. (They're supposedly two sword-lengths apart, to prevent a literal clashing of swords.) Between the benches is the canopied Speaker's Chair, for the chairman who keeps order and chooses who can speak next. A green bag on the back of the chair holds petitions from the public. The clerks sit at a central table that holds the ceremonial mace, a symbol of the power given Parliament by the monarch, who is not allowed in the Commons Chamber. When the prime minister visits, his ministers (or cabinet) join him on the front bench, while lesser MPs (the "backbenchers") sit behind. It's often a fiery spectacle, as the prime minister defends his policies, while the opposition grumbles and harrumphs in displeasure. It's not unheard of for MPs to get out of line and be escorted out by the Serjeant at Arms and his Parliamentary bouncers.

Nearby: Across the street from the Parliament building's St. Stephen's Gate, the **Jewel Tower** is a rare remnant of the old Palace of Westminster, used by kings until Henry VIII. The crude stone tower (1365-1366) was a guard tower in the palace wall, overlooking a moat. It contains an exhibit on the medieval Westminster Palace and the tower (£5.70, daily 10:00-18:00, shorter hours and closed Mon-Fri in off-season; tel. 020/7222-2219). Next to the tower is a quiet courtyard with picnic-friendly benches.

Big Ben, the 315-foot-high clock tower at the north end of the Palace of Westminster, is named for its 13-ton bell, Ben. The light above the clock is lit when Parliament is in session. The face of the clock is huge—you can actually see the minute hand moving. For a good view of it, walk halfway over Westminster Bridge.

▲▲▲Churchill War Rooms

This excellent sight offers a fascinating walk through the underground headquarters of the British government's WWII fight

against the Nazis in the darkest days of the Battle of Britain. It has two parts: the war rooms themselves, and a top-notch museum dedicated to the man who steered the war from here, Winston Churchill. Allow 1-2 hours for your visit.

Affording London's Sights

London is one of Europe's most expensive cities, with the dubious distinction of having some of the world's steepest admission prices. But with its many free museums and affordable plays, this cosmopolitan, cultured city offers days of sightseeing thrills without requiring you to pinch your pennies (or your pounds).

Free Museums: Free sights include the British Museum, British Library, National Gallery, National Portrait Gallery, Tate Britain, Tate Modern, Wallace Collection, Imperial War Museum, Victoria and Albert Museum, Natural History Museum, Science Museum, Sir John Soane's Museum, the Museum of London, the Museum of the Home, and the Guildhall. About half of these museums request a donation of about £5, but whether you contribute is up to you. If you feel like supporting these museums, renting audioguides, using their café, and buying a few souvenirs all help.

Free Churches: Smaller churches let worshippers (and tourists) in free, although they may ask for a donation. The big sightseeing churches—Westminster Abbey and St. Paul's—charge higher admission fees, but offer free evensong services nearly daily (though you can't stick around afterward to sightsee). Westminster Abbey also offers free organ recitals most Sundays.

Other Freebies: London has plenty of free performances, such as lunch concerts at St. Martin-in-the-Fields (see page 87). For other freebies, check out www.whatsfreeinlondon.co.uk. There's no charge to enjoy the pageantry of the Changing of the Guard, rants at Speakers' Corner in Hyde Park (on Sun afternoon), displays at Harrods, the people-watching scene at Covent Garden, and the colorful streets of the East End. It's free to view the legal action at the Old Bailey and the legislature at work in the Houses of Parliament. You can get into the chapels at the Tower of London and Windsor Castle by attending Sunday services. And, Greenwich is an inexpensive outing. Many of its sights are free, and the DLR journey is cheap.

Good-Value Tours: The London Walks tours with professional guides (£12) are one of the best deals going. (Note that the guides for the "free" walking tours are unpaid by their companies, and they expect tips—I'd pay up front for an expertly guided tour instead.) Hop-on, hop-off big-bus tours, while expensive (around £30-40), provide a great overview and include free boat tours as well as city walks. (Or, for the price of a transit ticket, you could

Cost and Hours: £22 for timed-entry ticket (buy online in advance), includes essential audioguide; daily 9:30-18:00, July-Aug until 19:00, last entry one hour before closing; on King Charles Street, 200 yards off Whitehall—follow signs, Tube: Westminster; tel. 020/7930-6961, www.iwm.org.uk/churchill-war-rooms. The museum's gift shop is great for anyone nostalgic for the 1940s.

get similar views from the top of a double-decker public bus.) A one-hour Thames ride to Greenwich costs about £12 one-way, but most boats come with entertaining commentary. A three-hour bicycle tour is about £27.

Buy Tickets Online: Tickets for many of London's most popular and expensive sights can be purchased online in advance, which will not only save you from standing in ticket-buying lines, but also will usually save you a few pounds per ticket.

Pricey...but Worth It? Big-ticket sights worth their hefty admission fees are the Tower of London, Kew Gardens, Shakespeare's Globe, and the Churchill War Rooms. The London Eye has become a London must-see—but you may feel differently when you see the price. St. Paul's Cathedral becomes more worthwhile if you climb the dome for the stunning view. Hampton Court Palace is well presented and a reasonable value if you have an interest in royal history. The Queen charges royally for a peek inside Buckingham Palace and her fine art gallery and carriage museum. Madame Tussauds Waxworks is pricey but still hard for many to resist (see page 106 for info on discounts). Harry Potter fans gladly pay the Hagrid-size fee to see the sets and props at the Warner Bros. Studio Tour (but those who wouldn't know a wizard from a Muggle needn't bother).

Totally Pants (Brit-speak for Not Worth It): The London Dungeon is gimmicky, overpriced, and a terrible value...despite the long line. The cost of the wallet-bleeding ride to the top of The Shard is even more breathtaking than the view from Western Europe's tallest skyscraper.

Theater: Compared with Broadway's prices, London's theater can be a bargain. Seek out the freestanding TKTS booth at Leicester Square to get discounts from 25 to 50 percent on good seats (and full-price tickets to the hottest shows with no service charges). Buying directly at the theater box office can score you a great deal on same-day tickets, and even popular shows may have some seats under £20 (possibly with restricted views). A £5 "groundling" ticket for a play at Shakespeare's Globe is the best theater deal in town. Tickets to the Open Air Theatre at north London's Regent's Park start at £25. For more on all of these options, see "Entertainment in London," later.

Advance Tickets Recommended: While you can buy a ticket on-site, ticket-buying lines can be long (1-2 hours), so it's smart to buy a timed-entry ticket online in advance. You still may have to wait up to 30 minutes in the security line. Note: London Pass holders do not get to skip the line here—they wait along with ticket buyers.

Cabinet War Rooms: The 27-room, heavily fortified nerve center of the British war effort was used from 1939 to 1945. Churchill's room, the map room, and other rooms are just as they were in 1945. As you follow the one-way route, the audioguide explains each room and offers first-person accounts of wartime happenings here. Be patient—it's well worth it. While the rooms are spartan, you'll see how British gentility survived even as the city was bombarded—posted signs informed those working underground what the weather was like outside, and a cheery notice reminded them to turn off the lights to conserve electricity.

Churchill Museum: Don't bypass this museum, which occupies a large hall amid the war rooms. It dissects every aspect of the man behind the famous cigar, bowler hat, and V-for-victory sign. It's extremely well presented and engaging, using artifacts, quotes, political cartoons, clear explanations, and interactive exhibits to bring the colorful statesman to life. You'll get a taste of Winston's wit, irascibility, work ethic, passion for painting, American ties, writing talents, and drinking habits. The exhibit shows Winston's warts as well: It questions whether his party-switching was just political opportunism, examines the basis for his opposition to Indian self-rule, and reveals him to be an intense taskmaster who worked 18-hour days and was brutal to his staffers (who deeply respected him nevertheless).

A long touch-the-screen timeline lets you zero in on events in his life from birth (November 30, 1874) to his first appointment as prime minister in 1940. When World War II broke out, Prime Minister Chamberlain's appeasement policies were discredited, and—on the day that Germany invaded the Netherlands—the king appointed Churchill prime minister. Many of the items on display—such as a European map divvied up in permanent marker, which Churchill brought to England from the postwar Potsdam Conference—drive home the remarkable span of history this man influenced. Imagine: Churchill began his military career riding horses in the cavalry and ended it speaking out against nuclear proliferation. Churchill guided the nation through its darkest hour. His greatest contribution may have been his stirring radio speeches that galvanized the will of the British people. It's all the more amazing considering that, in the 1930s, the man I regard as the greatest statesman of the 20th century was seen as a washed-up loony ranting about the growing threat of fascist Germany.

Eating: Rations are available at the **$$ museum café** or, better, get a pub lunch at the nearby **$$ Westminster Arms** (food served downstairs, on Storey's Gate, a couple of blocks south of the museum).

Horse Guards

Mounted sentries change at the top of every hour, courtyard guards change Monday-Saturday at 11:00 (Sun at 10:00), and a colorful dismounting ceremony takes place daily at 16:00. The rest of the day, they just stand there—making for boring video (at Horse Guards Parade on Whitehall, directly across from the Banqueting House, between Trafalgar Square and 10 Downing Street, Tube: Westminster, www.changing-guard.com). Buckingham Palace pageantry is canceled when it rains, but the Horse Guards change regardless of the weather.

▲Banqueting House

England's first Renaissance building (1619-1622) is still standing. Designed by Inigo Jones, built by King James I, and decorated by his son Charles I, the Banqueting House came to symbolize the Stuart kings' "divine right" management style—the belief that God himself had anointed them to rule. The house is one of the few London landmarks spared by the 1698 fire and the only surviving part of the original Palace of Whitehall. Today it opens its doors to visitors, who enjoy a restful 10-minute audiovisual history, a 45-minute audioguide, and a look at the exquisite banqueting hall itself. As a tourist attraction, it's basically one big room, with sumptuous ceiling paintings by Peter Paul Rubens. At Charles I's request, these paintings drove home the doctrine of the legitimacy of the divine right of kings. Ironically, in 1649—divine right ignored—King Charles I was famously executed right here.

Cost and Hours: £7, includes audioguide, daily 10:00-17:00, may close for government functions—though it's always open at least until 13:00 (call ahead for recorded info), immediately across Whitehall from the Horse Guards, Tube: Westminster, tel. 020/3166-6155, www.hrp.org.uk.

ON TRAFALGAR SQUARE

Trafalgar Square, London's central square, worth ▲▲, is at the intersection of Westminster, The City, and the West End. It's the climax of most marches and demonstrations, and is a thrilling place to simply hang out. A remodeling of the square has rerouted car traffic, helping reclaim the area for London's citizens. At the top of Trafalgar Square (north) sits the domed National Gallery with its grand staircase, and to the right, the steeple of St. Martin-in-

LONDON

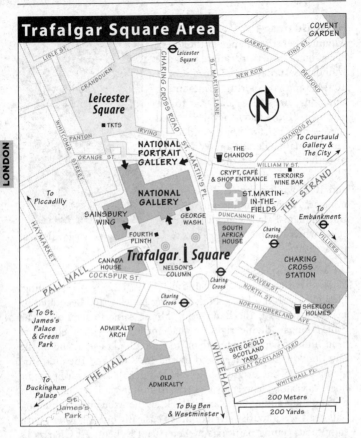

Trafalgar Square Area

COVENT GARDEN

Leicester Square

LISLE ST.

CRANBOURN

GARRICK KING ST.

BEDFORD

NEW ROW

CHARING CROSS ROAD

ST. MARTIN'S LANE

Leicester Square

■ TKTS

WHITCOMB STREET

PANTON

ORANGE ST.

IRVING

NATIONAL PORTRAIT GALLERY

THE CHANDOS

CHANDOS PL.

To Courtauld Gallery & The City

WILLIAM IV ST.

CRYPT, CAFÉ & SHOP ENTRANCE

TERROIRS WINE BAR

ST. MARTIN'S PL.

THE STRAND

NATIONAL GALLERY

ST. MARTIN-IN-THE-FIELDS

To Piccadilly

To Embankment

SAINSBURY WING

GEORGE WASH.

DUNCANNON

VILLIERS

FOURTH PLINTH

SOUTH AFRICA HOUSE

Charing Cross

Trafalgar Square

CANADA HOUSE

HAYMARKET

COCKSPUR ST.

NELSON'S COLUMN

CHARING CROSS STATION

PALL MALL

Charing Cross

CRAVEN ST.

NORTH. ST.

Charing Cross

NORTHUMBERLAND AVE.

SHERLOCK HOLMES

To St. James's Palace & Green Park

ADMIRALTY ARCH

WHITEHALL

SITE OF OLD SCOTLAND YARD

GREAT SCOTLAND YARD

To Buckingham Palace

THE MALL

OLD ADMIRALTY

WHITEHALL PL.

St. James's Park

To Big Ben & Westminster ↓

200 Meters

200 Yards

---

the-Fields, built in 1722, inspiring the steeple-over-the-entrance style of many town churches in New England. In the center of

the square, Lord Nelson stands atop his 185-foot-tall fluted granite column, gazing out toward Trafalgar, where he lost his life but defeated the French fleet. Part of this 1842 memorial is made from his victims' melted-down cannons. He's surrounded by spraying fountains, giant lions, hordes of people, and—until recently—even more pigeons. A former London mayor decided that London's "flying rats" were a public nuisance and evicted Trafalgar Square's venerable seed salesmen (Tube: Charing Cross).

▲▲▲National Gallery

Displaying an unsurpassed collection of European paintings from 1250 to 1900—including works by Leonardo, Botticelli, Velázquez, Rembrandt, Turner, Van Gogh, and the Impressionists—this is one of Europe's great galleries. You'll peruse 700 years of art—from gold-backed Madonnas to Cubist bathers.

Cost and Hours: Free, £5 suggested donation, special exhibits extra; daily 10:00-18:00, Fri until 21:00, last entry to special exhibits 45 minutes before closing; floor plan-£2; on Trafalgar Square, Tube: Charing Cross or Leicester Square, tel. 020/7747-2885, www.nationalgallery.org.uk.

Tours: Free one-hour overview tours leave from the Sainsbury Wing info desk Mon-Fri at 14:00 (no tours Sat-Sun); excellent £5 audioguides—choose from one-hour highlights tour, several theme tours, or an option that lets you dial up info on any painting in the museum.

Eating: Consider splitting afternoon tea at the **$$$ National Dining Rooms,** on the first floor of the Sainsbury Wing (see page 194). The **$$$ National Café,** located near the Getty Entrance, has a table-service restaurant and café. Seek out the **$ Espresso Bar,** near the Portico and Getty entrances, for sandwiches and pastries.

Visiting the Museum: Enter through the Sainsbury Entrance (facing Trafalgar Square), in the modern annex to the left of the classic building, and climb the stairs.

Medieval: In Room 51 (and nearby rooms), shiny gold paintings of saints, angels, Madonnas, and crucifixions float in an ethereal gold never-never land. Art in the Middle Ages was religious, dominated by the Church. The illiterate faithful could meditate on an altarpiece and visualize heaven. It's as though they couldn't imagine saints and angels inhabiting the dreary world of rocks, trees, and sky they lived in.

One of the finest medieval altarpieces, *The Wilton Diptych*, is tucked in the small alcove in Room 51. Two saint/kings and St. John the Baptist present King Richard II (left panel) to the Virgin Mary and her rosy-cheeked baby (right panel), who are surrounded by angels with flame-like wings. Despite the gold-leaf background, the kings have distinct, down-to-earth faces.

Italian Renaissance: In painting, the Renaissance meant realism. Artists rediscovered the beauty of nature and the human body. In Room 63, find Van Eyck's *The Arnolfini Portrait* (1434),

LONDON

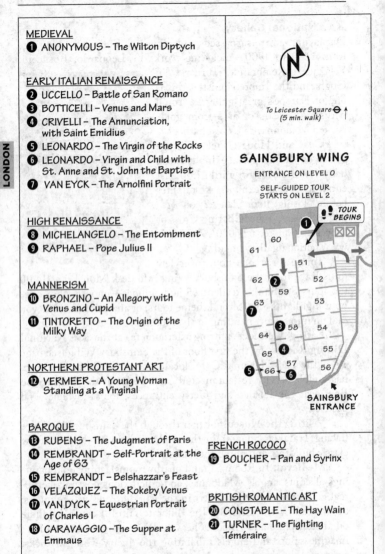

MEDIEVAL
1 ANONYMOUS – The Wilton Diptych

EARLY ITALIAN RENAISSANCE
2 UCCELLO – Battle of San Romano
3 BOTTICELLI – Venus and Mars
4 CRIVELLI – The Annunciation, with Saint Emidius
5 LEONARDO – The Virgin of the Rocks
6 LEONARDO – Virgin and Child with St. Anne and St. John the Baptist
7 VAN EYCK – The Arnolfini Portrait

HIGH RENAISSANCE
8 MICHELANGELO – The Entombment
9 RAPHAEL – Pope Julius II

MANNERISM
10 BRONZINO – An Allegory with Venus and Cupid
11 TINTORETTO – The Origin of the Milky Way

NORTHERN PROTESTANT ART
12 VERMEER – A Young Woman Standing at a Virginal

BAROQUE
13 RUBENS – The Judgment of Paris
14 REMBRANDT – Self-Portrait at the Age of 63
15 REMBRANDT – Belshazzar's Feast
16 VELÁZQUEZ – The Rokeby Venus
17 VAN DYCK – Equestrian Portrait of Charles I
18 CARAVAGGIO –The Supper at Emmaus

To Leicester Square ⊖ ↑ (5 min. walk)

SAINSBURY WING

ENTRANCE ON LEVEL 0

SELF-GUIDED TOUR STARTS ON LEVEL 2

TOUR BEGINS

SAINSBURY ENTRANCE

FRENCH ROCOCO
19 BOUCHER – Pan and Syrinx

BRITISH ROMANTIC ART
20 CONSTABLE – The Hay Wain
21 TURNER – The Fighting Téméraire

once thought to depict a wedding ceremony forced by the lady's swelling belly. Today it's understood as a portrait of a solemn, well-dressed, well-heeled couple, the Arnolfinis of Bruges, Belgium (the woman likely is not pregnant—the fashion of the day was to gather up the folds of one's extremely full-skirted dress).

Michelangelo's (unfinished) *The Entombment* is inspired by ancient statues of balanced, anatomically perfect, nude Greek gods. Renaissance balance and symmetry reign. Christ is the center of the composition, flanked by two people leaning equally, who sup-

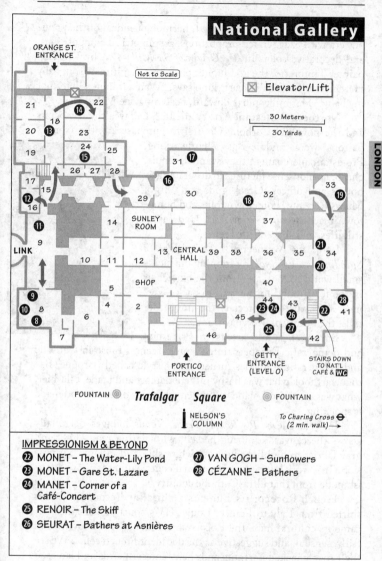

National Gallery

ORANGE ST. ENTRANCE

Not to Scale

⊠ Elevator/Lift

30 Meters
30 Yards

LINK

SUNLEY ROOM

CENTRAL HALL

SHOP

PORTICO ENTRANCE

GETTY ENTRANCE (LEVEL 0)

STAIRS DOWN TO NAT'L CAFÉ & WC

FOUNTAIN ◉ *Trafalgar Square* ◉ FOUNTAIN

NELSON'S COLUMN

To Charing Cross ⊖ (2 min. walk)→

IMPRESSIONISM & BEYOND

- **22** MONET – The Water-Lily Pond
- **23** MONET – Gare St. Lazare
- **24** MANET – Corner of a Café-Concert
- **25** RENOIR – The Skiff
- **26** SEURAT – Bathers at Asnières
- **27** VAN GOGH – Sunflowers
- **28** CÉZANNE – Bathers

port his body with strips of cloth. They, in turn, are flanked by two others.

Raphael's *Pope Julius II* gives a behind-the-scenes look at this complex leader. On the one hand, the pope is an imposing pyramid of power, with a velvet shawl, silk shirt, and fancy rings boasting of wealth and success. But at the same time, he's a bent and broken man, his throne backed into a corner, with an expression that seems to say, "Is this all there is?"

Mannerism: Developed in reaction to the High Renaissance,

Mannerism subverts the balanced, harmonious ideal of the previous era with exaggerated proportions, asymmetrical compositions, and decorative color. In *The Origin of the Milky Way* by Venetian painter Tintoretto, the god Jupiter places his illegitimate son, baby Hercules, at his wife's breast. Juno says, "Wait a minute. That's not my baby!" Her milk spurts upward, becoming the Milky Way.

Northern Protestant Art: While Italy had wealthy aristocrats and the powerful Catholic Church to purchase art, the North's patrons were middle-class, hardworking, Protestant merchants. They wanted simple, cheap, no-nonsense pictures to decorate their homes and offices. Greek gods and Virgin Marys were out, hometown folks and hometown places were in—portraits, landscapes, still lifes, and slice-of-life scenes.

Look for Vermeer's *A Young Woman Standing at a Virginal.* By framing off such a small world to look at—from the blue chair in the foreground to the wall in back—Vermeer forces us to appreciate the tiniest details, the beauty of everyday things.

Baroque: While artists in Protestant and democratic Europe painted simple scenes, those in Catholic and aristocratic countries turned to the style called Baroque. Baroque art took what was flashy in Venetian art and made it flashier, what was gaudy and made it gaudier, what was dramatic and made it shocking.

In Velázquez's *The Rokeby Venus,* Venus lounges diagonally across the canvas, admiring herself, with flaring red, white, and gray fabrics to highlight her rosy white skin and inflame our passion. This work by the king's personal court painter is a rare Spanish nude from that ultra-Catholic country.

French Rococo: As Europe's political and economic center shifted from Italy to France, Louis XIV's court at Versailles became its cultural hub. The Rococo art of Louis' successors was as frilly, sensual, and suggestive as the decadent French court. We see their rosy-cheeked portraits and their fantasies: lords and ladies at play in classical gardens, where mortals and gods cavort together. One of the finest examples is the tiny *Pan and Syrinx* by Boucher.

British Romantic Art: The reserved British were more comfortable cavorting with nature than with the lofty gods. Come-as-you-are poets like Wordsworth found the same ecstasy just in being outside. John Constable set up his easel out-of-doors, making quick sketches to capture the simple majesty of billowing clouds, spreading trees, and everyday rural life. Even British portraits (by Thomas Gainsborough and others) placed refined lords and ladies amid idealized greenery. The simple style of Constable's *The Hay Wain*—believe it or not—was considered shocking in its day.

Impressionism and Beyond: At the end of the 19th century, a new breed of artists burst out of the stuffy confines of the studio. They donned scarves and berets and set up their canvases in farmers' fields or carried their notebooks into crowded cafés, dashing off quick sketches in order to catch a momentary...impression. Check out Impressionist and Post-Impressionist masterpieces such as Van Gogh's *Sunflowers*. Van Gogh was the point man of his culture. He added emotion to Impressionism, infusing life even into inanimate objects. These sunflowers, painted with characteristic swirling brushstrokes, shimmer and writhe in either agony or ecstasy—depending on your own mood.

Cézanne's *Bathers* are arranged in strict triangles. He uses the Impressionist technique of building a figure with dabs of paint (though his "dabs" are often larger-sized "cube" shapes) to make solid, 3-D geometrical figures in the style of the Renaissance. In the process, his cube shapes helped inspire a radical new style—Cubism—bringing art into the 20th century.

▲▲National Portrait Gallery

A selective walk through this 500-year-long *Who's Who* of British history is quick and free, and puts faces on the story of England. The collection is well-described, not huge, and in historical sequence, from the 16th century on the second floor to today's royal family, usually housed on the ground floor. Some highlights: Henry VIII and wives; portraits of the "Virgin Queen" Elizabeth I, Sir Francis Drake, and Sir Walter Raleigh; the only real-life portrait of William Shakespeare; Oliver Cromwell and Charles I with his head on; portraits by Gainsborough and Reynolds; the Romantics (William Blake, Lord Byron, William Wordsworth, and company); Queen Victoria and her era; and the present royal family, including the late Princess Diana and the current Duchess of Cambridge—Kate.

Cost and Hours: Free, £5 suggested donation, special exhibits extra; daily 10:00-18:00, Fri until 21:00; excellent audioguide-£3, floor plan-£2; entry 100 yards off Trafalgar Square (around the corner from National Gallery, opposite Church of St. Martin-in-the-Fields), Tube: Charing Cross or Leicester Square, tel. 020/7306-0055, www.npg.org.uk.

▲St. Martin-in-the-Fields

The church, built in the 1720s with a Gothic spire atop a Greek-type temple, is an oasis of peace on wild and noisy Trafalgar Square. St. Martin cared for the poor. "In the fields" was where the first church stood on this spot (in the 13th century), between Westminster and The City. Stepping inside, you still feel a compassion for

the needs of the people in this neighborhood—the church serves the homeless and houses a Chinese community center. The modern east window—with grillwork bent into the shape of a warped cross—was installed in 2008 to replace one damaged in World War II.

A freestanding glass pavilion to the left of the church serves as the entrance to the church's underground areas. There you'll find the concert ticket office, a gift shop, brass-rubbing center, and the recommended support-the-church Café in the Crypt.

Cost and Hours: Free, donations welcome; Mon-Fri 8:30-18:00, Sat-Sun from 9:00, closed to visitors during services—listed at the entrance and on the website; Tube: Charing Cross, tel. 020/7766-1100, www.stmartin-in-the-fields.org. The church is famous for its concerts, including a free lunchtime concert several days a week and evening concerts (for details, see "Entertainment in London," later, as well as the church's website).

THE WEST END AND NEARBY
▲Piccadilly Circus

Although this square is slathered with neon billboards and tacky attractions (think of it as the Times Square of London), the surrounding streets are packed with great shopping opportunities and swimming with youth on the rampage.

Nearby Shaftesbury Avenue and Leicester Square teem with fun-seekers, theaters, Chinese restaurants, and street singers. To the northeast is London's Chinatown and, beyond that, the funky Soho neighborhood. And curling to the northwest from Piccadilly Circus is genteel Regent Street, lined with exclusive shops.

▲Soho

North of Piccadilly, once-seedy Soho has become trendy—with many recommended restaurants—and is well worth a gawk. It's the epicenter of London's thriving, colorful youth scene, a fun and funky *Sesame Street* of urban diversity.

▲▲Covent Garden

This large square is filled with people and street performers—jugglers, sword swallowers, magicians, and guitar players. London's buskers (including those in the Tube) are auditioned, licensed, and assigned times and places where they are allowed to perform.

The square's centerpiece is a covered marketplace. A market has been here since medieval times, when it was the "convent" garden owned by Westminster Abbey. In the 1600s, it became a housing development with this courtyard as its center, done in the Palladian style by Inigo Jones. Today's fine iron-and-glass structure was built in 1830 (when such buildings were all the Industrial Age rage) to house the stalls of what became London's chief produce market. Covent Garden remained a produce market until 1973, when its venerable arcades were converted to boutiques, cafés, and antique shops. A tourist market thrives here today (for details, see page 152).

The "Actors' Church" of St. Paul, the Royal Opera House, and the London Transport Museum (described next) all border the square, and theaters are nearby. The area is a people-watcher's delight, with cigarette eaters, Punch-and-Judy acts, food that's not good for you (or your wallet), trendy crafts, and row after row of boutique shops and market stalls. Better Covent Garden lunch deals can be found by walking a block or two away from the eye of this touristic hurricane (check out the places north of the Tube station, along Endell and Neal Streets).

▲London Transport Museum

This modern, well-presented museum is fun for kids and thought-provoking for adults (if a bit overpriced). Whether you're cursing or marveling at the buses and Tube, the growth of Europe's third-biggest city (after Istanbul and Moscow) has been made possible by its public transit system.

Cost and Hours: £18, kids under 18 free, daily 10:00-18:00, last entry 45 minutes before closing; pleasant upstairs café with Covent Garden view; in southeast corner of Covent Garden courtyard, Tube: Covent Garden, tel. 020/7379-6344, www.ltmuseum.co.uk.

Visiting the Museum: Take the elevator up to the top floor... and the year 1800, when horse-drawn vehicles ruled the road. Next, you descend to the first floor and the world's first under-

LONDON

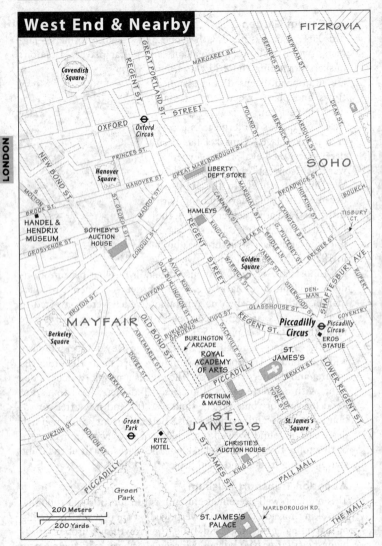

ground Metro system, which used steam-powered locomotives (the Circle Line, c. 1865). On the ground floor, horses and trains are replaced by motorized vehicles (cars, taxis, double-decker buses, streetcars), resulting in 20th-century congestion. How to deal with it? In 2003, car drivers in London were slapped with a congestion charge, and today, a half-billion people ride the Tube every year.

▲Courtauld Gallery

This gallery, part of the Courtauld Institute of Art, may be closed for a multiyear renovation when you visit. If it is open, you'll see

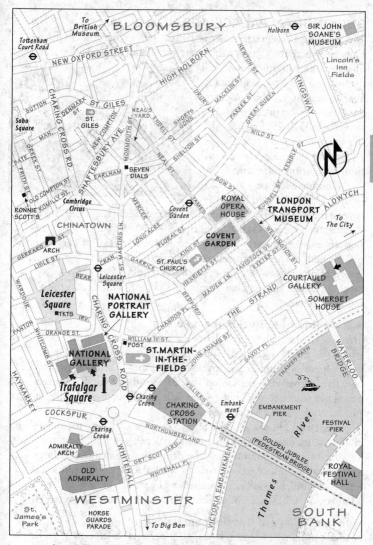

medieval European paintings and works by Rubens, the Impressionists (Manet, Monet, and Degas), Post-Impressionists (Cézanne and an intense Van Gogh self-portrait), and more. The gallery is located within the grand Somerset House; enjoy the riverside eateries and the courtyard featuring a playful fountain.

Cost and Hours: £7, price can change with exhibit; generally daily 10:00-18:00 but may be closed for renovation; in Somerset House on the Strand, Tube: Temple or Covent Garden, recorded info tel. 020/7848-2526, www.courtauld.ac.uk.

LONDON

BUCKINGHAM PALACE AREA

The working headquarters of the British monarchy, Buckingham Palace is where the Queen carries out her official duties as the head of state. She and other members of the royal family also maintain apartments here. The property hasn't always been this grand—James I (1603-1625) first brought the site under royal protection as a place for his mulberry plantation, for rearing silkworms.

Combo-Tickets: A £45 "Royal Day Out" combo-ticket covers the three palace sights that charge admission: the State Rooms, the Queen's Gallery, and the Royal Mews; the £20.70 version covers the Queen's Gallery and Royal Mews. You can also pay for each of these sights separately (prices listed later). For more information or to book online, see www.rct.uk. Many tourists are more interested in the Changing of the Guard, which costs nothing at all to view.

▲State Rooms at Buckingham Palace

This lavish home has been Britain's royal residence since 1837, when the newly ascended Queen Victoria moved in. When today's Queen is at home, the royal standard flies (a red, yellow, and blue flag); otherwise, the Union Jack flaps in the wind. The Queen opens her palace to the public—but only for a couple of months in summer, when she's out of town.

Cost and Hours: £25 for State Rooms and throne room, includes audioguide; late July-Sept only, daily 9:30-19:30, Sept until 18:30, last entry 75 minutes before closing; limited to 8,000 visitors a day by timed entry; come early to the palace's Visitor Entrance (opens at 9:00), or book ahead in person, by phone, or online; Tube: Victoria, tel. 0303/123-7300—but Her Majesty rarely answers.

Queen's Gallery at Buckingham Palace

A small sampling of Queen Elizabeth's personal collection of art is on display in five rooms in a wing adjoining the palace. Her 7,000 paintings, one of the largest private art collections in the world, are actually a series of collections built upon by each successive monarch since the 16th century. The exhibits change two or three times a year and are lovingly described by the included audioguide. Because the gallery is small and security is tight (involving lines), visit this gallery only if you're a patient art lover interested in the current exhibit.

Cost and Hours: £12 but can change depending on exhibit, daily 10:00-17:30, from 9:30 late July-Sept, last entry 75 minutes before closing, Tube: Victoria, tel. 0303/123-7301. Men shouldn't miss the mahogany-trimmed urinals.

Royal Mews

A visit to the Queen's working stables is likely to be disappointing unless you follow the included audioguide or the hourly guided tour (April-Oct only, 45 minutes), in which case it's fairly entertaining—especially if you're interested in horses and/or royalty. You'll see only a few of the Queen's 30 horses (most active between 10:00 and 12:00), a fancy car, and a bunch of old carriages, finishing with the Gold State Coach (c. 1760, 4 tons, 4 mph). Queen Victoria said absolutely no cars. When she died, in 1901, the mews got its first Daimler. Today, along with the hay-eating transport, the stable is home to five Bentleys and Rolls-Royce Phantoms, with at least one on display.

Cost and Hours: £12; daily 10:00-17:00, off-season until 16:00, closed Sun in Nov and all of Dec-Jan; last entry 45 minutes before closing, generally busiest immediately after Changing of the Guard, guided tours on the hour in summer; Buckingham Palace Road, Tube: Victoria, tel. 0303/123-7302.

▲▲Changing of the Guard at Buckingham Palace

This is the spectacle every London visitor has to see at least once: stone-faced, bearskin-hatted guards changing posts with much

fanfare, accompanied by a brass band. (This is also where you'll see nearly every tourist in London gathered in one place at the same time.)

The most famous part takes place right in front of Buckingham Palace at 11:00. But before and after that, over the course of about an hour, several guard-changing ceremonies and parades converge within a few hundred yards of Buckingham Palace in a perfect storm of red-coated pageantry, more or less simultaneously. Most tourists just show up near the palace gate and get lost in the crowds, but if you're savvy, you can catch a satisfying glimpse from less crowded locations with much less wait than if you station yourself at the palace gate (see the "Changing of the Guard Timeline" sidebar). Once it's all over, unwind with a stroll through nearby St. James's Park.

Cost and Hours: Free, May-July daily at 11:00, Aug-April Sun-Mon, Wed, and Fri, no ceremony in very wet weather; exact schedule subject to change—call 020/7766-7300 for the day's plan, or check www.householddivision.org.uk (search "Changing the Guard"); Buckingham Palace, Tube: Victoria, St. James's Park, or

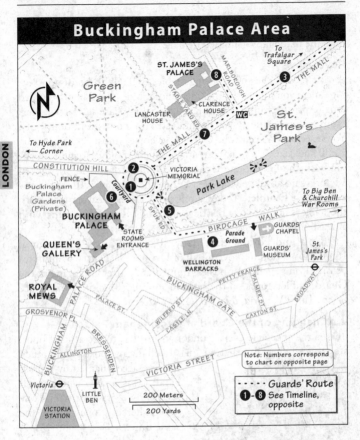

Buckingham Palace Area

Green Park

ST. JAMES'S PALACE ❽

To Trafalgar Square ❸ THE MALL

MARLBOROUGH ROAD

STABLE YARD RD.

LANCASTER HOUSE

CLARENCE HOUSE

WC

St. James's Park

CONSTITUTION HILL ❷ ❶ VICTORIA MEMORIAL ❼

To Hyde Park Corner ←

FENCE

Buckingham Palace Gardens (Private)

Courtyard

❻

Park Lake

To Big Ben & Churchill War Rooms →

SPUR RD.

❺

BUCKINGHAM PALACE

STATE ROOMS ENTRANCE

BIRDCAGE WALK

❹ Parade Ground

GUARDS' CHAPEL

St. James's Park

QUEEN'S GALLERY

WELLINGTON BARRACKS

GUARDS' MUSEUM

ROYAL MEWS

PETTY FRANCE

PALMER ST.

BROADWAY

GROSVENOR PL.

PALACE RD.

PALACE ST.

WILFRED ST.

BUCKINGHAM GATE

CASTLE LN.

CAXTON ST.

BUCKINGHAM PALACE RD.

BRESSENDEN

ALLINGTON

VICTORIA STREET

Victoria ⊖

LITTLE BEN

VICTORIA STATION

200 Meters

200 Yards

Note: Numbers correspond to chart on opposite page

- - - - Guards' Route

❶-❽ See Timeline, opposite

Green Park. Or hop into a big black taxi and say, "Buck House, please."

Tips: Download the official app for maps and background on the pageantry (www.rct.uk). The only public WC in the area is near St. James's Palace, just inside the gate to the park from Marlborough Road.

Viewing the Official Ceremony: The center of all this fanfare is the half-hour ceremony that takes place in the forecourt (between the palace and the fence) in front of Buckingham Palace. At 11:00 a batch of fresh guards meets the Old Guard in the courtyard, where the captain of the Old Guard hands over the keys. As the band plays, soldiers parade regimental flags (or "colours"), get counted and inspected—all with a lot of shouting—and finally exchange compliments before the tired guards return to Wellington Barracks, and a subset of the New Guard heads off to take over at St. James's Palace.

By the Palace Fence: If the actual changing of the Buckingham

Changing of the Guard Timeline

When	What
10:00	Tourists gather by the ❶ fence outside Buckingham Palace and the ❷ Victoria Memorial.
10:45	Cavalry guards, headed up ❸ The Mall back from their Green Park barracks, pass Buckingham Palace en route to the Horse Guards (except on Sundays).
10:57	❹ The New Guard, led by a band, marches in a short procession from Wellington Barracks down ❺ Spur Road to Buckingham Palace.
11:00	Guards converge around the Victoria Memorial before entering the ❻ fenced courtyard of Buckingham Palace for the main Changing of the Guard ceremony. (Meanwhile, farther away along Whitehall, the Horse Guard changes guard—except on Sundays, when it's at 10:00.)
11:10	Relief guards leave from Buckingham Palace along The Mall to Clarence House, via ❼ Stable Yard Road.
11:25	The remaining Old Guard leaves St. James's Palace for Buckingham Palace.
11:37	Cavalry guards, headed down The Mall back to their Green Park barracks from Horse Guards, pass Buckingham Palace.
11:40	The entire Old Guard, led by a band, leaves Buckingham Palace and heads up Spur Road for Wellington Barracks, while a detachment of the New Guard leaves Buckingham Palace to march up The Mall to take over at ❽ St. James's Palace (arriving around 11:45).

Palace guards is a must-see for you, show up at least an hour early to get a place front and center, next to the fence (shorter travelers should aim for two hours ahead in high season).

Near the Victoria Memorial: If you can't get a spot right by the gates, try the high ground on the circular Victoria Memorial, which can give you good (if more distant) views of the palace as well as the arriving and departing processions along The Mall and Spur Road. If grabbing an early spot, think about whether you'll still have a view once the crowds fill in—balustrades and other raised spots go quickly.

Following the Procession: If the main ceremony doesn't seem worth all the waiting and jostling, you can still enjoy plenty of fun fanfare—and the thrill of participating in the action—by planting yourself on the route of a string of processions that happen before, during, and after the official guard changing at Buckingham Palace.

To catch as much as possible, here's what I'd do:

Show up at St. James's Palace by 10:30 to see its soon-to-be-off-duty guards mobilizing in the courtyard (grab a spot just across Marlborough Road from the courtyard; people grouped on the palace side of the street will be asked to move when the inspection begins).

Just before they prepare to leave (at 10:43), march ahead of them down Marlborough Road to The Mall and pause at the corner to watch them parade past, possibly with a band, on their way to Buckingham Palace.

Then cut through the park and head to the Wellington Barracks—where a fresh batch of guards is undergoing inspection before they leave (at 10:57) for Buckingham Palace.

March along with the New Guard and their full military band, from the barracks to Buckingham Palace.

If it's too packed to see any of the action behind the palace gates, snap a few photos of the passing guards—and the crowds—before making your way back up The Mall, to where it meets Stable Yard Road, in time to watch several more processions: relief guards coming from Buckingham Palace at 11:10 for a switch of sentries at Clarence House (Prince Charles' official home), then other guards heading down The Mall *toward* Buckingham Palace at 11:25, and, at 11:37, a procession of cavalry guards en route from the Horse Guards to their barracks in Green Park.

Finally, at about 11:45, plant yourself back at the corner of The Mall and Marlborough Road for a great photo op as one last procession, the bulk of St. James's Palace New Guard, makes its way from Buckingham Palace to start its shift.

Join a Tour: Local tour companies such as **Fun London Tours** more or less follow the route above but add in history and facts about the guards, bands, and royal family to their already entertaining march. These walks add color and good value to what can otherwise seem like a stressful mess of tourists (£17, Changing of the Guard tour starts at Piccadilly Circus at 9:40, must book online in advance, www.funlondontours.com).

Sights in North London

▲▲▲British Museum

Simply put, this is the greatest chronicle of civilization...anywhere. A visit here is like taking a long hike through *Encyclopedia Britannica* National Park. The vast British Museum wraps around its Great Court (the huge entrance hall), with the

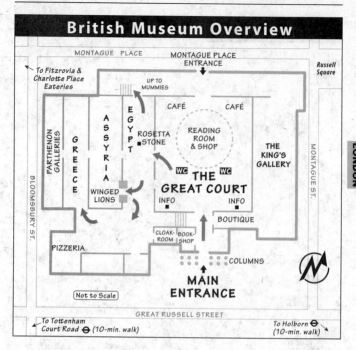

British Museum Overview

MONTAGUE PLACE

MONTAGUE PLACE ENTRANCE

Russell Square

To Fitzrovia & Charlotte Place Eateries

UP TO MUMMIES

CAFÉ   CAFÉ

EGYPT

ASSYRIA

ROSETTA STONE

READING ROOM & SHOP

THE KING'S GALLERY

PARTHENON GALLERIES

GREECE

WC   WC

THE GREAT COURT

WINGED LIONS

INFO   INFO

BOUTIQUE

BLOOMSBURY ST.

MONTAGUE ST.

CLOAK-ROOM   BOOK-SHOP

PIZZERIA

COLUMNS

MAIN ENTRANCE

Not to Scale

GREAT RUSSELL STREET

To Tottenham Court Road ⊖ (10-min. walk)

To Holborn ⊖ (10-min. walk)

LONDON

most popular sections filling the ground floor: Egyptian, Assyrian, and ancient Greek, with the famous frieze sculptures from the Parthenon in Athens. The museum's stately Reading Room—famous as the place where Karl Marx hung out while formulating his ideas on communism and writing *Das Kapital*—sometimes hosts special exhibits.

Cost and Hours: Free, £5 donation requested, special exhibits usually extra (and with timed ticket); daily 10:00-17:30, Fri until 20:30 (select galleries only), least crowded late on weekday afternoons, especially Fri; free guided tours offered, multimedia guide–£7; Great Russell Street, Tube: Tottenham Court Road, ticket desk tel. 020/7323-8181, www. britishmuseum.org.

Tours: Free 40-minute EyeOpener tours by volunteers focus on select rooms (daily 11:00-15:45, generally every 15 minutes). More in-depth 90-minute tours are offered Fri-Sun at 11:30 and 14:00. Ask about other specialty tours and lectures.

The £7 multimedia guide offers dial-up audio commentary

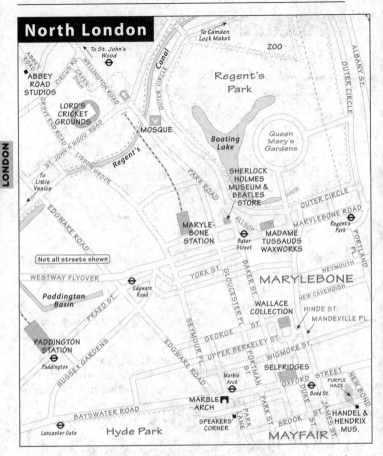

North London

To Camden Lock Maket

ZOO

ALBANY ST.

ABBEY ROAD

To St. John's Wood

CIRCUS RD.

WELLINGTON ROAD

CAVENDISH

Canal

OUTER CIRCLE

Regent's Park

ABBEY ROAD STUDIOS

LORD'S CRICKET GROUNDS

GROVE END ROAD

ST. JOHN'S WOOD ROAD

TISSON GROVE

MOSQUE

Regent's

Boating Lake

Queen Mary's Gardens

To Little Venice

EDGWARE ROAD

PARK ROAD

SHERLOCK HOLMES MUSEUM & BEATLES STORE

OUTER CIRCLE

MARYLEBONE ROAD

Regent's Park

Not all streets shown

WESTWAY FLYOVER

Paddington Basin

Edgware Road

YORK ST.

ALLSOP

MARYLE-BONE STATION

Baker Street

MADAME TUSSAUDS WAXWORKS

PORTLAND PL.

GLOUCESTER PL.

BAKER ST.

MARYLEBONE

WEYMOUTH

NEW CAVENDISH

PRAED ST.

SEYMOUR PL.

EDGWARE ROAD

GEORGE ST.

WALLACE COLLECTION

HINDE ST.

MANDEVILLE PL.

PADDINGTON STATION

Paddington

SUSSEX GARDENS

UPPER BERKELEY ST.

PORTMAN ST.

WIGMORE ST.

SELFRIDGES

Marble Arch

OXFORD STREET

DUKE

PURPLE HAZE

NEW BOND

MARBLE ARCH

Bond St.

BAYSWATER ROAD

PARK LANE

SPEAKERS' CORNER

BROOK ST.

JAMES ST.

HANDEL & HENDRIX MUS.

Lancaster Gate

Hyde Park

MAYFAIR

and video on 200 objects, as well as several substantial and cerebral theme tours (must leave photo ID). There's also a fun family multi-media guide offering various themed routes.

🎧 Download my free British Museum audio tour.

Visiting the Museum: From the Great Court, doorways lead to all wings. To the left are the exhibits on Egypt, Assyria, and Greece—the highlights of your visit.

Egypt: Start with the Egyptian Gallery. Egypt was one of the world's first "civilizations"—a group of people with a government, religion, art, free time, and a written language. The Egypt we think of—pyramids, mummies, pharaohs, and guys who walk funny—lasted from 3000 to 1000 BC with hardly any change in the government, religion, or arts.

The first thing you'll see in the Egypt section is the **Rosetta Stone.** When this rock was unearthed in the Egyptian desert in 1799, it was a sensation in Europe. This black slab, dating from 196

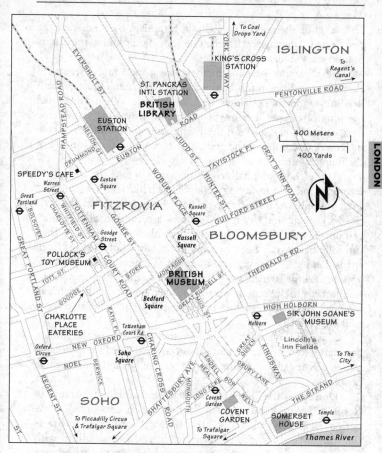

BC, caused a quantum leap in the study of ancient history. Finally, Egyptian writing could be decoded.

The hieroglyphic writing in the upper part of the stone was indecipherable for a thousand years. Did a picture of a bird mean "bird"? Or was it a sound, forming part of a larger word, like "burden"? As it turned out, hieroglyphics are a complex combination of the two, surprisingly more phonetic than symbolic. (For example, the hieroglyph that looks like a mouth or an eye is the letter "R.")

The Rosetta Stone allowed linguists to break the code. It contains a single inscription repeated in three languages. The bottom third is plain old

Greek, while the middle is medieval Egyptian. By comparing the two known languages with the one they didn't know, translators figured out the hieroglyphics.

Next, wander past the many **statues,** including a seven-ton Ramesses, with the traditional features of a pharaoh (goatee, cloth headdress, and cobra diadem on his forehead). When Moses told the king of Egypt, "Let my people go!" this was the stony-faced look he got. You'll also see the Egyptian gods as animals—these include Amun, king of the gods, as a ram, and Horus, the god of the living, as a falcon.

At the end of the hall, climb the stairs or take the elevator to **mummy** land. Mummifying a body is much like following a recipe. First, disembowel it (but leave the heart inside), then pack the cavities with pitch, and dry it with natron, a natural form of sodium carbonate (and, I believe, the active ingredient in Twinkies). Then carefully bandage it head to toe with hundreds of yards of linen strips. Let it sit 2,000 years, and...voilà! The mummy was placed in a wooden coffin, which was put in a stone coffin, which was placed in a tomb. (The pyramids were supersized tombs for the rich and famous.) The result is that we now have Egyptian bodies that are as well preserved as Larry King.

Many of the mummies here are from the time of the Roman occupation, when fine memorial portraits painted in wax became popular. X-ray photos in the display cases tell us more about these people.

Don't miss the animal mummies. Cats (near the entrance to Room 62) were popular pets. They were also considered incarnations of the cat-headed goddess Bastet. Worshipped in life as the sun god's allies, preserved in death, and memorialized with statues, cats were given the adulation they've come to expect ever since.

Assyria: Long before Saddam Hussein, Iraq was home to other palace-building, iron-fisted rulers—the Assyrians. They conquered their southern neighbors and dominated the Middle East for 300 years (c. 900-600 BC).

Their strength came from a superb army (chariots, mounted cavalry, and siege engines), a policy of terrorism against enemies ("I tied their heads to tree trunks all around the city," reads a royal inscription), ethnic cleansing and mass deportations of the vanquished, and efficient administration (roads and express postal service). They have been called the "Romans of the East."

The British Museum's valuable collection of Assyrian artifacts has become even more priceless since the recent destruction of ancient sites in the Middle East by ISIS terrorists.

Two human-headed winged stone lions guarded an Assyrian palace (11th-8th century BC). With the strength of a lion, the wings of an eagle, the brain of a man, and the beard of an ancient hipster, they protected the king from evil spirits and scared the heck out of foreign ambassadors and left-wing newspaper reporters. (What has five legs and flies? Take a close look. These winged quintupeds, which appear complete from both the front and the side, could guard both directions at once.)

Carved into the stone between the bearded lions' loins, you can see one of civilization's most impressive achievements—writing. This wedge-shaped **(cuneiform)** script is the world's first written language, invented 5,000 years ago by the Sumerians (of southern Iraq) and passed down to their less-civilized descendants, the Assyrians.

The **Nimrud Gallery** is a mini version of the throne room and royal apartments of King Ashurnasirpal II's Northwest Palace at Nimrud (9th century BC). It's filled with royal propaganda reliefs, 30-ton marble bulls, and panels depicting wounded lions (lion-hunting was Assyria's sport of kings).

Greece: The history of ancient Greece (600 BC–AD 1) could be subtitled "making order out of chaos." While Assyria was dominating the Middle East, "Greece"—a gaggle of warring tribes roaming the Greek peninsula—was floundering in darkness. But by about 700 BC, these tribes began settling down, experimenting with democracy, forming self-governing city-states, and making ties with other city-states.

During its Golden Age (500-430 BC), Greece set the tone for all of Western civilization to follow. Democracy, theater, literature, mathematics, philosophy, science, gyros, art, and architecture as we know them, were virtually all invented by a single generation of Greeks in a small town of maybe 80,000 citizens.

Your walk through Greek history starts with pottery—from the earliest, with geometric patterns (8th century BC), to painted black silhouettes on the natural orange clay, and then a few crudely done red human figures on black backgrounds. Later, find a vase painted with frisky figures **(Wine Cooler Signed by Douris as Painter),** which shows a culture really into partying, as well as an evolution into more realistic and three-dimensional figures.

The highlight is the **Parthenon Sculptures**—taken from the temple dedicated to Athena, the crowning glory of an enormous urban-renewal plan during Greece's Golden Age.

While the building itself remains in Athens, many of the Parthenon's best sculptures are right here in the British Museum—the

so-called Elgin Marbles, named for the shrewd British ambassador who had his men hammer, chisel, and saw them off the Parthenon in the early 1800s.

These much-wrangled-over bits of the Parthenon (from about 450 BC) are indeed impressive. The marble panels you see lining the walls of this large hall are part of the frieze that originally ran around the exterior of the Parthenon, under the eaves. The statues at either end of the hall once filled the Parthenon's triangular-shaped pediments and showed the birth of Athena. The relief panels known as metopes tell the story of the struggle between the forces of human civilization and animal-like barbarism.

Rest of the Museum: Be sure to venture upstairs to see artifacts from Roman Britain that surpass anything you'll see at Hadrian's Wall or elsewhere in the country. Also look for the Sutton Hoo Ship Burial artifacts from a seventh-century royal burial on the east coast of England (Room 41). A rare Michelangelo cartoon (preliminary sketch) is in Room 90 (level 4).

▲Sir John Soane's Museum

Architects love this quirky place, as do fans of interior decor, eclectic knickknacks, and Back Door sights. Tour this furnished home on a bird-chirping square and see 19th-century chairs, lamps, wood-paneled nooks and crannies, sculptures, and stained-glass skylights just as they were when the owner lived here. As professor of architecture at the Royal Academy, Soane created his home to be a place of learning, cramming it floor to ceiling with ancient relics, curios, and famous paintings, including several excellent Canalettos and Hogarth's series on *The Rake's Progress* (which is hidden behind a panel in the Picture Room and opened randomly at the museum's discretion, usually twice an hour). Soane even purchased the Egyptian sarcophagus of King Seti I (Ramesses II's father, on display in the basement) after the British Museum turned it down—at the time, they couldn't afford the £2,000 sticker price.

In 1833, just before his death, Soane established his house as a museum, stipulating that it be kept as nearly as possible in the state he left it. If he visited today, he'd be entirely satisfied by the diligence with which the staff safeguards his treasures. You'll leave wishing you'd known the man.

Cost and Hours: Free, but donations much appreciated; Wed-Sun 10:00-17:00, closed Mon-Tue; often long entry lines (especially Sat), knowledgeable volunteers in most rooms, guidebook-£5; free 30-minute tour of private apartment at 13:15 and 14:00, £15 one-hour highlights tour must be booked ahead online and runs Thu-Sun at 12:00 plus Sat-Sun at 11:00; 13 Lincoln's Inn Fields, quarter-mile southeast of British Museum, Tube: Holborn, tel. 020/7405-2107, www.soane.org.

▲▲▲British Library

Here, in just two rooms, are the literary treasures of Western civilization, from early Bibles to Shakespeare's *Hamlet* to Lewis Carroll's *Alice's Adventures in Wonderland* to the *Magna Carta*. The British Empire built its greatest monuments out of paper; it's through literature that England made her most lasting and significant contribution to civilization and the arts.

Cost and Hours: Free, £5 suggested donation, admission charged for special exhibits; Mon-Thu 9:30-20:00, Fri until 18:00, Sat until 17:00, Sun 11:00-17:00; 96 Euston Road, Tube: King's Cross St. Pancras or Euston, tel. 019/3754-6060, info tel. 020/7412-7676, www.bl.uk.

Tours: There are no guided tours or audioguides for the permanent collection. There are, however, guided tours of the building itself—the archives and reading rooms (for details, call 019/3754-6546 or see the website). Touch-screen computers in the permanent collection let you page virtually through some of the rare books.

♠ Download my free British Library audio tour.

Visiting the Library: Entering the library courtyard, you'll see a big statue of a naked Isaac Newton bending forward with a compass to measure the universe. The statue symbolizes the library's purpose: to gather all knowledge and promote humanity's endless search for truth.

Stepping inside, you'll find in the middle of the building a 50-foot-tall wall of 65,000 books teasingly exposing its shelves. In 1823 King George III gifted his collection to the people under the condition the books remain on display for all to see. The high-tech bookshelf—with moveable lifts to reach the highest titles—sits behind glass, inaccessible to commoners but ever visible. Likewise, the reading rooms upstairs are not open to the public.

Everything that matters for your visit is in a tiny but exciting area variously called "The Sir John Ritblat Gallery," "Treasures of the British Library," or just "The Treasures." We'll concentrate on a handful of documents—literary and historical—that changed the

LONDON

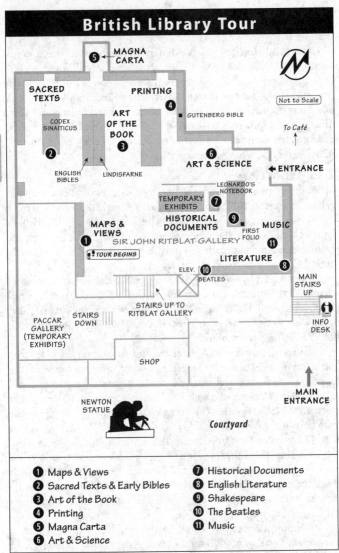

British Library Tour

1. Maps & Views
2. Sacred Texts & Early Bibles
3. Art of the Book
4. Printing
5. Magna Carta
6. Art & Science
7. Historical Documents
8. English Literature
9. Shakespeare
10. The Beatles
11. Music

course of history. Note that exhibits change often, and many of the museum's old, fragile manuscripts need to "rest" periodically in order to stay well preserved. Upon entering the Ritblat Gallery, start at the far side of the room with the display case showing historic ❶ **maps and views,** illustrating humans' shifting perspective of the world. Next, move into the area dedicated to ❷ **sacred texts and early Bibles,** including the Codex Sinaiticus (or the Codex Alexandrinus that may be on display instead). This bound book from around AD 350 is one of the oldest complete Bibles in existence—one of the first attempts to collect various books by different authors into one authoritative anthology.

In the display cases called ❸ **Art of the Book,** you'll find various medieval-era books, some beautifully illustrated or "illuminated." The lettering is immaculate, but all are penned by hand. The most magnificent of these medieval British "monk-uscripts" is the **Lindisfarne Gospels,** from AD 698. The text is in Latin, the language of scholars ever since the Roman Empire, but you can read an electronic copy of these manuscripts by using one of the touchscreen computers scattered around the room.

In the glass cases featuring early ❹ **printing,** you'll see the Gutenberg Bible—the first book printed in Europe using movable type (c. 1455). Suddenly, the Bible was available for anyone to read, fueling the Protestant Reformation.

Through a doorway is a small room with the ❺ **Magna Carta.** Though historians talk about *the* Magna Carta, several different versions of the document exist, some of which are kept in this room. The basis for England's constitutional system of government, this "Great Charter" listing rules about mundane administrative issues was radical because of the simple fact that the king had agreed to abide by them as law. Until then, kings had ruled by God-given authority, above the laws of men. Now, for the first time, there were limits—in writing—on how a king could treat his subjects.

Return to the main room to find display cases featuring trailblazing ❻ **art and science** documents by early scientists such as Galileo, Isaac Newton, and many more. Pages from Leonardo da Vinci's notebook show his powerful curiosity, his genius for invention, and his famous backward and inside-out handwriting. Nearby are many more ❼ **historical documents.** You may see letters by Henry VIII, Queen Elizabeth I, Darwin, Freud, Gandhi, and others.

Next, trace the evolution of ❽ **English literature.** Check out the AD 1000 manuscript of Beowulf, the first English literary masterpiece, and *The Canterbury Tales* (c. 1410), Geoffrey Chaucer's bawdy collection of stories. This display is often a greatest-hits sampling of literature in English, from Brontë to Kipling to Woolf to Joyce to Dickens. The most famous of England's writers—❾ **Shakespeare**—generally gets his own display case. Look for the First Folio—one of the 750 copies of 36 of the 37 known Shakespeare plays, published in 1623. If the First Folio is not out for viewing, the library should have other Shakespeare items on display.

Now fast-forward a few centuries to ❿ **The Beatles.** Look for photos of John Lennon, Paul McCartney, George Harrison, and Ringo Starr. Among the displays, you may find manuscripts of song lyrics written by Lennon and McCartney. In the ⓫ **music** section, there are manuscripts by Mozart, Beethoven, Chopin, and others (kind of an anticlimax after the Fab Four, I know). George Frideric Handel's famous oratorio, the *Messiah* (1741), is often on display and marks the end of our tour. Hallelujah.

▲Wallace Collection

Sir Richard Wallace's fine collection of 17th-century Dutch Masters, 18th-century French Rococo, medieval armor, and

assorted aristocratic fancies fills the sumptuously furnished Hertford House on Manchester Square. From the rough and intimate Dutch lifescapes of Jan Steen to the pink-cheeked Rococo fantasies of François Boucher, a wander through this little-visited mansion makes you nostalgic for the days of the empire. This collection would be a big deal in a midsize city, but here in London it gets pleasantly lost. Because this is a "closed collection" (nothing new is acquired and nothing permanent goes on loan), it feels more like visiting a classic English manor estate than a museum. It's thoroughly enjoyable.

Cost and Hours: Free, £5 suggested donation, daily 10:00-17:00, audioguide-£4, just north of Oxford Street on Manchester Square, Tube: Bond Street, tel. 020/7563-9500, www.wallacecollection.org.

▲Madame Tussauds Waxworks

This waxtravaganza is gimmicky, crass, and crazy expensive, but dang fun...a hit with the kind of tourists who skip the British

Museum. The original Madame Tussaud did wax casts of heads lopped off during the French Revolution (such as Marie-Antoinette's). She took her show on the road and ended up in London in 1835. Now it's all about singing with Lady Gaga and partying with The Beatles. In addition to posing with all the eerily realistic wax dummies—from the Queen and Will and Kate to the Beckhams—you'll have the chance to learn how they created this waxy army; hop on a people-mover and cruise through a kid-pleasing "Spirit of London" time trip; and visit with Marvel superheroes. A nine-minute "4-D" show features a 3-D movie heightened by wind, "back ticklers," and other special effects.

Cost and Hours: £35, kids-£30 (free for kids under 3), up to

Beatles Sights

London's city center is surprisingly devoid of sights associated with the famous '60s rock band. To see much of anything, consider taking a guided walk (see page 59).

For a photo op, go to Abbey Road and walk the famous crosswalk pictured on the *Abbey Road* album cover (north-

west of Regent's Park, Tube: St. John's Wood, get information and buy Beatles memorabilia at the small kiosk in the station). From the Tube station, it's a five-minute walk west down Grove End Road to the intersection with Abbey Road. The Abbey Road recording studio is the low-key white building to the right of Abbey House (it's still a working studio, so you can't go inside). Ponder the graffiti on the low wall outside, and...imagine. To re-create the famous cover photo, shoot the crosswalk from the roundabout as you face north up Abbey Road. Shoes are optional.

Nearby is **Paul McCartney's current home** (7 Cavendish Avenue): Continue down Grove End Road, turn left on Circus Road, and then right on Cavendish. Please be discreet.

The **Beatles Store** is at 231 Baker Street (Tube: Baker Street). It's small—some Beatles-logo T-shirts, mugs, pins, and old vinyl like you might have in your closet—and has nothing of historic value (open eight days a week, 10:00-18:30, tel. 020/7935-4464, www.beatlesstorelondon.co.uk; another rock memorabilia store is across the street).

25 percent cheaper online; combo-deal with the London Eye. Very flexible hours (check online), but roughly July-Aug and school holidays daily 8:30-18:00, Sept-June Mon-Fri 10:00-16:00, Sat-Sun 9:00-17:00, these are last entry times—it stays open roughly two hours later; Marylebone Road, Tube: Baker Street, tel. 0871-894-3000, www.madametussauds.com.

Crowd-Beating Tips: The ticket-buying line can be an hour or more (believe the posted signs about the wait). To avoid the ticket line, book a Priority Entrance ticket and reserve a time slot at least a day in advance. Or, pay royally for a Fast Track ticket in advance (available from souvenir stands and shops or at the TI), which gives you access to a dedicated entrance with shorter lines. The place is less crowded (for both buying tickets at the door and for simply enjoying the place) if you arrive after 15:00.

LONDON

Sherlock Holmes Museum

Around the corner from Madame Tussauds, this meticulous re-creation of the (fictional) apartment of the (fictional) detective sits at the (real) address of 221b Baker Street. The first-floor replica (so to speak) of Sherlock's study delights fans with the opportunity to play Holmes and Watson while sitting in authentic 18th-century chairs. The second and third floors offer fine exhibits on daily Victorian life, showing off furniture, clothes, pipes, paintings, and chamber pots; in other rooms, models are posed to enact key scenes from Sir Arthur Conan Doyle's famous books.

Cost and Hours: £15, daily 9:30-18:00, expect to wait 15 minutes or more—up to 2 hours in peak season; buy tickets inside the gift shop first, then get in line outside the museum (if you're traveling with a partner, send one person in to buy tickets while the other waits in the entrance line); large gift shop for Holmes connoisseurs, including souvenirs from the BBC-TV series; Tube: Baker Street, tel. 020/7935-8866, www.sherlock-holmes.co.uk.

Nearby: Fans of BBC-TV's *Sherlock* series starring Benedict Cumberbatch—which this museum doesn't cover—may want to grab a bite or snap a photo at Speedy's Café, the filming location for the show's 221b exterior (located near Euston Station at 187 North Gower Street, Tube: Euston Square).

Sights in The City

When Londoners say "The City," they mean the one-square-mile business center in East London that 2,000 years ago was Roman Londinium. The outline of the Roman city walls can still be seen in the arc of roads from Blackfriars Bridge to Tower Bridge. Within The City are 23 churches designed by Sir Christopher Wren, mostly just ornamentation around St. Paul's Cathedral. Today, while home to only 10,000 residents, The City thrives with around 400,000 office workers coming and going daily. It's a fascinating district to wander on weekdays, but since almost nobody actually lives there, it's dull in the evening and on Saturday and Sunday.

You can 🎧 download my free audio tour of The City, which peels back the many layers of history in this oldest part of London.

▲▲▲St. Paul's Cathedral

Wren's most famous church is the great St. Paul's, its elaborate interior capped by a 365-foot dome. Since World War II, St. Paul's has been Britain's symbol of resilience. Despite 57 nights of bombing,

the Nazis failed to destroy the cathedral, thanks to St. Paul's volunteer fire watchmen, who stayed on the dome. Today you can climb the dome for a great city view. The crypt (included with admission) is a world of historic bones and memorials, including Admiral Nelson's tomb and interesting cathedral models.

LONDON

Cost and Hours: £20, cheaper online, includes church entry, dome climb, crypt, tour, and audioguide; Mon-Sat 8:30-16:30 (dome opens at 9:30), closed Sun except for worship; Tube: St. Paul's, tel. 020/7246-8350, www.stpauls.co.uk.

Avoiding Lines: Purchasing online tickets in advance saves a little time (and a little money); otherwise the wait can be 15-45 minutes in summer and on weekends. To avoid crowds in general, arrive first thing in the morning.

Music and Church Services: Worship times are available on the church's website. Communion is generally Mon-Sat at 8:00 and 12:30. On Sunday, services are held at 8:00, 10:15 (Matins), 11:30 (sung Eucharist), 15:15 (evensong), and 18:00. The rest of the week, evensong is at 17:00 (Mon evensong is occasionally spoken, not sung). If you come 20 minutes early for evensong worship (under the dome), you may be able to grab a big wooden stall in the choir, next to the singers. On some Sundays, there's a free organ recital at 16:45.

Tours: There are 1.5-hour **guided tours** Mon-Sat at 10:00, 11:00, 13:00, and 14:00 (call to confirm or ask at church). Free 30-minute **"highlights" tours** are offered throughout the day. The **audioguide** (included with admission) contains video clips that show the church in action.

🎧 Download my free St. Paul's Cathedral **audio tour**.

Visiting the Cathedral: Even now, as skyscrapers encroach, the 365-foot-high dome of St. Paul's rises majestically above the rooftops of the neighborhood. The tall dome is set on classical columns, capped with a lantern, topped by a six-foot ball, and iced with a cross. As the first Anglican cathedral built in London after the Reformation, it is Baroque: St. Peter's in Rome filtered through clear-eyed English reason. Though often the site of historic funerals (Queen Victoria and Winston Churchill),

LONDON

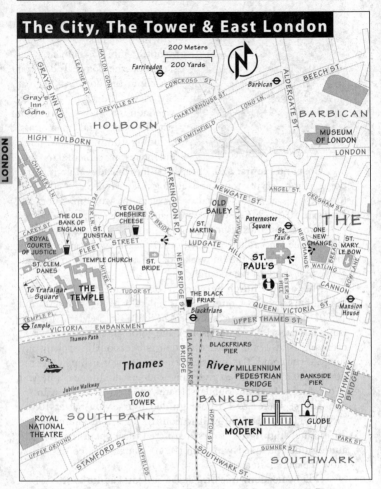

The City, The Tower & East London

St. Paul's most famous ceremony was a wedding—when Prince Charles married Lady Diana Spencer in 1981.

Start at the far back of the ❶ **nave,** behind the font. This big church feels big. At 515 feet long and 250 feet wide, it's Europe's fourth largest, after those in Rome (St. Peter's), Sevilla, and Milan. The spaciousness is accentuated by the relative lack of decoration. The simple, cream-colored ceiling and the clear glass in the windows light everything evenly. Wren wanted this: a simple, open church with nothing to hide. Unfortunately, only this entrance area keeps his original vision—the rest was encrusted with 19th-century Victorian ornamentation.

Ahead and on the left is the towering, black-and-white ❷ **Wellington Monument.** Wren would have been appalled, but his church has become so central to England's soul that many

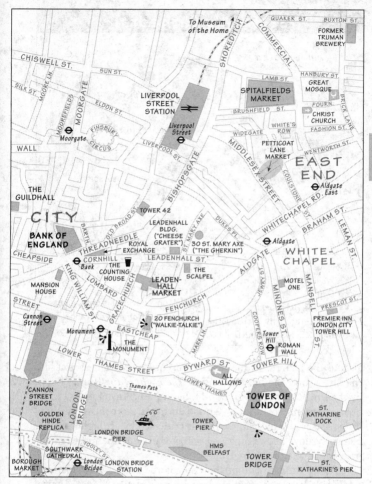

national heroes are buried here (in the basement crypt). General Wellington, Napoleon's conqueror at Waterloo (1815) and the embodiment of British stiff-upper-lippedness, was honored here in a funeral packed with 13,000 fans.

The ❸ **dome** you see from here, painted with scenes from the life of St. Paul, is only the innermost of three. From the painted interior of the first dome, look up through the opening to see the light-filled lantern of the second dome. Finally, the whole thing is covered on the outside by the third and final dome, the shell of lead-covered wood that you see from the street. Wren's ingenious three-in-one design was psychological as well as functional—he wanted a low, shallow inner dome so worshippers wouldn't feel diminished.

The ❹ **choir** area blocks your way, but you can see the altar at the far end under a golden canopy. Do a quick clockwise spin

LONDON

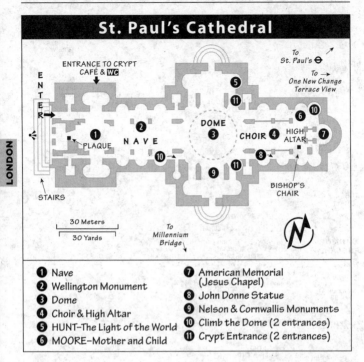

St. Paul's Cathedral

ENTRANCE TO CRYPT
CAFÉ & WC

To St. Paul's ⊖

To → One New Change Terrace View

E N T E R

5

11

DOME
3

10

6

PLAQUE

1

2

NAVE

CHOIR

4

HIGH ALTAR

7

10

8

11

9

BISHOP'S CHAIR

STAIRS

30 Meters
30 Yards

To Millennium Bridge

1 Nave
2 Wellington Monument
3 Dome
4 Choir & High Altar
5 HUNT–The Light of the World
6 MOORE–Mother and Child

7 American Memorial (Jesus Chapel)
8 John Donne Statue
9 Nelson & Cornwallis Monuments
10 Climb the Dome (2 entrances)
11 Crypt Entrance (2 entrances)

around the church. In the north transept (to your left as you face the altar), find the big painting **5** *The Light of the World* (1904), by the Pre-Raphaelite William Holman Hunt. Inspired by Hunt's own experience of finding Christ during a moment of spiritual crisis, the crowd-pleasing work was criticized by art highbrows for being "syrupy" and "simple"—even as it became the most famous painting in Victorian England.

Along the left side of the choir is the statue **6** *Mother and Child* (1983), by the great modern sculptor Henry Moore. Typical of Moore's work, this Mary and Baby Jesus—inspired by the sight of British moms nursing babies in WWII bomb shelters—renders a traditional subject in an abstract, minimalist way.

The area behind the main altar, with three stained-glass windows, is the **7** **American Memorial Chapel,** honoring the Americans who sacrificed their lives to save Britain in World War II. In brightly colored panes that arch around the big windows, spot the American eagle (center window, to the left of Christ), George Washington (right window, upper-right corner), and symbols of all 50 states (find your state seal). The Roll of Honor, a 500-page book under glass (immediately behind the altar), lists the names of 28,000 US servicemen and women based in Britain who gave their lives during the war.

Around the other side of the choir is a shrouded statue honoring
❽ **John Donne** (1573-1631), a passionate preacher in old St. Paul's,
as well as a great poet ("never wonder for whom the bell tolls—it tolls
for thee.") In the south transept are monuments to military greats
❾ **Horatio Nelson,** who fought Napoleon, and **Charles Cornwallis,**
who was finished off by George Washington at Yorktown.

Climb the Dome: The 528-step climb is worthwhile, and each
level (or gallery) offers something different. First you get to the
Whispering Gallery (257 shallow steps, with views of the church
interior). Whisper sweet nothings into the wall, and your partner
(and anyone else) standing far away can hear you. For best effects,
try whispering (not talking) with your mouth close to the wall,
while your partner stands a few dozen yards away with his or her
ear to the wall.

After another set of (steeper, narrower) stairs, you're at the
Stone Gallery, with views of London. Finally, a long, tight metal
staircase takes you to the very top of the cupola, the **Golden Gallery,**
with stunning, unobstructed views of the city. Looking west, you'll
see the London Eye, and you might be able to make out the towers
of Westminster Abbey. To the south, across the Thames, is the
rectangular smokestack of the Tate Modern, with Shakespeare's
Globe nestled nearby. To the east sprouts a glassy garden of
skyscrapers, including the 600-foot-tall, black-topped Tower 42, the
bullet-shaped 30 St. Mary Axe building (nicknamed "The Gherkin"),
and two more buildings easily ID'd by their nicknames—"The
Cheese Grater" and "The Walkie-Talkie." Farther in the distance,
the cluster of skyscrapers marks Canary Wharf. Just north of that
was the site of the 2012 Olympic Games, now a pleasant park.

Crypt: The crypt is a world of historic bones and interesting
cathedral models. Many legends are buried here—Horatio Nelson,
who wore down Napoleon; the Duke of Wellington, who finished
off Napoleon; and even Wren himself. Wren's actual tomb is marked
by a simple black slab with no statue, though he considered this
church to be his legacy. Back up in the nave, on the floor directly
under the dome, is Christopher Wren's name and epitaph (written
in Latin): "Reader, if you seek his monument, look around you."

▲Old Bailey

To view the British legal system in action—lawyers in little blond
wigs speaking legalese with an upper-crust accent—spend a few
minutes in the visitors' gallery at the Old Bailey courthouse, called
the "Central Criminal Court." Don't enter under the dome; continue up the block about halfway to the modern part of the building—the entry is at Warwick Passage.

Cost and Hours: Free, generally Mon-Fri 10:00-13:00 &
14:00-17:00 depending on caseload, last entry at 12:40 and 15:40

London's Best Views

Though London is a height-challenged city, you can get lofty per-spectives on it from several high-flying places. For some view-points, you need to pay admission, and at the bars or restaurants, you'll need to buy a drink.

London Eye: Ride the giant Ferris wheel for stunning London views. See page 123.

St. Paul's Dome: You'll earn a striking, unobstructed view by climbing hundreds of steps to the cramped balcony of the church's cupola. See page 113.

One New Change: Get fine, free views of St. Paul's Cathedral and surroundings—nearly as good as those from St. Paul's Dome—from the rooftop terrace of the One New Change shopping mall just behind and east of the church.

Tate Modern: One of the best, easiest, and cheapest views (free) is to head to the Tate Modern's annex—the Blavatnik Building—and ride the elevator to floor 10, where you'll enjoy sweeping views of the skyline (plus the Tate's own tower in the foreground). You can also ride to floor 6 of the main building. See page 126.

20 Fenchurch (a.k.a. "The Walkie-Talkie"): Get 360-degree views of London from the mostly enclosed Sky Garden, complete with a thoughtfully planned urban garden, bar, restaurants, and lots of locals. It's free to access but you'll need to make reservations in

but often closes an hour or so earlier, closed Sat-Sun, fewer cases in Aug; no kids under 14; 2 blocks northwest of St. Paul's on Old Bailey Street (down a tunnel called Warwick Passage, follow signs to public entrance), Tube: St. Paul's, tel. 020/7248-3277 www.cityoflondon.gov.uk.

Bag Check: Old Bailey has a strictly enforced policy of no bags, mobile phones, cameras, computers, or food. Small purses are OK (but no phones or cameras inside). You can check bags at many nearby businesses, including the Capable Travel agency just down the street at 4 Old Bailey (£5/bag).

The Guildhall

Hiding out in The City, the Guildhall offers visitors a grand medieval hall and a delightful painting gallery for free (Mon-Sat 10:00-17:00, Sun 12:00-16:00). This served as the meeting spot for guilds in medieval times, and still hosts about 100 professional as-sociations today. The **Guildhall Art Gallery** gives insight into old London society with mostly Victorian paintings.

▲Museum of London

This regular stop for local school kids gives the best overview of London history in town. Scale models and costumes help advance and bring photo ID (Mon-Fri 10:00-18:00, Sat-Sun 11:00-21:00, 20 Fenchurch Street, Tube: Monument, https://skygarden.london/sky-garden). If you can't get a reservation, try arriving before 10:00 (or 11:00 on weekends) and ask to go up. Once in, you can stay as long as you like.

National Portrait Gallery: A mod top-floor restaurant peers over Trafalgar Square and the Westminster neighborhood. See page 87.

Waterstones Bookstore: Its hip, low-key, top-floor café/bar has reasonable prices and sweeping views of the London Eye, Big Ben, and the Houses of Parliament (see page 45, on Sun bar closes one hour before bookstore, www.5thview.co.uk).

The Shard: The observation decks that cap this 1,020-foot-tall skyscraper offer London's most commanding views, but at an outrageously high price. See page 129.

Primrose Hill: For dramatic 360-degree city views, head to the huge grassy expanse at the summit of Primrose Hill, just north of Regent's Park (off Prince Albert Road, Tube: Chalk Farm or Camden Town, www.royalparks.org.uk/parks/the-regents-park).

The Thames River: Various companies run boat trips on the Thames, offering a unique vantage point and unobstructed, ever-changing views of great landmarks (see page 61).

you visualize everyday life in the city through history—from Neanderthals, to Romans, to Elizabethans, to Victorians, to Mods, to today. The displays are chronological, spacious, and informative without being overwhelming, with enough whiz-bang multimedia displays (including the Plague and the Great Fire) to spice up otherwise humdrum artifacts.

Cost and Hours: Free, daily 10:00-18:00, last entry one hour before closing, see the day's events board for special talks and tours, café, lockers, 150 London Wall at Aldersgate Street, Tube: Barbican or St. Paul's plus a 5-minute walk, tel. 020/7001-9844, www.museumoflondon.org.uk.

▲▲▲Tower of London

The Tower has served as a castle in wartime, a king's residence in peacetime, and, most notoriously, as the prison and execution site of rebels. You can see the crown jewels, take a witty Beefeater tour, and ponder the executioner's block that dispensed with troublesome heirs to the throne and a couple of Henry VIII's wives.

Cost and Hours: £30.30, cheaper online, family ticket available; Tue-Sat 9:00-17:30, Sun-Mon from 10:00; Nov-Feb closes one hour earlier; free Beefeater tours available, skippable audioguide-£5, Tube: Tower Hill, tel. 0844-482-7788, www.hrp.org.uk.

Advance Tickets: To avoid the long ticket-buying lines and save a few pounds off the gate price, buy tickets in advance for a specific day on the Tower website (print at home or collect on-site at group ticket office—see map).

Alternatively, you can buy a voucher on your way to the Tower at the Trader's Gate gift shop, located down the steps from the Tower Hill Tube stop (look for the blue awning down in the stairway, between the Tube station and the busy street). The voucher is good any day and can be exchanged for a ticket at the group ticket office.

Visiting the Tower: Even an army the size of the ticket line couldn't storm this castle. The ❶ **entrance gate** where you'll show your ticket was just part of two concentric rings of complete defenses.

As you enter, consult the daily event schedule, and consider catching a Beefeater tour.

When you're all set, go 50 yards straight ahead to the ❷ **traitors' gate.** This was the boat entrance to the Tower from the Thames. Princess Elizabeth, who was a prisoner here before she became Queen Elizabeth I, was carried down the Thames and through this gate on a barge, thinking about her mom, Anne Boleyn, who had been decapitated inside just a few years earlier. Many English leaders who fell from grace entered through here—Elizabeth was one of the lucky few to walk out.

Turn left to pass underneath the archway into the inner courtyard. The big, white tower in the middle is the ❸ **White Tower,** the original structure that gave this castle complex its name. William the Conqueror built it more than 950 years ago to put 15 feet of stone between himself and those he conquered. Over the centuries, the other walls and towers were built around it. Standing high above the rest of old London, the White Tower provided a gleaming reminder of the monarchy's absolute power over its subjects. If you made the wrong move here, you could be feasting on roast boar in the Banqueting Hall one night and chained to the walls of the prison the next. Torture ranged from stretching on the rack to the full monty: hanging by the neck until nearly dead, then "drawing" (cut open to be gutted), and finally quartering, with your giblets displayed on the walls as a warning.

Inside the White Tower is a ❹ **museum** with exhibits re-creating medieval life and the Tower's bloody history of torture and executions. The first suits of armor you see belonged to Henry

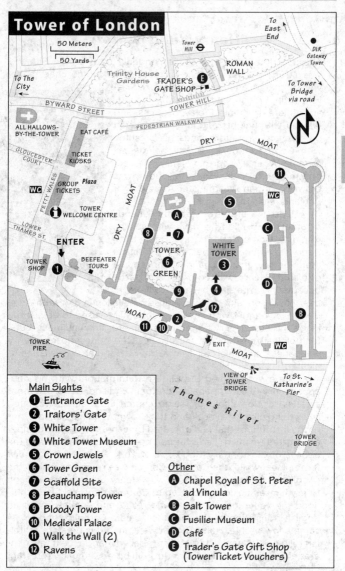

Tower of London

50 Meters
50 Yards

To East End

Tower Hill

DLR Gateway Tower

ROMAN WALL

Trinity House Gardens

TRADER'S GATE SHOP → **E**

To The City

To Tower Bridge via road

BYWARD STREET

TOWER HILL

PEDESTRIAN WALKWAY

ALL HALLOWS-BY-THE-TOWER

EAT CAFÉ

DRY MOAT

N

GLOUCESTER COURT

TICKET KIOSKS

WC

GROUP TICKETS

Plaza

DRY MOAT

WC

11

PETTY WALES

TOWER WELCOME CENTRE

A

5

WC

LOWER THAMES ST.

8

7

WHITE TOWER

C

ENTER

TOWER SHOP **1**

BEEFEATER TOURS

TOWER **6** GREEN

3

4

D

9

B

MOAT

2

12

11 **10**

TOWER PIER

EXIT

MOAT

WC

VIEW OF TOWER BRIDGE

To St. Katharine's Pier

Thames River

TOWER BRIDGE

Main Sights
1 Entrance Gate
2 Traitors' Gate
3 White Tower
4 White Tower Museum
5 Crown Jewels
6 Tower Green
7 Scaffold Site
8 Beauchamp Tower
9 Bloody Tower
10 Medieval Palace
11 Walk the Wall (2)
12 Ravens

Other
A Chapel Royal of St. Peter ad Vincula
B Salt Tower
C Fusilier Museum
D Café
E Trader's Gate Gift Shop (Tower Ticket Vouchers)

LONDON

VIII—on a horse, slender in his youth (c. 1515), then more heavyset by 1540 (with his bigger-is-better codpiece). Upstairs, St. John's Chapel (1080) is the oldest surviving part of the original Tower—and the oldest church in London. On the top floor are the Tower's actual execution ax and chopping block.

Across from the White Tower is the entrance to the **5 crown jewels.** You'll pass through a series of rooms with videos and ex-

Henry VIII (1491-1547)

The notorious king who single-handedly transformed England was a true Renaissance Man—six feet tall, handsome, charismatic, well-educated, and brilliant. He spoke English, Latin, French, and Spanish. A legendary athlete, he hunted, played tennis, and jousted with knights and kings. He played the lute and wrote folk songs; his "Pastime with Good Company", is still being performed. When 17-year-old Henry, the second monarch of the House of Tudor, was crowned king in Westminster Abbey, all of England rejoiced.

Henry left affairs of state in the hands of others, and filled his days with sports, war, dice, women, and the arts. But in 1529, Henry's personal life became a political atom bomb, and it changed the course of history. Henry wanted a divorce, partly because his wife had become too old to bear him a son, and partly because he'd fallen in love with Anne Boleyn, a younger woman who stubbornly refused to be just the king's mistress. Henry begged the pope for an annulment, but—for political reasons, not moral ones—the pope refused. Henry went ahead and divorced his wife anyway, and he was excommunicated.

The event sparked the English Reformation. With his defiance, Henry rejected papal authority in England. He forced monasteries to close, sold off some church land, and confiscated everything else for himself and the Crown. Within a decade, monastic institutions that had operated for centuries were left empty and gutted (many ruined sites can be visited today, including the abbeys of Glastonbury, St. Mary's at York, Rievaulx, and Lindisfarne). Meanwhile, the Catholic Church was reorganized into the (Anglican) Church of England, with Henry as its head. Though Henry himself basically adhered to Catholic doctrine, he discouraged the veneration of saints and relics, and commissioned an English translation of the Bible. Hard-core Catholics had to assume a low profile. Many English welcomed this break from Italian religious influence, but others rebelled. For the next few generations, England would suffer through bitter Catholic-Protestant differences.

Henry famously had six wives. The issue was not his love life (which could have been satisfied by his numerous mistresses), but the politics of royal succession. To guarantee the Tudor family's dominance, he needed a male heir born by a recognized queen.

Henry's first marriage, to Catherine of Aragon, had been arranged to cement an alliance with her parents, Ferdinand and Isabel of Spain. Catherine bore Henry a daughter, but no sons. Next came Anne Boleyn, who also gave birth to a daughter. After a turbulent few years with Anne and several miscarriages, a frustrated Henry had her beheaded at the Tower of London. His next wife, Jane Seymour, finally had a son (but Jane died soon after giving birth). A blind marriage with Anne of Cleves ended quickly when she proved to be both politically useless and ugly—the "Flanders Mare." Next, teen bride Catherine Howard ended up cheating on Henry, so she was executed. Henry finally found comfort—but no children—in his later years with his final wife, Catherine Parr.

In 1536 Henry suffered a serious accident while jousting. His health would never be the same. Increasingly, he suffered from festering boils and violent mood swings, and he became morbidly obese, tipping the scales at 400 pounds with a 54-inch waist.

Henry's last years were marked by paranoia, sudden rages, and despotism. He gave his perceived enemies the pink slip in his signature way—charged with treason and beheaded. (Ironically, Henry's own heraldic motto was "Coeur Loyal"—true heart.) Once-wealthy England was becoming depleted, thanks to Henry's expensive habits, which included making war on France, building and acquiring palaces (he had 50), and collecting fine tapestries and archery bows.

Henry forged a large legacy. He expanded the power of the monarchy, making himself the focus of a rising, modern nation-state. Simultaneously, he strengthened Parliament—largely because it agreed with his policies. He annexed Wales, and imposed English rule on Ireland (provoking centuries of resentment). He expanded the navy, paving the way for Britannia to soon rule the waves. And—thanks to Henry's marital woes—England would forever be a Protestant nation.

When Henry died at age 55, he was succeeded by his nine-year-old son by Jane Seymour, Edward VI. Weak and sickly, Edward died six years later. Next to rule was Mary, Henry's daughter from his first marriage. A staunch Catholic, she tried to brutally reverse England's Protestant Reformation, earning the nickname "Bloody Mary." Finally came Henry's daughter with Anne Boleyn—Queen Elizabeth I, who ruled a prosperous, expanding England, seeing her father's seeds blossom into the English Renaissance.

London abounds with "Henry" sights. He was born in Greenwich (at today's Old Royal Naval College) and was crowned in Westminster Abbey. He built a palace along Whitehall and enjoyed another at Hampton Court. At the National Portrait Gallery, you can see portraits of some of Henry's wives, and at the Tower you can see where he executed them. Henry is buried alongside his third wife, Jane Seymour, at Windsor Castle.

hibits showing the actual coronation items in the order that they're used whenever a new king or queen is crowned. The Sovereign's Scepter is encrusted with the world's largest cut diamond—the 530-carat Star of Africa, beefy as a quarter-pounder. The orb symbolizes how Christianity rules over the earth, a reminder that even a "divine monarch" is not above God's law. The Crown of the Queen Mother (Elizabeth II's famous mum, who died in 2002) has the 106-carat Koh-I-Noor diamond glittering on the front (considered unlucky for male rulers, it adorns the crown of the king's wife). The Imperial State Crown is what the Queen wears for official functions such as the State Opening of Parliament. Among its 3,733 jewels are Queen Elizabeth I's former earrings (the hanging pearls, top center), a stunning 13th-century ruby look-alike in the center, and Edward the Confessor's ring (the blue sapphire on top, in the center of the Maltese cross of diamonds).

Exiting the tower, turn right and walk past the White Tower, straight ahead to the grassy field called ❻ **Tower Green.** In medieval times, this was the "town square" for those who lived in the castle. Knights exercised and jousted here, and it was the last place of refuge in troubled times.

Near the middle of Tower Green is a granite-paved square, the ❼ **Scaffold Site.** It was here that enemies of the Crown would kneel before the king for the final time. On the left as you face the chapel is the ❽ **Beauchamp Tower** (pronounced "BEECH-um"), one of several places in the complex that housed Very Important Prisoners.

Down toward the river, at the bottom corner of the green is ❾ **Bloody Tower,** where Sir Walter Raleigh was imprisoned for 13 years and wrote the first volume of his *History of the World*.

Walk under the Bloody Tower, cross the cobbled road, and bear right a few steps to find the stairs up onto the wall to reach the ❿ **Medieval Palace,** built around 1240 by Henry III, the king most responsible for the expansive Tower of London complex we see today. From the throne room, continue up the stairs to ⓫ **walk the wall** for a fine view of Tower Bridge. Between the White Tower and the Thames are cages housing the ⓬ **ravens.** According to tradition, the Tower and the British throne are only safe as long as ravens are present here. Other sights at the Tower include the Salt Tower and the Fusilier Museum.

Tower Bridge

The iconic Tower Bridge (often mistakenly called London Bridge) was built in 1894 to accommodate the growing East End. While fully modern and hydraulically powered, the drawbridge was designed with a retro Neo-Gothic look.

The bridge is most interesting when the drawbridge lifts to let ships pass, as it does a thousand times a year (best viewed from the

Tower side of the Thames). For the bridge-lifting schedule, check the website or call.

You can tour the bridge at the **Tower Bridge Exhibition,** with a history display and a peek at the Victorian-era engine room that lifts the span. Included in your entrance is the chance to cross the bridge—138 feet above the road along a partially see-through glass walkway. As an exhibit, it's overpriced, though the adrenaline rush and spectacular city views from the walkway may help justify the cost.

Cost and Hours: £9.80, daily 10:00-18:00 in summer, 9:30-17:30 in winter, enter at northwest tower, Tube: Tower Hill, tel. 020/7403-3761, www.towerbridge.org.uk.

Nearby: The best remaining bit of London's **Roman Wall** is just north of the Tower (at the Tower Hill Tube station). The chic **St. Katharine Dock,** just east of Tower Bridge, has private yachts and mod shops. Across the bridge, on the South Bank, is the upscale Butlers Wharf area, as well as City Hall, museums, the Jubilee Walkway, and, towering overhead, the Shard.

Sights in East London

▲The East End

Immediately east of The City (and Liverpool Street Station), London's East End is a vibrant neighborhood with great eateries, lively markets, and interesting street art. It's also known as "Banglatown" for its Bangladeshi communities and curry houses along Brick Lane. Anchoring the area is Old Spitalfields Market, filled with merchants and creative food counters (see pages 151 and 191).

In medieval times, this was the less desirable end, in part because it was downwind from the noxious hide-tanning district. London's east/west disparity was exacerbated in Victorian times, when the wind carried the pollution of a newly industrialized London. And it was during this time that Jack the Ripper terrorized this neighborhood.

This area has also long been the city's arrival point for new immigrants, from the French Protestant Huguenots (late 16th century), to Ashkenazi Jews (late 19th century), to Bangladeshi refugees (1970s). This mixing of cultures—along with a spirit of

LONDON

East End

To Museum of the Home
To Columbia Flower Market
QUAKER ST.
CALVIN ST.
BUXTON ST.
COMMERCIAL
TRUMAN BREWERY (MARKETS) **7**
WOOD-SEER
SHOREDITCH
FOLGATE ST.
GREY EAGLE ST.
FOOD TRUCKS ☠
EAST END
LAMB ST.
HANBURY ST.
SPITALFIELDS MARKET **1**
TEN BELLS
MOSQUE
STREET ART **6**
BECK
PRINCELET ST.
APPOLD ST.
4
FOURNIER
BANGLA-TOWN
NATWEST
(NEW) (OLD)
BRUSHFIELD ST.
CRISPIN
☠ CHRIST CHURCH
HENEAGE ST.
LIVERPOOL STREET STATION
#149 & 242 **B**
Liverpool Street
ARTILLERY LN.
3
WHITE'S ROW
FASHION ST.
WIDEGATE
ARTILL PSG.
2
TOYNBEE
COMMERCIAL
MOORISH BUILDING
LIVERPOOL ST.
SWEDELAND COURT
MIDDLESEX ST.
5
STREET
BISHOPSGATE
WENTWORTH
IBIS STYLES CITY SHOREDITCH
WHITECHAPEL RD.
200 Meters
200 Yards
N
PETTICOAT LANE MARKET
Aldgate East
WHITE-CHAPEL

1 Old Spitalfields Market Eateries
2 Ottolenghi Spitalfields
3 The English Restaurant
4 St. John Bread & Wine Restaurant
5 Gunpowder
6 Meraz Café
7 Old Truman Brewery & Café 1001
☠ Ripper murder site

redevelopment—has given this area a wonderful energy that's well worth exploring.

▲Museum of the Home

This low-key but well-organized museum (formerly the Geffrye Museum) is housed in an 18th-century almshouse north of Liverpool Street Station. Its rooms are furnished, themed to everyday life in different times and all very well described. It's an intimate peek at the middle class as its comforts evolved from 1600 to 2000. In summer, explore the fragrant herb garden. The museum has been closed for renovation but should be reopened by the time you visit; check locally.

Cost and Hours: Free, £3 suggested donation, Tue-Sun 10:00-17:00, closed Mon, garden open April-Oct, 136 Kingsland Road, tel. 020/7739-9893, www.museumofthehome.org.uk.

Getting There: Take the Tube to Liverpool Street, then ride the bus 10 minutes north (bus #149 or #242—leave station through Bishopsgate exit and head left a few steps to find stop; hop off at the Pearson Street stop, just after passing the brick museum on the right). Or take the East London line on the Overground to the Hoxton stop, which is right next to the museum.

Sights on the South Bank

▲Jubilee Walkway

This riverside path is a popular pub-crawling pedestrian promenade that stretches all along the South Bank, offering grand views of the Houses of Parliament and St. Paul's. On a sunny day, this is the place to see  Londoners out strolling. The Walkway hugs the river except just east of London Bridge, where it cuts inland for a couple of blocks. It has been expanded into a 60-mile "Greenway" circling the city, including the 2012 Olympics site.

▲▲London Eye

This giant Ferris wheel, towering above London opposite Big Ben, is one of the world's highest observational wheels and London's answer to the Eiffel Tower. Riding it is a memorable experience, even though London doesn't have much of a skyline, and the price is borderline outrageous. Whether you ride or not, the wheel is a sight to behold.

The experience starts with an engaging, four-minute show combining a 4-D movie with wind and water effects. Then it's time to spin around the Eye. Twenty-eight people ride in each of its 32 air-conditioned capsules (representing the boroughs of London) for the 30-minute rotation (you go around only once). From the top of this 443-foot-high wheel—the second-highest public viewpoint in the city—even Big Ben looks small. Built to celebrate the new millennium, the Eye has become a permanent fixture on the London skyline and inspired countless other cities to build their own wheels.

Cost and Hours: £30, cheaper online, family ticket and combo-ticket with Madame Tussauds and other attractions available; daily 10:00-20:30 or later, Sept-May generally 11:00-18:00, check website for latest schedule, these are last-ascent times, Tube: Waterloo or Westminster. Thames boats come and go from London Eye Pier at the foot of the wheel.

Advance Tickets and Crowd-Beating Tips: The London

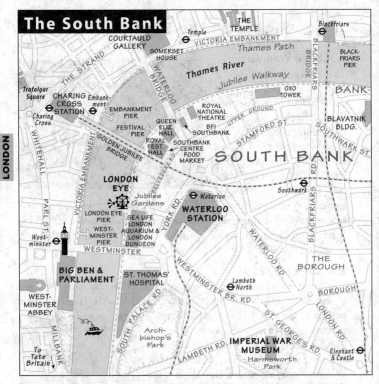

Eye is busiest between 11:00 and 17:00, especially on weekends year-round and every day in July and August. For visits during these times, buy timed-entry tickets online in advance at www. londoneye.com or in person at the box office (in the corner of the County Hall building nearest the Eye); day-of tickets can sell out. You can present your advance ticket on your phone; otherwise print it at home, retrieve it from an onsite ticket machine (bring your payment card and confirmation code), or stand in the "Ticket Collection" line. Even if you buy in advance, you may wait 30-45 minutes to board your capsule. The Fast Track ticket may still entail a wait up to 30 minutes—it's probably not worth the expense.

▲▲Imperial War Museum

This impressive museum covers the wars and conflicts of the 20th and 21st centuries. You can walk chronologically through World War I, to the rise of fascism, World War II, the Cold War, the Troubles in Northern Ireland, the wars in Iraq and Afghanistan, and terrorism. Rather than glorify war, the museum explores the human side of the wartime experience and its effect on people back home. It raises thoughtful questions about one of civilization's

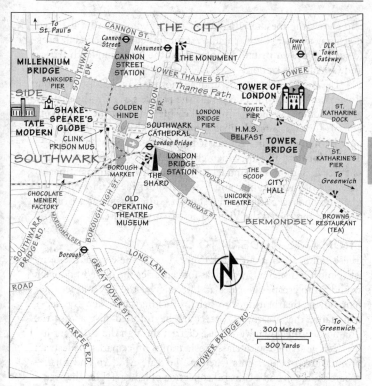

more uncivilized, persistent traits. Allow plenty of time; lots of artifacts, interactive experiences, and multimedia exhibits can be engrossing.

Cost and Hours: Free, £5 suggested donation, special exhibits extra, daily 10:00-18:00, last entry one hour before closing, Tube: Lambeth North or Elephant and Castle; buses #3, #12, and #159 from Westminster area; tel. 020/7416-5000, www.iwm.org.uk.

Visiting the Museum: Start in the atrium to grasp the massive scale of warfare as you wander among and under notable battle machines. The Spitfire plane overhead flew in the Battle of Britain. From here, the displays unfold chronologically as you work your way up from floor to floor. On level 0, enter **The First World War,** with hundreds of fascinating items. The highlight of the exhibit is a reconstructed trench, with a massive tank rearing overhead, where you're bombarded with the sounds of war. Climb the stairs for exhibits on **World War II.** A video clip shows the mesmerizing Adolf Hitler, who roused a defeated Germany to rearm for war again. At the museum shop, double back to see displays on Britain's fight against the Nazis in North Africa and Operation Overlord—i.e., D-Day.

Level 2, which may be under renovation in 2020, covers the **Post-War Years,** which began (as the plaque says) "In the shadow of The Bomb" (alongside an actual casing made for the Hiroshima bomb). Level 3 generally has **temporary exhibits** shedding light on why humans fight. The most powerful exhibit is on level 4— **The Holocaust.** Photos, video clips, and a few artifacts trace the sad story. A room-size model of the Auschwitz camp testifies to the scale of the slaughter and its banal orderliness. Crowning the museum on level 5, the **Lord Ashcroft Gallery** celebrates Britain's heroes who received the Victoria and George Crosses.

FROM TATE MODERN TO CITY HALL

These sights are in Southwark (SUTH-uck), the core of the tourist's South Bank. Southwark was for centuries the place Londoners would go to escape the rules and decency of the city and let their hair down. Bearbaiting, brothels, rollicking pubs, and theater— you name the dream, and it could be fulfilled just across the Thames. A run-down warehouse district through the 20th century, it's been gentrified with classy restaurants, office parks, pedestrian promenades, major sights (such as the Tate Modern and Shakespeare's Globe), and a colorful collection of lesser sights. The area is easy on foot and a scenic—though circuitous—way to connect the Tower of London with St. Paul's.

▲▲Tate Modern

This striking museum fills a former power station across the river from St. Paul's with a powerhouse collection including Dalí, Picasso, Warhol, and much more.

Cost and Hours: Free, £5 suggested donation, fee for special exhibits; daily 10:00- 18:00, Fri-Sat until 22:00, last entry to special exhibits 45 minutes before closing, especially crowded on weekend days (crowds thin out Fri and Sat evenings); view restaurant on top floor, across the Millennium Bridge from St. Paul's; Tube: Southwark, London Bridge, St. Paul's, Mansion House, or Blackfriars plus a 10-15-minute walk; or connect by Tate Boat museum ferry from Tate Britain—see page 63; tel. 020/7887-8888, www.tate.org.uk.

Tours: Free 45-minute guided tours are offered at the top of each hour between 11:00 and 16:00; free 10-minute gallery talks take place on occasion (see info desk for details).

Visiting the Museum: The permanent collection is generally on levels 2, 4, and part of level 3 of the Natalie Bell Building. Paintings are arranged according to theme, not artist. Paintings by Picasso, for example, might be scattered in different rooms on different levels. To help you get started, find the "Start Display" room on level 2—highlighting a range of artworks.

Since 1960, London has rivaled New York as a center for the visual arts. You'll find British artists displayed here—look for work by David Hockney, Henry Moore, and Barbara Hepworth. American art is also prominently represented—keep an eye out for abstract expressionist works by Mark Rothko and Jackson Pollock, and the pop art of Andy Warhol and Roy Lichtenstein. After you see the Old Masters of Modernism (Matisse, Picasso, Kandinsky, and so on), push your mental envelope with works by Pollock, Miró, Bacon, Picabia, Beuys, Twombly, and beyond.

You'll find temporary exhibits throughout the museum—some free, some requiring a special admission. Additionally, the main hall features a different monumental installation by a prominent artist each year. The museum's newer twisted-pyramid, 10-story Blavatnik Building also hosts changing themed exhibitions, performance art, experimental film, and interactive sculpture incorporating light and sound.

▲Millennium Bridge

The pedestrian bridge links St. Paul's Cathedral and the Tate Modern across the Thames. This is London's first new bridge in a century. When it opened, the $25 million bridge wiggled when people walked on it, so it promptly closed for repairs; 20 months and $8 million later, it reopened. Nicknamed the "blade of light" for its sleek minimalist design (370 yards long, four yards wide, stainless steel with teak planks), its clever aerodynamic handrails deflect wind over the heads of pedestrians.

▲▲Shakespeare's Globe

This replica of the original Globe Theatre was built, half-timbered and thatched, as it was in Shakespeare's time. (This is the first thatched roof constructed in London since they were outlawed after the Great Fire of 1666.) It serves as a working theater by night and offers tours by day. The original Globe opened in 1599, debuting Shakespeare's play *Julius*

Caesar. The Globe originally accommodated 2,200 seated and another 1,000 standing. Today, slightly smaller and leaving space for reasonable aisles, the theater holds 800 seated and 600 groundlings.

Its promoters brag that the theater melds "the three A's"—actors, audience, and architecture—with each contributing to the play. The working theater hosts authentic performances of Shakespeare's plays with actors in period costumes, modern interpretations of his works, and some works by other playwrights. For details on attending a play, see page 155.

The complex's smaller Sam Wanamaker Playhouse—an indoor, horseshoe-shaped Jacobean theater—allows the show to go on in the winter, when it's too cold for performances in the outdoor Globe. Seating fewer than 350, the playhouse is more intimate and sometimes uses authentic candle lighting for period performances. While the Globe mainly presents Shakespeare's works, the playhouse tends to focus on the works of his contemporaries (Jonson, Marlow, Fletcher) and some new plays, though there's some crossover.

Touring the Globe: Tours depart from the box office every half hour and last for 40 minutes (£17, £10 for kids 5-15; during outdoor theater season—April-mid-Oct—last tours depart Mon at 17:00, Tue-Sat at 12:30, Sun at 11:30; off-season last tours at 17:00; Tube: Mansion House or London Bridge plus a 10-minute walk; tel. 020/7902-1400, www.shakespearesglobe.com).

Eating: The **$$$ Swan at the Globe** café offers a sit-down restaurant (for lunch and dinner, reservations recommended, tel. 020/7928-9444, www.swanlondon.co.uk), a drinks-and-plates bar, and a sandwich-and-coffee cart (Mon-Fri 8:00-closing, depends on performance times, Sat-Sun from 10:00).

▲Southwark Cathedral

While made a cathedral only in 1905, this has been the neighborhood church since the 13th century, and comes with some interesting history. The enthusiastic docents give impromptu tours if you ask.

Cost and Hours: Free, £1 map serves as photo permit, Mon-Fri 8:00-18:00, Sat-Sun from 8:30, Tube: London Bridge, tel. 020/7367-6700, www.cathedral.southwark.anglican.org.

Music: The cathedral hosts evensong Sun at 15:00, Tue-Fri at

17:30, and some Sat at 16:00; organ recitals are Mon at 13:15 and music recitals Tue at 15:15 (call or check website to confirm times).

▲Old Operating Theatre Museum and Herb Garret

Climb a tight and creaky wooden spiral staircase to a church attic where you'll find a garret used to dry medicinal herbs, a fascinating exhibit on Victorian surgery, cases of well-described 19th-century medical paraphernalia, and a special look at "anesthesia, the defeat of pain." Then you stumble upon Britain's oldest operating theater, where limbs were sawed off way back in 1821.

Cost and Hours: £6.50, Tue-Sun 10:30-17:00, Mon from 14:00, 9a St. Thomas Street, Tube: London Bridge, tel. 020/7188-2679, oldoperatingtheatre.com.

The Shard

Rocketing dramatically 1,020 feet above the south end of the London Bridge, this addition to London's skyline is by far the tallest building in Western Europe...for now. Designed by Renzo Piano (best known as the co-architect of Paris' Pompidou Center), the glass-clad pyramid shimmers in the sun and its prickly top glows like the city's nightlight after dark. Its uppermost floors are set aside as public viewing galleries, but the ticket price is as outrageously high as the building itself, especially given that it's a bit far from London's most exciting landmarks. (For cheaper view opportunities in London, see the sidebar on page 114.)

Cost and Hours: £39—book online in advance, advance ticket includes free return ticket in case of bad weather, otherwise pay 25 percent more on-site; family ticket available, least crowded on weekday mornings, but perhaps better photo opportunities in the early evening (less haze); daily 10:00-22:00, shorter hours Oct-March; Tube: London Bridge—use London Bridge exit and follow signs, tel. 0844-499-7111, www.theviewfromtheshard.com.

HMS *Belfast*

This former Royal Navy warship, a veteran of World War II that took part in the D-Day invasion, clogs the Thames just upstream from the Tower Bridge. The huge vessel—now manned with wax sailors—thrills kids who always dreamed of sitting in a turret shooting off their imaginary guns. If you're into WWII warships, this is the ultimate. Otherwise, it's just an expensive opportunity to get lots of exercise with a nice view of the Tower Bridge.

Cost and Hours: £18, cheaper online, kids 5-15—£9, kids under 5—free, family ticket available, includes audioguide; daily 10:00-18:00, Nov-Feb until 17:00, last entry one hour before closing; Tube: London Bridge, tel. 020/7940-6300, www.iwm.org.uk/visits/hms-belfast.

LONDON

City Hall

The glassy, egg-shaped building near the south end of Tower Bridge is London's City Hall, designed by Sir Norman Foster, the architect who worked on London's Millennium Bridge and Berlin's Reichstag. Nicknamed "the Armadillo," City Hall houses the office of London's mayor—it's here that the mayor consults with the Assembly representatives of the city's 25 districts. An interior spiral ramp allows visitors to watch and hear the action below in the Assembly Chamber— ride the lift to floor 2 (the highest visitors can go) and spiral down. On the lower ground floor is a large aerial photograph of London and a handy cafeteria. Next to City Hall is the outdoor amphitheater called The Scoop (see page 158 for info on performances).

Cost and Hours: Free, open to visitors Mon-Thu 8:30-18:00, Fri until 17:30, closed Sat-Sun; Tube: London Bridge Station plus 10-minute walk, or Tower Hill Station plus 15-minute walk; tel. 020/7983-4000, www.london.gov.uk.

Sights in West London

▲▲Tate Britain

One of Europe's great art houses, Tate Britain specializes in British painting from the 16th century through modern times. The museum has a good representation of William Blake's religious sketches, the Pre-Raphaelites' naturalistic and detailed art, Gainsborough's aristocratic ladies, and the best collection anywhere of J. M. W. Turner's swirling works.

Cost and Hours: Free, £4 suggested donation, fee for special exhibits; daily 10:00-18:00, last entry 45 minutes before closing; free tours generally daily; on the Thames River, south of Big Ben and north of Vauxhall Bridge, Tube: Pimlico, Tate Boat museum ferry goes directly to the museum from Tate Modern— see page 63; tel. 020/7887-8888, www.tate.org.uk.

Tours: Free guided tours are generally offered daily at 11:00 (the best overview tour), with specialty tours at 12:00, 14:00, and 15:00.

Visiting the Museum: Works from the early centuries are

located in the west half of the building (to your left), and 20th-century art is in the east half. Also to the east, in the adjacent Clore Gallery, are the works of J. M. W. Turner, John Constable, and William Blake. The Tate rotates its vast collection of paintings, so it's difficult to predict exactly which works will be on display. Pick up a map as you enter (£1 suggested donation) or download the museum's helpful app for a room-by-room guide.

1700-1800—Art Blossoms: With peace at home (under three King Georges), a strong overseas economy, and a growing urban center in London, England's artistic life began to bloom. As the English grew more sophisticated, so did their portraits. Painters branched out into other subjects, capturing slices of everyday life (find William Hogarth's unflinchingly honest portraits, and Thomas Gainsborough's elegant, educated women).

1800-1850—The Industrial Revolution: Newfangled inventions were everywhere, but along with technology came factories coating towns with soot, urban poverty, regimentation, and clock-punching. Many artists rebelled against "progress" and the modern world. They escaped the dirty cities to commune with nature. Or they found a new spirituality in intense human emotions, expressed in dramatic paintings of episodes from history. In rooms dedicated to the 1800s, you may see a number of big paintings devoted to the power of nature.

1837-1901—The Victorian Era: In the world's wealthiest nation, the prosperous middle class dictated taste in art. They admired paintings that were realistic (showcasing the artist's talent and work ethic), depicting slices of everyday life. Some paintings tug at the heartstrings, with scenes of parting couples, the grief of death, or the joy of families reuniting.

Overdosed with the gushy sentimentality of their day, a band of 20-year-old artists—including Sir John Everett Millais, Dante Gabriel Rossetti, and William Holman Hunt—said "Enough!" and dedicated themselves to creating less saccharine art (the Pre-Raphaelites). Like the Impressionists who followed them, they donned their scarves, barged out of the stuffy studio, and set up outdoors, painting trees, streams, and people, like scientists on a field trip. Still, they often captured nature with such a close-up clarity that it's downright unnatural.

British Impressionism: Realistic British art stood apart from the modernist trends in France, but some influences drifted across the Channel (Rooms 1890 and 1900). John Singer Sargent (American-born) studied with Parisian Impressionists, learning the thick, messy brushwork and play of light at twilight. James Tissot used Degas' snapshot technique to capture a crowded scene from an odd angle. And James McNeill Whistler (born in America, trained

LONDON

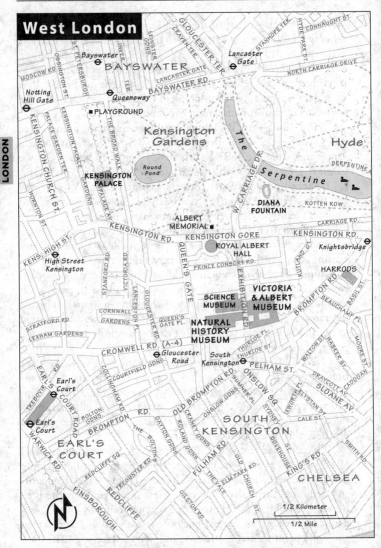

in Paris, lived in London) composed his paintings like music—see some of his paintings' titles.

1900-1950—World Wars: As two world wars whittled down the powerful British Empire, it still remained a major cultural force. British art mirrored many of the trends and "-isms" pioneered in Paris (Room 1930). You'll see Cubism like Picasso's, abstract art like Mondrian's, and so on. But British artists also continued the British tradition of realistic paintings of people and landscapes.

If British painters were less than avant-garde, their sculptors were cutting edge. Henry Moore's statues—mostly female, mostly

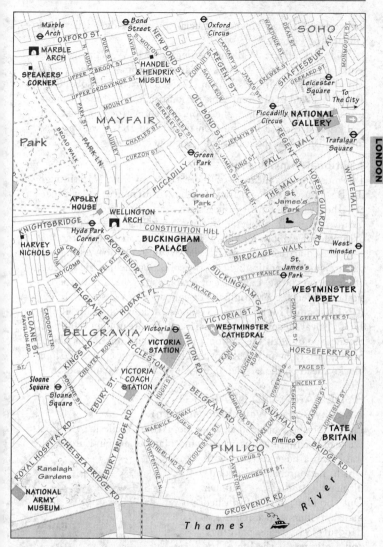

LONDON

reclining—capture the human body in a few simple curves, with minimal changes to the rock itself. Francis Bacon has become Britain's best-known 20th-century painter, exemplifying the angst of the early post-WWII years. His deformed half-humans/half-animals express the existential human predicament of being caught in a world not of your making, isolated and helpless to change it.

1950-2000—Modern World: No longer a world power, Britain in the Swinging '60s became a major exporter of pop culture. British art's traditional strengths—realism, portraits, landscapes, and slice-of-life scenes—were redone in the modern style. Look for works by David Hockney, Lucian Freud, Bridget Riley, and Gilbert and George.

Clore Gallery: Walking through J. M. W. Turner's life's work, you can watch Turner's style evolve from clear-eyed realism to hazy proto-Impressionism (1775-1851). You'll also see how Turner dabbled in different subjects: landscapes, seascapes, Roman ruins, snapshots of Venice, and so on. The corner room of the Clore Gallery is dedicated to John Constable (1776-1837), who painted the English landscape realistically, without idealizing it.

▲National Army Museum

This museum tells the story of the British army from 1415 through the Bosnian conflict and Iraq, and how it influences today's society. The five well-signed galleries are neatly arranged by theme—"Army," "Battle," "Soldier," "Society," and "Insight"—with plenty of interactive exhibits for kids. History buffs appreciate the carefully displayed artifacts, from 17th-century uniforms to Wellington's battle cloak. Other highlights of the collection include the skeleton of Napoleon's horse, Lawrence of Arabia's silk robe, and Burberry's signature trench coat (originally designed for WWI soldiers).

Cost and Hours: Free, £5 suggested donation, daily 10:00-17:30; Royal Hospital Road, Chelsea, Tube: 10-minute walk from Sloane Square, exit the station and head south on Lower Sloane Street, turn right on Royal Hospital Road, the museum is two long blocks ahead on the left, tel. 020/7730-0717, www.nam.ac.uk.

HYDE PARK AND NEARBY
▲Apsley House (Wellington Museum)

Having beaten Napoleon at Waterloo, Arthur Wellesley, the First Duke of Wellington, was once the most famous man in Europe. He was given a huge fortune, with which he purchased London's ultimate address, Number One London. His refurbished mansion offers a nice interior, a handful of world-class paintings, and a glimpse at the life of the great soldier and two-time prime minister. The highlight is the large ballroom, the Waterloo

Gallery, decorated with Anthony van Dyck's *Charles I on Horseback* (over the main fireplace), Diego Velázquez's earthy *Water-Seller of Seville* (to the left of Van Dyck), and Jan Steen's playful *Dissolute Household* (to the right). Just outside the door, in the Portico Room, is a large portrait of the Duke of Wellington by Francisco Goya. The place is well described by the included audioguide, which has sound bites from the current Duke of Wellington (who still lives at Apsley).

Cost and Hours: £10.30, Wed-Sun 11:00-17:00, closed Mon-Tue, shorter hours Nov-March, open only Sat-Sun in Jan-March, 20 yards from Hyde Park Corner Tube station, tel. 020/7499-5676, www.english-heritage.org.uk.

▲Hyde Park and Speakers' Corner

London's "Central Park," originally Henry VIII's hunting grounds, has more than 600 acres of lush greenery, Santander Cycles rental stations, the huge man-made Serpentine Lake (with rental boats and a lakeside swimming pool), the royal Kensington Palace (described next), and the ornate Neo-Gothic Albert Memorial across from the Royal Albert Hall (for more about the park, see www.royalparks.org.uk/parks/hyde-park). The western half of the park is known as Kensington Gardens. The park is huge—study a Tube map to choose the stop nearest to your destination.

On Sundays, from just after noon until early evening, **Speakers' Corner** offers soapbox oratory at its best (northeast corner of the park, Tube: Marble Arch).

Characters climb their stepladders, wave their flags, pound emphatically on their sandwich boards, and share what they are convinced is their wisdom. Regulars have resident hecklers who know their lines and are always ready with a verbal jab or barb. "The grass roots of democracy" is actually a holdover from when the gallows stood here and the criminal was allowed to say just about anything he wanted to before he swung. I dare you to raise your voice and gather a crowd—it's easy to do.

The Princess Diana Memorial Fountain honors the "People's Princess," who once lived in nearby Kensington Palace. The low-key circular stream, great for cooling off your feet on a hot day, is in the south-central part of the park, near the Albert Memorial and Serpentine Gallery (Tube: Knightsbridge). A similarly named but different sight, the Diana, Princess of Wales Memorial Playground, in the park's northwest corner, is loads of fun for kids (Tube: Queensway).

Kensington Palace

For nearly 150 years (1689-1837), Kensington was the royal residence, before Buckingham Palace became the official home of the monarch. Sitting primly on its pleasant parkside grounds, the palace gives a barren yet regal glimpse into royal life—particularly that of Queen Victoria, who was born and raised here.

After Queen Victoria moved the monarchy to Buckingham Palace, lesser royals bedded down at Kensington. Princess Diana lived here both during and after her marriage to Prince Charles (1981-1997). More recently, Will and Kate moved in. However—as many disappointed visitors discover—none of these more recent apartments are open to the public. The palace hosts a revolving series of temporary exhibits, some great, others not so. To see what's on during your visit, check online.

Cost and Hours: £17.50; daily 10:00-18:00, Nov-Feb until 16:00, last entry one hour before closing; a long 10-minute stroll through Kensington Gardens from either High Street Kensington or Queensway Tube stations, tel. 0844-482-7788, www.hrp.org.uk.

Outside: Garden enthusiasts enjoy popping into the secluded Sunken Garden, 50 yards from the exit. Consider afternoon tea at the nearby Orangery (see page 194), built as a greenhouse for Queen Anne in 1704.

▲▲▲Victoria and Albert Museum

The world's top collection of decorative arts encompasses 2,000 years of art and design (ceramics, stained glass, fine furniture, clothing, jewelry, carpets, and more), displaying a surprisingly interesting and diverse assortment of crafts from the West, as well as Asian and Islamic cultures. There's much to see, including Raphael's tapestry cartoons, Leonardo da Vinci's notebooks, the huge Islamic Ardabil Carpet (4,914 knots in every 10 square centimeters), a cast of Trajan's Column that depicts the emperor's conquests, and pop culture memorabilia, including the jumpsuit Mick Jagger wore for the Rolling Stones' 1972 world tour.

Cost and Hours: Free, £5 donation requested, fee for some special exhibits, daily 10:00-17:45, some galleries open Fri until 22:00, free tours daily, much-needed map-£1 donation; on Cromwell Road in South Kensington, Tube: South Kensington, from the Tube station a long tunnel leads directly to museum, tel. 020/7942-2000, www.vam.ac.uk.

Visiting the Museum: In the Grand Entrance lobby, look up into the rotunda to see the ❶ **Dale Chihuly chandelier,** epitomizing the spirit of the V&A's collection—beautiful manufactured objects that demonstrate technical skill and innovation, wedding the old with the new, and blurring the line between arts and crafts.

Now look up to the balcony (above the shop) and see the pointed arches of the ❷ **Hereford Screen,** a 35-by-35-foot, eight-ton rood screen (built for the Hereford Cathedral's sacred altar area). It looks medieval, but it was created with the most modern materials the Industrial Revolution could produce. George Gilbert Scott (1811-1878), who built the screen, redesigned much of London in the Neo-Gothic style, restoring old churches such as Westminster Abbey, renovating the Houses of Parliament, and building new structures like St. Pancras Station and the Albert Memorial—some 700 buildings in all.

LONDON

The V&A has (arguably) the best collection of Italian Renaissance sculpture outside Italy. One prime example is ❸ *Samson Slaying a Philistine,* by Giambologna (c. 1562), carved from a single block of marble, which shows the testy Israelite warrior rearing back, brandishing the jawbone of an ass, preparing to decapitate a man who'd insulted him.

The ❹ **Medieval and Renaissance Galleries** display 1,200 years of decorative arts, showing how the mix of pagan-Roman and medieval-Christian elements created modern Europe. In Room 8 is a glass case displaying the blue-and-gold, shoebox-sized ❺ **Becket Casket,** which contains the mortal remains (or relics) of St. Thomas Becket, who was brutally murdered. The enamel-and-metal work box is a specialty of Limoges, France. In Room 10a, you'll run into the ❻ **Boar and Bear Hunt Tapestry.** Though most medieval art depicted the Madonna and saints, this colorful wool tapestry—woven in Belgium—provides a secular slice of life.

Two floors up, you'll see the tiny, pocket-size ❼ **notebook by Leonardo da Vinci** (Codex Forster III, 1490-1493), which dates from years when he was living in Milan, shortly before undertaking his famous *Last Supper* fresco. The book's contents are all over the map: meticulous sketches of the human head, diagrams illustrating nature's geometrical perfection, a horse's leg for a huge equestrian statue, and even drawings of the latest ballroom fashions. The adjacent computer lets you scroll through three of his notebooks and even flip his backwards handwriting to make it readable.

Back on level 0, enter Room 46b, and find ❽ **Michelangelo casts** and other replica statues. These plaster-cast versions of famous Renaissance statues allowed 19th-century art students who

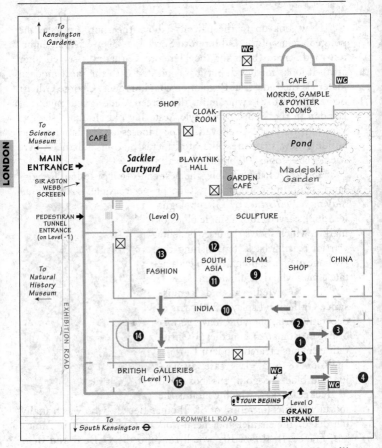

couldn't afford a rail pass to study the classics. In Room 42, you'll see **⑨ Islamic art,** reflecting both religious influences and a sophisticated secular culture. Many Islamic artists expressed themselves with beautiful but functional objects, such as the 630-square-foot Ardabil Carpet (1539-1540), which likely took a dozen workers years to make. Also in the room are ceramics and glazed tile—all covered top to bottom in similarly complex patterns. The intricate interweaving, repetition, and unending lines suggest the complex, infinite nature of God (Allah).

In the hallway (technically "Room" 47b) is a glass case with a statue of **⑩ Shiva Nataraja,** one of the hundreds, if not thousands, of godlike incarnations of Hinduism's eternal being, Brahma. As long as Shiva keeps dancing, the universe will continue. In adjoining Room 41, a glass case in the center of the room contains **⑪ possessions of Emperor Shah Jahana,** including a cameo portrait, thumb ring, and wine cup (made of white nephrite jade, 1657). Shah Jahan—or "King of the World"—ruled the largest empire of

Victoria & Albert Museum Tour

1. Dale Chihuly Chandelier
2. Hereford Screen (above lobby)
3. GIAMBOLOGNA – Samson Slaying a Philistine
4. Medieval & Renaissance Galleries
5. Becket Casket
6. Boar & Bear Hunt Tapestry
7. Stairs to Leonardo Notebook
8. Michelangelo Casts
9. Islamic Art
10. Shiva Nataraja Statue
11. Possessions of Emperor Shah Jahan
12. Tipu's Tiger
13. Fashion Galleries
14. RAPHAEL – Tapestry Cartoons
15. British Galleries
16. Stairs up to Jewelry, Theater & British Silver

TEMPORARY EXHIBITS

To 16

JAPAN

CAST COURT

ROOM 46

CAST COURT

8

WC

KOREA

STAIRS TO CAST COURTS VIEW

7

5

6

ELEVATOR/LIFT

Not to Scale

To Harrods & Hyde Park Corner →

BROMPTON ROAD

LONDON

the day, covering northern India, Pakistan, and Afghanistan. At the far end of Room 41 is the huge wood-carved **12 Tipu's Tiger,** a life-size robotic toy, once owned by an oppressed Indian sultan. When you turned the crank, the Brit's left arm would flail, and both he and the tiger would roar through organ pipes. (The mechanism still works.)

The **13 Fashion Galleries** display centuries of English fashion, from ladies' underwear, hoop skirts, and rain gear to high-society evening wear, men's suits, and more. Across the hall are **14 Raphael's tapestry cartoons.** The V&A owns seven of these full-size designs (approximately 13 by 17 feet, done in tempera on paper, now mounted on canvas). The cartoons were sent to factories in Brussels, cut into strips (see the lines), and placed on the looms.

Upstairs, Room 57 is the heart of the **15 British Galleries,** which cover the era of Queen Elizabeth I. Find rare miniature portraits—a popular item of the day—including Hilliard's oft-reproduced *Young Man Among Roses* miniature, capturing the romance of a Shakespeare sonnet. Back in the Grand Entrance lobby, climb the staircase to level 2 to see ⓰ **jewelry, theater artifacts, silver,** and more.

▲▲Natural History Museum

Across the street from the Victoria and Albert, this mammoth museum is housed in a giant and wonderful Victorian, Neo-Romanesque building. It was built in the 1870s specifically for the huge collection (50 million specimens). Exhibits are wonderfully explained, with lots of creative, interactive displays. It covers everything from life ("creepy crawlies," human biology, our place in evolution, and awe-inspiring dinosaurs) to earth science (meteors, volcanoes, and earthquakes).

Cost and Hours: Free, £5 donation requested, fee for special exhibits, daily 10:00-18:00, helpful £1 map, long tunnel leads directly from South Kensington Tube station to museum (follow signs), tel. 020/7942-5000, exhibit info and reservations tel. 020/7942-5011, www.nhm.ac.uk. Free visitor app available via the "Visit" section of the website.

▲Science Museum

Next door to the Natural History Museum, this sprawling wonderland for curious minds is kid-perfect, with themes such as measuring time, exploring space, climate change, the evolution of modern medicine, and the Information Age. It offers hands-on fun, with trendy technology exhibits, a state-of-the-art IMAX theater (shows—£11, £9 for kids, family ticket avail-

able), the Garden—a cool play area for children up to age seven, plus several other pay-to-enter attractions, including a virtual-reality spacecraft descent to Earth (£7) and Wonderlab kids area (£8, £6 for kids). Look for the family "What's On" brochure and ask about tours and demonstrations at the info desk.

Cost and Hours: Free, £5 donation requested, daily 10:00-18:00, last entry 45 minutes before closing, Exhibition Road, Tube: South Kensington, tel. 0333-241-4000, www.sciencemuseum.org.uk.

Sights in Greater London

EAST OF LONDON
▲▲Greenwich

This borough of London is an easy, affordable boat trip or DLR (Docklands Light Railway) journey from downtown. Along with majestic, picnic-perfect parks are the stately trappings of Britain's proud nautical heritage (the restored *Cutty Sark* clipper, the over-the-top-ornate retirement home for sailors at the Old Royal Naval College, and the comprehensive National Maritime Museum). It's also home to the Royal Observatory Greenwich, with a fine museum on how Greenwich Mean Time came to be and a chance to straddle the eastern and western hemispheres at the prime meridian. Boasting several top-notch museums (including some free ones), Greenwich is worth considering and easy to combine with a look at the Docklands (described later).

Getting There: For maximum efficiency and sightseeing, take the boat there for the scenery and commentary, and take the DLR back to avoid late-afternoon boat crowds (this plan also allows you to stop at the Docklands on the way home).

Various tour boats—with commentary and open-deck seating (2/hour, 30-75 minutes)—and faster Thames Clippers (every 20-30 minutes, 20-55 minutes) depart from several piers in central London. Thames Clippers also connects Greenwich to the Docklands' Canary Wharf Pier (2-3/hour, 15 minutes).

Docklands Light Railway (DLR) runs from the Bank-Monument Station to Cutty Sark Station in central Greenwich; it's one stop before the main—but less central—Greenwich Station (departs at least every 10 minutes, 20-minute ride, all in Zone 2).

Or, catch bus #188 from Russell Square near the British Museum (about 45 minutes to Greenwich).

Eating: Greenwich's parks are picnic perfect, especially around the National Maritime Museum and Royal Observatory. Greenwich Market offers an international variety of tasty food stalls. Greenwich has almost 100 pubs. **$$$ The Old Brewery,** in the Discover Greenwich center, is a gastropub decorated with all things beer.

Markets: The Greenwich Market is an entertaining mini Covent Garden, located in the middle of the block between the Cutty Sark DLR station and the Old Royal Naval College (farmers market, arts and crafts, and food stands; daily 10:00-17:30; antiques Mon-Tue and Thu-Fri, www.greenwichmarketlondon.com).

▲▲*Cutty Sark*

When first launched in 1869, the Scottish-built *Cutty Sark* was the last of the great China tea clippers and the queen of the seas. She

LONDON

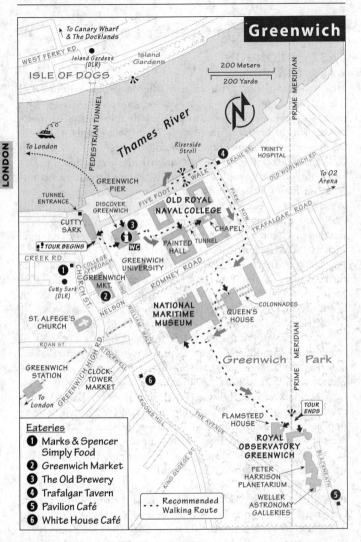

Greenwich

To Canary Wharf & The Docklands

WEST FERRY RD.
ISLE OF DOGS
Island Gardens (DLR)
Island Gardens
200 Meters
200 Yards

PRIME MERIDIAN

Thames River

To London

PEDESTRIAN TUNNEL

Riverside Stroll

CRANE ST.
TRINITY HOSPITAL
OLD WOOLWICH RD.
To O2 Arena

FIVE FOOT WALK
PARK ROW

GREENWICH PIER

TUNNEL ENTRANCE

DISCOVER GREENWICH

OLD ROYAL NAVAL COLLEGE

CHAPEL
TRAFALGAR ROAD

CUTTY SARK

TOUR BEGINS

WC

PAINTED HALL

TUNNEL

CREEK RD.

COLLEGE APPROACH

GREENWICH UNIVERSITY

ROMNEY ROAD

Cutty Sark (DLR)

GREENWICH MKT.

CHURCH ST.
KING WILLIAM WALK
NELSON

ST. ALFEGE'S CHURCH

NATIONAL MARITIME MUSEUM

QUEEN'S HOUSE

COLONNADES

ROAN ST.

GREENWICH HIGH RD.

PRIME MERIDIAN

Greenwich Park

GREENWICH STATION

CLOCK-TOWER MARKET

STOCKWELL

CROOMS HILL

THE AVENUE

FLAMSTEED HOUSE

TOUR ENDS

To London

KING GEORGE ST.

ROYAL OBSERVATORY GREENWICH

PETER HARRISON PLANETARIUM

BLACKHEATH

WELLER ASTRONOMY GALLERIES

Eateries
1. Marks & Spencer Simply Food
2. Greenwich Market
3. The Old Brewery
4. Trafalgar Tavern
5. Pavilion Café
6. White House Café

- - - Recommended Walking Route

was among the fastest clippers ever built, the culmination of centuries of ship design. With 32,000 square feet of sail—and favorable winds—she could travel 300 miles in a day. But as a new century dawned, steamers began to outmatch sailing ships for speed, and by the mid-1920s the *Cutty Sark* was the world's last operating clipper ship.

In 2012, the ship was restored and reopened with a spectacular new glass-walled display space (though one critic groused that the ship now "looks like it has run aground in a giant greenhouse"). Displays explore the *Cutty Sark*'s 140-year history and the cargo she carried—everything from tea to wool to gunpowder—as she raced between London and ports all around the world.

Cost and Hours: £15, cheaper online, kids ages 4-15—£7.50, free for kids under age 4, family tickets available, combo-ticket with Royal Observatory—£26.25, kids combo-ticket—£17.60; daily 10:00-17:00; to skip the ticket-buying line reserve timed-entry tickets online or by phone, or show up around 13:00; unnecessary £6 guidebook, reservation tel. 020/8312-6608, www.rmg.co.uk.

Old Royal Naval College

Despite the name, these grand structures were built (1692) as a veterans' hospital to house disabled and retired sailors who'd served their country. In 1873, the hospital was transformed into one of the world's most prestigious universities for training naval officers. Today, the buildings host university students, music students, business conventions, concerts, and film crews drawn to the awe-inspiring space.

▲Painted Hall

Originally intended as a dining hall for pensioners, this sumptuously painted room was deemed too glorious (and, in the winter, too cold) for that purpose. So almost as soon as it was completed, it became simply a showcase for visitors. Impressive as it is, the admission is quite steep to see gigantic paintings by an artist you've never heard of, featuring second-rate royals. But those who appreciate artistic spectacles and picking out lavish details will find it worthwhile.

Cost and Hours: £12, daily 10:00-17:00, sometimes closed for private events, www.ornc.org. Ticket includes audioguide and a 45-minute guided tour of the Old Royal Naval College grounds, not including the Painted Hall (departs from Discover Greenwich at the top of each hour.

▲National Maritime Museum

Great for anyone interested in the sea, this museum holds everything from a giant working paddlewheel to the uniform Admiral Horatio Nelson wore when he was killed at Trafalgar. A big glass roof tops three levels of slick, modern, kid-friendly exhibits about all things seafaring.

Cost and Hours: Free, daily 10:00-17:00, tel. 020/8858-4422, www.rmg.co.uk. The museum hosts frequent family-oriented events—singing, treasure hunts, and storytelling—particularly on weekends; ask at the desk. Listen for announcements alerting visitors to free tours on various topics.

▲▲Royal Observatory Greenwich

Located on the prime meridian (0° longitude), this observatory is famous as the point from which all time and distances on earth are measured. It was here that astronomers studied the heavens in order to help seafarers navigate. In the process, they used the constancy of the stars to establish standards of measurement for time and distance used by the whole world.

Cost and Hours: £16, includes audioguide, combo-ticket with *Cutty Sark*—£26.25; daily 10:00-17:00; tel. 020/8858-4422, reservations tel. 020/8312-6608, www.rmg.co.uk.

Visiting the Observatory: A visit here gives you a taste of the sciences of astronomy, timekeeping, and seafaring—and how they all meld together—along with great views over Greenwich and the distant London skyline. In the courtyard, snap a selfie straddling the famous prime meridian line in the pavement. In the museum, there's the original 1600s-era observatory and several early telescopes. You'll see the famous clocks from the 1700s that first set the standard of global time, as well as more recent timekeeping devices.

The **Weller Astronomy Galleries** has interactive, kid-pleasing displays allowing you to guide a space mission and touch a 4.5-billion-year-old meteorite (free, daily 10:00-17:00). And the state-of-the-art, 120-seat **Peter Harrison Planetarium** offers entertaining and informative shows several times a day where they project a view of the heavens onto the interior of the dome (£10, shows about every 45 minutes during the observatory's opening times, no morning shows on school days, check schedule online).

▲The Docklands

Nestled around a hairpin bend in the Thames, this area was Lon-

don's harbor and ware-
house district back in the
19th century, when Bri-
tannia ruled the waves.
Today, glittering new skyscrapers rise from those
historic canals and docks.

The heart of the
Docklands is the Isle of
Dogs, a marshy peninsula
in the river's curve. But don't expect Jolly Olde England here. The
Docklands is more about businesspeople in suits, creatively planned
parks, art-filled plazas, and chain restaurants. Even so, traces of its
rugged dockworker past survive. You'll see canals, former docks,
brick warehouses, and a fine history museum. Most impressive of
all, there's not a tourist in sight.

WEST OF LONDON

Because these two sights are in the same general direction, you
can visit both in one day. Take the train from London Waterloo
to Hampton Court Palace, then taxi to Kew Gardens (£20, about
30 minutes). If you're on a tight budget, the transit connection between Hampton Court and Kew is long but doable: Take bus #R68
from Hampton Court Station to the West Park Road stop (about
one hour), then walk about a half-mile to the Kew Gardens gate
(walk up West Park Road to, then through, the Kew Gardens train
station).

▲▲Kew Gardens

For a fine riverside park and a palatial greenhouse jungle to swing
through, take the Tube or the boat to every botanist's favorite escape, Kew Gardens. While to most visitors the Royal Botanic Gardens of Kew are simply a delightful opportunity to wander among
50,000 different types of plants, to the hardworking organization
that runs them, the gardens are a way to promote the understanding and preservation of the botanical diversity of our planet.

Cost and Hours: £18, June-Aug £11 after 16:00, kids 4-16—
£6, kids under 4—free; Mon-Thu 10:00-19:00, Fri-Sun until
20:00, closes earlier Sept-March—check schedule online, glass-
houses close at 17:30 in high season—earlier off-season, free one-
hour walking tours daily at 11:00 and 13:30, tel. 020/8332-5000,
www.kew.org.

Getting There: By Tube, ride to Kew Gardens station, then
cross the footbridge over the tracks, which drops you in a little
community of plant-and-herb shops, a two-block walk from Vic-

toria Gate (the main garden entrance). Boats also run to Kew Gardens from Westminster Pier (April-Oct; see page 63).

Eating: For a sun-dappled lunch or snack, walk 10 minutes from the Palm House to the **$$ Orangery Cafeteria** (Mon-Thu 10:00-17:30, Fri-Sun until 18:30, until 15:15 in winter, closes early for events).

Visiting the Gardens: Pick up a map brochure and check at the gate for a monthly listing of the best blooms. Garden lovers could spend days exploring Kew's 300 acres. For a quick visit, spend a fragrant hour wandering through three buildings: the Palm House, a humid Victorian world of iron, glass, and tropical plants that was built in 1844; a Waterlily House that Monet would swim for; and the Princess of Wales Conservatory, a meandering modern greenhouse with many different climate zones growing countless cacti, bug-munching carnivorous plants, and more. Check out the Xstrata Treetop Walkway, a 200-yard scenic steel walkway that puts you high in the canopy 60 feet above the ground.

▲▲Hampton Court Palace

Fifteen miles up the Thames from downtown, the 500-year-old palace of Henry VIII, William and Mary, and other royals is worth ▲▲▲ for palace aficiona-
dos. The stately brick-and-stone palace stands overlooking the Thames and includes some fine Tudor halls and Georgian-era rooms, all made engaging by a sharp, well-produced, included audioguide.

Cost and Hours: £23.70, cheaper online, family ticket available, daily 10:00-18:00, Nov-March until 16:30, last entry one hour before closing—but you'll need 2-3 hours to see the place; café, tel. 0844-482-7777, www.hrp.org.uk.

Getting There: From London's Waterloo Station, take a South West train. The train will drop you on the far side of the river from the palace—just walk across the bridge (2/hour, 35 minutes). Consider arriving at or departing from the palace by boat (connections with London's Westminster Pier, see page 62); it's a relaxing and scenic three- to four-hour cruise past two locks and a fun new/old riverside mix.

Background: Hampton Court was originally the palace of Henry VIII's minister and right-hand man, Cardinal Thomas Wolsey. When Wolsey realized Henry VIII was experiencing a little palace envy, he gave the mansion to his king...clever guy. The Tudor palace was also home to Elizabeth I and Charles I. Later, when William and Mary moved in, they renovated about one-third of the palace (with help from Christopher Wren).

Visiting the Palace: Use the free map to find your way to the audioguide tour routes. Red-vested docents throughout the complex are happy to answer questions.

Henry VIII's apartments feature a breathtaking Great Hall, with a marvelous hammerbeam ceiling, precious Abraham tapestries that kept this huge room warm and cozy, and a portrait of Henry VIII's family. His private balcony looks down into the stunning Chapel Royal. His kitchens were capable of keeping 600 schmoozing courtiers well fed. At the end of the kitchens, dip into the Chapel Royal for a closer look at the wood-carved decor and the starry-sky-and-gold-beam ceiling.

The Young Henry VIII's Story exhibit introduces you to the dashing, athletic, young Henry VIII, from the perspective of Henry himself; his first wife, Catherine of Aragon; and his right-hand man, Thomas Wolsey. At the end of the Young Henry VIII section, stairs lead up to William III's apartments, from about 150 years after Henry's time.

Before leaving, stroll in the gardens. Don't miss the easy-to-overlook entrance (immediately on the right) to William and Mary's walled privy garden, like a mini-Versailles.

NORTH OF LONDON
The Making of Harry Potter:
Warner Bros. Studio Tour London

While you can visit several real-life locations where the Harry Potter movies were filmed, there's only one way to see imaginary places like Hogwarts' Great Hall, Diagon Alley, Dumbledore's office, and #4 Privet Drive: Visit the Warner Bros. Studio in Leavesden 20 miles northwest of London.

Attractions include the actual sets, costumes, and props used for the films; video interviews with the actors and filmmakers; and exhibits about how the films' special effects were created.

The visit culminates with a stroll down Diagon Alley and a room-sized 1:24-scale model of Hogwarts.

Plan Ahead: It's essential to buy a ticket far in advance (entry possible only with reserved time slot). Allow about three hours at the studio, plus nearly three hours to get there and back.

Cost and Hours: £45—purchase timed-entry ticket online in advance, kids ages 5 to 15—£37, family ticket available; opening hours flex with season—first tour at 9:00 or 10:00, last tour as early as 14:30 or as late as 18:30, audio/videoguide-£5, café, tel. 0345-084-0900, www.wbstudiotour.co.uk.

Getting There: Take the frequent train from London Euston to Watford Junction (about 5/hour, 20 minutes), then catch the Mullany's Coaches shuttle bus (instantly recognizable by its bright paint job) to the studio tour (2-4/hour, 15 minutes, £2.50 round-trip—cash only, buy ticket from driver).

More direct (and more expensive), Golden Tours runs multiple daily **buses** between their office near Victoria Station and the studio (price includes round-trip bus and studio entrance: adults—£75-90, kids—£70-85; reserve ahead at www.goldentours.com).

Shopping in London

Most stores are open Monday through Saturday from roughly 9:00 or 10:00 until 17:00 or 18:00, with a late night on Wednesday or Thursday (usually until 19:00 or 20:00). Many close on Sundays. Large department stores stay open later during the week (until about 21:00 Mon-Sat) with shorter hours on Sundays. If you're looking for bargains, visit one of the city's many street markets.

SHOPPING STREETS

The best and most convenient shopping streets are in the West End and West London (roughly between Soho and Hyde Park).

You'll find midrange shops along **Oxford Street** (running east from Tube: Marble Arch), and fancier shops along **Regent Street** (stretching south from Tube: Oxford Circus to Piccadilly Circus) and **Knightsbridge** (where you'll find Harrods and Harvey Nichols; Tube: Knightsbridge). Other streets are more specialized, such as **Jermyn Street** for old-fashioned men's clothing (just south of Piccadilly) and **Charing Cross Road** for books. **Floral Street,** connecting Leicester Square to Covent Garden, is lined with boutiques.

Another fine street, which runs between Oxford Street and Marylebone Road, is **Marylebone High Street** (ending near Regent's Park and Madame Tussauds). It feels more quaint and less ritzy than some of the streets described above, and it's fun to browse for its combination of high-end chain stores, local one-off shops, art concept stores, clothing boutiques, and sleek home decor...all under handsome red-brick turreted townhouses. Along this street is the unique **Daunts Books,** filling an old townhouse with titles organized geographically (for details, see page 45), and an outpost of **Emma Bridgewater,** a country-charming home decor store (sort of the English Martha Stewart, www.emma-bridgewater.co.uk).

FANCY DEPARTMENT STORES

Harrods

Harrods is London's most famous and touristy department store. With more than four acres of retail space covering seven floors, it's a place where some shoppers could spend all day. (To me, it's still just a department store.) Big yet classy, Harrods has everything from elephants to toothbrushes (Mon-Sat 10:00-21:00, Sun 11:30-18:00, Brompton Road, Tube: Knightsbridge, tel. 020/7730-1234, www.harrods.com).

Harvey Nichols

Once Princess Diana's favorite and later Duchess Kate's, "Harvey Nick's" remains the department store *du jour* (Mon-Sat 10:00-20:00, Sun 11:30-18:00, near Harrods, 109 Knightsbridge, Tube: Knightsbridge, tel. 020/7235-5000, www.harveynichols.com). The store's fifth floor is a veritable food fest, with a gourmet grocery store, a fancy restaurant, a sushi bar, and a lively café.

Fortnum & Mason

The official department store of the Queen, Fortnum & Mason embodies old-fashioned, British upper-class taste. While some feel it is too stuffy, you won't find another store with the same storybook atmosphere. With rich displays and deep red carpet, Fortnum's feels classier and more relaxed than Harrods (Mon-Sat 10:00-21:00, Sun 11:30-18:00, elegant tea served in their Diamond Jubilee Tea Salon—see page 193, 181 Piccadilly, Tube: Green Park, tel. 020/7734-8040, www.fortnumandmason.com.

Liberty

Designed to make well-heeled shoppers feel at home, this half-timbered, mock-Tudor emporium is a 19th-century institution that thrives today. Known for its gorgeous "Liberty Print" floral fabrics, well-stocked crafts department, and castle-like interior, this iconic shop was a favorite of writer Oscar Wilde, who called it "the chosen resort of the artistic shopper" (Mon-Sat 10:00-20:00, Sun 11:30-18:00, Great Marlborough Street, Tube: Oxford Circus, tel. 020/7734-1234, www.liberty.co.uk.

STREET MARKETS

Those who appreciate antiques, artisan goods, and a fine bargain love London's street markets. There's good early-morning market activity somewhere any day of the week. The best markets—which combine lively stalls and a colorful neighborhood with cute and characteristic shops of their own—are Portobello Road and Camden Lock Market. Hagglers will enjoy the no-holds-barred bargaining encouraged in London's street markets. **Greenwich** (a quick DLR ride from central London) also has its share of great markets, especially lively on weekends. **Warning:** Markets attract two kinds of people—tourists and pickpockets.

Portobello Road Market (Notting Hill)

Arguably London's best street market, Portobello Road stretches for several blocks through the delightful, colorful, funky-yet-quaint Notting Hill neighborhood. Charming streets lined with pastel-painted houses and offbeat antique shops are enlivened on Fridays and Saturdays with 2,000 additional stalls (9:00-19:00), plus food, live music, and more. (The best strategy is to come on Friday; most stalls are open, with half the crowds of Saturday.) If you start at Notting Hill Gate and work your way north, you'll find these general sections: antiques, new goods, produce, vintage clothing, more new goods, a flea market, and more food. While Portobello Road is best on Fridays and Saturdays, you can still enjoy this street's quirky shops on most other days as well (Tube: Notting Hill Gate, near recommended accommodations, tel. 020/7727-7684, www.portobelloroad.co.uk).

Camden Lock Market (Camden Town)

This huge, trendy arts-and-crafts market is divided into three areas, each with its own vibe (but all of them fresh and funky). The whole complex sprawls around an old-fashioned, still-functioning lock (used mostly for leisure boats) and its retro-chic, yellow-brick industrial buildings. The main market, set alongside the picturesque canal, features a mix of shops and stalls selling boutique crafts and artisanal foods. The market on the opposite side of Chalk Farm Road is edgier, with cheap ethnic food stalls, lots of canalside seating, and punk crafts. The Stables, a sprawling, incense-scented complex, is decorated with fun statues of horses and squeezed into tunnels under the old rail bridge just behind the main market. It's a little lowbrow and wildly creative, with cheap clothes, junk jewelry, and loud music (daily 10:00-19:00, busiest on weekends, tel. 020/3763-9999, www.camdenmarket.com).

Leadenhall Market (The City)

One of London's oldest, Leadenhall Market stands on the original Roman center of town. Today, cheese and flower shops nestle between pubs, restaurants, and boutiques, all beneath a beautiful Victorian arcade (Harry Potter fans may recognize it as Diagon Alley). This is not a "street market" in the true sense, but more a hidden gem in the midst of London's financial grind (Mon-Fri 10:00-18:00, tel. 020/7332-1523, Tube: Monument or Liverpool; off Gracechurch Street near Leadenhall Street and Fenchurch).

East End Markets

These East End markets are busiest and most interesting on Sundays. See the map on page 122 for locations.

Petticoat Lane Market: Just a block from Spitalfields Market, this line of stalls sits on the otherwise dull, glass-skyscraper-filled Middlesex Street; adjoining Wentworth Street is grungier and more characteristic. Expect budget clothing, leather, shoes, watches, jewelry, and crowds (Sun 9:00-14:00, sometimes later; smaller market Mon-Fri on Wentworth Street only; no market Sat; Middlesex Street and Wentworth Street).

Spitalfields Market: This huge, mod-feeling market hall combines a shopping mall with old brick buildings and sleek modern ones, all covered by a giant glass roof. The shops, stalls, and a rainbow of restaurant options are open every day, tempting you with ethnic eateries, crafts, trendy clothes, bags, and an antiques-and-junk market (Mon-Fri 10:00-17:30—but vendors begin shutting down around 17:00, Sat from 11:00, Sun from 9:00; from the Tube stop, take Bishopsgate East exit, turn left, walk to Brushfield Street, and turn right; www.spitalfields.co.uk).

Truman Markets: Housed in the former Truman Brewery on Brick Lane, this cluster of markets is in the heart of the "Banglatown" Bangladeshi community. Of the East End market areas, these are the grittiest and most avant-garde. The markets are in full swing on Sundays, though you'll see some action on Saturdays and possibly other days (see hours below).

From Liverpool Street, head a few blocks east to Brick Lane and turn left. As you work your way north along Brick Lane through the Truman complex, you'll first come to the **Boiler House Food Hall** (on the left, filling an old warehouse with food stands and loud music), then the entrance to the **Vintage Market,** which occupies the basement with what claims to be London's largest assortment of vintage vendors (Mon-Sat 11:00-18:00, Sun from 10:00, www.vintage-market.co.uk). Just beyond, on the left, follow the crowds into the **Backyard Market,** with stylish clothing, arts, and crafts (Sat 11:00-18:00, Sun 10:00-17:00). Just beyond on the right, the **House of Vegan** fills yet another warehouse with exclusively vegetarian and vegan food stalls (Sat-Sun 11:00-18:00). Surrounding shops and eateries, including a fun courtyard of food trucks tucked off Brick Lane, are open all week.

LONDON

Brick Lane Market: If you leave the Truman Brewery complex and continue north along Brick Lane, the action flows into a more casual assortment of food and arts stands and street performers called the Brick Lane Market. This spans several short blocks, from about Buxton Street to Bethnal Green Road—about a 10-minute walk. Continuing another 10 minutes north, then turning right onto Columbia Road, takes you to the next market.

Columbia Road Flower Market: This colorful shopping street is made even more lively by the Sunday-morning commotion of shouting flower vendors (Sun 8:00-15:00, www.columbiaroad. info). Halfway up Columbia Road, be sure to loop left up little Ezra Street, with characteristic eateries, boutiques, and antique vendors.

West End Markets
Covent Garden Market: Originally the convent garden for Westminster Abbey, the iron-and-glass market hall hosted a produce market until the 1970s (earning it the name "Apple Market"). Now it's a mix of fun shops, eateries, markets, and a more modern-day Apple Store on the corner. Mondays are for antiques, while arts and crafts dominate the rest of the week. Yesteryear's produce stalls are open daily 10:30-18:00, and on Thursdays, a food market brightens up the square (Tube: Covent Garden, tel. 020/7395-1350, www. coventgardenlondonuk.com).

Jubilee Market: This market features antiques on Mondays (5:00-17:00); a general market Tuesday through Friday (10:30-19:00); and arts and crafts on Saturdays and Sundays (10:00-18:00). It's located on the south side of Covent Garden (tel. 020/7379-4242, www.jubileemarket.co.uk).

Entertainment in London

For the best list of what's happening and a look at the latest London scene, check www.timeout.com/london. The free monthly *London Planner* covers sights, events, and plays, though generally not as well as the Time Out website.

THEATER (A.K.A. "THEATRE")
London's theater scene rivals Broadway's in quality and often beats it in price. Choose from 200 offerings—Shakespeare, musicals,

comedies, thrillers, sex farces, cutting-edge fringe, revivals starring movie celebs, and more. London does it all well.

Seating Terminology: Just like at home, London's theaters sell seats in a range of levels—but the Brits use different terms: stalls (ground floor), dress circle (first balcony), upper circle (second balcony), balcony (sky-high third balcony), and slips (cheap seats on the fringes). Discounted tickets are called "concessions" (abbreviated as "conc" or "s"). "Restricted view" seats can be a bargain, but you won't be able to see all (or even most) of the stage. For floor plans of the various theaters, see www.theatremonkey.com.

Big West End Shows

Nearly all big-name shows are hosted in the theaters of the West End, clustering around Soho (especially along Shaftesbury Avenue) between Piccadilly and Covent Garden. With a centuries-old tradition of pleasing the masses, they present London theater at its grandest.

Well-known musicals may draw the biggest crowds, but the West End offers plenty of other crowd pleasers, from revivals of classics to cutting-edge works by the hottest young playwrights. These productions tend to have shorter runs than famous musicals. Many productions star huge-name celebrities—London is a magnet for movie stars who want to stretch their acting chops.

You'll see the latest offerings advertised all over the city. The *Official London Theatre Guide,* a free booklet that's updated every two weeks, is a handy tool (find it at hotels, box offices, the City of London TI, and online at www.officiallondontheatre.co.uk). You can check reviews at www.timeout.com/london.

Most performances are nightly except Sunday, usually with two or three matinees a week. The few shows that run on Sundays are mostly family fare (such as *The Lion King*).

Buying Tickets for West End Shows

For most visitors, it makes sense to simply buy tickets in London. Most shows have tickets available on short notice—likely at a discount. But if your time in London is limited—and you have your heart set on a particular show that's likely to sell out (usually the newest shows, and especially on weekends)—you can buy peace of mind by booking tickets from home.

Advance Tickets: It's generally cheapest to buy your tickets directly from the theater, either through its website or by calling the theater box office. In most cases, a theater will reroute you to a third-party ticket vendor such as Ticketmaster (which usually comes with a booking fee of around £3/ticket). You can have your tickets emailed to you or pick them up before show time at Will Call. Note that many third-party websites sell all kinds of London theater tickets, but these generally charge higher prices and fees. It's best to try the theater's website or box office first.

Discount Tickets from the TKTS Booth: This famous outlet at Leicester Square sells discounted tickets (25-50 percent off) for many shows (£3/ticket service charge included, open Mon-Sat 10:00-19:00, Sun 11:00-16:30). TKTS offers a wide variety of shows on any given day, though they may not always have the hottest shows in town. You must buy in person at the kiosk, and the best deals are same-day only.

The list of shows and prices is continually updated and posted outside the booth and on their website (www.tkts.co.uk). For the best choice and prices, come early in the day—the line starts forming even before the booth opens (it moves quickly).

Take note: The real TKTS booth (with its prominent sign) is a freestanding kiosk at the south edge of Leicester Square. Several dishonest outfits nearby advertise "official half-price tickets"—avoid these, where you'll rarely pay anything close to half price.

Tickets at the Theater Box Office: Even if a show is "sold out," there's usually a way to get a seat. Many theaters offer various discounts or "concessions": same-day tickets, cheap returned tickets, standing room, matinee, senior or student standby deals, and more. Start by checking the show's website, then call the box office or simply drop by (many theaters are right in the tourist zone).

Same-day tickets (called **"day seats"**) can be an excellent deal. These generally go on sale *only in person* when the box office opens (typically at 10:00; for popular shows, people start lining up well before then). These tickets (£20 or less) tend to be single seats either in the nosebleed rows or with a restricted view—but sometimes they can be front-row seats.

Very popular shows don't bother with "day seats," but a few distribute tickets through a lottery (for instance, via the show's website or a drawing for hopefuls who show up in person during a certain time window on the day of the show). The more popular the show, the lower your chances are, but it's fun to give it a shot. Look up details on each show's website.

Another strategy is to show up at the box office shortly before show time (best on weekdays) and—before paying full price—ask about cheaper options. Last-minute return tickets are often sold at great prices as curtain time approaches.

For a helpful guide to "day seats"—including recent user reports on how early you need to show up—consult www.theatremonkey.

com/dayseatfinder.htm; for tips on getting cheap and last-minute tickets, visit www.londontheatretickets.org and www.timeout.com/london/theatre.

Booking Through Other Agencies: Although booking through a middleman such as your hotel or a ticket agency is quick and easy (and may be your last resort for a sold-out show), prices are greatly inflated. Ticket agencies and third-party websites are often just scalpers with an address. If you do buy from an agency, choose one who is a member of the Society of Ticket Agents and Retailers (look for the STAR logo—short for "secure tickets from authorized retailers"). These legitimate resellers normally add a maximum 25 percent booking fee to tickets.

Scalpers (or "Touts"): As at any event, you'll find scalpers hawking tickets outside theaters. And, just like at home, those people may either be honest folk whose date just happened to cancel at the last minute...or they may be unscrupulous thieves selling forgeries. London has many of the latter.

Theater Beyond the West End

Tickets for lesser-known shows tend to be cheaper (figure £15-30), in part because most of the smaller theaters are government-subsidized. Remember that plays don't need a familiar title or famous actor to be a worthwhile experience—read up on the latest offerings online; *Time Out*'s website is a great place to start. Major noncommercial theaters include the National Theatre, Barbican Centre, Royal Court Theatre, Menier Chocolate Factory, and Bridge Theatre. The Royal Shakespeare Company performs at various theaters around London.

Shakespeare's Globe

To see Shakespeare in a replica of the theater for which he wrote his plays, attend a play at the Globe. In this round, thatched-roof, open-air theater, the plays are performed much as Shakespeare intended—under the sky, with no amplification.

The play's the thing from late April through mid-October (usually Tue-Sat 14:00 and 19:30, Sun either 13:00 and/or 18:30, tickets can be sold out months in advance). You'll pay £5 to stand and £23-47 to sit, usually on a backless bench (only a few rows and the pricier Gentlemen's Rooms have seats with backs, £2 cushions and £4 add-on backrests a good investment; dress for the weather).

The £5 "groundling" or "yard" tickets—which are open to rain—are most fun. Scurry in early to stake out a spot on the stage's edge, where the most interaction with the actors occurs. You're a crude peasant. You can lean your elbows on the stage, munch a snack (yes, you can bring in food—but bag size is limited), or walk around. I've never enjoyed Shakespeare as much as here, performed as it was meant to be in the "wooden O." If you can't get a ticket, consider waiting around. Plays can be long, and many groundlings leave before the end. Hang around outside and beg or buy a ticket from someone leaving early (groundlings are allowed to come and go). A few non-Shakespeare plays are also presented each year. If you can't attend a show, you can take a guided tour of the theater and museum by day (see page 127).

At the indoor Sam Wanamaker Playhouse, the season is designed to complement the Globe's summer season, though a few summer performances may take place here. In winter, the Playhouse hosts Shakespeare, Shakespearean-era plays, new works by up-and-coming playwrights, and early-music concerts. Many of the productions in this intimate venue (about 350 seats) are one-offs and can be more expensive.

To reserve tickets for plays at the Globe or Playhouse, drop by the box office (daily 10:00-18:00, open one hour later on performance days, New Globe Walk entrance, box office tel. 020/7401-9919; info tel. 020/7902-1400). You can also reserve online (www.shakespearesglobe.com, £2.50 booking fee). If the tickets are sold out, don't despair; a few often free up at the last minute. Try calling around noon the day of the performance to see if the box office expects any returned tickets. If so, they'll advise you to show up a little more than an hour before the show, when these tickets are sold (first-come, first-served).

The theater is on the South Bank, directly across the Thames over the Millennium Bridge from St. Paul's Cathedral (Tube: Mansion House or London Bridge). The Globe is inconvenient for public transport, but during theater season a regular supply of black cabs waits nearby, or you could try to order an Uber.

Outdoor and Fringe Theater

In summer, enjoy Shakespearean drama and other plays under the stars at the **Open Air Theatre,** in leafy Regent's Park in north London. You can bring your own picnic, order à la carte from the theater menu, or preorder a picnic supper from the theater at least 24 hours in advance (tickets from £25, available beginning in mid-Jan, season runs mid-May-mid-Sept; book at www.openairtheatre.org or—for an extra booking fee—by calling 0333-400-3562; grounds open 1.5 hours before performances; only one small bag permitted per person; 10-minute walk north of Baker Street Tube, near Queen Mary's Gardens within Regent's Park; detailed directions and more info at www.openairtheatre.org).

London's rougher evening-entertainment scene is thriving. Choose from a wide range of **fringe theater** and comedy acts (find posters in many Tube stations, or search for "fringe theater" on www.timeout.com; tickets can start as cheap as £5-10).

Evensong

One of my favorite experiences in Britain is to attend evensong at a great church. Evensong is an evening worship service that is typically sung rather than said (though some parts—including scripture readings, a few prayers, and a homily—are spoken). It follows the traditional Anglican service in the Book of Common Prayer, including prayers, scripture readings, canticles (sung responses), and hymns that are appropriate for the early evening—traditionally the end of the working day and before the evening meal. In major churches with resident choirs, this service is filled with quality, professional musical elements. A singing or chanting priest leads the service, and a choir—usually made up of both men's and boys' voices (to sing the lower and higher parts, respectively)—sings the responses. The choir usually sings a cappella, or is accompanied by an organ. While regular attendees follow the service from memory, visitors—who are welcome—are given an order of service or a prayer book to help them follow along.

The most impressive places for evensong include London (Westminster Abbey, St. Paul's, Southwark Cathedral, or St. Bride's Church), Cambridge (King's College Chapel), York Minster, and Durham Cathedral. While this list includes many of the grandest churches in England, be aware that evensong typically takes place in the small choir area—which is far more intimate than the main nave. (To see the full church in action, a concert is a better choice.) Evensong generally occurs daily between 17:00 and 18:00 (often two hours earlier on Sun)—check with individual churches for specifics. At smaller churches, evensong is sometimes spoken, not sung.

Note that evensong is not a performance—it's a somewhat somber worship service. If you enjoy worshipping in different churches, attending evensong can be a trip-capping highlight. Most major churches also offer organ or choral concerts—look for posted schedules or ask at the information desk or gift shop.

CONCERTS AT CHURCHES

For easy, cheap, or free concerts in historic churches, attend a **lunch concert,** especially:

- St. Bride's Church, with free half-hour lunch concerts twice a week at 13:15 (usually Tue and Fri—confirm in advance, church tel. 020/7427-0133, www.stbrides.com).
- Temple Church, also in The City, with free organ recitals weekly (Wed at 13:15, www.templechurch.com).
- St. James's at Piccadilly, with 50-minute concerts on Mon, Wed, and Fri at 13:10 (suggested £5 donation, info tel. 020/7734-4511, www.sjp.org.uk).
- St. Martin-in-the-Fields, offering concerts on Mon, Tue, and

Fri at 13:00 (suggested £3.50 donation, church tel. 020/7766-1100, www.stmartin-in-the-fields.org).

St. Martin-in-the-Fields also hosts fine **evening concerts** by candlelight (£9-29, several nights a week at 19:30) and live jazz in its underground Café in the Crypt (£8-15, Wed at 20:00).

Evensong services are held at several churches, including St. Paul's Cathedral (see page 109), Westminster Abbey (see page 69), Southwark Cathedral (see page 128), and St. Bride's Church (Sun at 17:30).

Free **organ recitals** are usually held on Sunday at 17:45 in Westminster Abbey (30 minutes, tel. 020/7222-5152). Many other churches have free concerts; ask for the *London Organ Concerts Guide* at the TI.

SUMMER EVENINGS ALONG THE SOUTH BANK

If you're visiting London in summer, consider hitting the South Bank neighborhood after hours.

Take a trip around the **London Eye** while the sun sets over the city (the wheel spins until late—last ascent at 20:30 or later in summer). Then cap your night with an evening walk along the pedestrian-only **Jubilee Walkway,** which runs east-west along the river. It's where Londoners go to escape the heat. This pleasant stretch of the walkway—lined with pubs and casual eateries—goes from the London Eye past Shakespeare's Globe to Tower Bridge (you can walk in either direction).

If you're in the mood for a movie, take in a flick at the **BFI Southbank,** located just across the river, alongside Waterloo Bridge. Run by the British Film Institute, the state-of-the-art theater shows mostly classic films, as well as art cinema (Tube: Waterloo or Embankment, check www.bfi.org.uk for schedules and prices).

Farther east along the South Bank is **The Scoop**—an outdoor amphitheater next to City Hall. It's a good spot for movies, concerts, dance, and theater productions throughout the summer—with Tower Bridge as a scenic backdrop. These events are free, nearly nightly, and family-friendly. For the latest event schedule, see www.morelondon.com and click on "Events" (next to City Hall, Riverside, The Queen's Walkway, Tube: London Bridge).

SPORTING EVENTS

Tennis, cricket, rugby, football (soccer), and horse races all take place within an hour of the city. In summer Wimbledon draws a half-million spectators (www.wimbledon.com), while big-name English Premier League soccer clubs—including Chelsea, Arsenal, Tottenham Hotspur, and West Ham United—take the pitch in London to sellout crowds (www.premierleague.com). The two biggest horse races of the year take place in June: the Royal Ascot Races (www.ascot.co.uk) near Windsor and the Epsom Derby (www.epsomderby.co.uk) in Surrey are both once-in-a-lifetime experiences.

Securing tickets to anything sporting-related in London can be difficult—and expensive. Check the official team or event website several months in advance; tickets can sell out within minutes of going on sale to the general public. Third-party booking companies such as SportsEvents 365 (www.sportsevents365.com) and Ticketmaster (www.ticketmaster.co.uk) often have tickets to popular events at a premium price—a godsend for die-hard fans. Many teams also offer affordable, well-run stadium tours—check your favorite side's official website for details. Even if you can't attend a sports event in person, consider cheering on the action in a London pub.

Sleeping in London

London is an expensive city for lodging. Focus on choosing the right neighborhood, which is as important as selecting the right hotel. I've picked a handful of my favorite neighborhoods (Victoria Station, South Kensington, Earl's Court, Bayswater, and North London) and recommend a range of options for each, from £20 bunks to deluxe £300-plus doubles with all the comforts. Because such comforts (and charm) come at a price, I've also listed big, modern, good-value chain hotels scattered throughout the city, along with hostels, dorms, and apartment rental information.

I rank accommodations from $ budget to $$$$ splurge. For the best deal, contact my family-run places directly by phone or email. When you book direct, the owner avoids a commission and may be able to offer a discount. Book well in advance for peak season or if your trip coincides with a major holiday or festival (see the appendix). For more details on reservations, short-term rentals, and more, see the "Sleeping" section in the Practicalities chapter.

Looking for Hotel Deals Online: Given London's high hotel prices, it's worth searching for a deal. For more options, browse these accommodation discount sites: www.londontown.com (an informative site with a discount booking service), www.athomeinlondon. co.uk and www.londonbb.com (both list central B&Bs), www. lastminute.com, www.visitlondon.com, and www.eurocheapo.com.

VICTORIA STATION NEIGHBORHOOD

The streets behind Victoria Station teem with little, moderately-priced-for-London B&Bs. It's a safe, surprisingly tidy, and decent area without a hint of the trashy, touristy glitz of the streets immediately surrounding the station. I've divided these accommoda-

LONDON

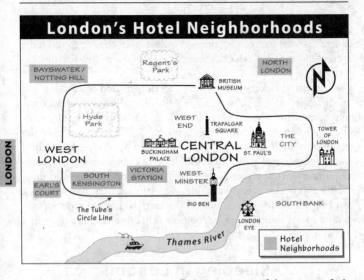

London's Hotel Neighborhoods

tions into two broad categories: Belgravia, west of the station, feels particularly posh, while Pimlico, to the east, is still upscale and dotted with colorful eateries. While I wouldn't go out of my way just to dine here, each area has plenty of good restaurants (see "Eating in London," later). All of my recommended hotels are within a five-minute walk of the Victoria Tube, bus, and train stations. In summer, request a quiet back room; most of these B&Bs lack airconditioning and may front busy streets.

Laundry: The nearest laundry option is **Pimlico Launderette,** about five blocks southwest of Warwick Square (self-service and same-day full service, daily 8:00-19:00, last wash at 17:30; 3 Westmoreland Terrace—go down Clarendon Street, turn right on Sutherland, and look for the launderette on the left at the end of the street; tel. 020/7821-8692).

Parking: The 400-space Semley Place **NCP parking garage** is near the hotels on the west/Belgravia side (£42/day, possible discounts with hotel voucher, just west of Victoria Coach Station at Buckingham Palace Road and Semley Place, tel. 0845-050-7080, www.ncp.co.uk). **Victoria Station car park** is cheaper but a quarter of the size; check here first, but don't hold your breath (£30/day on weekdays, £15/day on weekends, entrance on Eccleston Bridge between Buckingham Palace Road and Bridge Place, tel. 0345-222-4224, www.apcoa.co.uk).

West of Victoria Station (Belgravia)

In Belgravia, the prices are a bit higher and your neighbors include some of the world's wealthiest people. These two places sit on tranquil Ebury Street, two blocks over from Victoria Station (or a slightly shorter walk from the Sloane Square Tube stop). You can cut the walk from Victoria Station to nearly nothing by taking a short ride on frequent bus #C1 (leaves from Buckingham Palace Road side of Victoria Station and drops you off on corner of Ebury and Elizabeth streets). Both places come with some street noise; light sleepers should request a room in the back.

$$$$ Lime Tree Hotel has 28 spacious, stylish, comfortable, thoughtfully decorated rooms, a helpful staff, a fun-loving breakfast room, and a delightful garden in back (135 Ebury Street, tel. 020/7730-8191, www.limetreehotel.co.uk, info@limetreehotel. co.uk, Charlotte and Matt, Laura manages the office).

$$$ B&B Belgravia comes with 26 bright, colorful rooms and high ceilings. It feels less than homey, but still offers good value for the location. Most of its rooms come with closets and larger-than-average space (family rooms, 66 Ebury Street, tel. 020/7259-8570, www.bb-belgravia.com, info@bb-belgravia.com).

East of Victoria Station (Pimlico)

This area feels a bit less genteel than Belgravia, but it's still plenty inviting, with eateries and grocery stores. Most of these hotels are on or near Warwick Way, the main drag through this area. Generally the best Tube stop for this neighborhood is Victoria (though the Pimlico works equally well for the Luna Simone). Bus #24 runs right through the middle of Pimlico, connecting the Tate Britain to the south with Victoria Station, the Houses of Parliament, Trafalgar Square, the British Museum, and much more to the north.

$$$ Luna Simone Hotel rents 36 fresh, spacious, remodeled rooms with modern bathrooms. It's a smartly managed place, run for more than 50 years by twins Peter and Bernard—and Bernard's son Mark—and they still seem to enjoy their work (RS%, family rooms, 47 Belgrave Road near the corner of Charlwood Street, handy bus #24 stops out front, tel. 020/7834-5897, www. lunasimonehotel.com, stay@lunasimonehotel.com).

$$ Best Western Victoria Palace offers modern, if slightly worn, business-class comfort compared with some of the other creaky old guesthouses in the neighborhood. Choose from the 43 rooms in the main building (at 60 Warwick Way), or pay about 20 percent less by booking a nearly identical room in one of the annexes, each a half-block away—an excellent value for this neighborhood if you skip breakfast (air-con, elevator in main building only, 17 Belgrave Road and 1 Warwick Way, reception at main building, tel. 020/7821-7113, www.bestwesternvictoriapalace.co.uk, info@ bestwesternvictoriapalace.co.uk).

$ Cherry Court Hotel, run by the friendly and industrious Patel family, rents 12 very small but bright and well-designed

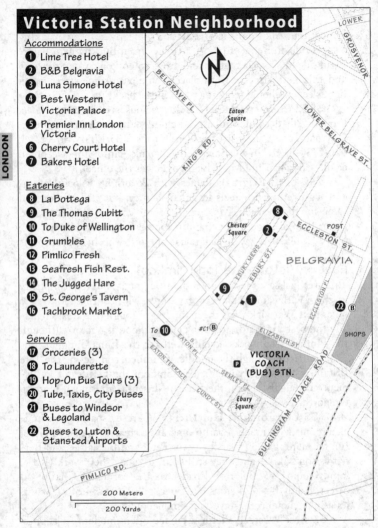

Victoria Station Neighborhood

Accommodations

1. Lime Tree Hotel
2. B&B Belgravia
3. Luna Simone Hotel
4. Best Western Victoria Palace
5. Premier Inn London Victoria
6. Cherry Court Hotel
7. Bakers Hotel

Eateries

8. La Bottega
9. The Thomas Cubitt
10. To Duke of Wellington
11. Grumbles
12. Pimlico Fresh
13. Seafresh Fish Rest.
14. The Jugged Hare
15. St. George's Tavern
16. Tachbrook Market

Services

17. Groceries (3)
18. To Launderette
19. Hop-On Bus Tours (3)
20. Tube, Taxis, City Buses
21. Buses to Windsor & Legoland
22. Buses to Luton & Stansted Airports

200 Meters
200 Yards

rooms with firm mattresses in a central location. Considering London's sky-high prices, this is an extraordinary budget choice (family rooms, fruit-basket breakfast in room, air-con, laundry, 23 Hugh Street, tel. 020/7828-2840, www.cherrycourthotel.co.uk, info@cherrycourthotel.co.uk, Neha answers emails and offers informed restaurant advice).

$$ OYO Hotels, an India-based chain that finances renovations for thousands of run-down budget hotels worldwide, has arrived in London. While they've salvaged some places that were at death's door, the standards are still pretty basic. If you're on

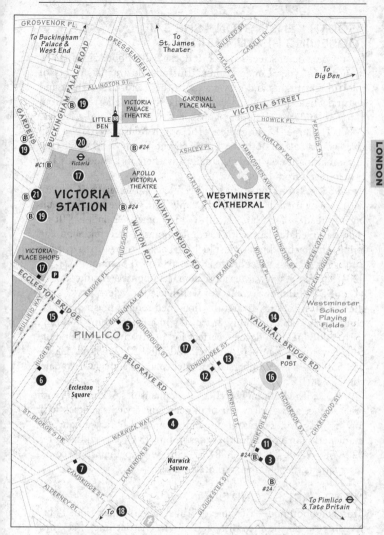

a very tight budget, OYO hotels may be worth considering—including several in the Victoria Station area (www.oyorooms.com/gb). One of these is **Bakers Hotel,** which shoehorns 12 brightly painted rooms into a tight building (cheaper single rooms with shared bath, family rooms, 126 Warwick Way, tel. 020/7834-0729, www.bakershotel.co.uk, reservations@bakershotel.co.uk, Amin Jamani).

If considering chain hotels, there's also a fine **$$$ Premier Inn** in this area (82 Eccleston Square, www.premierinn.com).

"SOUTH KENSINGTON," SHE SAID, LOOSENING HIS CUMMERBUND

To stay on a quiet street so classy it doesn't allow hotel signs, make "South Ken" your London home. This upscale area has plenty of colorful restaurants and easy access to the Victoria & Albert and Natural History museums; shoppers like being a short walk from Harrods and the designer shops of King's Road and Chelsea. When I splurge, I splurge here. The South Kensington Tube stop gives you access to both the handy Piccadilly and Circle/District lines, making it easy to get virtually anywhere in London; it's also easy to reach from Heathrow.

$$$$ Aster House, in a lovely Victorian town house, is run with care by friendly Simon and Leonie Tan, who've been welcoming my readers for years (I call it "my home in London"). It's a stately and sedate place, with 13 comfy rooms, a cheerful lobby, and lounge. Enjoy breakfast or just kicking back in the whisper-elegant Orangery, a glassy greenhouse (RS%, air-con, 3 Sumner Place, tel. 020/7581-5888, www.asterhouse.com, asterhouse@gmail.com).

$$$$ Number Sixteen, for well-heeled travelers, packs over-the-top class into its 41 artfully imagined rooms, plush designer-chic lounges, and tranquil garden. It's in a labyrinthine building, with boldly modern decor—perfect for an urban honeymoon (air-con, elevator, 16 Sumner Place, tel. 020/7589-5232, US tel. 1-888-559-5508, www.numbersixteenhotel.co.uk, sixteen@firmdale.com).

$$$$ The Pelham Hotel, a 52-room business-class hotel with crisp service and a pricey mix of pretense and style, is genteel, with low lighting and a pleasant drawing room and library among the many perks (air-con, elevator, fitness room, 15 Cromwell Place, tel. 020/7589-8288, US tel. 1-888-757-5587, www.pelhamhotel.co.uk, reservations.thepelham@starhotels.com).

NEAR EARL'S COURT

This neighborhood—a couple of Tube stops farther from South Kensington on the Piccadilly and Circle/District lines—is a nice compromise between local-feeling and accessible to travelers. It has a stately residential feel, and a high concentration of high-capacity, relatively expensive hotels. Solo travelers might consider one of the several quality chains here. The main drag that runs in front of the Tube station—Earl's Court Road—is lined with easy chain eateries.

$$$$ K+K Hotel George occupies a grand Georgian building on a quiet street just behind the Earl's Court Tube station. With spacious public areas, a wellness center, and 154 well-appointed rooms, it feels polished and professional (air-con, elevator,

LONDON

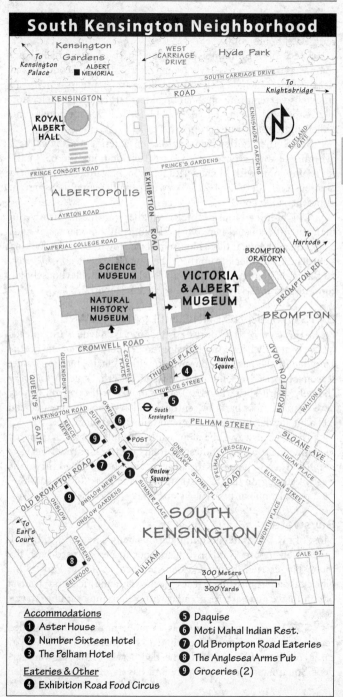

South Kensington Neighborhood

Kensington Gardens
To Kensington Palace
ALBERT MEMORIAL

WEST CARRIAGE DRIVE

Hyde Park

SOUTH CARRIAGE DRIVE

To Knightsbridge

KENSINGTON ROAD

ROYAL ALBERT HALL

ENNISMORE GARDENS

RUTLAND GATE

N

PRINCE CONSORT ROAD

PRINCE'S GARDENS

EXHIBITION ROAD

ALBERTOPOLIS

AYRTON ROAD

IMPERIAL COLLEGE ROAD

To Harrods

BROMPTON ORATORY

SCIENCE MUSEUM

VICTORIA & ALBERT MUSEUM

BROMPTON RD.

NATURAL HISTORY MUSEUM

BROMPTON

BROMPTON ROAD

CROMWELL ROAD

WALTON ST.

QUEEN'S GATE

QUEENSBURY PL.

CROMWELL PLACE

THURLOE PLACE

Thurloe Square

HARRINGTON ROAD

GWEN PL.

BUTE ST.

REECE MEWS

THURLOE STREET

❹

❸

❺ South Kensington

PELHAM STREET

SLOANE AVE.

❻

POST

❾

❷

❼

OLD BROMPTON ROAD

ONSLOW MEWS E.

❶

Onslow Square

ONSLOW GARDENS

SUMNER PLACE

SYDNEY PL.

Onslow Square

PELHAM CRESCENT

ROAD

LUCAN PLACE

ELYSTAN STREET

To Earl's Court

❾

ONSLOW GDNS.

SOUTH KENSINGTON

IXWORTH PLACE

CALE ST.

❽

SELWOOD

FULHAM

300 Meters

300 Yards

Accommodations
❶ Aster House
❷ Number Sixteen Hotel
❸ The Pelham Hotel

Eateries & Other
❹ Exhibition Road Food Circus

❺ Daquise
❻ Moti Mahal Indian Rest.
❼ Old Brompton Road Eateries
❽ The Anglesea Arms Pub
❾ Groceries (2)

1 Templeton Place, tel. 020/7598-8700, www.kkhotels.com, hotel. george@kkhotels.com).

$$$$ NH London Kensington, part of a Spanish hotel chain, has 121 business-style rooms offering reliable comfort and class. Bonuses include a pleasant garden patio, a fitness center, and an extensive, tempting optional breakfast buffet (air-con, elevator, 202 Cromwell Road, tel. 020/7244-1441, www.nh-hotels.com, nhkensington@nh-hotels.com).

$$$$ The Nadler Kensington, on a residential block, is a five-minute walk from Earl's Court Tube station. The 65 small-ish rooms come with kitchenettes (air-con, elevator, 25 Courtfield Gardens, tel. 020/7244-2255, www.thenadler.com, kensington.info@thenadler.com).

$$$ Henley House Hotel is smaller and more warmly run than the others listed here, with 21 rooms in a modern, red-and-black color scheme. It fills a handsome brick townhouse overlooking a garden, a half-block from the Tube stop (RS%, air-con, elevator, 30 Barkston Gardens, tel. 020/7370-4111, www.henleyhousehotel.com, reservations@henleyhousehotel.com, Roberta).

BAYSWATER, NOTTING HILL, AND NEARBY

From the core of the tourist's London, vast Hyde Park spreads west, eventually becoming Kensington Gardens. Along the northern edge of the park sits Bayswater, with a cluster of good-value, reasonably priced accommodations in an area that's sleepy and very "homely" (Brit-speak for cozy). Your money will take you farther here than in most parts of central London—though the area can feel a bit sterile, and the hotels tend to be impersonal.

The Queensway Tube stop, while a couple of blocks from my recommendations, is handiest as it sits on the Central Line. I've also listed a few choices in the adjacent areas of Notting Hill (to the west), Paddington (to the east) and Holland Park (to the south)—each one just one or two Tube stops away.

Bayswater

Most of my Bayswater accommodations flank a peaceful, tidy park called Kensington Gardens Square (not to be confused with the much bigger Kensington Gardens adjacent to Hyde Park). One block east is the bustling street Queensway, a multicultural festival of commerce and eateries popular with young international travelers.

$$$ Vancouver Studios has 45 modern, tastefully furnished rooms that come with fully equipped kitchenettes, or you can pay for a continental breakfast. It's nestled between Kensington Gardens Square and Prince's Square and has its own tranquil garden patio out back (laundry, 30 Prince's Square, tel. 020/7243-1270, www.vancouverstudios.co.uk, info@vancouverstudios.co.uk).

$$$ Phoenix Hotel offers spacious, stately public spaces and 125 modern-feeling rooms with classy decor. While the rates can vary wildly, it's a good choice if you can get a deal (elevator, 1 Kensington Gardens Square, tel. 020/7229-2494, www.phoenixhotel.co.uk, reservations@phoenixhotel.co.uk).

$$$ London House Hotel has 103 spiffy, modern, cookie-cutter rooms at reasonable prices (family rooms, air-con, elevator, 81 Kensington Gardens Square, tel. 020/7243-1810, www.londonhousehotels.com, reservations@londonhousehotels.com).

$$$ Princes Square Guest Accommodation is a crisp (if impersonal) place renting 50 businesslike rooms with pleasant, modern decor. It's well located, practical, and a very good value, especially if you can score a good rate (elevator, 23 Prince's Square, tel. 020/7229-9876, www.princessquarehotel.co.uk, info@princessquarehotel.co.uk).

$$$ Garden Court Hotel is understated, with 40 simple, homey-but-tasteful rooms (family rooms, elevator, 30 Kensington Gardens Square, tel. 020/7229-2553, www.gardencourthotel.co.uk, info@gardencourthotel.co.uk).

$$ Kensington Gardens Hotel, with the same owners as the Phoenix Hotel, laces 17 rooms together in a tall, skinny building (breakfast served at Phoenix Hotel, 9 Kensington Gardens Square, tel. 020/7243-7600, www.kensingtongardenshotel.co.uk, info@kensingtongardenshotel.co.uk).

Notting Hill

Just west of Bayswater (Tube: Notting Hill Gate), spreading out from the northwest tip of Kensington Gardens, this area is famous for two things: It's the site of the colorful Portobello Road Market (see page 150), and was the setting of the 1999 Hugh Grant/Julia Roberts film of the same name. The **$$$$ Portobello Hotel** is on a quiet residential street in the heart of the neighborhood. Its 21 rooms are funky yet elegant—both the style and location give it an urban-fresh feeling (elevator, 22 Stanley Gardens, tel. 020/7727-2777, www.portobellohotel.com, stay@portobellohotel.com).

Paddington

The streets and squares around Paddington Station teem with "budget" (but still overpriced) hotels handy to the Heathrow Express train and useful Tube lines. The well-run **$$ Stylotel** feels like the stylish, super-modern, aluminum-clad big sister of the EasyHotel chain. While the 42 rooms can be cramped, the beds have space for luggage underneath (RS%, family rooms, air-con,

LONDON

Earl's Court, Bayswater & Notting Hill

Accommodations

1. K+K Hotel George
2. NH London Kensington
3. Nadler Kensington
4. Henley House Hotel
5. Vancouver Studios
6. Phoenix & Kensington Gardens Hotels
7. London House Hotel
8. Princes Square Guest Accommodation
9. Garden Court Hotel
10. Portobello Hotel
11. Stylotel
12. Norwegian YWCA

Eateries

13. Cocotte
14. Farmacy
15. Hereford Road
16. Taqueria
17. The Prince Edward
18. Geales
19. Mazi
20. The Fish House of Notting Hill
21. Maggie Jones's
22. The Shed
23. The Churchill Arms Pub & Thai Kitchen
24. Café Diana
25. Groceries (5)
26. The Orangery (Afternoon Tea)

elevator, 160 Sussex Gardens, tel. 020/7723-1026, www.stylotel. com, info@stylotel.com, Andreas).

NORTH LONDON

These hotels are north of Regent Street, a long walk or quick Tube or bus ride from the lively Soho area and Hyde Park. These are my closest hotels to the center of London, and some of my most expensive. The wide streets and grand homes (including Sherlock Holmes') gives this area an elegant aura...which is only slightly compromised by the hordes of tourists flocking through to reach Madame Tussauds.

$$$$ The Sumner Hotel rents 19 rooms in a 19th-century Georgian townhouse sporting large contemporary rooms and a lounge with fancy modern Italian furniture. This swanky place packs in all the amenities and is conveniently located north of Hyde Park and near Oxford Street, a busy shopping destination—close to Selfridges and a Marks & Spencer (RS%, air-con, elevator, 54 Upper Berkeley Street, a block and a half off Edgware Road, Tube: Marble Arch, tel. 020/7723-2244, www.thesumner.com, hotel@ thesumner.com).

$$$$ Charlotte Street Hotel, in the Fitzrovia neighborhood close to the British Museum, has inviting public spaces and 52 bright, elegant rooms (connecting family rooms, air-con, elevator, 15 Charlotte Street, Tube: Tottenham Court Road, tel. 020/7806-2000, www.charlottestreethotel.com, reservations@ charlottestreethotel.com).

$$$$ The Mandeville Hotel, at the center of the action just one block from Bond Street Tube station, has a genteel British vibe, with high ceilings, tasteful art, just-vibrant-enough colors, and 142 rooms. It's a worthy splurge for its amenities and location, especially if you score a good deal (air-con, elevator, Mandeville Place, tel. 020/7935-5599, www.mandeville.co.uk, info@mandeville.co.uk).

$$$ The 22 York Street B&B offers a casual alternative in the city center, with an inviting lounge and 10 traditional, hardwood, comfortable rooms, each named for a notable London landmark (near Marylebone/Baker Street: From Baker Street Tube station, walk 2 blocks down Baker Street and take a right to 22 York Street—no sign, just look for #22; tel. 020/7224-2990, www.22yorkstreet.co.uk, mc@22yorkstreet.co.uk, energetically run by Liz and Michael Callis).

Near Covent Garden

These two hotels—pricey but oh so central—are a short walk from Covent Garden, in the heart of the action.

$$$$ The Fielding Hotel is a simple and slightly more affordable place lodged in the center of all the action on a quiet lane.

They rent 25 basic rooms, serve no breakfast, and have almost no public spaces (family rooms, air-con, 4 Broad Court off Bow Street, Tube: Covent Garden, tel. 020/7836-8305, www.thefieldinghotel. co.uk, reservations@thefieldinghotel.co.uk).

$$ Seven Dials Hotel's 38 no-nonsense rooms are plain and fairly tight, but they're also clean, reasonably priced, and incredibly well located (some, but not all, have air-con). Since doubles here all cost the same, request a larger room when you book (family rooms, elevator, 7 Monmouth Street, Tube: Leicester Square or Covent Garden, tel. 020/240-0823, www.sevendialshotel.co.uk, sevendialshotel@gmail.com, run by friendly and hardworking Hanna).

LONDON

OTHER SLEEPING OPTIONS
Big, Good-Value, Modern Hotels
If you can score a double for £100 (or less—often possible with promotional rates) and don't mind a modern, impersonal, American-style hotel, one of these can be a decent value in pricey London (for details on chain hotels, see page 1042).

I've listed a few of the dominant chains, along with a quick rundown on their more convenient London locations (see the map earlier to find chain hotels in North London). Quality can vary wildly so check online reviews. Some of these branches sit on busy streets in dreary train-station neighborhoods. While I wouldn't necessarily rule these out, ask for a quieter room, use common sense when exploring after dark, and wear a money belt.

I've focused on affordable options here. Pricier London hotel chains include Millennium/Copthorne, Grange, Firmdale, Thistle, InterContinental/Holiday Inn, Radisson, Hilton, and Red Carnation.

$$ Motel One, the German chain that specializes in affordable style, has a branch at Tower Hill, a 10-minute walk north of the Tower of London (24 Minories—see map on page 110, tel. 020/7481-6420, www.motel-one.com, london-towerhill@motel-one.com).

$$ Premier Inn has more than 70 hotels in greater London. Convenient locations include a branch inside London County Hall (next to the London Eye), at Southwark/Borough Market (near Shakespeare's Globe, 34 Park Street), Southwark/Tate Modern (15 Great Suffolk Street), Kensington/Earl's Court (11 Knaresborough Place), Victoria (82 Eccleston Square), and Leicester Square (1 Leicester Place). In North London, the following branches cluster between King's Cross St. Pancras and the British Museum: King's Cross, St. Pancras, and Euston. Avoid the Tower Bridge location, south of the bridge and a long walk from the Tube—but London City Tower Hill, north of the bridge on Prescot Street (see map on page 110)—works fine (www.premierinn.com).

LONDON

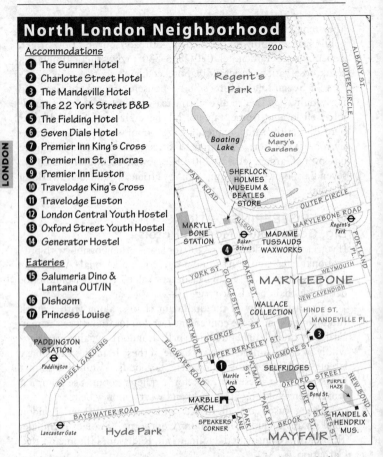

North London Neighborhood

Accommodations
1. The Sumner Hotel
2. Charlotte Street Hotel
3. The Mandeville Hotel
4. The 22 York Street B&B
5. The Fielding Hotel
6. Seven Dials Hotel
7. Premier Inn King's Cross
8. Premier Inn St. Pancras
9. Premier Inn Euston
10. Travelodge King's Cross
11. Travelodge Euston
12. London Central Youth Hostel
13. Oxford Street Youth Hostel
14. Generator Hostel

Eateries
15. Salumeria Dino & Lantana OUT/IN
16. Dishoom
17. Princess Louise

$$ Travelodge has close to 70 locations in London, including at King's Cross (200 yards in front of King's Cross Station, Gray's Inn Road) and Euston (1 Grafton Place). Other handy locations include King's Cross Royal Scot, Marylebone, Covent Garden, Liverpool Street, Southwark, and Farringdon; www.travelodge.co.uk.

$$ Ibis, the budget branch of the AccorHotels group, has a few dozen options across the city, with a handful of locations convenient to London's center, including London Blackfriars (49 Blackfriars Road) and London City Shoreditch (5 Commercial Street). The more design-focused Ibis Styles has branches near Earl's Court (15 Hogarth Road) and Southwark, with a theater theme (43 Southwark Bridge Road; https://ibis.accorhotels.com).

$ EasyHotel, with several branches in good neighborhoods, offers generally tiny, super-efficient, no-frills rooms that feel popped out of a plastic mold, down to the prefab ship's head-type "bathroom pod." Rates can be surprisingly low (with doubles as

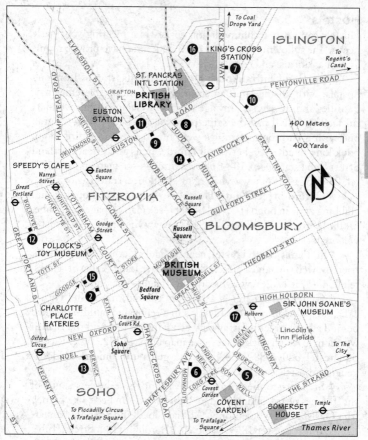

cheap as £30 if you book early enough)—but you'll pay à la carte for expensive add-ons, such as TV use, Wi-Fi, luggage storage, fresh towels, and daily cleaning (breakfast, if available, comes from a vending machine). If you go with the base rate, it's like hosteling with privacy—a hard-to-beat value. But you get what you pay for (thin walls, flimsy construction, noisy fellow guests, and so on). They're only a good deal if you book far enough ahead to get a good price and skip the many extras. Locations include Victoria (34 Belgrave Road), South Kensington (14 Lexham Gardens), and Paddington (10 Norfolk Place); www.easyhotel.com.

$ Hub by Premier Inn—the budget chain's no-frills, pod-style division—offers extremely small rooms (just a little bigger than the bed) in convenient locations for low prices (as affordable as £69; www.premierinn.com/gb/en/hub.html).

Hostels

Hostels can slash accommodation costs while meeting your basic needs. The following places are open 24 hours, have private rooms as well as dorms, and come with Wi-Fi.

¢ **London Central Youth Hostel** is the flagship of London's hostels, with all the latest in security and comfortable efficiency. Families and travelers of any age will feel welcome in this wonderful facility. You'll pay the same price for any bed—so try to grab one with a bathroom (families welcome to book an entire room, book long in advance; between Oxford Circus and Great Portland Street Tube stations at 104 Bolsover Street—see map on page 172, tel. 0345-371-9154, www.yha.org.uk, londoncentral@yha.org.uk).

¢ **Oxford Street Youth Hostel** is right in the shopping and clubbing zone in Soho (14 Noel Street—see map on page 172, Tube: Oxford Street, tel. 0345-371-9133, www.yha.org.uk, oxfordst@yha.org.uk).

¢ **St. Paul's Youth Hostel,** near St. Paul's Cathedral, is modern, friendly, well run, and a bit scruffy (36 Carter Lane, Tube: St. Paul's, tel. 0345-371-9012, www.yha.org.uk, stpauls@yha.org.uk).

¢ **Generator Hostel** is a brightly colored, hip hostel with a café and a DJ spinning the hits. It's in a renovated building tucked behind a busy street halfway between King's Cross and the British Museum (37 Tavistock Place—see map on page 172, Tube: Russell Square, tel. 020/7388-7666, http://staygenerator.com, ask.london@generatorhostels.com).

¢ **St. Christopher's Inn,** a cluster of three hostels south of the Thames near London Bridge, has cheap dorm beds; one branch (the Oasis) is for women only. All have loud and friendly bars attached (must be over 18 years old, 161 Borough High Street, Tube: Borough or London Bridge, reservations tel. 020/8600-7500, www.st-christophers.co.uk).

¢ **Norwegian YWCA** (Norsk K.F.U.K.) is open to all Norwegian women and to non-Norwegian women under 30. (Men must be under 30 with a Norwegian passport.) On a quiet street near Holland Park in the Kensington area, it offers an open-face Norwegian ambience (private rooms available, 52 Holland Park—see map on page 168, Tube: Holland Park, tel. 020/7727-9346, www.kfukhjemmet.org.uk, kontor@kfukhjemmet.org.uk).

Apartment Rentals

Consider this option if you're traveling as a family, in a group, or staying several days. Websites such as Airbnb and VRBO let you correspond directly with property owners or managers, or consider one of the sites listed next. For more information on short-term rentals, see the Practicalities chapter.

LondonConnection.com rents several properties around

London. **OneFineStay.com** offers stylish, contemporary flats (most of them part-time residences) in desirable London neighborhoods. **SuperCityUk.com** rents chic, comfortable aparthotels and serviced apartments in four buildings. Other options include **Cross-Pollinate.com, Coach House Rentals** (www.chsrentals. com), VisitApartmentsLondon.co.uk, HomeFromHome.co.uk, and **APlaceLikeHome.co.uk.**

Eating in London

Far from the dated stereotypes of dreary British food, London is one of Europe's great food cities. Whether it's dining well with the

upper crust, sharing hearty pub fare with the blokes, or venturing to a fringe neighborhood to try the latest hotspot or street food at a market, eating out is an essential part of the London experience. The sheer variety of foods—from every corner of Britain's former empire and beyond—is astonishing.

I rank eateries from **$** budget to **$$$$** splurge. For more advice on eating in London, including ordering, tipping, and British cuisine and beverages, see the "Eating" section of the Practicalities chapter.

CENTRAL LONDON

Central London is absolutely packed—with both locals and tourists—and restaurants are overflowing, even on a "quiet" night. On weekends and later in the evenings, sidewalks and even the streets become congested with people out barhopping and clubbing. If you're looking for peace and quiet and a calm meal, avoid Friday and Saturday evenings here and come early on other nights.

Many popular chain restaurants permeate this area (for a description of some reliable chains, see page 1055). There's no need to clutter up my listings and maps with these—like Starbucks or McDonald's, you can count on seeing them wherever you go.

Heart of Soho

With its many theaters, reputation as a rollicking nightspot, and status as *the* place where budding restaurateurs stake their claim on London's culinary map, the Soho neighborhood is a magnet for diners. As it's close to London's must see's and do's, you could find yourself eating here a lot (convenient for dinner after a day of sightseeing, or before going to the theater). Even if Soho isn't otherwise on your radar, make a point to dine here at least once.

LONDON

Central London Restaurants

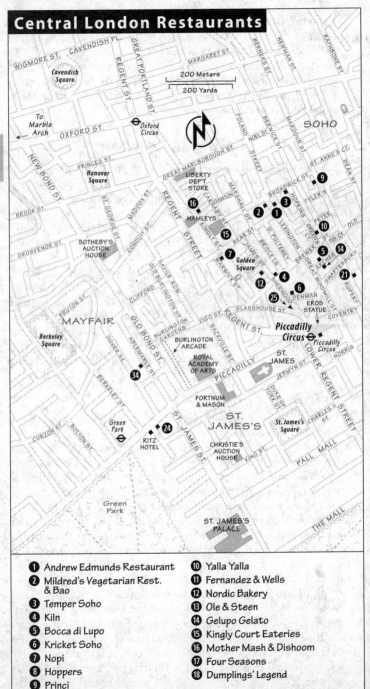

1. Andrew Edmunds Restaurant
2. Mildred's Vegetarian Rest. & Bao
3. Temper Soho
4. Kiln
5. Bocca di Lupo
6. Kricket Soho
7. Nopi
8. Hoppers
9. Princi
10. Yalla Yalla
11. Fernandez & Wells
12. Nordic Bakery
13. Ole & Steen
14. Gelupo Gelato
15. Kingly Court Eateries
16. Mother Mash & Dishoom
17. Four Seasons
18. Dumplings' Legend

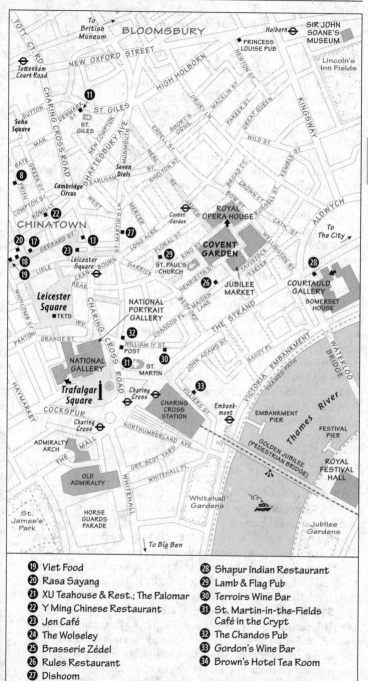

19 Viet Food

20 Rasa Sayang

21 XU Teahouse & Rest.; The Palomar

22 Y Ming Chinese Restaurant

23 Jen Café

24 The Wolseley

25 Brasserie Zédel

26 Rules Restaurant

27 Dishoom

28 Shapur Indian Restaurant

29 Lamb & Flag Pub

30 Terroirs Wine Bar

31 St. Martin-in-the-Fields Café in the Crypt

32 The Chandos Pub

33 Gordon's Wine Bar

34 Brown's Hotel Tea Room

$$$ Andrew Edmunds Restaurant is a tiny candlelit space where you'll want to hide your guidebook and not act like a tourist. This little place—with a loyal clientele—is the closest I've found to Parisian quality in a cozy restaurant in London. The extensive wine list, modern European cooking, and creative seasonal menu are worth the splurge (daily 12:30-15:30 & 17:30-22:45, these are last-order times, come early or call ahead, request ground floor rather than basement, 46 Lexington Street, tel. 020/7437-5708, www.andrewedmunds.com).

$$ Mildred's Vegetarian Restaurant, across from Andrew Edmunds, has a creative, fun menu and a tight, high-energy interior filled with happy herbivores (daily 12:00-23:00, vegan options, 45 Lexington Street, tel. 020/7494-1634).

$$$ Bao is a minimalist eatery selling top-quality Taiwanese cuisine, specializing in delicate and delectable steamed-bun sandwiches (portions are small so order more than one). This is a popular spot, often with a line across the street; try to arrive early or late (Mon-Sat 12:00-15:00 & 17:30-22:00, Sun 12:00-17:00, 53 Lexington Street).

$$$ Temper Soho pleases well-heeled carnivores. From the nondescript office-block entrance, you'll descend to a cozy, stylish cellar filled with rich smoke from meat grilling on open fires. They carve off chunks for tacos and *parathas* (Indian-style flatbreads). The portions are small and pricey (order multiple courses), but meat lovers willing to pay leave satisfied (Mon-Sat 12:00-22:30, Sun until 21:00, 25 Broadwick Street, tel. 020/3879-3834).

$$$ Kiln invigorates the taste buds with the explosive flavors of Northern Thailand. Squeeze along the long, stainless-steel counter—peering into the wood-fired kilns where the frantic staff does all the cooking—or grab a table in the cramped cellar dining room. The menu skews slightly to the adventurous (i.e., organ meat and strong sauces and curries), with delicious results (daily 12:00-15:00 & 17:00-23:00, 58 Brewer Street).

$$$ Bocca di Lupo, a stylish and popular option, serves half and full portions of classic regional Italian food. Dressy but with a fun energy, it's a place where you'll be glad you made a reservation. The counter seating, on cushy stools with a view into the lively open kitchen, is particularly memorable, or you can take a table in the snug, casual back end (daily 12:30-15:00 & 17:15-23:00, 12 Archer Street, tel. 020/7734-2223, www.boccadilupo.com).

$$$ Kricket Soho serves upmarket Indian fare a few steps from Piccadilly Circus. Opt for the tight, stylish, unpretentious main floor (with counter seating surrounding an open kitchen) or the dining room in the cellar. The small-plates menu is an education in Indian cuisine beyond the corner curry house, with *kulchas* (miniature naan breads with toppings), *kheer* (rice pudding), and

KFC—Keralan fried chicken (Mon-Sat 12:00-14:30 & 17:15-22:30, closed Sun, 12 Denman Street, tel. 020/7734-5612).

$$$$ Nopi is one of a handful of restaurants run by London celebrity chef Yotam Ottolenghi. The cellar features communal tables looking into the busy kitchen, and the cuisine is typical of Ottolenghi's masterful Eastern Mediterranean cooking, with an emphasis on seasonal produce. If you want to splurge in Soho, do it here (Mon-Sat 10:00-15:00 & 17:30-22:30, Sun until 16:00, 21 Warwick Street, tel. 020/7494-9584, www.ottolenghi.co.uk).

$$ Hoppers is an easy entry into Sri Lankan cuisine—reminiscent of Indian but with more tropical flourishes. You'll be glad the menu comes with a glossary of key terms—for example, hopper (a spongy yet firm rice-and-coconut pancake, shaped like a bowl), *kari* (Tamil for "curry"), and *roti* (flatbread). Be adventurous, and seek the waitstaff's advice (Mon-Sat 12:00-14:30 & 17:30-22:30, closed Sun, 49 Frith Street, tel. 020/3319-8110).

$$ Princi is a vast, bright, efficient, wildly popular Italian deli/bakery with Milanese flair. Along one wall is a long counter with display cases offering a tempting array of *pizza rustica*, panini, focaccia, pasta dishes, and desserts. Order your food at the counter, then find a space to share at a long table; or get it to go. They also have a classy restaurant section with reasonable prices if you'd rather have table service (daily 8:00-24:00, 135 Wardour Street, tel. 020/7478-8888).

$$ Yalla Yalla is a bohemian-chic hole-in-the-wall serving up high-quality Beirut street food—hummus, baba ghanoush, tabbouleh, and *shawarmas*. Eat in the cramped and cozy interior or at one of the few outdoor tables (daily 10:00-24:00, 1 Green's Court—just north of Brewer Street, tel. 020/7287-7663).

Between Soho and Covent Garden: Cozy and convivial, **$$ Fernandez & Wells** is a delightfully simple wine, cheese, and ham bar. Grab a stool as you belly up to the big wooden bar. Share a plate of tapas, top-quality cheeses, and/or Spanish, Italian, or French hams with fine bread and oil, all while sipping a nice glass of wine (generally Mon-Sat 10:00-22:00, Sun until 17:00, quality sandwiches at lunch, 1 Denmark Street, tel. 020/ 3302-9799).

Coffee and Pastries: Nordic Bakery is Scandinavian-sleek and faces the green and lovely Golden Square. They serve up good coffee, as well as delicious cinnamon buns and dark rye bread, among other light bites (Mon-Fri 7:30-20:00, Sat-Sun 9:00-19:00, 14A Golden Square, tel. 020/7487-5877). Similarly, keep an eye out for **Ole & Steen,** a chain of coffee shops with generous free samples of cinnamon buns (one location near Soho at 67 Charing Cross Road).

Gelato: Across the street from Bocca di Lupo (listed earlier) is its sister *gelateria,* **Gelupo,** with a wide array of ever-changing but always creative and delicious dessert favorites. Take away or enjoy their homey interior (daily 11:00-23:00, 7 Archer Street, tel. 020/7287-5555).

Near Carnaby Street

The area south of Oxford Circus between Regent Street and Soho Gardens entices hungry shoppers with attention-grabbing, gimmicky restaurants that fill the niche between chains and upscale eateries. Stroll along Ganton, Carnaby, Kingly, and Great Marlborough streets for something that fits your budget and appetite, or consider these.

Kingly Court, with three levels of international restaurants overlooking a convivial courtyard, is a handy place to comparison-shop for a meal. Favorites include **Le Bab,** serving elevated kebabs, and **Señor Ceviche,** with Peruvian raw fish fare (long hours daily, enter either at 9 Kingly Street or at 49 Carnaby Street).

$$$ Dishoom, the super-popular Indian restaurant (see full listing later, under "Near Covent Garden") also has a branch on Kingly Street, with the same top-notch fare and the same long lines (daily 8:00-23:00, 22 Kingly Street, tel. 020/7420-9322).

$$ Mother Mash is a bangers-and-mash version of a fish-and-chips shop. Choose your mash, meat, and gravy and enjoy this simple, satisfying, and thoroughly British meal (daily 10:00-22:00, 26 Ganton Street, tel. 020/7494-9644).

Chinatown

Chinatown is just next door to Soho. These listings straddle the two districts.

On the Main Drag, near the Archways: The intersecting main streets of Chinatown—Wardour Street and Gerrard Street, with the ornamental archways—are lined with touristy, interchangeable Chinese joints. **$$ Four Seasons** is a cheap, reliable, traditional standby (12 Gerrard Street; second location at 23 Wardour). A bit more appealing is **$$ Dumplings' Legend.** The draw here is their dumplings—particularly *siu long bao* (soup dumplings), which you can see being made fresh through the glassed-in kitchen as you enter (no reservations; on pedestrian main drag, 15 Gerrard Street). Other options worth considering include **$$$ Viet Food,** featuring tapas-style Vietnamese small plates with a busy chef in the window (34 Wardour Street); and **$ Rasa Sayang,** a hole-in-the-wall serving Malaysian wok dishes (5 Macclesfield Street).

On Rupert Street: These places are on easy-to-miss Rupert Street, one block over from Wardour. **$$$ XU Teahouse and Restaurant**—more sedate and sophisticated than the eateries in the heart of Chinatown—has a retro-feeling interior, genteel tea counter, and a short, well-curated Taiwanese menu. Come here to escape the bustle and enjoy a quality meal (daily 12:00-23:00, at #30, tel. 020/3319-8147). **$$$ The Palomar,** next door, serves well-respected Israeli and Middle Eastern small plates in a cozy atmosphere (daily 12:00-14:30 & 17:30-23:00, at #34, tel. 020/7439-8777).

On the Edge of Chinatown: $$ Y Ming Chinese Restaurant—across Shaftesbury Avenue from the ornate gates, clatter, and dim sum of Chinatown—has dressy, porcelain-blue European decor, serious but helpful service, and authentic Northern Chinese cooking. It's worth the short walk from the heart of Chinatown for food that's a notch above (good £15 meal deal offered 12:00-18:00, open Mon-Sat 12:00-23:30, closed Sun, 35 Greek Street, tel. 020/7734-2721, run for more than 20 years by William). **$ Jen Café,** across the little square called Newport Place from the main Chinatown strip, is a humble Chinese corner eatery appreciated for its homemade dumplings. It's just stools and simple seating, with fast service, a fun and inexpensive menu, and a devoted following (Mon-Wed 11:00-20:30, Thu-Sun until 21:30, cash only, 4 Newport Place, tel. 020/7287-9708).

Swanky Splurges in Central London

$$$$ The Wolseley is the grand 1920s showroom of a long-defunct British car. The last Wolseley drove out with the Great Depression, but today this old-time bistro bustles with formal waiters serving traditional Austrian and French dishes in an elegant black-marble-and-chandeliers setting fit for its location next to the Ritz. Although the food can be unexceptional, prices

are reasonable considering the grand presentation and setting. Reservations are a must (cheaper soup, salad, and sandwich "café menu" available in all areas of restaurant, daily 11:30-23:00, 160 Piccadilly, tel. 020/7499-6996, www.thewolseley.com). They're popular for their fancy cream tea or afternoon tea (details later, under "Taking Tea in London").

$$$ Brasserie Zédel is the former dining hall of the old Regent Palace Hotel, the biggest hotel in the world when built in 1915. Climbing down the stairs from street level, you're surprised by a gilded grand hall that feels like a circa-1920 cruise ship, filled with a boisterous crowd enjoying big, rich French food—old-fashioned brasserie dishes. With vested waiters, fast service, and paper tablecloths, it's great for a group of friends. After 21:30, the lights dim, the candles are lit, and it gets more romantic with live jazz (nightly inexpensive *plats du jour,* daily 11:30-24:00, 20 Sherwood Street, tel. 020/7734-4888). Across the atrium is the hotel's original Bar Américain (which feels like the 1930s) and the Crazy Coqs venue—busy with "Live at Zédel" music, theater, comedy, and literary events (see www.brasseriezedel.com for schedule).

$$$$ **Rules Restaurant,** established in 1798, is as traditional as can be—extremely British, classy yet comfortable. It's a big, stuffy place, where you'll eat in a plush Edwardian atmosphere with formal service and plenty of game on the menu. (A warning reads, "Game birds may contain lead shot.") This is the place to dress up and splurge for classic English dishes (daily 12:00-23:00, between the Strand and Covent Garden at 34 Maiden Lane, tel. 020/7836-5314, www.rules.co.uk).

Near Covent Garden

Covent Garden bustles with people and touristy eateries. The area feels overrun, but if you must eat around here, you have some good choices.

$$$ **Dishoom** is London's hotspot for upscale Indian cuisine. The dishes seem familiar, but the flavors are a revelation. People line up early (starting around 17:00) for a seat, either on the bright, rollicking, brasserie-like ground floor or in the less appealing basement. Reservations are possible only until 17:45. With its oversized reputation, long lines of tourists, and multiple locations, it's easy to think it's overrated. But the food is simply phenomenal (daily 8:00-23:00, 12 Upper St. Martin's Lane, tel. 020/7420-9320, www.dishoom.com). Other locations include near King's Cross Station and Carnaby Street (listed earlier).

$$$ **Shapur Indian Restaurant** is a well-respected place serving classic Indian dishes from many regions, fine fish, and a tasty and filling *thali* combination platter (including a vegetarian version). It's small, low energy, and dressy, with good service (Mon-Fri 12:00-14:30 & 17:30-23:30, Sat 15:00-23:30, closed Sun, next to Somerset House at 149 Strand, tel. 020/7836-3730, Syed Khan).

$$ **Lamb and Flag Pub** is a survivor—a spit-and-sawdust pub serving traditional grub (like meat pies) two blocks off Covent Garden, yet seemingly a world away. Here since 1772, this pub was a favorite of Charles Dickens and is now a hit with local workers. At lunch, it's all food. In the evening, the ground floor is for drinking and the food service is

upstairs (long hours daily, 33 Rose Street, go up the narrow alley from Floral Street, tel. 020/7497-9504).

Near Trafalgar Square

$$$ Terroirs Wine Bar is an enticing place with a casual but classy ambience that exudes happiness. It's a few steps below street level, with a long zinc bar that has a kitchen view and two levels of tables. The fun menu is mostly Mediterranean and designed to share. The meat-and-cheese plates complement the fine wines available by the glass (Mon-Sat 12:00-23:00, small bites only from 15:00-17:30, closed Sun, reservations smart, two blocks from Trafalgar Square but tucked away at 5 William IV Street, tel. 020/7036-0660, www. terroirswinebar.com).

$$ St. Martin-in-the-Fields Café in the Crypt is just right for a tasty meal on a monk's budget—maybe even on a monk's tomb. You'll dine sitting on somebody's gravestone in an ancient crypt. Their enticing buffet line is kept stocked all day, serving breakfast, lunch, and dinner (hearty traditional desserts, free jugs of water). They also serve a restful £11 afternoon tea (daily 12:00-18:00). You'll find the café directly under St. Martin-in-the-Fields, facing Trafalgar Square—enter through the glass pavilion next to the church (generally daily 10:00-19:30, profits go to the church, Tube: Charing Cross, tel. 020/7766-1158). On Wednesday evenings you can dine to the music of a live jazz band at 20:00 (food available until 21:00, band plays until 22:00, £8-15 tickets). While here, check out the concert schedule for the busy church upstairs (or visit www.stmartin-in-the-fields.org).

$$ The Chandos Pub's Opera Room floats amazingly apart from the tacky crush of tourism around Trafalgar Square. Look for it opposite the National Portrait Gallery (corner of William IV Street and St. Martin's Lane) and climb the stairs—to the left or right of the pub entrance—to the Opera Room. This is a fine Trafalgar rendezvous point and wonderfully local pub. They serve sandwiches and a better-than-average range of traditional pub meals for around £10—meat pies and fish-and-chips are their specialty. The ground-floor pub is stuffed with regulars and offers snugs (private booths) and more serious beer drinking. To eat on that level, you have to order upstairs and carry it down (kitchen open daily 11:30-21:00, Fri until 18:00, order and pay at the bar, 29 St. Martin's Lane, Tube: Leicester Square, tel. 020/7836-1401).

$$ Gordon's Wine Bar is a candlelit 15th-century wine cellar filled with dusty old bottles, faded British memorabilia, and nine-to-fivers. At the "English rustic" buffet, choose a hot meal or cold meat dish with a salad; the cheese plate comes with two big hunks of cheese (from your choice of 20), bread, and a pickle. Then step up to the wine bar and consider the many varieties of wine and port

London Pubs

Historic pubs still dot the London cityscape. The only place to see the very oldest-style tavern is at **$$ Ye Olde Cheshire Cheese,** which was rebuilt in 1667 (after the Great Fire) from a 16th-century tavern. Imagine this mazelike place, with three separate bars, in the pre-Victorian era: With no bar, drinkers gathered around the fireplaces, while tap boys shuttled tankards up from the cellar (pub grub, pricier meals in the restaurant, open daily, 145 Fleet Street, Tube: Blackfriars, tel. 020/7353-6170).

Late-Victorian pubs are more common, such as the lovingly restored **$$ Princess Louise,** dating from 1897 (open daily, no food Sat-Sun, 208 High Holborn, see map on page 172; Tube: Holborn, tel. 020/7405-8816). These places are fancy, often with heavily embossed wallpaper ceilings, decorative tile work, fine-etched glass, ornate carved stillions (the big central hutch for storing bottles and glass), and even urinals equipped with a place to set your glass.

London's best Art Nouveau pub is **$$ The Black Friar** (c. 1900-1915), with fine carved capitals, lamp holders, and quirky phrases worked into the decor. While now operated by a chain, it retains its period charm (open daily, outdoor seating, 174 Queen Victoria Street, Tube: Blackfriars, tel. 020/7236-5474).

These days, former banks are being repurposed as trendy, lavish pubs with elegant bars and freestanding stillions, which provide a fine centerpiece. Three such places are **$$ The Old**

available by the glass (this place is passionate about port—even the house port is excellent). The low carbon-crusted vaulting deeper in the back seems to intensify the Hogarth-painting atmosphere. Although it's crowded—often downright packed with people sitting at shared tables—you can normally find a spot. When sunny, the crowd spills out onto the tight parkside patio (daily 11:00-22:30, 2 blocks from Trafalgar Square, bottom of Villiers Street at #47—the door is locked but it's just around the corner to the right, Tube: Embankment, tel. 020/7930-1408, manager Gerard Menan).

VICTORIA STATION NEIGHBORHOOD

These restaurants are within a few blocks of Victoria Station. As with the accommodations in this area, I've grouped them into east and west of the station (for locations, see the map on page 160).

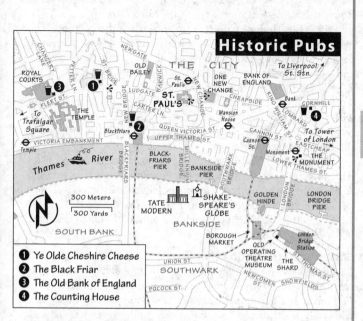

Historic Pubs

❶ Ye Olde Cheshire Cheese
❷ The Black Friar
❸ The Old Bank of England
❹ The Counting House

Bank of England (closed Sun, 194 Fleet Street, Tube: Temple, tel. 020/7430-2255), **$$ The Jugged Hare** (open daily, 172 Vauxhall Bridge Road—see map on page 160, Tube: Victoria, tel. 020/7614-0134), and **$$ The Counting House,** with great sandwiches, homemade meat pies, fish, and fresh vegetables (closed Sat-Sun; gets really busy with the buttoned-down 9-to-5 crowd after 12:15, especially Thu-Fri; 50 Cornhill, Tube: Bank, tel. 020/7283-7123).

Cheap Eats: For groceries, try the following places (all open long hours daily). Inside Victoria Station you'll find an **M&S Simply Food** (near the front, by the bus terminus) and a **Sainsbury's Local** (at rear entrance, on Eccleston Street). A larger **Sainsbury's** is on Wilton Road near Warwick Way, a couple of blocks southeast of the station (closes early on Sun). A string of diverse restaurants lines Wilton Road. For affordable if forgettable meals, try the row of cheap little eateries on Elizabeth Street.

West of Victoria Station (Belgravia)

$ La Bottega is an Italian delicatessen that fits its upscale Belgravia neighborhood. It offers tasty, freshly cooked pastas, lasagnas, and salads, great sandwiches, and a good coffee bar with Italian pastries. It's fast (order at the counter). Grab your meal to go, or enjoy the Belgravia good life with locals, either sitting inside or at a sidewalk table (Mon-Fri 7:30-19:00, Sat-Sun 9:00-18:00, on corner of Ebury and Eccleston Streets, tel. 020/7730-2730).

$$$ The Thomas Cubitt, named for the urban planner who designed much of Belgravia, is a trendy neighborhood gastropub packed with young professionals. It's pricey, a pinch pretentious, and popular for its modern English cooking. With a bright but slightly cramped interior and fine sidewalk seating, it's great for a drink or meal. Upstairs is a more refined and pricier **restaurant** with the same kitchen (food served daily 12:00-22:00, reservations recommended, 44 Elizabeth Street, tel. 020/7730-6060, www.thethomascubitt.co.uk).

$$ Duke of Wellington pub is a classic neighborhood place with forgettable grub, sidewalk seating, and an inviting interior. A bit more lowbrow than my other Belgravia listings, this may be your best glimpse of ye olde London (food served Mon-Sat 12:00-15:00 & 18:00-21:00, Sun lunch only, 63 Eaton Terrace, tel. 020/7730-1782).

East of Victoria Station (Pimlico)

$$ Grumbles brags it's been serving "good food and wine at non-scary prices since 1964." Offering a delicious mix of "modern eclectic French and traditional English," this unpretentious little place with cozy booths inside (on two levels) and a few nice sidewalk tables is the best spot to eat well in this otherwise workaday neighborhood. Their traditional dishes are their forte (early-bird specials, open daily 12:00-14:30 & 18:00-23:00, reservations wise, half a block north of Belgrave Road at 35 Churton Street, tel. 020/7834-0149, www.grumblesrestaurant.co.uk).

$ Pimlico Fresh's breakfasts and lunches feature fresh, organic ingredients, served up with good coffee and/or fresh-squeezed juices. This place is heaven if you need a break from your hotel's bacon-eggs-beans routine (takeout lunches, vegetarian options; Mon-Fri 7:30-18:00, breakfast served until 15:00; Sat-Sun 8:30-18:00; 86 Wilton Road, tel. 020/7932-0030).

$$$ Seafresh Fish Restaurant is the neighborhood place for plaice—and classic and creative fish-and-chips cuisine. You can either step up to the cheaper **takeout counter,** or eat in—enjoying a white-fish ambience. Though Mario's father started this place in 1965, it feels like the chippy of the 21st century (Mon-Sat 12:00-15:00 & 17:00-22:30, closed Sun, 80 Wilton Road, tel. 020/7828-0747).

$$ The Jugged Hare, a 10-minute walk from Victoria Station, fills a lavish old bank building, with vaults replaced by kegs of beer and a kitchen. They have a traditional menu and a plush, vivid pub scene good for a meal or just a drink (food served Mon-Fri

11:00-21:00, Sat-Sun until 20:00, 172 Vauxhall Bridge Road, tel. 020/7828-1543).

$$ St. George's Tavern is the neighborhood's best pub for a full meal. They serve dinner from the same menu in three zones: on the sidewalk to catch the sun and enjoy some people-watching (mostly travelers with wheelie bags), in the ground-floor pub, and in a classier downstairs dining room with full table service. The scene is inviting for just a beer, too (food served daily 12:00-22:00, corner of Hugh Street and Belgrave Road, tel. 020/7630-1116).

$ Tachbrook Market, filling a short traffic-free block near several recommended hotels, is a delightful place to browse a variety of food stalls. Sit on a nearby curb with the locals for a quick lunch. There's also a row of produce, fish, and meat vendors, making this more local-feeling than most London street markets (Mon-Sat 8:00-18:00, closed Sun, on Tachbrook Street just off Warwick Way).

SOUTH KENSINGTON

These places are close to several recommended hotels and just a couple of blocks from the Victoria and Albert Museum and Natural History Museum (Tube: South Kensington; for locations see the map on page 165). The Anglesea Arms pub is a bit farther, but well worth the walk.

Exhibition Road Food Circus: This one-block-long pedestrian zone (on the Victoria and Albert Museum side of the South Kensington Tube station) is lined with enticing little **$-$$** eateries. Facing down Exhibition Road is the best-regarded place in the area, **$$$ Daquise**—serving elevated Polish cuisine in a sophisticated but unstuffy atmosphere. With so many chain restaurants in this area, Daquise is a rare "destination" restaurant (daily 12:00-23:00, 20 Thurloe Street, tel. 020/7589-6117).

Indian: $$ Moti Mahal, with minimalist-yet-upscale ambience and attentive service, serves delicious, mostly Bangladeshi cuisine. Consider chicken *jalfrezi* if you like spicy, and butter chicken if you don't (daily 12:00-14:30 & 17:30-23:30, 3 Glendower Place, tel. 020/7584-8428).

Old Brompton Road Eateries: This street, just one block from the South Kensington Tube station, is lined with a variety of good eateries. These two **$** places are good for a quick bite: **Bosphorus Kebabs** (Turkish food, at #59) and **Beirut Express** (Lebanese, #65). **$$ Rocca,** at #73, is a bright and dressy Italian place with a heated terrace (daily 11:30-23:30, tel. 020/7225-3413).

Classic London Pub: $$ The Anglesea Arms, with a great terrace buried in a classy South Kensington residential area, is a destination pub that feels like the classic neighborhood favorite. It's a thriving and happy place, with a woody ambience. While the food is the main draw, this is also a fine place to just have a beer. Don't let the crowds here put you off. Behind all the drinkers, in back, is an elegant, mellow step-down dining room a world away from any tourism (meals served daily 12:00-15:00 & 18:00-22:00; heading west from Old Brompton Road, turn left at Onslow Gardens and go down a few blocks to 15 Selwood Terrace; tel. 020/7373-7960).

Supermarkets: Tesco Express (50 Old Brompton Road) and **Little Waitrose** (99 Old Brompton Road) are both open long hours daily.

BAYSWATER, NOTTING HILL, AND NEARBY

These are close to my recommended Bayswater and Notting Hill accommodations (for locations, see the map on page 168).

Near Bayswater Tube Station

$$ Cocotte is a "healthy rotisserie" restaurant specializing in delectable roast chicken, plus tempting sides and healthy salads (dine in or take away; daily 12:00-22:00, 95 Westbourne Grove, tel. 020/3220-0076).

$$$ Farmacy is focused on organic vegan fare...with a side of pretense. The menu includes earth bowls, meatless burgers and tacos, and superfood smoothies. With an all-natural, wood-grain vibe, it feels like a top-end health-food store (daily 9:00-16:00 & 18:00-22:00, 74 Westbourne Grove, tel. 020/7221-0705).

$$$ Hereford Road is a cozy, mod eatery tucked away on Leinster Square, serving heavy, meaty English cuisine made with modern panache. Cozy two-person booths face the open kitchen up top; the main dining room is down below under skylights. There are also a few sidewalk tables (daily 18:00-22:00, also open for lunch Thu-Sun 12:00-14:30, reservations smart, 3 Hereford Road, tel. 020/7727-1144, www.herefordroad.org).

$$ Taqueria turns out tasty tacos, quesadillas, and other Mexican fare a short walk from my recommended Bayswater accommodations (daily 12:00-23:00, 141 Westbourne Grove, tel. 020/7229-4734).

$$ The Prince Edward serves good grub in a comfy, family-friendly, upscale-pub setting and at its sidewalk tables (Mon-Sat 10:30-23:00, Sun 12:00-22:30, 2 blocks north of Bayswater Road at the corner of Dawson Place and Hereford Road, 73 Prince's Square, tel. 020/7727-2221).

Supermarkets: Queensway is home to several supermarkets, including **Sainsbury's Local** and **Tesco Express** (both next to Bayswater Tube stop; a larger **Tesco** is near the post office farther along Queensway), and **Marks & Spencer** (inside Whiteleys Shopping Centre). All of these open early and close late (except on Sundays).

Notting Hill

$$$ Geales, which opened its doors in 1939 as a fish-and-chips shop, has been serving Notting Hill ever since. Today, while the menu is more varied, the emphasis is still on fish. The interior is casual, but the food is upscale. The crispy battered cod that put them on the map is still the best around (£15 two-course express menu for lunch and until 20:00 Tue-Fri; open Tue-Sun 12:00-15:00 & 18:00-22:00, closed Mon, reservations smart, 2 Farmer Street, just south of Notting Hill Gate Tube stop, tel. 020/7727-7528, www. geales.com).

$$$$ Mazi is a highly regarded Greek restaurant serving refined renditions of classic dishes, including Greek salad, grilled octopus, and *loukoumades* (doughnuts) in a contemporary, sophisticated setting. Since ordering several small plates can add up, the £15 two-course lunch is a good deal (daily 18:30-22:30, also Tue-Sun 12:00-15:00, 12 Hillgate Street, tel. 020/7229-3794).

$ The Fish House of Notting Hill is an old-fashioned and well-loved chippie, with takeaway on the ground floor and a more expensive **table service** section upstairs (daily 11:30-22:00, 29 Pembridge Road, tel. 020/7229-2626).

Supermarkets: Tesco Metro is a half-block from the Notting Hill Gate Tube stop (near intersection with Pembridge Road at 114 Notting Hill Gate).

Near Kensington Gardens

$$$$ Maggie Jones's has been feeding locals for over 50 years. Its countryside antique decor and candlelight make a visit a step back in time. It's a longer walk than most of my recommendations, but you'll get solid English cuisine. The portions are huge (especially the meat-and-fish pies, their specialty), and prices are a bargain at lunch. You're welcome to split your main course. The candlelit upstairs is the most romantic, while the basement is lively (daily 12:00-14:00 & 18:00-22:30, reservations recommended, 6 Old Court Place, east of Kensington Church Street, near High Street Kensington Tube stop, tel. 020/7937-6462, www.maggie-jones. co.uk).

$$$$ The Shed offers farm-to-table dishes in a rustic-chic setting. Owned by three brothers—a farmer, a chef, and a restaurateur—The Shed serves locally sourced modern English dishes. The portions are hearty, with big, meaty flavors—a change of pace from London's delicate high-end dining scene. It's tucked a block off busy Notting Hill Gate (Mon-Sat 18:00-24:00, also open for lunch Tue-Sat 12:00-15:00, closed Sun, reservations smart, 122 Palace Gardens Terrace, tel. 020/7229-4024, www.theshed-restaurant. com).

$$ The Churchill Arms Pub and Thai Kitchen is a combo

establishment that's a hit in the neighborhood. It offers good beer and a thriving old-English ambience in front and hearty Thai dishes in an enclosed patio in the back. You can eat the Thai food in the tropical hideaway (table service) or in the atmospheric pub section (order at the counter). Bedecked with flowers on the exterior, it's festooned with Churchill memorabilia and chamber pots on the inside (including one with Hitler's mug on it—hanging from the ceiling farthest from Thai Kitchen—sure to cure the constipation of any Brit during World War II). Arrive by 18:00 or after 21:00 to avoid a line (food served daily 12:00-22:00, 119 Kensington Church Street, tel. 020/7727-4242 for the pub or 020/7792-1246 for restaurant, www.churchillarmskensington.co.uk).

$ Café Diana is a healthy little eatery serving sandwiches, salads, and Middle Eastern food. It's decorated—almost shrine-like—with photos of Princess Diana, who used to drop by for pita sandwiches (daily 8:00-23:00, cash only, 5 Wellington Terrace, on Bayswater Road, opposite Kensington Palace Garden gates, where Di once lived, tel. 020/7792-9606, Abdul).

NORTH LONDON

To avoid the touristy crush right around the British Museum, head a few blocks west to the Fitzrovia area. Here, tiny Charlotte Place is lined with small eateries (including my first two listings); nearby, the much bigger Charlotte Street has several more good options (Tube: Goodge Street). See the map on page 172 for locations.

$ Salumeria Dino serves up hearty £5 sandwiches, pasta, and Italian coffee. Dino, a native of Naples, has run his little shop for more than 30 years and has managed to create a classic-feeling Italian deli (cheap takeaway cappuccinos, Mon-Sat 7:30-18:00, closed Sun, 15 Charlotte Place, tel. 020/7580-3938).

$ Lantana OUT, next door to Salumeria Dino, is an Australian coffee shop that sells modern soups, sandwiches, and salads at their takeaway window (£8 daily hot dish). **Lantana IN** is an adjacent sit-down café that serves pricier meals (both Mon-Fri 8:00-18:00, Sat-Sun 9:00-17:00, 13 Charlotte Place, tel. 020/7637-3347).

Near the British Library: Farther north, in the Coal Drops Yard development just behind King's Cross Station, is a branch of the renowned Indian restaurant **$$$ Dishoom** (see description for Covent Garden branch, earlier). Not only is the food excellent, but it's a fun excuse to explore this development—a repurposing of an old industrial site on Regent's Canal.

EAST LONDON

Once known as *the* place to get authentic Indian and Bangladeshi food, the East End is now where lively restaurants, food trucks, and "pop-ups" come to get a toehold in an ever-evolving culinary scene. For locations, see the "East End" map on page 122.

Spitalfields Market Eateries

A few blocks east of Liverpool Street Station, this cavernous hall is filled with a festival of eateries. The modern part of the market—to the west, closer to the train station—has big, brassy outposts of all the predictable London chains. It's much better to focus on the historic, Victorian-age Old Spitalfields Market section, where you'll find a more interesting array of small, one-off **$-$$** eateries and pop-ups. Hours vary, but most places open around 10:00 (11:00 on Sat) and start closing down around 17:00. On weekdays, some stay open until 20:00, but selection is limited (www.oldspitalfieldsmarket.com).

Near Spitalfields Market

These places are burrowed in the tight streets near Spitalfields, a couple of blocks east of Liverpool Street Station.

$$$$ Ottolenghi Spitalfields showcases the big flavors of celebrity chef Yotam Ottolenghi's modern Israeli/Eastern Mediterranean dishes. It's squeezed along tiny Artillery Lane, one of the East End's narrowest and most atmospheric streets. Its little shop in front displays its appetizers and desserts, and sells a few Ottolenghi products, such as preserves, cookbooks, and so on (Mon-Sat 8:00-22:30, Sun 9:00-18:00, reservations recommended, 50 Artillery Lane, tel. 020/7247-1999, www.ottolenghi.co.uk).

$$$$ The English Restaurant, across from Spitalfields Market, started out as a Jewish bakery in the 17th century. It feels traditional for this trendy district, and is perhaps the best place to capture the ambience of the old East End. They serve up traditional British cuisine with a Belgian flair—like updated bread-and-butter pudding—in a snug dining room or a bistro-style bar area (Mon-Fri 8:00-23:00, Sat-Sun 9:30-18:00, 52 Brushfield Street, tel. 020/7247-4110).

$$$ St. John Bread and Wine Restaurant, with a "nose to tail" philosophy, is especially popular at breakfast—served until noon and featuring their award-winning bacon sandwich on thick bread with homemade ketchup (see if you can guess the special seasoning). They also have good lunches and dinners (daily 8:00-23:00, 94 Commercial Street, tel. 020/7251-0848).

$$$ Gunpowder—a modern alternative to the traditional curry houses on nearby Brick Lane—offers a short and carefully crafted menu of updated Indian fare in a tight, noisy, cozy brick space (Mon-Sat 12:00-15:00 & 17:30-22:30, closed Sun, 11 White's Row, www.gunpowderlondon.com).

LONDON

On and near Brick Lane

Once synonymous with curry houses, historic Brick Lane now has many more options (though curry is still what many come here for).

$$ Brick Lane's Famous Curry Houses: This "Curry Row" comes with its own subculture—it's one of the only places in London where curbside hawkers pitch each eatery's "award-winning" pedigree and are eager to offer a discount. Ultimately, little distinguishes the options along here. Compare menus and deals, and take your pick. For something a notch above, head a half-block off Brick Lane to **Meraz Café**, offering a small, simple menu of Indian, Pakistani, and Bangladeshi dishes and homemade chutney (daily 11:00-23:00, 56 Hanbury Street, tel. 020/7247-6999).

Other Brick Lane Delights: The **Old Truman Brewery** hosts a fun courtyard of **$ food trucks** surrounded by prominent street art. Inside the brewery, **Café 1001** is a good place for coffee and cheap cafeteria fare.

FOOD MARKETS

In this expensive city, one of the most cost-effective ways to sample local dishes is to graze through a food market. You'll find English classics (meat pies, bangers and mash, grilled English cheddar cheese sandwiches) and cuisine from every corner of the globe. Most vendors accept credit cards. Keep track of which day of the week the various markets thrive, coordinate your sightseeing accordingly, and suddenly you're a temporary Londoner.

South London

Some of the best food markets in London are South of the Thames.

Borough Market: London's oldest fruit-and-vegetable market has been serving the Southwark community for more than 800 years. Today, it's the granddaddy of all London food halls. There are as many people taking photos as buying fruit, cheese, and beautiful breads, but it's still a fun carnival atmosphere with fantastic food stalls.

For maximum market and minimum crowds, join the locals on Thursdays (full market open Wed-Sat generally 10:00-17:00, surrounding food stalls also open Mon-Tue; south of London Bridge, where Southwark Street meets Borough High Street; Tube: London Bridge, tel. 020/7407-1002, www.boroughmarket.org.uk).

Southbank Centre Food Market: You'll find some of the city's most popular vendors in this paradise of street food near the London Eye. Food vendors are wedged between ugly concrete buildings and elevated train tracks, but the selection is enticing and the location is handy (Fri-Sat 12:00-20:00, Sun-Mon until 18:00, closed midweek; between the Royal Festival Hall and BFI Southbank at Hayward Gallery—from the river, go around behind the buildings to find it; Tube: Waterloo, or Embankment and cross the Jubilee Bridge; tel. 020/3879-9555, www.southbankcentre.co.uk). The market also hosts various festivals throughout the year (German Christmas, coffee, and chocolate are among the favorites).

Ropewalk (Maltby Street Market): This short-but-sweet, completely untouristy food bazaar bustles on weekends under a nondescript rail bridge in the shadow of the Shard. Two dozen vendors fill the narrow passage—about as long as a football field—with a festival of hipster/artisan carts selling a fun array of foods. Tucked among the carts are some good sit-down eateries, including The Walrus & The Carpenter for seafood and Spanish tapas bar Tozino (Sat 9:00-17:00, Sun 11:00-16:00, www.maltby.st). A short walk southeast of Tower Bridge, this youthful area has several rustic microbreweries tucked between self-storage shops and auto-repair garages.

TAKING TEA IN LONDON

While visiting London, consider partaking in this most British of traditions. While some tearooms—such as the wallet-draining tea service at Claridges and the finicky Fortnum & Mason—still require a jacket and tie, most others that I list happily welcome tourists in jeans and sneakers (and cost, on average, £35-50). Most tearooms are usually open for lunch and close about 17:00. At all the places listed next, it's perfectly acceptable for two people to order one afternoon tea and one cream tea and share the afternoon tea's goodies. At many places, you can spring an extra £10 or so to upgrade to a boozy "champagne tea." For details on afternoon tea, see page 1057.

Traditional Tea Experiences

$$$ The Wolseley serves a good afternoon tea between their meal service. Split one with your companion and enjoy two light meals at a great price in classic elegance (generally served 15:00-18:30 daily, see full listing on page 181).

$$$$ The Capital Hotel, a luxury hotel a half-block from Harrods, caters to weary shoppers with its intimate five-table, linen-tablecloth tearoom. It's where the ladies-who-lunch meet to decide whether to buy that Versace gown they've had their eye on. Even so, casual clothes, kids, and sharing plates are all OK (daily 14:00-17:30, book ahead—especially on weekends, 22 Basil Street—see the "West London" color map at the back of this book, Tube: Knightsbridge, tel. 020/7591-1202, www.capitalhotel.co.uk).

$$$$ Fortnum & Mason department store offers tea at several different restaurants within its walls. You can "Take Tea in the Parlour" for a reasonably priced experience (including ice cream and scones; Mon-Sat 10:00-19:30, Sun 11:30-17:00). The pièce de resistance is their Diamond Jubilee Tea Salon, named in honor of the Queen's 60th year on the throne. At royal prices, consider it dinner (Mon-Sat 12:00-19:00, Sun until 18:00, dress up a bit—no shorts, "children must be behaved," 181 Piccadilly—see the "West London" color map at the back of this book, smart to reserve at least a week in advance, tel. 020/7734-8040, www.fortnumandmason.com).

$$$$ **Brown's Hotel** in Mayfair serves a fancy afternoon tea in its English tearoom (you're welcome to ask for second helpings of your favorite scones and sandwiches). Said to be the inspiration for Agatha Christie's *At Bertram's Hotel,* the wood-paneled walls and inviting fire set a scene that's more contemporary-cozy than pinky-raising classy (daily 12:00-18:00, reservations smart, no casual clothing, 33 Albemarle Street—see the "Central London Restaurants" map, Tube: Green Park, tel. 020/7518-4155, www.roccofortehotels.com).

$$$$ **The Orangery at Kensington Palace** may be closed for restoration when you visit. If so, you can take tea next door at the Kensington Palace Pavilion (daily 12:00-16:00, a 10-minute walk through Kensington Gardens from either Queensway or High Street Kensington Tube stations—see the map on page 168; tel. 020/3166-6113, www.hrp.org.uk).

Other Places to Sip Tea

Taking tea is not just for tourists and the wealthy—it's a true English tradition. If you want the teatime experience but are put off by the price, consider these options, more in the £15-30 range.

$$$ **Browns Restaurant** at Butler's Wharf serves an affordable afternoon tea with brioche sandwiches, traditional scones, and sophisticated desserts (daily 15:00-17:00, 26 Shad Thames facing Tower Bridge—see the map on page 176, tel. 020/7378-1700, www.browns-restaurants.co.uk).

$$ **The Restaurant at Sotheby's,** on the ground floor of the auction giant's headquarters, gives shoppers a break from fashionable New Bond Street (tea served Mon-Fri 15:00-16:45, reservations smart, 34 New Bond Street—see the map on page 176, Tube: Bond Street or Oxford Circus, tel. 020/7293-5077, www.sothebys.com).

At $ **Waterstones** bookstore you can put together a spread for less than £10 in their fifth-floor view café (203 Piccadilly).

Museum Cafés: Many museum restaurants offer a fine inexpensive tea service. The $$$ **National Dining Rooms,** within the Sainsbury Wing of the National Gallery on Trafalgar Square, serves a £7.50 cream tea and £22.50 afternoon tea with a great view from 14:30 to 16:30 (tea also served in National Café at the museum's Getty entrance, from 14:30 to 17:30; Tube: Charing Cross or Leicester Square, tel. 020/7747-2525). The **$$ Victoria and Albert Museum** café serves a classic cream tea in an elegant setting that won't break your budget, and the **$$$ Wallace Collection** serves reasonably priced afternoon tea and cream tea in its atrium (see page 106).

Shop Cafés: You'll find good-value teas at various cafés in shops and bookstores across London. Most department stores on Oxford Street (including those between Oxford Circus and Bond Street Tube stations) offer an afternoon tea.

London Connections

BY PLANE

London has six airports; I've focused my coverage on the two most widely used—Heathrow and Gatwick—with a few tips for using the others (Stansted, Luton, London City, and Southend). For more on flights within Europe, see the "Transportation" section of the Practicalities chapter.

Heathrow Airport

Heathrow Airport is one of the world's busiest airports. Consider this: 75 million passengers a year on 500,000 flights from 200 destinations traveling on 80 airlines, like some kind of global maypole dance. For Heathrow's airport, flight, and transfer information, call the switchboard at 0844-335-1801, or visit the helpful website www.heathrow. com (code: LHR).

Heathrow's terminals are numbered T-2 through T-5. Each terminal is served by different airlines and alliances; for example, T-5 is exclusively for British Air and Iberia Air flights, while T-2 serves mostly Star Alliance flights, such as United and Lufthansa.

You can walk between T-2 and T-3. From this central hub (called "Heathrow Central"), T-4 and T-5 split off in opposite directions (and are not walkable). The easiest way to travel between the T-2/T-3 cluster and either T-4 or T-5 is by Heathrow Express train (free to transfer between terminals, but tickets are required—hold onto your ticket even once you've passed through the turnstile—train departs every 15-20 minutes). You can also take a shuttle bus (free, serves all terminals), or the Tube (requires a ticket, serves all terminals).

If you're flying out of Heathrow, it's critical to confirm which

LONDON

London's Airports

Luton

Luton

Stansted

#75 & A1

Southend

ST. PANCRAS

PADDINGTON

LIVERPOOL STREET

Southend

Reading

Windsor
#71 & 77

Tube

VICTORIA

D.L.R.

London City

To Bath

Rail Air Link

Heathrow

VICTORIA COACH STN.

London

Thames

Guildford

Gatwick

Ashford

To Paris, Amsterdam & Brussels

- - - - - Rail
━━━━━ Eurostar Rail
──────── Tube & D.L.R.
- - - - Bus

ALL BUSES ARE NATIONAL EXPRESS UNLESS NOTED

↓To Brighton

English Channel

terminal your flight will use (look at your ticket/boarding pass, check online, or call your airline in advance)—if it's T-4 or T-5, allow extra time. Taxi drivers generally know which terminal you'll need based on the airline, but bus drivers may not.

Services: Each terminal has an airport information desk (open long hours daily), car-rental agencies, exchange bureaus, ATMs, a pharmacy, a VAT refund desk (tel. 0845-872-7627), and pay baggage storage (long hours daily, www.left-baggage.co.uk). Heathrow offers both free Wi-Fi and pay internet access points (in each terminal, check map for locations). You'll find a post office on the first floor of T-3 (departures area). Each terminal also has cheap eateries.

Heathrow's small **"TI"** (tourist info shop), even though it's a for-profit business, is worth a visit if you're nearby and want to pick up free information, including the *London Planner* visitors guide (long hours daily, 5-minute walk from T-3 in Tube station, follow signs to Underground; bypass queue for transit info to reach window for London questions).

Getting Between Heathrow and Downtown London

You have several options for traveling the 14 miles between Heathrow Airport and downtown London: Tube (about £6/person), bus (£8-10/person), express train with connecting Tube or taxi (£22-25, price does not include connecting Tube fare), or most expensive—taxi or car service. The one that works best for you will depend on your arrival terminal, your destination in central London, and your budget.

By Tube (Subway): The Tube takes you from any Heathrow terminal to downtown London in 50-60 minutes on the Piccadilly

Line (6/hour, buy ticket at Tube station self-service machine). Depending on your destination in London, you may need to transfer (for example, if headed to the Victoria Station neighborhood, transfer at Hammersmith to the District line and ride six more stops).

If you plan to use the Tube in London, it makes sense to buy a pay-as-you-go Oyster card (possibly adding a 7-Day Travelcard) at the airport's Tube station ticket machines. (For details on these passes, see page 45.) If you add a Travelcard that covers only Zones 1-2, you'll need to pay a small supplement for the initial trip from Heathrow (Zone 6) to downtown.

If you're taking the Tube from downtown London *to* the airport, note that Piccadilly Line trains don't stop at every terminal. Trains either stop at T-4, then T-2/T-3 (also called Heathrow Central), in that order; or T-2/T-3, then T-5. When leaving central London on the Tube, allow extra time if going to T-4 or T-5, and check the reader board in the station to make sure that the train goes to the right terminal before you board.

By Bus: Most buses depart from the outdoor common area called the Central Bus Station, a five-minute walk from the T-2/T-3 complex. To connect between T-4 or T-5 and the Central Bus Station, ride the free Heathrow Express train or the shuttle buses.

National Express has regular service from Heathrow's Central Bus Station to Victoria Coach Station in downtown London, near several of my recommended hotels. While slow, the bus is affordable and convenient for those staying near Victoria Station (£8-10, 1-2/hour, less frequent from Victoria Station to Heathrow, 45-75 minutes depending on time of day, tel. 0871-781-8181, www.nationalexpress.com). A less-frequent National Express bus goes from T-5 directly to Victoria Coach Station.

By Train: The **Heathrow Express** runs between Heathrow Airport and London's Paddington Station. At Paddington, you're in the thick of the Tube system, with easy access to any of my recommended neighborhoods—my Paddington hotels are just outside the front door, and Notting Hill Gate is just two Tube stops away.

The Heathrow Express is fast but pricey (£22-25 one-way, price depends on time of day, £37 round-trip, cheaper if purchased online in advance, covered by BritRail pass; 4/hour, Mon-Sat 5:00-24:00, Sun from 6:00, 15 minutes to downtown from Heathrow Central Station serving T-2/T-3, 21 minutes from T-5; for T-4 take free transfer to Heathrow Central, tel. 0345-600-1515, www.heathrowexpress.co.uk).

All Heathrow Express stations have ticket barriers, which require a mobile or paper train ticket to pass through (required even for free transfers between terminals; well-marked machines located near barriers). Tickets can be purchased through the Heathrow Express website or app, or at ticket machines and windows at stations. You can also use funds on an Oyster card, but only for same-day fares (not for buying in advance).

A cheaper alternative to the Heathrow Express—the new **Crossrail Elizabeth line**—may not yet be operational by the time you visit, but when it opens, it will be faster (and more expensive) than the Tube; see www.tfl.gov.uk for updates.

By Car Service: Just Airports offers a private car service between five London airports and the city center (see website for price quote, tel. 020/8900-1666, www.justairports.com).

By Taxi or Uber: Taxis from the airport cost £45-75 to west and central London (one hour). For four people traveling together, this can be a reasonable option. Hotels can often line up a cab back to the airport for about £50. If running, Uber also offers London airport pickup and drop-off.

Gatwick Airport

Gatwick Airport is halfway between London and the south coast (code: LGW, tel. 0844-892-0322, www.gatwickairport.com). Gatwick has two terminals, North and South, which are easily connected by a free monorail (two-minute trip, runs 24 hours). Note that boarding passes say "Gatwick N" or "Gatwick S" to indicate your terminal. The Gatwick Express trains (described next) stop only at Gatwick South. Schedules in each terminal show only arrivals and departures from that terminal.

Getting Between Gatwick and Downtown London: Gatwick Express trains are the best way into London from this airport. They shuttle conveniently between Gatwick South and London's **Victoria Station,** with many of my recommended hotels close by (£20 one-way, £35 round-trip, at least 10 percent cheaper if purchased online, Oyster cards accepted but no discount offered, 4/hour, 30 minutes, runs 5:00-24:00 daily, a few trains as early as 3:30, tel. 0845-850-1530, www.gatwickexpress.com). If you buy your tickets at the station before boarding, ask about possible group deals. (If you see others in the ticket line, you could suggest buying your tickets together.) When going *to* the airport, at Victoria Station note that Gatwick Express has its own ticket windows right by the platform (tracks 13 and 14). You'll also find easy-to-use ticket machines nearby.

A train also runs between Gatwick South and **St. Pancras International Station** (£12.10, 3-5/hour, 45-60 minutes, www. thetrainline.com)—useful for travelers taking the Eurostar train (to Paris, Amsterdam, or Brussels) or staying in the St. Pancras/King's Cross neighborhood.

While even slower, the **bus** is a cheap and handy option to the Victoria Station neighborhood. National Express runs a bus from Gatwick directly to Victoria Station (£10, at least hourly, 1.5 hours, tel. 0871-781-8181, www.nationalexpress.com); EasyBus has one that stops near the Earl's Court Tube stop (£4-10 depending on how far ahead you book, 2-3/hour, www.easybus.com).

London's Other Airports

Stansted Airport: From Stansted (code: STN, tel. 0844-335-1803, www.stanstedairport.com), you have several options for getting into or out of London. Two different **buses** connect the airport and London's Victoria Station neighborhood: National Express (£9-12, every 15 minutes, 2 hours, runs 24 hours a day, picks up and stops throughout London, ends at Victoria Coach Station or Liverpool Street Station, tel. 0871-781-8181, www.nationalexpress.com) and Airport Bus Express (£9, 2/hour, 1.5-2 hours). Or you can take the faster, pricier Stansted Express **train** (£19, cheaper if booked online, connects to London's Tube system at Tottenham Hale or Liverpool Street, 2-4/hour, 45 minutes, 4:30-23:00, www.stanstedexpress.com). Stansted is expensive by **cab**; figure £100-120 one-way from central London.

Luton Airport: For Luton (code: LTN, tel. 01582/405-100, www.london-luton.co.uk), the fastest way to get into London is by **train** to St. Pancras International Station (£14-17 one-way, 1-5/hour, 35-45 minutes—check schedule to avoid slower trains, tel. 0345-712-5678, www.eastmidlandstrains.co.uk); catch the 10-minute shuttle bus (every 10 minutes) from outside the terminal to the Luton Airport Parkway Station. You can purchase a shuttle bus and train combo-ticket from kiosks or ticket machines inside the airport. When buying your train ticket *to* Luton, make sure you select "Luton Airport" as your destination rather than "Parkway Station" to ensure the shuttle fare is included.

The **National Express bus** A1 runs from Luton to Victoria Coach Station (£7-11 one-way, 2/hour, 1-1.5 hours, runs 24 hours, tel. 0871-781-8181, www.nationalexpress.com). The **Green Line express bus** #757 runs to Buckingham Palace Road, just south of Victoria Station, and stops en route near the Baker Street Tube station—best if you're staying near Paddington Station or in North London (£10 one-way, 2-4/hour, 1-1.5 hours, runs 24 hours, tel. 0344-800-4411, www.greenline.co.uk). If you're sleeping at Luton, consider EasyHotel's Luton location.

London City and Southend Airports: To get into the city center from London City Airport (code: LCY, tel. 020/7646-0088, www.londoncityairport.com), take the Docklands Light Railway (DLR) to the Bank Tube station, which is one stop east of St. Paul's on the Central Line (less than £6 one-way, covered by Travelcard, a bit cheaper with an Oyster card, 20 minutes, www.tfl.gov.uk/dlr). Some EasyJet flights land farther out, at Southend Airport (code: SEN, tel. 01702/538-500, www.southendairport.com). Trains connect this airport to London's Liverpool Street Station (£16.20 one-way, 3-8/hour, 55 minutes, www.abelliogreateranglia.co.uk).

Connecting London's Airports by Bus

A handy **National Express bus** runs between Heathrow, Gatwick, Stansted, and Luton airports—easier than having to cut through the center of London—although traffic can be bad and can increase travel times (tel. 0871-781-8181, www.nationalexpress.com).

From Heathrow Airport to: Gatwick Airport (£25, 1-6/hour, about 1.5 hours—but allow at least three hours between flights), **Stansted Airport** (£27, 1-2/hour direct, 1.5 hours), **Luton Airport** (£27, roughly hourly, 1 hour).

BY TRAIN

London has a different train station for each region of Britain. There are nine main stations (see the map):

Euston: Serves northwest England, North Wales, and Scotland.

St. Pancras International: Serves north and south England, plus the Eurostar to Paris, Amsterdam, or Brussels (see "Crossing the Channel by Eurostar Train," later).

King's Cross: Serves northeast England and Scotland, including York and Edinburgh.

Liverpool Street: Serves east England, including Essex and Harwich.

London Bridge: Serves south England, including Brighton.

Waterloo: Serves south England, including Salisbury and Southampton.

Victoria: Serves Gatwick Airport, Canterbury, Dover, and Brighton.

Paddington: Serves south and southwest England, including Heathrow Airport, Windsor, Bath, Oxford, South Wales, and the Cotswolds.

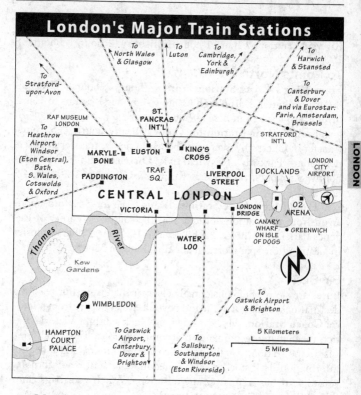

London's Major Train Stations

To North Wales & Glasgow

To Luton

To Cambridge, York & Edinburgh

To Harwich & Stansted

To Stratford-upon-Avon

To Canterbury & Dover and via Eurostar: Paris, Amsterdam, Brussels

RAF MUSEUM LONDON

To Heathrow Airport, Windsor (Eton Central), Bath, S. Wales, Cotswolds & Oxford

ST. PANCRAS INT'L

MARYLE-BONE

EUSTON

KING'S CROSS

STRATFORD INT'L

PADDINGTON

TRAF. SQ.

LIVERPOOL STREET

DOCKLANDS

LONDON CITY AIRPORT

CENTRAL LONDON

VICTORIA

LONDON BRIDGE

O2 ARENA

CANARY WHARF ON ISLE OF DOGS

GREENWICH

Thames River

WATER-LOO

Kew Gardens

WIMBLEDON

HAMPTON COURT PALACE

To Gatwick Airport, Canterbury, Dover & Brighton

To Salisbury, Southampton & Windsor (Eton Riverside)

To Gatwick Airport & Brighton

5 Kilometers

5 Miles

LONDON

Marylebone: Serves southwest and central England, including Stratford-upon-Avon.

In addition, London has several smaller train stations that you're less likely to use, such as **Charing Cross** (serves southeast England, including Dover) and **Blackfriars** (serves Brighton).

Any train station has schedule information, can make reservations, and can sell tickets for any destination. Most stations offer a baggage-storage service (look for *left luggage* signs); because of long security lines, it can take a while to check or pick up your bag (www.left-baggage.co.uk). For more details on the services available at each station, see www.nationalrail.co.uk/stations. UK train and bus info is available at www.traveline.org.uk. For information on tickets and rail passes, see the Practicalities chapter.

Train Connections from London
To Points West
From Paddington Station to: Windsor (Windsor & Eton Central Station, 2/hour, 35 minutes, easy change at Slough), **Bath** (2/hour, 1.5 hours), **Moreton-in-Marsh** (hourly, 1.5 hours), **Cardiff** (2/hour, 2 hours).

From Waterloo Station to: Windsor (to Windsor & Eton Riverside Station, 2/hour, 1 hour), **Salisbury** (2/hour, 1.5 hours).

To Points North

From King's Cross Station: York (3/hour, 2 hours), **Durham** (hourly, 3 hours), **Edinburgh** (2/hour, 4.5 hours). Trains to **Cambridge** also leave from here (4/hour, 1 hour).

From Euston Station to: Conwy (nearly hourly, 3.5 hours, transfer in Chester), **Liverpool** (hourly, 3 hours, transfer at Liverpool South Parkway), **Keswick/Lake District** (train to Penrith—hourly, 3.5 hours, then bus at Keswick), **Glasgow** (1-2/hour, 4.5 hours).

From Marylebone Station: Trains leave for Stratford-upon-Avon from this station, located near the southwest corner of Regent's Park (2/day direct, 2.5 hours; also 1-2/hour, 2 hours, transfer in Leamington Spa, Dorridge, or Birmingham Moor).

BY BUS

Buses are slower but considerably cheaper than trains for reaching destinations around Britain and beyond. Most depart from **Victoria Coach Station,** which is one long block south of Victoria Station (near many recommended accommodations, Tube: Victoria). Inside the station, you'll find basic eateries, kiosks, and a helpful information desk stocked with schedules and staff ready to point you to your bus or answer any questions. Watch your bags carefully—thieves thrive at the station.

Ideally you'll buy your tickets online (for tips on buying tickets and taking buses, see page 1070 of the Practicalities chapter). But if you must buy one at the station, arrive an hour before the bus departs, or drop by the day before. Ticketing machines are scattered around the station (separate machines for National Express/Eurolines and Megabus; you can buy either for today or for tomorrow); there's also a ticket counter near gate 21. For UK train and bus info, check www.traveline.info.

National Express buses go to: **Bath** (hourly, 3 hours), **Cambridge** (every 60-90 minutes, 2 hours), **Cardiff** (hourly, 3.5 hours), **Stratford-upon-Avon** (3/day, 3.5 hours), **Liverpool** (8/day direct, 5.5 hours, overnight available), **York** (3/day direct, 6 hours), **Durham** (3/day direct, 7 hours, train is better), **Glasgow** (2-4/day direct, 10 hours, train is much better), **Edinburgh** (2/day direct, 10 hours, go by train instead).

To Dublin, Ireland: This bus/boat journey, operated by Eurolines, takes 10-12 hours (£45, 1/day, departs Victoria Coach Station at 18:00, check in with passport one hour before). Consider a cheap 1-hour Ryanair flight instead.

To the Continent: Especially in summer, buses run to desti-

Public Transportation near London

Rail ------
Bus - - - -
Boat ....

Area covered by London Plus Pass

30 Kilometers
30 Miles (approx. scale)

Note: Bus Lines Follow Most Rail Lines

nations all over Europe, including Paris, Amsterdam, Brussels, and Germany (sometimes crossing the Channel by ferry, other times through the Chunnel). For any international connection, you need to check in with your passport one hour before departure. For details, call 0871-781-8181 or visit www.nationalexpress.com.

CROSSING THE CHANNEL BY EUROSTAR TRAIN

The Eurostar zips you (and up to 800 others in 18 sleek cars) from downtown London to downtown **Paris** (1-2/hour, 2.5 hours), **Brussels** (9/day, 2 hours), or **Amsterdam** (3/day, 4 hours; more with transfer in Brussels). The train travels at 190 mph, and the tunnel crossing is a 20-minute, silent, 100 mph nonevent. Your ears won't even pop.

Currently, trains only run direct from London to Amsterdam—those traveling *from* Amsterdam will need to change trains in Brussels and go through passport control. (Direct service from Amsterdam is in the works.)

Eurostar Tickets and Fares: A one-way ticket between London and Paris, Brussels, or Amsterdam can vary widely in price; for instance, $45-200 (Standard class), $160-310 (Standard Premier), and $400 (Business Premier). Fares depend on how far ahead you reserve and whether you're eligible for any discounts—available for children (under 12), youths (under 26), and adults booking months ahead or purchasing round-trip. You can book tickets 4-9 months in advance. Tickets can be exchanged before the scheduled departure for a fee (about $45 plus the cost of any price increase), but only Business Premier class allows any refund.

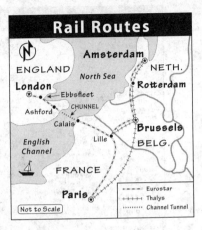

Buy tickets online using the print-at-home eticket option (see www.ricksteves.com/eurostar or www.eurostar.com). You can also order by phone through Rail Europe (US tel. 800-387-6782) for home delivery before you go, or through Eurostar (tel. 0843-218-6186, priced in euros) to pick up at the station. In Britain, tickets are issued only at the Eurostar office in St. Pancras. In continental Europe, you can buy tickets at any major train station in any country or at any travel agency that handles train tickets (expect a booking fee). If you have a Eurail Global Pass, seat reservations are available at Eurostar departure stations, through US agents, or by phone with Eurostar (generally harder to get at other train stations and travel agencies; $35 in Standard, $45 in Standard Premier, can sell out, no benefit with BritRail or other single-country pass).

Taking the Eurostar: Trains depart from and arrive at St. Pancras International Station. Check in at least 30 minutes early (times listed on tickets are local; Britain is one hour earlier than continental Europe). Pass through airport-like security, show your passport to customs officials, and locate your departure gate. The waiting area has shops, newsstands, horrible snack bars and cafés (get food beforehand), free Wi-Fi, and a currency-exchange booth.

WINDSOR & CAMBRIDGE

Windsor and Cambridge are two very different but equally enjoyable day-trip possibilities near London.

The primary residence of Her Majesty the Queen, Windsor hosts a castle that's regally lived-in, yet open to the public. This is simply a charming town to relax in—and its proximity to Heathrow Airport (60 minutes by train west of London) makes Windsor easy to combine with a flight into or out of London. Nearby is an oddball collection of intriguing sights, including Legoland Windsor, Eton College (Britain's most elite

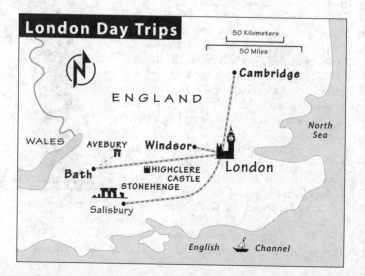

London Day Trips

high school), Ascot Racecourse (for horse racing), and Highclere Castle, where *Downton Abbey* was filmed.

Britain's venerable University of Cambridge is mixed into the delightful town of Cambridge, north of London, which offers a mellow, fun-to-explore townscape with a big-league university.

Other destinations that make for a practical day trip from London include Stonehenge and Salisbury (covered in the Avebury, Stonehenge & Salisbury chapter).

GETTING AROUND

By Train: If day-tripping from London, take advantage of British Rail's discounts. The "off-peak day return" ticket is a round-trip fare that costs virtually the same as one-way, provided you depart London outside rush hour (usually after 9:30 on weekdays and anytime Sat-Sun). Be sure to get the "day return" ticket (round-trip within a single day) rather than the more expensive, standard "return" ticket. You can also save a little money if you purchase tickets before 18:00 the day before your trip.

By Train Tour: London Walks offers a variety of "Daytrips from London" tours year-round by train, including a Cambridge itinerary (see page 59 for more on London Walks).

Windsor

Windsor, a compact and easy walking town of about 30,000 people, originally grew up around the royal residence. In 1070, William the Conqueror continued his habit of kicking Saxons out of their various settlements, taking over what the locals called "Windlesora" (meaning "riverbank with a hoisting winch")—which eventually became "Windsor." William built the first fortified castle on a chalk hill above the Thames; later kings added on to his early designs, rebuilding and expanding the castle and surrounding gardens.

By setting up their primary residence here, modern monarchs increased Windsor's popularity and prosperity—most notably, Queen Victoria, whose stern statue glares at you as you approach the castle. After her death, Victoria rejoined her beloved husband, Albert, in the Royal Mausoleum at Frogmore House, a mile south of the castle in a private section of the Home Park (house and mausoleum rarely open). Within the grounds of

Frogmore House is Frogmore Cottage—the home of Prince Harry, the Duchess of Sussex (Meghan Markle), and wee Master Archie.

The current Queen considers Windsor her primary residence; she generally hangs her crown here on weekends, using it as an escape from her workaday grind at Buckingham Palace in the city. You can tell if Her Majesty is in residence by which flag is flying above the round tower: If it's the royal standard (a red, yellow, and blue flag) instead of the Union Jack, the Queen is at home.

While 99 percent of visitors just come to tour the castle and go, some enjoy spending the night. Daytime crowds trample Windsor's charm, which is most evident when the tourists are gone. Consider overnighting here—parking and access to Heathrow Airport are easy, and an evening at the horse races (on Mondays) is hoof-pounding, heart-thumping fun.

GETTING TO WINDSOR

By Train: Windsor has two train stations—Windsor & Eton Central and Windsor & Eton Riverside. London's Paddington Station connects with Windsor & Eton Central (2-3/hour, 35 minutes, easy change at Slough—typically just across the platform, www.gwr.com). London's Waterloo Station connects with Windsor & Eton Riverside (2/hour, no changes but slower—55 minutes, www.nationalrail.co.uk). Either trip costs about £11 one-way (a few pounds more for same-day return).

By Bus: Green Line buses #702 and #703 run—very slooooowly—from London's Victoria Colonnades (between the Victoria train and coach stations) to the Parish Church stop on Windsor's High Street, before continuing on to Legoland (1-2/hour, 1.5 hours to Windsor, prices typically £6-10 each way, tel. 0871-200-2233, www.firstgroup.com).

By Car: Windsor is about 20 miles from London. The town (and then the castle and Legoland) is well signposted from the M-4 motorway. It's a convenient first stop if you're arriving at Heathrow and renting a car there.

From Heathrow Airport: You have two public transit options, both around £11. The train requires two changes (first take the Heathrow Express to Hayes & Harlington station, transfer to a train to Slough, then transfer again to Windsor, 50 minutes total). Or you can take First Bus Company's bus #8 or #9 from Terminal 5 (2/hour, 1 hour). London black cabs can (and do) charge whatever they like from Heathrow to Windsor; avoid them by calling a local cab company, such as Windsor Cars (tel. 01753/677-677, www.windsorcars.com).

Orientation to Windsor

Windsor's pleasant pedestrian shopping zone litters the approach to its famous palace with fun temptations. You'll find most shops and restaurants around the castle on High and Thames streets, and down the pedestrian Peascod Street (PESS-cot), which runs perpendicular to High Street.

TOURIST INFORMATION

The TI is in the Windsor Royal Shopping Centre's Old Booking Hall, immediately adjacent to Windsor & Eton Central Station (daily 10:00-16:00, sells discounted tickets to Legoland; tel. 01753/743-900, www.windsor.gov.uk).

ARRIVAL IN WINDSOR

By Train: Whichever train station you arrive at, you're only a five-minute walk to the castle. From Windsor & Eton Central, walk through the Windsor Royal Shopping Centre (which houses the TI), and up the hill to the castle. From Windsor & Eton Riverside, you'll see the castle as you exit—just follow the wall up and around to the ticket office.

By Car: Follow signs from the M-4 motorway for pay-and-display parking in the center. River Street Car Park is closest to the castle, but it's pricey and often full. The cheaper, bigger Alexandra Car Park (near the riverside Alexandra Gardens) is farther west, just below the central train station (find the stairs up to the station platform, and exit into the Windsor Royal Shopping Centre with the TI). The cheapest parking option is the King Edward VII Avenue car-park-and-ride, northeast of the castle on the B-470 (includes shuttle bus into town).

HELPFUL HINTS

Supermarkets: Pick up picnic supplies at **Marks & Spencer** (on the pedestrian shopping street near the TI, at 130 Peascod Street) or at **Waitrose** (bigger but a bit farther, buried in the King Edward Court Shopping Centre behind the central station). Just outside the castle, you'll find long benches near the statue of Queen Victoria—great for people-watching while you munch.

Hiking and Biking: Windsor and Eton occupy a lovely area on the Thames that's ideal for a pleasant walk or bike ride—get

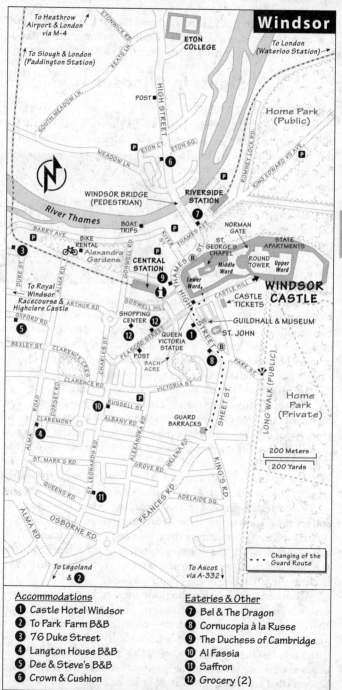

Windsor

To Heathrow Airport & London via M-4

To Slough & London (Paddington Station)

ETON COLLEGE

To London (Waterloo Station)

POST

ETONWICK RD.
KEATS LN.
HIGH STREET
SOUTH MEADOW LN.
MEADOW LN.
ETON CT.
ETON SQ.

Home Park (Public)

ROMNEY LOCK RD.
KING EDWARD VII AVE.

WINDSOR BRIDGE (PEDESTRIAN)

River Thames

BARRY AVE.

BIKE RENTAL
Alexandra Gardens

BOAT TRIPS

RIVERSIDE STATION

RIVER ST.
THAMES AVE.

NORMAN GATE
ST. GEORGE'S CHAPEL
STATE APARTMENTS
ROUND TOWER
Middle Ward
Upper Ward
Lower Ward

WINDSOR CASTLE

DUKE ST.
ALMA RD.
GOSWELL RD.

CENTRAL STATION

GOSWELL HILL

To Royal Windsor Racecourse & Highclere Castle

ARTHUR RD.

OXFORD RD.

BEXLEY ST.

CLARENCE CRES.
CHARLES ST.
CLARENCE RD.

ALMA ROAD
DORSET RD.

CLAREMONT

ST. MARK'S RD.

QUEENS RD.

ST. LEONARDS RD.

ALMA RD.

OSBORNE RD.

THAMES ST.
HIGH STREET
CASTLE HILL
CASTLE TICKETS

GUILDHALL & MUSEUM
ST. JOHN

SHOPPING CENTER

QUEEN VICTORIA STATUE

PEASCOD STREET

POST

BACHELORS ACRE

VICTORIA ST.

RUSSELL ST.
ALBANY RD.
ALEXANDRA RD.

GUARD BARRACKS

GROVE RD.
HELENA RD.

FRANCES RD.

ADELAIDE SQ.

PARK ST.
SHEET ST.
KING'S RD.
LONG WALK (PUBLIC)

Home Park (Private)

200 Meters
200 Yards

To Legoland & ❷

To Ascot via A-332

Changing of the Guard Route

Accommodations
❶ Castle Hotel Windsor
❷ To Park Farm B&B
❸ 76 Duke Street
❹ Langton House B&B
❺ Dee & Steve's B&B
❻ Crown & Cushion

Eateries & Other
❼ Bel & The Dragon
❽ Cornucopia à la Russe
❾ The Duchess of Cambridge
❿ Al Fassia
⓫ Saffron
⓬ Grocery (2)

WINDSOR & CAMBRIDGE

suggestions at the TI. You can rent bikes at **Extreme Motion,** near the river in Alexandra Gardens (summer daily 10:00-18:00, Sat-Sun only off-season, tel. 01753/830-220).

Sights in Windsor

▲▲WINDSOR CASTLE

Windsor Castle, the official home of England's royal family for 900 years, claims to be the largest and oldest occupied castle in

the world. Thankfully, touring it is simple. You'll see sprawling grounds, lavish staterooms, a crowd-pleasing dollhouse, and an exquisite Perpendicular Gothic chapel. Allow at least two hours for a complete visit.

Cost: £22.50, includes entry to castle grounds and all exhibits inside.

Hours: Grounds and most interiors open daily 10:00-17:15, Nov-Feb until 16:15, except St. George's Chapel, which is closed Sun to tourists (but open to worshippers; wait at the exit gate to be escorted in). Last entry to grounds and St. George's Chapel is 75 minutes before closing. Last entry to State Apartments and Queen Mary's Dolls' House is 45 minutes before closing.

Information: Tel. 020/7766-7324, www.rct.uk.

Crowd Control: Ticket lines can be quite long in summer. You can expect the worst crowds from opening until 13:00 any time of year. Avoid the wait by purchasing tickets in advance at www.rct.uk (collect them at the prepaid ticket window), or in person at the Buckingham Palace ticket office in London. (There's nowhere in Windsor to buy advance tickets.) All visitors must go through a security checkpoint, which can further slow entry at busy times.

Possible Closures: On rare occasions when the Queen is entertaining guests, the State Apartments close (and tickets are slightly reduced). Sometimes the entire castle closes. It's smart to call ahead or check the website (especially in mid-June) to make sure everything is open when you want to go. While you're at it, confirm the Changing of the Guard schedule.

Tours: An included **audioguide** (dry, reverent, informative) covers both the grounds and interiors. For a good overview—and an opportunity to ask questions—consider the free 30-minute **guided walk** around the grounds (about 5/day, schedule posted on path up to the main gate). The official £5 guidebook is full of gorgeous images and makes a fine souvenir but adds no information beyond what is covered in the audioguide and tour.

Changing of the Guard: The Changing of the Guard usually takes place Tuesday, Thursday, and Saturday at 11:00 (confirm schedule on website; canceled in very bad weather). The fresh guards, led by a marching band, leave their barracks on Sheet Street and march up High Street, hanging a right at Victoria, then a left into the castle's Lower Ward, arriving at about 11:00.

After about a half-hour, the tired guards march back the way the new ones came. If you want to view the ceremony from inside the castle, it's smart to arrive as early as possible (no later than 10:30 on quiet days) to have time to buy tickets, clear security, and stake out a spot with a clear view. If you arrive late, you could just wait for them to march by on High Street or on the lower half of Castle Hill.

Evensong: An evensong takes place in the chapel nightly at 17:15 (free for worshippers, line up at exit gate to be admitted).

Best View: While you can get great views of the castle from any direction, the classic views are from the wooded avenue called the Long Walk, which stretches south of the palace and is open to the public.

Eating: There are no real eateries inside (other than shops selling gifty boxes of chocolates and bottled water), so consider bringing a snack with you.

◑ Self-Guided Tour

After buying your ticket and going through security, pick up your audioguide and start strolling along the path through...

The Grounds

Head up the hill, enjoying the first of many fine castle views you'll see today. The tower-topped conical hill on your left represents the historical core of the castle. William the Conqueror built this motte (artificial mound) and bailey (fortified stockade around it) in 1080—his first castle in England. Among the later monarchs who spiffed up Windsor were Edward III (flush with French war booty, he made it a palace fit for a 14th-century king), Charles II (determined to restore the monarchy properly in the 1660s), and George IV (Britain's "Bling King," who financed many such vanity projects in the 1820s). On your right, the circular bandstand platform has a seal of the Order of the Garter, which has important ties to Wind-

The Order of the Garter

In addition to being the royal residence, Windsor is the home of the Most Noble Order of the Garter—Britain's most prestigious chivalrous order. The castle's history is inexorably tied to this order.

Founded in 1348 by King Edward III and his son (the "Black Prince"), the Order of the Garter was designed to honor returning Crusaders. This was a time when the legends of King Arthur and the Knights of the Round Table were sweeping England, and Edward III fantasized that Windsor could be a real-life Camelot. (He even built the Round Tower as an homage to the Round Table.)

The order's seal illustrates the story of the order's founding and unusual name: a cross of St. George encircled with a belt and a French motto loosely translated as "Shame be upon he who thinks evil of it." Supposedly while the king was dancing with a fair maiden, her garter slipped off onto the floor; in an act of great chivalry, he rescued her from embarrassment by picking it up and uttering those words.

The Order of the Garter continues to the present day as the single most prestigious honor in the United Kingdom. There can be only 24 knights at one time (perfect numbers for splitting into two 12-man jousting teams), plus the sitting monarch and the Prince of Wales. Aside from royals and the nobility, past Knights of the Garter have included Winston Churchill, Bernard "Monty" Montgomery, and Ethiopian Emperor Haile Selassie. In 2008, Prince William became only the 1,000th knight in the order's history. Other current members include various ex-military officers, former British Prime Minister John Major, and a member of the Colman's Mustard family.

The patron of the order is St. George—the namesake of the State Apartments' most sumptuous hall and of the castle's own chapel. Both of these spaces—the grandest in Windsor—are designed to celebrate and honor the Order of the Garter.

sor (see sidebar). This is where free guided tours depart (look for the posted schedule).

Passing through the small gate, you approach the stately St. George's Gate. Peek through here to the Upper Ward's **Quadrangle,** which is surrounded by the State Apartments (across the field) and the Queen's private apartments (to the right).

Turn left and follow the wall. Step into the long **exhibit** that traces the history of the castle, including models of how the structure evolved over time and illustrations of St. George's Hall in different historical periods.

Back outside, continue up the path. On your right-hand side, you enjoy great views of the **Round Tower** atop that original motte; running around the base of this artificial hill is the delightful, peaceful garden of the castle governor. The unusual design of this castle has not one "bailey" (castle yard), but three, which today make up Windsor's Upper Ward (where the Queen lives, which you just saw), Middle Ward (the ecclesiastical heart of the complex, with St. George's Chapel, which you'll soon pass on the left), and Lower Ward (residences for castle workers).

Continue all the way around this mini moat to the **Norman Gate,** which once held a prison. Carry on past the gate for even finer views of the Quadrangle.

Do a 180 and head back toward the Norman Gate, but before you reach it, go down the staircase on the right. You'll emerge onto a fine **terrace** overlooking the flat lands all around. It's easy to understand why this was a strategic place to build a castle. That's Eton College across the Thames. Imagine how handy it's been for royals to be able to ship off their teenagers to an elite prep school so close they could easily keep an eye on them...literally. The power-plant cooling towers in the distance mark the workaday burg of Slough (rhymes with "plow," immortalized as the setting for Britain's original version of *The Office*).

• *Note that this area may be torn up during your visit, as they are carrying out a years-long renovation of this part of the castle. Some of the items mentioned in the next part of the tour may be closed, and you may visit things in a different order than described.*

Turn right and wander along the terrace. You'll likely see two lines. The long one leads to Queen Mary's Dolls' House, then to the State Apartments. The short line skips the dollhouse and heads directly to the apartments. Read the following descriptions and decide if the dollhouse is worth the wait (or try again later in the day, when the line sometimes eases up).

Queen Mary's Dolls' House

This palace in miniature (1:12 scale, from 1924) is "the most famous dollhouse in the world." It was a gift for the adult Queen Mary (the wife of King George V, and the current Queen's grandmother), who greatly enjoyed miniatures. It's basically one big, dimly lit room with the large dollhouse in the middle, executed with an astonishing level of detail. Each fork, knife, and spoon on the expertly set banquet table is perfect and made of real silver—and the tiny pipes of its plumbing system actually have running water. But you're kept a few feet away by a glass wall, and constantly jostled by fellow sightseers in this crowded space, making it difficult to fully appreciate. Unless you're a dollhouse devotee, it's not worth waiting half an hour for a five-minute peek, but if the line is short it's worth a look.

State Apartments

Dripping with chandeliers, finely furnished, and strewn with history and the art of a long line of kings and queens, they're the best I've seen in Britain. This is where Henry VIII and Charles I once lived, and where the current Queen wows visiting dignitaries. Remember to take advantage of the talkative docents in each room, who are happy to answer your questions.

On your way in, you may pass through the **China Museum,** featuring items from the Queen's many exquisite settings for royal shindigs.

You'll climb the Grand Staircase up to the peach-colored **Grand Vestibule,** decorated with exotic items seized by British troops during their missions to colonize various corners of the world. Immediately to the left of the door into the next room, look for the bullet that killed Lord Nelson at Trafalgar.

In the next room, the magnificent wood-ceilinged **Waterloo Chamber** is wallpapered with portraits of figures from the pan-European alliance that defeated Napoleon. Find the Duke of Wellington (high on the far wall, in red) who outmaneuvered him at Waterloo, and Pope Pius VII (right wall, in red and white) whom Napoleon befriended...then imprisoned.

A highlight is **St. George's Hall,** decorated with emblems representing the knights of the prestigious Order of the Garter (see sidebar, earlier). This is the site of some of the most elaborate royal banquets—imagine one long table stretching from one end of the hall to the other and seating 160 VIPs. At the end of the hall, you enter the Queen's Guard Chamber, with more weapons and busts of English war heroes, from Nelson to Marlborough to Churchill.

At some point, you'll pass through a **series of living rooms**—bedchambers, dressing rooms, and drawing rooms of the king and queen (who traditionally maintained separate quarters). Many rooms are decorated with canvases by Rubens, Van Dyck, and Holbein. You may also tour some rooms that were restored after a fire in 1992, including the "Semi-State Apartments."

The **Garter Throne Room** is where new members of the Order of the Garter are invested (ceremonially granted their titles).

• *Exiting the State Apartments, you have one more major sight to see. Head back out the way you came in, but bear right/downhill toward (or follow signs to find)...*

St. George's Chapel

This church is known for housing numerous royal tombs, and is an exquisite example of the Perpendicular Gothic style (dating from about 1500). More recent-

ly, it's where Prince Harry and Meghan Markle tied the knot in 2018. Enter at the bottom end, pick up a free map, and circle the interior clockwise, finding these highlights:

Stand at the back and look down the **nave,** with its classic fan-vaulting spreading out from each slender pillar and nearly every joint capped with an elaborate and colorful roof boss. Most of these emblems are associated with the Knights of the Garter, who consider St. George's their "mother church." Under the upper stained-glass windows, notice the continuous frieze of 250 angels, lovingly carved with great detail, ringing the church.

In the back-left corner (#4 on your church-issued map), take in the melodramatic monument to **Princess Charlotte of Wales,** the only child of King George IV. Heir to the throne, her death in 1817 (at 21, in childbirth) devastated the nation. Head up the left side of the nave and find the simple chapel (#6, just past the wooden gate) containing the tombs of the current Queen's parents, **King George VI and "Queen Mum" Elizabeth;** the ashes of her younger sister, Princess Margaret, are also kept here (see the marble slab against the wall). Farther up the aisle is the tomb of **Edward IV** (#8, past the door into the choir), who expanded St. George's Chapel.

Stepping into the **choir area** (#12), you're immediately aware that you are in the inner sanctum of the Order of the Garter. The banners lining the nave represent the knights, as do the fancy helmets and half-drawn swords topping the spire of each wood-carved seat. These symbols honor only living knights; on the seats are some 800 golden panels memorializing departed knights. Under your feet lies the **Royal Vault** (#13), burial spot of Mad King George III (nemesis of American revolutionaries). Strolling farther up the aisle, notice the marker in the floor: You're walking over the burial site of **King Henry VIII** (#14) and Jane Seymour, Henry's favorite wife (perhaps because she was the only one who died before he could behead her). The body of King Charles I, who was beheaded by Oliver Cromwell's forces at the Banqueting House, was also discovered here...with its head sewn back on.

Exiting the choir area at the far end, loop around to the left and head to the back of the church. Leaving the church proper in the far corner, you'll pass the gift shop. On your way out, pause at the door of the sumptuous 13th-century **Albert Memorial Chapel** (#28), redecorated in 1861 after the death of Queen Victoria's husband, Prince Albert, and dedicated to his memory.

• *After exiting the chapel, you come into the castle's...*

Lower Ward

This area is a living town where some 160 people who work for the Queen reside; they include clergy, military, and castle administrators. Just below the chapel, you may be able to enter a tranquil little horseshoe-shaped courtyard ringed with residential doorways—all of them with a spectacular view of the chapel's grand entrance.

MORE SIGHTS IN WINDSOR
Legoland Windsor

Paradise for Legomaniacs under age 12, this huge, kid-pleasing park has dozens of tame but fun rides (often with very long lines) scattered throughout its 150 acres. The impressive Miniland has 40 million Lego pieces glued together to create 800 tiny buildings and a mini tour of Europe. Several of the more exciting rides involve getting wet, so dress accordingly or buy a cheap disposable poncho in the gift shop. While you may be tempt-ed to hop on the Hill Train at the entrance, it's faster and more convenient to walk down into the park.

Cost: £64 but varies by day, significant savings when booked online at least 7 days in advance, 10 percent discount at Windsor TI, free for ages 3 and under, optional Q-Bot ride-reservation gadget allows you to bypass lines (£25-90 depending on when you go and how much time you want to save).

Hours: Generally Mon-Fri 10:00-17:00, until 18:00 in summer and on Sat-Sun; often closed Tue-Wed outside of summer; closed entirely in winter. Check website for exact schedule, tel. 0871-222-2001, www.legoland.co.uk.

Getting There: A £5 round-trip shuttle bus runs from the Parish Church stop on High Street (2/hour). If day-tripping from London, ask about rail/shuttle/park admission deals from Paddington or Waterloo train stations. For drivers, the park is on the

B-3022 Windsor/Ascot road, two miles southwest of Windsor and 25 miles west of London. Legoland is clearly signposted from the M-3, M-4, and M-25 motorways (easy paid parking).

Eton College

Across the bridge from Windsor Castle is the most famous "public" (the equivalent of our "private") high school in Britain. Eton was founded in 1440 by King Henry VI; today it educates about 1,300 boys (ages 13-18), who live on campus. Eton has molded the characters of 19 prime ministers as well as members of the royal family—most recently princes William and Harry. Sparse on actual sights, the college is officially closed to visitors except via guided tour, where you may get a glimpse of the schoolyard, chapel, cloisters, and the Museum of Eton Life. However, curious and discreet visitors can often poke around the other grounds on their own—including the gardens, playing fields, and surrounding parks. For more information visit www.etoncollege.com or call 01753/370-100.

Eton High Street

Even if you're not touring the college, it's worth the few minutes it takes to cross the pedestrian bridge and wander straight up Eton's High Street. A bit more cutesy and authentic-feeling than Windsor (which is given over to shopping malls and chain stores), Eton has a charm that's fun to sample.

Windsor and Royal Borough Museum

Tucked into one room beneath the Guildhall (where Prince Charles remarried), this little museum does its best to give some insight into the history of Windsor and the surrounding area. They also have lots of special activities for kids. Ask at the desk whether tours are running to the Guildhall itself (visits only possible with a guide, leave sporadically, about 20-30 minutes); if not, it's probably not worth the admission—you can see most of the museum with a sweep of your head from the door.

Cost and Hours: £2, includes audioguide, Tue-Sat 10:00-16:00, Sun from 12:00, closed Mon, located in the Guildhall on High Street, tel. 01628/685-686, www.rbwm.gov.uk.

Boat Trips

Cruise up and down the Thames River for classic views of the castle, the village of Eton, Eton College, and the Royal Windsor Racecourse. Boats leave from the riverside promenade adjacent to Barry Avenue, and run from early spring through late fall.

Cost and Hours: 40-minute tour—£9.50, 1-2/hour daily 10:00-17:00; 2-hour tour—£14.55, 1-2/day; tel. 01753/851-900, www.frenchbrothers.co.uk.

Visiting Highclere Castle

If you're a fan of *Downton Abbey,* consider a day trip from London to Highclere Castle, the stately house where much of the show was filmed. Though the hugely popular series was set in Yorkshire, the actual house is located in Hampshire, about an hour's train ride west of London. Highclere has been home to the Earls of Carnarvon since 1679, but the present Jacobean-style house was rebuilt in the 1840s by Sir Charles Barry, who also designed London's Houses of Parliament. Noted landscape architect Capability Brown laid out the traditional gardens in the mid-18th century. The castle's Egyptian exhibit features artifacts collected by Highclere's fifth Earl, George Herbert, a keen amateur archaeologist. When Howard Carter discovered King Tut's tomb in 1922, he waited three weeks for his friend and patron Herbert to join him before looking inside. The Earl died unexpectedly a few months later, giving birth to the legend of a "mummy's curse."

Cost and Hours: £23 for castle, garden, and Egyptian exhibit; £16 for garden plus either castle or Egyptian exhibit; £7 for garden only. Open in summer Sun-Thu 10:30-17:00, grounds open from 9:00, last entry one hour before closing, closed Fri-Sat; generally closed mid-Sept-mid-July except for special events. Reserve timed-entry tickets well in advance—tickets available several months ahead; 24-hour info tel. 01635/253-204, www.highclerecastle.co.uk.

Getting There: Highclere is 6 miles south of Newbury, about 70 miles west of London, off the A-34.

By Train and Taxi: Great Western trains run from London's Paddington Station to Newbury (1-2/hour, 50-70 minutes, tel. 0345-7000-125, www.gwr.com). From Newbury train station, you can take a taxi (about £20 one-way, taxis wait outside station) or reserve a car and driver (must arrange in advance, £12.50/person round-trip; £25 minimum, tel. 07818/430-095, mapeng@msn.com).

By Tour: Brit Movie Tours offers an all-day bus tour of *Downton Abbey* filming locations, including Highclere Castle and the fictional village of Downton (sells out early, £80, includes transport and castle/garden entry, £5 extra for Egyptian exhibit, 9 hours, depart London from outside Gloucester Road Tube Station, reservations required, tel. 0844-247-1007, from the US or Canada call 011-44-20-7118-1007, www.britmovietours.com).

Horse Racing

The horses race every Monday at the Royal Windsor Racecourse (£25 entry, online discounts, under age 18 free with an adult, April-Oct except no races in Sept and sporadic in Aug, off the A-308 between Windsor and Maidenhead, tel. 01753/498-400, www.windsor-racecourse.co.uk). The romantic way to get there from Windsor is by a 10-minute shuttle boat (£7.50 round-trip, www.frenchbrothers.co.uk). The famous Ascot Racecourse (described next) is also nearby.

NEAR WINDSOR
Ascot Racecourse

Located seven miles southwest of Windsor and just north of the town of Ascot, this royally owned track is one of the most famous horse-racing venues in the world. The horses first ran here in 1711, and the course is best known for June's five-day Royal Ascot race meeting, attended by the Queen and 299,999 of her loyal subjects. For many, the outlandish hats worn on Ladies Day (Thu) are more interesting than the horses. Royal Ascot is usually the third week in June. The pricey tickets go on sale the preceding November; while the Friday and Saturday races tend to sell out far ahead, tickets for the other days are often available close to the date (check website). In addition to Royal Ascot, the racecourse runs the ponies year-round—funny hats strictly optional.

Cost: Regular tickets generally start from £20 and go as high as £80—may be available at a discount at TI, dress code enforced in some areas and on certain days, tel. 0844-346-3000, www.ascot.co.uk.

Sleeping in Windsor

$$$$ Castle Hotel Windsor, part of the boutique division of Accor Hotels, offers 108 rooms and elegant public spaces in a central location just down the street from Her Majesty's weekend retreat (air-con, elevator in main building, parking-£25/day, 18 High Street, tel. 01753/851-577, www.castlehotelwindsor.com, h6618@accor.com).

$$ Park Farm B&B, bright and cheery, is most convenient for drivers. But even if you're not driving, this beautiful place is such a good value, and the welcome is so warm, that you're unlikely to mind the bus ride into town (no kids under 12, cash only—credit card solely for reservations, shared fridge and microwave, free off-street parking, no kids under 12, 1 mile from Legoland on St. Leonards Road near Imperial Road, 5-minute bus ride or 1-mile walk to castle, £5 taxi ride from station, tel. 01753/866-823, www.parkfarm.com, stay@parkfarm.com, Caroline and Drew Youds).

$$ 76 Duke Street has two nice rooms, but only hosts one set of guests at a time. While the bathroom is (just) outside your bedroom, you have it to yourself (15-minute walk from station at—you guessed it—76 Duke Street, tel. 01753/620-636 or 07884/222-225, www.76dukestreet.co.uk, bandb@76dukestreet.co.uk, Julia).

$$ Langton House B&B is a stately Victorian home with five spacious, well-appointed rooms (continental breakfast included but full English breakfast extra, family rooms, guest kitchen, 46 Alma Road, tel. 01753/858-299, www.langtonhouse.co.uk, bookings@langtonhouse.co.uk, Paul and Sonja Fogg with help from Chris).

$$ Dee and Steve's B&B is a friendly four-room place above a window shop on a quiet residential street about a 10-minute walk from the castle and station. The rooms are cozy, Dee and Steve are pleasant hosts, and breakfast is served in the contemporary kitchen/lounge, with bricks and beams. They have two affordable singles that share a bathroom (169 Oxford Road, tel. 01753/854-489, www.deeandsteve.com, dee@deeandsteve.com).

$$ Crown and Cushion is a good option on Eton's High Street, just across the pedestrian bridge from Windsor's waterfront (a short uphill walk to the castle). While the pub it's situated over is worn and drab, you're right in the heart of charming Eton, and the eight creaky rooms—with uneven floors and old-beam ceilings—are nicely furnished (free parking, 84 High Street in Eton, tel. 01753/861-531, www.thecrownandcushioneton.co.uk, info@thecrownandcushioneton.com).

Eating in Windsor

Elegant Spots with River Views: Several places flank Windsor Bridge, offering romantic dining after dark. The riverside promenade, with cheap takeaway stands scattered about, is a delightful place for a picnic lunch or dinner with the swans. If you don't see anything that appeals, continue up Eton's High Street, which is also lined with characteristic eateries.

In the Tourist Zone Around the Palace: Strolling the streets and lanes around the palace entrance—especially in the shopping zone near Windsor & Eton Station—you'll find countless inviting eateries. The central area also has a sampling of dependable British chains. Residents enjoy a wide selection of unpretentious little eateries just past the end of pedestrian Peascod Street, where it becomes St. Leonards Road. These include Saffron (recommended on next page) and a fire station turned pub-and-cultural center (The Old Court Artspace).

$$$ Bel & The Dragon is the place to splurge on high-quality classic British food in a charming half-timbered building with an upscale-rustic dining space (food served daily 12:00-15:00 & 18:00-22:00, afternoon tea served between lunch and dinner, bar open longer hours, on Thames Street near the bridge to Eton, tel. 01753/866-056).

$$$ Cornucopia à la Russe, with a cozy, woody atmosphere, serves elegant French and international dishes (two- and three-course lunch deals, open Mon 18:00-21:30, Tue-Sat 12:00-14:30 & 18:00-21:30, closed Sun, 6 High Street, tel. 01753/833-009).

$$ The Duchess of Cambridge's friendly staff serves up the normal grub in a pub that's right across from the castle walls. It feels big and modern, but tasteful, and with an open fireplace to boot. While the pub predates Kate, it was named in her honor following a recent remodel, and has the photos to prove her endorsement (daily 11:00-23:00 or later, 3 Thames Street, tel. 01753/864-405).

$$ Al Fassia—just beyond the end of the pedestrian zone—has authentic Moroccan cuisine, including tagines served in pottery (Mon-Fri 18:00-22:00, Sat-Sun from 12:00, 27 St. Leonards Road, tel. 01753/855-370).

$$ Saffron restaurant, while a fairly long walk from the castle, is the local choice for South Indian cuisine, with a modern interior and tasty dishes. Their vegetable *thali* is a treat (daily 12:00-14:30 & 17:30-23:30, 99 St. Leonards Road, tel. 01753/855-467).

Cambridge

Cambridge, 60 miles north of London, is world-famous for its prestigious university. William Wordsworth, Isaac Newton, Charles Darwin, Alan Turing, Jane Goodall, and Prince Charles are only a few of its illustrious alumni. The university dominates—and owns—most of Cambridge, a historic town of about 125,000 people. Cambridge is the epitome of a university town, with busy bikers, stately residence halls, plenty of bookshops, and proud locals who can point out where DNA was originally modeled, the atom first split, and electrons discovered.

In medieval Europe, higher education was the domain of the Church and was limited to ecclesiastical schools. Scholars lived in

WINDSOR & CAMBRIDGE

"halls" on campus, which came to be known as "colleges." The first at Cambridge, Peterhouse, was founded in the 1280s. By 1350, Cambridge had eight separate colleges, each one a self-contained world in itself—enclosed behind walls, with a monastic-type courtyard, chapel, library, and lodgings. These colleges allied in a federation known as the University of Cambridge. That same arrangement survives to this day. Today, Cambridge has 31 colleges, totaling about 12,000 undergrads, scattered around the town center.

For travelers, Cambridge offers a pleasant medieval-era town, art-filled churches and museums, and—most of all—a chance to see some of the colleges (many are open to visitors—some free; others require a ticket at the gate). You can stroll the grounds and pop into a few public areas (mainly chapels and dining halls).

The town is easy to sort out. There's a small and youthful commercial center—quiet and traffic free (except for lots of bikes), one important museum (the Fitzwilliam), and lots of minor museums (all generally free). The River Cam has boat tours, three public bridges, and a strip of six colleges, which have gardens that basically own the river through the center of town and make it feel like an exclusive park. Trinity College has its famous Wren
Library, and King's College has a famous ornate chapel. The city is filled with students year-round—scholars throughout the regular terms and visiting students enjoying summer programs.

PLANNING YOUR TIME

Cambridge can easily be seen as a day trip from London. A good five-hour plan is to follow my self-guided walk, spend an hour on a punt ride, tour the Fitzwilliam Museum (closed Mon), and see the Wren Library at Trinity College (open Mon-Sat for only two hours a day, so plan ahead). For a little extra color, consider joining a walk through town with a local guide from the TI (2 hours, repeats much of my self-guided walk but splices in local flavor). Confirm which sights are covered on the TI's walk, so you don't duplicate those on your own.

Your visit will be affected somewhat by the university schedule. Cambridge has three terms: Lent term from mid-January to mid-March, Easter term from mid-April to mid-June, and Michaelmas term from early October to early December. During exams (roughly the month of May), the colleges are closed to visitors, which can impede access to some of the town's picturesque little corners. When class is in session, Cambridge is a bustling town of students buzzing to class on bikes. Between terms there's less going on, but the main sights—King's College Chapel and the Wren Library at Trinity College—stay open, and Cambridge is never sleepy. On good-weather weekends, the town overflows with visitors—many of them trying their hand, unsuccessfully, at punting the Cam.

If you're in town for the evening, the evensong service at King's College Chapel (Mon-Sat at 17:30, Sun at 15:30) is a must. And if you like plays and music, events are always happening in this thriving cultural hub.

GETTING TO CAMBRIDGE

By Train: It's an easy 50-minute trip from London's King's Cross Station (hourly express trains). Cheaper direct trains also run from London's Liverpool Street Station, but take longer (2/hour, 1.5 hours). Rail information: tel. 0845-748-4950, www.nationalrail. co.uk.

By Bus: National Express X90 coaches run from London's Victoria Coach Station to the Parkside stop in Cambridge (every 60-90 minutes, 2 hours, tel. 0871-781-8181, www.nationalexpress. co.uk).

Orientation to Cambridge

Cambridge is small. Everything is within a pleasant walk. The main colleges form a north-south row, bordered on one side by the River Cam and on the other by the town. The town center, brimming with tearooms, has a TI and a colorful open-air market square. The train station is about a mile to the southeast.

TOURIST INFORMATION

Cambridge's TI is well run and well signposted, just off Market Hill Square in the town center. They offer walking tours and store bags (both described later), and sell bus tickets and an inexpensive map/guide (Mon-Sat 9:30-17:00, Sun 11:00-15:00, closed Sun in off-season, Peas Hill, tel. 01223/791-500, www.visitcambridge. org). In the same building as the TI, kids love the elaborate Harry Potter gift shop in a former courtroom.

ARRIVAL IN CAMBRIDGE

By Train: Cambridge's train station is about a mile southeast of the center. To get downtown, you can **walk** for about 25 minutes (exit straight ahead on Station Road, bear right at the war memorial onto Hills Road, and follow it into town); take public **bus** #1, #3, or #7 (referred to as "Citi 1," "Citi 3," and so on in schedules, but buses are marked only with the number; £1, pay driver, runs every

5-10 minutes, turn left when exiting station, cross the street, and walk half a block to find bus stands—near the far end of the many bus stops; since stops are unmarked, ask driver which stop is best for the city center and TI); pay about £6 for a **taxi;** or take a City Sightseeing **bus tour** (described later).

By Car: To park in the middle of town, follow signs from the M-11 motorway to any of the central (but expensive) short-stay parking lots—including one at the Lion Yard shopping mall. Or leave your car at one of six park-and-ride lots outside the city, then take the shuttle into town (parking-£1/day; shuttle-£3 round-trip).

HELPFUL HINTS

Live Theater and Entertainment: With all the smart and talented students in town, there is always something going on. Make a point of enjoying a play or concert. The **Cambridge University Amateur Dramatic Club (ADC)** is Britain's oldest university playhouse, offering a steady stream of performances since 1855. It's lots of fun and casual, with easy-to-get and inexpensive tickets. This is your chance to see a future Emma Thompson or Ian McKellen—alumni who performed here as students—before they become stars (tel. 01223/300-085, www.adctheatre.com).

> **Cambridge Live Tickets** is a very helpful service, offering event info and ticket sales in person and online (Mon-Fri 12:00-18:00, Sat from 10:00, Sun from 18:00 until 30 minutes before show time, 2 Wheeler Street, tel. 01223/357-851 answered Mon-Sat 10:00-18:00, www.cambridgelive.org.uk). The TI also has lists of what's on.

Festivals: The **Cambridge Folk Festival** gets things humming and strumming in late July or early August (tickets go on sale several months ahead and often sell out; www.cambridgefolkfestival.co.uk). From mid-July through August, the town's **Shakespeare Festival** attracts 25,000 visitors for outdoor performances in some of the college's gardens (www.cambridgeshakespeare.com).

Baggage Storage: The TI (see listing earlier) stores luggage for £6 per bag.

Bike Rental: At the Lion Yard shopping mall, **Rutland Cycling** rents bikes (Mon-Fri 8:00-18:00, Sat from 9:00, Sun 10:00-17:00, look for it underground in the Grand Arcade, tel. 01223/307-655, www.rutlandcycling.com.

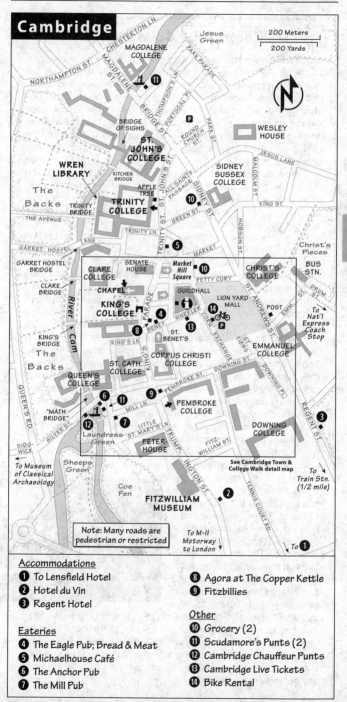

Cambridge

WINDSOR & CAMBRIDGE

Note: Many roads are pedestrian or restricted

<u>Accommodations</u>
① To Lensfield Hotel
② Hotel du Vin
③ Regent Hotel

<u>Eateries</u>
④ The Eagle Pub; Bread & Meat
⑤ Michaelhouse Café
⑥ The Anchor Pub
⑦ The Mill Pub
⑧ Agora at The Copper Kettle
⑨ Fitzbillies

<u>Other</u>
⑩ Grocery (2)
⑪ Scudamore's Punts (2)
⑫ Cambridge Chauffeur Punts
⑬ Cambridge Live Tickets
⑭ Bike Rental

Cambridge Colleges 101

Colleges, where students spend most of their time, are central to life at Cambridge. Cambridge has 31 colleges, which are not really schools as much as they are lodgings and social communities. They house, feed, and parent the students (including a "home professor" who coaches students), while the overall university offers formal teaching and lectures. Over the centuries, each college has developed a reputation: the rich elites, the partiers, the science nerds, the political progressives, and so on.

How to Visit: Some colleges are free to visit and welcoming to the public, some are closed off and very private, and others are famous and make money by charging for visits. Most are open only in the afternoons, and all have a similar design and etiquette. At their historic front gates, you'll find a porter's lodge where the porter delivers mail, monitors who comes and goes, and keeps people off the grass. Only fellows (senior professors) can walk on the grassy courts, which are the centerpiece of each college campus. Other than that, you can relax and roam freely, so long as an area is not locked or blocked with a "for members only" sign. Whether a college is open to visitors or private, you can usually at least pop in through the gate, chat with the porter, and enjoy the view of the court.

What You Will (and Won't) See: The court is ringed by venerable buildings, with a library, dormitories, a dining hall, and a chapel. The dining halls are easy to identify because they have big bay windows that mark the location of a "high table" where VIPs eat. A portrait of the college's founder usually hangs above the high table, and paintings of rectors and important alumni also decorate the walls. Students still eat in these halls, which is why they are rarely open to the public (but you can look in from the main door).

A college's chapel is the building that most often allows visitors (including at evensong services, usually at 17:30 or 18:00). In the chapel, seating is usually arranged in several rows of pews that face each other to allow for antiphonal singing and chanting—where one side starts and the other responds. The chapels often contain memorials to students who died in World Wars I and II. Libraries are treasured and generally not open to the  public. There's also a Senior Common Room (like a teachers' lounge but much fancier), where fellows share ideas in an exclusive social hall, creating a fertile intellectual garden. Student rooms are never open to the public during school terms, though some are available as vacation rentals when classes are not in session.

Tours in Cambridge

▲▲Walking Tour of the Colleges

A walking tour is the best way to understand Cambridge's mix of "town and gown." The walks can be more educational (read: dry) than entertaining, but they do provide a good rundown of the historic and scenic highlights of the university, some fun local gossip, and plenty of university trivia.

The TI offers **daily walking tours** of various lengths, subjects, and prices; Monday through Saturday, there's usually a tour at 11:00, 13:00 (also runs Sun), and 14:00. Check their website for the specific schedule (tel. 01223/791-500, www.visitcambridge. org). One good choice is the tour that includes King's College Chapel and Queens' College (£25, includes admission, 2 hours, usually Mon-Sat at 11:00). Groups are limited to 20, so it's smart to book online or drop in at the TI in advance to reserve a spot.

Private guides are available through the TI and affordable if you can assemble a group to share the cost (2-hour tour—£101; does not include individual college entrance fees, tel. 01223/791-500, tours@visitcambridge.org).

Walking Ghost Tour

If you're in Cambridge on the weekend, consider an £8 "ghost walk" to where spooky sightings have been reported (typically only in winter—when it's dark enough to be spooky, Fri-Sat at 18:00, organized by the TI, tel. 01223/791-500).

Bus Tours

City Sightseeing hop-on, hop-off bus tours are informative and cover the outskirts, including the American WWII Cemetery. But keep in mind that buses can't go where walking tours can—right into the center (£16.50, 80 minutes for full 19-stop circuit, 2-3/hour 10:00-17:30, recorded commentary, tel. 01223/433-250, www.city-sightseeing.com). If arriving by train, you can buy your ticket from the kiosk directly in front of the station, then ride the bus into town.

Cambridge Town and College Walk

This self-guided walk covers the essential sights. We start in the old market square, visit a couple of typical (if less-visited) colleges, pause at the dreamy River Cam, and finish at the glory of King's College Chapel. Although we won't go as far as Trinity College (Wren Library) or the Fitzwilliam Museum, they're close by and you can visit them on your own (covered in "Sights in Cambridge," later).

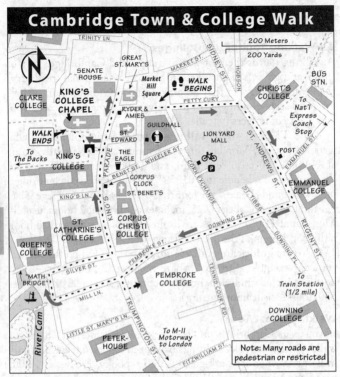

Cambridge Town & College Walk

• *Start on Market Hill Square in front of the Guildhall (the brick building with a big clock up top).*

Market Hill Square

This square has been a center of commerce for more than a thousand years. At a glance, you can see the elements that combined to make Cambridge: church (Great St. Mary's rear end), university (those modern buildings are student lodgings), and trade (the open-air market and Guildhall).

Think of the history this place has seen: Romans first built a bridge over the Cam in AD 43, Anglo-Saxons and Danes established a market here in the Dark Ages, and Normans built a castle here (now gone) in the 11th century. The city's coat of arms (above the Guildhall door) shows medieval boats flocking to trade at the newly built bridge over the River Cam, which established "Cambridge."

But the big year was 1209. After scuffles in Oxford between its scholars and townsfolk, many of Oxford's academics fled here and started their own university. Where's "the university"? Everywhere, mixed into the town, with the 31 individual colleges, university halls, and student dorms scattered about.

Cambridge suffered no bomb damage in World War II, so the older buildings you see are original. As you walk, notice how peaceful the town is, with almost no cars, but bikes everywhere.

The Guildhall facing this square (the seat of the city council today) overlooks market stalls. The really big market is on Sunday (9:30-16:30) and features produce, arts, and crafts. On other days, you'll find mostly clothes and food stands (Mon-Sat generally 9:30-16:00).

• *Let's get started by exploring a bit of modern Cambridge. Facing the Guildhall, exit the square to your left down Petty Cury Lane, a modern pedestrian shopping street. At the end of the street, turn right, walking down St. Andrews Street (which connects the town center to the train station).*

On the left side of the street is our first college: Christ's College. Its elaborate 16th-century gatehouse proudly displays the college's coat of arms and colors; look for others around town. Step inside to enjoy the classic court, next to a portrait of alum Charles Darwin (free, open daily 9:00-16:00). Don't linger—we'll see a better one in a minute.

Continue down St. Andrews Street two long blocks toward the steeple, then pause at the college on the left...

Emmanuel College

This college offers a classic peek at a typical Cambridge college (free, open 9:00-18:00). Emmanuel was founded in 1584 as a Protestant college on land that had once been a Dominican friary. Like many monasteries and convents in the 16th century, the friary had been dissolved by the English king in an epic power struggle that left England with its own version of Christianity and the government with lots of land once owned by the Catholic Church.

Entering the courtyard, take in the layout. On the left is the dining hall, marked by its big bay window. Directly ahead (behind the big clock) is the Senior Common Room, a social hall for college fellows. Below the big clock is the entrance to the chapel. Go inside.

The **chapel** was designed by the famed architect Christopher Wren, who built many churches in the late 1600s, culminating in St. Paul's Cathedral. Wren gave this his typical two-toned treatment: white walls above and carved-wood below, all lit brilliantly. On the ceiling is a typical Wren design (all in white) of circles in squares, adorned with garlands. In the stained glass (left wall) find the portrait of John Harvard—the Emmanuel College student who went to America and founded a prestigious school of his own.

Explore more of the college grounds. You can look through the doorway into the dining hall (find it in the near-left corner of the courtyard, from where you came in); enjoy the garden behind the chapel, with its fish pond (dating back to monastic days when this was a source of their food); or chat with the porter.

• *Leaving Emmanuel College, walk straight ahead along Downing Street (which becomes Pembroke Street). Stop when you reach the intersection with King's Parade. Notice the recommended Fitzbillies Café on the right (famous for its local cinnamon roll, the Chelsea Bun), then turn left and walk a few steps to the entrance (on the left) to...*

Pembroke College

Founded in 1347, Pembroke is the third-oldest college in Cambridge. Step into the court, past the porter's lodge—it's polite to say hello and ask whether you can wander around. Survey the court. Ahead of you is the medieval dining hall. The fancy building with the pointed clock tower is the library (the statue in front is alumnus William Pitt the Younger—a great 18th-century prime minister), with a charming garden beyond.

The highlight here is the chapel, to the right. It dates from about 1660 and is the first building (of any kind, anywhere) Christopher Wren completed. Before stepping inside to enjoy the interior, pause for a moment at the somber WWI and WWII memorial under the arcade. During the Great War, one in four students and faculty was killed.

• *From Pembroke College, cross King's Parade and follow Mill Lane directly down to the River Cam and its mill pond.*

River Cam, the Mill Pond, and Punting

From this perch you see the "harbor action" of Cambridge. The city was an important port in medieval times: Trading vessels from the North Sea (40 miles away) could navigate to here. Today a weir divides the River Cam from one of its tributaries, sometimes called the River Granta (on the left)—which leads through idyllic countryside from the town of Grantchester. Filling the mill pond is a commotion of the iconic Cambridge boats called punts. Students hustle to take visitors on a 45-minute trip with fun commentary (see "Punting on the Cam," later in this chapter). Skilled residents rent boats for themselves, as do not-so-skilled tourists—much to the amusement of locals who sip their beer while watching clumsy visitors fumble with the boats (which are tougher to maneuver than they look). If you'd like a detour from this sometimes-chaotic scene, simply cross the weir and walk along the River Granta into the countryside—it quickly becomes sleepy and idyllic.

But to continue this town walk, turn right and follow the narrow walkway along the harbor past the recommended Anchor Pub, then up the stairs to the Silver Street Bridge. From the bridge, you can watch more punt action and check out the famous "Mathematical Bridge," which links the old and new buildings of Queens' College. This wooden bridge, although curved, is made entirely of straight boards.

Gazing upstream past the wooden bridge, you see the start of the park known as "the Backs"—the backs of six colleges that line the river, with their fine architecture and most with bridges connecting campus grounds or buildings on both sides of the river.
• *From the Silver Street Bridge, walk up Silver Street, back to King's Parade, and turn left. You'll follow this about one block (passing the stately Corpus Christi College on your right). At the first corner, find the fancy gilded clock on your right.*

The Corpus Clock, Benet Street, and Eagle Pub

Designed and commissioned by Corpus Christi College alum John Taylor, this **clock** was unveiled by Cambridge physicist Stephen Hawking in a 2008 ceremony. Perched on top is the Chronophage—the "time eater"—a grotesque giant grasshopper that keeps the clock moving and periodically winks at passersby. The message? Time is passing, so live every moment to the fullest. It's a real clock—one blue light marks the hour, the other the minutes. At the top of the hour, it chimes with the sound of rattling chains.

The Eagle Pub, a venerable joint, is just down Benet Street on the left. This is Cambridge's oldest pub and a sight in itself. Poke into the courtyard and atmospheric rooms even if you don't eat or drink here. From the courtyard, look up at the balcony of second-floor guest rooms that date back to when this was a coachmen's inn as well as a pub. (It's said that in Shakespeare's time, plays were performed from this perch to entertain guests below.)

Back inside the pub, find the fireplace with a photo and plaque that remember two esteemed regulars—Francis Crick and James Watson—the scientists who first described the structure of DNA. They announced their finding here in 1953.

At the back of the Eagle is an annex called the RAF Bar. During World War II, US Army Air Corps pilots famously hung out here before missions over Germany. The fun interior is plastered with stickers of air crews and WWII memorabilia.

St. Benet's Church, across the street from the pub, is the oldest surviving building in Cambridgeshire. The rough stone tower dates from 1020. The Saxons who built the church included circular holes in its bell tower to encourage owls to roost there and keep the mouse population under control.

• *Return to the creepy grasshopper clock and turn right, continuing down King's Parade past the regal front facade of King's College Chapel (we'll return here shortly) to the...*

Senate House

This stately classical building with triangular pediments is the ceremonial heart of the University of Cambridge. It's where the university's governing body meets. And it's where graduation ceremonies are held. In June, you might notice green boxes lining the front of this house. Traditionally, at the end of the term, students came to these boxes to see whether they had earned their degree; those not listed knew they had flunked. Until 2010 this was the only notification students received about their status.

Looming across the street from the Senate House is **Great St. Mary's Church** (a.k.a. the University Church), with a climbable

bell tower (£5, Mon-Sat 9:30-16:30, Sun 12:30-16:00, 123 stairs). On the corner nearby is **Ryder & Amies** (22 King's Parade), which has been the official university outfitter for 150 years. It's a great shop for college gear: sweaters, ties, and so on.

• *Backtrack to the entrance to King's College, buy your ticket, and enter through the grand gateway to the spacious grounds. In the courtyard, you're surrounded by buildings from every era of the college's long history. To the right is the famous chapel; straight ahead is the Neoclassical fellows hall; and to the left is the Neo-Gothic dining hall. The statue in the center is Henry VII, the man most responsible for the wonder we'll see next. Head for the chapel and step inside.*

▲▲King's College Chapel

Built from 1446 to 1515 by Henrys VI through VIII, this is England's best example of Perpendicular Gothic architecture and the most impressive building in Cambridge.

Cost and Hours: £9, erratic hours depending on school events; during academic term usually Mon-Fri 9:30-15:30, Sat until 15:15, Sun 13:15-14:30; during breaks (see page 222) usually daily 9:30-16:30; recorded info tel. 01223/331-1212. Buy tickets at the King's College visitors center at 13 Kings Parade, across the street from the main entrance gate.

Evensong: When school's in session, you're welcome to enjoy an evensong service in this glorious space, with a famous choir made up of men and boys (free, Mon-Sat at 17:30, Sun at 15:30; for more on evensong, see page 157). Line up at the front entrance (on King's Parade) by 17:00 if you want prime seats in the choir.

Visiting the Chapel: Inside, stand and look down the nave, with its tunnel-like effect that accentuates both its length (290 feet) and height. It's exactly twice as tall (80 feet) as it is wide. Look up and marvel, as Christopher Wren did, at what was then the largest single span of **vaulted roof** anywhere. Built between 1512 and 1515, its 2,000 tons of incredible fan vaulting—held in place by the force of gravity—are a careful balancing act resting delicately on the buttresses visible outside the building. The round bosses in the center, each weighing nearly two tons, are what hold the structure together.

While Henry VI—who began work on the chapel—wanted it to be austere, his descendant Henry VII decided it should glorify the House of Tudor. So, lining the cream-colored walls are the personal symbols of Henry VII and his wife. There's the giant **Tudor coats-of-arms** supported by a dragon (symbolizing Henry's dad) and greyhound (from

his mom's side of the family). The Tudor double rose (of red and white roses) symbolizes the end of the bitter War of the Roses. The portcullis (the iron grate) honors the family of Henry VII's mother, Lady Margaret Beaufort. And the fleur-de-lis kept alive the fading hope that someday they might reclaim their place as rulers of France.

The 26 **stained-glass windows** date from the 16th century. It's the most Renaissance stained glass anywhere in one spot. (Most of the stained glass in English churches dates from Victorian times, but this glass is three centuries older.) The lower panes show scenes from the New Testament, while the upper panes feature corresponding stories from the Old Testament. Considering England's turbulent history, it's miraculous that

these windows have survived for half a millennium in such a pristine state. After Henry VIII separated from the Catholic Church in 1534, many such windows and other Catholic features around England were destroyed. However, since Henry had just paid for these windows, he couldn't bear to destroy them. A century later, in the days of Oliver Cromwell, another wave of iconoclasm destroyed more windows around England. Though these windows were slated for removal, they stayed put. Finally, during World War II, the windows were taken out and hidden away for safekeeping, then painstakingly replaced after the war ended. The only nonmedieval windows are on the west wall (opposite the altar). These are in the Romantic style from the 1880s; when Nazi bombs threatened the church, all agreed they should be left in place.

The **choir screen** that bisects the church was added by Henry VII's son, King Henry VIII—see his "H.R." monogram carved into it, for Henry Rex. He commissioned the oak screen to commemorate his marriage to Anne Boleyn. By the time it was finished, so was she (beheaded). But it was too late to remove her initials, which were already carved into the screen (look on the far upper left and right for "R.A.," for Regina Anna—"Queen Anne"). Behind the screen is the **choir** area, elaborately carved with the crests of the college and university. This is where the renowned King's College Choir performs. There's a daily evensong (during school terms), with students in the front-row stalls, the choir in the middle, and fellows in back. On Christmas Eve, a special service is held here and broadcast around the world on the BBC—a tradition near and dear to British hearts.

At the far end of the church is Rubens' masterful *Adoration of the Magi* (1634). It's actually a family portrait: The admirer in the front (wearing red) is a self-portrait of Rubens, Mary looks an awful lot like his much-younger wife, and the Baby Jesus resembles their own newborn at the time. In typical Rubens style, there's a diagonal line (running from the lower left) throwing the focus onto the main figures: Jesus and Mary.

Finally, check out the long and fascinating **series of side rooms** that run the length of the nave. Dedicated to the history and art of the church, these are a great little King's College Chapel museum.

• *Exit the church opposite where you entered, into the college court. From here you can stroll the rich grounds all the way to the River Cam and then back, passing through the grand entry gate and onto King's Parade.*

Sights in Cambridge

My self-guided walk takes you to most of the main sights in Cambridge, but not all. Visiting the following places in and near town is also worthwhile.

▲▲Trinity College and Wren Library

Of the more than 100 Nobel Prize winners affiliated with Cambridge, about a third come from this richest and biggest of the town's colleges, founded in 1546 by Henry VIII. The college has three sights to see: the entrance gate, the grounds, and the magnificent Wren Library.

Cost and Hours: Grounds—£3, daily 10:00-16:30, closes earlier off-season; library—free, Mon-Fri 12:00-14:00, during full term also Sat 10:30-12:30, closed Sun year-round; only 20 people allowed in at a time, tel. 01223/338-400, www.trin.cam.ac.uk.

Free Entrance to the Library: To see the Wren Library without paying for the grounds, access it from the riverside entrance (a long walk around the college via the Garret Hostel Bridge).

Trinity Gate: You'll notice gates like these adorning facades of colleges around town. Above the door is a statue of **King Henry VIII,** who founded Trinity because he feared that Cambridge's existing colleges were too cozy with the Church. Notice Henry's right hand holding a chair leg instead of the traditional scepter with the crown jewels. This is courtesy of Cambridge's Night Climbers, who first replaced the scepter a century ago. According to campus legend, decades ago some of the world's most talented mountaineers enrolled at Cambridge...in one of the flattest parts of England. (Cambridge was actually a seaport until Dutch engineers drained the surrounding swamps.) Lacking opportunities to practice their skill, they began scaling the frilly facades of Cambridge's college buildings under cover of darkness (if caught, they'd have been expelled). In the 1960s, climbers actually managed to haul an entire automobile onto the roof of the Senate House. The university had to bring in the army to cut it into pieces and remove it. Only 50 years later, at a class reunion, did the guilty parties finally fess up.

In the little park to the right, notice the lone **apple tree.** Supposedly, this tree is a descendant of the very one that once stood in the garden of Sir Isaac Newton (who spent 30 years at Trinity). According to legend, Newton was inspired to investigate gravity when an apple fell from the tree onto his head. This tree stopped bearing fruit long ago; if you do see apples, they've been tied on by mischievous students.

Beyond the gate are the Trinity grounds. Note that there's often a fine and free view of Trinity College courtyard—if the gate is open—from Trinity Lane (leading, under a uniform row of old chimneys, around the school to the Wren Library).

Trinity Grounds: The grounds are enjoyable to explore. Inside the **Great Court,** the clock (on the tower on the right) double-rings

at the top of each hour. It's a college tradition to take off running from the clock when the high noon bells begin (it takes 43 seconds to clang 24 times), race around the courtyard, touching each of the four corners without setting foot on the cobbles, and try to return to the same spot before the ringing ends. Supposedly only one student (a young lord) ever managed the feat—a scene featured in *Chariots of Fire* (but filmed elsewhere).

The **chapel** (entrance to the right of the clock tower)—which pales in comparison to the stunning King's College Chapel—feels like a shrine to thinking, with statues honoring great Trinity minds both familiar (Isaac Newton, Alfred Tennyson, Francis Bacon) and unfamiliar. Who's missing? The poet Lord Byron, who was such a hell-raiser during his time at Trinity that a statue of him was deemed unfit for Church property; his statue stands in the library instead.

Wren Library: Don't miss the 1695 Christopher Wren-designed library, with its wonderful carving and fascinating original manuscripts. Just outside the library entrance, Sir Isaac Newton clapped his hands and timed the echo to measure the speed of sound as it raced down the side of the cloister and back. Inside, admire Wren's design—long, white, and aglow with the bright light of the Enlightenment. Wren designed the whole ensemble, including the bookshelves topped with busts of great thinkers. (The one thing he didn't design is the stained-glass window showing him being honored by George III.) Unlike the other libraries at Cambridge, Wren designed Trinity's on the upper floor, not the damp, dark ground floor. As a result, Wren's library is flooded with light, rather than water (and it's also brimming with students during exam times).

In the library's 12 display cases (covered with cloth that you flip back), you'll see a (rotating) display of medieval manuscripts, first editions, letters, and documents. You might see works by William Shakespeare, John Milton, Samuel Taylor Coleridge, and A. A. Milne's original *Winnie the Pooh* (the real Christopher Robin attended Trinity College). Don't miss the case with Newton's memorabilia—a lock of his hair, notebook, pocket watch, walking stick, a prism he used to see how light bent, and a 1687 edition of his landmark book *Principia Mathematica* that changed forever the way humans viewed the physical world.

▲Fitzwilliam Museum

One of Britain's best museums of antiquities and art outside London is the Fitzwilliam. Housed in a grand Neoclassical building a 10-minute walk south of Market Hill Square, it's a palatial celebration of beauty and humankind's ability to create it.

Cost and Hours: Free but £5 donation suggested; Tue-Sat 10:00-17:00, Sun from 12:00, closed Mon; lockers, Trumpington Street, tel. 01223/332-900, www.fitzmuseum.cam.ac.uk.

Visiting the Museum: The Fitzwilliam's broad collection is like a mini British Museum/National Gallery rolled into one.

The ground floor features an extensive range of antiquities and applied arts—everything from Greek vases, Mesopotamian artifacts, and Egyptian sarcophagi to Roman statues, fine porcelain, and suits of armor.

Upstairs is the painting gallery, with works that span art

history: Italian Venetian masters (such as Titian and Canaletto), a worthy English section (featuring Gainsborough, Reynolds, Hogarth, and others), a notable array of French Impressionist art (including Monet, Renoir, Pissarro, Degas, and Sisley), and even a few small Picassos. Rounding out the collection are old manuscripts, including some musical compositions from Handel.

Museum of Classical Archaeology

Although this museum contains no originals, it offers a unique chance to study accurate copies (19th-century casts) of virtually every famous ancient Greek and Roman statue. More than 450 statues are on display.

Cost and Hours: Free; Mon-Fri 10:00-17:00, Sat until 13:00 during term, closed Sun year-round; Sidgwick Avenue, tel. 01223/330-402, www.classics.cam.ac.uk/museum.

Getting There: The museum is a five-minute walk west of Silver Street Bridge; after crossing the bridge, continue straight until you reach a sign reading *Sidgwick Site*.

▲▲Punting on the Cam

For a little levity and probably more exercise than you really want, try renting one of the traditional flat-bottom punts at the river.

You'll use a giant pole to push yourself up and down (or around and around, more likely) the lazy Cam. The water's only about six or seven feet deep, so you move by literally pushing off from the river floor (someone in front can use a little paddle to help out). This is one of the best memories the town has to offer, and once you get the hang of it, it's a fine way to enjoy the scenic side of Cambridge. It's less crowded in late afternoon (and less embarrassing).

Better yet, let someone else do the punting while you enjoy the ride. The 45-minute lazy punting trips are a delight—informatively narrated by your punter, who tries to avoid the clueless tourists creating a moving, aquatic obstacle course. Watching amateurs struggle with their massive poles, playing bumper cars in the busy river, you'll be happy someone else is at the helm. On a nice-weather day, there are few more relaxing activities.

Several companies rent punts and also offer tours. Both are open daily from about 9:00 until dusk when the weather's decent (typically March-Nov). **Scudamore's** has two locations: on Mill Lane, just south of the central Silver Street Bridge, and at the less convenient Quayside at Magdalene Bridge, at the north end of town (rental—£33/hour, 45-minute tour—£22/person, tel. 01223/359-750, www.scudamores.com). **Cambridge Chauffeur Punts,** just under the Silver Street Bridge, is a cheaper outfit (rental—£26/hour, 45-minute tour—£18/person, tel. 01223/354-164, www.punting-in-cambridge.co.uk). When it's not too busy, prices can be soft at either place for the guided tours—try asking for a discount.

If renting a punt in the Silver Street Bridge area, be clear on whether you're punting on the River Cam (the lovely but crowded stream that runs behind the pretty college campuses) or on the other side of the weir, at the River Granta (less crowded, it runs through idyllic countryside, but you won't see the famous landmarks). Most prefer the Cam.

NEAR CAMBRIDGE
Imperial War Museum Duxford

This former airfield, nine miles south of Cambridge, is popular with aviation fans and WWII history buffs. Wander through seven exhibition halls housing 200 vintage aircraft (including Spitfires, B-17 Flying Fortresses, a Concorde, and a Blackbird, some of which you can enter) as well as military land vehicles and special displays on Normandy and the Battle of Britain. The American Air wing thoughtfully portrays the achievements and controversies of British/US wartime collaboration, including the stories of American airmen based at Duxford.

Cost and Hours: £18, show local bus ticket for discount; daily 10:00-18:00, off-season until 16:00, last entry one hour before closing; tel. 01223/835-000, www.iwm.org.uk/visits/iwm-duxford.

Getting There: The museum is located off the A-505 in Duxford. On Sundays, direct Myalls bus #132 runs to the museum from the train station (4/day, 45 minutes, www.travelineeastanglia.org.uk). The rest of the week, it's best to take a taxi from Cambridge: Catch one at the taxi stand on St. Andrews Street next to the Lion Yard shopping mall (about £25 one-way).

Sleeping in Cambridge

While Cambridge is an easy side-trip from London (and you can enjoy an evening here before catching a late train back), its subtle charms might convince you to spend a night or two. Cambridge has few accommodations in the city center, and none in the tight maze of colleges and shops where you'll spend most of your time. These recommendations are about a 10- to 15-minute walk south of the town center, toward the train station.

$$$ Lensfield Hotel, popular with visiting professors, has 40 comfortable rooms—some old-fashioned, some refurbished (spa

and fitness room, 53 Lensfield Road, tel. 01223/355-017, www.
lensfieldhotel.co.uk, enquiries@lensfieldhotel.co.uk).

$$$ Hotel du Vin is an upscale place that rents 41 spiffy rooms
at a high price. It has a crooked-floors, duck-your-head historical
character and a whiff of pretense (air-con, elevator to some rooms,
light sleepers ask for quieter room in back, Trumpington Street 15,
tel. 01223/928 991, www.hotelduvin.com, reception.cambridge@
hotelduvin.com).

$$$ Regent Hotel has 22 modern, colorful rooms on the
main road between the town center and train station. Half of the
rooms overlook a giant park in back (air-con, elevator, 41 Regent
Street, tel. 01223/351-470, www.regenthotel.co.uk, reservations@
regenthotel.co.uk).

Eating in Cambridge

$$ The Eagle, near the TI and described earlier in my town walk,
is the oldest pub in town. While the food is mediocre, the pub
is a Cambridge institution—
with a history so rich that a
visit here practically qualifies as
sightseeing (food served daily
11:00-22:00, 8 Benet Street, tel.
01223/505-020).

$ Michaelhouse Café is a
heavenly respite from the crowds,
tucked into the repurposed St.
Michael's Church, just north of
Great St. Mary's Church. At lunch, choose from salads and sand-
wiches, as well as a few hot dishes and a variety of tasty baked goods
(Mon-Sat 8:00-17:00, breakfast served until 11:30, lunch served
11:30-15:50, closed Sun, occasional free lunchtime concerts, Trinity
Street, tel. 01223/309-147). Between 15:00 and 17:00 whatever they
have left from lunch is half-price.

$$ The Anchor Pub has a place in rock-and-roll history as a
spot where Pink Floyd band members hung out in their early days.
Today it's known for the best people-watching—and some locals
say best food—in Cambridge. Choose from its outdoor riverside
terrace, inside bar, or more romantic upstairs restaurant (all seating
areas serve the same menu, but the upstairs menu has a few added
specials; daily 12:00-21:30, on the riverfront at Silver Street, tel.
01224/353-554).

$$ The Mill Pub is a livelier, less formal alternative to The
Anchor, but enjoys a similar location right on the river. The clien-
tele is a mixture of students and tourists; the tipples are craft brews,

local ales, and ciders; and the food is updated pub standards (daily 11:00-23:00, 14 Mill Lane, tel. 01223/311-829).

$ Bread & Meat serves simple soups and hearty sandwiches. Grab a signature *porchetta* sandwich to take away or snag a rustic table in the small dining room (Mon-Thu 11:30-20:00, Fri-Sat until 21:00, Sun until 17:00, 4 Benet Street, tel. 0791/808-3057).

$$ Agora at The Copper Kettle is a popular place for Greek and Turkish *meze*, beautifully situated facing King's College on King's Parade (also fish-and-chips at lunch, daily 8:00-20:30, later in summer, 4 King's Parade, tel. 01223/308-448).

$$ Fitzbillies, long a favorite for cakes (Chelsea buns) and coffee, offers inviting lunch and afternoon tea menus (daily, 51 Trumpington Street, tel. 01223/352-500).

$ Street Food on Market Hill Square: For an interesting lunch on the go, browse the many food carts tucked into the tight aisles of the open-air market that fills the historic old market square (daily 9:00-16:00). There's no real seating, but people squeeze along the wall around the stone fountain in the middle of the square.

$ Fast Food: For healthy fast-food chains, the corner of Petty Cury Lane and Sidney Street (a long block east of Market Hill Square) has several good options.

Supermarkets: There's a **Marks & Spencer Simply Food** at the train station (long hours daily) and a larger **Marks & Spencer Foodhall** on Market Hill Square (Mon 9:00-18:00, Tue-Sat 8:00-20:00, closed Sun). **Sainsbury's** supermarket is open later (Mon-Sat 8:00-23:30, Sun 11:00-17:00, 44 Sidney Street, at the corner of Green Street).

A good picnic spot is Laundress Green, a grassy park on the river, at the end of Mill Lane near the Silver Street Bridge punts. There are no benches, so bring something to sit on. Remember, the college lawns are private property, so walking or picnicking on the grass is generally not allowed. When in doubt, ask at the college's entrance.

Cambridge Connections

From Cambridge by Train to: York (hourly, 2.5 hours, transfer in Peterborough), **London** (King's Cross Station: 2/hour, 45 minutes; Liverpool Street Station: 2/hour, 1.5 hours). Train info: Tel. 0345-748-4950, www.nationalrail.co.uk.

By Bus to: London (every 60-90 minutes, 2 hours), **Heathrow Airport** (1-2/hour, 3 hours). Bus info: Tel. 0871-781-8181, www.nationalexpress.com.

BATH

The best city to visit within easy striking distance of London is Bath—just a 1.5-hour train ride away. If ever a city enjoyed looking in the mirror, Bath's the one. Bath's narcissism is justified. It has more "government-listed" or protected historic buildings per capita than any other town in England. Built of the creamy warm-tone limestone called "Bath stone," it beams in its cover-girl complexion. Two hundred years ago, this city of 90,000 was the trendsetting Tinseltown of Britain. An architectural chorus line, it's a triumph of the Neoclassical style of the Georgian era—named for the four Georges who sat as England's kings from 1714 to 1830. Proud locals remind visitors that the town is routinely banned from the "Britain in Bloom" urban-beautification contest to give other towns a chance to win. Even with its mobs of tourists (2 million per year) and greedy prices, Bath is a joy to visit.

PLANNING YOUR TIME

Bath deserves two nights even on a quick trip. On a three-week England getaway, spend three nights in Bath, with one day for the city and one or two days for side trips to Wells, Glastonbury, or your pick of stone circles. Ideally, use Bath as your jet-lag recovery pillow (easy access from Heathrow Airport), and do London at the end of your trip.

Consider starting your English vacation this way:

Day 1: Land at Heathrow. Connect to Bath either by train via London Paddington, direct bus, or bus/train combination via Reading (for details, see page 282). You can also consider flying into Bristol, which has easy bus connections with Bath. While you don't need or want a car in Bath, those who land early and pick up their cars at the airport can visit Windsor Castle (near Heathrow) on their way to Bath. If you have the evening free in Bath, take a walking tour.

Day 2: 9:00—Tour the Roman Baths; 10:30—Catch the free city walking tour; 12:30—Picnic on the open deck of a tour bus; 14:00—Visit the abbey, then free time in the shopping center of old Bath; 15:30—Tour the No. 1 Royal Crescent Georgian house and Fashion Museum or Museum of Bath at Work. At night, consider seeing a play, take the evening walking tour (unless you did it last night), enjoy the Bizarre Bath comedy walk, or go for an evening soak in the Thermae Bath Spa.

Day 3 (and Possibly 4): Bath is a practical home base for visits to nearby sights. By car or bus, explore the mystical town of Glastonbury, the cathedral city of Wells, or the stone circles of Stonehenge and Avebury (see the next two chapters). Without a car or to go farther afield, consider a one-day Avebury/Stonehenge/ cute towns minibus tour from Bath (Mad Max tours are best; see "Tours in Bath," later.

Continuing from Bath: Consider linking Bath to the Cotswolds via South Wales (see the South Wales chapter).

BATH

Orientation to Bath

Think of Bath as three sightseeing neighborhoods. In the center of town is the main cluster of sights: the Roman Baths, Pump Room, and Bath Abbey. A few blocks northeast is another group of sights around Pulteney Bridge. And a 10-minute walk to

the northwest are the Georgian-era sights: the Circus, Royal Crescent, Assembly Rooms, and several museums. Bath is hilly. In general, you'll gain elevation as you head north.

TOURIST INFORMATION

The TI is next to The Huntsman Inn pub and a block south of the abbey (Mon-Sat 9:30-17:30, Sun 10:00-16:00, Bridgwater House, 2 Terrace Walk, tel. 01225/614-420, www.visitbath.co.uk). It houses the Bath Box Office, where you can check for events going on all around town (see listing below, under "Helpful Hints").

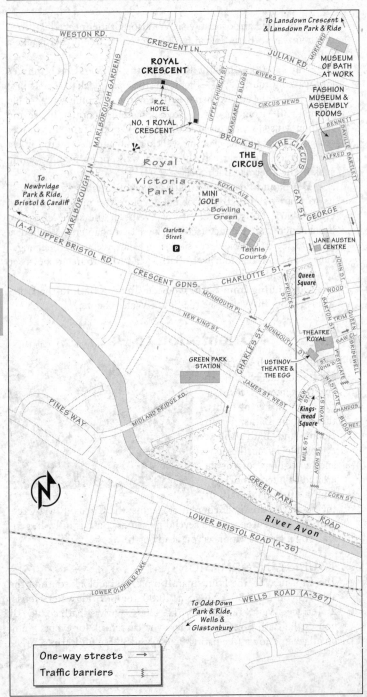

BATH

WESTON RD.

CRESCENT LN.

JULIAN RD.

MUSEUM OF BATH AT WORK

ROYAL CRESCENT

RIVERS ST.

FASHION MUSEUM & ASSEMBLY ROOMS

R.C. HOTEL

CIRCUS MEWS

NO. 1 ROYAL CRESCENT

BENNETT

BROCK ST.

THE CIRCUS

SAVILLE

ALFRED

THE CIRCUS

GAY ST.

Royal

To Newbridge Park & Ride, Bristol & Cardiff

Victoria Park

MINI GOLF

ROYAL AVE.

GEORGE

(A-4) UPPER BRISTOL RD.

Bowling Green

Charlotte Street P

Tennis Courts

JANE AUSTEN CENTRE

CRESCENT GDNS.

CHARLOTTE ST.

Queen Square

JOHN ST.

WOOD

BARTON ST.

TRIM

NEW KING ST.

MONMOUTH PL.

PRINCES ST.

QUEEN

THEATRE ROYAL

SAW CL.

BRIDEWELL

ST. JOHN'S

GREEN PARK STATION

CHARLES ST.

MONMOUTH ST.

USTINOV THEATRE & THE EGG

WESTGATE BLDGS

WESTGATE

NEW ST.

CHANDOS

JAMES ST. WEST

Kingsmead Square

PINES WAY

MIDLAND BRIDGE RD.

MILK ST.

AVON ST.

CORN ST.

N

GREEN PARK

River Avon

ROAD

LOWER BRISTOL ROAD (A-36)

LOWER OLDFIELD PARK

WELLS ROAD (A-367)

To Odd Down Park & Ride, Wells & Glastonbury

To Lansdown Crescent & Lansdown Park & Ride

MORFORD

UPPER CHURCH ST.

MARGARET'S BLDGS

MARLBOROUGH GARDENS

MARLBOROUGH LN.

One-way streets →
Traffic barriers

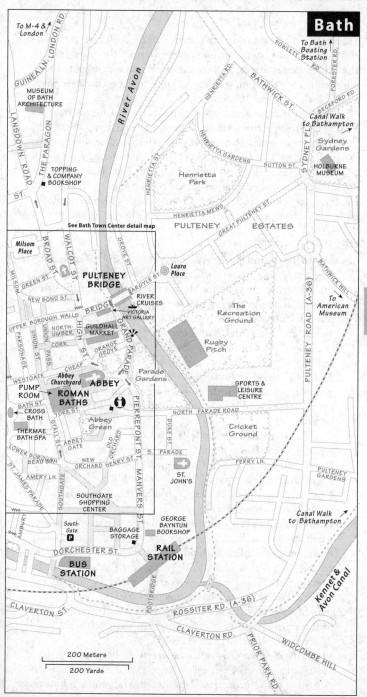

Bath

To M-4 &
London

GUINEA LN. LONDON RD.

POWLETT RD.

To Bath
Boating
Station

FORESTER RD.

BECKFORD RD.

MUSEUM
OF BATH
ARCHITECTURE

HENRIETTA RD.

BATHWICK ST.

SYDNEY PL.

Canal Walk
to Bathampton

LANSDOWN ROAD

THE PARAGON

River Avon

Sydney
Gardens

HOLBURNE
MUSEUM

TOPPING
& COMPANY
BOOKSHOP

ST.

HENRIETTA ST.

Henrietta
Park

HENRIETTA GARDENS

SUTTON ST.

HENRIETTA MEWS

GREAT PULTENEY ST.

PULTENEY   ESTATES

See Bath Town Center detail map

Milsom
Place

BROAD ST.

WALCOT ST.

GREEN ST.

GROVE ST.

PULTENEY
BRIDGE

Laura
Place

MILSOM

NEW BOND ST.

BRIDGE

ARGYLE ST.

The
Recreation
Ground

BATHWICK HILL (A-36)

To
American
Museum

UPPER BOROUGH WALLS

UNION ST.

HIGH ST.

RIVER CRUISES

VICTORIA
ART GALLERY

GUILDHALL
MARKET

Rugby
Pitch

PARSONAGE

NORTH-
UMBER.
CORR.

ORANGE
GROVE

GRAND PARADE

PULTENEY ROAD (A-36)

WESTGATE

CHEAP

Abbey
Churchyard

ABBEY

Parade
Gardens

SPORTS &
LEISURE
CENTRE

PUMP
ROOM

ROMAN
BATHS

PIERREPONT ST.

NORTH PARADE ROAD

BATH ST.

CROSS
BATH

YORK ST.

STALL ST.

Abbey
Green

DUKE ST.

Cricket
Ground

THERMAE
BATH SPA

ABBEY-
GATE

OLD
ORCHARD

S. PARADE

FERRY LN.

PULTENEY
GARDENS

LOWER BOROUGH

BEAU

NEW
ORCHARD

HENRY ST.

MANVERS ST.

AMERY LN.

ST. JAMES PARADE

SOUTHGATE

SOUTHGATE
SHOPPING
CENTER

ST.
JOHN'S

Canal Walk
to Bathampton

AMBURY

South-
Gate
P

BAGGAGE
STORAGE

GEORGE
BAYNTUN
BOOKSHOP

DORCHESTER ST.

RAIL
STATION

BUS
STATION

FOOTBRIDGE

Kennet &
Avon Canal

CLAVERTON ST.

ROSSITER RD. (A-36)

CLAVERTON RD.

WIDCOMBE HILL

PRIOR PARK RD.

200 Meters

200 Yards

BATH

ARRIVAL IN BATH

The Bath Spa **train station** has a staffed ticket desk and ticket machines. The **bus station** is immediately west of the train station, along Dorchester Street. Drivers can **park** at the Southgate shopping center near the train station. A handy luggage-check service is a half block away (see "Helpful Hints," next).

The best route into the town center is the 10-minute walk up Southgate Street. Exiting the train station, turn left on Dorchester, then right onto pedestrian-only Southgate, Bath's main modern shopping street. Continue uphill as Southgate changes names to Stall Street, glance right at a photogenic arch, then keep going another block to a row of columns on the right. Stepping through the columns, you enter Abbey Churchyard—Bath's historic center—with Bath Abbey, the Roman Baths, and the Pump Room.

HELPFUL HINTS

Getting to Bath and Stonehenge by Tour: Several companies offer guided bus tours from London to Stonehenge, Salisbury, and Bath; you can abandon the tour in Bath, essentially using the tour as one-way transport; see page 313.

Festivals: In late May, the 10-day **Bath Festival** celebrates art, music, and literature (bathfestivals.org.uk/the-bath-festival), overlapped by the eclectic **Bath Fringe Festival** (theater, walks, talks, bus trips; www.bathfringe.co.uk). The **Jane Austen Festival** unfolds genteelly in late September (www.janeausen.co.uk/festival). And for three weeks in December, the squares around the abbey are filled with a **Christmas market.**

    The **Bath Box Office** sells tickets for festivals and most events (except those at the Theatre Royal), and can tell you exactly what's on tonight (inside the TI, tel. 01225/463-362, www.bathfestivals.org.uk). The city's weekly paper, the *Bath Chronicle,* publishes a "What's On" events listing each Thursday (www.thisisbath.com).

Bookstore: Topping & Company, an inviting bookshop, has frequent author readings, free coffee and tea, a good selection of maps, and tables filled with tidy stacks, including lots of books on the Bath region (daily 8:30-19:30, near the bottom of the street called "The Paragon"—where it meets George Street, tel. 01225/428-111, www.toppingbooks.co.uk).

Baggage Storage: @Internet & Luggage is a half block in front of the train station (£2.50/bag per day, daily 8:00-22:00, 13 Manvers Street, tel. 01225/312-685).

Laundry: The **Spruce Goose Launderette** is between the Circus and the Royal Crescent, near several recommended restaurants on the pedestrian lane called Margaret's Buildings (bring coins, self-service, daily 8:00-20:00, last load at 19:00). **Speedy Wash** picks up your laundry anywhere in town on weekdays before 9:30 for same-day service (no pickup Sat, closed Sun, most hotels work with them, tel. 01225/427-616).

Bike Rental: You can rent a pricey bike or e-bike at **Green Park Bike Station** (£30/24 hours, includes lock and map, helmet extra; daily 10:00-16:00, Sept-April Tue-Sat only; must book in advance and leave cash security deposit and photo ID, at Green Park Station—enter through Sainsbury's on Lower Bristol Road, tel. 01225/920-148, www.greenparkbikestation. info).

Car Rental: Ideally, take the train or bus from downtown London to Bath, and rent a car as you leave Bath. Most offices close Saturday afternoon and all day Sunday, which complicates weekend pickups.

    Enterprise provides a pickup service for customers to and from their hotels (extra fee for one-way rentals, at Lower Bristol Road outside Bath, tel. 01225/443-311, www.enterprise. com). Others include **Thrifty** (pickup service and one-way rentals available, in the Burnett Business Park in Keynsham—between Bath and Bristol, tel. 01179/867-997, www.thrifty. co.uk), **Hertz** (one-way rentals possible, at Windsor Bridge, tel. 0843-309-3004, www.hertz.co.uk), and **National/Europcar** (one-way rentals available, about £15 by taxi from the train station, at Brassmill Lane—go west on Upper Bristol Road, tel. 0871-384-9985, www.europcar.co.uk). Skip **Avis**—it's a mile from the Bristol train station; you'd need to rent a car to get there.

Parking: As Bath becomes increasingly pedestrian friendly, city-center street parking is disappearing. For a stress-free, time- and money-saving option, park for free at one of the big **Park & Ride lots** just outside of Bath at Newbridge, Lansdown, or Odd Down, and ride a shuttle bus 10 minutes into town (look for the *P&R* signs as you approach; shuttles run daily every 15 minutes, £3.40 round-trip, £6/group round-trip; tel. 0345-602-0121, www.firstgroup.com/bath-park-and-ride).

    If you drive into town, be aware that short-term lots fill up fast (£2/hour, 2-4-hour maximum). You'll find more spots in long-stay lots for about the same cost. The Southgate shopping center lot on the corner of Southgate and Dorchester streets is a five-minute walk from the abbey (£5/up to 3 hours, £14/24 hours, open 24/7); the Charlotte Street car park is the biggest and most convenient. For more info on parking (including Park & Ride service), see the "Maps and Guides" section of http://visitbath.co.uk.

Tours in and near Bath

IN THE CITY

▲▲▲Free City Walking Tours

Free two-hour tours are led by the **Mayor of Bath's Honorary Guides,** volunteers who share their love of Bath with its many visitors (as the city's mayor first did when he took a group on a guided walk back in the 1930s). These chatty, historical, and gossip-filled walks give you the lay of the land while you learn about the evolution of the city, its architecture, and its amazing Georgian social scene. Tours leave from outside the Pump Room in the Abbey Churchyard (free, no tips, year-round Sun-Fri at 10:30 and 14:00, Sat at 10:30 only; additional evening walks May-Aug Tue and Thu at 18:00; www.bathguides.org.uk). Tip for theatergoers: When your guide stops to talk outside the Theatre Royal, skip out for a moment, pop into the box office, and see about snaring a great deal on a play for tonight.

Private Tours

For a private tour, call the local guides' bureau, **Bath Parade Guides** (£100/2 hours, tel. 01225/337-111, www.bathparadeguides.co.uk, bathparadeguides@yahoo.com). **Mike James** is a good Blue Badge Bath guide (£150/half-day, £270/day, mike@mikejames.org). Mike also does food tours (see below).

▲▲City Bus Tours

City Sightseeing's hop-on, hop-off bus tours zip through Bath. Jump on a bus at one of 17 signposted pickup points, pay the driver, climb upstairs, and hear recorded commentary about Bath. City Sightseeing has two 45-minute routes: the City Tour of Bath's center and the Skyline Tour outside town. Try to get one with a live guide; otherwise, bring your own earbuds for better sound. Save money by doing the bus tour first—your ticket gets you minor discounts at many sights (£16.50, ticket valid for 24 hours and both tour routes; City Tour generally 4/hour daily in summer 9:30-17:30, in winter 10:00-17:00, no buses Dec-Feb; Skyline Tour runs less frequently but year-round; tel. 01225/330-444, www. bathbuscompany.com).

Food Tours

Savouring Bath Food Tour is worth considering for a three-hour movable feast with eight tasty stops (£55, most weekdays and Sat at 9:45 and 14:00, no Sun tours, book online, RS%—10 percent discount with code "ricksteves," www.savouringbath.com, tel. 01225/425-843, Mike James).

BATH

NEARBY SIGHTS

Bath is a good launch pad for visiting nearby Glastonbury, Wells, Avebury, Stonehenge, and more.

Mad Max Minibus Tours

Operating daily from Bath, Maddy offers thoughtfully organized, informative tours run with entertaining guides and limited to 16 people per group. Book as far ahead as possible in summer. The **Stonehenge, Avebury, and Villages** full-day tour covers 110 miles and visits Stonehenge, the Avebury Stone Circles, photogenic Lacock (LAY-cock), and the southernmost Cotswold village, Castle Combe (£42 plus £20 Stonehenge entry, tours depart daily at 8:30 and return at 17:30). Check their website for other tours: Stonehenge's inner circle, Cotswold villages (£38/half-day, £45/full day, daily at 8:30), and Wells, Glastonbury, and Cheddar Gorge (£45, Tue and Sat at 9:00).

All tours depart from downtown Bath near the abbey (outside the Abbey Hotel on 1 North Parade, arrive 15 minutes early, book at least 48 hours in advance; RS%—£10 rebate with online purchase of two separate tour itineraries, request when booking second tour, discount refunded to credit card; mobile 07990-505-970, phone answered daily 8:00-18:00, www.madmaxtours.co.uk, maddy@madmaxtours.co.uk).

Lion Tours

This well-run outfit runs full-day tours of Cotswold villages and "King Arthur's Realm" (£45 each), and gets you to Stonehenge with half- or full-day tours (Stonehenge and Lacock tour-£49; Stonehenge, Salisbury, and Cotswold villages-£61; Stonehenge inner circle access-£130; these prices include Stonehenge admission; RS%—£10/adult discount when you book any two full-day tours online, £5 discount for half-day tours—email after booking first tour for code; mobile 07769-668-668, www.liontours.co.uk, see website for details). If you ask in advance, you can bring your luggage along and use this tour to get to the Cotswolds (£5/person, minimum two people).

Other Tour Options

Scarper Tours runs four-hour narrated minibus tours to Stonehenge, giving you two hours at the site. This is basically a shuttle bus service from Bath with tickets (£25 transportation only, £40 including Stonehenge entry fee and reservation, departs from outside the Abbey Hotel on Terrace Walk, daily mid-March-Oct at 9:30 and 14:00, Nov-mid-March at 13:00, www.scarpertours.com, sally@scarpertours.com).

Celtic Horizons is a car service offering tours from Bath to destinations such as Stonehenge, Avebury, and Wells. They also

Bath at a Glance

▲▲▲Free City Walking Tours Top-notch tours helping you make the most of your visit, led by the Mayor of Bath's Honorary Guides. **Hours:** Sun-Fri at 10:30 and 14:00, Sat at 10:30 only; additional evening walks offered May-Aug Tue and Thu at 18:00. See page 248.

▲▲▲Roman Baths Ancient baths that gave the city its name, tourable with good audioguide. **Hours:** Daily 9:00-18:00, July-Aug until 22:00, Nov-Feb 9:30-18:00. See page 252.

▲▲Bath Abbey 500-year-old Perpendicular Gothic church, graced with beautiful fan vaulting and stained glass. **Hours:** Mon-Sat 9:30-17:30, Sun 13:00-14:30 & 16:30-17:30. See page 257.

▲▲The Circus and Royal Crescent Stately Georgian (Neoclassical) buildings from Bath's 18th-century glory days. See pages 261 and 262.

▲▲No. 1 Royal Crescent Your best look at the interior of one of Bath's high-rent Georgian beauties. **Hours:** Daily 10:00-17:00. See page 262.

▲▲Canalside Walk to Bathampton This easy, hour-long stroll along an Industrial Age canal is a delightful escape from the busy town. See page 266.

▲Pump Room Swanky Georgian hall, ideal for a spot of tea or

provide a convenient transfer service (to or from London; Heathrow, Bristol, and other airports; the Cotswolds, and so on), with or without a tour itinerary en route. Allow about £35/hour for a group (comfortable minivans seat up to 8 people) and £150 for Heathrow-Bath transfers (1-3 people). Make arrangements and get pricing by email at info@celtichorizons.com (tel. 01373/800-500, US tel. 855-407-3200, www.celtichorizons.com).

Sights in Bath

IN THE TOWN CENTER

Abbey Churchyard

Ground zero for sightseeing is Abbey Churchyard, a vibrant square surrounded by the Roman Baths, Pump Room, and Bath Abbey. The Parade Gardens, Guildhall Market, Victoria Art Gallery, Pulteney Bridge, and River Avon are beyond the left corner of the a taste of unforgettably "healthy" spa water. **Hours:** Daily 9:30-16:00 for breakfast, lunch, and afternoon tea (open 18:00-21:00 for dinner July-Aug). See page 256.

▲**Pulteney Bridge and Parade Gardens** Shop-strewn bridge and relaxing riverside gardens. **Hours:** Bridge—always open; gardens—daily 10:00-18:00, Oct-April open 24 hours. See page 259.

▲**Victoria Art Gallery** Paintings from the late 17th century to today. **Hours:** Daily 10:30-17:00. See page 259.

▲**Fashion Museum** 400 years of clothing under one roof, plus the opulent Assembly Rooms. **Hours:** Daily 10:30-18:00, Nov-Feb until 17:00. See page 264.

▲**Museum of Bath at Work** Gadget-ridden circa-1900 engineer's shop, foundry, factory, and office. **Hours:** Daily 10:30-17:00, Nov and Jan-March weekends only, closed Dec. See page 264.

▲**American Museum and Gardens** Insightful look primarily at colonial/early-American lifestyles, with 18 furnished rooms and eager-to-talk guides. **Hours:** Tue-Sun 10:00-17:00, late Nov-mid-Dec until 16:30, closed Mon, closed early Nov and mid-Dec-mid-March. See page 265.

▲**Thermae Bath Spa** Relaxation center that put the bath back in Bath. **Hours:** Daily 9:00-21:30. See page 265.

BATH

abbey, a couple of minutes' walk away. Behind you, a block down Bath Street, is the Thermae Bath Spa.

Here in Abbey Churchyard, you can see the layers of Bath's history in a glance. The Roman Baths put the city on Europe's radar 2,000 years ago. The abbey made it an important medieval destination. The elegant Pump Room captures the city in its 18th-century heyday. And today's lively street performers show the city hasn't let up since.

The churchyard is also a showcase for Bath's distinctive Georgian architecture. The Pump Room's facade has a faux Greek-temple entrance: four tall columns support a triangular pediment with an inscription in Greek letters ("The greatest blessing is water"). Below that, the doorway is topped with a characteristic Georgian semicircular fanlight window. Five round windows and a fetching balustrade across the roofline complete the Neoclassical look.

▲▲▲Roman Baths

For thousands of years, humans have marveled at the hot water that bubbles out of the earth on this spot. In ancient Roman times, high

society enjoyed soaking in the mineral springs, and they built a large bathhouse around it. From Londinium, Romans traveled so often to Aquae Sulis, as the city was called, to "take a bath" that finally it became known simply as Bath. Today, a fine museum surrounds the ancient bathhouse. With the help of a great audioguide, you'll wander past Roman artifacts, a temple pediment with an evocative bearded face, a bronze head of the goddess Sulis Minerva, excavated ancient foundations, and the actual mouth of the health-giving spring. At the end, you'll have a chance to walk around the big, steaming pool itself, where Romans once lounged, splished, splashed, and thanked the gods for the gift of therapeutic hot water.

Cost and Hours: £22, £20 off-peak days—see website, includes audioguide; daily 9:00-18:00, July-Aug until 22:00, Nov-Feb 9:30-18:00, last entry one hour before closing; tel. 01225/477-784, www.romanbaths.co.uk.

Combo-Ticket: If you plan to see both the Roman Baths and the Fashion Museum, you can save a little with the £25 Museums Saver combo-ticket, which also covers the temporary exhibit at the Victoria Art Gallery. If you buy the combo-ticket online, you'll save more—it's £22.50—and avoid ticket lines at both sights. Family Saver tickets are also available.

Crowd-Beating Tips: Long ticket lines are typical in the summer. You can use the "fast track" lane by buying a ticket online in advance, or by purchasing a combo-ticket at the Fashion Museum or Victoria Art Gallery. On any day, try to visit early or late; peak time is between 13:00 and 15:00. If you're here in July or August, after 19:00 the baths are romantic, gas-lit, and all yours.

Tours: Take advantage of the excellent, included **audioguide.** For those with a big appetite for Roman history, in-depth 30-minute **guided tours** leave from the end of the museum at the edge of the actual bath (included with ticket, on the hour, a poolside clock shows the next departure time). You can revisit the museum after the tour.

◑ Self-Guided Tour: This brief tour follows the baths' one-way route; for more in-depth commentary, make ample use of the audioguide.

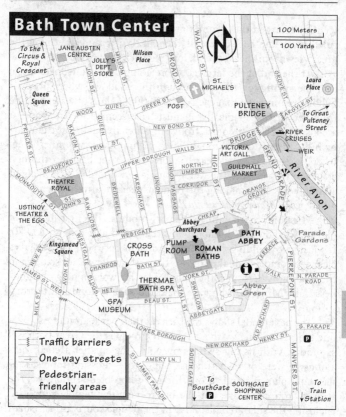

Bath Town Center

Begin by walking around the upper terrace, overlooking the swimming-pool–like Great Bath.

Terrace: Lined with **statues** of VIRs (Very Important Romans), the terrace evokes ancient times but was built in the 1890s. The terrace sits atop the remarkably well-preserved lower story, which was actually built by the Romans: The bases of the columns, the pavement, and the lead-lined pool are all original from the first century AD. Those ancient ruins had sat undisturbed for centuries before finally being excavated in the 1870s and turned into this museum. The terrace statues help put a face on the baths' history: Julius Caesar first set foot in Britain (55 BC). Claudius conquered the Celts in Bath (AD 43) and enclosed the first bathing pool with oak pilings. Hadrian

(c. 120) enlarged the complex around it, and Constantine (c. 325) ruled when the baths were at their peak of grandeur. Enjoy the great **view** from the west end, looking back toward the abbey.

At the end of the terrace, before going downstairs, peer down into the **spring** (on the left through the window), where little air bubbles remind you that each day 240,000 gallons of water emerge from the earth—magically, it must have seemed to Romans—at a constant 115°F. It comes from rainwater that falls on the nearby hills, filters down through layers of limestone two miles deep, where it's heated by the earth's core, then rises back up through cracks to the surface. The water you see now first fell as rain about 10,000 years ago...making the Romans seem relatively recent.

• *Now you'll head downstairs to the...*

Museum: Start with its helpful **models.** The first model (of plexiglass) shows the humble baths that stood here around AD 70. It's just two buildings, with the spring in between, but it makes clear the complex's dual purpose: The bathhouse was for soaking in the healing waters, and the temple was for worshipping the goddess Sulis Minerva, who gave mankind such a wondrous thermal spring.

The next model shows the baths at their peak, around AD 325. The tallest building (with a barrel-arch roof) is the Great Bath you see today, with its big swimming pool. The smaller arched roofs alongside were other bathhouse buildings—dressing rooms, saunas, cold plunges, and so on. The red-tile-roofed section was the temple. You can make out the big rectangular temple courtyard enclosing the small temple. Also in the temple courtyard is a small altar where sacrifices were offered. Get a close look at the temple's colorful pediment (the triangular gable atop its four columns). Now, let's see that actual pediment, displayed nearby.

The fragments of the **temple pediment**—carved by indigenous Celtic craftsmen but with Roman themes—represent a remarkable cultural synthesis. Sit and watch for a while as a slide projection fills in historians' best guesses as to what once occupied the missing bits. The identity of the circular face in the middle puzzles researchers. (God? Santa Claus?) It could be the head of Medusa, the Gorgon monster, after it was slain by Perseus—are those snakes peeking through its hair and beard? And yet, the Gorgon was traditionally depicted as female. Perhaps instead it's Neptune, the god of the sea—appropriate for this aquatic site.

The next exhibits examine every day **Roman life**—living, dying, and worshipping here in Aquae Sulis. You'll see vases, coins, and a stone head of a big-haired woman with her trendy first-century 'fro. The Beau Street Hoard—more than 17,500 Roman coins dating from 32 BC to AD 274 that were found near the Baths—emphasizes just how well visited this area was.

Next up are a couple of rooms dedicated to **Roman worship.** You'll see some of the small but extremely heavy stone altars that pilgrims hauled here as an offering to the goddess.

• *Next you'll walk through the ruins of the...*

Temple Courtyard: Imagine being a Roman arriving here to worship at the temple, which would have stood at the far end of the room. You'd pause to sacrifice an animal atop the great **altar** (on the right); note the nicely carved statue of Hercules adorning the altar's left corner. Then you'd continue on to the temple itself, where you'd come face-to-face with a gilded-bronze **statue** of the goddess Sulis Minerva (the surviving head is on display). The statue once wore a helmet (see the tiny holes for the rivets) and stood before a flaming cauldron. The goddess was a powerful multicultural hybrid of the Celtic goddess Sulis (who presided over the Aquae Sulis, or "waters of Sulis" in prehistoric times) and Minerva (a Roman life-giving mother-goddess), with hints of the Greek warrior-goddess Athena. Downstairs, enjoy a close-up look at the spring **overflow,** part of the original drain system built two millennia ago that still carries excess water to the River Avon.

• *Now head down a hall (with more exhibits), until you emerge outside in the...*

Great Bath: Take a slow lap (by foot) around the perimeter, imagining the frolicking Romans who once immersed themselves in this five-foot-deep pool. (These days, the water has turned greenish because of algae—don't touch it.) Originally, this pool was housed in a spacious hall with a three-story-tall arched ceiling, and sunlight filtered in through vast windows.

Romans had bathhouses in all major cities and went to the baths almost daily. Besides a way to keep clean, baths were also fitness clubs and social centers. This bath had the added feature of a natural thermal spring whose sulfurous content purportedly leeched out impurities, cured arthritis, and restored vigor. Role-playing actors are generally lounging around happy to talk (in Latin or English).

• *Now explore more of the...*

Bath Complex: The **East Baths** is a series of rooms showing how Romans typically bathed (with naked bodies artfully and modestly projected). You'd undress in the first room, warm up in the next room, get a massage in another, then start the cool-down process in another room. The large **central hall** was a sauna, heated by the Romans' famed hypocaust system: Stubby brick columns (which you can see) supported the floor, allowing the space in between to be filled with hot air to heat the room above.

Nearby is a giant red brick chunk of **roof span,** from when this was a cavernous covered swimming hall. At the corner, you'll see a length of original **lead pipe** (on the right, remarkably preserved since ancient times) and step over a small **canal** where hot water still trickles into the main pool. The water emerges from the spring at 115 degrees Fahrenheit—about 10 degrees too hot for most people—but it quickly cools to a perfect hot-tub temperature. In modern times, Britons bathed in this swimming pool up until the 1970s, then opened the Thermae Spa a block away—fed by the same spring.

When you're ready to cool down, follow the route away from the big pool and into the **West Baths** with its big round *frigidarium,* or "cold plunge" pool sparkling with coins. Across the hall (up a few steps) you have a close-up look at the source of this entire complex—the **sacred spring.**

• *After returning your audioguide, pop over to the **fountain** for a free taste of the spa water, which purportedly has health benefits (see minerals listed on the wall). Then pass the WC, head up the stairs, go through the gift shop, and exit via (or stop for tea in) the Pump Room (described next).*

▲Pump Room

The Pump Room, an elegant Georgian hall just above the Roman Baths, offers visitors their best chance to raise a pinky in Neoclassical grandeur. Above the clock, a statue of Beau Nash—who promoted Bath as an aristocratic playground in the 1700s—sniffles down at you. Come for tea or a light meal (see hours in listing on page 280), or to try a famous (but forgettable) "Bath bun" with your spa water (the same water that's in the fountain at

the end of the baths tour; also free in the Pump Room if you present your ticket). The spa water is served by an appropriately attired waiter, who will tell you the water is pumped up from nearly 100 yards deep and marinated in 43 wonderful minerals. Or for just the price of a coffee, drop in anytime—except during lunch—to enjoy live music (string trio or piano; times vary) and the atmosphere.

Even if you don't eat here, you're welcome to enter the foyer for a view of the baths and dining room.

▲▲Bath Abbey

The town of Bath wasn't much in the Middle Ages, but an important church has stood on this spot since Anglo-Saxon times. King Edgar I was crowned here in 973, when the church was much bigger (before the bishop packed up and moved to Wells). Dominating the town center, today's abbey—the last great church built in medieval England—is 500 years old and a fine example of

the Late Perpendicular Gothic style, with breezy fan vaulting and enough stained glass to earn it the nickname "Lantern of the West."

Cost and Hours: £4 suggested donation, Mon-Sat 9:30-17:30, Sun 13:00-14:30 & 16:30-17:30, handy flier narrates a self-guided tour, ask about events—including concerts, services, and evensong, schedule also posted on the door and online, tel. 01225/422-462, www.bathabbey.org.

Evensong: Choral evensong generally takes place twice a week (Thu at 17:30 and Sun at 15:30, 45 minutes); spoken evening prayers on other days are also a beautiful 20 minutes of worship (17:30).

Tower Climb: You can reach the top of the tower only with a worthwhile 50-minute guided tour (212 steps; £8, generally at the top of each hour when abbey is open, more often during busy times; Mon-Sat 10:00-16:00, no tours Sun, tour times usually posted outside abbey entrance, buy tickets in abbey gift shop).

Visiting the Abbey: This impressive church encapsulates Bath's long history in stone. It stands near the mineral springs where, even in pagan times, people came to worship. When Christianity arrived, a monastery was built here (8th century), then a larger church (11th century). The present church was begun in 1499.

No sooner was the church finished than it was stripped of its furnishings by King Henry VIII (1539), who dissolved the monastery and sold off its valuable lead roof and glass windows. (At the same time, the statue of Peter lost its head to mean-spirited iconoclasts; it was re-carved out of Peter's once supersized beard.)

For the next phase of the abbey's story, step inside and admire the **nave.** Queen Elizabeth I began repairing the abbey her father had plundered. In 1608, Bishop James Montague (see his

BATH

large **tomb** on the left side of the nave) took over. One rainy day, he saw water dripping down inside the church, and vowed to finish the ceiling. Thanks to Montague we have one of the abbey's most splendid features—the fan vaulting. Montague's coat of arms, with three diamonds and eagles, are symbols found throughout the church. Next to the tomb, the stained-glass **window** depicts coats of arms of other donors who financed the church's windows. On the wall beneath the window are several **gravestones** honoring Bath's notable citizens (there are more than 600 memorials to the deceased found in the church).

Cross to the opposite side of the nave toward the right transept. Just before entering the transept, find a gravestone on the wall for "Ricardi Nash"—better known as Beau Nash, Bath's 18th-century master of festivities. In the right transept is the 15-foot-tall stone **Waller Memorial.** It depicts the renowned English Civil War general Sir William Waller relaxing after liberating Bath from royalists. But the focus here is on his wife Jane, who died young. Now they gaze into each other's eyes for all eternity.

Before leaving the church, stand once again in the nave and appreciate the intricacy of the **fan vaulting** and brilliance of the windows. The glass, red-iron **lamps** and the **heating grates** on the floor are all remnants of the 19th century. (In a sustainable, 21st-century touch, the heat now comes from the baths' hot run-off water.) Note that a WWII bomb blast destroyed the medieval glass; what you see today is from the 1950s.

At the far end of the church (above the altar), the large **window** shows 52 scenes from Christ's life—good for weekly sermons for a year. The window to the left of the altar shows **King Edgar** being crowned. Edgar (in red) sits on a throne clutching the orb and scepter while the Archbishop of Canterbury (in purple) places the crown on his head. Edgar was one of the first monarchs of what we now call England. His coronation in AD 973

established the protocols used by all future English monarchs up to the present—and it all started here in Bath.

ALONG THE RIVER AND PULTENEY ESTATES

These pleasant, low-key sights are located along the River Avon behind Bath Abbey. Taken together, they create an enjoyable scene of shops, cafés, galleries, and people-watching.

Parade Gardens

This riverside park has manicured lawns, knockout flowerbeds, a café, and good views of the Pulteney Bridge. In season there's a small fee to enter the park, which was designed by prolific 18th-century architect John Wood the Elder (£2, fee includes deck chairs, daily 10:00-18:00, Oct-April free and open 24 hours, ask about summer concerts some Sun at 15:00, entrance a block south of Pulteney Bridge).

Guildhall Market

The little old-school shopping mall just north of the Parade Gardens is a frumpy time warp in this affluent town. In the 12th century the king gave Bath the right to have a market and that market moved from the abbey to here in the 18th century. Stand under the central dome and feel the surviving character. The historic negotiating table (or "nail") dates from 1768.

▲Victoria Art Gallery

This small gallery, between the Guildhall Market and Pulteney Bridge, was opened in 1897 to celebrate the 60th anniversary of Queen Victoria's reign. Today it's a delightful space with two parts: The ground floor houses temporary exhibits, while the upstairs is filled with paintings from the late 15th century to the present, along with a small collection of decorative arts, including 187 porcelain and pottery dog figures.

Cost and Hours: Free, £2 suggested donation, temporary exhibits-£5, covered by combo-ticket with Roman Baths and Fashion Museum, daily 10:30-17:00, tel. 01225/477-233, www.victoriagal. org.uk.

▲Pulteney Bridge

The shop-lined Pulteney Bridge was designed in 1770 by Scottish architect Robert Adam in the same Georgian, or "Palladian," style that John Wood the Younger was applying to the row of townhouses known as Bath's Royal Crescent.

The best view of the bridge is from its downstream side. The most Palladian feature is the center of the bridge with the outline of a Greek temple seemingly stamped into the stone. The temple's pediment is "broken"—that is, the triangle's base is purposely left incomplete. The bridge has grid windows, a few round medallions, and a central window that's bigger than the others,

BATH

with an arched top. The view from the upstream side lets you see a few shops jutting out (cantilevered) from the bridge.

Pulteney Estates

Pulteney Estates, the section of Bath stretching from Pulteney Bridge across the river, was open farmland owned by the Earl of Bath until the 18th century. Inherited by Frances Pulteney (cousin to the earl) in 1762, she started a project to develop this land as a grand neighborhood in 1788. But with the French Revolution in 1789, England fell into an economic recession and construction ground to a halt. All that she built was the

Pulteney Bridge (a classy way to bridge the old town with this new zone over the river) and Great Pulteney Street—intended to be the central axis of this new Georgian Bath.

Looking at Great Pulteney Street and a Bath map, you can imagine what was planned. Georgian England was all about appearances. The grand, uniform facade was key—everything behind that was higgledy-piggledy (a great metaphor for social life in the 18th century). If Great Pulteney Street looks like a movie set to you, it did to the producers of the 2004 movie *Vanity Fair* too, who used it as 18th-century London.

NORTHWEST OF THE TOWN CENTER

This area—a 10-minute uphill walk northwest of the town center—was a palatial housing development built during Bath's Golden Age of the 1700s. It's the masterpiece of the visionary father-and-son architects John Wood the Elder and John Wood the Younger. As visitors poured into the city, Bath was running out of suitable accommodations. The Woods bought large tracts of land northwest of downtown and built attractive vacation rentals for the rich and famous. In the process they helped forge the Georgian style of architecture soon found all over Britain.

Queen Square

This rectangular park surrounded by townhouses was Wood the Elder's first great real-estate development. He ringed the square with symmetrical facades in the classical style pioneered by the influential Italian architect Andrea Palladio. The north (uphill) side has a Greek-temple look to it, made of six columns topped with a triangular pediment. The windows are large, symmetrically placed, and topped with Palladian pediments and arches. The writer Jane Austen lived in the corner apartment to the right of the Francis

Hotel (#13). Completing the square's classical look is a 70-foot-tall obelisk in the middle, generously donated by Beau Nash.

▲▲The Circus

True to its name, this is a circular housing complex. It was Wood the Elder's next great expansion, consisting of 30 symmetrical townhouses arranged in a perfect circle. The best views are from the middle of the Circus among the grand plane trees, on the capped old well. Imagine the days before indoor plumbing, when servant girls gathered here to fetch water—this was gossip central. If you stand on the well, your clap echoes three times around the circle—try it.

The circle of houses is broken into three segments, so that anyone approaching from the street has a great view of the crescent-shaped facades. Each residence has five stories. You'd enter at street level into the workaday public rooms. The entrances were made large enough that aristocrats could be carried right through the door in their sedan chairs, and women could enter  without disturbing their sky-high hairdos. The next floor up (with bigger windows) generally had ballrooms and dining rooms for hosting parties. The floor above that held bedrooms. The top floor (the tiny dormer windows in the roof) had servant bedrooms, and the basement (below street level) held the kitchen and workrooms. Wood united it all with a symmetrical facade, but the arrangement of the actual rooms behind the facade was left to the owner's discretion. If you circled around, you'd see that the backs are a jumble, infamous for their "hanging loos" (bathrooms added years later).

Note the frieze—a continuous band of sculpted reliefs—located just above the ground floor. There are 525 different panels, each one unique, depicting everything from dogs to eagles to roses, scrolls, guitars, anchors, leaves, and roosters.

In its mid-1700s heyday, the Circus was home to Britain's elite. Prime Minister William Pitt the Elder (who oversaw the American colony's French and Indian War) lived at #11. Baron Robert Clive (who brought India under British control) vacationed here at #14 (on the sunny side of the Circus). Thomas Gainsborough set up shop at #17 to paint portraits of fashionable lords and ladies to take home as souvenirs.

Created at the height of Wood's creative powers, the Circus shows off the architect's mature style. There's Palladio's Greco-

Roman classicism—Doric columns on the ground floor, Ionic in the middle, and Corinthian on top—like Rome's Colosseum. For more Georgian effects, Wood added a balustrade and ornamental acorns on the roofline. The circular shape was likely inspired by Stonehenge, representing Britain's druid roots. And the symbolism in the frieze is distinctly Masonic. By combining the three styles—Roman, Celtic, and Masonic—Wood was creating his personal vision of Bath as the "new Rome."

▲▲Royal Crescent

This long, graceful arc of buildings evokes the wealth and gentility of Bath's glory days. The Royal Crescent was the majestic showpiece of John Wood the Younger. He took the Georgian style his father had pioneered and supersized it. The Crescent is a semicircular row of 30 townhouses 500 feet long and 50 feet tall. It's lined with 114 Ionic columns that span the middle two stories. A ground floor of large blocks and a balustrade across

the roofline unites it all. In typical Georgian style, the only deviation from the symmetry is in the very center of the crescent, which has two pairs of columns and a taller arched window. The building's warm golden color is typical of the city, made of limestone from the surrounding hills that began forming hundreds of millions of years ago when an ocean covered Bath.

Completed in 1774, the Royal Crescent quickly became the trendiest address in Bath. It offered stunning views of a park—a novel idea at the time that gave city dwellers a slice of the country. Like his father, Wood the Younger designed only the facade, allowing each resident to build whatever home they wanted behind it.

As you cruise the Crescent, strut like an aristocrat. Now imagine you're poor: Notice the "ha ha fence," a dropoff in the front yard that acted as a barrier, invisible from the windows, for keeping out sheep and peasants. The refined and stylish **Royal Crescent Hotel** sits virtually unmarked in the center of the Crescent (with the giant magnolia growing up its wall). You're welcome to (politely) drop in to explore its fine ground-floor public spaces and back garden, where a gracious and traditional tea is served (see page 280).

▲▲No. 1 Royal Crescent

This former residence at the east end of the Crescent is now a museum, taking visitors behind the classy Georgian facade for a glimpse into the everyday life of wealthy residents during the mid-1700s.

At the time, Britain was on the leading edge of global exploration and scientific discovery, and the period artifacts show the wide-ranging interests of the educated rich. Take the time to talk with the helpful docents (who almost give you no option but to learn), or you'll miss fascinating details like how high-class women shaved their eyebrows and pasted on carefully trimmed strips of mouse fur in their place.

Cost and Hours: £10.60, half-price after 16:00, daily 10:00-17:00, tel. 01225/428-126, http://no1royalcrescent.org.uk.

Visiting the Museum: Start on the ground floor with the **Parlour,** the main room of the house used for breakfast in the mornings, business affairs in the afternoon, and various other everyday activities throughout the evening. The Chippendale bookcase, with its octagonal woodwork, is typical, as is the (modern-looking but Georgian-era) design of the carpet.

The **Gentleman's Retreat**—an educated fellow's man-cave—has various proto-scientific objects, like a globe, telescope, and clock. In the **Dining Room,** refined 18th-century gentlemen ate with elegant dinnerware, drank, smoked, talked business, and relieved themselves behind the folding screen. Before going upstairs, pause at the **Cabinet of Curiosities**—a collection of odd and precious objects that a host would show his guests: fossils, tribal masks, and exotic weapons.

Upstairs, the **Withdrawing Room** (later called simply a "drawing" room) is where the ladies would withdraw from the rude company of men to play the harpsichord and take tea on the sofa. Note the fake door, to maintain the Georgian symmetry of the room. In the **Lady's Bedroom,** you can picture her ladyship waking from her canopied bed, attended by her maid (who arrived through the hidden door), dressing at her table, and donning her big-hair wig. Up another flight is the **Gentleman's Bedroom,** with his wig, engravings of old cityscapes, and a great view out the window of the Royal Crescent.

The visit ends (down the servants' back stairs) in the basement with the **Servants Hall and Kitchen.** Find Fido on a treadmill. The wooden rack hanging from the ceiling kept the bread, herbs, and ham away from the mice. Notice also the coal chute adjacent to the kitchen. Remember, the servants lived way up in the attic, worked in the basement, and served the family on the middle floors—lots of upstairs and downstairs. The kind of English class system seen at the Royal Crescent reached its peak in the 1700s. But by the next century, a middle class was on the rise, and the era of harpsichords and linen doilies would soon be consigned to museums.

▲Fashion Museum

Housed underneath Bath's Assembly Rooms, this museum displays four centuries of fashion on one floor. The fact-filled audioguide can

stretch a visit to an informative and enjoyable hour. Like fashion itself, the exhibits change all the time, but there's always a section on historical trends. You'll see how fashion evolved—just like architecture and other arts— from Georgian to Regency, Victorian, the Swinging '60s, and so on. A major feature is the "Dress of the Year" display: Since 1963 a fashion expert has anointed a new look to add to this collection. If you're intrigued by all those historic garments, go ahead and lace up your own trainer corset (which looks more like a life jacket) and try on a hoop underdress.

Cost and Hours: £9.50, includes audioguide; £25 combo-ticket includes Roman Baths and Victoria Art Gallery temporary exhibits, 10 percent cheaper online, family ticket available; daily 10:30-18:00, Nov-Feb until 17:00, last entry one hour before closing; free 30-minute guided tour in summer at 12:00 and 16:00, in winter at 12:00 and 13:00; self-service café, Bennett Street, tel. 01225/477-789, www.fashionmuseum.co.uk.

▲Museum of Bath at Work

This modest but informative museum north of the Assembly Rooms explains the industrial history of Bath. If you want to learn

about the unglamorous workaday side of the spa town, this is the place. The core of the museum is the well-preserved, circa-1900 fizzy-drink business of one Mr. Bowler, including a Dickensian office, engineer's shop, brass foundry, essence room lined with bottled flavorings (see photo), and factory floor. You'll then explore exhibits on more Bath creations, such as the traditional methods for cutting the local "Bath stone."

Cost and Hours: £8, includes audioguide, daily 10:30-17:00, Nov and Jan-March weekends only, closed Dec, last entry one hour before closing, Julian Road, 2 steep blocks up Russell Street from Assembly Rooms, tel. 01225/318-348, www.bath-at-work.org.uk.

OUTER BATH
▲American Museum and Gardens

The UK's sole museum dedicated to American history has thoughtful exhibits on the history of Native Americans and the Civil War, but the museum's heart is with the decorative arts and cultural artifacts that reveal how Americans lived from colonial times to the mid-19th century. The 18 completely furnished rooms (from a bare-bones 1600s Massachusetts dining/living room to a Rococo Revival explosion in a New Orleans bedroom) are hosted by eager guides waiting to fill you in on the everyday items that make domestic Yankee history surprisingly interesting. On a nice day, the surrounding gardens (including a replica of George Washington's garden at Mount Vernon) and view of the hills might be the best reasons to visit.

Cost and Hours: Museum and gardens—£13, gardens only—£7.50, Tue-Sun 10:00-17:00, late Nov-mid-Dec until 16:30, closed Mon, closed early Nov and mid-Dec-mid-March, last entry one hour before closing, at Claverton Manor, café, tel. 01225/460-503, www.americanmuseum.org.

Getting There: The museum is just east of town. From the city center take the #U1 bus to The Avenue stop (£2.90 one-way, £4.50 day ticket, 15-minute ride, 4/hour, stop is just before Bath University) and follow the tree-lined path (left of stone wall) 15 minutes. You could also hop a taxi for about £16. By car, it's well signed from A-36 and the city center.

Activities in Bath

▲Thermae Bath Spa

After simmering unused for a quarter-century, Bath's natural thermal springs once again offer R&R for the masses. The state-of-the-art spa is housed in a complex of three buildings that combine historic structures with new glass-and-steel architecture.

Is the Thermae Bath Spa worth the time and money? The experience is pricey and humble compared to similar German and Hungarian spas. The tall, modern building in the city center lacks any old-time elegance. Jets in the pools are limited, and the only water toys are big foam noodles. There's no cold plunge—the only way to cool off between steam rooms is to step onto a small, unglamorous balcony. The Royal Bath's two pools are essentially the same, and the water isn't particularly hot in either—in fact, the main attraction is the rooftop view from the top one.

All that said, this is the only natural thermal spa in the UK and your one chance to actually bathe in Bath. Consider an evening visit, when—on a chilly day—Bath's twilight glows through the steam from the rooftop pool.

Cost: The cheapest spa pass is £36 for two hours (£40 on weekends), which includes towel, robe, and slippers and gains you access to the Royal Bath's large, ground-floor "Minerva Bath"; four steam rooms and a waterfall shower; and the view-filled, open-air, rooftop thermal pool. Longer stays are £10 for each additional hour. The much-hyped £49 Twilight Package includes three hours and a meal (one plate, drink, robe, towel, and slippers). Bring your own swimsuit.

Thermae has all the "pamper thyself" extras (not included): massages, scrubs, and facials, including "watsu"—water shiatsu. Book treatments in advance by phone.

Hours: Daily 9:00-21:30, last entry at 19:00, pools close at 21:00. No kids under 16.

Information: It's 100 yards from the Roman Baths, on Beau Street (tel. 01225/331-234, www.thermaebathspa.com).

The Cross Bath: Operated by Thermae Bath Spa, this renovated circular Georgian structure across the street from the main spa provides a simpler and less-expensive bathing option. It has a hot-water fountain that taps directly into the spring, making its water hotter than the spa's (£20/1.5 hours, daily 10:00-19:30, last entry at 18:00, check in at Thermae Bath Spa's main entrance across the street—you'll be escorted to the Cross Bath, changing rooms, no access to Royal Bath, no kids under 12). If you're not comfortable playing footsie with strangers, it can feel cramped.

Spa Visitor Center: Also across the street, in the Hetling Pump Room, is a free one-room exhibit that explains the spring water's role in the founding of Bath (Mon-Sat 10:00-17:30, Sun 11:00-16:00, closed Oct-March). The visitor center rents a £2 audioguide for those wanting to explore the neighborhood around the baths.

▲▲Canalside Walk to Bathampton

An idyllic towpath leads three miles from Bath along the Kennet and Avon Canal to the sleepy village of Bathampton. For an unforgettable hour getting you totally out of the city, don't miss this memorable little walk. You can do it as a round-trip or do it one-way in either direction with a taxi or boat connection. Or you can do it on a rental bike.

From Pulteney Bridge walk straight down Great Pulteney Street to the Holburne Museum with its fine modern café facing

Sydney Gardens. Continue straight a hundred yards through the gardens, over the train tracks (which put canals, built for Industrial Age cargo transport, out of business shortly after they were opened) to the Kennet and Avon Canal. At the canal, turn left and walk the towpath (being thankful you're not a horse pulling a barge) for about an hour to Bathampton. Consider the classic **George pub** there for a nice meal and a beer (reservations smart, tel. 01225/425-079, www.chefandbrewer.com). The canal, while pristine and idyllic, gives you a sense of the Industrial Age.

From The George you can hike back to Bath, or walk (on the left) along the road for five more minutes to the River Avon. There you'll find the bigger **Bathampton Mill pub,** with garden tables overlooking the Avon (tel. 01225/469-758, www.thebathamptonmill.co.uk) and the pier for the *Pulteney Princess* river cruise that glides back to Bath (see below). From here it's a £10 taxi back to Bath.

River Cruise to Bathampton

The *Pulteney Princess* cruises to the neighboring village of Bathampton about hourly from Pulteney Weir. The river is like a Huck Finn dream—with trees encroaching on it, derelict old warehouses, and no riverside path. The cruise is a sleepy float with sporadic commentary, but it's certainly relaxing, and the boat has picnic-friendly sundecks. The Bathampton Mill pub awaits at the dock in Bathampton (£5 one-way, up to 12/day in good weather, one hour to Bathampton and back, WCs on board, mobile 07791-910-650, www.pulteneyprincess.co.uk). Consider combining the cruise with a walk along the parallel canal towpath (explained above). If stopping for a meal, between The Bathampton Mill (on the river) and The George (on the canal, a 5-minute walk from the river), I prefer The George.

Boating

The **Bath Boating Station,** in an old Victorian boathouse, rents rowboats, canoes, and punts (£8/person for first hour, then £4/hour; all day for £20; Wed-Sun 10:00-18:00, closed Mon-Tue and Oct-Easter, intersection of Forester and Rockcliffe roads, one mile northeast of center, tel. 01225/312-900, www.bathboating.co.uk).

Nightlife in Bath

For an up-to-date list of events, pick up the local weekly newspaper, the *Bath Chronicle,* which includes a "What's On" schedule (www.bath.live).

▲▲Bizarre Bath Street Theater

For an entertaining walking-tour comedy act "with absolutely no history or culture," follow Toby or Noel on their creative and lively Bizarre Bath walk. This 1.5-hour "tour," which combines stand-up comedy with cleverly executed magic tricks, plays off unsuspecting passersby as well as tour members.

Cost and Hours: £10, RS%—£8 with this book, April-Oct nightly at 20:00, smaller groups Mon-Thu, promises to insult all nationalities and sensitivities, just racy enough but still good family fun, leaves from the Huntsman Inn, North Parade Passage, next to the TI, www.bizarrebath.co.uk.

▲Theatre Royal Performance

The restored 18th-century, 800-seat Theatre Royal, one of England's loveliest, offers a busy schedule of London West End-type plays, including many "pre-London" dress-rehearsal runs. The Theatre Royal also oversees performances at two other theaters around the corner from the main box office: Ustinov Studio (edgier, more obscure titles, many of which are premier runs in the UK) and "the egg" (for children, young people, and families).

Cost and Hours: £23-48; shows generally start at 19:30 or 20:00, matinees at 14:30, box office open Mon-Sat 10:00-20:00, Sun from 12:00 if there's a show; book in person, online, or by phone; on Saw Close, tel. 01225/448-844, www.theatreroyal.org.uk.

Ticket Deals: Forty nosebleed spots on a bench (misnamed "standbys") go on sale at noon Monday through Saturday for that day's evening performance in the main theater (£7.50, 2 tickets maximum). If the show is sold out, same-day "standing places" go on sale at 18:00 (12:00 for matinees) for £4 (cash only). Also at the box office, you can snatch up any "last minute" seats for £15-20 a half-hour before "curtain up." Shows in the Ustinov Theatre go for around £20, with no cheap-seat deals.

Sightseeing Tip: During the free Bath walking tour, your guide stops here. Pop into the box office, ask what's playing, and see if there are many seats left for that night. If plenty of seats remain unsold, you're fairly safe to come back 30 minutes before curtain time to buy a ticket at the cheaper price.

Evening Walks

Take your choice: comedy (Bizarre Bath, described earlier), history, or ghost tour. Free city walking tours are offered on some evenings in high season (described on page 248). Ghost Walks are a popular way to pass the after-dark hours (£8, cash only, 1.5 hours, year-round Thu-Sat at 20:00, leave from The Garrick's Head pub—to the left and behind Theatre Royal as you face it, tel. 01225/350-512, www.ghostwalksofbath.co.uk).

Pubs

Most pubs in the center are very noisy, catering to a rowdy twenty-something crowd. But on the top end of town, you can still find some classic old places with inviting ambience and live music. See the map on page 277 for locations.

The Old Green Tree, conveniently right in the town center, is a rare traditional pub offering a warm welcome (locally brewed real ales, no TVs, 12 Green Street, tel. 01225/448-259).

The Star Inn is much appreciated by locals for its fine ale and "no machines or music to distract from the chat." It's a throwback to the manly pubs of yesteryear, and its long bench, nicknamed "death row," still comes with a complimentary pinch of snuff on request. Try the Bellringer Ale, made just up the road (daily 12:00-14:30 & 17:30-late, no food served, 23 The Vineyards, top of The Paragon/A-4 Roman Road, tel. 01225/425-072, Jon). Guests are welcome to play the pub's piano.

The Bell has a jazzy, pierced-and-tattooed, bohemian feel, but with a mellow older crowd. Some kind of musical activity brews nearly nightly, such as jazz, blues, DJs, and open-mike (Mon-Sat 11:30-23:00, Sun 12:00-22:30, 103 Walcot Street, tel. 01225/460-426, www.thebellinnbath.co.uk). There's an inviting garden out back, often with a pizza oven fired up.

Summer Nights at the Baths or Along the Canal

In July and August, you can stretch your sightseeing day at the Roman Baths, open nightly until 22:00 (last entry 21:00), when the gas lamps flame and the baths are far less crowded and more atmospheric. To take a dip yourself, consider popping over to the Thermae Bath Spa (last entry at 19:00). And on long, warm summer evenings, the canal walk to Bathampton where a pub dinner awaits (described earlier) can be delightful.

Sleeping in Bath

Bath is a busy tourist town. Reserve in advance, and keep in mind B&Bs favor those lingering longer. Accommodations are expensive and can be about 25 percent more on Fridays and Saturdays. At B&Bs, it's worth asking for a weekday, three-nights-in-a-row, or off-season deal. If you're driving to Bath, stowing your car near the center will cost you (though some less-central B&Bs have parking):

Take advantage of the Park & Ride lots outside of town or ask your hotelier for the best option.

NEAR THE ROYAL CRESCENT

These listings are all a 5- to 10-minute walk from the town center, and an easy 15-minute walk from the train station. With bags in tow you may want to either catch a taxi (£5-7) or (except for Brocks Guest House) hop on bus #4 (direction: Weston, catch bus inside bus station, pay driver £2.90, get off at the Comfortable Place stop—just after the park starts on the right, cross the street and backtrack 100 yards).

Except for Brocks, these B&Bs all face a busy arterial street (Upper Bristol Road, also known as Crescent Gardens); while the noise is minimal by urban standards and these B&Bs have well-insulated windows, light sleepers should request a rear- or side-facing room.

$$$ **Marlborough House,** exuberantly run by hands-on owner Peter, mixes modern style with antique furnishings and features a welcoming breakfast room with an open kitchen. Each of the six rooms comes with a sip of sherry (RS%, family room, air-con, minifridges, free parking, 1 Marlborough Lane, tel. 01225/318-175, www.marlborough-house.net, mars@manque.dircon.co.uk).

$$ **Brocks Guest House** rents six rooms in a Georgian townhouse built by John Wood in 1765. Located between the prestigious Royal Crescent and the courtly Circus, it's been redone in a way that would make the great architect proud. Each room has its own Bath-related theme (little top-floor library, 32 Brock Street, tel. 01225/338-374, www.brocksguesthouse.co.uk, brocks@brocksguesthouse.co.uk, Marta and Rafal).

$$ **Brooks Guesthouse** is the biggest and most polished of the bunch, albeit the least personal, with 22 modern rooms and classy public spaces, including an exceptionally pleasant breakfast room (limited pay parking, 1 Crescent Gardens, Upper Bristol Road, tel. 01225/425-543, www.brooksguesthouse.com, info@brooksguesthouse.com). They also rent two apartments.

$$ **2 Crescent Gardens,** owner Giacomo's former family home, has six attractive rooms—some with views—and a bright, open breakfast room and homey living room (family room, limited free parking, closed Jan, 2 Crescent Gardens, tel. 01225/331-186, www.2crescentgardens.co.uk, 2crescentgardens@gmail.com, managed by Monika).

$$ **Cornerways B&B** is centrally located, simple, and pleasant, with three rooms and old-fashioned homey touches (RS%, cheaper without breakfast, DVD library, free parking, 47 Crescent Gardens, tel. 01225/422-382, www.cornerwaysbath.co.uk, info@cornerwaysbath.co.uk, Sue Black).

EAST OF THE RIVER

These listings are a 5- to 10-minute walk from the city center. From the train station, it's best to take a taxi, as there are no good bus connections.

$$$$ The Roseate Villa rents 21 stately yet modern rooms in a freestanding Victorian townhouse, with a park on one side and an extensive lawn on the other. In a city that's so insistently Georgian, it's fun to stay in a mansion that's Victorian (family rooms, free parking for those booking direct, in quiet residential area on Henrietta Street, tel. 01225/466-329, http://roseatehotels.com/bath/theroseatevilla, reception.trvb@roseatehotels.com).

$$$ The Kennard is a short walk from the Pulteney Bridge. Each of the 12 rooms is colorfully and elaborately decorated (free street parking permits, peaceful little Georgian garden out back, 11 Henrietta Street, tel. 01225/310-472, www.kennard.co.uk, reception@kennard.co.uk, Priya and Ajay).

$$$ Henrietta House, with large rooms, hardwood floors, and daily homemade biscuits and jam, is cloak-and-cravat cozy. Even the name reflects English aristocracy, honoring the daughter of the mansion's former owners, Lord and Lady Pulteney. Now it's smartly run by Peter and another Henrietta (family-size suites, limited free parking, 33 Henrietta Street, tel. 01225/632-632, www.henriettahouse.co.uk, reception@henriettahouse.co.uk).

$$$ The Ayrlington, next door to a bowling green, rents 19 spacious rooms, each decorated with panache. Though this well-maintained hotel fronts a busy street, it's reasonably quiet and tranquil. Rooms in the back have pleasant views of sports greens and Bath beyond. For the best value, request a standard top-floor double with a view of Bath (fine garden, free and easy parking, 24 Pulteney Road, tel. 01225/425-495, www.ayrlington.com, theayrlington@gmail.com).

$$ At **Apple Tree Guesthouse,** near a shady canal, hostess Ling rents five comfortable rooms sprinkled with Asian decor (family rooms, 2-night minimum Fri-Sat nights, free parking, 7 Pulteney Gardens, tel. 01225/337-642, www.appletreebath.com, enquiries@appletreebath.com).

IN THE TOWN CENTER

Since Bath is so pleasant and manageable by foot, a downtown location isn't essential, but these options are close to the baths and abbey.

$$$ Three Abbey Green Guest House offers 10 spacious rooms off a quiet, traffic-free courtyard just 50 yards from the abbey and the Roman Baths. There's a different breakfast special every day (family rooms, 2-night minimum on weekends, limited free parking, 2 ground-floor rooms work well for those with limited

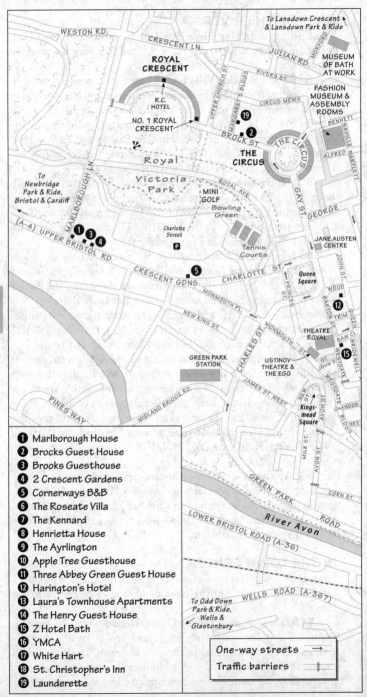

1. Marlborough House
2. Brocks Guest House
3. Brooks Guesthouse
4. 2 Crescent Gardens
5. Cornerways B&B
6. The Roseate Villa
7. The Kennard
8. Henrietta House
9. The Ayrlington
10. Apple Tree Guesthouse
11. Three Abbey Green Guest House
12. Harington's Hotel
13. Laura's Townhouse Apartments
14. The Henry Guest House
15. Z Hotel Bath
16. YMCA
17. White Hart
18. St. Christopher's Inn
19. Launderette

One-way streets →
Traffic barriers

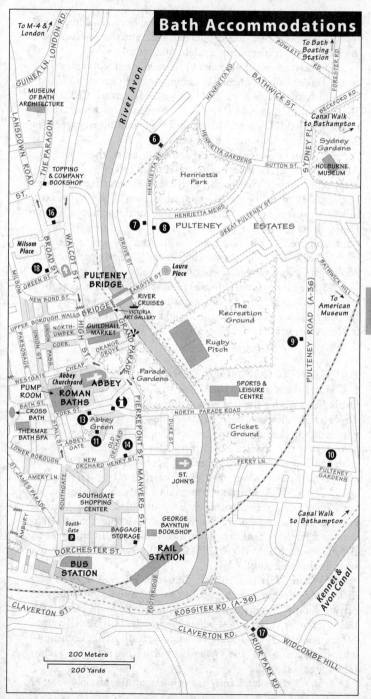

Bath Accommodations

mobility, tel. 01225/428-558, https://threeabbeygreen.com, stay@
threeabbeygreen.com, Sue, daughter Nicola, and son-in-law Alan).
They also rent an apartment (2-night minimum).

$$ Harington's Hotel rents 13 fresh, modern rooms on a quiet
street. This stylish place feels like a boutique hotel, but with a friend-
lier, laid-back vibe (pay parking, 8 Queen Street, tel. 01225/461-
728, www.haringtonshotel.co.uk, post@haringtonshotel.co.uk,
manager Julian). Owners Melissa and Peter rent nine apartments
nearby (2-night minimum on weekends).

$$ Laura's Townhouse Apartments rents three flats on
Abbey Green and others scattered around the city. The apart-
ment called Abbey View comes with a washer/dryer and has views
of the abbey from its nicely equipped kitchen. Laura provides a
simple breakfast, but it's fun and cheap to stock the fridge. When
Laura meets you to give you the keys, you become a local (2-night
minimum, rooms can sleep four with Murphy and sofa beds,
tel. 01225/464-238, www.laurastownhouseapartments.co.uk,
bookings@laurastownhouseapartments.co.uk).

$$ The Henry Guest House is a simple, vertical place, renting
seven clean rooms. It's friendly, well run, and just two blocks from
the train station (family room, 2-night minimum on weekends,
6 Henry Street, tel. 01225/424-052, www.thehenry.com, stay@
thehenry.com, Christina).

BARGAIN ACCOMMODATIONS

$ Z Hotel Bath (the Brits say "zed") rents spare, modern rooms
just big enough for the bed—your suitcase slides in a nook below.
Though tight on space, hotel frills include organic linen and a daily
wine-and-cheese buffet—and best of all, it's right in the center, just
across from the Theatre Royal (breakfast extra, cheaper "inside"
rooms lack windows, air-con, elevator, 7 Saw Close, tel. 01225/613-
160, www.thezhotels.com, bath@thezhotels.com).

¢ The YMCA, centrally located on a leafy square, is safe, se-
cure, quiet, and efficiently run with a youthful dorm vibe (private
en suite rooms and family rooms available, includes continental
breakfast, laundry facilities, down a tiny alley off Broad Street on
Broad Street Place, tel. 01225/325-900, www.bathymca.co.uk,
stay@bathymca.co.uk).

¢ White Hart is a friendly and colorful place in need of a
little updating, but offering good, cheap stays in a dorm or four
private rooms (fine garden out back, 5-minute walk behind the
train station at Widcombe—where Widcombe Hill hits Claverton
Street, tel. 01225/338-053, www.whitehartbath.co.uk, enquiries@
whitehartbath.co.uk). The White Hart also has a pub with a repu-
tation for good food.

¢ St. Christopher's Inn, in a prime central location, is part of a chain of high-energy hubs for backpackers looking for beds and brews. Rooms are basic, clean, and cheap because they know you'll spend money on their beer. The inn sits above the lively, youthful Belushi's pub, which is where you'll find the reception (cheaper to book online, private rooms and family rooms available, laundry facilities, lounge, 9 Green Street, tel. 01225/481-444, www. st-christophers.co.uk, bath@st-christophers.co.uk).

Eating in Bath

Bath is bursting with eateries. A picnic dinner in the Royal Crescent Park or down by the river is ideal for aristocratic hoboes. The restaurants I recommend are mostly small and popular—reserve a table for dinner, especially on Friday and Saturday. Most pricey little bistros offer big savings with their two- and three-course lunches and "pre-theatre" specials. Vegetarianism is trendy here; any serious restaurant offers a veggie course.

UPSCALE ENGLISH

$$$$ The Circus Restaurant is a relaxing eatery serving well-executed seasonal dishes with European flair. Choose between the modern interior—with seating on the main floor or in the less-charming cellar—and a few tables on the peaceful street connecting the Circus and the Royal Crescent (Mon-Sat 12:00-late, closed Sun, 34 Brock Street, tel. 01225/466-020, www. thecircusrestaurant.co.uk).

$$$ Eight Restaurant looks simple—like a tidy living room with six tables crowded into it. But each dish is a beautifully presented work of edible art, the price is right, and the service is perfectly attentive. The eight seasonal Italian/French/English dishes (at around £14 each) are small, and while you can make it a light meal, a couple could enjoy trying three or four dishes family-style (daily 17:30-21:30, 3 North Parade Passage, tel. 01225/724-111, https://eightinbath.co.uk).

$$$$ Clayton's Kitchen is where Michelin-star chef Rob Clayton aims to offer affordable British cuisine without pretense. The food is artfully prepared and presented (daily from 12:00 and 18:00, a few outside tables, 15 George Street, tel. 01225/585-100, www.claytonskitchen.com).

$$$ The Chequers is so nice I raised it out of the pub category. It's pubby gourmet, serving a small menu of creative, beautifully presented British dishes to enjoy in their handsome bar on the ground floor or refined upstairs restaurant (with open kitchen). Reasonable fixed-price lunches are available from 17:30-18:30 except Sunday (daily, just above the Royal Crescent at 50 Rivers Street, tel. 01225/360-017, www.thechequersbath.com). To enjoy

BATH

1 The Circus Restaurant
2 Eight Restaurant & Acorn Vegetarian Kitchen
3 Clayton's Kitchen
4 The Chequers
5 The Garrick's Head
6 Crystal Palace
7 The Raven
8 The Scallop Shell
9 Loch Fyne Fish Restaurant
10 Martini Restaurant
11 Rustico Bistro Italiano
12 Dough Pizza Restaurant
13 Olé Tapas
14 Eastern Eye
15 Thai Balcony Restaurant
16 Yak Yeti Yak
17 Hands Georgian Tearooms
18 Dower House
19 Market Café & Guildhall Market
20 Boston Tea Party
21 Chandos Deli
22 The Cornish Bakehouse
23 Gong Fu Noodle Bar; Seafoods Fish & Chips; Swoon
24 Chai Walla
25 Mission Burrito
26 Supermarket (3)
27 The Old Green Tree
28 The Star Inn
29 The Bell

One-way streets
Traffic barriers

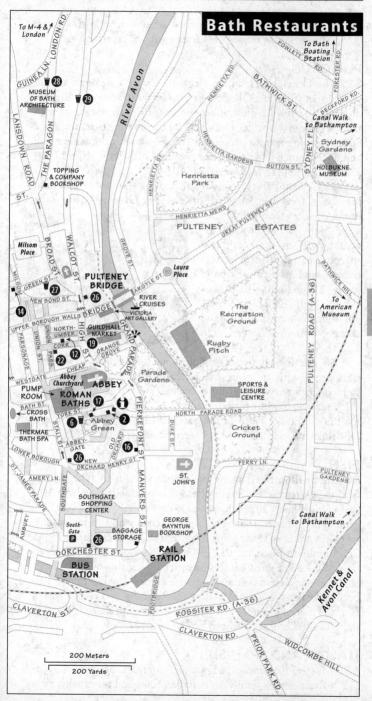

Bath Restaurants

To M-4 & London

GUINEA LN.

LANSDOWN ROAD

N. LONDON RD.

THE PARAGON

28

29

MUSEUM OF BATH ARCHITECTURE

River Avon

FOWLETT

To Bath Boating Station

BATHWICK ST.

FORESTER RD.

BECKFORD RD.

Canal Walk to Bathampton

Sydney Gardens

SYDNEY PL.

HENRIETTA RD.

HOLBURNE MUSEUM

HENRIETTA ST.

HENRIETTA GARDENS

SUTTON ST.

Henrietta Park

TOPPING & COMPANY BOOKSHOP

BROAD ST.

WALCOT ST.

GROVE ST.

HENRIETTA MEWS

PULTENEY ESTATES

GREAT PULTENEY ST.

Milsom Place

MILSOM

GREEN ST.

NEW BOND ST.

PULTENEY BRIDGE

BRIDGE

27

26

Laura Place

RIVER CRUISES

BRIDGE

The Recreation Ground

BATHWICK HILL

To American Museum

PULTENEY ROAD (A-36)

14

UPPER BOROUGH WALLS

PARSONAGE

UNION ST.

HIGH ST.

VICTORIA ART GALLERY

GUILDHALL MARKET

NORTH-UMBER.

CORK.

12

22

CHEAP

19

ORANGE GROVE

GRAND PARADE

Rugby Pitch

WESTGATE

PUMP ROOM

ROMAN BATHS

Abbey Churchyard

ABBEY

17

Parade Gardens

PIERREPONT ST.

SPORTS & LEISURE CENTRE

BATH ST.

CROSS BATH

YORK ST.

6

STALL ST.

Abbey Green

2

NORTH PARADE ROAD

DUKE ST.

Cricket Ground

THERMAE BATH SPA

LOWER BOROUGH

ABBEY-GATE

OLD ORCHARD

16

NEW ORCHARD

HENRY ST.

ST. JOHN'S

FERRY LN.

PULTENEY GARDENS

ST. JAMES PARADE

AMERY LN.

SOUTHGATE

MANVERS ST.

SOUTHGATE SHOPPING CENTER

GEORGE BAYNTUN BOOKSHOP

Canal Walk to Bathampton

AMBURY

South-Gate P

26

BAGGAGE STORAGE

RAIL STATION

DORCHESTER ST.

BUS STATION

FOOTBRIDGE

Kennet & Avon Canal

CLAVERTON ST.

ROSSITER RD. (A-36)

CLAVERTON RD.

WIDCOMBE HILL

PRIOR PARK RD.

200 Meters

200 Yards

BATH

the kitchen to the max, consider their seven-course tasting menu (£55, Mon-Fri only, request in advance with reservation).

PUB GRUB

$$$ The Garrick's Head, an elegantly simple gastropub around the corner from the Theatre Royal, serves traditional English dishes with a few Mediterranean options. There's a restaurant with table service on one side, a more casual bar on the other, and some tables outside great for people-watching—all with the same menu and prices (lunch and pre-theater specials until 19:00, daily 12:00-23:00, 8 St. John's Place, tel. 01225/318-368).

$$ Crystal Palace, a casual and inviting standby a block from the abbey, faces the delightful little Abbey Green. With a focus on food rather than drink, they serve "pub grub with a Continental flair" in three different spaces: a bar, a full-service restaurant, and an airy back patio (daily 11:00-23:00, 10 Abbey Green, tel. 01225/482-666). Their lunch menu, a simpler and cheaper option, is served until 17:00.

$$ The Raven attracts a boisterous local crowd. It emphasizes beer—with an impressive selection of real ales—but serves some delicious savory pies for nourishment. The ground floor has thick pub vibes while upstairs feels more like a restaurant (Mon-Fri 12:00-15:00 & 17:00-21:00, Sat-Sun 12:30-20:30, open longer for drinks; no kids under 10, 6 Queen Street, tel. 01225/425-045).

FISH

$$ The Scallop Shell is my top choice for fish in Bath. Hard-working Garry and his family offer grilled seafood along with fish-and-chips. Their £10 lunch special is served daily until 15:00. The ground floor is energized by the open kitchen while upstairs is quieter with a breezy terrace (Mon-Sat 12:00-21:30, Sun until 16:00, 22 Monmouth Place, tel. 01225/420-928).

$$$ Loch Fyne Fish Restaurant is an inviting outpost of this chain, serving fresh fish at reasonable prices. The big dining hall occupies what was once a lavish bank building and comes with a fun and family-friendly energy (two-course special until 18:00, daily 12:00-22:00, 24 Milsom Street, tel. 01225/750-120).

ITALIAN AND SPANISH

$$$ Martini Restaurant, a hopping, purely Italian place with jovial waiters, serves family-style Italian food and pizza with class (daily 12:00-14:30 & 18:00-22:30, daily fish specials, extensive wine list, 9 George Street, tel. 01225/460-818; Nunzio, Franco, and chef Luigi).

$$$$ Rustico Bistro Italiano, nestled between the Circus and the Royal Crescent, is precisely what its name implies. Franco and his staff are kept busy by a local crowd (no pizza, check chalkboard for specials, Tue-Sat 12:00-14:30 & 18:00-22:00, closed Sun-Mon, off Brock Street at 2 Margaret's Buildings, tel. 01225/310-064). If it's hot, they have delightful sidewalk seating.

$$ Dough Pizza Restaurant serves the best pizza in town in a fun and casual atmosphere with an open oven adding to the energy (daily 12:00-22:00, 14 The Corridor, tel. 01255/443-686).

$$ Olé Tapas bounces to a flamenco beat, turning out tasty tapas from their minuscule kitchen. If you're hungry for a trip to Spain, arrive early or make a reservation, as it's both tiny and popular (Sun-Thu 12:00-22:00, Fri-Sat until 23:00, up the stairs at 1 John Street, tel. 01225/424-274, www.oletapas.co.uk).

VEGETARIAN AND ASIAN

$$$$ Acorn Vegetarian Kitchen is pricey but highly rated (with an impressive tasting menu) and ideal for the well-heeled vegetarian. Its tight interior is elegant with a quiet and understated vibe (completely vegan menu, daily 12:00-15:00 & 17:30-21:30, 2 North Parade Passage, tel. 01225/446-059).

$$$ Eastern Eye serves large portions of Indian and Bangladeshi dishes in an impressive, triple-domed Georgian hall (Mon-Fri 12:00-14:30 & 18:00-23:30, Sat-Sun 12:00-23:30, RS%—free glass of wine or beer for those dining with this book, 8A Quiet Street, tel. 01225/422-323).

$$ Thai Balcony Restaurant has an open, spacious interior so plush, it'll have you wondering, "Where's the Thai wedding?" While residents debate which of Bath's handful of Thai restaurants serves the best food or value, there's no doubt that Thai Balcony's fun and elegant atmosphere makes for a memorable and enjoyable dinner (daily 12:00-14:30 & 18:00-22:00, Saw Close, tel. 01225/444-450).

$$ Yak Yeti Yak is a basic and earnest Nepalese restaurant with both Western and sit-on-the-floor seating. Sera and his wife, Sarah, along with their cheerful, hardworking Nepali team, cook up great traditional food (including plenty of vegetarian plates). It's a simple and honest place with prices that would delight a Sherpa (daily 12:00-14:00 & 18:00-22:00, downstairs at 12 Pierrepont Street, tel. 01225/442-299).

EVER SO ENGLISH AFTERNOON TEA

A tradition for anyone feeling both English and aristocratic is a formal "afternoon tea"—with a three-tiered trolley: delicate finger sandwiches, scones with clotted cream and jam, and cakes, accompanied by a fancy pot of tea. (A "cream tea" is just tea with scones, jam, and clotted cream.) While many places serve afternoon tea, the setting is critical for the experience.

$$$ The Pump Room sits above the Roman baths and for over two centuries has been Bath's iconic Georgian gathering place. The food comes with live music—piano or a string trio (£27 afternoon tea from noon; also open daily 9:30-16:00 for breakfast, tea/coffee and selection of pastries also available in the afternoon, dinner July-Aug 18:00-21:00 only; tel. 01225/444-477).

$ Hands Georgian Tearoom is an understated, family-run place a stone's throw from the abbey and the baths. With an elegant Georgian interior and traditional dishes, it's a good option for breakfast, lunch, or an economic afternoon tea in the center of the tourist bustle (cash only, Tue-Sat 9:30-17:00, Sun-Mon from 11:00, 1 Abbey Street, tel. 01225/463-928).

$$$ Dower House at the Royal Crescent Hotel is my choice on a sunny day as tea is served in an elegant garden—and they allow you to split one order, making the experience more affordable (£38 afternoon tea, daily 13:30-16:30, reserve a day ahead—a week ahead for Sat-Sun, 16 Royal Crescent, tel. 01225/823-333, www.royalcrescent.co.uk).

SIMPLE LUNCH AND BREAKFAST OPTIONS

For an olde tyme market experience, get breakfast at the Market Café. Chandos Deli is a more upscale foodie option. The Boston Tea Party is understandably packed with enthusiastic breakfasters. And bakeries and cafés all over town compete hard for the many Airbnb travelers that don't get that second "B" included.

$ Market Café, in the Guildhall Market, is where you can munch cheaply on a homemade meat pie or sip tea while surrounded by stacks of used books and old-time locals (traditional English meals including fried breakfasts all day, cash only, Mon-Sat 8:00-17:00, closed Sun, tel. 01225/461-593 a block north of the abbey, on High Street).

$ Boston Tea Party is what Starbucks aspires to be—the neighborhood coffeehouse and hangout. Its extensive breakfasts, bakery items, light lunches, and salads are fresh and healthy. They're popular with vegetarians and famously ethical in their business practices (daily 7:00-18:00, across from the Assembly Rooms at 8 Alfred Street, tel. 01225/476-465).

$ Chandos Deli has good coffee, breakfast pastries, and tasty £4 sandwiches made on artisan breads—plus meats, cheese, baguettes, and wine for assembling a gourmet picnic. Upscale yet casual, this place satisfies dedicated foodies who don't want to pay too much (Mon-Fri 8:00-17:30, Sat from 9:00, Sun from 10:00, 12 George Street, tel. 01225/314-418).

$ The Cornish Bakehouse has freshly baked takeaway pasties (Mon-Sat 7:30-18:00, Sun 9:00-17:30, off High Street at 11A The Corridor, tel. 01225/426-635). Munch your goodies at the nearby Parade Gardens or Abbey Churchyard.

$ Kingsmead Square is a shady space with a grand tree and inviting benches, surrounded by several ethnic joints where you can grab a bite and sit outside. **Gong Fu Noodle Bar** is a favorite with Chinese students studying in Bath (daily 11:00-23:00); **Chai Walla** serves up satisfying, simple Indian street food (no seating, Sun-Thu 12:00-17:00, Fri-Sat until late, Niraj); **Mission Burrito** is good if you crave Mexican (daily until 22:00); **Seafoods Fish & Chips** is a greasy standby but Scallop Shell, described above, is a better value (daily until 21:00); and **Swoon** has the best gelato in town.

Supermarkets: Waitrose has a café upstairs and racks of inexpensive picnic-type meals to go on the ground level. There are some stools inside and a few tables on the street out front (Mon-Fri 7:30-21:00, Sat until 20:00, Sun 11:00-17:00, just west of Pulteney Bridge and across from post office on High Street). **Marks & Spencer,** near the bottom end of town, has a grocery at the back of its department store and the M&S Café on the top floor (Mon-Sat 8:30-19:00, Sun 11:00-17:00, 16 Stall Street). **Sainsbury's Local,** across the street from the bus station, has the longest hours (daily 7:00-23:00, 2 Dorchester Street).

Bath Connections

Bath's train station is called Bath Spa (tel. 0345-748-4959). The National Express bus station is just west of the train station (bus info tel. 0871-781-8181, www.nationalexpress.com). For all public bus services in southwestern England, see www.travelinesw.com.

From Bath to London: You can catch a **train** to London's Paddington Station (2/hour, 1.5 hours, best deals for travel after 9:30 and when purchased in advance, www.gwr.com), or save money—but not time—by taking the National Express **bus** to Victoria Coach Station (direct buses nearly hourly, 3.5 hours, avoid those with layover in Bristol, one-way-£7-12, cheapest to purchase online several days in advance).

Connecting Bath with London's Airports: To get to or from **Heathrow,** it's fastest and most pleasant to take the **train via London;** it takes about three hours total (airport to London Paddington-4/hour, Paddington to Bath-2/hour). With a rail pass, it's also the cheapest option, as the whole trip is covered. Without a rail pass, it's the most expensive way to go (£60 total for off-peak travel, cheaper bought in advance, up to £60 more for full-fare peak-time ticket; 2/hour, 2.25 hours depending on airport terminal, easy change between First Great Western train and Heathrow Express at London's Paddington Station).

The **National Express bus** is direct and often much cheaper for those without a rail pass, but it's less frequent and can take nearly twice as long as the train (nearly hourly, 3.5 hours, £24-40 one-way depending on time of day, tel. 0871-781-8181, www.nationalexpress.com). Doing a **train-and-bus combination** via the town of Reading can make sense for travelers without a rail pass, as it's more frequent, can take less time than the direct bus—allow 2.5 hours total—and can be much cheaper than the train via London (RailAir Link shuttle bus to Reading: 2-3/hour, 45 minutes; train from Reading to Bath: 2/hour, 1 hour; £31-41 for off-peak, nonrefundable travel booked in advance—but up to double for peak-time trains; tel. 0118-957-9425, buy bus ticket from www.railair.com, train ticket from www.gwr.com). Another option is the **minibus** operated by recommended tour company Celtic Horizons (see page 249).

You can get to or from **Gatwick** by train with a transfer in Reading (hourly, 3 hours, £55-75 one-way depending on time of day, cheaper in advance; avoid transfer in London, where you'll have to change stations; www.gwr.com) or by bus with a transfer at Heathrow (6/day, 4-5 hours, about £35 one-way, transfer at Heathrow Airport, www.nationalexpress.com).

Connecting Bath and Bristol Airport: Located about 20 miles west of Bath, this airport is closer than Heathrow and has good connections by bus. From Bristol Airport, your most convenient option is the Bristol Air Decker bus #A4 (£14, 2/hour, 1.25 hours, www.airdecker.com). Otherwise, you can take a taxi (£40) or call Celtic Horizons (see page 249).

From Bath by Train to: Salisbury (hourly direct, 1 hour), **Moreton-in-Marsh** (hourly, 2.5 hours, 1 transfer, more with additional transfers), **York** (hourly with transfer in Bristol, 4.5 hours, more with additional transfers), **Cardiff** (hourly, 1.5 hours), and **points north** (via Birmingham, a major transportation hub, trains depart for Scotland and North Wales; use a train/bus combination to reach Ironbridge Gorge and the Lake District).

From Bath by Bus to: Salisbury (hourly, 3 hours), **Avebury** (hourly, 2-2.5 hours, transfer in Devizes), **Stratford-upon-Avon** (1/day, 4 hours, transfer in Bristol). For bus connections to **Glastonbury** and **Wells,** see the next chapter.

GLASTONBURY & WELLS

The countryside surrounding Bath holds two particularly fine cathedral towns. Glastonbury (perhaps a.k.a. Avalon) is the ancient resting place of King Arthur, and home (maybe) to the Holy Grail. It can be covered well in two to three hours: See the abbey, climb the tor, and ponder your hippie past (and where you are now). Nearby, medieval Wells gathers around its grand cathedral. Wells is simply a cute small town, much smaller and more medieval than Bath, with a uniquely beautiful cathedral that's best experienced at its evensong service.

GETTING AROUND THE REGION

By Car: Glastonbury and Wells are each about 20-25 miles from Bath and 140 miles from London. Drivers can do a 51-mile loop from Bath to Glastonbury (25 miles) to Wells (6 miles) and back to Bath (20 miles). Extend the trip to a 131-mile loop that includes two places covered in the next chapter: Drive from Bath to Avebury (25 miles) to Stonehenge (30 miles) to Glastonbury (50 miles) to Wells (6 miles) and back to Bath (20 miles).

By Bus and Train: The nearest train station is in Bath, served by regular trains from London's Paddington Station (2/hour, 1.5 hours). Wells and Glastonbury are both easily accessible by bus from Bath. Bus #173 goes direct from Bath to **Wells** (nearly hourly, less frequent on Sun, 75 minutes), where you can continue on to

Glastonbury & Wells Area

To Cardiff
M-49
Patchway
M-5
Yate
River Severn
M-4
Portishead
M-32
A-46
Portbury
A-38
Kingswood
A-420
M5
Tickenham
Pennsylvania
Bristol
Bristol
Keynsham
A-4
A-370
Pensford
Corston
Bath
A-38
A-37
A-39
Combe
Down
Congresbury
Farmborough
Clutton
A-368
Bishop
Sutton
Peasdown
St. John
A-367
Banwell
Blagdon
West
Harptree
Farington
Gurney
Radstock
A-366
CHEDDAR
GORGE
M5
Axbridge
A-39
A-367
A-562
A-38
Cheddar
A-37
Buckland
Dinham
Wedmore
A-371
Green
Ore
Oakhill
Nunney
Wells
SOMERSET
Shepton
Mallet
A-361
A-359
WILKINS
CIDER FARM
A-39
Cranmore
Wanstrow
GLASTONBURY
TOR
Pilton
Prestleigh
Glastonbury
A-361
A-371
A-39
West
Pennard
Ashcott
A-39
Kilometers
Walton
Miles
A-361
SCOTLAND
A-372
A-359
A-37
ENGLAND
WALES
London
Langport
A-372
Sparkford
A-303
A-378
To
Stonehenge
Ilchester

Glastonbury by catching bus #376 (2/hour, 20 minutes, drops off directly in front of abbey entrance on Magdalene Street). To return to Bath, you'll likely go back through Wells (as direct bus service from Glastonbury to Bath is very limited). First Bus Company's £11 day pass is a good deal if you plan on connecting Glastonbury and Wells from your Bath home base.

By Bike: A 10-mile path connects Wells and Glastonbury.

Glastonbury

Marked by its hill, or "tor," and located on England's most powerful line of prehistoric sites, the town of Glastonbury gurgles with history and mystery.

In AD 37, Joseph of Arimathea—Jesus' wealthy uncle—reputedly brought vessels containing the blood of Jesus to Glastonbury, and with him, Christianity came to England. (Joseph's visit is plausible—long before Christ, locals traded lead and tin to merchants from the Levant.)

While this story is "proven" by fourth-century writings and accepted by the Church, the King-Arthur-and-the-Holy-Grail legends it inspired are not. Those medieval tales came when England needed a morale-boosting folk hero for inspiration during a war with France. They pointed to the ancient Celtic sanctuary at Glastonbury as proof enough of the greatness of the fifth-century warlord Arthur. In 1191, after a huge fire, Arthur's supposed remains (along with those of Queen Guinevere) were dug up from the abbey garden. Reburied in the abbey choir, Arthur and Guinevere's gravesite is a shrine today. Many think the Grail trail ends at the bottom of the Chalice Well, a natural spring at the base of the Glastonbury Tor.

By the 10th century, Glastonbury Abbey was England's most powerful and wealthy, and was part of a nationwide network of monasteries that by 1500 owned one-quarter of all English land and had four times the income of the Crown. Then Henry VIII dissolved the abbeys in 1536. He was particularly harsh on Glastonbury—he not only destroyed the abbey but also hung and quartered the abbot, sending the parts of his body on four different national tours...at the same time. This was meant as a warning to other religious clerics, and it worked.

But Glastonbury rebounded. In an 18th-century publicity campaign, thousands signed affidavits stating that they'd been healed by water from the Chalice Well, and once again Glastonbury was on the tourist map. Today, Glastonbury and its tor are a center for "searchers"—too creepy for the mainstream Church but just right for those looking for a place to recharge their crystals. Glastonbury is also synonymous with its summer music-and-arts festival, a long-hair-and-mud Woodstock re-creation that's a rite of passage for young music lovers in Britain.

Part of the fun of a visit to Glastonbury is just being in a town where every other shop and eatery is a New Age place. Locals who are not into this complain that on High Street, you can buy any kind of magic crystal or incense—but not a roll

of TP. But, as this counterculture is their town's bread and butter, they do their best to sit in their pubs and go "Ommmmm."

Orientation to Glastonbury

TOURIST INFORMATION

The TI, located in St. Dunstan's House near the abbey, sells several booklets about area walks and bike rides, including the *Glastonbury and Street Town Guide,* and a £1.50 map (Mon-Sat 10:00-17:00, Sun until 16:00, shorter hours Oct-March, 1 Magdalene Street, tel. 01458/832-954, www.glastonburytic.co.uk). The TI also **rents bikes** (£20/day, £50 deposit).

HELPFUL HINTS

Market Day: Tuesday is market day for crafts, knickknacks, and local produce on the main street. There's also a country market Tuesday mornings in the Town Hall.

Glastonbury Festival: Nearly every summer (generally around the June solstice), the gigantic Glastonbury Festival—billing itself as the "largest music and performing arts festival in the world"—brings all manner of postmodern flower children to its notoriously muddy "Healing Fields." Music fans and London's beautiful people make the trek to see the hottest British and American bands. Anticipate increased traffic and crowds (especially on public transit; more than 165,000 tickets generally sell out), even though the actual music venue—practically a temporary city of its own—is six miles east of town (www. glastonburyfestivals.co.uk).

Sights in Glastonbury

I've listed these sights in the order you'll reach them, moving from the town center to the tor.

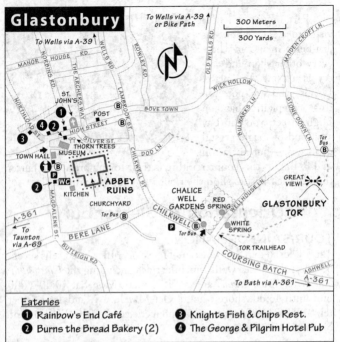

Eateries
1. Rainbow's End Café
2. Burns the Bread Bakery (2)
3. Knights Fish & Chips Rest.
4. The George & Pilgrim Hotel Pub

Glastonbury Town

The tiny town itself is worth a pleasant stroll. The abbey came first, and Glastonbury grew up to serve it. For example, the George and Pilgrim Hotel was originally a freestanding structure built in the 15th century to house pilgrims. And St. John's Church, which dates from the same century, was constructed to give townsfolk a place to worship, as they weren't allowed in the abbey. The Market Cross at the base of High Street dates from around 1800.

Though Glastonbury is much older, its vibe dates to 1970, when the town hosted its first rock festival. Like Woodstock, it was held on a farm. Unlike Woodstock, the Glastonbury Festival had legs—it's been held on the same farm almost every year since. You'll still see many hippie and New Age shops in town.

▲▲Glastonbury Abbey

The massive and evocative ruins of the first Christian sanctuary in the British Isles stand mysteriously alive in a lush 36-acre park. Because it comes with a small museum, a dramatic history, and enthusiastic guides dressed in period costumes, this is one of the most engaging to visit of England's many ruined abbeys.

Cost and Hours: £8.25; daily 9:00-18:00, June-Aug until 20:00, Nov-Feb until 16:00.

Information: Tel. 01458/832-267, www.glastonburyabbey.com.

Getting There: Enter the abbey from Magdalene Street (around the corner from High Street, near the St. Dunstan's parking lot). Pay parking is nearby.

Tours and Demonstrations: Costumed guides offer 30-minute tours (generally daily March-Oct on the hour from 10:00). As you enter, confirm these times, and ask about other tour and show times.

Eating: Picnicking is encouraged—bring something from one of the shops in town (see "Eating in Glastonbury," later), or buy food at the small café on site (open May-Sept).

Background: The space that these ruins occupy has been sacred ground for centuries. The druids used it as a pagan holy site, and during Joseph of Arimathea's supposed visit here, he built a simple place of worship. In the 12th century—because of that legendary connection—Glastonbury was the leading Christian pilgrimage site in all of Britain. The popular abbey  grew powerful and very wealthy, employing a thousand people to serve the needs of the pilgrims.

In 1184, there was a devastating fire in the monastery, and in 1191, the abbot here "discovered"—with the help of a divine dream—the tomb and bodies of King Arthur and Queen Guinevere. Of course, this discovery boosted the pilgrim trade in Glastonbury, and the new revenues helped to rebuild the abbey.

Then, in 1539, King Henry VIII ordered the abbey's destruction. When Glastonbury Abbot Richard Whiting questioned the king's decision, he was branded a traitor, hung at the top of Glastonbury Tor (after carrying up the plank that would support his noose), and his body cut into four pieces. His head was stuck over the gateway to the former abbey precinct. After this harsh example, the other abbots accepted the king's dissolution of England's abbeys, with many returning to monastic centers in France. Glastonbury Abbey was destroyed. With the roof removed, it fell into ruin and was used as a quarry.

Today, the abbey attracts both the curious and pious. Tie-dyed, starry-eyed pilgrims seem to float through the grounds, naturally high. Others lie on the grave of King Arthur, whose burial site is marked off in the center of the abbey ruins.

◑ Self-Guided Tour: After buying your ticket, pick up a

GLASTONBURY & WELLS

map and tour the informative **museum** at the entrance building. A model shows the abbey in its pre-Henry VIII splendor, and exhibits tell the story of a place "grandly constructed to entice the dullest minds to prayer." Knowledgeable costumed guides are eager to share the site's story and might even offer an impromptu tour.

Next, head out to explore the green park, dotted with bits of the **ruined abbey.** You come face-to-face with the abbey's Lady Chapel, the site of the first wattle-and-daub church, possibly dating to the first century. Today, the crypt is dug out and exposed; posted information helps you imagine its 12th-century splendor.

The Lady Chapel became the abbey's west entry when the church expanded. The abbey was long and skinny, but vast. Measuring 580 feet, it was the longest in Britain (larger than York Minster is today) and Europe's largest building north of the Alps.

Before poking around the ruins, circle to the left behind the entrance building to find the two **thorn trees.** According to legend, when Joseph of Arimathea came here, he climbed nearby Wearyall Hill and stuck his staff into the soil. A thorn tree sprouted, and its descendant still stands there today; the trees here in the abbey are its offspring. In 2010, vandals hacked off the branches of the original tree on Wearyall Hill, but miraculously, the stump put out small green shoots the following spring. The trees inside the abbey grounds bloom twice a year, at Easter and at Christmas. If the story seems far-fetched to you, don't tell the Queen—a blossom from the abbey's trees sits proudly on her breakfast table every Christmas morning.

Ahead and to the left of the trees, inside what was the north wall, look for two trap doors in the ground. Lift up the doors to see surviving fragments of the abbey's original tiled floor.

Now hike through the remains of the ruined complex to the far end of the abbey. You can stand and, from what was the altar, look down at what was the gangly nave. Envision the longest church nave in England. In this area, you'll find the tombstone (formerly in the floor of the church's choir) marking the spot where the supposed relics of **Arthur and Guinevere** were interred.

Continue around the far side of the abbey ruins, feeling free to poke around the park. Imagine all of this green space— just a tiny part of the lands the abbey owned—bustling with the daily business of a powerful monastic community.

All those monks needed to eat. Take a look at the abbot's conical **kitchen,** the only surviving intact building on the grounds.

Its size, and its simple exhibit about life in the abbey, gives you an idea of how big the community once was.

NEAR GLASTONBURY TOR

The tor is a steep hill at the southeastern edge of the town (it's visible from just about everywhere). The other two sights (the gardens and springs) are on your way to/from the tor.

Getting There: The garden and springs are about a 15-minute **walk** from the town center, toward the tor. The base of the tor is an additional five minutes. Climbing the tor is another 15-20 minutes.

If you don't want to walk, you have two options: The **Tor Bus** shuttles visitors from the town center to the base of the tor, stopping at the Chalice Well en route (£3.30 round-trip, 2/hour, departs on the half-hour from St. Dunstan's parking lot, near the TI and abbey, daily 10:00-12:30 & 14:00-17:00, doesn't run Oct-March). If you have a **car**, you won't find much parking nearby, so expect a bit of a hike (try the pay lot at the Draper sheepskin shop, near the Chalice Well on Chilkwell Street). A **taxi** to the tor trailhead costs about £7 one-way. Remember, these take you only to the bottom of the tor; to reach the top, you have to hike.

A good plan is to ride the shuttle bus to the tor, climb to the top, hike down, drop by Chalice Well Gardens, and stroll back into town from there.

Chalice Well Gardens

According to tradition, Joseph of Arimathea brought the chalice from the Last Supper to Glastonbury in AD 37. Supposedly it ended up in the bottom of a well, which is now the centerpiece of a peaceful and inviting garden. Even if the chalice is not at the bottom of the well (another legend says it made the trip to Wales), and the water is red from iron ore and not Jesus' blood, the tranquil setting attracts pilgrims still. If you're a fan of gardens—or want to say you've completed your grail quest— this place is worth a visit. To find the well itself, follow the well-marked path uphill alongside the gurgling stream, passing several places where you can  drink from or wade in the healing water, as well as areas designated for silent reflection. The stones of the well shaft date from the 12th century and are believed to have come from the church in Glastonbury Abbey (which was destroyed by fire). In the 18th century, pilgrims flocked to Glastonbury for the well's healing powers.

Have a drink or take some of the precious water home—they sell empty bottles to fill.

Cost and Hours: £4.50, daily 10:00-18:00, Nov-March until 16:30, on Chilkwell Street/A-361, tel. 01458/831-154, www.chalicewell.org.uk.

Red and White Spring Waters

If you'd just like to sample the fabled water, two waterspouts are just around the corner from the Chalice Well Gardens entrance (just beyond the trailhead to the tor, where the bus drops off). The spout on the Chalice Well side comes from the Red Spring; the other spout's source is the White Spring. Try both and see which you prefer.

▲Glastonbury Tor

Seen by many as a Mother Goddess symbol, the Glastonbury Tor—a natural plug of sandstone on clay—has an undeniable geological charisma. Climbing the tor is the essential activity on a visit to Glastonbury. A fine Somerset view rewards those who hike to its 520-foot summit.

Climbing the Tor: From the base of the tor, a trail leads up to the top (about 15-20 uphill minutes, if you keep a brisk pace). While you can hike up the tor from either end, the less-steep approach (which most people take) starts next to the Chalice Well.

Hiking up to the top of the tor, survey the surrounding land— a former swamp, inhabited for 12,000 years, which is still below sea level at high tide. Up until the 11th century you could actually sail to the tower. The ribbon-like man-made drainage canals that glisten as they slice through the farmland are the work of engineers—Huguenot refugees who turned the marshy wasteland into something arable.

Looking out, find Glastonbury (at the base of the hill) and Wells (marked by its cathedral) to the right. Above Wells, a TV tower marks the 996-foot-high point of the Mendip Hills. It was lead from these hills that attracted the ancient Romans (and, perhaps, Jesus' uncle Joe) so long ago. Stretching to the left, the Mendip Hills define what was the coastline before those Huguenot engineers arrived.

The tor-top tower is the remnant of a chapel dedicated to St. Michael. Early Christians often employed St. Michael, the warrior angel, to combat pagan gods. When a church was built upon a pagan holy ground like this, it was frequently dedicated to Michael. But apparently those pagan gods fought back: St. Michael's Church was destroyed by an earthquake in 1275.

Eating in Glastonbury

$ Rainbow's End is one of several fine, healthy, vegetarian lunch cafés for hot meals (different every day), salads, herbal teas, soups, yummy homemade sweets, and New Age people-watching. If you're looking for a midwife or a male-bonding tribal meeting, check their notice board (vegan and gluten-free options, counter service, daily 10:00-16:00, 17 High Street, tel. 01458/833-896).

$ Burns the Bread has two convenient locations in town, making hearty pasties (savory meat pies) as well as fresh pies, sandwiches, delicious cookies, and pastries. Ask for a sample of the Torsy Moorsy Cake (a type of fruitcake made with cheddar), or try a gingerbread man made with real ginger. Grab a pasty and picnic with the ghosts of Arthur and Guinevere in the abbey ruins (Mon-Sat 7:00-17:00, Sun 10:00-16:00, main location at 14 High Street; smaller shop in St. Dunstan's parking lot next to the abbey, tel. 01458/831-532).

$ Knights Fish and Chips Restaurant has been in the same family since 1909 and is the town's top chippy. It's another fine option for a picnic at the abbey (more for table service, Mon-Sat 12:00-21:30, Sun until 19:30, closed Sun off-season, 5 Northload Street, tel. 01458/831-882, Kevin and Charlotte).

$$ The George & Pilgrim Hotel's wonderfully Old World pub might be exactly what the doctor ordered for visitors suffering a New Age overdose. The local owners serve up a traditional pub-grub menu (food served daily 12:00-14:45 & 18:00-20:45, 1 High Street, tel. 01458/831-146). They also rent **$$** rooms.

Glastonbury Connections

The nearest train station is in Bath. Local buses are run by First Bus Company (tel. 0845-602-0156, www.firstgroup.com).

From Glastonbury by Bus to: Wells (2/hour, 20 minutes, bus #376 headed to Bristol), **Bath** (nearly hourly, allow 2 hours, take bus to Wells, transfer to bus #173 to Bath, 1.5 hours between Wells and Bath). Buses are sparse on Sundays (generally one bus every other hour). If you're heading to points west, you'll likely connect through **Taunton** (which is a transfer point for westbound buses from Bristol).

Wells

Because this well-preserved little town has a cathedral, it can be called a city. It's England's smallest cathedral city (pop. just under 12,000), with one of its most interesting cathedrals and a wonderful evensong service (generally not offered July-Aug). Of all the towns you'll visit, Wells has the most buildings still operating as originally intended. You'll spot a number of the wells, water, and springs that helped give the town its name. Markets fill the town square on Wednesday (farmers market) and Saturday (general goods).

Orientation to Wells

TOURIST INFORMATION

The TI is in the lobby of the Wells & Mendip Museum, across the green from the cathedral. Consider picking up their free town map or buying the £1 *Wells City Trail* booklet (Mon-Sat 10:00-17:00, Nov-March until 16:00, closed Sun year-round, 8 Cathedral Green, tel. 01749/671-770, www.wellssomerset.com). The TI's attached museum houses displays on the archaeology and geology of nearby Mendip Hills and Wookey Caves, along with an exhibit on World War I (£3, same hours as TI).

Walking Tour: If you're here on a Wednesday, consider a town walking tour (£7, departs 11:00 in peak season, 1.5 hours, leaves from The Crown on Market Place, www.wellswalkingtours.co.uk).

ARRIVAL IN WELLS

If you're coming by **bus,** you can get off in the city center at the Sadler Street stop, around the corner from the cathedral (tell the

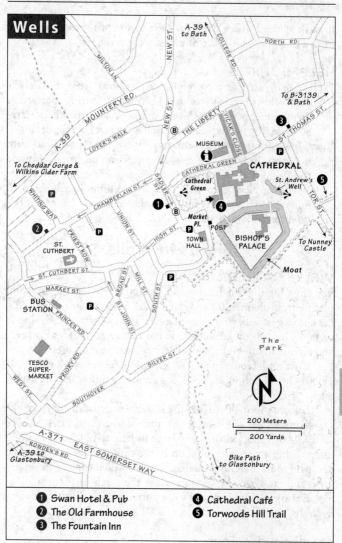

Wells

A-39 to Bath

NORTH RD.

NEW ST.

COLLEGE RD.

MILTON LN.

MOUNTERY RD.

LOYER'S WALK

To B-3139 & Bath

ST. THOMAS ST.

3

The Liberty

VICAR'S CLOSE

NEW ST.

B

SADLER ST.

MUSEUM

CATHEDRAL GREEN

CATHEDRAL

To Cheddar Gorge & Wilkins Cider Farm

WHITING WAY

CHAMBERLAIN ST.

UNION ST.

Cathedral Green

St. Andrew's Well

5

TOR ST.

1

B

4

Market Pl.

POST

2

PRIEST ROW

HIGH ST.

TOWN HALL

BISHOP'S PALACE

To Nunney Castle

ST. CUTHBERT

ST. CUTHBERT ST.

Moat

MARKET ST.

BROAD ST.

MILL ST.

SOUTH ST.

BUS STATION

PRINCES RD.

ST. JOHN ST.

The Park

TESCO SUPER-MARKET

PRIORY RD.

SOUTHOVER

SILVER ST.

N

WEST ST.

200 Meters

200 Yards

A-371

EAST SOMERSET WAY

ROWDEN'S RD.

A-39 to Glastonbury

Bike Path to Glastonbury

1 Swan Hotel & Pub
2 The Old Farmhouse
3 The Fountain Inn

4 Cathedral Café
5 Torwoods Hill Trail

GLASTONBURY & WELLS

driver that's your stop). Or you can disembark at the big, well-organized bus station/parking lot (staffed Mon-Fri 9:30-13:30, closed Sat-Sun), about a five-minute walk from the town center at the south end of town. Find the Wells map at the head of the stalls to get oriented (the big church tower you see is *not* the cathedral); the signpost at the main pedestrian exit directs you downtown.

Drivers will find pay parking right on the main square, but because of confusing one-way streets, it's hard to reach; it's simpler to park at the Princes Road lot next to the bus station (enter on Priory Road) and walk five minutes to the cathedral.

HELPFUL HINTS

Wells Carnival: Every November Wells hosts what it claims is the world's biggest illuminated carnival, featuring spectacular floats, street performers, and a market fair (carnival also travels to nearby towns; see www.wellssomerset.com for details).

Best Views: It's hard to beat the grand views of the cathedral from the green in front of it...but the reflecting pool tucked inside the Bishop's Palace grounds tries hard. For a fine cathedral-and-town view from your own leafy hilltop bench, hike 10 minutes up Torwoods Hill. The trail starts on Tor Street behind the Bishop's Palace.

Sights in Wells

WELLS CATHEDRAL

The city's highlight is England's first completely Gothic cathedral (dating from about 1200 and rated ▲▲). Locals claim this church has the largest collection of medieval statuary north of the Alps. It certainly has one of the widest and most elaborate facades I've seen, and unique figure-eight "scissor arches" that are unforgettable.

Cost and Hours: Free, £6 donation requested; daily 7:00-19:00, Oct-March until 18:00; for evensong times, see the listing later.

Information: Tel. 01749/674-483, www.wellscathedral.org.uk.

Tours: Free one-hour tours run Mon-Sat at 10:00, 11:00, 13:00, 14:00, and 15:00; Nov-March usually at 12:00 and 14:00—unless other events are going on in the cathedral. Additional free and paid tours are also available, some of which explore the upper areas and the 17th-century library; see their website for details.

Eating: A café is right by the entrance (described in "Eating in Wells," later).

◉ Self-Guided Tour

Begin on the large, inviting **green** in front of the cathedral. In the Middle Ages, the cathedral was enclosed within "The Liberty," an area free from civil jurisdiction until the 1800s. The Liberty included the green on the west side of the cathedral, which, from the 13th to the 17th century, was a burial place for common folk, including 17th-century plague victims. The green became a cricket pitch, then a field for grazing animals and picnicking people. Today, it's the perfect spot to marvel at an impressive cathedral.

Peer up at the magnificent **facade.** The west front displays almost 300 original 13th-century carvings of kings and the Last Judgment. The bottom row of niches is empty, too easily reached by Cromwell's men, who were hell-bent on destroying "graven images." Stand back and imagine it as a grand Palm Sunday welcome with a cast of hundreds—all gaily painted back then, choristers singing boldly from holes above the doors and trumpets tooting through the holes up by the 12 apostles.

Now head **inside.** Visitors enter by going to the right, through the door under the small spire, into the lobby and welcome center.

At the **welcome center,** you'll be warmly greeted and reminded how expensive it is to maintain the cathedral. Pay the donation and pick up a map of the cathedral's highlights. Then head through the cloister and into the cathedral.

At your first glance down the nave, you're immediately struck by the general sense of light and the unique "scissors" or hourglass-shaped **double arch** (added in 1338 to transfer weight from the south—where the foundations were sinking under the tower's weight—to the east, where they were firm). Until Henry VIII and the Reformation, the interior was opulently painted in golds, reds, and greens. Later it was whitewashed. Then, in the 1840s, the church experienced the Victorian "great scrape," as locals peeled moldy whitewash off and revealed the bare stone we see today. The floral ceiling painting is based on the original medieval design: A single pattern was discovered under the 17th-century whitewash and repeated throughout.

Small, ornate, 15th-century pavilion-like chapels flank the

altar, carved in lacy Gothic for church VIPs. On the right, the **pulpit** features a post-Reformation, circa-1540 English script—rather than the standard Latin (see where the stonemason ran out of space when carving the inscription—we've all been there). Since this was not a monastery church, the Reformation didn't destroy it as it did the Glastonbury Abbey church.

We'll do a quick clockwise spin around the cathedral's interior. First walk down the left aisle until you reach the north transept. The medieval **clock** does a silly but much-loved joust on the quarter-hour. If you get to watch the show, notice how—like clockwork—the same rider gets clobbered, as he has for hundreds of years. The clock's face, which depicts the earth at the center of the universe, dates from 1390. The outer ring shows hours, the middle ring shows minutes, and the inner ring shows the dates of the month and phases of the moon. Above and to the right of the clock is Jack Blandiver, a chap carved out of wood in the 14th century. Beneath the clock, the fine **crucifix** (1947) was carved out of a yew tree. Also in the north transept is a door with well-worn steps leading up to the **Chapter House,** a grand space for huddles among church officials. Its sublime "tierceron" vaulting—a forerunner of the fan vaults you can see in later English Gothic style—make this one of the most impressive medieval ceilings in the country.

Now continue down the left aisle. On the right is the entrance to the **choir** (or "quire," the central zone where the daily services are sung). Go in and take a close look at the embroidery work on the cushions, which celebrate the hometowns of important local church leaders. Up above the east end of the choir is "Jesse's Window," depicting Jesus' family tree. It's also called the "Golden Window," because it's bathed in sunlight each morning.

Head back out to the aisle the way you came in, and continue to the end of the church. On the outside wall, on the left, is the entry to the undercroft, now a cathedral history exhibit worth a look. In the apse you'll find the **Lady Chapel.** Examine the medieval stained-glass windows. Do they look jumbled? In the 17th century, Puritan troops trashed the precious original glass. Much was repaired, but many of the broken panes were like a puzzle that was never figured out. That's why today many of the windows are simply kaleidoscopes of colored glass.

Next to the chapel is the oldest known piece of wooden furniture in England: a **"cope chest,"** which is still used to store the clergy's garments. It is so large it can't be moved out through any of the cathedral's doors. Historians theorize the chest is older than the existing building, and was originally installed around AD 800, in the Saxon church that predated the cathedral.

Now circle around and head up the other aisle. As you walk, notice that many of the black **tombstones** set in the floor have decorative recesses that aren't filled with brass (as they once were). After the Reformation in the 1530s, the church was short on cash, so they sold the brass lettering to raise money for roof repairs.

Once you reach the south transept, you'll find several items of interest. The **old Saxon font** survives from the previous church (AD 705) and has been the site of Wells baptisms for more than a thousand years. (Normans added its carved arches in the 12th century, and the cover is from the 17th century.) In the far end of this transept (in the shade of the fancy chapels), a little of the original green and red wall painting, which wasn't white-washed, survives.

Nearby, notice the **carvings** in the capitals of the freestanding pillars,

with whimsical depictions of medieval life. On the first pillar, notice the man with a toothache and another man with a thorn in his foot. The second pillar tells a story of medieval justice: On the left, we see thieves stealing grapes; on the right, the woodcutter (with an ax) is warning the farmer (with the pitchfork) what's happening. Circle around to the back of the pillar for the rest of the story: On the left, the farmer chases one of the thieves, grabbing him by the ear. On the right, he clobbers the thief over the head with his pitchfork—so hard the farmer's hat falls off.

Also in the south transept, you'll find the entrance to the cathedral **Reading Room** and **Chained Library** (free, Mon-Fri 11:00-13:00 & 14:00-16:00, closed in winter; it's also often possible to step in for a quick look on Sat mornings). Housing a few old manuscripts, it offers a peek into a real 16th-century library. At the back of the Reading Room, peer through the doors and notice the irons chaining the books to the shelves—a reflection perhaps of the trust in the clergy at that time.

Head out into the cloister, then cross the courtyard back to the welcome center, shop, café, and exit. Go in peace.

MORE CATHEDRAL SIGHTS
▲▲Cathedral Evensong Service

The cathedral choir takes full advantage of heavenly acoustics with a nightly 45-minute evensong service. You'll sit right in the old "quire" as you listen to a great pipe organ and the world-famous Wells Cathedral choir.

Cost and Hours: Free, Mon-Sat at 17:15, Sun at 15:00, generally no service when school is out July-Aug unless a visiting choir

performs, to check call 01749/674-483 or visit www.wellscathedral.
org.uk. At 17:05 (Sun at 14:50), the verger ushers visitors to their
seats. There's usually plenty of room.

Returning to Bath After the Evensong: Confirm the departure time for the last direct bus to Bath in advance—it's usually
around 19:45; 19:20 on Sundays (10-minute walk from cathedral
to station, bus may also depart from The Liberty stop—a 4-minute
walk away).

Other Cathedral Concerts: The cathedral hosts several evening concerts each month (most £20-30, generally Thu-Sat at
19:00 or 19:30, buy tickets by phone or at box office in cathedral
gift shop; Mon-Sat 10:30-16:30, Sun 11:30-16:30; tel. 01749/672-
773). Concert tickets are also sometimes available at the TI, along
with pamphlets listing what's on.

Vicars' Close

Lined with perfectly pickled 14th-century houses, this is the oldest
continuously occupied complete street in Europe (since 1348; just

a block north of the cathedral—
go under the big arch and look
left). It was built to house the
vicar's choir, and it still houses
church officials and choristers.
These dwellings were bachelor
pads until the Reformation allowed clerics to marry; they
were then redesigned to accommodate families. Notice how the
close gets narrower at the top, creating the illusion that it is a longer lane than it is. Notice also the elevated passageway connecting
these choristers' quarters with the church.

▲Bishop's Palace

Next to the cathedral stands the moated Bishop's Palace, built in
the 13th century and still in use today as the residence of the bishop

of Bath and Wells. While
the interior of the palace
itself is dull, the grounds
and gardens surrounding
it are the most tranquil
and scenic spot in Wells,
with wonderful views of
the cathedral. It's just the
place for a relaxing walk in
the park. Watch the swans
ring the bell—hanging over the water just left of the entry gate—
when they have an attack of the munchies.

Cost and Hours: £8; daily 10:00-18:00, Nov-March until 16:00, includes guided tour at set times, see schedule online or call; often closed on Sat for special events—call to confirm; multimedia guide available for small fee; tel. 01749/988-111, www.bishopspalace.org.uk.

Visiting the Palace and Gardens: The palace's spring-fed moat was built in the 14th century to protect the bishop during squabbles with the borough. Bishops would generously release this potable water into the town during local festivals. Now the moat serves primarily as a pool for mute swans. The bridge was last drawn in 1831. Crossing that bridge, you'll buy your ticket and enter the grounds (past the old-timers playing a proper game of croquet—several times a week after 13:30). On your right, pass through the evocative ruins of the Great Hall (which was deserted and left to gradually deteriorate), and stroll through the chirpy south lawn. If you're feeling energetic, hike up to the top of the ramparts that encircle the property.

Circling around the far side of the mansion, walk through a door in the rampart wall, cross the wooden bridge, and follow a path to a smaller bridge and the wells (springs) that gave the city its name. Surrounding a reflecting pool with the cathedral towering overhead, these flower-bedecked pathways are idyllic. Nearby are an arboretum, picnic area, and sweet little pea-patch gardens.

After touring the gardens, the mansion's interior is a let-down—despite the borrowable descriptions that struggle to make the dusty old place meaningful. Have a spot of tea in the café (with outdoor garden seating—free access), or climb the creaky wooden staircase to wander long halls lined with portraits of bishops past.

SIGHTS NEAR WELLS

The following stops are best for drivers.

Cheddar Cheese

If you're in the mood for a picnic, drop by any local aromatic cheese shop for a great selection of tasty Somerset cheeses. Real farmhouse cheddar puts Velveeta to shame. The **Cheddar Gorge Cheese Company,** eight miles west of Wells, gives guests a chance to see the cheese-making process and enjoy a sample (£2, daily

GLASTONBURY & WELLS

10:00-15:00; take the A-39, then the A-371 to Cheddar Gorge; tel. 01934/742-810, www.cheddargorgecheeseco.co.uk).

Scrumpy Farms

Scrumpy is the wonderfully dangerous hard cider brewed in this part of England. You don't find it served in many pubs because of the unruly crowd it attracts. Scrumpy, at around 7 percent alcohol, will rot your socks—this is potent stuff. "Scrumpy Jack," carbonated mass-produced cider, is not real scrumpy. The real stuff is "rough farmhouse cider." It's said some farmers throw a side of beef into the vat, and when fermentation is done only the teeth remain. (Some use a pair of old boots, for the tannin from the leather.)

TIs list cider farms open to the public, such as **Wilkins Cider Farm** (also known as Land's End Farm)—a great Back Door travel experience (free, Mon-Sat 10:00-20:00, Sun until 13:00; west of Wells in Mudgley, take the B-3139 from Wells to Wedmore, then the B-3151 south for 2 miles, farm is a quarter-mile off the B-3151—tough to find, get close and ask locals; tel. 01934/712-385, www.wilkinscider.com).

Apples are pressed from August through December. Hard cider, while not quite scrumpy, is also typical of the West Country, but more fashionable, "decent," and accessible. You can get a pint of hard cider at nearly any pub, drawn straight from the barrel—dry, medium, or sweet.

Nunney Castle

The centerpiece of the charming and quintessentially English village of Nunney (between Bath and Glastonbury, off the A-361) is a striking 14th-century castle surrounded by a fairy-tale moat. Its rare, French-style design brings to mind the Paris Bastille. The year 1644 was a tumultuous one for Nunney. Its noble family was royalist (and likely closet Catholics). They defied Parliament, so Parliament ordered their castle "slighted" (deliberately destroyed) to ensure that it would threaten the order of the land no more. Looking at this castle, so daunting in the age of bows and arrows, you can see how it was no match for the modern cannon. The pretty Mendip village of Nunney, with its little brook, is also worth a wander.

Cost and Hours: Free, visitable at "any reasonable time;" tel. 0370/333-1181, www.english-heritage.org.uk.

Sleeping and Eating in Wells

Sleeping: Wells is a pleasant overnight stop, with a few accommodation options.

$$$ Swan Hotel, a Best Western Plus facing the cathedral, is a big, comfortable, 50-room hotel. Prices for their Tudor-style rooms vary based on whether you want extras like a four-poster bed or a cathedral view. They also rent five apartments in the village (Sadler Street, tel. 01749/836-300, www.swanhotelwells.co.uk, info@swanhotelwells.co.uk).

$$ The Old Farmhouse, a five-minute walk from the town center and cathedral, welcomes you with a secluded front garden and two tastefully decorated rooms (2-night minimum, secure parking, next to the gas station at 62 Chamberlain Street, tel. 01749/675-058, theoldfarmhousewells@hotmail.com, charming owners Felicity and Christopher Wilkes).

Eating: Downtown Wells is tiny. A fine variety of eating options is within a block or two of its market square, including classic pubs and little delis, bakeries, and takeaway places serving light meals.

$$ The Fountain Inn, on a quiet street 50 yards behind the cathedral, serves good pub grub (daily 12:00-14:00 & 18:00-21:00 except no dinner on Sun or lunch on Mon, pub open later, St. Thomas Street, tel. 01749/672-317).

$ The **café** in the cathedral welcome center offers a handy if not heavenly lunch (Mon-Sat 10:00-16:00, Sun from 11:00, may close earlier in winter, tel. 01749/676-543).

$$ The **Swan Hotel** has a pub that serves lunches in their garden across the street with a view over the green and cathedral (Sadler Street, tel. 01749/836-300).

Wells Connections

The nearest train station is in Bath. The bus station in Wells is at a well-organized bus parking lot at the intersection of Priory and Princes roads. Local buses are run by First Bus Company (for Wells, tel. 0845-602-0156, www.firstgroup.com), while buses to and from London are run by National Express (tel. 0871-781-8181, www.nationalexpress.com).

From Wells by Bus to: Bath (nearly hourly, less frequent on Sun, 75 minutes; if you miss the last direct bus to Bath, catch the bus to Bristol—runs hourly and takes one hour, then a 15-minute train ride to Bath), **Glastonbury** (2/hour, 20 minutes, take bus #376 toward the town of Street), **London**'s Victoria Coach Station (1/day direct, 4 hours; otherwise hourly with a change in Bristol).

GLASTONBURY & WELLS

AVEBURY, STONEHENGE & SALISBURY

Ooooh, mystery, history. England's southwest countryside holds some of the country's most goose-pimply prehistoric sites, as well as a particularly fine cathedral town. Get Neolithic at every druid's favorite stone circles, Avebury and Stonehenge. Then stop by Salisbury for its colorful markets and soaring cathedral.

PLANNING YOUR TIME

Avebury, Stonehenge, and Salisbury make a wonderful day out from Bath. With a car, you can do all three in a day if you're selective with your sightseeing.

Everybody needs to see Stonehenge, but I'll tell you now: It looks just like it looks (though the visitors center makes it a well-worthwhile visit). Avebury is the connoisseur's stone circle: more subtle and welcoming.

Just an hour from Bath, Salisbury makes a pleasant stop, particularly on a market day (Tue, Sat, every other Wed, plus more), though its cathedral is striking any time. Salisbury is also the logical launchpad for visiting nearby Stonehenge (particularly if you lack a car).

GETTING AROUND THE REGION

By Car: Avebury, Stonehenge, and Salisbury are each about 35-40 miles from Bath and 85-90 miles from London. Drivers can do a 104-mile loop from Bath to Avebury (25 miles) to Stonehenge (30

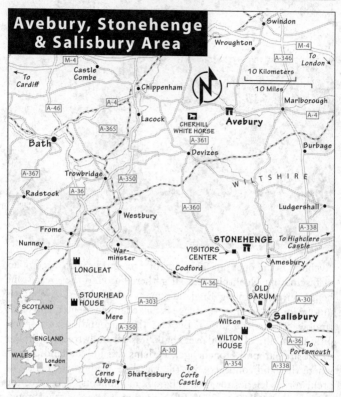

miles) to Salisbury (9 miles) and back to Bath (40 miles). For tips on incorporating Glastonbury and Wells, see the previous chapter.

By Bus and Train: The nearest train station is in Bath, with regular service from London's Paddington Station (2/hour, 1.5 hours). Many buses run between Bath and **Avebury,** all requiring one or two transfers (hourly, 2.5 hours, transfer at Trowbridge or Devizes). There's no bus between Avebury and Stonehenge.

A one-hour train trip connects Bath to **Salisbury** (hourly direct). With the best public transportation of all these towns, Salisbury is a good jumping-off point for **Stonehenge** or Avebury by bus or car. Stonehenge Tour buses run between Salisbury, Old Sarum, and Stonehenge (see "Getting to Stonehenge," later). Buses also run from Salisbury to **Avebury** (see "Salisbury Connections," later). For fares and schedules, check Traveline South West's easy-to-use website (www.travelinesw.com, tel. 0871-200-2233).

By Tour: From Bath, if you don't have a car, the most convenient and quickest way to see Avebury and Stonehenge is with a minibus tour. Mad Max is the liveliest of the tours leaving from Bath (see "Tours in and near Bath" on page 248).

Avebury

Avebury is an open-air museum of prehistory, with a complex of fascinating Neolithic sites all gathered around the great stone henge (circle). Among England's many stone circles, Avebury is unique for its vast size—a village is tucked into its center, and roads rumble between its stones. Because the surrounding area sports only a thin skin of topsoil over chalk, it is naturally treeless (similar to the area around Stonehenge). Perhaps this unique landscape—where the land connects with the big sky—made it the choice of prehistoric societies for their religious monuments. Whatever the case, Avebury dates to 2800 BC—six centuries older than Stonehenge. This complex, the St. Peter's Basilica of Neolithic civilization, makes for a fascinating visit. Some visitors enjoy it even more than Stonehenge.

Orientation to Avebury

Avebury is the name of a huge stone circle, as well as the tiny village that sits surrounded by its stones. It's easy to reach by car, but more difficult by public transportation (see "Getting Around the Region," earlier).

Tourist Information: There's no TI, but there's a National Trust information center in the Old Farmyard, and maps and booklets are sold in shops in the village. For more information on the Avebury sights, see www.nationaltrust.org.uk.

Parking: There's no public parking in the village center. Visitors park in a flat-fee National Trust lot along the A-4361—a five-minute walk from the village (£7, £4 after 15:00 and in winter, pay with coins or credit card at the machine, open summer 9:30-18:30, off-season until 16:30).

Stone Circles: The Riddle of the Rocks

Britain is home to roughly 800 stone circles, most of them rudimentary, jaggedly sparse boulder rings that lack the iconic

upright-and-lintel form of Stonehenge. But their misty, mossy settings provide curious travelers with an intimate and accessible glimpse of the mysterious people who lived in prehistoric Britain.

Bronze Age Britain (2000-600 BC) was populated by farming folk who had mastered the craft of smelting heated tin and copper together to produce bronze, which was used to make durable tools and weapons. Late in the Bronze Age, many of these clannish communities also put considerable effort into gathering huge rocks and arranging them into circles, perhaps for use in rituals with long-forgotten meanings. Some scholars believe the circles may have been used as solar observatories—used to calculate solstices and equinoxes to help plan life-sustaining seasonal crop-planting cycles. A few human remains have been discovered in the centers of some circles, but their primary use seems to have been ceremonial, not as burial sites. The superstitious people of the Middle Ages believed Stonehenge was arranged by giants (makes sense to me); nearby circles were thought to be petrified partiers who had dared to dance on the Sabbath.

Britain's stone circles generally lie in Scotland, Wales, and at the fringes of England. You'll find them marked in the Ordnance Survey atlas and signposted along rural roads. Ask a local farmer for directions—and savor the experience. I've highlighted my favorites in this book, and described each one in case you're being selective:

Stonehenge is by far the most famous, the only one with horizontal "lintels" connecting the monoliths, and comes with the most insightful visitors center.

Avebury is by far the biggest—so large that a small village was built inside it. Less crowded and easier to visit than Stonehenge, it's easy and fun to explore on your own.

Castlerigg is a pretty standard-issue stone circle, but it's handy for those going to the Lake District (just off the main road into Keswick; see page 485).

Clava Cairns (in Scotland just outside Inverness—see page 993) is quite different, with a collection of stone enclosures in a forest clearing (the inspiration for the stone circle in *Outlander*).

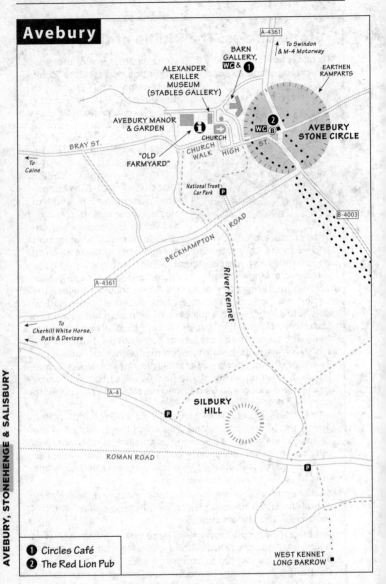

Avebury

ALEXANDER KEILLER MUSEUM (STABLES GALLERY)

BARN GALLERY, WC & ①

To Swindon & M-4 Motorway

EARTHEN RAMPARTS

AVEBURY MANOR & GARDEN

BRAY ST.

To Caine

CHURCH

"OLD FARMYARD"

CHURCH WALK HIGH ST.

WC ② B

AVEBURY STONE CIRCLE

National Trust Car Park

BECKHAMPTON ROAD

River Kennet

B-4003

A-4361

To Cherhill White Horse, Bath & Devizes

A-4

SILBURY HILL

ROMAN ROAD

WEST KENNET LONG BARROW

① Circles Café
② The Red Lion Pub

AVEBURY, STONEHENGE & SALISBURY

Sights in Avebury

All of Avebury's prehistoric sights—which spread over a wide area—are free to visit and always open. The underwhelming museum and mansion charge admission and have limited hours. I've linked the sights with directions for drivers who want to make a targeted visit to all that Avebury has to offer.

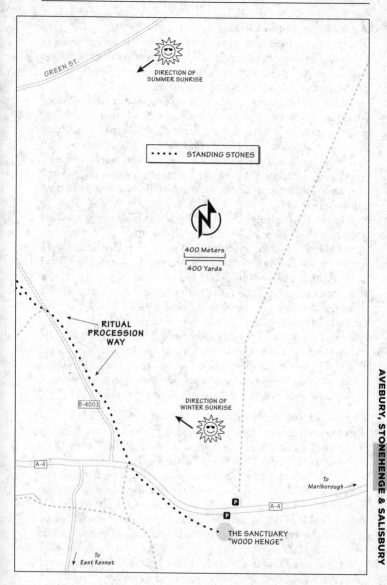

GREEN ST.

DIRECTION OF
SUMMER SUNRISE

· · · · · STANDING STONES

400 Meters
400 Yards

RITUAL
PROCESSION
WAY

B-4003

DIRECTION OF
WINTER SUNRISE

A-4

To
Marlborough →

P
P
A-4

THE SANCTUARY
"WOOD HENGE"

To
East Kennet

AVEBURY, STONEHENGE & SALISBURY

• From the National Trust parking lot, follow the path five minutes through fields to the village center. On your right, you'll see the first access point to the big stone circle. (To pass through the gate, slide the handle sideways rather than lifting it.) Take some time exploring the remarkable...

▲▲Avebury Stone Circle

The Neolithic stone circle at Avebury is 1,400 feet wide—that's 16 times as big as Stonehenge. It's so vast that it dwarfs the village that grew up in its midst. You're free to wander among 100 stones, ditches, mounds, and curious patterns from the past.

In the 14th century, in a frenzy of ignorance and religious paranoia, Avebury villagers buried many of these mysterious pagan stones. Their 18th-century descendants hosted social events in which they broke up the remaining pagan stones (topple, heat up, douse with cold water, and scavenge broken stones as building blocks). In modern times, the buried stones were dug up and re-erected. Concrete markers show where the missing broken-up stones once stood.

Explore. Touch a chunk of prehistory. While even just a short walk to a few stones is rewarding, you can stroll the entire half-mile around the circle, much of it along an impressive earthwork henge—a 30-foot-high outer bank surrounding a ditch 30 feet deep, making a 60-foot-high rampart. This earthen rampart once had stones standing around the perimeter, placed about every 30 feet, and four grand causeway entries. Originally, two smaller circles made of about 200 stones stood within the henge.

• *Directly across from the parking-lot trail, follow signs into the* Old Farmyard—*a little courtyard of rustic buildings near Avebury Manor. Today these house museums, WCs, the National Trust information center, a shop, a recommended café, and the two sights described next. (Note: These sights pale in comparison to the prehistoric sights.)*

Alexander Keiller Museum

This museum, named for the archaeologist who led excavations at Avebury in the late 1930s, is housed in two buildings (covered by the same ticket). The 17th-century **Barn Gallery** illustrates 6,000 years of Avebury history, with kid-friendly interactive exhibits about the landscape and the people who've lived here—from the Stone Age to Victorian times. Across the farmyard, the small, old-school **Stables Gallery** displays artifacts and skeletons from past digs and a re-creation of what Neolithic people might have looked like.

Cost and Hours: £5, daily 10:00-18:00, Nov-March until 16:00, tel. 01672/539-250, www.nationaltrust.org.uk.

• *Behind the Stables Gallery is the...*

Avebury Manor and Garden

Archaeologist Alexander Keiller's former home, a 500-year-old estate, was restored by a team of historians and craftspeople in collaboration with the BBC (for their 2011 documentary *The Manor Reborn*). Nine rooms were decorated in five different period styles showing the progression of design, from a Tudor wedding chapel to a Queen Anne-era bedroom to an early-20th-century billiards room. The grounds were also spruced up with a topiary and a Victorian kitchen garden. While it's fun to tour—and the docents enjoy explaining how each room was painstakingly researched and re-created—it's pricey and far from authentic...and it has nothing to do with Avebury's impressive circle.

Cost and Hours: £11, limited number of timed tickets sold per day; daily 11:00-17:00, shorter hours off-season, closed Jan-mid-Feb, last entry one hour before closing; buy tickets at Alexander Keiller Museum's Barn Gallery, tel. 01672/539-250, www.nationaltrust.org.uk.

• *The following sights are a long walk or a short drive from the center of Avebury.*

First, from the Avebury village center, the road southeast toward West Kennet and Malborough (B-4003, a.k.a. West Kennet Avenue) is evocatively lined with an "avenue" of stones. This is known as the...

▲Ritual Procession Way

This double line of stones provided a ritual procession way leading from Avebury to a long-gone wooden circle dubbed "The Sanctuary." This "wood henge," thought to have been 1,000 years older than everything else in the area, is considered to have been the genesis of Avebury and its big stone circle. (You can see the site of the former Sanctuary—turn left onto the A-4, look for the marked pullout on the left, and walk across the road—but all you'll see is an empty field with concrete blocks marking where the circle once stood.) Most of the stones standing along the procession way today were reconstructed in modern times.

• *From the end of the Ritual Procession Way, you can turn right (west) on the A-4. After a mile or so, watch on the right for the dome-shaped green hill. Just beyond it is a handy parking lot. (Walkers can reach this in about 20 minutes from the National Trust parking lot.)*

▲Silbury Hill

This pyramid-shaped hill (reminiscent of Glastonbury Tor) is a 130-foot-high, yet-to-be-explained mound of chalk just outside of Avebury. More than 4,000 years old, this mound is considered the largest man-made object in prehistoric Europe (with the surface area of London's Trafalgar Square and the height of the Nelson Column). It's a reminder that we've only

just scratched the surface of England's mysterious and ancient religious landscape.

Inspired by a legend that the hill hid a gold statue in its center, locals tunneled through Silbury Hill in 1830, undermining the structure. Work is underway to restore the hill, which remains closed to the public. Archaeologists (who date things like this by carbon-dating snails and other little critters killed in its construction) figure Silbury Hill took only 60 years to build, in about 2200 BC. This makes Silbury Hill the last element built at Avebury and contemporaneous with Stonehenge. Some think it may have been an observation point for all the other bits of the Avebury site. You can still see evidence of a spiral path leading up the hill and a moat at its base.

The Roman road detoured around Silbury Hill. (Roman engineers often used features of the landscape as visual reference points when building roads. Their roads would commonly kink at the crest of hills or other landmarks, where they realigned with a new visual point.) Later, the hill sported a wooden Saxon fort, which likely acted as a lookout for marauding Vikings. And in World War II, the Royal Observer Corps stationed men up here to count and report Nazi bombers on raids.

Nearby: Across the road from Silbury Hill (a 15-minute walk through the fields) is **West Kennet Long Barrow.** This burial chamber, the best-preserved Stone Age chamber tomb in the UK, stands intact on a ridge. It lines up with the rising sun on the summer solstice. You can walk inside the barrow, or sit on its roof and survey the Neolithic landscape around you.

• *The final sight is about four miles west of Avebury, along the A-4 toward Calne (and Bath), just before the village of Cherhill. Pull over at the Avebury end of the village and look for the hill-capping obelisk; below it, carved into the hillside, is the...*

Cherhill White Horse

Throughout southern England, you'll see horses (and other objects) like this one carved into the downs (chalk hills). There is one genuinely prehistoric white horse in England (the Uffington White Horse); the Cherhill White Horse is an 18th-century creation. Prehistoric discoveries were all the rage in the 1700s, and it was a fad to make fake ones by cutting into the thin layer of topsoil to expose the chalk beneath. Nowadays, figures like this are cemented and painted white so that the design doesn't need to be weeded. Above the horse are the remains of an Iron Age hill fort known as Oldbury Castle—described on an information board at the pullout.

Eating in Avebury

$ Circles Café is practical and pleasant, serving healthy lunches, including vegan and gluten-free dishes, and cream teas on most days (daily 10:00-17:30, Nov-March until 16:00, no hot food after 14:30, in the Barn Gallery on the Old Farmyard, tel. 01672/539-250).

$$ The Red Lion—a classic thatched-roof pub right in the heart of Avebury village—has updated but unpretentious pub grub; a creaky, well-worn, dart-throwing ambience; a medieval well in its dining room; and ample outdoor seating (daily 10:00-22:00, High Street, tel. 01672/539-266).

Stonehenge

As old as the pyramids, and far older than the Acropolis and the Colosseum, this iconic stone circle amazed medieval Europeans, who figured it was built by a race of giants. And it still impresses visitors today. As one of Europe's most famous sights, Stonehenge, worth ▲▲▲, does a valiant job of retaining an air of mystery and majesty (partly because cordons, which keep hordes of tourists from trampling all over it, foster the illusion that it stands alone in a field). Although cynics manage to be underwhelmed by Stonehenge, most of its almost one million annual visitors agree that it's well worth the trip. At few sights in Europe will you overhear so many awe-filled comments.

GETTING TO STONEHENGE

Stonehenge is about 90 miles southwest of central London. To reach it from London, you can take a bus tour; go on a guided tour that uses public transportation; or do it on your own using public transit, connecting via Salisbury. It's not worth the hassle or expense to rent a car just for a Stonehenge day trip.

By Bus Tour from London: Several companies offer big-bus day trips to Stonehenge from London, often with stops in Bath,

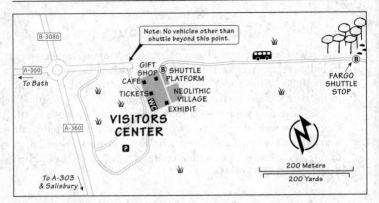

Windsor, Salisbury, and/or Avebury. These generally cost about £50-100 (including Stonehenge admission), last 8-12 hours, and pack a 45-seat bus. Some include hotel pickup, admission fees, and meals; understand what's included before you book. The more destinations listed for a tour, the less time you'll have at any one stop. Well-known companies are **Evan Evans** (their barebones Stonehenge Express gets you there and back for £54, tel. 020/7950-1777 or US tel. 800-422-9022, www.evanevanstours.co.uk) and **Golden Tours** (£53, tel. 020/7630-2028 or US toll-free tel. 800-509-2507, www.goldentours.com). **International Friends** runs pricier but smaller 16-person tours that include Windsor and Bath (£145, tel. 01223/244-555, www.internationalfriends.co.uk).

By Bus Tour from Bath: I prefer **Mad Max**'s minibus tour and **Scarper Tours'** shuttle bus service. For details and additional options, see page 249.

By Guided Tour on Public Transport from London: The "Stonehenge and Salisbury Excursion" from **London Walks** travels by train and bus on Tuesdays from mid-May through early October (£93, includes all transportation, Salisbury walking tour, entry fees, and guided tours of Stonehenge and Salisbury Cathedral; pay guide, cash only, Tue at 8:45, meet at Waterloo Station's main ticket office, opposite Platform 16, verify price and schedule online, advance booking not required, tel. 020/7624-3978, www.walks.com).

On Your Own on Public Transport via Salisbury: From London, you can catch a train to Salisbury, then go by tour bus or taxi to Stonehenge. **Trains** to Salisbury run from London's Waterloo Station (around £42 for same-day return leaving weekdays after 9:30, 2/hour, 1.5 hours, tel. 0345-600-0650, www.southwesternrailway.com or tel. 03457-484-950, www.nationalrail.co.uk). For details on trains to Salisbury from Bath, see "Getting Around the Region" at the beginning of this chapter.

From Salisbury, take the **Stonehenge Tour bus** to the site. These distinctive double-decker buses leave from the Salisbury train

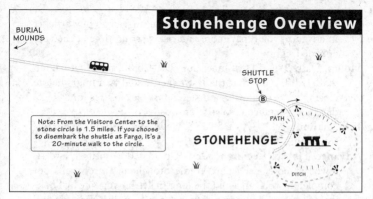

Stonehenge Overview

BURIAL MOUNDS

SHUTTLE STOP

B

PATH

Note: From the Visitors Center to the stone circle is 1.5 miles. If you choose to disembark the shuttle at Fargo, it's a 20-minute walk to the circle.

STONEHENGE

DITCH

station, stop in Salisbury's center, then make a circuit to Stonehenge and Old Sarum, with lovely scenery and a decent light commentary along the way (£15, £30 includes Stonehenge as well as Old Sarum—whether you want it or not; tickets good all day, order online or pay driver; daily June-Aug 10:00-17:00, 2/hour; may not run June 21 because of solstice crowds, shorter hours and hourly departures off-season; 30 minutes from station to Stonehenge, tel. 01202/338-420, timetable at www.thestonehengetour.info).

A **taxi** from Salisbury to Stonehenge can make sense for groups (about £40-60). Try On-Line City Cabs (tel. 01722/509-090, onlinecitycabs.co.uk) or Value Cars Taxis (tel. 01722/505-050, www.salisbury-valuecars.co.uk).

By Car: Stonehenge is well signed just off the A-303, about 15 minutes north of Salisbury, an hour southeast of Bath, an hour east of Glastonbury, and an hour south of Avebury.

Stonehenge is about 70 miles and 1.5 hours west of **London Heathrow** (barring traffic). From the M-25 ring road, connect with the M-3 toward Southampton. Past Basingstoke, exit to the A-303. Continue west past Andover to Amesbury. In 3.5 miles, turn onto northbound A-360 at the roundabout, and follow "From Salisbury" directions from that point (see next).

From **Salisbury,** head north on the A-360 (at the St. Paul's roundabout, take the second exit, direction: Devizes). Continue for eight miles, crossing the A-303 roundabout. In one more mile you'll encounter another roundabout; follow it around to the exit for the well-marked visitors center.

ORIENTATION TO STONEHENGE

The visitors center, located 1.5 miles west of the circle, is a minimalist steel structure with a subtly curved roofline, evoking the landscape of Salisbury Plain.

Cost: £19, purchase timed-entry ticket in advance online, ticket includes shuttle-bus ride to stone circle, covered by English

Heritage Pass (see page 1036). If you neglect to buy a ticket in advance, you'll pay more and risk wasting time at the very crowded sight.

Hours: Daily 9:30-19:00, June-Aug 9:00-20:00, mid-Oct-March 9:30-17:00. Note that the last ticket is sold two hours before closing. Expect shorter hours and possible closures June 20-22 due to huge, raucous solstice crowds.

Information: Tel. 0370-333-1181, www.english-heritage.org.uk/stonehenge.

Advance Tickets Recommended: Up to 9,000 visitors are allowed to enter each day. While Stonehenge rarely sells out completely, you can avoid the long ticket-buying line by booking at least 24 hours in advance at www.english-heritage.org.uk/stonehenge. When booking, you'll be asked to select a 30-minute entry window. Try to be on time, but if you're late you can generally sweet talk your way in. Even those with a timed entry may have to wait in line for the shuttle bus to and from the stones.

Crowd-Beating Tips: For a less crowded, more mystical experience, come early or late. Things are pretty quiet before about 10:30 (head out to the stones first, then circle back to the exhibits); at the end of the day, aim to arrive just before the "last ticket" time (two hours before closing). Stonehenge is most crowded when school's out: summer weekends (especially holiday weekends) and anytime in August.

Tours: Worthwhile audioguides are available behind the ticket counter (included with Heritage Pass, otherwise £3). Or you can use the visitors center's free Wi-Fi to download the free "Stonehenge Audio Tour" app.

Visiting the Inner Stones: For the true Stonehenge fan, special one-hour access to the stones' inner circle is available early in the morning (times vary depending on sunrise; the earliest visit is at 5:00 in June and July) or after closing to the general public. Touching the stones is not allowed. Only 30 people are allowed at a time, so reserve well in advance (£45, allows you to revisit the site the same day at no extra charge, tel. 0370-333-0605). For details see the English Heritage website (select "Plan Your Visit," then "Stone Circle Access").

Length of This Tour: Allow at least two hours to see everything.

Services: The visitors center has WCs and a large gift shop. Services at the circle itself are limited to emergency WCs. Even in summer, carry a jacket, as there are no trees to act as a windbreak and there's a reason Salisbury Plain is so green.

Eating: A large **$ café** within the visitors center serves hot drinks, soup, sandwiches, and salads.

◗ SELF-GUIDED TOUR

This commentary is designed to supplement the sight's audioguide. Start by touring the visitors center, then take a shuttle (or walk) to the stone circle. If you arrive early in the day, do the stones first—before they get crowded—then circle back to the visitors center.

• *As you enter the complex, on the right is the...*

Permanent Exhibit

This excellent, state-of-the-art exhibit uses an artful combination of multimedia displays and actual artifacts to provide context for the stones.

You'll begin by standing in the center of a virtual Stonehenge, watching its evolution through 5,000 years—including simulated solstice sunrises and sunsets.

Then you'll head into the exhibits, where prehistoric bones, tools, and pottery shards tell the story of the people who built Stonehenge, how they lived, and why they might have built the stone circle. Find the forensic reconstruction of a Neolithic man, based on a skeleton unearthed in 1863. Small models illustrate how Stonehenge developed from a simple circle of short, stubby stones to the stout ring we know today. And a large screen shows the entire archaeological area surrounding Stonehenge (which is just one of many mysterious prehistoric landmarks near here). In 2010, within sight of Stonehenge, archaeologists discovered another 5,000-year-old henge, which they believe once encircled a wooden "twin" of the famous circle. Recent excavations revealed that people had been living on the site since around 3,000 BC—about five centuries earlier than anyone had realized.

In the small side room, an exhibit examines the iconic status of Stonehenge, including its frequent appearances in popular culture (strangely, no Spinal Tap) and its history as a tourist destination. See the vintage Guinness ad showing smiling people having a picnic on the rocks.

Then step outside and explore a village of reconstructed **Neolithic huts** modeled after the traces of a village discovered just northeast of Stonehenge. Step into the thatched-roof huts to see primitive "wicker" furniture and straw blankets. Docents demonstrate Neolithic tools—made of wood, flint, and antler. You'll also see a huge, life-size replica of the rolling wooden sledge thought to have been used to slo-o-owly roll the stones across

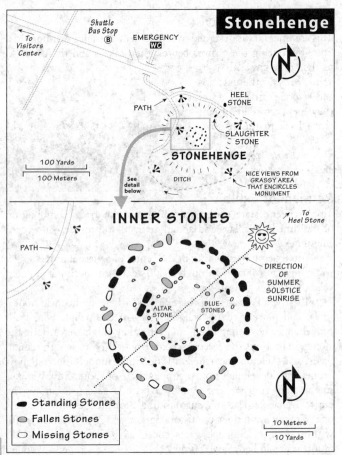

Stonehenge

Shuttle Bus Stop (B)

To Visitors Center

EMERGENCY WC

PATH

HEEL STONE

SLAUGHTER STONE

STONEHENGE

100 Yards
100 Meters

See detail below

DITCH

NICE VIEWS FROM GRASSY AREA THAT ENCIRCLES MONUMENT

INNER STONES

To Heel Stone

PATH →

DIRECTION OF SUMMER SOLSTICE SUNRISE

ALTAR STONE

BLUE-STONES

● Standing Stones
● Fallen Stones
○ Missing Stones

10 Meters
10 Yards

Salisbury Plain. While you can't touch the stones at the site itself, you can touch the one loaded onto this sledge.

• Shuttle buses to the stone circle depart every 5-10 minutes from behind the gift shop (there may be a wait). The trip takes six minutes. If you'd prefer, you can walk 1.5 miles through the fields to the site (use the map you receive with your ticket, or ask a staff member for directions).

Along the way, you have the option of stopping at **Fargo Plantation**, where you can see several burial mounds (tell the shuttle attendant when you first get on if you want to disembark here). After wandering through the burial mounds, you'll need to walk the rest of the way to the stone circle (about 20 minutes).

Stone Circle

As you approach the massive structure, walk right up to the knee-high cordon and let your fellow 21st-century tourists melt away. It's just you and the druids...

England has hundreds of stone circles, but Stonehenge—which literally means "hanging stones"—is unique. It's the only one that has horizontal crosspieces (called lintels) spanning the vertical monoliths, and the only one with stones that have been made smooth and uniform. What you see here is a bit more than half the original structure—the rest was quarried centuries ago for other buildings.

Now do a slow **clockwise spin** around the monument, and ponder the following points. As you walk, mentally flesh out the missing pieces and re-erect the rubble. Knowledgeable guides posted around the site are happy to answer your questions.

It's now believed that Stonehenge, which was built in phases between 3000 and 1500 BC, was originally used as a cremation cemetery. But that's not the end of the story, as the monument was expanded over the millennia. This was a hugely significant location to prehistoric peoples. There are several hundred burial mounds within a three-mile radius of Stonehenge—some likely belonging to kings or chieftains. Some of the human remains are of people from far away, and others show signs of injuries—evidence that Stonehenge may have been used as a place of medicine or healing.

Whatever its original purpose, Stonehenge still functions as a celestial calendar. As the sun rises on the summer solstice (June 21), the **"heel stone"**—the one set apart from the rest, near the road—lines up with the sun and the altar at the center of the stone circle. A study of more than 300 similar circles in Britain found that each was designed to calculate the movement of the sun, moon, and stars, and to predict eclipses in order to help early societies know when to plant, harvest, and party. Even in modern times, as the summer solstice sun sets in just the right slot at Stonehenge, pagans boogie.

Some believe that Stonehenge is built at the precise point where six **"ley lines"** intersect. Ley lines are theoretical lines of magnetic or spiritual power that crisscross the globe. Belief in the power of these lines has gone in and out of fashion over time. They are believed to have been very important to prehistoric peoples, but then were largely ignored until the early 20th century, when the English writer Alfred Watkins popularized them (to the scorn of serious scientists). More recently, the concept has been embraced by the New Age movement. Without realizing it, you follow these ley lines all the time: Many of England's modern highways follow prehistoric paths, and most churches are built over prehistoric monuments—placed where ley lines intersect. If you're a skeptic, ask one of the guides at Stonehenge to explain the mystique of this paranormal tradition that continued for centuries; it's creepy...and convincing.

Notice that two of the stones (facing the shuttle bus stop) are blemished. At the base of one monolith, it looks like someone has pulled back the stone to reveal a concrete skeleton. This is a clumsy **repair job** to fix damage done long ago by souvenir seekers, who actually rented hammers and chisels to take home a piece of Stonehenge. Look to the right of the repaired stone: The back of another stone is missing the same thin layer of protective lichen that covers the others. The lichen—and some of the stone itself—was sandblasted off to remove graffiti. (No wonder they've got Stonehenge roped off now.) The repairs were intentionally done in a different color, so as not to appear like the original stone.

Stonehenge's builders used two different types of stone. The tall, stout monoliths and lintels are sandstone blocks called

sarsen stones. Most of the monoliths weigh about 25 tons (the largest is 45 tons), and the lintels are about 7 tons apiece. These sarsen stones were brought from "only" 20 miles away. Scientists have chemically matched the shorter stones in the middle—called **bluestones**—to outcrops on the south coast of Wales...240 miles away (close if you're taking a train, but far if you're packing a megalith). Imagine the logistical puzzle of floating six-ton stones across Wales' Severn Estuary and up the River Avon, then rolling them on logs about 20 miles to this position...an impressive feat, even in our era of skyscrapers.

Why didn't the builders of Stonehenge use what seem like perfectly adequate stones nearby? This, like many other questions about Stonehenge, remains shrouded in mystery. Think again about the ley lines. Ponder the fact that many experts accept none of the explanations of how these giant stones were transported. Then imagine congregations gathering here 5,000 years ago, raising thought levels, creating a powerful life force transmitted along the ley lines. Maybe a particular kind of stone was essential for maximum energy transmission. Maybe the stones were levitated here. Maybe psychics really do create powerful vibes. Maybe not. It's as unbelievable as electricity used to be.

Salisbury

Salisbury, an attractive small city set in the middle of the expansive Salisbury Plain, is the natural launch pad for visiting nearby Stonehenge. But it's also  a fine destination in its own right, with a walkable core, a famously soaring cathedral (with England's tallest spire and largest green), and a thriving twice-weekly market (Tue and Sat). While well cared for, practical Salisbury isn't particularly cute or quaint. But that's part of its charm.

As the city most associated with Stonehenge, it's no surprise that Salisbury also has a very long history: It was originally settled during the Bronze Age—possibly as early as 600 BC—and later became a Roman town called Sarum (located on a hill above today's city). When the old settlement outgrew its boundaries, the townspeople relocated to the river valley below.

Today, sightseers flow through Salisbury on their way to Stonehenge. But if you have time to spare, spend some of it exploring this fine town.

Orientation to Salisbury

Salisbury (pop. 45,000) stretches along the River Avon in the shadow of its huge landmark cathedral. The heart of the city clusters around the vast Market Place. A few short blocks to the south is the walled complex of the Cathedral Close.

TOURIST INFORMATION

The TI is just off Market Place. If you're headed to Stonehenge, you can buy tickets here (Mon-Fri 9:00-17:00, Sat 10:00-16:00, Sun 10:00-14:00, corner of Fish Row and Queen Street, tel. 01722/342-860, www.visitwiltshire.co.uk).

Ask the TI about the 1.5-hour **city walking tours** (£6, April-

AVEBURY, STONEHENGE & SALISBURY

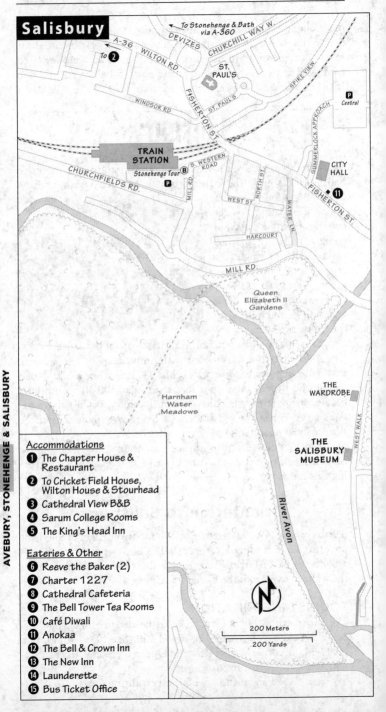

Salisbury

To Stonehenge & Bath via A-360

DEVIZES
CHURCHILL WAY W.
A-36
WILTON RD.
To 2
ST. PAUL'S
SPIRE VIEW
WINDSOR RD.
FISHERTON ST.
ST. PAUL'S

P Central

CHURCHFIELDS RD.
TRAIN STATION
S. WESTERN ROAD
SUMMERLOCK APPROACH
CITY HALL
Stonehenge Tour B
P
MILL RD.
WEST ST.
NORTH ST.
WATER LN.
FISHERTON ST.
♦ 11

HARCOURT

MILL RD.

Queen Elizabeth II Gardens

THE WARDROBE

Harnham Water Meadows

WEST WALK

THE SALISBURY MUSEUM

River Avon

N

200 Meters
200 Yards

<u>Accommodations</u>
1. The Chapter House & Restaurant
2. To Cricket Field House, Wilton House & Stourhead
3. Cathedral View B&B
4. Sarum College Rooms
5. The King's Head Inn

<u>Eateries & Other</u>
6. Reeve the Baker (2)
7. Charter 1227
8. Cathedral Cafeteria
9. The Bell Tower Tea Rooms
10. Café Diwali
11. Anokaa
12. The Bell & Crown Inn
13. The New Inn
14. Launderette
15. Bus Ticket Office

AVEBURY, STONEHENGE & SALISBURY

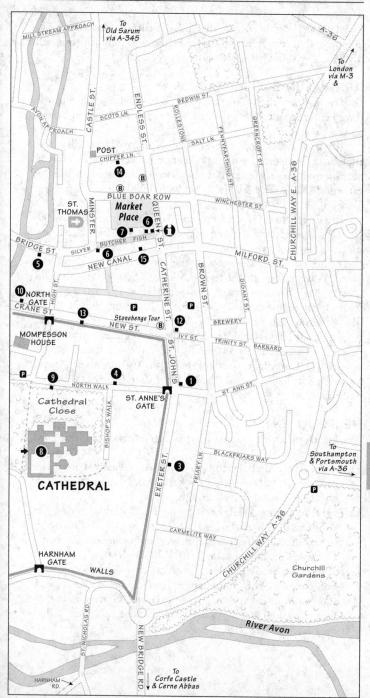

Oct daily at 11:00) or the weekly **Ghost Walk** (£6, May-Sept Fri at 20:00); both depart from the TI. For walking-tour information call 07873/212-941 or visit www.salisburycityguides.co.uk.

ARRIVAL IN SALISBURY

By Train: From the train station, it's a 10-minute walk into the town center: Exit to the left, then bear right on Fisherton Street, and follow it into town.

By Bus: Buses stop at several points along Market Place (on Blue Boar Row) and around the corner on Endless Street. A handy bus information and ticket office is between Market Place and the cathedral (Mon-Fri 8:30-17:00, Sat 9:00-15:00, closed Sun, New Canal 6).

By Car: Drivers will find several pay parking lots. Follow the blue *P* signs (specific parking options, and available spaces, are noted on signs as you approach). To get as close as possible to the cathedral, look for a space at the corner of High Street and North Walk, just inside the cathedral's High Street Gate. The Old George Mall parking garage, between Market Place and the cathedral, is handy, but closes Mon-Sat at 20:00 and Sun at 17:00. The "Central" lot, behind the giant red-brick Sainsbury's store, is farther out but walkable, and has plenty of spaces—even when others are full (enter from Churchill Way West or Castle Street, open 24/7). Overnight, your best bet is the Culver Street garage, located a few blocks east of Market Place (free after 15:00 and all day Sun).

HELPFUL HINTS

Market Days: Don't miss Salisbury's market days (see listing on next page).

Festivals: The **Salisbury International Arts Festival** normally runs for just over two weeks at the end of May and beginning of June (www.salisburyfestival.co.uk).

Laundry: Washing Well has two-hour full service (Mon-Sat 8:00-16:00) as well as self-service (Mon-Sat 15:00-20:30, Sun from 7:00, last self-service wash one hour before closing; bring £1 coins, 28 Chipper Lane, tel. 01722/421-874).

Getting to the Stone Circles: You can get to Stonehenge from Salisbury on **The Stonehenge Tour** double-decker bus in summer or (more expensively) by **taxi** (see "Getting to Stonehenge," earlier). For buses to Avebury's stone circle, see "Salisbury Connections," later.

Sights in Salisbury

ON MARKET PLACE

▲Market Days

For centuries, Salisbury has been known for its lively markets. And today, the big "charter market" still fills the vast Market Place each Tuesday and Saturday (8:00-16:00). This all-purpose market has everything from butchers, fishmongers, and spices to hardware, clothes, and shoes. A little "food court" of international stands is in the center. While fun to browse, this is decidedly not a tourist-oriented market—but it's great for people-watching an age-old tradition still going on in a modern English city. At the top of the square is a handy row of bars and coffee shops with outdoor tables.

Every other Wednesday is the farmers market. And increasingly, the city council has been hosting a variety of other themed markets: Fridays alternate between vintage French products, and "Foodie Friday" (typically once monthly each, 10:00-16:00). And if you brake for garage sales, you'll pull a U-turn for the occasional "Car Boot Sundays." For the latest schedule, see www.salisburycitycouncil.gov.uk.

▲St. Thomas's Church

This Gothic space—short and squat, but still airy and light-filled—boasts an unusual feature: A fully restored "Doom Painting" (illustration of the Last Judgment, c. 1475, over the choir). While these are commonplace in Continental churches, England's were whitewashed and forgotten during the Reformation. But St. Thomas's—long hidden behind the painted wooden coat-of-arms of Queen Elizabeth I, which is now displayed over the red door on the right—was uncovered and restored in the late 19th century. Examine the exquisite, Flemish-style details: Angels pulling the dead from their graves (on the left) to stand before the judgment of Jesus (at the top); some unfortunate souls are sent to the jaws of Hell (on the right)—past the Prince of Darkness, whose toe crosses the edge of the Gothic arch.

Cost and Hours: Free but donation requested, Mon-Sat 9:00-17:00, Sun from 12:00, just west of Market Place on St. Thomas's Square.

ON AND NEAR CATHEDERAL CLOSE

▲▲Salisbury Cathedral

This magnificent cathedral is visible for miles around because of its huge spire (the tallest in England at 404 feet). The surrounding enormous grassy field (called a "close") makes the Gothic master-piece look even larger. What's more impressive is that all this was built in a mere 38 years. When the old hill town of Sarum was

AVEBURY, STONEHENGE & SALISBURY

moved down to the valley, its cathedral had to be replaced in a hurry. So, in 1220, the townspeople began building, and in 1258 their sparkling-new cathedral was ready for ribbon-cutting. Since the structure was built in just a few decades, its style is uniform, rather than the centuries-long patchwork common in cathedrals of the time. The cathedral also displays a remarkably well-preserved original copy of the Magna Carta (in the Chapter House).

Cost and Hours: £7.50 suggested donation, Mon-Sat 9:00-17:00, Sun 12:00-16:00, can be closed for special events. This working cathedral opens early for services: Be respectful if you arrive when one is in session.

Information: Tel. 01722/555-156, www.salisburycathedral.org.uk.

Tours: Free guided tours of the cathedral nave are offered every hour or so, when enough people assemble. Free stained-glass tours run every Monday at 12:00.

Tower Tours: Imagine building a cathedral on this scale before the invention of cranes, bulldozers, or modern scaffolding. An excellent tower tour (1.5-2 hours) helps visitors understand how it was done. You'll climb in between the stone arches and the roof to inspect the vaulting and trussing; see a medieval winch that was used in the construction; and finish with the 332-step climb up the narrow tower for a sweeping view of the Wiltshire countryside. Because only 12 people are allowed on each tour, it's smart to reserve by phone or online a few days ahead—or even longer on summer weekends (£13.50; Mon-Sat hourly 10:15-15:15, Sun at 13:15 and 14:15, fewer tour times Oct-March; tel. 01722/555-156, www.salisburycathedral.org.uk/visit/tower-tours).

Evensong: Salisbury's daily choral evensong (Mon-Sat at 17:30, Sun at 16:30, about 45 minutes) is just as beautiful as the one in Wells Cathedral. Arrive up to 15 minutes early and enter through the north door. Spectators can sit in the nave, or you can ask to be seated in the wood-carved seats of the choir.

Eating: The cathedral has two fine eating options: a glassed-in cafeteria and an outdoor café with prime views (see "Eating in Salisbury," later).

Visiting the Cathedral: Enter through the cloister, around the west side of the building. Entering the church, you'll instantly feel the architectural harmony. Volunteer guides posted strategically throughout the church stand ready to answer your questions. Step into the center of the **nave,** noticing how the stone col-

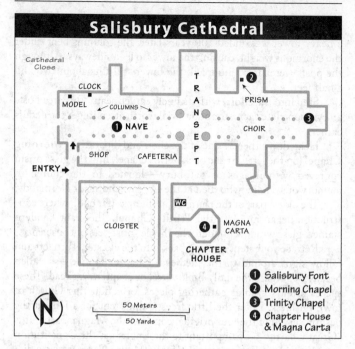

Salisbury Cathedral

Cathedral Close

CLOCK

MODEL

← COLUMNS →

T R A N S E P T

PRISM **2**

1 NAVE

CHOIR

3

SHOP

CAFETERIA

ENTRY →

CLOISTER

WC

4 MAGNA CARTA

CHAPTER HOUSE

50 Meters

50 Yards

1 Salisbury Font
2 Morning Chapel
3 Trinity Chapel
4 Chapter House & Magna Carta

umns march identically down the aisle—like a thick, gray forest of tree trunks. The arches overhead soar to grand heights, helping churchgoers appreciate the vast and amazing heavens. Now imagine the interior surfaces painted in red, blue, green, and gold, as they would have been prior to the whitewashing of the English Reformation.

Head to the far wall (the back-left corner), where an interesting **model** shows how this cathedral was built so quickly in the 13th century. A few steps toward the front of the church is the "oldest working clock in existence," dating from the 14th century (the hourly bell has been removed, so as not to interrupt worship services). On the wall by the clock is a bell from the decommissioned ship HMS *Salisbury*. Look closely inside the bell to see the engraved names of crew members' children who were baptized on the ship.

Wander down the aisle past monuments and knights' tombs, as well as tombstones set into the floor. About halfway down the nave, you'll see (and hear) the gurgling **Salisbury Font**—a modern, oxidized-bronze baptismal font dedicated in 2008 to honor the cathedral's 750th birthday. While it looks like a modern sculpture, it's also used for baptisms—one of many ways in which it's clear that this church is full of life.

When you reach the transept, gape up at the **columns.** These posts were supposed to support a more modest bell tower, but when a heavy tower was added 100 years later, the columns bent under the enormous weight, causing the tower to lean sideways. Although the posts were later reinforced, the tower still tilts about two and a half feet.

Step into the **choir,** with its finely carved seats. This area hosts an evensong late each afternoon (well worth attending—see details earlier).

Head down the left side of the choir and dip into the **Morning Chapel** (on the left). At the back of this chapel, find the glass prism engraved with images of Salisbury—donated to the church in memory of a soldier who died at the D-Day landing at Normandy.

The oldest part of the church is at the apse (far end), where construction began in 1220: the **Trinity Chapel.** The giant, modern stained-glass window ponders the theme "prisoners of conscience."

Retrace your steps and exit back into the cloister. Turn left and follow signs around to the medieval **Chapter House**—so called because it's where the daily Bible verse, or chapter, was read. These spaces often served as gathering places for conducting church or town business. Enter the little freestanding tent for a look at the best preserved of the four original copies of the Magna Carta. This "Great Charter" is as important to the English as the Constitution is to Americans. Dating from 1215, the Magna Carta settled a dispute between England's King John and some powerful barons by guaranteeing that the monarch was not above the law. To this day, lawyers and political scientists admire this very early example of "checks and balances"—a major victory in the centuries-long tug-of-war between monarchs and nobles. Notice the smudge marks on the glass case, where historians have bumped their noses squinting at the minuscule script.

▲Cathedral Close

The enormous green surrounding the cathedral is the largest in England, and one of the loveliest. It's cradled in the elbow of the

River Avon and ringed by row houses, cottages, and grand mansions. The church owns the houses on the green and rents them to lucky people with holy connections. A former prime minister, Edward Heath, lived on the green, not because of his political influence, but because he was once the church organist.

The benches scattered around the green are an excellent place for having a romantic moonlit picnic or for gazing thoughtfully at the leaning spire. Although you may be tempted to linger until it's late, don't—this is still private church property...and the heavy medieval gates of the close shut at about 22:00.

A few houses are open to the public, such as the overpriced Mompesson House and the medieval Wardrobe. The most interesting is...

▲The Salisbury Museum

Occupying the building just opposite the cathedral entry, this eclectic and sprawling collection was heralded by American expat travel writer Bill Bryson as one of England's best. While that's a stretch, the museum does offer a little something for everyone.

Cost and Hours: £8; Mon-Sat 10:00-17:00, Sun from 12:00 except closed Sun Oct-May; check with desk about occasional tours, 65 The Close, tel. 01722/332-151, www.salisburymuseum.org.uk.

Visiting the Museum: The highlight is the Wessex Gallery (to the left as you enter), with informative, interactive exhibits covering this area's rich prehistory—from Neanderthal ax heads to Iron Age cremation urns. Check out the ancient Roman mosaic floor and sarcophagus, and the sculpture fragments from the original Old Sarum cathedral. One exhibit details the excavation of Stonehenge, which began as early as 1620—back when it was believed to be Roman rather than druid.

The museum continues to the right of the entry, with a musty, dimly lit but endearing collection of Salisbury's historic bric-a-brac—including the true-to-its-name "Salisbury Giant" puppet once used by the tailors' guild during parades, and some J. M. W. Turner paintings of the cathedral interior. Upstairs is a historical clothing exhibit and a collection of exquisite Wedgwood china and other ceramics.

JUST OUTSIDE SALISBURY

These two rewarding sights are practically on Salisbury's doorstep—within a 10-minute drive of Market Place. While neither is worth planning your day around, either can easily be combined with a trip to or from Stonehenge.

Old Sarum

Today, little remains of the original town of Old Sarum, but a little imagination can transport you back to *very* Olde England. The city was originally founded on a slope overlooking the plain below. Uniquely, it combined both a castle and a cathedral within an Iron Age fortification. Old Sarum was eventually abandoned, leaving only a few stone foundations. The grand views of Salisbury from here have in-"spired" painters for ages and provided countless picnickers with a scenic backdrop (bring lunch or snacks).

Cost and Hours: £5.40; daily 10:00-18:00, Oct until 17:00, Nov-March until 16:00; tel. 01722/335-398, www.english-heritage.org.uk.

Getting There: It's on the edge of Salisbury, two miles north of the city center off the A-345. The Stonehenge Tour bus stops here (see "Getting to Stonehenge," earlier), or you can take either bus #X5 or the Activ8 bus, both run by Salisbury Reds (www.salisburyreds.co.uk).

Background: Human settlement in this area stretches back to the Bronze Age, and the Romans, Saxons, and Normans all called this hilltop home. From about 500 BC through AD 1220, Old Sarum flourished, giving rise to a motte-and-bailey castle, a cathedral, and scores of wooden homes along the town's outer ring. The town grew so quickly that by the Middle Ages, it had outgrown its spot on the hill. In 1220, the local bishop successfully petitioned to move the entire city to the valley below, where space and water were plentiful. So, stone by stone, Old Sarum was packed up and shipped to New Sarum, where builders used nearly all the rubble from the old city to create a brand-new town with a magnificent cathedral.

Visiting the Site: From the parking lot or bus stop, you'll cross over the former moat to reach the core of Old Sarum. Inside you'll find a few scant walls and foundations. Colorful information plaques help resurrect the rubble. Additional ruins line the road between the site and the main road.

▲Wilton House and Garden

This sprawling estate, with a grand mansion and tidy gardens, has been owned by the Earls of Pembroke since King Henry VIII's time. The Pembrokes are a classy clan, and—unlike the many borderline-scruffy aristocratic homes in Britain—their home and garden are in exquisite repair and oozing with pride. Jane Austen fans particularly enjoy this stately home, where parts of 2005's Oscar-nominated *Pride and Prejudice* were filmed. But, alas, Mr. Darcy has checked out. Note the unusual weekend closure—the Pembrokes like to have the place to themselves on Fridays and Saturdays.

Cost and Hours: House and gardens—£15.50, gardens only—£6.50; open Easter weekend and Sun-Thu in May-Aug (house open 11:30-17:00, gardens 11:00-17:30), closed Fri-Sat and all of Sept-April; tel. 01722/746-728, www.wiltonhouse.co.uk.

Getting There: It's five miles west of Salisbury via the A-36, to Wilton's Minster Street. You can also reach it on Salisbury Reds bus #R3, park-and-ride bus #PR3, or—on Sundays—Salisbury Reds bus #3.

Visiting the Estate: The first stop is the **Old Riding School,**

which houses a faintly interesting (but skippable) 15-minute film about the family and their house, and a fine collection of luxury cars old and new.

Inside the **mansion,** you'll tour several gorgeous rooms decorated with classical sculpture and paintings by Rubens, Rembrandt, Van Dyck, and Brueghel. You'll also see plenty of family portraits and some quirky odds and ends, such as a series of paintings of the Spanish Riding School, and a lock of Queen Elizabeth I's hair. The perfectly proportioned Double Cube Room has served as everything from a 17th-century state dining room to a secret D-Day planning room during World War II...if only the portraits could talk. Fortunately, the docents posted in each room do—since there's no posted information, be sure to ask plenty of questions.

You'll exit to the garden—flat and perfectly tended, with pebbly paths and a golf course-quality lawn, stretching along the gurgling River Nadder and decorated with a few Neoclassical ornaments.

Nearby: The village of Wilton itself is a proud, workaday burg that's fun to explore. It boasts the Wilton House at one end of town, a cozy green at its center, and at the far end of town, the Italianate **Church of Sts. Mary and Nicholas**—dating from the Romantic period of the mid-19th century, when world travelers brought some of their favorite styles back home. The can't-miss-it church, along West Street, looks like it'd be more at home in the Veneto than on Salisbury Plain.

Sleeping in Salisbury

Salisbury's town center has very few accommodations. Noisy roads rumble past most of these places: Light sleepers can try asking for a quieter room in back (or pack earplugs). Drivers should ask about parking when reserving. The town gets particularly crowded during the arts festival (late May through early June). If you're in a pinch, there's a **Premier Inn** two miles outside of town.

$$$ The Chapter House is a boutique hotel with 17 stylish, modern rooms in a creaky old shell. The rooms are above their trendy restaurant, immediately across from the side entrance to the Cathedral Close (9 St. John's Street, tel. 01722/341-277, www. thechapterhouseuk.com).

$$$ Cricket Field House, a cozy little compound just outside of town on the A-36 toward Wilton, overlooks a cricket pitch and golf course. It has 10 large, comfortable rooms, its own gorgeous garden, and plenty of parking (Wilton Road, tel. 01722/322-595, www.cricketfieldhouse.co.uk, cricketfieldcottage@btinternet.com; Brian and Margaret James). While this place works best for drivers, it's a 20-minute walk from the train station or a five-minute bus ride from the city center.

$$ Cathedral View B&B is a classic, traditional B&B renting four rooms just off the Cathedral Close. Wenda and Steve are generous with travel tips, and Steve is an armchair town historian with lots of insights (cash only, 2-night minimum on weekends, no kids under age 10, 83 Exeter Street, tel. 01722/502-254, www.cathedral-viewbandb.co.uk, info@cathedral-viewbandb.co.uk).

$$ Sarum College is a theological college that rents 40 rooms in its building right on the peaceful Cathedral Close. Much of the year, it houses visitors to the college, but it usually has rooms for tourists as well. The well-worn, slightly institutional but clean rooms share hallways with libraries, bookstores, and offices; the five attic rooms come with dramatic cathedral views from their dormer windows (meals available, elevator, limited free parking, 19 The Close, tel. 01722/424-800, www.sarum.ac.uk, hospitality@sarum.ac.uk).

$$ The King's Head Inn rents 33 modern rooms above a chain Wetherspoon pub. While impersonal, it's a decent value and conveniently located—in a handsome old sandstone building between Market Place and the train station—and likely to have room when others are full (breakfast extra, deeply discounted Sun nights, aircon, elevator to some rooms, 1 Bridge Street, tel. 01722/438-400, www.jdwetherspoon.com, kingsheadinn@jdwetherspoon.co.uk).

Eating in Salisbury

There are plenty of atmospheric pubs all over town. For the best variety of restaurants, head to the Market Place area. Some places offer "early bird" specials before 19:00.

$ Reeve the Baker crafts an array of high-calorie delights and handy pick-me-ups for a fast and affordable lunch. Peruse the long cases of pastries and savory treats, and notice the locals waiting patiently at the fresh bread counter in back (Mon-Sat 7:30-17:30, Sun 10:00-16:00, tel. 01722/320-367). The main branch, on Market Place (at 2 Butcher Row), has seating both upstairs and out on the square—either with a nice view of the busy market. A much smaller second branch is at the corner of Market and Bridge streets at 61 Silver Street.

$$$ The Chapter House is a lively and popular restaurant with an enticing menu of British, South African, and international fare in a trendy setting (Mon-Sat 12:00-15:00 & 18:00-22:00, Sun until 20:00, 9 St. John's Street, tel. 01722/341-277).

$$$$ Charter 1227 is a high-end splurge (by Salisbury standards) filling a contemporary dining room upstairs, overlooking Market Place. The short, selective menu is much more affordable at lunch for their midweek "early bird" specials (open Tue-Sat 12:00-14:30 & 18:00-21:30, closed Sun-Mon, lunch specials Tue-Thu, reservations smart, 6 Ox Row, enter from Market Place, tel. 01722/333-118, www.charter1227.co.uk).

At the Cathedral: For lunch near the cathedral, you have two great choices. The **$ cafeteria** has a full menu and fills a winter garden squeezed between the buttresses and the cloister, with additional seating in the cloister itself (open same hours as cathedral). But on a sunny day, it's hard to imagine a nicer setting than **$ The Bell Tower Tea Rooms,** with outdoor tables on England's biggest close, peering up at its tallest cathedral tower (drinks, deli sandwiches, and affordable teas—£5.50 cream tea, afternoon tea is £24/2 people; choose a table, then order at the counter; daily 10:00-17:00).

Indian: If you're going to try Indian food, do it in Salisbury. These two excellent options both serve creative variations on the typical "curry house" fare: **$$$ Café Diwali** takes an "Indian street food" approach, with delicious, creative dishes served thali-style, on big silver platters (daily 12:00-14:00 & 18:00-22:30, 90 Crane Street, tel. 01722/329-700). And **$$$ Anokaa** serves updated Indian cuisine in a dressy, contemporary setting (daily 12:00-14:00 & 17:30-23:00, 60 Fisherton Street, tel. 01722/414-142). ·

Pubs: $$ The Bell & Crown Inn is the best all-around choice, with reliable pub fare and atmosphere, and leather couches under heavy beams (daily 11:00-23:00, 83 Catherine Street, tel. 01722/338-102). **$$ The New Inn,** the local rugby pub, fills a creaky, atmospheric, 15th-century house rumored to have a tunnel leading directly into the cathedral—perhaps dug while the building housed a brothel? On a sunny day, their back garden is pleasant (daily 12:00-15:00 & 18:00-21:00, 41 New Street, tel. 01722/326-662).

Salisbury Connections

From Salisbury by Train to: London's Waterloo Station (2/hour, 1.5 hours), **Bath** (hourly direct, 1 hour). Train info: tel. 0345-748-4950, www.nationalrail.co.uk.

By Bus to: Bath (hourly, 3 hours, www.travelinesw.com), **Avebury** (hourly, 2 hours, transfer in Devizes, www.travelinesw.com). Many of Salisbury's long-distance buses are run by Salisbury Reds (tel. 01722/336-855 or 01202/338-420, www.salisburyreds.co.uk).

Near Salisbury

The most appealing sights in the Salisbury area are Stonehenge and Avebury. But if you have extra time here (or en route to your next stop), these attractions are worth considering. While best for drivers, and not worth going out of your way to see, they may appeal if you have a special interest in gardens, ruined castles, or cute villages.

Stourhead House and Gardens

Stourhead, designed by owner Henry Hoare II in the mid-18th century, is a sprawling 2,650-acre estate of rolling hills, meandering paths, placid lakes, and colorful trees, punctuated by classically inspired bridges and monuments. The creaky old mansion strains to make its obscure aristocratic owners interesting (with eager docents in each room), but the gardens are the real highlight: Take a two-mile loop hike around the lake.

Cost and Hours: £17.50 includes house and garden; house open daily 11:00-16:30, garden open daily 9:00-18:00, closes earlier off-season; parking-£4, tel. 01747/841-152, www.nationaltrust.org.uk. It's 28 miles (40 minutes) west of Salisbury in the village of Stourton.

Corfe Castle

Built by William the Conqueror in the 11th century, this castle was a favorite residence for medieval kings until it was destroyed by a massive gunpowder blast during a 17th-century siege. Today its jagged ruins cap a steep, conical hill, offering a fun excuse for a hike and sweeping views over the Dorset countryside. Park at the Castle View visitors center, then follow the path that curls around the back of the castle to the village (about 10 minutes). There you can buy your ticket, cross the drawbridge, and hike up. The castle is mostly an empty husk, with little to bring its dramatic history to life, but it's fun to scramble along its rocky remnants.

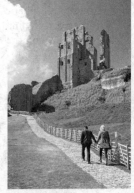

Cost and Hours: £10, daily 10:00-18:00, closes earlier off-season, tel. 01929/481-294, www.nationaltrust.org.uk. It's 44 miles (about one hour) south of Salisbury.

▲Cerne Abbas

Dorset County's most adorable village is cuddly, one-street Cerne Abbas (surn AB-iss)—about 45 miles (one hour) southwest of Salisbury. It's lined with half-timbered buildings and draped with ivy and wisteria. Park your car and go for a walk. Head up Abbey Street, passing the lovely St. Mary's Church on your way up to the village's namesake abbey. Let yourself in the gate and explore the mysterious, beautiful grounds. If you need a break, the town has some appealing pubs and the fine Abbots Tearoom (7 Long Street, tel. 01300/341-349).

The village is best known for the large chalk figure that's scraped into a nearby hillside: the famous **Cerne Abbas Giant.**

(To find it, head up the street just past Abbots Tearoom—by car or by foot; you can also follow brown road signs to *Giant Viewpoint*.) Chalk figures such as this one can be found in many parts of the region. Because the soil is only a few inches deep, the overlying grass and dirt can easily be removed to expose the bright white chalk bedrock beneath, creating the outlines. While nobody is sure exactly how old this figure is, or what its original purpose was, the giant is faithfully maintained by the locals, who mow and clear the fields at least once a year. This particular figure, possibly a fertility god, looks friendly...maybe a little too friendly. Locals claim that if a woman who's having trouble getting pregnant sleeps on the giant for one night, she will soon be able to conceive a child.

The area around Cerne Abbas can be fun to explore—with names seemingly invented on a bet by pub patrons on tuppence-ale night. Piddle Lane leads out of town to villages with names like Piddletrenthide, Piddlehinton (both on the aptly named River Piddle), Plush, Mappowder, Ansty, Lower Ansty, and, of course, Higher Ansty. More entertainment rewards careful map-readers in the surrounding hills: King's Stag, Fifehead Neville, Maiden Newton, Hazelbury Bryan, Poopton-upon-Piddle, Stock Gaylard, Bishop's Caundle, Alton Pancras, Melbury Bubb, Beer Hackett, Sturminster Newton, Nether Cerne, and Margaret Marsh. Believe it or not, only one of these names is made up.

THE COTSWOLDS

Chipping Campden • Stow-on-the-Wold •
Moreton-in-Marsh • Blenheim Palace

The Cotswold Hills, a 25-by-90-mile chunk of Gloucestershire, are dotted with enchanting villages and graced with Britain's greatest countryside palace, Blenheim. As with many fairy-tale regions of Europe, the present-day beauty of the Cotswolds is the result of an economic disaster. Wool was a huge industry in medieval England, and Cotswold sheep grew the best wool. (The famed Cotswold Lion breed goes back to ancient times when Romans bred one of their sheep with the indigenous breed to make a hybrid version that was big, bad for meat, and great for wool.) A 12th-century saying bragged, "In Europe the best wool is English. In England the best wool is Cotswold." The region prospered. Wool money built fine towns and houses. Local "wool" churches are called "cathedrals" for their scale and wealth. Stained-glass slogans say things like "I thank my God and ever shall, it is the sheep hath paid for all."

But with the rise of cotton and the Industrial Revolution, the woolen industry collapsed. The wealthy Cotswold towns fell into a depressed time warp; the homes of impoverished nobility became gracefully dilapidated. Today, visitors enjoy a harmonious blend of man and nature—the most pristine of English countrysides decorated with time-passed villages, rich wool churches, tell-me-a-story stone fences, and "kissing gates" you

wouldn't want to experience alone. Appreciated by throngs of 21st-century Romantics, the Cotswolds are enjoying new prosperity as rural-rooted citizens have been joined by wealthy retirees, London executives who don't mind a lengthy commute, and celebrities.

The north Cotswolds are best. Two of the region's coziest towns, Chipping Campden and Stow-on-the-Wold, are eight and four miles, respectively, from Moreton-in-Marsh, which has the best public transportation connections. Any of these three towns makes a fine home base for your exploration of the thatch-happiest of Cotswold villages and walks.

PLANNING YOUR TIME

The Cotswolds are an absolute delight by car and, with a well-organized plan—and patience—are enjoyable even without one. Do your homework in advance; read this chapter carefully. Then decide if you want to rent a car, rely on public transportation (budgeting for an inevitable taxi ride), or reserve a day with a tour company or private driver. Whatever you choose, on a three-week countrywide trip, I'd spend at least two nights and a day in the Cotswolds—its charm has a softening effect on many uptight itineraries. You could enjoy days of walking from a home base here.

Home Bases: Quaint without being overrun, **Chipping Campden** and **Stow-on-the-Wold** both have good accommodations. Stow has a bit more character for an overnight stay and offers the widest range of choices. The plainer town of **Moreton-in-Marsh** is the only one of the three with a train station, and only worth visiting as a transit hub. While Moreton has the most convenient connections, it's possible for nondrivers to home-base in Chipping Campden or Stow—especially if you don't mind sorting through bus schedules or springing for the occasional taxi to connect towns. (This becomes even more challenging on Sundays, when there is essentially no bus service.) These three towns are a 10- to 15-minute drive apart from each other.

Tourist Traps (Broadway, Bourton-on-the-Water, and Bibury): Mass tourism is channeled to a handful of towns that cater to big buses and their groups. Known as "The Bs," this trio of village cuteness has invested in convenient coach lots (the *terra firma* equivalent of cruise-ship docks), and they're capitalizing on their over-the-top quaintness and fame. Expect traffic congestion and lots of crowds during the day as most visitors are day-tripping from London or Stratford. If flexible, enjoy these towns at the end of the day when they're relaxed and quiet.

Nearby Sights: Britain's top countryside palace, **Blenheim**, is located at the eastern edge of the Cotswolds, between Moreton and Oxford (see the end of this chapter). For drivers, Blenheim fits well on the way into or out of the region. If you want to take in some Shakespeare, note that Stow, Chipping Campden, and Moreton are only a 30-minute drive from **Stratford,** which offers a great evening of world-class entertainment (see next chapter).

One-Day Driver's Cotswold Blitz: Use a good map and re-shuffle this plan to fit your home base:

9:00   Browse through Chipping Campden, following my self-guided walk.

10:30   Joyride through Snowshill, Stanway, and Stanton, sightseeing at your choice of several worthwhile stops in the area.

13:00   Have lunch in Stow-on-the-Wold, then follow my self-guided walk there.

16:00   Drive to the Slaughters and Bourton-on-the-Water or Northleach; or, if you're up for a hike instead of a drive, walk from Stow to the Slaughters to Bourton, then catch the bus back to Stow.

19:00   Have dinner at a countryside gastropub (reserve in advance), then head home; or drive 30 minutes to Stratford-upon-Avon for a Shakespeare play.

Two-Day Plan by Public Transportation: This plan is best for any day except Sunday—when virtually no buses run—and assumes you're home-basing in Moreton-in-Marsh.

Day 1: Take the morning bus to Chipping Campden (likely departing around 9:30) to explore that town. Hike up Dover's Hill and back (about one hour round-trip), or take the bus to Mickleton and walk (uphill, 45 minutes) to Hidcote Manor Garden for a visit there. Eat lunch in Chipping Campden, then squeeze in either Broad Campden or Broadway before returning directly from Broadway (bus #1 only) or Chipping Campden (bus #1 or #2) to Moreton.

Day 2: Take a day trip to Blenheim Palace via Hanborough (train to Hanborough, bus to palace—explained on page 392). Or take a morning bus to Stow. After poking around the town, hike from Stow through the Slaughters to Bourton-on-the-Water (about 3 hours at a relaxed pace), then return by bus or taxi to Moreton for dinner.

TOURIST INFORMATION

Local TIs stock a wide array of helpful resources and can tell you about any local events during your stay. Ask for the *Cotswold Lion* (or download the PDF from www.cotswoldsaonb.org.uk/about-us), the biannual magazine that includes listings for guided walks and hikes, events, and festivals. Each village also has its own assortment of brochures, often for a small fee. While being asked to pay for these items seems chintzy, realize that Cotswold TIs have lost much of their government funding and are struggling to make ends meet (some are run by volunteers). Most also sell Ordnance Survey maps prepared by the British government that are ideal for hiking. The "OS Maps" app has free basic maps of the region, and any purchase of a paper OS map comes with a code for a free digital version through the app.

GETTING AROUND THE COTSWOLDS
By Car

Joyriding here truly is a joy. Winding country roads seem designed to spring bucolic village-and-countryside scenes on the driver at every turn. Distances are wonderfully short, and easily navigable with GPS. As a backup, you could invest in the Ordnance Survey map of the Cotswolds, sold locally at TIs and newsstands (the £9 Explorer OL #45 map is excellent but geared toward hiking and is too detailed for drivers; a £5 tour map covers a wider area in less detail). Here are driving distances from Moreton: **Stow-on-the-Wold** (4 miles), **Chipping Campden** (8 miles), **Broadway** (10 miles), **Stratford-upon-Avon** (17 miles), **Warwick** (23 miles), **Blenheim Palace** (20 miles).

Car hiking is great. In this chapter, I cover the postcard-perfect (but discovered) villages. With a car and a good map (either GPS or the local Ordnance Survey), you can easily ramble about and find your own gems. The problem with having a car is that you are less likely to walk. Consider taking a taxi or bus somewhere, so that you can walk back to your car and enjoy the scenery (see suggestions next).

By Bus

The Cotswolds are so well preserved, in part, because public transportation to and within this area has long been miserable. Fortunately, trains link the region to larger towns, and a few key buses connect the more interesting villages. Centrally located Moreton-in-Marsh is the region's transit hub—with the only train station and several bus lines.

To explore the towns, use the bus routes that hop through the Cotswolds about every 1.5 hours, lacing together main stops and ending at train stations. In each case, the entire trip takes about an hour. Individual fares are around £4. If you plan on taking more than two rides in a day, consider the Cotswolds Discoverer pass, which offers unlimited travel on most buses including those listed next (£10/day, www.escapetothecotswolds.org.uk/discoverer).

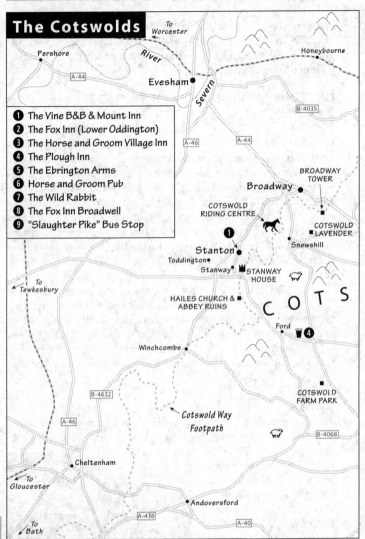

The Cotswolds

1. The Vine B&B & Mount Inn
2. The Fox Inn (Lower Oddington)
3. The Horse and Groom Village Inn
4. The Plough Inn
5. The Ebrington Arms
6. Horse and Groom Pub
7. The Wild Rabbit
8. The Fox Inn Broadwell
9. "Slaughter Pike" Bus Stop

The TI hands out easy-to-read bus schedules for the key lines described here (or check www.traveline.info, or call the Traveline info line, tel. 0871-200-2233). Put together a one-way or return trip by public transportation, making for a fine Cotswold day. If you're traveling one-way between two train stations, remember that the Cotswold villages—generally pretty clueless when it comes to the needs of travelers without a car—have no official baggage-check services. You'll need to improvise; ask sweetly at the nearest TI or business.

Note that no single bus connects the three major towns de-

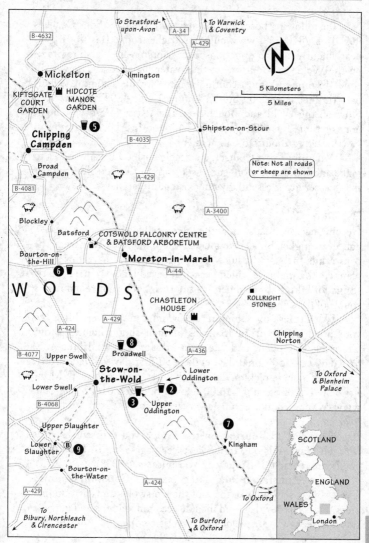

scribed in this chapter (Chipping Campden, Stow, and Moreton); to get between Chipping Campden and Stow, you'll have to change buses in Moreton. Since buses can be unreliable and connections aren't timed, it may be better to call a driver or taxi to go between Chipping Campden and Stow.

The following bus lines are operated by Johnsons Excelbus (tel. 01564/797-070, www.johnsonscoaches.co.uk): Buses **#1** and **#2** run from Moreton-in-Marsh to Blockley (#1 also stops in Broadway) on their way to Chipping Campden, and pass through Mickleton before ending at Stratford-upon-Avon.

The following buses are operated by Pulham & Sons Coaches (tel. 01451/820-369, www.pulhamscoaches.com): Bus **#801** goes nearly hourly in both directions from Moreton-in-Marsh to Stow-on-the-Wold to Bourton-on-the-Water (connecting towns in about 15 minutes); most continue on to Northleach and Cheltenham (limited service on Sun in summer). Bus **#802** runs between Stow-on-the-Wold and Bourton-on-the-Water (4-5/day, 1 hour, none on Sun). Bus **#855** goes from Moreton-in-Marsh and Stow to Northleach to Bibury to Cirencester.

Warning: Leave yourself a sizeable cushion if using buses to make another connection (such as a train to London). Remember that bus service is essentially nonexistent on Sundays.

By Bike

Despite narrow roads, high hedgerows (blocking some views), and even higher hills, bikers enjoy the Cotswolds free from the constraints of bus schedules. For each area, TIs have fine route planners that indicate which peaceful, paved lanes are particularly scenic for biking. In summer, it's smart to book your rental bike a couple of days ahead.

TY Cycles in Chipping Norton can deliver bikes to your hotel if it's within 15 miles of their shop (includes Stow, Chipping Campden, and Moreton-in-Marsh; hybrid bike-£25/first day, £15/additional day; ebike-£50/first day, £30/additional day; rates include pickup, delivery, helmet, lock, and map; Mon-Fri 8:30-17:00, Sat until 16:00, closed Sun, tel. 01608/238 150, www.tycycles.co.uk, enquiries@tycycles.co.uk, Tom and Rob Yeatman,).

If you make it to **Bourton-on-the-Water,** you can rent bicycles through **Hartwells** on High Street (see page 380). In **Broadway,** ebikes are rentable at **Broadway Tower** (see page 358).

If you're interested in a biking vacation, **Cotswold Country Cycles** offers self-led bike tours of the Cotswolds and surrounding areas (tours last 3-7 days and include accommodations and luggage transfer, see www.cotswoldcountrycycles.com).

By Foot

Walking guidebooks and leaflets abound, giving you a world of choices for each of my recommended stops. If you're doing any hiking whatsoever, get the excellent Ordnance Survey Explorer OL #45 map, which shows every road, trail, and ridgeline (£9 at local TIs). Nearly every hotel and B&B offers hiking advice and has a box or shelf of local walking guides and maps, including Ordnance Survey #45. Don't hesitate to ask for a loaner. For a quick **circular hike** from a particular village, peruse the books and brochures offered by that village's TI, or search online for maps and route descriptions; one good website is www.nationaltrail.co.uk—select "Cotswold Way," then "Be Inspired," then "Circular Walks." Villages are generally no more than three miles apart, and most have pubs that would love to feed and water you.

For a list of **guided walks,** ask at any TI for the free *Cotswold Lion* magazine or visit www.cotswoldsaonb.org.uk. The walks range from 2 to 12 miles, and often involve a stop at a pub or tearoom.

Another option is to leave the planning to a company such as **Cotswold Walking Holidays,** which can help you design a walking vacation, provide route instructions and maps, transfer your bags, and even arrange lodging. They also offer six-night walking tours that come with a local guide. Walking through the towns allows you to slow down and enjoy the Cotswolds at their very best—experiencing open fields during the day and arriving into towns just as the day-trippers depart (www.cotswoldwalks.com).

There are many options for hikers, ranging from the "Cotswold Way" path that leads 100 miles from Chipping Campden all the way to Bath, to easy loop trips to the next village. Serious hikers enjoy doing a several-day loop, walking for several hours each day and sleeping in a different village each night.

One popular route is the **"Cotswold Ring":** Day 1—Moreton-in-Marsh to Stow-on-the-Wold to the Slaughters to Bourton-on-the-Water (12 miles); Day 2—Bourton-on-the-Water to Winchcombe (13 miles); Day 3—Winchcombe to Stanway to Stanton (7 miles), or all the way to Broadway (10.5 miles total); Day 4—On to Chipping Campden (just 5.5 miles); Day 5—Chipping Campden to Broad Campden, Blockley, Bourton-on-the-Hill, or Batsford, and back to Moreton (7 miles).

Realistically, on a short visit, you won't have time for that much hiking. But if you have a few hours to spare, consider venturing across the pretty hills and meadows of the Cotswolds. Each of the home-base villages I recommend has several options. Stow-on-the-Wold, immersed in pleasant but not-too-hilly terrain, is within easy walking distance of several interesting spots and is probably the best starting point. Chipping Campden sits along a ridge, which means that hikes from there are extremely scenic, but also more strenuous. Moreton—true to its name—sits on a marsh, offering flatter and less picturesque hikes.

Recommended Hikes

Here are a few hikes to consider, in order of difficulty (easiest first). I've selected these for their convenience to the home-base towns and because the start and/or end points are on bus lines, allowing you to hitch a ride back to where you started (or on to the next town) rather than backtracking by foot.

Cotswold Appreciation 101

History can be read into the names of the area. *Cotswold* could come from the Saxon phrase meaning "hills of sheep's cotes" (shelters for sheep). Or it could mean shelter ("cot" like cottage) on the open upland ("wold").

In the Cotswolds, a town's main street (called High Street) needed to be wide to accommodate the sheep and cattle being marched to market. Some of the most picturesque cottages were once humble row houses of weavers' cottages, usually located along a stream for their waterwheels (good examples in Bibury and Lower Slaughter). The towns run on slow clocks and yellowed calendars.

Fields of yellow (rapeseed) and pale blue (linseed) separate pastures dotted with black and white sheep. In just about any B&B, when you open your window in the morning, you'll hear sheep baa-ing. The decorative "toadstool" stones dotting front yards throughout the region are medieval staddle stones, which buildings were set upon to keep the rodents out.

Cotswold walls and roofs are made of the local limestone. The limestone roof tiles hang by pegs. To make the weight more bearable, smaller and lighter tiles are higher up. An extremely strict building code keeps towns looking what many locals call "overly quaint."

Stow, the Slaughters, and Bourton-on-the-Water: Walk from Stow to Upper and Lower Slaughter, then on to Bourton-on-the-Water (which has bus service back to Stow on #801 or #802). One big advantage of this walk is that it's mostly downhill (4 miles, about 2-3 hours one-way). For details, see page 372.

Chipping Campden, Broad Campden, Blockley, and Bourton-on-the-Hill: From Chipping Campden, it's an easy mile walk into charming Broad Campden, and from there, a more strenuous hike to Blockley and Bourton-on-the-Hill (Blockley is connected by buses #1 and #2 to Chipping Campden and Moreton). For more details, see page 349.

Winchcombe, Stanway, Stanton, and Broadway: You can reach the charming villages of Stanway and Stanton by foot, but it's tough going—lots of up and down. The start and end points (Winchcombe and Broadway) have limited bus connections, and in a pinch some buses do serve Stanton (but carefully check schedules before you set out).

While you'll still see lots of sheep, the commercial wool industry is essentially dead. It costs more to shear a sheep than the 50 pence the wool will fetch. In the old days, sheep lived long lives, producing lots of wool. When they were finally slaughtered, the meat was tough and eaten as "mutton." Today, you don't find mutton much because the sheep are raised primarily for their meat, and slaughtered younger. When it comes to Cotswold sheep these days, it's lamb (not mutton) for dinner (not sweaters).

Towns are small, and everyone seems to know everyone. The area is provincial yet ever-so-polite, and people commonly rescue themselves from a gossipy tangent by saying, "It's all very...mmm...yaaa."

In contrast to the village ambience are the giant manors and mansions whose private gated driveways you'll drive past. Many of these now belong to A-list celebrities, who have country homes here. If you live in the Cotswolds, you can call Madonna, Elizabeth Hurley, and Kate Moss your neighbors.

This is walking country. The English love their walks and vigorously defend their age-old right to free passage. Once a year the Ramblers, Britain's largest walking club, organizes a "Mass Trespass," when each of the country's 50,000 miles of public footpaths is walked. By assuring that each path is used at least once a year, they stop landlords from putting up fences. Any paths found blocked are unceremoniously unblocked.

Questions to ask locals: Do you think foxhunting should have been banned? Who are the Morris men? What's a kissing gate?

Broadway to Chipping Campden: The hardiest hike of those I list here, this takes you along the Cotswold Ridge. Attempt it only if you're a serious hiker (5.5 miles).

Bibury and the Coln Valley are pretty, but limited bus access makes hiking there less appealing.

By Taxi or Private Driver

Two or three town-to-town taxi trips can make more sense than renting a car. While taking a cab cross-country seems extravagant, the distances are short (Stow to Moreton is 4 miles, Stow to Chipping Campden is 10), and one-way walks are lovely. If you call a cab, confirm that the meter will start only when you are actually picked up. Consider hiring a private driver at the hourly "touring rate" (generally around £35), rather than the meter rate. For a few more bucks than taking a taxi, you can have a joyride peppered with commentary. Whether you book a taxi or a private driver,

The Cotswolds at a Glance

Chipping Campden and Nearby

▲▲**Chipping Campden** Picturesque market town with finest High Street in England, accented by a 17th-century Market Hall, wool-tycoon manors, and a characteristic Gothic church. See page 348.

▲▲**Stanway House** Grand, aristocratic home of the Earl of Wemyss, with the tallest fountain in Britain and a 14th-century tithe barn. **Hours:** June-Aug Tue and Thu only 14:00-17:00, closed Sept-May. See page 359.

▲**Stanton** Classic Cotswold village with flower-filled exteriors and 15th-century church. See page 361.

▲**Hidcote Manor Garden** Fragrant garden organized into color-themed "outdoor rooms" that set a trend in 20th-century garden design. **Hours:** Daily 10:00-18:00; Oct until 17:00; Nov-mid-Dec Sat-Sun 11:00-16:00, closed Mon-Fri; closed mid-Dec-Feb. See page 364.

▲**Broad Campden, Blockley, and Bourton-on-the-Hill** Trio of villages with sweeping views and quaint homes, far from the madding crowds. See page 365.

Stow-on-the-Wold and Nearby

▲▲**Stow-on-the-Wold** Convenient Cotswold home base with charming shops and pubs clustered around town square, plus popular day hikes. See page 365.

▲**Lower and Upper Slaughter** Inaptly named historic villages—home to a working waterwheel, peaceful churches, and a folksy museum. See page 378.

expect to pay about £25 between Chipping Campden and Stow and about £20 between Chipping Campden and Moreton.

Note that the drivers listed here are not typical city taxi services (with many drivers on call), but are mostly individuals—it's smart to call ahead if you're arriving in high season, since they can be booked in advance on weekends.

To scare up a taxi in Moreton, try Stuart and Stephen at **ETC,** "Everything Taken Care of" (tel. 01608/650-343, www. cotswoldtravel.co.uk); see also the taxi phone numbers posted outside the Moreton train station office. In Stow, try **Tony Knight** (mobile 07887-714-047, anthonyknight205@btinternet.com). In Chipping Campden, call James at **Cotswold Private Hire** (mo-

▲**Bourton-on-the-Water** The "Venice of the Cotswolds," touristy yet undeniably striking, with petite canals and impressive Cotswold Motoring Museum. See page 379.

▲**Cotswold Farm Park** Kid-friendly park with endangered breeds of native British animals, farm demonstrations, and tractor rides. **Hours:** Daily 10:30-17:00, Nov-Dec until 16:00, closed Jan-Feb. See page 381.

▲**Bibury** Extremely touristy village of antique weavers' cottages, best for outdoor activities like fishing and picnicking. See page 384.

▲**Cirencester** Ancient 2,000-year-old city noteworthy for its crafts center and museum, showcasing artifacts from Roman and Saxon times. See page 385.

Moreton-in-Marsh and Nearby

▲▲▲**Blenheim Palace** Fascinating, sumptuous, still-occupied aristocratic abode—one of Britain's best. **Hours:** Daily 10:30-17:30, Nov-mid-Dec generally closed Mon-Tue, park open but palace closed mid-Dec-mid-Feb. See page 391.

▲**Moreton-in-Marsh** Relatively flat and functional home base with the best transportation links in the Cotswolds and a bustling Tuesday market. See page 386.

▲**Chastleton House** Lofty Jacobean-era home with a rich family history. **Hours:** Wed-Sun 13:00-17:00, closed Nov-mid-March and Mon-Tue year-round. See page 389.

bile 07980-857-833), or **Les Proctor,** who offers village tours and station pick-ups (mobile 07580-993-492, Les also co-runs Cornerways B&B—see page 356). Tim Harrison at **Tour the Cotswolds** specializes in tours of the Cotswolds and its gardens, but will also do tours outside the area (mobile 07779-030-820, www.tourthecotswolds.co.uk). Peter Shelley at **Cotswolds by Car** offers custom tours in a comfy Range Rover (mobile 07968-330-485, www.cotswoldsbycar.com).

By Minibus Tour

Go Cotswolds offers a fast blitz of the most famous stops. It's an efficient way to see some of the Cotswold's most picturesque places (with seven stops in a 16-seat bus). Energetic Tom or Colin will pick you up from Stratford-upon-Avon, Chipping Campden, or Moreton-in-Marsh for a jam-packed day including about an hour each in Chipping Campden, Stow-on-the-Wold, and Bourton-on-the-Water (£40/person, Wed-Sun 9:45-17:00, tel. 07786-920-166, www.gocotswolds.co.uk, info@gocotswolds.co.uk). Handy option: check out of your hotel, stow bag on bus, and catch the evening train in Moreton for your next stop.

Secret Cottage Cotswold Tours doesn't give you the famous stops; it's an intimate look at offbeat villages in a seven-seat minibus. You get short guided visits to a selection of lesser-known villages, and tours include a cream tea served in a private cottage. Meet Becky at Moreton-in-Marsh's train station at 10:00 and you'll return to the station by 16:20 (£95/person, must reserve ahead online, tel. 01608/674-700, www.cotswoldtourismtours.co.uk).

Other Cotswold Tours

Lion Tours, which departs from Bath, offers a Cotswold Discovery full-day tour, and can drop you and your luggage off in Stow (see page 249 of the Bath chapter).

Town Walks: While none of the Cotswold towns offers regularly scheduled walks, many have voluntary **warden groups** who love to meet visitors and give walks for a small donation (see specific contact information below for Chipping Campden).

Chipping Campden

Just touristy enough to be convenient, the north Cotswold town of Chipping Campden (CAM-den) is a ▲▲ sight. This market town, once the home of the richest Cotswold wool merchants, has some incredibly beautiful thatched roofs. Both the great British historian G. M. Trevelyan and I call Chipping Campden's High Street the finest in England.

Orientation to Chipping Campden

TOURIST INFORMATION

Chipping Campden's TI is tucked away in the old police station on High Street. Buy the cheap town guide with map, or the local *Footpath Guide* (daily 9:30-17:00; off-season Mon-

Thu until 13:00, Fri-Sun until 16:00; tel. 01386/841-206, www. chippingcampdenonline.org).

HELPFUL HINTS

Festivals: The **Cotswold Olimpicks** are a series of tongue-in-cheek countryside games (such as competitive shin-kicking) held atop Dover's Hill, just above town (generally in late spring; check www.olimpickgames.co.uk). Chipping Campden also has a **music festival** in May.

Taxi: Try **Cotswold Private Hire, Les Proctor,** or **Tour the Cotswolds** (see page 346).

Parking: Find a spot anywhere along High Street and park for free with no time limit. There's also a pay-and-display lot on High Street, across from the TI (2-hour maximum). If those are full, there is free parking on the street called Back Ends. On weekends, you can also park for free at the school (see map).

Tours: The local members of the **Cotswold Voluntary Wardens** are happy to show you around town for a small donation to the Cotswold Conservation Fund (suggested donation-£4/person, 1.5-hour walks run May-Sept Tue at 14:00 and Thu at 10:00, meet at Market Hall; mobile 07761-565-661, Vin Kelly).

Walks and Hikes from Chipping Campden: Since this is a particularly hilly area, long-distance hikes are challenging. The easiest and most rewarding stroll is to the thatch-happy hobbit village of **Broad Campden** (about a mile, mostly level). From there, you can walk or take the bus (#2) back to Chipping Campden.

Or, if you have more energy, continue from Broad Campden up over the ridge and into picturesque **Blockley**—and, if your stamina holds out, all the way to **Bourton-on-the-Hill** (Blockley is connected by buses #1 and #2 to Chipping Campden and Moreton).

Alternatively, you can hike up to **Dover's Hill,** just north of the village. Ask locally about this easy circular one-hour walk that takes you on the first mile of the 100-mile-long Cotswold Way (which goes from here to Bath).

For more about hiking, see "Getting Around the Cotswolds—By Foot," earlier.

Chipping Campden Walk

This self-guided stroll through "Campden" (as locals call their town) takes you from the Market Hall west to the old silk mill, and then back east the length of High Street to the church. It takes about an hour.

Market Hall: Begin at Campden's most famous monument—

the Market Hall. It stands in front of the TI, marking the town center. The Market Hall was built in 1627 by the 17th-century Lord of the Manor, Sir Baptist Hicks. (Look for the Hicks family coat of arms on the east end of the building's facade.) Back then, it was an elegant shopping hall for the townsfolk

who'd come here to buy their produce. In the 1940s, it was almost sold to an American, but the townspeople heroically raised money to buy it first, then gave it to the National Trust for its preservation.

The timbers inside are true to the original. Study the classic Cotswold stone roof, still held together with wooden pegs nailed

in from underneath. (Tiles were cut and sold with peg holes, and stacked like waterproof scales.) Buildings all over the region still use these stone shingles. Today, the hall, which is rarely used, stands as a testimony to the importance of trade to medieval Campden.

Adjacent to the Market Hall is the sober WWI monument—a reminder of the huge price paid by nearly every little town. Walk around it, noticing how 1918 brought the greatest losses.

Between the Market Hall and the WWI monument you'll find a limestone disc embedded in the ground marking the ceremonial start of the Cotswold Way (you'll find its partner in front of the abbey in Bath—100 miles away—marking the southern end).

The TI is across the street, in the old police courthouse. If it's open, you're welcome to climb the stairs and peek into the **Magistrate's Court** (free, same hours as TI, ask at TI to go up). Under the open-beamed courtroom is a humble little exhibit on the town's history.

• *Walk west, passing the Town Hall (with the cute little bell tower) and the parking lot that was originally the sheep market, until you reach the Red Lion Inn. Across High Street (and a bit to the right), look for the house with a sundial and sign over the door reading...*

"Green Dragons": The house's decorative black cast-iron fixtures (originally in the stables) once held hay and functioned much like salad bowls for horses. Fine-cut stones define the door, but "rubble stones" make up the rest of the wall. The pink stones

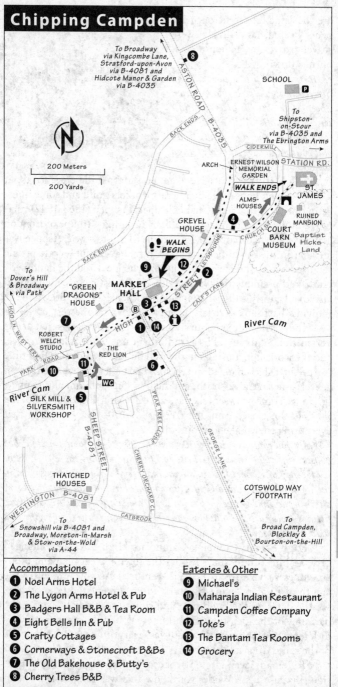

Chipping Campden

To Broadway
via Kingcombe Lane,
Stratford-upon-Avon
via B-4081 and
Hidcote Manor & Garden
via B-4035

8

SCHOOL

P

To
Shipston-
on-Stour
via B-4035 and
The Ebrington Arms

CIDERMILL

ASTON ROAD B-4035

BACK ENDS

ARCH

ERNEST WILSON
MEMORIAL
GARDEN

STATION RD.

WALK ENDS

ST.
JAMES

ALMS-
HOUSES

4

RUINED
MANSION

GREVEL
HOUSE

COURT
BARN
MUSEUM

Baptist
Hicks
Land

CHURCH ST.

200 Meters

200 Yards

To
Dover's Hill
& Broadway
via Path

"GREEN
DRAGONS"
HOUSE

WALK BEGINS

9   **12**

**MARKET
HALL**

2

SHEEP STREET LE BOURNE

CALF'S LANE

P

B

3

13

BACK ENDS

HOO LN. WEST TERR.

7

River Cam

1

14

i

ROBERT
WELCH
STUDIO

PARK ROAD

THE
RED LION

11

10

6

River Cam

5

WC

SILK MILL &
SILVERSMITH
WORKSHOP

SHEEP STREET B-4081

PEAR TREE CLOSE

CHERRY ORCHARD CL.

GEORGE LANE

THATCHED
HOUSES

COTSWOLD WAY
FOOTPATH

WESTINGTON B-4081

CATBROOK

To
Snowshill via B-4081 and
Broadway, Moreton-in-Marsh
& Stow-on-the-Wold
via A-44

To
Broad Campden,
Blockley &
Bourton-on-the-Hill

COTSWOLDS

Accommodations

1 Noel Arms Hotel

2 The Lygon Arms Hotel & Pub

3 Badgers Hall B&B & Tea Room

4 Eight Bells Inn & Pub

5 Crafty Cottages

6 Cornerways & Stonecroft B&Bs

7 The Old Bakehouse & Butty's

8 Cherry Trees B&B

Eateries & Other

9 Michael's

10 Maharaja Indian Restaurant

11 Campden Coffee Company

12 Toke's

13 The Bantam Tea Rooms

14 Grocery

are the same limestone but have been heated, and likely were scavenged from a house that burned down.

• *At the Red Lion, leave High Street and walk a block down Sheep Street. At the little creek just past the public WC, a 30-yard-long lane on the right leads to an old Industrial-Age silk mill (and the Hart silversmith shop).*

Silk Mill: The tiny River Cam powered a mill here since about 1790. Today it houses the handicraft workers guild and some interesting history. In 1902, Charles Robert Ashbee (1863-1942) revitalized this sleepy hamlet of 2,500 by bringing a troupe of London artisans and their families (160 people in all) to town. Ashbee was a leader in the romantic Arts and Crafts movement—craftspeople repulsed by the Industrial Revolution who idealized the handmade crafts and preindustrial ways. Ashbee's idealistic craftsmen's guild lasted only until 1908, when it ran into financial difficulties and the individual artisans were left to run their own businesses.

Today, the only shop surviving from the originals is that of **silversmith David Hart.** His grandfather came to town with Ashbee, and the workshop (upstairs in the mill building) is an amazing time warp—little has changed since 1902. Hart is a gracious elderly man as well as a fine silversmith, and he, his son William, and nephew Julian welcome browsers six days a week (Mon-Fri 9:00-17:00, Sat until 12:00, closed Sun, tel. 01386/841-100). They're proud that everything they make is a "one-off."

• *While you could continue 200 yards farther to see some fine thatched houses, this walk instead returns to High Street. On the corner is the studio shop of **Robert Welch**, a local industrial designer who worked in the spirit of the Arts and Crafts movement. His son and daughter carry on his legacy in the fine shop with sleek tableware, glassware, and bath fittings (with a little museum case in the back). Now turn right, and walk through town.*

High Street: Chipping Campden's High Street has changed little architecturally since 1840. (The town's street plan and property lines survive from the 12th century.) As you now walk the length of England's finest historic High Street, study the skyline, see the dates on the buildings, and count the sundials. Notice the harmony of the long rows of buildings. While the street comprises different styles through the centuries, everything you see was made of the same Cotswold stone—the only stone allowed today.

To remain level, High Street arcs with the contour of the hillside. Because it's so wide, you know this was a market town. In past centuries, livestock and packhorses laden with piles of freshly shorn fleece would fill the streets. Campden was a sales and distribution center for the wool industry, and merchants from as far away as Italy would come here for the prized raw wool.

High Street has no house numbers: Locals know the houses by their names. In the distance, you'll see the town church (where this walk ends). Notice that the power lines are buried underground, making the scene delightfully uncluttered.

As you stroll High Street, you'll find the finest houses on the uphill side. Decorative features (like the Ionic capitals near the TI) are added for nonstructural touches of class. Most High Street buildings are half-timbered, but with cosmetic stone facades. You may see some exposed half-timbered walls. Study the crudely beautiful framing, made of hand-hewn oak (you can see the adze marks) and held together by wooden pegs.

Peeking down alleys, you'll notice how the lots are narrow but very deep (33 x 330 feet). Called "burgage plots," this platting goes back to 1170. In medieval times, rooms were lined up long and skinny like train cars: Each building had a small storefront, followed by a workshop, living quarters, staff quarters, stables, and a garden at the very back. Now the private alleys that still define many of these old lots lead to comfy gardens. While some of today's buildings are wider, virtually all the widths are exact multiples of that basic first unit (for example, a modern building may be three times wider than its medieval counterpart).

• *Hike the length of High Street toward the church. After a couple hundred yards, just before Church Street, there's a fine mansion on the left.*

Grevel House: In 1367, William Grevel built what's considered Campden's first stone house. Sheep tycoons had big homes. Imagine back then, when this fine building was surrounded by humble wattle-and-daub huts. It had newfangled chimneys, rather than a crude hole in the roof. (No more rain inside!) Originally a "hall house" with just one big, tall room, it got its upper floor in the 16th century. The finely carved central bay window is a good early example of the Perpendicular Gothic style. The gargoyles scared away bad spirits—and served as rain spouts. The boot scrapers outside the door were fixtures in that muddy age—especially in market towns, where the streets were filled with animal dung.

• *Continue up High Street for about 100 yards. Go past Church Street (which we'll walk up later). On the right, at a big tree behind a low stone wall, you'll find a small Gothic arch leading into a garden.*

Ernest Wilson Memorial Garden: Once the church's vegetable patch, this small and secluded garden is a botanist's delight today. Pop inside if it's open. The garden is filled with well-labeled plants that the Victorian botanist Ernest Wilson brought

back to England from his extensive travels in Asia. There's a complete history of the garden on the board to the left of the entry.
• *Backtrack to Church Street. Turn left, walk past the recommended Eight Bells pub, and hook left with the street. Along your right-hand side stretches...*

Baptist Hicks Land: Sprawling adjacent to the town church, the area known as Baptist Hicks Land held Hicks' huge estate and manor house. This influential Lord of the Manor was from "a family of substance," who were merchants of silk and fine clothing as well as money-lenders. Beyond the ornate gate (which you'll see ahead, near the church), only a few outbuildings and the charred corner of his **mansion** survive. The mansion

was burned by royalists in 1645 during the Civil War—notice how Cotswold stone turns red when burned. Hicks housed the poor, making a show of his generosity, adding a long row of almshouses (with his family coat of arms) for neighbors to see as they walked to church. These almshouses (lining Church Street on the left) house pensioners today, as they have since the 17th century. Across the street is a ditch built as a "cart wash"—it was filled with water to soak old cart wheels so they'd swell up and stop rattling.

On the right, filling the old **Court Barn,** is a small, fussy museum about crafts and designs from the Arts and Crafts movement, with works by Ashbee and his craftsmen (£5, Tue-Sun 10:00-17:00, Oct-March until 16:00, closed Mon, tel. 01386/841-951, www.courtbarn.org.uk).
• *Next to the Hicks gate, a scenic lane leads to the front door of the church. It's lined with 11 linden trees: Planted in about 1760, there used to be one for each of the apostles. But recently one of the trees died.*

St. James Church: One of the finest churches in the Cotswolds, St. James Church graces one of its leading towns. Both the town and the church were built by wool wealth. Go inside. The church is Perpendicular Gothic, with lots of light and strong verticality. Notice the fine vestments and altar hangings (intricate c. 1460 embroidery) behind protective blue curtains (near the back of the church). Tombstones pave the floor in the chancel (often under protective red carpeting)—memorializing great wool merchants through the ages.

At the altar is a brass relief of William Grevel, the first owner of the Grevel House (described earlier), and his wife. But it is Sir Baptist Hicks who dominates the church. His huge canopied tomb is the ornate final resting place for Hicks and his wife, Elizabeth.

Study their faces, framed by fancy lace ruffs (trendy in the 1620s). Adjacent—as if in a closet—is a statue of their daughter, Lady Juliana, and her husband, Lutheran Yokels. Juliana commissioned the statue in 1642, when her husband died, but had it closed up until *she* died in 1680. Then, the doors were opened, revealing these two people holding hands and living happily ever after—at least in marble. The hinges were likely used only once.

Just outside as you leave the church, look immediately around the corner to the right of the door. A small tombstone reads "Thank you Lord for Simon, a dearly loved cat who greeted everyone who entered this church. RIP 1986."

Sleeping in Chipping Campden

In Chipping Campden—as in any town in the Cotswolds—B&Bs offer a better value than hotels. Most of my listings are centrally located on the main street (or just off it). Try to book well in advance, as rooms are snapped up early in the spring and summer by happy hikers heading for the nearby Cotswold Way. Rooms are also generally tight on Saturdays (when many charge a bit more and are reluctant to rent to one-nighters) and in September, another peak month. Parking is never a problem. Always ask for a discount if staying longer than one or two nights.

$$$ Noel Arms Hotel, the characteristic old hotel on the main square, has welcomed guests for 600 years. Its lobby was remodeled in a medieval-meets-modern style, and its 27 rooms are well furnished with antiques (some ground-floor doubles, attached restaurant/bar and café, free parking, High Street, tel. 01386/840-317, www.noelarmshotel.com, reception@noelarmshotel.com).

$$$ The Lygon Arms Hotel (pronounced "lig-un"), attached to the popular pub of the same name, has small public areas and 10 cheery, open-beamed rooms (family rooms available, free parking, High Street, go through archway and look for hotel reception on the left, tel. 01386/840-318, www.lygonarms.co.uk, sandra@lygonarms.co.uk, Sandra Davenport).

$$$ Badgers Hall, above a tearoom, rents four somewhat overpriced rooms with antique furnishings beneath wooden beams (2-night minimum, no kids under 18, High Street, tel. 01386/840-839, www.badgershall.com, karen@badgershall.com, Karen). Their delightful half-timbered tearoom (open to guests only Thu-Sat) offers a selection of savory dishes, homemade cakes, tarts, and scones.

$$$ Eight Bells Inn rents six old-school rooms with modern en suite baths above a recommended pub (Church Street, tel. 01386/840-371, wwww.eightbellsinn.co.uk, info@eightbellsinn.co.uk).

$$$ Crafty Cottages, run by helpful lifelong Cotswolds residents Sally and Paul, supply home-away-from-home modern amenities in three cottages—two one-bedroom and one two-bedroom—right next to the silk mill (3-night minimum, Sheep Street, tel. 01386/849-079, www.craftycottages.com, enquiries@craftycottages.com).

$$ Cornerways B&B is a fresh, bright, and comfy home a block off High Street. It's run by the delightful Carole Proctor, who can "look out the window and see the church where we were married." The two huge, light, airy loft rooms are great for families with children over 10 (2-night minimum, cash only, off-street parking, George Lane—walk through the arch beside Noel Arms Hotel, tel. 01386/841-307, www.cornerways.info, carole@cornerways.info). For a fee, Les can pick you up from the train station, or take you on village tours.

$$ Stonecroft B&B, next to Cornerways, has three polished, well-maintained rooms (one with low, slanted ceilings—unfriendly to tall people). The lovely garden with a patio and small stream is a tranquil place for meals or an early-evening drink (family rooms but no kids under 12, George Lane, tel. 01386/840-486, www.stonecroft-chippingcampden.co.uk, info@stonecroft-chippingcampden.co.uk, Roger and Lesley Yates).

$$ The Old Bakehouse, run by energetic young mom Zoe, rents two small-but-pleasant rooms in a 600-year-old home with exposed beams and cottage charm (cash only, Lower High Street, near intersection with Sheep Street, tel. 01386/840-979, mobile 07717-330-838, www.theoldbakehouse.org.uk, zoegabb@yahoo.co.uk).

$$ Cherry Trees B&B, set well off the road, is bubbly Angie's spacious, modern home, with three king rooms, one with balcony (2-night minimum, cash only, 10-minute walk from Market Hall or take bus to Aston Road, tel. 01386/840-873, www.cherrytreescampden.com, sclrksn7@tiscali.co.uk).

Eating in Chipping Campden

This town—filled with wealthy residents and tourists—comes with several good choices. I've listed some local favorites below. If you have a car, consider driving to one of the excellent countryside pubs mentioned in the sidebar on page 376.

$$$ Eight Bells pub is a charming 14th-century inn. It's the best deal going for top-end pub dining in town, with English dishes both classic and modern. They serve a daily special, summer salads, and always have a good vegetarian dish. The restaurant, classy pub, and terrace out back (lunch only) all have the same menu. Reservations are smart (daily 12:00-14:00 & 18:30-21:00, Church Street, tel. 01386/840-371, www.eightbellsinn.co.uk).

$$$ Michael's, a fun Mediterranean restaurant on High Street, serves hearty portions and breaks plates at closing every Saturday night. Michael, who runs his place with a contagious love of life, is from Cyprus: The forte here is Greek, with plenty of *mezes*—small dishes. "The Meze" special gives you the works with a hearty selection of small plates (Tue-Sun 18:45-22:00, closed Mon, tel. 01386/840-826).

$$ Maharaja Indian Restaurant, filling the back end of the down-and-dirty Volunteer Inn pub, serves decent Indian standards (daily 18:00-22:30, grassy courtyard out back, Lower High Street, tel. 01386/849-281).

LIGHT MEALS

If you want a quick takeaway sandwich, consider these options. Munch your lunch on the benches on the little green near the Market Hall.

$ Butty's is a practical little eatery offering salads, tasty sandwiches, and wraps made to order (Mon-Fri 7:00-14:00, Sat 8:00-13:00, closed Sun, Lower High Street, tel. 01386/840-401).

$ Campden Coffee Company is a cozy little café with local goodies including salads, sandwiches, and homemade sweets (Sat-Mon 10:00-16:00, Tue-Fri from 9:00, on the ground floor of the Silk Mill, tel. 01386/849-251).

$ Toke's has a tempting selection of cheeses, meats, and wine for a make-your-own ploughman's lunch (Mon-Fri 9:00-18:00, Sat 10:00-17:00, Sun 10:00-16:00, just past the Market Hall, tel. 01386/849-345).

Afternoon Tea: The Bantam Tea Rooms (daily 9:30-17:00) and **Badgers Hall** (Thu-Sat 10:00-16:00), each a scone's throw from the Market Hall, are sweet and pastel places popular for their cakes, bakery goods, lunches, and afternoon tea.

Picnic and Groceries: The **Co-op grocery** (daily 7:00-22:00, next to TI on High Street) is handy for a picnic, with a good selection of sandwiches and takeaway items.

COTSWOLDS

Near Chipping Campden

Because the countryside around Chipping Campden is particularly hilly, it's also especially scenic. This is a very rewarding area to poke around and discover little thatched villages.

WEST OF CHIPPING CAMPDEN

Due west of Chipping Campden lies the famous and touristy town of Broadway. Just south of that, you'll find my nominations for the cutest Cotswold villages. Like marshmallows in hot chocolate, Stanway, Stanton, and Snowshill nestle side by side, awaiting your arrival. (Note the Stanway House's limited hours when planning your visit.)

Broadway

This postcard-pretty town, a couple of miles west of Chipping Campden, is filled with inviting shops and fancy teahouses. With a "broad way" indeed running through its middle, it's one of the bigger towns in the area. This means you'll likely pass through at some point if you're driving—but, since all the big bus tours seem to stop here, I usually give Broadway a miss. However, with a new road that allows traffic to skirt the town, Broadway has gotten cuter than ever. If driving, check out the top end of High Street (which is a dead end, residential, and a classic/modern Cotswolds neighborhood). Broadway has limited bus connections with Chipping Campden.

Ebike Rental and More: Follow *Tower Barn* signs from the Broadway Tower ticket office to a slick café and shop with fine Cotswolds goods and ebike rentals. From here, it's an easy pedal over country lanes to the nearby lavender fields (£9/hour, £35/day, daily 10:00-16:00, tel. 01386/852-390, https://broadwaytower.co.uk). There's also a nuclear bunker open on weekends (£4.50, closed Nov-March).

Broadway Tower ornaments a hill above Broadway. Just outside of town, on the road to Chipping Campden, signs direct you to the tower, which looks like a turreted castle fortification stranded in the countryside without a castle in sight. This 55-foot-tall observation tower is a "folly"—a uniquely English term for a quirky, outlandish novelty erected as a giant lawn ornament by some aristocrat with more money than taste. If you're also weighted down with too many pounds, you can relieve yourself of £5 to climb to its top for a view over the pastures. But the view from the tower's parklike perch is free, and almost as impressive (daily 10:00-17:00). A short hike beyond the tower just before sunset can be unforgettable.

Stanway

More of a humble crossroads community than a true village, sleepy Stanway is worth a visit mostly for its manor house, which offers an intriguing insight into the English aristocracy today. If you're in the area when it's open, it's well worth visiting.

▲▲Stanway House

The Earl of Wemyss (pronounced "weemz"), whose family tree charts relatives back to 1202, opens his melancholy home and grounds to visitors two days a week in the summer. Walking through his house offers a unique glimpse into the lifestyles of England's eccentric and fading nobility.

Cost and Hours: £9 ticket covers house and fountain, includes a wonderful and intimate audioguide narrated by the lordship himself; June-Aug Tue and Thu only 14:00-17:00, closed Sept-May, tel. 01386/584-469, www.stanwayfountain.co.uk.

Getting There: By car, leave the B-4077 at a statue of (the Christian) George slaying the dragon (of pagan superstition); you'll round the corner and see the manor's fine 17th-century Jacobean gatehouse. Park in the lot across the street. There's no public transportation to Stanway.

Visiting the Manor: The 14th-century **Tithe Barn** (near where you enter the grounds) predates the manor. It was originally

where monks—in the days before money—would accept one-tenth of whatever the peasants produced. Peek inside: This is a great hall for village hoedowns. While the Tithe Barn is no longer used to greet motley peasants and collect their feudal "rents," the lord still gets rent from his vast landholdings, and hosts village fêtes in his barn.

Stepping into the obviously very lived-in **manor house,** you're free to wander around pretty much as you like, but keep in mind that a family does live here. His lordship is often roaming about as well. The place feels like a time warp. Ask a staff member to demonstrate the spinning rent-collection table. In the great hall, marvel at the one-piece oak shuffleboard table and the 1780 Chippendale

COTSWOLDS

exercise chair (half an hour of bouncing on this was considered good for the liver).

The manor dogs have their own cutely painted "family tree," but the Earl admits that his last dog, C. J., was "all character and no breeding." Poke into the office. You can psychoanalyze the lord by the books that fill his library, the DVDs stacked in front of his bed (with the mink bedspread), and whatever's next to his toilet.

The place has a story to tell. And so do the docents stationed in each room—modern-day peasants who, even without family trees, probably have relatives going back just as far in this village. Talk to these people. Probe. Learn what you can about this side of England.

Wandering through the expansive backyard you'll see the earl's pet project: restoring "the tallest **fountain** in Britain"—300 feet tall, gravity-powered, and running for 30 minutes twice a day (at 14:45 and 16:00).

Signs lead to a working **watermill,** which produces flour from wheat grown on the estate (about 100 yards from the house, requires separate £4 ticket to enter).

Hailes Church and Abbey

A three-mile drive or pleasant two-and-a-half-mile walk from Stanway House along the Cotswold Way leads you to a fine Norman church and tranquil abbey ruins. There's also an adjacent museum displaying the abbey's surviving artifacts. While little remains of the abbey, just being here can be a moving experience.

Cost and Hours: Church—free, abbey and museum—£7, daily 10:00-17:00, until 18:00 in summer, closed Nov-March, free parking, tel. 01242/602-398, www.english-heritage.org.uk.

Visiting the Abbey: Richard, Earl of Cornwall (and younger brother of King Henry III) founded the abbey after surviving a shipwreck. His son Edmund turned it into a pilgrimage site after buying a vial of holy blood and bringing the relic to Hailes around 1270. Because of Henry VIII's dissolution of monasteries in the 16th century, not much remains of the abbey today.

The church—which predates the abbey by about a century— houses some of its original tiles and medieval stained glass. It's worth a look for its 800-year-old baptismal font and faded but evocative murals (including St. Christopher, patron saint of travelers, and a hunting scene attributed to a local knight). Check out the wooden screen added long after the original construction—notice how the arch had to be cut away in order for the screen to fit.

From Stanway to Stanton

These towns are separated by a row of oak trees and grazing land, with parallel waves echoing the furrows plowed by medieval farm-

ers. Centuries ago, farmers were allotted long strips of land called "furlongs." The idea was to dole out good and bad land equitably. (One square furlong equals 10 acres.) Over centuries of plowing these, furrows were formed. Let someone else drive, so you can hang out the window under a canopy of oaks, passing stone walls and sheep. Leaving Stanway on the road to Stanton, the first building you'll see (on the left, just outside Stanway) is a thatched cricket pavilion overlooking the village cricket green. Originally built for *Peter Pan* author J. M. Barrie, it dates from 1930 and is raised up (as medieval buildings were) on rodent-resistant staddle stones. Stanton is just ahead; follow the signs.

▲Stanton

Pristine Cotswold charm cheers you as you head up the main street of the village of Stanton, served by a scant few buses. Go on a photo safari for flower-bedecked doorways and windows.

Stanton's **Church of St. Michael** (with the pointy spire) betrays a pagan past. It's safe to assume any church dedicated to St. Michael (the archangel who fought the devil) sits upon a sacred pagan site. Stanton is actually at the intersection of two ley lines (a line connecting prehistoric or ancient sights). You'll see St. Michael's well-worn figure (and, above that, a sundial) over the door as you enter. Inside, above the capitals in the nave, find the pagan symbols for the sun and

the moon (see photo). While the church probably dates back to the ninth century, today's building is mostly from the 15th century, with 13th-century transepts. On the north transept (far side from entry), medieval frescoes show faintly through the 17th-century whitewash. (Once

COTSWOLDS

upon a time, these frescoes were considered too "papist.") Imagine the church interior colorfully decorated throughout. Original medieval glass is behind the altar. The list of rectors (at the very back of the church, under the organ loft) goes back to 1269. Finger the grooves in the back pews, worn away by sheepdog leashes. (A man's sheepdog accompanied him everywhere.)

Horse Riding: Jill Carenza's **Cotswolds Riding Centre,** set just outside Stanton village, is in the most scenic corner of the re-

gion. The facility's horses can take anyone from rank beginners to more experienced riders on a scenic "hack" through the village and into the high country (per-hour prices: £34/person on a group hack, £44/person semiprivate hack, £54 private one-person hack; lessons, longer/expert rides, and pub tours available; tel. 01386/584-250, www.cotswoldsriding.co.uk, info@cotswoldsriding.co.uk). From Stanton, head toward Broadway and watch for the riding center on your right after about a third of a mile.

Sleeping in Stanton: $$ The Vine B&B has four rooms in a lovingly worn family home near the center of town, next to the cricket pitch (ask if any matches are on if you're there on a Saturday in summer). While it suffers from absentee management, the Vine is convenient if you want to ride all day (most rooms share a WC but have a private shower, one room en suite, family room available, some stairs; for contact info, see listing for riding center, above).

Eating in Stanton: High on a hill at the far end of Stanton's main drag, nearest to Broadway, the aptly named **$$$ Mount Inn** serves upscale meals on its big, inviting terrace with grand views of Stanton rooftops and the Cotswold hills (daily 12:00-15:00 & 18:00-23:00, may be closed Mon-Tue off-season, Old Snowshill Road, tel. 01386/584-316).

Snowshill

Another nearly edible little bundle of cuteness, the village of Snowshill (SNAH-zul) has a photogenic triangular square with a characteristic pub at its base.

Snowshill Manor

Dark and mysterious, this old manor house is stuffed with the lifetime collection of Charles Paget Wade (its management made me promise not to promote it as an eccentric collector's pile of curi-

osities). It's one big, musty celebration of craftsmanship, from finely carved spinning wheels to frightening samurai armor to tiny elaborate figurines carved by prisoners from the bones of meat served at dinner. Taking seriously his family motto, "Let Nothing Perish," Wade dedicated his life and fortune to preserving things finely crafted.

Cost and Hours: £12.20; manor house open daily 11:00-17:30, closed Nov-March; gardens and ticket window open at 11:00, last entry one hour before closing, restaurant, tel. 01386/852-410, www.nationaltrust.org.uk/snowshillmanor.

Getting There: There's no direct access from the square; instead, the entrance and parking lot are about a half-mile up the road toward Broadway. Park there and follow the long walkway through the garden to get to the house. A golf-cart-type shuttle to the house is available for those who need assistance.

Getting In: This popular sight strictly limits the number of entering visitors by doling out entry times. No reservations are possible; to get a slot, you must report to the ticket desk. It can be up to an hour's wait—even more on busy days, especially weekends (when they can sell out for the day as early as 14:00). Tickets go on sale and the gardens open at 11:00. A good strategy is to arrive close to the opening time, and if there's a wait, enjoy the gardens (it's a 10-minute walk to the manor). If you have more time to kill, head into the village of Snowshill itself (a half-mile away) to wander and explore—or get a time slot for later in the day, and return in the afternoon.

Cotswold Lavender

In 2000, farmer Charlie Byrd realized that tourists love lavender. He planted his farm with 250,000 plants, and now visitors come to wander among his 53 acres, which burst with gorgeous lavender blossoms from mid-June through late August. His fragrant fantasy peaks late each July. Lavender—so famous in France's Provence—is not indigenous to this region, but it

fits the climate and soil just fine. A free flier in the shop explains the variations of blooming flowers. Farmer Byrd produces lavender oil (an herbal product valued since ancient times for its healing, calming, and fragrant qualities) and sells it in a delightful shop, along with many other lavender-themed items. In the café, enjoy a pot of lavender-flavored tea with a lavender scone.

Cost and Hours: Free to enter shop and café, £4 to walk through the fields and the distillery; generally open June-Aug daily 10:00-17:00, closed Sept-May, schedule changes annually depending on when the lavender blooms—call ahead or check their website; tel. 01386/854-821, www.cotswoldlavender.co.uk.

Getting There: It's a half-mile out of Snowshill on the road toward Chipping Campden (easy parking). Entering Snowshill from the road to the manor (described earlier), take the left fork, then turn left again at the end of the village.

EAST OF CHIPPING CAMPDEN

Hidcote Manor Garden is just northeast of Chipping Campden, while Broad Campden, Blockley, and Bourton-on-the-Hill lie roughly between Chipping Campden and Stow (or Moreton)—handy if you're connecting those towns.

▲Hidcote Manor Garden

This is less "on the way" between towns than the other sights in this section—but the grounds around this manor house are well worth a detour if you like gardens. Hidcote is where garden designers pioneered the notion of creating a series of outdoor "rooms," each with a unique theme (such as maple room, red room, and so on) and separated by a yew-tree hedge. The garden's design, inspired by the Arts and Crafts movement, is most formal near  the house and becomes more pastoral as it approaches the countryside. Follow your nose through a clever series of small gardens that lead delightfully from one to the next. Among the best in England, Hidcote Gardens are at their fragrant peak from May through August. But don't expect much indoors—the manor house has only a few rooms open to the public.

Cost and Hours: £13.50; daily 10:00-18:00, Oct until 17:00; Nov-mid-Dec Sat-Sun 11:00-16:00, closed Mon-Fri; closed mid-Dec-Feb; last entry one hour before closing, café, restaurant, tel. 01386/438-333, www.nationaltrust.org.uk/hidcote.

Getting There: If you're driving, it's four miles northeast of Chipping Campden—roughly toward Ilmington. The gardens are accessible by bus, then a 45-minute country walk uphill. Buses #1 and #2 take you to Mickleton (one stop past Chipping Campden), where a footpath begins next to the churchyard. Continuing more or less straight, the path leads through sheep pastures and ends at Hidcote's driveway.

Nearby: Gardening enthusiasts will also want to stop at **Kiftsgate Court Garden,** just across the road from Hidcote. While not as impressive, these private gardens are a fun contrast since they were designed at the same time and influenced by Hidcote (£9; May-July Sat-Wed 12:00-18:00, Aug from 14:00, closed Thu-Fri; April and Sept Sun-Mon and Wed only 14:00-18:00; closed Oct-March; tel. 01386/438-777, www.kiftsgate.co.uk).

▲Broad Campden, Blockley, and Bourton-on-the-Hill

This trio of pleasant villages lines up along an off-the-beaten-path road between Chipping Campden and Moreton or Stow. **Broad**

Campden, just on the outskirts of Chipping Campden, has some of the cutest thatched-roof houses I've seen. **Blockley,** nestled higher in the picturesque hills, is a popular setting for films. The same road continues on to **Bourton-on-the-Hill** (pictured), with fine views looking down into a valley and an excellent gastropub (Horse and Groom, described on page 376). Blockley is connected to Chipping Campden by bus #1 and #2, or you can walk (easy to Broad Campden, more challenging to the other two—see page 341).

Stow-on-the-Wold

Located 10 miles south of Chipping Campden, Stow-on-the-Wold—with a name that means "meeting place on the uplands"—is the highest town in the Cotswolds. Despite its crowds, it retains its charm, and it merits ▲▲. Most of the tourists are day-trippers, so nights—even in the

peak of summer—are peaceful. Stow has no real sights other than the town itself, some good pubs, antiques stores, and cute shops draped seductively around a big town square. Visit the church, with its evocative old door guarded by ancient yew trees and the tombs of wool tycoons. A visit to Stow is not complete until you've locked your partner in the stocks on the village green.

Orientation to Stow-on-the-Wold

TOURIST INFORMATION

A small visitor information center—little more than a rack of brochures staffed by volunteers—is run out of the library in St. Edwards Hall on the main square (hours generally Mon-Sat 10:00-14:00, sometimes as late as 19:00, closed Sun; Oct-April Sat 10:00-14:00 only, tel. 01451/870-998). The TI in Moreton-in-Marsh is more serious (see page 386).

HELPFUL HINTS

Services: Pay WCs are located at the north and south ends of town.

Taxi: See "Getting Around the Cotswolds—By Taxi," earlier in the chapter.

Parking: Park anywhere on Market Square free for two hours, and overnight between 18:00 and 9:00 (combining overnight plus daily 2-hour allowances means you can park free 16:00-11:00—they note your license, so you can't just move to another spot after your time is up; £50 tickets for offenders). You can also park for free on some streets farther from the center (such as Park Street and Well Lane) for an unlimited amount of time. A convenient pay-and-display lot is at the bottom of town (toward the Oddingtons), and there's free long-stay parking adjacent to the lot at Tesco Supermarket—an easy five-minute walk north of town (follow the signs).

Sunday Morning Town Walk: Volunteers give charming guided town walks once a week to raise a little money for community projects. It's fun to mix with English visitors as a local tells the town's story (£5, April-Sept Sun at 10:30, just show up at the stocks on Market Square).

Stow-on-the-Wold Walk

This six-stop self-guided walk covers about 500 yards and takes about 45 minutes. We'll start in the small park on the main square.

The Stocks on Market Square

Imagine this village during the 17th century when people were publicly ridiculed in stocks like this as a punishment. (Lock up

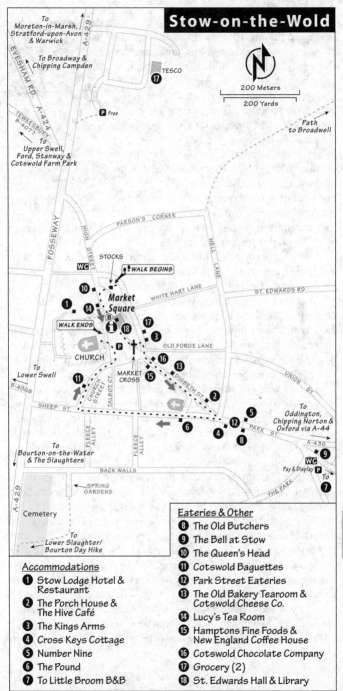

Stow-on-the-Wold

To Moreton-in-Marsh,
Stratford-upon-Avon
& Warwick

To Broadway &
Chipping Campden

TESCO

200 Meters
200 Yards

Path
to Broadwell

EVESHAM RD.

A-429

TEWKESBURY B-4077

A-424

To
Upper Swell,
Ford, Stanway &
Cotswold Farm Park

P Free

FOSSEWAY

HIGH STREET

PARSON'S CORNER

WELL LANE

ST. EDWARDS RD.

WC

STOCKS

WALK BEGINS

Market
Square

WHITE HART LANE

WALK ENDS

CHURCH

P

OLD FORGE LANE

MARKET
CROSS

DIGBETH ST.

UNION ST.

To
Lower Swell

B-4068

SHEEP ST.

CHURCH STREET

TALBOT CT.

To
Oddington,
Chipping Norton &
Oxford via A-44

PARK ST.

A-436

FLEECE ALLEY

FLEECE ALLEY

To
Bourton-on-the-Water
& The Slaughters

WC

P
Pay & Display

To

BACK WALLS

SPRING
GARDENS

A-429

Cemetery

To
Lower Slaughter/
Bourton Day Hike

THE PARK

Accommodations

1 Stow Lodge Hotel &
Restaurant
2 The Porch House &
The Hive Café
3 The Kings Arms
4 Cross Keys Cottage
5 Number Nine
6 The Pound
7 To Little Broom B&B

Eateries & Other

8 The Old Butchers
9 The Bell at Stow
10 The Queen's Head
11 Cotswold Baguettes
12 Park Street Eateries
13 The Old Bakery Tearoom &
Cotswold Cheese Co.
14 Lucy's Tea Room
15 Hamptons Fine Foods &
New England Coffee House
16 Cotswold Chocolate Company
17 Grocery (2)
18 St. Edwards Hall & Library

COTSWOLDS

your travel partner for a fun photo op.) Stow was born in pre-Roman times; it's where three trade routes crossed at a high point in the region (altitude: 800 feet). This square was the site of an Iron Age fort, and then a Roman garrison town. Starting in 1107, Stow was the site of an international fair, and people came from as far away as Italy to shop for wool fleeces on this vast, grassy expanse. Picture it in the Middle Ages (minus all the parked cars, and before the buildings in the center were added): a public commons and grazing ground, paths worn through the grass, and no well. Until the late 1800s, Stow had no running water; women fetched water from the "Roman Well" a quarter-mile down the hill.

With as many as 20,000 sheep sold in a single day, this square was a thriving scene. And Stow was filled with inns and pubs to keep everyone housed, fed, and watered.

Most of the buildings you see date from the 17th and 18th centuries. A thin skin of topsoil covers the Cotswold limestone, from which these buildings were made. The local limestone is easy to cut, hardens after contact with the air, and darkens with age. Many buildings were made of stone quarried right on site—with the mini quarries becoming their cellars.

That's why the **Stow Lodge** (next to the church) lies a little lower than the church. It sits on the spot where locals quarried stones for the church. That building, originally the rectory, is now a hotel. The church (where we'll end this little walk) is made of Cotswold stone, and marks the summit of the hill upon which the town was built.

Enjoy the stonework and the crazy rooflines. Observe the cheap signage on solid stone facades and think how shops have been coming and going for centuries in buildings that never change.

The **Stag Inn,** ahead on the left, was a typical coaching inn from a time before trains and cars, when land transport was literally horsepower. As horses could manage about 25 miles without a rest, coaches stopped at coaching inns to swap teams of horses. Taking advantage of such a relay of horses, travelers could go from London to Liverpool in 10 days.

As you walk, notice how locals stop to chat with each other to catch up on local news: This is a tight-knit little community.

• *Walk around the right of the building in the middle of the square and enter the library.*

St. Edwards Hall

The stately building in the square with the wooden steeple is St. Edwards Hall. Back in the 1870s, a bank couldn't locate the owner of an account containing a small fortune, so it donated the funds to the town to build this civic center. It serves as a City Hall, library, TI, and meeting place. When it's open, you can wander around upstairs to see the largest collection of Civil War portrait paintings in England—well described and an education in local 17th-century history. The library offers a candid peek at town life: community bulletin board, volunteers, history in a glass case, and historic town photos.

• *Beyond the library, at the far end of the square find the freestanding stone cross.*

The Market Cross

For 500 years, the Market Cross stood in the market reminding all Christian merchants to "trade fairly under the sight of God." Notice the stubs of the iron fence in the stone base—a reminder of how countless wrought-iron fences were cut down and given to the government to be melted down during World War II. (Recently, it's been disclosed that all that iron ended up in junk heaps—frantic patriotism just wasted.) One of the plaques on the cross honors the Lord of the Manor, who donated money back to his tenants, allowing the town to finally finance running water in 1878. Panels at the top of the cross feature St. Edward, the Crucifixion, the wool trade, and a memorial to the Battle of Stow.

This is the site of the 1646 Battle of Stow. During the English Civil War, which pitted Parliamentarians against Royalists, Stow-on-the-Wold remained staunchly loyal to the king. The final battle of England's first Civil War was fought on this square as about 3,000 troops loyal to the king made their last stand. About 200 Royalist troops were killed (and survivors were locked up in the church). Ultimately, this cleared the way for the beheading of King Charles I and the rise of Oliver Cromwell.

Scan the square for **The Kings Arms,** with its great gables and spindly chimney. This square was where travelers parked their horses before spending the night at the inn. In the 1600s, this inn was considered the premium "posting house" between London and Birmingham. Because of its allegiance to the king, the town has an abundance of pubs with royal names (King's This and Queen's That).

Today, The Kings Arms cooks up pub grub and rents rooms upstairs. It's the opposite of a "free house"—it's part of a big chain owned by a national brewery and therefore does not offer any of the local beers on tap.

• *Walk down Digbeth Street.*

Digbeth Street

This street is lined with workaday shops, cute gift shops, many good little eateries, and beautiful Cotswold stone. It starts with a handy ATM. Then, from top to bottom you'll find: Hampton's Fine Foods (local gifty edibles), Cotswold Chocolate Company (pop in to watch Tony working in the back kitchen and his wife, Heidi, decorating his concoctions), the New England Coffee House (which feels like a village Starbucks with cozy lounge rooms upstairs), a "saddlery" for the many local horse enthusiasts, Lambournes (a traditional butcher), Cotswold Cheese Company (with old milk churns flanking the door), and the Old Bakery Tearoom (good for a cream tea or lunch; see "Eating in and near Stow," later).

Digbeth ends at a little triangular park in front of the former Methodist Church and across from the Porch House Hotel, with timbers that date from 947 (it claims—along with about 20 others—to be the oldest in England).

Just beyond the small grassy triangle was the place where locals gathered for bloody cockfights and bearbaiting (watching packs of hungry dogs tear at bears).

Today this is where—twice a year, in May and October—the Stow Horse Fair attracts thousands of nomadic Roma (called Gypsies by the less politically correct locals) and Travellers from far and wide. Thousands of people, who are determined not to be "miserable clock punchers," congregate down the street on the Maugersbury Road. Locals paint a colorful picture of the Roma, Travellers, and horses inundating the town. The young women dress up to distract the men because the horse fair—with its "grabbing" ritual—also functions as a marriage market. (It's a challenging time for the town, and many shops and pubs actually close up for the fair.)

• *Hook right and hike up the wide street.*

Sheep Street

As you head up Sheep Street, you'll pass a boutique-filled former brewery yard (on the left). Notice the old brewery's fancy street-front office, with its striking Welsh flint facade. This was the bad side of town (with the "smelly trades"). Across the street from the brewery was the slaughterhouse. And Sheep Street was originally not a street, but a staging place for medieval sheep markets. The

COTSWOLDS

sheep would be gathered here, then paraded into the market on the main square.

You'll notice narrow lanes on either side of the street. There are two explanations: one I like to believe (paths just wide enough for a single file of sheep to walk down, making it easier for merchants to count them) and another that's more likely true (practical walks between the long, narrow, medieval strips of land allotments). You'll see several of these so-called "fleece alleys" as you walk up the street.

• *Walk a couple of blocks until you're one block from the traffic light and the highway, then make a right onto cute little Church Street, which leads to the church.*

St. Edwards Church

Before entering the church, circle it. On the back side, a wooden door is flanked by two ancient yew trees. While many see the

door and think of the Christian scripture, "Behold, I stand at the door and knock," J. R. R. Tolkien fans see something quite different. Tolkien hiked the Cotswolds, and had a passion for sketching evocative trees such as this. *Lord of the Rings* enthusiasts are convinced this must be the inspiration for the Doors of Durin, leading into Moria.

Notice the two "bale tombs" (10 steps to the right of the door). Wool-merchant gravestones were topped with a carved image of a tightly bound bale of wool.

Enter the church (usually open 9:00-17:00, except during services). While a wooden Saxon church stood here in the 10th century, today's structure is mostly from the 15th century. Its history is played up in leaflets and plaques just inside the door. The floor is paved with the tombs of big shots who made their money from wool and are still boastful in death. (Find the tombs crowned with the bales of wool.) Most of the windows are traditional Victorian (19th century) designs, but the two sets high up in the clerestory are from the dreamier Pre-Raphaelite school.

On the right wall, as you approach the altar, a monument remembers the many boys from this small town who were lost in World War I (50 out of a population of 2,000). There were far fewer in World War II. The biscuit-shaped plaque remembers an admiral from Stow who lost four sons defending the realm. It's sliced from an ancient fluted column (which locals believe is from Ephesus, Turkey).

During the English Civil War in the mid-1600s, the church was ransacked, and hundreds of soldiers were imprisoned here. The tombstone on the floor in front of the altar remembers the Royalist Captain Francis Keyt. His long hair, lace, and sash indicate he was a "cavalier," and true-blue to the king (Cromwellians were called "round heads"—named for their short hair). Study the crude provincial art—childlike skulls and (in the upper corners) symbols of his service to the king (armor, weapons).

Finally, don't miss the kneelers tucked in the pews. These are made by a committed band of women known as "the Kneeler Group." And with Reverend Martin Short for the pastor, the services could be pretty lively.

Hiking from Stow

Stow/Lower Slaughter/Bourton Day Hike

Stow is made to order for day hikes. The most popular is the downhill stroll to Lower Slaughter (3 miles), then on to Bourton-on-the-Water (about 1.5 miles more).
It's a two-hour walk if you keep up a brisk pace and don't stop, but dawdlers should allow three to four hours. At the end, from Bourton-on-the-Water, a bus can bring you back to Stow. While those with keen eyes can follow this walk by spotting trail signs, it can't hurt to download or bring a map (ask to borrow one at your B&B). Note that these three towns are described in more detail starting on page 378.

To reach the trail from Stow, walk to the top of Sheep Street. At the busy A-429 highway, turn left. Head south of town on a footpath alongside the busy highway, past the gas station for a couple hundred yards. Leave the highway on a well-marked trail (on the right) at Quarwood Cottage. You'll see a gravel lane with a green sign noting *Public Footpath/Gloucestershire Way/Monarch's Way*).

Follow this trail for a delightful hour across farms, through romantic gates, across a fancy driveway, and past Gainsborough-painting vistas. You'll enjoy an intimate backyard look at local farm life. Although it seems like you could lose the trail, tiny easy-to-miss signs (yellow *Public Footpath* arrows—sometimes also marked *Gloucestershire Way* or *The Monarch's Way*—usually embedded in fence posts) keep you on target—watch for these very carefully to avoid getting lost. Finally, passing a cricket pitch, you reach **Lower Slaughter,** with its fine church and a mill creek leading up to its mill. (The people at the mill can call a taxi for a quick return to Stow.)

From Lower Slaughter, you can continue 30 minutes on Monarch's Way (follow green signs) into touristy Bourton-on-the-Water. Enjoy some time in Bourton itself and—when ready—catch the bus from in front of the Edinburgh Woolen Mill back to Stow (bus #801 departs roughly hourly, none on Sun, 10-minute ride; bus #802 also connects to Stow).

Sleeping in Stow

$$$ Stow Lodge Hotel fills the historic church rectory with lots of old English charm. Facing the town square, with its own sprawling and peaceful garden, this lavish old place offers 21 large, thoughtfully appointed rooms with soft beds, stately public spaces, and a cushy-chair lounge (closed Jan, free parking, The Square, tel. 01451/830-485, www.stowlodge.co.uk, info@stowlodge.co.uk, helpful Hartley family).

$$ The Porch House rents 13 updated rooms with stonewall and wood-beam accents (Digbeth Street, tel. 01451/870-048, www.porch-house.co.uk, info@porch-house.co.uk).

$$ The Kings Arms, with 10 rooms above a pub, manages to keep its historic Cotswold character while still feeling fresh and modern in all the right ways (steep stairs, three slightly shabby "cottages" out back, free parking, Market Square, tel.  01451/830-364, www.kingsarmsstow.co.uk, info@kingsarmsstow. co.uk, Chris).

$$ Cross Keys Cottage offers four smallish but smartly updated rooms—some bright and floral, others classy white—with modern bathrooms. Kindly Margaret and Roger Welton take care of their guests in this 17th-century beamed cottage (RS%, call ahead to confirm arrival time, Park Street, tel. 01451/831-128, www.crosskeyscottage.co.uk, rogxmag@hotmail.com).

$ Number Nine has three large, bright, refurbished, and tastefully decorated rooms. This 200-year-old home comes with watch-your-head beamed ceilings and beautiful old wooden doors (9 Park Street, tel. 01451/870-333, mobile 07779-006-539, www.

number-nine.info, enquiries@number-nine.info, James and Carol Brown).

$ The Pound is the quaint, centuries-old, slanty, cozy, and low-beamed home of Patricia Whitehead. She offers two bright, inviting rooms and a classic old fireplace lounge (cash only, downtown on Sheep Street next to the inn with the *Sheep* sign, tel. 01451/830-229, patwhitehead1@live.co.uk).

NEAR STOW

$ Little Broom B&B hides out in the neighboring hamlet of Maugersbury, which enjoys the peace Stow once had. It rents three cozy rooms and a studio apartment that share a lush garden and pool (cash only, tel. 01451/830-510, www.cotswolds.info/webpage/little-broom.htm, brendarussell1@hotmail.co.uk). Brenda has racehorses, and her greenhouse keeps the pool warm throughout the summer (guests welcome). It's a hilly half-mile walk from Stow: Head east on Park Street and stay right toward Maugersbury. Turn right into Chapel Street and take the first right uphill to the B&B.

Eating in and near Stow

While Stow has several good dining options, consider venturing out of town for a meal. You can walk to the pub in nearby Broadwell, or—better yet—drive to one of several enticing gastropubs in the surrounding villages (see sidebar on page 376).

IN STOW

These places are all within a five-minute walk of each other, either on the main square or downhill on Queen and Park streets. For good sit-down fish-and-chips, go to either pub on the main square: The Queen's Head or The Kings Arms. For dessert, consider munching a locally made treat under the trees on the square's benches and watching the sky darken, the lamps come on, and visitors having their photo fun in the stocks.

Restaurants and Pubs

$$$ The Old Butchers, named for its location rather than its menu, specializes in fish. Serving oysters, scallops, and fish along with steak and burgers, they offer both indoor and outdoor tables and a good wine list (daily 12:00-14:30 & 18:30-21:30, 7 Park Street, tel. 01451/831-700).

$$ Stow Lodge is *the* choice of the town's proper ladies. There are two parts: The formal but friendly bar serves fine pub grub (daily 12:00-14:00 & 19:00-20:30); the restaurant serves a popular £30 three-course dinner (nightly, veggie options, good wines, just off main square, tel. 01451/830-485, Val). On a sunny day, the pub serves lunch in the well-manicured garden, where you'll feel quite aristocratic.

$$$ The Bell at Stow, at the end of Park Street (on the edge of town), has a youthful pub energy for a drink or a full meal. They serve up classic English dishes with seasonal, locally sourced ingredients (daily 12:00-21:00, reservations recommended, tel. 01451/870-916, www.thebellatstow.com).

$$ The Queen's Head faces Market Square, near Stow Lodge. With a classic pub vibe, it's a great place to bring your dog and watch the eccentrics while you eat pub grub and drink the local Cotswold brew, Donnington Ale. They have a meat pie of the day and good fish-and-chips (beer garden out back, Mon-Sat 12:00-14:30 & 18:30-21:00, Sun 12:30-16:00, tel. 01451/830-563).

Cheaper Options

The grassy triangle where Digbeth hits Sheep Street has takeout fish-and-chips, Chinese, and Indian food. You can picnic at the triangle, or on the benches by the stocks on Market Street.

$ Cotswold Baguettes Take-Out has a line out the door for tasty takeout jacket potatoes, pasties, made-to-order sandwiches, and soup (Mon-Fri 9:00-16:00, Sat until 13:00, closed Sun, Church Street, tel. 01451/831-362).

$ Greedy's Fish and Chips, on Park Street, is the go-to place for takeout. There's no seating, but they have benches out front (Mon-Sat 12:00-14:00 & 16:30-20:30, closed Sun, tel. 01451/870-821).

$ Jade Garden Chinese Take-Away is appreciated by locals who don't want to cook (Wed-Mon 17:00-23:00, closed Tue, 15 Park Street, tel. 01451/870-288).

$$ The Prince of India, with a pleasant dining room, offers good Indian food to take out or eat in (nightly 18:00-23:00, 5 Park Street, tel. 01451/830-099).

$ The Old Bakery Tearoom is a local favorite hidden away in a tiny mall at the bottom of Digbeth Street with traditional cakes and light lunches (Mon-Wed & Fri-Sat 10:30-16:00, closed Thu and Sun, Digbeth Street, Alan and Jackie). Come here for soup, salad, sandwiches, and tea and scones (£6 cream tea is splittable).

$ The Hive is a quality modern café, where Jane and Sally offer breakfast, lunch, and tea with a warm welcome (Thu-Mon 9:00-17:00, closed Tue-Wed, Digbeth Street, tel. 01451/831-087).

$ Lucy's Tea Room is a nice option if you fancy a light lunch or cream tea on Market Square (daily 9:00-16:00, next to Stow Lodge).

Groceries: The **Co-op,** a small grocery store, faces the main square next to the Kings Arms (daily 7:00-22:00) and a big **Tesco** supermarket is 400 yards north of town.

Great Country Gastropubs

These places—known for their high-quality meals and fine settings—are popular. Arrive early or phone in a reservation. (If you show up at 20:00, it's unlikely they'll be able to seat you for dinner if you haven't called first.) These pubs allow "well-behaved children," have overnight accommodations, and are practical only for those with a car. If you have wheels, make a point to dine at one of these—no matter where you're sleeping. For locations, see the map on page 340.

Near Stow

The first two (in Oddington, about three miles from Stow) are trendier and fresher, yet still in a traditional pub setting. The Plough (in Ford, a few miles farther away) is your jolly olde dark pub.

$$$$ The Fox Inn, a different Fox Inn than the one in Broadwell (see "Pub Dinner Hike from Stow"), has a long history but a fresh approach. It's a popular choice among local foodies for its updated pub classics and more creative, modern English dishes. They've perfected their upmarket rustic-chic vibe, with a genteelly Old World interior that's fresh and candlelit with a delightful back terrace and garden (extensive wine list, Mon-Sat 12:00-14:30 & 18:30-21:30, Sun 12:00-19:00, in Lower Oddington, tel. 01451/870-555, http://thefoxatoddington. com).

$$$$ The Horse and Groom Village Inn in Upper Oddington is a smart place in a 16th-century inn, serving modern English and Continental food with plenty of vegetarian options, a good wine list (12 wines by the glass), and serious attention to beer. It boasts a wonderful fireplace and lots of meat on the menu (daily 12:30-14:30 & 18:00-21:00, tel. 01451/830-584, www. horseandgroomoddington. com).

Between Stow and Chipping Campden

$$$ The Plough Inn, in the hamlet of Ford, fills a fascinating 16th-century building— once a coaching inn, later a courthouse, and now a tribute to all things horse racing (it sits across from the Jackdaws Castle racehorse training facility). Eat from the same traditional English menu in the restaurant, bar, or garden. They are serious about their beer (owned by the local brewery), seasonal ingredients, and serving up heaping portions of stick-to-your-ribs pub-grub classics—a bit more traditional and less refined than others listed here (daily 12:00-14:00 & 18:00-21:00, all day Fri-Sun and June-Aug, 6 miles from Stow on the road to Tewkesbury, reservations smart, tel. 01386/584-215, www.theploughinnford.co.uk).

Near Chipping Campden
$$$$ The Ebrington Arms is a quintessential neighborhood pub with 21st-century amenities: modern British cuisine, home-brewed beer, an extensive wine list, and friendly (if occasionally slow) service. Rub elbows with locals in the crowded bar—energetic any day of the week. The restaurant and rotating menu are classy without being pretentious, and owners Jim and Claire make you feel welcomed (daily 12:00-14:30 & 18:00-21:00, Sun until 15:30 and 20:30, 3 miles from Chipping Campden, reservations smart, tel. 01386/593-223, www.theebringtonarms.co.uk).

Near Moreton-in-Marsh, in Bourton-on-the-Hill
The hill-capping Bourton—about a five-minute drive (or two-mile uphill walk) above Moreton—offers sweeping views over the Cotswold countryside. Perched at the top of this steep, picturesque burg is an enticing destination pub.

    $$$$ Horse and Groom Pub melds a warm welcome with a tempting menu of delicious modern English fare. They hit a good balance of old and new, combining unassumingly delicious food with a convivial spit-and-sawdust spirit. Choose between the lively, light, spacious interior or—in good weather—the terraced picnic-table garden out back (daily 12:00-15:00 & 18:00-21:00 except Sun until 20:30, tel. 01386/700-413, www.horseandgroom.info). Don't confuse this with The Horse and Groom Village Inn in Upper Oddington, near Stow (described earlier).

Other Gastropubs Worth a Drive
$$$ Eight Bells in Chipping Campden (described on page 357) and **$$$ The Mount Inn** in Stanton (described on page 362) are both upscale options. **$$$$ The Wild Rabbit** in Kingham, five miles from Chipping Norton, is quiet, gourmet, and the most expensive of all. It's urbane-pub-meets-California, serving traditional British with a modern twist. The £65 tasting menu is a hit with foodies (on Church St. in Kingham, tel. 01608/658-389, www.thewildrabbit.co.uk).

COTSWOLDS

PUB DINNER HIKE FROM STOW

From Stow, consider taking a half-hour countryside walk to the village of Broadwell, where you'll find a traditional old pub facing the village green that serves good basic grub in a convivial atmosphere.

$$ The Fox Inn Broadwell serves pub dinners (fish, meat pies, basic grub) and draws traditional ales—including the local Donnington ales. It's a classic, family-friendly pub (food served Mon-Sat 12:00-14:30 & 18:00-21:00, Sun 12:00-15:30 only, outdoor tables in garden out back, reservations smart, tel. 01451/870-909, www.thefoxinnbroadwell.com). They'll happily drive diners back up to Stow when finished.

Getting There: It's 30 minutes downhill from Stow. While the walk is not particularly scenic (it's one-third paved lane, and the rest on an arrow-straight bridle path), it is peaceful, and the exercise is a good way to stoke your appetite. The trail is poorly marked, but it's hard to get lost: Leave Stow at Parson's Corner, continue downhill, pass the town well, follow the bridle path straight until you hit the next road, then turn right at the road and walk downhill into the village of Broadwell.

Near Stow-on-the-Wold

These sights are all south of Stow: Some are within walking distance (the Slaughters and Bourton-on-the-Water), and one is 20 miles away (Cirencester). The Slaughters and Bourton are tied together by the countryside walk described on page 372.

▲Lower and Upper Slaughter

"Slaughter" has nothing to do with lamb chops. It likely derives from an Old English word, perhaps meaning sloe tree (the one used to make sloe gin).

Lower Slaughter is a classic village, with ducks, a charming little church, a picturesque water mill, and usually an artist busy at her easel somewhere. The Old Mill Museum is a folksy ensemble with a tiny museum, shop, and café complete with a delightful terrace overlooking the mill pond, enthusiastically run by Gerald and his daughter Laura, who just can't resist giving generous tastes of their homemade ice cream (£1 for museum, daily 10:00-18:00, Nov-Feb until dusk, tel. 01451/822-127, www.oldmill-lowerslaughter.com). Just behind the Old Mill, two kissing gates lead to the path that goes to nearby Upper Slaughter, a 15-minute walk or 2-minute drive away (leaving the Old Mill, take two lefts, then follow sign for *Wardens Way*). And if you follow the mill creek downstream, a bridle path leads to Bourton-on-the-Water (described next).

In **Upper Slaughter,** walk through the yew trees (sacred in

COTSWOLDS

pagan days) down a lane through the raised graveyard (a buildup of centuries of graves) to the peaceful church. In the far back of the fine cemetery, the statue of a wistful woman looks over the tomb of an 18th-century rector (sculpted by his son). Notice the town is missing a war memorial—that's because every soldier who left Upper Slaughter for World War I and World War II survived the wars. As a so-called "Doubly Thankful Village" (one of only 13 in England and Wales), the town instead honors those who served in war with a simple wood plaque in the Town Hall.

Getting There: Though the stop is not listed on schedules, you should be able to reach these towns on bus #801 (from Moreton or Stow) by requesting the "Slaughter Pike" stop (along the main road, near the villages). Confirm with the driver before getting on. If driving, the small roads from Upper Slaughter to Ford and Kineton (and the Cotswold Farm Park, described later) are some of England's most scenic. Roll your window down and joyride slowly.

▲Bourton-on-the-Water

I can't figure out whether they call this "the Venice of the Cotswolds" because of its quaint canals or its miserable crowds. Either way, this town—four miles south of Stow and a mile from Lower Slaughter—is very pretty. But it can be mobbed with tour groups during the day: Sidewalks become jammed with disoriented tourists wearing nametags.

If you can avoid the crowds, it's worth a drive-through and maybe a short stop. It's pleasantly empty in the early evening and after dark.

Bourton's attractions are tacky tourist traps, but the three listed below might be worth considering. All are on High Street in the town center. In addition to these, consider Bourton's **leisure center** (big pool and sauna, a five-minute walk from town center off Station Road; Mon-Fri 6:30-22:00, Sat-Sun 8:00-20:00; shared with the school—which gets priority for use, tel. 01451/824-024).

Getting There: It's conveniently connected to Stow and Moreton by bus #801. Bus #802 also connects to Stow.

Parking: Finding a spot here can be tough. Even during the

COTSWOLDS

busy business day, rather than park in the pay-and-display parking lot a five-minute walk from the center, you can drive right into town and wait for a spot on High Street just past the village green. (Where the road swings left, turn a hard right (watch for signs for museums and TI) to go along the babbling brook and down High Street; there's a long row of free 1.5 hour spots starting just past the brook in front of the Edinburgh Woolen Mills Shop, on the right). After 18:00 you can park free just along the brook.

Tourist Information: The TI is tucked across the stream a short block off the main drag, on Victoria Street, behind The Victoria Hall (Mon-Sat 9:30-17:00, Sun 10:00-14:00 except closed Sun Oct-April, tel. 01451/820-211).

Bike Rental: Hartwells on High Street rents bikes by half-day or day and includes a helmet, map, and lock (£11/3 hours; £16/day, Mon-Sat 9:00-18:00, Sun from 10:00, tel. 01451/820-405, www.hartwells.supanet.com).

▲Cotswold Motoring Museum

Lovingly presented, this good, jumbled museum shows off a lifetime's accumulation of vintage cars, old lacquered signs, threadbare toys, prewar memorabilia, and sundry British pop-culture knickknacks. If you appreciate old cars, this is nirvana. Wander the car-and-driver displays, which range from the automobile's early days to slick 1970s models, including period music to set the mood. Talk to an elderly Brit who's touring the place for some personal memories.

Cost and Hours: £6.25, daily 10:00-18:00, closed mid-Dec-mid-Feb, in the mill facing the town center, tel. 01451/821-255, www.cotswoldmotoringmuseum.co.uk.

Model Railway Exhibition

This exhibit of three model railway layouts is impressive only to train buffs (£3, June-Aug daily 11:00-17:00; closed Jan and Mon-Fri off-season; located in the back of a hobby shop, in the center of town, www.bourtonmodelrailway.co.uk).

Model Village

This light but fun display re-creates the town on a 1:9 scale in a tiny outdoor park, and has an attached room full of tiny models showing off various bits of British domestic life (£4.25, daily 10:00-18:00, until 16:00 in winter, at the edge of town, behind The Old New

Inn, a few minutes' walk from the center, www.themodelvillage.com).

Walk to the Slaughters

From Bourton-on-the-Water, it's about a 30-minute walk (or a two-minute drive) to Upper and Lower Slaughter (described previously); taken together, they make for an easy two-hour round-trip walk from Bourton. (You could also walk from Stow through the Slaughters to Bourton—hike described on page 372.)

▲Cotswold Farm Park

Here's a delight for young and old alike. This park is the private venture of the Henson family, who are passionate about preserving ing rare and endangered breeds of native British animals. While it feels like a kids' zone (with all the family-friendly facilities you can imagine), it's a fascinating chance for anyone to get up close and (very) personal with piles of mostly cute animals,

including the sheep that made this region famous—the big and woolly Cotswold Lion. The "listening posts" deliver audio information on each rare breed.

Check the events board for seasonal demonstrations of farm life—such as milking, bottle-feeding, shearing, sheep shows (meet the seven local breeds), and more. Buy a bag of seed upon arrival, or have your map eaten by munchy goats as I did. Tykes love the "farm safari" tractor rides, maze, and zip line, and especially the "discovery barn"—where they can (carefully) handle wee chicks and bunnies.

Cost and Hours: £10.50, kids-£9, daily 10:30-17:00, Nov-Dec until 16:00, closed Jan-Feb, good guidebook (£5), restaurant and café, tel. 01451/850-307, www.cotswoldfarmpark.co.uk.

Getting There: It's well signposted about halfway between Stow and Stanway (15 minutes from either). A visit here makes sense if you're traveling from Stow to Chipping Campden.

Northleach

While other towns may be cuter with more tourist-oriented sights, Northleach (nine miles south of Stow-on-the-Wold) is the best of the "untouched and untouristed" Cotswold villages. Officials made sure the main road didn't pass through town back in the 1980s, and

COTSWOLDS

today there's no TI and no place to park a big bus. It's invisible to mass tourism...and I like it.

The town's impressive main square (Market Place) and church attest to its position as a major wool center in the Middle Ages. Along with the Cotswolds Discovery Centre (on the big road at the edge of town), the town mostly consists of a main street leading to a fine old square facing a glorious church.

Drivers can park in the square called The Green or the adjoining Market Place. Bus #801 (with good Stow and Moreton connections) stops on the square, where there's an outdated map posted by the WC. For better information, find the nicely done Northleach map/guide (free at the church, post office, or Black Cat Community Café). Information is also online (www.northleach.gov.uk). Your best bet for a friendly and knowledgeable local might be the volunteer greeters at the church.

Eating: Three good options are all on or near Market Place. **$ Black Cat Community Café,** where the church lane hits the square, is run by the church and raises money for its charity work (Mon-Sat 9:00-16:30, closed Sun). Also facing the square is the **$$ Sherborne Arms** pub (long hours daily). It's a classic, family- and pet-friendly locale, with a big fireplace, pool table, traditional ales and pub grub, outdoor seating, and a sloppy vibe.

$$$$ The Wheatsheaf Inn is the foodie's favorite for fine dining. With a pleasantly traditional dining room and a gorgeous sprawling garden, they offer modern English cuisine (long hours daily, on the main street into town one block before Market Place, tel. 01451/860-244, www.cotswoldswheatsheaf.com).

Market Place

Standing on the main square, you sense this was a fine medieval town. In fact, Northleach is a good example of a medieval "New Town." Hundreds of planned market towns like this were "planted" around England after the Norman conquest in 1066. Part of the Norman vision of creating a strong and centralized England was a land of logical towns, each with a triangular market place (likely symbolic of the Trinity) and a long High Street lined with standard and skinny "burgage plots"—parcels of land (from front-to-back: storefront, warehouse, living quarters, servants' quarters, stables, garden) all 33 feet wide and reaching back to a service lane 330 feet behind the High Street. The Northleach economy got a boost in 1227 when the king granted it a market charter. Back then, traders came from far and wide...you could hear Italian-speaking wool importers in the streets. Nine centuries later, you can still see these skinny units (now either 33 or 66 feet wide) surviving.

While the market hall and the stocks may be gone, the square still has all the essentials of a town: bus stop, post office, pub, and so on, overseen by its church tower.

Church of Saints Peter and Paul

This fine Perpendicular Gothic church has been called the "cathedral of the Cotswolds." It's one of the Cotswolds' two finest "wool" churches (along with Chipping Campden's), paid for by 15th-century wool tycoons. And, with

its enthusiastic corps of volunteer greeter/guides, it's the most welcoming place in town.

Pick up a flier and the fine town map/guide. Find the baptismal font with carved devils being crushed at its base (which

dates from the 14th century and was part of the previous church). Ponder the brass plaques on the floor that memorialize big shots, showing sheep and sacks of wool at their long-dead feet, and inscriptions mixing Latin and Old English. Imagine the stained glass filling the windows before being destroyed—likely in the 17th-century civil war. And don't miss the wonderful little exhibit about planned towns throughout medieval England in the north transept (daily 9:00-17:00 or until dusk, tel. 01451/861-132).

Cotswolds Discovery Centre at the Old Prison

This 18th-century building hosts displays about Cotswolds geology and history; pre-industrial farming including two shepherds' huts; and cell blocks and a courtroom from the building's previous uses. The on-site modern and glassy Cotswold Lion Café has indoor and outdoor seating (free, daily 9:30-16:30, on the A-429—Fosse Way—at the edge of Northleach, tel. 01451/862-000).

Coln Valley

Drivers will enjoy exploring the scenic Coln Valley, linking Northleach to Bibury as you pass through the enigmatic villages of Coln St. Dennis, Coln Rogers, Coln Powell, and Winson.

Chedworth Roman Villa

Secluded in thick woods in the Coln Valley are the remains of one of the finest aristocratic villas of fourth-century Roman Britain. Though well off the beaten path now, in its heyday of the late fourth

COTSWOLDS

century this wealthy farmstead was not far from a major Roman thoroughfare. You'll find a small museum and visitors center, and extensive, well-preserved floor mosaics. Rounding out the site are the remains of a small bath complex and a mossy spring once surrounded by an ostentatious water shrine. For history buffs with their own transportation, this is worth seeking out.

Cost and Hours: £11, daily 10:00-17:00, until 16:00 off-season, audioguide-£1, free guided tours daily, tel. 01242/890-256, www.nationaltrust.org.uk/chedworth.

Getting There: A half-mile beyond Northleach on the A-429, turn right and follow brown *Roman Villa* signs another 4 miles to the villa. Note: Don't follow *Chedworth* signs; these lead to Chedworth village.

▲Bibury

Six miles northeast of Cirencester, this village—long a favorite with British fond of strolling and fishing—is now so touristy I'd

only visit after hours. Bibury (BYE-bree) caters to tour buses, and lately has become a stop on the Instagram circuit and can be overwhelmed by selfie-stick tourists. After about 17:00, the light is warm and the masses are gone. The town offers some relaxing sights, including a row of very old weavers' cottages, a trout farm, a stream teeming with fat fish and proud ducks, and a church surrounded by rosebushes. A protected wetlands area on the far side of the stream hosts newts and water voles.

From the small parking lot, check out the posted map and information. Then walk the loop: up the main street (enjoying achingly beautiful homes with gardens and signs in Chinese that say keep out), then turn right along the old weavers' Arlington Row and back along the made-for-tour-groups paved path on the far side of the marsh, peeking into the rushes for wildlife.

For a closer look at the fish, cross the little bridge to the 15-acre **Trout Farm,** where you can feed them—or catch your own (£4.50 to walk the grounds, fish food-£0.60; daily 8:00-18:00, shorter hours off-season; catch-your-own only on weekends March-Oct 10:00-17:00, no fishing in winter, call or email to confirm fishing schedule, tel. 01285/740-215, www.biburytroutfarm.co.uk).

Getting There: Take bus #801 from Moreton-in-Marsh or Stow, then change to #855 in Northleach or Bourton-on-the-Water (3/day, 1 hour total).

Sleeping in Bibury: To spend the night in tiny Bibury, consider **$$ The William Morris B&B,** named for the 19th-century designer and writer (2 rooms, tearoom, 200 yards from the bridge toward the church at 11 The Street, tel. 01285/740-555, www. thewilliammorris.com, 11tearoom@gmail.com).

▲Cirencester

Almost 2,000 years ago, Cirencester (SIGH-ren-ses-ter) was the ancient Roman city of Corinium. Today it's the largest town of

the Cotswold district. It's less cute and feels more bustling than surrounding towns, but has a pleasant and pedestrianized historic center. It's 20 miles from Stow down the A-429, which was called Fosse Way in Roman times. The **TI,** in the shop at the Corinium Museum, answers questions and sells a town map and a town walking-tour brochure (same hours as museum, tel. 01285/654-180).

Getting There: By bus, take #801 from Moreton-in-Marsh or Stow, then change to #855 in Northleach or Bourton-on-the-Water for Cirencester (3/day, 1.5 hours total). Drivers follow *Town Centre* signs and find parking right on the market square; if it's full, retreat to the Waterloo pay-and-display lot (a 5-minute walk away).

Visiting Cirencester: Stop by the impressive **Corinium Museum** to find out why they say, "If you scratch Gloucestershire,

you'll find Rome." The museum chronologically displays well-explained artifacts from the town's rich history, with a focus on Roman times—when Corinium was the second-biggest city in the British Isles (after Londinium). You'll see column capitals and fine mosaics before moving on to the Anglo-Saxon and Middle Ages exhibits (£6, Mon-Sat 10:00-17:00, Sun from 14:00, shorter hours off-season, Park Street, tel. 01285/655-611, www. coriniummuseum.org).

Cirencester's **church,** built in about 1490, is the largest of the Cotswold "wool" churches. The cutesy **New Brewery Arts** crafts center entertains visitors with traditional weaving and potting, workshops, an interesting gallery, and a good coffee shop (www.newbreweryarts.org.uk). Monday and Friday are general-**market** days, Friday features an antique market, and a crafts market is held every Saturday.

Moreton-in-Marsh

This workaday town—worth ▲—is like Stow or Chipping Campden without the touristy sugar. Rather than gift and antique shops, you'll find streets lined with real shops: ironmongers selling cottage name-plates and carpet shops strewn with the re-markable patterns that decorate B&B floors. A traditional market of 100-plus stalls fills High Street each Tuesday, as it has for the last 400 years (9:00-15:00, handicrafts, farm produce, clothing, books, and people-watch-ing; best if you go early). The Cotswolds has an economy aside from tourism, and you'll feel it here.

Orientation to Moreton-in-Marsh

Moreton has a tiny, sleepy train station two blocks from High Street, lots of bus connections, and the best **TI** in the region. Pe-ruse the racks of fliers, confirm rail and bus schedules, and consider the £0.50 *Town Trail* self-guided walking tour leaflet. Ask about discounted tickets for Blenheim Palace, easily visited between here and Oxford (TI open Mon-Fri 8:45-17:00, Sat 10:00-13:00, closed Sat Nov-Easter and Sun year-round, good public WC, tel. 01608/650-881).

HELPFUL HINTS

Laundry: The handy launderette is a block in front of the train station on New Road (daily 7:00-19:00, last self-service wash at 17:00, drop-off service options available—call ahead to ar-range, tel. 01608/650-888).

Bike Rental and Taxis: See "Getting Around the Cotswolds," ear-lier.

Parking: It's easy—anywhere on High Street is fine any time, as long as you want, for free (though there is a 2-hour parking limit for the small lot in the middle of the street). On Tues-days, when the market makes parking tricky, try the **Budgens** supermarket, where you can park for two hours.

Hikes and Walks from Moreton-in-Marsh: As its name implies,

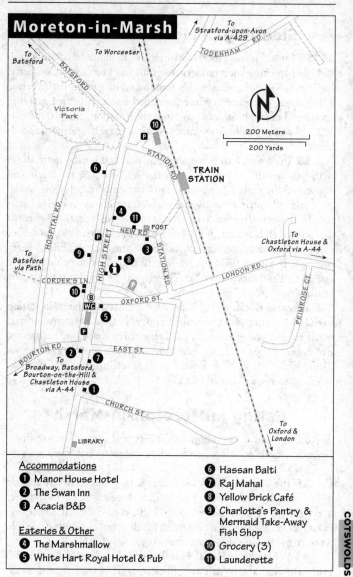

Moreton-in-Marsh

Accommodations
1. Manor House Hotel
2. The Swan Inn
3. Acacia B&B

Eateries & Other
4. The Marshmallow
5. White Hart Royal Hotel & Pub
6. Hassan Balti
7. Raj Mahal
8. Yellow Brick Café
9. Charlotte's Pantry & Mermaid Take-Away Fish Shop
10. Grocery (3)
11. Launderette

Moreton-in-Marsh sits on a flat, boggy landscape, making it a bit less appealing for hikes; I'd bus to Chipping Campden or to Stow, both described earlier, for a better hike (this is easy, since Moreton is a transit hub). If you do have just a bit of time to kill in Moreton, consider taking a fun and easy walk a mile out to the arboretum and falconry center in **Batsford** (described later).

Sleeping in Moreton-in-Marsh

$$$$ Manor House Hotel is Moreton's big old hotel, dating from 1545 but sporting such modern amenities as toilets and electricity. Its 35 classy-for-the-Cotswolds rooms and its garden invite relaxation (elevator, log fire in winter, attached restaurants, free parking, on far end of High Street away from train station, tel. 01608/650-501, www.cotswold-inns-hotels.co.uk, info@manorhousehotel.info).

$$ The Swan Inn is wonderfully perched on the main drag, with 10 en-suite rooms. Though the halls look a bit worn and you enter through a bar/restaurant that can be noisy on weekends, the renovated rooms themselves are classy and the bathrooms modern (free parking, restaurant gives guests 10 percent discount, High Street, tel. 01608/650-711, www.swanmoreton.co.uk, info@swanmoreton.co.uk, Sara and Terry Todd). Terry can pick up guests from the train station and may be able to drive guests to destinations within 20 miles if no public transport is available.

$ Acacia B&B, on the short road connecting the train station to the town center, is a convenient budget option. Dorothy has four small rooms: one is en suite, the other three share one bathroom. Rooms are bright and tidy, and most overlook a lovely garden (tel. 01608/650-130, 2 New Road, www.acaciainthecotswolds.co.uk, acacia.guesthouse@tiscali.co.uk).

Eating in Moreton-in-Marsh

A stroll up and down High Street lets you survey your options. Nobody travels to Moreton for its restaurants, but you won't go hungry.

$$ The Marshmallow is a dainty little place, relatively upscale but affordable, with a menu that includes traditional English dishes and afternoon tea (Sun-Tue 10:00-17:00, Wed-Sat until 20:00, reservations smart, shady back garden for dining, tel. 01608/651-536, www.marshmallow-tea-restaurant.co.uk).

$$ White Hart Royal Hotel and Pub is a solid bet for pub grub with a characteristic bar, finer restaurant seating, and a terrace out back—all with the same menu (daily, tel. 01608/650-731).

$$ Hassan Balti, with tasty Bangladeshi food, is a fine value for sit-down or takeout (daily 12:00-14:00 & 17:30-23:30, tel. 01608/650-798). **Raj Mahal,** at the other end of town (on High Street, just past the White Hart), is also good.

$$ Yellow Brick Café, run by Tom and Nicola, has a delightful outdoor patio, cozy indoor seating, cheap and cheery menu, and a tempting display of homemade cakes (daily 9:00-17:00, just off High Street at 3 Old Market Way, tel. 01608/651-881).

$ Charlotte's Pantry serves fresh soups, salads, sandwiches, and pastries for lunch in a cheerful spot on High Street across from the TI (good cream tea, Mon-Sat 9:00-17:00, Sun from 10:00, tel. 01608/650-000).

$ Mermaid Take-Away Fish Shop is popular for its takeout fish and tasty selection of traditional savory pies (Mon-Sat 11:30-14:00 & 17:00-22:00, closed Sun, tel. 01608/651-391).

Picnic: There's a small **Co-op** grocery on High Street (daily 7:00-20:00), and a **Tesco Express** two doors down (Mon-Fri 6:00-23:00, Sat-Sun from 7:00). The big **Budgens** supermarket is at the far end of High Street (Mon-Sat 7:00-22:00, Sun 10:00-16:00). You can picnic across the street in pleasant Victoria Park (with a playground).

Nearby: The excellent **$$$$ Horse and Groom** gastropub in Bourton-on-the-Hill is two miles away on the A-44 toward Chipping Campden (see page 377).

Moreton-in-Marsh Connections

Moreton, the only Cotswold town with a train station, is also the best base for exploring the region by bus (see "Getting Around the Cotswolds" on page 339).

From Moreton by Train to: London's Paddington Station (every 1-2 hours, 2 hours), **Bath** (hourly, 3 hours, 1-2 transfers), **Oxford** (hourly, 40 minutes), **Ironbridge Gorge** (hourly, 3 hours, 2 transfers; arrive Telford, then catch a bus or cab 5 miles to Ironbridge Gorge—see page 423), **Stratford-upon-Avon** (hourly, 3 hours, 2 transfers, slow and expensive, better by bus). Train info: Tel. 0345-748-4950, www.nationalrail.co.uk.

From Moreton by Bus to: Stratford-upon-Avon (#1 and #2 go via Chipping Campden: Mon-Sat 5/day, none on Sun, 1.5 hours, Johnsons Excelbus, tel. 01564/797-070, www.johnsonscoaches. co.uk).

Near Moreton-in-Marsh

▲Chastleton House

This stately home, located about five miles southeast of Moreton-in-Marsh, was lived in by the same family from 1607 until 1991. It offers a rare peek into a Jacobean gentry house. (Jacobean, which comes from the Latin for "James," indicates the style from the time of King James I—the early 1600s.) Built, like most Cotswold palaces, with wool money, it gradually declined with the fortunes of

COTSWOLDS

its aristocratic family, who lost much of their wealth in the war—not World War II, but the English Civil War in the 1640s. They stuck it out for centuries until, according to the last lady of the house, the place was "held together by cobwebs." It came to the National Trust on the condition that they would maintain its musty Jacobean ambience. It's so authentic that the BBC used it to film scenes from its adaptation of *Wolf Hall* (a best-seller about Henry VIII's chief minister, Thomas Cromwell, who masterminded Henry's divorce, marriage to Anne Boleyn, and break with Rome). Wander on creaky floorboards, many of them original, chat with the knowledgeable volunteer guides, and understand this frozen-in-time relic revealing the lives of nobles who were land rich but cash poor. The docents are proud to play on one of the best croquet teams in the region (the rules of croquet were formalized in this house in 1868—if you fancy a round, the ticket counter can lend you a set). Page through the early-20th-century family photo albums in the room just off the entry.

Cost and Hours: £10.50; Wed-Sun 13:00-17:00, closed Nov-mid-March and Mon-Tue year-round; last entry one hour before closing, tel. 01608/674-355, www.nationaltrust.org.uk/chastleton. They let in 15 people every 10 minutes; when it's busy you may have a short wait.

Getting There: Chastleton House is well signposted (be sure you follow signs to the house, not the town), about a 10-minute drive southeast of Moreton-in-Marsh off the A-44. It's a five-minute hike to the house from the free parking lot.

Batsford

This village has two side-by-side attractions that might appeal if you have a special interest or time to kill.

Getting There: Batsford is an easy 45-minute, 1.5-mile country walk west of Moreton-in-Marsh. By request, buses #1 and #2 will stop on the A-44, which is walking distance to Batsford Arboretum. You could also book a taxi in advance (see page 345).

Cotswold Falconry Centre

Along with the Cotswolds' hunting heritage comes falconry—and this place, with dozens of specimens of eagles, falcons, owls, and other birds, gives a sample of what these deadly birds of prey can do. You can peruse the cages to see all the different birds, but the demonstration, with vultures or falcons swooping inches over your head, is what makes it fun.

Cost and Hours: £10; daily mid-Feb–mid-Nov 10:30-17:30, closed rest of the year; flying displays at 11:30, 13:30, and 15:00, plus in summer at 16:30; Batsford Park, tel. 01386/701-043, www.cotswold-falconry.co.uk.

Batsford Arboretum and Garden Centre

This sleepy grove, with 2,800 trees from around the world, pales in comparison to some of the Cotswolds' genteel manor gardens. But it's next door to the Falconry Centre, and handy to visit if you'd enjoy strolling through a diverse wood. The arboretum's café serves lunch and tea on a terrace with sweeping views of the Gloucestershire countryside.

Cost and Hours: £9, Mon-Sat 9:00-17:00, Sun from 10:00, Dec-Feb same hours but last entry at 15:00, tel. 01386/701-441, www.batsarb.co.uk.

Blenheim Palace

Conveniently located halfway between the Cotswolds and Oxford, Blenheim Palace is one of Britain's best—worth ▲▲▲. Too many palaces can send you into a furniture-wax coma, but as a sightseeing experience and in simple visual grandeur, this palace is among Europe's finest. The Duke of Marlborough's home—one of the largest in England—is still lived in, which is wonderfully obvious as you prowl through it. The 2,000-acre yard, well designed by Lancelot "Capability" Brown, is as majestic to some as the palace itself. Note: Americans who pronounce the place "blen-HEIM" are the butt of jokes. It's "BLEN-em."

John Churchill, first duke of Marlborough, achieved Europe-wide renown with his stunning victory over Louis XIV of France's armies at the Battle of Blenheim in 1704. This was a major turning point in the War of the Spanish Succession—one of Louis's repeated attempts to gain hegemony over the continent. A thankful Queen Anne rewarded Churchill by building him this nice home, perhaps the finest Baroque building in England. Eleven dukes of Marlborough later, the palace is as impressive as ever. In 1874, a later John Churchill's American daughter-in-law, Jennie Jerome, gave birth at Blenheim to another historic baby in that line...and named him Winston.

GETTING TO BLENHEIM PALACE

Blenheim Palace sits at the edge of the cute cobbled town of Woodstock.

From the Cotswolds by Train: Your easiest train connection is from Moreton-in-Marsh to Hanborough—just 1.5 miles from the palace (£10, hourly, 30 minutes). From Hanborough station, take bus #233 (£3, buy on bus, 2/hour, 10 minutes, Mon-Sat only). Taxis don't wait at the station, but you can book one in advance (try A2B Taxis, tel. 07767/685-257; or Cabs 4U, tel. 07919/675-150).

From the Cotswolds by Car: Head for Woodstock (from the Cotswolds, follow signs for *Oxford* on the A-44); the palace is well signposted once in town, just off the main road. Buy your ticket at the gate, then drive up the long driveway to park near the palace.

ORIENTATION TO BLENHEIM PALACE

Cost: £27, includes audioguide; park and gardens only-£17, 30% discount when you buy on site and show your train or bus ticket, discount palace tickets are available at TIs in surrounding towns—including Oxford and Moreton-in-Marsh; family ticket available, £6.50 guidebook.

Hours: Daily 10:30-17:30, Nov-mid-Dec generally closed Mon-Tue, park open but palace closed mid-Dec-mid-Feb. Doors to the palace close at 16:45, it's "everyone out" at 17:30, and the park closes at 18:00. Late in the afternoon the palace is relaxed and quiet (even on the busiest of days).

Information: Tel. 0199/381-0530, www.blenheimpalace.com.

Tours: Audioguides are available for the **state rooms** (included in admission). Guided tours are available for the duke's **private apartment**—a.k.a. "Upstairs" Tour (£5, 2/hour, about 40 minutes, generally runs mid-Feb-Sept daily 11:00-16:30, tickets are limited), the **servants quarters**—a.k.a. "Downstairs" Tour (£5, generally daily 10:30-16:00, about 40 minutes), and the **gardens** (included in admission).

Eating and Sleeping near the Palace: The **$$ Water Terrace Café** at the garden exit is delightful for basic lunch and tea-time treats. The fancier **$$$ Orangery Restaurant,** serving afternoon tea and lunch, should be reserved in advance at the palace website (may be closed for renovation). There's also a $ café with lighter fare in the East Courtyard Visitors Center and a $ pizza café at the Pleasure Gardens.

In the pleasant, posh town of Woodstock just outside the palace gates, **$ Hampers Deli** is a good place to pick up provisions for a picnic on the palace grounds (31 Oxford Street, tel. 01993/811-535, www.hampersfoodandwine.co.uk). If you need a bed, consider a room in the characteristic old half-timbered **$$ Blenheim Buttery** (7 Market Place, tel. 01865/811-950, www.theblenheimbuttery.co.uk, info@theblenheimbuttery.co.uk).

VISITING THE PALACE

From the parking lot, you'll enter through the Visitors Center (shop, café, and WCs). Pick up a free map and daily tour program, consider signing up at the welcome desk for tours of the private apartment and the gardens, and head through the small courtyard. You'll emerge into a grand courtyard in front of the palace's columned yellow facade.

Facing the palace's steps, consider your six options: the state rooms, the Winston Churchill Exhibition, a skippable multimedia exhibit called The Untold Story, the private apartment tour, the gardens, and the Churchills' Destiny exhibit. The first three of these starts in the Great Hall, directly ahead. The palace state rooms and Winston Churchill Exhibition are substantial and most important (allow 1.5 hours total for both). The private apartment tour, an excellent behind-the-scenes peek at the palace, requires a special ticket and meets in the corner of the courtyard to the left. The gardens, through the wing on the right, are simply enchanting. And the Churchills' Destiny exhibit, worth a 15-minute walkthrough, is in the stables (West Courtyard) farther to the right.

State Rooms: The state rooms are the fancy halls the dukes use to impress visiting dignitaries. These most sumptuous rooms in the palace are ornamented with fine porcelain, gilded ceilings, portraits of past dukes, photos of the present duke's family, and "chaperone" sofas designed to give courting couples just enough privacy...but not *too* much.

Enjoy the series of 10 Brussels tapestries that commemorate military victories of the First Duke of Marlborough, including the Battle of Blenheim. After winning that pivotal conflict, he scrawled a quick note on the back of a tavern bill notifying the queen of his victory (you'll see a replica). The tour offers insights into the quirky ways of England's fading nobility—for example, in exchange for this fine palace, the duke still pays "rent" to the Queen in the form of one ornamental flag per year.

Finish with the remarkable "long library"—with its tiers of books and stuccoed ceilings—before exiting through the chapel, near the entrance to the gardens.

Winston Churchill Exhibition: This is a fascinating display of letters, paintings, and other artifacts of the great statesman who was born here. You'll either be instructed to see this before touring the main state rooms or directed into this exhibition from the library—the last room of the state rooms tour—before leaving the palace.

A highlight of your visit, the exhibit gives you an appreciation for this amazing leader and how blessed Britain was to have him when it did. Along with lots of intimate artifacts from his life, you'll see the bed in which Sir Winston was born in 1874 (prematurely...his mother went into labor suddenly while attending a party here).

The Untold Story: Upstairs, to the left as you enter the Great Hall, is a modern, 40-minute multimedia program with stories covering 300 years of palace history (this is skippable).

Private Apartment ("Upstairs" Tour): For a more extensive visit, book a spot to tour the duke's private digs (see "Tours," earlier). You'll see the chummy billiards room, luxurious china, the servants quarters with 47 bells—one for each room to call the servants, private rooms, 18th-century Flemish tapestries, family photos, and so on.

Churchills' Destiny: In the "stables block" (under the gateway to the right as you face the main palace entrance) is an exhibit that traces the military leadership of two great men who shared the name Churchill: John, who defeated Louis XIV at the Battle of Blenheim in the 18th century, and in whose honor this palace was built; and Winston, who was born in this palace, and who won the Battle of Britain and helped defeat Hitler in the 20th century. It's remarkable that arguably two of the most important military victories in the nation's history were overseen by distant cousins. (Winston Churchill fans can visit his tomb, just over a mile away to the south in the Bladon town churchyard—the church is faintly visible from inside the palace. Look for the footpath across from the White House pub.)

Gardens: The palace's expansive gardens stretch nearly as far as the eye can see in every direction. From the main courtyard follow signs through a little door (to the right as you face the main palace entrance). You'll emerge into the **Water Terraces;** from there, you can loop around to the left, behind the palace, to see (but not enter) the Italian

Garden. Or, head down to the lake to walk along the waterfront trail; going left takes you to the rose gardens and arboretum, while turning right brings you to the Grand Bridge.

On the way out of the palace complex, stop in at **Pleasure Gardens,** where a lush and humid greenhouse flutters with butterflies. A kid zone with the "world's largest symbolic hedge maze" is worth a look if you haven't seen one and want some exercise. If driving, you'll pass these gardens on the way to the exit; otherwise, you can take the tiny train from the palace parking lot (2/hour).

STRATFORD-UPON-AVON

Stratford is Shakespeare's hometown. To see or not to see? Stratford is a must for every big bus tour in England, and one of the most popular side-trips from London. English majors and actors are in seventh heaven here. Sure, it's touristy, and nonliterary types might find it's much ado about nothing. But nobody back home would understand if you skipped Shakespeare's house.

Shakespeare connection aside, the town's riverside and half-timbered charm, coupled with its hardworking tourist industry, make Stratford a fun stop. But the play's the thing to bring the Bard to life—and you've arrived just in time to see the Royal Shakespeare Company (the world's best Shakespeare ensemble) making the most of their state-of-the-art theater complex. If you'll ever enjoy a Shakespeare performance, it'll be here...even if you flunked English Lit.

PLANNING YOUR TIME

If you're just passing through Stratford, it's worth a half-day—stroll the charming core, visit your choice of Shakespeare sights (Shakespeare's Birthplace is best and easiest), and watch the swans along the river. But if you can squeeze it in, it's worth it to stick around to see a play; in this case, you'll need to spend the night here or drive in from the Cotswolds (just 30 minutes away; see previous chapter).

By Train or Bus: It's easy to stop in Stratford for a wander or an overnight. Stratford is well connected by train to London and Oxford, and linked by bus and train to nearby towns (Warwick and Coventry to the north, and Moreton in the Cotswolds to the south).

By Car: Stratford, conveniently located at the northern edge of the Cotswolds, is made to order for drivers connecting the Cotswolds with points north (such as Ironbridge Gorge or North Wales).

Orientation to Stratford

Stratford, with around 30,000 people, has a compact old town, with the TI and theater along the riverbank, and Shakespeare's Birthplace a few blocks inland; you can easily walk to everything except Mary Arden's Farm. The core of the town is lined with half-timbered houses. The River Avon has an idyllic yet playful feel, with a park along both banks, rowboats, swans, and a fun old crank-powered ferry.

TOURIST INFORMATION

The TI is in a small brick building on Bridgefoot, where the main street hits the river (Mon-Sat 9:00-17:30, Sun 10:00-16:00, tel. 01789/264-293, www.shakespeare-country.co.uk). In addition to selling combo-tickets for the Shakespeare Birthplace Trust sights (cheaper here, see "Shakespearean Sights," later), the TI also sells discount tickets for Warwick Castle (£18 here, £29 on-site).

ARRIVAL IN STRATFORD

By Train: Don't get off at the Stratford Parkway train station—you want Stratford-upon-Avon. Once there, exit straight ahead from the train station, bear right up the stairs, then turn left and follow the main drag straight to the river. (For the Grove Road B&Bs, turn right at the first big intersection.)

By Car: If you're sleeping in Stratford, ask your B&B for arrival and parking details (many have a few free parking spaces, but it's best to reserve ahead). If you're just here for the day, you'll find plenty of lots scattered around town. The Bridgefoot garage is big, easy, and cheap—coming from the south (i.e., the Cotswolds), cross the big bridge and veer right, following *Through Traffic, P,* and *Wark* (Warwick Road) signs. Go around the block—turning right and right and right—and enter the multistory garage; first hour free, £6/9 hours, £10/24 hours. The City Sightseeing bus stop and the TI are a block away. Parking is £1-3 at the park-and-ride near the Stratford Parkway train station, just off the A-46—from here you can ride a shuttle bus into town (£2 round-trip, 4/hour until

STRATFORD-UPON-AVON

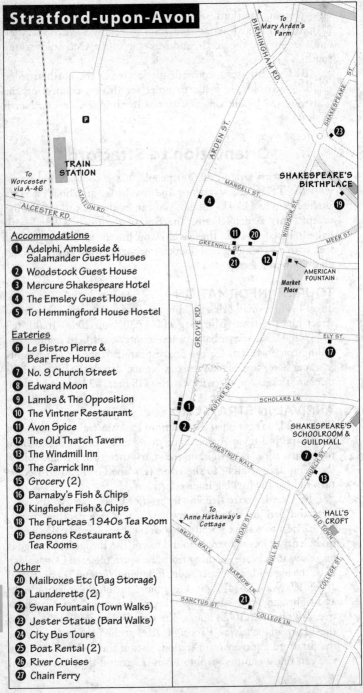

Stratford-upon-Avon

P

To Mary Arden's Farm

BIRMINGHAM RD.

SHAKESPEARE ST.

23

SHAKESPEARE'S BIRTHPLACE

ARDEN ST.

TRAIN STATION

To Worcester via A-46

STATION RD.

ALCESTER RD.

MANSELL ST.

4

19

WINDSOR ST.

MEEK ST.

11 20

GREENHILL ST.

21

12

AMERICAN FOUNTAIN

Market Place

GROVE RD.

ELY ST.

17

ROTHER ST.

SCHOLARS LN.

1

2

SHAKESPEARE'S SCHOOLROOM & GUILDHALL

CHESTNUT WALK

7

CHURCH ST.

13

To Anne Hathaway's Cottage

HALL'S CROFT

OLD TOWN

BROAD WALK

BROAD ST.

BULL ST.

COLLEGE ST.

21

SANCTUS ST.

NARROW LN.

COLLEGE LN.

Accommodations
1 Adelphi, Ambleside & Salamander Guest Houses
2 Woodstock Guest House
3 Mercure Shakespeare Hotel
4 The Emsley Guest House
5 To Hemmingford House Hostel

Eateries
6 Le Bistro Pierre & Bear Free House
7 No. 9 Church Street
8 Edward Moon
9 Lambs & The Opposition
10 The Vintner Restaurant
11 Avon Spice
12 The Old Thatch Tavern
13 The Windmill Inn
14 The Garrick Inn
15 Grocery (2)
16 Barnaby's Fish & Chips
17 Kingfisher Fish & Chips
18 The Fourteas 1940s Tea Room
19 Bensons Restaurant & Tea Rooms

Other
20 Mailboxes Etc (Bag Storage)
21 Launderette (2)
22 Swan Fountain (Town Walks)
23 Jester Statue (Bard Walks)
24 City Bus Tours
25 Boat Rental (2)
26 River Cruises
27 Chain Ferry

STRATFORD-UPON-AVON

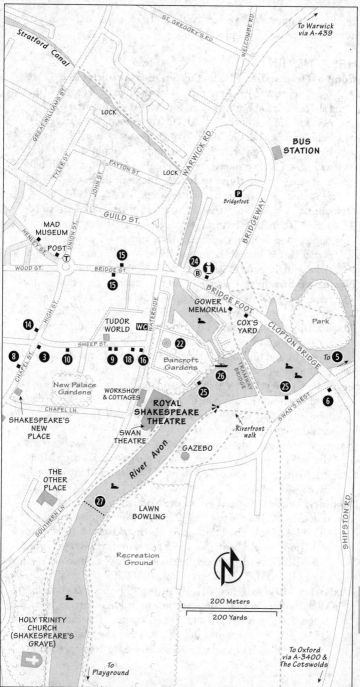

18:45, drops off at Wood Street NatWest Bank and Windsor Street near Shakespeare's Birthplace).

HELPFUL HINTS

Combo-Tickets: The TI and the Shakespeare Birthplace Trust sights sell combo-tickets that cover the five Trust sights (see "Shakespearean Sights," later, for details). A different combo-ticket for £13.10 covers the MAD Museum and Shakespeare's Schoolroom and Guildhall (which is not one of the Trust sights). City Sightseeing offers a range of combo-tickets that will save a little money if you combine a hop-on, hop-off bus tour with a boat cruise or rental, Shakespeare houses (3- or 5-house ticket), or the whole shebang.

Discounts: A ticket stub from a Stratford town walk (described under "Tours in Stratford," later) gets you a discount at many sights, shops, and restaurants. Also, ask the TI or your B&B owner if they have discount vouchers. Many sights sell online tickets for 10 percent less than the in-person price.

Name That Stratford: If you're coming by train or bus, be sure to request a ticket for "Stratford-upon-Avon," not just "Stratford" (to avoid a mix-up with Stratford Langthorne, near London.

Market Days: A local crafts and food market runs along the center of Bridge Street on Sundays from 10:00 to 17:00 (closed Jan-Feb), and on Rother Street on Fridays and Saturdays from 9:00 to 16:00.

Festival: Every year, on the weekend nearest to Shakespeare's birthday (traditionally considered to be April 23—also the day he died), Stratford celebrates. The town hosts free events, including activities for children.

Baggage Storage: Mailboxes Etc., a five-minute walk from the train station, can store your luggage (£2.50/bag, Mon-Fri hours vary, closed Sat-Sun, 12a Greenhill Street, tel. 01789/294-968).

Laundry: Laundry Quarter is on the road between the train station and the river (daily 8:00-20:00, 34 Greenhill Street, tel. 01789/417-766). The other option is **Sparklean,** a 10-minute walk from the city center, or about five minutes from the Grove Road B&Bs (daily 8:00-21:00, full-service option sometimes available—call, 74 Bull Street, tel. 01789/269-075).

Taxis: Try **007 Taxis** (tel. 01789/414-007) or the taxi stand on Woodbridge, near the intersection with High Street. To arrange for a private car and driver, contact **Platinum Cars** (£250/half-day tour, also does airport transfers from Heathrow and Birmingham, tel. 01789/264-626, www.platinum-cars.co.uk).

Tours in Stratford

Stratford Town Walks

These entertaining, award-winning two-hour walks introduce you to the town and its famous playwright. Tours run daily year-round, rain or shine. Just show up at the Swan fountain (on the waterfront, opposite Sheep Street) in front of the Royal Shakespeare Theatre and pay the guide (£6, ticket stub offers discounts to some sights, shops, and restaurants; daily at 11:00, Sat also at

14:00, mobile 07855-760-377, www.stratfordtownwalk.co.uk). They also run an evening ghost walk (£7, Sat at 19:30, 1.5 hours, must book in advance).

Tudor World

This attraction offers 1.5-hour Shakespeare tours and one-hour ghost tours; see the listing under "Sights in Stratford."

Bard Walks

A group of trained, costumed actors describe the city with Shakespearean flair, incorporating some of the Bard's most famous speeches and sonnets (£10, cash only, 1.5 hours, generally April-Oct Thu-Sun 14:00, book in advance, leaves from jester statue on Henley Street, mobile 07932-336-593, www.bardwalk.co.uk).

City Sightseeing Bus Tours

Open-top buses let you hop on and hop off at stops within the compact town, and head out to Anne Hathaway's Cottage and Mary Arden's Farm. The full 11-stop circuit takes about an hour and comes with entertaining and informative commentary (£15, ticket valid 24 hours, discount with town walk ticket stub, buy tickets on bus or at the TI; buses leave from the TI every 20 minutes, mid-April-Oct 9:30-17:00, no buses off-season, some weekend buses have live guides; tel. 01789/412-680, www.citysightseeing-stratford.com).

STRATFORD-UPON-AVON

Shakespearean Sights

Stratford's five biggest Shakespeare sights are run by the Shakespeare Birthplace Trust (www.shakespeare.org.uk). While these sights are promoted like tacky tourist attractions—and designed to be crowd-pleasers rather than to tickle academics—they're well run and genuinely interesting. Shakespeare's Birthplace, Shakespeare's New Place, and Hall's Croft are in town; Mary Arden's Farm and Anne Hathaway's Cottage are just outside Stratford. Each has a tranquil garden and helpful, eager docents who love to tell a story; and yet, each is quite different, so visiting all five gives you a well-rounded look at the Bard and his influences. (A sixth sight, Shakespeare's Schoolroom and Guildhall, is run by a separate organization, with a separate ticket.)

If you're here for Shakespeare sightseeing—and have time to venture to the countryside sights—you might as well buy a combo-ticket and drop into all five Shakespeare Birthplace Trust sights (described next). If your time is limited, visit only Shakespeare's Birthplace, which is the most convenient to reach (right in the town center) and offers the best historical introduction to the playwright.

Combo-Tickets: A combo-ticket that covers all five Shakespeare Birthplace Trust sights is called the **Full Story ticket**—a.k.a. the "five-house ticket"—and is sold at the TI and covered sights (£21 at the TI, £22.50 if purchased at a covered sight).

Another option is the £18 **any-three combo-ticket.** This ticket lets you choose three of the five Shakespeare Birthplace Trust sights—for instance, the birthplace, Anne Hathaway's Cottage, and Mary Arden's Farm (sold only at the TI; you'll get a receipt, then show it at the first sight you visit to receive your three-sight card).

Booking online saves you 10 percent; tickets are valid for one year.

IN STRATFORD
▲▲Shakespeare's Birthplace
While the birthplace itself is a bit underwhelming, it's rewarding to stand in the bedroom where Shakespeare was born, and helpful docents make this a good introduction to the Bard. A modern exhibit and live mini performances emphasize how his work continues to inspire.

Cost and Hours: £17.50, covered by combo-tickets, daily 9:00-17:00, Nov-March 10:00-16:00, in town center on Henley Street, tel. 01789/204-016, www.shakespeare.org.uk.

Visiting Shakespeare's Birthplace: An introductory **exhibit** shows Shakespeare's enduring influence, with a video mash-up ranging from *The Simpsons* to the Hip-Hop Shakespeare Company. Check out the timeline of Shakespeare's plays, information about his upbringing and family life, and career in London. A few historical artifacts, including an original 1623 First Folio of Shakespeare's work, are also on display.

I find the **half-timbered Elizabethan building** where young William grew up a bit disappointing, as if millions of visitors have rubbed it clean of anything authentic. It was restored in the

1800s, and the furnishings are true to 1575, when William was 11. To liven up the otherwise dead-feeling house, chat up the well-versed, often-costumed attendants posted in many of the rooms, eager to engage with travelers and answer questions.

Shakespeare's father, John—who came from humble beginnings, but bettered himself by pursuing a career in glove-making (you'll see the window where he sold them to customers on the street)—provided his family with a comfortable upper-middle-class existence. The guest bed in the parlor was a major status symbol: They must have been rich to afford such a nice bed that wasn't used every day. This is also the house where Shakespeare and his bride, Anne Hathaway, began their married life together. Upstairs are the rooms where young Will, his siblings, and his parents slept (along with their servants). Look for the window etched with the names of important visitors, from Sir Walter Scott to actor Henry Irving. After Shakespeare's father died and William inherited the building, the thrifty playwright converted it into a pub to make a little money.

Exit into the fine **garden** where Shakespearean **actors** often perform brief scenes (they may even take requests). Pull up a bench and listen, imagining the playwright as a young boy stretching his imagination in this very place.

Shakespeare's New Place

While nothing remains of the house the Bard inhabited when he made it big (it was demolished in the 18th century), its manicured grounds are a tranquil spot to soak up some history. Today, modern sculptures and traditional gardens adorn the grounds of the mansion Shakespeare called home for nearly 20 years. It's hard to imagine a house on this site, but vivid docent descriptions and visual aids bring the history to life. The expansive lawn is a pleasant respite from the hubbub of town, and the perfect place to sip a coffee or compose sonnets. Next door, Nash's House (which belonged to Shakespeare's granddaughter and her husband) hosts a model of Shakespeare's house, domestic artifacts, period clothing, and a balcony view of the knot garden.

William Shakespeare (1564-1616)

To many, William Shakespeare is the greatest author, in any language, period. In one fell swoop, he expanded and helped define modern English—the unrefined tongue of everyday people—and granted it a beauty and legitimacy that put it on par with Latin. In the process, he gave us phrases like "one fell swoop," which we quote without knowing that no one ever said it before Shakespeare wrote it.

Shakespeare was born in Stratford-upon-Avon in 1564 to John Shakespeare and Mary Arden. Though his parents were probably illiterate, Shakespeare is thought to have attended Stratford's grammar school, finishing his education at age 14. When he was 18, he married 26-year-old Anne Hathaway (she was three months pregnant with their daughter Susanna).

The very beginnings of Shakespeare's writing career are shrouded in mystery: Historians have been unable to unearth any record of what he was up to in his early 20s. We only know that seven years after his marriage, Shakespeare was living in London as a budding poet, playwright, and actor. He soon hit the big time, writing and performing for royalty, founding (along with his troupe) the Globe Theatre (a functioning replica of which now stands along the Thames' South Bank—see page 127), and raking in enough dough to buy New Place, a swanky mansion back in his hometown. Around 1611, the rich-and-famous playwright retired from the theater and moved back to Stratford, where he died at the age of 52.

With plots that entertained both the highest and the lowest minds, Shakespeare taught the play-going public about human nature. His tool was an unrivaled linguistic mastery of English. Using borrowed plots, outrageous puns, and poetic language, Shakespeare wrote comedies (c. 1590—*Taming of the Shrew, As You Like It*), tragedies (c. 1600—*Hamlet, Othello, Macbeth, King Lear*), and fanciful combinations (c. 1610—*The Tempest*), exploring the full range of human emotions and reinventing the English language.

Perhaps as important was his insight into humanity. His father was a glove-maker and wool merchant, and his mother was the daughter of a landowner from a Catholic family. Some scholars speculate that Shakespeare's parents were closet Catholics,

Cost and Hours: £12.50, covered by combo-tickets, daily 10:00-17:00, Nov-March until 16:00, 22 Chapel Street, tel. 01789/338-536.

Hall's Croft

This former home of Shakespeare's eldest daughter, Susanna, gives a good idea of how the wealthy lived in the 17th century, with finer furnishings compared to the other Shakespeare practicing their faith during the rise of Protestantism. It is this tug-of-war between two worlds, some think, that helped enlighten Shakespeare's humanism. Think of his stock of great characters and great lines: Hamlet ("To be or not to be, that is the question"), Othello and his jealousy ("It is the green-eyed monster"), ambitious Mark Antony ("Friends, Romans, countrymen, lend me your ears"), rowdy Falstaff ("The better part of valor is discretion"), and the star-crossed lovers Romeo and Juliet ("But soft, what light through yonder window breaks"). Shakespeare probed the psychology of human beings 300 years before Freud. Even today, his characters strike a familiar chord.

The scope of his brilliant work, his humble beginnings, and the fact that no original Shakespeare manuscripts survive raise a few scholarly eyebrows. Some have wondered if Shakespeare had help on several of his plays. After all, they reasoned, how could a journeyman actor with little education have written so many masterpieces? And he was surrounded by other great writers, such as his friend and fellow poet, Ben Jonson. Most modern scholars, though, agree that Shakespeare did indeed write the plays and sonnets attributed to him.

His contemporaries had no doubts about Shakespeare—or his legacy. As Jonson wrote in the preface to the First Folio, "He was not of an age, but for all time!"

properties. Since Susanna married a doctor, exhibits focus on Elizabethan-era medicine, leaving visitors grateful to live in modern times. Hall appears to have been a conscientious physician: He kept notes in Latin of all his cures. His treatment for scurvy—watercress and scurvy grass—are both now known to contain vitamin C.

Cost and Hours: £8.50, covered by combo-tickets, daily 10:00-

Shakespearean Plays 101

Shakespeare's 38 plays span (and often intertwine) three genres: comedy, history, and tragedy. Brush up on some of the Bard's greatest hits before enjoying a performance in Stratford.

Comedy

As You Like It: Two brothers, a banished duke, noblemen, and a duke's daughter (Rosalind) fight and fall in love in the Forest of Arden, contemplating life, love, and death.

Much Ado About Nothing: Soldier Claudio and a nobleman's daughter, Hero, fall in love and play matchmakers to their unsuspecting friends. Trickery, slander, and heartbreak are overcome in an ultimately happy ending.

A Midsummer Night's Dream: Four Athenian lovers, two eloping, follow each other into the woods, where fairy King Oberon enchants them with a love potion. A mistaken identity leaves Lysander and Demetrius both pining after Helena, and Hermia without a groom.

The Tempest: Prospero, duke of Milan, is overthrown by his brother and Alonso (the king of Naples) and dwells on an enchanted island with daughter Miranda. When his old enemies wash ashore, Prospero enlists island spirits to seek his revenge—and Miranda falls in love with Alonso's son Ferdinand.

History

The Henriad: A series of four plays chronicles the demise of England's King Richard II, the rule of successor King Henry IV, and his relationship with rebellious son Prince Harry (eventually King

17:00, Nov-March 11:00-16:00, on-site tearoom, between Church Street and the river on Old Town Street, tel. 01789/338-533.

Shakespeare's Grave (Holy Trinity Church)

Shakespeare was a rector for Holy Trinity Church when he died. While the church is surrounded by an evocative graveyard, the Bard is entombed in a place of honor, right in front of the altar inside. The church marks the ninth-century birthplace of the town, which was once a religious settlement.

Cost and Hours: £4 donation, Mon-Sat 9:00-17:00 (Oct-March until 16:00), Sun from 12:30; no access to grave

Henry V). War across England and France forms the backdrop for Shakespeare's exploration of honor, nationalism, and power.

Tragedy

Romeo and Juliet: Lovers from rival families seek to marry, but are torn apart by their families. When Juliet fakes her death to avoid an arranged marriage, misunderstanding breeds heartbreak.

Macbeth: Three witches prophesize Macbeth's ascension from nobility to the throne of Scotland, leading Macbeth, aided by his ambitious wife, to embark on a violent mission to become king. Plagued by paranoia and hallucinations, he commits heinous crimes to gain—and maintain—power.

Othello: General Othello promotes Cassio to lieutenant over officer Iago. After Othello elopes with senator Brabantio's daughter Desdemona, a bitter Iago seeks revenge, manipulating the couple and Cassio by pitting them against each other.

Hamlet: Haunted by his father's ghost, Prince Hamlet plots to kill his father's murderer, King Claudius. But when Hamlet inadvertently causes his lover Ophelia's death, her brother Laertes vows to kill Hamlet, with Claudius' help. A climactic duel between Laertes and Hamlet leads to a bloodbath.

King Lear: King Lear banishes daughter Cordelia to France, while daughters Regan and Goneril secretly plot his death. Lear's ally the Earl of Gloucester, at odds with his own sons, warns Lear of the vengeful plot, and Lear drifts into madness. Both men succumb to the political chaos created by their families' greed and betrayal.

13:00-14:30; 10-minute walk past the theater—see its graceful spire as you gaze down the river, tel. 01789/266-316, www.stratford-upon-avon.org.

Shakespeare's Schoolroom and Guildhall

The guildhall and the guild's schoolhouse help visitors imagine Shakespeare's childhood years. Built between 1418 and 1420, the guildhall was the headquarters for the Guild of the Holy Cross, where everyone from Stratford and nearby towns—from tradesmen to craftsmen to clergy and nobility—networked and struck deals. Anyone could join for a small fee; in return, the guild supported members' families, even employing priests to pray for their souls. It also provided social services, such as town infrastructure—and established Stratford's first school.

Cost and Hours: £8.50, £13.10 combo-ticket with MAD

Museum, daily 11:00-17:00, Church Street, tel. 01789/203-170, www.shakespearesschoolroom.org.

Visiting the Guildhall and Schoolroom: The guildhall's priest's chapel and the Guild Chapel next door both contain fragments of medieval wall paintings that were probably whitewashed during Reformation efforts—during William's father's tenure as chamberlain here. (The paintings were uncovered when the chapel was restored in 1804 and are barely visible.)

In the very room where Shakespeare attended school for seven years, six days a week, you'll see a wood table with centuries-old student-carved graffiti, and you can try out a quill pen as you conjugate Latin. A costumed docent describes student life. Wood benches face each other so that kids could easily help each other learn. Since paper was so expensive, students were taught verbally, likely boosting young Will's flair for storytelling. Groups of traveling actors performed at the guildhall several times while Will attended school here. In the days before TV, movies, or social media, these productions were the pinnacle of entertainment, and likely inspired him.

JUST OUTSIDE STRATFORD

To reach either of these sights, it's best to drive or take the hop-on, hop-off bus tour (see "Tours in Stratford," earlier)—unless you're staying at one of the Grove Road B&Bs, which are an easy 20-minute walk from Anne Hathaway's Cottage. Both sights are well signposted (with brown signs) from the major streets and ring roads around Stratford. If driving between the sights, ask for directions at the sight you're leaving.

▲▲Mary Arden's Farm

Along with Shakespeare's Birthplace, this is my favorite of the Shakespearean sights. Famous as the girlhood home of William's mom, this homestead is in Wilmcote (about three miles from Stratford). Built around two historic farmhouses, it's an open-air folk museum depicting 16th-century farm life...which happens to have ties to Shakespeare.

Cost and Hours: £15, covered by combo-tickets, daily 10:00-17:00, everyone's shooed out at 17:30, closed Nov-mid-March, on-site café and picnic tables, tel. 01789/338-535.

Getting There: It's most convenient by car (free parking) or hop-on, hop-off bus, but also easy to reach by train. The Wilmcote train station is a five-minute walk up the street (two stops from Stratford-upon-Avon on Birmingham- and London-bound trains, 1-2/hour, 5-minute trip, call London Midland to confirm departure time—tel. 0844-811-0133, www.londonmidland.com).

Visiting Mary Arden's Farm: The museum hosts many special **events**—check the board by the entry. There are always plenty of active, hands-on activities to engage kids. Save some time for a walk: There are 23 acres of bucolic trails, orchards, and meadows to explore.

Pick up a map (and handful of organic animal feed) at the entrance and wander the grounds and buildings. Throughout the complex, you'll see interpreters in Tudor costumes performing daily 16th-century chores, such as milking the sheep and cutting wood to do repairs on the house. They answer questions and provide fun, gossipy insight into what life was

like at the time. Look out for heritage breeds of farmyard animals including goats, woolly pigs, and friendly donkeys.

The first building, **Palmer's farm** (mistaken for Mary Arden's home for hundreds of years, and correctly identified in 2000), holds a kitchen where food is prepared over an open fire; at 13:00 each day the "servants" (employees) sit down in the adjacent dining room for a traditional dinner.

Mary Arden actually lived in the neighboring **farmhouse,** covered in brick facade and less impressive. The house is filled

with kid-oriented activities, including period dress-up clothes, board games from Shakespeare's day, and a Tudor alphabet so kids can write their names in fancy lettering.

Of the many events here, the most enjoyable is the daily **bird of prey display,** with lots of mean-footed birds (call ahead for times). Chat with the falconers about their methods for earning the birds' trust: Like Katherine in *The Taming of the Shrew*—described as "my falcon" by husband Petruchio—the birds are motivated by food. Their hunger sets them to flight (a round-trip earns the bird a bit of food; the birds fly when hungry—but don't have the energy if they're *too* hungry). You may be given a bit of meat to feed the bird yourself.

▲Anne Hathaway's Cottage

Located 1.5 miles out of Stratford (in Shottery), this home is a 12-room farmhouse where the Bard's wife grew up. William courted Anne here—she was 26, he was only 18—and his tactics proved successful. (Maybe a little too much, as she was several months pregnant at their wedding.) Their 34-year marriage produced two more children, and lasted until his death in 1616 at age 52. The Hathaway family lived here from the 1500s until 1911, and much of the family's 92-acre farm remains part of the sight.

Cost and Hours: £12.50, covered by combo-tickets, daily 9:00-17:00, Nov-March 10:00-16:00, tearoom, tel. 01789/338-532.

Getting There: It's a 30-minute walk from central Stratford (20 minutes from the Grove Road B&Bs), a stop on the hop-on, hop-off tour bus, or a quick taxi ride from downtown Stratford (around £7). Drivers will find it well signposted entering Stratford from any direction, with easy cheap parking.

Visiting Anne Hathaway's Cottage: The thatched-roof **cottage** looks cute enough to eat, and it's fun to imagine the writer of some of the world's greatest romances wooing his favorite girl right here during his formative years. (If the place shakes, a tourist has thunked his or her head on the low beams.) The docent talks provide an intimate peek at life in Shakespeare's day.

Maybe even more interesting than the cottage are the **gardens,** which have several parts (including a prizewinning "traditional cottage garden"). Follow the signs to the "Woodland Walk" (look for the music-note willow sculpture on your way), along with a fun sculpture garden littered with modern interpretations of Shakespearean characters (such as Falstaff's mead gut, and a great photo-op statue of the British Isles sliced out of steel). From April through June, the gardens are at their best, with birds chirping, bulbs in bloom, and a large sweet-pea display. You'll also find a music trail, a butterfly trail, and various exhibits, like a teepee built of sticks that is rigged up to play a selection of Shakespeare's love sonnets when you press a button.

THE ROYAL SHAKESPEARE COMPANY

The Royal Shakespeare Company (RSC), undoubtedly the best Shakespeare company on earth, performs year-round in Stratford and in London. Seeing a play here in the Bard's birthplace is a must for Shakespeare fans, and a memorable experience for anybody. Between its excellent acting and remarkable staging, the RSC makes Shakespeare as accessible and enjoyable as it gets.

The RSC makes it easy to take in a play, thanks to their very user-friendly website, painless ticket-booking system, and chock-a-block schedule that fills the summer with mostly big-name

> ## Stratford Thanks America
>
> Residents of Stratford are thankful for the many contributions Americans have made to their city and its heritage. Along with pumping up the economy day in and day out with tourist visits, Americans paid for half the rebuilding of the Royal Shakespeare Theatre after it burned down in 1926. The Swan Theatre renovation was funded entirely by American aid. Harvard University inherited—you guessed it—the Harvard House, and it maintains the house today. London's much-loved theater, Shakespeare's Globe, was the dream (and gift) of an American. And there's even an odd but prominent "American Fountain" overlooking Stratford's market square on Rother Street, which was given in 1887 to celebrate the Golden Jubilee of the rule of Queen Victoria.

Shakespeare plays (plus a few more obscure titles to please the die-hard aficionados).

The RSC is enjoying renewed popularity after the update of its Royal Shakespeare Theatre. Even if you're not seeing a play, exploring this cleverly designed theater building is well worth your time. The smaller attached Swan Theatre hosts plays on a more intimate scale, with only about 400 seats.

▲▲▲Seeing a Play

Performances take place most days (Mon-Sat generally at 19:15 at the Royal Shakespeare Theatre or 19:30 at the Swan, matinees around 13:15 at the RST or 13:30 at the Swan, sporadic Sun shows). Shows generally last three hours or more, with one intermission; for an evening show, don't count on getting back to your B&B much before 23:00. There's no strict dress code—nice jeans and short-sleeve shirts are fine—but shorts are discouraged. If you're feeling bold, buy a £10 standing ticket and slip into an open seat as the lights dim—if nothing is available during the play's first half, something might open up after intermission.

Getting Tickets: Tickets range from £5 (standing) to £75, with most around £45 (discounts for families). Saturday-evening shows—the most popular—are the most expensive. You can book tickets as you like it: online (www.rsc.org.uk), by phone (tel. 01789/331-111, Mon-Sat 10:00-18:00, Sun until 17:00) or in person at the box office (Mon-Sat 10:00-20:00, until 18:00 on non-performance days, Sun until 17:00). Print tickets at home, pick them up at the theater 30 minutes before "curtain up," or just show them on your phone. Because it's so easy to get tickets online or by phone, it makes absolutely no sense to pay extra to book tickets through any other source.

The Look of Stratford

There's much more to Stratford than Shakespeare sights. Take time to appreciate the look of the town itself. While the main street goes back to Roman times, the key date for the city was 1196, when the king gave the town "market privileges." Stratford was shaped by its marketplace years. The market's many "departments" were located on logically named streets, whose names still remain: Sheep Street, Corn Street, and so on. Today's street plan—and even the 57' 9" width of the lots—survives from the 12th century. (Some of the modern store-fronts in the town center are still that exact width.)

Starting in about 1600, three great fires gutted the town, leaving very few buildings older than that era. After those fires, tinderbox thatched roofs were prohibited—the Old Thatch Tavern on Greenhill Street is the only remaining thatched roof in town, predating the law and grandfathered in.

The town's main drag, Bridge Street, is the oldest street in town, but looks the youngest. It was built in the Regency style—a result of a rough little middle row of wattle-and-daub houses being torn down in the 1820s to double the street's width. Today's Bridge Street buildings retain that early-19th-century style.

Throughout Stratford, you'll see striking black-and-white half-timbered buildings, as well as half-timbered structures that were partially plastered over and covered up in the 19th century. During Victorian times, the half-timbered style was considered low-class, but in the 20th century—just as tourists came, preferring ye olde style—timbers came back into vogue, and the plaster was removed on many old buildings. But any black and white you see is likely to be modern paint. The original coloring was "biscuit yellow" and brown.

Tickets go on sale 10 months in advance. Saturdays and very famous plays (such as *Romeo and Juliet* or *Hamlet)*—or any play with a well-known actor—sell out the fastest. Before your trip, check the website, and consider buying tickets if something strikes your fancy. But demand is difficult to predict, and some tickets do go unsold. On a past visit, on a sunny Friday in June, the riverbank was crawling with tourists. I stepped into the RSC on a lark to see if they had any tickets. An hour later, I was watching King Lear lose his marbles.

Even if there aren't any seats available, you may be able to buy a returned ticket on the same day of an otherwise sold-out show. Also, the few standing-room tickets in the main theater are sold only on the day of the show. While you can check at the box office anytime during the day, it's best to go either when it opens at 10:00 (daily) or between 17:30 and 18:00 (Mon-Sat). Be prepared to wait.

STRATFORD-UPON-AVON

Visiting the Theaters
▲▲The Royal Shakespeare Theatre

The RSC's flagship theater is one of Stratford's most fascinating sights. If you're seeing a play here, come early to poke around the building and check out interesting tidbits of theater history. You need to take a guided tour (explained later) to see the backstage areas, but you're welcome to wander the theater's public areas any time the building is open.

Cost and Hours: Free entry, £8.50 for *The Play's the Thing* exhibit; Mon-Sat 10:00-23:00, Sun until 17:00.

Information: Tel. 01789/331-111, www.rsc.org.uk.

Guided Tours: Well-informed RSC volunteers lead entertaining one-hour tours (£9; behind-the-scenes tour and front-of-the-house tours are at Royal Shakespeare Theatre; audition tours and From Page-to-Stage tours are at The Other Place—described later; tour schedule varies by day, depends on performances; call, check online, or go to box office to confirm schedule; best to book ahead).

Tour Combo-Ticket: The £15 Explorer Pass includes a theater tour of your choice, the tower climb, and *The Play's the Thing* exhibit (described later, book at box office or online).

Background: The original Victorian-style theater was built in 1879 to honor the Bard, but it burned down in 1926. The big Art Deco-style building you see today was erected in 1932 and outfitted with a stodgy Edwardian "picture frame"-style stage, even though a more dynamic "thrust"-style stage—better for engaging the audience—was the actors' choice. (It would also have been closer in design to Shakespeare's original Globe stage, which jutted into the crowd.)

The latest renovation in 2011 addressed this ill-conceived design, adding an updated thrust-style stage. They've left the shell of the 1930s theater, but given it an unconventional deconstructed-industrial style, with the seats stacked at an extreme vertical pitch. Though smaller, the redesigned theater can seat about the same size audience as before (1,048 seats), and now there's not a bad seat in the house—no matter what, you're no more than 50 feet from the stage (the cheapest "gallery" seats look down right onto Othello's bald spot). Productions are staged to play to all of the seats throughout the show. Those sitting up high appreciate different details from those at stage level, and vice versa.

Visiting the Theater: From the main lobby and box office/gift shop area, there's plenty to see. First head left. In the circular **atrium** between the brick wall of the modern theater and fragments of the previous theater, notice the ratty old floorboards. These were pried up from the 1932 stage and laid down here—so as you wait for your play, you're treading on theater history. Upstairs on level 2, find the **Paccar Room,** with generally excellent temporary exhibits assembled from the RSC's substantial collection of historic costumes, props, manuscripts, and other theater memorabilia. Continue upstairs to level 3 to the Rooftop Restaurant (described later). High on the partition that runs through the restaurant, facing the brick theater wall, notice the four **chairs** affixed to the wall. These are original seats from the earlier theater, situated where the back row used to be (90 feet from the stage)—illustrating how much more audience-friendly the new design is.

Back downstairs, pass through the box office/gift shop area to find the **Swan Wing**—an old, Gothic-style Victorian space that survives from the original 1879 Memorial Theatre and hosts *The Play's the Thing,* an immersive exhibit that lets you digitally try on costumes, design sets, and grace a Shakespearean stage.

Back outside, across the street from the theater, notice the building with the steep gable and huge door (marked *CFE 1887*). This was built as a **workshop** for building sets, which could be moved in large pieces to the main theater. To this day, all the sets, costumes, and props are made here in Stratford. The row of **cottages** to the right is housing for actors. The RSC's reputation exerts enough pull to attract serious actors from all over the UK and beyond, who live here for the entire season. The RSC uses a repertory company approach, where the same actors appear in multiple shows concurrently. Today's Lady Macbeth may be tomorrow's Rosalind.

Tower View: For a God's-eye view of all of Shakespeare's houses, ride the elevator to the top of the RSC's tower (£3, £1 with tour ticket, buy ticket at box office or book online; tower open daily 10:00-17:00; Oct-March Sun-Fri 10:00-16:30, Sat until 12:15; closed 12:00-14:00 year-round during matinees). Aside from a few sparse exhibits, the main attraction here is the 360-degree view over the theater building, the Avon, and the lanes of Stratford.

The Food's the Thing: The main theater has a casual **$ café** with a terrace overlooking the river (sandwiches, daily 10:00-21:00), as well as the fancier **$$ Rooftop Restaurant**—though I'd dine elsewhere (Mon-Sat 11:30 until late, Sun 10:30-18:15, dinner reservations smart, tel. 01789/403-449, www.rsc.org.uk/rooftop).

The Swan Theatre

Adjacent to the RSC Theatre is the smaller (about 400 seats), Elizabethan-style Swan Theatre, named not for the birds that fill the park out front, but for the Bard's nickname—the "sweet swan of Avon." It has a vertical layout and a thrust stage similar to the RSC Theatre, but its wood trim and railings give it a cozier, more traditional feel. The Swan is used for lesser known Shakespeare plays and alternative works. Occasionally, the lowest level of seats is removed to accommodate "groundling" (standing-room-only) tickets, much like at the Globe Theatre in London.

The Other Place (Former Courtyard Theatre)

A two-minute walk down Southern Lane from the original Royal Shakespeare Theatre, the Courtyard Theatre (affectionately called the "rusty shed" by locals) was built as a replacement venue while the RSC was being renovated. Now called The Other Place, it serves as a space for rehearsal, research, and development, and educates theater buffs about play production through its "From Page to Stage" tours, where you'll learn about everything from rehearsals to costumes to props. The venue also hosts a bar/café, plus monthly music nights, spoken-word nights, and family activities.

Cost and Hours: Music nights-free, tours-see Royal Shakespeare Theater guided tours earlier, café open Mon-Wed 9:30-18:00, Thu-Sat until 21:00, closed Sun, tel. 01789-403-493, www.rsc.org.uk.

The Dell

Summer open-air Shakespeare performances at Avonbank Gardens near Holy Trinity Church are easy, free, and fun: Just bring something to sit on and a picnic. These are not RSC productions; the company invites university and amateur groups to perform (June-Aug weekends, schedule posted on garden gates, www.rsc.org.uk/thedell).

Other Stratford Sights

Avon Riverfront

The River Avon is a playground of swans and canal boats. The swans have been the mascots of Stratford since 1623, when, seven years after the Bard's death, Ben Jonson's poem in the First Folio dubbed him "the sweet swan of Avon."

For a nice **riverfront walk,** consider crossing over the Tramway Footbridge and following the trail to the right (west) along the south bank of the Avon. To your left is the **Stratford Big Wheel,** not as big as the London Eye, but much cheaper (£5). From here, you'll get a great view of the Royal Shakespeare Theater across the river. Continuing down the path, you'll pass the local lawn-bowling club (guest players welcome, £4, Tue and Thu 14:00-16:00) and Lucy's Mill Weir, an area popular with fishers and kayakers, where you can turn around. On the way back, cross the river by the chain ferry (described later) and return to the town center via the north bank for a full loop.

In the water you'll see colorful **canal boats.** These boats saw their workhorse days during the short window of time between the start of the Industrial Revolution and the establishment of the railways. Today they're mostly pleasure boats. The boats are long and narrow, so two can pass in the slim canals. There are 2,000 miles of canals in England's Midlands, built to connect centers of industry with seaports and provide vital transportation during the early days of the Industrial Revolution. Stratford was as far inland as you could sail on natural rivers from Bristol; it was the terminus of the man-made Birmingham Canal, built in 1816. Even today you can motor your canal boat all the way to London from here. Along the

embankment, look for the signs indicating how many hours it'll take—and how many locks you'll traverse—to go by boat to various English cities.

For a little bit of mellow river action, rent a **rowboat** (£7/hour per person) or, for more of a challenge, pole yourself around

on a Cambridge-style **punt** (the canal is only 4-5 feet deep; same price as the rowboat and more memorable/embarrassing if you do the punting—don't pay £10 for a waterman to do the punting for you). You can rent boats at the Swan's Nest Boathouse across the Tramway Footbridge; another rental station, along the river next to the theater, has higher prices but is more conveniently located.

You can also try a sleepy 40-minute **river cruise** (£7, includes commentary, Avon Boating, board boat in Bancroft Gardens near the RSC Theater, tel. 01789/267-073, www.avon-boating.co.uk), or jump on the oldest surviving **chain ferry** in Britain (c. 1937, £0.50), which shuttles people across the river just beyond the theater.

The old **Cox's Yard,** a riverside timber yard until the 1990s, is a rare physical remnant of the days when Stratford was an

industrial port. Today, Cox's has been taken over by a restaurant complex, with a café, lots of outdoor seating, and occasional live music. Upstairs is the Attic Theatre, which puts on fringe theater acts (www.treadtheboardstheatre.co.uk).

In the riverfront park, roughly between Cox's Yard and the TI, the **Gower Memorial** honors the Bard and his creations. Named for Lord Ronald Gower, the man who paid for and sculpted the memorial, this 1888 work shows Shakespeare up top ringed by four of his most indelible creations, each representing a human pursuit: Hamlet (philosophy), Lady Macbeth (tragedy), Falstaff (comedy), and Prince Hal (history). Originally located next to the theater, it was moved here following the theater's destruction by fire in 1926.

▲MAD Museum

A refreshing change of pace in Bard-bonkers Stratford, this museum's name stands for "Mechanical Art and Design." It celebrates machines as art, showcasing a changing collection of skillfully constructed robots, gizmos, and Rube-Goldberg machines that spring to entertaining life with the push of a button. Engaging for anyone, riveting for engineers, it's pricey but conveniently located near Shakespeare's Birthplace.

Cost and Hours: £7.80, £13.10 combo-ticket also covers Shakespeare's Schoolroom and Guildhall, Mon-Fri 10:00-17:00, Sat-Sun until 17:30, last entry 45 minutes before closing, 4 Henley Street, tel. 01789/269-356, www.themadmuseum.co.uk.

Tudor World at the Falstaff Experience

This attraction is tacky, gimmicky, and more about entertainment than education. (And, while it's named for a Shakespeare character, the exhibit isn't about the Bard.) Filling Shrieve's House Barn with mostly kid-oriented exhibits (mannequins and descriptions, but few real artifacts), it sweeps through Tudor history from the plague to Henry VIII's privy chamber to a replica 16th-century tavern. If you're into ghost-spotting, their nightly ghost tours may be your best shot.

Cost and Hours: Museum—£6,

daily 10:30-17:30; Shakespeare tour—£5, Sat at 14:00; ghost tours—£7.50, daily at 18:00, additional tours possible Fri-Sat; 40 Sheep Street, tel. 01789/298-070, www.tudorworld.com.

Sleeping in Stratford

If you want to spend the night after you catch a show, options abound. Ye olde timbered hotels are scattered through the city center. Most B&Bs are a short walk away on the fringes of town, right on the busy ring roads that route traffic away from the center. (The recommended places below generally have double-paned windows for rooms in the front, but still get some traffic noise.)

In general, the weekend on or near Shakespeare's birthday (April 23) is particularly tight, but Fridays and Saturdays are busy throughout the season. This town is so reliant upon the theater for its business that some B&Bs have insurance covering their loss if the Royal Shakespeare Company ever stops performing in Stratford.

ON GROVE ROAD

These accommodations are at the edge of town on busy Grove Road, across from a grassy square, and come with free parking when booked in advance. From here, it's about a 10-minute walk either to the town center or to the train station (opposite directions).

$$ Adelphi Guest House is run by Shakespeare buffs Sue and Simon, who pride themselves on providing a warm welcome, homemade gingerbread, and original art in every room (RS%, 39 Grove Road, tel. 01789/204-469, www.adelphi-guesthouse.com, info@adelphi-guesthouse.com).

$$ Ambleside Guest House is run with quiet efficiency and attentiveness by owners Peter and Ruth. The place has six rooms and a homey, airy feel with no B&B clutter (ground-floor room, family room, 41 Grove Road, tel. 01789/297-239, www.amblesideguesthouse.com, peter@amblesideguesthouse.com—include your phone number in your request, since they like to call you back to confirm with a personal touch).

$ Woodstock Guest House is a friendly, family-run, and classy place with five comfortable rooms (RS%, ground-floor room, 30 Grove Road, tel. 01789/299-881, www.woodstock-house.co.uk, jackie@woodstock-house.co.uk, bubbly Jackie).

$ Salamander Guest House, run by gregarious Frenchman Pascal and his wife, Anna, rents eight simple rooms that are a bit cheaper than their neighbors (family room, free parking, 40 Grove Road, tel. 01789/205-728, www.salamanderguesthouse.co.uk, p.delin@btinternet.com).

ELSEWHERE IN STRATFORD

$$ Mercure Shakespeare Hotel, centrally located in a black-and-white building just up the street from Shakespeare's New Place, has 78 business-class rooms, each one named for a Shakespearean play or character. Some of the rooms are old-style Elizabethan higgle-dy-piggledy (with modern finishes), while others are contemporary style—note your preference when you reserve (breakfast extra, pay parking, Chapel Street, tel. 01789/294-997, www.mercure.com, h6630@accor.com).

$$ The Emsley Guest House, with Victorian style and modern comfort, holds five bright rooms named after different counties in England—plus a cozy guest library (family rooms, no kids under 5, free off-street parking, 5 minutes from train station at 4 Arden Street, tel. 01789/299-557, www.theemsley.co.uk, stay@theemsley.co.uk, Liz and Chris).

¢ Hostel: Family-friendly **Hemmingford House** has 32 rooms in a Georgian mansion, half of them en suite. It's a 10-minute bus ride from town (private rooms, family rooms, camping pods and tents, breakfast extra, take bus #X18 or #15 two miles to Alveston, hostel is on Wellesbourne Road, tel. 01789/297-093, www.yha.org.uk/hostel/stratford-upon-avon, stratford@yha.org.uk).

Eating in Stratford

RESTAURANTS

Stratford's numerous restaurants vie for your pre-theater business, with special hours and meal deals. (Most offer light two- and three-course menus before 19:00.) You'll find many hardworking places on Sheep Street and Waterside. Unfortunately, post-theater dinners are more challenging, as most places close early.

$$$ Le Bistro Pierre, across the river near the boating station, is a French eatery that's been impressing Stratford residents and tourists alike. They have indoor or outdoor seating and French (read: slow) service (Mon-Fri 12:00-15:00 & 17:00-22:30, Sat until 16:00 & 23:00, Sun 12:30-16:30 & 18:00-22:00, Swan's Nest Hotel, Bridgefoot, tel. 01789/264-804). The pub next door, **Bear Free House,** is owned by the same people and shares the same kitchen, but offers a different menu.

$$$ No. 9 Church Street earns raves for its modern take on British classics, with an emphasis on seasonal and local ingredients, all served in a 400-year-old building with exposed beams and brick. Their tasting and pre-theater menus are good deals; Saturday reservations are recommended (Tue-Sat 12:00-14:00 & 17:00-21:30, closed Sun-Mon, 9 Church Street, tel. 01789/415-522, www.no9churchst.com).

$$$ **Edward Moon** is an upscale English brasserie serving signature dishes like steak-and-ale pies and roasted lamb shank in a setting reminiscent of *Casablanca* (Mon-Fri 12:00-14:30 & 17:00-21:30, Sat until 15:00 & 22:00, Sun until 15:00 & 21:00, 9 Chapel Street, tel. 01789/267-069, www.edwardmoon.com).

$$$ **Sheep Street Eateries:** The next three places, part of the same chain, line up along Sheep Street, offering trendy ambience and modern English cuisine at relatively high prices (all three have good-value pre-theater menus before 19:00). **Lambs** is intimate and serves meat, fish, and veggie dishes with panache. The upstairs feels dressy, under low half-timbered beams (daily 17:00-21:00, lunch served Tue-Sun, 12 Sheep Street, tel. 01789/292-554). **The Opposition,** next door, has a less formal "bistro" ambience (Mon-Thu 12:00-14:00 & 17:00-21:00, Fri-Sat until 22:30, closed Sun, tel. 01789/269-980; book in advance for post-theater dinner here Fri-Sat). **The Vintner,** just up the street, is known for their burgers (daily 9:30-22:00, Sun until 21:30, 4 Sheep Street, tel. 01789/297-259).

Indian: $$ **Avon Spice** has a good reputation and good prices for takeout or dine-in meals (daily 17:30-23:30, 7 Greenhill Street, tel. 01789/267-067).

PUBS

$$ **The Old Thatch Tavern** is, according to locals, the best place in town for beer, serving up London-based Fuller's brews. The atmosphere is cozy, and the food is a cut above what you'll get in other pubs; enjoy it either in the bar, in the tight, candlelit restaurant, or out on the quiet patio (daily 12:00-21:00, on Greenhill Street overlooking the market square, tel. 01789/295-216).

$$ **The Windmill Inn** serves decent, modestly priced fare in a 17th-century inn. It combines old and new styles, and—since it's a few steps beyond the heart of the tourist zone—actually attracts some locals as well. Order drinks and food at the bar, then either settle into a comfy chair or head out to the half-timbered courtyard to wait for your meal (daily 12:00-21:00, Church Street, tel. 01789/297-687).

$$ **The Garrick Inn** bills itself as the oldest pub in town, and comes with a cozy, dimly lit restaurant vibe. Choose between the pub or table-service section; either way, you'll dine on bland, pricey pub grub (daily 11:00-22:00, 25 High Street, tel. 01789/292-186).

PICNICS

With its sprawling and inviting riverfront park, Stratford is a particularly pleasant place to picnic. Choose a bench and enjoy views of the river and vacation houseboats while munching your meal. It's a fine way to spend a midsummer night's eve. For groceries or prepared foods, find **Marks & Spencer** on Bridge Street (Mon-Sat 8:00-18:00, Sun 10:30-16:30, small coffee-and-sandwiches café upstairs). Across the street, **Sainsbury's Local** stays open later than other supermarkets (daily 7:00-22:00).

For fish-and-chips, you have a couple of options: **$ Barnaby's** is a greasy fast-food joint near the waterfront—but convenient if you want takeout for the riverside park just across the street (cash only, daily 11:00-19:30, at Sheep Street and Waterside). For better food (but a less convenient location—closer to my recommended B&Bs than to the park), queue up with the locals at **$ Kingfisher,** then ask for the freshly battered haddock (Mon-Sat 11:30-13:45 & 17:00-22:00, closed Sun, a long block up at 13 Ely Street, tel. 01789/292-513).

TEAROOMS

$$ The FourTeas 1940s Tea Room transports diners to another era, with period details ranging from the servers' housedresses to the ration-card menu to the Glenn Miller-era soundtrack. There's even an air-raid shelter beyond the terrace garden. Don't be fooled by the theme: This place eludes kitsch with high-quality pastry, classic sandwiches, all-day breakfast, and locally sourced ingredients (Mon-Sat 9:30-17:00, Sun 11:00-16:00, 24 Sheep Street, tel. 01789/293-908).

$$ Bensons Restaurant and Tea Rooms, across the street from Shakespeare's Birthplace, has indoor seating, outdoor tables right on the main pedestrian mall, and friendly service (teas available all day, daily 9:00-17:30, 40 Henley Street, tel. 01789/415-572).

Stratford Connections

Remember: When buying tickets or checking schedules, ask for "Stratford-upon-Avon," not just "Stratford."

From Stratford-upon-Avon by Train to: London (3/day direct, more with transfers, 2-2.5 hours, to Marylebone Station), **Moreton-in-Marsh** (almost hourly, 3 hours, 2-3 transfers, slow and expensive, better by bus). Train info: tel. 0345-748-4950, www.nationalrail.co.uk.

By Bus to: Cotswolds towns (bus #1 or #2, Mon-Sat 5/day, none on Sun, 50 minutes to **Chipping Campden,** 1.5 hours to **Moreton-in-Marsh,** some also stop at Broadway and/or Blockley,

Johnsons Excelbus, tel. 01564/797-070, www.johnsonscoaches. co.uk; on Sundays #606 provides service to Chipping Campden and Broadway, 2/day, 30 minutes, Marchants Coaches, tel. 01242/257-714, www.marchants-coaches.com). Most intercity buses stop on Stratford's Bridge Street (a block up from the TI). For bus info that covers all the region's companies, call Traveline at tel. 0871-200-2233 (www.travelinemidlands.co.uk).

By Car: Driving is easy and distances are short: **Chipping Campden** (12 miles), **Stow-on-the-Wold** (22 miles).

ROUTE TIPS FOR DRIVERS

These tips assume you're heading north from Stratford.

Leaving the Bridgefoot garage in downtown Stratford, circle to the right around the same block, but stay on "the Wark" (Warwick Road, A-439).

To the Northeast: Heading toward York, Durham, and other destinations northeast of Stratford, take the Wark to the A-46. Just past Coventry, it merges into the M-69 toward Leicester, which intersects with a major north-south route, the M-1.

To the Northwest: When heading toward Ironbridge Gorge, North Wales, Liverpool, or the Lake District, take A-46 toward Warwick then exit onto the M-40 north toward Birmingham. You want to avoid driving through Birmingham. After Warwick, take the M-42 to the west; the sign will read *The Southwest (M5), Birmingham (S & W), Redditch*. When the M-42 ends at the M-5, follow M-5 north, the sign will read *The Northwest, B'ham, Stourbridge*.

After Birmingham, for Ironbridge Gorge, take the M-54 toward Telford. For specifics on getting to Ironbridge Gorge, see page 435. For other destinations, take the M-6.

IRONBRIDGE GORGE

The Industrial Revolution was born in the Severn River Valley. In its glory days, this valley—blessed with abundant deposits of iron ore and coal, and a river for transport—gave the world its first iron wheels, steam-powered locomotive, and cast-iron bridge (begun in 1779). Other industries flourished here, too—from mass-produced clay pipes to delicate porcelain and colorful decorative tiles. The museums in Ironbridge Gorge, which capture the flavor of the Victorian Age, take you back into the days when Britain was racing into the modern era—and pulling the rest of the West with her.

Near the end of the 20th century, the valley went through a second transformation: Photos taken just a few decades ago show an industrial wasteland. Today the Severn River Valley is lush and lined with walks and parkland. Even its bricks, while still smoke-stained, seem warmer and more inviting. Those who come for its "industrial" sights are pleasantly surprised to find an extremely charming corner of England—with wooded hillsides and tidy, time-warp brick villages.

PLANNING YOUR TIME

Without a car, Ironbridge Gorge isn't worth the headache for most (though I've included some tips at the end of this chapter). Drivers can slip it in between the Cotswolds/Stratford and points north (such as the Lake District or North Wales). Speed demons zip in for a midday tour of the Blists Hill Victorian Town, look at the famous Iron Bridge and quaint Industrial Age town that sprawls around it, and head out. For an overnight visit, arrive in the early evening to browse the town, see the bridge, and walk along the river. Spend the morning touring the Blists Hill Victorian Town, have lunch there, and head to your next destination.

Those with more time (or a healthy interest in the Industrial Revolution) can spend two nights and a leisurely day strolling the town and exploring Blists Hill and the many museums, capped by dinner at one of my recommended restaurants.

Orientation to Ironbridge Gorge

The village of Ironbridge is just a few blocks gathered around the Iron Bridge, which spans the peaceful, tree-lined River Severn.

While the smoke-belching bustle is long gone, knowing that this wooded, sleepy river valley was the "Silicon Valley" of the 19th century makes wandering its brick streets almost a pilgrimage. Other villages—including Coalbrookdale, Jackfield, and Coalport—are scattered along the valley, all within a short drive or a long walk. The museum sights are scattered over three miles. The modern cooling towers (for coal, not nuclear energy) that you'll see west of town, looming ominously over these red-brick remnants, seem strangely appropriate.

TOURIST INFORMATION

The TI is in the Museum of the Gorge, just west of the town center (daily 10:00-16:00, tel. 01952/433-424, www.ironbridge.org.uk). In summer, you may also find an information desk inside the Iron Bridge tollbooth.

GETTING AROUND IRONBRIDGE GORGE

For connections from the Telford train or bus stations to the sights, see the end of this chapter.

By Bus: Link the area's museums with **Gorge Connect** buses, which run on busy summer weekends when school's out—including Easter and the two May Bank Holidays (Sat-Mon), plus every weekend from late July through mid-September (every 30 minutes 9:30-17:00, £2.50 day ticket—discounted to £1 with Passport Ticket—described in "Sights in Ironbridge Gorge"; see schedule at www.telford.gov.uk—search for "Gorge Connect"; tel. 01952/384-384). If you're waiting for the Gorge Connect bus on the main road by the bridge, or at a stop for one of the less-popular museums, make sure the driver sees you.

Bus **#19,** operated by Arriva, connects the Coalbrookdale

Museum of Iron (stop: Coalbrookdale Post Office) and the TI in Ironbridge, but runs infrequently (roughly 7/day, www.arrivabus. co.uk).

By Car: Routes to the attractions are well signed, so driving is a snap (museum parking described later).

By Taxi: Taxis will pick up at the museums and are a good option if you don't have a car and the bus is not convenient. Call Go Carz at tel. 01952/501-050.

Sights in Ironbridge Gorge

Ten museums clustered within a few miles focus on the Iron Bridge and all that it represents—but not all are worth your time. The Blists Hill Victorian Town is by far the best. The Museum of the Gorge attempts to give a historical overview, but the displays are humble—its most interesting feature is a short video that helps give context to other area sights. The Coalbrookdale Museum of Iron is interesting to metalheads. Enginuity is just for kids. The original Abraham Darby Furnace (free to view, located across from the Museum of Iron) is a shrine to 18th-century technology. And the Jackfield Tile Museum, Coalport China Museum, and Broseley Pipeworks delve into industries that picked up the slack when the iron industry shifted away from the Severn Valley in the 1850s.

Cost: Individual admission charges vary (£4.50-18.50); the £26.50 **Passport Ticket** covers admission to all area sights and gives a discount on the Gorge Connect bus. Even if you visit only the Blists Hill Victorian Town and the Coalbrookdale Museum of Iron, the Passport Ticket (which is good for a year) pays for itself.

Hours: All museums open daily 10:00-16:00 unless otherwise noted; closed Mon Oct-mid-March.

Information: Tel. 01952/433-424, www.ironbridge.org.uk.

Parking: To see the most significant sights by car, you'll park three times: once in town (either in the pay-and-display lot just over the bridge or at the Museum of the Gorge—the Iron Bridge and Gorge Museum are connected by an easy, flat walk); once at the Blists Hill parking lot; and once outside the Coalbrookdale Museum of Iron (Enginuity is across the lot, and the Darby Houses are a three-minute uphill hike away). While you'll pay separately to park at the Museum of the Gorge, a single £3 ticket is good for pay-and-display lots at all other sights.

IRONBRIDGE VILLAGE
▲▲Iron Bridge

While England was at war with her American colonies, this first cast-iron bridge was built in 1779 to show off a wonderful new building material. Lacking experience with cast iron, the builders

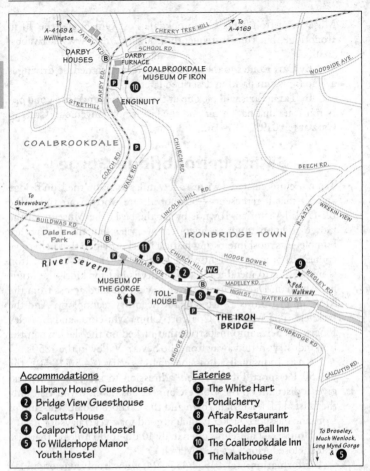

Accommodations
1 Library House Guesthouse
2 Bridge View Guesthouse
3 Calcutts House
4 Coalport Youth Hostel
5 To Wilderhope Manor Youth Hostel

Eateries
6 The White Hart
7 Pondicherry
8 Aftab Restaurant
9 The Golden Ball Inn
10 The Coalbrookdale Inn
11 The Malthouse

erred on the side of sturdiness and constructed it as if it were made of wood. Notice that the original construction used traditional timber-jointing techniques rather than rivets. (Rivets are from later repairs.) The valley's centerpiece is free, open all the time, and thought-provoking... cars still used it into the 1960s. Walk across the bridge to the tollhouse. Inside, read the fee

schedule and notice the subtle slam against royalty. (England was not immune to the revolutionary sentiment inhabiting the colonies at this time.) Pedestrians paid half a penny to cross; poor people crossed cheaper by coracle—a crude tub-like wood-and-canvas

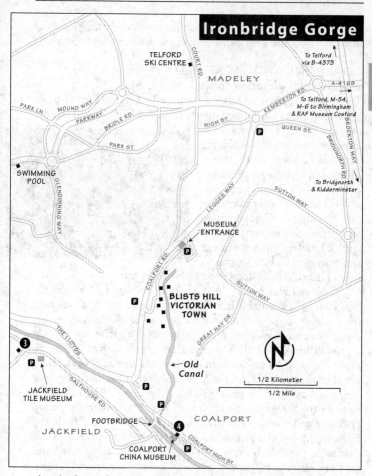

shuttle ferry. Cross back to the town and enjoy a pleasant walk downstream along the towpath. Where horses once dragged boats laden with Industrial Age cargo, locals now walk their dogs.

Museum of the Gorge

Orient yourself to the valley at this simple museum, filling the Old Severn Warehouse. It's worthwhile merely for the 12-minute introductory video (on a continuous loop), which lays the groundwork for what you'll see in the other museums. You'll also see exhibits on local geology and ecology, some of the items that were produced here, and a well-explained 30-foot model of the entire valley in its heyday.

Cost: £4.50, 500 yards upstream from the bridge, parking-£3 (3-hour maximum).

Nearby: Farther upstream from the museum parking lot is the fine riverside **Dale End Park,** with picnic areas and a playground.

COALPORT AND JACKFIELD
▲▲Blists Hill Victorian Town

This immersive open-air folk museum thrills kids and kids-at-heart by re-creating a fully formed society from the 1890s. You'll wander through 50 acres of commerce, industry, and chatty locals. It's particularly lively (with every-thing open and lots of docents—and engaged kids) on weekends and in summer; off-peak times can be sleepy. Compared to other open-air museums in Brit-ain, it's refreshingly compact and manageable. Pick up the £5

Blists Hill guidebook for a good step-by-step rundown.

Cost and Hours: £18.50, daily until 16:30 mid-March–Sept.

Eating in Blists Hill: Several places serve lunch: a café near the entrance, the New Inn Pub for beer and pub snacks, a tradi-tional fish-and-chips joint, and the Forest Glen cafeteria.

Visiting Blists Hill: The experience begins with a 360-degree movie showing Victorians at (noisy, hot, and difficult) work. Then you'll walk through a door and be transported back in time. The map you're given when entering is very important—it shows which stops in the big park are staffed with energetic docents in period clothes. Pop in to say hello to the banker, the post office clerk, the blacksmith, and the girl in the candy shop. Maybe the boys are singing in the pub. It's fine to take photos. Asking questions and chatting with the villagers is encouraged. How's the pay? What's a shilling? How about 1800s health care?

Stop by the pharmacy and check out the squirm-inducing setup of the dentist's chair—it'll make you appreciate modern den-tal care. Check the hands-on activities in the barn across the way. Down the street, kids like watching a candlemaker at work, as he explains the process and tells how candles were used back in the day. You'll find out what a "spinning donkey" is, why candles have two wicks, and why miners used green candles instead of white ones.

Just as it would've in Victorian days, the village has a working pub, a greengrocer's shop, a fascinating squatter's cottage, and a snorty, slippery pigsty. On your way down to the ironworks, drop in on the high-end mine manager's house, with a doctor's surgery tucked in the back. Don't miss the explanation of the "winding engine" at the Blists Hill Mine (demos throughout the day).

At the back of the park, you can hop aboard a train and enter a clay mine, complete with a sound-and-light show illustrating the dangers of working in this type of environment (small charge, 15 minutes). Nearby, the Hay Inclined Plane was used to haul loaded tub boats between the river and the upper canal. Today, a passenger-operated lift hauls visitors instead (just press the button to call for it). At the top, you can walk along the canal back to the town.

Coalport China Museum

This museum fills an old porcelain factory directly downhill from Blists Hill, along the river. You'll see a few fine samples of china that was made here (the Caughley porcelain, at the end, is top quality); walk through a long workshop, where workers demonstrate various aspects of porcelain production (molds, flowers, printing, glazing, painting, and gilding); peek into a working glassblower's shop; and walk around inside a cavernous "botte kiln." While a bit less engaging than most of Ironbridge's museums, it's informative and rounds out your look at the area.

Cost: £9.50.

▲Jackfield Tile Museum

While most area museums focus on the grit and brawn of the Industrial Revolution—iron, coal, that sort of thing—the Jackfield Tile Museum looks at the softer side of Severn Valley innovation. Located in the village of Jackfield (across the river from Ironbridge), here you can walk through several buildings in an old brick industrial complex where tiles are still produced. The highlight is seeing the wide range of uses and styles of tile—a material so versatile (and so beautiful) that it looks equally good in bathrooms and in churches, and even in London's Tube (much of the Underground tile came from right here). The modern Fusion facility next door suggests that tile's heyday isn't over.

Cost: £9.50.

COALBROOKDALE

Note that the Darby Houses close an hour before the other sights here; if visiting later in the day, go there first.

▲Coalbrookdale Museum of Iron and Abraham Darby's Old Furnace

The Coalbrookdale neighborhood is the birthplace of modern technology—locals like to claim it's where mass production was invented. The museum and furnace are located on either side of a parking lot, tucked under a rail trestle. There's a café on-site, and the Coalbrookdale Inn—a classic pub—is just up the hill in front of the museum.

Cost: Museum—£9.50, £11.50 combo-ticket includes the

How to Smelt Iron...
and Change the World

The Severn Valley had an abundance of ingredients for big industry: iron ore, top-grade coal (processed into coke), and water for power and shipping. And the person who finally put all the pieces together was a clever Quaker brassmaker from Bristol named Abraham Darby.

Before Darby's time, iron ore was laboriously melted by charcoal—they couldn't use coal because sulfur made the iron brittle. Darby experimented with higher-carbon coke instead. With huge waterwheel-powered bellows, Darby burned coke at super-hot temperatures and dumped iron ore into the furnace. Impurities floated to the top, while the pure iron sank to the bottom of a clay tub in the bottom of the furnace.

Twice a day, the plugs were knocked off, allowing the "slag" to drain away on the top and the molten iron to drain out on the bottom. The low-grade slag was used locally on walls and paths. The high-grade iron trickled into molds formed in the sand below the furnace. It cooled into pig iron (named because the molds look like piglets suckling their mother). The pig-iron "planks" were broken off by sledgehammers and shipped away.

The River Severn became one of Europe's busiest, shipping pig iron to distant foundries, where it was melted again and made into cast iron (for projects such as the Iron Bridge), or to forges, where it was worked like toffee into wrought iron.

Once Darby cracked the coke code, iron became *the* go-to building material. Versatile and ubiquitous, iron became the plastic of the Victorian age. To this day, many of the icons of Britain—post boxes, frilly benches, fences in front of tidy houses—are made of iron. All thanks to the innovation that took place centuries ago, right here in the Severn Valley.

Darby Houses; Furnace—free, volunteers sometimes lead free guided walks to the furnace (ask at museum info desk for times).

Visiting the Museum: The fresh, well-presented museum works hard to explain all facets of iron—which has been used to make tools since ancient times and makes up 95 percent of all industrial metal. You'll get a quick primer on the history of iron tools, then head up to the top floor and work your way down, chronologically, through the role iron played here in the Severn Valley. You'll see original items from Coalbrookdale's boom time (including a little three-legged pot created by Abraham Darby, c. 1714) and learn about the critical role Quakers (like Darby) played in the Industrial Revolution—several important individuals are profiled. You'll also see a detailed model of the Iron Bridge, and—on the middle floor—several Victorian Age items made possible by this innovation, from a gigantic cast-iron anchor to delicately crafted benches and sculptures.

Abraham Darby Furnace: Across from the museum, standing like a shrine to the Industrial Revolution, is Darby's blast furnace, sitting inside a big glass pyramid and surrounded by evocative Industrial Age ruins. It was here that in 1709 Darby first smelted iron, using coke as fuel. To me, "coke" is a drink, and "smelt" is the past tense of smell... but around here, these  words recall the event that kicked off the modern Industrial Age and changed the world (see the sidebar).

Enginuity

Enginuity is a hands-on funfest for kids. Riffing on Ironbridge's engineering roots, this converted 1709 foundry is full of entertaining-to-kids water contraptions, pumps, magnets, and laser games. Build a dam, try your hand at earthquake-proof construction, navigate a water maze, operate a remote-controlled robot, or power a turbine with your own steam. Mixed in among all this entertainment is a collection of vintage machines.

Cost: £9.50, across the parking lot from the Coalbrookdale Museum of Iron.

Darby Houses

Abraham Darby, who kicked off the Industrial Age when he figured out how to smelt iron in his big furnace, lived with his family  in these two homes up on a ridge overlooking the Coalbrookdale Museum (go under the rail bridge and head uphill). Although Quakers, they were the area's wealthiest residents by far. Touring their homes, you'll learn a bit about their lifestyles, and about Quakers in general.

The 18th-century Darby mansion, **Rosehill House,** is decorated and furnished as the family home would have been in 1850. It features a collection of fine china, furniture, and trinkets from various family members. If the gilt-framed mirrors and fancy china seem a little ostentatious for wealth-shunning Quakers, keep in mind that these folks were rich beyond reason, and—as docents will assure you—considering their vast wealth, this was relatively modest. At the end of the tour is a collection of period clothes: You're welcome to dress up as a humble Quaker or a fashionable dandy.

Skip the adjacent **Dale House.** Dating from the 1710s, it's older than Rosehill, but almost completely devoid of furniture, and its exhibits are rarely open.

Cost and Hours: £5.95, £11.50 combo-ticket includes Coalbrookdale Museum of Iron, closes earlier than other museums—at 16:00—and closed entirely Oct-mid-March.

MORE SIGHTS AND EXPERIENCES IN AND NEAR IRONBRIDGE GORGE

Skiing and Swimming

A small brush-covered **ski and snowboarding slope** with two Poma lifts is at Telford Snowboard and Ski Centre in Madeley, two miles from Ironbridge Gorge; you'll see signs for it as you drive into Ironbridge Gorge (open practice times vary by day—schedule posted online, tel. 01952/382-621, www.telfordandwrekinleisure. co.uk). A public **swimming pool,** the Abraham Darby Sports and Leisure Centre, is near Madeley (5-minute drive from town on Ironbridge Road, tel. 01952/382-770).

Royal Air Force (RAF) Museum Cosford

This Red Baron magnet displays more than 80 aircraft, from warplanes to rockets. Get the background on ejection seats and a primer on the principles of propulsion (free, daily 10:00-17:00, Nov-Feb until 16:00, last entry one hour before closing, parking-£3/3 hours, Shifnal, Shropshire, on the A-41 near junction with the M-54, tel. 01902/376-200, www.rafmuseum.org.uk/cosford).

More Sights

If you're looking for reasons to linger in Ironbridge Gorge, these sights are all within a short drive: the **medieval town** of Shrewsbury, the **abbey village** of Much Wenlock, the **scenic Long Mynd gorge** at Church Stretton, the **castle** at Ludlow, and the **steam railway** at the river town of Bridgnorth. Shoppers like Chester (en route to points north). **Brosely Pipeworks,** in the town of Brosley Wood, offers a fascinating look at the mass-production of clay pipes, but its opening hours are limited (£5.95, open mid-May-Sept 10:30-16:00, tours required, at 10:30, 12:00, 13:30, and 15:00, closed off-season).

Sleeping in Ironbridge Gorge

$$ Library House Guesthouse is *Town and Country*-elegant. Located in the town center, a half-block downhill from the bridge, it's a classy, friendly gem that once served as the village library. Each of its three rooms is a delight, and the public spaces are decorated true to the Georgian period. The Chaucer Room, which includes a small garden, is the smallest and least expensive. Tim and Sarah will make you feel right at home (free parking just up the road, 11 Severn Bank, tel. 01952/432-299, www.libraryhouse.com, info@ libraryhouse.com).

$$ Bridge View Guesthouse rents seven tidy but uninspired rooms over a tearoom directly at the Iron Bridge; true to its name, four rooms have bridge views. While less personal than Library House or Calcutts, they may have a room when those are full (free parking nearby, 10 Tontine Hill, tel. 01952/432-541, www. ironbridgeview.co.uk, bookings@ironbridgeview.co.uk).

OUTSIDE OF TOWN

$$ Calcutts House rents seven rooms in an 18th-century iron-master's home and adjacent coach house. Rooms in the main house are elegant, while the coach-house rooms are bright, modern, and less expensive. Their inviting garden is a plus. Ask the owners, James and Sarah Pittam, how the rooms were named (free parking, Calcutts Road, tel. 01952/882-631, www.calcuttshouse.co.uk, info@calcuttshouse.co.uk). From Calcutts House, it's a delightful 15-minute stroll down a former train track into town.

¢ Coalport Youth Hostel, plush for a hostel, fills an old factory at the China Museum in Coalport (reception open 7:30-23:00, no lockout, High Street, tel. 0345-371-9325, www.yha.org.uk, coalport@yha.org.uk). Don't confuse this hostel with another area hostel, Coalbrookdale, which is only available for groups.

¢ Wilderhope Manor Youth Hostel, a beautifully remote Elizabethan manor house from 1586, is one of Europe's best hostels (it even has a bridal suite). On Sunday afternoons, tourists actually pay to see what hostelers get to sleep in (family rooms, reservations recommended, reception closed 10:00-15:00, restaurant open 18:00-20:30, tel. 0345-371-9149, www.yha.org.uk, wilderhope@ yha.org.uk). It's in Longville-in-the-Dale, six miles from Much Wenlock, down the B-4371 toward Church Stretton.

Eating in Ironbridge Gorge

$$$$ The White Hart has a split personality—the woody pub section is Brit-rustic, while the two-level restaurant is white-tablecloth chic. Prices make this a splurge, but the food is creative and tasty (Mon-Sat 11:00-21:30, Sun from 9:30, food served until 21:00, reservations smart on weekends, 10 Wharfage, tel. 01952/432-901, www.whitehartironbridge.com).

$$$ Pondicherry, in a former police station, serves Indian meals that gild the lily. The basement holding cells are now little plush lounges—a great option if you'd like your pre-dinner drink "in prison" (daily 17:30-23:00, 57 Waterloo Street, tel. 01952/433-055). For cheaper (but still good) Indian food, look for **$$ Aftab,** a bit closer to the Iron Bridge.

$$ The Golden Ball Inn is a classic countryside pub high on the hill above Ironbridge. You can dine with the friendly local crowd in the "bar," eat in back with the 18th-century brewing gear in the quieter—and more formal—dining room, or munch out on the lush garden patio. This place is serious about beer, listing featured ales daily (food served Mon-Sat 12:00-21:00, Sun until 19:00, reservations smart on weekends, 10-minute hike up Madeley Road from the town roundabout, look for sign to pedestrian shortcut, 1 Newbridge Road, tel. 01952/432-179, www.goldenballironbridge. co.uk).

$$ The Coalbrookdale Inn is filled with locals enjoying excellent ales and simple pub grub—nothing fancy. This former "best pub in Britain" has a tradition of offering free samples from a lineup of featured beers. Ask which real ales are available (Mon-Fri 16:00-23:00, Sat-Sun from 12:00, lively ladies' loo, across street from Coalbrookdale Museum of Iron, 1 mile from Ironbridge, 12 Wellington Road, tel. 01952/432-166).

$$ The Malthouse, located in an 18th-century beer house, is popular with local twenty-somethings. The menu includes pub standards, plus a few pricier, high-end dishes (food served daily 11:30-22:00, near Museum of the Gorge, 5-minute walk from center, The Wharfage, tel. 01952/433-712). For nighttime action, The Malthouse is *the* vibrant spot in town, with live rock music and a fun crowd (generally Fri-Sat).

Ironbridge Gorge Connections

Ironbridge Gorge is five miles southwest of Telford, which has the nearest train station.

Getting Between Telford and Ironbridge Gorge: It's easiest to take a **taxi** from Telford train station to Ironbridge Gorge (about £5.50 to Blists Hill, £9 to the Iron Bridge; call Go Carz at tel. 01952/501-050). If the Gorge Connect bus is running (described earlier, under "Getting Around Ironbridge Gorge"), you could take **bus** #4 (2-5/hour) from the Telford train station to High Street in the town of Madeley. This is where the Gorge Connect bus originates and ends. Hop on it to ride to one of the museums, the TI, or the bridge.

By Train from Telford to: Birmingham (2/hour, 45 minutes), **Stratford-upon-Avon** (2/hour, 2.5 hours, 1-2 changes), **Moreton-in-Marsh** (hourly, 3 hours, 2 transfers), **Conwy** in North Wales (3/day direct, 2.5 hours, more with transfer), **Keswick/Lake District**

(hourly, 4 hours total; 3 hours to Penrith with 1-2 changes, then catch a bus to Keswick—see page 501). **Train info:** Tel. 0345-748-4950, www.nationalrail.co.uk.

ROUTE TIPS FOR DRIVERS

From the South to Ironbridge Gorge: From the Cotswolds and Stratford, you want to avoid going through Birmingham; see page 422 for the best route.

After Birmingham, follow signs to *Telford* via the M-54. Leave the M-54 at the Telford/Ironbridge exit (Junction 4). Follow the brown *Ironbridge* signs through several roundabouts to Ironbridge Gorge. (Note: On maps, Ironbridge Gorge is often referred to as "Iron Bridge" or "Iron-Bridge.")

From Ironbridge Gorge to North Wales: The drive is fairly easy, with clear signs and good roads all the way. From Ironbridge Gorge, follow signs to the M-54. Get on the M-54 in the direction of Telford, and then Shrewsbury, as the M-54 becomes the A-5; then follow signs to North Wales. In Wales, the A-483 (direction Wrexham, then Chester) takes you to the A-55, which leads to Conwy.

LIVERPOOL

Wedged between serene North Wales and the even-more-serene Lake District, Liverpool provides an opportunity to sample the "real" England. It's the best look at urban England outside of London.

Beatles fans flock to Liverpool to learn about the Fab Four's early days, but the city has much more to offer—most notably, a wealth of quality, free museums, a pair of striking cathedrals, a dramatic skyline mingling old red-brick maritime buildings and glassy new skyscrapers, and—most of all—the charm of the Liverpudlians.

Sitting at the mouth of the River Mersey in the metropolitan county of Merseyside, Liverpool has long been a major shipping center. Its port played a key role in several centuries of world history—as a point in the "triangular trade" of African slaves, a gateway for millions of New World-bound European emigrants, and a staging ground for the British Navy's Battle of the Atlantic against the Nazi's U-boat fleet. But Liverpool was devastated physically by WWII bombs, and then economically by the advent of container shipping in the 1960s. Liverpudlians looked on helplessly as postwar recovery resources were steered elsewhere, the city's substantial wartime contributions seemingly ignored.

Despite the pride and attention garnered in the 1960s by a certain quartet of favorite sons, Liverpool continued to decline through the 1970s and '80s. The Toxteth Riots of 1981, sparked by the city's dizzyingly high unemployment, brought worldwide attention to Liverpool's troubles.

But, finally, things started looking up. The city's status as the 2008 European Capital of Culture spurred major gentrification, EU funding, development of the "Liverpool ONE" commercial

On the Scouse

Nicknamed "Scousers" (after a traditional local stew, originally brought here by Norwegian immigrants), the people of Liverpool have a reputation for being relaxed, easygoing, and welcoming to visitors. The Scouse dialect comes with a distinctive lilt and quick wit (the latter likely a means of coping with long-term hardship)—think of The Beatles' familiar accents, and all their famously sarcastic off-the-cuff remarks, and you get the picture. Many Liverpudlians attribute these qualities to the Celtic influence here: Liverpool is a melting pot of not only English culture, but also loads of Irish and Welsh, as well as arrivals from all over Europe and beyond (Liverpool's diverse population includes many of African descent and the oldest Chinese community in Britain). Liverpudlians are also famous for their passion for football (soccer), and the Liverpool FC team—as locals will be quick to tell you—is one of England's best. And, along with the city, scouse stew is on the rise as well—you'll see it on menus all over town.

complex in the once bombed-out center, and a cultural renaissance. And, with some 50,000 students attending three universities in town, Liverpool is also a youthful city, with a pub or nightclub on every corner. Anyone who still thinks of Liverpool as a depressed industrial center is behind the times.

PLANNING YOUR TIME

Liverpool can easily fill a day of sightseeing. For the quickest visit, focus your time around the Albert Dock area, home to The Beatles

Story, Merseyside Maritime Museum, Museum of Liverpool, and the British Music Experience. If time allows, consider a Beatles bus tour (departs from the Albert Dock).

A full day buys you time either to delve into the rest of the city (the rejuvenated urban core, the cathedrals, and the Walker Art Gallery near the train station), to binge on more Beatles sights (the Magical

Beatles Museum or the boyhood homes of John and Paul), or a bit of both.

If you're here just for the Beatles, you can easily fill a day with Fab Four sights: Do the tour of John's and Paul's homes in the morning, then return to the Albert Dock area to visit The Beatles Story and/or the British Music Experience. Take an afternoon bus tour from the Albert Dock to the other Beatles sights in town, winding up at the Cavern Quarter to tour the Magical Beatles Museum and enjoy a Beatles cover band in the reconstructed Cavern Club. (Beatles bus tours zip past the John and Paul houses from the outside, but visiting the interiors takes more time and should be reserved well in advance.)

International Beatles Week, celebrated in late August, is a very busy time in Liverpool, with lots of live musical performances.

Orientation to Liverpool

With nearly half a million people, Liverpool is Britain's fifth-biggest city. But for visitors, most points of interest are concentrated in the generally pedestrian-friendly downtown area. You can walk from one end of this zone to the other in half an hour. Since interesting sights and colorful neighborhoods are scattered throughout this area, it's enjoyable to connect your sightseeing on foot. (Beatles sights, however, are spread far and wide—it's most efficient to connect them with a tour.)

Tourist Information: Liverpool's TIs are just tiny desks free-loading in the Central Library (near the train station) and at the Magical Beatles Museum on Mathew Street (tel. 0151/707-0729, www.visitliverpool.com).

Private Guide: Paul Beesley, a local guide who runs the Liverpool Tour Guide Service with the help of others, is a good source for private guiding (£140/half-day, tel. 0151/374-2374, www.liverpooltgs.weebly.com, office@ltgs.co.uk).

ARRIVAL IN LIVERPOOL

By Train: The main **Lime Street train station** has eateries, shops, car rentals, and pay baggage storage (daily 7:00-21:00, weekends until 23:00, tel. 0151/909-3697, www.left-baggage.co.uk).

Getting to the Albert Dock: From Lime Street Station to the Albert Dock is about a 20-minute walk or a quick trip by subway or taxi.

To **walk,** exit straight out the front door. On your right, you'll see the giant Neoclassical St. George's Hall; the Walker Art Gallery is just beyond it. To reach the Albert Dock, go straight ahead across the street, then head down the hill between St. George's Hall (on your right) and the big blob-shaped mall (on your left). Turn left onto Whitechapel Street and walk straight ahead all the way until you see the big red-brick warehouses of Albert Dock.

You can also take a **subway** from Lime Street Station to James Street Station, then walk about five minutes to the Albert Dock (£2.05, also covered by BritRail pass, www.merseyrail.org).

A **taxi** from Lime Street Station to the Albert Dock costs about £6. Taxis wait outside either of the side doors of the station.

By Plane: Liverpool John Lennon Airport (tel. 0871-521-8484, www.liverpoolairport.com, airport code: LPL) is about eight miles southeast of downtown, along the river. Buses to the airport depart regularly from Liverpool ONE Bus Station. Bus #500 is quickest (2/hour, 35 minutes, £2.30, covered by all-day ticket).

By Car: Most drivers approach Liverpool on the M-62 motorway, which dies at the edge of town. Just follow signs to *City Centre* and *Waterfront*, then brown signs to *Albert Dock*, where you'll find a huge pay parking lot. There's a bigger central garage at the Liverpool ONE commercial complex. If coming from Wales, take the toll tunnel under the River Mersey (£2) and follow signs for *Albert Dock*.

Tours in Liverpool

BEATLES BUS TOURS

If you want to see as many Beatles-related sights as possible in a short time, these tours are the way to go. Each drives by the houses where the Fab Four grew up (exteriors only), places they performed, and spots made famous by the lyrics of their hits ("Penny Lane," "Strawberry Fields," the Eleanor Rigby graveyard at St. Peter's Church, and so on). Even lukewarm fans will enjoy the commentary and seeing the shelter on the roundabout, the barber who shaves another customer, and the banker who never wears a mack in the pouring rain. (Very strange.)

LIVERPOOL

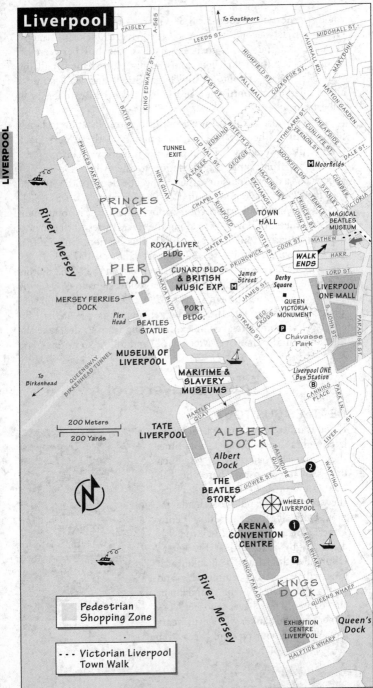

Liverpool

To Southport

PAISLEY
LEEDS ST.
A-565
HIGHFIELD ST.
COCKSPUR ST.
PALL MALL
VAUXHALL RD.
MIDGHALL ST.
MARYBONE
HATTON GARDEN
KING EDWARD ST.
BATH ST.
EAST ST.
OLD HALL ST.
EDMUND BIXTETH ST.
TITHEBARN ST.
CHEAPSIDE
VERNON ST.
CUNLIFFE ST.
DALE ST.
CUMBER.
STANLEY

TUNNEL EXIT

NEW QUAY
FAZAKER ST.
GEORGE
HACKINS HEY
MOORFIELDS
EXCHANGE
N. JOHN ST.
PRINCES ST.
TEMPLE
VICTORIA

M Moorfields

PRINCES DOCK

PRINCES PARADE

River Mersey

CHAPEL ST.
RUMFORD
WATER ST.
CASTLE ST.
COOK ST.
MATHEW
HARR.

TOWN HALL

ROYAL LIVER BLDG.

PIER HEAD

CANADA BLVD.

MERSEY FERRIES DOCK

CUNARD BLDG. & BRITISH MUSIC EXP. M

James Street

BRUNSWICK ST.

JAMES ST.

Derby Square

WALK ENDS

LORD ST.

MAGICAL BEATLES MUSEUM

LIVERPOOL ONE MALL

Pier Head

PORT BLDG.

BEATLES STATUE

QUEENSWAY BIRKENHEAD TUNNEL

To Birkenhead

MUSEUM OF LIVERPOOL

STRAND ST.
RED CROSS
Queen Victoria Monument

P Chavasse Park

S. JOHN ST.
PARADISE ST.

MARITIME & SLAVERY MUSEUMS

HARTLEY QUAY

Liverpool ONE Bus Station B
CANNING PLACE
PARK LN.

200 Meters
200 Yards

TATE LIVERPOOL

ALBERT DOCK

Albert Dock

SALTHOUSE QUAY

LIVER ST.
WAPPING

N

THE BEATLES STORY

GOWER ST.

2

WHEEL OF LIVERPOOL

ARENA & CONVENTION CENTRE

1

KEEL WHARF

P

KINGS PARADE

KINGS DOCK

QUEENS WHARF

River Mersey

EXHIBITION CENTRE LIVERPOOL

HALFTIDE WHARF

Queen's Dock

Pedestrian Shopping Zone

- - - Victorian Liverpool Town Walk

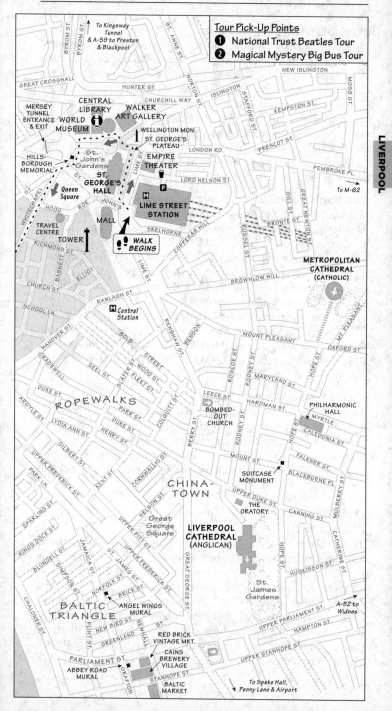

LIVERPOOL

Magical Mystery Big Bus Tour

Beatles fans enjoy loading onto this old, psychedelically painted bus for a spin past Liverpool's main Beatles landmarks, with a few photo ops off the bus. With an enthusiastic live commentary and Beatles tunes cued to famous landmarks, it leaves people happy. The tour ends at the Cavern Club and includes general admission when the club charges a cover (£20, 5-8/day, fewer on Sun and in off-season, 2 hours, buses depart from the Albert Dock near The Beatles Story, tel. 0151/703-9100, www.cavernclub.org). As these tours often fill up, you'd be wise to book at least a day ahead by phone or online.

Phil Hughes Minibus Beatles and Liverpool Tours

For something more extensive, fun, and intimate, consider a five-hour (can be made shorter) minibus Beatles tour from Phil Hughes. It's longer because it includes information on historic Liverpool, along with The Beatles stuff and a couple of *Titanic* and *Lusitania* sights. Phil organizes his tour to fit your schedule and will do his best to accommodate you (£150 for private group tour with 1-5 people; £30/person in peak season if he can assemble a group of 5-8 people; can coordinate tour to include pickup from end of National Trust tour of Lennon and McCartney homes, also does door-to-door service from your hotel or train station, 8-seat minibus, tel. 0151/228-4565, mobile 07961-511-223, www.tourliverpool.co.uk, tourliverpool@hotmail.com).

Jackie Spencer Private Tours

To tailor a visit to your schedule and interests, Jackie Spencer is at your service...just say when and where you want to go (up to 5 people in her chauffeur-driven minivan-£240, 3 hours, longer tours available, will pick you up at hotel or train station, mobile 0799-076-1478, www.jackiespencerbeatleguide.com, jackie@beatleguide.com).

OTHER TOURS

City Bus Tour

Two different hop-on, hop-off bus tours cruise around town, offering a quick way to get an overview that links all the major sights. Liverpool City Sights (red buses) generally have recorded tours, so I prefer **City Explorer** (yellow buses), because they come with live guides (£11, 13 stops, tel. 0151/933-2324, www.cityexplorerliverpool.co.uk). On either bus, your ticket is valid 24 hours and can be purchased from the driver (both run 4/hour at peak times, 2/hour after 15:00, daily April-Oct, generally 10:00-17:00; shorter hours and less frequent in winter).

Liverpool at a Glance

▲▲**Museum of Liverpool** Three floors of intriguing exhibits, historical artifacts, and fun interactive displays tracing the port city's history, culture, and contributions to the world. **Hours:** Daily 10:00-17:00. See page 449.

▲▲**British Music Experience** Immersive and interactive museum on the history of British music from 1945 to current times. **Hours:** Daily 10:00-18:00. See page 450.

▲▲**Liverpool Cathedral** Huge Anglican house of worship—the largest cathedral in Great Britain—with cavernous interior and tower climb. **Hours:** Daily 8:00-18:00. See page 457.

▲▲**Magical Beatles Museum** Offers the best historic artifacts of the group with a special focus on the very early days. **Hours:** Daily 10:00-18:00. See page 454.

▲**The Beatles Story** Well-done if overpriced exhibit about the Fab Four, with a great audioguide narrated by John Lennon's sister, Julia Baird. **Hours:** Daily 9:00-19:00, Nov-March 10:00-18:00. See page 444.

▲**Merseyside Maritime Museum** and **International Slavery Museum** Duo of thought-provoking museums exploring Liverpool's seafaring heritage and the city's role in the African slave trade. **Hours:** Daily 10:00-17:00. See page 445.

▲**Walker Art Gallery** Enjoyable, easy-to-appreciate collection of European paintings, sculptures, and decorative arts. **Hours:** Daily 10:00-17:00. See page 453.

▲**Metropolitan Cathedral of Christ the King** Striking, daringly modern Catholic cathedral with a story as fascinating as the building itself. **Hours:** Daily 7:30-18:00. See page 455.

▲**Lennon and McCartney Homes** Guided visit to their 1950s boyhood homes, with restored interiors. **Hours:** Tours run three times daily in peak season. See page 459.

LIVERPOOL

Ferry Cruise

Mersey Ferries offers cruises with recorded commentary that depart from the Pier Head ferry terminal, a 10-minute walk north of the Albert Dock. The 50-minute cruise makes two brief stops on the other side of the river. While you're welcome to hop off and on, there's little reason to get off across the river as city views are just as good from the boat (£10 round-trip, leaves Pier Head at top of hour, daily 10:00-15:00, Sat-Sun until 18:00 in April-Oct, café, WCs onboard, tel. 0151/330-1000, www.merseyferries.co.uk).

Sights in Liverpool

ON THE WATERFRONT

In its day, Liverpool was England's greatest seaport. It was along here (in front of the Cunard Building) that great ships embarked for America. For millions of people in the 19th century, this was their last stop before a new life in the New World.

But trade declined after 1890, as the port wasn't deep enough for the big new ships. The advent of mega container ships in the 1960s put the final nail in the port's coffin, and by 1972 the central port was closed entirely.

Today, it's once again full of energy and a busy hub of harbor traffic: the harbor tour boat, ferries to Belfast and the Isle of Man, and just beyond, in a tented structure, the Liverpool cruise port (each year about a hundred ships stop here).

Over the past couple of decades, this formerly derelict and dangerous area has been the focus of the city's rejuvenation efforts. Liverpool's waterfront is now a venue for some of the city's top attractions. Three zones interest tourists (from south to north): the Kings Dock, with Liverpool's futuristic arena, conference center, and adjacent Ferris wheel; the red-brick Albert Dock complex, with some of the city's top museums and lively restaurants and nightlife; and Pier Head, with the Museum of Liverpool, ferries across the River Mersey, and buildings both old/stately and new/glassy. Below are descriptions of the main sights at the Albert Dock and Pier Head.

At the Albert Dock

Opened in 1846 by Prince Albert and enclosing seven acres of water, the Albert Dock is surrounded by five-story brick warehouses. A half-dozen trendy eateries are lined up here, protected from the rain by arcades and padded by lots of shopping mall-type distractions. There's plenty of pay parking.

▲The Beatles Story

The Beatles are becoming a bigger and bigger attraction in Liverpool these days. This exhibit—while overpriced and a bit small—is well done. The story's a fascinating one, and even an avid fan will pick up some new information.

Cost and Hours: £17, includes audioguide; daily 9:00-19:00, Nov-March 10:00-18:00; tel. 0151/709-1969, www.beatlesstory. com.

Visiting the Museum: Start with a chronological stroll through the evolution of The Beatles, focusing on their Liverpool years: meeting as school-

boys, performing at (and helping decorate) the Cas-bah Coffee Club, making a name for themselves in Hamburg's red light district, meeting their man-ager Brian Epstein, and the advent of worldwide Beatlemania (with some help from Ed Sullivan). There are many actual artifacts (from George Harrison's first boyhood guitar to John Lennon's orange-tinted "Imagine" glasses), as well as large dioramas celebrating landmarks in Beatles lore (a reconstruction of the Cavern Club, a life-size re-creation of the *Sgt. Pepper* album cover, and a walk-through yellow submarine). The last rooms trace the members' solo careers, and the reverence for John's peace work, including a replica of the white room he used while writing "Imagine." A sepa-rate room shows the history of The Beatles in India, where they practiced transcendental meditation (along with singer Donovan, actress Mia Farrow, and the Beach Boys' Mike Love) and worked on songs for the *White Album*. Rounding out the exhibits are a "Discovery Zone" for kids and (of course) the "Fab 4 Store," with an impressive pile of Beatles buyables.

The great audioguide, narrated by Julia Baird (John Lennon's little sister), captures The Beatles' charm and cheekiness in a way the stiff wax mannequins can't.

While this is a fairly sanitized look at the Fab Four (LSD and Yoko-related conflicts are glossed over), the exhibits remind listen-ers of all that made the group earth-shattering—and even a little edgy—at the time. You'll find that it's strong on Beatles' history, but you'll have to go elsewhere to understand why Beatlemania happened.

▲Merseyside Maritime Museum and International Slavery Museum

These museums tell the story of Liverpool, once the second city of the British Empire. The third floor covers slavery, while the first, second, and basement handle other maritime topics.

LIVERPOOL

The Beatles in Liverpool

The most iconic rock-and-roll band of all time was made up of four Liverpudlians who spent their formative years amid the bombed-out shell of WWII-era Liverpool. The city has become a pilgrimage site for Beatlemaniacs, but even those with just a passing interest in the Fab Four are likely to find themselves humming their favorite tunes around town. Most Beatles sights in Liverpool relate to their early days, before the psychedelia, transcendental meditation, Yoko, and solo careers. Because these sights are so spread out, the easiest way to connect all of them in one go is by tour (see "Tours in Liverpool," earlier).

All four of The Beatles were born in Liverpool, and any tour of town glides by the **home** most identified with each one's childhood: John Lennon at "Mendips," Paul McCartney at 20 Forthlin Road, George Harrison at 12 Arnold Grove, and Ringo Starr (a.k.a. Richard Starkey) at 10 Admiral Grove.

Behind John's house at Mendips is a wooded area called **Strawberry Field** (he added the "s" for the song). This surrounds a Victorian mansion that was, at various times, a Salvation Army home and an orphanage. John enjoyed sneaking into the trees around the mansion to play. Today visitors pose in front of Strawberry Field's red gate (a replica of the original).

During The Beatles' formative years in the mid-1950s, skiffle music (American-inspired rockabilly/folk) swept through Liverpool. As a teenager, John formed a skiffle band called the Quarrymen. Paul met John for the first time when he saw the Quarrymen on July 6, 1957, at **St. Peter's Church** in the suburb of Woolton. After the show, in the social hall across the street, Paul noted that John played only banjo chords (his mother had taught him to play on a banjo rather than a guitar—he didn't even know how to tune a guitar), and improvised many lyrics. John, two years older, realized he was a better improviser than a musician, so he was impressed when Paul borrowed a guitar, tuned it effortlessly, and played a note-perfect rendition of Eddie Cochran's "Twenty Flight Rock." Before long, Paul had joined the band.

The boys went to school on **Mount Street** in the center of Liverpool (near Hope Street, between the two cathedrals). John and his friend Stuart Sutcliffe attended the Liverpool College of Art, and Paul and his pal George Harrison went to Liverpool Institute High School for Boys. (When Paul introduced George to John as a possible new member for the band, John dismissed him as being too young...until he heard George play. He immediately became the lead guitarist.) Paul later bought his old school building and turned it into the Liverpool Institute for Performing Arts.

As young men, the boys rode the bus together to school— waiting at a bus stop in the **Penny Lane** neighborhood. Later they wrote a nostalgic song about the things they would observe while waiting there: the shelter by the roundabout, the barbershop, and the fireman with the clean machine.

By 1960 the group had officially become The Beatles: John Lennon, Paul McCartney, George Harrison, and...Pete Best and Stu Sutcliffe. The quintet gradually built a name for themselves in Liverpool's "Merseybeat" scene, performing at local clubs. While the famous **Cavern Club** is gone (the one you see advertised is a reconstruction, but does offer similar ambience and good cover bands), the original **Casbah Coffee Club**—which the group felt more attached to—still exists and is open for tours (3.5 miles northwest of downtown in Pete Best's former basement, book by calling the TI at tel. 0151/707-0729 or online at www.petebest.com).

The group went to Hamburg, Germany, to cut their teeth in the thriving music scene there. They wound up performing as the backing band for Tony Sheridan's single "My Bonny." When this caught on back in Liverpool, promoter Brian Epstein took note, and signed the act. His shrewd management would eventually propel the Beatles to superstardom.

Many people could be considered the "Fifth Beatle." John's friend Stu, who performed with the group in Hamburg, left to pursue his own artistic interests. Pete Best was the band's original drummer, but he was a loner and producers questioned his musical chops, so he was replaced with Ringo Starr. (John later said, "Pete Best was a great drummer, but Ringo was a Beatle.") Brian Epstein, the manager who marketed the Beatles brilliantly before his untimely death, is another candidate. But—in terms of long-term musical influence—it's hard to ignore the case for George Martin, who produced all The Beatles' albums except *Let It Be*, and was instrumental in both forging and developing The Beatles sound.

By early 1964, The Beatles were already world-famous—but, as evidenced by their songs about Penny Lane and Strawberry Fields, they never forgot their Merseyside home.

Cost and Hours: Free, donations accepted, daily 10:00-17:00, café, tel. 0151/478-4499, www.liverpoolmuseums.org.uk.

Background: Liverpool's port prospered in the 18th century as one corner of a commerce triangle with Africa and America. British shippers profited greatly through exploitation: About 1.5 million enslaved African people were taken to the Americas on Liverpool's ships (that's 10 percent of all African slaves). From Liverpool, the British exported manufactured goods to Africa in exchange for enslaved Africans; the slaves were then shipped to the Americas, where they were traded for raw material (cotton, sugar, and tobacco); and the goods were then brought back to Britain. While the merchants on all three sides made money, the big profit came home to England (which enjoyed substantial income from customs, duties, and a thriving smugglers' market). As Britain's economy boomed, so did Liverpool's.

After participation in the slave trade was outlawed in Britain in the early 1800s, Liverpool kept its port busy as a transfer point for emigrants. If your ancestors came from Scandinavia, Ukraine, or Ireland, they likely left Europe from this port. Between 1830 and 1930, nine million emigrants sailed from Liverpool to find their dreams in the New World.

Visiting the Museums: Begin by riding the elevator up to floor 3—we'll work our way back down.

On floor 3, three galleries make up the **International Slavery Museum.** First is a description of life in West Africa, which re-creates traditional domestic architecture and displays actual artifacts. Then comes a harrowing exhibit about enslavement and the Middle Passage (as the voyage to the Americas was called). The tools of the enslavers—chains, muzzles, and a branding iron—and the intense film about the Middle Passage drive home the horrifying experience of being abducted from your home and taken in life-threatening conditions thousands of miles away to toil for a wealthy stranger. Finally, the museum examines the legacy of slavery—both the persistence of racism in contemporary society and the substantial positive impact that people of African descent have had on European and American cultures.

Continue down the stairs to the **Maritime Museum,** on floor 2. This celebrates Liverpool's shipbuilding heritage and displays actual ship components, model boats, and a gallery of nautical paintings. There's also good coverage of emigration. Part of that heritage is covered in an extensive exhibit on the *Titanic.* The shipping line and its captain were based in Liverpool, and 89 of the crew members who died were from the city.

Floor 1 shows footage and artifacts from another maritime disaster—the 1915 sinking of the *Lusitania,* which was torpedoed by a German U-boat. She sank off the coast of Ireland in under

20 minutes; 1,191 people died in the tragedy, including 405 crew members from Liverpool. The attack on an unarmed passenger ship sparked riots in Liverpool and almost thrust the US into the war. Also on this floor, an extensive exhibit traces the **Battle of the Atlantic** (during World War II, Nazi U-boats attacked merchant ships bringing supplies to Britain, in an attempt to cripple this island nation). You'll see how crew members lived aboard merchant ships.

In the last room, three different exhibits overlap each other. *Carrying Passengers* covers Liverpool as a passenger port and gives an overview of passenger traffic in Britain today. *Carrying Cargos* focuses on cargo ships, imports, and exports, and has an impressive figurehead from the HMS *Hastings*. *Life of a Seafarer* depicts life aboard ship, from leisure activities to diets and living conditions. From the early 1900s to the 1960s, most merchant fleet sailors came from towns like Liverpool.

A last section is dedicated to the MV *Derbyshire*, an oil tanker that disappeared in the South China Sea in 1980. The wreck was eventually found in 1994.

Make your way to the basement, where exhibits describe the tremendous wave of **emigration** through Liverpool's port. And the *Seized!* exhibit looks at the legal and illegal movement of goods through that same port, including thought-provoking displays on customs, taxation, and smuggling.

At Pier Head, North of the Albert Dock

A five-minute walk across the bridge north of the Albert Dock takes you to the Pier Head area, with a popular statue of The Beatles on the harborfront and the sights listed next.

▲▲Museum of Liverpool

This museum, in the blocky white building just across the bridge north of the Albert Dock, does a good job of fulfilling its goal to "capture Liverpool's vibrant character and demonstrate the city's unique contribution to the world." The museum is full of interesting items, fun interactive displays (great for kids), and fascinating facts that bring a whole new depth to your Liverpool experience.

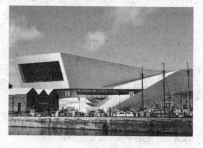

Cost and Hours: Free, donations encouraged, daily 10:00-

17:00, guidebook-£1, café, Mann Island, Pier Head, tel. 0151/478-4545, www.liverpoolmuseums.org.uk.

Ground Floor: On this level, *The Great Port* details the story of Liverpool's defining industry and how it developed through the Industrial Revolution. On display is an 1838 steam locomotive that was originally built for the Liverpool and Manchester Railway. The *Global City* exhibit focuses on how Liverpool's status as a major British shipping center made it the gateway to a global empire and features a 20-minute video, *Power and the Glory*, about Liverpool's role within the British Empire.

First Floor: Don't miss the *Liverpool Overhead Railway* exhibit, which features the only surviving car from this 19th-century elevated railway. You can actually jump aboard and take a seat to watch 1897 movie footage shot from the train line. A huge interactive model shows the railway's route. Also on this floor is the *History Detectives* exhibit, which covers Liverpool's archaeology and history, including the story of the Liverpool Blitz (bombings by the German Luftwaffe in 1940-41—only London was bombed more than Liverpool during WWII raids over Britain).

Second Floor: If you're short on time, spend most of it here. The *People's Republic* exhibit examines what it means to be a Liverpudlian (a.k.a. "Scouser") and covers everything from housing and health issues to military and religious topics. As industrialized Liverpool has long been a hotbed of the labor movement, exhibits here also detail the political side of the city, including child labor issues and women's suffrage.

Music is the other big focus here, with plenty of fun interactive stops that include quizzes, a karaoke booth, and listening stations featuring artists with ties to Liverpool (from Elvis Costello to Echo & the Bunnymen). And, of course, you'll see plenty of Beatles mania, including their famous suits, the original stage from St. Peter's Church (where John Lennon was performing the first time Paul McCartney laid eyes on him; located in the theater), and an eight-minute film on the band.

Finally, in the **Skylight Gallery,** look for Ben Johnson's painting *The Liverpool Cityscape, 2008,* a remarkable and fun-to-examine melding of old and new art styles. At first glance, it's a typical skyline painting, but Johnson used computer models to create perfect depictions of each building before he put brush to canvas. This method allows for a photorealistic, highly detailed, but completely sanitized portrait of a city. Notice there are no cars or people.

▲▲British Music Experience

This museum, located in the Cunard Building at Pier Head, goes beyond Liverpool's Beatlemania, immersing visitors in the history of British music of all genres from 1945 until today. The multimedia exhibits include costumes, instruments, recordings, and memorabilia from artists and bands such as David Bowie, Queen, Amy Winehouse, Coldplay, and Adele, plus the chance to play professional-grade instruments in a sound studio. You could easily spend hours here, but plan for at least 90 minutes.

Cost and Hours: £14, daily 10:00-18:00, last entry 1.5 hours before closing, multimedia guide-£2; tel. 0344-335-0655, www. britishmusicexperience.com.

Visiting the Museum: The museum is one big room with a stage dominating the center that's flanked by eight zones cover-

ing different eras. Music videos and holographic performances play on the stage. You can work your way around the hall chronologically from 1945 (when, with the help of pop music culture, children began freeing themselves from being "little adults who dressed and acted like their parents").

Each section displays interesting facts about well-known artists, billboard art, costumes, instruments, and more. Your multimedia guide provides interviews, videos, and picture galleries. The first two sections (1945-1962, which covers jazz, skiffle, and rock-and-roll, and 1962-1966, covering R&B, Merseybeat, and The Beatles) have well-done interactive tables explaining the origin of these music genres and how the UK and US music scenes influenced each other. Timelines place the music in historical context, describing its relation to the politics and culture of each decade.

The final section is a studio where you can exercise your musical skills: take interactive instrument lessons (I learned to play a set of drums.); record your singing; or learn (and then record on video) dance moves that have been popular over the decades.

DOWNTOWN

Stepping away from the waterfront, you find Liverpool's workaday commercial center stretching east up to the train station and Walker Art Gallery and south past the massive Liverpool ONE shopping and residential complex. Take a moment with the map to get the lay of this easily walkable land: The older part of downtown stretches from Liverpool Town Hall down Castle Street to the huge Queen Victoria monument. Beyond the Victoria monument is Liverpool ONE. Next to that complex is the Ropewalks District stretching to Liverpool's "bombed-out church." Uphill from there you'll find the cathedral neighborhood, with the Catholic cathedral to the left and Chinatown and the Anglican cathedral to the right.

Victorian Liverpool Town Walk

If you're arriving at Lime Street Station, here's a stately way to get from the station into the city center. We'll start by walking through St. George's Plateau, past the Walker Art Gallery, and then down-hill past St. John's Gardens to Beatles sights along Mathew Street. Along the way, the only sight of real importance is the Walker Gallery (free and well worth a look, see listing, later). But the walk gives you a feel for the grand side of 19th-century Liverpool.

St. George's Hall is the big, temple-like Neoclassical building facing the station. It originally contained courts and a concert hall; now it's a venue for conferences, civic events, and the performing arts. Between the hall and train station is **St. George's Plateau,** a gathering place for the community with equestrian statues of Prince Albert and a youthful Queen Victoria that flank a somber memorial to the World Wars. Walk all around the memorial to appreciate the royal faces and the huge wartime losses Liverpool, like any British city, endured.

When John Lennon was shot, 25,000 gathered here for a candlelight vigil...probably recalling the last live Beatles performance here in December 1965, in the **Empire Theatre** across the street. Take a look up Lord Nelson Street to the right of the theater to spot the recommended **Ma Egerton's Stage Door** pub, where many an artist went for a pint (and still do) after their performances.

The towering monumental column honors the Duke of Wellington, who beat Napoleon at the Battle of Waterloo in 1815. Behind him is the **Walker Art Gallery,** which is like a mini version of London's National Gallery.

Now turn left and work your way downhill. The Neoclassical building adjacent to the Walker Gallery is the **Central Library,** containing a modern atrium (free, with TI open Mon-Sat 10:00-16:30) and, upstairs, the impressive Victorian Picton Reading Room. In front of the entrance, notice the long walkway engraved with famous book, movie, and music titles. Here and there you can see red letters sprinkled among the words, forming a puzzle to a secret code that the museum has yet to reveal.

The next grand building houses the **World Museum,** a catch-all family museum with five floors of kid-oriented exhibits. You'll see dinosaurs, an aquarium, artifacts from the ancient world, a planetarium, and theater (free, daily 10:00-17:00).

Continue strolling downhill along **St. John's Gardens** (across the street). Filled with statues, it celebrates influential locals—politicians and philanthropists. (With all the slave wealth, big shots here felt a need to be philanthropic.)

At the foot of the park, find a round bronze memorial to the Hillsborough Stadium tragedy when 96 local fans (most quite young) were crushed during a 1989 soccer game in Sheffield. That tragedy led to a big change in how stadium seating is built in Britain.

The gaping tunnel below (with statues of the king and queen flanking its entry) is the mouth to the **Mersey Tunnel,** the first road under the river, that was opened in 1934. Movie buffs might recognize it from a *Fast and Furious* car chase or from a Harry Potter flying-broom chase.

From here, head downhill to the left on Whitechapel for about six blocks. A block into the pedestrian zone you'll have entered the heart of Liverpool's commercial center. At Stanley Street go right and then left onto **Mathew Street**—historic for Beatles fans. Lined with bars and souvenir shops, it's super-touristy by day and sloppy and rowdy at night, often overrun with stag and hen parties on weekends (see listing, below).

▲Walker Art Gallery

Though it has few recognizable works, Liverpool's main art gallery offers an enjoyable walk through an easy-to-digest collection

of European (mostly British) paintings, sculpture, and decorative arts. There's no audioguide, but many of the works are well explained by posted descriptions. You'll see a sculpture gallery with works by John Gibson, a Welshman who grew up in Liverpool and later studied under the Italian master Antonio Canova; and a painting gallery including Baroque, Pre-Raphaelite, 20th-century, and Impressionist works.

Cost and Hours: Free, donations accepted, daily 10:00-17:00, William Brown Street, tel. 0151/478-4199, www.liverpoolmuseums.org.uk.

Mathew Street

The narrow, bar-lined Mathew Street, right in the heart of downtown, is ground zero for Beatles fans. The Beatles frequently performed in their early days together at the original Cavern Club, deep in a cellar along this

street. While that's long gone, a mock-up of the historic nightspot (built with many of the original bricks) lives on a few doors down. Still billed as "the **Cavern Club**," this noisy bar is worth a visit to see the reconstructed cellar that's often filled by Beatles cover bands. While just a touristy pub draped in memorabilia, dropping by in the afternoon for a live Beatles tribute act in the Cavern Club somehow just feels right. You'll have Beatles songs stuck in your head all day anyway, so you might as well see John and Paul wannabes strumming and harmonizing a close approximation of the original (open daily 10:00-24:00; live music daily from noon until late evening, free admission most of the time, small entry fee Thu-Sun evenings; tel. 0151/236-9091, www.cavernclub.org).

Across the street and run by the same owners, the **Cavern Pub** lacks its sibling's troglodyte aura, but makes up for it with walls lined with old photos and memorabilia from The Beatles and other bands who've performed here. Like the Cavern Club, the pub features frequent performances by Beatles cover bands and other acts (no cover, daily 11:00-24:00, tel. 0151/236-4041).

Out front is the Cavern's **Wall of Fame,** with a too-cool-for-school bronze John Lennon leaning up against a wall of bricks engraved with the names of musical acts that have graced the Cavern stage. Adjacent, notice the 57 number-one singles from 1953 to 2018 by Liverpool bands.

At the corner is the recommended **Hard Day's Night Hotel,** decorated inside and out to honor the Fab Four. Notice the statues of John, Paul, George, and Ringo on the second-story corners, and the Beatles gift shop (one of many in town) on the ground floor.

▲▲Magical Beatles Museum

Claiming to be "the world's most authentic Beatles museum," this fascinating-to-Beatles-fans collection is spread chronologically over three floors with thoughtful descriptions. Neil Aspinall, a roadie-hoarder, collected this memorabilia during the early years as if he knew The Beatles would make history. Filled with a trove of artifacts (letters, clothing, photos, and so on), each floor covers an era: before they were famous, the touring years, and the studio/psychedelic years. Beatle-geek staffers are standing by to tell stories and answer questions. It's strong on pre-Ringo days, because Neil was "a kind of stepfather" to Pete Best (the original drummer)...it's complicated.

Cost and Hours: £15, RS%—Roag Best (the owner and

half-brother of Pete) promises 20 percent off with this book; daily 10:00-18:00, last entry one hour before closing, 50 yards from the Cavern Club at 23 Mathew Street, tel. 0151/236-1337, www. magicalbeatlesmuseum.com.

CATHEDRALS NEIGHBORHOOD

Liverpool has not one but two notable cathedrals—one Anglican, the other Catholic. (As the Spinners song puts it, "If you want a cathedral, we've got one to spare.") Both are huge, architecturally significant, and well worth visiting. Near the eastern edge of downtown, they're connected by a 10-minute, half-mile walk on pleasant Hope Street, which is lined with theaters and good restaurants (see "Eating in Liverpool," later).

Liverpudlians enjoy pointing out that they have not only the world's only Catholic cathedral designed by a Protestant architect, but also the only Protestant one designed by a Catholic. With its large Irish-immigrant population, Liverpool suffered from tension between its Catholic and Protestant communities for much of its history. But during the city's darkest stretch of the depressed 1970s, the bishops of each church—Anglican Bishop David Sheppard and Catholic Archbishop Derek Worlock—came together and worked hard to reconcile the two communities for the betterment of Liverpool. (Liverpudlians nicknamed this dynamic duo "fish and chips" because they were "always together, and always in the newspaper.") It worked: Liverpool is a bold new cultural center, and relations between the two faiths remain healthy here. Join in this ecumenical spirit by visiting and appreciating the lively energy of both churches.

▲Metropolitan Cathedral of Christ the King (Catholic)

This daringly modern building, a cone topped with a crowned cylinder, seems almost out of place in its workaday Liverpool neigh-

borhood. But the cathedral you see today bears no resemblance to Sir Edwin Lutyens' original 1930s plans for a stately Neo-Byzantine cathedral, which was to take 200 years to build and rival St. Peter's Basilica in Vatican City. (Lutyens was desperate to one-up the grandiose plans of Sir Giles Gilbert Scott, who was building the Anglican Cathedral down the street.) The crypt for the ambitious church was excavated in the 1930s, but World War II (during which the crypt was used as an air-raid shelter) stalled progress for decades. In the 1960s, the plans were scaled back, and

LIVERPOOL

this smaller (but still impressive) house of worship was completed in 1967.

Cost and Hours: Cathedral—free entry but donations accepted, daily 7:30-18:00—but after 17:15 (during Mass), you won't be able to walk around; crypt—£3, Mon-Sat 10:00-16:00, closed Sun, last entry 45 minutes before closing, enter from inside church near organ; visitors center and an inviting café, Mount Pleasant, tel. 0151/709-9222, www.liverpoolmetrocathedral.org.uk.

Visiting the Cathedral: On the stepped plaza in front of the church, you'll see the entrance to the cathedral's visitors center and café (on your right). You're standing on a big concrete slab that provides a roof to the massive Lutyens Crypt underfoot. The existing cathedral occupies only a small part of the would-be cathedral's footprint. Because of its tent-like appearance and ties to the local Irish community, some Liverpudlians dubbed it "Paddy's Wigwam."

Climb up the stairs to the main doors, step inside, and let your eyes adjust to this magnificent, dimly lit space. Unlike a typical nave-plus-transept cross-shaped church, this cathedral has a round footprint, with seating for a congregation of 3,000 surrounding the white marble altar. Like a theater-in-the-round, it was designed to involve worshippers in the service. Suspended above the altar is a stylized crown of thorns.

Spinning off from the round central sanctuary are 13 smaller chapels, many of them representing stages of Jesus' life. Each chapel is different. Explore, tuning into the symbolic details in each one. Also keep an eye out for the 14 exquisite bronze Stations of the Cross by local artist Sean Rice (on the wall).

The massive **Lutyens Crypt** (named for the ambitious original architect)—the only part of the originally planned cathedral to be completed—has huge vaults and vast halls lined with six million bricks. The crypt contains a chapel—with windows by Lutyens—that's still used for Sunday Mass, the tombs of three archbishops, a treasury, and an exhibit about the cathedral's construction.

Hope Street

The street connecting the cathedrals is the main artery of Liverpool's "uptown," a lively and fun-to-explore district loaded with dining and entertainment options. At the intersection with Mount Street is a monument consisting of concrete suitcases (explained by a nearby info plaque); just down this street is John's art school and Paul and George's high school—with the four grand columns. In addition to well-respected theaters, this street is home to the Liverpool Philharmonic and its namesake pub.

The **Philharmonic Dining Rooms,** kitty-corner from the Philharmonic Hall on Hope Street, must be the most flamboyantly Victorian pub in town. It's amazingly elaborate, the pink-marble urinals (while stinky) are downright genteel, and the cozy sitting areas on the ground floor will entice you to sip a pint. John Lennon said that his biggest regret about fame was "not being able to go to the Phil for a drink."

▲▲Liverpool Cathedral (Anglican)

The largest cathedral in Great Britain, this gigantic house of worship hovers at the south end of downtown. Tour its cavernous interior and consider scaling its tower.

Cost and Hours: Free, £5 suggested donation, daily 8:00-18:00; £5.50 ticket includes tower climb (sold in the gift shop, 2 elevators and 108 steps), audioguide, and 10-minute *Great Space* film; tower—Mon-Sat 10:00-17:00 (Thu until sunset March-Oct), Sun 12:00-16:00 (changes possible depending on bell-ringing schedule); St. James Mount, tel. 0151/709-6271, www.liverpoolcathedral.org.uk.

Visiting the Cathedral: Over the main door is a modern *Risen Christ* statue by Elisabeth Frink. Liverpudlians, not thrilled with the featureless statue and always quick with a joke, have dubbed it **"Frinkenstein."**

Stepping inside, pick up a floor plan at the information desk, go into the main hall, and take in the size of the place. When Liverpool was officially designated a "city" (seat of a bishop), they wanted to build a huge house of worship as a symbol of Liverpudlian pride. Built in bold Neo-Gothic style (like London's Parliament), it seems to trumpet with modern bombast the importance of this city on the Mersey. Begun in 1904, the cathedral's construction was interrupted by the tumultuous 20th century and not completed until 1978.

Go to the big circular tile in the very center of the cathedral, under the highest tower. This is a plaque for the building's architect, **Sir Giles Gilbert Scott** (1880-1960). While the church you're surrounded by may seem like his biggest legacy, he also designed an icon that's synonymous with Britain: the classic red telephone box. Notice the highly detailed sandstone carvings flanking this aisle.

Take a counterclockwise spin around the church interior. Head up the right aisle until you find the **model** of the original plan for the cathedral (press the button to light it up).

Nearby, the **"whispering arch"** spanning the monument has remarkable acoustics, carrying voices from one end to the other. Try it.

Continuing down the church, notice the very colorful, modern painting of *The Good Samaritan* (by Adrian Wiszniewski, 1995), high above on the right. The naked crime victim (who has been stabbed in his side, like the Crucifixion wound of Jesus) has been ignored by the well-dressed yuppies in the foreground, but the female Samaritan is finally taking notice. The canvas is packed with symbolism (for example, the Swiss Army knife, in a pool of blood in the left foreground, is open in the 3 o'clock position—the time that Jesus was crucified).

Proceeding to the corner, you'll reach the entrance to the oldest part of the church (1910): the **Lady Chapel,** with stained-glass windows celebrating important women. (Sadly, the original windows were destroyed in World War II; these are replicas.)

Back up in the main part of the church, continue behind the main altar to the **Education Centre,** with a fun, sped-up video showing all of the daily work it takes to make this cathedral run.

Circling around the far corner of the church, you'll pass the children's chapel and chapterhouse, and then pass under another modern Wiszniewski painting *(The House Built on Rock).* Across from that painting, go into the choir to get a good look at the Last Supper altarpiece above the **main altar.**

Continuing back up the aisle, you'll come to the **war memorial transept.** At its entrance is a book listing Liverpudlians lost in war. Battle flags fly high on the wall above.

You'll wind up at the gift shop, where you can buy a ticket to climb to the top of the tower. The cathedral's café is up the stairs, above the gift shop.

AWAY FROM THE CENTER
▲Lennon and McCartney Homes

John's and Paul's boyhood homes are now owned by the National Trust and have both been restored to how they looked during the lads' 1950s childhoods.

The proud family home of the McCartney family; **Jim, Mary, Paul** and **Mike**
Accessible via The National Trust
Tickets available from:
www.nationaltrust.org.uk/beatles
Telephone: 0151 427 7231
(There is no direct access inside the house)

While some Beatles bus tours stop here for photo ops, only the National Trust minibus tour gets you inside the homes. This isn't Graceland—you won't find an over-the-top rock-and-roll extravaganza here. If you don't know the difference between John and Paul, you'll likely be bored. But for die-hard Beatles fans who want to get a glimpse into the time and place that created these musical masterminds, the National Trust tour is worth ▲▲▲.

Because the houses are in residential neighborhoods—and still share walls with neighbors—the National Trust runs only a few tours per day, limited to 15 or so Beatlemaniacs each.

Cost: £25, £31 includes a guidebook.

Reservations: Advance booking is strongly advised, especially in summer and on weekends or holidays. Book online or by phone as soon as you know your Liverpool plans—or at least two weeks ahead (tel. 0344-249-1895, www.nationaltrust.org.uk/beatles). If you haven't reserved ahead, you can try to book a same-day tour; the last tour of the day is least likely to be full.

Visitor Information: Tours run daily from the Albert Dock at 10:00, 11:00, and 14:10 (tours do not run Mon-Tue in mid-Feb-mid-March and Nov; no tours at all Dec-mid-Feb). They depart from the Jurys Inn (south across the bridge from The Beatles Story, near the Ferris wheel—meet in hotel lobby). The entire visit takes about 2.5 hours.

Visiting the Homes: A minibus takes you to the homes of John and Paul, with about 45 minutes inside each (no photos allowed inside either home). Each home has a caretaker who acts as your guide. These folks give an entertaining, insightful-to-fans talk that lasts about 30 minutes. You then have 10-15 minutes to wander through the house on your own. Ask lots of questions if their spiel peters out early—these docents are a wealth of information.

Mendips (John Lennon's Home): Even though he sang about being a working-class hero, John grew up in the suburbs of Liverpool, surrounded by doctors, lawyers, and—beyond the back fence—Strawberry Field.

This was the home of John's Aunt Mimi, who raised him in this house from the time he was five years old and once told him, "A guitar's all right, John, but you'll never earn a living by it." (John later bought Mimi a country cottage with those fateful words etched over the fireplace.) John moved out at age 23, but his first wife, Cynthia, bunked here for a while when John made his famous first trip to America. Yoko Ono bought the house in 2002 and gave it as a gift to the National Trust (generating controversy among the neighbors). The house's stewards make this place come to life.

On the surface, it's just a 1930s house carefully restored to how it would have been in the past. But delve deeper. It's been lovingly cared for—restored to be the tidy, well-kept place Mimi would have recognized (down to dishtowels hanging in the kitchen). It's a lucky quirk of fate that the house's interior remained mostly unchanged after the Lennons left: The bachelor who owned it decades after them didn't upgrade much, so even the light switches are true to the time.

20 Forthlin Road (Paul McCartney's Home): In comparison to Aunt Mimi's house, the home where Paul grew up is simpler, much less "posh," and even a little ratty

around the edges. It's been intentionally scuffed up around the edges to preserve the historical accuracy. Notice the differences—Paul has said that John's house was vastly different and more clearly middle class; at Mendips, there were books on the bookshelves—but Paul's father had an upright piano. He also rigged up wires and headphones that connected the boys' bedrooms to the living room radio so they could listen to rock-and-roll on Radio Luxembourg.

More than a hundred Beatles songs were written in this house (including "I Saw Her Standing There") during days Paul and John spent skipping school. The photos from Michael, taken in this house, help make the scene of what's mostly a barren interior much more interesting. Ask your guide how Paul would sneak into the house late at night without waking up his dad.

Nightlife in Liverpool

Liverpool hops after hours, especially on weekends. If you're out after dinner, here are a few suggestions.

Ropewalks and Nearby

A particularly lively zone is the area called Ropewalks, just east of the downtown shopping district and Albert Dock. Part of the protected historic area of Liverpool's docklands, the redeveloped Ropewalks area is now filled with pubs, nightclubs, and lounges—some of them rough around the edges, others posh and sleek. While this area is aimed primarily at the college-age crowd, it's still worth a stroll, and has a few eateries worth considering.

The Bridewell bar fills a circa-1850 police station with a lively pub atmosphere and a beer garden. Inside, past the bar, several jail cells have been converted into cozy seating areas (1 Campbell Square).

The Grapes, an artsy pub between Hope Street and Ropewalks, has a cracking atmosphere with a hardworking staff and a good selection of ales and cocktails. Upstairs is a cozy outdoor terrace (live music on Sun, 60 Roscoe Street).

Peter Kavanagh's, near the Anglican Cathedral, is worth the trek. It's a proper pub with no food but plenty of good ales, cocktails, and friendly locals. The interior is richly decorated with memorabilia from its various owners. Enjoy a pint on the outside terrace or in the comfy leather seating inside. There's a late-night quiz every Thursday at 22:00, and live music Tuesday and Saturday evenings (8 Egerton Street, cash only).

Downtown

The pubs listed here are best for serious drinkers and beer aficionados—the food is an afterthought.

Thomas Rigby's has hard-used wooden floors in the taproom that spill out into a rollicking garden courtyard. Its atmosphere is laid back, and chances are good you'll meet locals, especially after work hours (21 Dale Street).

Ye Hole in Ye Wall, around the corner and much more sedate, brags that it's Liverpool's oldest pub, from 1726. Notice the men's room on the ground floor—the women's room, required by law to be added in the 1970s, is upstairs (just off Dale Street on Hackins Hey).

The Globe, a few blocks over, right in the heart of downtown and surrounded by modern mega-malls, is a tight, cozy, local-feeling pub with five real ales and sloping floors (17 Cases Street).

The Cavern Quarter, with the Cavern Club and neighboring music bars, covers a one-block stretch of Mathew Street. Filled with Beatles bars and Beatles memories, it's packed with curious tourists by day and gets rowdier after dark—especially with hen and stag parties on weekend nights. You can always drink and dance to cover bands playing Beatles classics on Mathew Street.

The Baltic Triangle

This area, just a short walk south from Albert Dock, is an up-and-coming, shabby-chic zone with street art, mod bars, trendy eateries, and an edgy night scene.

The most interesting part starts on **Jamaica Street** where Paul Curtis, "Liverpool's Banksy," (along with other local artists) has decorated the Baltic Triangle with creative murals. The main attractions are his fun-loving *Angel Wings* and *Abbey Road* (painted for the 50th anniversary of that album) on Grafton Street. Both are just waiting for you as photo ops. On Jordan Street, check out the rotating statue exhibition, always good for a selfie. Across the street is a mural of Liverpool's soccer coach Jürgen Klopp, a native of Germany who's made Liverpool a top contender in England's Premier League.

At the end of Jamaica Street is the popular **Camp and Furnace,** a cultural hub hosting events such as "Bongo's Bingo," singalongs, concerts, and a Beatles disco (67 Greenland Street, tel. 0151/708-2890, www.campandfurnace.com).

Across busy Parliament Street you'll find **Cains Brewery Village** with a surprisingly good secondhand mall called **Red Brick Vintage Market.** For food, head to the **Baltic Market,** a warehouse full of alternative pop-up eateries that has done a lot to put the neighborhood on the map (closed Mon-Wed, 107 Stanhope Street).

Sleeping in Liverpool

Your best budget options in this thriving city are the boring, predictable, and central chain hotels—though I've listed a couple more colorful options also worth considering. Many hotels, including the ones listed below, charge more on weekends (particularly Sat), especially when the Liverpool FC soccer team plays a home game. Rates shoot up even higher two weekends a year: during the Grand National horse race (long weekend in April), and during Beatles Week in late August—avoid these times if you can. Prices plummet on Sunday nights.

$$ Hope Street Hotel is a class act that sets the bar for Liverpool's hotels. Located across from the Philharmonic on Hope Street (midway between the cathedrals, in a fun dining neighborhood), this stylish and contemporary hotel has 89 luxurious rooms with lots of hardwood, exposed brick, and elegant little extras. An extension, located in the former School for the Blind, has 50 additional rooms, a roof garden, a spa with a pool, and a cinema (breakfast extra—book ahead, elevator, some rooms handicap accessible, pay parking, 40 Hope Street, tel. 0151/709-3000, www. hopestreethotel.co.uk, sleep@hopestreethotel.co.uk).

$$ Hard Day's Night Hotel is ideal for Beatles pilgrims. Located in a carefully restored old building smack in the heart of the Cavern Quarter, its contemporary  decor is purely Beatles, from its public spaces (lobby, lounge, bar, restaurant) to its 110 rooms, each with a different original Beatles portrait by New York artist Shannon. There's often live music in the afternoons in the lobby bar—and it's not all Beatles covers. What could have been a tacky travesty is instead tasteful, with a largely black-and-white color scheme and subtle nods to the Fab Four (some rates include breakfast, elevator, Internet-enabled TVs with music playlists, pay parking, Central Building, North John Street, tel. 0151/668-0479, www.harddaysnighthotel.com, enquiries@harddaysnighthotel. com).

$$ Sir Thomas Hotel is a centrally located hotel that was once a bank. The lobby has been redone in a trendy style, and the 39 rooms are comfortable. As windows are thin and it's a busy neighborhood, ask for a quieter room (some rates include breakfast, elevator, pay parking, 10-minute walk from station, 24 Sir Thomas Street at the corner of Victoria Street, tel. 0151/236-1366, www. thesirthomas.co.uk, reservations@thesirthomas.co.uk).

$ Aachen Guest Accommodations is a family-run hotel with 15 modern, straightforward rooms in an old Georgian townhouse. The hotel is situated on a pleasant street just uphill from the heart of downtown (includes breakfast, a few rooms have shared baths, 89 Mount Pleasant, tel. 0151/709-3477, www.aachenhotel.co.uk, aachenhotel@btconnect.com).

$ Hallmark Inn Liverpool, nearly next door in a stately old Georgian building, has tight hallways and 82 small rooms with mod decor and amenities (breakfast extra—book ahead, no elevator and six floors, pay parking, 115 Mount Pleasant, tel. 0330-028-

LIVERPOOL

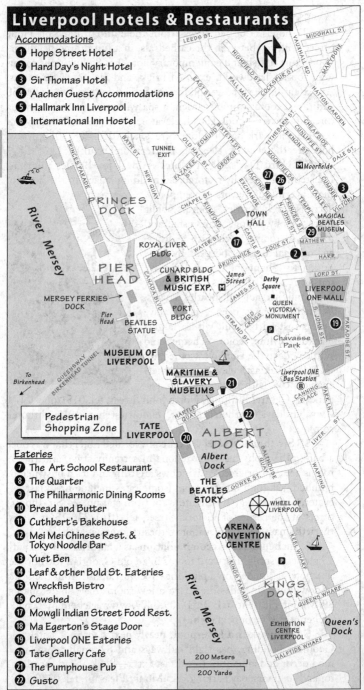

Liverpool Hotels & Restaurants

Accommodations
1. Hope Street Hotel
2. Hard Day's Night Hotel
3. Sir Thomas Hotel
4. Aachen Guest Accommodations
5. Hallmark Inn Liverpool
6. International Inn Hostel

Eateries
7. The Art School Restaurant
8. The Quarter
9. The Philharmonic Dining Rooms
10. Bread and Butter
11. Cuthbert's Bakehouse
12. Mei Mei Chinese Rest. & Tokyo Noodle Bar
13. Yuet Ben
14. Leaf & other Bold St. Eateries
15. Wreckfish Bistro
16. Cowshed
17. Mowgli Indian Street Food Rest.
18. Ma Egerton's Stage Door
19. Liverpool ONE Eateries
20. Tate Gallery Cafe
21. The Pumphouse Pub
22. Gusto

Pedestrian Shopping Zone

200 Meters
200 Yards

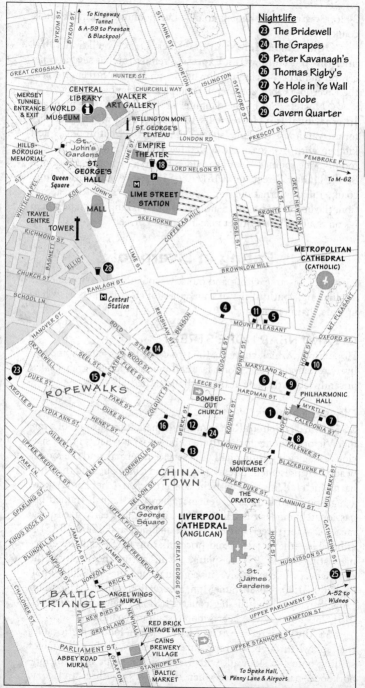

Nightlife
- 23 The Bridewell
- 24 The Grapes
- 25 Peter Kavanagh's
- 26 Thomas Rigby's
- 27 Ye Hole in Ye Wall
- 28 The Globe
- 29 Cavern Quarter

3426, www.hallmarkhotels.co.uk, liverpoolinn@hallmarkhotels.co.uk).

Other Chain Hotels: At the Albert Dock, you'll find a **Premier Inn** and **Holiday Inn Express.** Premier Inn has several other central branches, including downtown on Vernon Street and near the Liverpool ONE commercial complex on Hanover Street.

¢ **Hostel:** Run by the daughter of The Beatles' first manager, **International Inn Hostel** rents 100 budget beds in a former Victorian warehouse (includes sheets, all rooms have bathrooms, guest kitchen with free toast and tea/coffee available 24 hours, laundry room, game room/TV lounge, video library, 24-hour reception, 4 South Hunter Street, tel. 0151/709-8135, www.internationalinn.co.uk, info@internationalinn.co.uk). From the Lime Street Station, the hostel is an easy 15-minute walk; if taking a taxi, tell them it's on South Hunter Street near Hardman Street.

Eating in Liverpool

Liverpool has an exciting and quickly evolving culinary scene. As a rollicking, youthful city, it's a magnet for creative chefs as well as upscale chain restaurants.

ON AND NEAR HOPE STREET

Hope Street, which connects the two cathedrals, is also home to a lively restaurant scene. For a fast and practical lunch, grab a salad or sandwich at the café at the Catholic cathedral.

Classic Eateries

$$$$ The Art School Restaurant fills the Lantern Room of a former Victorian home for destitute children with what is now a spacious and elegant dining hall. The service is formal, and the food is beautifully presented. Dressy, elegant, and a block behind the Philharmonic Hall, it's a hit with the concert crowd. Chef Paul Askew, a high-powered bundle of gourmet energy, is French-trained but passionately modern English in the kitchen. The early fixed-price meal (£34 for three courses, served at lunch and 17:00-18:15) is affordable—the regular fixed-price offering (£75) and the enticing tasting menu (£95) are splurges. Considering the quality of the experience, while expensive, it's a good value (Tue-Sat 12:00-14:30 & 17:00-21:30, closed Sun-Mon, reservations smart, a block off Hope Street, behind the big concert hall at 1 Sugnall Street, tel. 0151/230-8600, www.theartschoolrestaurant.co.uk).

$$ The Quarter serves up Mediterranean food at rustic tables that sprawl through several connected houses, with a few tables spilling onto the sidewalk with views of the Hope Street neighborhood—particularly nice when sunny. It's youthful and cozy, serving pasta, pizza, and boards of meats and cheeses meant to be shared. They also do breakfast and have carryout coffee, homemade cakes, and sandwiches in their attached deli (daily 8:00-23:00, deli open 12:00-15:00 only, 7 Falkner Street, tel. 0151/707-1965).

$$ The Philharmonic Dining Rooms, kitty-corner from the Philharmonic Hall, is actually a pub—but what a pub. This place wins the "atmosphere award" for its old-time elegance. The bar is a work of art, and the three sitting areas on the ground floor (including the giant hall) are enticing places to tip back a pint. While primarily a drinking pub, I'd eat here for the atmo-

sphere. The restaurant seating is upstairs, but the ambience is on the ground floor (food served daily 11:00-22:00, bar open until late, corner of Hope and Hardman streets, tel. 0151/707-2837).

$$ Bread and Butter is a cozy little restaurant serving a French-inspired menu. Look for daily specials and enjoy a cold pint in their beer garden (Tue-Sat 12:00-23:00, Sun 13:00-19:00, closed Mon, 23 Hope Street, tel. 0151/709-7612).

$$ Cuthbert's Bakehouse is a charming café and teahouse located two blocks down from the Liverpool Science Park. This is your best bet for an afternoon tea (£18 Cuthbert's classic, reserve in advance by phone). They also have an impressive range of tasty homemade cakes and sweets; check out their specialty—red velvet cake (Mon-Sat 10:00-18:00, Tue until 20:00, Sat until 19:00, Sun from 11:00, 103 Mount Pleasant, tel. 0151/709-9912).

Asian Cuisine

A few blocks southwest of Hope Street is Liverpool's thriving Chinatown neighborhood, with the world's biggest Chinese arch. Lots of enticing options dishing up Asian cuisine line up along Berry Street in front of the arch and Cornwallis Street behind it.

$$ Mei Mei Chinese Restaurant serves Cantonese to an enthusiastic local Chinese clientele. It's dressy, with a big, enticing menu and a hardworking staff (daily 12:00-22:30, 9 Berry Street, tel. 0151/707-2888).

$$ Yuet Ben is one of Liverpool's most established Chinese restaurants (Wed-Sun 17:00-23:00, closed Mon-Tue, facing the arch at 1 Upper Duke Street, tel. 0151/709-5772).

$ Tokyo Noodle Bar is a cheap and simple diner featuring tasty noodle and rice dishes (Cantonese, Japanese, Malaysian, and so on) with service that's fast and furious (daily 12:00-22:45, 7 Berry Street, tel. 0151/708-6286).

ROPEWALKS

While primarily a nightlife zone, this gentrified area (between the pedestrian Liverpool ONE and the Hope Street neighborhood) also has a smattering of unique restaurants. Focus on Bold Street, lined with fun eateries.

$$ Leaf, with a wonderful energy, is my favorite on the street. Like Liverpool, it's a little bit of everything—sharing dishes, fresh bakery items, salads, vegetarian plates, soups, sandwiches, fun cocktails, and lots of tea—all driven by the simple philosophy: When there's tea, there's hope. It's a chaotic, industrial-minimalist space with noisy acoustics. Grab a table and then order at the counter (daily 9:00-22:00, 65 Bold Street, tel. 0151/707-7747).

Other Bold Street Eateries: Along with trendy tapas, Middle Eastern, and Italian restaurants, look for these **$** places: **The Cat Café** (where you can actually munch and sip with a cuddly cat, #10 at the bottom of the street), **Johnny English** for traditional fish-and-chips (at #60), and the wildly popular **Mowgli Indian Street Food** (at #69 next to Leaf, also downtown location).

$$$ Wreckfish Bistro is dynamic and friendly with an open kitchen and a small, woody, and romantic dining area serving modern British cuisine. Despite its name, the menu is not particularly fishy. The food, while unpretentious, is beautiful in its fresh simplicity. The meals will entice you to come back—and back (daily 12:00-14:30 & 18:00-22:00, reservations smart, corner of Slater and Seel streets, tel. 0151/707-1960, www.wreckfish.co).

$$ Cowshed does chargrilled steaks and ice-cold cocktails in a rustic townhouse. You can eat at the bar or at a table in an inviting room in back. The service is refreshingly efficient (Tue-Thu 17:00-22:00, Fri until 22:30, Sat 12:00-22:30, Sun 12:00-22:00, 104 Seel Street, tel. 0151/708-7580).

DOWNTOWN

$ Mowgli Indian Street Food Restaurant, a phenom in town, hustles delicious traditional Indian dishes on little tin plates. Eat family-style, enjoying two or three plates per person. While it's trendy and set in an elegant location across from Town Hall, the prices are great—and the service is fun (daily 12:00-22:00, 3 Water Street, tel. 0151/236-6366). They have a second location the Rope-walks District.

$ Ma Egerton's Stage Door is an enjoyable pub tucked away next to Lime Street Station. In addition to good ales, this place also serves well-priced pizzas and a tasty homemade beef scouse (the traditional stew brought to Liverpool by Norwegians, known as *lapskaus* in Norway). With its proximity to the Empire Theatre's stage door, the pub has been frequented by artists such as Tom Jones, Frank Sinatra, The Rolling Stones, and, of course, The Beatles (daily 11:00-late, 9 Pudsey Street, tel. 0151/345-3525).

Liverpool ONE: This huge modern shopping center, right in the heart of town, is filled with British chain restaurants. The upper Leisure Terrace has a row of some popular chains, all with outdoor seating. If you want to dine on predictable mass-produced food, you'll have a wide selection here.

AT THE ALBERT DOCK

The eateries at the Albert Dock aren't high cuisine, but they're handy to your sightseeing. A slew of trendy restaurants come alive with club energy at night, but are sedate and pleasant in the afternoon and early evening. For lunch near the sights, consider the **$ Tate Gallery** café (daily 10:00-16:30). **$ The Pumphouse Pub,** with the tall brick chimney overlooking Canning Dock at the north edge of Albert Dock, is a touristy place for pub grub with a noisy interior and great harborside tables outside (£8 lunch deals, daily 11:00-21:00). **$$ Gusto** is a chain restaurant with a fancy and spacious interior, serving a wide selection of pasta, pizzas, steaks, and fish. Best seats on a warm day are on the back side overlooking the Albert Dock (Mon-Fri 12:00-23:00, Sat 10:00-23:30, Sun 10:00-23:00, Edward Pavilion).

Liverpool Connections

BY TRAIN

Note that many connections from Liverpool transfer at the Wigan North Western Station, which is on a major north-south train line.

From Liverpool by Train to: Keswick/Lake District (train to Penrith—2/hour with change in Wigan or Lancaster, 2.5 hours; then bus to Keswick), **York** (hourly direct, 2 hours), **Edinburgh** (at least 2/hour, 4 hours, most change in Preston, Wigan, or York), **Glasgow** (1-2/hour, 4 hours, change in Preston and possibly elsewhere), **London's** Euston Station (3/hour, 2.5 hours, more with changes), **Crewe** (3/hour, 45 minutes), **Chester** (4/hour, 45 minutes). Train info: Tel. 0345-748-4950, NationalRail.co.uk.

BY FERRY

By Ferry to Dublin, Republic of Ireland: P&O Irish Sea Ferries runs a car ferry only—no foot passengers (up to 5/day, 8.5-hour trip, prices vary widely—roughly £150 for car and 2 passengers, overnight ferry includes berth and meals—roughly £290, 20-minute drive north of the city center at Liverpool Freeport—Gladstone dock, check in 1-2 hours before departure, tel. 01304/448-888, www.poferries.com). Those without cars can take a ferry to Dublin via the Isle of Man (runs mid-June-Aug, www.steam-packet.com), or ride the train to North Wales and catch the Dublin ferry from Holyhead (www.stenaline.co.uk).

By Ferry to Belfast, Northern Ireland: Ferries sail from nearby Birkenhead roughly twice a day (8.5 hours, fares vary widely, tel. 0344-770-7070, www.stenaline.co.uk). Birkenhead's dock is a 15-minute walk from Hamilton Square Station on Merseyrail's Wirral Line.

THE LAKE DISTRICT

Keswick & the North Lake District • Ullswater Lake •
South Lake District

The Lake District is nature's lush green playground. Here, William Wordsworth's poems still shiver in trees and ripple on ponds. Nature rules this pristine land, and humanity keeps a wide-eyed but low profile. Relax, recharge, take a cruise or a hike, and maybe even write a poem. Renew your poetic license at Wordsworth's famous Dove Cottage.

Located in the northwestern county of Cumbria, the Lake District is about 30 miles long and 30 miles wide. Explore it by foot, bike, bus, or car. Locals are fond of declaring that their mountains are older than the Himalayas and were once as tall, but have been worn down by the ages (Scafell Pike, the tallest peak in England, is only 3,206 feet). There's a walking-stick charm about the way nature and the culture mix here. Hiking along a windblown ridge or climbing over a rock fence to look into the eyes of a ragamuffin sheep, even tenderfeet get a chance to feel very outdoorsy. The tradition of staying close to the land remains true in the 21st century; restaurants serve organic food and you'll see stickers in home windows advocating for environmental causes.

Dress in layers, and expect rain mixed with "bright spells" (pubs offer atmospheric shelter at every turn). Drizzly days can be followed by delightful evenings.

Plan to spend the majority of your time in the unspoiled North Lake District. In this chapter, I focus on the town of Keswick, the lake called Derwentwater, and the vast, time-passed Newlands Valley. The North Lake District works great by car or by bus (with easy train access via Penrith), delights nature lovers, and has good accommodations to boot.

The South Lake District—slightly closer to London—is

known primarily for its sights related to Wordsworth and Beatrix Potter (of Peter Rabbit fame), and gets the promotion, tour crowds, and tackiness that comes with them. While the slate-colored towns (Ambleside, Windermere, Bowness-on-Windermere, and so on) are cute, they're also touristy—which means crowded and over-priced. I strongly recommend that you buck the trend and focus on the north.

Ideally, make your home base in or near Keswick, and side-trip from there into the South Lake District only if you're inter-ested in the Wordsworth and Beatrix Potter sights. Dipping into the South Lake District also works well en route if you're driving between Keswick and points south.

PLANNING YOUR TIME

I'd suggest spending two days and two nights in this area. Penrith is the nearest train station, 45 minutes by bus or car from Keswick. Those without a car will use Keswick as a springboard: Cruise the lake and take a hike in the Catbells area, or hop on a minibus tour. If great scenery is commonplace in your life, the Lake District can be more soothing (and rainy) than exciting. If you're rushed, you could make this area a one-night stand—or even a quick drive-through. But since the towns themselves are unexceptional, a visit here isn't worth it unless you have time to head up into the hills at least once.

Two-Day Driving Plan: Here's the most exciting way for drivers coming from the south to max out their time here and see some South Lake District sights en route to the north:

Day 1: Leave the motorway at Kendal by 10:30; drive along Lake Windermere and through the town of Ambleside.

11:30	Tour Wordsworth Grasmere, the site of Dove Cottage.
13:00	Backtrack to Ambleside, where a small road (Kirkstone) leads up to the dramatic Kirkstone Pass and down (on route A-592) to Glenridding on Lake Ullswater.
15:00	Catch the next Ullswater boat and ride to Howtown. Depending on the available daylight, you can hike six miles (3-4 hours) from Howtown back to Glenridding. Or, with less time, ride the boat as far as Aira Force to hike up to the waterfall (1 hour) or skip the boat and walk to Lanty's Tarn (2 hours) right from the Glenridding parking lot.
19:00	Drive to your Keswick hotel or farmhouse B&B, with a stop as the sun sets at Castlerigg Stone Circle.

Day 2: Spend the morning (3-4 hours) splicing the Catbells high-ridge hike into a boat trip around Derwentwater. In the after-

noon, make the circular drive from Keswick through the Newlands Valley, Buttermere, Honister Pass, and Borrowdale. You could tour the Honister Slate Mine en route (last tour at 15:30) and/or pitch-and-putt nine holes in Keswick before a late dinner.

GETTING AROUND THE LAKE DISTRICT
By Car

Nothing is very far from Keswick and Derwentwater. Pick up a good map (any hotel can loan you one), get off the big roads, and leave the car, at least occasionally, for some walking. In summer, the Keswick-Ambleside-Windermere-Bowness corridor (A-591) suffers from congestion. Back lanes are far less trampled and lead you through forgotten villages, where sheep outnumber people.

To **rent a car** here, try Enterprise in Penrith. They'll transport you between Keswick and their office when you're picking up and dropping off the car (Mon-Fri 8:00-18:00, Sat 9:00-12:00, closed Sun, requires drivers license and second ID, reserve a day in advance, located at the David Hayton Peugeot dealer, Haweswater Road, tel. 01768/893-840). Larger outfits are more likely to have a branch in Carlisle, which is a bit to the north but well served by train (on the same Glasgow-Birmingham line as Penrith) and only a few minutes farther from the Keswick area.

Parking is tight throughout the region. It's easiest to park in the pay-and-display lots (generally about £1/hour; have coins on hand; most machines also take credit cards). If you're parking for free on the roadside, don't block vital turnouts. Never park on double yellow lines.

Without a Car

Those based in Keswick without a car manage fine. Because of the region's efforts to "green up" travel and cut down on car traffic, the bus service can be quite efficient for hiking and sightseeing. (Even with a car, consider leaving it in town and using the bus—that way you don't need to limit yourself to round-trip hikes.)

By Bus: Keswick has no real bus station; buses stop in front of the Booths supermarket where well-designed maps and posted schedules make your bus options very clear. Local buses take you quickly and easily (if not always frequently) to most nearby points of interest. Check the schedule carefully to make sure you can catch

LAKE DISTRICT

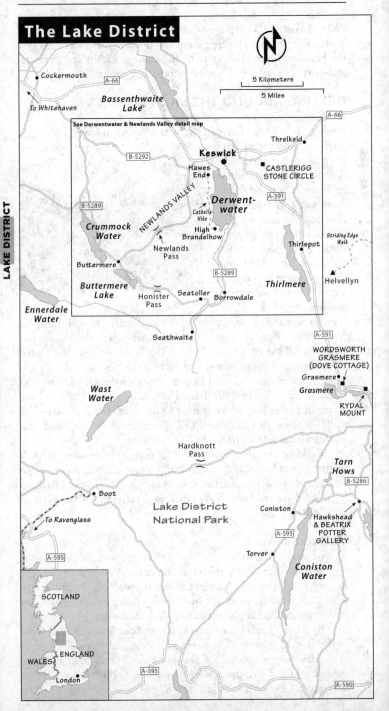

The Lake District

N

5 Kilometers

5 Miles

Cockermouth

A-66

To Whitehaven

Bassenthwaite Lake

A-66

Threlkeld

See Derwentwater & Newlands Valley detail map

B-5292

Keswick

Hawes End

• CASTLERIGG STONE CIRCLE

A-591

B-5289

NEWLANDS VALLEY

Catbells Hike

Derwentwater

Striding Edge Walk

Crummock Water

High Brandelhow

Newlands Pass

Thirlspot

Buttermere

B-5289

Helvellyn

Buttermere Lake

Honister Pass

Seatoller

Borrowdale

Thirlmere

Ennerdale Water

Seathwaite

A-591

WORDSWORTH GRASMERE (DOVE COTTAGE)

Grasmere

Grasmere

Wast Water

RYDAL MOUNT

Hardknott Pass

Tarn Hows

B-5286

Boot

Lake District National Park

Coniston

Hawkshead & BEATRIX POTTER GALLERY

To Ravenglass

A-593

A-595

Torver

Coniston Water

SCOTLAND

ENGLAND

WALES

London

A-595

A-590

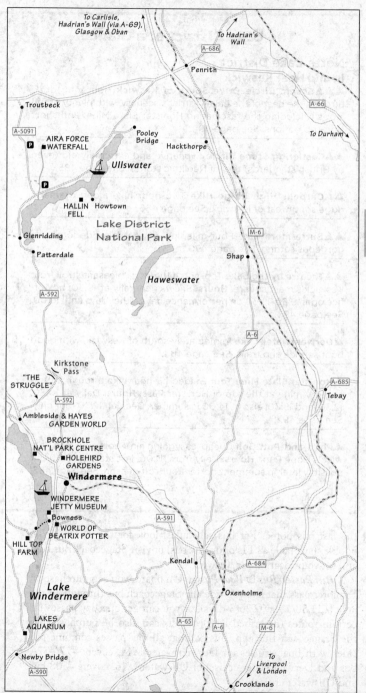

The Lake District at a Glance

North Lake District
In and Near Keswick

▲▲▲**Scenic Circle Drive South of Keswick** Hour-long drive through the best of the Lake District's scenery, with plenty of fun stops (including the fascinating Honister Slate Mine) and short side-trip options. See page 491.

▲▲**Castlerigg Stone Circle** Evocative and extremely old (even by British standards) ring of Neolithic stones. See page 485.

▲▲**Catbells High Ridge Hike** Two-hour hike along dramatic ridge southwest of Keswick. See page 486.

▲▲**Buttermere Hike** Four-mile, low-impact lakeside loop in a gorgeous setting. See page 490.

▲▲**Theatre by the Lake** Top-notch theater a pleasant stroll from Keswick's main square. **Hours:** Shows generally at 19:30; box office open 9:30-19:30 on performance days, other days until 18:00. See page 493.

▲**Derwentwater Lake** Immediately south of Keswick, with good boat service and trails. See page 484.

▲**Honister Slate Mine Tour** Guided 1.5-hour hike through a 19th-century mine at the top of Honister Pass. **Hours:** Daily at 10:30, 12:30, and 15:30; also at 14:00 in summer; Dec-Jan 12:30 tour only. See page 492.

▲**Pitch-and-Putt Golf** Cheap, easygoing nine-hole course in Keswick's Hope Park. **Hours:** Daily from 10:00, last start at 18:00 but possibly later in summer, shorter hours off-season. See page 485.

the last bus home. For bus schedules, look for the *Lakes by Bus* booklet (available at TIs or on any bus) or visit StagecoachBus.com and set your location for Keswick.

Bus Passes/Bus & Boat Passes: On board, you can purchase an Explorer pass that lets you ride any Stagecoach bus throughout the area (£11.50/1 day, £26/3 days), or you can get one-day passes for certain routes (described later); tickets can also be purchased via the Stagecoach Bus app. Bus & Boat all-day passes combine bus rides with boat cruises on Derwentwater (£14, covers #77/#77A bus and Derwentwater cruise) or Ullswater (£16, covers #508 bus and Ullswater cruise).

Ullswater Lake Area

▲▲Ullswater Hike and Boat Ride Long lake best enjoyed via steamer boat and seven-mile walk. **Hours:** Boats generally daily 9:45-16:55, 6-9/day April-Oct, fewer off-season. See page 502.

▲▲Lanty's Tarn and Keldas Hill Moderately challenging 2.5-mile loop hike from Glenridding with sweeping views of Ullswater. See page 502.

▲Aira Force Waterfall Easy uphill hike to picturesque waterfall. See page 503.

South Lake District

▲▲Dove Cottage at Wordsworth Grasmere The poet's humble home, with a museum that tells the story of his remarkable life. **Hours:** Daily 9:30-17:30, Nov-Feb 10:00-16:30 except closed Jan and for events in Dec and Feb (call ahead). See page 505.

▲Rydal Mount and Gardens Wordsworth's later, more upscale home. **Hours:** Daily 9:30-17:30; Nov-Dec and Feb 10:00-16:30 and closed Mon-Tue; closed Jan. See page 507.

▲Hill Top Farm Beatrix Potter's painstakingly preserved cottage. **Hours:** June-Aug daily 10:00-17:30; mid-Feb-May and Sept-Oct until 16:30 and closed Fri; house closed Nov-Dec but gardens and shop open Sat-Sun, closed Jan-mid-Feb; often a long wait to visit—call ahead. See page 508.

▲Beatrix Potter Gallery Collection of artwork by and background on the creator of Peter Rabbit. **Hours:** Daily 10:30-16:00, closed Nov-mid-Feb. See page 510.

Bus routes: Buses **#X4** and **#X5** connect Penrith train station to Keswick (April-Oct hourly, every 2 hours on Sun, 45 minutes).

Bus **#77/#77A,** the Honister Rambler, makes the gorgeous circle from Keswick around Derwentwater, over Honister Pass, through Buttermere, and down the Whinlatter Valley (5-7/day clockwise, 4/day "anticlockwise," daily Easter-Oct, 1.75-hour loop). Bus **#78,** the Borrowdale Rambler, goes topless in the summer, affording a wonderful sightseeing experience in and of itself, heading from Keswick to Lodore Hotel, Grange Bridge, Rosthwaite, and Seatoller at the base of Honister Pass (hourly, daily Easter-Oct, 2/hour July-Sept, 30 minutes each way). Both of these routes are covered by the £8.50 Keswick and Honister Dayrider all-day pass.

Bus **#508,** the Kirkstone Rambler, runs between Penrith and Patterdale Hotel (near the bottom of Ullswater), stopping in Pooley Bridge (5/day, more frequent June-Aug with open-top buses, 50 minutes). Bus #508 also connects Glenridding and Windermere (1 hour).

Bus **#505,** the Coniston Rambler, connects Windermere with Hawkshead (about hourly, daily Easter-Oct, 35 minutes).

Bus **#555** connects Keswick with the south and Windermere (hourly, 2/hour July-Sept, 1 hour to Windermere).

Bus **#599,** the open-top Lakeland Experience, runs along the main Windermere corridor, connecting the big tourist attractions in the south: Grasmere and Dove Cottage, Rydal Mount, Ambleside, Brockhole (National Park Visitors Centre), Windermere, and lake cruises from Bowness Pier (3/hour June-Sept, 2/hour May and Oct, 50 minutes each way, £8.50 Central Lakes Dayrider all-day pass).

By Bike: Keswick works well as a springboard for several fine days out on a bike; consider a three-hour loop trip up Newlands Valley. Ask about routes at the TI or your bike-rental shop. You cannot take bikes on local boats or buses. E-bikes are a boon for those who like biking but would enjoy a little help.

Several shops in Keswick rent road and mountain bikes (£20-25/day) and e-bikes (£30-50/day); rentals come with helmets and advice for good trips. Try **Whinlatter Bikes** (best prices, daily 10:00-17:00, free touring maps, 82 Main Street, tel. 017687/73940, www.whinlatterbikes.com); **E-Venture** (happy to store bags while you rent for no cost, daily 9:00-17:00, Elliot Park—facing the Keswick bus stop, tel. 017687/71363, www.e-venturebikes.co.uk); or **Keswick Bikes** (daily 9:00-17:30, 133 Main Street, tel. 017687/73355, www.keswickbikes.co.uk).

By Boat: A circular boat service glides you around Derwentwater, with several hiker-aiding stops along the way (for a cruise/hike option, see "Derwentwater Lakeside Walk" on page 484).

By Foot: Hiking information is available everywhere. Don't hike without a good, detailed map (wide selection at Keswick TI and at the many outdoor gear stores, or borrow one from your B&B). Helpful fliers at TIs and B&Bs describe the most popular routes. For an up-to-date weather report, check LakeDistrictWeatherLine.co.uk or call the local weather line: 0844-846-2444. Wear suitable clothing and footwear (you can rent boots in town), and plan for rain. Watch your footing—every year, several people die in hiking accidents in the area.

By Tour: For organized bus tours that run the roads of the Lake District, see "Tours in Keswick," later.

Keswick and the North Lake District

As far as touristy Lake District towns go, Keswick (KEZ-ick, population 5,000) is far more enjoyable than Windermere, Bowness, or Ambleside. Many of the place names around Keswick have Norse origins, inherited from the region's 10th-century settlers. Notice that most lakes in the region end in either *water* (e.g., Derwentwater) or *mere* (e.g., Windermere), which is related to the Dutch word for lake, *meer*.

An important mining center for slate, copper, and lead through the Middle Ages, Keswick became a resort in the 19th century. Its fine Victorian buildings recall the days when city slickers first learned about "communing with nature," inspired by the Romantic poets (Wordsworth, Coleridge) who wandered the trails here. Today, the compact town is lined with tearooms, pubs, gift shops, and hiking-gear shops. The shore of the lake called Derwentwater is a pleasant 10-minute walk from the town center.

Orientation to Keswick

Keswick is an ideal home base, with plenty of good B&Bs, an easy bus connection to the nearest train station at Penrith, and a prime location near the best lake in the area, Derwentwater. In Keswick, everything is within a 10-minute walk of everything else: the pedestrian town square, the TI, recommended B&Bs, grocery stores, the wonderful municipal pitch-and-putt golf course, the main bus stop, a lakeside boat dock, and a central parking lot. Thursdays and Saturdays are market days in the town square, but the square is lively every day throughout the summer.

TOURIST INFORMATION

The National Park Visitors Centre/TI is in Moot Hall, right in the middle of the town square (daily 9:30-17:30, Nov-Easter until 16:30, tel. 0845-901-0845, www.keswick.org; you'll also find helpful planning info at www.lakedistrict.gov.uk, tel. 01539/724-

LAKE DISTRICT

555). Staffers are pros at advising you about hiking routes. They can also help you figure out public transportation to outlying sights and tell you about the region's various adventure activities.

The TI sells theater tickets, Keswick Launch tickets (at a £1 discount), fishing licenses, and brochures and maps that outline nearby hikes (including a series of *Lap Maps* featuring sights, walks, and driving/cycling tours). The TI and shops all over town also have books and maps for hikers, cyclists, and drivers.

The boards inside the TI's foyer are filled with posted information (about walks, talks, movies, theater, weather forecasts, and bus schedules). For information about the TI's guided walks, see "Tours in Keswick," later.

HELPFUL HINTS

Book in Advance: It's smart to book ahead if you'll be visiting during the summer or over a festival or bank-holiday weekend (see "Holidays and Festivals" in the appendix). If you have trouble finding a room (or a B&B that accepts small children), try www.keswick.org to search for available rooms.

Laundry: The town's launderette is on Bank Street, just up the side street from the post office (full- and self-service; Mon-Fri 8:00-19:00, Sat-Sun 9:00-18:00, tel. 017687/75448).

Weather Info: Hikers should always check the daily forecast by calling weather tel. 0844-846-2444 or visiting LakeDistrictWeatherLine.co.uk.

Midges: Tiny biting insects called midges might bug you in this region from late May through September, particularly at dawn and dusk. The severity depends on the weather since wind and sunshine can deter them, and insect repellant fends them off: Ask the locals what works if you'll be hiking.

Local Candy: Be sure to try Kendal mint cakes, which are basically flat, mint-flavored sugar cubes. You'll find them in area supermarkets and gift stores.

Groceries and More: Booths, a huge, modern supermarket (facing the Keswick bus stop), has a fine cafeteria (with inside and outside seating), handy food to-go, a great book and map section, and a public WC (daily 7:00-22:00, shorter Sun hours, Tithebarn Street, tel. 017684/73518).

Tours in Keswick

Walking Tours

The **Keswick TI** offers guided walks several times weekly, some free and others £5-10, led by "Voluntary Rangers" in summer (depart from Keswick TI; check the Events and Guided Walks page at www.lakedistrict.gov.uk for schedule, descriptions, and advance booking; optional contribution welcome at the end of a free walk).

Private Guides

Show Me Cumbria Private Tours, run by Andy, offers personalized tours all around the Lake District. He's based in Penrith but can pick up in Keswick and other locations (£140/half-day for 3-6 people, tel. 017688/64825, mobile 07809-026-357, www.showmecumbria.co.uk, andy@showmecumbria.co.uk).

Discover Lakeland, led by friendly and experienced Blue Badge guide Anna Grey, gives tours all over Cumbria and beyond. She specializes in the Lake District but also gives tours at Hadrian's Wall (£160/half-day, £260/full day, mobile 07557-915-855, www.discoverlakeland.uk, anna@discoverlakeland.co.uk).

Keswick Rambles Guided Walks, led by Pete and Lynn Armstrong, offers private guided hikes of varying difficulty, including the popular Catbells trail. They'll meet you at your B&B and ride with you on public transport (not included) to the trailhead (cost depends on hike but typically £90/day or £20-25/person if more than 4, Easter-Oct, wear suitable clothing and footwear, bring lunch and water, must book in advance, tel. 017687/71302, mobile 07342-637-813, keswickrambles.blogspot.co.uk, armstrongps1@gmx.com).

Bus Tours

For those who want to see the area without lots of hiking or messing with public transport, a bus tour can be the answer. **Mountain Goat Tours** is the region's dominant tour company and runs half- and full-day minibus excursions nearly every morning and afternoon from Keswick to all the scenic highlights. Customizable private tours are also available. For details, see their website (£22-40/half-day, £48/full day, tours run April-Oct, maximum of 16 persons, book in advance, tel. 015394/45161, www.mountain-goat.com, tours@mountain-goat.com).

LAKE DISTRICT

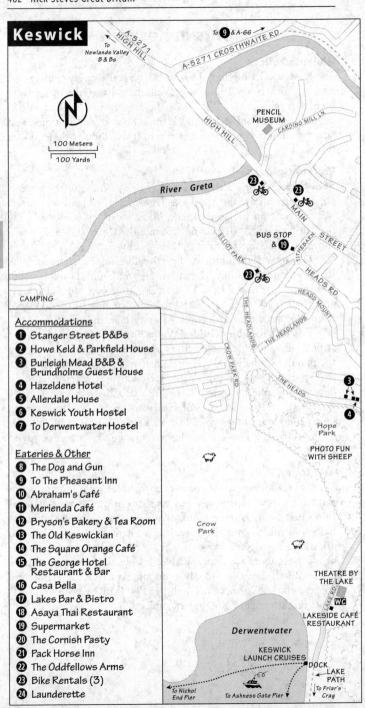

Keswick

100 Meters
100 Yards

<u>Accommodations</u>
1. Stanger Street B&Bs
2. Howe Keld & Parkfield House
3. Burleigh Mead B&B & Brundholme Guest House
4. Hazeldene Hotel
5. Allerdale House
6. Keswick Youth Hostel
7. To Derwentwater Hostel

<u>Eateries & Other</u>
8. The Dog and Gun
9. To The Pheasant Inn
10. Abraham's Café
11. Merienda Café
12. Bryson's Bakery & Tea Room
13. The Old Keswickian
14. The Square Orange Café
15. The George Hotel Restaurant & Bar
16. Casa Bella
17. Lakes Bar & Bistro
18. Asaya Thai Restaurant
19. Supermarket
20. The Cornish Pasty
21. Pack Horse Inn
22. The Oddfellows Arms
23. Bike Rentals (3)
24. Launderette

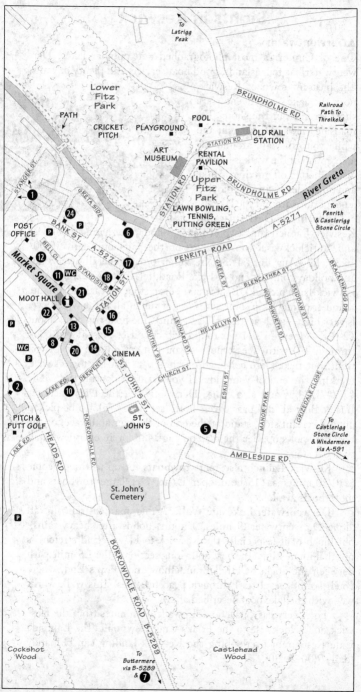

LAKE DISTRICT

Sights in Keswick

▲Derwentwater

One of Cumbria's most photographed and popular lakes, Derwentwater has four islands, good boat service, and plenty of trails. The pleasant town of Keswick, near the lake's north end, is a short stroll from the shore. The roadside views aren't much, and while you can walk around the lake, much of the walk is boring. You're better off mixing a hike and boat ride, or simply enjoying a boat cruise around the lake.

Boating on Derwentwater: Keswick Launch runs two **cruises** an hour, alternating clockwise and "anticlockwise" (boats depart on the half-hour, daily 10:00-16:30, July-Aug until 17:30, in winter 6/day generally weekends and holidays only, at end of Lake Road, tel. 017687/72263, www.keswick-launch.co.uk). Boats make seven stops on each 50-minute round-trip (may skip some stops or not run at all if the water level is very high—such as after a heavy rain). The boat trip costs about £2 per segment or £11 per round-trip circuit (£1 less if you book through TI) with free stopovers; you can get on and off all you want, but tickets are collected on the boat's last leg to Keswick, marking the end of your ride. If you want to hop on the scenic #77/#77A bus and also cruise Derwentwater, the Derwentwater Bus & Boat all-day pass covers both (see page 476). To be picked up at a certain stop, stand at the end of the pier and wave, or the boat may not stop. See the map on page 488 for an overview of all the boat stops.

Keswick Launch also rents **rowboats** for up to three people (£10/30 minutes, £15/hour, open Easter-Oct, larger rowboats and motorboats available).

Derwentwater Lakeside Walk: A fine, marked trail runs all along Derwentwater (9 miles, 4 hours, floods after heavy rains), but much of it (especially the Keswick-to-Hawes End stretch) is not that interesting. The best hour-long section is the 1.5-mile path between the docks at High Brandelhow and Hawes End, where you'll stroll a level trail through peaceful trees. This walk works well with the lake boat described above.

For a very easy, paved stroll, walk 10 minutes from the Keswick dock clockwise to the Friar's Crag viewpoint. The Lakeside Café Restaurant overlooking the Keswick landing can be handy (daily 9:00-20:30).

Derwent Pencil Museum

Graphite was first discovered centuries ago in Keswick. A hunk of the stuff proved great for marking sheep in the 15th century. In 1832, the first crude Keswick pencil factory opened, and the rest is history (which is what you'll learn about here). While the factory that made the famous Derwent pencils is closed, a small modern building tells the story in a kid-friendly exhibit filling one small room.

Cost and Hours: £5, daily 9:30-17:00, last entry one hour before closing, humble café, 3-minute walk from town center, sign-posted off Main Street, tel. 017687/73626, www.pencilmuseum. co.uk.

Fitz Park

An inviting grassy park stretches alongside Keswick's tree-lined, duck-filled River Greta. There's a playground and plenty of room for kids to burn off energy. Consider an after-dinner stroll on the footpath. You may catch men in white (or frisky schoolboys in uniform) playing a game of cricket. There's the serious bowling green (where you're welcome to watch the experts play and enjoy the cheapest cuppa—i.e., tea—in town), and the public one where tourists are welcome to give lawn bowling a go. You can try tennis on a grass court or enjoy the putting green. Find the rental pavilion across the road from the art museum (open daily Easter-Sept 10:00-17:30, longer hours July-Aug, Station Road, mobile 07976-573-785).

Golf and Hope Park

A nine-hole ▲ pitch-and-putt golf course near the lush gardens in Hope Park separates the town from the lake and offers a classy, cheap, and convenient chance to golf near the birthplace of the sport. This is a fun and inexpensive experience—just right after a day of touring (£5 for pitch-and-putt, £3.50 for putting, £4.50 for 18 tame holes of "obstacle golf," £3 for *boules,* daily from 10:00, last round starts around 18:00, possibly later in summer, shorter hours off-season, café, tel. 017687/73445, www. hopeleisure.com).

Even if you're not a golfer, Hope Park is a fine place to walk among grazing sheep, with great photo ops.

NEAR KESWICK

▲▲Castlerigg Stone Circle

For some reason, 70 percent of England's stone circles are here in Cumbria. Castlerigg is one of the best and oldest in Britain, and an easy stop for drivers. The circle—90 feet across and 5,000 years old—has 38 stones mysteriously laid out on a line between the two tallest peaks on the horizon. They may have served as a celestial calendar for ritual celebrations. Imagine the ambience here, as ancient people filled this clearing in spring to celebrate fertility, in late summer to commemorate the harvest, and in the winter to celebrate the winter solstice and the coming renewal of light. Festival dates may have been dictated by how the sun

rose and set in relation to the stones. The more that modern academics study this circle, the more meaning they find in the placement of the stones. The two front stones face due north, toward a cut in the mountains. The rare-for-stone-circles "sanctuary" lines up with its center stone to mark certain celestial events. (Party!) For maximum "goose pimples" (as they say here), show up at sunset.

Cost and Hours: Free, always open, located 1.5 miles east of Keswick on Eleventrees Road—see map on page 488; about 30 minutes from town on foot; by car, follow brown signs—it's 3 minutes off the A-66, limited but easy parking, www.english-heritage.org.uk.

Hikes and Drives in the North Lake District

FROM KESWICK

For an easy, flat stroll, consider the trail that runs alongside Derwentwater (see "Sights in Keswick," earlier). More strenuous options are described next (for more detailed hike info, stop in at the Keswick TI).

▲▲Catbells High Ridge Hike

For a great "king of the mountain" feeling, 360-degree views, and a close-up look at the weather blowing over the ridge, take a two-

hour hike above Derwentwater from Hawes End up along the ridge to Catbells (1,480 feet) and down to High Brandelhow. Because the mountaintop is basically treeless, you're treated to dramatic panoramas the entire way up. From High Brandelhow, you can catch the boat back to Keswick or take the easy path

along the Derwentwater shore to your Hawes End starting point. (Extending the hike farther around the lake to Lodore takes you to a waterfall, rock climbers, a fine café, and another boat dock for a convenient return to Keswick—for more about Lodore, see page 492). Note: When the water level is very high (for example, after a heavy rain), boats can't stop at Hawes End—ask at the TI or boat dock before setting out.

Catbells is probably the most dramatic family walk in the area (but wear sturdy shoes, bring a raincoat, and watch your footing). From Keswick, the lake, or your farmhouse B&B, you can see silhouetted figures—what locals call "crag rats"—hiking along this ridge.

Getting There: To reach the trailhead from Keswick, catch the "anticlockwise" boat (see "Boating on Derwentwater," earlier) and ride for 10 minutes to the second stop, Hawes End. (You can also ride to High Brandelhow and take this walk in the other direction, but I don't recommend it—two rocky scrambles along the way are easier and safer to navigate going uphill from Hawes End.) Note the schedule for your return boat ride. If driving, there's free but limited parking at Hawes End, and the road can be hard to find—get clear directions in town before heading out. (Hardcore hikers can walk to the foot of Catbells from Keswick via Portinscale, which takes about 40 minutes—ask your B&B or the TI for directions.)

The Route: The path is not signposted, but it's easy to follow, and you'll see plenty of other walkers. From Hawes End, walk away from the lake through a kissing gate to the turn just before the car park. Then turn left and go up, up, up. After about 20 minutes, you'll hit the first of two short scrambles (where the trail vanishes into a cluster of steep rocks), which leads

to a bluff. From the first little summit (great for a picnic break), and then along the ridge, you'll enjoy sweeping views of the lake on one side and of Newlands Valley on the other. The bald peak in the distance is Catbells. Broken stones crunch under each step, wind buffets your ears, clouds prowl overhead, and the sheep baa comically. To anyone looking up from the distant farmhouse B&Bs, you are but a stick figure on the ridge. Just below the summit, the trail disintegrates into another short, steep scramble. Your reward is just beyond: a magnificent hilltop perch.

After the Catbells summit, descend along the ridge to a saddle ahead. The ridge continues much higher, and while it may look like your only option, at its base a small, unmarked lane with comfortable steps leads left. Unless you're up for extending the hike

LAKE DISTRICT

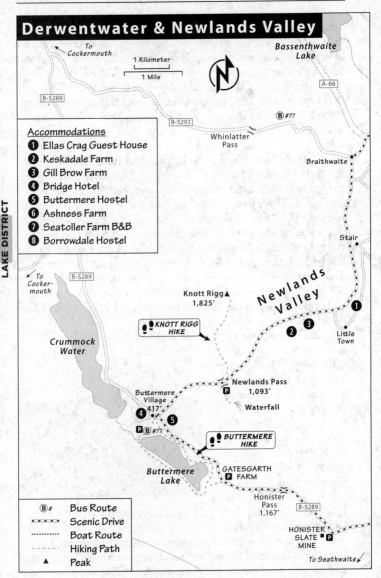

Derwentwater & Newlands Valley

Accommodations
1. Ellas Crag Guest House
2. Keskadale Farm
3. Gill Brow Farm
4. Bridge Hotel
5. Buttermere Hostel
6. Ashness Farm
7. Seatoller Farm B&B
8. Borrowdale Hostel

To Cockermouth

1 Kilometer
1 Mile

Bassenthwaite Lake

A-66

B-5289

B-5292

Whinlatter Pass

Ⓑ #77

Braithwaite

Stair

To Cockermouth

B-5289

Newlands Valley

Knott Rigg ▲ 1,825'

KNOTT RIGG HIKE

Little Town

Crummock Water

Newlands Pass 1,093'

Waterfall

Buttermere Village 417'

BUTTERMERE HIKE

Buttermere Lake

GATESGARTH FARM

Honister Pass 1,167'

B-5289

HONISTER SLATE MINE

To Seathwaite

Ⓑ # Bus Route
••••• Scenic Drive
••••• Boat Route
– – – Hiking Path
▲ Peak

(see "Longer Catbells Options," next), take this path down to the lake. To get to High Brandelhow Pier, take the first left fork you come across down through a forest to the lake. When you reach Abbot's Bay, go left through a swinging gate, following a lakeside trail around a gravelly bluff to the idyllic High Brandelhow Pier, a peaceful place to wait for your boat back to Keswick. (You can pay your fare when you board.)

Note, after coming down from Catbells here, rather than re-

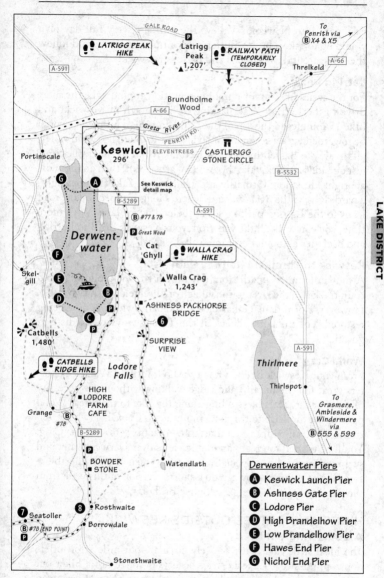

LAKE DISTRICT

turn to the lake you can carry on to the charming little village of Grange, from where bus #78 travels back to Keswick (2/hour, the stop is over the Grange bridge on the main road).

Longer Catbells Options: Catbells is just the first of a series of peaks, all connected by a fine ridge trail. Hardier hikers can continue for nine miles along this same ridge, enjoying valley and lake views as they arc around the Newlands Valley toward (and even down to) Buttermere. After High Spy, you can descend an easy path into Newlands Valley. The ultimate, very full day-plan would be to take a bus to Buttermere, climb Robinson, and follow the ridge around to Catbells and back to Keswick.

Latrigg Peak

For the easiest mountain-climbing sensation around, take the short drive to the Latrigg Peak parking lot just north of Keswick, and hike 15 minutes to the top of the 1,200-foot-high hill, where you'll be rewarded with a commanding view of the town, lake, and valley, all the way to Bassenthwaite, the next lake over. At the traffic circle just outside Keswick, take the A-591 Carlisle exit, then an immediate right (direction: Ormathwaite/Underscar). Take the next right, a hard right, at the *Skiddaw* sign, where a long, steep, one-lane road leads to the Latrigg parking lot at the end of the lane. With more time, you can walk all the way from your Keswick B&B to Latrigg and back (it's a popular evening walk for locals).

Keswick to Threlkeld Railway Path

A four-mile railway path from downtown Keswick follows an old train track and the river to the village of Threlkeld (with two pubs). However, storm damage has closed the path, which is now being restored. For the latest, check at the TI or see www.lakedistrict. gov.uk.

Walla Crag

From your Keswick B&B, a fine two-hour walk to Walla Crag offers great fell (mountain) and ridge walking without the necessity of a bus or car. Start by strolling along the lake to the Great Wood parking lot (or drive to this lot), and head up Cat Ghyl (where "fell runners"—trail-running enthusiasts—practice) to Walla Crag. You'll be treated to great panoramic views over Derwentwater and surrounding peaks—especially beautiful when the heather blossoms in the summer. You can do a shorter version of this walk from the parking lot at Ashness Packhorse Bridge.

HIKES AND DRIVES OUTSIDE KESWICK
▲▲Buttermere Hike

The ideal little lake with a lovely circular four-mile stroll offers nonstop, no-sweat Lake District beauty. If you're not a hiker but wish you were, take this walk. If you're short on time, at least stop here and get your shoes dirty.

Buttermere is connected with Borrowdale and Derwentwater by a dramatic road that runs over rugged Honister Pass. Buses #77/#77A make a 1.75-hour round-trip loop between Keswick and Buttermere that includes a trip over this pass. The two-pub hamlet of Buttermere has two pay-and-display parking lots and free parking along the roadside by the church. There's also a pay parking lot at the Honister Pass end of the lake (at Gatesgarth Farm). The Syke Farm Tea Room in Buttermere is popular for its enticing farm-made ice cream (daily 11:30-17:00, light lunches, box lunches for hikers). See "Eating in the Newlands Valley," later, for more Buttermere eateries.

While you can circumnavigate the entire lake, the side opposite the road is nicest. You can walk from one end to the other—Buttermere to Gatesgarth Farm—in about an hour (using a pay-and-display lot at either end and/or bus #77). In Buttermere the trail starts at The Fish Hotel.

▲▲▲Scenic Circle Drive South of Keswick

This hour-long drive, which includes Newlands Valley, Buttermere, Honister Pass, and Borrowdale, offers the North Lake District's best scenery. (To do a similar route without a car from Keswick, take loop bus #77/#77A and use it as a do-it-yourself, hop-on, hop-off tour.) Distances are short, roads are narrow and have turnouts, and views are rewarding. Get a good map and ask your B&B host for advice.

Keswick to Newlands Pass: From Keswick, leave town on Crosthwaite Road, then, at the roundabout, head west on Cockermouth Road (A-66, following *Cockermouth* and *Workington* signs). Don't take the first Newlands Valley exit (to Grange), but do take the second one (through Braithwaite), and follow signs up the majestic Newlands Valley (also signed for *Buttermere*).

If the **Newlands Valley** had a lake, it would be packed with tourists. But it doesn't—and it isn't. The valley is dotted with 500-year-old family-owned farms. Shearing day is reason to rush home from school. Sons get school out of the way ASAP and follow their dads into the family business. Neighbor girls marry those sons and move in. Grandparents retire to the cottage next door. With the price of wool depressed, most of the wives supplement the family income by running B&Bs (virtually every farm in the valley rents rooms). The road (six miles to the pass) has one lane, with turnouts for passing. From the Newlands Pass summit, notice the glacial-shaped wilds, once forested, now not.

At **Newlands Pass** (unmarked, but you'll see a waterfall on the left and a parking pullout), an easy 300-yard hike leads to a little waterfall. On the other side of the road, a one-mile hike climbs up to **Knott Rigg,** which offers lots of TPCB (thrills per calorie burned). If you don't have time for even a short hike, at least get out of the car, hike a couple of minutes to your own private bluff, and get a feel for the setting.

Newlands Pass to Honister Pass and Slate Mine: From the pass, descend to **Buttermere** (scenic lake, tiny hamlet with pubs and an ice-cream store—see "Buttermere Hike," earlier), turn left, drive the length of the lake, and climb over rugged **Honister Pass**—strewn with glacial debris, remnants from the old slate mines, and curious shaggy sheep (the local breed, with their curly horns, looks more like goats). The U-shaped valleys you'll see are textbook examples of those carved out by glaciers. Look high on the hillsides for small "hanging valleys"—they were cut off by the huge flow of the much larger glacier that swept down the main valley floor.

The **Honister Slate Mine,** England's last still-functioning slate mine (and worth ▲), stands at the summit of Honister Pass. The youth hostel next to it was built to house miners in the 1920s.

The mine offers worthwhile tours (perfect for when it's pouring outside): You'll put on a hard hat, load onto a bus for a short climb, then hike into a shaft to learn about the region's slate industry. It's a long, stooped hike into the mountain, made interesting by the guide and punctuated by the sound of your helmet scraping against low bits of the shaft. Standing deep in the mountain, surrounded by slate scrap and the beams of 30 headlamps fluttering around like fireflies, you'll learn of the hardships of miners' lives and how "green gold" is trendy once again, making the mine viable. Even if you don't have time to take the tour, stop here for the slate-filled shop (£17.50, 1.5-hour tour; departs daily at 10:30, 12:30, and 15:30; additional tour at 14:00 in summer; Dec-Jan 12:30 tour only; reserve online or call ahead to confirm times and to book a spot, helmets and lamps provided, wear good walking shoes and bring warm clothing even in summer, café and nice WCs, tel. 017687/77230, www.honister.com, Roland).

From Honister Slate Mine to Lodore: From the mine, you'll drop into the sweet and homey **Borrowdale Valley,** with a few lonely hamlets. Circling past Borrowdale, you'll turn north onto the B-5289 (a.k.a. the Borrowdale Valley Road), which takes you past the following popular attractions:

The house-size **Bowder Stone,** thought to have cleaved from the top of a nearby cliff, sits about 15 minutes off the main road (signposted); a ladder lets you climb to the top. For a great lunch or snack, including tea and homemade quiche and cakes, drop in to the much-loved **$ High Lodore Farm Café** (daily 9:00-18:00, closed Nov-Easter, short drive uphill from the main road and over a tiny bridge, tel. 017687/77221).

Nearby is the village of **Grange,** which must be the cutest hamlet in the area. It's built of locally quarried Lakeland Green slate, and mostly by one builder, which adds to the tidy feel. Grange has a couple of inviting cafés and two tiny churches—one vibrant and welcoming; the other home to the free "Borrowdale Story" history exhibit.

Farther along, **Lodore Falls** is a short walk from the road, behind the Lodore Hotel (a nice place to stop for tea and beautiful views). **Shepherds Crag,** a cliff overlooking Lodore, was made famous by pioneering rock climbers as far back as the 1890s. (Their descendants hang from little ridges on its face today.)

From Lodore, with a Detour, to Keswick: A very hard right off the B-5289 at the Ashness Gate Pier (signposted *Ashness Bridge, Watendlath*) and a steep half-mile climb on a narrow lane takes you to the postcard-pretty **Ashness Packhorse Bridge,** a quintessential Lake District scene (parking lot just above on right). A half-mile farther up, park the car and hop out (parking

lot on left, no sign). You'll be startled by the "surprise view" of Derwentwater—great for a lakes photo op. Continuing from here, the road gets extremely narrow en route to the hamlet of **Watendlath,** which has a tiny lake and lazy farm animals.

Return to the B-5289 and head back to Keswick. If you have yet to see it, cap your drive with a short detour from Keswick to the Castlerigg Stone Circle (described earlier).

Nightlife in Keswick

For a small and remote town, Keswick has lots going on in the evening. Remember, at this latitude it's light until 22:00 in midsummer.

▲▲Theatre by the Lake

Keswickians brag that they enjoy "London theater quality at Keswick prices." Their theater offers events year-round on two stages and a wonderful rotation of six plays from late May through October (plays vary throughout the week, with music concerts on Sun in summer). Attending a play here is a fine opportunity to enjoy a classy night out.

Cost and Hours: £10-36, discounts for those under 26; shows generally at 19:30; café, restaurant (pre-theater dinners start at 17:30 and must be booked 24 hours ahead by calling 017687/81102), located off Lake Road with parking in adjacent lot. It's smart to buy tickets in advance—book at box office (daily 9:30-19:30 on performance days, other days until 18:00), by phone (tel. 017687/74411), at TI, or at www.theatrebythelake.com.

Pub Events

To socialize with locals, head to a pub for one of their special evenings. **Quiz nights** are popular at many local pubs, and tourists are more than welcome. Drop in, say you want to join a team, and you're in. If you like trivia, it's a great way to get to know people here (the Pack Horse Inn, on Packhorse Court, hosts quiz nights most Wed at 21:30).

The Oddfellows Arms has free **live music** (often classic rock) in summer (April-Oct Thu-Sun from 21:30, 19 Main Street). The Square Orange occasionally has live music on Wednesday evenings (20 St. John's Street) and the Pack Horse Inn on weekends.

Sleeping in Keswick

The Lake District abounds with attractive B&Bs, guesthouses, and hostels. It needs them all when the summer hordes threaten the serenity of this Romantic-era mecca.

Reserve your room in advance in high season. From November through March, you should have no trouble finding a room, but to get a particular place (especially on Saturdays), book ahead. If you're using public transportation, sleep in Keswick. Most of my recommended B&Bs and small hotels are within three blocks of the bus station and town square. If you're driving, staying outside Keswick is your best chance for a remote farmhouse experience.

Many Keswick listings charge extra for a one-night stay and most won't book one-night stays on weekends. Most don't welcome young children. None have elevators and all have lots of stairs—ask about a ground-floor unit if steps are a problem. Owners are enthusiastic about offering advice to get you on the right walking trail. Most accommodations have inviting lounges with libraries of books on the region and loaner maps.

This is still the countryside—expect huge breakfasts (often with a wide selection, including vegetarian options) and shower systems that might need to be switched on to get hot water. Parking is generally easy.

ON STANGER STREET

This street, quiet but just a block from Keswick's town center, is lined with B&Bs situated in Victorian slate townhouses. Each of these places is small and family run. They all offer comfortably sized rooms, free parking, and a friendly welcome.

$$ Ellergill Guest House has four spic-and-span rooms with an airy, contemporary feel—several with views (2 percent surcharge for credit cards, 2-night minimum, no children under age 10, 22 Stanger Street, tel. 017687/73347, www.ellergill.co.uk, stay@ellergill.co.uk, Clare and Robin Pinkney).

$$ Badgers Wood B&B, at the top of the street, has six modern, bright, unfrilly view rooms, each named after a different tree (3 percent surcharge for credit cards, 2-night minimum, no children under age 12, special diets accommodated, 30 Stanger Street, tel. 017687/72621, www.badgers-wood.co.uk, enquiries@badgers-wood.co.uk, chatty Scotsman Andrew and his charming wife, Anne).

$$ Abacourt House, with a daisy-fresh breakfast room, has five pleasant doubles (2-night minimum on weekends, no children, sack lunches available, 26 Stanger Street, tel. 017687/72967, www.abacourt.co.uk, abacourt.keswick@btinternet.com, John and Heather).

$ Dunsford Guest House rents four updated rooms at bargain prices. Stained glass and wooden pews give the bright breakfast room a country-chapel vibe (RS%, cash only, 16 Stanger Street, tel. 017687/75059, www.dunsfordguesthouse.co.uk, info@dunsfordguesthouse.co.uk, Deb and Keith).

ON THE HEADS

The classy area known as The Heads has B&Bs with bigger and grander Victorian architecture and great views overlooking the pitch-and-putt range and out into the hilly distance. The golf-course side of The Heads has free parking, if you can snare a spot (easy

at night). A single yellow line on the curb means you're allowed to park for free, but only overnight (16:00-10:00).

$$$ Howe Keld has the polished feel of a boutique hotel, but offers all the friendliness of a B&B. Its 12 contemporary-posh rooms are spacious and tastefully decked out in native woods and slate. It's warm, welcoming, and family-run, with an à la carte breakfast cooked to order by chef Jerome (cash and 2-night mini-

LAKE DISTRICT

mum preferred, sack lunches available, tel. 017687/72417, www.
howekeld.co.uk, laura@howekeld.co.uk, run with care by Laura
and Jerome Bujard).

$$ Parkfield House, thoughtfully run and decorated by John
and Susan Berry, is a big Victorian house with a homey lounge.
Its six rooms, some with fine views, are bright and classy (RS%,
2-night minimum, no children under age 16, free parking, tel.
017687/72328, www.parkfieldkeswick.co.uk, parkfieldkeswick@
hotmail.co.uk).

$$ Burleigh Mead B&B is a slate mansion from 1892. Gill
(pronounced "Jill," short for Gillian) rents seven lovely rooms and
offers a friendly welcome, as well as a lounge and peaceful front-
yard sitting area that's perfect for enjoying the view (cash only, discount for longer stays, no children under age 8, tel. 017687/75935,
www.burleighmead.co.uk, info@burleighmead.co.uk).

$$ Hazeldene Hotel, on the corner of The Heads, rents 10
spacious rooms, many with commanding views. There's even a "boot
room" that doubles as a guest rec room with a ping-pong table. It's
run with care by delightful Helen and Howard (ground-floor unit
available, free parking, tel. 017687/72106, www.hazeldene-hotel.
co.uk, info@hazeldene-hotel.co.uk).

$$ Brundholme Guest House has four bright and comfy
rooms, most with sweeping views at no extra charge—especially
from the front side—and a friendly and welcoming atmosphere
(minifridge, free parking, tel. 017687/73305, mobile 07739-435-
401, www.brundholme.co.uk, bazaly@hotmail.co.uk, Barry and
Allison Thompson).

ON ESKIN STREET

Just southeast of the town center, the area around Eskin Street is
still within easy walking distance and has stress-free parking.

$$ Allerdale House, a classy, nicely decorated stone mansion
with five rooms, is well run by Mat and Leigh Richards (RS%, 1.5
percent surcharge for credit cards, free parking, 1 Eskin Street, tel.
017687/73891, www.allerdale-house.co.uk, reception@allerdale-
house.co.uk).

HOSTELS IN AND NEAR KESWICK

The Lake District's inexpensive hostels, mostly located in great old
buildings, are handy sources of information and social fun.

¢ Keswick Youth Hostel, with a big lounge and a great river-
side balcony, fills a converted mill. Travelers of all ages feel at home
here, but book ahead—family rooms book up July through Sep-
tember (breakfast extra, café, bar, office open 7:00-23:00, center of
town just off Station Road before river, tel. 017687/72484, www.
yha.org.uk, keswick@yha.org.uk).

¢ **Derwentwater Hostel,** in a 220-year-old mansion on the shore of Derwentwater, is two miles south of Keswick (breakfast extra, family rooms; follow the B-5289 from Keswick—entrance is 2 miles along the Borrowdale Valley Road about 150 yards after Ashness exit—look for cottage and bus stop at bottom of the drive; tel. 017687/77246, www.derwentwater.org, contact@ derwentwater.org).

IN THE NEWLANDS VALLEY

If you have a car, drive 10 minutes west and south of Keswick into the majestic Newlands Valley (described earlier, under "Scenic Circle Drive South of Keswick") to find accommodations with easy parking, grand views, and perfect tranquility. Rooms here tend to be plainer and more dated than those in town and come with steep and gravelly roads, plenty of dogs, and an earthy charm. Don't expect mobile-phone service—even your B&B's satellite Wi-Fi can be spotty. Traditionally, farmhouses lacked central heating, and while they are now heated, you can still request a hot-water bottle to warm up your bed.

Getting to the Newlands Valley: Leave Keswick via the roundabout at the end of Crosthwaite Road, and then head west on Cockermouth Road (A-66). Take the Newlands Valley exit through Braithwaite (B-5292), and follow signs toward Buttermere and Newlands. All my recommended B&Bs are on this road, a 10- to 15-minute drive from Keswick. The one-lane road is tight but has turnouts for passing.

$$ Ellas Crag Guest House, with three rooms—each with a great view—is a comfortable stone house with a contemporary feel and tranquil terrace overlooking the valley. This homey B&B offers a good mix of modern and traditional decor, including beautifully tiled bathrooms (RS%, singles available Mon-Thu only, 2-night minimum, local free-range meats and eggs for breakfast, sack lunches available, huge DVD library, laundry, tel. 017687/78217, www.ellascrag.co.uk, info@ellascrag.co.uk, run by friendly Jane and Ed Ma).

$ Keskadale Farm is another good farmhouse experience, with Ponderosa hospitality. One of the valley's oldest, the house—with two guest rooms and a cozy lounge—is made from 500-year-old ship beams. This working farm is an authentic slice of Lake District life and is your chance to get to know lots of curly-horned sheep and the dogs that herd them. While her husband and sons work in the fields, Margaret Harryman runs the B&B (cash only, sack lunches available, closed Nov-May, tel. 017687/78544, www. keskadalefarm.co.uk, info@keskadalefarm.co.uk). They also rent a one-bedroom apartment that sleeps two (£450/week).

$ Gill Brow Farm is a rough-hewn working farmhouse more

than 300 years old where Anne Wilson rents two simple but fine rooms, one with an en-suite bathroom, the other with a private bathroom down the hall (self-catering cottage that sleeps up to 6 also available, tel. 017687/78270, www.gillbrow-keswick.co.uk, info@gillbrow-keswick.co.uk).

IN BUTTERMERE

$$$$ Bridge Hotel, just beyond the Newlands Valley at Buttermere, offers 21 beautiful rooms—most of them quite spacious—and a classic Old World countryside-hotel experience. On Fridays and Saturdays, dinner is required (apartments available, minimum 2-night stay on weekends, tel. 017687/70252, www.bridge-hotel.com, enquiries@bridge-hotel.com). There are no shops within 10 miles—only peace and quiet a stone's throw from one of the region's most beautiful lakes. The hotel has a dark-wood pub/restaurant on the ground floor.

¢ Buttermere Hostel, a quarter-mile south of Buttermere village on Honister Pass Road, has good food and a peacefully rural setting (private and family rooms, breakfast extra, inexpensive dinners and packed lunches, office open 8:30-10:00 & 17:00-22:00, reservation tel. 0345-371-9508, www.yha.org.uk, buttermere@yha.org.uk).

NEAR BORROWDALE

$$ Ashness Farm, ruling its valley high above Derwentwater, immerses guests in farm sounds and lakeland beauty. On this 750-acre working farm, now owned by the National Trust, people have raised sheep and cattle for centuries. Today, Anne and her family are "tenant farmers," keeping this farm operating and renting five rooms to boot (cozy lounge, farm-fresh eggs and sausage for breakfast, sack lunches available, just above Ashness Packhorse Bridge, tel. 017687/77361, www.ashnessfarm.co.uk, enquiries@ashnessfarm.co.uk).

$$ Seatoller Farm B&B is a rustic 16th-century house on another working farm owned by the National Trust. Ruby rents three rooms in her B&B, one of five buildings in this hamlet. The lounge has a toasty fireplace, and while the old windows are small, the abundant flower boxes keep things bright (closed Dec-mid-Jan, tel. 017687/77232, www.seatollerfarm.co.uk, info@seatollerfarm.co.uk). There's also a farm cottage for rent by the week.

¢ Borrowdale Hostel, in the secluded Borrowdale Valley just south of Rosthwaite, is a well-run place surrounded by many ways to immerse yourself in nature. The hostel offers cheap dinners and sack lunches (private and family rooms, breakfast extra, office open 7:30-23:00, game room, reservation tel. 0845-371-9624, hostel tel. 017687/77257, www.yha.org.uk, borrowdale@yha.org.uk). To reach this hostel from Keswick by bus, take #78, the Borrowdale Rambler. Note that the last bus from Keswick departs around 18:00 most of year (see page 473 for bus details).

Eating in Keswick

Keswick has a variety of good, basic eateries, but nothing particularly outstanding. Most places stop serving by 21:00.

$$ The Dog and Gun serves good pub food (their rump of lamb is a hit) with great pub ambience. Upon arrival, muscle up
to the bar to order your beer or meal. Then snag a table as soon as one opens up. Mind your head and tread carefully: Low ceilings and wooden beams loom overhead, while paws poke out from under tables below, as Keswick's canines wait patiently for

their masters to finish their beer (food served daily 12:00-21:00, famous goulash, dog treats, 2 Lake Road, tel. 017687/73463).

$$ The Pheasant Inn is a walk outside town, but locals trek here regularly for the food. The menu offers Lake District pub standards (fish pie, Cumberland sausage, guinea fowl) as well as more inventive choices. Check the walls for caricatures of pub regulars, sketched at these tables by a Keswick artist. There's a small restaurant section, but I much prefer eating in the bar (food served daily 12:00-14:00 & 18:00-21:00, bar open until 23:00, Crosthwaite Road, tel. 017687/72219). From the town square, walk past the Pencil Museum, hang a right onto Crosthwaite Road, and walk 10 minutes. For a more scenic route, cross the river into Fitz Park, go left along the riverside path until it ends at the gate to Crosthwaite Road, turn right, and walk five minutes.

$ Abraham's Café, popular with townspeople, is a fine value for lunch. It's tucked away on the upper floor of the giant George Fisher outdoor store (Mon-Sat 10:00-17:00, Sun 10:30-16:30, on the corner of Borrowdale and Lake streets, tel. 017687/71811).

$$ Merienda Café, with a friendly staff and a contemporary space, can be a welcome break from pub grub, serving up an inviting menu of international, North African, and vegetarian dishes (daily 9:00-21:00, 10 Main Street, tel. 017687/72024).

$$ Bryson's Bakery and Tea Room has an enticing ground-floor bakery, with sandwiches and light lunches. The upstairs is a popular tearoom. Order lunch to go from the bakery, or for a few pence more, eat in, either sitting on stools or at a sidewalk table.

Upstairs, consider their Cream Tea made with local ingredients; it's a good deal for what most would consider "afternoon tea," with sandwiches, scones, and little cakes served on a three-tiered platter (daily 9:00-17:00, 42 Main Street, tel. 017687/72257).

$ The Old Keswickian, a fish-and-chips shop, is a fixture on the main square, with an old-fashioned takeaway bar on the ground floor and 70 seats upstairs in a proper dining room (£10 plates and meat pies, daily 11:00-19:30, takeaway until 20:00, on Market Square, tel. 017687/73861).

$$ The Square Orange Café—small and very orange—is a quirky place that just makes you want to smile. It's popular—and they take no reservations, so grab one of their eight little tables when you can and then order at the bar. The eclectic menu features Spanish tapas, Neapolitan pizzas, fun cocktails, and fine European beers (daily 12:00-15:00 & 17:00-21:00, 20 St. John's Street, tel. 017687/73888).

$$ The George Hotel Restaurant and Bar, with a good solid pub and a large hotel dining room adjacent, is a warm and cozy Old World place. They offer the same extensive and very English menu in both the restaurant and bar (order at the pub's bar or wait to be served in the restaurant, tel. 017687/72076, St. John's Street, reservations in dining room only).

Eateries on Station Street: The street leading from the town square to the leisure center has several restaurants, including **$$ Casa Bella,** a popular and well-priced Italian place that's good for families—reserve ahead (daily 12:00-15:30 & 17:00-21:00, 24 Station Street, tel. 017687/75575, www.casabellakeswick.co.uk). **$$ Lakes Bar and Bistro** is popular for its burgers, meat pies, and good fixed-price meal deals (daily 10:00-23:00, 25 Station Street, tel. 017687/74080). **$ Asaya Thai Restaurant,** a hardworking, bright-and-mellow place, is a solid, inexpensive bet (daily 17:00-22:00, 21 Station Street, tel. 017687/75111).

Picnic Food: $ The Cornish Pasty offers an enticing variety of fresh meat pies to go (daily 9:00-17:00 or until the pasties are all gone, across from The Dog and Gun on Borrowdale Road, tel. 017687/72205). Or stop by the huge **Booths** grocery store (see "Helpful Hints," earlier).

EATING IN THE NEWLANDS VALLEY

The farmhouse B&Bs of Newlands Valley don't serve dinner, but guests have two good options for an evening meal: Go into Keswick, or take the lovely 10-minute drive to Buttermere. In Buttermere you have three choices: **$$ The Fish** pub has fine indoor and outdoor seating, but takes no reservations (food served daily 12:00-14:00 & 18:00-21:00, family-friendly, good fish and daily specials with fresh vegetables, tel. 017687/70253). The neighboring **$$ Bridge Hotel Pub,** a bit cozier and more expensive, takes a modern approach to classic pub grub. If you want fancy service, you can eat in the more formal hotel restaurant (food served daily 9:00-21:30, tel. 017687/70252). For lunch, also consider the **$ Croft House Farm Café,** which serves freshly made soups and sandwiches to eat on their sunny deck or to take away (daily 10:00-16:00, tel. 017687/70235).

Keswick Connections

The nearest train station to Keswick is in Penrith (no lockers). For train and bus info, check at a TI, visit Traveline.info, or call 0345-748-4950 (for train). Most routes run less frequently on Sundays.

From Keswick by Bus: For bus routes and connections, see "Getting Around the Lake District/Without a Car," earlier.

From Penrith by Bus to: Keswick (hourly, every 2 hours on Sun in Nov-April, 45 minutes, pay driver, Stagecoach bus #X4 or #X5), **Ullswater** and **Glenridding** (5/day, more frequent June-Aug with open-top buses, 50 minutes, bus #508). The Penrith bus stop is just outside the train station (bus schedules posted inside and outside station).

From Penrith by Train to: Liverpool (2/hour, 2.5 hours, change in Wigan or Preston), **Durham** (hourly, 3 hours, 1-2 transfers), **York** (roughly 2/hour, 4 hours, 1-2 transfers), **London**'s Euston Station (hourly, 3.5 hours), **Edinburgh** (8/day direct, more with transfer, 1.5 hours), **Glasgow** (hourly direct, 1.5 hours), **Oban** (5/day, 6 hours, transfer in Glasgow).

ROUTE TIPS FOR DRIVERS

From Points South to the Lake District: From Liverpool or North Wales, the direct, easy way to Keswick is to leave the M-6 at Penrith and take the A-66 motorway for 16 miles to Keswick. For a scenic sightseeing drive through the south lakes to Keswick, exit the M-6 on the A-590/A-591 through the towns of Kendal and Windermere to reach Brockhole National Park Visitors Centre. From Brockhole, the A-road to Keswick is fastest, but the high road—the tiny road over Kirkstone Pass to Glenridding and lovely Ullswater—is much more dramatic.

Coming from (or Going to) the West: Only 1,300 feet above sea level, Hardknott Pass is still a thriller, with a narrow, winding, steeply graded road. Just over the pass are the scant but evocative remains of the Hardknott Roman fortress. The great views can come with miserable rainstorms, and it can be very slow and frustrating when the one-lane road with turnouts is clogged by traffic. Avoid it on summer weekends.

Ullswater Lake Area

Long, narrow Ullswater, which some consider the loveliest lake in the area, offers miles of diverse and grand Lake District scenery. The main town on Ullswater is the stony village of **Glenridding,** which is little more than a few pubs and shops along the bank of a spritely stream. Visit the **TI** there for advice on the Ullswater area (daily 9:30-17:30, Nov-March weekends only until 15:30, located in the village's pay parking lot, tel. 017684/82414, www.visiteden. co.uk). For locations of Ullswater sights, see the "Lake District" map earlier in this chapter.

▲▲Ullswater Hike and Boat Ride

While you can drive it or cruise the lake, I'd ride the boat from the south tip halfway up (to Howtown—which is nothing more than a dock) and hike back. Or walk first, then enjoy an easy boat ride back.

An old-fashioned **"steamer" boat** (actually diesel-powered) leaves Glenridding regularly for Howtown (departs daily generally 9:45-16:55, 6-9/day April-Oct, fewer off-season, 40 minutes; £7.30 one-way, £12 round-trip, £17 round-the-lake ticket lets you hop on and off, covered by Ullswater Bus & Boat day pass, family rates, drivers can use safe pay-and-display parking lot, by public transit take bus #508 from Penrith, café at dock, tel.

017684/82229, www.ullswater-steamers.co.uk).

From Howtown, spend three to four hours hiking and dawdling along the well-marked path by the lake south to Patterdale, and then along the road back to Glenridding. This is a serious seven-mile walk with good views, varied terrain, and a few bridges and farms along the way. For a shorter hike from the Howtown pier, consider a three-mile loop around Hallin Fell. A rainy-day plan is to ride the covered boat up and down the lake to Howtown and Pooley Bridge at the northern tip of the lake (2 hours). Boats don't run in bad weather—call ahead if it looks iffy.

If you'd rather get out on the water on your own, you can rent **canoes and kayaks** just south of Glenridding—ask locally for details.

▲▲Lanty's Tarn and Keldas Hill

If you like the idea of an Ullswater-area hike but aren't up for the long huff from Howtown, consider this shorter (but still moderately challenging and plenty scenic) loop that leaves right from the TI's pay parking lot in Glenridding (about 2.5 miles, allow 2 hours; before embarking, buy the leaflet at the TI that describes this walk).

From the parking lot, head to the main road, turn right to cross the Glenridding Beck river, then turn right again immediately and follow the river up into the hills. After passing a row of cottages, turn left, cross the wooden bridge, and proceed up the hill through the swing gate. Just before the next swing gate (set in a stone wall—do not go through this gate), turn left (following *Grisedale* signs) and head to yet another gate. From here you can see the small lake called Lanty's Tarn.

While you'll eventually go through this gate and walk along the lake to finish the loop, first you can detour to the top of the adjacent hill, called Keldas, for sweeping views over the near side of Ullswater (to reach the summit, climb over the step gate and follow the faint path up the hill). Returning to—and passing through— the swing gate, you'll walk along Lanty's Tarn on your left, then begin your slow, steep, and scenic descent into the Grisedale Valley. Reaching the valley floor (and passing a noisy dog-breeder's farm), cross the stone bridge, then turn left and follow the road all the way back to the lakefront, where a left turn returns you to Glenridding.

▲Aira Force Waterfall

On the north bank of Ullswater, there's a delightful little park with parking, a ranger trailer, and easy trails leading a half-mile uphill to a powerful 60-foot-tall waterfall. At the falls a little loop trail takes you over two romantic stone arched bridges. Wordsworth was inspired to write three poems here...and after taking this little walk, you'll know why. Park at the pay-and-display lot just where the A-5091 from Troutbeck hits the lake and the A-592. To get to the falls with a much shorter walk (10 minutes), drivers can find the Park Brow pay-and-display lot above the lake on A-5091 (direction: Troutbeck).

Helvellyn

Considered by many the best high-mountain hike in the Lake District, this breathtaking 7.5-mile round-trip route from Glenridding includes the spectacular Striding Edge—about a half-mile knife's edge along the ridge. (If this is too scary, there is a detour trail.) Be careful; this is a demanding six-hour hike with some scrambling, and should be done only in good weather, since the wind can be fierce. While it's not the shortest route, the Glenridding ascent is best. Get advice from the Ullswater TI in Glenridding or look for various books on this hike at any area TI.

▲Kirkstone Pass

Heading south from Ullswater to Windermere, you drive over the 1500-foot Kirkstone Pass. The stark Ullswater Valley is famous for its old dry-stone walls, built without mortar. Back in the 18th century, the British parliament passed a series of "enclosures acts," which allowed private ownership of what had been communal farmland. Landowners began squabbling about boundaries and set about establishing clear property lines with stone walls. But because the walls were expensive, the feuding landowners began collaborating and sharing the cost...and they began getting along. To this day, these fine walls still define the valley's family farms. If you look carefully, you can see "sheep creeps"—small holes in the walls to allow sheep to be moved conveniently from one field to the next.

At the summit, stop to enjoy the view and check out the Kirkstone Pass Inn, a 500-year-old coaching stop. The steep road just across from the inn is called "The Struggle" for the work it took for those long-ago coaches to climb it.

▲Holehird Gardens

South of Kirkstone Pass on the Ullswater-Windermere road, Holehird is a haven for gardeners. Run by Lakeland Horticultural Society volunteers for 50 years, it's one of the most enjoyable gardens in England. Stop first at the reception to take advantage of the info desk and pick up a map. Adjacent are the walled garden and several greenhouses. Of particular interest are several National Plant Collections, a scheme to systematically collect and preserve particular plant families cultivated in the UK. The Holehird examples are well worth seeking out.

Cost and Hours: Free, donations welcome, open dawn to dusk, car park, WC, on the A-592 one mile north of Windermere, tel. 105394/46008, www.holehirdgardens.org.uk.

South Lake District

The South Lake District has a cheesiness that's similar to other popular English resort destinations. Here, piles of low-end vacationers suffer through terrible traffic, slurp ice cream, and get candy floss caught in their hair. The area around Windermere is worth a drive-through if you're a fan of Wordsworth or Beatrix Potter, but you'll still want to spend the majority of your Lake District time (and book your accommodations) up north.

GETTING AROUND THE SOUTH LAKE DISTRICT

By Car: Driving is your best option to see the small towns and sights clustered here; consider combining your drive with the bus trip mentioned next. If you're coming to or leaving the South Lake District from the west, you could take the Hardknott Pass for a scenic introduction to the area (see "Keswick Connections," earlier, for route tips).

By Bus: Buses #599 and #555 are a fine and stress-free way to lace together the gauntlet of sights in the congested Lake Windermere area. Consider leaving your car at Grasmere and enjoying the breezy and extremely scenic bus #599, hopping off and on as you like (see page 478 for details).

By Boat: Windermere Lake Cruises run from Bowness to Ambleside and other points on the lake all year (several itineraries offered, some are seasonal; tel. 015394/43360, www.windermere-lakecruises.co.uk).

Sights in the South Lake District

WORDSWORTH SIGHTS

William Wordsworth was one of the first writers to reject fast-paced city life. During England's Industrial Age, hearts were muz-

zled and brains ruled. Science was in, machines were taming nature, and factory hours were taming humans. In reaction to these brainy ideals, a rare few—dubbed Romantics—began to embrace untamed nature and undomesticated emotions.

Back then, nobody climbed a mountain just because it was there—but Wordsworth did. He'd "wander lonely as a cloud" through the countryside, finding inspiration in "plain living and high thinking." Today the Romantic appreciation of the natural world thrives as visitors continue to inundate the region.

▲▲Dove Cottage at Wordsworth Grasmere

Following a yearlong renovation, Dove Cottage reopened in the spring of 2020 with a new name (Wordsworth Grasmere) and new galleries and displays to celebrate the 250th anniversary of Wordsworth's birth. For literary types, this visit is the top sight of the Lake District. Take a short tour of William Wordsworth's humble cottage; get inspired in its excellent museum, which displays original writings, sketches, personal items, and fine paintings; and wander the garden/orchard.

The poet whose appreciation of nature and a back-to-basics lifestyle put this area on the map spent his most productive years (1799-1808) in this well-preserved stone cottage on the edge of Grasmere. After functioning as the Dove and Olive Bow pub for

Wordsworth at Dove Cottage

William Wordsworth (1770-1850) was a Lake District home-boy. Born in Cockermouth (in a house now open to the public), he was schooled in Hawkshead. In adulthood, he married a local girl, settled down in Grasmere and Ambleside, and was buried in Grasmere's St. Oswald's churchyard.

But the 30-year-old man who moved into Dove Cottage in 1799 was not the carefree lad who'd once roamed the district's lakes and fields. At Cambridge University, he'd been a C student, graduating with no job skills and no interest in a nine-to-five career. Instead, he and a buddy hiked through Europe, where Wordsworth had an epiphany of the "sublime" atop Switzerland's Alps. He lived a year in France, watching the Revolution rage. It stirred his soul. He fell in love with a Frenchwoman who bore his daughter, Caroline. But lack of money forced him to return to England, and the outbreak of war with France kept them apart.

Pining away in London, William hung out in the pubs and coffeehouses with fellow radicals, where he met poet Samuel Taylor Coleridge. They inspired each other to write, edited each other's work, and jointly published a groundbreaking book of poetry.

In 1799, his head buzzing with words and ideas, William and his sister (and soul mate), Dorothy, moved into the white-washed, slate-tiled former inn now known as Dove Cottage. He came into a small inheritance, and dedicated himself to poetry full time. In 1802, during a break in the war with France, William returned there to finally meet his daughter. (He wrote of the rich experience: "It is a beauteous evening, calm and free... / Dear child! Dear Girl! that walkest with me here, / If thou appear untouched by solemn thought, / Thy nature is not therefore less divine.")

Having achieved closure, Wordsworth returned home to marry a former kindergarten classmate, Mary. She moved into Dove Cottage, along with an initially jealous Dorothy. Three of their five children were born here, and the cottage was also home to Mary's sister, the family dog Pepper (a gift from Sir Walter Scott; see Pepper's portrait), and frequent house-guests who bedded down in the pantry: Scott, Coleridge, and Thomas de Quincey, the Timothy Leary of opium.

The time at Dove Cottage was Wordsworth's "Golden Decade," when he penned his masterpieces. But after almost nine years here, Wordsworth's family and social status had outgrown the humble cottage. They moved first to a house in Grasmere before settling down in Rydal Hall. Wordsworth was changing. After the Dove years, he would write less, settle into a regular government job, quarrel with Coleridge, drift to the right politically, and endure criticism from old friends who branded him a sellout. Still, his poetry—most of it written at Dove—became increasingly famous, and he died honored as England's Poet Laureate.

almost 200 years, Wordsworth's family bought it. This is where Wordsworth got married, had kids, and wrote much of his best poetry. The place comes with some amazing artifacts, including the poet's passport and suitcase (he packed light) and his own furniture. Even during his lifetime, Wordsworth was famous, and Dove Cottage was turned into a museum in 1891—it's now protected by the Wordsworth Trust.

Cost and Hours: £9, daily 9:30-17:30, Nov-Feb 10:00-16:30 except closed Jan and for events in Dec and Feb (call ahead), café, bus #555 from Keswick, bus #555 or #599 from Windermere, tel. 015394/35544, www.wordsworth.org.uk. Pay parking in the Dove Cottage lot off the main road (A-591), 50 yards from the site.

Visiting the Cottage and Museum: Wordsworth's appreciation of nature, his Romanticism, and the ways his friends unleashed their creative talents with such abandon are appealing. The cottage tour and adjoining museum, with lots of actual manuscripts handwritten by Wordsworth and his illustrious friends, are both excellent. In dry weather, the garden where the poet was much inspired is lovely. (Visit this after leaving the cottage tour and pick up the description at the back door. The garden is closed when wet.) Allow 1.5 hours for this visit.

Poetry Readings: The Wordsworth Trust puts on poetry readings of Wordsworth's works written at Dove Cottage. Readings are held in the museum library in a relaxed and friendly setting (£5, confirm schedule in advance, same contact info as above).

▲Rydal Mount and Gardens

Located just down the road from Dove Cottage, this sight is worthwhile for Wordsworth fans. The poet's final, higher-class home, with a lovely garden and view, lacks the humble charm of Dove Cottage, but still evokes the creative spirit of the literary giant who lived here for 37 years. His family repurchased it in 1969 (after a 100-year gap), and his great-great-great-

granddaughter still calls it home on occasion, as shown by recent family photos sprinkled throughout the house. After a short intro by the attendant, you are free to roam. Wander through the garden William himself designed, which has changed little since then. Surrounded by his nature, you can imagine the poet enjoying them with you. "O happy garden! Whose seclusion deep hath been so friendly to industrious hours; and to soft slumbers, that did gently steep our spirits, carrying with them dreams of flowers, and wild notes warbled among leafy bowers."

Cost and Hours: £7.50; daily 9:30-17:30, Nov-Dec and Feb 11:00-16:30 and closed Mon-Tue, closed Jan; occasionally closed for private functions—check website; tearoom, 1.5 miles north of Ambleside, well-signed, free and easy parking, bus #555 from Keswick, tel. 015394/33002, www.rydalmount.co.uk.

BEATRIX POTTER SIGHTS

Author and illustrator Beatrix Potter, of Peter Rabbit fame, lived and worked in the Lake District for years. Of the many attractions in the area that claim a connection to her, there are two serious sights: Hill Top, her farm, and the Beatrix Potter Gallery, filled with her sketches and paintings. The sights are two miles apart: Beatrix Potter Gallery is in Hawkshead, an extremely cute but extremely touristy town that's a 20-minute drive south of Ambleside; Hill Top Farm is south of Hawkshead, in Near Sawrey village.

On busy summer days, the wait to get into Hill Top Farm can last several hours. If you like quaint towns engulfed in Potter tourism (Hawkshead), this extra waiting time can be a blessing. Otherwise, you'll wish you were in the woods somewhere with Wordsworth.

To reach Hawkshead from Windermere, take bus #505 or catch the little 15-car ferry from Bowness (runs continually except when it's extremely windy, 10-minute trip, £5 car fare includes all passengers). If going straight to the farm, it's a 5-minute drive or 40-minute walk from the ferry landing. If you have questions, visit the Hawkshead TI inside the Ooh-La-La gift shop across from the parking lot (tel. 015394/36946). To reach Hill Top Farm from Hawkshead, see the directions on the next page.

▲Hill Top Farm

A hit with Beatrix Potter fans (and skippable for others), this dark and intimate cottage, swallowed up in the inspirational and rough nature around it, provides an enjoyable if quick experience. The six-room farm was left just as it was when Potter died in 1943. At her request, the house

Beatrix Potter (1866-1943)

As a girl growing up in London, Beatrix Potter vacationed in the Lake District, where she became inspired to write her popular children's books. Unable to get a publisher, she self-published the first two editions of *The Tale of Peter Rabbit* in 1901 and 1902. When she finally landed a publisher, sales of her books were phenomenal. With the money she made, she bought Hill Top Farm, a 17th-century cottage, and fixed it up, living there sporadically from 1905 until she married in 1913. Potter was more than a children's book writer; she was a fine artist, an avid gardener, and a successful farmer. She married a lawyer and put her knack for business to use, amassing a 4,000-acre estate. An early conservationist, she used the garden-cradled cottage as a place to study nature. She willed it—along with the rest of her vast estate—to the National Trust, which she enthusiastically supported.

is set as if she had just stepped out—flowers on the tables, fire on, low lights. While there's no printed information here, guides in each room are eager to explain things. Fans of the classic *Tale of Samuel Whiskers* will recognize the home's rooms, furniture, and views—the book and its illustrations were inspired by an invasion of rats when Potter bought this place. If exasperated by long lines, remember you can enjoy the garden and see the house from outside for free at any time.

Cost and Hours: Farmhouse—£12, gardens—free; June-Aug daily 10:00-17:30; mid-Feb-May and Sept-Oct until 16:30 and closed Fri; house closed Nov-Dec but gardens and shop open Sat-Sun; closed Jan-mid-Feb; tel. 015394/36269, www.nationaltrust. org.uk/hill-top.

Getting In: Admission is by timed tickets, which cannot be booked in advance (only eight people are let in every five minutes). To beat the lines, get to the ticket office 15 minutes before it opens. Otherwise, call the farm for the current wait times (if no one answers, leave a message for the administrator; if the office is attended, someone will call you back). Big bus or student groups (common in late July and Aug) can book up several hours of entries at any moment if you're unlucky.

Getting There: Mountain Goat Tours runs a shuttle bus (Mountain Goat #525) from across the Hawkshead TI to the farm every 20-40 minutes (tel. 015394/45161). Drivers can take the B-5286 and B-5285 from Ambleside or the B-5285 from Coniston—be prepared for extremely narrow roads with no shoulders that are often lined with stone walls. You'll find the museum parking lot and ticket office about 150 yards down the road from the farm.

▲Beatrix Potter Gallery

Located in the cute town of Hawkshead, this gallery fills the one-time law office of Potter's husband with the wonderful and intimate drawings and watercolors she made to illustrate her books. Each year the museum highlights a new theme and brings out a different set of Potter's paintings, drawings, and other items. Unlike Hill Top, the gallery has plenty of explanation about her life and work, including touchscreen displays and information panels. Anyone will find this museum rather charming and her art surprisingly interesting.

Cost and Hours: £6.80, daily 10:30-16:00, closed Nov-mid-Feb, Main Street, drivers use the nearby Hawkshead pay-and-display lot and walk 200 yards to the town center, tel. 015394/36355, www.nationaltrust.org.uk/beatrix-potter-gallery.

The World of Beatrix Potter

This exhibit, a hit with children, is gimmicky, with all the historical value of a Disney ride. The 45-minute experience begins with a five-minute film introducing Potter and her characters. From there, you'll tour through a series of Lake District tableaux starring Mrs. Tiggy-winkle, Peter Rabbit, Mr. Jeremy Fisher, and company. In July and August, there's often a daily theater show ("Where is Peter Rabbit?")—check event schedule online and reserve ahead.

Cost and Hours: £8, kids-£4, daily 10:00-17:30, last entry one hour before closing, tearoom, on Crag Brow in Bowness-on-Windermere, tel. 015394/88444, www.hop-skip-jump.com.

MORE SIGHTS AT LAKE WINDERMERE

Brockhole National Park Visitors Centre

This visitors center (between Ambleside and Windermere on the A-591) is set in a lakeside park and surrounded by lots of touristic kitsch. It offers a free video on life in the Lake District, an information desk, exhibits, a shop (with maps and guidebooks), gardens, and nature walks. It's a popular place to bring kids for its adventure playground with slides, swings, nets, and swinging bridges. Other family activities include an aerial treetop trek, a zip line, and mini golf. Boat and bike rentals are also available.

Cost and Hours: Free entry but you'll pay to park; daily 10:00-17:00, Nov-March until 16:00; tel. 015394/46601, www.lakedistrict.gov.uk.

Cruise: For a joyride around famous Lake Windermere, you can catch the Brockhole "Green" cruise here (£9, runs daily April-Oct 10:20-17:45, hourly, 2/hour in summer, 50-minute circuit, scant narration, passengers can hop on and off on one ticket, tel. 015394/43360, www.windermere-lakecruises.co.uk).

Windermere Jetty Museum

On the east shore of Windermere, this museum offers a fun opportunity to learn about the boating history of the lake over the past 200 years. Brush up on your maritime vocabulary with the display of mooring warps, splicing fids, fenders, and more. Then view the museum's collection of 40 boats (about half are exhibited at any one time). You'll find rowing skiffs (including one belonging to Beatrix Potter), motorboats, and steam launches, including *Dolly*, a 19th-century example salvaged from the bottom of the lake in 1962. At the adjacent conservation workshop, watch the ongoing restoration of the old boats (there's a "conservation conversation" daily at 11:00); other vintage boats are berthed in the lakeside boathouse (daily presentation at 14:00). Kids will enjoy the model boat pond.

Cost and Hours: £9, £19 includes trip on the steam launch *Osprey*, daily 10:00-17:30; Nov-Feb 10:30-16:00; last entry one hour before closing, free parking, view café, tel. 01539/637-940, www.windermerejetty.org.

Getting There: The museum is just off the A-592, near Bowness Pier. Bus #599 from Ambleside (daily mid-July-Aug) stops at Bowness Pier (8-minute walk), where Windermere Lake Cruises also stop (www.windermere-lakecruises.co.uk).

YORK

Historic York is loaded with world-class sights. Marvel at the York Minster, England's finest Gothic church. Ramble The Shambles, York's wonderfully preserved medieval quarter. Enjoy a walking tour led by an old Yorker. Hop a train at one of the world's greatest railway museums, travel to the 1800s in the York Castle Museum, head back 1,000 years to Viking times at the Jorvik Viking Centre, or dig into the city's buried past at the Yorkshire Museum.

York has a rich history. In AD 71 it was Eboracum, a Roman provincial capital—the northernmost city in the empire. Constantine was proclaimed emperor here in AD 306. In the fifth century, as Rome was toppling, the Roman emperor sent a letter telling England it was on its own, and York—now called Eoforwic—became the capital of the Anglo-Saxon kingdom of Northumbria.

The city's first church was built in 627, and the town became an early Christian center of learning. The Vikings later took the town, and from the 9th through the 11th century, it was a Danish trading center called Jorvik. The invading and conquering Normans destroyed and then rebuilt the city, fortifying it with a castle and the walls you see today.

Medieval York, with 9,000 inhabitants, grew rich on the wool trade and became England's second city. Henry VIII used the city's fine Minster as the northern capital of his Anglican Church. (In today's Anglican Church, the Archbishop of York is second only to the Archbishop of Canterbury.)

In the Industrial Age, York was the railway hub of northern England. When it was built in 1877, York's train station was the world's largest. During World War II, the station suffered an aerial bombardment. (In response to Allied bombing of historic German towns, the Nazis unleashed the "Baedeker raids," bombing English cities—including York—that were described as the most historic and beautiful in the leading German guidebook of the day.)

Today, York feels like a big, traffic-free amusement park for adults. Its leading industry is tourism. It seems like everything that's great about Britain finds its best expression in this manageable town. While the city has no single claim to fame, York is more than the sum of its parts. With its strollable cobbles and half-timbered buildings, grand cathedral and excellent museums, thriving restaurant scene and welcoming locals, York delights.

PLANNING YOUR TIME

After London, York is the best sightseeing city in England. On even a 10-day trip through Britain, it deserves two nights and a day. For the best 36 hours, follow this plan: Arrive early enough to catch the 17:15 evensong service at the Minster, then take the free city walking tour at 18:15 (evening tours offered June-Aug only). Enjoy dinner (which you reserved in advance) at one of the city's bistros. The next morning at 9:00, take my self-guided walk, interrupting it midway with a tour of the Minster. Finish the walk and grab lunch. To fill your afternoon, choose among the town's many important sights (such as the York Castle Museum or the Railway Museum). Spend the evening enjoying a ghost walk of your choice and another memorable dinner.

This is a packed day; as you review this chapter, you'll see that there are easily two days of sightseeing fun in York.

Orientation to York

There are roughly 200,000 people in York and its surrounding area; about one in ten is a student. But despite the city's size, the sightseer's York is small. Virtually everything is within a few minutes' walk: sights, train station, TI, and B&Bs. The longest walk a visitor might take (from a B&B across the old town to the York Castle Museum) is about half an hour.

Bootham Bar, a gate in the medieval town wall, is the hub of your York visit. (In York, a "bar" is a gate and a "gate" is a street. Blame the Vikings.) At Bootham Bar and on Exhibition Square, you'll find the starting points for most walking tours and bus tours, handy access to the medieval town wall, a public WC, and Bootham Street (which leads to my recommended B&Bs). To find your way around York, use the Minster's towers as a navigational landmark, or follow the strategically placed signposts, which point out all places of interest to tourists.

TOURIST INFORMATION

York's TI is a block in front of the Minster (Mon-Sat 9:00-17:00, Sun 10:00-16:00, 1 Museum Street, tel. 01904/550-099, www.visityork.org). They sell a quality £1 map.

York Pass: The TI sells a £45 one-day pass that covers all the sights in York, the City Sightseeing bus, river-boat ride, and a few regional sights. You'd have to be a very busy sightseer to make this pass worth the cost (it's good for a calendar day, not 24 hours; multi-day options available, www.yorkpass.com).

ARRIVAL IN YORK

By Train: The train station is a 10-minute walk from downtown. Day-trippers can pay to store baggage at the small hut next to the Europcar office just off Queen Street—as you exit the station, turn right and walk along a bridge to the first intersection, then turn right (daily 8:00-20:00). Baggage storage is also available near Bootham Bar—see "Helpful Hints," next page.

Recommended B&Bs are a 5- to 15-minute walk or a £7-9 taxi ride from the station. For walking directions to the B&Bs, see page 549.

To walk downtown from the station, exit straight, crossing the street through the bus stops, and turn left down Station Road, keeping the wall on your right. At the first intersection, turn right through the gap in the wall and then left across the river, and follow the crowd toward the Gothic towers of the Minster. After the bridge, a block before the Minster, you'll see the TI on your right.

By Car: Driving and parking in York is maddening. Those day-tripping here should follow signs to one of several park-and-ride lots ringing the perimeter. At these lots, parking is free, and cheap shuttle buses go every 10 minutes into the center. (But, oddly, they generally don't allow overnight parking.)

If you're sleeping here, park your car where your B&B advises and walk. As you near York (and your B&B), you'll hit the A-1237 ring road. Follow this to the A-19/Thirsk roundabout (next to river on northwest side of town). From the roundabout, follow signs for *York,* traveling through Clifton into Bootham. All recommended B&Bs are four or five blocks before you hit the medieval city gate (see the map on page 553). If you're approaching York from the south, take the M-1 until it becomes the A-1M, exit at junction

45 onto the A-64, and follow it for 10 miles until you reach York's ring road (A-1237), which allows you to avoid driving through the city center.

HELPFUL HINTS

Festivals: Book a room well in advance during festival times and on weekends any time of year. The **Viking Festival** features *lur* horn-blowing, warrior drills, and re-created battles in mid-February (www.jorvikvikingfestival.co.uk). The **Early Music Festival** (medieval minstrels, Renaissance dance, and so on) zings its strings in early July (www.ncem.co.uk/yemf.shtml). The **Great Yorkshire Fringe Festival** keeps the city entertained the last two weeks of each July (www.greatyorkshirefringe.com). York claims to be the "Ascot of the North," and the town fills up on horse-race weekends (once a month May-Oct, check schedules at www.yorkracecourse.co.uk); it's especially busy during the **Ebor Races** in mid-August. (Many avoid York during this period, as prices go up and the streets are filled with drunken revelers. Others find that attractive.) The **York Food and Drink Festival** takes a bite out of late September (www.yorkfoodfestival.com). And the **St. Nicholas Fair** Christmas market jingles its bells from mid-November through Christmas. For a complete list of festivals, see www.visityork.org/whats-on/festivals.

Baggage Storage: Yorbag Left Luggage has a tiny office at 20 High Petergate (daily 9:00-19:00, just inside Bootham Bar near the Minster, 10-minute walk to train station, mobile 07561-852-654).

Laundry: Some B&Bs will do laundry for a reasonable charge. Otherwise the nearest place is **Haxby Road Launderette,** a long 15-minute walk north of the town center (or you can take a bus—ask your B&B for directions, 124 Haxby Road, call ahead for prices and hours—tel. 01904/623-379).

Bike Rental: With the exception of the pedestrian center, the town's not great for biking. But there are several fine countryside rides from York, and the riverside New Walk bike path is pleasant. **Cycle Heaven** is at the train station (£10/2 hours, £15/5 hours, £20/24 hours, includes helmet and lock, Mon-Fri 8:30-17:30, Sat 9:00-17:00, Sun 11:00-16:00, closed Sun off-season, to the left as you face the main station entrance from outside, tel. 01904/622-701). For location, see map on the next page.

Taxi: From the train station, taxis zip new arrivals to their B&Bs for £7-9. Queue up at the taxi stand, or call 01904/623-332; cabbies don't start the meter until you get in.

YORK

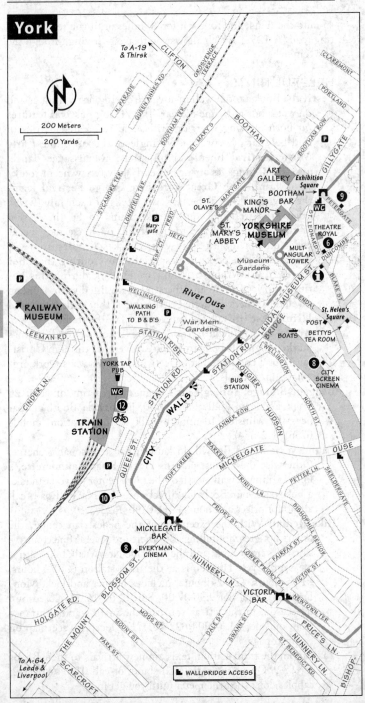

York

To A-19 & Thirsk

CLIFTON

GROSVENOR TERRACE

CLAREMONT

PORTLAND

N

200 Meters
200 Yards

N. PARADE

QUEEN ANNE'S RD.

BOOTHAM TER.

ST. MARY'S

BOOTHAM

BOOTHAM ROW

GILLYGATE

P

SYCAMORE TER.

LONGFIELD TER.

ESP. CT.

FRED

HETH.

MARYGATE

ART GALLERY

ST. OLAVE'S

KING'S MANOR

Exhibition Square

BOOTHAM BAR

WC

PETERGATE

⑨

Marygate

P

ST. MARY'S ABBEY

YORKSHIRE MUSEUM

ST. LEONARD'S

THEATRE ROYAL

⑥

DUNCOMBE

P

RAILWAY MUSEUM

Museum Gardens

MULT-ANGULAR TOWER

ℹ

BLAKE ST.

WELLINGTON

River Ouse

LENDAL MUSEUM ST.

LENDAL BRIDGE

St. Helen's Square

POST

BETTYS TEA ROOM

LEEMAN RD.

CINDER LN.

WALKING PATH TO B & B'S

P

War Mem. Gardens

STATION RISE

STATION RD.

ROUGIER

WELLINGTON

BOATS

⑧

CITY SCREEN CINEMA

NORTH ST.

OUSE

YORK TAP PUB

WC

⑫

STATION RD.

BUS STATION

HUDSON

TRAIN STATION

CITY WALLS

QUEEN ST.

TOFT GREEN

TANNER ROW

BARKER

MICKELGATE

TRINITY LN.

FETTER LN.

SPEEDERGATE

P

⑩

MICKLEGATE BAR

PRIORY ST.

LOWER PRIORY ST.

FAIRFAX ST.

BISHOPHILL SENIOR

⑧ Everyman Cinema

NUNNERY LN.

VICTORIA BAR

NEWTON TER.

HOLGATE RD.

BLOSSOM ST.

MOSS ST.

DALE ST.

SWANN ST.

VICTOR ST.

NUNNERY LN.

PRICE'S LN.

ST. BENEDICT RD.

BISHOP.

THE MOUNT

MOUNT ST.

PARK ST.

SCARCROFT

To A-64, Leeds & Liverpool

⬛ WALL/BRIDGE ACCESS

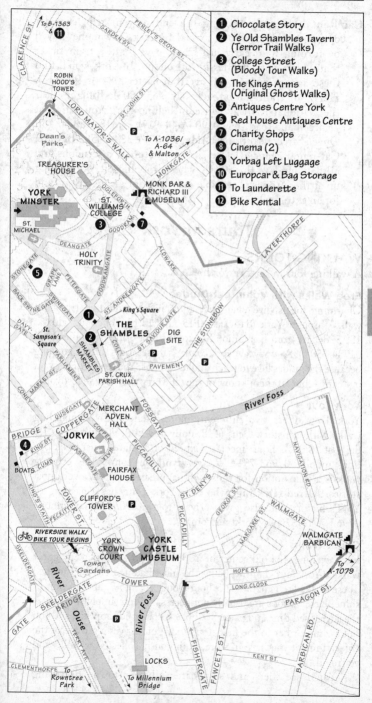

1. Chocolate Story
2. Ye Old Shambles Tavern (Terror Trail Walks)
3. College Street (Bloody Tour Walks)
4. The Kings Arms (Original Ghost Walks)
5. Antiques Centre York
6. Red House Antiques Centre
7. Charity Shops
8. Cinema (2)
9. Yorbag Left Luggage
10. Europcar & Bag Storage
11. To Launderette
12. Bike Rental

YORK

Car Rental: If you're nearing the end of your trip, consider dropping your car upon arrival in York. The money saved by turning it in early just about pays for the train ticket that whisks you effortlessly to London. In York, you'll find these agencies: **Avis** (3 Layerthorpe, tel. 0844-544-6117); **Hertz** (at train station, tel. 0843-653-503); **Budget** (near the National Railway Museum behind the train station at 75 Leeman Road, tel. 01904/644-919); and **Europcar** (off Queen Street near train station, tel. 0371-384-3458). Beware: Car-rental agencies close early on Saturday afternoons and all day Sunday. This is OK when dropping off, but picking up at these times is possible only by prior arrangement (and for an extra fee).

Tours in York

WALKING TOURS

A walking tour in York is worth ▲▲▲.

Free Walks with Volunteer Guides

Charming locals give energetic, entertaining, and free two-hour walks through York (daily at 10:15 and 13:15, June-Aug also at 18:15; depart from Exhibition Square in front of the art gallery, tel. 01904/550-098, www.avgyork.co.uk). These tours often go long because the guides love to teach and tell stories. You're welcome to cut out early—but let them know, or they'll worry that they've lost you.

York Tour

York Tour offers two different, more intellectually demanding walks with a history focus (£18, daily at 14:00, 90 minutes; £15, daily at 18:00, 1 hour; meet at Exhibition Square, must book on-line, mobile 07963-791-937, www.yorktour.com). The evening walk is a nice option for those who appreciate history over ghost stories. **Alfred Hickling,** who runs York Tour, has a passion for York's history and also gives private tours (£90/half-day, mobile 07963-791-937www.yorktour.com).

Ghost Walks

Each evening, the old center of York is crawling with creepy ghost walks. (York lays claim to being the most haunted city in Europe.) These walks are generally 1.5 hours long, cost £5-7, and go rain or shine. Reservations are usually not necessary. You simply show up at the advertised time and place, your black-clad guide appears, and you follow him or her to the first stop. Your guide gives a sample of the entertainment you have in store, humorously collects the "toll," and you're off.

You'll see fliers and signboards all over town advertising

the many ghost walks. Companies come and go, but I find there are three general styles of walks: street theater, historic, and storytelling. Here are three reliably good walks, one for each style (discount for children under 14).

The **Terror Trail Walk** has entertaining guides with backgrounds in the performing arts. The tours are both thought provoking and historic. A good mix of horrifying stories, historical (fun) facts, humor, and role-play makes the tour playful and engaging (£5, daily at 18:45, meet in front of Ye Old Shambles Tavern on The Shambles, www.yorkterrortrail.co.uk).

The **Bloody Tour of York,** led by Mad Alice (an infamous figure in York lore), is an engaging walk with captivating descriptions about the plague, martyred saints, the torturing of regicide-wannabe Guy Fawkes, and other bloody tales. Alice may be mad, but she provides a fine blend of history, violence, and mayhem (£7, Thu-Sat at 18:00, also at 20:00 in April-Oct, no tours Sun-Wed, Dec-Jan by reservation only, meet outside St. Williams College behind the Minster on College Street, www.thebloodytourofyork.co.uk).

The **Original Ghost Walk,** said to be the first of its kind, dates to the 1970s. The walk covers some of the supposedly haunted places in York, where old dukes, Vikings, and Roman soldiers are still seen at night. The walk is more classic spooky storytelling than comedy, and you may learn that your B&B is haunted—or that it sits atop an old graveyard (£5, daily at 20:00, meet outside The Kings Arms at Ouse Bridge, www.theoriginalghostwalkofyork.co.uk).

OTHER TOURS IN YORK
Food Tour

Tours in a Dish, led by Marion Martinez, makes five stops in three hours that can also serve as lunch. The tour visits small eateries offering both savory and sweet cuisine, mostly modern and eclectic rather than traditional English, where you meet the artisan (£50/person, 2-8 people, vegan options, departs at 11:30 from the Minster, book online, mobile 07588-773-647, www.toursinadish.com).

Hop-on, Hop-off Bus Tour

City Sightseeing's half-enclosed, double-decker hop-on, hop-off buses circle York, taking tourists past secondary sights that the city walking tours skip—the mundane perimeter of town. While you can hop on and off all day, York is so compact that these have no real transportation value. If taking a bus tour, I'd catch either one at Exhibition Square (near Bootham Bar) and ride it for an orientation all the way around. Consider getting off at the National Railway Museum, skipping the last five minutes. In the summer, several

York at a Glance

▲▲▲**York Minster** York's pride and joy, and one of England's finest churches, with stunning stained-glass windows, textbook Decorated Gothic design, and glorious evensong services. **Hours:** Mon-Sat 9:00-18:30, Sun 12:30-15:00; shorter hours for tower and undercroft; evensong services Tue-Sat and some Mon at 17:15, Sun at 16:00. See page 529.

▲▲▲**Walking Tours** Variety of guided town walks and evening ghost walks covering York's history. **Hours:** Various times daily; fewer off-season. See page 518.

▲▲**York Castle Museum** Far-ranging collection displaying everyday objects from Victorian times to the present. **Hours:** Daily 9:30-17:00. See page 543.

▲▲**National Railway Museum** Train buff's nirvana, tracing the history of all manner of rail-bound transport. **Hours:** Daily 10:00-18:00. See page 544.

▲**Yorkshire Museum** Archaeology and natural history museum with York's best Viking exhibit, plus Roman, Saxon, Norman, and Gothic artifacts. **Hours:** Daily 10:00-17:00. See page 537.

▲**Merchant Adventurers' Hall** Vast medieval guildhall with displays recounting life and commerce in the Middle Ages. **Hours:** Sun-Fri 10:00-16:30, Sat until 13:30. See page 540.

▲**Jorvik Viking Centre** Entertaining and informative Disney-style exhibit/ride exploring Viking lifestyles and artifacts. **Hours:** Daily 10:00-17:00, Nov-March until 16:00. See page 541.

▲**Fairfax House** Glimpse into an 18th-century Georgian family house, with enjoyably chatty docents. **Hours:** Tue-Sat 10:00-17:00, Sun 11:00-16:00, Mon by tour only at 11:00 and 14:00, closed Jan-mid-Feb. See page 542.

▲**The Shambles** Atmospheric old butchers' quarter, with colorful, tipsy medieval buildings. See page 528.

▲**Ouse Riverside Walk** Bucolic path along river to a mod pedestrian bridge. See page 546.

YORK

departures come with a live guide (£15, pay driver, cash only, ticket valid 24 hours, Easter-Oct departs every 10-15 minutes, daily 9:00-17:30, less frequent off-season, about 1 hour, tel. 01904/633-990, www.yorkbus.co.uk).

Boat Cruise

City Cruise York does a lazy, narrated 45-minute lap along the River Ouse (£10, April-Sept daily 10:30-16:30, runs every 30 minutes, off-season 4/day, no cruises Dec-Jan; leaves from Lendal Bridge, also 1-hour evening cruise at 19:30 and 21:15 for £12, leaves from King's Staith near Skeldergate Bridge; tel. 01904/628-324, www.citycruisesyork.com).

Yorkshire Day Trips

Two reliable companies run all-day minibus (16 passenger) tours with various routes covering the nearby North York Moors, Yorkshire Dales, and Whitby on the coast. Tours cost around £40 and are an efficient way to get a taste of this scenic and charming region without the headache and expense of a rental car (**Mountain Goat Tours,** tel. 01904/405-341, www.mountain-goat.com; and **Bob Holiday's Day Trips from York,** tel. 01609/779-933, www.bobholidays.com).

York Walk

Get a taste of Roman and medieval York on this easy, self-guided stroll. The walk begins in the gardens just in front of the Yorkshire Museum, covers a stretch of the medieval city walls, and then cuts through the middle of the old town. Start at the

ruins of St. Mary's Abbey in the Museum Gardens (see the "York Walk" map).

❶ St. Mary's Abbey

This abbey dates to the age of William the Conqueror—whose harsh policies (called the "Harrowing of the North") consisted of massacres and destruction, including the burning of York's main church. His son Rufus, who tried to improve relations in the 11th century, established a great church here. The church became an abbey that thrived from the 13th century until the Dissolution of the Monasteries in the 16th century. The Dissolution, which

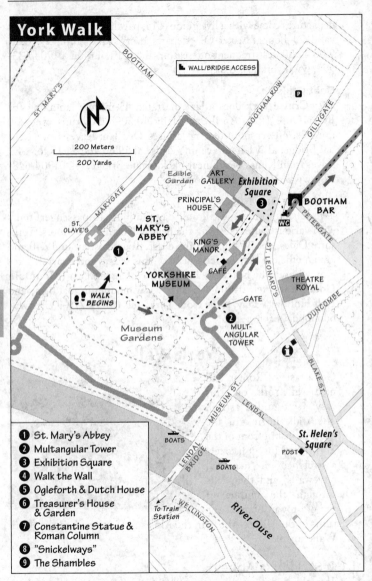

York Walk

WALL/BRIDGE ACCESS

200 Meters
200 Yards

Edible Garden
ART GALLERY
Exhibition Square ❸
BOOTHAM BAR
WC
PRINCIPAL'S HOUSE
ST. OLAVE'S
ST. MARY'S ABBEY
MARYGATE
❶
PETERGATE
KING'S MANOR
CAFÉ
ST. LEONARD'S
THEATRE ROYAL
YORKSHIRE MUSEUM
WALK BEGINS
GATE
❷ MULTI-ANGULAR TOWER
DUNCOMBE
Museum Gardens
ℹ
BLAKE ST.
MUSEUM ST.
BOATS
LENDAL
St. Helen's Square
POST◆
LENDAL BRIDGE
BOATS
To Train Station
WELLINGTON
River Ouse

❶ St. Mary's Abbey
❷ Multangular Tower
❸ Exhibition Square
❹ Walk the Wall
❺ Ogleforth & Dutch House
❻ Treasurer's House & Garden
❼ Constantine Statue & Roman Column
❽ "Snickelways"
❾ The Shambles

accompanied the Protestant Reformation and break with Rome, was a power play by Henry VIII. The king wanted much more than just a divorce: He wanted the land and riches of the monasteries. Upset with the pope, he demanded that his subjects pay him taxes rather than give the Church tithes. (For more information, see the sidebar on page 533.)

As you gaze at this ruin, imagine magnificent abbeys like

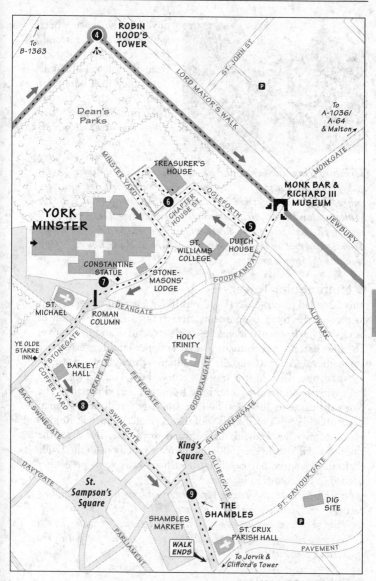

this scattered throughout the realm. Henry VIII destroyed most of them, taking the lead from their roofs and leaving the stones to scavenging townsfolk. Scant as they are today, these ruins still evoke a time of immense monastic power. The one surviving wall was the west half of a very long, skinny nave. The tall arch marked the start of the transept. Stand on the nearby plaque that reads *Crossing beneath central tower,* and look up at the air that

now fills the space where a huge tower once stood. (Fine carved stonework from the ruined abbey is on display in a basement room of the adjacent Yorkshire Museum.)

• *With your back to the abbey, see the fine Neoclassical building housing the* **Yorkshire Museum** *(worth a visit and described later, under "Sights in York"). Walk in front of this building and circle left down a tree-covered lane. On your right is a corner of the* **Roman Wall** *with the* **Multangular Tower.** *After 30 yards, a lane on the right leads through a garden, past yew trees (York means "place of the yew trees"), and through a small gated arch in the wall. Step through the wall and look right for a peek into the ruined tower.*

❷ Multangular Tower

This 12-sided tower (c. AD 300) was likely a catapult station built to protect the town from enemy river traffic. The red ribbon of bricks was a Roman trademark—both structural and decorative. The lower stones are Roman, while the upper (and bigger) stones are medieval. After Rome fell, York suffered through two centuries of a dark age. Then, in the ninth century, the Vikings ruled. They built with wood, so almost nothing from that period remains. The Normans came in 1066 and built in stone, generally atop Roman structures (like this wall). The wall that defined the ancient Roman garrison town worked for the Norman town, too. But after the English Civil War in the 1600s and Jacobite rebellions in the 1700s (Britain's last internal conflicts), fortified walls were no longer needed in the country's interior.

• *Now, return to the tree-covered lane and turn right, walking between the museum and the Roman wall. Continuing straight, the lane goes between the abbot's palace and the town wall. This is a "snickelway"—a small, characteristic York lane or footpath. The snickelway pops out on...*

❸ Exhibition Square

With Henry VIII's Dissolution of the Monasteries, the abbey was destroyed and the Abbot's Palace became the **King's Manor** (from the snickelway, make a U-turn to the left and through the gate). Enter the building under the coat of arms of Charles I, who stayed here during the English Civil War in the 1640s. Today, the building is part of the University of York. Because the northerners were slow to embrace the king's reforms, Henry VIII came here to personally enforce the Dissolution. He stayed 17 days in this mansion and brought along 1,000 troops to make his determination clear. You can wander into the grounds and building. A few stairs lead to the King's Manor Refectory café serving cheap cakes, soup, and sandwiches to students, professors, and visitors like you (Mon-Fri 9:30-15:00, closed Sat-Sun).

Exhibition Square is the departure point for various walking and bus tours. The venerable York Art Gallery (£8, minor collection of paintings and ceramics) overlooks it. The square's centerpiece is a statue of William Etty. With the Industrial Age most great cities had their walls torn down and railway lines laid right through their hearts. With leadership from Etty, York saved its

walls and parked the station outside, thus retaining the character that so many visitors enjoy today.

From Exhibition Square you can see the towers of the Minster in the distance. Travelers in the Middle Ages could see the Minster from miles away as they approached the city. Across the street is a pay WC and **Bootham Bar**—one of the fourth-century Roman gates in York's wall (this one faced Scotland)—with access to the best part of the city walls (free, walls open 8:00-dusk).

• *Climb up the bar.*

❹ Walk the Wall

Hike along the top of the wall behind the Minster to the first corner. (While there may be a padlock on an entry gate, it's generally open. Just push.) York's 13th-century walls are three miles long. This stretch follows the original Roman wall. Norman kings built up the walls to assert control over northern England. Notice the pivots in the crenellations (square notches at the top of a

medieval wall), which once held wooden hatches to provide cover for archers. The wall was extensively renovated in the 19th century. (Victorians may have saved the walls, but the fortifications were not "medieval" enough for their taste, so they ornamented them with fanciful extras, adding little touches such as Romantic arrow slits.)

At the corner with the benches—**Robin Hood's Tower**—you can lean out and see the moat outside. This was originally the Roman ditch that surrounded the fortified garrison town. (Looking at a town map, you can still make out the rectangular footprint of that original occupiers' green zone.) Continue walking for a fine view of the Minster, with its truncated main tower and the pointy rooftop of its chapter house.

Continue on to the next gate, **Monk Bar.** This fine medieval gatehouse is the home of the little **Richard III Museum** (described later, under "Sights in York").

• *Descend the wall at Monk Bar, and step outside the city's protective wall. Pass the portcullis (last lowered in 1953 for the Queen's coronation). Take 10 paces and gaze up at the tower. Imagine 10 archers behind the arrow slits. Keep an eye on the 17th-century guards, with their stones raised and primed to protect the town.*

Return through the city wall. After a short block, turn right on Ogleforth. ("Ogle" is the Norse word for owl, hence our word "ogle"—to look at something fiercely.)

York's Old Town

Walking down ❺ **Ogleforth,** ogle (on your left) a charming little brick house from the 17th century called the **Dutch House.** It was designed by an apprentice architect who was trying to show off for his master, and was the first entirely brick house in town—a sign of opulence. Next, also of brick, is a former brewery, with a 19th-century industrial feel.

Ogleforth jogs left and becomes **Chapter House Street** which leads on to the Minster. On your way you'll pass the ❻ **Treasurer's House** on the right, where a short detour to a tranquil garden awaits. While admission is charged to visit the stately house (daily 11:00-16:30), it's free to visit its garden and café. Pass through the ornate iron gate into the hallway and take a sharp left into the garden. Find a bench and pause to enjoy this pint-sized walled oasis before exiting onto Minster Yard with the pointed tower of the octagonal Chapter House looming in front of you.

Then, circle left around the back side of the Minster, past the stonemasons' lodge (where craftsmen are chiseling local limestone for the church, as has been done here since the 13th century), to the statue of Roman Emperor Constantine and an ancient Roman column.

Take a good look at the lounging ❼ **Constantine.** Five emperors visited York when it was the Roman city of Eboracum. Constantine was here when his father died. The troops declared him the Roman emperor in AD 306 at this site, and six years later, he went to Rome to claim his throne. In AD 312, Constantine legalized Christianity, and in AD 314, York got its first bishop.

The **ancient column,** across the street from Constantine, is a reminder that the Minster sits upon the site of the Roman head-quarters, or *principia.* The city placed this column here in 1971, just before celebrating the 1,900th anniversary of the founding of Eboracum—a.k.a. York.

• *If you want to visit the* **York Minster** *now, find the entrance on its west side, ahead and around the corner (see description on page 529). Otherwise, head into the town center. From opposite the Minster's south transept door (the door by Constantine), take a narrow pedestrian walkway—which becomes Stonegate—into the tangled commercial center of medieval York. Walk straight down Stonegate, a street lined with fun and inviting cafés, pubs, and restaurants. Just before the Ye Old Starre Inne banner hanging over the street, turn left down the snickelway called Coffee Yard. (It's marked by a red devil.) Enjoy strolling another of York's...*

❽ "Snickelways"

This is a made-up York word combining "snicket" (a passageway between walls or fences), "ginnel" (a narrow passageway between buildings), and "alleyway" (any narrow passage)—snickelway. York—with its population packed densely inside its protective walls—has about 50 of these public passages. In general, when exploring the city, you should duck into these—both for the adventure and to take a shortcut. While some of York's history has been bulldozed by modernity, bits of it hide and survive in the snickelways.

Coffee Yard leads past Barley Hall (look through the big window on the left to see its fine old interior), popping out at the corner of Grape Lane and Swinegate. Medieval towns named streets for the business done there. Swinegate, a lane of pig farmers, leads to the market. Grape Lane is a polite version of that street's original crude name, Gropec*nt Lane. If you were here a thousand years ago, you'd find it lined with brothels. Throughout England, streets for prostitutes (rife with men groping women) were called by this graphic name. Today, if you see a street named Grape Lane, that's usually its heritage.

Skip Grape Lane and turn right down Swinegate to a market (which you can see in the distance). The **Shambles Market,** popular for cheap produce and clothing, was created in the 1960s with the demolition of a bunch of colorful medieval lanes. Despite the rise of suburban shopping malls, it's good to see a bit of the old commercial zone with its medieval heritage thriving after all those centuries in the heart of York. (The collection of food trucks at the far end is a popular place for a fast, cheap, and memorable little lunch.)

• In the center of the market, tiny "Little Shambles" lane (on the left) dead-ends into the most famous lane in York.

❾ The Shambles

This colorful old street (rated ▲) was once the "street of the butchers." The name was derived from "shammell"—a butcher's

bench upon which he'd cut and display his meat. In the 16th century, this lane was dripping with red meat. You can still see the hooks—once used to hang rabbit, pheasant, beef, lamb, and pigs' heads—under the eaves. Fresh slabs were displayed on the fat sills, while people lived above the shops. All the garbage and sewage flushed down the street to a mucky pond at the end—a favorite hangout for the town's cats and dogs. Tourist shops now fill these fine, half-timbered Tudor buildings. Look above the modern crowds and storefronts to appreciate the classic old English architecture. While fires gutted most old English town centers, York's old town survives intact. (London would have looked like this before its devastating fire in 1666.) The soil here isn't great for building; notice how the structures have settled in the absence of a solid foundation.

Turn right and slalom down The Shambles. Just past the tiny sandwich shop at #37, pop in to the snickelway and look for very old **woodwork.** Study the 16th-century carpentry: mortise-and-tenon joints with wooden plugs rather than nails, and the wattle-and-daub construction (timber frames filled in with rubble and plastered over).

Next door (back on The Shambles) is the **shrine of St. Margaret Clitherow,** a 16th-century Catholic crushed by Protestants under her own door (as was the humiliating custom when a city wanted to teach someone a lesson). She was killed for refusing to testify about hiding priests in her home. Step into the tiny shrine for a peaceful moment to ponder Margaret, who in 1970 was sainted for her faith.

The Shambles reminds many of Diagon Alley in Harry Potter films. While this lane inspired the set design (and the establishment of several Harry Potter shops at the bottom end of the lane), no filming was ever done here.

At the bottom of The Shambles is the cute, tiny **St. Crux Parish Hall,** which charities use to raise funds by selling light meals (see "Eating in York," later). Take some time to chat with the volunteers.

With blood and guts from The Shambles' 20 butchers all draining down the lane, it's no wonder The Golden Fleece, just below, is considered the most haunted pub in town.

• *Your town walk is finished. From here, you're just a few minutes from plenty of fun: street entertainment and lots of cheap eating options on King's Square, good restaurants on Fossgate, the York Castle Museum (a few blocks farther downhill), and the starting point for my Ouse Riverside Walk (see page 546).*

Sights in York

▲▲▲YORK MINSTER

The pride of York, this largest Gothic church north of the Alps (540 feet long, 200 feet tall) brilliantly shows that the High Middle Ages were far from dark. The word "minster" means an important church chartered with a mission to evangelize. As it's the seat of a bishop, York Minster is also a cathedral. While Henry VIII destroyed England's great abbeys, this was not part of a monastery (and Henry needed an ecclesiastical center for  his Anglican Church in the north), so it was left standing. It seats 2,000 comfortably; on Christmas and Easter, at least 4,000 worshippers pack the place. Today, more than 250 employees and 500 volunteers work to preserve its heritage and welcome more than a million visitors each year. It costs £11,000 a day to maintain the great church, and they just about break even with the revenue generated by tourism.

Cost: £12, includes guided tour, undercroft museum, and crypt; free for kids under age 16. If you buy your ticket online in advance, you can skip the ticket line. Ask a staff member where to enter.

Hours: The cathedral is open for sightseeing Mon-Sat 9:00-18:30, Sun 12:30-15:00. It opens for worship daily at 7:30. Closing time flexes with activities, but last entry is generally at 16:30. Sights

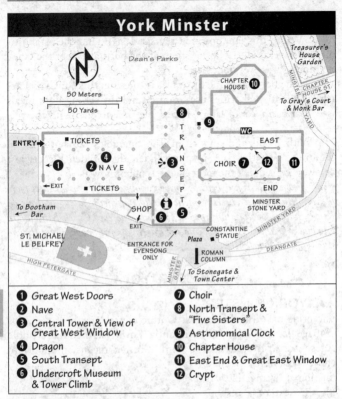

York Minster

1 Great West Doors
2 Nave
3 Central Tower & View of Great West Window
4 Dragon
5 South Transept
6 Undercroft Museum & Tower Climb
7 Choir
8 North Transept & "Five Sisters"
9 Astronomical Clock
10 Chapter House
11 East End & Great East Window
12 Crypt

YORK

within the Minster have shorter hours (listed below). The Minster may close for special events (check calendar on website).

Information: Tel. 01904/557-217 or 0844-393-0011, www. yorkminster.org.

Visitor Information: You'll get a free map with your ticket. For more information, pick up the inexpensive *York Minster Short Guide.* Helpful Minster guides stationed throughout are happy to answer your questions (but not on Sundays).

Tower Climb: It costs £5 for 30 minutes of exercise (275 steps) and forgettable views. The tower opens at 9:30 (13:15 on Sun), with ascents every 45 minutes; the last ascent is generally at 17:00, earlier in winter (no children under 8, not good for acrophobes, closes in extreme weather). Get your timed-entry ticket upon arrival, as only 50 visitors are allowed up at once. It's a tight, spiraling, claustrophobic staircase with an iron handrail. You'll climb about 150 steps to the top of the transept, step outside to cross a narrow walkway, then go back inside for more than 100 steps to the top of the central tower. From here, you'll have caged-in views of rooftops and the flat countryside.

Undercroft Museum: This museum focuses on the history of the site and its origins as a Roman fortress (Mon-Sat 10:00-17:00, Sun 13:00-16:00).

Tours: Free, guided hour-long tours depart from the ticket desk every hour on the hour (Mon-Sat 10:00-15:00, can be more frequent during busy times, none on Sun, they go even with just one or two people). You can join a tour in progress.

Evensong: To experience the cathedral in musical and spiritual action, attend an evensong (Tue-Sat at 17:15, Sun at 16:00, Mon spoken service at 17:15, enter at south door). Visiting choirs perform when the Minster's choir is on summer break (mid-July-Aug). Arrive 15 minutes early and wait just outside the choir in the center of the church. You'll be ushered in and can sit in one of the big wooden stalls. As evensong is a worship service, attendees enter the church free of charge. For more on evensong, see page 157.

Church Bells: If you're a fan of church bells, you'll experience ding-dong ecstasy Sunday morning at about 10:00 and during the Tuesday practice session between 19:00 and 22:00. These performances are especially impressive, as the church holds a full carillon of 35 bells (it's the only English cathedral to have such a range). Stand in front of the church's west portal and imagine the gang pulling on a dozen ropes (halfway up the right tower—you can actually see the ropes through a little window) while a talented carillonneur plays 22 more bells with a keyboard and foot pedals.

YORK

➋ Self-Guided Tour

Before entering, stand before the great west portal (under the twin towers). You'll notice this facade has lots of empty niches. These were potential "advertising" spaces, built to entice rich donors, but never filled. An exception is in the center, where a bishop stands flanked by two wealthy dukes—one who gave stone (on the left, holding a stone) and another who gave timber (on the right, holding a beam).

Upon entering, decide whether you're climbing the tower. If so, get a ticket (with an assigned time). Also consider visiting the Undercroft Museum (described later) if you want to get a comprehensive history and overview of the Minster before touring the church.

• *Entering the church, turn 180 degrees and look back at the...*

➊ **Great West Doors:** These are used only on special occasions. Flanking the doors is a list of archbishops (and other church officials) that goes unbroken back to the 600s. The statue of Peter with the key and Bible (between the doors) is a reminder that the church is dedicated to St. Peter, and the key to heaven is found through the word of God. While the Minster sits on the remains of a Romanesque church (c. 1100), today's church was begun in 1220 and took 250 years to complete. Up above, look for the female, headless "semaphore saints" (from 2004), using semaphore flag code to spell out a message with golden discs: "Christ is here."

• *Grab a chair and enjoy the view down the...*

❷ **Nave:** Your first impression might be of its spaciousness and brightness. One of the widest Gothic naves in Europe, it

was built between 1280 and 1360—the middle period of the Gothic style, called "Decorated Gothic." Rather than risk a stone roof, builders spanned the space with wood. Colorful shields on the arcades are the coats of arms of nobles who helped tall and formidable Edward I, known as "Longshanks," fight the Scots in the 13th century.

The coats of arms in the clerestory (upper-level) glass represent the nobles who helped Edward I's son, Edward II, in the same fight. There's more medieval glass in this building than in the rest of England combined. This precious glass (including the Great East Window) survived World War II—hidden in stately homes throughout Yorkshire.

While originally a Roman Catholic church, it has been a Protestant church for 500 years—ever since the Reformation. Thankfully, rather than destroying the church, the practical Anglicans just purged it of its Roman iconography. You'll find no hint of the original pope-celebrating elements that ornamented it before the days of Henry VIII.

Walk to the very center of the church, under the ❸ **central tower.** Look up. An exhibit in the undercroft explains how gifts and skill saved this 197-foot tower from collapse. Use the neck-saving mirror to marvel at it.

Look back at the west end to marvel at the **Great West Window,** especially the stone tracery. While its nickname is the "Heart of Yorkshire," it represents the sacred heart of Christ, meant to remind people of his love for the world.

Find the ❹ **dragon** on the right of the nave (two-thirds of the way up the wall, affixed to the top of a pillar). While no one is sure of its purpose, it pivots and has a hole through its neck—so it was likely a mechanism designed to raise a lid of a saint's coffin. Carved

England's Anglican Church

The Anglican Church (a.k.a. the Church of England) came into existence in 1534, when Henry VIII declared that he, and not Pope Clement VII, was the head of England's Catholics. The pope had refused to allow Henry to divorce his wife to marry his mistress Anne Boleyn (which Henry did anyway, resulting in the birth of Elizabeth I). Still, Henry regarded himself as a faithful Catholic—just not a *Roman* Catholic—and made relatively few changes in how and what Anglicans worshipped.

It's interesting to think of the Dissolution of the Monasteries in 1534 as "the first Brexit." It was spearheaded by a much-married, arrogant, overweight, egomaniacal Henry VIII—matched today by the Conservative Party's Boris Johnson. Henry (like Boris) wanted "to be free" from European meddling (the pope then, the EU today). The local sentiment (then as now) was no more money to Europe (tithes to the pope then, taxes to Brussels today) and no more intrusions into English life from the Continent.

Henry's son, Edward VI, later instituted many of the changes that Reformation Protestants were bringing about in continental Europe: an emphasis on preaching, people in the pews actually reading the Bible, clergy being allowed to marry, and a more "Protestant" liturgy in English from the revised Book of Common Prayer (1549). The next monarch, Edward's sister Mary I, returned England to the Roman Catholic Church (1553), earning the nickname "Bloody Mary" for her brutal suppression of Protestant elements. When Elizabeth I succeeded Mary (1558), she soon broke from Rome again. Today, many regard the Anglican Church as a compromise between the Catholic and Protestant traditions. In the US, Anglicans split off from the Church in England after the American Revolution, creating the Episcopal Church.

Ever since Henry VIII's time, the York Minster has held a special status within the Anglican hierarchy. After a long feud over which was the leading church, the archbishops of Canterbury and York agreed that York's bishop would have the title "Primate of England" and Canterbury's would be the "Primate of All England," directing all Anglicans and Episcopalians throughout the world.

out of a piece of Scandinavian oak, it's considered part of the earlier church built during Viking times. The statue, directly across the nave, is likely of St. George—the slayer of dragons and protector against pagan religious malpractice.

• *Facing the altar, turn right and head into the...*

❺ **South Transept:** Look up. The new "bosses" (carved medallions decorating the point where the ribs meet on the ceiling) are a reminder that the roof of this wing of the church was destroyed by fire in 1984, caused when lightning hit an electricity box. Some believe the lightning was God's angry response to a new bishop, David Jenkins, who questioned the literal truth of Jesus' miracles. (Jenkins had been interviewed at a nearby TV studio the night before, leading locals to joke that the lightning occurred "12 hours too late, and 17 miles off-target.") Regardless, the entire country came to York's aid. *Blue Peter* (England's top kids' show at the time) conducted a competition among its young viewers to design new bosses. Out of 30,000 entries, there were six winners (the blue ones—e.g., man on the moon, feed the children, save the whales).

Two other sights can be accessed through the south transept: the ❻ **Undercroft Museum** (explained later) and the **tower climb** (explained earlier). But for now, stick with this tour; we'll circle back to the south transept at the end, before exiting the church.

• *Head back into the middle of the nave and face the front of the church. You're looking at the...*

❼ **Choir:** Examine the choir screen—the ornate wall of carvings separating the nave from the choir. It's lined with all the English kings from William I (the Conqueror) to Henry VI (during whose reign it was carved, in 1461). Numbers indicate the years each reigned. It is literally covered in gold leaf,

which sounds impressive, but the gold is very thin...a nugget the size of a sugar cube can be pounded into a foil-like sheet the size of a driveway.

Step into the choir, where a service is held daily. All the carving was redone after an 1829 fire, but its tradition of glorious evensong services (sung by choristers from the Minster School) goes all the way back to the eighth century.

• *To the left as you face the choir is the...*

❽ **North Transept:** In this transept, the grisaille windows—dubbed the **"Five Sisters"**—are dedicated to British servicewomen who died in war. They were made in 1260, before colored glass was produced in England. Notice that the design has no figures, perhaps inspired by Islamic art seen by Christian Crusaders in the 13th century. The windows were originally much lighter but became darker after countless cracked panes were fixed over the centuries by added leading.

The 18th-century ❾ **astronomical clock** is worth a look (the sign helps you make sense of it). It's dedicated to the heroic Allied aircrews from bases here in northern England who died in World War II. The Book of Remembrance below the clock contains 18,000 names.

• A corridor leads to the Gothic, octagonal...

⓪ Chapter House: This was the traditional meeting place of the governing body (or chapter) of the Minster. On the pillar in the middle of the doorway, the Virgin holds Baby Jesus while standing on the devilish serpent. The Chapter House, without an interior support, is remarkable (almost frightening) for its breadth. A model of the wooden construction (in the hallway just outside the door) illustrates the impressive 1285 engineering: with a wooden frame from which the ceiling actually hangs.

The fanciful carvings decorating the canopies above the stalls date from 1280 (80 percent are originals) and are some of the Minster's

finest. Stroll slowly around the entire room and imagine that the tiny sculpted heads are a 14th-century parade—a fun glimpse of medieval society. Grates still send hot air up robes of attendees on cold winter mornings.

The Chapter House was the site of an important moment in England's parliamentary history. In the late 1200s, the Scots under William Wallace and Robert the Bruce were threatening London. Fighting the Scots in 1295, Edward I (the "Longshanks" we met earlier) convened his parliament (a war cabinet) here, rather than down south in London. The government met here through the 20-year reign of Edward II, before moving to London during Edward III's rule in the 14th century (as then foreign policy was focused on fighting the French—in the Hundred Years' War—rather than the Scots).

• Return to the main part of the church, turn left, and continue all the way down the nave (behind the choir) to the...

⓫ East End and Great East Window: This part of the church is square, lacking a semicircular apse, typical of England's Perpendicular Gothic style (15th century). Monuments (almost no graves) were once strewn throughout the church, but in the Victorian Age, they were gathered into the east end, where you see them today.

The Great East Window, the size of a tennis court, is one of the great treasures of medieval art in Europe. It's all original, recently cleaned and restored with its stone tracery, leadings, and painted glass (not stained) looking today as it did when finished in 1408.

Imagine being a worshipper here the day it was unveiled—mesmerized by this sweeping story told in more than 300 panels of painted glass climaxing with the Apocalypse. It's a medieval disaster movie—a blockbuster back in 1408—showing the end of the world in fire and flood and pestilence...vivid scenes from the book of Revelation. Angels trumpet disaster against blood-red skies. And there it is, the fifth panel up on the far left side...the devil giving power to the Beast of the Apocalypse, a seven-headed, ten-crowned lion, just as it was written in the Bible.

This must have terrified worshippers. A hundred years before Michelangelo frescoed the story of the beginning and end of time at the Sistine Chapel in Rome, this was unprecedented in its epic scale, and done by one man: John Thornton of Coventry.

Because of the Great East Window's immense size, the east end has an extra layer of supportive stonework, parts of it wide enough to walk along. In fact, for special occasions, the church choir has been known to actually sing from the walkway halfway up the window.

• *Looking under the central altar and choir (or going down a flight of steps) you can see the...*

⑫ Crypt: Here you can view the boundary of the much smaller, but still huge, Norman church from 1100 that stood on this spot (look for the red dots, marking where the Norman church ended, and note how thick the wall was). You can also see some of the old columns and additional remains from the Roman fortress that once stood here, the tomb of St. William of York (actually a Roman sarcophagus that was reused), and the modern concrete save-the-church foundations (much of this church history is covered in the undercroft museum).

• *You'll exit the church through the gift shop in the south transept. If you've yet to climb the* **tower,** *the entrance is in the south transept before the exit. Also before leaving, look for the entrance to the...*

Undercroft Museum: Well-described exhibits follow the history of the site from its origins as a Roman fortress to the founding of an Anglo-Saxon/Viking church, the shift to a Norman place of worship, and finally the construction of the Gothic structure that stands today. The museum fills a space that was excavated following the near collapse of the central tower in 1967.

Videos re-create how the fortress and Norman structure would have been laid out, and various artifacts provide an insight into each period. Highlights include:

• The actual remains of the Roman fort's basilica (its hall of justice), which are viewable through a see-through floor including patches of Roman frescoes from what was the basilica's anteroom.

• The Horn of Ulf, the finest Viking treasure in York. This intricately carved elephant's tusk was presented to the Minster in 1030 by Ulf, a Viking nobleman, as a symbol that he was dedicating his land to God and the Church. Consider the horn's travels: From Indian elephant, to Islamic carvers in southern Italy, to a Viking lord, to this church.

- The personal effects of Archbishop Walter de Gray who, in the 13th century, started the current church.

- The York Gospels manuscript, a thousand-year-old text containing the four gospels. Made by Anglo-Saxon monks at Canterbury, it's the only book in the Minster's collection that dates prior to the Norman Conquest. It is still used to this day to swear in archbishops.

- *This finishes your visit. Before leaving, take a moment to just be in this amazing building. Then, go in peace.*

Nearby: As you leave through the south transept, notice the people-friendly plaza created here and how effectively it ties the church in with the city that stretches before you. To your left is the Roman column from the ancient headquarters, which stood where the Minster stands today (and from where Rome administered the northern reaches of Britannia 1,800 years ago); a statue of Emperor Constantine (for more details, see page 526); and the York Minster Stone Yard, where masons are chiseling stone—as they have for centuries—to keep the religious pride and joy of York standing strong and looking good.

OTHER SIGHTS INSIDE YORK'S WALLS

I've listed these roughly in geographical order, from near the Minster at the northwest end of town to the York Castle Museum at the southeast end.

Note that several of York's glitzier and most heavily promoted sights (including Jorvik Viking Centre, Dig, and Barley Hall) are run by the York Archaeological Trust (YAT). While rooted in real history, YAT attractions are geared primarily toward kids and work hard (some say too hard) to make the history entertaining. If you like their approach and plan to visit several, ask about the various combo-ticket options.

▲Yorkshire Museum

Located in a lush, picnic-perfect park next to the stately ruins of St. Mary's Abbey (described in my "York Walk," earlier), the Yorkshire Museum is the city's serious "archaeology of York" museum. You can't dig a hole in York without hitting some remnant of the city's long past, and most of what's found ends up here. While the hordes line up at Jorvik Viking Centre, this museum has no crowds and provides a broader historical context, with more real artifacts. The three main collections—Roman, medieval, and natural history—are well described, bright, and kid friendly.

Cost and Hours: £8, kids under 16 free with paying adult, daily 10:00-17:00, within Museum Gardens, tel. 01904/687-687, www.yorkshiremuseum.org.uk.

Visiting the Museum: At the entrance, you're greeted by an original, early-fourth-century Roman statue of the god Mars. If he could talk, he'd say, "Hear me, mortals. There are three sections here: Roman (on this floor), medieval (downstairs), and natural history (a kid-friendly, fossil-based archaeology wing on this floor opposite the Roman stuff)."

The **Roman** collection starts with a large map of the Roman Empire, set on the floor. Then, in a series of rooms, you'll see slice-of-life exhibits about Roman baths, a huge floor mosaic, and skulls accompanied by artists' renderings of how the people originally looked. (One man was apparently killed by a sword blow to the head—making it graphically clear that the struggle between Romans and barbarians was a violent one.) These artifacts are particularly interesting when you consider that you're standing in one of the farthest reaches of the Roman Empire.

The **medieval** collection is in the basement. During the Middle Ages, York was England's second city. One large room is dominated by ruins of the St. Mary's Abbey complex (described on page 521; one wall of the abbey still stands just out front—be sure to see it before leaving). In the center of the rooms is the Vale of York Hoard, displaying a silver cup and the accompanying treasures it held—more than 600 silver coins as well as silver bars and jewelry. A father-and-son team discovered the hoard (thought to have been buried by Vikings in 927) while out for a day of metal detecting in 2007. You'll also see old weapons, glazed vessels, and a well-preserved 13th-century leather box.

The museum's prized pieces, a helmet and a pendant, are housed in this section. The eighth-century Anglo-Saxon helmet (known as the York Helmet or the Coppergate Helmet) shows a bit of barbarian refinement. Examine the delicate carving on its brass trim. The exquisitely etched 15th-century pendant—called the

Middleham Jewel—is considered the finest piece of Gothic jewelry in Britain. The noble lady who wore this on a necklace believed that it helped her worship and protected her from illness. The back of the pendant, which rested near her heart, shows the Nativity. The front shows the Holy Trinity crowned by a sapphire (which people believed put their prayers at the top of God's to-do list).

In addition to the Anglo-Saxon pieces, the Viking collection is one of the best in England. Looking over the artifacts, you'll find that the Vikings (who conquered most of the Anglo-Saxon lands) wore some pretty decent shoes and actually combed their hair. The Cawood Sword, nearly 1,000 years old, is one of the finest surviving swords from that era.

Barley Hall

Uncovered behind a derelict office block in the 1980s, this medieval house has been restored to replicate a 1483 dwelling. It's designed to resurrect the Tudor age for visiting school groups—but with no historic artifacts other than its half-timbered wall, it feels soulless to adults.

Cost and Hours: £6, combo-tickets with Jorvik Viking Centre and/or Dig, daily 10:00-17:00, Nov-March until 16:00, 2 Coffee Yard off Stonegate, tel. 01904/615-505, www.barleyhall. co.uk.

Holy Trinity Church

Built in the late Perpendicular Gothic style, this church has windows made of precious clear and stained glass from the 13th to 15th century. It holds rare box pews, which rest atop a floor that is sinking as bodies of "the stinking rich" rot and coffins collapse. Enjoy its peaceful picnic-friendly gardens.

Cost and Hours: Free, daily 11:00-15:30, 70 Goodramgate, www.holytrinityyork.org.

Richard III Museum

The last king of England's Plantagenet dynasty got a bad rap from Shakespeare (the Tudors took over after Richard was killed in 1485, so Shakespeare followed the party line and demonized him as a hunchbacked monster). With the discovery of Richard's remains in Leicester in 2013, interest in him has skyrocketed, and this exhibit tries to excite visitors with all the blood and gore of that era, but it lacks any historic artifacts. Richard III groupies find it worth the time and money.

Cost and Hours: £3.50, daily 10:00-17:00, Monk Bar, tel. 01904/615-505, http://richardiiiexperience.com.

King's Square

This lively people-watching zone, with its inviting benches, once hosted a church. Then it was the site for the town's gallows. Today, it's prime real estate for buskers and street performers. Just hanging out here can be entertaining. Beyond is the most characteristic and touristy street in old York: The Shambles. Within sight of this lively square are plenty of cheap eating options (for tips, see "Eating in York," later).

York's Chocolate Story

Though known mainly for its Roman, Viking, and medieval past, York also has a rich history in chocolate. Throughout the 1800s and 1900s, York was home to three major confectionaries—including Rowntree's, originators of the venerable Kit Kat. This chocolate "museum" is childish and overpriced, with no historic artifacts and in a building with no significance. If you visit, you'll join a tour, which pairs generous samples with the history of York's confectionary connections—and you'll have a chance to make your own chocolate lolly.

Cost and Hours: £13, one-hour tours run every 15 minutes daily starting at 10:00, last tour at 16:00, King's Square, tel. 01904-527-765, www.yorkchocolatestory.com.

Dig

This hands-on, kid-oriented archaeological site gives young visitors an idea of what York looked like during Roman, Viking, medieval, and Victorian eras. Sift through "dirt" (actually shredded tires), dig up reconstructed Roman wall plaster, and take a look at what archaeologists have found recently. Entry is possible only with a one-hour guided tour (departures every 30 minutes); pass waiting time by looking at the exhibits near the entry. The exhibits fill the haunted old St. Saviour's Church.

Cost and Hours: £6.50, combo-tickets with Jorvik Viking Centre and/or Barley Hall, daily 10:00-17:00, Saviourgate, tel. 01904/615-505, www.digyork.com.

▲Merchant Adventurers' Hall

The word "adventurers" refers to investors of the day, and this was a kind of merchants' corporate headquarters/early stock exchange.

Claiming to be the finest surviving medieval guildhall in Britain (built from 1357 to 1361), the vast half-timbered building with marvelous exposed beams contains interesting displays about life and commerce in the Middle Ages when the economy revolved around guilds. You'll see three original, large rooms that are still intact: the great hall itself, where meetings took place;

the undercroft, which housed a hospital and almshouse; and a chapel. Several smaller rooms are filled with exhibits about guilds in this 14th-century world trade center. Sitting by itself in its own little picnic-friendly park, the classic old building is worth a stop even just to see it from the outside. Remarkably, the hall is still owned by the same Merchant Adventurers society that built it 660 years ago (now a modern charitable organization).

Cost and Hours: £7, includes audioguide, Sun-Fri 10:00-16:30, Sat until 13:30, inviting café, south of The Shambles between Fossgate and Piccadilly, tel. 01904/654-818, www.merchantshallyork.org.

▲Jorvik Viking Centre

Take the "Pirates of the Caribbean," sail them northeast and back in time 1,000 years, sprinkle in some real artifacts, and you get Jorvik (YOR-vik). In the late 1970s, more than 40,000 artifacts were dug out of the peat bog right here in downtown York—the UK's largest archaeological dig of Viking-era artifacts. When the archaeologists were finished, developers were allowed to build the big Fenwick Department store next door, and the dig site was converted into this attraction, opened in 1984.

Jorvik blends museum exhibits with a 16-minute ride on theme-park-esque "time capsules" that glide through the re-created Viking street of Coppergate as it looked circa the year 975. Animatronic characters and modern-day interpreters bring the scenes to life. Innovative when it first opened, the commercial success of Jorvik inspired copycat rides/museums all over England. Some love Jorvik, while others call it gimmicky and overpriced. If you think of it as Disneyland with a splash of history, Jorvik's fun. To me, Jorvik is a commercial venture designed for kids, with too much emphasis on its gift shop. But it's also undeniably entertaining, and—if you take the time to peruse its exhibits and substantial museum with a rich trove of Viking artifacts—it can be quite informative.

Cost and Hours: £13, daily 10:00-17:00, Nov-March until 16:00, these are last-entry times, tel. 01904/615-505, www.jorvik-viking-centre.co.uk.

Crowd-Beating Tips: This popular attraction can come with long lines—especially during school breaks and mid-July through August. At the busiest times (roughly 11:00-15:00), you may have to wait an hour or more. For £2 extra, you can book a slot in advance, either over the phone or on their website. Or avoid the worst lines by coming early or late in the day.

▲Fairfax House

This well-furnished home, one of the first Georgian townhouses in England, is perfectly Neoclassical inside. Its seven rooms on two floors are each staffed by pleasant docents eager to talk with you. They'll explain how the circa-1760 home was built as the dowry for an aristocrat's daughter. The house is compact and bursting with stunning period furniture (the personal collection of a local chocolate magnate), gorgeously restored woodwork, and lavish stucco ceilings that offer clues as to each room's purpose. For example, stucco philosophers look down on the library, while the goddess of friendship presides over the drawing room. Taken together, this house provides fine insights into aristocratic life in 18th-century England.

Cost and Hours: £7.50, Tue-Sat 10:00-17:00, Sun 11:00-16:00, Mon by one-hour guided tour only at 11:00 and 14:00, closed Jan-mid-Feb, near Jorvik Viking Centre at 29 Castlegate, tel. 01904/655-543, www.fairfaxhouse.co.uk.

Clifford's Tower

Perched high on a knoll across from the York Castle Museum, this ruin is all that's left of York's 13th-century castle. It's a textbook example of the basic Norman castle "motte-and-bailey" design: a manmade hill with a fort (motte) with a circular stockade (bailey) at its foot. The bailey's footprint can be seen today, nearly a thousand years later, in the grassy, circular Eye of York courtyard across from Clifford's Tower (and surrounded by Georgian buildings).

Cost and Hours: £5, daily 10:00-18:00, closes earlier off-season, tel. 01904/646-940, www.english-heritage.org.uk.

Background: Clifford's Tower is a memorial to medieval anti-Semitism. Throughout European history, moneylenders were often Jews. During bad times, frustrated Christians vented (and wiped clean their debts) by massacring those they called "Christ-killers" in their town.

In 1190, after the coronation of Richard I, anti-Semitism was considered patriotic. (Nobles encouraged angry racism—calling England's Jews something akin to "rapists and murderers"— to stoke their base.) Taking the convenient cue, the angry mobs of York chased local Jews into the tower. An estimated 150 Jews locked themselves inside and, rather than face forced conversion or death at the hands of the bloodthirsty mob, they committed ritual suicide. The crowd then set the tower ablaze. (Read the whole story on the sign at the base of the hill.) Today, daffodils, with their six-pointed flowers recalling the Star of David, are planted as a memorial on the slopes leading to the tower.

The present tower was built 60 years after the massacre, but historians think the earthen mound may still hold evidence from the tragedy. If you go inside, you'll see a model of the original castle complex as it looked in the Middle Ages, and you can climb up to enjoy fine city views from the top of the ramparts—but neither is worth the cost of admission.

▲▲York Castle Museum

This fascinating social-history museum is a Victorian home show, one of the closest things to a time-tunnel experience England has to offer. The one-way plan ensures that you'll see everything, including remakes of rooms from the 17th to 20th century, a re-creation of a Victorian street, a heartfelt WWI exhibit, and eerie prison cells.

Cost and Hours: £10, kids under 16 free with adult, daily 9:30-17:00, roaming guides happily answer your questions (no audioguide), cafeteria at entrance, tel. 01904/687-687, www.yorkcastlemuseum.org.uk. It's at the bottom of the hop-on, hop-off bus route. The museum can call you a taxi (worthwhile if you're hurrying to the National Railway Museum, across town).

Visiting the Museum: The exhibits are divided between two wings: the North Building (the former women's prison, to the left as you enter) and the South Building (former debtors' prison, to the right).

Follow the one-way route, starting in the **North Building**. You'll first visit the Period Rooms, illuminating Yorkshire lifestyles during different time periods (1600s-1950s) and among various walks of life. Toy Stories is an enchanting review of toys through the ages. Next is the Shaping the Body exhibit, detailing diet and fashion trends over the last 400 years. Check out the codpieces, bustles, and corsets that used to "enhance" the human form, and ponder some of the odd diet fads that make today's craziest diets seem normal. For foodies and chefs, the exhibit showcasing fireplaces and kitchens from the 1600s to the 1980s is especially tasty.

YORK

Next, stroll down the museum's re-created Kirkgate, a street from the Victorian era (1890s), when Britain was at the peak of its power. It features old-time shops and storefronts, including a pharmacist, sweet shop, school, and grocer for the working class, along with roaming live guides in period

dress. Around the back is a slum area depicting how the poor lived in those times.

Circle back to the entry and cross over to the **South Building**. In the WWI exhibit you can follow the lives of five York citizens as they experience the horrors and triumphs of the war years. One room plunges you into the gruesome world of trench warfare, where the average life expectancy was six weeks (and if you fell asleep during sentry duty, you'd be shot). A display about the home front notes that York suffered from Zeppelin attacks in which six died. At the end you're encouraged to share your thoughts in a room lined with chalkboards.

Exit outside and cross the castle yard. A detour to the left leads to a flour mill (open sporadically). Otherwise, your tour continues through the door on the right, where you'll find another reconstructed historical street, this one capturing the spirit of the swinging 1960s—"a time when the cultural changes were massive but the cars and skirts were mini." Slathered with DayGlo colors, this street scene examines fashion, music,

and television (including clips of beloved kids' shows and period news reports).

Finally, head into the York Castle Prison, which recounts the experiences of actual people who were thrown into the clink here. Videos, eerily projected onto the walls of individual cells, show actors telling tragic stories about the cells' one-time inhabitants.

ACROSS THE RIVER
▲▲National Railway Museum

If you like model railways, this is train-car heaven. The thunderous museum—displaying 200 illustrious years of British railroad history—is one of the biggest and best railroad museums anywhere.

Cost and Hours: Free but £5 suggested donation, daily 10:00-

18:00, lockers-£3, café, restaurant, tel. 0333-016-1010, www. railwaymuseum.org.uk.

Getting There: It's about a 15-minute walk from the Minster (southwest of town, behind the train station). From the TI walk

down Museum Street and cross the Lendal Bridge, then take a right and follow the signs. To skip the walk, a cute little "road train" shuttles you more quickly between the Minster and the Railway Museum (£3 one-way, runs daily Easter-Oct, leaves museum every 30 minutes 11:00-16:00 at :00 and :30 past each hour; leaves town—from Duncombe Place, 100 yards in front of the Minster—at :15 and :45 past each hour).

Visiting the Museum: Pick up the floor plan to locate the various exhibits, which sprawl through several gigantic buildings on both sides of the street. Throughout the complex are info stands with staff eager to talk trains and give directions.

The museum's most impressive room is the **Great Hall** (head right from the entrance area and take the stairs to the underground passage). Fanning out from this grand

roundhouse is an array of historic cars and engines, starting with the very first "stagecoaches on rails," with a crude steam engine from 1830. You'll trace the evolution of steam-powered transportation, from a replica of the Rocket (one of the first successful steam locomotives) to the era of the aerodynamic Mallard (famous as the first train to travel at a startling two miles per minute—a marvel back in 1938) and the striking Art Deco-style Duchess of Hamilton. The collection spans to the present day, with a replica of the Eurostar (Chunnel) train and the Shinkansen Japanese bullet train. Other exhibits include a steam engine that's been sliced open to show its cylinders, driving wheels, and smoke box, as well as a working turntable that's put into action twice a day. The Mallard Experience simulates a ride on the Mallard.

In the **North Shed** you find **The Works**—an actual workshop where engineers scurry about, fixing old trains. Live train switch-boards show real-time rail traffic on the East Coast Main Line.

Next to the diagrammed screens, you can look out to see the actual trains moving up and down the line. **The Warehouse** is loaded with more than 10,000 items relating to train travel (including dinnerware, signage, and actual trains). Exhibits feature dining cars, post cars, sleeping cars, train posters, and info on the Flying Scotsman (the first London-Edinburgh express rail service, now running all over Britain in private tours).

Crossing back to the entrance side, continue to the Station Hall, with a collection of older trains, including ones that the royals have used to ride the rails. One of these includes Queen Victoria's lavish royal car and a WWII royal carriage reinforced with armor. Behind the hall are the South Yard and the Depot, with actual working trains in storage. Families and die-hard train fans can hop on a steam train for a 10-minute ride (£4, daily 11:30-16:00, every 30 minutes).

OUTSIDE TOWN
▲Ouse Riverside Walk or Bike Ride

The New Walk is a mile-long, tree-lined riverside lane created in the 1730s as a promenade for York's dandy class to stroll, see, and be seen—and is a fine place for today's visitors to walk or bike. This hour-long walk is a delightful way to enjoy a dose of countryside away from York. It's paved, illuminated in the evening, and a popular jogging route any time of day.

Start from the riverside under Skeldergate Bridge (near the York Castle Museum) and walk south away from town for a mile. Notice modern buildings across the river, with their floodwalls. Shortly afterward, you cross the tiny River Foss on Blue Bridge, originally built in 1738. The easily defended confluence of the Foss and the Ouse is the reason the Romans founded York in AD 71. Look back to see the modern floodgate (built after a flood in 1979) designed to stop the flooding Ouse from oozing up the Foss. At the bridge, a history panel describes this walk to the Millennium Bridge.

Stroll until you hit the striking, modern **Millennium Bridge.** Sit a bit on its reclining-lounge-chair fence and enjoy the vibrations of bikes and joggers as they pass. There's a strong biking trend in Britain. The British have won many Olympic gold medals in cycling. In 2012, Bradley Wiggins became Sir Bradley Wiggins by winning the Tour de France; his countryman Chris Froome won it in several subsequent years, and Mark Cavendish has won 30 Tour de France stages. You'll see lots of locals riding fancy bikes and wearing high-tech gear while getting into better shape. (Energetic bikers can continue past the Millennium Bridge 14 miles to the market town of Selby.)

Cross the river and take a right to walk back home. Continue along the river until you come to the skateboard court. Here you can enter **Rowntree Park** through its fine old gate. This park was financed by Joseph Rowntree, a wealthy chocolate baron with a Quaker ethic of contributing to his community. In the 19th century, life for the poor was a Charles Dickens-like struggle. A rich man building a park for the working class, which even had a swimming pool, was quite progressive. Victorian England had a laissez-faire approach to social issues. Then, like now, many wealthy people believed things would work out for the poor if the government just stayed out of it. However, others, such as the Rowntree family, felt differently. Their altruism contributed to the establishment of a society that now takes much better care of its workers and poor.

Walk directly into the park toward the evocative Industrial Age housing complex capping the hill beyond the central fountain. In the park's brick gazebo are touching memorial plaques to WWI and WWII deaths. Rowntree also gave this park to York to remember those lost in the "Great War." Stroll along the delightful, duck-filled pond near the Rowntree Park Café, return to the riverside lane, and continue back into York. You're almost home.

YORK

Shopping in York

With its medieval lanes lined with classy as well as tacky little shops, York is a hit with shoppers. I find two kinds of shopping in York particularly interesting: antique malls and charity shops.

Antique Malls: Two places within a few blocks of each other are filled with stalls and cases owned by antique dealers from the countryside (all open daily). The malls, a warren of rooms on three floors with cafés buried deep inside, sell the dealers' bygones on commission. Serious shoppers do better heading for the country, but if you brake for garage sales you'll love these: The **Antiques Centre York** (41 Stonegate, www.theantiquescentreyork. co.uk), and the **Red House Antiques Centre** (a block from the Minster at Duncombe Place, www.redhouseyork.co.uk).

Charity Shops: In towns all over Britain, it seems one low-rent street is lined with charity shops, allowing locals to both donate their junk and buy the junk of others in the name of a good cause. (Talk about a win-win.) It's great for random shopping. And, as the people working there are often volunteers involved in that cause, it can lead to some interesting conversations. In York, on Goodramgate (stretching a block or so from the town wall), you'll find "thrift shops" run by the British Heart Foundation, Mind, and Oxfam. Good deals abound on clothing, purses, accessories, children's toys, books, CDs, and maybe even a guitar. If you buy something, you're getting a bargain and at the same time helping the poor, mentally ill, elderly, or even a pet in need of a vet (stores generally open between 9:00 and 10:00 and close between 16:00 and 17:00, with shorter hours on Sun).

Nightlife in York

PUBS

Even more than chocolate, York likes its beer. Many pubs serve inexpensive plates at lunch, then focus on selling beer in the evening.

Others offer lunch and early dinner. You can tell by their marketing how enthusiastic they are about cooking versus drawing pints. While I've listed good eating pubs under "Eating in York," later, here are a few pubs I'd recommend to give your beer drinking an atmospheric kick:

The Maltings, just over Lendal Bridge, has classic pub ambience. While local beer purists swear by this place, the owners don't allow swearing or music... which shapes the clientele. The pub's fine local and international beers and light-and-mellow vibe are conducive to drinking and talking. They do serve light lunches (simple salads and sandwiches only 12:00-14:00; cross the bridge and look down and left to Tanners Moat, tel. 01904/655-387).

The Blue Bell is one of my favorites for old-school York vibes. This tiny, traditional establishment with a time-warp Edwardian interior is the smallest pub in York. It has two distinct and inviting little rooms (no music, east end of town at 53 Fossgate, tel. 01904/654-904).

The House of the Trembling Madness is another fine watering hole with a cozy atmosphere; it sits above a "bottle shop" that sells a stunning variety of beers by the bottle to go (48 Stonegate).

Evil Eye Lounge, a hit with York's young crowd, is a creaky, funky, hip space famous for its strong cocktails and edgy ambience. There are even beds to drink in. You can order downstairs at the bar (with a small terrace out back) or head upstairs (42 Stonegate, tel. 01904/640-002).

The Golden Fleece claims to be the oldest and most haunted coaching inn in York (music nightly at 21:00, 16 Pavement, see listing in "Eating in York," later).

    Riverside Eating and Drinking: On sunny days, there are several pubs with riverside tables just below Ouse Bridge, starting with **The Kings Arms,** which boasts flood marks inside its door and has a rougher local crowd than other recommended pubs. For a cheap thrill, grab a pint indoors and sit outside at their rustic picnic tables (3 King's Staith, tel. 01904/659-435).

ENTERTAINMENT
Theatre Royal
This spiffed-up theater sporting an 18th-century facade offers a full variety of dramas, comedies, and works by Shakespeare. The locals are proud of the state-of-the-art main theater and little 100-seat theater-in-the-round (tickets £15-35, shows usually Tue-Sat at 19:30, tickets easy to get, on St. Leonard's Place near Bootham Bar and a 5- to 10-minute walk from recommended B&Bs, booking tel. 01904/623-568, www.yorktheatreroyal.co.uk). Those under 18 and students of any age can get tickets for £10-15.

Ghost Tours
You'll see fliers, signs, and promoters hawking a variety of entertaining after-dark tours. For a rundown on this scene, see page 518.

Movies
The centrally located **City Screen Cinema,** right on the river, plays both art-house and mainstream flicks. They also have an enticing café/bar overlooking the river that serves good food (13 Coney Street, tel. 0871-902-5726). The Art Deco **Everyman Cinema** is another good option (near the train station on Blossom Street, tel. 0872-436-9060).

Sleeping in York

July through October are the busiest (and usually most expensive) months. B&Bs often charge more for weekends and sometimes turn away one-night bookings, particularly for peak-season Saturdays. (York is worth two nights anyway.) Prices may spike for horse races and Bank Holidays (about 20 nights a season). Remember to book ahead during festival times (see "Helpful Hints" on page 515) and weekends year-round.

B&Bs AND GUESTHOUSES
These places are all small and family-run. They come with plenty of steep stairs (and no elevators) but no traffic noise. Rooms can be tight; if maneuverability is important, say so when booking. For a good selection, contact them well in advance. Most have permits to lend for street parking.

    The handiest B&B neighborhood is the quiet residential area

just outside the old town wall's Bootham Bar, along the road called Bootham. All of these are within a 10-minute walk of the Minster and TI, and a 5- to 15-minute walk from the station. If driving, head for the cathedral and follow the medieval wall to Bootham Bar. The street called Bootham leads away from Bootham Bar.

Getting There: From the train station it's an easy five-minute walk to the B&B neighborhood: Head to the north end of the station along track 2 (past the York Tap pub and racks of bicycles) and into the short-stay parking lot. You'll continue essentially straight along the tracks, never taking any stairs, over the river and along a footpath ultimately to a short stairway (on the right) that leads to the base of St. Mary's Street.

On or near Bootham Terrace

$$ St. Raphael Guesthouse, run by Fran and Jamie, has seven comfy rooms. Each is themed after a different York street, and lovingly accented with a fresh rose and home-baked banana bread. For more space, ask for their small apartment with a private entrance and courtyard (RS%, family rooms, 44 Queen Annes Road, tel. 01904/645-028, www.straphaelguesthouse.co.uk, info@straphaelguesthouse.co.uk).

$$ Alcuin Lodge, run by welcoming Darren and Mark, is a cozy place, with five rooms that feel personal (look for Darren's grandmother's vase and dresser) yet up to date (one room with private WC in the hallway just outside; 15 Sycamore Place, tel. 01904/629-837, www.alcuinlodge.com, darren@alcuinlodge.com).

$$ Bronte Guesthouse is a modern B&B with five airy, bright rooms and a lovely back garden. Little extras like a communal fridge stocked with water, ice, and milk and a room for playing cards make it easy to relax (family room available, 22 Grosvenor Terrace, tel. 01904/621-066, www.bronte-guesthouse.com, enquiries@bronte-guesthouse.com, Mick and Mandy).

$$ Arnot House, run by a hardworking daughter-and-mother team, is old-fashioned, homey, and lushly decorated with Victorian memorabilia. The three well-furnished rooms even have little libraries (2-night minimum preferred, no children, huge DVD library, 17 Grosvenor Terrace, tel. 01904/641-966, www.arnothouseyork.co.uk, kim.robbins@virgin.net, Kim and her cats Pickle and Tabitha).

$$ Bootham Guest House features creamy walls and contemporary furniture that are a break from more traditional York B&B decor. Of the eight rooms, six are en suite, while two share a bath (RS%, 56 Bootham Crescent, tel. 01904/672-123, www.boothamguesthouse.co.uk, boothamguesthouse1@hotmail.com, Andrew).

$ Number 34, run by Jason, has five simple, light rooms at fair prices. It has a clean, uncluttered feeling, with modern decor (RS%, ground-floor room, 5-person apartment next door, 34 Bootham Crescent, tel. 01904/645-818, www.number34york.co.uk, enquiries@number34york.co.uk).

$ Queen Annes Guest House has nine basic rooms in two adjacent houses. While it doesn't have the plushest beds or richest decor, this is a respectable, affordable, and clean place to sleep (RS%, family room, lounge, 24 and 26 Queen Annes Road, tel. 01904/629-389, www.queen-annes-guesthouse.co.uk, info@ queen-annes-guesthouse.co.uk, Phil).

On the River

$$ Abbey Guest House is a peaceful refuge overlooking the River Ouse, with five cheerful, beautifully updated, contemporary-style rooms and a cute little garden. A tasty homemade breakfast is served, and the riverview rooms will ramp up your romance with York (RS%, pay laundry service, 13 Earlsborough Terrace, tel. 01904/627-782, www.abbeyguesthouseyork.co.uk, info@ abbeyguesthouseyork.co.uk, welcoming couple Jane and Kingsley).

On St. Mary's Street

$$ Number 23 St. Mary's B&B, run by Simon and his helpful staff, has nine extravagantly decorated and spaciously comfortable rooms, plus a classy lounge and all the doily touches (discount for longer stays, family room, honesty box for drinks and snacks, lots of stairs, 23 St. Mary's, tel. 01904/622-738, www.23stmarys.co.uk, stmarys23@hotmail.com).

$$ Crook Lodge B&B, with six tight but elegantly charming rooms, serves breakfast in an old Victorian kitchen. The 21st-century style somehow fits this old house (one ground-floor room, free parking, quiet, 26 St. Mary's, tel. 01904/655-614, www. crooklodgeguesthouseyork.co.uk, crooklodge@hotmail.com, David and Caroline).

$$ Airden House rents nine nice, mostly traditional rooms, though the two basement-level rooms are more mod—one has a space age-looking hot tub and a separate room with single bed (RS%, lounge, free parking, 1 St. Mary's, tel. 01904/638-915, www.airdenhouse.co.uk, info@airdenhouse.co.uk, Emma and Heather).

$$ Alhambra Court is a family-run hotel with 24 charmingly appointed rooms. Relax outside in the quiet courtyard or inside in the two splendidly decorated lounges (elevator, pay laundry service, free parking, 31 St. Mary's, tel. 01904/628-474, www. alhambracourt.co.uk, stay@alhambracourt.co.uk)

YORK

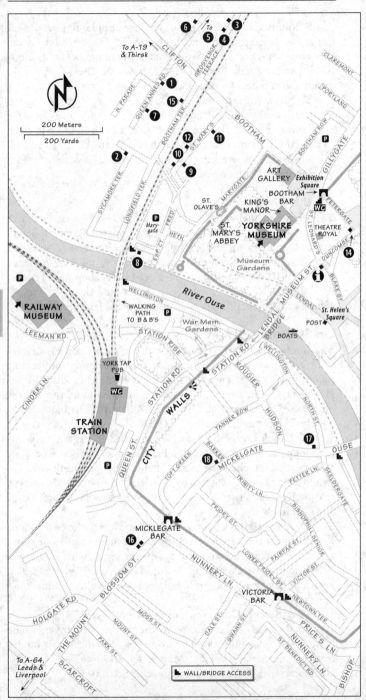

YORK

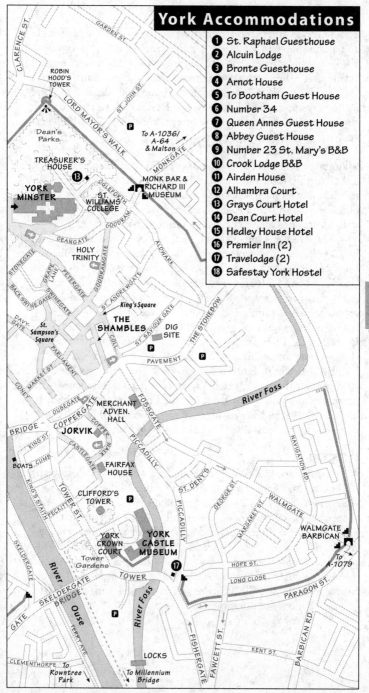

York Accommodations

1. St. Raphael Guesthouse
2. Alcuin Lodge
3. Bronte Guesthouse
4. Arnot House
5. To Bootham Guest House
6. Number 34
7. Queen Annes Guest House
8. Abbey Guest House
9. Number 23 St. Mary's B&B
10. Crook Lodge B&B
11. Airden House
12. Alhambra Court
13. Grays Court Hotel
14. Dean Court Hotel
15. Hedley House Hotel
16. Premier Inn (2)
17. Travelodge (2)
18. Safestay York Hostel

YORK

HOTELS

$$$$ Grays Court Hotel is a historic mansion—the home of dukes and archbishops since 1091—that now rents 12 rooms to travelers. While its public spaces and gardens are lavish, its rooms are elegant yet modest. The creaky, historic nature of the place makes for a memorable stay. If it's too pricey for lodging, consider coming here for its fine-dining **$$$$ Bow Room Restaurant** serving modern English cuisine (Chapter House Street, tel. 01904/612-613, www.grayscourtyork.com).

$$$ Dean Court Hotel, a Best Western facing the Minster, is a big stately hotel with classy lounges and 37 comfortable rooms. It has a great location and friendly vibe for a business-class establishment. A few rooms have views for no extra charge—try requesting one (elevator, restaurant, Duncombe Place, tel. 01904/625-082, www.deancourt-york.co.uk, sales@deancourt-york.co.uk).

$$$ Hedley House Hotel, well run by a wonderful family, has 30 clean and spacious rooms. The outdoor hot tub/sauna is a fine way to end your day, or you can sign up for yoga or Pilates (ask for a deal with stay of three or more nights, family rooms, good two-course evening meals, in-house massage and beauty services, free parking, 3 Bootham Terrace, tel. 01904/637-404, www.hedleyhouse.com, greg@hedleyhouse.com, Greg and Louise Harrand). They also have three luxury studio apartments—see their website for details.

Budget Chain Hotels: If looking for something a little less spendy than the hotels listed above, consider several chains with central locations in town. These include **Premier Inn** (two branches side-by-side) and **Travelodge** (one location near the York Castle Museum at 90 Piccadilly; second location on Micklegate).

HOSTEL

¢ Safestay York is a boutique hostel on a rowdy street (especially on Fridays and Saturdays). Located in a big old Georgian house, they rent 158 beds in 4- to 12-bed rooms, with great views, private prefab "pod" bathrooms, and reading lights for each bed. They also offer fancier, hotel-quality doubles (family room for up to four, continental breakfast extra, 4 floors, no elevator, air-con, Wi-Fi in public areas only, self-service laundry, TV lounge, game room, bar, lockers, no curfew, 5-minute walk from train station at 88 Micklegate, tel. 01904/627-720, www.safestay.com/ss-york-micklegate.html, reception-yk@safestay.com).

YORK

Eating in York

York is a great food city, with a wide range of ethnic options and foodie bistros. Thanks to the local high-tech industry, the university, and tourism, there's a demand that sustains lots of creative and fun eateries.

If you're in a hurry or on a tight budget, picnic and light-meals-to-go options abound, and it's easy to find a churchyard, bench, or riverside perch where you can munch. On a sunny day, perhaps the best picnic spots in town are under the evocative 12th-century ruins of St. Mary's Abbey in the Museum Gardens (near Bootham Bar), in the park surrounding the Minster, or in the yard of little Holy Trinity Church (on Goodramgate).

Most bistros have good-quality, creative vegetarian options and offer economical lunch specials and early dinners (generally order by 18:30). After 19:00 or so, main courses cost £16-26 and fixed-price meals (two or three courses) go for around £25. If you're set on a particular place for dinner, reservations are often smart.

IN THE CITY CENTER
Fine Dining
$$$$ Skosh serves a smart local clientele gourmet tapas—modern, creative, and sharable small dishes that are a fusion of English and international cuisine. Its bright dining room is loud and fun, with an open kitchen adding energy to the mix. It's top quality with no pretense. The four stools at the bar are nice if you like watching the chef at work (£10 plates—three or four per person makes a meal, Wed-Sat 12:00-14:00 & 17:30-22:00, closed Sun-Tue, 98 Micklegate, tel. 01904/634-849).

Cheap Eats Around King's Square
King's Square is about as central as can be for sightseers. And from here, you can actually see several fine quick-and-cheap lunch options. After buying your takeout food, sit on the square and enjoy the street entertainers. Or, for a peaceful place to eat more prayerfully, find the Holy Trinity Church yard, with benches amid the old tombstones on Goodramgate (half a block to the right of York Roast Company).

$ York Roast Company is a local fixture, serving their Yorkshire pudding wrap (a kind of old English burrito) and hearty pork sandwiches with applesauce, stuffing, and "crackling" (roasted bits of fat and skin). If Henry VIII wanted fast food, he'd have eaten here (daily 10:00-23:00, order at counter then eat upstairs or take away for the same price, 74 Low Petergate, tel. 01904/629-197, second location at 4 Stonegate).

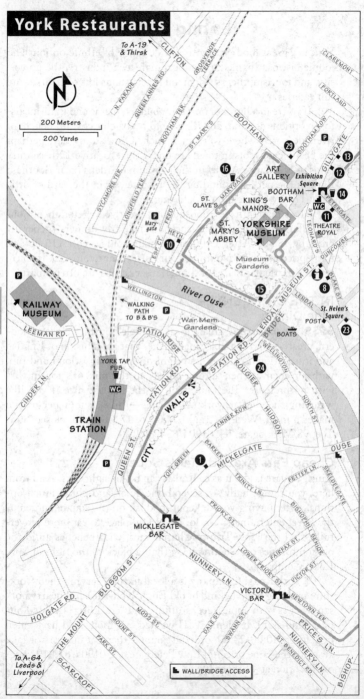

York Restaurants

YORK

Map labels:

To A-19 & Thirsk

CLIFTON

GROSVENOR TERRACE

CLAREMONT

PORTLAND

N. PARADE

QUEEN ANNE'S RD.

BOOTHAM TER.

ST. MARY'S

BOOTHAM

BOOTHAM ROW

GILLYGATE

200 Meters
200 Yards

SYCAMORE TER.

LONGFIELD TER.

MARYGATE

16

ART GALLERY

Exhibition Square

29

13

12

ST. OLAVE'S

KING'S MANOR

BOOTHAM BAR

WC

PETERGATE

14

11

ESP. CT.

FRED.

HETH.

Marygate

10

ST. MARY'S ABBEY

YORKSHIRE MUSEUM

ST. LEONARD'S

DUNCOMBE

THEATRE ROYAL

P

RAILWAY MUSEUM

WELLINGTON

River Ouse

Museum Gardens

15

LENDAL MUSEUM ST.

i

8

BLAKE ST.

LENDAL

St. Helen's Square

LEEMAN RD.

CINDER LN.

WALKING PATH TO B & B'S

War Mem. Gardens

STATION RISE

BRIDGE

POST

23

BOATS

WELLINGTON

NORTH ST.

OUSE

YORK TAP PUB

WC

STATION RD.

STATION RD.

ROUGIER

24

TRAIN STATION

QUEEN ST.

CITY

WALLS

TANNER ROW

HUDSON

QUEEN ST.

P

BARKER

TOFT GREEN

1

MICKELGATE

FETTER LN.

SKELDERGATE

TRINITY LN.

PRIORY ST.

BISHOPHILL SENIOR

MICKLEGATE BAR

HOLGATE RD.

NUNNERY LN.

LOWER PRIORY ST.

FAIRFAX ST.

VICTOR ST.

THE MOUNT

BLOSSOM ST.

MOSS ST.

DALE ST.

SWANN ST.

VICTORIA BAR

NEWTOWN TER.

PRICE'S LN.

To A-64, Leeds & Liverpool

SCARCROFT

PARK ST.

MOUNT ST.

NUNNERY LN.

ST. BENEDICT RD.

BISHOP.

WALL/BRIDGE ACCESS

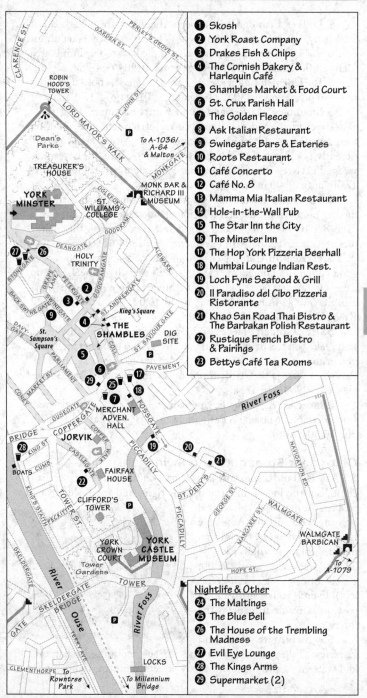

1. Skosh
2. York Roast Company
3. Drakes Fish & Chips
4. The Cornish Bakery & Harlequin Café
5. Shambles Market & Food Court
6. St. Crux Parish Hall
7. The Golden Fleece
8. Ask Italian Restaurant
9. Swinegate Bars & Eateries
10. Roots Restaurant
11. Café Concerto
12. Café No. 8
13. Mamma Mia Italian Restaurant
14. Hole-in-the-Wall Pub
15. The Star Inn the City
16. The Minster Inn
17. The Hop York Pizzeria Beerhall
18. Mumbai Lounge Indian Rest.
19. Loch Fyne Seafood & Grill
20. Il Paradiso del Cibo Pizzeria Ristorante
21. Khao San Road Thai Bistro & The Barbakan Polish Restaurant
22. Rustique French Bistro & Pairings
23. Bettys Café Tea Rooms

YORK

Nightlife & Other
24. The Maltings
25. The Blue Bell
26. The House of the Trembling Madness
27. Evil Eye Lounge
28. The Kings Arms
29. Supermarket (2)

$ Drakes Fish & Chips, across the street from York Roast Company, is a local favorite chippy. While it's mostly takeout, for £3 extra you can sit and eat in their simple backroom dining area (daily 11:00-22:30, 97 Low Petergate, tel. 01904/624-788).

$ The Cornish Bakery, facing King's Square, cooks up pasties to eat in or take away (30 Colliergate, tel. 01904/671-177).

$ Shambles Market and Food Court has many food stalls and street-food vendors—like a corral of food trucks—offering fun, nutritious, and ethnic light meals. The Moros stand is particularly popular for its North African plates. This lively scene is wedged between The Shambles and Parliament Street (daily 7:00-17:00, until 16:00 in winter).

$ St. Crux Parish Hall is a medieval church now used by a medley of charities that sell tea, homemade cakes, and light meals (Tue-Sat 10:00-16:00, closed Sun-Mon, at bottom of The Shambles at its intersection with Pavement, tel. 01904/621-756).

$ Harlequin Café, a charming place, is appreciated for its good coffee and homemade cakes, as well as its light meals. It's up a creaky staircase overlooking King's Square. On weekend nights it morphs into a gin bar (Mon-Sat 10:00-16:00, Sun 11:00-15:00, 2 King's Square, tel. 01904/630-631).

$$ The Golden Fleece is a sloppy, dingy place with tilty floors that make you feel drunk even if you aren't. It's a good bet for casual pub grub in a characteristic setting, with music nightly at 21:00 (16 Pavement, across the street from the southern end of The Shambles, tel. 01904/625-171).

Groceries: A Marks & Spencer Food Hall is a block away from Shambles Market on Parliament Street (Mon-Sat 8:00-18:30, Sun 10:30-17:00).

On or near Stonegate and Swinegate

$$ Ask Italian Restaurant is part of a cheap and cheery Italian chain, but the food's fine, the price is right, and you'll slurp your pasta in the majestic Neoclassical hall of York's Grand Assembly Rooms, lined with Corinthian marble columns (daily 11:00-22:00, weekends until 23:00; Blake Street, tel. 01904/637-254). Even if you're just walking past, peek inside to gape at the interior.

$$ Swinegate Bars and Eateries: Take your pick of the various tempting restaurants and watering holes on this touristy street. Some are trendy, with thumping music, while others are tranquil; some have elaborately decorated dining rooms, while others emphasize heated courtyards.

NEAR BOOTHAM BAR AND RECOMMENDED B&Bs

$$$$ Roots Restaurant feels formal and romantic, with a classy dining room and small gourmet dishes designed to be enjoyed family-style. To fully appreciate esteemed chef Tommy Banks' modern English cuisine, I'd opt for the £55 tasting menu (lots of fine wine by the glass, lunch from noon, dinner 17:30-21:00, closed Tue, 68 Marygate, no phone, reserve at info@rootsyork. co.uk or www.rootsyork.com).

$$ Café Concerto, a casual and cozy bistro with wholesome food and a charming musical theme, has an understandably loyal following. The fun menu features updated English favorites with some international and vegetarian options (daily 9:30-17:00, facing the Minster at 21 High Petergate, tel. 01904/610-478, www. cafeconcerto.biz).

$$$ Café No. 8 is a romantic and modern little bistro. Grab one of the tables in front or in the sunroom, or enjoy a shaded little garden out back if the weather's good. Chef Chris Pragnell uses what's fresh in the market to shape his simple, elegant, and creative modern British menu. There's an early dinner special Tuesday through Thursday until 18:30 (Mon 12:00-16:00, Tue-Fri 12:00-22:00, Sat 9:00-22:00, Sun until 16:00, 8 Gillygate, tel. 01904/653-074, www.cafeno8.co.uk).

$$ Mamma Mia Italian Restaurant is a popular choice for its pizza, pasta, and a full menu of Italian *secondi*. The casual, garlicky eating area features a tempting gelato bar, and in nice weather the back patio is *molto bello* (Tue-Sun 11:30-14:00 & 17:30-23:00, closed Mon, 20 Gillygate, tel. 01904/622-020).

$$ Hole-in-the-Wall Pub is the place if you're looking for a ye olde pub with good grub and a £10 dinner. They have an extensive menu with light bites, burgers, fish-and-chips, meat pies, and veggie dishes—and it's a fine spot for a traditional Yorkshire pudding. The atmosphere is your English pub dream come true (daily 11:30-22:00, on High Petergate just inside Bootham Bar, tel. 01904/634-468).

$$$ The Star Inn the City has a quality reputation for modern Yorkshire cuisine and a dressy dining hall. Lunch is served on its enticing riverside terrace, but in the evening that's for drinks only (daily 12:00-22:00, next to the river in Lendal Engine House, Museum Street, tel. 01904/619-208, www.starinnthecity.co.uk).

$$ The Minster Inn, an Edwardian alehouse serving stonebaked pizzas, tapas, and a good selection of cask ales and wines, is a friendly neighborhood hangout with an open courtyard

YORK

that's fun in the summer (daily 12:00-23:00, 24 Marygate, tel. 01904/849-240).

Groceries: Sainsbury is handy for picnic provisions or a simple cheap dinner in your B&B room (daily 6:00-24:00, 50 yards outside Bootham Bar, on Bootham).

AT THE EAST END OF TOWN

This neighborhood is across town from my recommended B&Bs, but still central (and a short walk from the York Castle Museum). These places are all hits with local foodies; reservations are smart for all. The emerging bohemian-chic axis of Fossgate/Walmgate is lined with quality restaurants and has an inviting, untouristy energy.

$$ The Hop York Pizzeria Beerhall is a favorite for its simple approach and winning combo: pizza and beer. The pub pulls real ales in the front, serves wood-fired pies in an inviting space in the back, and offers live music featuring rock and pop covers (daily 12:00-23:00, food served until 21:00—Sun until 20:00, music Wed-Sun at 21:00; 11 Fossgate, tel. 01904/541-466).

$$ Mumbai Lounge Indian Restaurant (named for its top-floor lounge) is a local choice for Indian food (daily 12:00-14:00 & 17:30-23:30, 47 Fossgate, tel. 01904/654-155, www.mumbailoungeyork.co.uk).

$$ Loch Fyne Seafood and Grill is a fine fish value with an inviting and affordable menu served in a classic and spacious old hall. While a national chain, it still feels smart and has a caring waitstaff. Their three-course, £13 lunch special is served until 18:00 (daily 12:00-22:30, Foss Bridge House, Walmgate, tel. 01904/650-910).

$$$ Il Paradiso del Cibo Pizzeria Ristorante, with its adorable chaos, just feels special. It's an eccentric little place with tight seating, few tourists, and a fun bustle, run by a Sardinian with attitude (cash only, daily 12:00-15:00 & 18:00-22:00, 40 Walmgate, tel. 01904/611-444, www.ilparadisodelciboyork.com).

$$ Khao San Road Thai Bistro hits the spot if you need a Thai fix (daily from 17:00, 52 Walmgate, tel. 01904/635-599).

$$ The Barbakan Polish Restaurant is run by a Krakow family offering an inviting little Polish dining room with a passion for homemade cakes (Mon-Sat 9:00-13:00 & 18:00-22:00, Sun 10:00-21:00, 58 Walmgate, tel. 01904/672-474, www.deli-barbakan.co.uk).

$$$ Rustique French Bistro has one big room of tight tables and walls decorated with simple posters. The place has good prices (£20 three-course meal) and is straight French—right down to the welcome (daily 12:00-22:00, across from Fairfax House at 28 Castlegate, tel. 01904/612-744, www.rustiqueyork.co.uk).

$$ Pairings is a stylish wine bar with small bites, an extensive list of drinks, and a patient and helpful waitstaff. Two travelers can make a meal out of the £23 deli platter (which includes the fun of choosing any three meats or cheeses) and their £14 white or red pairing boards (daily 12:00-23:00, 28 Castlegate, tel. 01904/848-909). For wine lovers, this place can also be a fun stop before or after dinner.

TEAROOM

$$ Bettys Café Tea Rooms is a destination restaurant for many. Choose between a Yorkshire Cream Tea (tea and scones with clotted Yorkshire cream and strawberry jam) or a full traditional English afternoon tea (tea, delicate sandwiches, scones, and sweets). With the afternoon tea, your table is so full of doily niceties that the food is served on a little three-tray  tower. While you'll pay a little extra here, the ambience and people-watching are hard to beat. There's generally a line, but it moves quickly except at dinnertime. (Those just wanting to buy a takeaway pastry can skip the line and go directly to the bakery counter.) They'll offer to seat you sooner in the bigger and less atmospheric basement, but I'd be patient and wait for a place upstairs—ideally by the window. It's permissible for travel partners on a budget to enjoy the experience for about half the price by one ordering a "full tea"—£20, with enough little sandwiches and sweets for two to share—and the other a simple cup of tea (daily 9:00-21:00, tel. 01904/659-142, www.bettys.co.uk, St. Helen's Square). During World War II, Bettys was a drinking hangout for Allied airmen based nearby. Downstairs near the WC is a mirror signed by bomber pilots—read the story.

York Connections

From York by Train to: Durham (4/hour, 50 minutes), **London**'s King's Cross Station (3/hour, 2 hours), **Bath** (hourly with change in Bristol, 4.5 hours, more with additional transfers), **Cambridge** (hourly, 2.5 hours, transfer in Stevenage or Peterborough), **Keswick/Lake District** (train to Penrith: roughly 2/hour, 4 hours,

1-2 transfers; then bus, allow about 5 hours total), **Manchester Airport** (2/hour, 2 hours), **Edinburgh** (2/hour, 2.5 hours). Train info: Tel. 0345-748-4950, www.nationalrail.co.uk.

Connections with London's Airports: Heathrow (allow 4 hours minimum; from airport take Heathrow Express train to London's Paddington Station, transfer by Tube to King's Cross, then take train to York; for details on cheaper but slower Tube or bus option from airport to London King's Cross, see page 196), **Gatwick** (allow 4 hours minimum; from Gatwick South, catch Thameslink train to London's St. Pancras International Station; from there, walk to neighboring King's Cross Station, and catch train to York).

DURHAM & NORTHEAST ENGLAND

Durham • Beamish Museum • Hadrian's Wall

Northeast England harbors some of the country's best historical sights. Go for a Roman ramble at Hadrian's Wall, a reminder that Britain was an important Roman colony 2,000 years ago. Marvel at England's greatest Norman church—Durham's cathedral—and enjoy an evensong service there. At the excellent Beamish Museum, travel back in time to the 19th and 20th centuries.

PLANNING YOUR TIME

For **train** travelers, Durham is the most convenient overnight stop in this region. But it can be problematic to see en route to another destination since there's limited baggage storage in Durham: Either stay overnight, check a baggage-storage website like Stasher. com, or do Durham as a day trip from York. If you like Roman ruins, visit Hadrian's Wall (tricky but doable by public transportation). The Beamish Museum is an easy day trip from Durham (less than an hour by bus).

By **car,** you can easily visit everything in this chapter. Spend a night in Durham and a night near Hadrian's Wall, stopping at the Beamish Museum on your way to Hadrian's Wall.

For the best quick visit to Durham, arrive by midafternoon, in time to tour the cathedral and enjoy the evensong service (Tue-Sat at 17:15, Sun at 15:30; limited access and no tours during June graduation ceremonies). Sleep in Durham. Visit Beamish the next morning before continuing on to your next destination.

Durham

Without its cathedral, Durham would hardly be noticed. But this magnificently situated structure is hard to miss (even if you're zooming by on the train). Seemingly happy to go nowhere, Durham sits along the tight curve of its river, snug below its castle and famous church. It has a medieval, cobbled atmosphere and a scraggly peasant's indoor market just off the main square. Durham is home to England's third-oldest university, with a student vibe jostling against its lingering working-class mining-town feel. You'll see tattooed and pierced people in search of job security and a good karaoke bar. Yet Durham has a youthful liveliness and a small-town warmth that shines—especially on sunny days, when most everyone is out licking ice-cream cones.

Orientation to Durham

As it has for a thousand years, tidy little Durham (pop. 65,000) clusters everything safely under its castle, within the protective hairpin bend of the River Wear.

Because of the town's hilly topography, going just about anywhere involves a lot of up and down...and back up again. The main spine through the middle of town (Framwellgate Bridge, Silver Street, and Market Place) is level to moderately steep, but walking in any direction from that area involves some serious uphill climbing. Take advantage of the handy Cathedral Bus to avoid the tiring elevation changes—especially up to the cathedral and castle area, or to the train station (perched high on a separate hill).

TOURIST INFORMATION

Durham does not have a physical TI, but the town does maintain a call center and a useful website (calls answered Mon-Fri 9:00-17:00, tel. 03000-262-626, www.thisisdurham.com, visitor@ thisisdurham.com).

During the summer, a group of 70 volunteers called **Durham Pointers** staff a tourist information cart in Market Place near the equestrian statue. They hand out free maps of the city and offer unbiased advice on Durham attractions—tell them Rick Steves sent you (late May-early Oct Mon-Fri 9:30-15:00, Sat 10:00-14:30, Sun 11:00-15:00, mobile 0758-233-2621, www.durhampointers.co.uk).

Though not an official TI, the **Durham World Heritage Site Visitor Centre** near the Palace Green can offer some guidance, including a short video on the town. They also sell tickets to tour the castle (center open daily 9:30-17:00, 7 Owengate, tel. 0191/334-3805, www.durhamworldheritagesite.com, visitor.centre@durham.ac.uk).

ARRIVAL IN DURHAM

By Train: From the train station, the fastest and easiest way to reach the cathedral is to hop on the **Cathedral Bus** (described later, under "Getting Around Durham"). But the town's setting—while steep in places—is enjoyable to stroll through (and you can begin my self-guided walk halfway through, at the Framwellgate Bridge).

To **walk** into town, follow the *walkway route to Durham city* signs exiting the station and head along the road downhill to the second pedestrian turnoff (the spiral one within sight of the railway bridge), which leads almost immediately over a bridge above busy road A-690. From here, you can bypass the bridge and continue straight down the hill to some of my recommended accommodations (using this chapter's map—and the giant rail bridge as a handy landmark). Or cross the pedestrian bridge and take North Road into town to reach other hotels, the river, and the cathedral.

By Car: Drivers simply surrender to the wonderful 400-space Prince Bishops Shopping Centre parking lot (coming from the A-1/M-1 exit, you'll run right into it at the roundabout at the base of the old town). It's perfectly safe, with 24-hour access. An elevator deposits you right in the heart of Durham (£3.30/up to 4 hours, £11.50/over 6 hours, £1.50/overnight 18:00-8:00, must enter license plate number to use payment machines, cash or credit card with chip, a short block from Market Place, tel. 0191/375-0416, www.princebishops.co.uk).

HELPFUL HINTS

Markets: The main square, known as Market Place, has an indoor market (generally Mon-Sat 9:00-17:00, closed Sun) and hosts outdoor markets (Sat retail market generally 9:30-16:30, farmers' market third Thu of each month 9:30-15:30, tel. 0191/384-6153, www.durhammarkets.co.uk).

Tours: Each Saturday at 14:00 in peak season, **Blue Badge guides** offer 1.5-hour city walking tours (£4, meet at Durham World Heritage Site Visitor Centre, contact TI call center to confirm schedule, tel. 03000-262-626).

GETTING AROUND DURHAM

While all my recommended hotels, eateries, and sights are doable by foot, if you don't feel like walking Durham's hills, hop on the

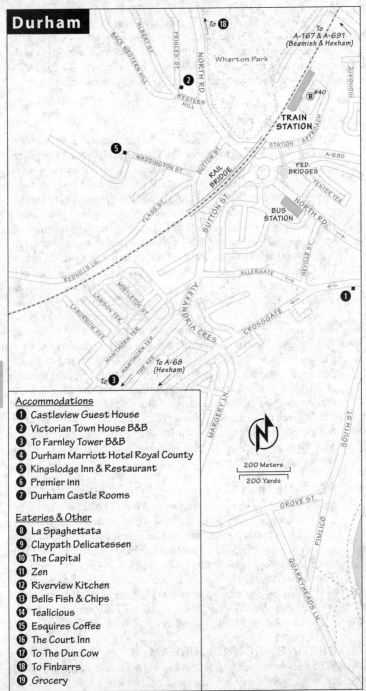

Durham

To 18

To A-167 & A-691 (Beamish & Hexham)

HIGHGATE

Wharton Park

ALBERT ST.

BACK WESTERN HILL

PRINCES ST.

NORTH RD.

2

WESTERN HILL

B #40

TRAIN STATION

STATION APPROACH

A-690

5

WADDINGTON ST.

SUTTON ST.

RAIL BRIDGE

PED. BRIDGES

FLASS ST.

SUTTON ST.

BUS STATION

NORTH RD.

TENTER TER.

KEDHILLS LN.

ALLERGATE

NEVILLE ST.

MISTLETOE ST.

LAWSON TER.

LABURNUM AVE.

HAWTHORN TER.

HAWTHORN TER.

ALEXANDRIA CRES.

CROSSGATE

1

THE AVE.

To A-68 (Hexham)

To **3**

MARGERY LN.

N

200 Meters

200 Yards

GROVE ST.

SOUTH ST.

PIMLICO

QUARRYHEADS LN.

Accommodations

1. Castleview Guest House
2. Victorian Town House B&B
3. To Farnley Tower B&B
4. Durham Marriott Hotel Royal County
5. Kingslodge Inn & Restaurant
6. Premier Inn
7. Durham Castle Rooms

Eateries & Other

8. La Spaghettata
9. Claypath Delicatessen
10. The Capital
11. Zen
12. Riverview Kitchen
13. Bells Fish & Chips
14. Tealicious
15. Esquires Coffee
16. The Court Inn
17. To The Dun Cow
18. To Finbarrs
19. Grocery

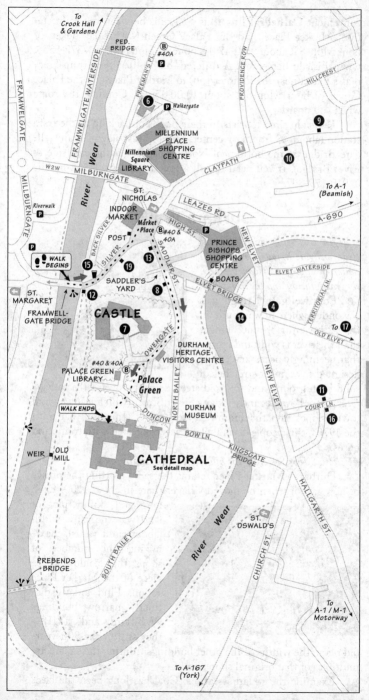

To Crook Hall & Gardens

PED. BRIDGE

FREEMAN'S PL.

(B) #40A

P

PROVIDENCE ROW

HILLCREST

FRAMWELGATE

FRAMWELGATE WATERSIDE

6

P Walkergate

9

10

MILLENNIUM PLACE SHOPPING CENTRE

River Wear

Millennium Square LIBRARY

CLAYPATH

To A-1 (Beamish)

W2W

MILBURNGATE

LEAZES RD.

A-690

MILLBURNGATE

P

Riverwalk

ST. NICHOLAS

INDOOR MARKET

Market Place

HIGH ST.

NEW ELVET

P

BACK SILVER

POST

SILVER

(B) #40 & 40A

PRINCE BISHOPS SHOPPING CENTRE

ELVET WATERSIDE

P

WALK BEGINS

15

19

13

SADDLER ST.

ELVET BRIDGE

BOATS

TERRITORIAL LN.

ST. MARGARET

12

SADDLER'S YARD

8

14

4

To 17

OLD ELVET

FRAMWELGATE BRIDGE

CASTLE

7

OWENGATE

DURHAM HERITAGE VISITORS CENTRE

NEW ELVET

11

COURT LN.

16

#40 & 40A

(B)

PALACE GREEN LIBRARY

Palace Green

NORTH BAILEY

DURHAM MUSEUM

WALK ENDS

DUNCOW

BOW LN.

KINGSGATE BRIDGE

HALLGARTH ST.

WEIR

OLD MILL

CATHEDRAL

See detail map

River Wear

ST. OSWALD'S

CHURCH ST.

SOUTH BAILEY

PREBENDS BRIDGE

To A-1 / M-1 Motorway

To A-167 (York)

DURHAM & NE ENGLAND

convenient **Cathedral Bus.** Bus #40 runs between the train station, Market Place, and the Palace Green (£1 all-day ticket, 3/hour Mon-Sat about 9:00-17:00, none on Sun; tel. 0191/372-5386, www.thisisdurham.com). A different bus (#40A) goes from Freeman's Place (near the Premier Inn) to Market Place and the Palace Green (2/hour Mon-Sat about 10:00-15:45). Confirm the route when you board.

Taxis zip tired tourists to their B&Bs or back up to the train station (about £5 from city center, wait on west side of Framwellgate Bridge at the bottom of North Road or on the east side of Elvet Bridge). If you need to call a taxi, try Polly's Taxis, mobile 07910-179-397.

Durham Walk

• *Begin this self-guided walk at Framwellgate Bridge (down in the center of town, halfway between the train station and the cathedral).*

Framwellgate Bridge was a wonder when it was built in the 12th century—much longer than the river is wide and higher than seemingly necessary. It was designed to connect stretches of solid high ground and to avoid steep descents toward the marshy river. Note how elegantly today's Silver Street (which leads toward town) slopes into the Framwellgate Bridge. (Imagine that until the 1970s, this people-friendly lane was congested with traffic and buses.)

• *Follow Silver Street up the hill to the town's main square.*

Durham's **Market Place** retains the same plotting the prince bishop gave it when he moved villagers here in about 1100. Each

long and skinny plot of land was the same width (about eight yards), maximizing the number of shops that could have a piece of the Market Place action. Find today's distinctly narrow buildings (Whittard and TUI)—they still fit the 900-year-old plan. The widths of the other buildings fronting the square are multiples of that original shop width.

Examine the square's **statues.** Coal has long been the basis

DURHAM & NE ENGLAND

of this region's economy. The statue of Neptune was part of an ill-fated attempt by a coal baron to bribe the townsfolk into embracing a canal project that would make the shipment of his coal more efficient. The statue of the fancy guy on the horse is of Charles Stewart Vane, the Third Marquess of Londonderry. He was an Irish aristocrat and a general in Wellington's army who married a local coal heiress. A clever and aggressive businessman, he managed to create a vast business empire by controlling every link in the coal business chain—mines, railroads, boats, harbors, and so on.

In the 1850s throughout England, towns were moving their markets off squares and into Industrial Age iron-and-glass market halls. Durham was no exception, and today its funky 19th-century **indoor market** (which faces Market Place) is a delight to explore (closed Sun). There are also outdoor markets here on Saturdays and the third Thursday of each month.

Do you enjoy the sparse traffic in Durham's old town? It was the first city in England to institute a "congestion fee." When drivers enter the town Monday through Saturday, a camera snaps a photo of their car's license plate, and the driver must pay £2 that day or face a £50 fine by mail. This has cut downtown traffic by more than 50 percent. Locals brag that London (which now has a similar congestion fee) was inspired by Durham's success.

• *Head up the hill on Saddler Street toward the cathedral, stopping where you reach the chunk of wall at the top of a stairway. On the left, you'll see a bridge.*

A 12th-century construction, **Elvet Bridge** led to a town market over the river. Like Framwellgate, it's very long (17 arches) and designed to avoid riverside muck and steep inclines. Even today, Elvet Bridge leads to an unusually wide road—once swollen to accommodate the market action. Shops lined the right-hand side of Elvet Bridge in the 12th century, as they do today. An alley separated the bridge from the buildings on the left. When the bridge was widened, it met the upper stories of the buildings on the left, which became "street level."

Turn back to look at the chunk of **wall** by the top of the stairs— a reminder of a once-formidable fortification. The Scots, living just 50 miles from here, were on the rampage in the 14th century. After their victory at Bannockburn in 1314, they pushed farther south and actually burned part of Durham. Wary of this new threat, Durham built thick city walls. As people settled within the walls, the population density soared. Soon, open lanes were covered by residences and became tunnels (called "vennels"). A classic vennel leads to Saddlers Yard, a fine little 16th-century courtyard (opposite the wall, look for the yellow Vennels Café sign). While the vennels are cute today, centuries ago they were Dickensian nightmares—the filthiest of hovels.

• *Continue up Saddler Street. Just before the fork at the top of the street, duck through the blue door next to the Georgian Window sign. You'll see a bit of the medieval wall incorporated into the brickwork of a newer building and a turret from an earlier wall. Back on Saddler Street, you can see the ghost of the old wall (picture it standing exactly the width of the building now housing the Salvation Army). Veer right at Owengate*

*as you continue uphill to the Palace Green. (The **Durham World Heritage Site Visitor Centre** is near the top of the hill, on the left.)*

The **Palace Green** was the site of the original 11th-century Saxon town, filling this green between the castle and an earlier church. Later, the town made way for 12th-century Durham's defenses, which now enclose the green. With the threat presented by the Vikings, it's no wonder people found comfort in a spot like this.

The **castle** still stands—as it has for a thousand years—on its motte (man-made mound). Like Oxford and Cambridge, Durham

University is a collection of colleges scattered throughout the town, and even this castle is now part of the school. Look into the old courtyard from the castle gate. It traces the very first and smallest bailey (protected area). As future bishops expanded the castle, they left their coats of arms as a way of "signing" the wing they built. Because the Norman kings appointed prince bishops here to rule this part of their realm, Durham was the seat of power for much of northern England. The bishops had their own army and even minted their own coins. The castle is accessible with a 45-minute guided tour, which includes the courtyard, kitchens, great hall, and chapel (£5, open most days when school is in session—but schedule varies so call ahead, buy tickets at Durham World Heritage Site Visitor Centre or Palace Green Library—

Durham's Early Years

Durham's location, tucked inside a tight bend in the River Wear, was practically custom-made for easy fortifications. But it wasn't settled until 995, with the arrival of St. Cuthbert's body (buried in Durham Cathedral). Shortly after that, a small church and fortification were built upon the site of today's castle and church to house the relic. The castle was a classic "motte-and-bailey" design (with the "motte," or mound, providing a lookout tower for the stockade encircling the protected area, or "bailey"). By 1100, the prince bishop's bailey was filled with villagers—and he wanted everyone out. This was *his* place! He provided a wider protective wall, and had the town resettle below (around today's Market Place). But this displaced the townsfolk's cows, so the prince bishop constructed a fine stone bridge (today's Framwellgate) to connect the new town to grazing land he established across the river. The bridge had a defensive gate, with a wall circling the peninsula and the river serving as a moat.

---

described next, ask about possible self-guided tour in summer only, tel. 0191/334-2932, www.dur.ac.uk/durham.castle).

• *Turning your back to the castle and facing the cathedral, on the right is the university's Palace Green Library.*

The **Palace Green Library** has a free permanent exhibit—*Living on the Hills*—that chronicles 10,000 years of human history on the site of Durham. It also hosts temporary exhibits in both its Wolfson Gallery and Dennyson Stoddart Gallery on everything from rare books to robots. Pop in or check online for current exhibits (temporary exhibits—generally £5, Tue-Sun 10:00-16:30, Mon 12:00-17:00, Palace Green, tel. 0191/334-2932, www.dur.ac.uk/library/asc).

• *This walk ends at Durham's stunning cathedral, described next.*

Sights in Durham

▲▲▲DURHAM'S CATHEDRAL

Built to house the much-venerated bones of St. Cuthbert from Lindisfarne (known today as Holy Island), Durham's cathedral offers the best look at Norman architecture in England. ("Norman" is British for "Romanesque.") In addition to touring the cathedral, try to fit in an evensong service.

Cost: Entry to the cathedral itself is free, though a £3 donation is suggested. You must pay to climb the tower and to enter the *Open Treasure* exhibit.

Hours: The cathedral is open to visitors Mon-Sat 9:00-18:00,

Sun 12:30-17:00, daily until 20:00 mid-July-Aug, sometimes closes for special services, opens daily at 7:15 for worship and prayer. Access is limited for a few days in June, when the cathedral is used for graduation ceremonies (check online).

Information: Tel. 0191/386-4266, www.durhamcathedral.co.uk.

Visitor Information: A shop, café, and WC are tucked away in the cloister. Their pamphlet, *A Short Guide to Durham Cathedral*, is inexpensive and informative but dull.

Evensong: For a thousand years, this cradle of English Christianity has been praising God. To really experience the cathedral, attend an evensong service. Arrive early and ask to be seated in the choir. It's a spiritual Oz, as the choristers (12 men and 40 youngsters—now girls as well as boys) sing psalms—a red-and-white-robed pillow of praise, raised up by the powerful pipe organ. If you're lucky and the service goes well, the organist will run a spiritual musical victory lap as the congregation breaks up (Tue-Sat at 17:15, Sun at 15:30, 1 hour, sometimes sung on Mon; visiting choirs nearly always fill in when choir is off on school break mid-July-Aug; tel. 0191/386-4266). For more on evensong, see page 157.

Organ Recitals: Noted organists play most Wednesday evenings from July to early September (£10, 19:30, advance tickets available on the cathedral website under "What's On").

Tours: Regular tours run Monday through Saturday. If one is already in session, you're welcome to join (£5; tours at 10:30, 11:00, and 14:00; fewer in winter, call or check website to confirm schedule; £10 combo-ticket for guided tour and the *Open Treasure* exhibit).

Tower Climb: The view from the tower will cost you 325 steps and £5 (Mon-Sat 10:00-16:00, closes at 15:00 in winter, sometimes open Sun outside of services; closed during services, events, and bad weather; must be at least eight years old, no high heels or backless shoes; enter through south transept).

Open Treasure **Exhibit:** This collection of the church's rare artifacts is housed in the former monks' quarters (£7.50, Mon-Sat 10:00-17:00, Sun from 12:30, last entry one hour before closing).

❷ Self-Guided Tour

Begin your visit outside the cathedral. From the Palace Green, notice how this fortress of God stands boldly opposite the Norman keep of Durham's fortress of man.

Look closely: The **exterior** of this awe-inspiring cathedral has

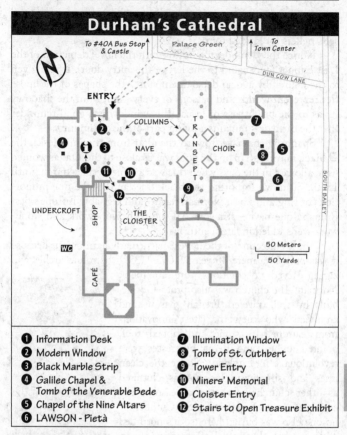

Durham's Cathedral

To #40A Bus Stop & Castle

Palace Green

To Town Center

DUN COW LANE

ENTRY

COLUMNS

TRANSEPT

CHOIR

NAVE

UNDERCROFT

SHOP

THE CLOISTER

CAFÉ

WC

SOUTH BAILEY

50 Meters
50 Yards

1 Information Desk
2 Modern Window
3 Black Marble Strip
4 Galilee Chapel &
   Tomb of the Venerable Bede
5 Chapel of the Nine Altars
6 LAWSON - Pietà

7 Illumination Window
8 Tomb of St. Cuthbert
9 Tower Entry
10 Miners' Memorial
11 Cloister Entry
12 Stairs to Open Treasure Exhibit

a serious skin problem. In the 1770s, as the stone was crumbling, they crudely peeled it back a few inches. The scrape marks give the cathedral a bad complexion to this day. For proof of this odd

"restoration," study the masonry 10 yards to the right of the door. The L-shaped stones in the corner would normally never be found in a church like this—they only became L-shaped when the surface was cut back.

At the cathedral **door,** check out the big, bronze, lion-faced knocker (this is a replica of the 12th-century original, which is in the *Open Treasure* exhibit). The knocker was used by criminals seeking sanctuary (read the explanation).

Inside, purple-robed church attendants are standing by to happily answer questions.

The handy ❶ **information desk** at the back (right) end of the nave sells tickets for guided tours.

Notice the ❷ **modern window** with the novel depiction of the Last Supper (above and to the left of the entry door). It was given to the church by a local department store. The shapes of the apostles represent worlds and persons of every kind, from the shadowy Judas to the brightness of Jesus. This window is a good reminder that the cathedral remains a living part of the community.

Spanning the nave (toward the altar from the info desk), the ❸ **black marble strip** on the floor was as close to the altar as women were allowed in the days when this was a Benedictine church (until 1540). Sit down (ignoring the black line) and let the fine proportions of England's best Norman nave—and arguably Europe's best Romanesque nave—stir you. All the frilly woodwork and stonework were added in later centuries.

The architecture of the **nave** is particularly harmonious because it was built in a mere 40 years (1093-1133). The round arches and zigzag-carved decorations are textbook Norman. The church was also proto-Gothic, built by well-traveled French masons and architects who knew the latest innovations from Europe. Its stone and ribbed roof, pointed arches, and flying buttresses were revolutionary in England. Notice the clean lines and simplicity. It's not as cluttered as other churches for several reasons: For centuries—out of respect for St. Cuthbert—no one else was buried here (so it's not filled with tombs). During Reformation times, sumptuous Catholic decor was removed. Subsequent fires and wars destroyed what Protestants didn't.

Head to the back of the nave and enter the ❹ **Galilee Chapel** (late Norman, from 1175). Find the smaller altar just to the left of the main altar. The paintings of St. Cuthbert and St. Oswald (seventh-century king of Northumbria) on the side walls of the niche are rare examples of Romanesque (Norman) paintings. Facing this altar, look above to your right to see more faint paintings on the upper walls above the columns. On the right side of the chapel, the upraised tomb topped with a black slab contains the remains of the **Venerable Bede,** an eighth-century Christian scholar who wrote the first history of England. We know this because the Latin reads, "In this tomb are the bones of the Venerable Bede."

Back in the main church, stroll down the nave to the center, under the highest **bell tower** in Europe (218 feet). Gaze up. The ropes turn wheels upon which bells are mounted. If you're stirred by the cheery ringing of church bells, tune in to the cathedral on Sunday (9:15-10:00 & 14:30-15:30) or Thursday (19:30-21:00 practice, trained bell ringers welcome, www.durhambellringers.org.uk), when the resounding notes tumble merrily through the entire town.

Continuing east (all medieval churches faced east), enter the **choir.** Monks worshipped many times a day, and the choir in the center of the church provided a cozy place to gather in this vast, dark, and chilly building. Mass has been said daily here in the heart of the cathedral for 900 years. The fancy wooden benches are from the 17th century. Behind the altar is the delicately carved Neville Screen from 1380 (made of Normandy stone in London, shipped to Newcastle by sea, then brought here by wagon). Until the Reformation, the niches contained statues of 107 saints. Exit the choir from the far-right side (south). Look for the stained-glass window (to your right) that commemorated the church's 1,000th anniversary in 1995. The colorful scenes depict England's history, from coal miners to cows to computers.

Step down behind the high altar into the east end of the church, which contains the 13th-century ❺ **Chapel of the Nine Altars.** Built later than the rest of the church, this is Gothic—taller, lighter, and relatively more extravagant than the Norman nave—but look up to see if you can spot an error in the symmetry. On the right, see the powerful modern ❻ **pietà** made of driftwood, with brass accents by local sculptor Fenwick Lawson.

Walk through the chapel to the north end where you will find an ❼ **illumination window** to your left. Designed by the glass artist Mel Howse, the window is a memorial to Sara Pilkington, a Durham University student who tragically died from a cardiac-related condition in 2012. The window casts vibrant colors onto the ❽ **tomb of St. Cuthbert.** Climb a few steps up to enter.

An inspirational leader of the early Christian Church in north England, St. Cuthbert lived in the Lindisfarne monastery (100 miles north of Durham, today called Holy Island). He died in 687. Eleven years later, his body was exhumed and found to be miraculously preserved. This stoked the popularity of his shrine, and pilgrims came in growing numbers. When Vikings raided Lindisfarne in 875, the monks fled with his body (and the famous illuminated Lindisfarne Gospels, now in the British Library in London). In 995, after 120 years of roaming, the monks settled in Durham on an easy-to-defend tight bend in the River Wear. This cathedral was built over Cuthbert's tomb.

Throughout the Middle Ages, a shrine stood here and was visited by countless pilgrims. In 1539, during the Reformation—whose proponents advocated focusing on God rather than saints—

the shrine was destroyed. But pilgrims still come, especially on St. Cuthbert's feast day (March 20).

Continue through the chapel and exit down the stairs. Walk down the **south transept** (to your left) to the ❾ **tower entry** (tower described earlier), as well as an astronomical clock and the Chapel of the Durham Light Infantry, a regiment of the British Army (1881-1968). The old flags and banners hanging above were actually carried into battle. On the right-hand side over the black door, look for a banner for the Durham Miners Association, one of many miners associations that existed—and still exist—in Durham today.

Return along the left side of the nave toward the entrance. Across from the entry is the door to the cloister. Along the wall by the cloister door, notice the ❿ **memorial honoring coal miners** who died, and those who "work in darkness and danger in those pits today." (This message is a bit dated. Durham's coal mines closed down in the 1980s.) The nearby book of remembrance lists mine victims. As an ecclesiastical center, a major university town, and a gritty, blue-collar coal-mining town, Durham's population has long been a complicated mix: priests, academics, and the working class.

After exiting the church, act like a monk and make a circuit of the Gothic ⓫ **cloister** (made briefly famous in a scene from the film *Harry Potter and the Sorcerer's Stone* in which Harry walks with his owl through a snowy courtyard). This area provides a fine view back up to the church towers.

Enter the ⓬ *Open Treasure* **exhibit** from the cloister, going upstairs to the Monks' Dormitory, a long, impressive room that stretches out under an original 14th-century timber roof. Formerly the monks' sleeping quarters, the room now holds artifacts from the cathedral treasury and monks' library. At the far end of the hall you'll find a door leading to the Collections Gallery. The double set of glass doors allows the cathedral to display more of its treasures in a climate-controlled environment—sometimes including a copy of the *Magna Carta* from 1216—as well as items from the Norman/medieval period (when the monks of Durham busily copied manuscripts), the Reformation, and the 17th century. The exhibit continues through the cloister's Great Kitchen, where the actual relics from St. Cuthbert's tomb are on view—his coffin, vestments, and cross—and ends in the undercroft, where you'll find a **shop** and a **café.**

MORE SIGHTS IN DURHAM

There's little to see in Durham beyond its cathedral, but it's a pleasant place to go for a stroll and enjoy its riverside setting.

Durham Museum

Situated in the old Church of St. Mary-le-Bow near the cathedral, this modest, somewhat hokey little museum does its best to illuminate the city's history, but it's worthwhile only on a rainy day. The exhibits, which are scattered willy-nilly throughout the old nave, include a reconstructed Victorian-era prison cell; a look at Durham industries past and present, especially coal mining (in Victorian times, the river was literally black from coal); and a 10-minute movie about 20th-century Durham. In the garden on the side of the church are two modern sculptures by local artist Fenwick Lawson, whose work is also in the cathedral.

Cost and Hours: £2.50; July-Sept daily 11:00-16:30, weekend afternoons only in off-season, closed Nov-March; corner of North Bailey and Bow Lane, tel. 0191/384-5589, www.durhammuseum. co.uk.

Riverside Path

For a 20-minute woodsy escape, walk Durham's riverside path from busy Framwellgate Bridge to sleepy Prebends Bridge.

Boat Cruise and Rental

Hop on the *Prince Bishop* for a relaxing one-hour narrated cruise of the river that nearly surrounds Durham (£10, Easter-Oct; for schedule, call 24-hour info line at 0191/386-9525, check their website, or go down to the dock at Brown's Boat House at Elvet Bridge, just east of old town; www.princebishoprc.co.uk). Sailings vary based on weather and tides. For some exercise with identical scenery, you can rent a rowboat at the same pier (£6.50/hour per person, £10 deposit, late-March-Oct daily 10:00-18:00, last rental at 17:00, tel. 0191/386-3779).

Crook Hall and Gardens

While most English gardens are in the countryside, Crook Hall is only a 10-minute walk from the city center, making it a convenient sight for travelers without a car. It has all the elements you'd expect in a classic English garden—walled "secret" gardens, a maze, a pool, and plenty of moss-covered statues. A map and witty signs take you on a self-guided tour.

Cost and Hours: £8, £6 off-season, March-Oct Sun-Wed 10:00-17:00, shorter hours off-season, closed Thu-Sat for weddings; café open daily 9:30-17:00, pay parking; from the city center, walk across the river and head north along the riverside path—it's on

Frankland Lane, just past the Radisson Blu Hotel; tel. 0191/384-8028, www.crookhallgardens.co.uk.

Sleeping in Durham

Close-in pickings are slim in Durham. Because much of the housing is rented to students, there are only a handful of B&Bs. Otherwise, there are a few hotels within easy walking distance of the town center. During graduation (typically the last two weeks of June), everything books up well in advance, and prices increase dramatically. Rooms can be tight on weekends any time of year.

B&BS

$$$ Castleview Guest House rents five airy, restful rooms in a well-located, 250-year-old guesthouse next door to a little church. If it's sunny, guests relax in the Eden-like backyard. Located on a charming cobbled street, it's just above Silver Street and the Framwellgate Bridge—take the stairs just after the church (free street-parking permit, 4 Crossgate, tel. 0191/386-8852, www.castle-view.co.uk, castle_view@hotmail.com, Anne).

$$ Victorian Town House B&B offers three spacious, boutique-like rooms in an 1853 townhouse. It's in a tidy residential area just down the hill from the train station and is handy to the town center. This is your best B&B option in Durham (family room, cash only, 2-night minimum preferred April-Oct, some view rooms, check-in 16:00-19:00 or by prior arrangement, 2 Victoria Terrace, 10-minute walk from train or bus station, tel. 0191/370-9963, www.durhambedandbreakfast.com, stay@durhambedandbreakfast.com, friendly Jill and Andy).

$$ Farnley Tower, a decent but impersonal B&B, has 16 large rooms and a quirky staff. On a quiet street at the top of a hill, it's a 15-minute hike up from the town center. Though you won't find the standard B&B warmth and service, this is a suitable alternative when the central hotels are booked (some rooms with cathedral view, family room, easy free parking, inviting yard, The Avenue—hike up this steep street and look for the sign on the right, tel. 0191/375-0011, www.farnley-tower.co.uk, enquiries@farnley-tower.co.uk, Raj and Roopal Naik). The Naiks also run the inventive Indian restaurant in the same building.

HOTELS

If the B&Bs are full, Durham could be a good place to resort to a bigger chain hotel, such as the Marriott (see below) or the centrally located **Premier Inn** (on Freemans Place).

$$ Durham Marriott Hotel Royal County scatters its 150 posh, four-star but slightly scruffy rooms among several buildings sprawling across the river from the city center. The Leisure Club has a pool, sauna, hot tub, spa, and fitness equipment (breakfast included in some rates, elevator, free Wi-Fi in public areas, pay Wi-Fi in rooms, restaurant, pay parking, Old Elvet, tel. 0191/386-6821 or tel. 0870-400-7286, www.marriott.co.uk).

$$ Kingslodge Inn & Restaurant is a slightly worn but comfortable 23-room place with charming terraces, an attached restaurant, and a pub. Located in a pleasantly wooded setting, it's convenient for train travelers (family room, free parking, Waddington Street, Flass Vale, tel. 0191/370-9977, http://kingslodgeinn. co.uk, enquiries@kingslodgeinn.co.uk).

STUDENT HOUSING OPEN TO ANYONE

$$ Durham Castle, a student residence actually on the castle grounds facing the cathedral, rents rooms during the summer break

(generally July-Sept). Request a room in the stylish main building, which is more appealing than the modern dorm rooms (includes breakfast in an elegant dining hall, Palace Green, tel. 0191/334-4106, www.dur.ac.uk/event. durham/tourism, durham. castle@durham.ac.uk). Note that the same office also rents rooms in other university buildings, but most are far less convenient to the city center—make sure to request the Durham Castle location when booking.

Eating in Durham

Durham is a university town with plenty of lively, inexpensive eateries. Especially on weekends, the places downtown are crowded with noisy college kids and rowdy townies, but as tourism increases, more good restaurants are popping up. Stroll down North Road, across Framwellgate Bridge, up through Market Place, and up Saddler Street, and consider the options suggested below. Some of the better choices are about a five-minute walk from this main artery—or a long hike to the suburbs—and worth the trek.

$$ La Spaghettata has some of the best Italian food in town. The hardworking staff serves pasta, pizza, and daily specials to hungry locals and tourists (Mon-Thu 17:00-22:30, Fri-Sun 11:30-14:00 & 17:00-22:30, 66 Saddler Street, tel. 0191/383-9290).

$ Claypath Delicatessen is worth the five-minute uphill walk above Market Place for lunch. Not just any old deli, this place assembles fresh ingredients and homemade bread into tasty sandwiches, salads, sampler platters, and more. They pride themselves on their killer espresso. While carryout is possible, most people eat in the casual, comfortable café setting (Tue-Fri 10:00-17:00, Sat until 16:00, closed Sun-Mon; from Market Place, cross the bridge and walk up Claypath to #57; tel. 0191/340-7209).

$$ The Capital, on the same stretch of road as Claypath Deli, has well-executed Indian food in a contemporary setting (daily 18:00-23:30, 69 Claypath, tel. 0191/386-8803).

$$ Zen is a modern, dark-wood place serving curries, noodles, fried rice, and other Asian fare. It's popular with students, so it's best to book a table or go early and sit in the bar (daily 11:00-22:00, Court Lane, tel. 0191/384-9588, www.zendurham.co.uk).

$$ Riverview Kitchen is a cozy place with a friendly staff and tables overlooking the river. They serve a wide variety of burgers, sandwiches, pancakes, salads, cakes, and more (Mon-Fri 9:30-17:00, Sat-Sun 9:00-17:00, 21 Silver Street, tel. 0191/384-5777).

$ Bells is a standby for carryout fish-and-chips just off Market Place toward the cathedral. I'd skip their fancier dining room (generally Mon-Thu 11:00-21:00, Fri-Sat 11:00-24:00, Sun 12:00-16:00, 11 Market Place, tel. 0191/384-8974).

$ Tealicious is run by mother-and-daughter team Alison and Jenny, who bake homemade cakes and scones for their all-day tea. They also offer fresh soups and sandwiches. Look for a tall, skinny teahouse at the end of Elvet Bridge (Tue-Sat 10:00-16:00, Sun from 12:00, closed Mon, 88 Elvet Bridge, tel. 0191/340-1393).

$ Esquires Coffee offers breakfast all day, tasty cakes, and good coffee. Outside seats are great for people-watching, and there are a few tables overlooking the river (daily 9:15-18:45, by the Framwellgate Bridge at 22 Silver Street, tel. 0191/375-7578).

Pubs Across the Elvet Bridge: Two good options are within a five-minute walk of the Elvet Bridge (just east of the old town). **$$ The Court Inn** offers an eclectic menu of pub grub and an open, lively atmosphere (food served daily 11:00-22:00; cross the Elvet Bridge, turn right, walk several blocks, and then look left; Court Lane, tel. 0191/384-7350). **$ The Dun Cow** is popular with locals and good for beer and ales. There's a cozy "snug bar" up front and a more spacious lounge in the back. Read the legend behind the pub's name on the wall along the outside corridor. More sedate than the student-oriented places in the town center, this pub serves only snacks and light meals—come here to drink and nibble, not to feast (daily 11:00-23:00; from the Elvet Bridge, walk five minutes straight ahead to Old Elvet 37; tel. 0191/386-9219).

Splurge Outside the Town Center: One of Durham's top restaurants, **$$$$ Finbarrs** is an untouristy splurge serving sophisticated meat and seafood dishes. You'll find inventive twists on regional standards—such as roasted venison or duck breast—and daily fish selections. More than a mile from the city center, it's practical only for drivers or hardy walkers staying near the train station who don't mind a 20-minute hike. The evening fixed-price meals are one of the best deals in town, but they're not offered on the weekend (lunch and dinner specials available, Tue-Sun 12:00-14:30 & 18:00-21:30, closed Mon, reservations smart on weekends, northwest of town, Aykley Heads, tel. 0191/307-7033, www.finbarrsrestaurant.co.uk).

Supermarket: Look for **Tesco Metro** in the old town, just off Market Place (Mon-Sat 7:00-22:00, Sun 11:00-17:00). You can **picnic** on Market Place, or on the benches and grass outside the cathedral entrance (but not on the Palace Green, unless the park police have gone home).

Durham Connections

From Durham by Train to: York (4/hour, 50 minutes), **Keswick/Lake District** (train to Penrith—hourly, 3 hours, 1-2 transfers, then bus to Keswick), **London** (hourly direct, 3 hours, more with transfers), **Hadrian's Wall** (take train to Newcastle—4/hour, 20 minutes, then a train/bus or train/taxi combination to Hadrian's Wall—see "Getting Around Hadrian's Wall" later in this chapter), **Edinburgh** (hourly direct, 2 hours, more with changes, less frequent in winter). Train info: Tel. 0345-748-4950, www.nationalrail.co.uk.

ROUTE TIPS FOR DRIVERS

As you head north from Durham on the A-1 motorway (beyond the junction for the Beamish Museum, described next), you'll pass a famous bit of public art: **The Angel of the North,** a modern, rusted-metal angel standing 65 feet tall with a wingspan of 175 feet (wider than a Boeing 757). While initially controversial when it was erected in 1998, it has since become synonymous with Northeast England, and is a beloved local fixture.

Beamish Museum

This huge, 300-acre open-air museum, which re-creates life in northeast England during the 19th and 20th centuries, is England's

best museum of its type. It takes at least three hours to explore its five sections: Pit Village (a coal-mining settlement with an actual mine); The Town (a 1913 street lined with actual shops); Pockerley Old Hall (the manor house of a "gentleman farmer"); Home Farm (a preserved farm and farmhouse); and the newest section, 1950s Town (mid-century street still under development). This isn't a wax museum. If you touch the exhibits, they may smack you. Attendants at each stop happily explain everything. In fact, the place is only really interesting if you talk to the attendants—who make it worth ▲▲▲.

GETTING THERE

By **car,** the museum is five minutes off the A-1/M-1 motorway (one exit north of Durham at Chester-le-Street/Junction 63, well signposted; it's a 12-mile, 25-minute drive northwest of Durham). You'll find free parking in the hills leading down to the main entrance.

Getting to Beamish from Durham by **bus** is an uncomplicated affair. Catch bus #21, #X21, or #50 from the Durham bus station (3-4/hour, 25 minutes) and transfer at Chester-le-Street to bus #8, #78A, #28, or #28A, which takes you right to the museum entrance (2/hour Mon-Sat, hourly Sun, 15 minutes, leaves from South Burns Stand L at the central bus kiosk, tel. 0191/420-5050, www.simplygo.com). Show your bus ticket for a 25 percent museum discount.

ORIENTATION TO BEAMISH MUSEUM

Cost and Hours: £19.50, children 5-16-£11.50, under 5-free; open Easter-Oct daily 10:00-17:00; off-season until 16:00, weekends only Dec-mid-Feb, and only The Town and Pit Village are open with vintage trams still running, last entry one hour before closing; check events schedule on chalkboard as you enter, tel. 0191/370-4000, www.beamish.org.uk.

Getting Around the Museum: Pick up a free map at the entry to help navigate the five zones; while some are side-by-side, others

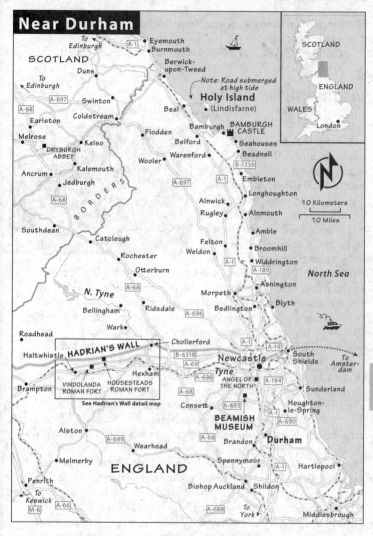

Near Durham

To Edinburgh
Eyemouth
Burnmouth

SCOTLAND

To Edinburgh
Duns

A-697

Swinton

A-68

Earlston

Melrose

DRYBURGH ABBEY

Kelso

Coldstream

Ancrum

Kalemouth

Jedburgh

A-68

BORDERS

Southdean

Catcleugh

Rochester

Otterburn

N. Tyne

A-68

Bellingham

Ridsdale

A-696

Wark

Roadhead

Haltwhistle

HADRIAN'S WALL

VINDOLANDA ROMAN FORT

HOUSESTEADS ROMAN FORT

See Hadrian's Wall detail map

Brampton

Alston

A-689

Wearhead

Melmerby

ENGLAND

Penrith

To Keswick

A-66

M-6

Berwick-upon-Tweed

Note: Road submerged at high tide
Holy Island
(Lindisfarne)

Beal

Flodden

Bamburgh
BAMBURGH CASTLE

Belford

Warenford

Seahouses
Beadnell

Wooler

B-1339

A-697

A-1

Embleton

Longhoughton

Alnwick

Rugley

Alnmouth

Felton

Amble

Weldon

Broomhill

A-1

Widdrington

A-189

Morpeth

Ashington

Bedlington

Blyth

Cholerford

B-6318

A-69

Hexham

A-696

Newcastle

Tyne

ANGEL OF THE NORTH

A-68

Consett

A-693

BEAMISH MUSEUM

Brandon

Spennymoor

Bishop Auckland

Shildon

To York

A-688

A-19

South Shields

To Amsterdam

A-194

Sunderland

Houghton-le-Spring

A-1

Durham

A-690

A-1

Hartlepool

Middlesbrough

North Sea

SCOTLAND

ENGLAND

WALES

London

10 Kilometers

10 Miles

DURHAM & NE ENGLAND

are up to a 15-minute walk apart. Vintage trams and cool, circa-

1910 double-decker buses shuttle visitors around the grounds, and their attendants are helpful and knowledgeable. Signs on the trams advertise a variety of 19th-century products, from "Borax, for washing everything" to "Murton's Reliable Travelling Trunks."

Eating: Several eateries are scattered around Beamish, including a pub and tearooms (in The Town), a fish-and-chips stand (in the Pit Village), and various cafeterias and snack stands. Or bring a picnic.

VISITING THE MUSEUM

I've described the five areas in counterclockwise order from the entrance.

From the entrance building, bear left along the road, then watch for the turnoff on the right to the **Pit Village & Colliery.** This is a company town built around a coal mine, with a schoolhouse, a Methodist chapel, and a row of miners' homes with long, skinny pea-patch gardens out front. Poke into some of the homes to see their modest interiors. In the Board School, explore the different classrooms, and look for the interesting poster with instructions for avoiding consumption (a.k.a. tuberculosis, a huge public-health crisis back then).

Next, cross to the adjacent colliery (coal mine), where you can take a fascinating—if claustrophobic—20-minute tour into the drift mine (check in at the "lamp cabin"—tours depart when enough people gather, generally every 5-10 minutes). Your guide will tell you stories about beams collapsing, gas exploding, and flooding; after that cheerful speech, you'll don a hard hat as you're led into the mine.

Notice in the lamp cabin how each lamp has a number. Miners arriving for work would yell out their number and be given a lamp and two tokens—one brass, one zinc—with that number. A "bankman" would collect each miner's zinc token as he entered the mine, returning it to the number board in the lamp cabin. When the miner exited at the end of the day, he would hang his brass token over the zinc one, signifying he'd safely left the mine. You'll also see a sign discouraging spitting. Miners would salivate a lot, primarily because of tuberculosis, but also from chewing tobacco.

Nearby (across the tram tracks) is the fascinating **mine elevator,** where you can see the actual steam-powered winding engine used to operate it. The "winderman" demonstrates how he skillfully eases both coal and miners up and down the tight mine shaft. This delicate, high-stakes job was one of the most sought-after at the entire colliery—passed down from father to son—and the winderman had to stay in this building for his entire shift (the seat of his chair flips up to reveal a built-in WC).

A path leads through the woods to Georgian-era **Pockerley,** which has two parts. First you'll see the **Waggonway,** a big barn filled with steam engines, including the re-created, first-ever passenger train from 1825. (Occasionally this train takes modern-day visitors for a spin on 1825 tracks—a hit with railway buffs.)

Then, walk back and climb the hill to **Pockerley Old Hall,** the manor house of a gentleman farmer and his family. The house dates

from the 1820s, and—along with the farmhouse described later—is Beamish's only vintage building still on its original site (other buildings at Beamish were relocated from elsewhere and reconstructed here). While not extremely wealthy, the farmer who lived here owned large tracts of land and could afford to hire help to farm it for him. This rustic home is no palace, but it was comfortable for the period. Costumed docents in the kitchen often bake delicious cookies from old recipes...and hand out samples.

The small garden terrace out front provides beautiful views across the pastures. From the garden, turn left and locate the narrow stairs up to the "old house." Actually under the same roof as the gentleman farmer's home, this space consists of a few small rooms that were rented by some of the higher-up workers to shelter their entire families of up to 15 children (young boys worked on the farm, while girls were married off early). While the parents had their own bedroom, the children all slept in the loft up above (notice the ladder in the hall).

From the manor house, hop on a vintage tram or bus or walk 10 minutes to the **1950s Town,** a new zone where the mid-century

buildings include a replica of a local welfare hall and community center. Visit the clinic tucked in the back to talk with a midwife who would offer advice to new parents and do pediatric check-ups. Next, move into the assembly hall to experience card games, dances, and crafts.

From here, a short tram ride or five-minute walk takes you back to the Edwardian era in **The Town** (c. 1913). This bustling street features several working shops and other buildings that are a delight to explore. In the Masonic Hall at the beginning of The Town, ogle the grand high-ceilinged meeting room. Farther on, check out the fun old metal signs inside the garage. Across the street, poke into the courtyard to find the stables, which are full of carriages (and sometimes horses). The heavenly-smelling candy store sells old-timey sweets and has an actual workshop in back with trays of free samples. The newsagent sells stationery, cards, and old toys, while in the grocery, you can see old packaging and the scales used for weighing out products. Other buildings include a clothing store, a working pub (The Sun Inn; don't expect 1913 prices), Barclays Bank, and a hardware store featuring a variety of "toilet sets" (not what you think).

For lunch, try the Tea Rooms cafeteria (upstairs); or, if the weather is good, picnic in the grassy park with the gazebo next to the tram stop. The row of townhouses includes both homes and offices (if the dentist is in, chat with him to hear some harrowing stories about pre-Novocain tooth extraction). At the circa-1913 railway station at the far end of The Town, you can stand on the bridge over the tracks to watch old steam engines go back and forth—along with a carousel of "steam gallopers."

Finally, walk or ride a tram or bus to the **Home Farm.** (This is the least interesting section—if you're running short on time, it's skippable.) Here you'll get to experience a petting zoo and see a

"horse gin" (a.k.a. "gin gan")—where a horse walking in a circle turned a crank on a gear to amplify its "horsepower," helping to replace human hand labor. Near the cafeteria, you can cross a busy road to the old farmhouse, still on its original site, where attendants sometimes bake goodies on a coal fire.

Hadrian's Wall

Cutting across the width of the isle of Britain, this ruined Roman wall is one of England's most thought-provoking sights. Once a towering 20-foot-tall fortification, these days "Hadrian's Shelf," as some cynics call it, is only about three feet wide and three to six feet high. (The conveniently precut stones of the wall were carried away by peasants during the post-Rome Dark Ages and now form the foundations of many local churches, farmhouses, and other structures.) In most places, what's left of the wall has been covered over by centuries of sod, making it effectively disappear into the landscape. But for those intrigued by Roman history, Hadrian's Wall provides a fine excuse to take your imagination for a stroll. These are the most impressive Roman ruins in Britain. Pretend you're a legionnaire on patrol in dangerous and distant Britannia, at the empire's northernmost frontier...with nothing but this wall protecting you from the terrifying, bloodthirsty Picts just to the north.

Today, several restored chunks of the wall, ruined forts, and museums thrill history buffs. While a dozen Roman sights cling along the wall's route, I've focused my coverage on an easily digestible six-mile stretch right in the middle, where you'll find the best museums and some of the most enjoyable-to-hike stretches of the wall. Three top sights are worth visiting: From east to west, Housesteads Roman Fort shows you where the Romans lived; Vindolanda's museum shows you how they lived; and the Roman Army Museum explains the empire-wide military organization that brought them here. If you plan to visit all three, the Roman Army Museum is an ideal place to start, as it sets the stage for what you're about to see; it's also next to the Walltown Visitor Centre, where you can get your bearings for the region.

A breeze for drivers, this area can also be seen fairly easily in summer by bus for those good at studying timetables (see "Getting Around Hadrian's Wall," later).

Hadrian's Wall is in vogue as a destination for multiday hikes through the pastoral English countryside. The Hadrian's Wall National Trail runs 84 miles, following the wall's route from coast to coast (for details, go to www.nationaltrail.co.uk/HadriansWall). Through-hikers (mostly British) can walk the wall's entire length in four to ten days. You'll see them bobbing along the ridgeline, drying out their socks in your B&B's mudroom, and recharging at local pubs in the evening. For those with less time, the brief ridge walk next to the wall from Steel Rigg to Sycamore Gap to Housesteads Roman Fort gives you a perfect taste of the scenery and history.

Orientation to Hadrian's Wall

The area described in this section is roughly between the midsize towns of Bardon Mill and Haltwhistle, which are located along the busy A-69 highway. Each town has a train station and some handy B&Bs, restaurants, and services. However, to get right up close to the wall, you'll need to head a couple of miles north to the adjacent villages of Once Brewed and Twice Brewed (along the B-6318 road).

TOURIST INFORMATION

For an overview of your options, visit the helpful website at www. HadriansWallCountry.co.uk.

Portions of the wall are in Northumberland National Park. The **Walltown Visitor Centre** lies along the Hadrian's Wall bus #AD122 route and has information on the area, including walking guides to the wall (Easter-Oct daily 10:00-17:00, closed Nov-Easter, just off the B-6318 next to the Roman Army Museum, follow signs to *Walltown Quarry*, pay parking, tel. 01434/344-396, www. northumberlandnationalpark.org.uk).

Visitor information may also be found at **The Sill National Landscape Discovery Centre,** next to the recommended Twice Brewed Inn and about a half-mile from the Steel Rigg trailhead. The Sill, with its unique grassland roof, also features interactive exhibits about the surrounding landscape and includes an 86-bed hostel, a local crafts shop, and a café (daily April-Oct 9:30-18:00, Nov-March 10:00-16:00, pay parking, served by bus #AD122, on the B-6318 near Bardon Mill, tel. 01434/341-200, www.thesill.org.uk).

The helpful TI in **Haltwhistle,** a block from the train station inside the library, has a good selection of maps and guidebooks and schedule information for Hadrian's Wall bus #AD122 (year-round Mon-Fri 10:00-13:00 & 13:30-16:30, Sat 10:00-13:00, closed Sun, The Library, Westgate, tel. 01434/321-863, www. visitnorthumberland.com).

GETTING AROUND HADRIAN'S WALL

Hadrian's Wall is anchored by the big cities of Newcastle to the east and Carlisle to the west. Driving is the most convenient way to see Hadrian's Wall. If you're coming by train, consider renting a car for the day at either Newcastle or Carlisle; otherwise, you'll need to rely on trains and a bus to connect the sights, hire taxis, or book a private guide with a car. If you're just passing through for the day using public transportation, it's challenging to stop and see more than just one or two of the sights—study the schedules carefully and prioritize. Nondrivers who want to see everything—or even hike part of the wall—will need to stay one or two nights along the bus route.

By Car

Zip to this "best of Hadrian's Wall" zone on the speedy A-69; when you get close, head a few miles north and follow the B-6318, which parallels the wall and passes several viewpoints, minor sights, and "severe dips." (These road signs add a lot to a photo portrait.) Buy a good local map to help you explore this interesting area more easily and thoroughly. Official Hadrian's Wall parking lots (including at the Walltown Visitor Centre, The Sill, Housesteads Roman Fort, and the trailhead at Steel Rigg) have pay-and-display machines.

Without a Car

To reach the Roman sights without a car, take the made-for-tourists Hadrian's Wall **bus #AD122** (named for the year the wall was built; runs only in peak season—see below). Essential resources for navigating the wall by public transit include the *Hadrian's Wall Country Map*, the bus #AD122 schedule, and a local train time-table for Northern Line #4—all available at local visitors centers and train stations (also see www.hadrianswallcountry.co.uk). If you arrive by train when the bus isn't running, you'll need to rely on taxis, a private guide, or long walks to visit the wall (see "Off-Season Options," later).

By Bus: Bus #AD122 connects the Roman sights (and several recommended accommodations) with train stations in **Haltwhistle** and **Hexham** (from £2/ride, £12.50 unlimited Day Rover ticket, buy tickets on board).

The bus runs between Haltwhistle and Hexham (8/day in each direction Easter-Sept, no service Oct-Easter). If you're coming from Carlisle or Newcastle, you'll need to take the train to Halt-whistle or Hexham and pick up the bus there (tel. 01434/322-002, www.gonortheast.co.uk/ad122).

By Train: Northern Line's train route #4 runs parallel to and a few miles south of the wall much more frequently than the bus. While the train stops at stations in larger towns—including (west to east) **Carlisle, Haltwhistle, Hexham,** and **Newcastle**—it

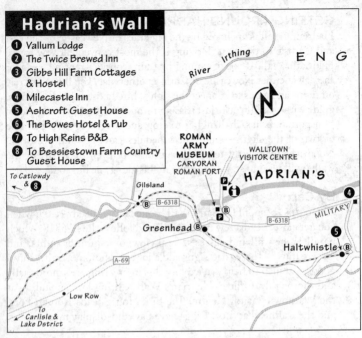

Hadrian's Wall

1 Vallum Lodge
2 The Twice Brewed Inn
3 Gibbs Hill Farm Cottages & Hostel
4 Milecastle Inn
5 Ashcroft Guest House
6 The Bowes Hotel & Pub
7 To High Reins B&B
8 To Bessiestown Farm Country Guest House

doesn't take you near the actual Roman sights. You can catch bus #AD122 at Hexham and Haltwhistle (no bus service Oct-Easter; train runs hourly; Carlisle to Haltwhistle—30 minutes; Haltwhistle to Hexham—20 minutes; Hexham to Newcastle—40 minutes; www.northernrail.org).

By Taxi: These Haltwhistle-based taxi companies can help you connect the dots: Sprouls (tel. 01434/321-064, mobile 07712-321-064) or Diamond (mobile 07597-641-222). It costs about £14 one-way from Haltwhistle to Housesteads Roman Fort (arrange for return pickup or have museum staff call a taxi). Note that on school days, all of these taxis are busy shuttling rural kids to class in the morning (about 8:00-10:00) and afternoon (about 14:30-16:30), so you may have to wait.

By Private Tour: Peter Carney, a former history teacher who waxes eloquently on all things Roman, offers tours with his car and also leads guided walks around Hadrian's Wall, including the Roman Army Museum, Vindolanda, and Housesteads. He customizes the tour to suit your time frame and interests and is happy to pick you up from your B&B or the train station in the Hexham or Haltwhistle area (£200/day for up to 4 people, £150/half-day, does not include museum admission, £100 extra for pickup at Carlisle or Durham, £75 extra at Newcastle train station, mobile 07585-139-016 or 07810-665-733, www.hadrianswall-

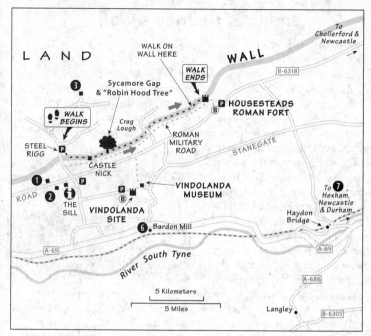

walk.com, petercarney@hadrianswall-walk.com). Peter also offers tours of medieval Durham.

Off-Season Options: Bus #AD122 doesn't run off-season (Oct-Easter). The only alternative for bus transportation is #185 from Haltwhistle, which takes you to the Roman Army Museum (3/day). Otherwise, you can only get as far as the train will take you (that is, Haltwhistle)—from there, you'll have to take a taxi or hire a local guide to take you to the other sights. Or, if you're a hardy hiker, take the Northern Line train to Bardon Mill, then walk about 2 miles to Vindolanda and another 2.5 miles to Housesteads Roman Fort.

Baggage Storage: It's difficult to bring your luggage along with you. If you're day-tripping, you can store your luggage in **Newcastle** at the bus station which is part of the Eldon Square Shopping Center, a five-minute walk north of the train station (credit card only, tel. 01912/611-891, www.intu.co.uk/eldonsquare). In **Carlisle** try a web-based service such as Stasher.com. If you must travel with luggage, Housesteads Roman Fort and Vindolanda will most likely let you leave your bags at the sight entrance while you're inside. If you want to walk the wall, a baggage-courier service will send your luggage ahead to your next B&B in the region for about £7 per bag (contact Hadrian's Haul, mobile 07967-564-823, www. hadrianshaul.com).

Sights at Hadrian's Wall

▲▲Hiking the Wall

It's enjoyable to hike along the wall speaking Latin, even if only for a little while. Note that park rangers forbid anyone from actually walking on top of the wall, except along a very short stretch at Housesteads. On the following hike, you'll walk alongside the wall.

For a good, craggy, three-mile, one-way, up-and-down walk along the wall, hike between Steel Rigg and Housesteads Roman Fort. For a shorter hike, begin at Steel Rigg (where there's a pay parking lot) and walk a mile to Sycamore Gap, then back again (described next; the Sill and Walltown visitors centers hand out a free description of this walk). These hikes are moderately strenuous and are best for those in good shape. You'll need sturdy

shoes and a windbreaker to comfortably overcome the often-blustery environment. As you would while driving in Britain, stay on the left side of the path when you meet other hikers.

To reach the trailhead for the short hike from **Steel Rigg to Sycamore Gap,** take the little road off the B-6318 near the Twice Brewed Inn and park in the pay-and-display parking lot on the right at the crest of the hill. Walk through the gate to the shoulder-high stretch of wall, go to the left, and follow the wall running steeply down the valley below you. Ahead of you are dramatic cliffs, creating a natural boundary made to order for this Roman fortification. Walk down the steep slope into

the valley, then back up the other side (watch your footing on the stone stairs). Following the wall, you'll do a similar up-and-down routine three more times, like a slow-motion human roller coaster.

In the second gap is one of the best-preserved milecastles, #39 (called Castle Nick because it sits in a nick in a crag). Each milecastle controlled a gate, and the gates meant income since the Roman Empire would take a cut every time goods passed through them. That may explain why Hadrian wanted so many gates, even when there were rugged hills and cliffs in the way.

Soon after Castle Nick, you'll reach the third gap, called Sycamore Gap for the large symmetrical tree in the middle. (Do

DURHAM & NE ENGLAND

you remember the 1991 Kevin Costner movie *Robin Hood: Prince of Thieves*? Locals certainly do—this tree was featured in it, and tourists frequently ask for directions to the "Robin Hood Tree.") You can either hike back the way you came or walk down a short stretch toward the main road to find a less strenuous path, which skirts lower down on the ridge (rather than following the wall up and down). The lower path leads back to the base of the Steel Rigg hill, where you can huff back up to your car.

If you continue on to Housesteads, you'll pass a traditional Northumbrian sheep farm, windswept lakes, and more ups and downs. The farther you go, the fewer people you'll encounter, making this hike even more magical. As you close in on Housesteads, you'll be able to actually walk on top of the wall.

▲▲Housesteads Roman Fort

With its respectable museum, powerful scenery, and the best-preserved segment of the wall, this is your single best stop at Hadrian's Wall. It requires a steep hike up from the parking lot, but once there it's just you, the bleating sheep, and memories of ancient Rome.

Cost and Hours: £8 for site and museum, discount with bus ticket; if the main entrance line is long, you can pay admission fee at the museum; daily April-Sept 10:00-18:00, Oct until 17:00, Nov-March until 16:00; last entry 45 minutes before closing, pay parking, bus #AD122 stops here; museum tel. 01434/344-363, info tel. 0870-333-1181, www.english-heritage.org.uk/housesteads.

Visitor Information: The parking lot has a visitors center with WCs, a snack bar, and a gift shop. They sell a low-cost guidebook about the fort and another one covering the entire wall. If you're traveling by bus and want to leave your luggage, ask at the visitors center if they'll stow it for a bit.

Visiting the Museum and Fort: From the visitors center, head outside and hike about a half-mile uphill to the fort. At the top of the hill, duck into the **museum** (on the left) before touring the site. While smaller and housing fewer artifacts than the museum at Vindolanda, it's interesting nonetheless. Look for the giant Victory statue, which

The History of Hadrian's Wall

In about AD 122, during the reign of Emperor Hadrian, the Romans constructed this great stone wall. Stretching 73 miles coast to coast across the narrowest stretch of northern England, it was built and defended by some 20,000 troops. Not just a wall, it was a military complex with forts, ditches, settlements, and roads. At every mile of the wall, a castle guarded a gate, and two turrets stood between

each castle. The milecastles are numbered (80 covering 73 miles, because a Roman mile was shorter than our mile).

In cross-section, Hadrian's Wall consisted of a stone wall—around 15 to 20 feet tall—with a ditch on either side. The flat-bottomed ditch on the south side of the wall, called the vallum, was flanked by earthen ramparts and likely demarcated the "no-man's-land" beyond which civilians were not allowed to pass. Between the vallum and the wall ran a service road called the Military Way. Another less-elaborate ditch ran along the north side of the wall. In some areas—including the region that I describe—the wall was built upon a volcanic ridgeline that provided a natural fortification.

The wall's actual purpose is still debated. While Rome ruled Britain for 400 years, it never quite ruled its people. The wall may have been used for any number of reasons: to protect Roman Britain from invading Pict tribes from the north (or at least cut down on pesky border raids); to monitor the movement of people as a show of Roman strength and superiority; or to simply give an otherwise bored army something to do. (Emperors understood that nothing was more dangerous than a bored army.) Or perhaps the wall represented Hadrian's tacit admission that the empire had reached its maximum extent; Hadrian was known for consolidating his territory, in some cases giving up chunks of land that had been conquered by his predecessor, Trajan, to create an easier-to-defend (if slightly smaller) empire. His philosophy of "defense before expansion" is embodied by the impressive wall that still bears his name.

once adorned the fort's East Gate; her foot is stepping on a globe, serving as an intimidating reminder to outsiders of the Romans' success in battle. A good seven-minute film shows how Housesteads (known back then as Vercovicium) would have operated.

Artifacts offer more insights into those who lived here. A cooking pot from Frisia (Northern Holland) indicates the presence of women, showing that soldiers came with their families in tow.

A tweezer, probe, spoons, and votive foot (that would have been offered to the gods in exchange for a cure for a foot ailment) reveal the type of medical care you could expect. And a weighted die and a coin mold—perhaps used to make counterfeit money—show what may have been the less-than-savory side of life at the fort.

After exploring the museum, head out to the sprawling ruins of the **fort.** Interpretive signs and illustrations explain what you're seeing. All Roman forts were the same rectangular shape and design, containing a commander's headquarters, barracks, and latrines (Housesteads has the best-preserved Roman toilets found anywhere—look for them at the lower-right corner). This fort also had a hospital, granary, and a bakery where the soldiers would bake bread and cook meals. The fort was built right up to the wall, which runs along its upper end.

Even if you're not a hiker, take some time to walk the wall here. (This is the one place along the wall where you're actually allowed to get up and walk on top of it for a photo op.) Visually trace the wall to the left to see how it disappears into a bank of overgrown turf. *Game of Thrones* fans may enjoy visualizing how author George R. R. Martin was inspired by Hadrian's Wall to create the famous ice wall in his books.

▲▲Vindolanda

This larger Roman fort (which actually predates the wall by 40 years) and museum are just south of the wall. Although

Housesteads has better ruins and the wall, Vindolanda has the more impressive museum, packed with artifacts that reveal intimate details of Roman life.

There are two entrances, an east entrance and the west main entrance. I recommend the main entrance for easy access. To get there, follow the signs to Vindolanda from the A-69 or the B-6318. (If you see a steep hill from the parking lot, you are at the east entrance.)

Cost and Hours: £8.25, £12.20 combo-ticket includes Roman Army Museum, discount with bus ticket; daily April-Sept 10:00-18:00, mid-Feb-March and Oct-Nov until 17:00, winter hours variable, last entry one hour before closing, call first during bad weather, free parking with entry, bus #AD122 stops here, café; tel. 01434/344-277, www.vindolanda.com.

Visitor Information: A free map and low-cost guidebook are available at the entrance.

Tours: Free guided tours are offered in high season (July-Aug

Sat-Sun 10:30, 11:00, 13:00, and 14:00; Mon-Fri 11:00 and 13:00; Apr-June and Sept Sat-Sun 11:00 and 13:00 only, call to confirm). Archaeological talks and tours may be offered on weekdays as well. Both are included in your ticket.

Archaeological Dig: The Vindolanda site is an active dig—from Easter through September, you'll see the excavation work in progress (usually Mon-Fri, weather permitting). Much of the work is done by volunteers, including armchair archaeologists from the US.

Visiting the Site and Museum: After entering, stop at the model of the entire site as it was in Roman times (c. AD 213-276). Notice that the site had two parts: the fort itself, and the *vicus* (town) just outside that helped to supply it.

Head out to the **site,** walking through 500 yards of grassy parkland decorated by the foundation stones of the Roman fort and a full-size replica chunk of the wall. Over the course of 400 years, at least nine forts were built on this spot. The Romans, by lazily sealing the foundations from each successive fort, left modern-day archaeologists with a 20-foot-deep treasure trove of remarkably well-preserved artifacts: keys, coins, brooches, scales, pottery, glass, tools, leather shoes, bits of cloth, and even a wig. Many of these are now displayed in the museum, well described in English, German, French, and...Latin.

At the far side of the site, pass through the pleasant riverside garden area on the way to the museum. The well-presented **museum** pairs actual artifacts with insightful explanations—such as a collection of Roman shoes with a description about what each one tells us about its wearer. The weapons (including arrowheads and spearheads) and fragments of armor are a reminder that Vindolanda was an important outpost on Rome's northern boundary—look for the Scottish skull stuck on a pike to discourage rebellion.

Thanks to Vindolanda's boggy grounds, trash tossed away by the Romans was preserved in an airless environment. You'll see the world's largest collection of Roman leather; tools that were used for building and expanding the fort; locks and keys (the fort had a password that changed daily—jotting it on a Post-It note wasn't allowed); a large coin collection; items imported here from the far corners of the vast empire (such as fragments of French pottery and amphora jugs from the Mediterranean); beauty aids such as combs, tools for applying makeup, and hairpins; and religious pillars and steles.

But the museum's main attraction is its collection of writing tablets. A good video explains how these impressively well-preserved examples of early Roman cursive were discovered here in 1973. Displays show some of the actual letters—written on thin pieces of wood—alongside the translations. These letters bring Romans to life in a way that ruins alone can't. The most famous piece (described but not displayed here) is the first known example of a woman writing to a woman (an invitation to a birthday party). A large interactive screen lets you choose and read tablets selected by Robin Birley, a British archaeologist and former leader of the excavations.

A separate room hosts the *Wooden Underworld* gallery. Although the Romans built in stone, many of their everyday personal objects were made of wood, and this gallery hosts a collection of 2,000 items. See if you can find the wooden toilet seat and the toy sword.

Finally, you'll pass through an exhibit about the history of the excavations, including a case featuring the latest discoveries, on your way to the shop and cafeteria.

▲▲Roman Army Museum

This museum, a few miles farther west at Greenhead (near the site of the Carvoran Roman fort), has cutting-edge, interactive exhibits illustrating the structure of the Roman Army that built and monitored this wall, with a focus on the everyday lifestyles of the Roman soldiers stationed here. Bombastic displays, life-size figures, and several different films—but few actual artifacts—make this entertaining museum a good complement to the archaeological emphasis of Vindolanda.

Cost and Hours: £7, £12.20 combo-ticket includes Vindolanda, discount with bus ticket; April-Sept daily 10:00-18:00, mid-Feb-March and Oct daily until 17:00, Nov-Dec Sat-Sun only until 16:00, closed Jan-mid-Feb; free parking with entry, bus #AD122 stops here. Tel. 01697/747-485; if no answer, call Vindolanda tel. 01434/344-277; www.vindolanda.com.

Visiting the Museum: In the first room, a video explains the complicated structure of the Roman Army—legions, cohorts, centuries, and so on. While a "legionnaire" was a Roman citizen, an "auxiliary" was a noncitizen specialist recruited for their unique skills (such as horsemen and archers). A video of an army-recruiting officer delivers an "Uncle Caesar wants YOU!" speech to prospective soldiers. A timeline traces the history of the Roman Empire, especially as it related to the British Isles.

The good 20-minute *Edge of Empire* 3-D movie offers an evocative look at what life was like for a Roman soldier marking time on the wall, and digital models show reconstructions of the wall and forts. In the exhibit on weapons, shields, and armor (mostly replicas), you'll learn how Roman soldiers trained with lead-filled wooden swords, so that when they went into battle, their metal swords felt light by comparison. Another exhibit explains the story of Hadrian, the man behind the wall, who stopped the expansion of the Roman Empire, declaring that the age of conquest was over.

Sleeping and Eating near Hadrian's Wall

If you want to spend the night near Hadrian's Wall, set your sights on the area of Once Brewed and Twice Brewed, with a few accommodations options, a good pub, and easy access to the most important sights. I've also listed some other accommodations scattered around the region.

IN AND NEAR ONCE BREWED AND TWICE BREWED

Although the use of these two names can be slightly confusing, they simply describe a handful of houses that sit at the base of the ridge along the B-6318. Many locals just refer to the area as "The Sill." The Twice Brewed Inn and Milecastle Inn are reachable with Hadrian's Wall bus #AD122. Bus drivers can drop you off at Vallum Lodge by request (but they won't pick you up).

$$ Vallum Lodge is a cushy, comfortable, nicely renovated base situated near the vallum (the ditch that forms part of the fortification a half-mile from the wall itself). Its six cheery rooms are all on the ground floor, along with a guest lounge, and a separate guesthouse called the Snug has one bedroom and a kitchen. It's just up the road from The Twice Brewed Inn—a handy dinner option (pay laundry service, evening meal on request, Military Road, tel. 01434/344-248, www.vallum-lodge.co.uk, stay@vallum-lodge.co.uk, Samantha).

$$ The Twice Brewed Inn, two miles west of Housesteads and a half-mile from the wall, rents 19 basic, workable rooms, all en-suite (ask for a room away from the road, Military Road, tel. 01434/344-534, www.twicebrewedinn.co.uk, info@twicebrewedinn.co.uk). The inn's friendly **$$ brewpub** serves as the community gathering place and is a hangout for hikers and the archaeologists digging at the nearby sites. It serves real ales and large portions of good pub grub (vegetarian options, fancier restaurant in back with same menu, food served daily 12:00-21:00, Sun until 20:00).

Rural and Remote, North of the Wall: A practical choice for drivers, **$$ Gibbs Hill Farm Cottages and Hostel** is a friendly working sheep-and-cattle farm set on 700 acres in the stunning valley on the far side of the wall. The three 6-bed dorm rooms are in a restored hay barn (no breakfast, coin-op laundry facilities, 5-minute drive from Twice Brewed Inn or 30-minute walk from Steel Rigg trailhead, tel. 01434/344-030, www.gibbshillfarm.co.uk, val@gibbshillfarm.co.uk, warm Val). They also rent two self-catering cottages for two to four people by the week or occasionally shorter periods.

West of Once/Twice Brewed: $$ Milecastle Inn cooks up

all sorts of exotic game and offers the best dinner around, according to hungry national park rangers. You can order food at the counter and sit in the pub, or take a seat in the table-service area. Make sure to finish off with their sticky toffee pudding with custard (food served daily Easter-Sept 12:00-20:45, Oct-Easter 12:00-14:30 & 18:00-20:30, smart to reserve in summer, North Road, tel. 01434/321-372, www.milecastle-inn.co.uk).

IN HALTWHISTLE

The larger town of Haltwhistle has a train station, along with stops for Hadrian's Wall bus #AD122 (at the train station and a few blocks east, at Market Place). It also has a helpful TI (see "Tourist Information," earlier), a launderette, several eateries, and a handful of B&Bs, including this one.

$$ Ashcroft Guest House, a large Victorian former vicarage, is 400 yards from the Haltwhistle train station and 200 yards from the Market Place bus stop. It has seven big, luxurious rooms, huge terraced gardens, and views from the comfy lounge, along with a two-bedroom apartment with kitchen, and ample free parking. If you want to indulge yourself after hiking the wall, this is the place (2-night minimum for apartment, family room, 1.5 miles from the wall, Lanty's Lonnen, tel. 01434/320-213, www.ashcroftguesthouse.co.uk, info@ashcroftguesthouse.co.uk, helpful Geoff and Christine James).

IN BARDON MILL

$$ The Bowes Hotel, with its friendly staff, is just a two-minute walk from the train station and has six attractive, shipshape rooms. The **$$ pub** downstairs has a good selection of ales and serves dinner Wed-Sat 12:00-20:00, Sun until 16:00 (tel. 01434/344-237, www.theboweshotel.uk, ian@theboweshotel.uk, Ian & Sar).

NEAR HEXHAM

$ High Reins offers four rooms in a stone house built by a shipping tycoon in the 1920s. The rooms are cushy and comfortable—there's a cozy feeling all over the place (cash only, 2-bedroom apartment also available in the house, lounge, 1 mile south of train station on the western outskirts of Hexham, Leazes Lane, tel. 01434/603-590, www.highreins.uk, bookings@highreins.uk, Jan and Peter Walton). They also rent an apartment in the town center; ask for details.

NEAR CARLISLE

$$ Bessiestown Farm Country Guest House, located far northwest of the Hadrian sights, is convenient for drivers connecting the Lake District and Scotland. It's a quiet and soothing stop in the middle of sheep pastures, with four bedrooms in the main house, a pair of two-bedroom apartments, and a honeymoon suite in the former stables. One apartment is on the ground floor, with an accessible bathroom (discount with 3-night stay, serves afternoon tea and an evening meal; in Catlowdy, midway between Gretna Green and Hadrian's Wall, a 30-minute drive north of Carlisle; tel. 01228/577-219, www.bessiestown.co.uk, info@bessiestown.co.uk, gracious Margaret and Jack Sisson).

WALES

WALES

Croeso! Welcome to Wales, a country with 750 miles of scenic, windswept coastline jutting out of the west coast of the Isle of Britain into the Irish Sea. Shaped somewhat like a miniature Britain, Wales is longer than it is wide (170 miles by 60 miles) and is roughly the size of Massachusetts. The north is mountainous, rural, and sparsely populated. It's capped by 3,560-foot Mount Snowdon, taller than any mountain in England. The south, with a less-rugged topography, is where two-thirds of the people live (including 350,000 in the capital of Cardiff).

The Welsh are proud of their, well, Welshness. Despite centuries of English imperialism, the Welsh language (a.k.a. Cymraeg, pronounced kum-RAH-ig) re-

mains alive and well—more so than its nearly dead Celtic cousin in Scotland, Gaelic. Though everyone in Wales speaks English, one in five can also speak the native tongue; for many, it's their first language. In the northwest, well over half the population is fluent in Welsh and uses it in everyday life. Listen in.

Most certainly *not* a dialect of English, the Celtic Welsh tongue sounds to foreign ears like Elvish from *The Lord of the Rings*. One of Europe's oldest languages, Welsh has been written down since about AD 600, and it was spoken 300 years before French or German. Today, the Welsh language is protected by law from complete English encroachment—the country is officially bilingual, and signs display both languages (e.g., *Cardiff/Caerdydd*). In schools, it's either the first or the required second language; in many areas, English isn't used in classes at all until middle school.

Though English has been the dominant language in Wales for many years (and most newspapers and media are in English), the Welsh people cherish their linguistic heritage as something that

Speaking Welsh

Welsh pronunciation is tricky. The common "ll" combination sounds roughly like "thl" (pronounced as if you were ready to make an "l" sound and then blew it out; it can also sound like "cl" or "tl"). As in Scotland, "ch" is a soft, guttural k, pro-

nounced in the back of the throat. The Welsh "dd" sounds like the English "th," f = v, ff = f, w = the "u" in "push," y = i. Non-Welsh people often make the mistake of trying to say a long Welsh name too fast, and inevitably trip themselves up. A local tipped me off: Slow down and say each syllable separately, and it'll come out right. For example, Llangollen

is thlang-GOTH-lehn. But it gets harder. Some words are a real mouthful, like Llanfairpwllgwyngyllgogerychwyrndrobwllllantysiliogogogoch, the 58-character name for a small town on the island of Angelsey (it's the longest single-word place name in Europe).

Although there's no need to learn any Welsh (because everyone also speaks English), without too much effort you can make friends and impress the locals by learning a few polite phrases. In a pub, toast the guy who just bought your drink with *Diolch* and *Yeach-hid dah* (YECH-id dah, "Good health to you").

English	Welsh
Hello	Helo (hee-LOH)
Goodbye	Hwyl (hoo-il)
Please	Os gwelwch yn dda (os GWELL-uck UN thah)
Thank you	Diolch (dee-olkh)
Wales	Cymru (KUM-ree)
England	Lloegr (THLOY-ger)

sets them apart. In fact, a line of the Welsh national anthem goes, "Oh, may the old language survive!"

You can psychoanalyze the English-Welsh relationship through the word for Wales. The Anglo-Saxon word for "enemy" is "wealas" (which became "Wales"), and that's what they called this wild and historically unrulable part of their island (from their point of view). By contrast, the Celtic word for Wales, "Cymru," means "comrade" in Welsh—the opposite of what eventually became the English name for this region.

Wales has some traditional foods worth looking for, par-

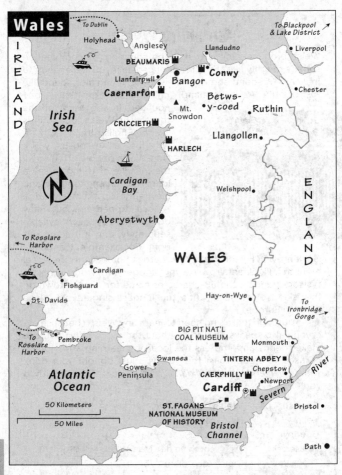

ticularly lamb dishes and leek soup *(cawl)*. In fact, the national symbol is the leek, ever since medieval warriors—who wore the vegetable on their helmets in battle—saved the land from Saxon invaders. Melted cheese on toast—kind of an open-faced grilled cheese sandwich—is known as "Welsh rarebit" (or "Welsh rabbit"; the name is a throwback to a time when the poor Welsh couldn't afford much meat in their diet). At breakfast, you might get some "Welsh cakes," basically a small squashed scone. Cockles and seaweed bread were once common breakfast items—but don't expect your B&B to serve them.

Wales' three million people are mostly white and Christian (Presbyterian, Anglican, or Catholic). Like their English and Scottish counterparts, they enjoy football (soccer), but rugby is the unofficial Welsh sport, more popular in Wales than in any country outside of New Zealand. Other big sports are cricket and snooker (similar to billiards).

The Welsh flag features a red dragon on a field of green and white. The dragon has been a symbol of Wales since at least the ninth century. According to legend, King Arthur's men carried the dragon flag to battle.

Welsh history stretches back into the mists of prehistoric Britain. In AD 43, Romans invaded Britain. Arriving in Wales about AD 50, they met stiff resistance from indigenous Welsh guerillas who harassed the Romans for 30 years. The Romans built a string of forts (each 12 miles—or a half-day's march— apart) along a military road, today's A-48 highway. You'll notice towns along this route that are still 12 miles apart.

The Welsh in South Wales ultimately became Romanized and Christian. When Rome checked out as the Empire fell, the Celts assumed power, adopting the Roman style of defense and the fortifications they left behind. (The dragon on the Welsh flag may originally have been a Roman military symbol.)

Saxon (Germanic) tribes like the Angles then stepped into the power vacuum, conquering what they renamed "Angle-land"—but they failed to penetrate Wales. Brave Welsh warriors, mountainous terrain, and the 177-mile manmade ditch-and-wall known as Offa's Dyke helped preserve the country's unique Celtic/Roman heritage.

A fixed border dividing England and Wales was established in about AD 780. Behind that border, Wales was a mosaic of small independent kingdoms. When the Normans beat the English at the Battle of Hastings in 1066, they moved rapidly to consolidate greater Norman rule, and Wales sank into three centuries of war with generations of Norman warlords.

In 1216, Wales' medieval kingdoms unified under Llywelyn Fawr ("the Great"). But in 1282, King Edward I of England invaded and conquered, putting an end to Wales' one era as a unified, sovereign nation. To solidify his hold on the country, Edward built a string of castles (see sidebar on page 624). He then named his son and successor the "Prince of Wales," starting the tradition of granting that ceremonial title to the heir to the English throne.

This was the age of castles—man-made earthen mounds crowned by wooden forts, eventually becoming the evocative stone wonders we climb through today. The big castles you can see

throughout Wales were designed to keep the angry Welsh locals under control. Just as the Normans built the Tower of London in their capital, they built castles in Cardiff, Conwy, and Caernarfon to protect their foothold in Wales. English settlers were imported to live within the walls of the garrison town (with gardens behind their houses) and to give the place a tax base. The indigenous Welsh people, outside the walls, were called "piss poor"—back then, very poor people sold their own urine (used to soak leather in Norman tanneries) to earn a few pennies.

Despite an unsuccessful rebellion in 1400, led by Owen Glendower (Owain Glyndwr), Wales has remained under English rule ever since Edward's invasion. In 1535, the annexation was formalized under Henry VIII.

By the 19th century, Welsh coal and iron stoked the engines of Britain's Industrial Revolution, and its slate was exported to shingle roofs throughout Europe. Wales became the first country on earth with the majority of its people working in industry. That's why the Welsh didn't emigrate to North America in droves like the Scottish and Irish. Rather, the big people movement here during that era was from villages and farms to mining valleys and seaports.

While this was a lucrative boom time for wealthy industrialists, the common working people of Wales toiled under very difficult conditions. The stereotype of the Welsh as poor, grimy-faced miners continued into the 20th century. Their economy has been slow to transition from mining, factories, and sheep farming to the service-and-software model of the global world.

In recent decades, the Welsh have consciously tried to preserve their local traditions and language. In 1999, Wales was granted its own parliament, the National Assembly, with powers to distribute its portion of the UK's national budget. Though still ruled by the UK government in London, Wales now has a measure of independence and self-rule. The Plaid Cymru party, which advocates for Welsh independence, has a small percentage of Welsh seats in parliament.

Less urbanized and less wealthy than England, Wales consists of miles of green land where sheep graze (because the soil is too poor for crops). It makes for wonderful hillwalking, but hikers should beware of midges. From late May through September, these tiny biting insects are very interested in dawn, dusk, dampness, and you—bring insect repellent along on any hike.

Singing the Praises of Welsh Choirs

The Welsh love their choirs. Nearly every town has a choir (men's or mixed) that practices weekly. Visitors are usually welcome to observe the session (lasting about 1.5-2 hours), and sometimes the choir heads to the pub afterward for a good old-fashioned, beer-lubricated sing-along.

As these choir rehearsals have become something of a tourist attraction, many choirs ask attendees for a small donation—fair enough. Note that some towns have more than one choir, and schedules are subject to change (especially in Aug, when most choirs take a break from practicing); confirm the schedule with a TI or your B&B before making the trip. Additionally, many choirs regularly perform concerts—inquire for the latest schedule.

Here are choir practices that occur in or near towns I recommend visiting: **Llandudno Junction,** near **Conwy** (men's choir Mon at 19:30 except Aug, tel. 01492/534-115, www.cormaelgwn.cymru); **Caernarfon** (men's choir Tue at 19:45, arrive by 19:30 in summer to guarantee a seat, no practice in Aug, in the Galeri Creative Enterprise Centre at Victoria Dock, tel. 01286/677-404, www.cormeibioncaernarfon.org); **Llangollen** (men's choir Fri at 19:30 at Hand Hotel, 21:30 pub singsong afterward, hotel tel. 01978/860-303); **Ruthin** (mixed choir Thu at 20:00 except Aug at Pwllglas Village Hall, three miles south of Ruthin in Pwllglas, mobile tel. 07724/112-984, www.corrhuthun.co.uk); and **Betws-y-Coed** (men's choir every other Sun in summer at 14:00, www.cantoriongogleddcymru.co.uk; other choruses most other Sun July-Sept; St. Anne's Church, check schedule online and/or book ahead at TI).

Because Wales is an affordable weekend destination for many English, the country is popular among avid English drinkers, who pour over the border on Friday nights for cheap beer before stumbling home on Sunday. Expect otherwise-sleepy Welsh border towns to be rowdy on Saturday nights.

I've focused most of my coverage of Wales on the north, which has the highest concentration of castles, natural beauty, and attractions. But I've also covered a few important sights in South Wales that are easy to combine with a visit to Bath or the Cotswolds (or as a quick stopover between them), including the

Welsh capital of Cardiff, its nearby top-notch open-air museum, and the picturesque Tintern Abbey.

Try to connect with Welsh culture on your visit. Clamber over a castle, eat a leek, count sheep in a field, catch a rugby match, or share a pint of bitter with a baritone. Open your ears to the sound of words as old as the legendary King Arthur. "May the old language survive!"

NORTH WALES

Conwy • Near Conwy • Caernarfon • Snowdonia National Park • Northeast Wales

Wales' top historical, cultural, and natural wonders are found in the north. From towering Mount Snowdon to lush forests to desolate moor country, North Wales is a poem written in landscape. For sightseeing thrills and diversity, North Wales is Britain's most interesting slice of the Celtic crescent. And it's remarkably compact: In a single day you can lie on a beach, conquer a castle, spelunk in a slate mine, hike on a mountain slope, ogle a grand garden, and settle in for dinner at one of Britain's most pleasant small towns, Conwy.

Wales is wonderful, but smart travelers sort through their options carefully. Tourism dominates the local economy, and sales pitches can be aggressive. Be careful not to be waylaid by the many gimmicky sights and bogus "best of" lists.

When choosing where to sleep, the most logical options are Conwy and Caernarfon—each an old walled town attached to a castle (the two best in Wales). Conwy, the more charming of the two, makes the region's best home base, with appealing B&Bs and restaurants, a fun-to-explore townscape within mighty walls, and manageable connections to many nearby sights. Caernarfon is bigger, more blue-collar, and slightly better connected.

At Conwy's doorstep are sumptuous Bodnant Garden and the interesting Trefriw Woolen Mills. And if two castles aren't enough, you have several more to choose from (I've also described Beaumaris, Harlech, and Criccieth).

Close by, Snowdonia National Park plunges you into some of Wales' top scenery—you can ride a train from Llanberis to the top of Mount Snowdon, learn more about the local industry at Llanberis' National Slate Museum, and explore the huggable villages

North Wales

To Dublin

Irish Sea

A-5025

Amlwch

A-5025

ANGLESEY

Holyhead

Holy Island

Valley   A-55

Rhosneigr

Aberffraw

MENAI BRIDGE

Beaumaris

Llanfairpwll   Bangor

A-55

A-5

Bethesda

Caernarfon   A-4086

NAT'L SLATE MUSEUM

Ogwen Valley

Llanberis

Pen-y-Pass

Caernarfon Bay

SNOWDON MTN. RAILWAY

Mt. Snowdon

N

10 Kilometers

10 Miles

SNOWDONIA

A-487

Bedd-gelert

NAT'L

Llanaelhaearn

Porthmadog

A-487

Nefyn

CRICCIETH

Twdweiliog

Portmeirion

Llanbedrog   Pwllheli

Tremadog Bay

Harlech

SCOTLAND

ENGLAND

Abersoch

WALES

Aberdaron

London

A-496

Llanaber

Fairbourne

Cardigan Bay

To Aberystwyth & Cardiff

Llangelynnin

of Beddgelert and Betws-y-Coed. The tongue-twisting industrial town of Blaenau Ffestiniog invites you to tour an actual slate mine. And on the way back to England are the appealing towns of Llangollen, strikingly set in a gorge, and Ruthin, with a relaxing market-town vibe.

There's so much variety in this region—and it's all so close—that there's no single "best plan" for seeing it all. Peruse this chapter, make a wish list, and weave together a North Wales itinerary that suits your interests.

PLANNING YOUR TIME

The absolute minimum is two nights and a day; if you can spare the time, you won't regret adding an extra night (or two). With two

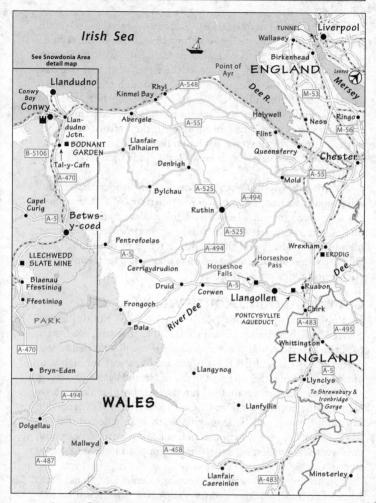

nights in Conwy, use your arrival and departure days to see the town and its castle, leaving your full day for side-tripping.

By Car: Drivers can try this "best of" North Wales itinerary:

9:30	Leave your Conwy home base after breakfast.
10:00	Visit Bodnant Garden.
12:00	Drive Pen-y-Pass to Llanberis (lunch on the way).
13:00	Tour the National Slate Museum, then drive to Caernarfon.
16:00	Tour Caernarfon Castle.
17:00	Scenic drive to Conwy via Beddgelert (allow 1.5 hours; consider dinner in Beddgelert) or head straight back to Conwy (45 minutes).
19:00	Dinner or my self-guided walk in Conwy.

By Public Transportation: For those relying on public transportation, Conwy is a good home base. Most of the region's destinations can be reached by bus or train from Conwy or nearby Llandudno Junction, just across the river. With just one day, leave Conwy in the morning for a loop through the Snowdonia sights (possibly including Betws-y-Coed, Beddgelert, or Llanberis, depending on bus and train schedules—check timetables and plan your route before heading out), then return to Conwy in the evening for the town walk and dinner. To pack more into your limited time, consider hiring a local guide for a private driving tour.

With a Second Day: Slow down and consider the region's other sights, such as the train from Llanberis up Mount Snowdon, the slate-mine tour in Blaenau Ffestiniog, Beaumaris or Harlech castles, the dreamy Italianate village of Portmeirion, the scenic hike to Cwm Idwal, and the charming towns of Ruthin or Llangollen. With more time and a desire to hike, consider the mountain village of Beddgelert as your base.

GETTING AROUND NORTH WALES

By Public Transportation: North Wales (except Ruthin) is well covered by a combination of buses and trains. That said, you'll want to get an early start and allow ample time if you plan to visit several destinations. TIs and B&B hosts can help you sort through your options to lace together an exciting day of North Wales sightseeing.

Trains: The main train line, run by Transport for Wales, travels along the north coast from Chester to Holyhead via Llandudno Junction, Conwy, and Bangor, with nearly hourly departures (tel. 0345-748-4950, www.nationalrail.co.uk, www.traveline.cymru, or www.tfwrail.wales; note that Virgin Trains to Holyhead do not stop in Conwy).

There are also several intersecting, scenic spur lines. From Llandudno Junction, the **Conwy Valley line** goes south to Betws-y-Coed and Blaenau Ffestiniog (see "Conwy Connections," on page 632). The old-fashioned **Welsh Highland Railway** steam train goes from Caernarfon to Beddgelert, then loops back to the coast and Porthmadog. Porthmadog is a terminus for the **Ffestiniog Railway** steam train, which heads into the mountains to Blaenau Ffestiniog, where it meets the Conwy Valley line. Both steam trains are described on page 643.

Buses: Public buses (run by various companies) pick up where trains leave off. Get the *Public Transport Information* booklet at any TI. Certain bus lines—dubbed "Sherpa" routes (bus numbers begin with #S)—circle Snowdonia National Park with the needs

North Wales at a Glance

▲▲**Conwy Castle** North Wales' best castle, in its most charming town, with stunning 360-degree views. **Hours:** Daily 9:30-17:00, July-Aug until 18:00; Nov-Feb Mon-Sat 10:00-16:00, Sun from 11:00. See page 623.

▲▲**Plas Mawr** Oldest house in Wales with a rare glimpse into 16th-century life within Conwy's walls. **Hours:** Daily 9:30-17:00, Oct until 16:00, closed Nov-March. See page 625.

▲▲**Caernarfon Castle** North Wales' best-known castle, with fine exhibits, and where Welsh princes are invested. **Hours:** Daily 9:30-17:00, July-Aug until 18:00; Nov-Feb Mon-Sat 10:00-16:00, Sun from 11:00. See page 642.

▲▲**Snowdon Mountain Railway** Britain's only rack-and-pinion railway chugs up to Mount Snowdon from Llanberis. **Hours:** Weather dependent but several daily late March-Oct generally 9:00-17:30, 10/day peak season. See page 652.

▲▲**National Slate Museum** 19th-century industrial workshop converted into an excellent museum. **Hours:** Daily 10:00-17:00; Nov-Easter Sun-Fri until 16:00, closed Sat. See page 653.

▲▲**Llechwedd Slate Caverns** Descend 500 feet into a working slate mine to learn harrowing tales of Victorian-era miners. **Hours:** Daily 9:00-17:30. See page 654.

▲▲**Plas Newydd** Tour the ornate manor home of two upper-class Irish women who ran off together and lived here in the 18th century. **Hours:** Daily 10:30-17:00, house interior closed Nov-March—but gardens open. See page 660.

▲**Bodnant Garden** One of Britain's best gardens, with 80 acres of flora amidst a craggy mountain backdrop. **Hours:** Daily 10:00-17:00 (Wed until 20:00 in summer); Nov-Feb daily until 16:00. See page 633.

▲**Harlech Castle** Compact castle built by Edward I, with expansive sea views. **Hours:** Daily 9:30-17:00, July-Aug until 18:00; Nov-Feb Mon-Sat 10:00-16:00, Sun from 11:00. See page 656.

▲**Portmeirion** Fun faux-Italian Riviera village that's a pastel-colored, flower-filled folly. **Hours:** Daily 9:30-19:30, Nov-March until 17:30. See page 656.

of hikers in mind (www.gwynedd.llyw.cymru, search "Snowdon Sherpa" for timetables).

Schedules get sparse late in the afternoon and on Sundays; plan ahead and confirm times carefully. For questions about public transportation, visit the Wales Travel Line website at www.traveline.cymru.

Your choices for money-saving public-transportation **passes** are confusing. The Red Rover Ticket—the simplest and probably the best bet for most travelers—covers all buses west of Llandudno, including Sherpa buses (£6.80/day, buy from driver). Sort through your choices at the TI to find the best deal for your itinerary.

By Car: Driving and parking throughout North Wales is easy and allows you to cover more ground. If you need to rent a car here, see "Helpful Hints," later.

By Private Tour: Donna Goodman leads private day trips of North Wales and walking tours of Conwy, Caernarfon, or Beaumaris, including the castles (from £180/day, book in advance, tel. 01286/677-059, mobile 07946-163-906, www.turnstone-tours.co.uk, info@turnstone-tours.co.uk).

Conwy

Along with Conwy Castle, this garrison town was built in the 1280s to give Edward I a toehold in Wales. As there were no real cities in 13th-century Wales, this was an English town, planted with settlers for the king's political purposes. What's left today are the best medieval walls in Britain, surrounding a humble town crowned by the bleak and barren hulk of a castle that was awesome in its day (and still is). Conwy's charming High Street leads down to a fishy harbor that permitted Edward to restock his castle safely. Because the modern highway was tunneled under the town, Conwy has a strolling ambience. I find it the perfect size—big enough to have a real vitality, but small enough to be cozy. It's one of the most purely delightful towns of its size in Britain.

Orientation to Conwy

Conwy is an enjoyably small community of 4,000 people. The walled old town center is compact and manageable. Lancaster Square marks the center, where you'll find the bus "station" (a blue-and-white bus shelter), the unstaffed train kiosk (the little white hut at the end of a sunken parking lot), and the start of the main drag—High Street—and my self-guided walk.

TOURIST INFORMATION

Conwy's TI is located across from the castle's short-stay parking lot on Rose Hill Street (Mon-Sat 9:30-17:00, Sun 10:30-16:30, tel. 01492/577-566, www.visitllandudno.org.uk). Because Conwy's train and bus "stations" are unstaffed, ask at the TI about train or bus schedules. Don't confuse the TI with the uninformative Conwy Visitors Centre, a big gift shop near the station.

ARRIVAL IN CONWY

By Bus or Train: Whether taking the bus or train, you need to tell the driver or conductor you want to stop at Conwy. Milk-run trains stop here only upon request; major trains don't stop here at all (instead, they stop at nearby Llandudno Junction—see next). For additional train info in town, ask at the TI, call tel. 0871-200-2233, or see www.traveline.cymru. If you're leaving Conwy by train, you can buy your ticket on board with no penalty.

For more frequent trains, use **Llandudno Junction,** visible a mile away beyond the bridges (to get into Conwy from here, catch bus #5, take a £6 taxi, or simply walk a mile if you've packed light—it's quite scenic, especially in good weather). Make sure to ask for trains that stop at Llandudno Junction, not Llandudno proper, which is a seaside resort farther from Conwy.

By Car: The easiest parking option for day-trippers is the pay lot just behind the castle, facing the TI.

HELPFUL HINTS

Festivals: The town is eager to emphasize its medieval history, with several events and festivals annually: Pirate Weekend (June, www.conwypirates.com), the River Festival (July/Aug, www.conwyriverfestival.org), and a food festival, which includes a laser light show projected onto the castle (Oct, www.conwyfeast.co.uk). The town also shuts down two days a year to host a pair of 700-year-old markets: the Seed Fair (March) and the Honey Fair (Sept). Ask the TI or your B&B what might be going on during your visit.

Laundry: In Llandudno Junction, **Junction Laundry Service** offers self- and full-service. Bus #5 from Conwy stops just outside (Mon-Sat 8:00-17:30, Sat 9:00-16:00, closed Sun, 161 Conway Road, tel. 01492/592-555).

Bike Rental: Conwy lacks its own bike-rental outfit, but **Buster's Cycles** in nearby Kinmel Bay has 10 pickup and drop-off spots, or can deliver a bike to you in Conwy for an extra charge (mountain, hybrid, and e-bikes available, tel. 07858/633-874, https://family-cyclehire.online, bustersholidaycyclehire@gmail.com).

Car Rental: Several car-rental agencies in the city of Llandudno (a mile north of Llandudno Junction) can generally deliver to you in Conwy; the Conwy TI has a list. The closest ones, in Llandudno Junction, are **Avis** (113a Conwy Road, tel. 0844-544-6075) and **Enterprise** (tel. 01492/593-380). Both close early on Saturday and all day Sunday.

Harbor Cruise: Two tour boats depart nearly hourly from the Conwy harborfront (£7/30 minutes, pay on boat, early Feb-Oct daily 10:30-17:00 or 18:00, may be cancelled for low tides, mobile 07917-343-058, http://sightseeingcruises.co.uk).

Conwy Walk

This brief self-guided orientation walk introduces you to essential Conwy in about an hour. As the town walls are open late, you can do this walk any time—evening is fine. For a shorter stroll, skip ahead to the harborfront's promenade, which is perfect for a peaceful half-mile shoreline walk (start at the Smallest House in Great Britain—listed later, under "Harborfront").

• *Start at the top of High Street on the main square.*

Lancaster Square: The square's centerpiece is a **column** honoring the town's red-cloaked founder, the Welsh prince Llywelyn the Great. Looking downhill, past the blue-and-white bus stop, find the cute pointed archway (possibly hidden behind the trees) built into the medieval wall so the train could get through. Turning 180 degrees and looking uphill, you can see Bangor Gate, built by the British engineer Thomas Telford in 1826 to accommodate traffic from his suspension bridge.

• *Walk uphill on York Place, past the recommended Alfredo Restaurant, to the end of the lane.*

Slate Memorials: This wall of various memorials includes one recalling the 1937 coronation of King George VI (the father of today's Queen Elizabeth II). Also find one offering a Welsh-language lesson, donated to the town by a citizen who never learned to read and wanted to inspire others to avoid his fate. It lists, in Welsh, the counties (shires, or *sir*), months (a few are vaguely recognizable), days, numbers, and the Welsh alphabet with its unique letters (CH, DD, FF, NG, LL, PH, and TH). Much has changed since this memorial was posted. Today more people speak Welsh, and all local children are taught Welsh in school until age 12.

• *Turn left and walk uphill on Upper Gate Street all the way to the wall, where steps lead to the ramparts. At the top of the stairs, head left and continue climbing to the very top of the town's tallest turret.*

Tallest Tower and Walls: You're standing atop the most complete set of medieval town walls in Britain. In 1283, workers started to build them in conjunction with the castle. Four years later, they sent a message to London declaring, "Castle habitable, town defensible." Edward then sent in English settlers. Enjoy the view from the top all the way down to Conwy Castle, at the

opposite corner of town (and the end point of this walk). From up here, guards could spot ships approaching by sea. Turn around 180 degrees to see Conwy Mountain, an enjoyable six-mile hike described later in this chapter.

• *Continue downhill around the ramparts.*

Ramparts: The turrets you see were positioned about every 50 yards, connected by ramparts, and each one had a drawbridge that could be raised to bottle up any breach. Passing the second turret, notice that its wall is cracked. When they tunneled underneath this turret for the train, the construction accidentally undermined the foundation, effectively taking the same tactic that invading armies would have. The huge crack makes plain why undermining was such a popular technique in medieval warfare. (Unlike the town walls, Conwy Castle was built upon solid rock, so it couldn't be undermined.)

• *At the first opportunity (just after walking above Bangor Gate), take the steps back down to street level. Then leave the old town by passing through Bangor Gate, heading downhill, and crossing the street for the best wide view of the walls. Behind you is the new **Conwy Culture***

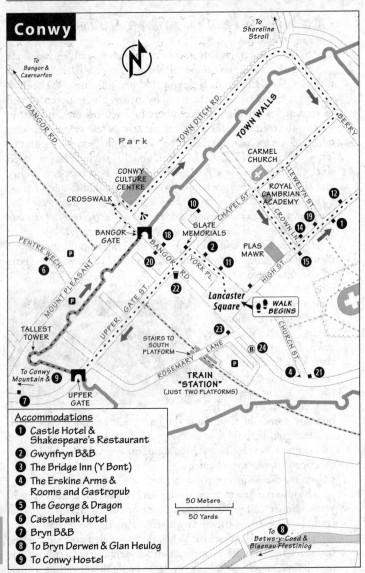

Conwy

Accommodations

1 Castle Hotel &
   Shakespeare's Restaurant
2 Gwynfryn B&B
3 The Bridge Inn (Y Bont)
4 The Erskine Arms &
   Rooms and Gastropub
5 The George & Dragon
6 Castlebank Hotel
7 Bryn B&B
8 To Bryn Derwen & Glan Heulog
9 To Conwy Hostel

NORTH WALES

Centre *containing a library, the Conwy archives, and interactive displays of historic collections.*

The Walls (from Outside): Walk down Town Ditch Road, named for the dry moat that was the first line of defense from the highest tower down to the riverbank. As was the case with most walled towns, there was a clear swath of "dead ground" outside the walls, so no one could sneak up. Once England centralized and consolidated its rule, there was no longer a use for all the walls and

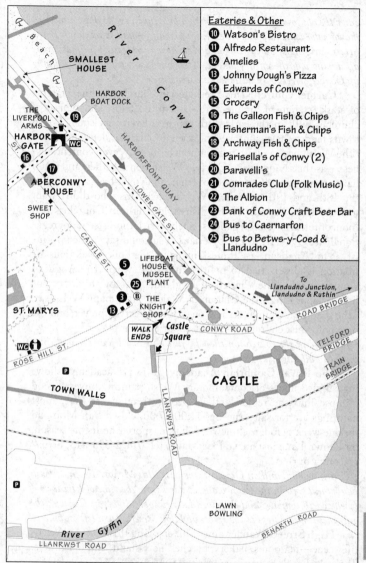

castles in Britain. Most fell into disrepair—ravaged by time and by scavengers who used them as quarries. During the Napoleonic Wars, English aristocrats were unable to make their Grand Tour of the Continent, so they explored the far reaches of their own land. That's when ruined castles such as Conwy's were "discovered" and began to be appreciated for their romantic allure.

• Stroll downhill to the bottom of Town Ditch Road. At the elderly-crossing sign (which also serves as a reminder to stand up straight), re-

enter the old town—crossing through a hole cut in the wall by a modern mayor who wanted better access from his land—and walk down Berry Street. Originally called "Burial Street," it was a big ditch for mass burials during a 17th-century plague. After one block, turn right, climbing up Chapel Street to an austere stone structure.

Carmel Church: This Presbyterian church is a fine example of stark "statement architecture"—stern, no frills, and typical of churches built in the early 20th century. Even very small Welsh towns tend to have churches for several Christian denominations. (The Welsh have a reputation for nonconformity, even contentiousness—as the saying goes, "Get two Welshmen together, and you'll have an argument. Get three together, and you'll have a fight.") In the 18th and 19th centuries, Welsh Christians who didn't want to worship in the official, English-style Anglican Church joined "nonconformist" congregations, such as Methodists, Congregationalists, Quakers, or Presbyterians. You could say "nonconformist" is to "Anglican" as "Protestant" is to "Catholic." Religious affiliation is closely tied to politics in Wales, where the Anglican Church, a.k.a. "The Church of England," goes by the more politically appealing "The Church in Wales." Still, many Welsh say, "The Anglican Church is the Conservative Party at prayer, and the nonconformist churches are the Labour Party at prayer."

• *Just beyond the church (on the left, just past Sea View Terrace), in a modern building, is...*

The Royal Cambrian Academy: This art academy, showing off two floors of contemporary Welsh painting, gives a good glimpse into the region and its people through art (free, most paintings are for sale; Tue-Sat 11:00-17:00, closed Sun-Mon and for one week before each new exhibition, shorter hours off-season; on Crown Lane just above Plas Mawr, tel. 01492/593-413, http://rcaconwy.org).

• *Continue downhill on Crown Lane past **Plas Mawr**. The first Welsh house built within the town walls, it dates from the time of Elizabeth I (well worth touring, and described later, under "Sights in Conwy"; the entrance is a few steps to the right, up High Street). Turn left onto...*

High Street: Wander downhill, enjoying this slice-of-Welsh-life scene—tearooms, bakery, butcher, newsstand, and old timers. The colorful flags you may see have no meaning—merchants fly them simply to pump up the town's medieval feel. **Aberconwy House** marks the bottom of High Street (the white house with the stone base, on your right). One of the oldest houses in town, it's now a skippable mu-

seum. In its garrison-town days, Conwy was filled with half-timbered buildings just like this one. At end of High Street, 20 yards to the right at 4 Castle Street, is the **Conwy Sweet Shop**—filled with old-fashioned candy.

• *Follow High Street through the gate and to the harbor.*

Harborfront: The Harbor Gate, one of three original gates in the town walls, leads to the waterfront. The harbor dates from the 13th century, when it served Edward's castle and town. (The harborfront street is still called King's Quay.) Conwy was once a busy slate port. Slate, barged downstream to here, was loaded onto big three-masted ships and transported to the Continent. Back when much of Europe was roofed with Welsh slate, Conwy was a boomtown. All the mud is new—the modern bridge caused this part of the river to silt up.

The actions of the European Union have had a mixed effect on this waterfront. EU money helped pay for the recently built promenade, but hygiene laws have forced Conwy's fishermen out: Now that fish must be transported in refrigerated vehicles, the fishermen had to set up shop a few miles away (since refrigerator trucks can't fit through the stone gate).

Conwy's harbor is now a laid-back area that locals treat like a town square. On summer evenings, the action is on the quay (pronounced "key"). The scene is mellow, multigenerational, and perfectly Welsh. It's a small town, and everyone is here enjoying the local cuisine—"chips," ice cream, and beer—and savoring that great British pastime: torturing little crabs. (If you want to do more than photograph the action, rent gear from the nearby lifeboat house. Mooch some bacon from others for bait, and join in. It's catch-and-release.)

The benches and knee-high walls all along here are ideal for a picnic (two recommended fish-and-chips shops are back through the gate). Just be wary of those noisy gulls taking an interest in your food: They're notorious for swooping in and stealing your lunch while you're distracted.

Just next to the Harbor Gate is **The Liverpool Arms** pub, built by a captain who ran a ferry service to Liverpool in the 19th century. Today it remains a salty and characteristic hangout—one of the few thriving pubs in town. In 1900, Conwy had about 40 pubs. Back when this harbor was busy with quarrymen shipping their slate, mussel men carting their catch, and small farmers with their goods, Conwy's pubs were all thriving. Today, times are tough on the pubs, and this one depends on tourism.

• *Facing the harbor in front of The Liverpool Arms, turn left and walk along the promenade.*

It's easy to miss the **Smallest House in Great Britain.** It's red, 72 inches wide, 122 inches high, and worth £1 to pop in and listen to the short audioguide tour. No WC—but it did have a bedpan (daily 10:00-16:00, closed Nov-March, mobile 07925-049-786).

• *Now do an about-face and walk along the promenade in the opposite direction, toward the bridges and castle.*

About 100 yards down, on your right, you'll find a **mussel-processing plant.** Mussels, historically a big "crop" for Conwy, are processed "in the months with an R." If there's a fresh catch, you'll find a little shop here; you can read information panels about mussels anytime.

The nearby **lifeboat house** welcomes visitors. Each coastal town has a house like this one, outfitted with a rescue boat suited to the area—in the shallow waters around Conwy, inflatable boats work best. You'll see *Lifeboats* stickers around town, marking homes of people who donate to the valuable cause of the Royal National Lifeboat Institution (RNLI)—Britain's all-volunteer and totally donation-funded answer to the Coast Guard.

Check out the striking **sculpture** on the quay—a giant clump of mussels carved from dark-gray limestone.

• *Walk past the sculpture and head up the stairs by the huge red-and-white buoy to the big street for a view of the castle and bridges. You can cross the road for a closer look at the...*

Bridges: Three bridges cross the river, side by side. Behind the modern 1958 highway bridge is the historic 1826 Telford Suspension Bridge. This was an engineering marvel in its day, part of a big infrastructure project to better connect Ireland with the rest of the realm (and, as a result, have more control over Ireland). In those days, Dublin was the number-two city in all of Britain. These two major landmarks—the castle and 19th-century bridge—are both symbols of English imperialism. Just beyond that is Robert Stephenson's tube bridge for the train line (built in 1848). These days, 90 percent of traffic passes Conwy underground, unseen and unheard, in a modern tunnel.

• *On the town side of the big road, follow the sidewalk away from the water, past the ivy and through an arch, to a tiny park around a well. Facing that square is...*

The Knight Shop: If you're in the market for a battle-axe or perhaps some chainmail, pop in here. Even if you're not, it's a fun place to browse. The manager, Toby, is evangelical about mead, an ancient drink made from honey. Most travelers just get the cheap stuff at tourist shops, but Toby offers free tastes to help you appreciate quality mead (daily 10:00-17:00, Castle Square, tel. 01492/596-142, www.theknightshop.com).

• *Now, with a belly full of mead, set your bleary eyes on the...*

View of Conwy Castle: Imagine this castle when it was newly built. Its eight mighty drum towers were brightly whitewashed, a statement of power from the English king to the Welsh—who had no cities and little more than bows and arrows to fight with. The castle is built upon solid rock—making it impossible for invaders to tunnel underneath the walls. The English paid dearly for its construction, through heavy taxes. And today, with the Welsh flag proudly flying from its top, the English pay again just to visit. Notice the remains of the castle entry, which was within the town walls. There was once a steep set of stairs (designed so no horse could approach) up to the drawbridge. The castle is by far the town's top sight (described next).

Sights in Conwy

▲▲Conwy Castle

Positioned on a rock overlooking the sea with eight linebacker towers, this castle has an interesting story to tell. Finished in just four

years, it had a water gate that allowed safe entry for English boats in a land of hostile Welsh subjects. This is my favorite of the many castles in North Wales—it's compact, fun to explore, and has the best views.

Cost and Hours: £9.90, £12.10 combo-ticket with Plas Mawr; daily 9:30-17:00, July-Aug until 18:00; Nov-Feb Mon-Sat 10:00-16:00, Sun from 11:00; tel. 01492/592-358, www.cadw.gov.wales.

Visiting the Castle: The exhibits are paltry, so just enjoy exploring the place and climbing its ramparts and towers. Entering the main courtyard, head to the far end (past the 91-foot-deep, spring-fed well) and go through the Middle Gate to access the main courtyard. Of the four perfectly round towers here, you can climb to the very top of three of them—each one with stunning 360-degree views over the entire area. In the base of the Chapel Tower is a scale model of the town as it might have looked around the year 1312.

Around the corner are stairs up to the wall walk. Head up and find a small chapel (with reconstructed stained-glass windows) and—up another flight of stairs—the king's "watching chamber"

King Edward's Castles

The castles of Wales hover in the mist as mysterious reminders of the country's hard-fought history. In the 13th century, the Welsh, unified by two great princes named Llywelyn, created a united and independent Wales. The English king, Edward I, fought hard to end this Welsh sovereignty. In 1282, Llywelyn the Last was killed (and went "where everyone speaks Welsh"). King Edward spent the next 20 years building or rebuilding 17 great castles to consolidate his English foothold in troublesome North Wales. The greatest of these

(such as Conwy Castle) were masterpieces of medieval engineering, with round towers (tough to undermine), castle-within-a-castle defenses (giving defenders a place to retreat and wreak havoc on the advancing enemy...or just wait for reinforcements), and sea access (safe to restock from England).

These castles were English islands in the middle of angry Wales. Most were built with a fortified grid-plan town attached and then filled with English settlers. (With this blatant abuse of Wales, you have to wonder, where was Greenpeace 700 years ago?) Edward I was arguably England's most successful monarch. By establishing and consolidating his realm (adding Wales to England), he made his kingdom big enough to compete with other rising European powers.

Edward I's "big five" border castles—listed next—are all within about an hour's drive of each other. Doing all five is overkill for most visitors. When choosing your castle, consider the town attached to each. Compared to Caernarfon, Conwy is more quaint, with a higgledy-piggledy medieval vibe and a modern workaday heart and soul. Conwy also has more accommodations and good eateries than Caernarfon, making it a better home base.

(for observing chapel services by himself...complete with a private toilet). From there, climb another flight of stairs to a room where videos are projected onto the wall. Continue up the last strenuous stairs to the top—definitely worth it for the view.

▲City Walls

Most of the walls, with 22 towers and castle and harbor views, can be walked for free. Start at Upper Gate (the highest point) or Berry Street (the lowest), or you can do the small section at the castle entrance. (My favorite stretch is described on my "Conwy Walk," earlier.) In the evening, most of the walkways stay open,

The castles themselves are mostly variations on the same theme, with modest, mildly interesting exhibits and lots of stony stairs to climb. You'll hike to the top of towers, stroll along ramparts, and peer into grassy, open courtyards. To help you choose, here's a quick rundown—listed roughly in my order of preference (and all described in this chapter):

▲▲**Conwy** is my favorite castle in North Wales. It's a bit more ruined and less slick than Caernarfon, but in a way, that makes it more evocative. It's compact and has the best views.

▲▲**Caernarfon** is the most famous of the castles. With several entertaining exhibits inside, it's probably the best presented.

▲**Harlech** has perhaps the most dramatic setting, perched on a hillside next to the cute town of Blaenau Ffestiniog, with sweeping views.

▲**Beaumaris,** surrounded by a moat on the Isle of Anglesey, is the last and largest of Edward's castles. It was never finished, but would've been the quintessential medieval castle if it had been.

Criccieth (KRICK-ith), the smallest of the five, is perched on a hilltop over the sea near Snowdonia National Park. The views *from* the castle are magnificent, but there's very little to see inside.

If you have a big appetite for castles, a car and two days gives you one of Europe's best castle tours. All five castles are operated by Cadw (KAH-dew), the Welsh version of England's National Trust, and share similar opening hours (daily 9:30-17:00, July-Aug until 18:00; Nov-Feb Mon-Sat 10:00-16:00, Sun from 11:00). Criccieth has slightly shorter hours (see listing).

If you're visiting at least three of the castles, consider Cadw's three-day Explorer Pass, which covers the castles plus many other sights in Wales (£23.10, £35.70 for 2 people, £47.25 for a family; 7-day pass available; buy at castle ticket offices). For more information on the castles and other Welsh historic monuments, see www.cadw.gov.wales.

though the section located near the castle closes 30 minutes before the castle does.

▲▲Plas Mawr

A rare house from 1580, built during the reign of Elizabeth I, Plas Mawr was the first Welsh home to be built within Conwy's walls. (The Tudor family had Welsh roots—and therefore relations between Wales and England warmed.) Billed as "the oldest house in Wales," it offers a delightful look at 16th-century domestic life, with gorgeous plasterwork throughout. Historically accurate household items bring the rooms to life, as does the refreshing lack of velvet ropes—you're free to wander as you imagine life in this house. Unlike the austere Welsh castles, here you'll feel like you're visiting a home where the 16th-century owner has just stepped out for a minute.

Cost and Hours: £7.30, £12.10 combo-ticket with Conwy Castle, includes audioguide; daily 9:30-17:00, Oct until 16:00, closed Nov-March; last entry 45 minutes before closing, tel. 01492/580-167, www.cadw.gov.wales.

Visiting the House: At the entry, pick up the included audioguide—it's engagingly narrated by family members who lived here. Docents, who are posted in some rooms, are happy to answer your questions—take advantage of their enthusiasm.

Guests stepping into the house in the 16th century were wowed by the heraldry over the fireplace. This symbol, now repainted in

its original bright colors, proclaimed the family's rich lineage and princely stock. The kitchen came with all the circa-1600 conveniences: hay on the floor to add a little warmth and soak up spills; a hanging bread cage to keep food safe from wandering critters; and a good supply of fresh meat in the pantry. Inside the parlor, an interactive display lets you take a closer virtual look at the different parts of the house. The brewhouse is where the family made their own ale.

Upstairs, the lady of the house's bedroom doubled as a sitting room—with a finely carved four-poster bed and a foot warmer by the chair. At night, the bedroom's curtains were drawn to keep in warmth. In the great chamber next door, hearty evening feasting was followed by boisterous gaming, dancing, and music. And fixed above all this extravagant entertainment was...more heraldry, pronouncing those important—if unproven—family connections, and leaving a powerful impact on impressed guests. On the same floor is a well-done exhibit on health and hygiene in medieval Britain—you'll be grateful you were born a few centuries later.

Don't bother climbing the many stairs to the top of the tower—the views from the castle and town wall are better.

St. Mary's Parish Church

Sitting lonely in the town center, Conwy's church was the centerpiece of a Cistercian abbey that stood here a century before the town or castle. The Cistercians were French monks who built their abbeys in places "far from the haunts of man." Popular here because they were French—that is, not English—the Cistercians taught locals farming and mussel-gathering techniques. Edward moved the monks 12 miles upstream but kept the church for his town. Out in the churchyard, find the tombstone of a survivor of the 1805 Battle of Trafalgar who died in 1860 (two feet left of the north transept). On the other side of the church, a tomb containing seven brothers and sisters is marked "We Are Seven." It inspired William Wordsworth to write his poem of the same name. The slate tombstones look new even though many are hundreds of years old; slate weathers better than marble.

Cost and Hours: Free; church generally open Mon-Fri 10:00-16:00 except Wed from 11:30, Sat 11:00-15:00, closed Sun though you can try visiting before or after the services at 11:00; tel. 01492/593-402, www.caruconwy.com.

JUST BEYOND CONWY
Conwy Mountain Hikes

For lovely views across the bay to Llandudno, take a pleasant walk (50 minutes one-way) along the footpath up Conwy Mountain (follow Sychnant Pass Road past the recommended Bryn B&B, look for fields on the right and a sign with a stick figure of a walker).

For an even more satisfying, extended version of this hike, begin at the top of the pass. Drivers should look for the pullout on the left with hiking signs, just past the Pensychnant Conservation Centre. Or, so that you don't have to backtrack to fetch your car later, take a taxi or bum a ride from a friendly local (such as your B&B host). From the parking lot, it's about an hour-long walk along a lovely ridgeline with gorgeous 360-degree views. After about 10 minutes, the official Wales Coastal Trail veers to the right; at this point, bear left and follow the gravel path over the peaks for a higher vantage point. Eventually you'll rejoin the official path and pop out into the suburbs of Conwy. The hike is easy to moderate, with a bit of steep climbing up and down on loose-gravel trails.

Llandudno

This genteel Victorian beach resort, a few miles away, is much bigger and better known than Conwy. It was built after the advent of railroads, which made the Welsh seacoast easily accessible to the English industrial heartland. In the 1800s, the notion that bathing in seawater was good for your health was trendy, and the bracing sea air was just what the doctor ordered. These days, Llandudno remains popular with the English, but you won't see many other foreigners strolling its long pleasure pier and line of old-time hotels. If the weather is nice, it's worth checking out if only to see how middle-class Brits like to holiday.

Nightlife in Conwy

No one goes to Conwy for wild nightlife. But you will find some typically Welsh diversions here.

In Town: The **Conwy Folk Music Club** plays at the Comrades Club off Church Street Mondays at 20:30. Note that this isn't local, Welsh-language folk music, but amateurs performing a variety of folk tunes from every region and era (free, doors open at 20:00, www.conwyfolkclub.org.uk).

To sample local brews, including some made in Conwy, head to **The Albion.** Managed by a coalition of four local breweries, the Albion has real ales and a fun communal pub atmosphere (Sun-Thu 12:00-23:00, Fri-Sat until 24:00, Upper Gate Street, tel. 01492/582-484).

Bank of Conwy Craft Beer Bar is a bustling place with live music Wednesdays and Fridays from 21:00. Enjoy one of their many beers either downstairs in the old vault or upstairs, where you'll still see remnants of the bank's interior (daily 9:00-23:00, Lancaster Square, tel. 01492/573-741).

Near Conwy: For an authentic Welsh experience, catch a performance of the **local choir.** The Maelgwn men's choir from nearby Llandudno Junction rehearses weekly, and visitors are welcome to watch (free, Mon 19:30-21:00 except Aug, call ahead to confirm, at Awel y Mynydd School, Pen Dyffryn, Llandudno Junction, tel. 01492/534-115, www.cormaelgwn.cymru).

Several churches in Llandudno hold regular **choir concerts** in summer. Concerts at St. John's Church feature a rotation of visiting choirs (£7, May-Oct Tue and Thu at 20:00, doors open at 19:15, between the two Marks & Spencer stores at 53 Mostyn Street, tel. 01492/860-439, www.stjohnsllandudno.org). The Llanddulas Choir performs weekly concerts at Gloddaeth Church (£6, April-Sept most Tue at 20:00, corner of Chapel Street and Gloddaeth Street, www.llanddulaschoir.co.uk).

Llandudno also has the **beach fun** you'd expect at a Coney-Island-type coastal resort.

Sleeping in Conwy

Conwy's hotels are overpriced, but its B&Bs include some good-value gems. Nearly all have free parking (ask when booking). There's no launderette; the closest one is in Llandudno Junction, a short drive (or bus or taxi ride) away.

INSIDE CONWY'S WALLED OLD TOWN

Note that on summer weekends, bar-hoppers and revelers can make the Old Town a bit noisy: Ask for a quieter room or pack earplugs.

NORTH WALES

$$$ Castle Hotel, along the main drag, rents 29 comfortable rooms where Old World antique furnishings mingle with modern amenities. The rec-ommended Shakespeare's restaurant is located in-side the hotel (RS%, High

Street, tel. 01492/582-800, www.castlewales.co.uk, castle@innmail. co.uk, Joe Lavin).

$$ Gwynfryn B&B is located dead center in town, a few steps off Lancaster Square. The four rooms in their main house are bright and airy, each with eclectic decor. In the old chapel next door, they've converted the vestry into four utilitarian, less-charm-ing but well-designed and comfortable rooms. The main part of the church, with pews and a big organ looming overhead, is now a striking breakfast room in the morning and a bar in the evening (no children under 15, free parking nearby, self-catering cottage for 4 available, 4 York Place, on the lane off Lancaster Square, tel. 01492/576-733, mobile 07947-272-821, www.gwynfrynbandb. co.uk, info@gwynfrynbandb.co.uk, energetic Monica and Colin).

Rooms Above Pubs and Restaurants

These old-town listings are a good option if my recommended B&Bs are full.

$$ The Bridge Inn (Y Bont) is located on top of the rec-ommended Johnny Dough's Pizza, near the castle. It has six straightforward rooms and lots of stairs, and its location—on a busy roundabout—makes traffic noise unavoidable (Rose Hill Street, tel. 01492/572-974, www.bridgeinnconwy.co.uk, info@ bridgeinnconway.co.uk).

$$ The Erskine Arms, a newer place, rents 10 clean and el-egant rooms and sits atop the gastropub with the same name (10 Church Street, tel. 01492/593-535, www.erskinearms.co.uk, info@ erskinearms.co.uk).

$$ The George and Dragon has seven modern rooms in the heart of town; while comfortable, they're not the best value (21 Castle Street, tel. 01492/584-232, www.georgeanddragonconwy. com).

BEYOND THE OLD TOWN
Just Outside the Wall

These options are just a few paces from Conwy's old town wall.

$$ Castlebank Hotel feels old-time plush, with nine exuber-antly decorated rooms (some quite spacious), a small bar, and an inviting lounge with a wood-burning fireplace that makes the Welsh winter warmer (family rooms, easy free parking, closed first 3 weeks in Jan, just outside town wall at Mount Pleasant, tel. 01492/593-888, www.castlebankhotel.co.uk, reservations@castlebankhotel.co.uk, Jo and Henrique).

$$ Bryn B&B offers four large, tastefully decorated rooms (and one small one) with castle or mountain views in a big 19th-century house with the city wall literally in the backyard. Owners Anne and Neil run the place with style, providing all the thoughtful touches—a library of regional guides and maps, a glorious garden, granny's Welsh cakes for breakfast, and a very warm welcome (one room with private bathroom next door, ground-floor room available, private parking, just outside Upper Gate of wall on Sychnant Pass Road, tel. 01492/592-449, www.bryn.org.uk, stay@bryn.org.uk).

Farther Out

The first two places, both good-value options with free parking, share a building overlooking Llanrwst Road on the way to Betws-y-Coed, about a 10-minute walk from the center.

$$ Bryn Derwen Guest House rents six modern rooms that feel tidy and contemporary. Friendly Andrew and Jill serve you breakfast with a view overlooking the garden (tel. 01492/596-134, www.conwybrynderwen.co.uk, info@conwybrynderwen.co.uk).

$ Glan Heulog Guest House offers seven bright rooms and a pleasant, enclosed sun porch (one room with private bathroom downstairs, family suite, will pick you up at the train station, tel. 01492/593-845, www.conwy-bedandbreakfast.co.uk, stay@conwy-bedandbreakfast.co.uk, Richard and Jenny Nash).

¢ Conwy Hostel, welcoming travelers of any age, has super views from all 25 rooms and a spacious garden. The airy dining hall and glorious rooftop lounge and deck make you feel like you're in the majestic midst of Wales (breakfast extra, packed lunches, dinner, bar, elevator, parking, staffed 24 hours, check-in at 15:00, Sychnant Pass Road in Larkhill, tel. 01492/593-571, www.yha.org.uk, conwy@yha.org.uk). It's a 10-minute uphill walk from the Upper Gate of Conwy's wall.

Eating in Conwy

RESTAURANTS IN THE WALLED OLD TOWN

For dinner, consider strolling down High Street, comparing the cute teahouses and workaday eateries. With limited options for a good sit-down meal, Conwy gets booked up on summer weekends: Reserve ahead on Friday or Saturday night.

$$$$ Watson's Bistro, tucked away on Chapel Street, serves freshly prepared modern and traditional Welsh cuisine in a warm wood-floor-and-exposed-beam setting. Dishes are made from locally sourced ingredients and well worth the splurge. It's more affordable if you get the early-bird special, served weekdays before 18:30 and on Sunday (Wed-Sun 17:30-20:30, also open Fri-Sat 12:00-14:00, closed Mon-Tue, reservations smart, tel. 01492/596-326, www.watsonsbistroconwy.co.uk).

$$$ Shakespeare's, in the recommended Castle Hotel, has a good selection of seafood and other dishes. The same menu is served in both the dressy restaurant (reservations recommended) and the more casual Dawson's Bar (daily 12:00-21:30, High Street, tel. 01492/582-800, www.castlewales.co.uk).

$$ The Erskine Arms, at the top of Rose Hill Street, has a classy setting with good food including a few Welsh specialties (daily 11:30-23:00, 10 Church Street, tel. 01492/593-535).

$$ Alfredo Restaurant, a thriving and family-friendly place right on Lancaster Square, serves decent, reasonably priced Italian food (daily 18:00-22:00, York Place, tel. 01492/592-381, Christine).

$$ Amelies, located in what used to be the old cinema, serves breakfast and lunch. Follow the stairs up to the friendly dining room. Amelie has a hardworking staff and an eclectic menu inspired by French and Welsh cuisine (Tue-Sun 10:00-17:00, closed Mon, 10 High Street, tel. 01492/583-142).

$ Johnny Dough's Pizza is a popular spot for inexpensive wood-fired pizza (food served daily 12:00-21:00, Rose Hill Street, tel. 01492/572-974).

TAKEAWAY AND PICNICS

$ Edwards of Conwy, a well-respected butcher right on High Street, has a deli counter serving top-quality and affordably priced meals to go, including hot or cold sandwiches and curries (Mon-Sat 7:00-17:30, Sun 10:00-16:00, 18 High Street, tel. 01492/581-111). The **Spar** grocery is conveniently located and well stocked (daily 7:00-23:00, middle of High Street).

$ Fish-and-Chips: At the bottom of High Street, on the intersecting Castle Street, are two chippies—**The Galleon** (daily 12:00-19:00 in summer, until 15:00 off-season weekdays, closed Nov-mid-March, mobile 07899-901-637) and **Fisherman's** (daily 11:30-20:00, closes earlier off-season, small sit-down area, tel. 01492/593-792). **Archway Fish & Chips,** at the top of town just inside Bangor Gate, is open later and has both a restaurant and takeaway service (takeout daily 11:30-22:00, restaurant daily until 20:00, 10 Bangor Road, tel. 01492/592-458). Consider taking your fish-and-chips down to the harbor and sharing it with the noisy seagulls.

Sweets: Parisella's of Conwy has some of the best ice cream I've enjoyed in Britain, including some unusual flavors. They have locations on High Street and along the harborfront (both typically daily 10:00-19:30 in summer). Near Lancaster Square, **Baravelli's** makes their own top-end chocolates, which have earned a national reputation (Mon-Sat 10:00-17:00, Sun 11:00-16:00, 13 Bangor Road, tel. 01492/330-0540).

Conwy Connections

If you want to leave Conwy by train, be sure the schedule indicates the train can stop there, then wave as it approaches; for more frequent trains, go to Llandudno Junction (see "Arrival in Conwy," earlier). Train schedules are posted at street level before you descend to the platforms. There's no ticket machine on the Conwy platform; buy your ticket from the conductor. For train info, see www.traveline.cymru. If hopping around by bus, simply buy the £6.80 Red Rover Ticket from the driver, and you're covered for the entire day on buses running west of Llandudno. Remember, all connections are less frequent on Sundays.

From Conwy by Bus to: Llandudno Junction (5/hour, 10 minutes), **Caernarfon** (3-4/hour, 1.5 hours), **Betws-y-Coed** (hourly, 45 minutes, fewer on Sun), **Blaenau Ffestiniog** (8/day, none on Sun, 1.5 hours, transfer in Llandudno Junction to bus #X19, also stops in Betws-y-Coed; train is better—see later), **Beddgelert** (6/day, 2 hours, requires 1 or 2 transfers—in Bangor and/or Caernarfon).

From Conwy by Train to: Llandudno Junction (nearly hourly, 10 minutes), **Chester** (nearly hourly, 1 hour), **Holyhead** (nearly hourly, 1 hour), **Llangollen** (5/day, 2 hours; take train to Ruabon, then change to bus #5 or #T3), **London**'s Euston Station (nearly hourly, 3.5 hours, transfer in Chester).

From Llandudno Junction by Train to the Conwy Valley: Take the train to Llandudno Junction, where you'll board the scenic little Conwy Valley line, which runs up the pretty Conwy Valley to **Betws-y-Coed** and **Blaenau Ffestiniog** (5/day Mon-Sat, 3/day on Sun in summer, no Sun trains in winter, 30 minutes to Betws-y-Coed, 1 hour to Blaenau Ffestiniog, www.conwyvalleyrailway.co.uk). If your train from Conwy to Llandudno Junction is late and you miss the Conwy Valley connection, tell a station employee at Llandudno Junction, who can arrange a taxi for you. Your taxi is free, as long as the missed connection is the Conwy train's fault *and* the next train doesn't leave for more than an hour (common on the infrequent Conwy Valley line).

From Llandudno Junction by Train to: **Chester** (3/hour, 1 hour), **Birmingham** (5/day direct, 3 hours, more with transfers), **London**'s Euston Station (5/day direct, 3 hours, many more with transfers).

Near Conwy

SOUTH OF CONWY

These sights are on the route to Betws-y-Coed and Snowdonia National Park. Note that Bodnant Garden is on the east side of the River Conwy, on the A-470, while Trefriw and Surf Snowdonia are on the west side, along the B-5106 (see the "Snowdonia Area" map, later). To see sights on both sides, you'll drive about 20 minutes and cross the river at Tal-y-Cafn.

▲Bodnant Garden

This sumptuous 80-acre display of floral color six miles south of Conwy is one of Britain's best gardens—it's worth ▲▲▲ for gar-

deners and nature lovers. Originally the private garden of the stately Bodnant Hall, this lush landscape was donated by the Aberconway family (who still live in the house) to the National Trust in 1949.

Cost and Hours: £15.40; daily 10:00-17:00 (Wed until 20:00 in summer), Nov-Feb daily until 16:00; WCs in parking lot and inside garden, best in spring, check online to see what's blooming and get a schedule of guided walks, tel. 01492/650-460, www.nationaltrust.org.uk/bodnant-garden.

Getting There: To reach the garden by public transportation from Conwy, first take a bus or train to Llandudno Junction, then catch bus #25 (6/day Mon-Sat, 30 minutes, direction: Eglwysbach; on Sun take bus #X19, 3/day, 15 minutes, direction: Betws-y-Coed or Dolwyddelan).

Eating: The garden has multiple cafés. Also, located next to the car park is the **Pavilion Tearoom**, offering locally produced wine and beer, and the opportunity to have home-baked cakes and a cup of tea in their tearooms (daily 9:00-17:00, closed in winter, www.bodnant-estate.co.uk).

Visiting the Gardens: The map you receive upon entering helps you navigate the sprawling grounds. The highlight for many is the famous Laburnum Arch—a 180-foot-long canopy made of

bright-yellow laburnum, hanging like stalactites over the heads of garden lovers who stroll beneath it (just inside the entry, blooms late May through early June).

The garden is also famous for its magnolias, rhododendrons, camellias, and roses—and for the way that the buildings of the estate complement the carefully planned landscaping—all with a backdrop of rolling hills and craggy Welsh mountains. The wild English-style plots seem to spar playfully with the more formal rose gardens along the terrace. Victorian explorers donated rare species to the owners—try to find an American redwood tree and Himalayan poppies. Consider your visit an extravagantly beautiful nature hike, and walk all the way to the old mill and waterfall. If you're going to devote substantial time to any garden in Britain, this one deserves serious consideration.

Nearby: About 1.5 miles south of Bodnant Garden off the A-470, the **Bodnant Welsh Food Centre** has a farm shop selling mostly food produced in Wales, a restaurant, an underwhelming tearoom, and a cooking school (Mon-Sat 9:00-17:00, Sun 10:00-16:00, tel. 01492/651-100, www.bodnant-welshfood.co.uk). It's also the home of the National Beekeeping Centre, which features an interesting exhibit on bees and honey production and offers paid tours of its beehives in nice weather (Tue-Sat 10:00-16:00, Sun from 11:00, closed Mon and all of Nov-March, tel. 01492/651-106, www.beeswales.co.uk).

Surf Snowdonia

The world's largest simulated wave pool is improbably located in a tranquil Welsh valley, where surfers and amateurs alike can pay to ride perfect waves in the "wave garden." They offer lessons for beginners, or experienced surfers can simply rent time in the pool (check website for specifics, and to book ahead). Even if you're not looking to surf, this can be a good spot to grab lunch while you watch the lagoon action. They also have a kids' activity pool, as well as "glamping" pods for a unique overnight experience.

Cost and Hours: Surf lessons—£55, one hour of time for experienced and novice surfers—£50, rentable boards and wetsuits, daily 8:30-23:00—waves run until sunset, tel. 01492/353-123, www.adventureparcsnowdonia.com.

Getting There: The complex is located three miles north of Trefriw in the village of Dolgarrog. Take bus #19 from Lancaster Square in Conwy to Y Ganolfan in Dolgarrog (hourly direct, fewer on Sun, 30 minutes).

Trefriw Woolen Mills

At Trefriw (TREV-roo), five miles north of Betws-y-Coed, you can peek into a working woolen mill. It's surprisingly interesting and rated ▲ if the machines are running (weekdays; machines don't run in winter).

Cost and Hours: Free, variable hours for different parts of mill (see below), tel. 01492/640-462, www.t-w-m.co.uk.

Getting There: Bus #19 goes from Conwy and Llandudno Junction right to Trefriw (hourly Mon-Sat, fewer on Sun, 30 minutes).

Visiting the Mill: This mill turns British wool (and some from New Zealand) into bedspreads, rugs, and tweeds. The highlight is the **mill museum** (Mon-Fri 10:00-13:00 & 14:00-17:00, closed Sat-Sun, closed Nov-Easter due to lack of heat). Pick up the self-guided tour brochure, then walk through both levels of the mill, following the 11 stages of wool transformation: blending, carding, spinning, doubling, hanking, spanking, warping, weaving, and so on (some, but not all, machines are likely running at any one time). Follow a matted glob of fleece on its journey to becoming a fashionable cap or scarf. It's impressive that this Rube Goldberg-type process was so ingeniously designed and coordinated in an age before computers (mostly the 1950s and 1960s)—each machine seems to "know" how to do its rattling, clattering duty with amazing precision. In summer, the **rug-making and hand-spinning house** (next to the WC) has a charming spinster as well as yarn and knitted goods for sale (only open Tue-Thu June-Sept).

You can peruse the finished products in the **shop** (Mon-Sat 9:30-17:30, Sun 11:00-17:00; shorter hours and closed Sun in off-season). The whole complex creates its own hydroelectric power; the "**turbine house**" in the cellar lets you glance at enormous, fiercely spinning turbines dating from the 1930s and 1940s, powered by streams that flow down the hillside above the mill (same hours as shop). Watch the **weaving looms,** with bobbin-loaded shuttles flying to and fro, to see a bedspread being created (Mon-Fri 10:00-13:00 & 14:00-17:00).

Nearby: The grade school next door is busy with rambunctious Welsh-speaking kids—fun to listen to at recess.

Thrill-Seeking in Wales

To further immerse yourself in North Wales' natural beauty—and inject some adrenaline into your travels—you can pick from a variety of outdoor activities. These are becoming increasingly popular with travelers, particularly those with teen-agers.

Zipline courses at two old slate mines—in Blaenau Ffestiniog and Bethesda—let you speed high above piles of discarded slate scraps. The same company also runs a zipline course through the woods near Betws-y-Coed, and a half-mile long "Fforest Coaster" luge ride twisting through the forest at up to 25 mph (www.zipworld.co.uk).

High-speed **RIB** (rigid inflatable boat) tours depart from the Isle of Anglesey, racing across the waters of the Menai Strait and nearby (www.ribride.co.uk).

At **Surf Snowdonia,** tucked in idyllic Welsh countryside just south of Conwy, the surf's always up—thanks to an artificial surf machine (see the listing in this chapter).

Whitewater rafting is another fun way to get up close and personal with Welsh nature (www.canoewales.com or www.nationalwhitewatercentre.co.uk).

ISLE OF ANGLESEY

The huge Isle of Anglesey ("Ynys Môn" in Welsh) looms just off-shore, about a 40-minute drive west from Conwy (connected by bridge to the mainland), and a short detour from the route to Caernarfon. While Anglesey—and its port-town Holyhead—is known primarily as the jumping-off point for ferries to Dublin (see "North Wales Connections" at the end of this chapter), from a sightseeing perspective it has one real sight: Beaumaris Castle.

Menai Suspension Bridge

The Isle of Anglesey is connected to the mainland by one of the engineering marvels of its day, the Menai Suspension Bridge. With the Act of Union of 1800, London needed to be better connected to Dublin. And, as the economy of the island of Anglesey was mainly cattle farming (cows had to literally swim the Straits of Menai to get to market), there was a local need for this bridge. Designed by Thomas Telford and finished in 1826, at 580 feet it was the longest bridge of that era. It was built to be 100 feet above sea level at high tide—high enough to let Royal Navy ships sail beneath. When it opened, the bridge cut the travel time from London to Holyhead from 36 to 27 hours. Most drivers today take the modern A-55 highway bridge, but the historic bridge still handles local traffic (on the A-5).

Beaumaris

This charming town originated, like other castle towns, as an English "green zone" in the 13th century, surrounded by Welsh guerrillas. Today, it feels workaday Welsh, with a fine harborfront, a simple pleasure pier (advertising boat trips around the bird sanctuary at Puffin Island), lots of colorful shops and eateries, a mothballed Victorian prison (now a museum), and the remains of an idyllic castle. Around the castle are putt-putt-type amusements for the family, including a fine little picnic-and-playground area tucked right against the castle wall.

Beaumaris' small, simple **TI** is staffed entirely by volunteers, and is stocked with helpful maps and brochures, even if no one's there to answer questions (hours vary, in the Town Hall on Castle Street, next to the Buckeley Hotel, www.visitanglesey.co.uk).

Getting There: If driving, simply follow signs for *Holyhead*. Immediately after crossing the big bridge onto the island, take the small coastal A-545 highway for 15 lovely minutes into Beaumaris. There's a vast, grassy pay-and-display lot at the point just beyond the end of town (and the castle).

▲Beaumaris Castle

Begun in 1295, Beaumaris was the last link in King Edward's "Iron Chain" of castles to enclose Gwynedd, the rebellious former kingdom of North Wales.

The site has no natural geological constraints like those that encumbered the castle designers at Caernarfon and Conwy, so its wall-within-a-wall design is almost perfectly concentric. If completed, the result would have been one of Britain's most beautiful castles, and medieval castle engineering at its best—four rings of defense, a moat, and a fortified dock. But problems in Scotland changed the king's priorities, construction stopped in 1330, and the castle was never finished. Today it looks ruined (and rather squat), but it was never ransacked or destroyed—it's simply unfinished. The site was overgrown until the last century, but now it's been uncovered and cleaned up to act as a park, with pristine lawns and a classic moat. Because it's harder to get here than the big, famous castles in Conwy and Caernarfon, it's less crowded—making your visit more enjoyable. In the south gatehouse (near where you enter), you can watch a brief film about the castle's history. The rest is mostly unexplained, with a few small information plaques and several hands-on activities for kids.

Cost and Hours: £7.30; daily 9:30-17:00, July-Aug until 18:00; Nov-Feb 10:00-16:00; tel. 01248/810-361, www.cadw.gov. wales.

Beaumaris Gaol

The jail opened in 1829 as a result of new laws designed to give prisoners more humane treatment; it remained in use until 1878. Under this "modern" ethic, inmates had their own cells, women prisoners were kept separate and attended by female guards, and prisoners worked to pay for their keep rather than suffer from jailers bilking their families for favors. This new standard of incarceration is the subject of this museum, where you'll see the prisoners' quarters, work yard, punishment cells, whipping rack, treadmill, and chapel. Explanations are limited, but it's interesting to explore the old space. (Ruthin has a similar but more engaging prison exhibit—described later.)

Cost and Hours: £5.55; daily 10:00-17:00, weekends only in Oct, closed most days Oct-Easter; to reach the jail, head down the main street from the castle, go right on Steeple Lane, then left on Bunkers Hill; tel. 01248/810-921.

Wildlife Cruises

Starida operates a fine Wildlife Cruise from Beaumaris (£10, daily—weather permitting, 75 minutes). You'll sail to Puffin Island to see puffins, cormorants, gray seals, and more. A crew of experienced locals provides helpful commentary. If you have time, opt for the Extended Cruise, combining the Wildlife Cruise with sightseeing along the Menai Strait (£17, daily 9:00-21:00, 2.5 hours; tel. 01248/810-379, www.starida.co.uk, book@starida.co.uk). They also offer fishing trips.

Llanfairpwllgwyngyllgogerychwyrndrobwllllanty -siliogogogoch

Proud owner of the second-longest place name in the world, this village is called "Llanfair Pwllgwyngyll" for short. To reach it, take the first exit after crossing the A-55 bridge—it's well marked. Follow the A-5, which leads past a Volvo dealership with a very long sign, to the train station, a popular place to take photos of the platform sign. The town itself is otherwise wholly unexceptional—but the "long name" gimmick is a huge draw for visitors. Next to the train station is the James Pringle Weavers shop, a souvenir superstore catering to big-bus tours. (You can ask nicely

inside if they'll stamp your passport with the village name.) It's tacky, but fun to see such a fuss made over a town name, and it's an easy detour from Beaumaris.

Caernarfon

The small, salty town of Caernarfon (kah-NAR-von) is famous for its striking castle—the place where the Prince of Wales is "invest-

ed" (given his title). Like Conwy, it has an Edward I garrison town marching out from the castle; it still follows the original medieval grid plan laid within its well-preserved ramparts.

Caernarfon is mostly a 19th-century town. In those days, the most important thing in town wasn't the castle or the adjacent walled town, but the seafront that sprawled below the castle (now a parking lot). This was once a booming slate port, shipping tidy bundles of the rock from North Wales mining towns to roofs all over Europe.

The statue of local boy David Lloyd George looks over the town square. A member of Parliament from 1890 to 1945, he was the most important politician Wales ever sent to London, and ultimately became Britain's prime minister during the last years of World War I. Young Lloyd George began his career as a noisy nonconformist Liberal advocating Welsh rights. He ended up an eloquent spokesperson for the nation of Great Britain, convincing his slate-mining constituents that only as part of the Union would their industry boom.

Caernarfon bustles with shops, cafés, and people. It's fun to explore—but compared to Conwy, it's noticeably scruffier (it experienced a heavy economic decline following the collapse of the mining industry). Locals, who seem self-conscious about their rival town, told me, "We're poor cousins to Conwy." But recent years have brought new initiatives and fresh investments to the town, such as the Welsh Highland Railway station and the Galeri Creative Enterprise Centre, which serves as a cultural hub for art exhibits, movies, and festivals. The newest rejuvenation project is Cei Llechi ("Slate Quay"), a set of refurbished buildings on the harborfront, hosting a number of artisan workshops (may be open by the time you visit).

Orientation to Caernarfon

The small walled old town of Caernarfon (pop. 10,000) spreads out from its waterfront castle, its outer flanks fringed with modern sprawl. The castle fronts the main square, called Castle Square ("Y Maes" in Welsh). Public WCs are off the main square, on the road down to the riverfront and parking lot.

TOURIST INFORMATION

Caernarfon's TI is located across from the castle entrance on Castle Street (Mon-Sat 9:30-16:30, closed Sun, www.visitcaernarfon. wales). The friendly staff happily gives out brochures and other info, and there's a small Welsh heritage exhibition upstairs.

ARRIVAL IN CAERNARFON

If you arrive by **bus,** walk straight ahead up to the corner at Bridge Street, turn left, and walk two short blocks until you hit the main square and the castle. **Drivers** can park in the staffed parking lot along the riverfront quay below the castle (£5 all day); other pay parking lots fill the moat-like area along Greengate Street. If lots in the center are full (or you prefer to park on the outskirts and avoid traffic), there's a big pay lot below the Morrisons Supermarket, near Victoria Dock.

HELPFUL HINTS

Market Day: Caernarfon's big main square hosts a market of varying size on Saturdays and Mondays year-round (better in summer).

Laundry: Pete's Launderette hides at the end of Skinner Street, a narrow lane branching off the main square (same-day full service, Mon-Thu 9:00-18:00, Fri-Sat until 17:30, Sun 11:00-16:00 in summer only, tel. 01286/678-395, Pete and Monica).

Bike Rental: Beics Antur Bikes rents good bikes at the end of High Street toward the water (Mon-Sat 9:30-17:00, closed Sun, Porth Yr Aur High Street, tel. 01286/802-222 or 07436/797-969, www.anturwaunfawr.org). One of their suggested routes is 12 miles down an old train track—now a bike path—through five villages to Bryncir and back (figure 4 hours for the 24-mile round-trip).

Harbor Cruise: Narrated cruises on the **Queen of the Sea** run daily in summer (£8; late May-late Sept 3-6/day—depending on weather, tides, and demand; 40 minutes, castle views, mobile 07979-593-483, www.menaicruises.co.uk).

Local Guide: The experienced **Emrys Llewelyn** gives a "My Town My Walk" tour starting at 10:00 by the statue of Lloyd George on the main square (£10, 1.5 hours, reserve in advance, tel.

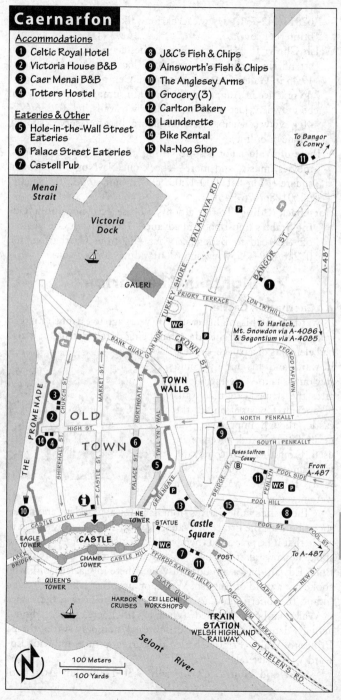

Caernarfon

Accommodations
1. Celtic Royal Hotel
2. Victoria House B&B
3. Caer Menai B&B
4. Totters Hostel

8. J&C's Fish & Chips
9. Ainsworth's Fish & Chips
10. The Anglesey Arms
11. Grocery (3)
12. Carlton Bakery
13. Launderette
14. Bike Rental
15. Na-Nog Shop

Eateries & Other
5. Hole-in-the-Wall Street Eateries
6. Palace Street Eateries
7. Castell Pub

NORTH WALES

07813/142-751, www.caernarfonwalks.com, melissahb98@
btinternet.com).

Welsh Choir: If you're spending a Tuesday night here, you can
attend the weekly practice of the local men's choir (Tue at
19:45 in Galeri Creative Enterprise Centre at Victoria Dock,
no practice in Aug, arrive by 19:30 in summer—practices can
be crowded; just outside the old town walls, tel. 01286/677-
404, www.cormeibioncaernarfon.org; best to reserve a spot by
phone or online).

A Taste of Wales: For a store selling all things Welsh—books,
movies, music, and more—check out **Na-Nog** on the main
square (Mon-Sat 9:00-17:00, closed Sun, 16 Castle Square,
tel. 01286/676-946).

Horseback Riding: To ride a pony or horse, try **Snowdonia Riding Stables** (must book in advance, 3 miles from Caernarfon,
off the road to Beddgelert, bus #S4 from Caernarfon, tel.
01286/479-435, www.snowdoniaridingstables.co.uk).

Sights in Caernarfon

▲▲Caernarfon Castle

Edward I built this mighty castle 700 years ago to establish English
rule over North Wales. Rather than being purely defensive, it also

had elements of a palace—where
Edward and his family could
stay on visits to Wales. Modeled
after the striped, angular walls
of ancient Constantinople, the
castle, though impressive, was
never finished and never really
used. From the inner courtyard,
you can see the notched walls
ready for more walls—which
were never built.

The castle's fame derives from its physical grandeur and its association with the Prince of Wales. Edward got the angry Welsh to
agree that if he presented them with "a prince, born in Wales, who
spoke not a word of English," they would submit to the Crown. In
time, Edward had a son born in Wales (here in Caernarfon), who
spoke not a word of English, Welsh, or any other language—as an
infant. In modern times, as another political maneuver, the Prince
of Wales has been "invested" (given his title) here. This "tradition"
actually dates only from the 20th century, and only two of the 21
Princes of Wales (Prince Charles, the current prince, and King Edward VIII) have taken part.

Cost and Hours: £9.90; daily 9:30-17:00, July-Aug until

18:00; Nov-Feb Mon-Sat 10:00-16:00, Sun from 11:00; tel. 01286/677-617, www.cadw.gov.wales.

Tours: Local guide **Martin de Lewandowicz** gives mind-bending tours of the castle (tel. 01286/674-369).

Visiting the Castle: In the huge **Eagle Tower** (to the far right as you enter), see the "Princes of Wales" exhibit, featuring a chess-board of Welsh and English princes as life-size chess pieces. You'll also see a model of the original castle and a video from the investiture of Prince Charles in 1969. The next level's skimpy exhibit covers the life of Eleanor of Castile, wife of Edward I. Be sure to climb the tower for a great view of the Menai Strait and the Irish Sea.

The **Chamberlain's Tower** and **Queen's Tower** (ahead and to the right as you enter the castle) house the mildly interesting Museum of the Royal Welsh Fusiliers—a military branch made up entirely of Welshmen. The museum shows off medals, firearms, uniforms, and information about various British battles.

The **Northeast Tower,** at the opposite end of the castle (to the left as you enter), has an eight-minute video covering the history of the castle. Nearby, the **Black Tower** has a small exhibit that psychoanalyzes Edward's decision to build such an important castle here—which, some believe, is rooted in a legend surrounding a Roman emperor who dreamed of marrying a Welsh princess (as shown in the video in the Northeast Tower)...and then did. You can step out onto the little balcony overlooking the seaside parking lot, where Prince Charles addressed the crowd moments after his royal investiture (an event that locals still recall fondly).

JUST BEYOND CAERNARFON
Narrow-Gauge Steam Train

The Welsh Highland Railway steam train billows scenically through the countryside south from Caernarfon along the original line that served a slate quarry, crossing the flanks of Mount Snowdon en route. The trip to Beddgelert makes a fine joyride; to save time, ride the train one-way, look around, and catch bus #S4 back to Caernarfon (40 minutes). Steam-train enthusiasts will want to ride all the way to Porthmadog—and can even loop from there back up to Conwy with a ride on the Ffestiniog Railway steam train from Porthmadog to Blaenau Ffestiniog, and then the Conwy Valley line from Blaenau Ffestiniog to Conwy (Caernarfon to Beddgelert—£21 one-way, £31 round-trip, 1.5 hours; Caernarfon to Porthmadog—£27 one-way, £41 round-trip, 2.5 hours; trains run 2-3 times per day on most days late March-Oct; Porthmadog to Blaenau Ffestiniog—£17 one-way, £26 round-trip, 2-6/day, 75 minutes; day passes available, tel. 01766/516-000, www.festrail.co.uk).

NORTH WALES

Segontium Roman Fort

Dating from AD 77, this ruin is the westernmost Roman fort in Britain. It was manned for more than 300 years to keep the Welsh and the coast quiet. Little is left but foundations (the stone was plundered to help build Edward I's castle at Caernarfon), and any artifacts that are found end up in Cardiff. This is only worth seeing if you have an unusual appetite for the footprints of Roman buildings (free, gate generally unlocked daily 12:30-16:30, 20-minute walk from town, atop a hill on the A-4085—drivers follow signs to *Beddgelert*).

Sleeping in Caernarfon

These choices (except the Celtic Royal) line a cozy, sleepy, narrow street just inside the town's seawall—you can't get more central. If you're looking for a bigger hotel farther out, try the Celtic Royal or—cheaper—Caernarfon's branches of **Premier Inn** (www.premierinn.com) or **Travelodge** (www.travelodge.co.uk).

$$ Celtic Royal Hotel rents 110 large, comfortable rooms and includes a restaurant, gym, pool, hot tub, and sauna; some top-floor rooms have castle views. Its grand, old-fashioned look comes with modern-day conveniences—but it's still overpriced (on Bangor Street, tel. 01286/674-477, www.celtic-royal.co.uk, reservations@celtic-royal.co.uk).

$$ Victoria House B&B rents four airy, fresh, large-for-Britain rooms with nice natural-stone bathrooms. Generous breakfasts are served in a pleasant woody room, and a complimentary drink is served upon arrival. Stairs from the courtyard lead to the top of the castle wall for a fine view (lounge, free parking, 13 Church Street, tel. 01286/678-263, mobile 07748/098-928, www.thevictoriahouse.co.uk, jan@thevictoriahouse.co.uk, friendly Jan Baker).

$ Caer Menai B&B ("Fort of the Menai Strait") rents seven modern, classy-for-the-price rooms (try requesting the one seaview room, free parking, 15 Church Street, tel. 01286/672-612, www.caermenai.co.uk, info@caermenai.co.uk, Karen and Mark).

¢ Totters Hostel is a creative little hostel run by Bob and Henryette. They have dorms as well as private rooms, including some in a building across the street (includes continental breakfast, cash only, open 24 hours, inviting living room, kitchen, 2 High Street, tel. 01286/672-963, www.totters.co.uk, totters.hostel@gmail.com).

Eating in Caernarfon

The streets near Caernarfon's castle teem with inviting eateries. The lineup seems to change often; rather than recommending specifics, here are some streets worth browsing.

In the Old Town: "**Hole-in-the-Wall Street**" (just inside the back wall of town) is a trendy strip lined with several charming cafés and bistros. **Palace Street,** a block toward the water, also has several choices (including the well-established, extremely atmospheric, but questionably named **$$ Black Boy** pub).

Near Palace Square: In nice weather, several places on the main square have outside tables from which you can watch the people scene while munching your toasted sandwich. **$$ Castell,** a big and bright pub inside Castle Hotel facing Palace Square, dishes up good food. Across the square, the pedestrianized but grubby **Pool Street** offers several budget options, including the popular **$ J&C's** fish-and-chips joint (#21). A couple of blocks away, **$ Ainsworth's** has arguably better fish-and-chips, but the wait can be longer (41 Bridge Street).

Along the Waterfront: **$ The Anglesey Arms** is a rough, old, characteristic pub serving basic pub grub at picnic benches on the harborfront (the only eating or drinking place along the water). It's lively in the evening with darts and well-lubricated locals; they host live folk music on some Thursdays and Fridays from about 21:00 (Harbour Front, tel. 01286/672-158).

Picnics: For groceries, you'll find a small **Spar** supermarket on the main square, an **Iceland** supermarket near the bus stop, and a huge **Morrisons** supermarket a five-minute walk from the city center on Bangor Street. **$ Carlton Bakery** has freshly made pies, salad rolls, and sandwiches (Mon-Thu 9:00-17:00, Sat until 16:00, closed Sun, 14 Bangor Street).

Caernarfon Connections

Caernarfon is a handy hub for buses into Snowdonia National Park (such as to Llanberis, Beddgelert, and Betws-y-Coed). Bus info: tel. 01766-771-000, www.gwynedd.llyw.cymru/en.

From Caernarfon by Bus to: Conwy (3-4/hour, 1.5 hours, transfer in Bangor), **Llanberis** (hourly, 30 minutes, bus #88), **Beddgelert** (bus #S4, 7/day Mon-Sat, 2/day on Sun, 40 minutes), **Betws-y-Coed** (hourly, 1-1.5 hours, 1 transfer), **Blaenau Ffestiniog** (hourly, 1.5 hours, 1 transfer).

The narrow-gauge steam **train** provides both sightseeing and transport from Caernarfon to **Beddgelert** (described earlier).

Snowdonia National Park

This is Britain's second-largest national park, and its centerpiece—taller than any other mountain in Wales or England—is Mount Snowdon. Each year, half a million people ascend one of seven different paths to the top of the 3,560-foot mountain. Hikes take from five to seven hours; if you're fit and the weather's good, it's an exciting day. Trail info abounds (local TIs sell maps and guidebooks, including the small £3 book *The Ascent of Snowdon*, by E. G. Bowland, which describes the routes). Even if you're not a hiker, the park offers plenty of cute towns and sights—and stunning scenery—to fill up a day. As you explore, notice the slate roofs—the local specialty—then visit the National Slate Museum and the Llechwedd Slate Caverns to learn about the up-and-down role the industry played in Welsh life. The towns of Beddgelert and Blaenau Ffestiniog are quintessentially Welsh.

Betws-y-Coed

The resort center of Snowdonia National Park, Betws-y-Coed (BET-oos-uh-coyd), bursts with tour buses and souvenir shops.

This picturesque town is cuddled by wooded hills, made cozy by generous trees, and situated along a striking waterfall-rippled stretch of the River Conwy. It verges on feeling overly manicured, with uniform checkerboard-stone houses yawning at each other from across a broad central green. There's little to do here except wander along the waterfalls (don't miss the old stone

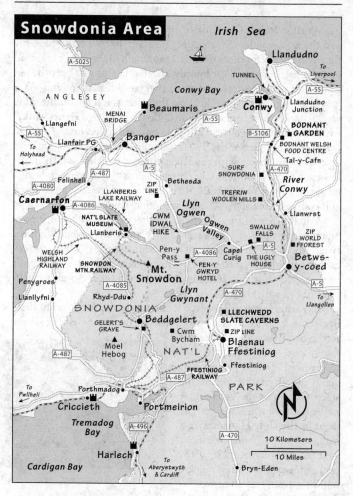

Snowdonia Area

Irish Sea

bridge—just up the river from the green—with the best waterfall views), have a snack or meal, and go for a walk in the woods.

Trains and buses arrive at the village green; with your back to the station, the TI is to the right of the green. There's also a short-stay pay-and-display parking lot along the green.

Betws-y-Coed's good **National Park Centre/TI** sells a variety of good maps for hiking in Snowdonia (daily 9:30-17:00, off-season 9:30-12:30 & 13:30-16:00, tel. 01690/710-426, www.snowdonia-npa.gov.uk. They show a free 13-minute video with bird's-eye views of the park, and offer a free downloadable audioguide tour of the park on their website (with maps and navigational aids). In summer, you might catch some live entertainment in the TI's courtyard.

Walks: Most of the "hikes" in Betws-y-Coed are along rivers and through woodland—certainly pleasant, but I'd rather save my time and energy for more dramatic mountain hikes. One easy stroll in town is the **Pont y Pair boardwalk** that begins just over the old stone bridge in the center of town (pay-and-display lot and WCs nearby) and runs a half-mile along the river; you'll return the same way. Another easy and enjoyable option is the **"two rivers walk,"** which begins through the white gate (marked *Private Road—Royal Oak Farm*) just outside the TI. You'll follow the Afon Llugwy river up to the confluence with the River Conwy, which you'll then follow back to St. Michael's Church and across the suspension bridge into town; most of this walk is through woods, circling the town golf course (allow about 45 minutes round-trip).

Music: St. Mary's Church, in the middle of town, opens practice for the local men's chorus, Cantorion Goledd Cymru, twice monthly in summer (June-Sept Sun at 14:00, www. cantoriongogleddcymru.co.uk). Most other Sunday evenings in summer, the church hosts a variety of other choruses (Sun at 19:30, book ahead with the TI).

Nearby: If you drive west out of town on the A-5 (toward Beddgelert or Llanberis), after two miles you'll see the parking lot for scenic **Swallow Falls,** a pleasant five-minute walk from the road (overpriced at £1.50/person; best views are from the top of the steep trail—not the bottom). A half-mile past the falls on the right is **The Ugly House** (with a café, see photo), built overnight to take advantage of a 15th-century law that let any quickie building avoid fees and taxes.

Betws-y-Coed Connections: The Conwy Valley train line connects Betws-y-Coed to **Llandudno Junction** near Conwy (north, 30 minutes) and **Blaenau Ffestiniog** (south, 30 minutes; 5/day Mon-Sat, 3/day Sun in summer, no Sun trains in winter). Buses connect Betws-y-Coed with **Conwy** (bus #19, hourly, 45 minutes, fewer on Sun), **Llanberis** (bus #S2, 7/day, more in summer, 40 minutes), **Beddgelert** (5/day, 1.5 hours; bus #S2 to Pen-y-Pass, then transfer to bus #S4 to Beddgelert), **Blaenau Ffestiniog** (bus #X19, 8/day, none on Sun, 25 minutes), and **Caernarfon** (hourly, 1-1.5 hours; ride bus #S2 to Llanberis, noted above, then transfer to frequent Caernarfon-bound bus).

▲Ogwen Valley (Dyffryn Ogwen)

Leaving Betws-y-Coed, road A-5 continues toward the village of

Capel Curig. Here, most visitors peel off on the A-4086 toward Beddgelert or Llanberis, but I'd continue on A-5 through the just-as-dramatic, less-touristed Ogwen Valley—a gorgeous glacial groove filled by the lake called Llyn Ogwen. The surrounding mountains are peppered with stone walls, stray sheep, and lonely farms.

One of my favorite easy-to-moderate Snowdonia hikes—called **Cwm Idwal**—begins from the pay-and-display lot at the far end of Llyn Ogwen (by a hostel

and a café). From the parking lot, follow the flagstone path that leads up to the left of the café. You'll hike about 15-20 minutes with some uphill sections (on an uneven but well-tended stone path) to the gorgeous mountain lake called Llyn Idwal, hemmed in on three sides—like a natural amphitheater—by sheer cliff walls. From here, you can either head back the way you came, or with more time, circle clockwise around the entire lake. Plan on about an hour to hike to the lake and back; add about 45 minutes if circling the lake.

Farther along the A-5, you'll see mountains of discarded slate before entering the blue-collar town of **Bethesda**—which, like Blaenau Ffestiniog—owes its existence to a now-defunct slate mine. (Also like Blaenau, there's a zipline course that sends you soaring over all that slate, www.zipworld.co.uk.)

Dropping down from Bethesda, you eventually rejoin the A-55, which zips you east to Conwy or west to Caernarfon.

▲▲Beddgelert

This quintessential Snowdon village, 17 miles from Betws-y-Coed, packs a scenic mountain punch without the tourist crowds. Bed-

dgelert (BETH-geh-lert) is a cluster of stone houses lining a babbling brook in the shadow of Mount Snowdon and her sisters. The stony homes, surrounding a stony bridge, seem to rise straight up from the Welsh landscape. (In a sense, they do.) Cute as a hobbit, Beddgelert will have you looking for The Shire around the next bend. Thanks to the fine variety of hikes from its doorstep and its decent bus service, Beddgelert is the ideal stop for those wanting to experience the peace of Snowdonia.

Getting There: The Welsh Highland Railway train serves Beddgelert. This narrow-gauge joyride (12 miles and 1.5 hours to or from Caernarfon) is a popular excursion (for details, see page 643). Most people ride the train one-way and return by bus (see "Beddgelert Connections," later).

Orientation: The village doesn't have real "sights," but it's a starting place for some great walks—ask locals for tips, or stop at the **National Park Centre/TI** at the far end of town (daily 9:30-17:00, along the main road a couple of blocks from the bridge toward Porthmadog, tel. 01766/890-615, www.snowdonia-npa.gov. uk). For town info, see www.beddgelerttourism.com.

Activities: For an easy stretch-your-legs **stroll,** simply take the path along the river and follow signs to "Gelert's Grave" (*Beddgelert* in Welsh). In about 10 minutes, you'll reach a small grove of trees in a field marking the spot where the 13th-century Prince Gelert honored the dog, Gelert, who saved his infant son from a wolf attack. To extend your walk, follow the flat path beside the river as far as you like (it's 3 miles round-trip if you go all the way to the end and back).

For a more serious **hike,** here are four options: Trek along the cycle path that goes from the center of Beddgelert, through the forest to the village of Rhyd-Ddu (4.5 miles); walk down the river and around the hill (3 hours, 6 miles, 900-foot elevation gain, via Cwm Bycham); hike along (or around) Llyn Gwynant Lake and four miles back to Beddgelert (ride the bus to the lake); or try the dramatic ridge walks on Moel Hebog (Hawk Hill).

For **mountain-bike rentals,** try Beddgelert Bikes (directly under Welsh Highland Railway station, tel. 01766/890-434, www. beddgelertbikes.co.uk).

Sleeping in Beddgelert: This little village has a few choices, mostly clustering around the bridge in the heart of town.

$$ Saracens Head is a newer, upmarket pub with 11 of the town's plushest rooms (tel. 01766/890-329, www.saracens-head. co.uk).

$$ Tanronnen Inn is an older choice, with seven rooms above a pub that's been renovated from its interior medieval timbers to its exterior stone walls (tel. 01766/890-347, www.tanronnen.co.uk, tanronnen@btconnect.com).

$$ Plas Gwyn Guest House rents six rooms in a cozy, cheery, 19th-century townhouse with a comfy lounge (RS%, cash only, tel. 01766/890-215, www.plas-gwyn.com, stay@plas-gwyn.com).

$ Colwyn Guest House has five tight but slick and new-feeling rooms (RS%, 2-night minimum on weekends, cash only, tel. 01766/890-276, mobile 07774/002-637, www. beddgelertguesthouse.co.uk, colwyn276@gmail.com, Colleen).

Sleeping near Beddgelert: Mountaineers appreciate that Sir Edmund Hillary and Sherpa Tenzing Norgay practiced here before the first successful ascent of Mount Everest. They slept at **$$ Pen-y-Gwryd Hotel,** at the base of the road leading up to the Pen-y-Pass by Mount Snowdon, and today the bar is strewn with fascinating memorabilia from Hillary's 1953 climb. The 18 rooms, with dingy old furnishings and crampon ambience, are a poor value—aside from the impressive history (old-time-elegant public rooms, some double rooms share museum-piece Victorian tubs and showers, natural pool and sauna for guests, dinners, tel. 01286/870-211, www.pyg.co.uk, reserve by phone).

Eating in Beddgelert: $$ Caffi Colwyn, just across the bridge from the B&Bs, serves nicely done home cookin' at good prices in a cozy one-room bistro, or in their back garden (long hours daily, tel. 01766/890-374). The **$$ Tanronnen Inn** serves up tasty food in an inviting pub setting, with several cozy, atmospheric rooms (lunch and dinner daily, tel. 01766/890-347). **$$$ Saracens Head** is an upscale choice, with a classy dining room and equally classy pub food (food served daily 12:00-15:00 & 18:00-20:30, tel. 01766/890-329).

For something sweet, the **Glaslyn Homemade Ice Cream** shop (up the road from the Tanronnen Inn) offers good quality and selection.

Beddgelert Connections: Beddgelert is connected to **Caernarfon** by the scenic Welsh Highland Railway (2-3/day on most days late March-Oct, 1.5 hours) and handy bus #S4 (7/day Mon-Sat, 2/day Sun, 40 minutes). Bus connections to **Betws-y-Coed** are much less convenient (5/day, 1.5 hours, 1 transfer). To reach **Conwy,** you'll need to transfer in Caernarfon and/or Bangor (6/day, 2 hours total). Buses to **Blaenau Ffestiniog** involve one or two transfers (7/day Mon-Sat, fewer on Sun, 1-2.5 hours).

Llanberis

Llanberis (THLAN-beh-ris) is a long, skinny, rugged, and functional town that feels like a frontier village. It's surrounded by dramatic, bald Welsh mountains—several of which are gouged by huge slate quarries. With 2,000 people and just as many tourists on a sunny day, Llanberis is a popular base for Snowdon activities. Most people prefer to take the train from

here to the Snowdon summit, but Llanberis is also loaded with hikers, as it's the launch pad for the longest (five miles) but least strenuous hiking route to the summit. (Routes from the nearby Pen-y-Pass, between here and Beddgelert, are steeper and even more scenic.)

Drivers approaching Llanberis will find pricey pay parking lots throughout town, including one next to the Electric Mountain/TI and another along the lake. For information, visit www. electricmountain.co.uk.

Getting There: Llanberis is easiest to reach from Caernarfon (hourly, 30 minutes, bus #88) or Betws-y-Coed (7/day, more in summer, 40 minutes); from Conwy, transfer in one of these towns (Caernarfon is generally best). While it's a quick 30-minute drive from Beddgelert to Llanberis, the bus connection is more complicated, requiring a transfer at Caernarfon or Pen-y-Pass, on the high road around Mount Snowdon (9/day, 1-1.5 hours).

▲▲Snowdon Mountain Railway

This is the easiest and most popular ascent of Mount Snowdon. You'll travel five miles from Llanberis to the summit on Britain's only rack-and-pinion railway (from 1896), climbing a total of 3,500 feet. Along with the views, there's a mountaintop visitors center and a café. You can take a diesel or steam train: the diesel-powered train with a 70-person car, or the steam train, carrying 34 passengers in a rebuilt Victorian carriage. Either trip takes 2.5 hours (one hour up, one hour down, 30 minutes free time at the summit).

Don't confuse this with the Welsh Highland Railway (described earlier under "Sights in Caernarfon") or the Llanberis Lake Railway, a different (and far less appealing) "Thomas the Tank Engine"-type steam train that fascinates kids and runs to the end of Padarn Lake and back.

Cost and Hours: Diesel train—£30 round-trip, £24 early-bird special for 9:00 departure (must book in advance); steam train—£39 round-trip. The first departure is often at 9:00, and the last trip can be as late as 17:30 in peak season (July-Aug). While the schedule flexes with weather and demand, several trips generally run each day from late March through October, with up to 10/day in peak season (steam train up to 4/day). Until May (or in bad weather), the train may not run all the way to the summit.

Buying Tickets: On sunny summer days—especially weekends, and any day in July and August—trains fill up fast so it's smart to reserve ahead. Originally designed for Victorian gentry, these days the train is overrun with commoners. You can buy tickets in advance either online or by calling after 13:00 the day before (£3.50 fee per group, tel. 01286/870-223, www.snowdonrailway. co.uk). Same-day tickets are only available in person. Show up early: The office opens at 8:30, and on very busy (read: sunny) days, tickets can sell out by midmorning; even if you get one, you may have to wait until afternoon for your scheduled departure time.

Getting There: The train departs from Llanberis Station, along the main road at the south end of Llanberis' town center. The closest parking lots are the pay-and-display lot located behind the station (off Victoria Terrace) or the pricier car park at Royal Victoria Hotel (across the street from the station). You can also park at one of the other pay lots in town (cheaper, about a 10-minute walk).

▲▲National Slate Museum

Across the lake from Llanberis yawns a giant slate quarry, which was a critical local industry until 1969. Slate from the hillsides above Llanberis was transported to the harbor in Caernarfon, where it was shipped all over the world.

Today, the 19th-century industrial workshops have been converted into an excellent and free museum, where you can learn more about processing slate. The highlight is the 30-minute slate-splitting demo. This museum is a nice comple-ment to the Llechwedd Slate Caverns in Blaenau Ffestiniog (described later): While that experience focuses on the lifestyles of the people who worked in underground mines (and is of general interest), this museum is primarily about the aboveground workshops (and is particularly thrilling for engineers).

Cost and Hours: Free; daily 10:00-17:00; Nov-Easter Sun-Fri until 16:00, closed Sat; last entry one hour before closing, pay-and-display parking, tel. 03001-112-333, www.museum.wales/slate.

Visiting the Museum: Entering the courtyard, note the time of the next slate-splitting demonstration, then work your way clockwise around the exhibits. A poetic 12-minute film provides context. Nearby, the "caban" is where workers would gather to socialize. Head through the passage at the far end of the courtyard to find a little row of impossibly modest quarrymen's houses from different eras—offering a thought-provoking glimpse into their hardy lifestyle. Nearby, look for the stairs or elevator up to take a look at a gigantic, 50-foot-high waterwheel, which turns a shaft that runs throughout the workshop. Walk through the different parts of the shop—the foundry, the blacksmiths' forge, the machine shop—noticing how that one shaft powers all the various belt-driven machinery. Stepping out of the museum, peer up at the gouged-out mountainside—and tip your hardhat to the 3,000 people who once worked here.

Electric Mountain

This visitors center, which may be closed for renovations when you visit, offers tours into a power plant burrowed into Elidir Mountain. After a 10-minute video, you'll board a bus and venture underground into Europe's biggest hydroelectric power station for a one-hour guided tour.

Cost and Hours: Visitors center—free, tour—£8.50; daily 9:30-17:30, tours run Easter-Oct about hourly (every 30 minutes when busy); off-season open 10:00-16:30, 3-5 tours/day—call or check online for times; wear warm clothes and sturdy shoes, reserve ahead online, no children under 4, tel. 01286/870-636, www.electricmountain.co.uk.

Blaenau Ffestiniog

High on a mountaintop, Blaenau Ffestiniog (BLEH-nigh FES-tin-yog) is a quintessential Welsh slate-mining town. The town seems to struggle on, oblivious to the tourists who nip in and out. Though it's tucked amidst a pastoral Welsh landscape, Blaenau Ffestiniog is surrounded by a gunmetal-gray wasteland of "tips," huge mountain-like piles of excess slate. While not technically inside the national park (thanks to its heavy industry and those giant slate heaps), Blaenau Ffestiniog is surrounded by Snowdonia on all sides, and is a short drive from the idyll of Betws-y-Coed or Beddgelert.

Take a walk. The shops are right out of the 1950s. Long rows of humble "two-up and two-down" houses (four rooms) feel a bit grim. The train station, bus stop, and parking lot all cluster along a one-block stretch in the heart of town. There's no TI.

Getting There: Blaenau Ffestiniog is conveniently connected by the Conwy Valley train to Betws-y-Coed and Conwy (5/day Mon-Sat, 3/day Sun in summer, no Sun trains in winter, 30 minutes to Betws-y-Coed, 1 hour to Conwy via Llandudno Junction) and by bus #X19 (8/day, none on Sun, 20 minutes to Betws-y-Coed, 1 hour to Llandudno Junction near Conwy). By bus, it's possible to connect with Beddgelert (7/day Mon-Sat, fewer on Sun, 1-2.5 hours, 1-2 transfers) or Caernarfon (hourly, 1.5 hours, transfer in Porthmadog).

▲▲Llechwedd Slate Caverns

Slate mining played a blockbuster role in Welsh heritage, and this working slate mine on the northern edge of Blaenau Ffestiniog does an excellent job of explaining the mining culture of Victorian Wales. The Welsh mined and split most of the slate roofs of Europe. When done right, a quality Welsh slate roof could last for up to 300 years. But it was hard work: 10 tons of slate were mined for every one ton of usable slate extracted. Miners would work 12-hour shifts, six days a week, with one 30-minute break every day. They'd latch themselves to the cliff face at an angle and slowly, one tap at a time, use a long metal rod to chip out four-foot-deep holes to fill with gunpowder. The guided tour will give you a new appreciation for all those slate roofs you'll see in your travels. Dress warmly—I mean it. You'll freeze underground without a sweater or jacket (you can borrow a coverall). Lines are longer when rain drives in the hikers—it's smart to book in advance.

Cost and Hours: £20; daily 9:00-17:30, tours run every 30 minutes, arrive 30 minutes before your tour, last tour generally at 17:00 (16:30 off-season); cafeteria, pub, tel. 01766/830-306, www.llechwedd.co.uk.

Getting There: The slate mine is about a mile from the town center. Buses leave from the Blaenau Ffestiniog rail station and drop you off near the mine. You can also walk 30 minutes to the mine or take a taxi (about £8, reserve in advance, tel. 01766/762-465 or 01766/831-781).

Visiting the Mine: The one-hour tour takes you into the mine with a live guide. You'll descend on a cable railway about 500 feet into the mountain for an audiovisual dramatization, set in the 1860s and centered around several relatives who work in the mine. You'll walk through several chambers, learning about the miners' primitive techniques and their (virtually nonexistent) safety measures. Sadly, despite the reassurances of doctors during that age, inhaling slate dust caused often-fatal cases of silicosis...where the inside of a miner's lung became coated with tiny chips of slate. You'll get to heft their tools (such as the pointed and weighted rod, called a

"jumper") and watch a brief slate-splitting demonstration. The tour requires a half-mile of walking through tunnels and caves with 60-plus stairs and some uneven footing.

▲Ffestiniog Railway

This 13-mile narrow-gauge train line was built in 1836 for small horse-drawn wagons to transport slate from the Ffestiniog mines to the port of Porthmadog. In the 1860s, horses gave way to steam trains. Today, hikers and tourists enjoy these tiny titans (tel. 01766/516-000, www.festrail.co.uk). This line connects to the narrow-gauge Welsh Highland Railway from Caernarfon via Porthmadog (see page 643). This is a novel steam-train experience, but the full-size Conwy Valley line from Llandudno to Blaenau Ffestiniog is more scenic and works a little better for hikers (see page 643 for info on both lines).

Near Blaenau Ffestiniog
▲Harlech Castle

Dramatically sited 14 miles south of Blaenau Ffestiniog, Harlech Castle is compact and fun to explore. When it was built by Edward

I in 1283, the sea lapped at the base of the castle wall (you can see the jagged dike since built in the distance, along with an old stone staircase that led down to the former water level, now the train tracks). During the War of the Roses, Queen Mary of Anjou hid out here for a time, and it was the last castle in Britain to fall (after a nine-month siege) during the Civil War. Before crossing the bridge to the castle, watch the seven-minute introductory film. At the gatehouse (where you enter the castle), climb to the top of the southwest tower, with panoramic views to the sea. Back down in the central courtyard, you can climb either tower flanking the gatehouse to reach the lower wall-top walkway and hike all the way around. The village of Harlech is cute and worth a wander.

Cost and Hours: £6.50; daily 9:30-17:00, July-Aug until 18:00; Nov-Feb Mon-Sat 10:00-16:00, Sun from 11:00; in the village of Harlech, just above the A-496; pay-and-display lot at castle entry, tel. 01766/780-552, www.cadw.gov.wales.

Near Snowdonia National Park

Tucked between Snowdonia and the North Sea is a sweeping, sandy tidal estuary called Tremadog Bay, with a faux Italian town (Portmeirion) and yet another castle, Criccieth. The sights here—about a half-hour's drive from Beddgelert, Blaenau Ffestiniog, or Caernarfon—can help round out a busy day exploring North Wales. The area's main town, Porthmadog, is the end point of two of the area's scenic rail lines (the Ffestiniog Railway and the Welsh Highland Railway). Portmeirion and Criccieth Castle are both within a 15-minute drive of Porthmadog, in different directions.

▲Portmeirion

File this under "Britain's offbeat sights." Tucked into a balmy microclimate, a short drive from the slag heaps of Blaenau Ffestiniog or the hobbit town of Beddgelert, is a faux-Italian Riviera village

NORTH WALES

modeled after Portofino. This flower-filled fantasy is extravagant: Surrounded by lush Welsh greenery and a windswept mudflat at low tide, Portmeirion is an artistic glob of palazzo arches, fountains, gardens, and promenades filled with cafés, souvenir shops,

two hotels, and local tourists who always wanted to go to Italy.

In 1925, Sir Clough Williams-Ellis began building this grand-scale folly—a pastel world of Italianate architecture. Soon this retreat began to attract celebrities seeking both novelty and privacy: H.G. Wells, Noel Coward, Prince Charles, and Beatles manager Brian Epstein were all repeat guests. The 1960s British TV series *The Prisoner*—which still has a big cult following—was filmed here, adding to the town's fame.

You'll pay admission at the tollhouse, then you're free to wander and explore. Free and helpful 20-minute orientation tours leave from the entrance every 30 minutes (10:30-15:30). Two 45-minute trails—the "Woodland Walk" and the "Coastal Walk"—provide structure for your meanderings, and a shuttle bus passes along the village and the Woodland trail every 20 minutes or so. If you'd like to completely forget you're in Wales...this is the place.

Cost and Hours: £12; daily 9:30-19:30, Nov-March until 17:30; tel. 01766/770-000, https://portmeirion.wales.

Criccieth Castle

Perched on a grassy bluff over the pretty seafront town of the same name, Criccieth (KRICK-ith) is the smallest, least historic, and least impressive of the "big five" border castles. Built by the Welsh around 1230, it was later seized, beefed up, and added to the castle ring by the English. The modern visitors center at the base of the hill has a small but well-presented exhibit on the castle's his-

tory...but there's not much to say. You can hike up and prowl the ruins, with great 360-degree views over Tremadog Bay and deep into Snowdonia. On a nice day, you can see all the way to Harlech Castle. Of the five Edward castles, this is the one where the views from the castle are better than the interior of the castle itself.

Cost and Hours: £5.80; daily 10:00-17:00; Nov-March Wed-Sat 10:00-16:00, Sun from 11:00, closed Mon-Tue; on the A-497 in the village of Criccieth; a few free street-parking spaces right in front of the ticket office and a pay-and-display lot nearby, tel. 01766/522-227, www.cadw.gov.wales.

Northeast Wales

If you're driving between North Wales and England, the Denbigh-shire towns of Llangollen and Ruthin are worth a stop. Llangollen is more engaging, with a dramatic setting and lots of ways to spend a few minutes or a few hours. Ruthin is appealing simply for its salt-of-the-earth character; while it has some good sights and a fine hotel, it's more of a place to melt into small-town Welsh life. Neither town is particularly well connected by public transportation, so they're effectively just for drivers. You can squeeze either or both into the drive from North Wales to England, but with more time, spend a night...or two.

While you're in the Denbighshire area, look for the free, engaging, wryly written "Town Trail" maps, detailing self-guided walks in Llangollen, Ruthin, and other towns (free at TIs).

Llangollen

Llangollen (thlang-GOTH-lehn) is a red-brick riverside town that's strikingly set in a gorge with a rushing river. It has an impressive history (thanks to its clever canal, a symbol of the Industrial Revolution) and a handful of great sights, including the fascinating manor house called Plas Newydd. It's also a popular launch pad for hikes, boat trips, and steam-train journeys. The town is famous for its weeklong International Musical Eisteddfod, a very popular and

crowded festival held every July, with dance competitions and evening concerts (tel. 01978/862-001, www.international-eisteddfod.co.uk). The town feels equal parts blue-collar and touristy.

With about 3,600 people, little Llangollen is easy to navigate. It has a big pay parking lot on Market Street, well signed as you enter town, and a helpful **TI** just around the corner on Castle Street (tel. 01978/860-828, www.llangollen.org.uk). A couple of blocks north, a bridge scenically crosses the River Dee, with the steam railway station and the canal just beyond. To the south, the

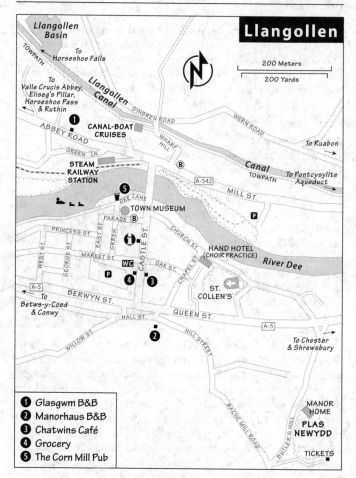

Llangollen

- **1** Glasgwm B&B
- **2** Manorhaus B&B
- **3** Chatwins Café
- **4** Grocery
- **5** The Corn Mill Pub

aptly named Hill Street climbs steeply up to a residential zone, where you'll find the town's best sight, Plas Newydd.

Llangollen Canal

At the turn of the 18th century, famed engineers Thomas Telford and William Jessop built this remarkable industrial canal, with a horse-drawn towpath for hauling cargo running its entire length. (It was originally intended to connect to a network of canals linking all the way to the big port at Liverpool, but the entire run was never completed.) The ingenious design—which begins at the River Dee's Horseshoe Falls two miles west of town, and crosses the towering Pontcysyllte Aqueduct four miles east of town—was engineered to drop less than 20 inches over its entire 11-mile length.

Today it's a tourist attraction (to find it, cross the bridge from the town center and head up the hill). You can go for an easy, level

NORTH WALES

stroll along its towpath, or take a lazy **canal-boat cruise.** The classic choice is by horse-drawn boat—either the basic, 45-minute version or the full-blown two-hour version all the way to Horseshoe Falls (tel. 01978/860-702, www.horsedrawnboats.co.uk). A two-hour motorized canal-boat trip goes all the way to—and across—the Pontcysyllte Aqueduct. As the longer tours (both horse-drawn and motorized) can sell out, it's smart to book ahead.

▲▲Plas Newydd

This is the manor home (pronounced "plass NEW-eth") of two 18th-century upper-class Irish women who ran off together and lived here as a couple for 50 years. Known as the "Ladies of Llan-

gollen," Lady Eleanor Butler and Sarah Ponsonby escaped from their families and settled here in 1778, causing a sensation in Georgian society. The rich and famous—inspired by the way the ladies' relationship epitomized the Romantic Age—beat a path to their door, including the Duke of Wellington, Josiah Wedgwood, William Wordsworth, and Sir Walter Scott. They were avid collectors of fine woodwork, which they incorporated into both the exterior and interior of their "cottage." These ornate wood carvings cover seemingly every surface of the many cozy rooms you'll see—living room, library, bedroom, guest room—which also display some of their personal belongings. Out front is the well-tended topiary garden. While there are plenty of old British manor houses to tour, this one is uniquely fascinating. Rent the essential audioguide, and take time to listen to its complete story.

Cost and Hours: £6; daily 10:30-17:00, house interior closed Nov-March—but gardens open; £1.50 audioguide, 10-minute walk from TI on Hill Street, free parking, café, tel. 01978/862-834, www.plasnewyddllangollen.co.uk.

Other Experiences in Llangollen

You'll see a steady stream of serious walkers huffing through town. Llangollen is a popular launch pad for both short and long-distance **walks** in the Welsh countryside. For an easy stroll, wander along the canal's towpath in either direction (Horseshoe Falls is 2 miles away). For a sturdier hike, head for Valle Crucis Abbey. (The falls and abbey are both described later.) Another popular choice is the steep huff up to Castell Dinas Brân, the ruined castle capping the bald mountain over the canal side of town (visible from various points in Llangollen). The TI can give advice on any of these hikes.

The **men's choir** practices traditional Welsh songs weekly on Friday nights (19:30 at the Hand Hotel on Bridge Street, 21:30 pub sing-along afterward, hotel tel. 01978/860-303).

Llangollen has its own little **steam-train line,** the Llangollen Railway, which putters up and down the Dee Valley to the town of Corwen and back (about 30 minutes each way, www.llangollen-railway.co.uk).

The humble, endearingly cluttered **town museum** fills a circular, bunker-like building between the TI and the river (on Parade Street, free, daily 10:00-16:00). It's worth ducking in on a rainy day. The centerpiece is a replica of the ninth-century Eliseg's Pillar (you can see the original on the way up to the Horseshoe Pass—see "Scenic Drive Between Llangollen and Ruthin," later).

Sleeping in Llangollen: $ Glasgwm B&B rents four spacious rooms in a Victorian townhouse—it's tidy, updated, and centrally located (evening meals and sack lunches available by request, free parking, Abbey Road, tel. 01978/861-975, www.glasgwm-llangollen.co.uk, glasgwm@llangollen.co.uk, friendly John and Heather). **$$ Manorhaus** is a luxurious boutique option with eight rooms. It's run by Christopher (who played piano in London's West End theaters for years) and Gavin (an architect and former mayor of Ruthin), who also run the recommended Manorhaus in Ruthin (Hill Street, tel. 01978/860-775, www.manorhaus.com, post@manorhaus.com).

Eating in Llangollen: You'll find no shortage of options for a quick lunch downtown. Several vendors sell savory pastries, called oggies. **Chatwins** (a local bakery/coffee-shop chain) sells tasty, filling, made-to-order sandwiches, and the **Spar** on the main drag is good for picnic supplies. A couple of blocks away, **$$ The Corn Mill** is a lively and tempting pub in an historic stone building along the water (a short walk upstream from the bridge). If the weather's nice, grab a seat on the deck hanging over the rapids (food served daily 12:00-21:30, Dee Lane, tel. 01978/869-555).

Llangollen Connections: To reach **Conwy,** you can take bus #5 or #T3 to Ruabon, where you can transfer to a train (5/day; 2 hours total).

Scenic Drive Between Llangollen and Ruthin

It's a fast (30 minutes), scenic, and satisfying drive between Llangollen and Ruthin on the A-542 over the **Horseshoe Pass** (1,367 feet). Allow more time if you stop on the way at the following points of interest.

From Llangollen's town center, cross the bridge and turn left on Abbey Road (A-542). About two miles out of town, watch for the Horseshoe Falls turnoff on the left. Follow this road and park in a pay-and-display lot, then walk five minutes steeply downhill through a meadow to reach **Horseshoe Falls** (and, nearby, the starting point of the Llangollen Canal).

Back on the main road, about a mile farther along on the right is the turnoff for **Valle Crucis Abbey.** This lovely Cistercian abbey, from 1201, was one of many "dissolved" by King Henry VIII. While not as striking as others—especially the much more famous and evocative Tintern Abbey in South Wales—it's worth stopping if it's your best chance to see a ruined abbey (£4.20; Wed-Sun 10:00-17:00, closed Mon-Tue, Nov-March daily until 16:00; tel. 01978/860-326, www.cadw.gov.wales).

A few hundred yards farther along the main road, look right for a green mound topped by **Eliseg's Pillar**—a weathered nub of a monument placed here by a Welsh king in the ninth century.

From here, over the next few miles you'll ascend past the tree line, zoom by an old slate mine (with a roadside mountain of unwanted slate fragments), and dodge some roadside sheep to reach the top of the pass, with sweeping views of the countryside. The scenery eventually changes from sheep to cows as you wind your way down to Ruthin.

Ruthin

Ruthin (RITH-in; "Rhuthun" in Welsh) is a low-key market town with charm in its ordinary Welshness. The people are the sights, and admission is free if you start the conversation.

Ruthin (pop. 5,000) is situated atop a gentle hill surrounded by undulating meadows. In this crossroads town, the central roundabout (at the former medieval marketplace, St. Peter's Square) is a busy pinwheel, with cars spinning off in every direction. The market square, jail, museum, arts center, bus station, and in-town accommodations are all within five blocks of one another. The town is so untouristy that it has no official TI (though the recommended Craft Center has handy brochures).

NORTH WALES

▲Ruthin Gaol

Get a glimpse into crime and punishment in 17th- to early-20th-century Wales in this 100-cell prison. You'll head down to the cellar to explore the "dark" and condemned cells, give the dreaded hand-crank a whirl, and learn about the men, women, and children who did time here before the prison closed in 1916. Head up into the bright and eerie "panopticon"—a design all British prisons adopted in the late 19th century to allow all prisoners to be watched at the same time.

Cost and Hours: £7; Wed-Mon 10:00-17:00, closed Tue and Oct-March, last entry one hour before closing; essential audioguide-£1.50, Clwyd Street, tel. 01824/708-281, www. ruthingaol.co.uk.

Nantclwyd y Dre

This Elizabethan-era "oldest timbered townhouse in Wales" underwent an award-winning £600,000 renovation (funded partly by the EU) to convert it into a museum. Seven decorated rooms give visitors a peek into the history of the house, which was built in 1435.

Cost and Hours: £7, call ahead or check website to confirm hours, last entry one hour before closing, Castle Street, tel. 01824/706-868, www.denbighshire.gov.uk.

Ruthin Craft Center

This state-of-the-art facility at the base of Ruthin's hill hosts contemporary art. Inside, you'll find an information desk (stocked with brochures about Ruthin and the surrounding region), as well as a series of galleries and studio spaces for Welsh artists.

Cost and Hours: Free, daily 10:00-17:30, café, Park Road, tel. 01824/704-774, www.ruthincraftcentre.org.uk.

Walks

For a scenic and interesting one-hour walk, try the Offa's Dyke Path to Moel Famau (the "Jubilee Tower," a 200-year-old war memorial on a peak overlooking stark moorlands). The trailhead is a 10-minute drive east of Ruthin on the A-494.

▲▲Welsh Choir

The Côr Rhuthun mixed choir usually rehearses weekly at the Pwllglas Village Hall, and welcomes visitors to observe. ("They sing better when they have an audience," the director told me.) Note that this is a practice—not a performance—but anyone who's sung in a choir (or anyone who's interested in the Welsh language) will find it an entertaining evening as it's entirely in Welsh (Thu at 20:00 except Aug, call or email in advance to confirm practice; located three miles south of Ruthin in the village of Pwllglas—follow the A-494 out of town in the direction of Blas; mobile 07724/112-984, www.corrhuthun.co.uk, cor@corrhuthun.co.uk).

Sleeping in Ruthin: $$ Manorhaus, filling a Georgian building, is Ruthin's classiest sleeping option. Its eight rooms are impeccably appointed with artsy-contemporary decor, and the halls serve as gallery space for local artists. Guests enjoy use of the sauna, steam room, library, and mini cinema in the cellar. In fact, you could have a vacation and never leave the place. Owned by the same people who run the recommended Manorhaus in Llangollen, it brings a splash of fun and style to Ruthin (no children under 9, recommended restaurant, Well Street, tel. 01824/704-830, www.manorhaus.com, post@manorhaus.com).

Eating in Ruthin: $$$ On the Hill serves hearty lunches and dinners made mostly with fresh, local ingredients. The Old World decor complements the quality cuisine (Tue-Fri 11:45-14:00 & 18:30-21:00, Sat lunch only, closed Sun-Mon; 1 Upper Clwyd Street, tel. 01824/707-736). **$$$ Manorhaus** serves inventive and locally sourced dinners in a mod art-gallery space. Eating here is an experience in itself (daily 18:30-21:00, reservations required, Well Street, tel. 01824/704-830). **$ Leonardo's Delicatessen** is *the* place to buy a top-notch gourmet picnic (made-to-order sandwiches, small salad bar, Mon-Sat 9:00-16:00, closed Sun, just off the main square at 4 Well Street, tel. 01824/707-161). **$ Finn's** is the local favorite for takeaway fish-and-chips (daily 11:30-14:00 & 16:30-21:30 except dinner only on Sun, near Ruthin Gaol at the bottom of Clwyd Street, tel. 01824/702-518).

North Wales Connections

Two major transfer points out of (or into) North Wales are Crewe and Chester. Figure out your complete connection at www.nationalrail.co.uk.

From Crewe by Train to: London's Euston Station (4/hour direct, 2 hours), Bristol, near **Bath** (2/hour, 3 hours, 1 transfer), **Cardiff** (hourly direct, 2.5 hours, more with transfer), **Holyhead** (5/day direct, 2 hours, more with transfer), **Blackpool** (hourly, 1.5 hours, transfer in Preston), **Keswick** in the Lake District (every 2 hours direct, 2 hours to Penrith, more with transfer; then bus to Keswick, 45 minutes), **Birmingham** (3/hour direct, 1 hour, more with transfer), **Glasgow** (roughly hourly direct, 3 hours, more with transfer).

From Chester by Train to: London's Euston Station (hourly, 2 hours direct, more with transfer), **Liverpool** (4/hour direct, 45 minutes), points in North Wales via **Llandudno Junction** (2-3/hour, 1 hour).

Ferry Connections Between North Wales and Ireland

Two companies make the crossing between Holyhead (in North Wales, beyond Caernarfon) and Dublin: **Stena Line** (www.

stenaline.co.uk) and **Irish Ferries** (www.irishferries.com; both roughly 4/day, 3-4 hours, book online for best fares).

Sleeping near Holyhead Dock: On the Isle of Anglesey, the fine **$ Monravon B&B** has five rooms a 15-minute uphill walk from the dock (includes continental breakfast, cooked breakfast-£4, Porth-Y-Felin Road, tel. 01407/762-944, www.monravon. co.uk, monravon@yahoo.co.uk, John and Joan).

SOUTH WALES

Cardiff • Near Cardiff • Wye Valley

South Wales offers a taste of Welsh flavor just an hour from major English destinations such as Bath and the Cotswolds. While the dramatic castles and scenery that many find quintessentially Welsh are in the north, spunky South Wales leaves you with great memories—from the revitalized capital city of Cardiff with its own castle ruins, to the lush Wye Valley with the romantic Tintern Abbey.

Cardiff—like so many Industrial Age giants—became a rundown rust-belt city, but has now reemerged with fresh vigor. Its castle has medieval intrigue as well as Victorian bling, its downtown is ruddy yet vibrant, and its port—which shipped 20 percent of the world's fuel when coal was king—is now a delightful place to stroll.

Just outside Cardiff, St. Fagans open-air museum celebrates the unheralded Welsh culture. The towns of Chepstow and Caerphilly both have stout castles designed by the British to keep the natives of this feisty little country in line. And the beloved Tintern Abbey, frequently immortalized in verse and on canvas, is the most spectacular of Britain's many ruined abbeys.

PLANNING YOUR TIME

South Wales could fill two or three days (overnight in Cardiff or near Tintern Abbey). To learn about Welsh history and culture, spend a few hours at the St. Fagans National Museum of History; for an urban Welsh experience, visit Cardiff. Castle lovers and romantics should consider seeing Tintern Abbey and the castles of Caerphilly and Chepstow (Caerphilly is best).

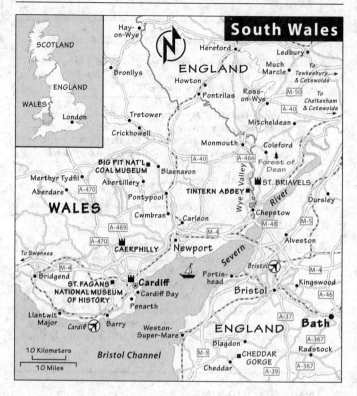

For a targeted visit, cherry-pick the best sights on a busy day between Bath and the Cotswolds:

9:00 Leave Bath for South Wales.

10:30 Tour St. Fagans (or visit Cardiff).

14:30 Head to Tintern Abbey and/or a castle of your choice, then drive to the Cotswolds.

18:00 Set up in your Cotswolds home base.

Cardiff

The Welsh capital of Cardiff (pop. 350,000) feels underrated. It has a fine castle, a freshly revitalized pedestrian core, a smattering of museums, and an impressively modern waterfront. While rugby and soccer fans know Cardiff as the home of Millennium Stadium, and sci-fi fans know it as the place where *Doctor Who* is filmed, the Welsh proudly view the city as their political and cultural capital.

South Wales at a Glance

▲▲**Cardiff Bay** People-friendly, rejuvenated harborfront brimming with attractions, striking architecture, entertainment, and dining options. See page 678.

▲▲**St. Fagans National Museum of History** One hundred acres dedicated to Welsh folk life, including a museum, castle, and more than 40 reconstructed houses demonstrating bygone Welsh ways. **Hours:** Daily 10:00-17:00. See page 685.

▲▲**Caerphilly Castle** Britain's second-largest castle, featuring a leaning tower inhabited by a heartbroken ghost. **Hours:** Daily 9:30-17:00, July-Aug until 18:00; Nov-Feb Mon-Sat 10:00-16:00, Sun from 11:00. See page 688.

▲▲**Tintern Abbey** Remains of a Cistercian abbey that once inspired William Wordsworth and J. M. W. Turner. **Hours:** Daily 9:30-17:00, July-Aug until 18:00; Nov-Feb Mon-Sat 10:00-16:00, Sun from 11:00. See page 692.

▲**Cardiff Castle** Sumptuous castle with a fanciful Victorian-era makeover, plus WWII tunnels, museum, and expansive walled grounds. **Hours:** Daily 9:00-18:00, Nov-Feb until 17:00. See page 676.

PLANNING YOUR TIME

If you're just passing through, Cardiff can be seen in a few hours: Visit the castle, follow my self-guided town walk, and take a quick look at the Cardiff Bay waterfront. But it's also worth considering as an overnight home base for exploring more of South Wales. Just outside Cardiff are two sights well worth visiting: St. Fagans National Museum of History (open-air folk museum) to the west, and Caerphilly (with its sturdy castle) to the north—all doable with just one night and a busy day on either side. If you're seeing other ruined castles in North Wales, Caerphilly is skippable (consider Tintern Abbey instead).

Orientation to Cardiff

Compact Cardiff can be seen quickly, with two main sightseeing zones: the castle and adjacent city center, and Cardiff Bay (a short bus or taxi ride away).

TOURIST INFORMATION

The TI is inside Cardiff Castle's visitors center (daily 9:00-17:00, just inside main castle gate to the right, tel. 029/2087-3573, www.visitcardiff.com).

ARRIVAL IN CARDIFF

By Train: Cardiff Central train station (with the bus station across the street) is at the southern edge of the town center. From here, it's about a 15-minute walk to the castle: Exit the station to the right, then bear left when you hit busy St. Mary Street. Follow this as it becomes High Street, which runs right into Cardiff Castle. The train station has no lockers; you can walk 10 minutes to the Old Library and use the lockers there (see "Helpful Hints," later).

By Car: Cardiff's city center has multiple parking garages. The most convenient, spacious, and reasonably priced are associated with St. David's mall, just southeast of the castle area. To get as close as possible to the castle, try finding pay-and-display street parking in the Civic Center area (near the National Museum, just east of the castle). If heading for Cardiff Bay, the Pierhead Street garage is handiest to the sights, while the Mermaid Quay garage is closer to restaurants. Warning: Cardiff's ridiculously high and jagged curbs seem designed to damage any car that challenges them... trust me.

HELPFUL HINTS

Getting Around: The only public transit you'll likely need is to connect the castle and downtown with the port zone. **Bus #6** and a small **boat service** both shuttle people efficiently from the castle to the port. For details, see page 678.

Welsh Crafts: The **Castle Welsh Crafts Shop** (directly across the street from the castle entrance) is an insanely touristy place offering every Welsh cliché, plus an impressive exhibition of traditional carved wooden love spoons (Mon-Sat 9:00-18:00, Sun 10:30-16:30, 1 Castle Street).

Baggage Storage: You'll find pay storage lockers in the **Old Library,** which hosts the Museum of Cardiff (see "Sights in Cardiff," later) in the pedestrian core of town, just behind the big church. It's a 5-minute walk from Cardiff Castle and a 10-minute walk from the train station (lockers open daily 10:00-15:30).

Walking Tours: Handy walking tours depart from the Castle Welsh Crafts Shop about every other day at 11:00 (£7/person, 2 hours, covers the city but not the castle, schedule posted in craft shop window, call to confirm dates and time, mobile 07849-067-449). Many of the tours are guided by **Bill O'Keefe,** a walking encyclopedia well versed in the history of

Cardiff's Rise, Fall, and Rise

Modern Cardiff, built as a coal port, was made a "city" only in 1905, but its local history goes back to ancient times. In AD 55, the Romans established Cardiff as a fort that could garrison up to 6,000 men to help sub-due the indigenous Welsh. The castle was further fortified (for much the same reason) by King Edward I of England in the late 13th century.

In 1800, Cardiff had fewer than 2,000 residents (two dozen other Welsh towns were bigger). But that all changed when the steam-powered In-dustrial Revolution hit, and fuel-hungry factories recognized Welsh coal as the world's fin-est. (Welsh coal provided more heat per ton, with less smoke and ash.) Cardiff built a suitable port to export the mainstay of Wales' new economy. By 1900 Cardiff was nicknamed "Coal-opolis," and the old town was suddenly industrialized. (There's little for the modern visitor to see that predates this building boom.)

Eventually, Britain began looking east for coal. Modern container ports on England's east coast (facing the continent), coupled with a Europe-wide emphasis on free trade, prompt-ed Britain to begin importing its coal rather than using coal from Wales. (Today, the port of Hull in eastern England im-ports nearly the same tonnage of coal as Cardiff exported in 1900.)

In 1964, the last shipment of coal left Cardiff, marking the end of its industrial port. Like many blue-collar British towns, Cardiff's economy slumped severely in the 1970s and 1980s as its steelworks and other heavy industry were shuttered.

Cardiff experienced a rebound in the 1990s and 2000s. Once a gloomy industrial wasteland, Cardiff's docklands were revitalized with state-of-the-art facilities (such as the impres-sive Wales Millennium Centre for the performing arts) that sit side by side with restored historic buildings and futuristic gov-ernment centers. Formerly traffic-choked downtown streets were pedestrianized and are today filled with modern shop-ping centers.

Cardiff's transformation echoes that of many "second cit-ies" in Britain and beyond that have emerged from dark eco-nomic times to a brighter future. And here, on the south coast of Wales, it comes with a lilting Welsh accent.

SOUTH WALES

Cardiff and South Wales, and a passionate, nonstop teacher. You can also book Bill for a private tour (£100/half-day, £200/day, £250/day with car for up to 4 people, www.planetwales.co.uk, tours@planetwales.co.uk).

Cardiff Walk

Ideally, visit the castle first (see "Sights in Cardiff," later). Then follow this brief self-guided walk from the castle, past just about

everything worth seeing in the town center, and ending near a bus stop for Cardiff Bay. Allow about an hour.

• *We'll begin at the castle gate, with the castle to your back. Look across the busy street to the start of High Street.*

Cardiff was a garrison town back when Wales was an English-ruled apartheid society. The English lived within the walls (now long gone), and the indigenous Welsh who lived beyond made the English thankful they had those walls. The medieval city was mostly built over during Cardiff's Victorian boom times. Pedestrianized **High Street** (which becomes St. Mary Street) is the spine, running from the castle's entrance through the center.

• *We'll head down High Street...eventually. But first, take a little detour. Cross the busy street and bear right (past the Castle Welsh Crafts Shop) to the entrance of the...*

Castle Arcade: This is the most impressive of the many Victorian-era arcades burrowing through the city center. During the late 1800s, when Cardiff was boom-

ing, there emerged a class of wealthy women who demanded climate-controlled, London-quality shopping. The city answered by developing several arcades with glass roofs, ensuring the ladies stayed warm in the winter, and didn't get a "working-class" tan in the summer. (The term "blue blooded" refers to the fact that their wrists were so lily white that the blue of the veins popped.) These long, narrow Victorian arcades—echoing the shape of farm plats from the days when people lived and farmed within the town's protective walls—were state of the

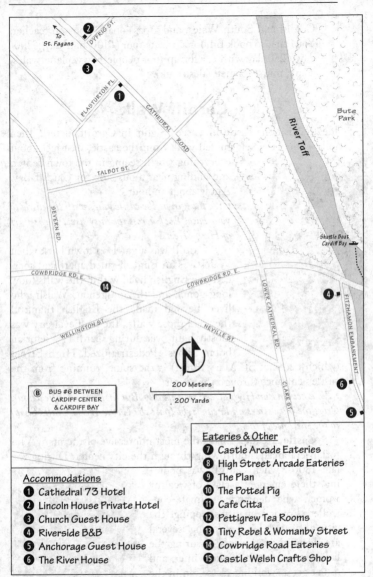

Eateries & Other
7 Castle Arcade Eateries
8 High Street Arcade Eateries
9 The Plan
10 The Potted Pig
11 Cafe Citta
12 Pettigrew Tea Rooms
13 Tiny Rebel & Womanby Street
14 Cowbridge Road Eateries
15 Castle Welsh Crafts Shop

Accommodations
1 Cathedral 73 Hotel
2 Lincoln House Private Hotel
3 Church Guest House
4 Riverside B&B
5 Anchorage Guest House
6 The River House

B BUS #6 BETWEEN CARDIFF CENTER & CARDIFF BAY

200 Meters
200 Yards

art when first constructed, with some of the first electric lighting anywhere.

Today, the joy of visiting these arcades lies in their characteristic shops and little cafés, the majority of which are family-run rather than chain stores. Stroll through Castle Arcade, noticing the fun liquid nitrogen ice cream being made at **Science Cream,** and (at the bend in the arcade) the recommended **Madame Fromage,**

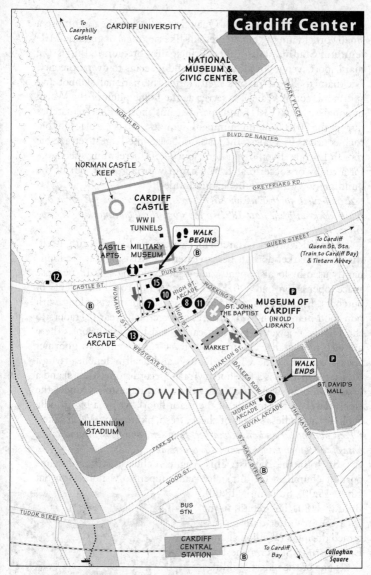

Cardiff Center

To Caerphilly Castle

CARDIFF UNIVERSITY

NATIONAL MUSEUM & CIVIC CENTER

NORTH RD

PARK PLACE

BLVD. DE NANTES

NORMAN CASTLE KEEP

CARDIFF CASTLE

GREYFRIARS RD.

WW II TUNNELS

QUEEN STREET

To Cardiff Queen St. Stn. (Train to Cardiff Bay) & Tintern Abbey

CASTLE APTS.

MILITARY MUSEUM

🚶 **WALK BEGINS**

ℹ️ 🅱️

CASTLE ST.

12 🅱️

WOMANBY ST.

DUKE ST.

15

10

HIGH ST. ARCADE

WORKING ST.

HIGH ST.

8

11

7

ST. JOHN THE BAPTIST

MUSEUM OF CARDIFF (IN OLD LIBRARY)

🅿️

CASTLE ARCADE

13

WESTGATE ST.

MARKET

WHARTON ST.

🚶 **WALK ENDS**

🅿️

D O W N T O W N

BAKERS ROW

ST. DAVID'S MALL

MILLENNIUM STADIUM

PARK ST.

MORGAN ARCADE

ROYAL ARCADE

9

THE HAYES

WOOD ST.

ST. MARY STREET

🅱️

BUS STN.

TUDOR STREET

CARDIFF CENTRAL STATION

🅱️

To Cardiff Bay

Callaghan Square

an upscale cheese-and-wine bar—one of many places on this walk ideal for a Welsh lunch. Look above to see the upper gallery (accessed via well-marked staircases).

• *Exiting out the far end of Castle Arcade, you'll pop out along...*

High Street (Heol Fawr): Cardiff's main street was pedestrianized in 2007, making it a delightful walking zone. Turn right and stroll down the street.

At the first corner with Quay Street, look right to glimpse a small corner (and the big, white, sail-like riggings) of gigantic **Millennium Stadium** (also called Principality Stadium). This is the main sports venue for all of Wales, and it seems to dwarf the city. Nicknamed "The Dragon's Den" (after the national symbol and sports mascot of Wales), it serves as the home pitch of the Welsh national rugby (WRU) and soccer teams, hosted soccer matches during the 2012 London Summer Olympics, and is *the* place for big rock concerts in Wales. The stadium boasts the largest retractable roof in Europe. Even if you don't join 74,500 screaming spectators for a rugby or soccer match, you can pay for a guided tour of the building (www.principalitystadium.wales).

• *A half-block farther down High Street, watch on the left for a big, white clock with the date 1891 in the stone threshold, marking the entrance to the...*

Cardiff Market (Marchnad Caerdydd): Like Cardiff itself, this lively market does its best to cater to tourists...but is predominantly used by locals. Spend some time exploring this all-purpose space (open Mon-Sat 8:00-17:30, closed Sun). You'll find plenty of butchers, fishmongers, fruits and veggies, and sweets, along with non-food items such as hardware, vintage menswear ("Traders to the Dandy"), jewelry, greeting cards, and hair extensions. There are also food stalls, ranging from basic snack stands to gourmet cheese counters (The Cheese Pantry) and healthy lunches (Migli Market). Upstairs is a top-notch vintage record store (Kelly's) and a few bric-a-brac shops. For a tasty treat, find Bakestones (under the clock tower in the middle of the main floor), where a big griddle cooks up an endless supply of cheap, fresh, piping-hot Welsh cakes.

• *Exit out the far end of the market, turn left, and hook around to the base of the church tower to enter the church of...*

St. John the Baptist: This Anglican church is the most important church in Cardiff's city center (open to visitors Mon-Sat 10:00-15:00, Sun until 18:00).

Built in 1180, then rebuilt in the 15th century after damage sustained during a rebellion against English rule, St. John the Baptist is one of the oldest buildings in Cardiff. Step inside to enjoy the Victorian stained glass and the Herbert family tomb (in the chapel to the left of the main altar). The Herberts ran the town in the 16th century like gangster Medicis.

As you face the altar, exit the church through the door on your right, emerging into the churchyard. Look for the tall, well-worn nub of a medieval **preaching cross.** Originally standing on High Street, this cross marked the site of official announcements and special preaching (e.g., "Join in on the newest crusade!").

• *With the church at your back, exit the churchyard through the gate, then continue past the fenced park to the...*

Old Library (Yr Hen Lyfrgell): This fine building dates from Cardiff's Victorian glory days—back when city leaders wanted to be sure the general public had access to good books. Today it contains a fine shop full of classy Welsh souvenirs, lockers for baggage storage, WCs, and a museum exhibit.

As you enter the library, turn left to find the gorgeously preserved, colorfully tiled **Victorian corridor**—evoking the spare-no-expense gentility of Cardiff's boom era.

The building houses the free, engaging **Museum of Cardiff** (daily 10:00-16:00, www.cardiffmuseum.com). Step into its one large room for a concise, vividly illustrated look at the full sweep of Cardiff's history—including a big model of its sprawling port circa 1913. More exhibits are in the basement, including a children's dress-up area and a reading nook with comfy couches and lots of Cardiff and Wales-related books to choose from.

• *Beyond the Old Library, at a plaza with tall trees, the street widens into a pedestrian boulevard called...*

The Hayes (Yr Aes): Like High Street, The Hayes was revitalized (in 2006) and transformed into the city's finest shopping zone. The trees mark a small food court called Hayes Island, with a venerable snack stand, fish-and-chips shop, and a noodle bar. Stroll beyond that, noticing the vast, sprawling, modern St. David's mall on your left. For more local browsing, watch on your right for the entrance to the **Morgan Arcade**—another classic Victorian shopping gallery. Step inside and poke your way into the center, where you'll find the recommended **Plan Café,** one of Cardiff's best coffee shops...and a good place to unwind at the end of this walk.

• *To continue to Cardiff's other main sightseeing zone—Cardiff Bay— find the nearby bus stop. Walk through Morgan Arcade to the far end. You'll pop out on St. Mary' Street, the southern part of High Street. Turn left and walk two blocks to the curve of a busy road. Here you'll see bus stops—hop on bus #6 or the "Baycar" for a ride to Cardiff Bay.*

Sights in Cardiff

I've listed Cardiff's main sights below. For two worthwhile sights within 30 minutes of the city (St. Fagans National Museum of History and Caerphilly Castle), see the "Near Cardiff" section, later.

IN THE CENTER
▲Cardiff Castle

Cardiff Castle (Castell Caerdydd in Welsh) is one of the town's top sights—a fun complex that contains within its big medieval wall bits of several fortresses erected here since Roman times. You'll ramble its ramparts, climb an impressive Norman keep built on a man-made mound, see a WWII bomb shelter, visit an impressive Welsh military museum, and tour a romantically rebuilt Victorian-era palace that is less than historic but dazzling just the same.

Cost and Hours: £11.50, includes audioguide; daily 9:00-18:00, Nov-Feb until 17:00, last entry one hour before closing; café, tel. 029/2087-8100, www.cardiffcastle.com.

Tours: For a 50-minute tour of the 19th-century palace, pay £3.75 extra as you enter and reserve a time. Tours depart at the top of each hour and cover the rooms you can see on your own plus a handful of otherwise inaccessible rooms (the nursery, bedroom, and rooftop garden).

Visiting the Castle: Your visit includes the following stops, which you can tour in any order. All are well explained in the included audioguide.

The **entrance building** has the ticket office, TI, shop, café, and WCs. Upstairs are the audioguide pickup and a brief movie about the castle. Downstairs is a fine **military exhibit** called "Firing Line: Museum of the Welsh Soldier." Illustrated with plenty of artifacts (uniforms, medals, and weapons), the exhibit zigzags chronologically through the cellar, from conflict to conflict. You'll learn why a goat always leads Welsh regiments into battle.

WWII Tunnels: Stepping out into the main courtyard, on your right (near the catapult) is a long, two-level stretch of passageways—the battlements and WWII tunnels. The old battlements are above, and underneath them is a tunnel that was used during WWII air raids as a bomb shelter. Cardiff was an important military port (20 percent of all American GIs who fought in Europe landed here), which made it a target of Nazi bombers. While the port was hit hard, the city center got off pretty lightly.

Keep: Dominating the castle grounds is the keep, a classic Norman motte-and-bailey construction, with a stout fortress on top of a man-made hill. The original structure, made of wood, was built by William the Conqueror in 1081. He was returning from what he called a "pilgrimage" to St. David's—a cathedral town in western Wales—which clearly included a little scouting for future military action. You can ascend the very steep steps into the keep's courtyard, then even more steps to reach the (empty) inner chamber, the (empty) jail, and the rest of this mostly empty shell.

Castle Apartments: Finally, on the left is the most interesting interior in the castle complex. This Neo-Gothic fantasy palace was rebuilt by John Crichton-Stuart, third marquess of Bute, whose income from the thriving coal trade flowing through his docklands made him one of Europe's wealthiest men in the late 1860s. He spared no expense. With his funds and architect William

Burges' know-how, the castle was turned into a whimsical, fantastical take on the Middle Ages. It's the Welsh equivalent of "Mad" King Ludwig's fairy-tale castles in Bavaria (built in the same romantic decade). In 1947, the family donated it to the city of Cardiff.

Heading upstairs, peek into the glittering **Arab Room,** slathered in gold, including a gold-leaf stalactite ceiling. Then you'll step into the highlight of the complex, the breathtaking **Banqueting Hall**—with every surface covered in the highly detailed, gilded imagery of medieval symbolism. This hall grandly evokes the age of chivalry, right down to the raised minstrel's gallery (where musicians could perform overhead but remain unseen). Farther along, the **small dining room** has a table designed for a grapevine to grow up through a hole in the middle—so that guests could pick their own dessert. And the **library** boasts rows of leather-bound books and desks that double as radiators.

Nearby: The lush Bute Park—the largest urban park in Britain (as big as New York's Central Park)—runs from the castle to the open valley beyond Cardiff. It offers a world of escapes for relaxing locals—formal gardens, rugby and cricket pitches, and a riverside path that leads through natural surroundings from the castle into the hills. On the River Taff, at the southeast end of the park (nearest the castle), you'll find the dock for the shuttle boats to the port. For more about the shuttle boat, see "Getting to Cardiff Bay," later.

National Museum and Civic Center

The National Museum focuses not on Welsh culture and history—that's at St. Fagans (see "Near Cardiff," later)—but on art (with a particularly strong Impressionist collection), natural history (dinosaurs and mammoths), and archaeology (scant fragments of prehistoric Wales).

The imposing Civic Center—a gathering of stately buildings—was erected just before Cardiff reached the end of its boom. A leading citizen sold the city some prime land at a great price on one condition: Grand London-class structures made of Portland stone must be built here, and remain forever open to the public. So, in 1910 the city built its Edwardian City Hall, law courts, National Museum, and the University of Wales just north of the castle on North Road.

Cost and Hours: Free, Tue-Sun 10:00-17:00, closed Mon, Cathays Park, tel. 0300-111-2333, www.museumwales.ac.uk/cardiff.

CARDIFF BAY

Cardiff Bay (worth ▲▲) was the city's industrial engine during its Golden Age—and its most miserable corner during its era of

precipitous decline. But today the bay has bounced back, with lots of new construction and some thoughtful refurbishment of historical sights. It's worth the short bus or boat ride from downtown to this lively area to get a glimpse of Cardiff's past, present, and future, and to see how a once-flailing city can right the ship.

Getting to Cardiff Bay: It's about 15 minutes by **bus** from downtown. While various routes get you close, your best bet is bus #6 (or another service, called the "Baycar," that follows the same route; if bus #X8 comes by, that will also get you here). You can catch bus #6 at various points from downtown: try the Wyndham Arcade stop (southern end of St. Mary Street, near the end of my self-guided walk); or the Kingsway stop in front of the Hilton Hotel, across the street from the side wall of Cardiff Castle (£2, exact change only; about every 10 minutes, www.cardiffbus.com). Hop off at the East Bute Street stop, just behind the Wales Millennium Centre (walk through the Millennium Centre to pop out on Roald Dahl Plass). For the return trip, you can catch the bus at the more convenient Millennium Centre stop, facing Roald Dahl Plass.

You can also get here by slightly-slower-yet-scenic **boat.** Two companies (Aquabus and Princess Katharine) leave from a dock in Bute Park not far from the castle, below the Castle Street bridge

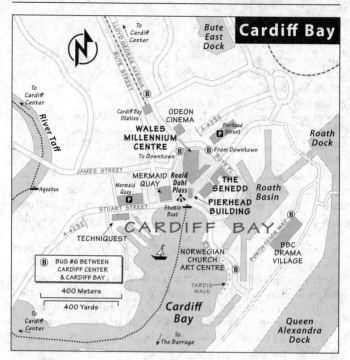

Cardiff Bay

To Cardiff Center

LLOYD GEORGE AVENUE
BUTE STREET

Bute East Dock

To Cardiff Center

River Taff

To Cardiff Center

Aquabus

Cardiff Bay Station

ODEON CINEMA

A-4232

WALES MILLENNIUM CENTRE

To Downtown

Pierhead Street

From Downtown

Roath Dock

BUTE PL

JAMES STREET

MERMAID QUAY

Mermaid Quay

Roald Dahl Plass

THE SENEDD

Roath Basin

PIERHEAD BUILDING

STUART STREET

Shuttle Boat

CARDIFF BAY

A-4232

TECHNIQUEST

BBC DRAMA VILLAGE

PORTH TEIGR WAY

B BUS #6 BETWEEN CARDIFF CENTER & CARDIFF BAY

400 Meters

400 Yards

NORWEGIAN CHURCH ART CENTRE

TARDIS WALK

Cardiff Bay

To Cardiff Center

To The Barrage

Queen Alexandra Dock

and Pettigrew Tea Rooms (£4, each company goes hourly—alternating on the half-hour, 25 minutes, www.cardiffboat.com).

Background: Cardiffians love to brag that in its heyday, the port of Cardiff shipped almost a quarter of the world's coal. Valleys rich with the best coal deposits anywhere funneled the black gold of the 19th century right into Cardiff. Capitalizing on the Industrial Revolution demand for steam power, the city built a massive port, ultimately with about 200 miles of train tracks lining its shipping piers. (There are none of the vast brick warehouses you'd expect in a 19th-century port; rather than being warehoused, the coal was simply piled next to the tracks and shipped almost immediately upon arrival.)

But with the advent of imported coal and oil, Cardiff's port declined. A generation ago, the port was derelict—a place no tourist would dream of visiting. But in the late 1980s, city leaders hatched a scheme for the "Cardiff Bay Barrage," designed to seal off the mouth of the port and create a permanent high-tide waterline. Their goal was to attract developers with the promise of an inviting new people zone on the waterfront. It worked. Today, as with rusty old ports all over Europe, Cardiff Bay is thriving—packed with sparkling bold architecture, sightseeing attractions, and fun entertainment.

▲▲Cardiff Bay Visual Tour

There's a lot to see at Cardiff Bay. Fortunately, you can see almost all of it with a strategic sweep of the head. To get your bearings, plant yourself on the little bridge at the harbor end of Roald Dahl Plass, and survey the bay.

• *Begin by facing straight out to sea.*

Cardiff Bay and the Barrage: Before 2002, one of biggest tides in the world literally emptied this bay twice a day. Now, the mouth of the harbor is dammed by "The Barrage" (BAH-rahzh), a high-tech dam marked by the grassy slope in the distance. While locks let in boats and a fish ladder lets in fish, the tide is kept out, and Cardiff Bay has become an inviting tourist zone. The bluff called Penarth Head (right of the Barrage) is a desirable residential zone, and on a clear day, you can spot the hills of West England in the far distance.

On the embankment below and in front of you, you'll see **boat docks** offering harbor cruises, or a boat ride up the River Taff to the city center (a scenic return if you came here by bus; see "Getting to Cardiff Bay," earlier). The giant, bronze circular sculpture (called the *Celtic Ring*) is the starting point for the **Taff Trail,** a beloved 55-mile walking and cycling riverside path that leads through the green core of Cardiff all the way to the village of Brecon, deep in the Welsh interior.

• *The stately, red-brick building on your left is the...*

Pierhead Building: Sometimes called the "Welsh Big Ben," this landmark is a symbol of the city. The building was originally the port authority for Cardiff Bay, which was later merged with the Cardiff Railway Company (logical, since this is where rails met ships). Note the evocative relief celebrating steamships and trains with the Welsh phrase *wrth ddŵr a thân* ("by water and fire")—still the motto of the Welsh railways. A history exhibit inside shows a free and interesting video (Mon-Fri 9:30-16:30, Sat-Sun from 10:30, www.pierhead.org).

Behind the Pierhead—but not visible from here—is the Welsh National Assembly (more on this later).

• *Looking just to the right from the Pierhead, you'll see a white shiplap church that seems like it would be more at home on a fjord. This is the...*

Norwegian Church Art Centre: This was originally built as a seamen's mission by the Norwegian merchant marines, in properly austere Lutheran style, during Cardiff's Industrial-Age boom. Originally, it sat where the Wales Millennium Centre is today, but in the 1970s and 1980s—when the docklands were a dangerous, derelict no-man's-land—the church was literally disassembled and mothballed for future use. Over the decades, it has been reassembled, reconsecrated, refurbished, and repurposed as a successful arts center (free, daily 11:00-16:00, café, www.norwegianchurchcardiff.com).

• *Beyond the Norwegian Church is a handful of other sights.*

More Bay Sights: Many popular BBC television shows are filmed in Cardiff, including the long-running science-fiction series *Doctor Who.* On Roath Lock sprawls the **BBC Drama Village,** the studio lot where shows such as *Doctor Who, Casualty,* and the Welsh-language soap opera *Pobol y Cwm* are filmed. *Torchwood* and the 2010-12 version of *Upstairs Downstairs* also filmed here.

In the bay beyond here, notice the rotting **wooden pilings** in the harbor. Nicknamed "dolphins," these were used to brace ships caught here by falling tides before the construction of the Barrage. (Captains would tie their boats to a dolphin and gently settle onto mud without toppling.)

• *Now turn with your back to the bay. You're looking right at the huge plaza at the center of this area called...*

Roald Dahl Plass: Visitors congregate on this expansive bowl-shaped main plaza named for the Cardiff-born children's author. You can see a seated statue of him on the right. (The Norwegian term plass—"square"—honors Dahl's Norwegian ancestry.) As this area was once a coal port, it angles down to the water. The pillars are illuminated with a light show after dark, and the 70-foot-tall silver water tower is always trickling.

• *On the left side of the square is **Mermaid Quay,** a sprawling outdoor-dining zone loaded with mostly chain restaurants. On the right side of the square is the dramatic...*

Wales Millennium Centre: Wales, a land famous for its love of music, had no national opera house until 2004. The Welsh fixed that with gusto when they built the 2,000-seat Wales Millennium Centre. It's a cutting-edge venue housing opera and theater, among other performances (funded mostly by lottery money). The enormous opera house anchors the entire Cardiff Bay district. Its facade—dominated by slate and steel, two important Welsh resources that have kept this small country humming—is carved with the words of one-time Welsh national poet Gwyneth Lewis: the English phrase "In these stones horizons sing," and the Welsh phrase *Creu gwir fel gwydr o ffwrnais awen* ("Creating truth like glass from the furnace of inspiration"). The expansive lobby holds shops, an enticing food court, and lots of activities, including occasional free lunch concerts (tel. 029/2063-6464, www.wmc.org.uk).

• *One more important sight nearby is not visible from here. Facing the water, walk to the left along the railing. Looking to your left, soon you'll see the big, modern...*

Senedd, The National Assembly of Wales: With its huge overhanging roof, this is essentially the Welsh capitol. While Wales—like Scotland and Northern Ireland—has a degree of autonomy from the United Kingdom, many matters are still decided in London. The National Assembly was created in 1999, moved into these new digs in 2006, and gained more authority in 2007. The building, with vast walls of glass symbolizing the ideal of an open and transparent govern-

ment, was designed by prominent architect Richard Rogers (best known for London's Millennium Dome and Lloyd's Building, and—with frequent collaborator Renzo Piano—Paris' Pompidou Centre).

In front of the Senedd, notice the modern sculpture that resembles the hull of a ship—but notice that its prow has the ghostly features of a human head. This is the **Merchant Marine Memorial,** built to remember the sailors who died keeping Britain supplied during the WWII Battle of the Atlantic.

• *Our tour is over. We've covered the main landmarks, but there's much more to see and do around this bay: bikes and boats for rent, a hands-on science museum (Techniquest), fake-yet-thrilling whitewater rafting, an open-air exhibit of boats from around the world, a multiplex (with Wales' only IMAX screen), and the nearby International Sports Village (with an ice arena and swimming pool). Enjoy!*

Sleeping in Cardiff

ALONG CATHEDRAL ROAD

This pleasant (but busy) tree-lined street—a one-mile walk or quick bus ride from the city center—feels classic and upscale, with rows of tidy Victorian homes...several of which host B&Bs. Expect some street noise. Street parking here is free but tight; I've noted places that offer private parking.

$$ Cathedral 73 Hotel is plush but loosely run, with eight rooms above a classy, contemporary lobby area (73 Cathedral Road, tel. 029/2023-5005, www.cathedral73.com, stay@cathedral73.com).

$$ Lincoln House Private Hotel feels classic and classy. Its 21 rooms are traditionally decorated and neatly maintained, and the public spaces—from a plush lounge to a convivial bar—are appealing (free parking, 118 Cathedral Road, tel. 029/2039-5558, www.lincolnhotel.co.uk, reservations@lincolnhotel.co.uk).

$ Church Guest House rents nine straightforward rooms with simple, contemporary style (includes continental breakfast,

109 Cathedral Road, tel. 029/2169-0033, www.churchguesthouse. co.uk, enquiries@churchguesthouse.co.uk).

FACING MILLENNIUM STADIUM

A quiet middle-class neighborhood of row houses lines up across the river from Millennium Stadium. It's a shorter walk to the center than the Cathedral Road options (about 10 minutes to the castle), and generally less "posh" and more affordable—making it a smart budget choice.

$ Riverside B&B, carefully run by Irena, has one en-suite double and three top-floor rooms that share a bathroom. Everything is neat as a pin, and guests gather around a big shared breakfast table (free parking, 1 Coldstream Terrace, tel. 029/2021-0378, mobile 029-2021-0378, www.riversidebandb.co.uk, irenahinc@ yahoo.co.uk).

$ Anchorage Guest House feels impersonal—there's no 24-hour reception, and you'll use a key code to come and go. The public spaces are a bit dated and scuffed, but its 14 rooms are comfortable, and the price is right (cheaper rooms with shared bath, includes continental breakfast, pay-and-display street parking, 45 Fitzhamon Embankment, tel. 029/2240-1888, www.anchorageguesthouse. co.uk, anchorageguesthousecardiff@gmail.com).

¢ The River House is a delightful hostel/backpackers' hotel, conscientiously run by brother-and-sister team Charlie and Abi. Their 12 rooms include doubles, as well as four- and six-bed dorms (all with shared bath). They pride themselves on offering good value and a welcoming, mellow home base in Cardiff. There's a shared kitchen, a small lounge, and delightful back garden. No wonder they've been voted best hostel in Wales (59 Fitzhamon Embankment, tel. 029/2010-5590, www.riverhousebackpackers.com).

CHAIN HOTELS IN THE CENTER

Cardiff's city center—where you'll be spending most of your sightseeing time—is full of big chain hotels at every price point. Midrange options include **$ Jurys Inn** (1 Park Place), **$ Travelodge** (St. Mary Street), **$ Ibis** (near the Queen Street train station on Churchill Way), and **$ Premier Inn** (also near the Queen Street train station, 10 Churchill Way). Generally, these are a good deal in a convenient location; when it's busy (such as when there's a big rugby match), prices skyrocket and the city center can feel rowdy. Either way, parking can be pricey.

Eating in Cardiff

All of my recommendations, except those on Cowbridge Road, are in the city center. Many are deep inside Cardiff's delightful shopping arcades, and most are lunch-only. If looking for a meal on Cardiff Bay, simply peruse the restaurants at Mermaid Quay.

In Castle Arcade: $$ Madame Fromage, right at the bend of the arcade, is a tempting choice for mostly cheese-focused light meals, such as Welsh rarebit (Mon-Sat 10:00-17:30, closed Sun, 21 Castle Arcade, tel. 029/2064-4888). **$$ Coffee Barker** is a sprawling yet cozy café, good for a beverage or a light meal either inside or out on the arcade (Mon-Sat 8:30-17:30, Sun 10:00-16:30).

In High Street Arcade: $ New York Deli dishes up good sandwiches (Mon-Fri 11:00-15:30, Sat 10:00-16:00...or until they run out of bread, closed Sun, 19 High Street Arcade, tel. 029/2038-8388). **$$ Barkers Tea Rooms** is an outpost of the popular Coffee Barker described above, with a similar menu (Mon-Sat 9:00-17:00, Sun 10:30-16:30, 8 High Street Arcade, tel. 029/2034-1390).

In Morgan Arcade: $$ The Plan may be Cardiff's most appealing coffee shop, filling a woody two-story space in a genteel arcade (light meals, Mon-Sat 8:45-17:00, Sun 9:45-16:00, food until one hour before closing, 28 Morgan Arcade, tel. 029/2039-8764).

Near the Castle: $$$$ The Potted Pig is *the* place for a fancy meal downtown. It's in a cellar with straightforward decor that doesn't compete with the menu: locally sourced, seasonal, and artfully composed modern Welsh dishes with French influences. Reservations are smart at dinnertime. While pricey to order à la carte, their lunch special—just £12 for two courses—is affordable (Mon-Sat 12:00-14:30 & 18:30-21:00, Sun lunch only, directly in front of Cardiff Castle at 27 High Street, tel. 029/2022-4817, www.thepottedpig.com).

$$ Cafe Citta, in the pedestrian zone in front of the castle, is a local favorite for Italian food. Tight and cozy (reserve ahead), the first language spoken here is Italian—and the food is authentically delicious (Tue-Sat 12:00-23:00, closed Sun-Mon, 4 Church Street, tel. 029/2022-4040).

Tea in the Park: $ Pettigrew Tea Rooms is a cozy space just inside Bute Park that feels like a visit to grandma's (Mon-Fri 8:30-17:30, Sat-Sun 9:00-18:00, between the castle and the river, tel. 029/2023-5486, www.pettigrew-tearooms.com).

Local Brews: An outpost of a brewery in nearby Newport, **$$ Tiny Rebel** fills a striking, classic red-brick building near the stadium. With youthful-but-mellow ambience and a basic menu of burgers and bar food, this is a good place to sample Welsh brews (flights available, long hours daily, food served Mon-Sat 12:00-21:00, Sun until 16:00, 25 Westgate Street). Tiny Rebel also marks the start of **Womanby Street,** a lively after-hours zone where bars and clubs fill formerly abandoned industrial buildings.

Cowbridge Road: This street just west of the river (and south of my recommended Cathedral Road hotels) is lined with a mishmash of blue-collar businesses and ethnic eateries. **$ Chai Street** (#153) serves Indian street food on silver thali platters.

Cardiff Connections

From Cardiff by Train to: Caerphilly (2-4/hour, 20 minutes), **Bath** (hourly, 1-1.5 hours), **Birmingham** (1/hour direct, more with change in Bristol, 2 hours), **London**'s Paddington Station (2/hour, 2 hours), **Chepstow** (2/hour, 35 minutes; then bus #69 to **Tintern**—runs every 1-2 hours, 20 minutes). Train info: tel. 0871-200-2233, www.traveline-cymru.info.

By Car: For driving directions from Bath to Cardiff, see "Route Tips for Drivers" at the end of this chapter.

Near Cardiff

▲▲St. Fagans National Museum of History

The best look anywhere at traditional Welsh folk life, St. Fagans is a 100-acre open-air museum with more than 40 carefully reconstructed and fully furnished historic buildings from all corners of Wales, as well as a "castle" (actually a Tudor-era manor house) that offers a glimpse of how the other half lived. Also known as *Amgueddfa Werin Cymru* (Museum of Welsh Life),

its workshops feature busy craftsmen eager to demonstrate their skills. Each house comes equipped with a local expert warming up beside a toasty fire, happy to tell you anything you want to know about life in this old cottage. Ask questions.

Cost and Hours: Free, parking-£5 (cash only), daily 10:00-17:00, tel. 030/0111-2333, www.museumwales.ac.uk/en/stfagans.

SOUTH WALES

Information: Pick up the essential map (small fee). Plaques by each building do an exceptional job of succinctly explaining where the building came from, its role in Welsh culture, and how it came to be here, all illustrated by a helpful timeline.

Getting There: From Cardiff's bus station (across the street from Cardiff Central train station), catch **bus #32A** (which stops right at the museum entrance; bus #320 takes you to St. Fagans village, a five-minute walk to the museum; buses run about 2/hour, 25 minutes, www.traveline-cymru.info). **Drivers** leave the M-4 at Junction 33 and follow the brown signs to *Museum of Welsh Life.* Leaving the museum, jog left on the freeway, take the first exit, and circle back, following signs to the M-4.

Eating at St. Fagans: Within the park are plenty of snack stands, as well as two bigger eateries: the Gwalia Tea Room in the heart of the traditional building zone, and The Buttery inside the castle. Derwen Bakehouse sells snacks and traditional fruit-studded bread, which is tasty and warm out of the oven. Back in the real world, The Plymouth Arms pub, just outside the museum, serves the best food.

Visiting the Museum: Buy the map and pick up the list of today's activities. Once in the park, you'll find most of the traditional buildings to your left, while to the right are the castle and its surrounding gardens. Here's a rough framework for seeing the highlights:

First, head left and do a clockwise spin around the traditional buildings, starting with the circa-1800, red-and-white **Kennix-ton Farmhouse.** Then swing left, go down past the mill, and hook left again down the path to the fine **Lywyn-yr-eos Farmhouse.** Along with the castle, this is the only building at the museum that stands in its original location. It's furnished as it would have been at the end of World War I—complete with

"welcome home" banner and patriotic portraits of stiff-upper-lip injured troops. From here you can side-trip five minutes to two Celtic **round houses,** which were farmhouses back in the Iron Age.

Head back up the main path and continue deeper into the park, turning left at the fork (toward *Church* and *Y Garieg Fawr*). Passing another farmhouse, then a small mill (used for grinding gorse—similar to scotch broom—into animal feed) and a Tudor-era trader's house, continue through the woods to **St. Teilos' Church,** surrounded by a whitewashed stone fence. The interior has been restored to the way it looked around 1520—including vibrantly colorful illustrations of Bible stories on all the walls.

Leaving the church, turn left and continue ahead to the **Oakdale Workmen's Institute**—basically a leisure club and community center for hardworking miners and their families. Poking around the building—from the library, reading room, and meeting hall downstairs to the concert hall upstairs—you can imagine how a space like this provided a humble community with a much-needed social space.

Next up, just past the tall red box (a **telephone booth** from the 20th century, where people would make "telephonic" calls) are the **Gwalia Stores,** a village general store where you could buy just about anything imaginable (poke around to see what locals may have shopped for). One section of the store still sells canned goods, local cheeses, sweets, and ice cream; upstairs is a full-service tearoom.

Pass the olde-tyme portrait studio on your way up to the museum's highlight, the **Rhyd-y-Car** terrace of row houses, which displays ironworker cottages as they might have looked in 1805, 1855, 1895, 1925, 1955, and 1985—offering a fascinating zip through Welsh domestic life from hearths to microwaves. Notice the pea patches in front, the outhouse, and the chicken coops in the back.

Just past the row houses is a large grassy expanse (with a penny arcade and period rides on the far side). Turn right and step into the one-room **St. Mary's Board Schoolhouse,** where the docent can explain the various items used to punish ill-behaved kids in the late 19th century. What looks like a wooden version of brass knuckles was used to force lefties to write right. The "Welsh not" was worn as a badge of shame by any student heard speaking Welsh rather than the required English. Students could pass it on to other kids they heard speaking Welsh, and whoever was wearing it at day's end was caned (spanked with a stick).

After exiting the schoolhouse, take a hard right at the tollhouse to reach the **bakery.** This is a fine place to break for coffee and cake—they sell *bara brith* (speckled bread), a kind of fruit bread, hot out of the oven. Sitting on the picnic benches, you can enjoy all the family fun around you. Listen for parents talking to their kids in Welsh.

Head back past the entrance area and continue to the castle and gardens. You'll dip down past a series of terraced ponds, then climb steeply up to the misnamed **"castle"**—so-called because it was built on the remains of a real, Norman-era castle that once stood here. This circa-1580 Elizabethan manor house boasts a stately interior decorated with antique period furnishing. It feels like the perfect setting for a murder mystery or a ghost tale. Entering, you'll walk through The Hall (a reception room for visitors), The Study (where the master of the house carried out his business), and The Drawing Room (where the ladies would convene for a post-dinner chat, à la *Downton Abbey*). Climb the funhouse stairs up to the long gallery, where you can dip into a series of bedrooms.

Leaving the castle, if it's nice out, turn left and explore the expansive manicured **gardens** that stretch out across the grounds. Near the far end is a woolen mill.

▲▲Caerphilly Castle

This impressive but gutted old castle—evocative but with no actual artifacts—is surrounded by lakes, gently rolling hills, and the town of Caerphilly. It's the most visit-worthy castle I've seen in South Wales—but if you're heading to the great castles of North Wales (such as Conwy and Caernar-fon) a visit here is redundant.

Cost and Hours: £8.90; daily 9:30-17:00, July-Aug until 18:00; Nov-Feb Mon-Sat 10:00-16:00, Sun from 11:00; tel. 029/2088-3143, www.cadw.wales.gov.uk.

Information: Scant explanations are offered by a few post-ed plaques; if you want the full story, invest in the £5 guidebook. Across the moat, Caerphilly's helpful town **TI** happily answers questions. It sells a variety of locally sourced, non-tacky Welsh souvenirs (daily 9:30-17:00, tel. 029/2088-0011, www.visitcaerphilly.com).

Getting There: The castle is located right in the center of the town of Caerphilly, nine miles north of Cardiff. To get there, take the **train** from Cardiff to Caerphilly (4/hour Mon-Sat, hourly Sun, 20 minutes) and walk five minutes. It's 20 minutes by **car** from St. Fagans (exit 32, following signs from the M-4). Once in town, follow signs to park in the pay lot right next to the TI, facing the castle.

Background: Spread over 30 acres, Caerphilly is the second-largest castle in Britain after Windsor. English Earl Gilbert de Clare erected this squat behemoth to try to establish a stronghold in Wales. With two concentric walls, it was considered to be a brilliant arrangement of defensive walls and moats. Attackers had to negotiate three drawbridges and four sets of doors and portcullises just to reach the main entrance. For the record, there were no known successful enemy forays beyond the current castle's inner walls. Later, this castle understandably became a favorite of Romantics, who often painted it in the shimmering Welsh mist. And in modern times, during the Great Depression of the 1930s, the castle's owner undertook a restoration of the then-mostly ruined structure (as a sort of private stimulus package), restoring it at least partway to its previous glory. Today it's surrounded by a picturesque, picnic-perfect park.

Visiting the Castle: Cross the first moat and enter the outer gate to buy your ticket. Then head across the second moat to reach the central keep of the castle.

You'll enter through the **Inner East Gatehouse,** with a short introductory video on the ground floor, and unfurnished but still stately residential halls  upstairs. The top-floor terrace offers great views between the crenellations of the castle complex and the town. On the way up and down, look for the little bathrooms. No need to flush—the chute beneath the hole drops several stories directly into the moat below. (Just one more disincentive for would-be attackers thinking of crossing that moat.)

From there, head into the **Inner Ward**—the central yard (or "bailey") that's ringed by thick walls and stout towers. The tower across the Inner Ward to the right features another short video about the castle. To the left as you enter the Inner Ward is the restored, cavernous **Great Hall,** with thick stony walls, a wood-beam ceiling, and a man-sized fireplace. This space helps you imagine a great medieval feast. (If you'd like to do more than imagine, you can rent out the hall for a banquet of your own.)

Hiding behind the Great Hall is the icon of the castle—a half-destroyed listing **tower** (which, they like to brag, "out-leans Pisa's"). Following the English Civil War, the Parliament decreed that many castles like this one be destroyed as a preventive measure; this tower was a victim. Some believe that the adjacent **Braose Gallery** has a resident ghost: Legend has it that de Clare, after learning of his wife Alice's infidelity, exiled her back to France and had her lover killed. Upon discovering her paramour's fate, Alice died of a broken heart. Since then, the "Green Lady," named for her husband's jealousy, has reportedly roamed the ramparts.

Before leaving, be sure to visit the strip of yard that stretches out in front of the ticket office (along the inner moat). The first tower has a replica (complete with sound effects) of the **latrines** that were used by the soldiers—again, these dumped right into the moat. Just beyond that tower is a collection of life-size replica **siege engines**—ingenious catapult-like devices and oversized crossbows designed to deter attackers (each one is well described).

Big Pit National Coal Museum

To learn just how important the coal industry was to the economic development of South Wales, venture 30 miles north of Cardiff to a former coal mine in Blaenavon. Now part of the National Museum of Wales, the mine operated from 1860 to 1980. You can wander the grounds to see machinery and visit old buildings and exhibits. The highlight is the hour-long miner-guided tour 300 feet underground (hard hats and headlamps provided).

Cost and Hours: Free, parking-£3, daily 9:30-17:00, underground tours run 10:00-15:30, shorter hours off-season, last entry one hour before closing, café and coffee shop; in Blaenavon on the A-4043, tel. 0300-111-2333, www.museumwales.ac.uk/bigpit.

The Wye Valley

From Chepstow, on the mouth of the River Severn, the River Wye cuts north, marking the border between Wales (Monmouthshire, on the west bank) and England (Gloucestershire, on the east bank). While everything covered here is in Wales, it's all within sight of England—just over the river.

This land is lush, mellow, and historic. Local tourist brochures explain the area's special dialect, its strange political autonomy, and its oaken ties to Trafalgar and Admiral Nelson (who harvested timbers for his ships in the Forest of Dean). The valley is home to the legendary Tintern Abbey, the ruined skeleton of a glorious church that's well worth a quick stop. The abbey sits partway between two pleasant, workaday towns with interesting sights of their own: Chepstow (with a fine castle) and Monmouth (a market town with some quirky sights). (Note that just to the east of the river, in England, is the heavily promoted but disappointing and skippable Forest of Dean, a 43-square-mile patch of "ancient woodland"—what Americans call "old-growth forest.)

If you've always dreamed of visiting Tintern Abbey—and wouldn't mind a quick taste of a stout castle and a couple of charming Welsh towns—the riverside A-466 traces the Wye and makes a detour between Bath and the Cotswolds that's worth considering (adding about an hour of driving compared with the less scenic, more direct route). I've listed these sights in the order you'll reach them as you move north up the Wye.

Chepstow

This historic burg enjoys a strategic location, for the same reason it may be your first stop in Wales: It marks the natural boundary between England and Wales. Driving into town, you'll pass through the town gate where, in medieval times, folks arriving to sell goods or livestock were hit up for tolls.

Park in the pay-and-display lot just below the castle, which is also convenient to the TI, museum, and free WCs. Everything worth seeing is within a short walk. To explore more of the town, buy the *Chepstow Town Trail* guide at the TI (daily 10:00-17:00, off-season until 15:00, Bridge Street, tel. 01291/623-772, www.visitmonmouthshire.com) or the Chepstow Museum. St. Mary's Street is lined with appealing little lunch spots (try the Lime Tree Café).

Chepstow Castle

Perched on a riverside ridge overlooking the pleasant village of Chepstow on one side and the River Wye on the other, this castle is

worth a short stop for drivers heading for Tintern Abbey, or it's a 10-minute walk from the Chepstow train station (follow signs; uphill going back).

Cost and Hours: £7.30; daily 9:30-17:00, July-Aug until 18:00; Nov-Feb Mon-Sat 10:00-16:00, Sun from 11:00; guidebook-£5, in Chepstow village a half-mile from train station, tel. 01291/624-065, www.cadw.wales.gov.uk.

Visiting the Castle: The stone-built Great Tower, dating from 1066, was among the first castles the Normans plunked down to secure their turf in Wales, and it remained in use through 1690. While many castles of the time were built first in wood, Chepstow, then a key foothold on the England-Wales border, was built from stone from the start for durability.

You'll work your way up through various towers and baileys (inner yards); a few posted plaques provide details, but you're mostly on your own. As you clamber along the battlements (with great views to town and over the river to England), you'll find architectural evidence of military renovations through the centuries, from Norman to Tudor right up through Cromwellian additions. You can tell which parts date from Norman days—they're the ones built from yellow sandstone instead of the grayish limestone that makes up the rest of the castle. While the castle would benefit from more exhibits (it's basically an empty shell), with a little imagination you can resurrect the skeletons of buildings and appreciate how formidable and strategic it must have been in its heyday.

▲Chepstow Museum

Highlighting Chepstow's history, this museum is in an 18th-century townhouse across the street from the castle. Endearingly earnest, jammed with artifacts, and well presented, it says just about everything that could possibly be said about this small town. Upstairs, the 1940 machine for giving women permanents will be etched in your memory forever.

Cost and Hours: Free; Thu-Tue 11:00-16:00, closed Wed; tel. 01291/625-981.

Riverfront Park

From the TI and parking lot, walk one block down Bridge Street to the River Wye. A graceful, white cast-iron bridge spans the river. If you walk across it to the ornate decorations in the middle (at the *Gloucester/Monmouth* sign), you can stand with one foot in Wales and the other in England (notice the *Gloucestershire* sign across the bridge). From the bridge, you'll also have great views back to the castle. Beneath your feet, the River Wye's banks and water are muddy because this is a tidal river, which can rise and fall about 20 feet twice a day.

Back in Wales, stroll 100 yards along the riverside park (with the river on your left), noticing that the English bank sits on a chalk cliff—into which has been painted a Union Jack (to celebrate King George V's Silver Jubilee in 1935). Near the standing stones is a large circular plaque marking the beginning of the Welsh Coast Path; from here, you can walk 870 miles all the way along the coast of Wales. Nearby is the 176-mile Offa's Dyke Path, which roughly traces the border between Wales and England. Together, these two paths go almost all the way around the country.

▲▲Tintern Abbey

Inspiring monks to prayer, William Wordsworth to poetry, J. M. W. Turner to a famous painting, and rushed tourists to a thoughtful mo-
ment, this verse-worthy ruined-castle-of-an-abbey merits a five-mile detour off the motorway. Founded in 1131 on a site chosen by Norman monks for its tranquility, it functioned as an austere Cistercian abbey until its dissolution in 1536. The monks followed a strict schedule. They rose several hours after midnight for the first  of eight daily prayer sessions and spent the rest of their time studying, working the surrounding farmlands, and meditating. Dissolved under Henry VIII's Act of Suppression in 1536, the magnificent

church moldered in relative obscurity until tourists in the Romantic era (late 18th century) discovered the wooded Wye Valley and abbey ruins. J. M. W. Turner made his first sketches in 1792, and William Wordsworth penned "Lines Composed a Few Miles Above Tintern Abbey..." in 1798.

With all the evocative ruined abbeys dotting the British landscape, why all the fuss about this one? Because few are as big, as remarkably intact, and as picturesquely situated. Most of the external walls of the 250-foot-long, 150-foot-wide church still stand, along with the exquisite window tracery and outlines of the sacristy, chapter house, and dining hall. The daylight that

floods through the roofless ruins highlights the Gothic decorated arches—in those days a bold departure from Cistercian simplicity. While the guidebook (see "Information," below) narrates a very detailed, architecture-oriented tour, the best visit is to simply stroll the cavernous interior and let your imagination roam, like the generations of Romantics before you.

In summer, the abbey is flooded with tourists, so visit early or late to miss the biggest crowds. The shop sells Celtic jewelry and other gifts. Take an easy 15-minute walk up to St. Mary's Church (on the hill above town) for a view of the abbey, River Wye, and England just beyond.

Cost and Hours: £7.30; daily 9:30-17:00, July-Aug until 18:00; Nov-Feb Mon-Sat 10:00-16:00, Sun from 11:00; occasional summertime concerts in the cloisters (check website for schedule or ask at the TI), tel. 01291/689-251, www.cadw.wales.gov.uk.

Information: Sparse informational plaques identify and explain each part of the complex. The dry, extensive £4.50 guidebook may be too much information, but it makes a fine souvenir (especially if you apply the refundable parking fee—described next—to the cost).

Getting There: Drivers park in the pay lot right next to the abbey (£3, refundable if you buy anything in the official shop or at The Anchor restaurant). By public transportation from Cardiff, catch a 35-minute train to Chepstow; from there, take bus #69 (every 1-2 hours, 20 minutes) or a taxi (about £10 one-way) the final six miles to the abbey.

Near Tintern Abbey: The villages of **Tintern** and **Tintern Parva** cluster in wide spots along the main riverside road, just north of the abbey. A couple of miles north, just beyond the last of the inns, you'll find the **Old Station**—a converted train station with old rail cars that house a regional TI, gift shop, and an exhibit on the local railway (closed Nov-March, pay parking lot, tel. 01291/689-566, www.visitmonmouthshire.com). Surrounding the train cars are a fine riverside park, a café, and a few low-key, kid-friendly attractions.

Monmouth

Another bustling market town—bookending the valley of the River Wye with Chepstow—Monmouth has a pleasant square, a few offbeat museums, and an impressive roster of past residents. The main square is called **Agincourt Square,** after the famous battle won by a king who was born right here: Henry V (you'll see a statue of him in the niche on the big building). The stately building on that square, which houses the TI, is **Shire Hall,** the historic home of the courts and town council. This was the site of a famous 1840 trial of John Frost, a leader of the Chartist movement (championing the rights of the working class in Victorian Britain).

Standing in front of Shire Hall is a statue of **Charles Rolls** (1877-1910), contemplating a model airplane. This descendant of a noble Monmouth family was a pioneer of ballooning and aviation, and—together with his business partner, Frederick Royce—revolutionized motoring with the creation of their company, Rolls-Royce. The airplane he's holding, which he purchased from the Wright Brothers, helped him become the first person to fly over the English Channel and back, in 1910. (Just over a month later, he also became the first British person to die in a plane crash, when that same Wright Flyer lost its tail midflight.)

Across the street from Shire Hall, angle right up the lane to the Regimental Museum and the scant ruins of **Monmouth Castle,** where Henry V was born in 1386. While there's not much to see, the site may wring out a few goose bumps for historians.

A block up Priory Street is the endearing **Nelson Museum** (a.k.a. Monmouth Museum). Admiral Horatio Nelson, who was considered in Victorian times (and still today, by many) to be the savior of England for his naval victories in the Napoleonic Wars, was a frequent visitor to Monmouth. This remarkable collection of Nelson-worship began as the personal collection of local noblewoman Lady Georgiana Llangattock, who was also the mother of Charles Rolls. You'll see several of Nelson's personal effects, a replica of his uniform, the actual sword he wore in the Battle of Trafalgar (as well as the two swords surrendered by the French and Spanish commanders), and some 800 letters by or to him (pull out the drawers to see them). There are also a few small exhibits about other aspects of town history, including the Rolls family (www.monmouthshire.gov.uk).

A few blocks downhill in the opposite direction (down Monnow Street from Agincourt Square) is the picturesque, 13th-century **Monnow Bridge,** with its graceful arches and stout defensive tower in the middle.

Sleeping in the Wye Valley

If you're seduced into spending the night in this charming area, you'll find plenty of B&Bs near Tintern Abbey or in the castle-crowned town of Chepstow, located just down the road (a one-hour drive from Bath). These places are near the abbey.

$$ Parva Farmhouse has eight old-fashioned rooms in a 400-year-old building right along the main road through Tintern. While a bit dated, it comes with Welsh charm and is within walking distance of the abbey, village, and local pubs (tel. 01291/689-411, www.parvafarmhouse.co.uk, parvahoteltintern@hotmail.co.uk, Roger and Marta).

¢ St. Briavels Castle Youth Hostel is housed in an 800-year-old Norman castle used by King John in 1215 (the year he signed the Magna Carta). The hostel is comfortable (as castles go), friendly, and in the center of the quiet village of St. Briavels just north of Tintern Abbey. Nonguests are welcome to poke around the courtyard; if you're in town and the gates are open, step inside (breakfast extra, private rooms possible, modern kitchen and medieval banquet hall, brown-bag lunches and evening meals available, tel. 0345-371-9042, www.yha.org.uk, stbriavels@yha.org.uk). The village of St. Briavels sits in a forest high above the river. From Tintern, head north on the A-466, watch for the St. Briavels turnoff on the right, and switchback up the steep road into town.

South Wales Connections

ROUTE TIPS FOR DRIVERS

Bath to Cardiff and St. Fagans: Leave Bath following signs for the A-4, then the M-4. It's 10 miles north (on the A-46 past a village called Pennsylvania) to the M-4 freeway. Zip westward, crossing a huge suspension bridge over the Severn, into Wales (£6.50 toll westbound only). Stay on the M-4 (not the M-48) past Cardiff, take exit 33, and follow the brown signs south to *St. Fagans National Museum of History /Amgueddfa Werin Cymru/ Museum of Welsh Life.*

Bath to Tintern Abbey: Follow the directions above to the M-4. Take the M-4 to exit 21 and get on the M-48. After crossing the northern bridge (£6.50 toll) into Wales, take exit 2 for the A-466 for six miles (follow signs to *Chepstow*, then *Tintern*). You'll see the Abbey on your right.

Cardiff to the Cotswolds via Forest of Dean: On the Welsh side of the big suspension bridge, take the Chepstow exit and follow signs up the A-466 to *Tintern Abbey* and the *Wye River Valley*. Continue on to Monmouth, and follow the A-40 and the M-50 to the Tewkesbury exit, where small roads lead to the Cotswolds.

SCOTLAND

SCOTLAND

One of the three countries that make up Great Britain, rugged, feisty, colorful Scotland stands apart. Whether it's the laid-back, less-organized nature of the people, the stony architecture, the unmanicured landscape, or simply the haggis, go-its-own-way Scotland is distinctive.

Scotland encompasses about a third of Britain's geographical area (30,400 square miles), but has less than a tenth of its population (about 5.4 million). This sparsely populated chunk of land stretches to Norwegian latitudes. Its Shetland Islands, at about 60°N (similar to Anchorage, Alaska), are the northernmost point of the British Isles. You may see Scotland referred to as "Caledonia" (its ancient Roman name) or "Alba" (its Gaelic name). Scotland's fortunes were long tied to the sea; all of its leading cities are located along firths (estuaries), where major rivers connect to ocean waters.

The southern part of Scotland, called the Lowlands, is relatively flat and urbanized. The northern area—the Highlands—features a wild, severely undulating terrain, punctuated by lochs (lakes) and fringed by sea lochs (inlets) and islands.

The geographical fault line that divides the Highlands from the Lowlands also divides Scotland culturally. Historically, the country had two distinct identities: rougher Highlanders in the northern wilderness and the more refined Lowlanders in the southern flatlands. Highlanders represented the stereotypical image of "true Scots," speaking Gaelic, wearing kilts, and playing bagpipes, while Lowlanders spoke languages of Saxon origin and wore trousers. After the 16th-century Scottish Reformation, the Lowlanders embraced Protestantism, while most Highlanders stuck to Catholicism. Although this Lowlands/Highlands division has faded over time, some Scots still cling to it.

Today the Lowlands are dominated by rival cities: bustling

Scotland

Orkney
Islands
Durness
John O'Groats
Thurso
Wick
Lewis
Harris
Ullapool
Isle of
Skye
Portree
Applecross
North
Atlantic
Mallaig
Fort
William
▲ Ben Nevis
Inverness
■ CULLODEN
■ CLAVA CAIRNS
Loch
Ness
H I G H L A N D S
BALMORAL
Ballater
Aberdeen
Iona
Mull
Glencoe
Pitlochry
North
Sea
Oban
Stirling
SCOTLAND
Dundee
St. Andrews
Loch
Lomond
FALKIRK
■ WHEEL
Glasgow
Edinburgh
Artan
L O W L A N D S
Irish
Sea
Ayr
Jedburgh
NORTHERN
IRELAND
Cairnryan
Dumfries
ENGLAND
Newcastle
Belfast

50 Kilometers
50 Miles

Edinburgh (on the east coast's Firth of Forth) and friendly Glasgow (on the west coast's Firth of Clyde). Edinburgh, the old royal capital, teems with Scottish history and is the country's most popular tourist attraction. Glasgow, once gloomy and industrial, is now a hip, laid-back city of art, music, and architecture. In addition to these two cities—both of which warrant a visit—the Lowlands' highlights include the medieval university town and golf mecca of St. Andrews, the small city of Stirling (with its castle and many nearby historic sites), and selected countryside stopovers.

The Highlands provide your best look at traditional Scotland. The sights are subtle, but the vivid traditional culture and friendly people are engaging. The Highlands are more rocky and harsh than other parts of the British Isles. Most of the "Munros"—Scotland's 282 peaks over 3,000 feet—are concentrated in the Highlands. Keep an eye out for shaggy Highland cattle (adorable "hairy coos," with their bangs falling in their eyes); bring bug spray in summer to thwart the tiny bugs called midges, which can make

life miserable; and plan your trip around trying to attend a Highland game (see sidebar on page 930).

Generally, the Highlands are hungry for the tourist dollar, and everything overtly Scottish is exploited to the kilt; you need to spend some time here to get to know the area's true character. You can get a feel for the Highlands with a quick drive to Oban, through Glencoe, then up the Caledonian Canal to Inverness. With more time, the Isles of Iona, Staffa, and Mull (an easy day trip from Oban); and countless brooding countryside castles will flesh out your Highlands experience.

At these northern latitudes, cold and drizzly weather isn't uncommon—even in midsummer. The blazing sun can quickly be covered over by black clouds and howling wind. Your B&B host will warn you to prepare for "four seasons in one day." Because Scots feel personally responsible for bad weather, they tend to be overly optimistic about forecasts. Take any Scottish promise of "sun by the afternoon" with a grain of salt—and bring your raincoat, just in case.

The major theme of Scottish history is the drive for independence, especially from England. (Scotland's rabble-rousing national motto is *Nemo me impune lacessit*—"No one provokes me with impunity.") Like Wales, Scotland is a country of ragtag Celts sharing an island with wealthy and powerful Anglo-Saxons. Scotland's Celtic culture is a result of its remoteness—the invading Romans were never able to conquer this rough-and-tumble people, and even built Hadrian's Wall to lock off this distant corner of their empire. The Anglo-Saxons, and their descendants the English, fared little better than the Romans did. Even King Edward I—who so successfully dominated Wales—was unable to hold on to Scotland for long, largely thanks to the relentlessly rebellious William Wallace a.k.a. "Braveheart" (see page 748).

Failing to conquer Scotland by the blade, England eventually absorbed it politically. In 1603, England's Queen Elizabeth I died without an heir, so her closest royal relative—Scotland's King James VI—took the throne, becoming King James I of England. It took another century or so of battles, both military and diplomatic,

British, Scottish, and English

Scotland and England have been tied together politically for more than 300 years, since the Act of Union in 1707. For a century and a half afterward, Scottish nationalists rioted for independence in Edinburgh's streets and led uprisings in the Highlands. In this controversial union, history is clearly seen through two very different filters.

If you tour a British-oriented sight, such as Edinburgh's National War Museum Scotland, you'll find things told in a "happy union" way, which ignores the long history of Scottish resistance—from the ancient Picts through the time of Robert the Bruce. The official line: In 1706-1707, it was clear to England and certain parties in Scotland (especially landowners from the Lowlands) that it was in their mutual interest to dissolve the Scottish government and fold it into the United Kingdom, to be ruled from London.

But talk to a cabbie or your B&B host, and you may get a different spin. Scottish independence is still a hot-button issue. Since 2007, the Scottish National Party (SNP) has owned the largest majority in the Scottish Parliament. During a landmark referendum in 2014, the Scots voted to remain part of the union—but many polls, right up until election day, suggested that things could easily have gone the other way.

The rift shows itself in sports, too. While the English may refer to a British team in international competition as "English," the Scots are careful to call it "British." If a Scottish athlete does well, the English call him "British." If he screws up... he's a clumsy Scot.

but the Act of Union in 1707 definitively (and controversially) unified the Kingdom of Great Britain. Meanwhile, the English parliament overthrew the grandson of James I when he became a Catholic, replacing him with a line of Protestant monarchs. In 1745, Bonnie Prince Charlie attempted to reclaim the throne on behalf of the deposed Stuarts, but his army was slaughtered at the Battle of Culloden (page 988). This cemented English rule over Scotland, and is seen by many Scots as the last gasp of the traditional Highlands clan system. Bagpipes, kilts, the Gaelic language, and other symbols of the Highlands were briefly outlawed.

Scotland has been joined to England ever since, and the Scots have often felt oppressed by their English countrymen (see sidebar). During the Highland Clearances in the 18th and 19th centuries, landowners (mostly English) decided that vast tracts of land were more profitable as grazing land for sheep than as farmland for people. Many Highlanders were forced to abandon their traditional homes and lifestyles and seek employment elsewhere, moving to the cities to work in Industrial Revolution-era factories. Large numbers ended up in North America, especially parts of eastern Canada, such as Prince Edward Island and Nova Scotia (literally, "New Scotland").

Travelers of Scottish descent enjoy coming "home" to Scotland. If you're Scottish, your surname will tell you which clan your

ancestors likely belonged to. The prefix "Mac" (or "Mc") means "son of"—so "MacDonald" means the same thing as "Donaldson." Tourist shops everywhere are happy to help you track down the distinctive plaid pattern of your clan's tartan. For more on how these "clan tartans" don't go back as far as you might think, see the sidebar on page 724.

Scotland shares a monarchy with the rest of the United Kingdom, though to Scots, Queen Elizabeth II is just "Queen Elizabeth"; the first Queen Elizabeth ruled England, but not Scotland. Scotland is not a sovereign state, but it is a "nation" in that it has its own traditions, ethnic identity, languages (Gaelic and Scots), and football league. To some extent, it even has its own government.

Recently, Scotland has enjoyed its greatest measure of political autonomy in centuries. The Scottish parliament convened in

Edinburgh in 1999 for the first time in almost 300 years; in 2004, it moved into its brand-new building near the foot of the Royal Mile. Though its powers are limited (most major decisions are still made in London), the Scottish people are enjoying increased self-governance. In a 2014 independence referendum,

the Scots favored staying in the United Kingdom by a margin of 10 percent. The question of independence will likely remain a pivotal issue in Scotland for many years to come.

Scotland even has its own currency...sort of. The country uses the same coins as England, Wales, and Northern Ireland, but Scotland also prints its own bills (featuring Scottish, rather than English, people and landmarks). Just to confuse tourists, three different banks print Scottish pound notes, each with a different design. In the Lowlands (around Edinburgh and Glasgow), you'll receive both Scottish and English pounds from ATMs and in change. But in the Highlands, you'll almost never see English pounds. Bank of

Outlander Locations in Scotland

American novelist Diana Gabaldon's *Outlander* series spans continents and centuries, but the origin story—that of a High-

lands laird and an English combat nurse caught up in the Jacobite rebellion—is grounded in Scotland. Much of the Starz television adaptation was filmed here. *Outlander* fans may enjoy seeing some of the following landmarks.

Outlander begins with Claire Randall on her honeymoon in 1945 Inverness—played on TV by **Falkland** village, near St. Andrews. Claire is mysteriously transported back in time to 1743 at Craig na Dun, a fictional stone circle inspired by **Clava Cairns** near Inverness. The TV version was filmed at **Dunalastair Estate,** between Pitlochry and Loch Rannoch.

Claire is rescued by the MacKenzie clan and tends to injured Highlander Jamie Fraser. They travel to the fictional Castle Leoch, seat of the Clan Mackenzie (the real-life Mackenzie home is Castle Leod, near Strathpeffer). Exterior scenes at Castle Leoch were filmed at **Doune Castle** near Stirling (page 889); the grounds—where Claire gathers herbs—were filmed in **Pollok County Park** (near Glasgow's Burrell Collection).

Claire meets the "witch" Geillis Duncan in fictional Cranesmuir village, but **Culross,** with its distinctive mercat cross is a fine onscreen stand-in. The stone-and-thatched village where the MacKenzies collect rents was filmed at the **Highland Folk Museum**. Claire and Jamie visit the fictional Fraser family homestead, Lallybroch (on TV the deserted country estate of **Midhope Castle**—closed to the public).

In the books, Black Jack Randall's stout stone fortress is at Fort William; for TV those scenes were filmed at **Blackness Castle** on the Firth of Forth. Nearby, **Linlithgow Palace** is the filming location for the fictional Wentworth Prison (where Black Jack imprisons—and Claire rescues—Jamie), and **Aberdour Castle** plays the monastery where Jamie recovers. Scenes at **Ardsmuir Prison,** where Jamie is interned after the Battle of Culloden, were filmed at **Craigmillar Castle,** on the outskirts of Edinburgh. Carfax Close, where A. Malcolm has his print shop, is fictional—and played on TV by Edinburgh's very real **Tweeddale Court** and **Bakehouse Close.**

Many of the show's interior scenes are filmed at Wardpark Studios, a former factory converted into Scotland's first permanent film studio for *Outlander*. For more *Outlander* locations, see VisitScotland.com/outlander.

England notes are legal and widely used; Northern Ireland bank notes are legal but less common.

The Scottish flag—a diagonal, X-shaped white cross on a blue field—represents the cross of Scotland's patron saint, the Apostle Andrew (who was crucified on an X-shaped cross). You may not realize it, but you see the Scottish flag every time you look at the Union Jack: England's flag (the red St. George's cross on a white field) superimposed on Scotland's (a blue field with a white diagonal cross). The diagonal red cross (St. Patrick's cross) over Scotland's white one represents Northern Ireland. (Wales gets no love on the Union Jack.)

Here in "English-speaking" Scotland, you may still encounter a language barrier. First is the lovely, lilting Scottish accent—which may take you a while to understand. You may also hear an impenetrable dialect of Scottish English that many linguists consider to be a separate language, called "Scots." You may already know several Scots words: lad, lassie, wee, bonnie, glen, loch, aye. On menus, you'll see neeps and tatties (turnips and potatoes). And in place names, you'll see ben (mountain), brae (hill), firth (estuary), and kyle (strait). And about one percent of the population, particularly in the Highlands, speaks the ancient Celtic language of Gaelic (pronounced "gallic").

While soccer ("football") is as popular here as anywhere, golf is Scotland's other national sport. But in Scotland, it's not necessarily considered an exclusively upper-class pursuit; you can generally play a round at a basic course for about £15. While Scotland's best scenery is along the west coast, its best golfing is on the east coast—home to many prestigious golf courses. Most of these are links courses, which use natural sand from the  beaches for the bunkers. For tourists, these links are more authentic, more challenging, and more fun than the regular-style courses (with artificial landforms) farther inland. If you're a golfer, St. Andrews—on the east coast—is a pilgrimage worth making.

Scottish cuisine is down to earth, often with an emphasis on local produce. Both seafood and "land food" (beef, chicken, lamb, and venison) are common. One Scottish mainstay—eaten more by tourists than by Scots these days—is the famous haggis, tastier than it sounds and worth trying...even before you've tucked into the whisky. Also look for cullen skink, a satisfying, chowder-like cream soup with smoked fish (see sidebar).

The "Scottish breakfast" is similar to the English version, but

SCOTLAND

Haggis and Other Traditional Scottish Dishes

Scotland's most unique dish, **haggis** began as a peasant food. Waste-conscious cooks wrapped the heart, liver, and lungs of  a sheep in its stomach lining, packed in some oats and spices, and then boiled the lot to create a hearty, if barely palatable, meal. Traditionally served with "neeps and tatties" (turnips and potatoes), haggis was forever immortalized in Robbie Burns' *Address to a Haggis*.

Today haggis has been refined almost to the point of high cuisine. You'll likely find it on many menus, including at breakfast. You can dress it up with anything from a whisky cream sauce to your basic HP brown sauce. To appreciate this iconic Scottish dish, think of how it tastes—not what it's made of.

The king of Scottish **black puddings** (blood sausage) is made in the Hebrides Islands. Called Stornoway, it's so famous that the European Union has granted it protected status to prevent imitators from using its name. A mix of beef suet, oatmeal, onion, and blood, the sausage is usually served as part of a full Scottish breakfast, but it also appears on the menus of top-class restaurants.

Be on the lookout for other traditional Scottish taste treats. **Cullen skink,** Scotland's answer to chowder, is a hearty, creamy fish soup, often made with smoked haddock. A **bridie** (or Forfar bridie) is a savory meat pastry similar to a Cornish pasty, but generally lighter (no potatoes). A **Scotch pie**—small, double-crusted, and filled with minced meat, is a good picnic food; it's a common snack at soccer matches and outdoor events. **Crowdie** is a dairy spread that falls somewhere between cream cheese and cottage cheese.

And for dessert, **cranachan** is similar to a trifle, made with whipped cream, honey, fruit (usually raspberries), and whisky-soaked oats. Another popular dessert is the **Tipsy Laird,** served at "Burns Suppers" on January 25, the annual celebration of national poet Robert Burns. It's essentially the same as a trifle but with whisky or brandy and Scottish raspberries.

they often add a potato scone (like a flavorless, soggy potato pancake) and haggis (best when served with poached eggs and HP brown sauce).

Breakfast, lunch, or dinner, the Scots love their whisky—and touring one of the country's many distilleries is a sightseeing treat. The Scots are fiercely competitive with the Irish when it comes to this peaty spirit. Scottish "whisky" is typically distilled twice, whereas Irish "whiskey" adds a third distillation (and an extra *e*). Some distilleries roast their barley over peat fires, giving many Scottish whiskies a smokier flavor than their Irish cousins. Also note that what we call "scotch"—short for "scotch whisky"—is just "whisky" here. I've listed a few of the most convenient and interesting distilleries to visit, but if you're a whisky connoisseur, make a point of tracking down and touring your favorite.

Some of Scotland's sights are subtle, but its misty glens, brooding countryside castles, and warm culture are plenty engaging. Whether toasting with beer, whisky, or Irn-Bru (Scotland's favorite soft drink), you'll enjoy meeting the Scottish people. It's easy to fall in love with the irrepressible spirit and beautiful landscape of this faraway corner of Britain.

EDINBURGH

Edinburgh is the historical, cultural, and political capital of Scotland. For nearly a thousand years, Scotland's kings, parliaments, writers, thinkers, and bankers have called Edinburgh home. Today, it remains Scotland's most sophisticated city.

Edinburgh (ED'n-burah—only tourists pronounce it like "Pittsburgh") is Scotland's showpiece and one of Europe's most entertaining cities. It's a place of stunning vistas—nestled among craggy bluffs and studded with a prickly skyline of spires, towers, domes, and steeples. Proud statues of famous Scots dot the urban landscape. The buildings are a harmonious yellow-gray, all built from the same local sandstone.

Culturally, Edinburgh has always been the place where Lowland culture (urban and English) met Highland style (rustic and Gaelic). Tourists will find no end of traditional Scottish clichés: whisky tastings, kilt shops, bagpipe-playing buskers, and gimmicky tours featuring Scotland's bloody history and ghost stories.

Edinburgh is two cities in one. The Old Town stretches along the Royal Mile, from the grand castle on top to the palace on the bottom. Along this colorful labyrinth of cobbled streets and narrow lanes, medieval skyscrapers stand shoulder to shoulder, hiding peaceful courtyards.

A few hundred yards north of the Old Town lies the New Town. It's a magnificent planned neighborhood (from the 1700s). Here, you'll enjoy upscale shops, broad boulevards, straight streets, square squares, circular circuses, and Georgian mansions decked out in Greek-style columns and statues.

Just to the west of the New Town, the West End is a prestigious and quieter neighborhood boasting more Georgian architecture, cobbled lanes, fine dining options, and a variety of concert and theater venues.

Today's Edinburgh is big in banking, scientific research, and scholarship at its four universities. Since 1999, when Scotland regained a measure of self-rule, Edinburgh reassumed its place as home of the Scottish Parliament. The city hums with life. Students and professionals pack the pubs and art galleries. It's especially lively in August, when the Edinburgh Festival takes over the town. Historic, monumental, fun, and well organized, Edinburgh is a tourist's delight.

PLANNING YOUR TIME

While the major sights can be seen in a day, I'd give Edinburgh two days and three nights.

Day 1: Tour the castle, then take my self-guided Royal Mile walk, stopping in at St. Giles' Cathedral and whichever shops and museums interest you. At the bottom of the Mile, consider visiting the Scottish Parliament, the Palace of Holyroodhouse, or both. If the weather's good and the trail is open, you could hike back to your B&B along the Salisbury Crags.

Day 2: Visit the National Museum of Scotland. After lunch, stroll through the Scottish National Gallery. Then follow my self-guided walk through the New Town, visiting the Scottish National Portrait Gallery and the Georgian House—or squeeze in a quick tour of the good ship *Britannia* (check last entry time before you head out).

Evenings: Options include various "haunted Edinburgh" walks, the literary pub crawl, or live music in pubs. Sadly, full-blown traditional folk performances are just about extinct, surviving only in excruciatingly schmaltzy variety shows put on for tour-bus groups. Perhaps the most authentic evening out is just settling down in a pub to sample the whisky and local beers while meeting the locals...and attempting to understand them through their thick Scottish accents.

Orientation to Edinburgh

A VERBAL MAP

With 500,000 people (835,000 in the metro area), Edinburgh is Scotland's second-biggest city (after Glasgow). But the tourist's Edinburgh is compact: Old Town, New Town, West End, and the B&B area south of the city center.

Edinburgh's **Old Town** stretches across a ridgeline slung between two bluffs. From west to east, this "Royal Mile" runs from the Castle Rock—which is visible from anywhere—to the base of the 822-foot extinct volcano called Arthur's Seat. For visitors, this east-west axis is the center of the action. Just south of the Royal Mile are the university and the National Museum of Scotland; farther to the south is a handy B&B neighborhood that lines up along **Dalkeith Road** and **Mayfield Gardens.** North of the Royal Mile ridge is the **New Town,** a neighborhood of grid-planned streets and elegant Georgian buildings, and the **West End,** near Charlotte Square—a posh, quiet neighborhood that's still close to the sightseeing action.

In the center of it all—in a drained lake bed between the Old and New Towns—sit the Princes Street Gardens park and Waverley Bridge, where you'll find the Waverley train station, Waverley Mall, bus info office (starting point for most city bus tours), Scottish National Gallery, and a covered dance-and-music pavilion.

TOURIST INFORMATION

The TI, branded "iCentre," is on the Royal Mile across from St. Giles' Cathedral (Mon-Sat 9:00-17:00, Sun from 10:00, June daily until 18:00, July-Aug daily until 19:00, 249 High Street, tel. 0131/473-3868, www.visitscotland.com). The staff is scattered at various tables with laptops on and ready to help.

For more information than what's included in the TI's free map, buy the excellent *Collins Discovering Edinburgh* map (which comes with opinionated commentary and locates almost every major sight). If you're interested in evening music, ask for the comprehensive entertainment listing, *The List.* Also consider buying Historic Scotland's Explorer Pass, which can save you some money if you visit the castles at both Edinburgh and Stirling, or are also visiting the Orkney Islands (for details, see page 1037).

ARRIVAL IN EDINBURGH

By Train: Most long-distance trains arrive at **Waverley Station** in the city center. For groceries to go, M&S Simply Food, near track 2, is economic and efficient (daily 7:00-22:00, Thu-Fri until 23:00, Sun from 8:00). Taxis line up outside, on Princes Street or Waverley Bridge. To catch a city bus, exit the train station via Princes Street and ride up several escalators (Waverley Mall is on your left). City buses #14, #30, and #33 stop around the corner to your right, along North Bridge, and are handy if you're staying in my recommended B&B neighborhood south of town. Those staying at one

EDINBURGH

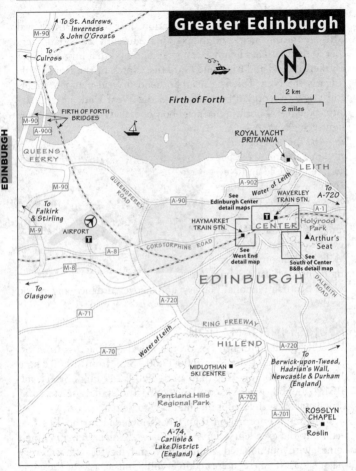

Greater Edinburgh

To St. Andrews, Inverness & John O'Groats

To Culross

M-90

M-90
A-900

FIRTH OF FORTH BRIDGES

QUEENS-FERRY

QUEENSFERRY ROAD

M-90

To Falkirk & Stirling

M-9

AIRPORT

A-8

CORSTORPHINE ROAD

M-8

To Glasgow

A-71

A-70

Water of Leith

A-720

Firth of Forth

N

2 km

2 miles

ROYAL YACHT BRITANNIA

LEITH

A-902   Water of Leith

To A-720

A-90

A-1

WAVERLEY TRAIN STN.

See Edinburgh Center detail maps

HAYMARKET TRAIN STN.

CENTER

Holyrood Park

Arthur's Seat

See West End detail map

See South of Center B&Bs detail map

EDINBURGH

DALKEITH ROAD

A-720

RING FREEWAY

HILLEND

A-720

To Berwick-upon-Tweed, Hadrian's Wall, Newcastle & Durham (England)

MIDLOTHIAN SKI CENTRE

A-702

Pentland Hills Regional Park

A-701

ROSSLYN CHAPEL

Roslin

To A-74, Carlisle & Lake District (England)

of my recommended West End accommodations might consider taking the train directly to **Haymarket Station** (rather than Waverley). For more specifics on linking to my recommended hotel neighborhoods, see the "Sleeping in Edinburgh" section, later.

By Bus: Scottish Citylink, Megabus, and National Express buses use the bus station (with luggage lockers) in the New Town, two blocks north of the train station on St. Andrew Square.

By Car: No matter where you're coming from, avoid needless driving in the city by taking advantage of Edinburgh's bypass road, A-720. To conveniently reach my recommended B&Bs, circle the city on the A-720 (direction: Edinburgh South), until the last roundabout, named *Sheriffhall*. Exit the roundabout at the first left *(A-7 Edinburgh)*. From here it's four miles to the B&B neighborhood. After a while, the A-7 becomes Dalkeith Road. If you see the huge Royal Commonwealth Pool, you've gone a couple of blocks too far.

By Plane: Edinburgh's airport is eight miles west of downtown—about a 30-minute tram or taxi ride. For information, see "Edinburgh Connections," at the end of this chapter.

HELPFUL HINTS

Festivals: August is a crowded, popular month to visit Edinburgh thanks to the multiple festivals hosted here, including the official Edinburgh International Festival, the Fringe Festival, and the Military Tattoo. Book ahead for hotels, events, and restaurant dinners if you'll be visiting in August, and expect to pay significantly more for your room. Many museums and shops have extended hours in August. For more festival details, see page 785.

Wi-Fi: The city-wide network **EdiFreeWiFi** is free and unlimited in the city center. Just enter your basic information where prompted, and connect.

Baggage Storage: At the train station, a luggage storage office is near platform 2 (£7.50/3 hours, daily 7:00-23:00). Cheaper lockers are at the bus station on St. Andrew Square, just two blocks north of the train station (£8/12 hours, daily 4:30-24:00). Apps like Stasher can also help you find convenient baggage storage locations around big cities like Edinburgh.

Laundry: The **Ace Cleaning Centre** launderette is located near my recommended B&Bs south of town. You can pay for full-service laundry (drop off in the morning for same-day service) or stay and do it yourself. For a small extra fee, they'll collect your laundry from your B&B and drop it off the next day (Mon-Fri 8:00-19:30, Sat 9:00-17:00, Sun 10:00-16:00, along bus route to city center at 13 South Clerk Street, opposite Queens Hall, tel. 0131/667-0549). In the West End, **Johnsons the Cleaners** will do your laundry (no hotel or B&B drop-off, Mon-Fri 9:30-18:00, Sat until 17:00, closed Sun, 5 Drumsheugh Place, tel. 0131/225-8077).

Bike Rental and Tours: The laid-back crew at **Cycle Scotland** happily recommends good bike routes with your rental (prices starting at £20/3 hours or £30/day, electric bikes available for extra fee, daily 10:00-18:00, may be closed in winter, just off Royal Mile at 29 Blackfriars Street, tel. 0131/556-5560, mobile 0779-688-6899, www.cyclescotland.co.uk, Peter). They also run guided three-hour bike tours daily at 11:00 (and sometimes at 15:00) that start on the Royal Mile and ride through Holyrood Park, Arthur's Seat, Duddingston Village, Doctor Neil's (Secret) Garden, and along the Innocent railway path (£45/person, extra fee for e-bike, book ahead).

EDINBURGH

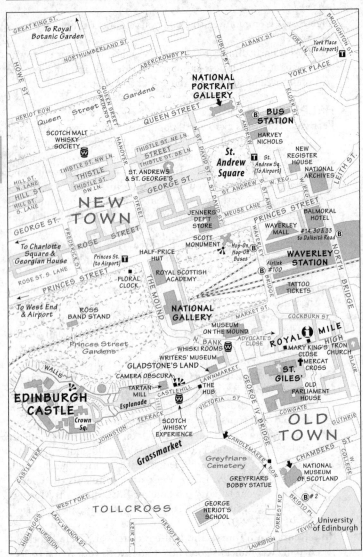

Car Rental: These places have offices both in the town center and at the airport: **Avis** (24 East London Street, tel. 0344-544-6059, airport tel. 0344-544-6004), **Europcar** (Waverley Station, near platform 2, tel. 0371-384-3453, airport tel. 0371-384-3406), **Hertz** (10 Picardy Place, tel. 0843-309-3026, airport tel. 0843-309-3025), and **Budget** (24 East London Street, tel. 0344-544-9064, airport tel. 0344-544-4605). Some downtown offices close or have reduced hours on Sunday, but the airport locations tend to be open daily. If you plan to rent a

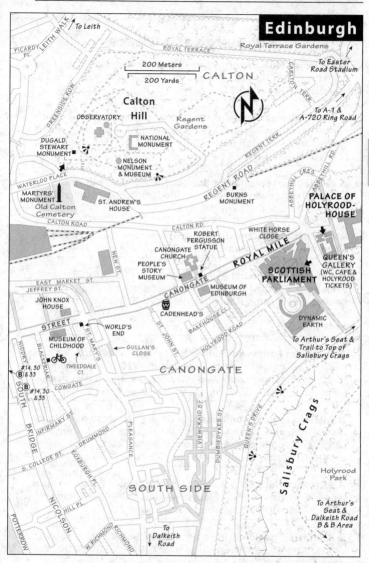

car, pick it up on your way out of Edinburgh—you won't need it in town.

Dress for the Weather: Weather blows in and out—bring your sweater and be prepared for rain.

GETTING AROUND EDINBURGH

By Bus: Many of Edinburgh's sights are within walking distance of one another, but buses come in handy—especially if you're staying at a B&B south of the city center (use buses #14, #30, or #33).

Edinburgh at a Glance

▲▲▲**Royal Mile** Historic road—good for walking—stretching from the castle down to the palace, lined with museums, pubs, and shops. See page 719.

▲▲▲**Edinburgh Castle** Iconic hilltop fort and royal residence complete with crown jewels, Romanesque chapel, memorial, and fine military museum. **Hours:** Daily 9:30-18:00, Oct-March until 17:00. See page 741.

▲▲▲**National Museum of Scotland** Intriguing, well-displayed artifacts from prehistoric times to the 20th century. **Hours:** Daily 10:00-17:00. See page 767.

▲▲**Gladstone's Land** Seventeenth-century Royal Mile merchant's residence. **Hours:** Daily 11:00-16:30. See page 754.

▲▲**St. Giles' Cathedral** Preaching grounds of Scottish Reformer John Knox, with spectacular organ, Neo-Gothic chapel, and distinctive crown spire. **Hours:** Mon-Fri 9:00-19:00, Sat until 17:00; Nov-March Mon-Sat 9:00-17:00; Sun 13:00-17:00 year-round. See page 756.

▲▲**Scottish Parliament Building** Striking headquarters for parliament, which returned to Scotland in 1999. **Hours:** Mon-Sat 10:00-17:00, longer hours Tue-Thu when parliament is in session (Sept-June), closed Sun year-round. See page 764.

▲▲**Palace of Holyroodhouse** The Queen's splendid official residence in Scotland, with lavish rooms, 12th-century abbey, and gallery with rotating exhibits. **Hours:** Daily 9:30-18:00, Nov-March until 16:30, closed during royal visits. See page 765.

▲▲**Scottish National Gallery** Choice sampling of European masters and Scotland's finest. **Hours:** Fri-Wed 10:00-17:00, Aug until 18:00; Thu 10:00-19:00 year-round. See page 772.

▲▲**Scottish National Portrait Gallery** Beautifully displayed Who's Who of Scottish history. **Hours:** Daily 10:00-17:00. See page 774.

▲▲**Georgian House** Intimate peek at upper-crust life in the late 1700s. **Hours:** Daily 10:00-17:00, March and Nov 11:00-16:00, closed Dec-Feb. See page 777.

▲▲**Royal Yacht *Britannia*** The Queen's former floating palace, with a history of distinguished passengers, a 15-minute trip out of town. **Hours:** Daily 9:30-16:30, Oct until 16:00, Nov-March 10:00-15:30. See page 777.

▲**Camera Obscura** Five floors of illusions, holograms, and gags, topped with the best view of the Royal Mile. **Hours:** Daily 9:00-21:00, Sat until 22:00, shorter hours off-season. See page 753.

▲**The Scotch Whisky Experience** Gimmicky but fun and educational introduction to Scotland's most famous beverage. **Hours:** Generally daily 10:00-18:30. See page 753.

▲**Writers' Museum at Lady Stair's House** Aristocrat's house, built in 1622, filled with artifacts from Robert Burns, Robert Louis Stevenson, and Sir Walter Scott. **Hours:** Daily 10:00-17:00. See page 754.

▲**The Real Mary King's Close** Underground street and houses last occupied in the 17th century, viewable by guided tour. **Hours:** Daily generally 9:00-21:45, Oct-April until 17:00 (these are last tour times). See page 761.

▲**Museum of Childhood** Five stories of nostalgic fun. **Hours:** Daily 10:00-17:00. See page 761.

▲**John Knox House** Medieval home with exhibits on the life of Scotland's great Protestant reformer. **Hours:** Mon-Sat 10:00-18:00, closed Sun except in July-Aug. See page 761.

▲**People's Story Museum** Everyday life from the 18th to 20th century. **Hours:** Daily 10:00-17:00. See page 762.

▲**Museum of Edinburgh** Historic mementos, from the original National Covenant inscribed on animal skin to early golf balls. **Hours:** Daily 10:00-17:00. See page 763.

▲**Queen's Gallery** Intimate museum with treasures from the royal art collection. **Hours:** Daily 9:30-18:00, Nov-March until 16:30. See page 766.

▲**Rosslyn Chapel** Small 15th-century church chock-full of intriguing carvings a short drive outside of Edinburgh. **Hours:** Mon-Sat 9:30-17:00, June-Aug until 18:00, Sun 12:00-16:45 year-round. See page 779.

Double-decker buses come with fine views upstairs. It's easy once you get the hang of it: Buses come by frequently and have free, fast Wi-Fi on board. The only hassle is that you must pay with exact change (£1.70/ride). As you board, tell your driver where you're going (or just say "single ticket") and drop your change into the box. The £4 all-day pass pays for itself in three rides and frees you from worrying about change. You can also use a payment app on your smartphone, such as ApplePay or Google Pay, to pay for your bus fare when you board. (For a day pass, tap the sensor each time you ride. If you ride three or more times, you'll be charged £4 at the end of the day.)

You can pick up a route map at the TI, in the train station, or at the transit office at the Old Town end of Waverley Bridge (tel. 0131/555-6363, www.lothianbuses.com).

By Tram: Edinburgh's single tram line (also £1.70/ride, buy at ticket machine before boarding, credit card or exact change) is designed more for locals than tourists. It's most useful for reaching the airport (£6 one-way; see "Edinburgh Connections" at the end of this chapter) or getting from my recommended West End hotels to Princes Street and St. Andrew Square, near the Waverley train station.

By Taxi or Uber: The 1,300 taxis cruising Edinburgh's streets are easy to flag down (a ride between downtown and the B&B neighborhood costs about £7; rates go up after 18:00 and on weekends). They can turn on a dime, so hail them in either direction. Uber also works very well here and is substantially cheaper than taxis (with quick pickups and most rides in town averaging £5-6).

Tours in Edinburgh

Royal Mile Walking Tours

Walking tours are an Edinburgh specialty; you'll see groups trailing entertaining guides all over town. Below I've listed good all-purpose walks; for **literary pub crawls** and **ghost tours,** see "Nightlife in Edinburgh" on page 792.

Edinburgh Tour Guides offers a good historical walk (without all the ghosts and goblins). Their Royal Mile tour is a gentle three-hour downhill stroll from the top of the Mile to the palace (£25; daily at 9:30 and 19:00—evening tour is only two hours; meet outside Gladstone's Land, near the top of the Royal Mile—see map on page 721, must reserve ahead, mobile 0785-888-0072, www.edinburghtourguides.com, info@edinburghtourguides.com). Their other offerings include *Outlander*-themed Edinburgh walks and day tours.

Mercat Tours offers a 1.5-hour "Secrets of the Royal Mile" walk that's more entertaining than intellectual (£14; £30 includes optional, 45-minute guided Edinburgh Castle visit; daily at 10:00 and 13:00, leaves from Mercat Cross on the Royal Mile, tel. 0131/225-5445, www.mercattours.com). The guides, who enjoy making a short story long, ignore the big sights and take you behind the scenes with piles of barely historical gossip, bully-pulpit Scottish pride, and fun but forgettable trivia. They also offer other tours, such as ghost walks, tours of 18th-century underground vaults on the southern slope of the Royal Mile, and *Outlander* sights (see their website for a rundown).

Sandemans New Edinburgh runs "free" tours multiple times a day; you won't pay upfront, but the guide will expect a tip (check schedule online, 2-3 hours, meet in front of Frankie & Benny's by Tron Kirk on High Street, www.neweuropetours.eu).

The **Voluntary Guides Association** offers free two-hour walks, but only during the Edinburgh Festival. You don't need a reservation—just show up (check website for times, generally depart from City Chambers across from St. Giles' Cathedral on the Royal Mile, www.edinburghfestivalguides.org). You can also hire their guides (for a small fee) for private tours outside of festival time.

Blue Badge Local Guides

The following guides charge similar prices and offer half-day and full-day tours: **Jean Blair** (a delightful teacher and guide, £230/day without car, £450/day with car, mobile 0798-957-0287, www.travelthroughscotland.com, scotguide7@gmail.com); **Sergio La Spina** (an Argentinean who adopted Edinburgh as his hometown more than 20 years ago, £250/day, tel. 0131/664-1731, mobile 0797-330-6579, www.vivaescocia.com, sergiolaspina@aol.com); **Ken Hanley** (who wears his kilt as if pants don't exist, £130/half-day, £250/day, extra charge if he uses his car—seats up to six, tel. 0131/666-1944, mobile 0771-034-2044, www.small-world-tours.co.uk, kennethhanley@me.com); **Liz Everett** (walking tours only—no car; £175/half-day, £265/day, mobile 0782-168-3837, liz.everett@live.co.uk); and **Maggie McLeod** (another top-notch guide, £175/half-day walking tour, £660 day trips with car to farther-flung destinations, mobile 0775-151-6776, www.scotlandandmore.com, margaret.mcleod@live.co.uk).

Hop-On, Hop-Off Bus Tours

The following one-hour hop-on, hop-off bus tour routes, all run by the same company, circle the town center, stopping at the major sights. **Edinburgh Tour** (green buses) focuses on the city center, with live guides (stay on for the entire 75-minute loop if you like your guide). **City Sightseeing** (red buses, focuses on Old Town) has recorded commentary, as does the **Majestic Tour** (blue-and-yellow buses, goes to the port of Leith and includes a stop at the *Britannia*

EDINBURGH

and Royal Botanic Garden). You can pay for just one tour (£16/24 hours), but most people pay a few pounds more for a ticket covering all buses (£24/48 hours). It's a great convenience to be able to hop on any bus that goes by with the same ticket (buses run April-Oct roughly 9:00-19:00, shorter hours off-season; about

every 10 minutes, buy tickets on board, tel. 0131/220-0770, www. edinburghtour.com). On sunny days the buses go topless. As is generally the case with such tours, there's patter the entire time but almost nothing of real importance other than identifying what you're driving by and a few random factoids (the live guides are little better than the recorded spiels).

The Royal Edinburgh Ticket costs £57 and covers 48 hours of unlimited travel on all three hop-on, hop-off buses, as well as admission at Edinburgh Castle, the Palace of Holyroodhouse, and *Britannia* (www.royaledinburghticket.co.uk). This is a good deal if you plan to use the buses and see all three sights. As you'll already have your ticket, you save time too, skipping ticket lines at the included sights.

The **3 Bridges Tour** combines a hop-on, hop-off bus to South Queensferry with a boat tour on the Firth of Forth (£25, 3 hours total).

Day Trips from Edinburgh

Many companies run a variety of day trips to regional sights, as well as multiday and themed itineraries. (Several of the local guides listed earlier have cars, too.)

The most popular tour is the all-day **Highlands trip**, which gives those with limited time a chance to experience the wonders of Scotland's wild and legend-soaked Highlands in a single long day (about £50, roughly 8:00-20:00). Itineraries vary but you'll generally visit/pass through the Trossachs, Rannoch Moor, Glencoe, Fort William, Fort Augustus on Loch Ness (some tours offer an optional boat ride), and Pitlochry. To save time, look for a tour that gives you a short glimpse of Loch Ness rather than driving its entire length or doing a boat trip. (Once you've seen a little of it, you've seen it all.) Also popular are all-day tours of locations from the *Outlander* novels and TV series (about £50, roughly 8:00-20:00); for more about *Outlander* sights, see page 703.

Larger outfits, typically using bigger buses, include **Timberbush Tours** (tel. 0131/226-6066, www.timberbush-tours.co.uk), **Gray Line** (tel. 0131/555-5558, www.graylinescotland.

com), **Highland Experience** (tel. 0131/226-1414, www. highlandexperience.com), **Highland Explorer** (tel. 0131/558-3738, www.highlandexplorertours.com), and **Scotline** (tel. 0131/557-0162, www.scotlinetours.co.uk). Other companies pride themselves on keeping group sizes small, with 16-seat minibuses; these include **Rabbie's** (tel. 0131/226-3133, www.rabbies.com) and **Heart of Scotland Tours: The Wee Red Bus** (RS%—10 percent Rick Steves discount on full-price day tours, mention when booking, does not apply to overnight tours or senior/student rates; may cancel off-season if too few sign up—leave a contact number; tel. 0131/228-2888, www.heartofscotlandtours.co.uk, run by Nick Roche).

For young backpackers, **Haggis Adventures** runs day tours plus overnight trips of up to 10 days (tel. 0131/557-9393, www. haggisadventures.com).

At **Discreet Scotland,** Matthew Wight and his partners specialize in tours of greater Edinburgh and Scotland in spacious SUVs—good for families (£380/2 people, 8 hours, mobile 0798-941-6990, www.discreetscotland.com).

Walks in Edinburgh

I've outlined two walks in Edinburgh: along the Royal Mile, and through the New Town. Many of the sights we'll pass on these walks are described in more detail later, under "Sights in Edinburgh."

THE ROYAL MILE

The Royal Mile is one of Europe's most interesting historic walks— it's worth ▲▲▲. The following self-guided stroll is also available as a free ∩ downloadable Rick Steves audio tour.

This 1.5-hour walk covers the Royal Mile's landmarks, but skips the many museums and indoor sights along the way (these are described in walking order under "Sights in Edinburgh" on page 753). Doing this walk as an orientation upon arrival in the morning or evening allows you to focus on the past without having to dodge crowds. You can return later to stroll the same walk during the much livelier business hours when shops, museums, and the cathedral are all open.

Another option is to review the sight descriptions beforehand, plan your walk around their open hours, and pop into those that interest you as you pass them. Several of the sights you'll pass on this walk are free to enter, including the Writers' Museum, St. Giles' Cathedral, Old Parliament House, People's Story Museum, Museum of Edinburgh, and Scottish parliament building.

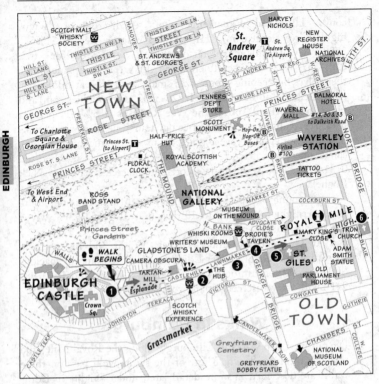

Overview

Start at Edinburgh Castle at the top and amble down to the Palace of Holyroodhouse. The street itself changes names—Castlehill, Lawnmarket, High Street, and Canongate—but it's a straight, downhill shot totaling just over one mile. And nearly every step is packed with shops, cafés, and lanes leading to tiny squares.

The city of Edinburgh was born on the rock at the top, where the castle stands today. Celtic tribes (and maybe the Romans) once occupied this site. As the town grew, it spilled downhill along the sloping ridge that became the Royal Mile. Because this strip of land is so narrow, there was no place to build but up. So in medieval times, it was densely packed with multistory "tenements"—large edifices under one roof that housed a number of tenants.

As you walk, you'll be tracing the growth of the city—its birth atop Castle Hill, its Old Town heyday in the 1600s, its expansion in the 1700s into the Georgian New Town (leaving the old quarter an overcrowded, disease-ridden Victorian slum), and on to the 21st century at the modern Scottish parliament building (2004).

Most of the Royal Mile feels like one long Scottish shopping mall, selling all manner of kitschy souvenirs (known locally as "tartan tat"), shortbread, and whisky. But the streets are also packed

Royal Mile Walk

- To Leith
- DUGALD STEWART MONUMENT
- NATIONAL MONUMENT
- NELSON MONUMENT & MUSEUM
- WATERLOO PLACE
- MARTYRS' MONUMENT
- Old Calton Cemetery
- ST. ANDREW'S HOUSE
- REGENT ROAD
- BURNS MONUMENT
- ABBEYHILL CRES
- ABBEYHILL
- PALACE OF HOLYROOD-HOUSE
- WALK ENDS
- CALTON ROAD
- CALTON RD.
- ROBERT FERGUSSON STATUE
- CANONGATE CHURCH
- PEOPLE'S STORY MUSEUM
- CLARINDA'S
- WHITE HORSE CLOSE
- ROYAL MILE
- SCOTTISH PARLIAMENT
- QUEEN'S GALLERY (WC, CAFE & HOLYROOD TICKETS)
- EAST MARKET ST.
- JEFFREY ST.
- NEW ST.
- CANONGATE
- MUSEUM OF EDINBURGH
- JOHN KNOX HOUSE
- PUBS
- STREET
- WORLD'S END
- ST. MARY'S
- CADENHEAD'S
- BAKEHOUSE CL.
- HOLYROOD ROAD
- DYNAMIC EARTH
- To Arthur's Seat & Trail to Top of Salisbury Crags
- NIDDRY ST.
- BLACKFRIAR
- MUSEUM OF CHILDHOOD
- GULLAN'S CLOSE
- ST. JOHN ST.
- CANONGATE
- #14, 30 & 33
- TWEEDDALE CT.
- COWGATE
- SOUTH
- INFIRMARY ST.
- DRUMMOND
- BRIDGE
- S. COLLEGE ST.
- FOXBURGH PL.
- To Dalkeith Road

200 Meters
200 Yards

EDINBURGH

1. Edinburgh Castle
2. Castlehill
3. Lawnmarket
4. Bank/High Streets Intersection
5. St. Giles' Cathedral
6. More of High Street
7. John Knox House
8. The World's End
9. Canongate
10. Scottish Parliament Building
11. Palace of Holyroodhouse

with history, and if you push past the postcard racks into one of the many side alleys, you can still find a few surviving rough edges of the old city.

Despite the drizzle, be sure to look up—spires, carvings, and towering Gothic "skyscrapers" give this city its unique urban identity.

As you stroll this mostly traffic-free tourist strip, you'll weave between big military-style barriers designed to frustrate terrorists, and navigate a can-can of low-grade souvenir shops and eateries, tourists with rolling suitcases, and cruise groups following their guides' umbrellas. Along the way, you'll be entertained by buskers, perused by pickpockets, hit up by beggars, and tempted by street merchants. Oh, and Edinburgh is quite haunted, you may feel the presence of a few ghosts.

• *We'll start at the castle esplanade, the big parking lot at the entrance to...*

EDINBURGH

❶ Edinburgh Castle

Edinburgh was born on the bluff—a big rock—where the castle now stands. Since before recorded history, people have lived on this strategic, easily defended perch.

The **castle** is an imposing symbol of Scottish independence (for a self-guided tour of Edinburgh Castle, see page 743). Its esplanade—built as a military parade ground (1816)—is now the site of the annual Military Tattoo. This spectacular massing of regimental bands fills the square nightly for most of August. Fans watch from temporary bleacher seats to see kilt-wearing dancers and bagpipers marching against the spectacular backdrop of the castle. TV crews broadcast the spectacle to all corners of the globe.

When the bleachers aren't up, there are fine views in both directions from the esplanade. Facing north, you'll see the body of water called the Firth of Forth, and Fife beyond that. (The Firth of Forth is the estuary where the River Forth flows into the North Sea.) Still facing north, find the lacy spire of the Scott Monument and two Neoclassical buildings housing art galleries. Beyond them, the stately buildings of Edinburgh's New Town  rise. Panning to the right, find the Nelson Monument and some faux Greek ruins atop Calton Hill (see page 783).

The city's many bluffs, crags, and ridges were built up by volcanoes, then carved down by glaciers—a city formed in "fire and ice," as the locals say. So, during the Ice Age, as a river of glaciers swept in from the west (behind today's castle), it ran into the super-hard volcanic basalt of Castle Rock and flowed around it, cutting valleys on either side and leaving a tail that became the Royal Mile you're about to walk.

At the bottom of the esplanade, where the square hits the road, look left to find a plaque on the wall above the tiny **witches' well** (now a planter). This memorializes 300 women who were accused of witchcraft and burned here. Below was the Nor' Loch, the swampy lake where those accused of witchcraft (mostly women) were bound and dropped into the lake. If they sank and drowned, they were innocent. If they floated, they were guilty, and were burned here in front of the castle, providing the city folk a nice afternoon out. The plaque shows two witches: one good and one bad. Tickle the serpent's snout to sympathize with the witches. (I just made that up.)

• *Start walking down the bustling Royal Mile. The first block is a street called...*

EDINBURGH

❷ Castlehill

The big squat, tank-like building immediately on your left was once the Old Town's reservoir. While it once held 1.5 million gallons of water, today it's filled with the tour-isty **Tartan Weaving Mill** (open daily 9:00-17:30), a massive complex of four floors selling every kind of Scottish cli-ché. At the bottom level (a long way down) is a floor of big looms and weav-ers sometimes at work.

The black-and-white tower ahead on the left has entertained visitors since the 1850s with its **camera obscura,** a darkened room where a mirror and a series of lenses capture live images of the city surroundings outside. (Giggle at the funny mirrors as you walk fatly by.) Across the street, filling the old Castlehill Primary School, is a gimmicky-if-intoxicating whisky-sampling exhibit called the **Scotch Whisky Experience** (a.k.a. "Malt Disney"). Both are de-scribed later, under "Sights in Edinburgh."

• *Just ahead, in front of the church with the tall, lacy spire, is the old market square known as...*

❸ Lawnmarket

During the Royal Mile's heyday, in the 1600s, this intersection was bigger and served as a market for fabric (especially "lawn," a linen-like cloth). The market would fill this space with hustle, bustle, and lots of commerce. The round white hump in the middle of the roundabout is all that remains of the official weighing beam called the Butter Tron—where all goods sold were weighed for honesty and tax purposes.

Towering above Lawnmarket, with the highest spire in the city, is the former Tolbooth Church. This impressive Neo-Gothic structure (1844) is now home to **the Hub,** Edinburgh's festival-ticket and information center. This is a handy stop for its WC, café, and free Wi-Fi, and for information on Edinburgh's many festivals: The world-famous Edinburgh Festival fills the month of August with cultural action, while other August festivals feature classical music, traditional and fringe theater (especially comedy), art, books, and more.

In the 1600s, this—along with the next

The Kilt

The kilt, Scotland's national dress, is intimately tied to the country's history. It originated in the 1500s as a multipurpose robe, toga, tent, poncho, and ground cloth. A wearer would lay a length of fabric (roughly 2 x 6 yards) on the ground, scrunch it up into pleats, then wrap it around the waist and belt it. Extra fabric was thrown over the shoulder or tucked into the belt, creating both a rakish sash and a rucksack-like pouch.

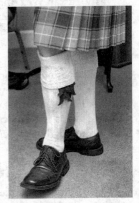

The colors and patterns of the first kilts depended on who wove them and what dyes were available in a locale (colors were muted, unlike later kilts). Because members of one clan tended to live in the same area, they often wore similar patterns—but they weren't specifically designed to represent a single clan.

The kilt became standard Highlands dress and a patriotic statement during conflicts with England. After the tragic-for-Scotland Battle of Culloden in 1746, the victorious English dismantled the Scottish clan system. Wearing the kilt, speaking Gaelic, and playing the bagpipes were all outlawed.

In 1782, kilts were permitted again, but by then the tradition had faded, and many Scots no longer wanted to wear one. Then, in 1822 King George IV visited Edinburgh (the first royal visit in 200 years). In a not-so-subtle assertion of his authority over Scotland, he wore a kilt. That bit of pageantry charmed Scottish

stretch, called High Street—was the city's main street. At that time, Edinburgh was bursting with breweries, printing presses, and banks. Tens of thousands of citizens were squeezed into the narrow confines of the Old Town.

Here on this ridge, they built tenements (multiple-unit residences) similar to the more recent ones you see today. These tenements, rising 10 stories and more, were some of the tallest domestic buildings in Europe. The living arrangements shocked class-conscious English visitors to Edinburgh because the tenements were occupied by rich and poor alike—usually the poor in the cellars and attics, and the rich in the middle floors.

• *Continue a half-block down the Mile.*

Gladstone's Land (at #477b, on the left), a surviving original tenement, was acquired by a wealthy merchant in 1617. Stand in front of the building and look up at this centuries-old skyscraper. This design was standard for its time: a shop or shops on the ground floor, with columns and an arcade, and residences on the floors noblemen, and the kilt was in vogue once more.

During the king's visit, Sir Walter Scott organized a Highland festival that reinvented and romanticized the image of traditional Scottish culture, giving it a newfound respectability. The brightly colored "clan tartans" you'll see in Scottish souvenir shops got their start at this time, as fabric salesmen hastily designed and assigned patterns to particular clans to capitalize on the newfound enthusiasm for kilts.

A generation later, Queen Victoria enhanced the cachet of the kilt even more. She loved Scotland and wallpapered her palace at Balmoral with tartan patterns and wore dresses made from tartan fabric. Since then, tartanry has been embraced as if it were historic. (By the way, Scots use these key terms differently than Americans do: "Tartan" is the pattern itself, while "plaid" is the piece of cloth worn over the shoulder with a kilt.)

If shopping for a kilt, consider where you'll wear it. Unless you want just a casual kilt for festivals and pubs, the rule of thumb is to get the best you can afford, since it never goes out of style. You'll choose a tartan and fabric weight (a heavier weight is considered higher quality, hangs well, and is easier to press). The kilt should sit high on the waist a couple of inches above the hip bone.

Kilt-related gear includes the kilt pin, worn on the front fringed side of the kilt; kilt hose (socks) and flashes (sock garters, with a decorative ribbon that peeks from the sock cuff); the sporran, the leather pouch worn around the waist; and the *sgian dubh* ("black knife"), the short blade worn in the top of the sock. Traditional shoes worn with kilts are ghillie brogues, with laces wrapped around the ankles and tied in front.

above. Because window glass was expensive, the lower halves of window openings were made of cheaper wood, which swung out like shutters for ventilation—and were convenient for tossing out garbage. Now a museum, Gladstone's Land is worth visiting for its intimate look at life here 400 years ago (see page 754).

Branching off the spine of the Royal Mile are a number of narrow alleyways that go by various local names. A "wynd" (rhymes with "kind") is a narrow, winding lane. A "pend" is an arched gateway. "Gate" is from an Old Norse word for street. And a "close" is a tiny alley between two buildings (originally with a door that "closed" at night). A "close" usually leads to a "court," or courtyard.

To explore one of these alleyways, head into Lady Stair's Close (on the left, 10 steps downhill from Gladstone's Land). This alley pops out in a small courtyard, where you'll find the **Writers' Museum** (described on page 754). It's free and well worth a visit for fans of Scotland's holy trinity of writers (Robert Burns, Sir Walter Scott, and Robert Louis Stevenson), but also for a glimpse of what a typical home might have looked like in the 1600s. Burns actually lived for a while in this neighborhood, in 1786, when he first arrived in Edinburgh.

Opposite Gladstone's Land (at #322), another close leads to **Riddle's Court.** Wander through here and imagine Edinburgh in the 17th and 18th centuries, when tourists came here to marvel at its skyscrapers. Some 40,000 people were jammed into the few blocks between here and the World's End pub (which we'll reach soon). Visualize the labyrinthine maze of the old city, with people scurrying through these back alleyways, buying and selling, and popping into taverns.

No city in Europe was as densely populated—or perhaps as filthy. Without modern hygiene, it was a living hell of smoke, stench, and noise, with the constant threat of fire, collapse, and disease. The dirt streets were soiled with sewage from bedpans emptied out windows. By the 1700s, the Old Town was rife with poverty and disease. The smoky home fires rising from tenements and the infamous smell (or "reek" in Scottish) that wafted across the city gave it a nickname that sticks today: "Auld Reekie."

• *Return to the Royal Mile and continue down it a few steps to take in some sights at the...*

❹ Bank/High Streets Intersection

Several sights cluster here, where Lawnmarket changes its name to High Street and intersects with Bank Street and George IV Bridge.

Begin with **Deacon Brodie's Tavern.** Read the "Doctor Jekyll and Mr. Hyde" story of this pub's notorious namesake on the wall facing Bank Street. Then, to see his spooky split personality, check out both sides of the hanging signpost. Brodie—a pillar of the community by day but a burglar by night—epitomizes the divided personality of 1700s Edinburgh. It was a rich, productive city—home to great philosophers and scientists, who actively contributed to the Enlightenment. Meanwhile, the Old Town was riddled with crime and squalor. The city was scandalized when a respected surgeon— driven by a passion for medical research and needing corpses—was accused of colluding with two lowlifes, named Burke and Hare,  to acquire freshly murdered corpses for dissection. (In the next century, in the late 1800s, novelist Robert Louis Stevenson would capture the dichotomy of Edinburgh's rich-poor society in his *Strange Case of Dr. Jekyll and Mr. Hyde.*)

In the late 1700s, Edinburgh's upper class moved out of the Old Town into a planned community called the New Town (a quarter-mile north of here). Eventually, most tenements were torn down and replaced with newer Victorian buildings. You'll see some at this intersection.

Look left down Bank Street to the green-domed **Bank of Scotland.** This was the headquarters of the bank, which had practiced modern capitalist financing since 1695. The building now houses the Museum on the Mound, a free exhibit on banking history (see page 754), and is also the Scottish headquarters for Lloyds Banking Group—which swallowed up the Bank of Scotland after the financial crisis of 2008.

If you detour left down Bank Street toward the bank, you'll find the recommended **Whiski Rooms Shop.** If you head in the opposite direction, down George IV Bridge, you'll reach the excellent **National Museum of Scotland,** the famous Greyfriars Bobby statue, photogenic Victoria Street, which leads to the pub-lined Grassmarket square (all described later in this chapter), and several recommended eateries. Victoria Street (to the left) is so dreamy, many Potterheads figure it must be the inspiration for J. K. Rowling's Diagon Alley.

Across the street (downhill) from Deacon Brodie's Tavern is a seated green statue of hometown boy **David Hume** (1711-1776)—

one of the most influential thinkers not only of Scotland, but in all of Western philosophy. The atheistic Hume was one of the towering figures of the Scottish Enlightenment of the mid-1700s. Thinkers and scientists were using the experimental method to challenge and investigate everything, including religion. Hume questioned cause and effect in thought puzzles such as this: We can see that when one billiard ball strikes another, the second one moves, but how do we know the collision "caused" the movement? Notice his shiny toe: People on their way to trial (in the high court just behind the statue) or students on their way to exams (in the nearby university) rub it for good luck.

Follow David Hume's gaze to the opposite corner, where a **brass H** in the pavement marks the site of the last public execution in Edinburgh in 1864. Deacon Brodie himself would have been hung about here (in 1788, on gallows whose design he had helped to improve—smart guy).

• *From the brass H, continue down the Royal Mile, pausing just before the church square at a stone wellhead with the pyramid cap.*

All along the Royal Mile, **wellheads** like this (from 1835) provided townsfolk with water in the days before buildings had plumbing. These neighborhood wells were served by the reservoir up at the castle. Imagine long lines of people in need of water standing here, gossiping and sharing the news. Eventually buildings were retrofitted with water pipes—the ones you see running along building exteriors.

• *Ahead of you (past the Victorian statue of some duke), embedded in the cobblestones near the street, is a big heart.*

The **Heart of Midlothian** marks the spot of the city's 15th-century municipal building and jail. In times past, in a nearby open space, criminals were hanged, traitors were decapitated, and witches were burned. Citizens hated the rough justice doled out here. Locals still spit on the heart in the pavement. Go ahead...do as the locals do—land one right in the heart of the heart. By the way, Edinburgh has two soccer teams—Heart of Midlothian (known as "Hearts") and Hibernian ("Hibs"). If you're a Hibs fan, spit again.

• *Make your way to the entrance of the church.*

❺ St. Giles' Cathedral

This is the flagship of the Church of Scotland (Scotland's largest denomination)—called the "Mother Church of Presbyterianism."

The interior serves as a kind of Scottish Westminster Abbey, filled with monuments, statues, plaques, and stained-glass windows dedicated to great Scots and moments in history.

A church has stood on this spot since 854, though this structure is an architectural hodgepodge, dating mostly from the 15th through 19th century. In the 16th century, St. Giles was a kind of national stage on which the drama of the Reformation was played out. The reformer John Knox (1514-1572) was the preacher here. His fiery sermons helped turn once-Catholic Edinburgh into a bastion of Protestantism. During the Scottish Reformation, St. Giles was transformed from a Catholic cathedral to a Presbyterian church. The spacious interior is well worth a visit (for a self-guided tour, see page 756).

• *Facing the church entrance, curl around its right side, into a parking lot.*

Sights Around St. Giles

The grand building across the parking lot from St. Giles is the **Old Parliament House.** Since the 13th century, the king had ruled a rubber-stamp parliament of nobles and bishops. But the Protestant Reformation promoted democracy, and the parliament gained real power. From the early 1600s until 1707, this building evolved to become the seat of a true parliament of elected officials. That came to an end in 1707, when Scotland signed an Act of Union, joining what's known today as the United Kingdom and giving up their right to self-rule. (More on that later in the walk.) If you're curious to peek inside, head through the door at #11 (described on page 761).

The great reformer **John Knox** is buried—with appropriate austerity—under parking lot spot #23. The statue among the cars shows King Charles II riding to a toga party back in 1685.

• *Continue through the parking lot, around the back end of the church.*

Every Scottish burgh (town licensed by the king to trade) had three standard features: a "tolbooth" (basically a Town Hall, with a courthouse, meeting room, and jail);

a "tron" (official weighing scale); and a "mercat" (or market) cross. The **mercat cross** standing just behind St. Giles' Cathedral has a slender column decorated with a unicorn holding a flag with the cross of St. Andrew. Royal proclamations have been read at this mercat cross since the 14th century. In 1952, a town crier heralded the news that Britain had a new queen—three days after the actual event (traditionally the time it took for a horse to speed here from London). Today, Mercat Cross is the meeting point for many of Edinburgh's walking tours—both historic and ghostly.

• *Circle around to the street side of the church.*

The statue to **Adam Smith** honors the Edinburgh author of the pioneering *Wealth of Nations* (1776), in which he laid out the economics of free-market capitalism. Smith theorized that an "invisible hand" wisely guides the unregulated free market. Stand in front of Smith and imagine the intellectual energy of Edinburgh in the mid-1700s, when it was Europe's most enlightened city. Adam Smith was right in the center of it. He and David Hume were good friends. James Boswell, the famed biographer of Samuel Johnson, took classes from Smith. James Watt, inventor of the steam engine, was another proud Scotsman of the age. With great intellectuals like these, Edinburgh helped create the modern world. The poet Robert Burns, geologist James Hutton (who's considered the father of modern geology), and the publishers of the first *Encyclopedia Britannica* all lived in Edinburgh. Steeped in the inquisitive mindset of the Enlightenment, they applied cool rationality and a secular approach to their respective fields.

• *Head on down the Royal Mile.*

❻ More of High Street

Continuing down this stretch of the Royal Mile, which is traffic-free most of the day (notice the bollards that raise and lower for permitted traffic), you'll see the Fringe Festival office (at #180), street musicians, and another wellhead (with horse "sippies," dating from 1675).

Notice those **three red boxes.** In the 20th century, people used these to make telephonic calls to each other. (Imagine that!) These cast-iron booths were produced in Scotland for all of Britain. As phone booths are decommissioned, some are finding new use as tiny shops and ATMs, and even showing up in residential neighborhoods as nostalgic garden decorations.

At the next intersection, on the left, is **Cockburn Street** (pronounced "COE-burn"), with a reputation for its eclectic independent shops and string of trendy bars and eateries. In the Middle Ages, only tiny lanes (like Fleshmarket Close just uphill) interrupted the long line of Royal Mile buildings. Cockburn Street was cut through High Street's dense wall of medieval skyscrapers in the 1860s to give easy access to the Georgian New Town and the train station. Notice how the sliced buildings were thoughtfully capped with facades that fit the aesthetic look of the Royal Mile.

• *When you reach the Tron Church (with a fine 17th-century interior, currently housing historic exhibits and shops), you're at the intersection of* **North and South Bridge** *streets. These major streets lead left to Waverley Station and right to the Dalkeith Road B&Bs. Several handy bus lines run along here.*

This is the halfway point of this walk. Stand on the corner diagonally across from the church. Look up to the top of the Royal Mile at the Hub and its 240-foot spire. In front of that, take in the spire of St. Giles' Cathedral—inspired by the Scottish crown and the thistle, Scotland's national flower.

With its faux turret and made-up 16th-century charm, the **Radisson Blu Hotel** just across the street is entirely new construction (1990), but built to fit in. The city is protecting its historic look. The **Inn on the Mile** next door was once a fancy bank with a lavish interior. As modern banks are moving away from city centers, their sumptuous buildings are being converted into ornate pubs and restaurants.

In the next block downhill are three **characteristic pubs** (The Mitre, Royal Mile, and Whiski), side by side, that offer free folk music many evenings. On the facing buildings, notice the chimneys. Tenement buildings shared stairways and entries, but held individual apartments, each with its own chimney.

• *Go down High Street another block, passing near the Museum of Childhood (on the right, at #42, and worth a stop; see page 761).*

Directly across the street, just below another wellhead, is the...

❼ John Knox House

Remember that Knox was a towering figure in Edinburgh's history, converting Scotland to a Calvinist style of Protestantism. His religious bent was "Presbyterianism," in which parishes are governed

by elected officials rather than appointed bishops. This more democratic brand of Christianity also spurred Scotland toward political
democracy. If you're interested in Knox or the Reformation, this
sight is worth a visit (see page 761). Full disclosure: It's not certain
that Knox ever actually lived here. Attached to the Knox House is
the Scottish Storytelling Centre, where locals with the gift of gab
perform regularly; check the posted schedule.

• *A few steps farther down High Street, at the intersection with St.
Mary's and Jeffrey streets, you'll reach...*

❽ The World's End

For centuries, a wall stood here, marking the end of the burgh of
Edinburgh. For residents within the protective walls of the city, this
must have felt like the "world's end," indeed. You can even pop in
for a pint at the recommended The World's End pub, to your right.
The area beyond was called Canongate, a monastic community
associated with Holyrood Abbey. At the intersection, find the brass
bricks in the street that trace the gate (demolished in 1764). Look to
the right down St. Mary's Street about 200 yards to see a surviving
bit of that old wall, known as the **Flodden Wall.** In the 1513 Battle
of Flodden, the Scottish king James IV made the disastrous decision
to invade northern England. James and 10,000 of his Scotsmen were
killed. Fearing a brutal English counterattack, Edinburgh scrambled
to reinforce its broken-down city wall. To the left, down Jeffrey
Street, you'll see Scotland's top tattoo parlor, and a supplier for a
different kind of tattoo (the Scottish Regimental Store).

Look left down Jeffrey Street past the train tracks for a good
view of the **Calton Cemetery** up on Calton Hill. The obelisk,
called Martyrs' Monument, remembers a group of 18th-century
patriots exiled by London to Australia for their reform politics. The
round building to the left is the grave of philosopher David Hume.
Today, the main reason to go up Calton Hill is for the fine views
(see page 783).

• *Continue down the Royal Mile—leaving old Edinburgh—as High
Street changes names to...*

❾ Canongate

A couple hundred yards
farther along (on the right
at #172) you reach **Cadenhead's,** a serious whisky
shop (see page 788). About
30 yards beyond that,
you'll pass two worthwhile
and free museums, the
People's Story Museum

(on the left, in the old tollhouse at #163) and the **Museum of Edinburgh** (on the right, at #142), with the entry to the characteristic Bakehouse Close next door (for more on all three, see page 762). But our next stop is the church just across from the Museum of Edinburgh.

The 1688 **Canongate Kirk** (Church)—located not far from the royal residence of Holyroodhouse—is where Queen Elizabeth II

and her family worship whenever they're in town. (So don't sit in the front pew, marked with her crown.) The gilded emblem at the top of the roof, high above the door, has the antlers of a stag from the royal estate of Balmoral. One of the Queen's granddaughters got married here in 2011.

The church is open only when volunteers have signed up to welcome visitors. Chat them up and borrow the description of the place. Then step inside the lofty blue and red interior, renovated with royal money; the church is filled with light and the flags of various Scottish regiments. In the narthex, peruse the photos of royal family events here, and find the list of priests and ministers of this parish—it goes back to 1143 (with a clear break with the Reformation in 1561).

Outside, turn right as you leave the church and walk up into the graveyard. The large, gated grave (abutting the back of the People's Story Museum) is the affectionately tended tomb of **Adam Smith**, the father of capitalism. (Throw him a penny or two.)

The statue on the sidewalk in front of the church is of the poet **Robert Fergusson.** One of the first to write verse in the Scots language, he so inspired Robert Burns that Burns paid for Fergusson's tombstone in the Canongate churchyard and composed his epitaph.

Now look across the street at the **gabled house** next to the Museum of Edinburgh. Scan the facade to see shells put there in the 17th century to defend against the evil power of witches yet to be drowned.

• *Walk about 300 yards farther along (past the recommended **Clarinda's** Tea Room). In the distance you can see the Palace of Holyroodhouse (the end of this walk) and soon, on the right, you'll come to the modern Scottish parliament building.*

Just opposite the parliament building is **White Horse Close** (on the left, in the white arcade that juts into the sidewalk).

Step into this 17th-century courtyard. It was from here that the Edinburgh stagecoach left for London. Eight days later, the horse-drawn carriage would pull into its destination: Scotland Yard. Note that bus #35 leaves in two directions from here—downhill for the Royal Yacht *Britannia*, and uphill along the Royal Mile (as far as South Bridge) and on to the National Museum of Scotland.

• *Now walk up around the corner to the flagpoles (flying the flags of Europe, Britain, and Scotland) in front of the...*

EDINBURGH

⑩ Scottish Parliament Building

Finally, after centuries of history, we reach the 21st century. And finally, after three centuries of London rule, Scotland has a

parliament building...in Scotland. When Scotland united with England in 1707, its parliament was dissolved. But in 1999, the Scottish parliament was reestablished, and in 2004, it moved into this striking new home. Notice how the eco-friendly building,

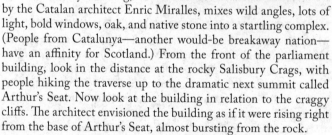

by the Catalan architect Enric Miralles, mixes wild angles, lots of light, bold windows, oak, and native stone into a startling complex. (People from Catalunya—another would-be breakaway nation—have an affinity for Scotland.) From the front of the parliament building, look in the distance at the rocky Salisbury Crags, with people hiking the traverse up to the dramatic next summit called Arthur's Seat. Now look at the building in relation to the craggy cliffs. The architect envisioned the building as if it were rising right from the base of Arthur's Seat, almost bursting from the rock.

Since it celebrates Scottish democracy, the architecture is not a statement of authority. There are no statues of old heroes. There's not even a grand entry. You feel like you're entering an office park. Given its neighborhood, the media often calls the Scottish Parliament "Holyrood" for short (similar to calling the US Congress "Capitol Hill"). For details on touring the building and seeing parliament in action, see page 764.

• *Across the street is the Queen's Gallery, where her majesty shares part of her amazing personal art collection in excellent revolving exhibits—each with a theme (see page 766). Finally, walk to the end of the road (Abbey Strand), and step up to the impressive wrought-iron gate of the Queen's palace. Look up at the stag with its holy cross, or "holy rood," on its forehead, and peer into the palace grounds. (The ticket office and palace entryway, a fine café, and a handy WC are just through the arch on the right.)*

EDINBURGH

⓫ Palace of Holyroodhouse

Since the 16th century, this palace has marked the end of the Royal Mile. An abbey—part of a 12th-century Augustinian

monastery—originally stood in its place. While most of that old building is gone, you can see the surviving nave behind the palace on the left. According to one legend, it was named "holy rood" for a piece of the cross, brought here as a relic by Queen (and later Saint) Margaret. (Another version of the story is that King David I, Margaret's son, saw the image of a cross upon a stag's head while hunting here and took it as a sign that he should build an abbey on the site.) Because Scotland's royalty preferred living at Holyroodhouse to the blustery castle on the rock, the palace grew over time. If the Queen's not visiting, the palace welcomes visitors (get tickets in the Queen's Gallery; see page 766 for details).

• *Your walk—from the castle to the palace, with so much Scottish history packed in between—is complete. But if your appetite is whetted, don't worry, there's much more to see. Enjoy the rest of Edinburgh.*

NEW TOWN WALK: GEORGIAN EDINBURGH

Many visitors, mesmerized by the Royal Mile, never venture to the New Town. And that's a shame. With the city's finest Georgian architecture (from its 18th-century boom period), the New Town has a completely different character than the Old Town. This self-guided walk—worth ▲▲—gives you a quick orientation in about one hour.

• *Begin on Waverley Bridge, spanning the gully between the Old and New towns; to get there from the Royal Mile, just head down the curved Cockburn Street near the Tron Church (or cut down any of the "close" lanes opposite St. Giles' Cathedral). Stand on the bridge overlooking the train tracks, facing the castle.*

❶ **View from Waverley Bridge:** From this vantage point, you can enjoy fine views of medieval Edinburgh, with its 10-story-plus

"skyscrapers." It's easy to imagine how miserably crowded this area was, prompting the expansion of the city during the Georgian period. Pick out landmarks along the Royal Mile, most notably the open-work "thistle steeple" of St. Giles.

A big lake called the **Nor'**

Loch once was to the north (nor') of the Old Town; now it's a valley between Edinburgh's two towns. The lake was drained around 1800 as part of the expansion. Before that, the lake was the town's water reservoir...and its sewer. Much has been written about the town's infamous stink. The town's nickname, "Auld Reekie," referred to both the smoke of its industry and the stench of its squalor.

The long-gone loch was also a handy place for drowning witches. With their thumbs tied to their ankles, they'd be lashed to dunking stools. Those who survived the ordeal were considered "aided by the devil" and burned as witches. If they died, they were innocent and given a good Christian burial. Edinburgh was Europe's witch-burning mecca—any perceived "sign," including a small birthmark, could condemn you. Scotland burned more witches per capita than any other country—17,000 souls between 1479 and 1722.

Visually trace the train tracks as they disappear into a tunnel below the **Scottish National Gallery** (with the best collection anywhere of Scottish paintings; you can visit it during this walk— see page 772). The two fine Neoclassical buildings of the National Gallery date from the 1840s and sit upon a mound that's called... **The Mound.** When the New Town was built, tons of rubble from the excavations were piled here (1781-1830), forming a dirt bridge that connected the new development with the Old Town to allay merchant concerns about being cut off from the future heart of the city.

Turning 180 degrees (and facing the ramps down into the train station), notice the huge, turreted building with the clock tower. (The clock is famously four minutes fast to help locals not miss their train.) **The Balmoral** was one of the city's two grand hotels during its glory days (its opposite bookend, the **Waldorf Astoria Edinburgh,** sits at the far end of the former

lakebed—near the end of this walk). Aristocrats arriving by train could use a hidden entrance to go from the platform directly up to their plush digs. (Today The Balmoral is known mostly as the place where J. K. Rowling completed the final Harry Potter book. She has a suite there that she uses when struggling with writer's block.)

• *Now walk across the bridge toward the New Town. Before the corner, enter the gated gardens on the left, and head toward the big, pointy monument. You're at the edge of...*

❷ **Princes Street Gardens:** This grassy park, filling the

EDINBURGH

New Town Walk: Georgian Edinburgh

200 Meters
200 Yards

To Leith

Water of Leith

RIVERSIDE PATH

Moray Place

1 View from Waverly Bridge
2 Princes Street Gardens
3 Scott Monument
4 Jenners Dep't Store
5 St. Andrew Square
6 George Street
7 St. Andrew's & St. George's Church
8 The Dome Restaurant
9 King George IV Statue
10 Thistle Street
11 William Pitt Statue
12 Rose Street
13 Charlotte Square
14 Georgian House

Ainslie Place

NEW

Queen

QUEEN

HILL ST.

GEORGIAN HOUSE 14

13

Charlotte Square

GEORGE STREET

ROSE ST. N. LANE

ROSE ST. 12

ROSE ST. S. LANE

PRINCES

QUEENSFERRY ST.

HOPE ST. LANE

ALVA ST.

SHANDWICK PL.

To Haymarket Station

WEST END

EDINBURGH GIN DISTILLERY

WALDORF ASTORIA

ST. CUTHBERT'S

EDINBURGH CASTLE

---

former lakebed, offers a wonderful escape from the bustle of the city. Once the private domain of the wealthy, it was opened to the public around 1870—not as a democratic gesture, but in hopes of increasing sales at the Princes Street department stores (Jenners is across the street). Join the office workers for a picnic lunch break.

• *Take a seat on the bench as encouraged by the Livingstone (Dr. Livingstone, I presume?) statue. (The Victorian explorer is well equipped with a guidebook but is hardly packing light—his lion skin doesn't even fit in his rucksack carry-on.)*

   Look up at the towering...

3 **Scott Monument:** Built in the early 1840s, this elaborate Neo-Gothic monument honors the great author Sir Walter Scott, one of Edinburgh's many illustrious sons. When Scott died in 1832, it was said that "Scotland never owed so much to one man." Scott almost singlehandedly created the image of the Scotland we know. Just as the country was in danger of being assimilated into England, Scott celebrated traditional songs, legends, myths, architecture, and kilts, thereby reviving the Highland culture and cementing a national identity. And, as the father of the Romantic historical novel, he contributed to Western literature in general.

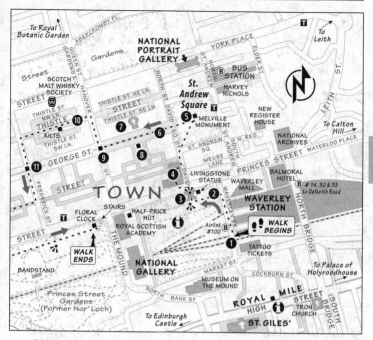

Nicknamed "the Gothic Rocket," this 200-foot-tall monument shelters a marble statue of Scott and his favorite pet, Maida, a deerhound who was one of 30 canines this dog lover owned during his lifetime. Climbing the tight, stony spiral staircase of 220 steps earns you a peek at a tiny museum midway and a fine city view at the top (£8, open daily 10:00-17:00, Oct-March until 16:00; 30-minute tours depart on the half hour, last tour 30 minutes before closing; tel. 0131/529-4068).

• Exit the park and head across busy Princes Street to the venerable...

❹ Jenners Department Store: As you wait for the light to change, notice how statues of women support the building—just as real women support the business. The arrival of new fashions here was such a big deal in the old days that they'd announce it by flying flags on the Nelson Monument atop Calton Hill (which you can see in the distance on the right).

Step inside and head upstairs into the grand, skylit atrium. The central space—filled with a towering tree at Christmas—is classic Industrial Age architecture. The Queen's coat of arms high

EDINBURGH

above the clock indicates she shops here. But Jenners, like most department stores, is struggling in the age of online shopping.

• *Walk through the atrium, turn right, and exit onto South St. David Street. Turn left and follow this street uphill one block up to...*

❺ **St. Andrew Square:** This green space is dedicated to the patron saint of Scotland. In the early 19th century, there were no shops around here—just fine residences; this was a private garden for the fancy people living here. Now open to the public, the square is a popular lunch hangout for workers. The Melville Monument honors a powermonger member of parliament who, for four decades (around 1800), was nicknamed the "uncrowned king of Scotland."

One block beyond the top of the park on Queen Street is the excellent **Scottish National Portrait Gallery,** which introduces you to all of the biggest names in Scottish history (described later, under "Sights in Edinburgh").

• *Follow the Melville Monument's gaze straight ahead out of the park. Cross the street and stand at the top of...*

❻ **George Street:** This is the main drag of Edinburgh's grid-planned New Town. Laid out in 1776, when King George III was busy putting down a revolution in a troublesome overseas colony, the New Town was a model of urban planning in its day. The architectural style is "Georgian"—British for "Neoclassical." And the street plan came with an unambiguous message: to celebrate the union of Scotland with England into the United Kingdom. (This was particularly important, since Scotland was just two decades removed from the failed Jacobite uprising of Bonnie Prince Charlie.)

If you look at a map, you'll see the politics in the street plan: St. Andrew Square (patron saint of Scotland) and Charlotte Square (George III's queen) bookend the New Town, with its three main streets named for the royal family of the time (George, Queen, and Princes). Thistle and Rose streets—which we'll see near the end of this walk—are named for the national flowers of Scotland and England.

The plan for the New Town was the masterstroke of the 23-year-old urban designer James Craig. George Street—20 feet wider than the others (so a four-horse carriage could make a U-turn)—was the main drag. Running down the high spine of the area, it afforded grand, unobstructed views. As you stroll down George Street, you'll notice that, with Craig's grid, grand cross streets come with fine Old Town and river views to the left and right, and monuments seem placed to accentuate the perspectives.

• *Halfway down the first block of George Street, on the right, is...*

❼ St. Andrew's and St. George's Church: Designed as part of the New Town plan in the 1780s, the church is a product of the Scottish Enlightenment. It has an elliptical plan (the first in Britain) so that all can focus on the pulpit. If it's open, step inside. The church conveys the idea that God is space, light, reason, and ordered beauty. A fine leaflet tells the story of the church, and a handy cafeteria downstairs serves cheap and cheery lunches.

❽ The Dome: Directly across the street from the church is another temple, this one devoted to money. This former bank building (now housing a recommended restaurant) has a pediment filled with figures demonstrating various ways to make money, which they do with all the nobility of classical gods. Consider scurrying across the street and ducking inside to view the stunning domed atrium.

❾ Statue of King George IV: Continue down George Street to the intersection with a statue commemorating the visit by George

IV. Notice the particularly fine axis formed by this cross-street: The National Gallery lines up perfectly with the Royal Mile's skyscrapers and the former Tolbooth Church, creating a Gotham City collage.

• *By now you've gotten your New Town bearings.*
Feel free to stop this walk here: If you were to turn left and head down Hanover Street, in a block you'd run into the Scottish National Gallery; the street behind it curves back up to the Royal Mile.

But to see more of the New Town—including the Georgian House, offering an insightful look inside one of these fine 18th-century homes—stick with me for a few more long blocks, zigzagging through side streets to see the various personalities that inhabit this rigid grid.

Turn right on Hanover Street; after just one (short) block, cross over and go left down...

❿ Thistle Street: Of the many streets in the New Town, this has perhaps the most vivid Scottish character. And that's fitting, as it's named after Scotland's national flower. At the beginning and end of the street, also notice that Craig's street plan included tranquil cul-de-sacs within the larger blocks. Thistle Street seems sleepy, but holds characteristic boutiques and good restaurants (see "Eating in Edinburgh," later). Halfway down the street on the left is a rare kilt-making artisan in action: Howie Nicholsby's shop,

EDINBURGH

21st Century Kilt, updates traditional Scottish menswear (though it's usually open by appointment only; for details see the listing on page 791).

• *You'll soon reach Frederick Street. Turn left and head toward the...*

⓫ Statue of William Pitt the Younger: Pitt was a prime minister under King George III during the French Revolution and the Napoleonic Wars. His father gave his name to the American city of Pittsburgh (which Scots pronounce as "Pitts-burrah"...I assume).

• *For an interesting contrast, we'll continue down another side street. Pass the statue of Pitt (heading toward Edinburgh Castle), and turn right onto...*

⓬ Rose Street: As a rose is to a thistle, and as England is to Scotland, so is brash, boisterous Rose Street to sedate, thoughtful Thistle Street. This stretch of Rose Street feels more commercialized, jammed with chain stores. The far end is packed with pubs and restaurants. As you walk, keep an eye out for the cobbled Tudor rose embedded in the brick sidewalk. When you cross the aptly named Castle Street, linger over the grand views to Edinburgh Castle. It's almost as if they planned it this way...just for the views.

• *Popping out at the far end of Rose Street, across the street and to your right is...*

⓭ Charlotte Square: The building of the New Town started cheap with St. Andrew Square, but finished well with this stately space. In 1791, the Edinburgh town council asked the prestigious Scottish architect Robert Adam to pump up the design for Charlotte Square. The council hoped that Adam's plan would answer criticism that the New Town buildings lacked innovation or ambition—and they got what they wanted. Adam's design, which raised the standard of New Town architecture to "international class," created Edinburgh's finest Georgian square. To this day, the fine garden filling the square is private, reserved for residents only.

• *Along the right side of Charlotte Square, at #7, you can visit the* **⓮ Georgian House,** *which gives you a great peek behind all of these harmonious Neoclassical facades (see page 777).*

When you're done touring the house, you can head back through the New Town grid, perhaps taking some different streets than the way you *came. If you're staying in the West End, you're just a few blocks away from your hotel. Or, for a restful return to our starting point, consider this...*

Return Through Princes Street Gardens: From Charlotte Square, drop down to busy Princes Street (noticing the red building to the right—the grand Waldorf Astoria Hotel and twin sister of The Balmoral at the start of our walk). But rather than walking along the busy bus-and-tram-lined shopping drag, head into **Princes Street Gardens** (cross Princes Street and enter the gate on the left). With the castle looming overhead, you'll pass a playground, a fanciful Victorian fountain, more monuments to great Scots, war memorials, and a bandstand (which hosts Scottish country dancing—see page 793). Finally, you'll reach a staircase up to the Scottish National Gallery (though access from this entrance may be limited); and the oldest **floral clock** in the world—perhaps telling you it's time for a spot of tea.

• *Our walk is over. From here, you can tour the gallery; head up Bank Street just behind it to reach the Royal Mile; hop on a bus along Princes Street to your next stop (or B&B); or continue through another stretch of the Princes Street Gardens to the Scott Monument and our starting point.*

Sights in Edinburgh

▲▲▲EDINBURGH CASTLE

The fortified birthplace of the city 1,300 years ago, this imposing symbol of Edinburgh sits proudly on a rock high above the town. The

home of Scotland's kings and queens for centuries, the castle has witnessed royal births, medieval pageantry, and bloody sieges. Today it's a complex of various buildings, the oldest dating from the 12th century, linked by cobbled roads that survive

from its more recent use as a military garrison. The castle—with expansive views, plenty of history, and the stunning crown jewels of Scotland—is a fascinating and multifaceted sight that deserves several hours of your time.

Cost and Hours: £20, daily 9:30-18:00, Oct-March until 17:00, last entry one hour before closing, tel. 0131/225-9846, www.edinburghcastle.scot.

Avoiding Lines: The castle is usually less crowded after 15:00 (cruise and bus-tour groups tend to come in the morning). To avoid

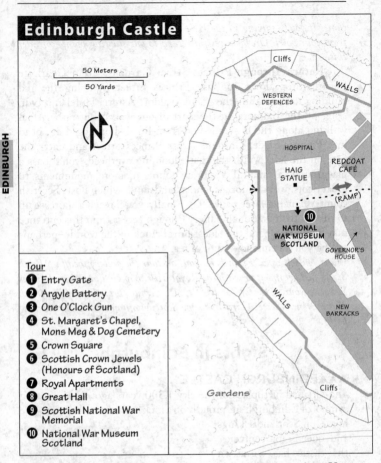

Edinburgh Castle

50 Meters
50 Yards

Cliffs

WALLS

WESTERN
DEFENCES

HOSPITAL

REDCOAT
CAFÉ

HAIG
STATUE

(RAMP)

10
NATIONAL
WAR MUSEUM
SCOTLAND

GOVERNOR'S
HOUSE

WALLS

NEW
BARRACKS

Gardens

Cliffs

Tour
1. Entry Gate
2. Argyle Battery
3. One O'Clock Gun
4. St. Margaret's Chapel, Mons Meg & Dog Cemetery
5. Crown Square
6. Scottish Crown Jewels (Honours of Scotland)
7. Royal Apartments
8. Great Hall
9. Scottish National War Memorial
10. National War Museum Scotland

ticket lines (worst in Aug), buy your ticket in advance online. You can print your ticket at home or pick it up at the black kiosk—with several nearby computer stations—just below the esplanade (facing the Tartan Weaving Mill) before joining the castle crowds. You can also pick up tickets at the machines just inside the castle entrance or at the visitor information desk a few steps uphill on the right.

You can skip the ticket line with a Historic Scotland Explorer Pass (see page 1037 for details) or the Royal Edinburgh Ticket (see "Tours in Edinburgh," earlier).

Getting There: Simply walk up the Royal Mile (if arriving by bus from the B&B area south of the city, get off at South

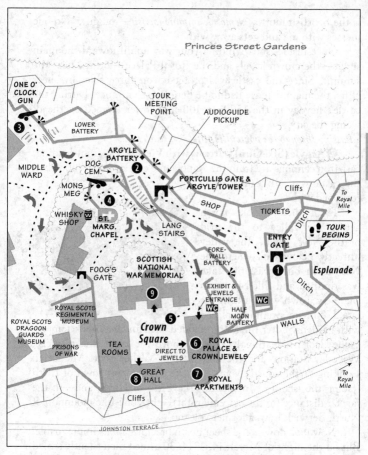

Bridge and huff up the Mile for about 15 minutes). Taxis get you closer, dropping you a block below the esplanade at the Hub/ Tolbooth Church.

Tours: Thirty-minute introductory guided tours are free with admission (2-4/hour, depart from Argyle Battery, see clock for next departure; fewer off-season). The informative audioguide provides four hours of descriptions, including the National War Museum Scotland (£3.50, pick up inside Portcullis Gate).

Eating: The **$ Redcoat Café**—just past the Argyle Battery— is a big, bright, efficient cafeteria with great views.

➋ Self-Guided Tour

❶ **Entry Gate:** Approaching from the esplanade, you're greeted by the two greatest Scottish heroes. Flanking the entryway are statues of the fierce warriors who battled English invaders, William Wallace (on the right) and Robert the Bruce (left). Between them is the Scottish motto, *Nemo me impune lacessit*—roughly, "No one messes with me and gets away with it."

Once inside, start winding your way uphill toward the main sights—the crown jewels and the Royal Palace—located near the summit. Since the castle was protected on three sides by sheer cliffs, the main defense had to be here at the entrance. During the castle's heyday in the 1500s, a 100-foot tower loomed overhead, facing the city.

• *Passing through the **portcullis gate**, you reach the...*

❷ **Argyle (Six-Gun) Battery, with View:** These front-loading, cast-iron cannons are from the Napoleonic era, around 1800, when the castle was still a force to be reckoned with.

From here, look north across the valley to the grid of the New Town. The valley (directly below) sits where the Nor' Loch once was; this lake was drained and filled in when the New Town was built in the late 1700s, its swamps replaced with gardens. Later the land provided sites for the Greek-temple-esque Scottish National Gallery (above the train line tunnels), Waverley Station, and the tall, lacy Sir Walter Scott Memorial. Looking farther north, you can make out the port town of Leith (facing the island of Inchkeith), the Firth of Forth, and—in the far, far distance (to the extreme right)—the cone-like mountain of North Berwick Law, a former volcano.

Now look down. The sheer north precipice looks impregnable. But on the night of March 14, 1314, 30 armed men silently scaled this rock face. They were loyal to Robert the Bruce and determined to recapture the castle, which had fallen into English hands. They caught the English by surprise, took the castle, and—three months later—Bruce defeated the English at the Battle of Bannockburn.

Looking back at the gate you just entered, the curved stairway to the right known as Lang Stairs leads steeply up to St. Margaret's Chapel and Crown Square—where we'll end up eventually. But we'll take a more gradual approach.

• *A little farther along, to the right of the Redcoat Café, is the...*

❸ **One O'Clock Gun:** Crowds gather for the 13:00 gun blast (which comes with a little military ceremony), a tradition that gives ships in the bay something to set their navigational devices by. Before the gun, sailors set their clocks with help from the Nelson Monument—that's the tall pillar in the distance on Calton Hill. The monument has a "time ball" affixed to the cross on top, which drops precisely at the top of the hour. But on foggy days, ships couldn't see the ball, so the cannon shot was instituted instead (1861). The tradition stuck, every day at 13:00. (Locals joke that the frugal Scots don't fire it at high noon, as that would cost 11 extra rounds a day.) For more information, there's a small exhibit just down the stairs.

• *Continue uphill, winding to the left and passing through* **Foog's Gate.** *At the very top of the hill, climb up the stairs on your left to reach...*

❹ St. Margaret's Chapel: This tiny stone chapel is Edinburgh's oldest building (around 1120) and sits atop its highest point (440

feet). It represents the birth of the city.

In 1057, Malcolm III murdered King Macbeth (of Shakespeare fame) and assumed the Scottish throne. Later, he married Princess Margaret, and the family settled atop this hill. Their marriage united Malcolm's Highland Scots with

Margaret's Lowland Anglo-Saxons—the cultural mix that would define Edinburgh.

Step inside the tiny, unadorned church—a testament to Margaret's reputed piety. The elegant-yet-simple stone structure is Romanesque. The nave is wonderfully simple, with classic Norman zigzags decorating the round arch that separates the tiny nave from the sacristy. You'll see a facsimile of St. Margaret's 11th-century gospel book. The small (19th-century Victorian) stained-glass windows feature St. Margaret herself, St. Columba, St. Ninian (who brought Christianity to Scotland in AD 397), St. Andrew (Scotland's patron saint), and William Wallace (the defender of Scotland). These days, the place is popular for weddings. (As it seats only 20, it's particularly popular with parents funding the festivities.)

Margaret died at the castle in 1093, and her son King David I built this chapel in her honor (she was sainted in 1250). David expanded the castle and also founded Holyrood Abbey, across town. These two structures were soon linked by a Royal Mile of buildings, and Edinburgh was born.

Mons Meg, in front of the church, is a huge and once-upon-a-time frightening 15th-century siege cannon that fired 330-pound stones nearly

EDINBURGH

two miles. Look at the huge granite cannon balls and imagine. It was a gift from Philip the Good, duke of Burgundy, to his great-niece's husband King James II of Scotland.

Nearby, belly up to the banister and look down to find the **Dog Cemetery,** a tiny patch of grass with a sweet little line of doggie tombstones, marking the graves of soldiers' faithful canines-at-arms.

• *Continue on, curving downhill into...*

❺ **Crown Square:** This courtyard is the center of today's Royal Castle complex. Get oriented. You're surrounded by the crown jewels, the Royal Palace (with its Great Hall), and the Scottish National War Memorial.

The castle has evolved over the centuries, and Crown Square is relatively "new." After the time of Malcolm and Margaret, the castle was greatly expanded by David II (1324-1371), complete with tall towers, a Great Hall, dungeon, cellars, and so on. This served as the grand royal residence for two centuries. Then, in 1571-1573, the Protestant citizens of Edinburgh laid siege to the castle and its Catholic/monarchist holdouts, eventually blasting an earlier castle to smithereens. The palace was rebuilt nearby—around what is today's Crown Square.

• *We'll tour the buildings around Crown Square. First up: the crown jewels. There are two entrances—both usually with a line. The one on Crown Square, only open in peak season, deposits you straight into the room with the crown jewels but usually comes with a longer line. The other entry, around the left side (near the WCs), takes you—at a shuffle—to the jewels the long way, through the interesting, Disney-esque "Honours of Scotland" exhibit, which tells the story of the crown jewels and how they survived the harrowing centuries, but lacks any actual artifacts.*

❻ **Scottish Crown Jewels:** For centuries, Scotland's monarchs were crowned in elaborate rituals involving three wondrous objects: a jewel-studded crown, scepter, and sword. These objects—along with the ceremonial Stone of Scone (pronounced "skoon")—are known as the "Honours of Scotland." Scotland's crown jewels may not be as impressive as England's, but locals treasure them as a symbol of Scottish nationalism. They're also older than England's; while Oliver Cromwell destroyed England's jewels, the Scots managed to hide theirs.

History of the Jewels: The Honours of Scotland exhibit that leads up to the Crown Room traces the evolution of the jewels, the ceremony, and the often-turbulent journey of this precious regalia. Here's the short version:

In 1306, Robert the Bruce was crowned with a "circlet of gold" in a ceremony at Scone—a town 40 miles north of Edinburgh, which Scotland's earliest kings had claimed as their capital. Around 1500, King James IV added two new items to the coronation ceremony—a scepter (a gift from the pope) and a huge sword (a gift from another pope). In 1540, James V had the

original crown augmented by an Edinburgh goldsmith, giving it the imperial-crown shape it has today.

These Honours were used to crown every monarch: nine-month-old Mary, Queen of Scots (she cried); her one-year-old son James VI (future king of England); and Charles I and II. But the days of divine-right rulers were numbered.

In 1649, the parliament had Charles I (king of both England and Scotland) beheaded. Soon Cromwell's rabid English antiroyalists were marching on Edinburgh. Quick! Legend says two women scooped up the crown and sword, hid them in their skirts, and buried them in a church far to the northeast until the coast was clear.

When the monarchy was restored, the regalia were used to crown Scotland's last king, Charles II (1660). Then, in 1707, the Treaty of Union with England ended Scotland's independence. The Honours came out for a ceremony to bless the treaty, and were then locked away in a strongbox in the castle. There they lay for over a century, until Sir Walter Scott—the writer and great champion of Scottish tradition—forced a detailed search of the castle in 1818. The box was found...and there the Honours were, perfectly preserved. Within a few years, they were put on display, as they have been ever since.

The crown's most recent official appearance was in 1999, when it was taken across town to the grand opening of the reinstated parliament, marking a new chapter in the Scottish nation. As it represents the monarchy, the crown is present whenever a new session of parliament opens. (And if Scotland ever secedes, you can be sure that crown will be in the front row.)

The Honours: Finally, you enter the Crown Room to see the regalia itself. The four-foot steel **sword** was made in Italy under orders of Pope Julius II (the man who also commissioned Michelangelo's Sistine Chapel and St. Peter's Basilica). The **scepter** is made of silver, covered with gold, and topped with a rock crystal and a pearl.

William Wallace (c. 1270-1305)

In 1286, Scotland's king died without an heir, plunging the prosperous country into a generation of chaos. As Scottish nobles bickered over naming a successor, the English King Edward I—nicknamed "Longshanks" because of his long legs—invaded and assumed power (1296). He placed a figurehead on the throne, forced Scottish nobles to sign a pledge of allegiance to England (the "Ragman's Roll"), moved the British parliament north to York, and took the highly symbolic Stone of Scone to London, where it would remain for centuries.

WILLIAM WALLACE.

A year later, the Scots rose up against Edward, led by William Wallace (popularized in the film *Braveheart*). A mix of history and legend portrays Wallace as the son of a poor-but-knightly family that refused to sign the Ragman's Roll. Exceptionally tall and strong, he learned Latin and French from two uncles, who were priests. In his teenage years, his father and older brother were killed by the English. Later, he killed an English sheriff to avenge the death of his wife, Marion. Wallace's rage inspired his fellow Scots to revolt.

In the summer of 1297, Wallace and his guerrillas scored a series of stunning victories over the English. On September 11, a well-equipped English army of 10,000 soldiers and 300 horsemen began crossing Stirling Bridge. Wallace's men attacked, and in the chaos, the bridge collapsed, splitting the English ranks in two. The ragtag Scots drove the confused English into the river. The Battle of Stirling Bridge was a rout, and Wallace was knighted and appointed guardian of Scotland.

All through the winter, King Edward's men chased Wallace, continually frustrated by the Scots' hit-and-run tactics. Finally, at the Battle of Falkirk (1298), they drew Wallace's men out onto the open battlefield. The English with their horses and archers easily destroyed the spear-carrying Scots. Wallace resigned in disgrace and went on the lam, while his successors negotiated truces with the English, finally surrendering unconditionally in 1304. Wallace alone held out.

In 1305, the English tracked him down and took him to London, where he was convicted of treason and mocked with a crown of oak leaves as the "king of outlaws." On August 23, they stripped him naked and dragged him to the execution site. There he was strangled to near death, castrated, and dismembered. His head was stuck on a spike atop London Bridge, while his body parts were sent on tour to spook would-be rebels. But Wallace's martyrdom only served to inspire his countrymen, and the torch of independence was picked up by Robert the Bruce (see page 752).

The gem- and pearl-encrusted **crown** has an imperial arch topped with a cross. Legend says the band of gold in the center is the original crown that once adorned the head of Robert the Bruce.

The **Stone of Scone** (a.k.a. the "Stone of Destiny") sits plain and strong next to the jewels. It's a rough-hewn gray slab of sandstone, about 26 by 17 by 10 inches. As far back as the ninth century, Scotland's kings were crowned atop this stone, when it stood at the medieval capital of Scone. But in 1296, the invading army of Edward I of England carried the stone off to Westminster Abbey. For the next seven centuries, English (and subsequently British) kings and queens were crowned sitting on a coronation chair with the Stone of Scone tucked in a compartment underneath.

In 1950, four Scottish students broke into Westminster Abbey on Christmas Day and smuggled the stone back to Scotland in an act of foolhardy patriotism. But what could they do with it? After three months, they abandoned the stone, draped in Scotland's national flag. It was returned to Westminster Abbey, where (in 1953) Queen Elizabeth II was crowned atop it. In 1996, in recognition of increased Scottish autonomy, Elizabeth agreed to let the stone go home, on one condition: that it be returned to Westminster Abbey for all British coronations. Assuming Scotland remains in the United Kingdom, one day, the next monarch of the UK—Prince Charles is first in line—will sit atop this stone, re-enacting a coronation ritual that dates back a thousand years.

· *Exit the crown jewel display, heading down the stairs. But just before exiting into the courtyard, turn left through a door that leads into the...*

❼ Royal Apartments: Scottish royalty lived in the Royal Palace only when safety or protocol required it (they preferred the Palace of Holyroodhouse at the bottom of the Royal Mile). Here you can see several historic but unimpressive rooms. The first one, labeled **Queen Mary's Chamber,** is where Mary, Queen of Scots (1542-1587) gave birth to James VI of Scotland, who

later became King James I of England. Nearby **Laich Hall** (Lower Hall) was the dining room of the royal family.

· *Head back outside, across the square, to find the entry on the left to the...*

❽ Great Hall: Built by James IV to host the castle's official banquets and meetings, the Great Hall is still used for such purposes today. Most of the interior—its fireplace, carved walls, pikes, and armor—is Victorian. But the well-constructed wood ceiling is original. This hammer-beam roof (constructed like the

EDINBURGH

hull of a ship) is self-supporting. The complex system of braces and arches distributes the weight of the roof outward to the walls, so there's no need for supporting pillars or long cross beams. Before leaving, look for the tiny iron-barred window above the fireplace, on the right. This allowed the king to spy on his subjects while they partied.

• Across the Crown Square courtyard is the...

❾ **Scottish National War Memorial:** This commemorates the 149,000 Scottish soldiers lost in World War I, the 58,000 who died in World War II, and the nearly 800 (and counting) lost in British battles since. Before entering, notice how the Art Deco facade (built in the 1920s with the historic stones of a church that once stood on this spot) fits perfectly with the surrounding buildings.

Inside, the main memorial is directly ahead, but you circulate counterclockwise. Since this structure was built after World War I, the scenes in the windows are from that war. Memorials honor regiments from each of the four branches of the British military with maroon remembrance books listing all the names of the fallen.

The main shrine, featuring a green Italian-marble memorial that contains the original WWI rolls of honor, sits on an exposed chunk of the castle rock. Above you, the archangel Michael is busy slaying a dragon. The bronze frieze accurately shows the attire of various wings of Scotland's military. The stained glass starts with Cain and Abel on the left and finishes with a celebration of peace on the right. To appreciate how important this place is, consider that Scottish soldiers died at twice the rate per capita of other British soldiers in World War I.

• There are several other exhibits (including "Prisons of War," covering the lives of POWs held in the castle in 1781), memorials, and regimental museums in the castle. If you have seen enough, the Lang Stairs near St. Margaret's Chapel are a shortcut leading down to the Argyle Battery and the exit.

But there is one more important stop—the **National War Museum.** Backtrack down the hill toward the Redcoat Café (and the One O'Clock

Gun). Just before the café head downhill to the left to the museum courtyard. (If you were in a horse-drawn carriage, you'd be thankful for the courtyard's cobblestone design—rough stones in the middle so your horse could get a grip, and smooth stones on the outside so your ride was even.) The statue in front of the museum is **Field Marshall Sir Douglas Haig**—*the Scotsman who commanded the British Army through the WWI trench warfare of the Battle of the Somme and in Flanders Fields.*

⑩ National War Museum Scotland: This thoughtful museum covers four centuries of Scottish military history. Instead of the usual musty, dusty displays of endless armor, there's a compelling mix of videos, uniforms, weapons, medals, mementos, and eloquent excerpts from soldiers' letters. Your castle audioguide includes coverage of this museum, and the introductory video in the theater is worth watching.

Here you'll learn the story of how the fierce and courageous Scottish warrior changed from being a symbol of resistance against Britain to being a champion of that same empire. Along the way, these military men received many decorations for valor and did more than their share of dying in battle. But even when fighting alongside—rather than against—England, Scottish regiments still promoted their romantic, kilted-warrior image.

Queen Victoria fueled this ideal throughout the 19th century. She was infatuated with the Scottish Highlands and the culture's untamed, rustic mystique. Highland soldiers, especially officers, went to great personal expense to sport all their elaborate regalia, and the kilted men fought best to the tune of their beloved bagpipes. For centuries the stirring drone of bagpipes accompanied Highland soldiers into battle—raising their spirits and announcing to the enemy that they were about to meet a fierce and mighty foe.

This museum shows the human side of war as well as the cleverness of government-sponsored ad campaigns that kept the lads enlisting. Two centuries of recruiting posters make the same pitch that still works today: a hefty signing bonus, steady pay, and job security with the promise of a manly and adventurous life—all spiked with a mix of pride and patriotism.

Leaving the castle complex, you're surrounded by cannons that no longer fire, stony walls that tell an amazing story, dramatic views of this grand city, and the clatter of tourists (rather than soldiers) on cobbles. Consider for a moment all the bloody history

EDINBURGH

Robert the Bruce (1274-1329)

In 1314, Robert the Bruce's men attacked Edinburgh's Royal Castle, recapturing it from the English. It was just one of many intense battles between the oppressive English and the plucky Scots during the Wars of Independence.

In this era, Scotland had to overcome not only its English foes but also its own divisiveness—and no one was more divided than Robert the Bruce. As earl of Carrick, he was born with blood ties to England and a long-standing family claim to the Scottish throne.

When England's King Edward I ("Longshanks") conquered Scotland in 1296, the Bruce family welcomed it, hoping Edward would defeat their rivals and put Bruce's father on the throne. They dutifully signed the "Ragman's Roll" of allegiance—and then Edward chose someone else as king.

Twentysomething Robert the Bruce (the "the" comes from his original family name of "de Bruce") then joined William Wallace's revolt against the English. As legend has it, he was the one who knighted Wallace after the victory at Stirling Bridge. When Wallace fell from favor, Bruce became a guardian of Scotland (caretaker ruler in the absence of a king) and continued fighting the English. But when Edward's armies again got the upper hand in 1302, Robert—along with Scotland's other nobles—diplomatically surrendered and again pledged loyalty.

In 1306, Robert the Bruce murdered his chief rival and boldly claimed to be king of Scotland. Few nobles supported him. Edward crushed the revolt and kidnapped Bruce's wife, the Church excommunicated him, and Bruce went into hiding on a distant North Sea island. He was now the king of nothing. Legend says he gained inspiration by watching a spider patiently build its web.

The following year, Bruce returned to Scotland and wove alliances with both nobles and the Church, slowly gaining acceptance as Scotland's king by a populace chafing under English rule. On June 24, 1314, he decisively defeated the English (now led by Edward's weak son, Edward II) at the Battle of Bannockburn. After a generation of turmoil (1286-1314), England was finally driven from Scotland, and the country was united under Robert I, king of Scotland.

As king, Robert the Bruce's priority was to stabilize the monarchy and establish clear lines of succession. His descendants would rule Scotland for the next 400 years, and even today, Bruce blood runs through the veins of Queen Elizabeth II, Prince Charles, Princes William and Harry, and wee George, Charlotte, Louis, and Archie.

and valiant struggles, along with British power and Scottish pride, that have shaped the city over which you are perched.

SIGHTS ON AND NEAR THE ROYAL MILE
▲Camera Obscura

A big deal when it was built in 1853, this observatory topped with a mirror reflected images onto a disc before the wide eyes of people

who had never seen a photograph or a captured image. Today, you can climb 100 steps for an entertaining 20-minute demonstration (3/hour). At the top, enjoy the best view anywhere of the Royal Mile. This sight is a goofy and entertaining break from all the heavy history and culture of the city's standard sights—it's just flat-out fun. You'll work your way down through five floors of illusions, holograms, and entertaining gags.

Cost and Hours: £16, book online one day in advance in peak season to skip the ticket line; open daily 9:00-21:00, Sat until 22:00, shorter hours off-season; tel. 0131/226-3709, www.camera-obscura.co.uk.

▲The Scotch Whisky Experience

This attraction seems designed to distill money out of your pocket. The 50-minute experience consists of a "Malt Disney"

whisky-barrel ride through the production process followed by an explanation and movie about Scotland's five main whisky regions. Though gimmicky, it does succeed in providing an entertaining yet informative orientation to the creation of Scottish firewater (things get pretty psychedelic when you hit the yeast stage). Your ticket also includes sampling a wee dram and the chance to stand amid the world's largest Scotch whisky collection (almost 3,500 bottles). At the end, you'll find yourself in the bar, with a fascinating wall of unusually shaped whisky bottles. Serious connoisseurs should stick with the more substantial shops in town, but this place can be worthwhile for beginners.

Cost and Hours: £16 "silver tour" includes one sample, £28 "gold tour" includes five samples—one from each main region, generally daily 10:00-18:30, last "silver tour" at 17:00, tel. 0131/220-0441, www.scotchwhiskyexperience.co.uk.

▲▲Gladstone's Land

This is a typical 16th- to 17th-century merchant's "land," or tenement building. These multistory structures—in which merchants ran their shops on the ground floor and lived upstairs— were typical of the time (the word "tenement" didn't have the slum connotation then that it has today). At six stories, this one was still just half the height of the tallest "skyscrapers."

Gladstone's Land comes complete with an almost-lived-in, furnished interior and 400-year-old Renaissance painted ceiling. You'll explore five rooms, each with a docent posted to answer your questions. Keep this place in mind as you stroll the rest of the Mile, imagining other houses as if they still looked like this on the inside. (For a comparison of life in the Old Town versus the New Town, also visit the Georgian House, described later.)

Cost and Hours: £7, daily 11:00-16:30, tel. 0131/226-5856, www.nts.org.uk/Visit/Gladstones-Land.

▲Writers' Museum at Lady Stair's House

This aristocrat's house, built in 1622, is filled with well-described manuscripts and knickknacks of Scotland's three greatest literary figures: Robert Burns, Robert Louis Stevenson, and Sir Walter Scott. If you'd like to see Scott's pipe and Burns' snuffboxes, you'll love this little museum. You'll wind up steep staircases through a maze of rooms as you peruse first editions and keepsakes of these celebrated writers. Edinburgh's high society gathered in homes like this in the 1780s to hear the great poet Robbie Burns read his work—it's meant to be read aloud rather than to oneself.

Cost and Hours: Free, daily 10:00-17:00, tel. 0131/529-4901, www.edinburghmuseums.org.uk.

Museum on the Mound

Located in the basement of the grand Bank of Scotland building, this exhibit tells the story of the bank, which was founded in 1695 (making it only a year younger than the Bank of England) and claims to be the longest operating bank in the world. Featuring lots of artifacts and displays on cash production, safe technology, and bank robberies, this museum (with a case holding £1 million in cash) makes banking almost interesting. It's worth popping in if you have extra time or find the subject appealing.

Cost and Hours: Free, Tue-Fri 10:00-17:00, Sat from 13:00, closed Sun-Mon, down Bank Street from the Royal Mile— follow the street around to the left and enter through the gate, tel. 0131/243-5464, www.museumonthemound.com.

Whisky 101

Whisky is high on the experience list of most visitors to Scotland—even for teetotalers. Whether at a distillery, a shop, or a pub, be sure to try a few drams. (From the Gaelic word for "drink," a dram isn't necessarily a fixed amount—it's simply a small slug.) While touring a distillery is a ▲▲▲ Scottish experience, many fine whisky shops (including Cadenhead's in Edinburgh) offer guided tastings and a chance to have a small bottle filled from the cask of your choice.

Types of Whisky

Scotch whiskies come in two broad types: **"single malt,"** meaning that the bottle comes from a single batch made by a single distiller; and **"blends,"** which master blenders mix and match from various whiskies into a perfect punch of booze. While single malts get the most attention, blended whiskies represent 90 percent of all whisky sales. They tend to be light and mild—making them an easier way to tiptoe into the whisky scene.

There are more than 100 distilleries in Scotland, each one proud of its unique qualities. The **Lowlands,** around Edinburgh, produce light and refreshing whiskies—more likely to be taken as an aperitif. Whiskies from the **Highlands** and **Islands** range from floral and sweet to smoky and robust. **Speyside,** southeast of Inverness, is home to half of all Scottish distilleries. Mellow and fruity, Speyside whiskies can be the most accessible for beginners. The **Isle of Islay** is just the opposite, specializing in the peatiest, smokiest whiskies—not for novices. Only a few producers remain to distill the smoky and pungent **Campbeltown** whiskies in the southwest Highlands, near Islay.

Tasting Whisky

Tasting whisky is like tasting wine; you'll use all your senses. First, swirl the whisky in the glass and observe its color and "legs"—the trail left by the liquid as it runs back down the side of the glass (quick, thin legs indicate light, young whisky; slow, thick legs mean it's heavier and older one). Then take a deep sniff—do you smell smoke and peat? And finally, taste it (sip!). Adding a few drops of water is said to "open up the taste"—look for a little glass of water with a dropper standing by, and try tasting your whisky before and after.

A whisky's flavor is most influenced by three things: whether the malt is peat-smoked; the shape of the stills; and the composition of the casks. Even local climate can play a role; some island distilleries tout the salty notes of their whiskies, as the sea air permeates their casks.

▲▲St. Giles' Cathedral

This is Scotland's most important church. Its ornate spire—the Scottish crown steeple from 1495—is a proud part of Edinburgh's skyline. The fascinating interior contains nearly 200 memorials honoring distinguished Scots through the ages.

Cost and Hours: Free, but consider the suggested £5 donation as a fair admission cost; Mon-Fri 9:00-19:00, Sat until 17:00; Nov-March Mon-Sat 9:00-17:00; Sun 13:00-17:00 year-round; info sheet-£1, guidebook-£6, tel. 0131/226-0677, www.stgilescathedral.org.uk.

Concerts: St. Giles busy concert schedule includes free organ recitals and visiting choirs (frequent events at 13:30 and concerts Sun at 18:00; also sometimes Wed, Thu, or Fri at 20:00; see schedule or ask for *Music at St. Giles* pamphlet at welcome desk or gift shop).

⊘ Self-Guided Tour: Today's facade is 19th-century Neo-Gothic, but most of what you'll see inside is from the 14th and 15th centuries. Engage the cathedral guides in conversation; you'll be glad you did.

Just inside the entrance, turn around to see the modern stained-glass **❶ Robert Burns window,** which celebrates Scotland's favorite poet (see sidebar, later). It was made in 1985 by the Icelandic artist Leifur Breidfjord. The green of the lower level symbolizes the natural world—God's creation. The middle zone with the circle shows the brotherhood of man—Burns was a great internationalist. The top is a rosy red sunburst of creativity, reminding Scots of Burns' famous line, "My love is like a red, red rose"—part of a song near and dear to every Scottish heart.

To the right of the Burns window is a fine **❷ Pre-Raphaelite window.** Like most in the church, it's a memorial to an important patron (in this case, John Marshall). From here stretches a great swath of war memorials.

As you walk along the north wall, find **❸ John Knox's statue** (standing like a six-foot-tall bronze chess piece). Look into his eyes for 10 seconds from 10 inches away, and think of the Reformation struggles of the 16th century. Knox, the great

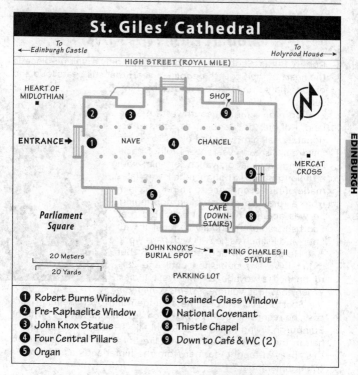

St. Giles' Cathedral

To ←Edinburgh Castle

To Holyrood House→

HIGH STREET (ROYAL MILE)

HEART OF MIDLOTHIAN

SHOP

❷ ❸ ❾

ENTRANCE→ ❶ NAVE ❹ CHANCEL

MERCAT CROSS

❾

❻ ❼

Parliament Square ❺ CAFÉ (DOWN-STAIRS) ❽

JOHN KNOX'S BURIAL SPOT ■→■ ■KING CHARLES II STATUE

20 Meters

20 Yards

PARKING LOT

❶ Robert Burns Window
❷ Pre-Raphaelite Window
❸ John Knox Statue
❹ Four Central Pillars
❺ Organ

❻ Stained-Glass Window
❼ National Covenant
❽ Thistle Chapel
❾ Down to Café & WC (2)

EDINBURGH

religious reformer and founder of austere Scottish Presbyterianism, first preached here in 1559. His insistence that every person should be able to personally read the word of God—notice that he's pointing to a book—gave Scotland an educational system 300 years ahead of the rest of Europe (for more on Knox, see "The Scottish Reformation" on page 898). Thanks partly to Knox, it was Scottish minds that led the way in math, science, medicine, and engineering. Voltaire called Scotland "the intellectual capital of Europe."

Knox preached Calvinism. Consider that the Dutch and the Scots both embraced this creed of hard work, frugality, and strict ethics. This helps explain why the Scots are so different from the English (and why the Dutch and the Scots—both famous for their thriftiness and industriousness—are so much alike).

The oldest parts of the cathedral—the ❹ **four massive central**

Robert Burns (1759-1796)

Robert Burns, Scotland's national poet, holds a unique place in the heart of the Scottish people—a heart that still beats loud and proud, thanks, in large part, to Burns himself.

Born on a farm in southwestern Scotland, Robbie (or "Rabbie," as Scots affectionately call him) was the oldest of seven children. His early years were full of back-breaking farm labor, which left him with a lifelong stoop. Though much was later made of his ascendance to literary acclaim from a rural, poverty-stricken upbringing, he was actually quite well educated (per Scottish tradition), equally as familiar with Latin and French as he was with hard work.

He started writing poetry at 15, but didn't have any published until age 28—to finance a voyage to the West Indies. When that first volume, *Poems, Chiefly in the Scottish Dialect*, became a sudden and overwhelming success, he reconsidered his emigration. Instead, he left his farm for Edinburgh, living just off the Royal Mile. He spent a year and a half in the city, schmoozing with literary elites, who celebrated this "heaven-taught" farmer from the hinterlands as Scotland's "ploughman poet."

His poetry, written primarily in the Scots dialect, drew on his substantial familiarity with both Scottish tradition and Western literature. By using the language of the common man to create works of beauty and sophistication, he found himself wildly popular among both rural folk and high society. Hearty poems such as "To a Mouse," "To a Louse," and "The Holy Fair" exalted the virtues of physical labor, romantic love, friendship, natural beauty, and drink—all of which he also pursued with vigor in real life. This further endeared him to most Scots, though considerably less so to Church fathers, who were particularly displeased with his love

pillars—are Norman and date from the 12th century. They supported a mostly wooden superstructure that was lost when an invading English force burned it in 1385. The Scots rebuilt it bigger and better than ever, and in 1495 its famous crown spire was completed.

During the Reformation—when Knox preached here (1559-1572)—the place was simplified and whitewashed. Before this, when the emphasis was on holy services provided by priests, there were lots of little niches. With the new focus on sermons rather than rituals, the grand pulpit took center stage.

Knox preached against anything that separated you from God, including stained glass (considered the poor man's Bible, as life (of Burns' dozen children, nine were by his eventual wife, the others by various servants and barmaids).

After achieving fame and wealth, Burns never lost touch with the concerns of the Scottish people, championing such radical ideas as social equality and economic justice. Burns bravely and loudly supported the French and American revolutions, which inspired one of his most beloved poems, "A Man's a Man for A' That," and even an ode to George Washington—all while other writers were being shipped off to Australia for similar beliefs. While his social causes cost him some aristocratic friends, it cemented his popularity among the masses, and not just within Scotland (he became, and remains, especially beloved in Russia).

Intent on preserving Scotland's rich musical and lyrical traditions, Burns traveled the countryside collecting traditional Scottish ballads. If it weren't for Burns, we'd have to come up with a different song to sing on New Year's Eve—he's the one who found, reworked, and popularized "Auld Lang Syne." His championing of Scottish culture came at a critical time: England had recently and finally crushed Scotland's last hopes of independence, and the Highland clan system was nearing its end. Burns lent the Scots dialect a new prestige, and the scrappy Scottish people a reinvigorated identity. (The official Burns website, www.robertburns. org, features a full collection of his works.)

Burns died at 37 of a heart condition likely exacerbated by hard labor (all the carousing probably hadn't helped, either). By that time, his fortune was largely spent, but his celebrity was going strong—around 10,000 people attended his burial. Even the Church eventually overcame its disapproval, installing a window in his honor at St. Giles' Cathedral. In 2009, his nation voted Burns "Greatest Ever Scot" in a TV poll. And every January 25 (the poet's birthday), on Burns Night, Scots gather to recite his songs and poems, tuck into some haggis ("chieftain o' the puddin' race," according to Burns), and raise their whisky to friendship, and to Scotland.

illiterate Christians could learn from its pictures). Knox had the church's fancy medieval glass windows replaced with clear glass, but 19th-century Victorians took them out and installed the brilliantly colored ones you see today.

Cross over to the ❺ **organ** (1992, Austrian-built, one of Europe's finest) and take in its sheer might.

Immediately to the right of the organ is a tiny chapel for silence and prayer. The dramatic ❻ **stained-glass window** above shows the commotion that surrounded Knox when he preached. The bearded, fiery-eyed Knox had a huge impact on this community. Notice how there were no pews back then. The church was so packed, people even looked through clear windows from across the street. With his hand on the holy book, Knox seems to conduct divine electricity to the Scottish faithful.

In the corner to the far left of the organ, find a copy of the ❼ **National Covenant** (behind small curtains). It was signed in blood in 1638 by Scottish heroes who refused to compromise their religion for the king's. Most who signed were martyred (their monument is nearby in Grassmarket). You can see the original National Covenant in the Edinburgh Museum, described later.

Head toward the east (back) end of the church, and turn right to see the Neo-Gothic ❽ **Thistle Chapel** (volunteer guide is a wealth of information). The interior is filled with intricate wood carving. Built in two years (1910-1911), entirely with Scottish materials and labor, it is the private chapel of the Order of the Thistle, the only Scottish chivalric order. It's used several times a year for the knights to gather (and, if one dies, to inaugurate a new member). Scotland recognizes its leading citizens by bestowing a membership upon them. The Queen presides over the ritual from her fancy stall, marked by her Scottish coat of arms—a heraldic zoo of symbolism. Are there bagpipes in heaven? Find the tooting stone angel at the top of a window to the left of the altar, and the wooden one to the right of the doorway you came in.

❾ **Downstairs** you'll find handy public WCs and an inviting **$ café**—a good place for paupers to munch prayerfully—quick, quaint, and supporting the church (simple, light lunches, coffee and cakes; Mon-Sat 9:00-17:00, Sun from 11:00, in basement on back side of church, tel. 0131/225-5147).

Old Parliament House

This space housed the Scottish parliament until the Act of Union in 1707. The building now holds the Scottish Supreme Court, so you'll need to go through security as you enter. Peruse the grand hall, with its fine 1639 hammer-beam ceiling and stained glass. The biggest stained-glass window depicts the initiation of the first Scottish High Court in 1532. The building is busy with wigged and robed lawyers hard at work in the old library (peek through the door) or pacing the hall deep in discussion. The basement café is literally their supreme court's restaurant (open to public until 14:30).

Cost and Hours: Free, public welcome Mon-Fri 9:00-16:30, closed Sat-Sun, no photos, enter behind St. Giles' Cathedral at door #11; open-to-the-public trials are just across the street at the High Court—the doorman has the day's docket.

▲The Real Mary King's Close

For an unusual peek at Edinburgh's gritty, plague-ridden past, join a costumed performer on an hour-long trip through an excavated underground street and buildings on the northern slope of the Royal Mile. Tours cover the standard goofy, crowd-pleasing ghost stories, but also focus on authentic and historical insight into a part of town entombed by later construction. Book ahead (online up to the day before, or by phone or in person for a same-day booking).

Cost and Hours: £16.50, book at least one day in advance during peak season; tours leave every 15-30 minutes, daily generally 9:00-21:45, Oct-April until 17:00; these are last tour times, across from St. Giles at 2 Warriston's Close—but enter through door on High Street, tel. 0131/225-0672, www.realmarykingsclose.com.

▲Museum of Childhood

This five-story playground of historical toys and games is rich in nostalgia and history. Each well-signed gallery is as jovial as a Norman Rockwell painting, highlighting the delights and simplicity of childhood. The museum does a fair job of representing culturally relevant oddities, such as ancient Egyptian, Peruvian, and voodoo dolls, and displays early versions of toys it's probably best didn't make the final cut (such as a grim snake-centered precursor to the popular board game Chutes and Ladders).

Cost and Hours: Free, daily 10:00-17:00, 42 High Street.

▲John Knox House

Intriguing for Reformation buffs, this fine medieval house dates back to 1470 and offers a well-explained look at the life of the

great 16th-century reformer. Although most contend he never actually lived here, preservationists called it "Knox's house" to save it from the wrecking ball in the 1840s. Regardless, the place has good information on Knox and his intellectual sparring partner, Mary, Queen of Scots. Imagine the Protestant firebrand John Knox and the devout Catholic Mary sitting face-to-face in old rooms like these, discussing the most intimate matters of their spiritual lives as they decided the course of Scotland's religious future. The sparsely furnished house contains some period furniture, an early 1600s hand-painted ceiling, information on the house and its

Scotland's Literary Greats

Edinburgh was home to Scotland's three greatest literary figures, pictured above: Robert Burns (left), Robert Louis Stevenson (center), and Sir Walter Scott (right).

Robert Burns (1759-1796), known as "Rabbie" in Scotland and quite possibly the most famous and beloved Scot of all time, moved to Edinburgh after achieving overnight celebrity with his first volume of poetry (staying in a house on the spot where Deacon Brodie's Tavern now stands). Even though he wrote in the rough Scots dialect and dared to attack social rank, he was a favorite of Edinburgh's high society, who'd gather in fine homes to hear him recite his works. For more on Burns, see the sidebar, earlier.

One hundred years later, **Robert Louis Stevenson** (1850-1894) also stirred the Scottish soul with his pen. An avid traveler who always packed his notepad, Stevenson created settings that are vivid and filled with wonder. Traveling through Scotland, Europe, and around the world, he distilled his adventures into Romantic classics, including *Kidnapped* and *Treasure Island* (as well as *The Strange Case of Dr. Jekyll and Mr. Hyde*). Stevenson, who was married in San Francisco and spent his last years in the South Pacific, wrote, "Youth is the time to travel—both in mind and in body—to try the manners of different nations." He said, "I travel not to go anywhere...but to simply go." Travel was his inspiration and his success.

Sir Walter Scott (1771-1832) wrote the *Waverley* novels, including *Ivanhoe* and *Rob Roy.* He's considered the father of the

resident John Mossman (goldsmith to Mary, Queen of Scots), and exhibits on printing—an essential tool for early reformers.

Cost and Hours: £6, Mon-Sat 10:00-18:00, closed Sun except in July-Aug, 43 High Street, tel. 0131/556-9579, www.scottishstorytellingcentre.com.

▲People's Story Museum

This engaging exhibit, which occupies the Canongate Tolbooth (built in 1591), traces the working and social lives of ordinary people through the 18th, 19th, and 20th centuries. You'll see tools, products, and objects related to important Edinburgh trades (printing, brewing), a wartime kitchen, and a small theater on the top floor with a video.

Romantic historical novel. Through his writing, he generated a worldwide interest in Scotland, and reawakened his fellow countrymen's pride in their heritage. His novels helped revive interest in Highland culture—the Gaelic language, kilts, songs, legends, myths, the clan system—and created a national identity. An avid patriot, he wrote, "Every Scottish man has a pedigree. It is a national prerogative, as unalienable as his pride and his poverty." Scott is so revered in Edinburgh that his towering Neo-Gothic monument dominates the city center. With his favorite hound by his side, Sir Walter Scott overlooks the city that he inspired, and that inspired him.

The best way to learn about and experience these literary greats is to visit the Writers' Museum at Lady Stair's House (see page 754) and to take Edinburgh's Literary Pub Tour (see page 792).

While just three writers dominate your Edinburgh sightseeing, consider also the other great writers with Edinburgh connections: J. K. Rowling (who captures the "Gothic" spirit of Edinburgh with her Harry Potter series); current resident Ian Rankin (with his "tartan noir" novels); J. M. Barrie (who attended University of Edinburgh and later created Peter Pan); Sir Arthur Conan Doyle (who was born in Edinburgh, went to medical school here, and is best known for inventing Sherlock Holmes); and James Boswell (who lived 50 yards away from the Writers' Museum, in James Court, and is revered for his biography of Samuel Johnson).

Cost and Hours: Free, daily 10:00-17:00, 163 Canongate, tel. 0131/529-4057, www.edinburghmuseums.org.uk.

▲Museum of Edinburgh

Another old house full of old stuff, this one is worth a stop for a look at its early Edinburgh history (and its handy ground-floor WC). Be sure to see the original copy of the National Covenant—written in 1638 on animal skin. Scottish leaders signed this, refusing to adopt the king's religion—and were killed because of it. Exploring the rest of the collection, keep an eye out for Robert Louis Stevenson's antique golf ball, James Craig's architectural plans for the Georgian New Town, an interactive kids' area with dress-up clothes, a sprawling top-floor exhibit on Edinburgh-born Field Marshall Sir David Haig (who led the British Western Front efforts in World War I and later became Earl Haig), and locally made glass and ceramics.

Cost and Hours: Free, daily 10:00-17:00, 142 Canongate, tel. 0131/529-4143, www.edinburghmuseums.org.uk.

Nearby: Next to the museum is the entry to **Bakehouse**

Close, a well-preserved 18th-century alleyway. It's worth a peek (and recognizable to fans of the *Outlander* TV series—the exterior of Jamie's print shop was filmed here).

▲▲Scottish Parliament Building

Scotland's parliament originated in 1293 and was dissolved when Scotland united with England in 1707. But after the Scottish elec-

torate and the British parliament gave their consent, in 1997 it was decided that there should again be "a Scottish parliament guided by justice, wisdom, integrity, and compassion." Formally reconvened by Queen Elizabeth in 1999 (note that, while she's "II" in England, she's only the first "QE" for the people of Scot-

land), the Scottish parliament now enjoys self-rule in many areas (except for matters of defense, foreign policy, immigration, and taxation). The current government, run by the Scottish Nationalist Party (SNP), is pushing for even more independence.

The innovative building, opened in 2004, brought together all the functions of the fledgling parliament in one complex. It's a people-oriented structure conceived by Catalan architect Enric Miralles. Signs are written in both English and Gaelic (the Scots' Celtic tongue).

For a peek at the building and a lesson in how the Scottish parliament works, drop in, pass through security, and find the visi-

tors' desk. You're welcome in the public parts of the building, including a small ground-floor exhibit on the parliament's history and function and, up the stairs, a viewing gallery overlooking the impressive Debating Chambers.

Cost and Hours: Free; Mon-Sat 10:00-17:00, Tue-Thu 9:00-18:00 when parliament

is in session (Sept-June), closed Sun year-round. For a complete list of recess dates or to book tickets for debates, check their website or call their visitor services line, tel. 0131/348-5200, www.parliament.scot.

Tours: Free worthwhile hour-long tours covering history, architecture, parliamentary processes, and other topics are offered by proud locals. Tours generally run throughout the day Mon and Fri-Sat in session (Sept-June) and Mon-Sat in recess (July-Aug). While you can try dropping in, these tours can book up—it's best to book ahead online or over the phone.

Seeing Parliament in Session: The public can witness the Scottish parliament's hugely popular debates (usually Tue-Thu 14:00-18:00, but hours can vary). Book ahead online no more than seven days in advance, over the phone, or at the info desk. You're not required to stay the whole session.

You can also watch parliamentary committees in session (usually Tue-Thu mornings). Topics are published the Friday before (see business bulletin on website), and you must book ahead just as you would for debates.

On Thursdays from 11:40 to 12:45 the First Minister is on the hot seat and has to field questions from members across all parties (reserve ahead for this popular session over the phone a week in advance; spots book up quickly—call at 9:00 sharp on Thu for the following week). If you don't get tickets over the phone, show up at 10:00 and ask if you can get in—they sometimes have standby tickets.

▲▲Palace of Holyroodhouse

Built on the site of the abbey/monastery founded in 1128 by King David I, this palace was the true home, birthplace, and coronation spot of Scotland's Stu-art kings in their heyday (James IV; Mary, Queen of Scots; and Charles I). It's particularly memorable as the site of some dramatic moments from the short reign of Mary, Queen of Scots—includ-ing the murder of her per-  sonal secretary, David Rizzio, by agents of her jealous husband. Today, it's one of Queen Elizabeth II's official residences. She usually manages her Scottish affairs here during Holyrood Week, from late June to early July (and generally stays at Balmoral in August). Holyrood is open to the public outside of the Queen's visits. Touring the interior offers a more polished contrast to Edinburgh Castle, and is particularly worth considering if you don't plan to go to Balmoral. The one-way audioguide route leads you through the fine apartments and tells some of the notable stories that played out here.

Cost: £15, includes quality one-hour audioguide; £20 combo-ticket includes the Queen's Gallery; £24.50 combo-ticket adds guided tour of palace gardens (April-Oct only); tickets sold in Queen's Gallery to the right of the castle entrance (see next listing).

Hours: Daily 9:30-18:00, Nov-March until 16:30, last entry 1.5 hours before closing, tel. 0131/556-5100, www.rct.uk. It's still a working palace, so it's closed when the Queen or other VIPs are in residence.

Eating: The **$$$ café** on the palace grounds, to the right of the palace entrance, has an inviting afternoon tea.

Visiting the Palace: The building, rich in history and decor, is filled with elegantly furnished Victorian rooms and a few darker, older rooms with glass cases of historic bits and Scottish pieces that locals find fascinating. Bring the palace to life with the audioguide. The tour route leads you into the grassy inner courtyard, then up to the royal apartments: dining rooms, *Downton Abbey*-style drawing rooms, and royal bedchambers. Along the way, you'll learn the story behind the 96 portraits of Scottish leaders (some real, others imaginary) that line the Great Gallery; why the king never slept in his official "state bed"; why the exiled Comte d'Artois took refuge in the palace; and how the current Queen puts her Scottish subjects at ease when she receives them here. Finally, you'll twist up a tight spiral staircase to the private chambers of Mary, Queen of Scots, where conspirators stormed in and stabbed her secretary 56 times.

After exiting the palace, you're free to stroll through the evocative **ruined abbey** (destroyed by the English during the time of

Mary, Queen of Scots, in the 16th century) and the **palace gardens** (closed Nov-March except some weekends). Some 8,000 guests—including many honored ladies sporting fancy hats—gather here every July when the Queen hosts a magnificent tea party. (She gets help pouring.)

Nearby: Hikers, note that the wonderful trail up Arthur's Seat starts just across the street from the gardens (see page 781 for details). From the palace, face parliament, turn left, and head straight.

▲Queen's Gallery, Palace of Holyroodhouse

Over more than five centuries, the royal family collected a wealth of art treasures. While the Queen keeps most of the royal collection in her many private palaces, she shares an impressive sampling of it in this small museum, with themed exhibits changing about every six months. Though the gallery occupies just a few rooms, its displays can be exquisite.

Cost and Hours: £8 includes excellent audioguide, £20 combo-ticket includes Palace of Holyroodhouse, daily 9:30-18:00, Nov-March until 16:30, last entry one hour before closing, www.rct.uk. Buses #35 and #36 stop outside, saving you a walk to or from Princes Street/North Bridge.

Dynamic Earth

Located about a five-minute walk from the Palace of Holyroodhouse, this immense exhibit tells the story of our planet, filling several underground floors under a vast, white Gore-Tex tent. It's pitched, appropriately, at the base of the Salisbury Crags. The exhibit is designed for younger kids and does the same thing an American science exhibit would do—but with a charming Scottish accent. You'll learn about the Scottish geologists who pioneered the discipline, then step into a "time machine" to watch the years rewind, from cave dwellers to dinosaurs to the Big Bang. After viewing several short films on stars, tectonic plates, ice caps, and worldwide weather (in a "4-D" exhibit), you're free to wander past salty pools and a re-created rain forest.

Cost and Hours: £16, kids-£10, daily 10:00-17:30, July-Aug until 18:00, closed Mon-Tue Nov-Feb, last entry 1.5 hours before closing, on Holyrood Road, between the palace and mountain, tel. 0131/550-7800, www.dynamicearth.co.uk.

SIGHTS SOUTH OF THE ROYAL MILE
▲▲▲National Museum of Scotland

This huge museum has amassed more historic artifacts than every other place I've seen in Scotland combined. It's all wonderfully displayed, with fine descriptions offering a best-anywhere hike through the history of Scotland.

Cost and Hours: Free, daily 10:00-17:00; two long blocks south of St. Giles' Cathedral and the Royal Mile, on Chambers Street off George IV Bridge, tel. 0131/123-6789, www.nms.ac.uk.

Tours: Free one-hour general tours are offered daily at 11:00

and 13:00; themed tours at 15:00 (confirm tour schedule at info desk or on TV screens). The National Museum of Scotland Highlights app provides thin coverage of select items but is free and downloadable using their free Wi-Fi. Scattered interactive kiosks help navigate the stories behind important artifacts and figures.

Services: Bag check is on the ground floor (£1.50).

Eating: A **$$ brasserie** is on the ground floor near the information desks, and a **$ café** with coffee, tea, cakes, and snacks is on the level 3 balcony overlooking the Grand Gallery. On the museum's fifth floor, the dressy and upscale **$$$$ Tower restaurant** serves good food with a castle view (lunch/early-bird special, afternoon tea, three-course dinner specials; daily 10:00-22:00, Fri-Sat until 10:30—use Tower entry if eating after museum closes, reservations recommended, tel. 0131/225-3003, www.tower-restaurant.com). A number of good eating options are within a couple of blocks of the museum (see page 812).

Overview: The museum can be confusing to navigate, so pick up the map when you enter for a color-coded guide to each wing. The place gives you several museums in one, with each gallery rising vertically up several floors: the Natural World galleries (T. Rex skeletons and other animals), the Science and Technology galleries, and a fashion, art, and design exhibit. The World Cultures galleries feature clothing, tools, textiles, and artifacts from ancient Egypt, China, Japan, and the Pacific Islands. With time and interest, these are all worth a look.

We'll focus on yet another wing, the Scotland galleries, which sweep you through Scottish history covering Roman and Viking times, Edinburgh's witch-burning craze and clan massacres, the struggle for Scottish independence, the Industrial Revolution, and right up to Scotland in the 21st century.

◆ Self-Guided Tour: Get oriented on level 1, in the impressive glass-roofed Grand Gallery right above the entrance hall. Just outside the Grand Gallery is the **millennium clock,** a 30-foot high clock with figures that move to a Bach concerto on the hour from 11:00 to 16:00. The clock has four parts (crypt, nave, belfry, and spire) and represents the turmoil of the 20th century, with a pietà at the top.

• *To reach the **Scottish history wing**, exit the Grand Gallery at the far right end, under the clock and past the statue of Scottish inventor James Watt.*

On the way, you'll pass through the science and technology wing. While walking through, on your left, look for **Dolly the sheep**—the world's first cloned mammal—born in

Edinburgh and now stuffed and on display. Continue into Haw-thornden Court (level 1, past the little snack bar), where our tour begins. (It's possible to detour downstairs from here to level -1 for Scotland's prehistoric origins—geologic formation, Celts, Romans, Vikings.)

• *Enter the door marked...*

Kingdom of the Scots (c. 900s-late 1600s): From its very start, Scotland was determined to be free. You're greeted with proud quotes from what's been called the Scottish Declaration of Independence—the Declaration of Arbroath, a defiant letter written to the pope in 1320. As early as the ninth century, Scotland's patron saint, Andrew (see the small statue in the next room), had—according to legend—miraculously intervened to help the Picts and Scots of Scotland remain free by defeating the Angles of England. Andrew's X-shaped cross still decorates the Scottish flag today.

Enter the first room on your right, with imposing swords and other objects related to Scotland's most famous patriots—William Wallace and Robert the Bruce. Bruce's descendants, the Stuarts, went on to rule Scotland for the next 300 years. Eventually, James VI of Scotland (see his baby cradle) came to rule England as well (as King James I of England). In the middle of the room, a massive banner of the royal arms of Britain is adorned with the motto of James VI: "Blessed are the peacemakers."

In the next room, a big guillotine recalls the harsh justice meted out to criminals, witches, and "Covenanters" (17th-century political activists who opposed interference of the Stuart kings in affairs of the Presbyte-rian Church of Scotland). Look for the creepy mask of Covenanter Alexander Peden, who preached il-legally in this disguise. Nearby, also check out the tomb (a copy) of Mary, Queen of Scots, the 16th-century Stuart monarch  who opposed the Presbyterian Church of Scotland. Educated and raised in Renaissance France, Mary brought refinement to the Scottish throne. After she was imprisoned and then executed by Elizabeth I of England in 1587, her supporters rallied each other by invoking her memory. Pendants and coins with her portrait stoked the irrepressible Scottish spirit (see display case next to tomb).

Browse the rest of level 1 to see everyday objects from that age: carved panels, cookware, and sculptures.

• *Backtrack to Hawthornden Court and head up to level 3.*

Scotland Transformed (1700s): You'll see artifacts related to

Bonnie Prince Charlie and the Jacobite rebellions as well as items related to the Treaty of Union document, signed in 1707 by the Scottish parliament. This act voluntarily united Scotland with England under the single parliament of the United Kingdom. For some Scots, this move was an inevitable step in connecting to the wider world, but for others it symbolized the end of Scotland's existence.

Union with England brought stability and investment to Scotland. In this same era, the advances of the Industrial Revolution were making a big impact on Scottish life. Mechanized textile looms (on display) replaced hand craftsmanship. The huge Newcomen steam-engine water pump helped the mining industry to develop sites with tricky drainage. Nearby is a model of a coal mine (or "colliery"); coal-rich Scotland exploited this natural resource to fuel its textile factories.

How the parsimonious Scots financed these new, large-scale enterprises is explained in an exhibit on the Bank of Scotland. Powered by the Scottish work ethic and the new opportunities that came from the Industrial Revolution, the country came into relative prosperity. Education and medicine thrived. With the dawn of the modern age came leisure time, the concept of "healthful sports," and golf—a popular Scottish pastime. On display (near the back, in a small corridor behind the machinery) are some early golf balls, which date from about 1820, made of leather and stuffed with feathers.

• *Leave this hall the way you came in, and journey up to level 5.*

Industry and Empire (1800s): Turn right and do a counterclockwise spin around this floor to survey Scottish life in the 19th century. Industry had transformed the country. Highland farmers left their land to find work in Lowland factories and foundries. Modern inventions—the phonograph, the steam-powered train, the kitchen range—revolutionized everyday life. In Glasgow near the turn of the century, architect Charles Rennie Mackintosh helped to define Scottish Art Nouveau. Scotland was at the forefront of literature (Robert Burns, Sir Walter Scott, Robert Louis Stevenson), science (Lord Kelvin, James Watt, Alexander Graham Bell...he was born here, anyway!), world exploration (John Kirk in Africa, Sir Alexander Mackenzie in Canada), and whisky production.

• *Climb the stairs to level 6.*

Scotland: A Changing Nation (1900s-present): Turn left and do a clockwise spin through this floor to bring the story to the present day. The two world wars decimated the population of this already wee nation. In addition, hundreds of thousands emigrated, especially to Canada (where one in eight Canadians has Scottish origins). Other exhibits include shipbuilding and the fishing industry; Scots in the world of entertainment (from folk singer Donovan to actor-comedian Billy Connolly); a look at the recent trend of devolution from the United Kingdom (1999 opening of Scotland's own parliament and the landmark 2014 referendum on Scottish independence); and a sports Hall of Fame (from tennis star Andy Murray to auto racers Jackie Stewart and Jim Clark).

• *Finish your visit on level 7, the rooftop.*

Garden Terrace: The well-described roof garden features grasses and heathers from every corner of Scotland and spectacular views of the city.

Greyfriars Bobby Statue and Greyfriars Cemetery

This famous **statue** of Edinburgh's favorite dog is across the street from the National Museum of Scotland. Every business nearby, it seems, is named for this Victorian Skye terrier, who is reputed to have

slept upon his master's grave in Greyfriars Cemetery for 14 years. The story was immortalized in a 1960s Disney flick, but recent research suggests that 19th-century businessmen bribed a stray to hang out in the cemetery to attract sightseers. If it was a ruse, it still works.

Just behind Greyfriars Bobby is the entrance to his namesake **cemetery** (open until late). Stepping through the gate, you'll see the pink-marble grave of Bobby himself. (Rather than flowers, well-wishers bring sticks to remember Bobby.) The well-tended cemetery is an evocative place to stroll, and a nice escape from the city's bustle. Harry Potter fans could turn it into a scavenger hunt: J. K. Rowling sketched out her saga just around the corner at The

Elephant House café—and a few of the cemetery's weather-beaten headstones bear familiar names, including McGonagall and Thomas Riddell. At the far end, past a stretch of the 16th-century Flodden Wall, peek through the black iron cemetery fence to see the frilly Gothic spires of posh George Heriot's

School, said to have inspired Hogwarts. And just a few short blocks to the east is a street called...Potterrow.

The cemetery just feels made for ghost walks. It's said that the tombs with iron cages over them were designed so thieves couldn't break into the grave and steal bodies to sell to the medical school across the street (which always needed cadavers). Hmmm.

Grassmarket

Once Edinburgh's site for hangings (residents rented out their windows—above the wryly named "Last Drop" pub—for the view), today Grassmarket is a people-friendly piazza. It was originally the city's garage, a depot for horses and cows (hence the name). It's rowdy here at night—a popular place for "hen dos" and "stag dos" (bachelorette and bachelor parties). In the early evening, the Literary Pub Tour departs from

here (see "Nightlife in Edinburgh," later). Some good shopping streets branch off from Grassmarket: Picturesque Victoria Street, built in the Victorian Age, is lined with colorful little shops and eateries; angling off in the other direction, Candlemaker's Row has a few interesting artisan shops (and leads, in just a couple minutes' walk, up to Greyfriars Bobby and the National Museum; for more shopping tips in this area, see "Shopping in Edinburgh," later).

At the top of Grassmarket is the round monument to the "Covenanters." These strict 17th-century Scottish Protestants were killed for refusing to accept the king's Episcopalian prayer book. To this day, Scots celebrate their national church's emphatically democratic government. Rather than big-shot bishops (as in the Anglican or Roman Catholic Church), they have a low-key "moderator" who's elected each year.

MUSEUMS IN THE NEW TOWN

These sights are linked by my "New Town Walk" on page 734.

▲▲Scottish National Gallery

This delightful, small museum has Scotland's best collection of paintings—both European and Scottish. In a short visit, you can admire well-described works by Old Masters (Raphael, Rembrandt, Rubens), Impressionists (Monet, Degas, Gauguin), and a few underrated Scottish painters. Although there are no iconic masterpieces, it's a surprisingly enjoyable collection that's truly world class. The museum is undergoing renovation until 2021, but it's still worthwhile.

Cost and Hours: Free; Fri-Wed 10:00-17:00, Aug until 18:00; Thu 10:00-19:00 year-round; café downstairs, The Mound (between Princes and Market streets), tel. 0131/624-6200, www.nationalgalleries.org.

Expect Changes: The museum is undergoing major renovation to increase the space of its Scottish collection and build a grand main entrance from Princes Street Gardens. As a result, some exhibits may be closed, and pieces may be relocated, on loan, or in storage. Ask one of the friendly tartan-sporting attendants or at the info desk downstairs (near the WCs and gallery shop) if you can't find a particular item.

Next Door: The skippable **Royal Scottish Academy** hosts temporary art exhibits and is connected to the Scottish National Gallery at the Gardens level (underneath the gallery) by the Weston Link building (same hours as gallery, fine café and restaurant).

Visiting the Museum: While it's tempting to give a painting-by-painting tour, the paintings on display here are always changing, there are few must-see masterpieces, and each painting is clearly labeled with a thoughtfully written description. It's easiest to simply wander through the collection. It's arranged chronologically, mostly on one floor with the more modern paintings (19th and early 20th century) upstairs.

The main-floor collection includes exquisite medieval altarpieces and works by the great masters (Botticelli, Raphael, Rubens, Rembrandt), as well as English artists (Gainsborough, Constable). Highlights of the more modern paintings (mostly upstairs) cover Celtic Revival, Pre-Raphaelites, Impressionists, and Post-Impressionists.

For the heart of the Scottish collection (on the main floor) look for the section labeled "Scottish, 1650-1850." But works by these homegrown artists are scattered throughout the museum:

Allan Ramsay, the son of the well-known poet of the same name, painted portraits of curly-wigged men of the Enlightenment era (the philosopher David Hume, King George III) as well as likenesses of his two wives. Ramsay's portrait of the duke of Argyll—founder of the Royal Bank of Scotland—appears on the front of notes printed by this bank.

Sir Henry Raeburn chronicled the next generation: Sir Walter Scott, the proud kilt-wearing Alastair MacDonell, and the ice-skating Reverend Robert Walker, minister of the Canongate Church.

Sir David Wilkie's forte was small-scale scenes of everyday life. *The Letter of Introduction* (1813) captures Wilkie's own experience of trying to impress skeptical art patrons in London; even the dog is sniffing the Scotsman out. *Distraining for Rent* (1815) shows the plight of a poor farmer about to lose his farm—a common occurrence during 19th-century industrialization.

William Dyce's *Francesca da Rimini* (1837) depicts star-crossed lovers—a young wife and her husband's kid brother—who can't help but indulge their passion. The husband later finds out and kills her; at the far left, you see his ominous hand.

William McTaggart's impressionistic landscape scenes from the late 1800s provide a glimpse of the unique light, powerful clouds, and natural wonder of the Highlands.

▲▲Scottish National Portrait Gallery

Put a face on Scotland's history by enjoying these portraits of famous Scots from the earliest times until today. From its Neo-Gothic facade to a grand entry hall highlighting Scottish history, to galleries showcasing the great Scots of each age, this impressive museum will fascinate anyone interested in Scottish culture. The gallery also hosts temporary exhibits highlighting the work of more contemporary Scots. Because of its purely Scottish focus, many travelers prefer this to the (pan-European) main branch of the National Gallery.

Cost and Hours: Free, daily 10:00-17:00, good cafeteria serving healthy meals, 1 Queen Street, tel. 0131/624-6490, www.nationalgalleries.org.

Visiting the Gallery: Start by studying the gallery map and the *What's On* quarterly, which gives you a rundown of special exhibits here (and at the National Gallery and Modern Art Gallery). While the entrance hall is stirring, its history frieze is better viewed from the balcony above (described later).

The meat of the collection is on the **top floor,** where Scottish history is illustrated by portraits and vividly described by information plaques next to each painting. With the 20th and 21st centuries, the chronological story spills down a level into Room 12 on the first floor. The rest of the gallery is devoted to special (and often very interesting) exhibits.

• *Start on the top floor, diving right into the thick of the struggle between Scotland and England over who should rule this land.*

Reformation to Revolution (Room 1): The collection starts with a portrait of **Mary, Queen of Scots** (1542-1587), her cross and rosary prominent. This controver-

sial ruler set off two centuries of strife. Mary was born with both Stuart blood (the ruling family of Scotland) and the Tudor blood of England's monarchs (Queen Elizabeth I was her cousin). Catholic and French-educated, Mary felt alienated from her own increasingly Protestant homeland. Her tense conversations with the reformer John Knox must have been epic. Then came a series of scandals: She married unpopular Lord Darnley, then (possibly) cheated on him, causing Darnley to (possibly) murder her lover, causing Mary to (possibly) murder Darnley, then (possibly) run off with another man, and (possibly) plot against Queen Elizabeth.

Amid all that drama, Mary was forced by her own people to relinquish her throne to her infant son, **James VI.** Find his portraits as a child and as a grown-up. James grew up to rule Scotland, and when Queen Elizabeth (the "virgin queen") died without an heir, he also became king of England (James I). But after a bitter civil war, James' son, **Charles I,** was arrested and executed in 1649: See the large *Execution of Charles I* painting, his blood-dripping head displayed to the crowd (in a section dedicated to his beheading and that tumultuous political time). His son, Charles II, restored the Stuarts to power. He was then succeeded by his Catholic brother James VII of Scotland (II of England), who was sent into exile in

France. There the Stuarts stewed, planning a return to power, waiting for someone to lead them in what would come to be known as the Jacobite rebellions.

The Jacobite Cause (a few rooms later, in Room 4): One of the biggest paintings in the room is *The Baptism of Prince Charles Edward Stuart*. Born in 1720, this Stuart heir to the thrones of Great Britain and Ireland is better known to history as "Bonnie Prince Charlie." (See his bonnie features in various portraits nearby, as a child, young man, and grown man.) Charismatic Charles convinced France to invade Scotland and put him back on the throne there. In 1745, he entered Edinburgh in triumph. But he was defeated at the tide-turning Battle of Culloden (1746). The Stuart cause died forever, and Bonnie Prince Charlie went into exile, eventually dying drunk and wasted in Rome, far from the land he nearly ruled.

The Age of Improvement (Room 7): The faces portrayed here belonged to a new society whose hard work and public spirit achieved progress with a Scottish accent. Social equality and the Industrial Revolution "transformed" Scotland—you'll see portraits of the great poet Robert Burns, the son of a farmer (Burns was heralded as a "heaven-taught ploughman" when his poems were first published), and the man who perfected the steam engine, James Watt.

• *Check out the remaining galleries, then head back down to the first floor for a good look at the...*

Central Atrium (first floor): Great Scots! The atrium is decorated in a parade of late-19th-century Romantic Historicism. The

frieze (below the bannister, working counterclockwise) is a visual encyclopedia, from an ax-wielding Stone Age man and a druid, to the early legendary monarchs (Macbeth), to warriors William Wallace and Robert the Bruce, to many kings (James I, II, III, and so on), to great thinkers, inventors, and artists (Allan Ramsay, Flora MacDonald, David Hume, Adam Smith, James Boswell, James Watt), the three greatest Scottish writers (Robert Burns, Sir Walter Scott, Robert Louis Stevenson), and culminating with the historian Thomas Carlyle, who was the driving spirit (powered by the fortune of a local newspaper baron) behind creating this portrait gallery.

Around the first-floor mezzanine are large-scale **murals** depicting great events in Scottish history, including the landing of St. Margaret at Queensferry in 1068, the Battle of Stirling Bridge in 1297, the Battle of Bannockburn in 1314, and the marriage procession of James IV and Margaret Tudor through the streets of Edinburgh in 1503.

• *Also on this floor you'll find the...*

Modern Portrait Gallery: This space is dedicated to rotating art and photographs highlighting Scots who are making an impact in the world today, such as Annie Lennox, Alan Cumming, and physicist Peter Higgs (theorizer of the Higgs boson, the so-called God particle). Look for the *Three Oncologists*, a ghostly painting depicting the anxiety and terror of cancer and the dedication of those working so hard to conquer it.

▲▲Georgian House

This refurbished Neoclassical house, set on Charlotte Square, is a trip back to 1796. It recounts the era when a newly gentrified and well-educated Edinburgh was nicknamed the "Athens of the North." Begin on the second floor, where you'll watch a fascinating 16-minute video dramatizing the upstairs/downstairs lifestyles of the aristocrats and servants who lived here. Try on

some Georgian outfits, then head downstairs to tour period rooms and even peek into the fully stocked medicine cabinet. Info sheets are available in each room, along with volunteer guides who share stories and trivia, such as why Georgian bigwigs had to sit behind a screen while enjoying a fire. A walk down George Street after your visit here can be fun for the imagination.

Cost and Hours: £8, daily 10:00-17:00, March and Nov 11:00-16:00, closed Dec-Feb, last entry 45 minutes before closing; 7 Charlotte Square, tel. 0131/225-2160, www.nts.org.uk.

SIGHTS NEAR EDINBURGH
▲▲Royal Yacht *Britannia*

This much-revered vessel, which transported Britain's royal family for more than 40 years on 900 voyages (an average of once around the world per year) before being retired in 1997, is permanently moored in Edinburgh's port of Leith. Queen Elizabeth II said of the ship, "This is the only place I can truly relax." Today it's open to the curious public, who have access to its many decks—from engine rooms to drawing rooms—and offers a fascinating time-warp look into the late-20th-century lifestyles of the rich and royal. It's worth the 20-minute bus or taxi ride from the center; figure on spending about 2.5 hours total on the outing.

Cost and Hours: £16.50, includes 1.5-hour audioguide, daily 9:30-16:30, Oct until 16:00, Nov-March 10:00-15:30, these are last-entry times, tearoom; at the Ocean Terminal Shopping Mall, on Ocean Drive in Leith; tel. 0131/555-5566, www.royalyachtbritannia.co.uk.

Getting There: From central Edinburgh, catch Lothian bus #11 or #22 from Princes Street (just above Waverley Station), or #35 from the bottom of the Royal Mile (alongside the parliament building) to Ocean Terminal (last stop). From the B&B neighborhood, you can either bus to the city center and transfer to one of the buses above, or take bus #14 from Dalkeith Road to Mill Lane, then walk about 10 minutes. The Majestic Tour hop-on, hop-off bus stops here as well. If you're getting off the bus, go through the shopping center and take the escalator to level 2 (top floor).

Drivers can park free in the blue parking garage—park on level E (same floor as visitors center).

Visiting the Ship: First, explore the **museum,** filled with engrossing royal-family-afloat history. You'll see lots of family photos that evoke the fine times the Windsors enjoyed on the *Britannia,* as well as some nautical equipment and uniforms. Then, armed with your audioguide, you're welcome aboard.

This was the last in a line of royal yachts that stretches back to 1660. With all its royal functions, the ship required a crew of more than 200. Begin in the captain's bridge, which feels like it's been preserved from the day it was launched in 1953. Then head down a deck to see the officers' quarters, then the garage, where a Rolls Royce was hoisted aboard to use in places where the local transportation wasn't up to royal standards. The Veranda Deck at the back of the ship was the favorite place for outdoor entertainment. Ronald Reagan, Boris Yeltsin, Bill Clinton, and Nelson Mandela all sipped champagne here. The Sun Lounge, just off the back Veranda Deck, was the Queen's favorite, with Burmese teak and the same phone system she was used to in Buckingham Palace. When she wasn't entertaining, the Queen liked it quiet. The crew wore sneakers, communicated in hand signals, and (at least near the Queen's quarters) had to be finished with all their work by 8:00 in the morning.

Take a peek into the adjoining his-and-hers bedrooms of the Queen and the Duke of Edinburgh (check out the spartan twin beds), and the honeymoon suite where Prince Charles and Lady Di began their wedded bliss.

Heading down another deck, walk through the officers' lounge (and learn about the rowdy games they played) and past the galleys (including custom cabinetry for the fine china and silver) on your way to the biggest room on the yacht, the state dining room. Now decorated with gifts given by the ship's many noteworthy guests, this space enabled the Queen to entertain a good-size crowd. The drawing room, while rather simple (the Queen specifically requested "country house comfort"), was perfect for casual relaxing among royals. Princess Diana played the piano, which is bolted to the deck. Note the contrast to the decidedly less plush crew's quarters, mail room, sick bay, laundry, and engine room.

EDINBURGH

▲Rosslyn Chapel

This small but fascinating countryside church, about a 20-minute drive outside Edinburgh, is a riot of carved iconography. The patterned ceiling and walls have left scholars guessing about the symbolism for centuries.

Cost and Hours: £9, Mon-Sat 9:30-17:00, June-Aug until 18:00, Sun 12:00-16:45 year-round, located in Roslin Village, tel. 0131/440-2159, www.rosslynchapel.com.

Getting There: Ride Lothian bus #37 from Princes Street (stop PJ), North Bridge, or Newington Road in the B&B neighborhood (1-2/hour, 45 minutes). By car, take the A-701 to Penicuik/Peebles, and follow signs for *Roslin;* once you're in the village, you'll see signs for the chapel.

Background: After it was featured in the climax of Dan Brown's 2003 bestseller *The Da Vinci Code,* the number of visitors to Rosslyn Chapel more than quadrupled. But the chapel's allure existed well before the books, and will endure long after they move from bargain bin to landfill. Founded in 1446 as the private mausoleum of the St. Clair family—who wanted to be buried close to God—the church's interior is carved with a stunning mishmash of Christian, pagan, family, Templar, Masonic, and other symbolism. After the Scottish Reformation, Catholic churches like this fell into disrepair. But in the 18th and 19th centuries, Romantics such as Robert Burns and Sir Walter Scott discovered these evocative old ruins, putting Rosslyn Chapel back on the map. Even Queen Victoria visited, and gently suggested that the chapel be restored to its original state. Today, after more than a century of refits and refurbishments, the chapel transports visitors back to a distant and mysterious age.

Visiting the Chapel: From the ticket desk and visitors center, head to the chapel itself. Ask about docent lectures (usually at the top of the hour—last talk at 17:00 in summer, 16:00 in winter). If you have time to kill, pick up the good laminated descriptions for a clockwise tour of the carvings. In the crypt—where the stonemasons worked—you can see faint architectural drawings engraved in the wall, used to help them plot out their master design.

Elsewhere, look for these fun details: In the corner to the left of the altar, find the angels playing instruments—including one with bagpipes. Nearby, you'll see a person dancing with a skeleton. This "dance of death" theme—common in the Middle Ages—is a reminder of mortality: We'll all die eventually, so we might as well whoop it up while we're here. On the other side of the nave are carvings of the seven deadly sins and the seven acts of mercy. One inscription reads: "Wine is strong. Kings are stronger. Women are stronger still. But truth conquers all."

Flanking the altar are two carved columns that come with a legend: The more standard-issue column, on the left, was executed by a master mason, who soon after (perhaps disappointed in his lack of originality) went on a sabbatical to gain inspiration. While he was gone, his ambitious apprentice carved the beautiful corkscrew-shaped column on the right. Upon returning, the master flew into an envious rage and murdered the apprentice with his carving hammer.

Scattered throughout the church, you'll also see the family's symbol, the "engrailed cross" (with serrated edges). Keep an eye out for the more than one hundred "green men"—chubby faces with leaves and vines growing out of their orifices, symbolizing nature. This paradise/Garden of Eden theme is enhanced by a smattering of exotic animals (monkey, elephant, camel, dragon, and a lion fighting a unicorn) and some exotic foliage: aloe vera, trillium, and corn. That last one (framing a window to the right of the altar) is a mystery: It was carved well before Columbus sailed the ocean blue, at a time when corn was unknown in Europe. Several theories have been suggested—some far-fetched (the father of the man who built the chapel explored the New World before Columbus), and others more plausible (the St. Clairs were of Norse descent, and the Vikings are known to have traveled to the Americas well before Columbus). Others simply say it's not corn at all—it's stalks of wheat. After all these centuries, Rosslyn Chapel's mysteries still inspire the imaginations of historians, novelists, and tourists alike.

Royal Botanic Garden

Britain's second-oldest botanical garden (after Oxford) was established in 1670 for medicinal herbs, and this 70-acre refuge is now one of Europe's best. A visitors center has temporary exhibits.

Cost and Hours: Gardens free, greenhouse-£7, daily 10:00-

18:00, Feb and Oct until 17:00, Nov-Jan until 16:00, greenhouse last entry one hour before closing, café and restaurant, a mile north of the city center at Inverleith Row, tel. 0131/248-2909, www.rbge. org.uk.

Getting There: It's a 10-minute bus ride from the city center: Take bus #8 from North Bridge, or #23 or #27 from George IV Bridge (near the National Museum) or The Mound. The Majestic Tour hop-on, hop-off bus also stops here.

Scottish National Gallery of Modern Art

This museum, set in a beautiful parkland, houses Scottish and international paintings and sculpture from 1900 to the present, including works by Matisse, Duchamp, Picasso, and Warhol. The grounds include a pleasant outdoor sculpture park and a café.

Cost and Hours: Free, daily 10:00-18:00, 75 Belford Road, tel. 0131/624-6200, www.nationalgalleries.org.

Getting There: It's about a 20-minute walk west from the city center. Or take the shuttle bus, which runs about hourly between this museum and the Scottish National Gallery (£1 donation requested, confirm times on website).

Experiences in Edinburgh

URBAN HIKES

▲▲Holyrood Park: Arthur's Seat and the Salisbury Crags

Rising up from the heart of Edinburgh, Holyrood Park is a lush green mountain squeezed between the parliament/Holyroodhouse (at the bottom of the Royal Mile) and my recommended B&B neighborhood. For an exhilarating hike, connect these two zones with a 30-minute walk along the Salisbury Crags—reddish cliffs with sweeping views over the city—but be aware that  the crags occasionally close due to falling rocks. Or, for a more serious climb, make the ascent to the summit of Arthur's Seat, the 822-foot-tall remains of an extinct volcano. You can run up like they did in *Chariots of Fire,* or just stroll. At the summit, you'll be rewarded with commanding views of the town and surroundings.

You can do this hike either from the bottom of the Royal Mile, or from the B&B neighborhood. A small road behind the bluff is accessible to taxis, so cheaters can ride halfway to the top. (Note that there are no facilities at the summit.)

From the Royal Mile: Begin in the parking lot below the Palace of Holyroodhouse. Facing the cliff, you'll see two trailheads. For the easier hike along the base of the **Salisbury Crags,** take the steps to the trail to the right. At the far end, you can descend into the Dalkeith Road area or continue steeply up the switchback trail to the Arthur's Seat summit. If you know you'll want to ascend **Arthur's Seat** from the start, take the wider path on the left from the Holyroodhouse parking lot (easier grade, through the abbey ruins and "Hunter's Bog").

From the B&B Neighborhood: If you're sleeping in this area, enjoy an early-morning or late-evening hike starting from the other side (in June, the sun comes up early, and it stays light until nearly midnight). From the Commonwealth Pool, take Holyrood Park Road, bear left at the first roundabout, then turn right at the second roundabout (onto Queen's Drive). Soon you'll see the trailhead, and make your choice: Bear right up the steeper "Piper's Walk" to **Arthur's Seat** (about a 20-minute hike from here, up a steep switchback trail), or bear left for an easier ascent up the "Radial Road" to the **Salisbury Crags,** which you can follow—with great views over town—all the way up and over to Holyroodhouse Palace.

Duddingston Village and Dr. Neil's Garden

This low-key, 30-minute walk goes from the B&B neighborhood to Duddingston Village—a former village that got absorbed by the city but still retains its old, cobbled feel, local church, and great old-time pub, the recommended Sheep Heid Inn. Also here is Dr. Neil's Garden, a peaceful, free garden on a loch.

Walk behind the Commonwealth Pool along Holyrood Park Road. Before the roundabout, just after passing through the wall/gate, take the path to your right. This path runs alongside the Duddingston Low Road all the way to the village and garden. Ignore the road traffic and enjoy the views of Arthur's Seat, the golf course, and eventually, Duddingston Loch. When you reach the cobbled road, you're in Duddingston Village, with the church on your right and the Sheep Heid Inn a block down on your left. Another 100 feet down the main road is a gate labeled *The Manse* with the number 5—enter here for the garden.

Dr. Neil's Garden (also known as the Secret Garden) was started by doctors Nancy and Andrew Neil, who traveled throughout Europe in the 1960s gathering trees and plants. They brought them back here, planted them on this land, and tended to them with the help of their patients. Today it offers a quiet, secluded break from the city, where you can walk among flowers and trees and over quaint bridges, get inspired by quotes written on chalkboards, or sit on a bench overlooking the loch (free, daily 10:00-dusk, charming café, mobile 0784-918-7995, www.drneilsgarden.co.uk).

▲Calton Hill

For an easy walk for fine views over all of Edinburgh and beyond, head up to Calton Hill—the monument-studded bluff that rises from the eastern end of the New Town. From the Waverley Station area, simply head east on Princes Street (which becomes Waterloo Place).

About five minutes after passing North Bridge, watch on the right for the gated entrance to the **Old Calton Cemetery**—worth a quick walk-through for its stirring monuments to great Scots. The can't-miss-it round monument honors the philosopher David Hume; just next to that is a memorial topped by Abraham Lincoln, honoring Scottish-American troops who were killed in combat. The obelisk honors political martyrs.

The views from the cemetery are good, but for even better ones, head back out to the main road and continue a few more minutes on Waterloo Place.  Across the street, steps lead up into **Calton Hill.** Explore the park, purchased by the city in 1724 and one of the first public parks in Britain. Informational plaques identify the key landmarks. At the summit of the hill is the giant, unfinished replica of the Parthenon, honoring those lost in the Napoleonic Wars. Donations to finish it never materialized, leaving it with the nickname "Edinburgh's Disgrace." Nearby, the old observatory holds an old telescope, and the back of the hillside boasts sweeping views over the Firth of Forth and Edinburgh's sprawl. Back toward the Old Town, the tallest tower (shaped like a 19th-century admiral's telescope) celebrates Admiral Horatio Nelson—the same honoree of the giant pillar on London's Trafalgar Square. There's an interesting, free exhibit about Nelson at the base of the tower. While you can pay to climb it for the view, it doesn't gain you much. The best views are around the smaller, circular Dugald Stewart Monument, with postcard panoramas overlooking the spires of the Old Town and the New Town.

More Hikes

You can hike along the river (called the Water of Leith) through Edinburgh. Locals favor the stretch between Roseburn and Dean Village, but the 1.5-mile walk from Dean Village to the Royal Botanic Garden is also good. For more information on these and other hikes, ask at the TI or your B&B.

WHISKY AND GIN TASTING

Whisky Tasting

One of the most accessible places to learn about whisky is at **The Scotch Whisky Experience** on the Royal Mile, an expensive but informative overview to whisky, including a tasting (see page 753). To get more into sampling whisky, try one of the early-evening tastings at the recommended **Cadenhead's Whisky Shop** (see page 788).

The Scotch Malt Whisky Society, in the New Town, is for more serious whisky fans. It serves glasses from numbered bottles of single malts from across Scotland and beyond. Each bottle—pure from the cask and not blended—is only described and not labeled. You read the description and make your choice...or enlist the help of the bartender, who will probe you on what kind of flavor profile you like. While this place's shrouded-in-mystery pretense could get lost on novices, aficionados enjoy it (daily 11:00-23:00, tastings listed on website, bar serves light dishes, on-site top-end restaurant, 28 Queen Street, tel. 0131/220-2044, www.smws.com).

Gin Distillery Tours

The residents of Edinburgh drink more gin per person than any other city in the United Kingdom. The city is largely responsible for the recent renaissance of this drink, so it's only appropriate that you visit a gin distillery while in town. Two distilleries right in the heart of Edinburgh offer hour-long tours with colorful guides who discuss the history of gin, show you the stills involved in the production process, and ply you with libations. Both tours are popular and fill up; book ahead on their websites.

Pickering's is located in a former vet school and animal hospital at Summerhall, halfway between the Royal Mile and the B&B neighborhood. The bar and funky distillery have a cool, young, artsy vibe with skeletons and X-rays still hanging around. The mellow bar also serves cheap pub grub (£10 includes welcome gin and tonic, tour, and 3 samples; 5/day Thu-Sun, meet at the Royal Dick Bar in the central courtyard at 1 Summerhall—for location see the map on page 805, tel. 0131/290-2901, www. pickeringsgin.com).

Edinburgh Gin is a showroom (not a distillery) in the West End, near the Waldorf Astoria Hotel. Besides the basic tour, there's a connoisseur tour with more tastings and a gin-making tour (basic tour £10, 3/day daily, reserve ahead to guarantee a spot, 1A Rutland Place, enter off Shandwick Place next to the Ghille Dhu bar—for location see the map on page 801, tel. 0131/656-2810, www.edinburghgin.com). If you can't get on to one of their tours, visit their Heads & Tales bar to taste their gins (Tue-Sun 17:00-24:00, closed Mon).

LEISURE ACTIVITIES

Several enjoyable activities cluster near the B&B area around Dalkeith Road. For details, check their websites.

The **Royal Commonwealth Pool** is an indoor fitness and activity complex with a 50-meter pool, gym/fitness studio, and kids' soft play zone (daily, 21 Dalkeith Road—see map on page 805, tel. 0131/667-7211, www.edinburghleisure.co.uk).

The **Prestonfield Golf Club,** also an easy walk from the B&Bs, has golfers feeling like they're in a country estate (dress code, 6 Priestfield Road North—see map on page 805, general tel. 0131/667-9665, reservation tel. 0131/667-8597, www.prestonfieldgolf.co.uk).

At the **Midlothian Snowsports Centre** (a little south of town in Hillend; better for drivers), you can try skiing without any pesky snow. It feels like snow-skiing on a slushy day, even though you're schussing over matting misted with water. Four tubing runs offer fun even for nonskiers (£13/first hour, £6/hour after that, includes gear, generally Mon-Fri 9:30-21:00, Sat-Sun until 19:00, shorter hours off-season, Biggar Road—see map on page 710, tel. 0131/445-4433, www.midlothian.gov.uk).

EDINBURGH'S FESTIVALS

Every summer, Edinburgh's annual festivals turn the city into a carnival of the arts. The season begins in June with the international film festival (www.edfilmfest.org.uk); then the jazz and blues festival in July (www.edinburghjazzfestival.com).

In August a riot of overlapping festivals known collectively as the **Edinburgh Festival** rages simultaneously—international, fringe, book, and art, as well as the Military Tattoo. There are enough music, dance, drama, and multicultural events to make even the most jaded traveler giddy with excitement. Every day is jammed with formal and spontaneous fun.

Many city sights run on extended hours. It's a glorious time to be in Edinburgh...*if* you have (and can afford) a room.

If you'll be in town in August, book your room and tickets for major events (especially the Tattoo) as far ahead as you can lock in dates. Plan carefully to ensure you'll have time for festival activities as well as sightseeing. Check online to confirm dates; the best overall website is www.edinburghfestivalcity.com. Several publications—including the festival's official schedule, the *Edinburgh Festivals Guide Daily, The List, Fringe Program,* and *Daily Diary*—list and evaluate festival events. The *Scotsman* newspaper reviews every show.

The official, more formal **Edinburgh International Festival** is the original. Major events sell out well in advance (ticket office at the Hub, in the former Tolbooth Church near the top of the Royal Mile, tel. 0131/473-2000, www.hubtickets.co.uk or www. eif.co.uk).

The less formal **Fringe Festival,** featuring edgy comedy and theater, is huge—with 2,000 shows—and has eclipsed the original festival in popularity (ticket/info office just below St. Giles' Cathedral on the Royal Mile, 180 High Street, bookings tel. 0131/226-0000, www.edfringe.com). Tickets may be available at the door, and half-price tickets for some events are sold on the day of the show at the Half-Price Hut, located at The Mound, near the Scottish National Gallery.

The **Military Tattoo** is a massing of bands, drums, and bagpipes, with groups from all over the former British Empire and beyond. Displaying military finesse with a stirring lone-piper finale, this grand spectacle fills the castle esplanade (nightly during most of Aug except Sun, performances Mon-Fri at 21:00, Sat at 19:15 and 22:30, £25-90, booking starts in Dec, Fri-Sat shows sell out first, all seats generally sold out by early summer, some scattered same-day tickets may be available; office open Mon-Fri 10:00-16:30, closed Sat-Sun, during Tattoo open until show time and closed Sun; 1 Cockburn Street, behind Waverley Station, tel. 0131/225-1188, www.edintattoo.co.uk). Some performances are filmed by the BBC and later broadcast as a big national television special. This broadcast has become an annual ritual for the people of Britain.

Other **summer festivals** cover books (mid-late Aug, www. edbookfest.co.uk) and art (late July-Aug, www.edinburghartfestival. com). The **Festival of Politics** is held in October in the Scottish parliament building. It's a busy weekend of discussions and lectures on environmentalism, globalization, terrorism, gender, and other issues (www.festivalofpolitics.scot).

Shopping in Edinburgh

Edinburgh is bursting with Scottish clichés for sale: kilts, short-bread, whisky...if they can slap a tartan on it, they'll sell it. Locals dismiss the touristy trinket shops, which are most concentrated along the Royal Mile, as "tartan tat." Your challenge is finding something a wee bit more authentic. If you want to be sure you are taking home local merchandise, check if the label reads: "Made in Scotland." "Designed in Scotland" actually means "Made in China." Shops are usually open around 10:00-18:00 (later on Thu, shorter hours or closed on Sun). Tourist shops are open longer hours.

SHOPPING STREETS AND NEIGHBORHOODS

Near the Royal Mile: The Royal Mile is intensely touristy, mostly lined with interchangeable shops selling made-in-China souvenirs. I've listed a few worthwhile spots along here later, under "What to Shop For." But in general, the area near Grassmarket, an easy stroll from the top of the Royal Mile, offers more originality. **Victoria Street,** which climbs steeply downhill from the Royal Mile (near the Hub/Tolbooth Church) to Grassmarket, has a fine concentration of local chain shops, including I.J. Mellis Cheesemonger and Walker Slater for designer tweed, plus Calzeat (scarves, throws, and other textiles), a Harry Potter store, and more clothing and accessory shops. On **Grassmarket,** the Hawico shop sells top quality cashmere milled in southern Scotland. Exiting Grassmarket opposite Victoria Street, **Candlemaker Row** is more artisan, with boutiques selling hats (from dapper men's caps to outrageous fascinators), jewelry, art, design items, and even fossils. The street winds a couple of blocks up toward the National Museum; Greyfriars Bobby awaits you at the top of the street.

In the New Town: For mass-market shopping, you'll find plenty of big chain stores along **Princes Street.** In addition to Marks & Spencer, H&M, Zara, Primark, and a glitzy Apple Store, you'll also see the granddaddy of Scottish department stores, Jenners (Mon-Wed 9:30-18:00, Thu-Sat until 17:00, Sun 11:00-18:00). Parallel to Princes Street, **George Street** has higher-end chain stores (including many from London, such as L.K. Bennett, Molton Brown, and Karen Millen). Just off St. Andrew Square is a branch of the high-end London department store Harvey Nichols.

For more local, artisan shopping, check out **Thistle Street,** lined with some fun eateries and a good collection of shops. You'll see some fun boutiques selling jewelry, shoes, and clothing. This is also the home of Howie Nicolsby's 21st Century Kilts (described later).

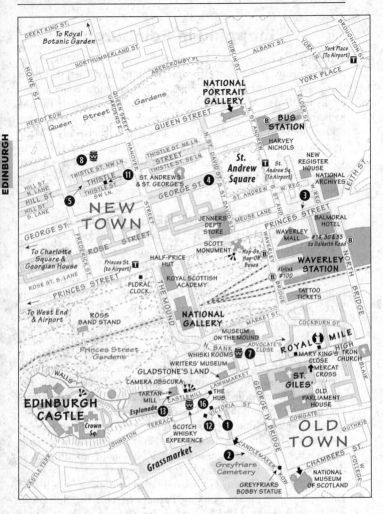

WHAT TO SHOP FOR
Whisky

You can order whisky in just about any bar in town, and whisky shops are a dime a dozen around the Royal Mile. But the places I've listed here distinguish themselves by their tradition and helpful staff. Before sampling or buying whisky, read all about Scotland's favorite spirit on page 755.

Cadenhead's Whisky Shop is not a tourist sight—don't expect free samples or a handholding shopping experience. Founded in 1842, this firm prides itself on bottling good whisky straight from casks at the distilleries, without all the compromises that come with profitable mass production (coloring with sugar to fit the

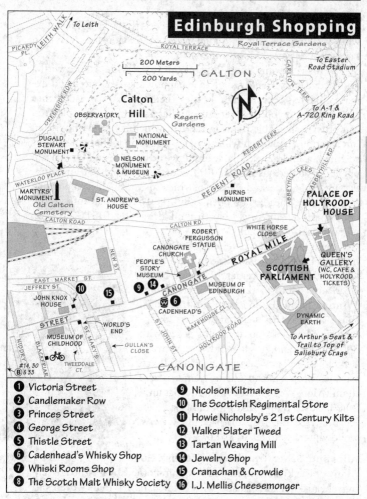

Edinburgh Shopping

To Leith

PICARDY PL.
LEITH WALK
GREENSIDE ROW

ROYAL TERRACE
Royal Terrace Gardens

To Easter
Road Stadium

200 Meters
200 Yards

CALTON

Calton Hill

OBSERVATORY

Regent
Gardens

DUGALD
STEWART
MONUMENT

NATIONAL
MONUMENT

To A-1 &
A-720 Ring Road

CARLTON TERR.

REGENT TERR.

ABBEYHILL RD.
ABBEYHILL CRES.

NELSON
MONUMENT
& MUSEUM

WATERLOO PLACE

MARTYRS'
MONUMENT

Old Calton
Cemetery

ST. ANDREW'S
HOUSE

CALTON ROAD

REGENT ROAD

BURNS
MONUMENT

PALACE OF
HOLYROOD-
HOUSE

CALTON RD.

NEW ST.

ROBERT
FERGUSSON
STATUE

CANONGATE
CHURCH

WHITE HORSE
CLOSE

ROYAL MILE

QUEEN'S
GALLERY
(WC, CAFE &
HOLYROOD
TICKETS)

PEOPLE'S
STORY
MUSEUM

CANONGATE

MUSEUM OF
EDINBURGH

SCOTTISH
PARLIAMENT

EAST MARKET ST.
JEFFREY ST.

JOHN KNOX
HOUSE

WORLD'S
END

CADENHEAD'S

BAKEHOUSE CL.

ST. JOHN ST.

HOLYROOD ROAD

DYNAMIC
EARTH

To Arthur's Seat &
Trail to Top of
Salisbury Crags

STREET

ST. MARY'S ST.

MUSEUM OF
CHILDHOOD

GULLAN'S
CLOSE

NIDDRY ST.
BLACKFRIARS

#14, 30
& 33

TWEEDDALE
CT.

CANONGATE

EDINBURGH

① Victoria Street
② Candlemaker Row
③ Princes Street
④ George Street
⑤ Thistle Street
⑥ Cadenhead's Whisky Shop
⑦ Whiski Rooms Shop
⑧ The Scotch Malt Whisky Society

⑨ Nicolson Kiltmakers
⑩ The Scottish Regimental Store
⑪ Howie Nicholsby's 21st Century Kilts
⑫ Walker Slater Tweed
⑬ Tartan Weaving Mill
⑭ Jewelry Shop
⑮ Cranachan & Crowdie
⑯ I.J. Mellis Cheesemonger

expected look, watering down to reduce the alcohol tax, and so on). Those drinking from Cadenhead-bottled whiskies will enjoy the

pure product as the distilleries' owners themselves do, not as the sorry public does. If you're serious about buying, the staff can explain the sometimes-complex whisky board and talk you through flavor profiles (prices start around £8.50 for about 3.5

ounces, open Mon-Sat 10:30-17:30, closed Sun, 172 Canongate,

EDINBURGH

tel. 0131/556-5864, www.cadenhead.scot). They host hour-long whisky tastings—a hit with aficionados (£25, Mon-Fri at 17:45, 6 tastes, not designed for beginners).

Whiski Rooms Shop, just off the Royal Mile, comes with a knowledgeable, friendly staff that happily assists novices and experts alike to select the right bottle. Their adjacent bar usually has about 400 open bottles: Serious purchasers can get a sample. You can order a shareable flight in the bar, which comes with written information about each whisky you're sampling (variety of options starting around £25, available anytime the bar is open). Or you can opt for a guided tasting (£30 introductory tasting, £50 premium tasting, chocolate and cheese pairings also available; about one hour, reserve ahead; shop open daily 10:00-18:00, bar until 24:00, both open later in Aug, 4 North Bank Street, tel. 0131/225-1532, www.whiskirooms.co.uk).

Near the B&B Neighborhood: Per-haps the most accessible place to learn about local whiskies is conveniently located in the B&B area south of the city center. **Wood-Winters** has a passion both for traditional spirits and for the latest innovations in Ed-inburgh's booze scene. It's well stocked with 300 whiskies and gins (a trendy alternative to Scotch), as well as wines and local craft beers. Curious browsers can ask to sample a wee dram (Mon-Wed 10:00-19:00, Thu-Sat until 20:00, closed Sun, 91 Newington Road—for location, see the map on page 805, www. woodwinters.com, tel. 0131/667-2760).

Kilts and Other Traditional Scottish Gear

Many of the kilt outfitters you'll see along the Royal Mile are sell-ing cheap knockoffs, made with printed rather than woven tar-tan material. If you want a serious kilt—or would enjoy window-shopping for one—try one of the places below. These have a few off-the-rack options, but to get a kilt in your specific tartan and size, they'll probably take your measurements, custom-make it, and ship it to you. For a good-quality outfit (kilt, jacket, and accessories), plan on spending about £1,000.

Nicolson Kiltmakers has a respect for tradition and qual-ity. Owner Gordon enlists and trains local craftspeople who

specialize in traditionally manufactured kilts and accessories. He prides himself on keeping the old ways alive (in the face of deeply discounted "tartan tat") and actively cultivates the next generation of kiltmakers (Mon-Sat 9:30-17:30, Sun 12:00-16:00, 189 Canongate, tel. 0131/558-2887, www.nicolsonkiltmakers.com).

The Scottish Regimental Store, run by Nigel, is the official outfitter for military regiments. They sell top-of-the-line, formal kiltwear, as well as medals and pins that can be a more affordable souvenir (Mon-Fri 10:00-16:00, Sat until 17:00, closed Sun, 9 Jeffrey Street, tel. 0131/557-0249, www.scottishregimentalstore. co.uk).

Howie Nicholsby's 21st Century Kilts, in the New Town, brings this traditional craft into the present day. It's fun to peruse his photos of both kilted celebrities (he's dressed everyone from Sam Heughan to Vin Diesel) and wedding albums—which make you wish you were Scottish, engaged, and wealthy enough to hire Howie to outfit your bridal party (Howie asks that you make an appointment, though you're welcome to drop in if he happens to be there; closed Sun-Mon and Wed, 48 Thistle Street, send text to 0777-475-7222, www.21stcenturykilts.com, howie@21stcenturykilts.com).

Tweed

Several places around town sell the famous Harris Tweed, the authentic stuff hand woven on the Isle of Harris in the far west of Scotland. Harris Tweed is a protected name, so if the label says "Harris," you know it's the real thing. **Walker Slater** is the place to go for top-quality tweed at top prices. They have three locations on Victoria Street, just below the Royal Mile near Grass-

market: menswear (at #16), womenswear (#44), and a sale shop (#5). You'll find a rich interior and a wide variety of gorgeous jackets, scarves, bags, and more. This place feels elegant and exclusive (Mon-Sat 10:00-18:00, Sun 11:00-17:00, www.walkerslater. com). Harris Tweed is also available at the **Tartan Weaving Mill** at the top of the Royal Mile (daily 9:00-17:30, 555 Castlehill, tel. 0131/220-2477).

Jewelry

Jewelry with Celtic designs, mostly made from sterling silver, is a popular and affordable souvenir. While you'll see it sold around town, **Celtic Design** (156 Canongate) offers a quality and tasteful selection.

Food and Treats

Cranachan & Crowdie is your one-stop shop for authentic Scottish goodies. They collect products (mostly edibles, some crafts) from more than 300 small, independent producers all over Scotland. The selection goes well beyond the mass-produced clichés, and American Beth and Scottish Fiona love to explain the story behind each item. They also offer up Scottish gin samples upon request (daily 11:00-18:00, on the Royal Mile at 263 Canongate, tel. 0131/556-7194).

I.J. Mellis Cheesemonger, tucked down Victoria Street just off the top of the Royal Mile, stocks a wide variety of Scottish, English, and international cheeses. They're as knowledgeable about cheese as they are generous with samples (Mon-Sat 9:30-19:00, Sun 11:00-18:00, 30A Victoria Street, tel. 0131/226-6215).

Nightlife in Edinburgh

▲▲Literary Pub Tour

This two-hour walk is interesting and a worthwhile way to spend an evening—even if you can't stand "Auld Lang Syne." Think of it as a walking theatrical performance, where you follow the witty dialogue of two actors as they debate the great literature of Scotland. (You may ask yourself if this is high art or the creative re-creation of fun-loving louts fueled by a passion for whisky.) You'll cover a lot of ground, wandering from Grassmarket over the Old Town and New Town, with stops in three to four pubs, as your guides share their takes on Scotland's literary greats. The tour meets at the Beehive Inn on Grassmarket (£16, just show up or book online and save £2, drinks extra; May-Sept nightly at 19:30, April and Oct Thu-Sun, Jan-March Fri and Sun, Nov-Dec Fri only; 18 Grassmarket, tel. 0800-169-7410, www.edinburghliterarypubtour.co.uk).

▲Ghost Walks

A variety of companies lead spooky walks around town, providing an entertaining and affordable night out (offered nightly, most around 19:00 and 21:00, easy socializing for solo travelers). These two options are the most established.

Auld Reekie Tours offers a scary array of walks daily and nightly. Auld Reekie intertwines the grim and gory aspects of Scotland's history with the paranormal, witch covens, and pagan temples. They take groups into the "haunted vaults" under the old bridges "where it was so dark, so crowded, and so squalid that the people there knew each other not by how they looked, but by how they sounded, felt, and smelt." The guides are passionate, and the stories are genuinely spooky. Even if you don't believe in ghosts, you'll be entertained (£12-16, 1-1.5 hours, all tours leave from the modern Bank of Scotland building on the Royal Mile, opposite Deacon Brodie's Tavern, tel. 0131/557-4700, www.auldreekietours. com).

The theatrical **Cadies & Witchery Tours,** the most established outfit, offers two different 1.25-hour walks led by costumed actors: "Ghosts and Gore" (April-Aug only, in daylight and following a flatter route) and "Murder and Mystery" (year-round, after dark, hillier, more surprises and corny scares). The balance of historical context and slapstick humor makes these a fun pick for families (£10, includes book of stories, leaves from top of Royal Mile, outside the Witchery Restaurant, near castle esplanade, reservations required, tel. 0131/225-6745, www.witcherytours.com).

Scottish Folk Evenings

These Scottish variety shows include a traditional dinner with all the edible clichés, followed by a full slate of swirling kilts, blaring bagpipes, storytelling, and Scottish folk dancing. As these are designed for tour groups, you'll sit in a big music hall, served en masse before enjoying the stage show with an old-time emcee. If you like Lawrence Welk, you're in for a treat. But for most travelers, these are painfully cheesy. You can sometimes see the show without dinner for about two-thirds the price.

Taste of Scotland at Prestonfield House, filling a kind of circus tent in a luxurious estate near the Dalkeith Road B&Bs, offers its kitschy folk evening with or without dinner Sunday to Friday. For £55, you get the show with two drinks and a wad of haggis; £70 buys you the same, plus a three-course meal and a half-bottle of wine (dinner at 19:00, show from 20:00-22:00, April-Oct only). It's in the stables of "the handsomest house in Edinburgh," which is now home to the recommended Rhubarb Restaurant (Priestfield Road—see map on page 805, tel. 0131/225-7800, www. scottishshow.co.uk).

Spirit of Scotland Show is essentially the same experience but in the city center (£65 for dinner and show, dinner at 19:00, show from 20:00-21:30, next to the National Portrait Gallery at 5 Queen Street, tel. 0131/618-9899, https://spiritofscotlandshow.com).

The Princes Street Gardens Dancers perform a range of Scottish country dancing each summer at the Princes Street Gardens. The volunteer troupe demonstrates each dance, then invites spectators to give it a try (£5, June-July Mon 19:30-21:30, at Ross Bandstand in Princes Street Gardens—in the glen just below Edinburgh Castle, tel. 0131/228-8616, www.princesstreetgardensdancing.org. uk). The same group offers summer programs in other parts of town (see website for details).

EDINBURGH

Theater

Even outside festival time, Edinburgh is a fine place for lively and affordable theater and live music. Pick up *The List* for a complete rundown of what's on (free at TI; online at www.list.co.uk).

▲▲Live Music in Pubs

While traditional music venues have been eclipsed by beer-focused student bars, Edinburgh still has a few good pubs that can deliver a traditional folk-music fix. These days, many places that advertise "live music" offer only a solo singer/guitarist rather than a folk group. The monthly *Gig Guide* (free at TI, accommodations, and various pubs, www.gigguide.co.uk) lists several places each night that have live music, divided by genre (pop, rock, world, and folk). For locations, see the "Edinburgh City Center Eateries" map on page 809.

South of the Royal Mile: Tight, stuffy **Sandy Bell's** is a pub with live folk music nightly from 21:30 (near the National Museum of Scotland at 25 Forrest Road, tel. 0131/225-2751). There's no food, drinks are cheap, tables are small, and the vibe is local. They also have a few sessions earlier in the day (Sat at 14:00, Sun at 16:00, Mon at 17:30 is for beginners).

Captain's Bar is a crowded-but-cozy, music-focused pub with live sessions of folk and traditional music nightly around 21:00—see website for lineup (4 South College Street, https://captainsedinburgh.webs.com).

The Royal Oak is another characteristic, snug place for a dose of folk and blues that feels like a friend's living room (just off South Bridge opposite Chambers Road at 1 Infirmary Street, tel. 0131/557-2976).

Grassmarket Neighborhood: This area below the castle bustles with live music and rowdy people spilling out of the pubs and into what was (once upon a time) a busy market square. While it used to be a mecca for Scottish folk music, today it's more youthful with a heavy-drinking, rowdy feel. It's fun to just wander through this area late at night and check out the scene. Thanks to the music and crowds, you'll know where to go...and where not to.

The Fiddlers Arms has a charming Grassmarket pub energy with live folk, pop, or rock, depending on the night (Thu-Sat from 21:00, at the far end of the square). Check out **Biddy Mulligans** or **White Hart Inn** (both on Grassmarket and both usually with a single Irish folk singer nightly). **Finnegans Wake,** on Victoria Street (which leads down to Grassmarket), is more of a down-and-dirty, classic rock bar with dancing. **The Bow Bar,** a couple of doors away on Victoria Street, has no music but offers a hard-to-resist classic pub scene.

On the Royal Mile: Three characteristic pubs within a few steps of each other on High Street (opposite the Radisson Blu Hotel) offer a fun setting, classic pub architecture and ambience, and live music (generally just a single loud folk guitarist) for the cost of a beer: **Whiski Bar** (mostly trad and folk; nightly at 22:00), **Royal Mile** (classic pop; nightly at 22:00), and **Mitre Bar** (acoustic pop/rock with some trad; Fri-Sat at 22:00).

Just a block away (on South Bridge) is **Whistlebinkies Live Music Bar.** While they rarely do folk or Scottish trad, this is the most serious of the music pubs, with an actual stage and several acts nightly (schedule posted inside the door makes the genre clear; most nights music starts at 19:00 or 21:30, young crowd, fun energy, sticky floors, no cover, tel. 0131/557-5114). **No. 1 High Street** is an accessible little pub with a love of folk and traditional music (Wed-Thu from about 21:00, 1 High Street, tel. 0131/556-5758). **World's End,** across the street, also has music starting about 21:00 (trad on Thu, other genres Fri-Sat, 4 High Street, tel. 0131/556-3628).

In the New Town: All the beer drinkers seem to head for the pedestrianized, west end of Rose Street, famous for having the most pubs per square inch anywhere in Scotland—and plenty of live music.

Pubs near the B&B Neighborhood

The pubs in the B&B area don't typically have live music, but some are fun evening hangouts (for locations, see the "B&Bs & Restaurants South of the City Center" map). **Leslie's Bar,** sitting between a working-class and an upper-class neighborhood, has two sides. Originally, the gang (men) would go in on the right to gather around the great hardwood bar, glittering with a century of *Cheers* ambience. Meanwhile, the more delicate folks (women) would slip in on the left, with its discreet doors, plush snugs (cozy private booths), and ornate ordering windows. Since 1896, this Victorian classic has been appreciated for both its real ales and its huge selection of fine whiskies (listed on a lengthy menu). Dive into the whisky mosh pit on the right, and let them show you how whisky can become "a very good friend" (daily 11:00-24:00, 49 Ratcliffe Terrace, tel. 0131/667-7205).

Other good pubs in this area include **The Old Bell** (uphill from Leslie's, popular and cozy, with big TV screens) and **The Salisbury Arms** (bigger, more sprawling, feels upscale); both are described later, under "Eating in Edinburgh."

Sleeping in Edinburgh

I've recommended accommodations in three areas: the city center, the West End, and a quieter neighborhood south of town.

To stay in the city center, you'll select from large hotels and mostly impersonal guesthouses. The West End (just a few blocks from the New Town, spanning from Haymarket to Charlotte Square) offers a few comfortable and more intimate hotels and guesthouses. These places provide a calm retreat in a central location.

For the classic B&B experience (friendly hosts and great cooked breakfasts), look south of town near Dalkeith Road or Mayfield Gardens. From either area, it's a long walk to the city center (about 30 minutes) or a quick bus or taxi/Uber ride. While the B&Bs here are not cheap (generally **$$**), they're less expensive than staying at a downtown hotel.

Note that during the Festival in August, prices skyrocket and most places do not accept bookings for one- or even two-night stays. If coming in August, book far in advance. Conventions, rugby matches, school holidays, and weekends can make finding a room tough at other times of year, too. In winter, when demand is light, some B&Bs close, and prices at all accommodations get soft.

I rank accommodations from **$** budget to **$$$$** splurge. For the best deal, contact smaller places directly by phone or email. When you book direct, the owner avoids a commission and may be able to offer a discount. For some travelers, short-term Airbnb-type rentals can be a good alternative to hotels; search for places in my recommended hotel and B&B neighborhoods. For more details on reservations, short-term rentals, and more, see the "Sleeping" section in the Practicalities chapter.

HOTELS IN THE CITY CENTER

These places are mostly characterless, but they're close to the sightseeing action and Edinburgh's excellent restaurant and pub scene. Prices are very high in peak season and drop substantially in off-season (a good time to shop around). In each case, I'd skip the institutional breakfast and eat out. You'll generally pay about £10 a day to park near these hotels.

$$$$ The Inn Place, part of a small chain, fills the former headquarters of The *Scotsman* newspaper—a few steep steps below the Royal Mile—with 48 classy, minimalist rooms ("bunk rooms" for 6-8 people, best deals on weekdays, breakfast extra, elevator serves some rooms, 20 Cockburn Street, tel. 0131/526-3780, www.theinnplaceedinburgh.co.uk, reception@theinnplaceedinburgh.co.uk).

$$$$ The Inn on the Mile is your trendy, central option, filling a renovated old bank building right in the heart of the Royal Mile (at North Bridge/South Bridge). The nine bright and stylish rooms are an afterthought to the busy upmarket pub, which is where you'll check in. If you don't mind some noise (from the pub and the busy street) and climbing lots of stairs, it's a handy home base (breakfast extra, complimentary drink, 82 High Street, tel. 0131/556-9940, www.theinnonthemile.co.uk, info@theinnonthemile.co.uk).

$$$$ **Grassmarket Hotel**'s 42 rooms are quirky and fun, from the Dandy comic-book wallpaper to the giant wall map of Edinburgh equipped with planning-your-visit magnets. The hotel is in a great location right on Grassmarket overlooking the Covenanters Memorial and above Biddy Mulligans Bar (family rooms, two-night minimum on some weekends, elevator serves half the rooms, 94 Grassmarket, tel. 0131/220-2299, www.grassmarkethotel.co.uk).

$$$ **The Place Hotel,** sister of the Inn Place listed earlier, has a fine New Town location 10 minutes north of the train station. It occupies three grand Georgian townhouses, with no elevator and long flights of stairs leading up to the 47 contemporary, no-frills rooms. Their outdoor terrace with retractable roof and heaters is a popular place to unwind (save money with a smaller city double, 34 York Place, tel. 0131/556-7575, www.yorkplace-edinburgh.co.uk, frontdesk@yorkplace-edinburgh.co.uk).

$$ **Ten Hill Place Hotel** is a seven-minute walk from the Royal Mile, down a quiet courtyard. It's run in conjunction with the 500-year-old Royal College of Surgeons and profits go toward funding student education. Its 129 rooms are classy, and some have views of the Salisbury Crags (family rooms, breakfast extra, elevator, 10 Hill Place, tel. 0131/662-2080, www.tenhillplace.com, reservations@tenhillplace.com).

$$ **Motel One Edinburgh Royal,** part of a stylish German budget-hotel chain, is between the train station and the Royal Mile; it feels upscale and trendy for its price range (208 rooms, pay more for a park view or less for a windowless "basic" room with skylight, breakfast extra, elevator, 18 Market Street, tel. 0131/220-0730, www.motel-one.com, edinburgh-royal@motel-one.com).

$$ **Motel One Edinburgh Princes** is a good deal for its location, with 140 rooms, some with nice views of Waverley Station and the Old Town. The rooms are cookie-cutter, but the sprawling ballroom-like lounge offers great views (family rooms, reception on first floor, breakfast extra, elevator, 10 Princes Street, enter around the corner on West Register Street, www.motel-one.com, edinburgh-princes@motel-one.com).

Chain Hotels in the Center: Besides my recommendations above, you'll find a number of cookie-cutter chain hotels close to the

EDINBURGH

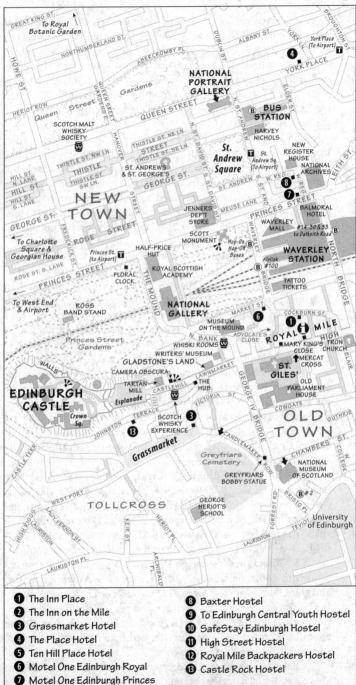

1 The Inn Place
2 The Inn on the Mile
3 Grassmarket Hotel
4 The Place Hotel
5 Ten Hill Place Hotel
6 Motel One Edinburgh Royal
7 Motel One Edinburgh Princes

8 Baxter Hostel
9 To Edinburgh Central Youth Hostel
10 SafeStay Edinburgh Hostel
11 High Street Hostel
12 Royal Mile Backpackers Hostel
13 Castle Rock Hostel

EDINBURGH

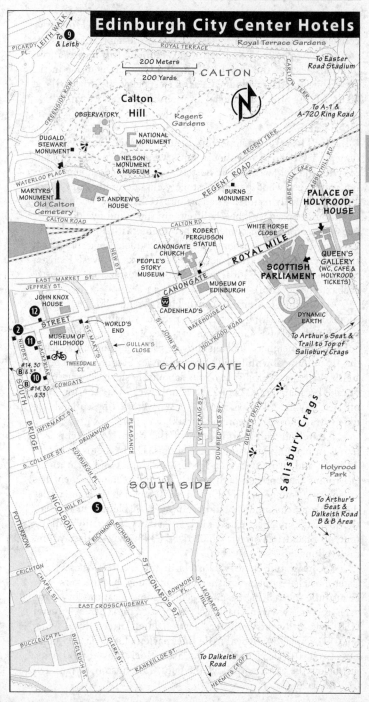

Edinburgh City Center Hotels

To 9 & Leith

PICARDY PL.

LEITH WALK

GREENSIDE ROW

ROYAL TERRACE

Royal Terrace Gardens

ROYAL TERRACE

CALTON

200 Meters

200 Yards

Calton Hill

CARLTON TERR.

To Easter Road Stadium

OBSERVATORY

Regent Gardens

N

To A-1 & A-720 Ring Road

DUGALD STEWART MONUMENT

NATIONAL MONUMENT

NELSON MONUMENT & MUSEUM

REGENT TERR.

WATERLOO PLACE

REGENT ROAD

ABBEYHILL CRES.

ABBEYHILL RD.

MARTYRS' MONUMENT

Old Calton Cemetery

ST. ANDREW'S HOUSE

BURNS MONUMENT

PALACE OF HOLYROOD-HOUSE

CALTON ROAD

CALTON RD.

NEW ST.

ROBERT FERGUSSON STATUE

WHITE HORSE CLOSE

QUEEN'S GALLERY (WC, CAFE, & HOLYROOD TICKETS)

CANONGATE CHURCH

ROYAL MILE

SCOTTISH PARLIAMENT

PEOPLE'S STORY MUSEUM

CANONGATE

MUSEUM OF EDINBURGH

EAST MARKET ST.

JEFFREY ST.

JOHN KNOX HOUSE

CADENHEAD'S

DYNAMIC EARTH

12

STREET

ST. MARY'S

WORLD'S END

BAKEHOUSE CL.

To Arthur's Seat & Trail to Top of Salisbury Crags

2

MUSEUM OF CHILDHOOD

ST. JOHN ST.

HOLYROOD ROAD

11

BLACKFRIARS

GULLAN'S CLOSE

CANONGATE

#14, 30 & 33

NIDDRY ST.

TWEEDDALE CT.

10

B

#14, 30 & 33

COWGATE

SOUTH BRIDGE

INFIRMARY ST.

S. COLLEGE ST.

DRUMMOND

ROXBURGH PL.

PLEASANCE

VIEWCRAIG ST.

DUMBIEDYKES ST.

QUEEN'S DRIVE

Salisbury Crags

Holyrood Park

SOUTH SIDE

NICOLSON

HILL PL.

5

W. RICHMOND RICHMOND

ST. LEONARD'S HILL

To Arthur's Seat & Dalkeith Road B & B Area

POTTERROW

CRICHTON

CHAPEL ST.

BOWMONT PL.

ST. LEONARD'S ST.

EAST CROSSCAUSEWAY

BUCCLEUCH PL.

BUCCLEUCH ST.

CLERK ST.

KANKEILLOR ST.

To Dalkeith Road

HERMITS CROFT

Royal Mile, including **Jurys Inn** (43 Jeffrey Street), **Ibis Hotel** (two convenient branches: near the Tron Church and another around the corner along the busy South Bridge), **Holiday Inn Express** (two locations: just off the Royal Mile at 300 Cowgate and one in the New Town), and **Travelodge Central** (just below the Royal Mile at 33 St. Mary's Street; additional locations in the New Town).

HOSTELS

¢ **Baxter Hostel** is an appealing boutique hostel. Occupying one floor of a Georgian townhouse (up several long, winding flights of stairs and below two more hostels), it has tons of ambience: tartan wallpaper, wood paneling, stone walls, decorative tile floors, and a beautifully restored kitchen/lounge that you'd want in your own house. Space is tight—hallways are snug, and five dorms (42 beds) share one bathroom. Another room, with four beds, has its own en-suite bathroom (includes scrambled-egg breakfast; small fee for towel, travel adapters, and locks; 5 West Register Street, tel. 0131/503-1001, www.thebaxterhostel.com, thehost@ thebaxterhostel.com).

¢ **Edinburgh Central Youth Hostel** rents 251 beds in 72 rooms accommodating three to six people (all with private bathrooms and lockers). Guests can eat cheaply in the cafeteria, or cook in the members' kitchen (private rooms available, pay laundry, 15-minute downhill walk from Waverley Station—head down Leith Walk, pass through two roundabouts, hostel is on your left—or take Lothian bus #22 or #25 to Elm Rowe, 9 Haddington Place off Leith Walk, tel. 0131/524-2090, www.hostellingscotland.org.uk, central@hostellingscotland.org.uk).

¢ **SafeStay Edinburgh,** just off the Royal Mile, rents 272 bunks in pleasing purple-accented rooms. Dorm rooms have 4 to 12 beds, and there are also a few private singles and twin rooms (all rooms have private bathrooms). Bar 50 in the basement has an inviting lounge. Half of the rooms function as a university dorm during the school year, becoming available just in time for the tourists (breakfast extra, kitchen, laundry, free daily walking tour, 50 Blackfriars Street, tel. 0131/524-1989, www.safestay.com, reservations-edi@safestay.com).

¢ **Cheap and Scruffy Hostels in the Center:** These three sister hostels—popular crash pads for young backpackers—are beautifully located in the noisy center (some locations have private rooms, www.macbackpackers.com): **High Street Hostel** (150 beds, 8 Blackfriars Street, just off High Street/Royal Mile, tel. 0131/557-3984); **Royal Mile Backpackers** (38 beds, 105 High Street, tel. 0131/557-6120); and **Castle Rock Hostel** (300 beds, just below the castle and above the pubs, 15 Johnston Terrace, tel. 0131/225-9666).

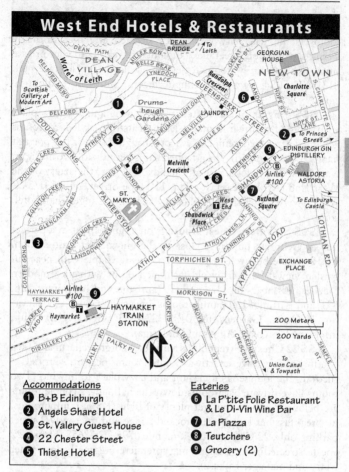

West End Hotels & Restaurants

EDINBURGH

Accommodations

1. B+B Edinburgh
2. Angels Share Hotel
3. St. Valery Guest House
4. 22 Chester Street
5. Thistle Hotel

Eateries

6. La P'tite Folie Restaurant & Le Di-Vin Wine Bar
7. La Piazza
8. Teutchers
9. Grocery (2)

THE WEST END

The area just west of the New Town and Charlotte Square is a quiet, classy, residential area of stately Georgian buildings. Hotels here can be pricey and ostentatious, catering mostly to business travelers. But my recommendations are central and offer character and hospitality. Though these places aren't as intimate as my recommended B&Bs south of town, the West End is convenient to most sightseeing. It's an easy 10- to 15-minute walk to bustling Princes Street.

To get here from the train station, take the Airlink #100 from Waverley Bridge to Shandwick Place, or take the train to Haymarket Station (depending on your hotel—confirm in advance). Coming from Princes Street, take the tram to the West End stop.

$$$$ B+B Edinburgh is a boutique hotel with 27 comfortable rooms (some with city views). It's situated on quiet Rothesay Terrace, where you'll feel like a diplomat retreating to your private suite (RS%, family rooms, elevator, 3 Rothesay Terrace, tel. 0131/225-5084, www.bb-edinburgh.com, info@bb-edinburgh.com).

$$$ Angels Share Hotel is an elegant and inviting place with a proud Scottish heritage. Each of its tidy, stylish 31 rooms is named after a contemporary Scottish figure (his or her portrait hangs above your bed). The attached bar is glitzy, with live music on weekends. The hotel is just off Shandwick Place, the artery of the West End (RS%, breakfast extra, 11 Hope Street, tel. 0131/247-7007, www.angelssharehotel.com, reception@angelssharehotel.com).

$$$ St. Valery Guest House is on a quiet street in a perfect line of Georgian buildings close to the Haymarket train station. Its 12 simple but well-maintained rooms (a couple with peaceful garden views) have frilly old-fashioned decor with nice modern touches. It's near the Haymarket tram stop and bus routes #26, #31, and Airlink #100 (family rooms, breakfast included, no elevator, 36 Coates Gardens, tel. 0131/337-1893, www.stvalery.co.uk, info@stvalery.co.uk, Agnes and Solveiga).

$$ 22 Chester Street offers a mix of Georgian charm and Ikea comfort, renting five smartly appointed rooms near St. Mary's Cathedral. The lounge is an elegant and cozy place to unwind. Two rooms have private bathrooms down the hall, and a couple rooms are below street level but get plenty of light (RS%, family rooms, no breakfast but lounge has stocked fridge and microwave, street parking only, 22 Chester Street, mobile 0795-755-8658, https://22chesterstreetedinburgh.co.uk, marypremiercru@gmail.com, owner Mary and manager Lukasz).

$$ Thistle Hotel is your no-frills budget option (albeit still expensive) in this otherwise fancy neighborhood. The 16 rooms are basic but functional, and many bathrooms are remodeled (and others need to be). Two rooms have castle views (RS%, family rooms, breakfast extra, no elevator, 59 Manor Place, tel. 0131/225-6144, www.edinburghthistlehotel.com, enquiries@edinburghthislehotel.com, Gregory).

B&Bs SOUTH OF THE CITY CENTER

A B&B generally provides more warmth and lower prices. At these not-quite-interchangeable places, character is provided by the personality quirks of the hosts and sometimes the decor. In general, cash is preferred and can lead to discounted rates. Book direct—you will pay a much higher rate through a booking website.

Near the B&Bs, you'll find plenty of fine eateries and some good, classic pubs. A few places have their own private parking; others offer access to easy, free street parking (ask when booking—or better yet, don't rent a car for your time in Edinburgh). The nearest launderette is Ace Cleaning Centre (see page 711).

Taxi or Uber fare between the city center and these B&Bs is about £7. If taking the bus from the B&Bs into the city, hop off at the South Bridge stop for the Royal Mile (see below—and "Getting Around Edinburgh," earlier—for more bus specifics).

Near Dalkeith Road

Most of my B&Bs near Dalkeith Road are located south of the Royal Commonwealth Pool. This comfortable, safe neighborhood is a ten-minute bus ride from the Royal Mile.

To get here from the train station, catch the bus around the corner on North Bridge: Exit the station onto Princes Street, turn right, continue around the corner onto North Bridge, cross the street, and walk up the bridge to the bus stop (lines #14, #30, or #33). About 10 minutes into the ride, after following South Clerk Street for a while, the bus makes a left turn onto East Preston Street, then a right onto Dalkeith Road. Depending on where you're staying, you'll get off at the first stop (Commonwealth Pool) or second stop (Marchhall Place) after the turn—confirm specifics with your B&B.

$$ Gil Dun Guest House, with eight rooms—some contemporary, others more traditional—is on a quiet cul-de-sac just off Dalkeith Road. It's comfortable, pleasant, and managed with care by Gerry and Bill; Maggie helps out occasionally (family rooms, two-night minimum in summer preferred, limited off-street parking, 9 Spence Street, tel. 0131/667-1368, www.gildun.co.uk, gildun.edin@btinternet.com).

$$ Gifford House, on busy Dalkeith Road, is a bright, flowery retreat with six peaceful, colorful rooms (some with ornate cornices and views of Arthur's Seat) and compact, modern bathrooms (RS%, family rooms, cash preferred, street parking, 103 Dalkeith Road, tel. 0131/667-4688, www.giffordhouseedinburgh.com, giffordhouse@btinternet.com, Melanie, David, and Margaret).

$$ Hotel Ceilidh-Donia is bigger (17 rooms) and more hotel-

EDINBURGH

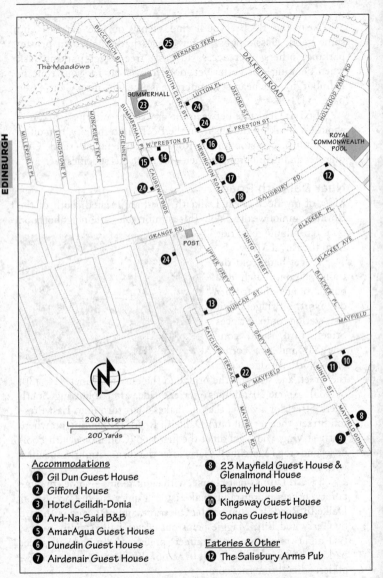

Accommodations
1. Gil Dun Guest House
2. Gifford House
3. Hotel Ceilidh-Donia
4. Ard-Na-Said B&B
5. AmarAgua Guest House
6. Dunedin Guest House
7. Airdenair Guest House

8. 23 Mayfield Guest House & Glenalmond House
9. Barony House
10. Kingsway Guest House
11. Sonas Guest House

Eateries & Other
12. The Salisbury Arms Pub

like than other nearby B&Bs, with a bar and a small reception area, but managers Kevin and Susan and their staff provide guesthouse warmth. The back deck is a pleasant place to relax on a warm day (family room, 2-night minimum on peak-season weekends, 14 Marchhall Crescent, tel. 0131/667-2743, www.hotelceilidh-donia. co.uk, reservations@hotelceilidh-donia.co.uk).

$$ Ard-Na-Said B&B, in an elegant 1875 Victorian house, has seven bright, spacious rooms with modern bathrooms, includ-

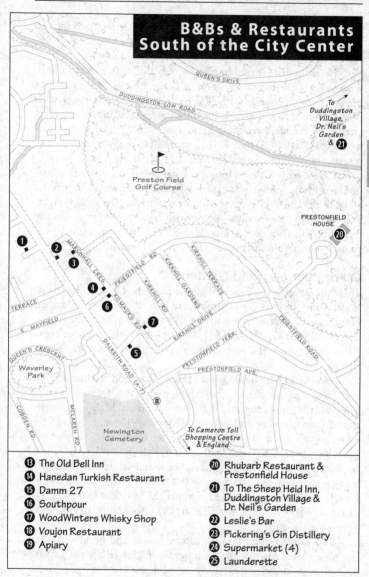

B&Bs & Restaurants South of the City Center

EDINBURGH

- ⑬ The Old Bell Inn
- ⑭ Hanedan Turkish Restaurant
- ⑮ Damm 27
- ⑯ Southpour
- ⑰ WoodWinters Whisky Shop
- ⑱ Voujon Restaurant
- ⑲ Apiary
- ⑳ Rhubarb Restaurant & Prestonfield House
- ㉑ To The Sheep Heid Inn, Duddingston Village & Dr. Neil's Garden
- ㉒ Leslie's Bar
- ㉓ Pickering's Gin Distillery
- ㉔ Supermarket (4)
- ㉕ Launderette

ing one ground-floor room with a pleasant patio and two with Ard-Na-Said (Arthur's Seat) views (2-night minimum preferred in summer, off-street parking, 5 Priestfield Road, tel. 0131/283-6524, mobile 0747-660-6202, www.ardnasaid.co.uk, info@ardnasaid. co.uk, Audrey Ballantine and her son Steven).

$$ AmarAgua Guest House is an inviting Victorian home away from home, with six welcoming rooms—a couple with four-poster beds—and eager hosts (one double has private bath down the hall, 2-night minimum, no kids under 12, street parking, 10 Kilmaurs Terrace, tel. 0131/667-6775, www.amaragua.co.uk, reservations@amaragua.co.uk, Lucia and Kuan).

$$ Dunedin Guest House (dun-EE-din) is bright and plush, with seven well-decorated rooms, a skylit atrium, and a spacious breakfast room/lounge with TV (family rooms, one room with private bath down the hall, includes continental breakfast, extra charge for cooked breakfast, limited off-street parking, 8 Priestfield Road, tel. 0131/668-4438, www.dunedinguesthouse.co.uk, reservations@dunedinguesthouse.co.uk, Mary and Tony).

$ Airdenair Guest House is a hands-off, bare-bones guesthouse, with no formal host greeting (you'll get an access code to let yourself in) and a self-serve breakfast buffet. But the price is right, and the five simple rooms—some with older bathrooms—do the trick (29 Kilmaurs Road, mobile 0781-731-3035, www.airdenair.co.uk, contact@airdenair-edinburgh.co.uk, Duncan).

On or near Mayfield Gardens

These places are just a couple of blocks from the Dalkeith Road options, along the busy Newington Road (which turns in to Mayfield Gardens). All have private parking. To reach them from the center, hop on bus #3, #7, #8, #29, #31, #37, or #49. Note: Some of these buses depart from the second bus stop, a bit farther along North Bridge.

$$$ At 23 Mayfield Guest House, Ross and Kathleen (with their wee helpers Ethan and Alfie) rent seven splurge-worthy, thoughtfully appointed rooms complete with high-tech bathrooms (rain showers and motion-sensor light-up mirrors). Little extras—such as locally sourced gourmet breakfasts, an inviting guest lounge outfitted with leather-bound Sir Arthur Conan Doyle books, an "honesty bar," and classic black-and-white movie screenings—make you feel like royalty (RS% with cash, family room, 2-night minimum preferred in summer, 23 Mayfield Gardens, tel. 0131/667-5806, www.23mayfield.co.uk, info@23mayfield.co.uk). They also rent an apartment.

$$$ Glenalmond House, run by Jimmy and Fiona Mackie, has nine smart rooms, two with garden patios (RS% with cash, discounts for longer stays, family room, no kids under 5, 25 Mayfield Gardens, tel. 0131/668-2392, www.glenalmondhouse.com, enquiries@glenalmondhouse.com).

$$ Barony House, the best value of all these places, is run with infectious enthusiasm by Aussies Paul and Susan. Their seven elegant doubles are lovingly decorated by Susan, who's made the beautiful friezes and fabric headboards (she also bakes welcome pastries for guests). Two of the rooms are next door, in a former servants' quarters, now a peaceful retreat with access to a shared kitchen (3-night minimum preferred in summer, no kids under 9, 20 Mayfield Gardens, tel. 0131/662-9938, www.baronyhouse. co.uk, booknow@baronyhouse.co.uk).

$$ Kingsway Guest House, with seven bright and stylish rooms, is owned by conscientious, delightful Gary and Lizzie, who have thought of all the little touches, such as a DVD library and in-room Internet radios, and offer good advice on neighborhood eats (RS% with cash, family rooms, one room with private bath down the hall, off-street parking, 5 East Mayfield, tel. 0131/667-5029, www.edinburgh-guesthouse.com, booking@kingswayguesthouse. com).

$$ Sonas Guest House is nothing fancy—just a simple, easy-going place with nine rooms, six of which have bathtubs (family room, 3 East Mayfield, tel. 0131/667-2781, www.sonasguesthouse. com, info@sonasguesthouse.com, Irene and Dennis).

Eating in Edinburgh

Edinburgh, with a strong economy and more tourism than ever, is thriving with dining options. Tourists clog the famous stretches where bottom-feeding eateries make easy money. But if you walk just a few blocks away from the chain restaurants and tacky strips, you'll find a different world. Things are very competitive, and you'll find even high-end places offer lunch and early dinner specials. Reservations are essential in August and on weekends, and a good idea anytime. Here are some favorites of mine, designed to fill the tank economically at lunch time or give you a great experience for dinner. With the ease and economy of Uber and the bus system, don't be too tied to your hotel or B&B neighborhood for dinner.

THE OLD TOWN
I prefer spots within a few minutes' walk of the tourist zone—just far enough to offer better value and a more local atmosphere.

Just off the Royal Mile on George IV Bridge
$$$ Le Bistrot is the tour guides' favorite—a delightful café hiding just steps off of the Royal Mile in the same building as the French consulate (as if put here by the consulate to promote a love of French culture). Its glowy ambience, authentic French menu, and great prices make this a welcoming spot to have dinner before an evening stroll down the Royal Mile—when all the crowds have gone to the pubs. Try their soup or fish of the day (£16 fixed-price lunch, daily 9:00-22:00, 59 George IV Bridge, tel. 0131/225-4021, www.lebistrot.co.uk).

$$$$ Ondine Seafood Restaurant is a dressy, top-end res-

EDINBURGH

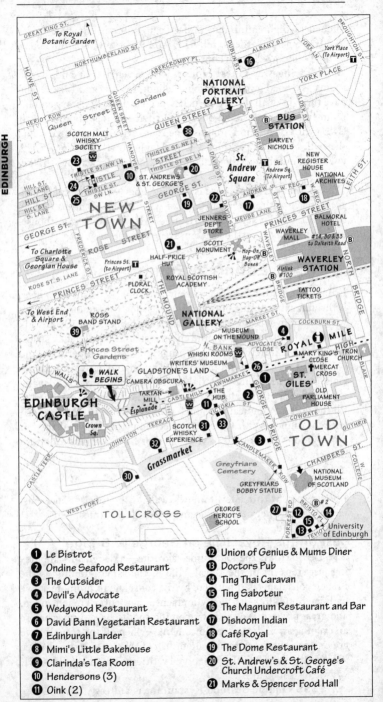

1 Le Bistrot
2 Ondine Seafood Restaurant
3 The Outsider
4 Devil's Advocate
5 Wedgwood Restaurant
6 David Bann Vegetarian Restaurant
7 Edinburgh Larder
8 Mimi's Little Bakehouse
9 Clarinda's Tea Room
10 Hendersons (3)
11 Oink (2)

12 Union of Genius & Mums Diner
13 Doctors Pub
14 Ting Thai Caravan
15 Ting Saboteur
16 The Magnum Restaurant and Bar
17 Dishoom Indian
18 Café Royal
19 The Dome Restaurant
20 St. Andrew's & St. George's
     Church Undercroft Café
21 Marks & Spencer Food Hall

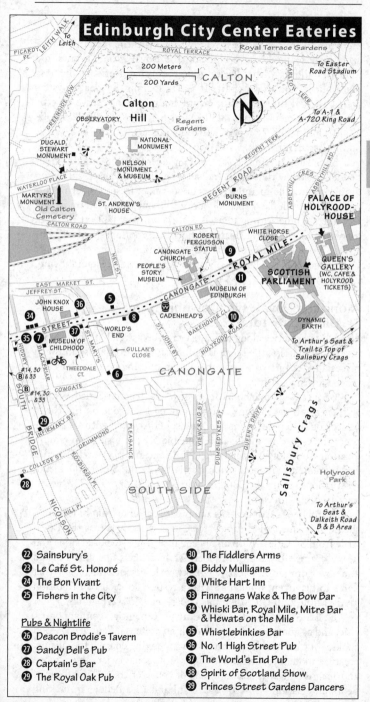

Edinburgh City Center Eateries

22 Sainsbury's
23 Le Café St. Honoré
24 The Bon Vivant
25 Fishers in the City

<u>Pubs & Nightlife</u>
26 Deacon Brodie's Tavern
27 Sandy Bell's Pub
28 Captain's Bar
29 The Royal Oak Pub

30 The Fiddlers Arms
31 Biddy Mulligans
32 White Hart Inn
33 Finnegans Wake & The Bow Bar
34 Whiski Bar, Royal Mile, Mitre Bar & Hewats on the Mile
35 Whistlebinkies Bar
36 No. 1 High Street Pub
37 The World's End Pub
38 Spirit of Scotland Show
39 Princes Street Gardens Dancers

taurant with a smart clientele and a quality, sophisticated vibe; it's known for some of the best seafood in town (the menu is almost exclusively seafood). It's a block off the Royal Mile, upstairs in a modern building with a sleek dining room that overlooks the busy road, but feels a world apart. If you're looking for deals, oysters are £1 each at the bar during happy hour, and they serve an economic lunch menu until 18:30 (Mon-Sat 12:00-15:00 & 17:30-22:00, closed Sun, 2 George IV Bridge, tel. 0131/226-1888, www.ondinerestaurant.co.uk).

$$$ **The Outsider** has a thriving energy. It's a proudly independent bistro with a social (noisy) vibe filling its sleek, sprawling dining room. The menu features good-value, fresh, modern Scottish cuisine with daily specials "until sold out" scribbled on it. You feel like a winner eating here. Ask for a window table at the back for views of the castle floating above the rooftops (daily 12:00-23:00, lunch specials until 17:00, reservations smart, 15 George IV Bridge, tel. 0131/226-3131, www.theoutsiderrestaurant.com, Eddie and partners).

Along the Royal Mile, Downhill from St. Giles' Cathedral

Though the eateries along this most-crowded stretch of the city are invariably touristy, the scene is fun. Sprinkled in this list are some places a block or two off the main drag offering better values and maybe fewer tourists.

$$$ **Hewats on the Mile,** next to the recommended Whiski Bar, is an intimate refuge wedged among the shops on the Royal Mile. You'll step down into an atmospheric cavern with tartan accents and enjoy fine dining at reasonable prices for such a premium location. Its colorful Scottish-Mediterranean dishes are flavorful, and ingredients are local (Mon-Sat 17:00-22:00, Sun 18:00-21:00, reservations required, 123b High Street, tel. 0131/557-5732, www.hewatsedinburgh.com).

$$$ **Devil's Advocate** is a popular gastropub that hides down the narrow lane called Advocates Close, directly across the Royal Mile from St. Giles. With an old cellar setting—exposed stone and heavy beams—done up in modern style, it feels like a mix of old and new Edinburgh. Creative whisky cocktails kick off a menu that dares to be adventurous, but with a respect for Scottish tradition (daily 12:00-22:00, 9 Advocates Close, tel. 0131/225-4465).

$$$$ **Wedgwood Restaurant** is romantic, contemporary, chic, and as gourmet as possible with no pretense. Paul Wedgwood cooks while his wife Lisa serves with appetizing charm. The cuisine: creative, modern Scottish with an international twist. The pigeon-and-haggis starter is scrumptious, or consider their "Wee Tour of Scotland" tasting *menu* for £55. Paul and Lisa believe in making

the meal the event of the evening—don't come here to eat and run (the table is yours). I like the ground level with the Royal Mile view and the busy kitchen ambience better than their basement seating (fine wine by the glass, daily 12:00-15:00 & 18:00-22:00, reservations smart, 267 Canongate on Royal Mile, tel. 0131/558-8737, www.wedgwoodtherestaurant.co.uk).

$$$ David Bann Vegetarian Restaurant is a worthwhile stop for well-heeled vegetarians in need of a break from traditional veggie grub. While vegetarian as can be, this place—with its candles and woody decor—doesn't have even a hint of hippie. It's upscale (it has a cocktail bar), sleek, minimalist, and stylish (gorgeously presented dishes), serious about quality, and organic. There's an enthusiastic local following—and decadent desserts (daily 12:00-22:00, vegan and gluten-free options, a long block off the Royal Mile at 56 St. Mary's Street, tel. 0131/556-5888, www.davidbann.co.uk).

EDINBURGH

Quick, Easy, and Cheap Breakfast and Lunch Options

$ Edinburgh Larder promises "a taste of the country" in the center of the city. They focus on high-quality, homestyle breakfast and lunches made from seasonal, local ingredients. The café, with table service, is a convivial space with rustic tables filled by local families. Their "Little Larder" sister outlet, next door, offers more of the same (Mon-Fri 8:00-16:00, Sat-Sun from 9:00, 15 Blackfriars Street, tel. 0131/556-6922).

$ Mimi's Little Bakehouse, a handy Royal Mile outpost of a prizewinning bakery, serves up baked goods—try the scones—and sandwiches in their cute and modern shop (daily 9:00-18:00, 250 Canongate, tel. 0131/556-6632).

$ Clarinda's Tea Room, near the bottom of the Royal Mile, is a charming time warp—a fine and tasty place to relax after touring the Mile or the Palace of Holyroodhouse. Stop in for a quiche, salad, or soup lunch. It's also great for sandwiches and tea and cake any time (Mon-Sat 9:00-16:30, Sun from 10:00, 69 Canongate, tel. 0131/557-1888).

$$ Hendersons is a bright and casual local chain with good vegetarian dishes to go or eat in (daily 9:00-17:00, 67 Holyrood Road—three minutes off Royal Mile near Scottish Parliament end, tel. 0131/557-1606).

$ Oink is handy for a cheap sandwich to go near the top (34 Victoria Street) or bottom (82 Canongate) of the Royal Mile. They carve from a freshly roasted pig each afternoon for sandwiches that come in "oink" or "grunter" sizes. Watch the pig shrink in the front window throughout the day (daily 11:00-18:00 or whenever they run out of meat, cash only, mobile 0777-196-8233).

Historic Pubs for Grub Along the Mile

To grab some forgettable pub grub in historic surroundings, consider one of these landmark pubs described on my self-guided walk. All serve basic pub meals for £10-20 (cheaper lunch deals) and serve food daily from about 12:00 to 21:00. Deacon Brodie's is the most touristy and famous. The others have better ambience and feature music at night (see "Live Music in Pubs" on page 794).

$$ Deacon Brodie's Tavern, at a dead-center location on the Royal Mile, has a sloppy pub on the ground floor with a sloppy restaurant upstairs (435 Lawnmarket).

$$ The Mitre Bar has a classic interior, and their menu includes good meat pies (131 High Street). The neighboring **$$$ Whiski Pub** and **$$ Royal Mile Pub** are also good options.

$$ The World's End Pub, farther down the Mile at Canongate, is a colorful old place dishing up hearty meals from a creative menu in a fun, dark, and noisy space (4 High Street).

Near the National Museum

These restaurants (all within about 100 yards of each other) are happily removed from the Royal Mile melee and skew to a youthful clientele with few tourists. After passing the Greyfriars Bobby statue and the National Museum, fork left onto Forrest Road. To get to the B&B neighborhood from here, take bus #2 from Bristo Place (across the street from Hotel du Vin).

$ Union of Genius is a creative soup kitchen with a strong identity. They cook up a selection of delicious soups with fun foodie twists each morning at their main location in Leith, then deliver them to this shop by bicycle (for environmental reasons). These are supplemented with good salads and fresh-baked breads. The "flight" comes with three small cups of soup and three types of bread. Line up at the counter, then either take your soup to go or sit in the cramped interior, with a couple of tables and counter seating (Mon-Fri 10:00-16:00, Sat from 12:00, closed Sun, 8 Forrest Road, tel. 0131/226-4436).

$$ Mums Diner, a kitschy Scottish diner, serves up comfort food just like mum used to make. The extensive menu offers huge portions of heavy, greasy Scottish/British standards—bangers (sausages), meat pies, burgers, and artery-clogging breakfasts (served until 12:00)—and vegetarian options. There's often a line out the door on weekends (Mon-Sat 9:00-22:00, Sun from 10:00, 4 Forrest Road, tel. 0131/260-9806).

$$ Doctors Pub is a big, inviting corner hangout with a wide-ranging menu of basic pub grub—along with an impressive array of gins, whiskies, and cask ales (kitchen open daily 12:00-14:00 & 18:00-21:00, 32 Forrest Road, where Forrest Road hits Teviot Place, tel. 0131/225-1819).

$$ Ting Thai Caravan, is a loud, industrial-mod eatery serving adventurous Thai street food (soups, noodles, and curries). It's a young, stark, and simple place with thumping music, communal tables, and great food (cash only, daily 11:30-22:00, Fri-Sat until 23:00, 8 Teviot Place, tel. 0131/225-9801).

$$ Ting Saboteur, just a few doors down from Ting Thai Caravan, serves Vietnamese and Southeast Asian cuisine in a slightly more casual (but equally hip), techy-chic space. The enticing menu of bao buns and creative bowls encourages a sense of adventure—consider ordering family-style (no reservations, daily 11:30-22:00, Fri-Sat until 23:00, 19 Teviot Place, tel. 0131/623-0384).

THE NEW TOWN

In the Georgian part of town, you'll find a bustling world of office workers, students, and pensioners doing their thing. These eateries are all within a 10-minute walk of Waverley Station.

Favorites on or near St. Andrew Square

$$$ The Magnum Restaurant and Bar is a relaxed, classy pub-gone-bistro serving beautifully presented Scottish dishes with smart service and no pretense. The appetizing menu is creative and inviting. A block beyond the tourist zone, it feels like a neighborhood favorite (£17-20 lunch specials, daily 12:00-14:30 & 17:30-22:00, 1 Albany Street, tel. 0131/557-4366).

$$ Dishoom is a sprawling, high-energy, Bombay Café phenom. The menu makes Indian food joyfully accessible (and affordable). You'll enjoy upscale South Asian cuisine in a bustling, dark, 1920s dining room on the second floor overlooking St. Andrew Square (I'd avoid the basement). It's a popular spot but no reservations are taken, so plan ahead (daily 12:00-23:00, 3A St. Andrew Square, tel. 0131/202-6406).

$$ Café Royal is a movie producer's dream pub—the perfect *fin de siècle* setting for a coffee, beer, or light meal. (In fact, parts of *Chariots of Fire* were filmed here.) Drop in, if only to admire the 1880 tiles featuring famous inventors. The menu is both traditional and modern with vegetarian dishes and lots of oysters (daily 12:00-22:00, 19 West Register Street, tel. 0131/556-1884, no reservations). The attached small, dressier **restaurant,** specializing in oysters, fish, and game—while stuffier and more expensive—is also good.

$$$$ The Dome Restaurant,

filling what was a fancy bank, serves modern international cuisine around a classy bar and under the elegant 19th-century skylight dome. With soft jazz and chic, white-tablecloth ambience, it feels a world apart. Come here not for the food, but for the opulent atmosphere (lunch deals, early-bird special until 18:30, daily 12:00-23:00, reserve for dinner, open for a drink any time under the dome, 14 George Street, tel. 0131/624-8624, www.thedomeedinburgh.com).

$ St. Andrew's and St. George's Church Undercroft Café, in the basement of a fine old church, is the cheapest place in town for soup, sandwiches, quiche, or scones for lunch. Your tiny bill helps support the Church of Scotland (Mon-Fri 10:00-14:00, closed Sat-Sun, just off St. Andrew Square at 13 George Street, tel. 0131/225-3847). It's run by sweet volunteers who love to chat.

Supermarkets: Marks & Spencer Food Hall offers an assortment of tasty hot foods, prepared sandwiches, fresh bakery items, a wide selection of wines and beverages, and plastic utensils at the checkout queue. It's just a block from the Scott Monument and the picnic-perfect Princes Street Gardens (Mon-Sat 8:00-19:00, Thu until 20:00, Sun 11:00-18:00, Princes Street 54—separate stairway next to main M&S entrance leads directly to food hall, tel. 0131/225-2301). **Sainsbury's** supermarket, a block off Princes Street, also offers grab-and-go items (daily 7:00-22:00, on corner of Rose Street on St. Andrew Square, across the street from Jenners).

Hip Eateries on and near Thistle Street

Peaceful little Thistle Street has a cluster of enticing eateries. Browse the options, but tune into these favorites.

$$$ Le Café St. Honoré, tucked away like a secret bit of old Paris, is a charming place with friendly service and walls lined with wine bottles. It serves French-Scottish cuisine in tight, Old World, cut-glass elegance to a dressy crowd (three-course lunch and dinner specials, daily 12:00-14:00 & 17:30-22:00, reservations smart—I'd ask to sit upstairs rather than in the basement, 34 Northwest Thistle Street Lane, tel. 0131/226-2211, www.cafesthonore.com).

$$$ The Bon Vivant is woody, youthful, and candlelit, with a rotating menu of French/Scottish dishes, lots of champagne by the glass, and a companion wine shop next door. They have fun tapas plates and heartier dishes, served either in the bar up front or in the restaurant in back (daily 12:00-22:00, 55 Thistle Street, tel. 0131/225-3275, www.bonvivantedinburgh.co.uk).

$$$ Fishers in the City, a good place to dine on seafood, has an inviting menu and a fine value lunch and early-bird dinner menu (served daily until 18:00). The energy is lively, the clientele is smart, and the room is bright and airy with a simple elegance (daily 12:00-

22:00, lots of nice wines by the glass, reservations smart, 58 Thistle Street, tel. 0131/225-5109, www.fishersrestaurants.co.uk).

$$ Hendersons Vegetarian has fed a generation of New Town vegetarians hearty cuisine and salads. Even carnivores love this place for its delectable salads, desserts, and smoothies. Their main restaurant, facing Hanover Street, is self-service by day but has table service after 17:00 (Mon-Sat 8:30-22:00, Sun 10:30-16:00, between Queen and George streets at 94 Hanover Street, tel. 0131/225-2131). Just around the corner on Thistle Street, **Hendersons Vegan** has a strictly vegan menu and feels a bit more casual (daily 12:00-21:30, tel. 0131/225-2605).

THE WEST END

In this posh neighborhood of high-end eateries, the following places have character, tasty food, and fair prices. For locations, see the map on page 801.

$$$ La P'tite Folie Restaurant occupies a beautiful, half-timbered Tudor house that once housed a Polish Catholic church. Its sophisticated, local clientele goes for flavorful specialties like steak and duck—all with a French flair (good-value two-course lunch, food served Mon-Thu 12:00-15:00 & 18:00-22:00, Fri-Sat until 23:00, closed Sun, reservations smart, 9 Randolph Place, tel. 0131/225-8678, www.laptitefolie.co.uk). Under the same roof, **$$ Le Di-Vin Wine Bar** is in the nave of the church, with an extensive wine list and nice cheese-and-meat boards (Mon-Sat 12:00-late, closed Sun, tel. 0131/538-1815).

$$$ La Piazza stands out among several Italian restaurants in this neighborhood. It's a welcoming place with solid pasta dishes, pizzas, and an Italian villa vibe. Pleasant terrace tables are out back (generally Mon-Sat 12:00-23:00, Sun 16:30-22:00, reservations strongly recommended, 97 Shandwick Place, tel. 0131/221-1150, www.lapiazzaedinburgh.com).

$$ Teutchers is a friendly joint on cute William Street, with a fun vibe and nice tables in a rustic space. The food is a cut above typical pub grub, and the downstairs restaurant serves Scottish specialties with local ingredients (daily 10:00-late, 26 William Street, tel. 0131/225-2973).

Supermarket: There's a handy **Sainsbury's** near my recommended West End accommodations (daily 6:00-23:00, 32 Shandwick Place). A **Marks & Spencer** is at the Haymarket train station (Mon-Fri 6:00-22:00, Sat 7:00-21:00, Sun from 9:00).

SOUTH OF THE CITY CENTER

These places are within a 10-minute walk of my recommended B&Bs. For locations, see the map on page 805. For a cozy drink after dinner, visit the recommended pubs in the area (see "Nightlife in Edinburgh," earlier). Except for the "memorable meals" places, I wouldn't eat here unless you're staying nearby.

Pub Grub

$$ The Salisbury Arms is a gastropub serving upscale, traditional classics with flair. While they have a bar area and a garden terrace, I'd dine in their elegant restaurant section. The menu ranges from burgers and salads to more sophisticated dishes (book ahead for restaurant, no reservations taken for pub, food served daily 12:00-22:00, across from the pool at 58 Dalkeith Road, tel. 0131/667-4518, www.thesalisburyarmsedinburgh.co.uk).

$$ The Old Bell Inn, with an old-time sports-bar ambience—fishing, golf, horses, lots of TVs—serves an extensive menu of pub meals with daily specials. This is a classic "snug pub"—all dark woods and brass beer taps, littered with evocative knickknacks (bar tables can be reserved, food served daily until 21:15, 233 Causewayside, tel. 0131/668-1573, www.oldbelledinburgh.co.uk).

Eateries Around Newington Road

$$ Hanedan serves fresh Turkish food at tiny tables in a cozy dining room. The lamb, fish, and vegetable dishes are all authentic and bursting with flavor, making this a welcome alternative to pub fare (Tue-Sun 12:00-15:00 & 17:30-late, closed Mon, 42 West Preston Street, tel. 0131/667-4242).

$$ Damm 27, tucked around the corner from Newington, is rustic-chic but unpretentious, with an appealing cocktail-and-wine list and attentive service. The menu features small plates, gourmet burgers, mussel pots, and good vegetarian and vegan options (daily 10:00-late, 27 Causewayside, tel. 0131/667-6693).

$$ Southpour is a nice place for a local beer, craft cocktail, or reliable meal from a menu of salads, sandwiches, meat dishes, and other comfort foods. The brick walls, wood beams, and giant windows give it a warm and open vibe (don't miss the specials board, daily 10:00-22:00, 1 Newington Road, tel. 0131/650-1100).

$$ Voujon Restaurant serves a fusion menu of Bengali and Indian cuisines. Vegetarians appreciate the expansive yet inexpensive offerings (daily 17:00-23:00, 107 Newington Road, tel. 0131/667-5046).

$$ Apiary has an inviting, casual interior and a hit-or-miss, eclectic menu that mingles various international flavors—they call it "local products with global spices" (early-bird specials, daily 10:00-15:00 & 17:30-21:00, 33 Newington Road, tel. 0131/668-4999).

Groceries: On the main streets near the restaurants you'll find **Sainsbury's Local** and **Co-op** (on South Clerk Road), and **Tesco**

Express and another **Sainsbury's Local** one block over on Causewayside (all open late—until at least 22:00).

Memorable Meals Farther Out

$$$$ **Rhubarb Restaurant** specializes in Old World elegance. It's in "Edinburgh's most handsome house"—an over-the-top riot of antiques, velvet, tassels, and fringe. The plush dark-rhubarb color theme reminds visitors that this was the place where rhubarb was first popularized in Britain. It's a short taxi ride past the other recommended eateries behind Arthur's Seat, in a huge estate with big, shaggy Highland cattle enjoying their salads al fresco. At night, it's a candlelit wonder. Most spend a ton here. Reserve in advance and dress up if you can (daily 12:00-14:00 & 18:00-22:00, afternoon tea served daily 12:00-19:00, in Prestonfield House, Priestfield Road, tel. 0131/662-2303, www.prestonfield.com). For details on their schmaltzy Scottish folk evening, see "Nightlife in Edinburgh," earlier.

$$ **The Sheep Heid Inn,** Edinburgh's oldest and most inviting public house, is equally notable for its history, date-night appeal, and hearty portions of affordable, classy dishes. It's a short cab ride or pleasant 30-minute walk from the B&B neighborhood, but it's worth the effort to dine in this dreamy setting in the presence of past queens and kings—choose between the bar downstairs, dining room upstairs, or outside in the classic garden courtyard (food served Mon-Fri 12:00-21:00, Sat-Sun 12:00-21:30, 43 The Causeway, tel. 0131/661-7974, www.thesheepheidedinburgh.co.uk).

Edinburgh Connections

BY TRAIN OR BUS

From Edinburgh by Train to: Glasgow (7/hour, 50 minutes), **St. Andrews** (train to Leuchars, 2/hour, 1 hour, then 10-minute bus into St. Andrews), **Stirling** (2/hour, 45 minutes), **Inverness** (6/day direct, 3.5 hours, more with transfer), **Oban** (roughly 6/day, 4.5 hours, change in Glasgow), **York** (3/hour, 2.5 hours), **London** (2/hour, 4.5 hours), **Durham** (2/hour direct, 2 hours, less frequent in winter), **Keswick/Lake District** (8/day to Penrith—more via Carlisle, 1.5 hours, then 40-minute bus ride to Keswick). Train info: Tel. 0345-748-4950, www.nationalrail.co.uk.

By Citylink Bus: Direct buses go to **Glasgow** (#900, 4/hour, 1.5 hours), **Inverness** (express #G90, 2/day, 4 hours; or #M90, 2/day, 4 hours, more with transfer), **Stirling** (every 2 hours on #909, 1.5 hours). To reach other destinations in the Highlands—including **Oban, Fort William,** or **Glencoe**—you'll have to transfer. It's usually fastest to take the train to Glasgow and change to a bus there. For details, see "Getting Around the Highlands" on page

EDINBURGH

914. For bus info, stop by the station or call Scottish Citylink (tel. 0871-266-3333, www.citylink.co.uk).

Additional long-distance routes may be operated by National Express (www.nationalexpress.com) or Megabus (www.megabus. com).

BY PLANE

Edinburgh Airport is located eight miles northwest of the center (code: EDI, tel. 0844-481-8989, www.edinburghairport.com). A **taxi** or **Uber** between the airport and city center costs about £30 (25 minutes to downtown, West End, or Dalkeith Road). The airport is also well connected to central Edinburgh by tram and bus. Just follow signs outside; the tram tracks are straight ahead, and the bus stop is to the right, along the main road in front of the terminal. **Trams** make several stops in town, including along Princes Street and at St. Andrew Square (£6, £8.50 round-trip, buy ticket from machine, runs every 5-10 minutes from early morning until 23:30, 35 minutes, www.edinburghtrams.com).

The Lothian **Airlink bus #100** drops you at Waverley Bridge (£4.50, £7.50 round-trip, runs every 10 minutes, 30 minutes, tel. 0131/555-6363, www.lothianbuses.com).

ROUTE TIPS FOR DRIVERS HEADING SOUTH

If you're linking by car to England, note that it's 100 miles south from Edinburgh to Hadrian's Wall; to Durham, it's another 50 miles.

To Hadrian's Wall: From Edinburgh, head south on Dalkeith Road (a handy Cameron Toll Shopping Center with a Sainsbury's grocery and cheap gas is off to your right as you head out of town; gas and parking behind store). Follow Dalkeith Road for about four miles (10 minutes) until you reach the *Sheriffhall* roundabout. Take the exit to A-68 (straight ahead). The A-68 road takes you to Hadrian's Wall in 2.5 hours. You'll pass Jedburgh and its abbey after one hour. (For one last shot of Scotland shopping, there's a bus tour's delight just before Jedburgh, with kilt makers, woolens, and a sheepskin shop.) Across from Jedburgh's lovely abbey is a free parking lot, a good visitors center, and pay WCs. The England/Scotland border is a fun, quick stop (great view, ice cream, and tea caravan). Just after the turn for Colwell, turn right onto the A-6079, and roller-coaster four miles down to Low Brunton. Then turn right onto the B-6318, and stay on it by turning left at Chollerford, following the Roman wall westward.

To Durham: If you're heading straight to Durham, you can take the scenic coastal route on the A-1 (a few more miles than the A-68, but similar time), which takes you near Holy Island and Bamburgh Castle.

GLASGOW

Glasgow (GLAZ-goh)—astride the River Clyde—is a surprising city. In its heyday, Glasgow was one of Europe's biggest cities and the second-largest in Britain, right behind London. A century ago it had 1.2 million people, twice the size (and with twice the importance) of today. It was an industrial powerhouse producing 25 percent of the world's oceangoing ships. But in the mid-20th century, tough times hit Glasgow, giving it a rough edge and a run-down image.

At the city's low point during the Margaret Thatcher years (1980s), its leaders embarked on a systematic rejuvenation designed to again make Glasgow appealing to businesses, tourists...and locals. Today the city feels revitalized and goes out of its way to offer a warm welcome. Glaswegians (rhymes with "Norwegians") are some of the chattiest people in Scotland—and have the most entertaining (and impenetrable) accent.

Many travelers give Glasgow a miss, but that's a shame: I consider it Scotland's most underrated destination. Glasgow is a workaday Scottish city as well as a cosmopolitan destination, with an unpretentious friendliness, an energetic and expanding dining and nightlife scene, top-notch museums (most of them free), and a unique flair for art and design. It's also a pilgrimage site for architecture buffs, thanks to a cityscape packed

with Victorian facades, early-20th-century touches, and bold and glassy new construction. Most beloved are the works by hometown boy Charles Rennie Mackintosh, the visionary—and now very trendy—architect who left his mark all over Glasgow at the turn of the 20th century.

Many more tourists visit Edinburgh, a short train trip away. But for a more complete look at urban Scotland, be sure to stop off in Glasgow. Edinburgh may have the royal aura, but Glasgow has down-to-earth appeal. In Glasgow, there's no upper-crust history, and no one puts on airs. In Edinburgh, people identify with the quality of the school they attended; in Glasgow, it's their soccer team allegiance. One Glaswegian told me, "The people of Glasgow have a better time at a funeral than the people of Edinburgh have at a wedding." Here, friendly locals do their best to introduce you to the fun-loving, laid-back Glaswegian way of life.

PLANNING YOUR TIME

While many visitors blitz Glasgow as a day trip from Edinburgh or Stirling (and a single day in Glasgow is certainly more exciting than a fourth day in Edinburgh), the city can easily fill two days of sightseeing.

On a quick visit, follow my "Get to Know Glasgow" self-guided walk, tying together the most important sights in the city's core. If your time is short, the interiors most worth considering are the Tenement House and the Kelvingrove Museum.

With additional time, your options open up. Follow my West End Walk to get a taste of Glasgow's appealing residential zone, which has some of the city's best restaurants as well as a number of worthwhile sights. Fans of Art Nouveau and Charles Rennie Mackintosh can lace together a busy day's worth of sightseeing (the TI has a brochure laying it out). At a minimum, those interested in Mackintosh should visit the Mackintosh House at the Hunterian Gallery (in the West End) and the Mackintosh exhibit at the Kelvingrove Museum.

Regardless of how long you're staying, consider the 1.5-hour hop-on, hop-off bus tour, which is convenient for getting the bigger picture and reaching three important sights away from the center (the Cathedral Precinct, the Riverside Museum, and the Kelvingrove Museum).

Day Trip from Edinburgh: For a full day, catch the 9:30 train to Glasgow (morning trains at least every 10 minutes; discount for same-day round-trip if traveling outside rush hours or on weekends); it arrives at Queen Street Train Station before 10:30. To fill your Glasgow hours smartly, I'd do the entire hop-on, hop-off bus tour circuit (1.5 hours), then follow my self-guided walk through downtown (finishing with the Tenement House). Next, check out the Kelvingrove Museum and have dinner nearby (in the Finnieston area). Catch a train that leaves around 21:00 to return to Edinburgh (evening trains depart every 10-20 minutes).

Orientation to Glasgow

Although it's often thought of as a "second city," Glasgow is actually Scotland's biggest (pop. 621,000, swelling to 1.2 million within Greater Glasgow—that's one out of every five Scots).

The tourist's Glasgow has two parts: the businesslike downtown (train stations, commercial zone, and main shopping drag) and the residential West End (B&Bs, restaurants, and nightlife). Both areas have good sights, and both are covered in this chapter by self-guided walks.

Glasgow's **downtown** is a tight grid of boxy office buildings and shopping malls, making it feel more like a midsize American city than a big Scottish one—like Cincinnati or Pittsburgh, but with shorter skyscrapers made of Victorian sandstone rather than glass and steel. The walkable city center has two main drags, both lined with shops and crawling with shoppers: Sauchiehall Street (pronounced "Sockyhall," running west to east) and Buchanan Street (running north to south). These two pedestrian malls—part of a shopping zone nicknamed the Style Mile—make a big zig and zag through the heart of town. The city is busy revamping both Sauchiehall and the third leg of the Style Mile, Argyle Street, in an effort to reduce car traffic and make the city more cycle- and pedestrian-friendly. You'll notice wide sidewalks and bike lanes (and very little parking).

The **West End** is a posh suburb, with big homes, upscale apartment buildings, and lots of green space. The area has three pockets of interest: near the Hillhead subway stop, with a lively restaurant scene and the Botanic Gardens; the University of Glasgow campus, with its stately buildings and fine museums; and, just downhill through a sprawling park, the area around the Kelvingrove Museum, with a lively nearby strip of trendy bars and restaurants (Finnieston).

TOURIST INFORMATION

The TI is on Buchanan Street, just across from Nelson Mandela Place and right behind the lower entrance to the Buchanan Street subway stop (good free Glasgow map; hours change seasonally but

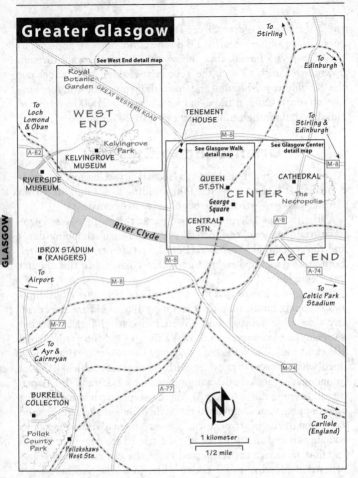

Greater Glasgow

GLASGOW

generally Mon-Sat 9:00-18:00, Sun 10:00-16:00; 156a Buchanan Street, www.visitscotland.com).

ARRIVAL IN GLASGOW

By Train: Glasgow, a major Scottish transportation hub, has two main train stations, which are just a few blocks apart in the heart of town: **Central Station** (with a grand, genteel interior under a vast steel-and-glass Industrial Age roof) and **Queen Street Station** (more functional, with better connections to Edinburgh—take the exit marked *Buchanan Street* to reach the main shopping drag). Both stations have pay WCs and baggage storage. If going between stations to change trains, you can walk five minutes or take the roundabout "RailLink" bus #398 (free with train ticket, otherwise

£1.20, 5/hour; also goes to the bus station). Either way, I'd allow at least 30 minutes to make a connection.

By Bus: Buchanan bus station is at Killermont Street, two blocks up the hill behind Queen Street Station (luggage lockers daily 6:00-23:00; travel center info desk daily 6:00-18:00; Citylink ticket office daily 9:00-17:00).

By Car: Glasgow's downtown streets are steep, mostly one-way, congested with buses and pedestrians, and a horrible place to drive. Ideally, do Glasgow without a car—for example, tour Edinburgh and Glasgow by public transit, then pick up your rental car on your way out of town. If you are stuck with a car in Glasgow, try to sleep in the West End, where driving and parking are easier (and use public transit or taxis as necessary). Parking downtown is a hassle: Metered street parking is expensive (£3/hour) and limited to two hours during the day; garages are even more expensive (figure £25/24 hours).

The M-8 motorway, which slices through downtown Glasgow, is the easiest way in and out of the city, and it connects well with other highways.

By Plane: For information on Glasgow's two airports, see "Glasgow Connections," at the end of this chapter.

HELPFUL HINTS

Safety: The city center, which is packed with ambitious career types during the day, can feel deserted at night. While the area between Argyle Street and the River Clyde has been cleaned up in recent years, parts can still feel sketchy. As in any big city, use common sense and don't wander alone down dark alleys. The Style Mile shopping drag, the Merchant City area (east of the train stations), and the West End all bustle with crowded restaurants well into the evening and feel well populated in the wee hours.

If you've picked up a football (soccer) jersey or scarf as a souvenir, don't wear it in Glasgow; passions run very high, and most drunken brawls in town are between supporters of Glasgow's two rival soccer clubs: Celtic in green, and Rangers in blue and red. (For more on the soccer rivalry, see page 830.)

Sightseeing: Almost every sight in Glasgow is free, but most request £3-5 donations (www.glasgowlife.org.uk/museums). While these donations are not required, I like to consider what the experience was worth and decide if and how much to donate as I leave. (Voluntary donations are a nice option—but only work if people actually donate.)

Sunday Travel: Bus and train schedules are dramatically reduced on Sundays and in the off-season. (If you want to get to the Highlands by bus on a Sunday in winter, forget it.)

Laundry: Call to arrange **Majestic Launderette** to pick up and drop off at your B&B or hotel; they also have a launderette near the Kelvingrove Museum in the West End (self-serve or full-serve, Mon-Fri 8:00-18:00, Sat until 16:00, Sun 10:00-16:00, 1110 Argyle Street, see map on page 838, tel. 0141/334-3433).

GETTING AROUND GLASGOW

By City Bus: Most city-center routes are operated by First Bus Company (£1.65 or £2.40/ride depending on destination—ask driver when you board, £4.60 for all-day ticket, pay driver, exact change required or use contactless payment like ApplePay). Buses run every few minutes down Glasgow's main thoroughfares (such as Hope Street) to the downtown core (train stations). You can also get around the city via hop-on, hop-off bus (see "Tours in Glasgow," next).

By Taxi or Uber: Taxis are affordable, plentiful, and often come with nice, chatty cabbies (if your driver has an impenetrable Glaswegian accent, just smile and nod). Most taxi rides within the downtown area cost about £6; to the West End is about £8. Uber works particularly well in Glasgow and lets you make quick connections for about £5.

By Subway: Glasgow's cute and clean little single-line subway system, nicknamed The Clockwork Orange, makes a six-mile circle that has 15 stops. While simple today, when it opened in 1896 it was a wonder (it's the world's third-oldest subway system, after those in London and Budapest). Though the subway is useless for connecting city-center sightseeing (Buchanan Street and St. Enoch are the only downtown stops), it's ideal for connecting to the West End for its sights (like the Kelvingrove Museum; Kelvinhall stop) and restaurants and nightlife (Hillhead stop). It's £1.75 for a single trip or £4.20 for an all-day ticket. The £3 Bramble card is reloadable and reduces your single-ride cost to £1.45, but is worthwhile only if you'll be in Glasgow for several days and/or riding the subway frequently (subway runs Mon-Sat 6:30-23:15, Sun 10:00-18:00, free Wi-Fi at each station, www.spt.co.uk/subway).

Tours in Glasgow

Hop-On, Hop-Off Bus

CitySightseeing connects Glasgow's far-flung historic sights in a 1.5-hour loop and lets you hop on and off as you like. Buses are frequent (every 10-20 minutes, daily 9:30-18:30, service ends earlier in off-season) and alternate between live guides and recorded narration (both are equally good). The route covers the city very well—it's a handy way to reach distant sights like the Riverside

Glasgow at a Glance

▲▲**Tenement House** Perfectly preserved 1930s-era middle-class row house offering a time-warp experience. **Hours:** Daily 10:00-17:00, Nov-Feb Sat-Mon 11:00-16:00, closed Tue-Fri. See page 844.

▲▲**Tennent's Brewery Tour** Scotland's biggest brewery, founded in 1740, offering hour-long tours of its 18-acre facility. **Hours:** Tours on the hour Mon-Sat 10:00-18:00, Sun 12:00-17:00. See page 848.

▲▲**Kelvingrove Art Gallery and Museum** Vast collection that includes the city's best Mackintosh works and paintings by the great masters. **Hours:** Mon-Thu and Sat 10:00-17:00, Fri and Sun from 11:00. See page 851.

▲▲**Riverside Museum** High-tech, kid-friendly museum along the River Clyde dedicated to all things transportation. **Hours:** Mon-Thu and Sat 10:00-17:00, Fri and Sun from 11:00. See page 852.

▲**National Piping Centre** Small but insightful bagpipe museum, with historic instruments and pipers sometimes on hand for demos. **Hours:** Mon-Thu 9:00-19:00, Fri until 17:00, Sat until 15:00, closed Sun. See page 844.

▲**Glasgow Cathedral** Rare example of intact pre-Reformation Scottish cathedral. **Hours:** Mon-Sat 9:30-17:30, Sun 13:00-17:00; Oct-March Mon-Sat 10:00-16:00, Sun from 13:00. See page 846.

▲**St. Mungo Museum of Religious Life and Art** Secular, city-run museum promoting religious understanding and offering a great view from the top floor. **Hours:** Tue-Thu and Sat 10:00-17:00, Fri and Sun from 11:00, closed Mon. See page 847.

▲**Necropolis** Burial hill with grand tombstones of eminent Glaswegians from the city's Victorian glory days. **Hours:** Always open. See page 848.

▲**Hunterian Gallery and Mackintosh House** Two-for-one museum featuring works of Scottish artists and the reconstructed home of the country's greatest architect. **Hours:** Tue-Sat 10:00-17:00, Sun 11:00-16:00, closed Mon. See page 849.

▲**Hunterian Museum** Natural science museum housing everything from ancient Roman artifacts to animal oddities in a gorgeous university building. **Hours:** Tue-Sat 10:00-17:00, Sun 11:00-16:00, closed Mon. See page 850.

GLASGOW

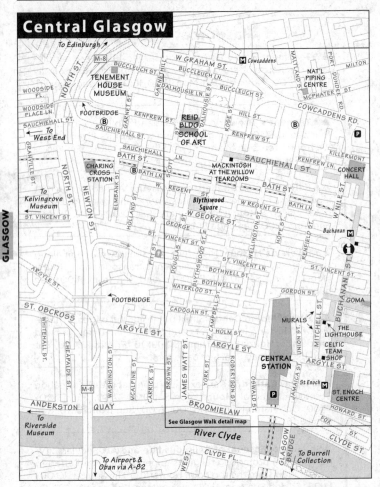

Central Glasgow

Museum—and the guide does a fine job of describing activities at each stop. While the first stop is on George Square (where you can buy your ticket from CitySightseeing staff), you can hop on and pay the driver anywhere along the route (one day-£16, two days-£17, cash only if buying ticket from driver, tel. 0141/204-0444, www.citysightseeingglasgow.co.uk).

Walking Tours

Walking Tours in Glasgow was started by Jenny and Liv, two University of Glasgow graduates who love their city. The city center tour starts in George Square and covers about 3 miles in 2.5 hours (daily at 10:30 and 14:00, off-season at 10:30 only); their street-art tour covers Glasgow's ever-growing mural scene (Fri-Sun at 14:00, off-season by request only). Ask about their West

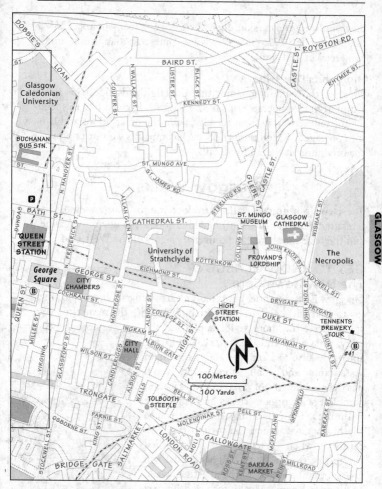

End tour (by request only; all tours £10, www.walkingtoursin.com, walkingtouringlasgow@gmail.com).

Trainspotters may enjoy the guided, behind-the-scenes tours of **Central Station,** including a spooky, abandoned Victorian train platform (£13, book ahead, www.glasgowcentraltours.co.uk).

Local Guides

Joan Dobbie, a native Glaswegian and registered Scottish Tourist Guide, will give you the insider's take on Glasgow's sights (£155/half-day, £205/day, tours on foot or by public transit—no tours by car, tel. 01355/236-749, mobile 07773-555-151, joan.leo100@gmail.com).

Ann Stewart is a former high-school geography teacher turned Blue Badge guide who is excited to show you around Glasgow or take you on an excursion outside the city (£165/4 hours, £265/8 hours, mobile 07716-358-997, www.comeseescotland.com, ann@comeseescotland.com).

Highlands Day Trips

Most of the same companies that do Highlands side-trips from Edinburgh also operate trips from Glasgow. If you'd like to spend an efficient day away from the city, skim the descriptions and listings on page 718, and then check each company's website or browse the brochures at the TI for details.

Glasgow Walks

These two self-guided walks introduce you to Glasgow's most interesting (and very different) neighborhoods: the downtown zone, and the residential area and university sights of the West End.

GET TO KNOW GLASGOW
The Downtown Core

Glasgow isn't romantic, but it has an earthy charm, its people are a joy to chat with, and architecture buffs love it. The more time you

spend here, the more you'll appreciate the edgy, artsy vibe and the quirky, fun-loving spirit. Be sure to look up—above the chain restaurants and mall stores—and you'll discover a wealth of imaginative facades, complete with ornate friezes and expressive sculptures. These buildings transport you to the heady days around the turn of the 20th century—when Victorianism enthralled the rest of Britain, but Glasgow set its own course, thanks largely to the artistic bravado of Charles Rennie Mackintosh and his Art Nouveau friends (the "Glasgow Boys"). This walking tour takes about 1.5 hours (plus sightseeing stops along the way).

• *Start at the St. Enoch subway station, at the base of the pedestrian shopping boulevard, Buchanan Street. (This is a short walk from Central Station, or a longer walk or quick cab ride from Queen Street Station.) Stand at the intersection of Argyle and Buchanan, where the square hits the street (with your back to the glassy subway entry). Take a moment to get oriented.*

❶ Argyle Street and Nearby

The grand pedestrian boulevard, Buchanan Street, leads uphill to the Royal Concert Hall. This is the start of the "Style Mile"—the

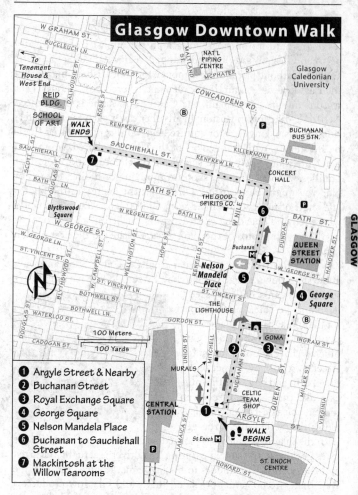

Glasgow Downtown Walk

W GRAHAM ST.

BUCCLEUCH LN.

To Tenement House & West End

REID BLDG

SCHOOL OF ART

WALK ENDS

NAT'L PIPING CENTRE

MCPHATER ST.

Glasgow Caledonian University

BUCCLEUCH ST.

HILL ST.

COWCADDENS RD.

RENFREW ST.

SAUCHIEHALL ST.

SAUCHIEHALL LN.

RENFREW LN.

KILLERMONT ST.

BUCHANAN BUS STN.

CONCERT HALL

BATH LN.

BATH ST.

Blythswood Square

W REGENT ST.

THE GOOD SPIRITS CO.

BATH ST.

DUNDAS ST.

QUEEN STREET STATION

W. GEORGE LN.

W. GEORGE ST.

Buchanan

ST. VINCENT ST.

W. VINCENT LN.

Nelson Mandela Place

W. GEORGE ST.

N. HANOVER ST.

BOTHWELL ST.

BOTHWELL LN.

ST. VINCENT ST.

THE LIGHTHOUSE

George Square

WATERLOO ST.

GORDON ST.

GOMA

INGRAM ST.

CADOGAN ST.

100 Meters

100 Yards

MURALS

CENTRAL STATION

UNION ST.

MITCHELL ST.

CELTIC TEAM SHOP

MILLER ST.

❶ Argyle Street & Nearby
❷ Buchanan Street
❸ Royal Exchange Square
❹ George Square
❺ Nelson Mandela Place
❻ Buchanan to Sauchiehall Street
❼ Mackintosh at the Willow Tearooms

ARGYLE ST.

VIRGINIA ST.

WALK BEGINS

JAMAICA ST.

St Enoch

HOWARD ST.

ST. ENOCH CENTRE

GLASGOW

---

nickname for a Z-shaped pedestrian zone made of three streets: Sauchiehall, Buchanan, and Argyle. While the city is always coming up with marketing slogans to goose its shopping metabolism, this district does have the top shops in town.

Look left (a long block away) to where Central Station (with its huge glass facade) makes a bridge over Argyle Street. This bridge was nicknamed "The Highlanders' Umbrella" from the days when poor Highlanders, who came to Glasgow to find work, would gather here to connect with their community.

Before heading up Buchanan Street, take a quick detour down Argyle to see a couple slices of Glasgow life. About halfway to the Highlanders' Umbrella, on the right, step into the extremely green sports store, the **Celtic Shop** (at #154).

Green is the color of Glasgow's dominant (for now) soccer team. It's hard for outsiders to fathom the intensity of the rivalry between Glasgow's Celtic and Rangers teams. Celtic, founded by an Irish Catholic priest to raise money for poor Irish immigrants in the East End, is—naturally—green and favored by Catholics. (For reasons no one can explain, the Celtic team name is pronounced "sell-tic"—like it is in Boston; in all other cases, such as when referring to music, language, or culture, this word is pronounced "kell-tic.") Rangers, with team colors of the Union Jack (red, white, and blue), are more likely to be supported by Unionist and Protestant families. Wander into the shop (minimizing or hiding any red or blue you might be wearing). Check out the energy in the photos and shots of the stadium filled with 60,000 fans. You're in a world where red and blue don't exist. Upstairs, tucked in a back room, is a gallery with photos of the 1967 team, considered the best in club history.

Now head around the corner from the Celtic Shop and walk a few steps down the alley (Mitchell Street). While it's usually deserted and can seem a bit seedy, it should be safe...but look out for giant magnifying glasses and taxis held aloft by balloons. City officials have cleverly co-opted street artists by sanctioning huge, fun, and edgy **graffiti murals** like these. (You'll see even more if you side-trip down alleys along the Style Mile.) The girl

with the magnifying glass is painted by graffiti artist Smug (see the girl's necklace). In the taxi painting, the driver is actually the artist and the license plate alludes to his tag name: Rogue-One. (By the way, there are no actual bricks on that wall.) Glasgow produces a free booklet, called City Center Mural Trail (also available at www. citycentremuraltrail.co.uk), which explains all this fun art around town. Some local companies offer tours of the murals (see "Tours in Glasgow," earlier).

• *Now return to the base of...*

❷ Buchanan Street

Buchanan Street has a friendly Ramblas-style vibe with an abundance of street musicians. As you stroll uphill, keep an eye out for a few big landmarks: Immediately on your left, **Frasers** (#45) is a vast and venerable

department store, considered the "Harrods of Glasgow." The **Argyll Arcade** (#30, opposite Frasers), dating from 1827 with a proud red-sandstone facade, is the oldest arcade in town. It's filled mostly with jewelry and plenty of security guards. **Princes Square** (at #48, just past Argyll Arcade) is a classic old building dressed with a modern steel peacock and foliage. Step inside to see the delightfully modernized Art Nouveau atrium.

Back on Buchanan Street, at your next left, peer down Mitchell Lane at **The Lighthouse.** This building was Charles Rennie Mackintosh's first public commission (built in 1895, when Mackintosh was in his late twenties). It was originally built to house the Glasgow Herald newspaper, but today the building hosts design exhibitions and a small exhibit on Mackintosh's contributions to Glasgow architecture (third floor). With the once-great Mackintosh-designed Glasgow School of Art gutted by a recent fire and years away from reopening, this is a good stop for a quick overview of his work. The Lighthouse's water tower (also designed by Mackintosh) has 135 spiral steps inside—consider climbing to the wraparound balcony for 360-degree views of the city (Mon-Sat 10:30-17:00, Sun from 12:00).

• *Just beyond Mitchell Lane, turn down the alley on the right, toward the large archway. This is Exchange Place. You'll pass the recommended Rogano restaurant on your right before emerging onto...*

❸ Royal Exchange Square

The centerpiece of this square—which marks the entrance to the shopping zone called Merchant City—is a stately, Neoclassical, bank-like building. This was once the **private mansion** of one of the tobacco lords, the super-rich businessmen who reigned here through the 1700s, stomping through the city with gold-tipped canes. During the port's heyday, these entrepreneurs helped Glasgow become Europe's sixth-biggest city—number two in the British Empire.

Today the mansion houses the **Glasgow Gallery of Modern Art,** nicknamed GoMA. Circle around the building to the main entry (at the equestrian statue of the Duke of Wellington, often creatively decorated as Glasgow's favorite cone-head), and step back to take in the full Neoclassical facade. On the pediment, notice the funky, mirrored mosaic celebrating the miracles of St. Mungo—an example of how Glasgow refuses to

take itself too seriously. The temporary exhibits and installations inside GoMA are generally forgettable, but they occasionally show works by well-known artists such as Andy Warhol (free, £2 suggested donation, Mon-Wed and Sat 10:00-17:00, Thu until 20:00, Fri and Sun 11:00-17:00, www.glasgowlife.org.uk).

• *Facing the fanciful GoMA facade, turn right up Queen Street. Within a block, you'll reach...*

❹ George Square

This square, the centerpiece of Glasgow, is filled with statues and lined with notable buildings, such as the Queen Street train station

and the Glasgow City Chambers. (It's the big Neoclassical building standing like a secular church to the east; pop in to see its grand ground floor.) In front of the City Chambers stands a monument to Glaswegians killed fighting in the World Wars. The square is decorated with a *Who's Who* of statues depicting great

Glaswegians. Find James Watt (sitting in a chair; he perfected the steam engine that helped power Europe into the Industrial Age), as well as Scotland's two top literary figures: Robert Burns and Sir Walter Scott (capping the tallest pillar in the center). The twin equestrian statues are of Prince Albert and a skinny Queen Victoria—a rare image of her in her more svelte youth.

• *Just past skinny Vic and Robert Peel, turn left onto West George Street, and cross Buchanan Street to the tall church in the middle of...*

❺ Nelson Mandela Place

This first public space named for Nelson Mandela honors the man who, while still in prison, helped bring down apartheid in South Africa. The square was renamed in the 1980s while apartheid was still in place—and when the South African consulate was here. Subsequently, anyone sending the consulate a letter had to address it with the name of the man who embodied the anti-apartheid spirit: Mandela. (Glasgow, nicknamed Red Clyde Side for its socialist politics and empathy for the working class, is quick to jump on progressive causes.)

The area around **St. George's Church** features some interesting bits of architectural detail. Facing the church's left side are the three circular friezes of the former **Stock Exchange** (with a Neo-Gothic facade, built in 1875). These idealized heads represent the industries that made Glasgow prosperous during its prime: building, engineering, and mining.

Around the back of the church, find the **Athenaeum,** the sandy-colored building at #8 (notice the low-profile label over the door). Now a law office, this was founded in 1847 as a school and city library during Glasgow's Golden Age. (Charles Dickens gave the building's inaugural address.) Like Edinburgh, Glasgow was at the forefront of the 18th-century Scottish Enlightenment, a celebration of education and intellectualism. The Scots were known for their extremely practical brand of humanism; all members of society, including the merchant and working classes, were expected to be well educated. Look above the door to find the symbolic statue of a reader sharing books with young children, an embodiment of this ideal.

• *Return to the big, pedestrianized Buchanan Street in front of the church. Head uphill (you'll pass the TI on your right).*

❻ Buchanan Street to Sauchiehall Street (More of the Style Mile)

A short distance uphill is the glass entry to Glasgow's subway. Soon after, on the right, you'll pass the Buchanan Galleries, an indoor mall that sprawls through several city blocks (filled with shopping temptations and offering a refuge in rainy weather).

Whisky Side Trip: For a fun education in whisky, take a little detour. At the Buchanan Galleries, head left down Bath Street a block and a half to #23, where stairs lead down on the left into **The Good Spirits Company** (note that as you cross West Nile Street you may first spot the Good Spirits beer-and-wine shop on the left—although tempting, continue down Bath Street to find the main whisky shop). This happy world of whisky is run by two young aficionados (Shane and Matthew) and their booze-geek staff. They welcome you to taste and learn (Mon-Wed and Sat 10:00-19:00, Thu until 20:00, Sun 12:00-17:00, tel. 0141/258-8427).

• *Returning to Buchanan Street, continue uphill to the top.*

At the top of Buchanan Street stands the **Glasgow Royal Concert Hall.** Its steps are a favorite perch where local office workers munch lunch and enjoy the street scene. The statue is of **Donald Dewar,** who served as Scotland's first-ever "First Minister"

GLASGOW

Charles Rennie Mackintosh (1868-1928)

Charles Rennie Mackintosh brought an exuberant Art Nouveau influence to the architecture of his hometown. His designs challenged the city planners of this otherwise practical, working-class port city to create beauty in the buildings they commissioned.

As a student traveling in Italy, Mackintosh ignored the paintings inside museums and set up his easel to paint the exteriors of churches and buildings instead. He rejected the architectural traditions of ancient Greece and Rome. In Venice and Ravenna, he fell under the spell of Byzantine design, and in Siena he saw a unified, medieval city design he would try to import—but with a Scottish flavor and palette—to Glasgow.

When Mackintosh was at the Glasgow School of Art, the Industrial Age dominated life. Factories belched black soot as they burned coal and forged steel. Mackintosh and his artist friends drew inspiration from nature and created some of the first Art Nouveau buildings, paintings, drawings, and furniture. His first commission came in 1893, to design an extension to the Glasgow Herald building. More work followed, including the Glasgow School of Art (recently gutted by fire) and the Willow Tea Rooms (now the Mackintosh at the Willow).

A radical thinker, Mackintosh shared credit with his artist wife, Margaret MacDonald (who specialized in glass and metalwork). He once famously said, "I have the talent...Margaret has the genius." The two teamed up with another husband-and-wife duo—Herbert MacNair and Margaret's sister, Frances MacDonald—to define a new strain of Scottish Art Nouveau, called the "Glasgow Style." These influential couples were known as "the Glasgow Four."

after the Scottish Parliament reconvened in 1999 (previously they'd been serving in London—as part of the British Parliament—since 1707).

• *From here, the Style Mile zags left, Buchanan Street becomes Sauchiehall Street, and the shopping gets cheaper and less elegant. While there's little of note to see, it's still an entertaining stroll. Walk a few blocks, passing "Pound Shops" (the equivalent of "dollar stores"), newspaper hawkers, beggars, buskers, souvenir shops, and a good bookstore. Enjoy the people-watching. Just before the end of the pedestrian zone, on the left side (at #217), is the...*

Mackintosh's works show a strong Japanese influence, particularly in his use of black-and-white contrast to highlight the idealized forms of nature. He also drew inspiration from the Arts and Crafts movement, with an eye for simplicity, clean lines, respect for tradition, and an emphasis on precise craftsmanship over mass production. While some of his designs appear to be repeated, no two motifs are exactly alike—just as nothing is exactly the same in nature.

Mackintosh insisted on designing every element of his commissions—even the furniture, curtains, and cutlery. As a furniture and woodwork designer, Mackintosh preferred to use cheaper materials, then paint them with several thick coats, hiding seams and imperfections and making the piece feel carved rather than built. His projects often went past deadline and over budget, but resulted in unusually harmonious spaces.

Mackintosh inspired other artists, such as painter Gustav Klimt and Bauhaus founder Walter Gropius, but his vision was not appreciated in his own time as much as it is now; he died poor. Now, a century after Scotland's greatest architect set pencil to paper, his hometown is at last celebrating his unique vision.

In Glasgow, locals favor five main Mackintosh sights (listed in order of importance and all described in this chapter): The Mackintosh House (a reconstruction of his 1906 home filled with his actual furniture, on the University of Glasgow campus); the Kelvingrove Art Gallery (with a wonderful exhibit of his work along with the other three of the "Glasgow Boys"); the Mackintosh at the Willow tearooms (a building designed by Mackintosh and currently a functioning tearoom entirely furnished in his style); the Glasgow School of Art (currently closed to tourists), and The Lighthouse (Mackintosh's first public commission—a water tower and modern glass-and-metal building). For the mildly interested traveler, the easiest way to "experience" Mackintosh is to focus on the Kelvingrove Art Gallery exhibit and perhaps pop into the Mackintosh at the Willow tearooms.

❼ Mackintosh at the Willow

This tearoom is in the old Willow Tea Rooms building, an Art Nouveau masterpiece designed by Charles Rennie Mackintosh. The original tearooms at this location were opened in 1903, and the restored version you see today is an exact replica of the original.

Tearooms were hugely popular during the industrial boom of the late 19th century. As Glasgow grew, more people moved to the suburbs, meaning that office workers couldn't easily return home for lunch. And during this age of Victorian morals, the temperance movement was trying to discourage the consumption of alcohol.

Tearooms were designed to be an appealing alternative to eating in pubs.

Mackintosh made his living from design commissions, including multiple tearooms for businesswoman Kate Cranston. He took his theme for the café from the name of the street it's on—*saugh* is Scots for willow.

In the design of these tearooms, there was a meeting of the (very modern) minds. In addition to giving office workers an al-

ternative to pubs, Cranston also wanted a place where women could gather while unescorted—in a time when traveling solo could give a woman a less-than-desirable reputation. An ardent women's rights supporter, Cranston requested that the rooms be bathed in white, the suffragettes' signature color.

The **tearooms** recently underwent a several-year restoration and have reopened as the new Mackintosh at the Willow tearooms, with an interior that perfectly replicates Mackintosh's original designs and decor. You can have a meal or tea, visit the gift shop, or pay to browse the **exhibit** about the history of this place, the tradition of afternoon tea, and Mackintosh's work for Cranston (tearooms daily 9:00-17:45; exhibit-£5.50, daily 10:00-17:30, last entry at 16:00, earlier on Sun; tours available at 10:00 and 11:00). The upstairs Salon de Luxe **dining room** is only accessible by guided tour or by reserving teatime in advance. It appears just as it did in Mackintosh's day, though most features (such as the chairs and the doors) are reproductions of the fragile originals.

You'll see two other "Willow Tea Rooms" locations around town (on Buchanan Street and in the Watt Brothers store on Sauchiehall Street), but these are not associated with the original tearooms.

• *Our walk ends here. Two additional sights (described later) lie within a five-minute stroll (in different directions). The remarkably preserved* **Tenement House** *offers a fascinating glimpse into Glasgow lifestyles in the early 1900s. And the* **National Piping Centre** *goes beyond the clichés and provides a better appreciation for the history and musicality of Scotland's favorite instrument.*

WEST END WALK

Glasgow's West End—just a quick subway, bus, or taxi ride from downtown—is the city's top residential neighborhood. The main drags are Byres Road running north-south and Great Western Road running east-west. As in so many British cities, the western part of town—upwind of industrial pollution—was historically the most desirable. Today this area has great restaurants and nightlife, and fine accommodations.

This walk begins at the Hillhead subway stop, meanders through dining and residential zones, explores some grand old university buildings (and related museums), and ends with a wander through the park to the Kelvingrove Museum—Glasgow's top museum (to trace the route of this walk, see the "Glasgow's West End" map, on the next page). Since this walk is most worthwhile as a scenic way to connect several important museums, it's best when they're open.

• *Start at the Hillhead subway station. Exiting the station, turn right and walk four short blocks up...*

Byres Road: A *byre* is a cowshed. So back when this was farmland outside the big city, cattle were housed along here. Today, Byres Road is a lively thoroughfare through this trendy district. A block before the big intersection, notice the **Waitrose** supermarket on the left. In Britain, this upscale grocery is a sure sign of a posh neighborhood.

Approaching the corner with Great Western Road, you'll see a church spire on the right. Dating from 1862, this church was converted into a restaurant and music venue called **Òran Mòr** (Gaelic for "The Great Music"). Step into the entryway to see the colorful murals (by Alasdair Gray, a respected Glaswegian artist and novelist). Consider a drink or meal in their pub (try some whisky—they have over 300 varieties). Also check what's on while you're in town, as this is a prime music and theater venue (take advantage of "a play, a pie, and a pint," described later under "Eating in Glasgow").

• *If the weather's good, cross Great Western Road and head into the...*

Glasgow Botanic Gardens: This inviting parkland is Glaswegians' favorite place to enjoy a break from the bustling city. And, like

so many things in Glasgow, it's free. Locals brag about their many parks, claiming that—despite their industrial reputation—they have more green space per capita than any other city in Europe. And even the city's name comes from the Gaelic for "the dear green place."

Before going into the park, pause at the red-brick entrance gate. On the gate on the left, look for Glasgow's quite-busy **city seal,** which honors St. Mungo, the near-legendary town founder. The jumble of symbols (a bird, a tree, a bell, and a salmon with

GLASGOW

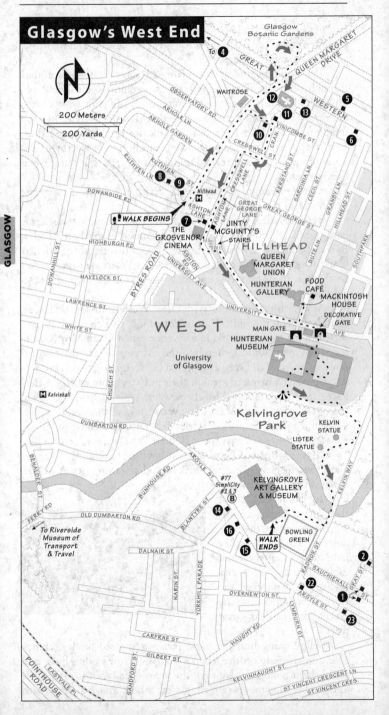

Glasgow's West End

N

200 Meters
200 Yards

Glasgow Botanic Gardens

To ④

GREAT

QUEEN MARGARET DRIVE

WESTERN

WAITROSE

⑫ ⑪ ⑬ ⑤

OBSERVATORY RD

ARHOLE LN.

ARHOLE GARDEN

⑩ ⑥

VINICOMBE ST.

CRESSWELL ST.

CRAN.

KERSLAND ST.

SARDINIA LN.

CECIL ST.

CRESSWELL LANE

GRANBY LN.

HILLHEAD ST.

SOUTHPARK

RUTHVEN LN.

RUTHVEN

⑧ ⑨

DOWANSIDE RD.

Hillhead
M

ASHTON LANE

WALK BEGINS

⑦

THE GROSVENOR CINEMA

ASHTON LANE

JINTY McGUINTY'S STAIRS

GREAT GEORGE LANE

GREAT GEORGE ST.

BUTE LN.

HILLHEAD

HIGHBURGH RD.

ASHTON RD.

UNIVERSITY AVE.

HAVELOCK ST.

BYRES ROAD

QUEEN MARGARET UNION

HUNTERIAN GALLERY

FOOD CAFÉ

MACKINTOSH HOUSE

DOWANHILL ST.

LAWRENCE ST.

WHITE ST.

CHURCH ST.

UNIVERSITY

DECORATIVE GATE

AVE.

WEST

MAIN GATE

HUNTERIAN MUSEUM

M Kelvinhall

University of Glasgow

DUMBARTON RD.

Kelvingrove Park

KELVIN STATUE

LISTER STATUE

KELVIN WAY

BENALDER RD.

FERRY RD.

BUNHOUSE RD.

ARGYLE ST.

OLD DUMBARTON RD.

To Riverside Museum of Transport & Travel

#77 SimpliCity #2 & 3
Ⓑ

⑭

KELVINGROVE ART GALLERY & MUSEUM

BLANTYRE ST.

⑯

DALNAIR ST.

NAKIN ST.

YORKHILL PARADE

⑮

WALK ENDS

BOWLING GREEN

RADNOR ST.

②

GRAY ST.

SAUCHIEHALL ST.

�22

①

OVERNEWTON ST.

ARGYLE ST.

LYMBURN ST.

⑳

CARFRAE ST.

HAUGHT RD.

GILBERT ST.

POINTHOUSE ROAD

EASTVALE PL.

SANDYFORD ST.

KELVINHAUGHT ST.

ST. VINCENT CRESCENT LN.

ST. VINCENT CRES.

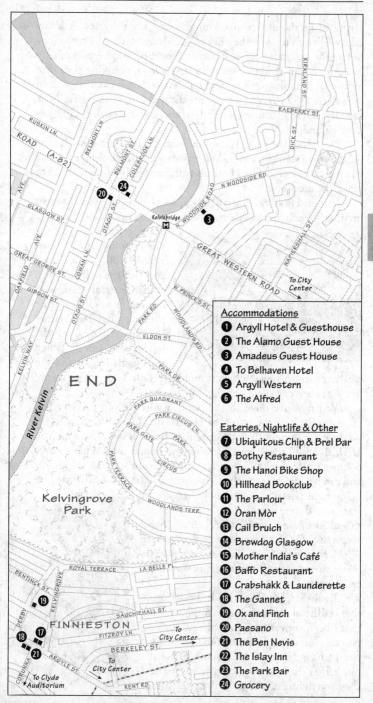

Accommodations
1. Argyll Hotel & Guesthouse
2. The Alamo Guest House
3. Amadeus Guest House
4. To Belhaven Hotel
5. Argyll Western
6. The Alfred

Eateries, Nightlife & Other
7. Ubiquitous Chip & Brel Bar
8. Bothy Restaurant
9. The Hanoi Bike Shop
10. Hillhead Bookclub
11. The Parlour
12. Òran Mòr
13. Cail Bruich
14. Brewdog Glasgow
15. Mother India's Café
16. Baffo Restaurant
17. Crabshakk & Launderette
18. The Gannet
19. Ox and Finch
20. Paesano
21. The Ben Nevis
22. The Islay Inn
23. The Park Bar
24. Grocery

a ring in its mouth) recalls Mungo's four key miracles. Ask any Glaswegian to tell you the tales of St. Mungo—they learn it all by heart. The city motto, "Let Glasgow Flourish," is apt—particularly given its recent rejuvenation following a long, crippling period of industrial rot. Glasgow's current renaissance was kicked off with an ambitious 1989 garden festival in a disused former shipyard. Now the city is one of Europe's trendiest success stories. Let Glasgow flourish, indeed.

Head into the park. If the sun's out, it'll be jammed with people enjoying some rare rays. Young lads wait all winter for the day when they can cry, "Sun's oot, taps aff!" and pull off their shirts to make the most of it.

In addition to the finely landscaped gardens, the park has two inviting greenhouse pavilions—both free and open to the public.

The big white one on the right (from 1873; open 10:00-18:00, winter until 16:15) is the most elegant, with a classical statue welcoming you among the palm fronds (but beware the killer plants, to the left as you enter). When the clouds roll in and the weather turns rotten—which is more the status quo—these warm, dry areas become quite popular.

When you're done in the park, head back out the way you came in. Back on the street, before crossing Great Western Road, go right a few steps to find the blue **police call box.** Once an icon of British life, these were little neighborhood mini offices where bobbies could store paperwork and equipment, use the telephone, and catch up with each other. These days, some of the call boxes are being repurposed as coffee shops, ice-cream stands, and time machines.

• *Cross back over Great Western Road and back-track (past the Òran Mòr church/restaurant) one block down Byres Road. Turn left down Vini-combe Street (across from the Waitrose). Now we'll explore...*

Back-Streets West End: Peek inside the **Hillhead Bookclub**—a former cinema that's been converted into a hipster bar/restaurant serving affordable food (described later, under "Eating in Glasgow"). A half-block after that, turn right (on poorly marked Cranworth Street) and walk along the row of red-sandstone **tenements.** While that word has negative connotations stateside, here a "tenement" is simply an apartment building. And judging from the grand size, bulging bay windows, and prime location of these, it's safe to say they're far from undesirable. Many are occupied by a single family, while others are subdivided into five or six rooms for students (the university is right around the corner). Across the street from this tenement row (at #12) is a **baths club**—a private swimming pool, like an exclusive health club. Historically, most people couldn't afford bathing facilities in their homes, so they came to central locations like this one to get clean every few days (or weeks). Today, it's the wealthy—not the poor—who come to places like this.

After the baths, turn right down Cresswell Street. A half-block down on the right, turn left down **Cresswell Lane**—an inviting, traffic-free, brick-lane shopping and dining zone. While the Style Mile downtown is packed with chain stores, this is where you'll find charming one-off boutiques.

Browse your way to the end of the lane, cross the street, and continue straight to the even more appealing **Ashton Lane,** strung with fairy lights. Scout this street and pick a place to return for dinner tonight. Fancy a film? Halfway down the street on the right, The Grosvenor Cinema shows both blockbusters and art-house fare (see listing on page 856).

• *When you reach the end of the lane, take a very sharp left up the stairs (with the idyllic beer garden for Brel on your left). At the top of the stairs, turn right along the road. You're now walking through the modern part of the...*

University of Glasgow Campus: Founded in 1451, this is Scotland's second-oldest university (after St. Andrews). Its 28,000 students sprawl through the West End. Unlike the fancy "old university" buildings, this area is gloomy and concrete. The ugly, gray building on your left is the Queen Margaret Union, with a music venue that has hosted several big-name bands before they were famous—from Nirvana to Franz Ferdinand. (If you think Franz Ferdinand is an Austrian archduke rather than a Scottish alternative rock band...you've been out of college too long.)

• *Eventually you'll reach a wide cross street, University Avenue. Turn left up this street and walk two more blocks uphill. At the traffic light, the Hunterian Gallery and Mackintosh House are just up the hill on your left, and the Hunterian Museum is across the street on the right.*

GLASGOW

Hunterian Gallery and Mackintosh House: First, stop in at the Hunterian Gallery to inquire about tours of the Mackintosh House. Ask if there's a wait, and if so, spend your time either in the adjacent gallery, the wonderful university cafeteria named Food (across the lane, cheap and cheery lunch), or the Hunterian Museum across the street. All three sights (the Mackintosh House, Hunterian Gallery, and Hunterian Museum) are important if you have the time and energy (all described later under "Sights in Glasgow" on page 849).

• *When you're done here, head for the Hunterian Museum in the university's big, old, main building across University Avenue. Instead of going through the main gate, go to the left end of the building facing the street to find a more interesting decorative gate.*

University of Glasgow Main Building: Take a good look at the gate, which is decorated with the names of illustrious alumni.

Pick out the great Scots you're familiar with: James Watt, King James II, Adam Smith, Lord Kelvin, William Hunter (the namesake of the university's museums), and Donald Dewar, a driving force behind devolution who became Scotland's first "First Minister" in 1999.

Go through the gate and face the main university building. Stretching to the left is Graduation Hall, where commencement takes place. Head straight into the building, ride the elevator to floor 4, and enjoy the **Hunterian Museum.**

After you visit the Hunterian Museum, find the grand staircase down (just off the main hall housing the Antonine Wall exhibit). You'll emerge into one of the twin quads enclosed by the enormous ensemble of university buildings. Veer right to find your way into the atmospheric, Neo-Gothic **cloisters** that support the wing separating the two quads. These are modeled after the Gothic cloisters in the lower chapel of Glasgow Cathedral, across town. On the other side, you'll pop out into the adjoining quad. Enjoy pretending you're a student for a few minutes, then head out the door at the bottom of the quad (to your left).

Leaving the university complex, head for the tall flagpole on a bluff overlooking a grand view. The turreted building just below is the Kelvingrove Museum, where this walk ends. (If you get turned around in the park, just head for those spires.)

• *From the flagpole, turn left and head to the end of the big building. Head down the stairs leading through the woods on your right (marked* James Watt Building*). When you reach the busy road, turn right along it for a few yards, then—as soon as you can—angle to the right back into the green space of...*

Kelvingrove Park: Another of Glasgow's favorite parks, this originated in the Victorian period, when there was a renewed focus on trying to get people out into green spaces. One of the first things you'll come to is a big statue of **Lord Kelvin** (1824-1907). Born William Thomson, he chose to take the name of the River Kelvin, which runs through Glasgow (and gives its name to many other things here, including the museum we're headed to). One of the most respected scientists of his time, Kelvin was a pioneer in the field of thermodynamics, and gave his name (or, actually, the river's) to a new, absolute unit of temperature measurement designed to replace Celsius and Fahrenheit.

Just past Kelvin, bear left at the statue of **Joseph Lister** (1827-1912, of "Listerine" fame—he pioneered the use of antiseptics to remove infection-causing germs from the surgical environment), and take the bridge across the River Kelvin. Once across the bridge, turn right toward the museum. You'll walk along a pleasant bowling green that was built for the Commonwealth Games that Glasgow hosted in 2014. They keep it free and open to anyone—hoping to create a popular interest in this very old and genteel sport (see page 852).

Now take some time to explore the Kelvingrove Museum, described on page 851.

• *When you're finished at the museum, exit out the back end, toward the busy road. Several recommended restaurants are ahead and to the left, in the Finnieston neighborhood (see page 865). Or, if you'd like to hop on the subway, just turn right along Argyle Street and walk five minutes to the Kelvinhall station.*

Sights in Glasgow

DOWNTOWN

▲▲Tenement House

Here's a chance to drop into a perfectly preserved 1930s-era middle-class residence. The National Trust for Scotland bought this otherwise ordinary row home, located in a residential neighborhood, because of the peculiar tendencies of Miss Agnes Toward (1886-1975). For five decades, she kept her home essentially unchanged. The kitchen calendar is still set for 1935, and canisters of licorice powder (a laxative) still sit on the bathroom shelf. It's a time-warp experience, where Glaswegian oldtimers enjoy coming to reminisce about how they grew up.

Cost and Hours: £7.50, daily 10:00-17:00; Nov-Feb Sat-Mon 11:00-16:00, closed Tue-Fri; guidebook-£3, 145 Buccleuch Street (pronounced "ba-KLOO"), down from the top of Garnethill, tel. 0141/333-0183, www.nts.org.uk.

Visiting the House: Buy your ticket on the main floor, and poke around the little museum. You'll learn that in Glasgow, a "tenement" isn't a slum—it's simply an apartment house. In fact, tenements like these were typical for every class except the richest. Then head upstairs to the apartment, which is staffed by caring volunteers. Ring the doorbell to be let in. Explore the four little rooms. Imagine a world without electricity (Miss Toward was a late adapter, making the leap to electricity only in 1960). Ask about the utility of the iron stove. Ponder the importance of that drawer full of coal and how that stove heated her entire world. Ask why the bed is in the kitchen. As you look through the rooms laced with Victorian trinkets—such as the ceramic dogs on the living room's fireplace mantle—consider how different they are from Mackintosh's stark, minimalist designs from the same period. Miss Toward's clothes and trinkets are switched up throughout the year to match the changing of the seasons.

▲National Piping Centre

If you consider bagpipes a tacky Scottish cliché, think again. At this small but insightful museum, you'll get a scholarly lesson in the proud and fascinating history of the bagpipe. For those with a healthy attention span for history or musical instruments—ideally both—it's fascinating. On Mondays, Thursdays, and Fridays at 12:00 and 14:00 (plus Saturdays at 12:00) a kilt-clad piper is on hand to perform, answer questions, and show you around the collection. He'll even give you a lesson on how to play. At other times, if it's quiet, ask the ticket-sellers to tell you more—some are bagpipe students at the music school across the street. The center also offers a shop, lessons, a restaurant, and accommodations.

Cost and Hours: £4.50, includes audioguide, Mon-Thu 9:00-19:00, Fri until 17:00, Sat until 15:00, closed Sun, 30 McPhater Street, tel. 0141/353-5551, www.thepipingcentre.co.uk.

Visiting the Museum: The collection is basically one big room packed with well-described exhibits, including several historic bagpipes. You'll learn that bagpipes from as far away as Italy, Spain, and Bo-hemia predated Scottish ones; that Lowlands bag-pipes were traditionally bellows-blown rather than lung-powered; and why bagpipes started being used to inspire Scottish  soldiers on the battlefield. You'll also learn about the tradition of bagpipe competitions around Scotland. The thoughtful, beautifully produced audioguide—which mixes knowledgeable commentary with sound bites of bagpipes being played and brief interviews with performers—feels like a 40-minute audio-documentary on the BBC. The 15-minute film shown at the end of the room sums up the collection helpfully. They also have chanters and a practice set of bagpipes in case you want to try your hand. The chanter finger-ing is easy if you play the recorder, but keeping the bag inflated is exhausting.

CATHEDRAL PRECINCT, WITH A HINT OF MEDIEVAL GLASGOW

Very little remains of medieval Glasgow, but a visit to the cathedral and the area around it—to the east of downtown—is a visit to the birthplace of the city (see the "Central Glasgow" map, earlier).

The first church was built here in the seventh century. To-day's towering **cathedral** is mostly 13th-century—the only great Scottish church to survive the Reformation intact. Nearby, the **Provand's Lordship** is Glasgow's only secular building dating from the Middle Ages. The **St. Mungo Museum** of Religious Life and Art, built on the site of the old Bishop's Castle, is a unique exhibit covering the spectrum of religions. And the **Necropolis,** blanketing the hill behind the cathedral, provides an atmospheric walk through a world of stately Victorian tombstones. From there you can scan the city and look down on the brewery where Tennent's Lager (a longtime Glasgow favorite) has been made since 1885. And, if the spirit moves you, hike on down and tour the brewery (described later).

As you face the cathedral, the St. Mungo Museum is on your right (with handy public WCs), the Provand's Lordship is across the street from St. Mungo, and the Necropolis is behind the cathedral and to the right. The brewery is a 10-minute walk away.

Getting Here: To reach these sights from Buchanan Street, turn east on Bath Street, which soon becomes Cathedral Street, and walk about 15 minutes (or hop a bus along the main drag—try bus #38 or #57, confirm with driver that the bus stops at the cathedral). To head to the Kelvingrove Museum after your visit, from the cathedral, walk two blocks up Castle Street and catch bus #19 (on the cathedral side).

▲Glasgow Cathedral

This blackened, Gothic cathedral is a rare example of an intact pre-Reformation Scottish cathedral. (It was once known as "the Pink Church" for the tone of its stone, but with Industrial Age soot and modern pollution, it blackened. Cleaning would damage the integrity of the stone structure, so it was left black.) The zealous Reformation forces of John Knox ripped out the stained glass and ornate chapels of the Catholic age, but they left the  church standing. The church is aching to tell its long and fascinating story and volunteers are standing by to do just that.

Cost and Hours: Free, £3 suggested donation; Mon-Sat 9:30-17:30, Sun 13:00-17:00; Oct-March Mon-Sat 10:00-16:00, Sun from 13:00; last entry to lower church 45 minutes before closing, request a free tour (Mon-Sat) or join one in progress, near junction of Castle and Cathedral Streets, tel. 0141/552-6891, www.historicenvironment.scot.

Visiting the Cathedral: Inside, look up to see the wooden barrel-vaulted ceiling, and take in the beautifully decorated section over the choir ("quire"). The choir screen is the only pre-Reformation screen surviving in Scotland. It divided the common people from the priests and big shots of the day, who got to

worship closer to the religious action. The cathedral's glass dates mostly from the 19th century. One window on the right side of the choir, celebrating the 14 trades of Glasgow (try to find them), dates from 1951. Left of that, a set of three windows tells the story of St. Mungo retrieving a ring from the mouth of a fish (it's a long story).

Step into the choir and enjoy the east end with the four evangelists presiding high above in stained glass. Two seats (with high backs, right of altar) are reserved for Queen Elizabeth II and her husband Prince Philip, the Duke of Edinburgh.

Move into the lower church (down stairs on right as you face the choir), where the central altar sits upon St. Mungo's tomb. Mungo was the seventh-century Scottish monk and mythical founder of Glasgow who established the first wooden church on this spot and gave Glasgow its name. Notice the ceiling bosses (decorative caps where the ribs come together) with their colorfully carved demons, dragons, and skulls.

Nearby: In front of the cathedral (near the street), you'll see an attention-grabbing statue of **David Livingstone** (1813-1873). Livingstone—the Scottish missionary/explorer/cartographer who discovered a huge waterfall in Africa and named it in honor of his queen, Victoria—was born eight miles from here.

▲St. Mungo Museum of Religious Life and Art

This secular, city-run museum, just in front of the cathedral, aims to promote religious understanding. Built in 1990 on the site of the

old Bishop's Castle, it provides a handy summary of major and minor world religions, showing how each faith handles various rites of passage across the human life span: birth, puberty, marriage, death, and everything in between and after. Start with the 10-minute video overview on the first floor, and finish with a great view from the top floor of the cathedral and Necropolis. Ponder the Zen Buddhist garden out back as you leave.

Cost and Hours: Free, £3 suggested donation, Tue-Thu and Sat 10:00-17:00, Fri and Sun from 11:00, closed Mon, free WCs downstairs, cheap ground-floor café, 2 Castle Street, tel. 0141/276-1625, www.glasgowlife.org.uk/museums.

Nearby: To view a modern-day depiction of St. Mungo, walk two minutes down High Street from the museum to a building-sized mural by the artist Smug.

Provand's Lordship

With low beams and medieval decor, this creaky home—supposedly the "oldest house in Glasgow"—is the only secular building surviving in Glasgow from the Middle Ages. On three floors it displays the *Lifestyles of the Rich and Famous*...circa 1471. First, sit down and watch the 10-minute video (ground floor). The interior, while sparse and stony, shows off a few pieces of furniture from the 16th, 17th, and 18th centuries. Out back, explore the St. Nicholas Garden, which was once part of a hospital that dispensed herbal remedies. The plaques in each section show the part of the body each plant is used to treat.

Cost and Hours: Free, small donation requested, Tue-Thu and Sat 10:00-17:00, Fri and Sun from 11:00, closed Mon, across the street from St. Mungo Museum at 3 Castle Street, tel. 0141/552-8819, www.glasgowlife.org.uk/museums.

▲Necropolis

From the cathedral, a lane leads over the "bridge of sighs" into the park filled with grand tombstones. Glasgow's huge burial hill has

a wistful, ramshackle appeal. A stroll among the tombstones of the eminent Glaswegians of the 19th century gives a glimpse of Victorian Glasgow and a feel for the confidence and wealth of the second city of the British Empire in its glory days.

With the Industrial Age (in the early 1800s), Glasgow's population tripled to 200,000. The existing churchyards were jammed and unhygienic. The city needed a beautiful place in which to bury its beautiful citizens, so this grand necropolis was established. Because Presbyterians are more into simplicity, the statuary is simpler than in a Catholic cemetery. Wandering among the disintegrating memorials to once-important people, I thought about how, someday, everyone's tombstone will fall over and no one will care.

The highest pillar in the graveyard is a memorial to John Knox. The Great Reformer (who's actually buried in Edinburgh) looks down at the cathedral he wanted to strip of all art, and even tear down. (The Glaswegians rallied to follow Knox, but saved the church.) If the cemetery's main black gates are closed, see if you can get in and out through a gate off the street to the right.

▲▲Tennent's Brewery Tour

Tennent's, founded in 1740, is now the biggest brewery in Scotland, spanning 18 acres. They give serious hour-long tours showing how they make "Scotland's favorite pint," and how they fill 750 kegs per hour and 2,000 cans per minute (you'll see more action Mon-Fri). It's hot and sweaty inside, with 100 steps to climb on your tour.

When you're done (surrounded by "the Lager Lovelies"—cans from 1965 to 1993 that were decorated with cover girls), you'll enjoy a pint (£12.50, tours depart on the hour Mon-Sat 10:00-18:00, Sun 12:00-17:00; call or book online; 161 Duke Street, 0141/202-7145, www.tennentstours.com). To head back downtown, bus #41 stops in front of the brewery on Duke Street and goes to George Square.

If you're still thirsty after your tour, head around the corner to **Drygate Brewing,** with good pub food and a wider selection of craft beers (85 Drygate, see "Central Glasgow Hotels & Restaurants" map, later).

THE WEST END

These sights are linked by my "West End Walk" on page 836.

▲Hunterian Gallery and Mackintosh House

Here's a sightseeing twofer: an art gallery offering a good look at some

Scottish artists relatively unknown outside their homeland, and the chance to explore the reconstructed home of Charles Rennie Mackintosh, decorated exactly the way he liked it. For Charles Rennie Mack fans—or anyone fascinated by the unique habitats of artists—it's well worth a visit.

Cost and Hours: Gallery—free, Tue-Sat 10:00-17:00, Sun 11:00-16:00, closed Mon, across University Avenue from the main university building, tel. 0141/330-4221, www.gla.ac.uk/hunterian. Mackintosh House—£6, same hours as gallery, last entry 45 minutes before closing. Only 12 people are allowed at a time, so there may be a short wait.

Visitor Information: First, check in at the reception desk to buy your ticket for the Mackintosh House and see if there's a wait to get in. You'll also need to check any bags (free lockers available). Spend your waiting time visiting the gallery, or, with a longer wait, head across the street to the Hunterian Museum (described later). If it's lunchtime, eat at **$ Food,** a cheap, healthy, fast, and modern student cafeteria across the lane from the museum that's open to the public. Inside the house, pick up the laminated guide as you enter.

Mackintosh House: In 1906, Mackintosh and his wife, Margaret MacDonald, moved into the end unit of a Victorian row house. Mackintosh gutted the place and redesigned it to his own liking—bathing the interior in his trademark style, a mix of curving, organic lines and rigid, proto-Art Deco functionalism. They moved out in 1914, and the house was demolished in the 1960s—but the university wisely documented the layout and carefully removed and preserved all of Mackintosh's original furnishings. In 1981, when respect for Mackintosh was on the rise, they built this replica house and reinstalled everything just as Mackintosh had designed it. You'll see the entryway, dining room, drawing room, and bedroom—each one offering glimpses into the minds of these great artists. You'll see original furniture and decorations by Mackintosh and MacDonald, providing insight into their creative process.

Hunterian Art Gallery: The adjacent gallery is manageable and worth exploring. Circling one floor, you'll enjoy thoughtfully described sections organized by theme. One highlight is the modern Scottish art, focusing on two groups: the "Glasgow Boys," who traveled to France to study during the waning days of Realism (1880s), and, a generation later, the Scottish Colourists, who found a completely different inspiration in circa-1910 France—bright, bold, with an almost Picasso-like exuberance. The gallery also has an extensive collection of portraits by American artist James Whistler—Whistler's wife was of Scottish descent, as was Whistler's mother. (Hey, that has a nice ring to it.) The painter always found great support in Scotland, and his heir donated his estate to the University of Glasgow. Another part of the gallery hosts temporary exhibits.

▲Hunterian Museum

The oldest public museum in Scotland was founded by William Hunter (1718-1783), a medical researcher. Today his natural science collection is housed in a huge and gorgeous space inside the university's showcase building. Everything is well presented and well explained. You'll see a perceptive exhibit on the Antonine Wall (the lesser-known cousin of Hadrian's Wall), built in AD 142 to seal off the Picts from the Roman Empire. Ancient Roman artifacts on display include leather shoes, plumbing, weapons, and carved reliefs. The eclectic collection also includes musical instruments, a display on the Glasgow-built *Lusitania*, and a fine collection of fossils, including the aquatic dinosaur called plesiosaur (possibly a distant ancestor of the Loch Ness monster). But to some, most fascinating are the many morbid examples of deformities—two-headed animals, body parts in jars, and so on (main hall, left of Romans). Ever the curious medical researcher,

Hunter collected these for study, and these intrigue, titillate, and nauseate visitors to this day.

Cost and Hours: Free, Tue-Sat 10:00-17:00, Sun 11:00-16:00, closed Mon, Gilbert Scott Building, University Avenue, tel. 0141/330-4221, www.gla.ac.uk/hunterian.

▲▲Kelvingrove Art Gallery and Museum

This "Scottish Smithsonian" displays everything from a stuffed elephant to paintings by the great masters and what, for me, is the city's best collection of work by Charles Ren-nie Mackintosh. The well-described contents are impressively displayed in a grand, 100-year-old, Spanish Baroque-style building. The Kelvingrove claims to be one of the most-visited museums in

Britain—presumably because of all the field-trip groups you'll see here. Watching all the excited Scottish kids—their imaginations ablaze—is as much fun as the collection itself.

Cost and Hours: Free, £5 suggested donation, Mon-Thu and Sat 10:00-17:00, Fri and Sun from 11:00, free tours at 11:00 and 14:30, Argyle Street, tel. 0141/276-9599, www.glasgowlife.org.uk/museums.

Getting There: My self-guided "West End Walk" leads you here from the Hillhead subway stop, or you can ride the subway to the Kelvinhall stop. When you exit, turn left and walk five minutes. Buses #2 and #3 run from Hope Street downtown to the museum. It's also on the hop-on, hop-off bus route. No matter how you arrive, just look for the huge, turreted red-brick building.

Organ Concerts: At the top of the main hall, the huge pipe organ booms with a daily 30-minute recital at 13:00 (15:00 on Sunday, 45 minutes).

Visiting the Museum: Built in 1901 to house the city collection, the museum is divided into two sections: Art ("Expression") and Natural ("Life"), each with two floors. The symmetrical floor plan can be confusing. Pick up a map and plan your strategy.

The "Expression" section, in the East Court, is marked by a commotion of heads—each with a different expression—raining down from the ceiling. This half of the museum focuses on artwork, including Dutch, Flemish, French, and Scottish Romanticism from the late 19th century. The exhibits on "Scottish Identity in Art" let you tour the country's scenic wonders and its history on canvas. The Mackintosh section, a highlight for many, demonstrates the Art

GLASGOW

Nouveau work of the "Glasgow Boys," including Charles Rennie Mackintosh. Upstairs, in the "south balcony," (above the "Glasgow Boys" section), you'll find the museum's most famous painting, Salvador Dalí's *Christ of St. John of the Cross*, which brought visitors to tears when it was first displayed here in the 1950s.

The "Life" section, in the West Court, features a menagerie of stuffed animals (including a giraffe, kangaroo, ostrich, and moose) with a WWII-era Spitfire fighter plane hovering overhead. Branching off are halls with exhibits ranging from Ancient Egypt to "Scotland's First People" to weaponry ("Conflict and Consequence").

Kelvingrove Lawn Bowling

For a fun and free activity surrounded by relaxed locals, try your hand at lawn bowling. There's a mission behind the perfectly manicured greens next to the Kelvingrove Museum (made beautiful to host the 2014 Commonwealth Games): Keep young people interested in the traditional sport. They'll provide balls (4 per person) and a court time. It's all free and tourists are welcome. While sunny weekends may be too busy, you'll always find a court on a cloudy weekday. It's a fine evening activity; you can bowl rain or shine (April-Sept Mon-Fri 9:00-21:00, Sat-Sun until 18:00, mobile 07920-048-945). Lawn bowling is a lot like *petanque* (popular in France); the object and scoring are the same. The balls are bigger and "biased" (lopsided on purpose to let experts throw curves). Let the attendant explain the rules if necessary. (They also rent tennis gear for the adjacent courts.) An efficient plan would be to end your sightseeing day at the huge Kelvingrove Museum (closes at 17:00), play an hour of "bowls," and have dinner a couple of blocks away at a recommended Finnieston restaurant of your choice. You could cap your night with a beer and live music at a Gaelic pub.

AWAY FROM THE CENTER

For general locations, see the "Greater Glasgow" map near the beginning of this chapter.

▲▲Riverside Museum

Located along the River Clyde, this high-tech, kid-friendly museum—nostalgic and modern at the same time—is dedicated to all things transportation-related. Named the European museum of the year in 2013, visiting is a must for anyone interested in transportation and how it has shaped society.

Cost and Hours: Free, £5 suggested donation, Mon-Thu and Sat 10:00-17:00, Fri and Sun from 11:00, ground-floor café with £6-9 meals, upstairs coffee shop with basic drinks and snacks, 100 Pointhouse Place, tel. 0141/287-2720, www.glasgowlife.org.uk/museums.

Getting There: It's on the riverfront promenade, two miles west of the city center. Bus #100 runs between the museum and George Square (1-2/hour, operated by Garelochhead Coaches), or you can take a taxi (£7-8, 10-minute ride from downtown). The museum is also included on the hop-on, hop-off sightseeing bus route (described earlier, under "Tours in Glasgow").

Visiting the Museum: Most of the collection is strewn across one huge, wide-open floor. Upon entering, visit the info desk (to the right as you enter, near the shop) to ask about today's free tours and activities—or just listen for announcements. Also pick up a map from the info desk, as the museum's open floor plan can feel a bit like a traffic jam at rush hour.

Diving in, explore the vast collection: stagecoaches, locomotives, double-decker trolleys, and an entire wall stacked with vin-

tage automobiles and another with motorcycles. Learn about the opening of Glasgow's old-timey subway (Europe's third oldest). Explore the collections of old toys and prams, and watch a film about 1930s cinema. Stroll the re-creation of a circa-1900 main street, with video clips bringing each shop to life (there's one about a little girl who discovers her daddy was selling things to the pawn shop to pay the rent).

Don't miss the much-smaller upstairs section, with great views over the River Clyde (cross the footbridge over the trains), additional exhibits about ships built here in Glasgow (see the sidebar), and what may be the world's oldest bicycle. The description explains how two different inventors have tried to take credit for the bike—and both of them are Scottish.

Nearby: Be sure to head to the River Clyde directly behind the museum (just step out the back door). The *Glenlee*, one of five remaining tall ships built in Glasgow in the 19th century (1896), invites visitors to

When the Great Ships of the World Were "Clyde-Built"

Glasgow's River Clyde shipyards were the mightiest in the world, famed for building the largest moving man-made objects on earth. The shipyards, once 50 strong, have dwindled to just three. Yet a few giant cranes still stand to remind locals and visitors that from 1880 to 1950, a quarter of the world's ships were built here and "Clyde-built" meant reliability and quality. For 200 years, shipbuilding was Glasgow's top employer—as many as 100,000 workers at its peak, producing a new ship every two days. The glamorous Cunard ships were built here—from the *Lusitania* in 1906 (infamously sunk by a German U-boat in World War I, which almost brought the US into the war) to the *Queen Elizabeth II* in 1967. People still talk about the day when over 200,000 Glaswegians gathered for the launch, the Queen herself smashed the champagne bottle on the prow, and the magnificent ship slid into the harbor. To learn lots more about shipbuilding in Glasgow, visit the excellent Riverside Museum.

come aboard (free, daily 10:00-17:00, Nov-Feb until 16:00, tel. 0141/357-3699, www.thetallship.com). Good exhibits illustrate what it was like to live and work aboard the ship. Explore the officers' living quarters, then head below deck to the café and more exhibits. Below that, the cargo hold has kids' activities and offers the chance to peek into the engine room. As you board, note the speedboat **river tour** that leaves from here each afternoon (£10, roughly hourly, 20 minutes).

Burrell Collection

This eclectic art collection of a wealthy local shipping magnate—which includes sculpture from Roman to Rodin, stained glass, tapestries, furniture, Asian and Islamic works, and halls of paintings starring Cézanne, Renoir, Degas, and a Rembrandt self-portrait—is closed for renovation until spring 2021 (three miles outside the city center in Pollok Country Park, tel. 0141/287-2550, www.glasgowlife.org.uk/museums).

Shopping in Glasgow

Downtown, the **"Style Mile"** has all the predictable chain stores, with a few Scottish souvenir stands mixed in. For more on this shopping area, see the start of my self-guided "Get to Know Glasgow" walk. The Glasgow Gallery of Modern Art (GoMA) has a quirky gift shop that many find enticing.

The West End also has some appealing shops. Many are concentrated on **Cresswell Lane** (covered in my self-guided West End Walk). Browsing here, you'll find an eclectic assortment of gifty shops, art galleries, design shops, hair salons, record stores, home-decor shops, and lots of vintage bric-a-brac. Be sure to poke into De Courcy's Arcade, a two-part warren of tiny offbeat shops.

Entertainment in Glasgow

Glasgow has a youthful vibe, and its nightlife scene is renowned. The city is full of live music acts and venues. Walking through the city center, you'll pass at least one club or bar on every block.

PUBS AND CLUBS

Downtown: Glasgow's central business and shopping district is pretty sleepy (and can be a little unsavory) after hours, but there are a few pockets of upbeat activity—each with its own personality. **Bath Street**'s bars and clubs are focused on young professionals as well as students; the recommended Pot Still is a perfect place to sample Scotch whisky (see "Eating in Glasgow," later). Nearby, **Sauchiehall Street** is younger, artsier, and more student-oriented. The recently revitalized **Merchant City** zone, stretching just east of the Buchanan Street shopping drag, has a slightly older crowd and a popular gay scene.

West End: You'll find fun bars and music venues in **Hillhead,** on Ashton Lane and surrounding streets. **Finnieston,** just below the Kelvingrove Museum, is packed with trendy bars and restaurants. But it also has an old-school selection of spit-and-sawdust Gaelic pubs, some of which have live music in the evenings (see next).

LIVE MUSIC

Glasgow has a great music scene, on its streets (talented buskers) and in its bars and clubs (including trad sessions). For the latest, *The Skinny* is Glasgow's information-packed alternative weekly (www.theskinny.co.uk). Or check out *The List* (www.list.co.uk) or the *Gig Guide* (www.gigguide.co.uk). All three are also available in print around town. Or check out what's going on at these bars:

Finnieston

The following pubs line up along Argyle Street. For locations, see the "Glasgow's West End" map on page 838.

The Ben Nevis hosts lively, toe-tapping sessions three times a week. It's a good scene—full of energy but crowded. Show up early to grab a seat in this tiny pub, or be ready to stand (Wed, Thu, and Sun at 21:00, no food service—just snacks, #1147).

The **Islay Inn** has bands twice weekly—some traditional, some doing contemporary covers. On nonmusic nights you'll find televisions blasting sports (music Fri and Sat at 21:00, food available, #1256, at corner with Radnor).

At **The Park Bar,** you'll find live music several nights a week, including traditional Scottish bands and sessions on Thursdays (Thu-Sun around 21:00, food available, #1202).

Hillhead

For locations, see the "Glasgow's West End" map on page 838.

The **Òran Mòr** (a former church, www.oran-mor.co.uk) and **Hillhead Bookclub** (a former cinema, www.hillheadbookclub. co.uk) are popular live music venues (both recommended later, under "Eating in Glasgow").

Jinty McGuinty's has acoustic music every night, ranging from chart hits to Irish classics to soul and blues (daily at 21:30, 29 Ashton Lane).

Downtown

For locations, see the "Central Glasgow Hotels & Restaurants" map on page 858.

Twice weekly at **Babbity Bowster,** musicians take over a corner of this cute, simple, and bright pub (under a recommended B&B) for a trad session. The music, energy, and atmosphere are top-notch (Wed and Sat at 15:00, solid pub grub, 16 Blackfriars Street).

Sloans, hidden away through a muraled tunnel off Argyle Street, is a fun pub with outdoor tables filling an alley. They have live traditional music on Wednesdays (21:00) and *ceilidh* dancing instruction on Fridays (£10, starts at 20:30, book ahead, food available, 108 Argyle Street, www.sloansglasgow.com).

Waxy O'Connor's is a massive, almost Disneyesque, multilevel Irish bar featuring a maze of dark, atmospheric rooms, a tree climbing up a wall, and lots of live music (usually acoustic—check their website for days/times) and trad sessions on Sundays at 15:00 (food available until 22:00, 44 West George Street, www. waxyoconnors.co.uk).

MOVIES

The Grosvenor Cinema, right on Ashton Lane in the heart of the bustling West End restaurant scene, is an inviting movie theater, with cushy leather seats in two theaters showing films big and small (most movies £10) and lots of special events. Wine and beer are available at the theater, or you can order cocktails and warm food at the bar next door and have it delivered to your seat (21 Ashton Lane, tel. 0141/341-1234, http://grosvenorwestend.co.uk).

Sleeping in Glasgow

For accommodations, choose between downtown (bustling by day, nearly deserted at night, close to main shopping zone and some major sights, very expensive parking and one-way streets that cause headaches for drivers) and the West End (neighborhoody, best variety of restaurants, easier parking, easy access to West End sights and parks but a bus or subway ride from the center and train station).

DOWNTOWN

These accommodations are scattered around the city center. For locations, see the "Central Glasgow Hotels & Restaurants" map. Glasgow also has all the predictable chains.

$$$ Pipers' Tryst has eight simple rooms enthusiastically done up in good tartan style above a restaurant in the National Piping Centre (described on page 844). It's in a grand, old former church building overlooking a busy intersection, across the street from the downtown business, shopping, and entertainment district. The location is handy, if not romantic, and it's practically a pilgrimage for fans of bagpipes (breakfast extra, 30 McPhater Street, tel. 0141/353-5551, www.thepipingcentre.co.uk, hotel@thepipingcentre.co.uk).

$$$ Z Hotel, part of a small "compact luxury" chain, offers 104 sleek, stylish rooms (some are very small and don't have windows). It's impersonal but handy to Queen Street Station, just a few steps off George Square (breakfast extra, air-con, elevator, free wine-and-cheese buffet each afternoon, 36 North Frederick Street, tel. 0141/212-4550, www.thezhotels.com, glasgow@thezhotels.com).

$$ Grasshoppers is a cheerful, above-it-all retreat on the sixth floor of a building overlooking Central Station. The street-level entry is minimal, but popping out of the elevator, you know you've arrived. The 29 rooms are bright and welcoming (some with small "efficiency" bathrooms), the welcome is warm, and there's 24-hour access to fresh cupcakes, shortbread, and ice cream (free breakfast when you book direct, optional buffet dinner Mon-Wed, elevator, 87 Union Street, tel. 0141/222-2666, www.grasshoppersglasgow.com, info@grasshoppersglasgow.com).

$$ Motel One, part of a stylish German budget hotel chain, has a grand, modern lobby, 374 cookie-cutter rooms, and is conveniently located right next to Central Station (breakfast extra, corner of Oswald and Argyle streets at 78 Oswald Street, tel. 0141/468-0450, www.motel-one.com).

$ Babbity Bowster, named for a traditional Scottish dance, is a pub and restaurant renting five simple, mod rooms up top. It's

Central Glasgow Hotels & Restaurants

located in the trendy Merchant City area on the eastern fringe of downtown, near several clubs and restaurants (lots of stairs and no elevator, 10-minute walk from either station, 16 Blackfriars Street, tel. 0141/552-5055, www.babbitybowster.com, info@babbitybowster.com). The ground-floor **$$** pub serves good grub (daily 12:00-23:00) and has twice-weekly sessions (see "Entertainment in Glasgow").

¢ The huge **Euro Hostel** is a well-run and well-located option for those on a tight budget (private rooms, family rooms, most rooms have en-suite bathrooms, some singles with shared bathrooms, very central on the River Clyde near Central Station, 318 Clyde Street, tel. 0845-539-9956, www.eurohostels.co.uk, glasgow@eurohostels.co.uk).

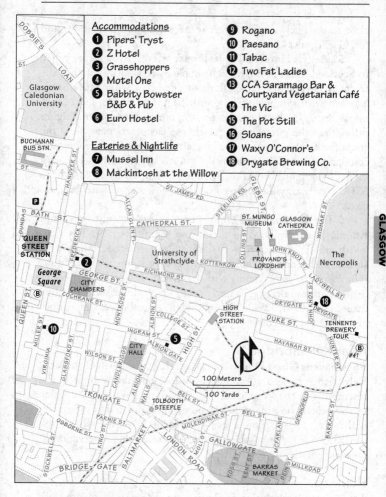

Accommodations
1. Pipers' Tryst
2. Z Hotel
3. Grasshoppers
4. Motel One
5. Babbity Bowster B&B & Pub
6. Euro Hostel

Eateries & Nightlife
7. Mussel Inn
8. Mackintosh at the Willow
9. Rogano
10. Paesano
11. Tabac
12. Two Fat Ladies
13. CCA Saramago Bar & Courtyard Vegetarian Café
14. The Vic
15. The Pot Still
16. Sloans
17. Waxy O'Connor's
18. Drygate Brewing Co.

GLASGOW

IN THE WEST END

For a more appealing neighborhood experience, bunk in the West End—the upper-middle-class neighborhood just a few subway stops (or a 15-minute, £8 taxi ride) from downtown. As this is also one of the city's best dining zones, you'll likely come here for dinner anyway—so why not sleep here? My favorites in this area are the Alamo and Amadeus, which have the most personality. For locations, see "Glasgow's West End" map, earlier.

Finnieston

These places are in an inviting residential area near the Kelvingrove Museum (not as handy to the subway, but easy by bus). They're close to the lively Argyle Street scene, with good restaurants and fun Gaelic pubs.

$$ Argyll Hotel and Guesthouse won't let you forget you're in Scotland. Each room, though simple, is accessorized with a different tartan and has info on the associated clan, while the halls are adorned with symbols of Scotland (bagpipes, thistle, local landmarks, etc.). The hotel has an elevator, breakfast room, and higher prices than the guesthouse (guesthouse customers must cross the street for breakfast and deal with stairs). Otherwise the rooms are comparable but a bit larger in the guesthouse (family rooms, save money by skipping breakfast, 973 Sauchiehall Street, tel. 0141/337-3313, www.argyllhotelglasgow.co.uk, info@argyllhotelglasgow.co.uk).

$ The Alamo Guest House, energetically run by Steve and Emma, faces the bowling green and tennis court. It has rich, lavish public spaces and 10 delicately decorated rooms with stylish bathrooms, including three luxury suites with bathtubs (family room, some rooms with bathroom down the hall, 2- or 3-night minimum stay on weekends in peak season, 46 Gray Street, tel. 0141/339-2395, www.alamoguesthouse.com, info@alamoguesthouse.com).

Near Kelvinbridge

$$ Amadeus Guest House is a classy refuge just north of the large Kelvingrove Park, a 10-minute walk (or one subway stop) to the restaurants in the West End, and a 20-minute walk to the sights in the center. Its nine modern rooms are quiet and comfortable, with some artistic flourishes (411 North Woodside Road, tel. 0141/339-8257, www.amadeusguesthouse.co.uk, reservations@amadeusguesthouse.co.uk, Alex).

Hillhead

These places, overlooking the busy Great Western Road, are close to the Botanic Gardens and Hillhead restaurant scene but farther from the center (10-minute walk to Hillhead subway stop or catch bus to center from Great Western Road).

$$ Belhaven Hotel, a little farther out (about 10 minutes past Byres Road), has 18 sizeable, refurbished rooms in an elegant four-floor townhouse with a pretty, tiled atrium (huge family room, save money by skipping breakfast, bar in breakfast room serves drinks to guests, no elevator, 15 Belhaven Terrace, tel. 0141/339-3222, www.belhavenhotel.com, info@belhavenhotel.com).

$$ Argyll Western, with 17 sleek and tartaned Scottish-themed rooms, feels modern, efficient, and a bit impersonal (family rooms, breakfast included when you book direct, 6 Buckingham Terrace, tel. 0141/339-2339, www.argyllwestern.co.uk, info@

argyllwestern.co.uk, same family runs the Argyll Hotel, listed earlier).

$$ The Alfred, run by the landmark Òran Mòr restaurant/pub (located in the former church just up the street), is dark, creaky, and traditional. Some of the 14 rooms are newer and stylish, while others feel tired (family room, 1 Alfred Terrace, tel. 0141/357-3445, www.thealfredhotelglasgow.co.uk, alfred@thealfredhotelglasgow. co.uk).

Eating in Glasgow

DOWNTOWN

For locations, see the "Central Glasgow Hotel and Restaurants" map on page 858.

$$$ Mussel Inn offers light, good-value fish dinners and seafood plates in an airy, informal environment. The restaurant is a cooperative, owned and run by shellfish farmers. Their "kilo pot" of Scottish mussels is popular with locals and big enough to share ("lunchtime quickie" deals, daily specials, Mon-Fri 12:00-14:30 & 17:00-22:00, Sat 12:00-22:00, Sun from 12:30, 157 Hope Street, tel. 0141/572-1405).

$$ Mackintosh at the Willow, designed by Charles Rennie Mackintosh, serves breakfast, light lunches, and tea in several dining areas spread across three floors. Each room comes with a unique feel. If you want to have afternoon tea in the classy Salon de Luxe dining room upstairs, you must book ahead (daily 9:00-17:00, reservations smart any time, 217 Sauchiehall Street, tel.  0141/204-1903, www.mackintoshatthewillow.com).

$$ Rogano is a time-warp Glasgow institution that retains much of the same classy Art Deco interior it had when it opened in 1935. The restaurant has three distinct sections (all with varying but similar hours—roughly daily 12:00-22:00): **Rogano Bar** in front is an Art Deco diner with dressy outdoor seating and serves inexpensive soups, sandwiches, and simple dishes; **Rogano Restaurant,** a fancy and pricey dining room at the back of the main floor that smacks of the officers' mess on the *Queen Mary,* focuses on seafood, classic Scottish dishes, and afternoon tea (their early menu—until 19:00—is a good deal); and **Rogano Café,** a more casual yet still dressy bistro in the cellar, is filled with 1930s-Hollywood posters and offers a similar menu to the fancy restaurant, but cheaper (11 Exchange Place—just before giant Merchant City archway just off Buchanan Street, reservations smart, tel. 0141/248-4055, www.roganoglasgow.com).

$$ Paesano is the city's favorite pizza place, serving authentic and reasonably priced Neapolitan-style pizzas at jam-packed, convivial communal tables (Sun-Thu 12:00-22:30, Fri-Sat until 24:00, 94 Miller Street, tel. 0141/258-5565). There's a second location on Great Western Road, near my recommended West End accommodations.

$$ Tabac is a dark, mod, and artsy cocktail bar with spacious seating on a narrow lane just off Buchanan Street. They serve pizza, burgers, and big salads (daily 12:00-24:00, food served until 21:00, across from "The Lighthouse" at 10 Mitchell Lane, tel. 0141/572-1448).

$$$ Two Fat Ladies is a hardworking and dressy little place with a focus on food rather than atmosphere and a passion for white fish (lunch and early-bird fixed-price menu at 18:00 are great values, daily 12:00-14:30 & 17:00-22:00, 118 Blythswood Street, tel. 0141/847-0088).

$$ CCA Saramago Bar and Courtyard Vegetarian Café, located on the first floor of Glasgow's edgy contemporary art museum, charges art-student prices for its designer vegetarian and vegan food. An 18th-century facade, discovered when the site was excavated to build the gallery, looms over the atrium restaurant (food served daily 12:00-22:00, 350 Sauchiehall Street, tel. 0141/352-4920).

$ The Vic is a hipster student hangout within the Glasgow School of Art facilities (around the corner from the fire-damaged Mackintosh building). Face the modern Reid Building and hook around the left side to find the easy-to-miss entrance to this funky bar/café, with a menu of salads, burgers, sandwiches, and a few heartier main dishes (Mon-Sat 12:00-late, closed Sun; Aug Tue-Fri 10:00-18:00, closed Sat-Mon).

For Your Whisky: The Pot Still is an award-winning malt whisky bar dating from 1835 that's also proud of its meat pies. You'll see locals of all ages sitting in its leathery interior, watching football (soccer), and discussing their drinks. Give the friendly bartenders a little background on your beverage tastes, and they'll narrow down a good choice for you from their list of over 750 whiskies (daily 11:00-24:00, food served 12:00-17:00, 154 Hope Street, tel. 0141/333-0980, Frank has the long beard).

IN THE WEST END

This hip, lively residential neighborhood/university district is worth exploring, particularly in the evening. The restaurant scene focuses on two areas (at opposite ends of my West End Walk): near the Hillhead subway stop and, farther down, in the Finnieston neighborhood near the Kelvingrove Museum. For locations, see the map on page 838. It's smart to book ahead at any of these places—and for some, it's critical.

Near Hillhead

There's a fun concentration of restaurants on the streets that fan out from the Hillhead subway stop (£8 taxi ride from downtown).

If it's a balmy evening, several have convivial gardens designed to catch the evening sun. Before choosing a place, take a stroll and scout the Ashton Lane scene, which has the greatest variety of places (including Ubiquitous Chip and Brel Bar, recommended next). Tucked away on Ruthven Lane (opposite the subway station) are Bothy Restaurant and The Hanoi Bike Shop. And a couple of blocks away (near the Botanic Gardens) are Hillhead Bookclub, The Parlour, Òran Mòr, and Cail Bruich.

$$$$ Ubiquitous Chip, aka "The Chip," is a beloved local landmark with a couple of inviting pubs and two great restaurant options. On the ground floor is their fine restaurant with beautifully presented contemporary Scottish dishes in a garden atrium. Their early-bird menu (order by 18:30) is a great value. Upstairs (looking down on the scene) is the less-formal, less-expensive, but still very nice brasserie (roughly Sun-Fri 12:00-22:00, Sat until 23:00, brasserie often open later, 12 Ashton Lane, tel. 0141/334-5007 www.ubiquitouschip.co.uk).

$$ Brel Bar is a fun-loving place with a happy garden and a menu with burgers, mussels, and quality bar food. On a nice evening, its backyard beer garden is hard to beat (daily 12:00-24:00, 37 Ashton Lane, tel. 0141/342-4966).

$$$ Bothy Restaurant is a romantic place offering tasty, traditional Scottish fare served by waiters in kilts. Sit outside in the inviting graveled alleyway or in the rustic-contemporary dining room (2- and 3-course dinner deals, Sun-Thu 12:00-21:00, Fri-Sat until 22:00, reservations recommended, down the lane opposite the subway station to 11 Ruthven Lane, tel. 0141/334-4040, www.bothyglasgow.co.uk).

$$ The Hanoi Bike Shop, a rare-in-Scotland Vietnamese "street food" restaurant, serves Asian tapas that are healthy and tasty, using local produce. With tight seating and friendly service, the place has a fun energy (daily 12:00-23:00, 8 Ruthven Lane, tel. 0141/334-7165).

$$ Hillhead Bookclub is a historic cinema building cleared out to make room for fun, good food, and lots of booze. It's a youthful and quirky art-school scene, with lots of beers on tap, creative cocktails, retro computer games, Ping-Pong, and theme evenings like "drag queen bingo" night. The menu features international-inspired dishes, from schnitzel to tacos to curry, plus the usual burgers and salads (daily 10:00-24:00, food served until 21:00, 17 Vinicombe Street, tel. 0141/576-1700).

$$ The Parlour, across from the Hillhead Bookclub, gets all the evening sun on its terrace seating. In bad weather, an open fire warms the spacious interior. It's young, fun, and pub-like, with tacos, burgers, and creative cocktails (daily 10:30-24:00, 28 Vinicombe Street, tel. 0141/560-8004).

$$ Òran Mòr fills a converted church from the 1860s with a classic pub. They offer basic pub grub either inside or on the front-porch beer garden—and have a good-value lunch deal ("a play, a pie, and a pint") for theater performances (daily 9:00-late, across from the Botanic Gardens at 731 Great Western Road, tel. 0141/357-6200).

$$$$ Cail Bruich serves award-winning classic Scottish dishes with an updated spin in an elegant and romantic setting. Reservations are smart (classy tasting menus for £60, lunch Wed-Sat 12:00-14:00, dinner Tue-Sat 18:00-21:00, closed Sun-Mon, 725 Great Western Road, tel. 0141/334-6265, www.cailbruich.co.uk).

Grocery: There's a **Co-op** supermarket between the Kelvinbridge subway stop and my recommended accommodations in the West End—handy for a quick grocery run on the walk back to your hotel (long hours daily, 470 Great Western Road).

Facing the Kelvingrove Museum

These three places are immediately across from the Kelvingrove Museum (which is likely to leave you hungry). They're more basic and less trendy than the Finnieston places (a few blocks away, listed next) that will leave you with better memories.

$$ Brewdog Glasgow is a beer-and-burgers joint. It's a great place to sample Scottish microbrews—from their own brewery in Aberdeen, as well as guest brews—in an industrial-mod setting reminiscent of American brewpubs (daily 12:00-24:00, 1397 Argyle Street, tel. 0141/334-7175).

$$ Mother India's Café is a busy joint with a line out the door on most nights (no reservations). It serves tasty Indian and is a good stop if you crave Scotland's national dish: "a good curry." The menu features small plates designed to enjoy family-style (about two plates per person makes a meal, Mon-Sat 12:00-22:30, Sun until 22:00, 1355 Argyle Street, tel. 0141/339-9145). They also run two nearby locations with the same name.

$ Baffo, a fun Italian place, serves up cheap pizzas and basic pastas. It's casual and buzzing with locals, and if you snag a window seat, you'll enjoy nice views of the Kelvingrove Museum (Sun-Thu 11:00–22:00, Fri-Sat 10:00-24:00, 1377 Argyle Street, tel. 0141/583-0000).

Trendy Finnieston Eateries on and near Argyle Street

This trendy neighborhood—with a hipster charm in this hipster city—stretches east from in front of the Kelvingrove Museum (a 10-minute walk from the Kelvinhall or Kelvinbridge subway stops). Each of these is likely to require a reservation. The Crabshakk started things off here and today it anchors a strip of similarly funky, foodie eateries.

$$$ Crabshakk, specializing in fresh, beautifully presented seafood, is a foodie favorite, with a very tight bar-and-mezzanine seating area and tables spilling out onto the sidewalk. It's casual but still respectable. If you can't reserve a table, ask to sit at the bar (daily 12:00-22:00, 1114 Argyle Street, tel. 0141/334-6127, www.crabshakk.com).

$$$$ The Gannet offers multicourse set menus of beautifully prepared Scottish ingredients with a modern spin. It's relaxed and stylish, but the owners/chefs are serious about the food (no à la carte, 4-course menu until 18:00, 6-course menu thereafter, open for lunch Thu-Sat 12:00-14:00, dinner Tue-Sat 17:00-21:30, Sun 13:00-15:00 & 17:30-21:00, closed Mon, 1155 Argyle Street, tel. 0141/204-2081, www.thegannetgla.com).

$$$ Ox and Finch is a trendy and bustling place with an open kitchen and an upscale, rustic, wood-meets-industrial atmosphere. They serve modern international cuisine in small, shareable portions (reservations strongly recommended, daily 12:00-22:00, 920 Sauchiehall Street, tel. 0141/339-8627, www.oxandfinch.com).

Glasgow Connections

Traveline Scotland's journey planner is linked to all of Scotland's train and bus schedule info. Go online (www.travelinescotland.com), call them at tel. 0871-200-2233, or use the individual websites listed below. If you're connecting with Edinburgh, note that the train is faster but the bus is cheaper.

BY TRAIN

Train info: Tel. 0345-748-4950, NationalRail.co.uk.

From Glasgow's Queen Street Station by Train to: Oban (6/day, fewer on Sun, 3 hours), **Fort William** (3/day, 4 hours), **Inverness** (4/day direct, 3 hours, more with change in Perth), **Edinburgh** (7/hour, 50 minutes), **Stirling** (3/hour, 45 minutes).

From Glasgow's Central Station by Train to: Keswick in England's Lake District (train to Penrith, hourly, 1.5 hours; then bus to Keswick, 40 minutes), **Cairnryan** for ferry to Belfast (train to Ayr, 2/hour, 1 hour; then bus to Cairnryan, 1 hour), **Liverpool** (2/hour, 4 hours, change in Wigan or Preston), **Durham** (2/hour, 3 hours, may require change in Edinburgh), **York** (hourly, 4 hours, more with change in Edinburgh), **London** (2/hour, 5 hours direct).

BY BUS

Glasgow's Buchanan bus station is a hub for reaching the Highlands. If you're coming from Edinburgh, you can take the bus to Glasgow and transfer here. Or, for a speedier connection, zip to Glasgow on the train, then walk a few short blocks to the bus station. (Ideally, try to arrive at Glasgow's Queen Street Station, which is closer to the bus station.) For more details on these connections, see "Getting Around the Highlands" on page 914. Unless otherwise noted, connections below are on Citylink buses (tel. 0871-266-3333, www.citylink.co.uk).

From Glasgow by Bus to: Edinburgh (#900, 4/hour, 1.5 hours), **Oban** (#976 and #977; 5/day, 3 hours), **Fort William** (#914/#915/916; 7-8/day direct, 3 hours), **Glencoe** (#914/#915/#916; 7-8/day, 2.5 hours), **Inverness** (express bus #G10, 5/day, 3 hours; 6/day direct on Megabus, 3.5 hours), **Portree** on the Isle of Skye (#915 and #916, 3/day, 7 hours), **Stirling** (#M8, hourly, 45 minutes).

BY PLANE

Glasgow International Airport: Located eight miles west of the city, this airport (code: GLA) has currency-exchange desks, a TI, luggage storage, and ATMs (www.glasgowairport.com). Taxis connect downtown to the airport for about £25. Your hotel can likely arrange a private taxi service for £15, or you can take Uber.

Bus #500 zips to central Glasgow (every 10 minutes, 5:00-23:00, £7.50 one-way, 25 minutes to both train stations and the bus station, catch at bus stop #1). Slow bus #77 goes to the West End, stopping at the Kelvingrove Museum and rolling along Argyle Street (departs every 30 minutes, £5 one-way, 50 minutes).

Prestwick Airport: A hub for Ryanair, this airport is 30 miles southwest of the city center (code: PIK, www.glasgowprestwick.com). The best connection is by train, which runs between the airport and Central Station (3/hour, 50 minutes, half-price with Ryanair ticket, trains also run to Edinburgh Waverley Station—about 2/hour, 2 hours). Stagecoach buses link the airport with Buchanan Bus Station (£10, 1-2/hour, 50 minutes, www.stagecoachbus.com).

ROUTE TIPS FOR DRIVERS

From England's Lake District to Glasgow: From Keswick, take the A-66 for 18 miles to the M-6 and speed north nonstop (via Penrith and Carlisle), crossing Hadrian's Wall into Scotland. The road becomes the M-74 just north of Carlisle. To slip through Glasgow quickly, leave the M-74 at Junction 4 onto the M-73, following signs to *M-8/Glasgow*. Leave the M-73 at Junction 2, exiting onto the M-8. Stay on the M-8 west through Glasgow, exit at Junction 30, cross Erskine Bridge, and turn left on the A-82, following signs to *Crianlarich* and *Loch Lomond*. (For a scenic drive through Glasgow, take exit 17 off the M-8 and stay on the A-82 toward Dumbarton.)

GLASGOW

STIRLING & NEARBY

Stirling • Wallace Monument • Bannockburn • Falkirk • Culross • Doune

The historic city of Stirling is the crossroads of Scotland: Equidistant from Edinburgh and Glasgow (less than an hour from both), and rising above a plain where the Lowlands meet the Highlands, it's no surprise that Stirling has hosted many of the biggest names (and biggest battles) of Scottish history. Everyone from Mary, Queen of Scots to Bonnie Prince Charlie has passed through the gates of its stately, strategic castle.

From the cliff-capping ramparts of Stirling Castle, you can see where each of the three pivotal battles of Scotland's 13th- and 14th-century Wars of Independence took place: the Battle of Stirling Bridge, where against all odds, the courageous William Wallace defeated the English army; the Battle of Falkirk, where Wallace was toppled by a vengeful English king; and the Battle of Bannockburn, when—in the wake of Wallace's defeat—Robert the Bruce rallied to kick out the English once and for all (well, at least for a few generations). The Wallace Monument and Battle of Bannockburn Visitors Centre—on the outskirts of Stirling, in opposite directions—are practically pilgrimage sites for patriotic Scots.

Stirling itself is sleepy, but it's a good home base for a variety of side-trips. In Falkirk, take a spin in a fascinating Ferris wheel for boats, and ogle the gigantic horse heads called The Kelpies. Sitting on the nearby estuary known as the Firth of Forth—on the way to Edinburgh or St. Andrews—is the gorgeously preserved time-warp village of Culross. To the north, fans of Monty Python and *Outlander* flock to Doune Castle.

PLANNING YOUR TIME

You'll likely pass near Stirling at least once as you travel through Scotland. Skim this chapter to learn about your options and select the stops that interest you. If you can't fit it all in on a pass-through, spend the night. Just as Stirling was ideally situated for monarchs and armies of the past, it's handy for present-day visitors: It's much smaller, and arguably even more conveniently located, than Edinburgh or Glasgow, and it has a variety of good accommodations. You'd need a solid three days to see all the big sights within an hour's drive of Stirling—but most people are (and should be) more selective.

Stirling

Every Scot knows the city of Stirling (pop. 41,000) deep in their bones. This patriotic heart of Scotland is like Bunker Hill, Gettysburg, and the Alamo, all rolled into one. Stirling perches on a ridge overlooking Scotland's most history-drenched plain: a flat expanse—cut through by the twisting River Forth and the meandering stream called Bannockburn—that divides the Lowlands from the Highlands. And

capping that ridge is Stirling's formidable castle, the seat of the final kings of Scotland.

From a traveler's perspective, Stirling is a pleasant mini-Edinburgh, with a steep spine leading up to that grand castle. It's busy with tourists by day, but sleepy at night. The town, and its castle, may lack personality—but both are striking and strategic.

Orientation to Stirling

Stirling's old town is situated along a long, narrow, steep hill. At its base are the train and bus stations and a thriving commercial district; at its apex is the castle. The old town feels like a steeper, shorter, less touristy, and far less characteristic version of Edinburgh's Royal Mile.

Tourist Information: The TI is a five-minute walk below the castle, just inside the gates of the Old Town Jail (June-Sept Wed-Mon 9:30-17:00, Tue from 10:00; Oct-May daily from 10:00; St. Johns Street, tel. 01786/475-019, www.yourstirling.com).

Getting Around: While the sights within Stirling nestle together at the top of the town, the Wallace Monument and Battle of Bannockburn Visitors Centre are an easy taxi ride, longer bus ride, or short drive away. From July through mid-September, **hop-on, hop-off bus #1314** loops from the train station, bus station, and castle esplanade to the Wallace Monument visitors center (£4.90, every 40 minutes, daily 10:10-16:50, these are first and last departure times from the train station).

A tacky green **tourist train** shuttles people up and down the ridge to Stirling Castle. Unfortunately, it zips past the town's strollable streets and artisan shops. I'd skip the train and explore the town on your way up to the castle.

Sights in Stirling

▲▲STIRLING CASTLE

"He who holds Stirling, holds Scotland." These fateful words have been proven, more often than not, to be true. Stirling Castle's prized position—perched on a volcanic crag overlooking a bridge over the River Forth, the primary passage between the Lowlands and the Highlands—has long been the key to Scotland. This castle was the preferred home of Scottish kings and queens in the Middle Ages; today it's one of the most historic—and most

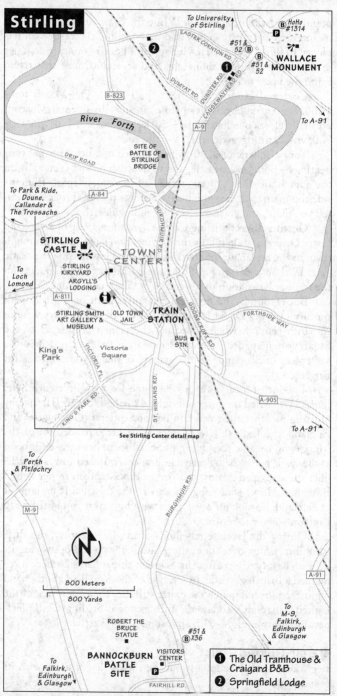

Stirling

To University of Stirling

EASTER CORNTON RD.

B HoHo #1314

P

#51 & 52

B #51 & 52

WALLACE MONUMENT

DUNSTER RD.

DUMYAT RD.

CAUSEWAYHEAD RD.

B-823

River Forth

A-9

To A-91

DRIP ROAD

SITE OF BATTLE OF STIRLING BRIDGE

To Park & Ride, Doune, Callander & The Trossachs

A-84

BURGHMUIR RD.

STIRLING CASTLE

TOWN CENTER

To Loch Lomond

STIRLING KIRKYARD

ARGYLL'S LODGING

A-811

STIRLING SMITH ART GALLERY & MUSEUM

OLD TOWN JAIL

TRAIN STATION

GOOSECROFT RD.

FORTHSIDE WAY

King's Park

VICTORIA PL.

Victoria Square

BUS STN.

A-905

KING'S PARK RD.

ST. NINIANS RD.

To A-91

See Stirling Center detail map

To Perth & Pitlochry

M-9

BURGHMUIR RD.

N

800 Meters

800 Yards

A-91

ROBERT THE BRUCE STATUE

#51 & X36

To M-9, Falkirk, Edinburgh & Glasgow

VISITORS CENTER

To Falkirk, Edinburgh & Glasgow

BANNOCKBURN BATTLE SITE

P

FAIRHILL RD.

❶ The Old Tramhouse & Craigard B&B

❷ Springfield Lodge

STIRLING & NEARBY

popular—castles in Scotland. While the compound is simple and its interiors are pretty empty and new-feeling, the castle still has plenty to offer: spectacular views over a gentle countryside, tales of the dynamic Stuart monarchs, and several exhibits that try to bring the place to life.

Cost and Hours: £16, daily 9:30-18:00, Oct-March until 17:00, last entry 45 minutes before closing, Regimental Museum normally closes one hour before castle, good café, tel. 01786/450-000, www.stirlingcastle.scot.

Tours: The included 40-minute guided tour helps you get your bearings—both to the castle, and to Scottish history (generally on the hour 10:00-16:00, often on the half-hour too, departs from inside the main gate near the well). Docents posted throughout can tell you more, and you can rent a £3 audioguide.

Getting There: Stirling Castle sits at the very tip of a steep old town. Drivers should follow the *Stirling Castle* signs uphill through town to the esplanade and park at the £4 lot just outside the castle gate. Without a car, you can hike the 20-minute uphill route from the train or bus station to the castle, or take a taxi (about £5).

Background: The first real castle was built here in the 12th century by King David I. But Stirling Castle's glory days were in the 16th century, when it became the primary residence of the Stuart (often spelled "Stewart") monarchs, who turned it into a showpiece of Scotland—and a symbol of one-upmanship against England.

The 16th century was a busy time for royal intrigues here: James IV married the sister of England's King Henry VIII, thereby knitting together the royal families of Scotland (the Stuarts) and England (the Tudors). Later, James V further expanded the castle. Mary (who became the Queen of Scots) spent her early childhood at the castle before being raised in France. As queen and as a Catholic, she struggled against the rise of Protestantism in her realm. But when Mary's son, King James VI, was crowned King James I of England, he took his royal court with him away from Stirling to London—never to return.

During the Jacobite rebellions of the 18th century, the British military took over the castle—bulking it up and destroying its delicate beauty. Even after the Scottish threat had subsided, it remained a British garrison, home base of the Argyll and Sutherland regiments. (You'll notice the castle still flies the Union Jack of the United Kingdom.) Today, the fully restored Stirling Castle feels new but fairly empty—with almost no historic artifacts.

● Self-Guided Tour

Begin on the esplanade, just outside the castle entrance, with its grand views.

STIRLING & NEARBY

The Esplanade: The castle's esplanade, a military parade ground in the 19th century, is a tour-bus parking lot today. As you survey this site, remember that Stirling Castle bore witness to some of the most important moments in Scottish history. To the right as you face the castle, a statue of **King Robert the Bruce** looks toward the plain called Bannockburn, where he defeated the English army in 1314. Squint off to the horizon on Robert's left to spot the pointy stone monument capping the hill called Abbey Craig. This is the **Wallace Monument,** marking the spot where the Scottish warrior William Wallace surveyed the battlefield before his victory in the Battle of Stirling Bridge (1297).

These great Scots helped usher in several centuries of home rule. In 1315, Robert the Bruce's daughter married into an on-the-rise noble clan called the Stuarts, who had distinguished themselves fighting at Bannockburn. When their son Robert became King Robert II of Scotland in 1371, he kicked off the Stuart dynasty. Over the next few generations, their headquarters—Stirling Castle—flourished. The fortified grand entry showed all who approached that James IV (r. 1488-1513) was a great ruler with a powerful castle.

• *Head through the first gate into Guardroom Square, where you can buy your ticket, check tour times, and consider renting the audioguide. Then continue up through the inner gate.*

Gardens and Battlements: Once through the gate, follow the passage to the left into a delightful grassy courtyard called the **Queen Anne Garden.** This was the royal family's playground in the 1600s. Imagine doing a little lawn bowling with the queen here.

In the casemates lining the garden is the **Castle Exhibition.** Its "Come Face to Face with  1,000 Years of History" exhibit provides an entertaining and worthwhile introduction to the castle. You'll meet each of the people who left their mark here, from the first Stuart kings to William Wallace and Robert the Bruce. The video leaves you thinking that re-enactors of Jacobite struggles are even more spirited than our Civil War re-enactors.

Leave the garden the way you came and make a hairpin turn up the ramp (twice) to the top of the **battlements.** From up here, the castle's strategic position is evident: Defenders had a 360-degree view of enemy armies approaching from miles away. These battlements were built in 1710, long after the castle's Stuart glory days, in response to early rebellions by the Jacobites (from the Latin word for "James"). By this time, the successes of William Wallace and Robert the Bruce were a distant memory; and through the 1707 Act of Union, Scotland had become welded to England. Bonnie Prince Charlie—descendant of those original Stuart "King Jameses" who built this castle—later staged a series of uprisings to try to reclaim the throne of Great Britain for the Stuart line, frightening England enough for it to further fortify the castle. And sure enough, Bonnie Prince Charlie found himself—ironically—laying siege to the fortress that his own ancestors had built: Facing the main gate (with its two round towers below the UK flag), notice the pockmarks from Jacobite cannonballs in 1746.

• Now head back down the top ramp and pass through that main gate, into the...

Outer Close: As you enter this courtyard, straight ahead is James IV's yellow **Great Hall.** To the left is his son **James V's**

royal palace, lined with finely carved Renaissance statues. In 1540, King James V, inspired by French Renaissance châteaux he'd seen, had the castle covered with about 200 statues and busts to "proclaim the peace, prosperity, and justice of his reign" and to validate his rule. Imagine the impression all these classical gods and goddesses made on visitors. The message: James' rule was a Golden Age for Scotland.

Guided tours of the castle depart from just to your right, near the well. Beyond that is the Grand Battery, with its cannons and rampart views and, underneath that, the Great Kitchens. We'll see both at the end of this tour.

• Hike up the ramp between James V's palace and the Great Hall (under the crenellated sky bridge connecting them). You'll emerge into the...

Inner Close: Standing at the center of Stirling Castle, you're surrounded by Scottish history. This courtyard was the core of the 12th-century castle. From here, additional buildings were added—each by a different monarch. Facing downhill, you'll see the Great Hall. To the left is the Chapel Royal—where Mary, Queen of Scots was crowned in 1543. Opposite that, to the right, is the royal palace (containing the Royal Apartments)—notice the "I5" monogram above the windows (for the king who built it: James, or Iacobus in Latin, V). Upstairs in this same palace is the Stirling Heads Gallery. And behind you is the Regimental Museum devoted to the Argyll and Sutherland Highlanders.

• *We'll visit each of these in turn. First, at the far-left end of the gallery with the coffee stand, step into...*

The Great Hall: This is the largest secular space in medieval Scotland. Dating from 1503, this was a grand setting for the great banquets of Scotland's Renaissance kings. One such party, to which all the crowned heads of Europe were invited, reportedly went on for three full days. This was also where kings and queens would hold court, earning it the nickname "the parliament." The impressive hammerbeam roof is a modern reconstruction, modeled on the early-16th-century roof at

Edinburgh Castle. It's made of 400 local oak trees, joined by wooden pegs. If you flipped it over, it would float.

• *At the far-right end of the hall, climb a few stairs and walk across the sky bridge into James V's palace. Here you can explore...*

The Royal Apartments: Six ground-floor apartments are colorfully done up as they might have looked in the mid-16th century, when James V and

his queen, Mary of Guise, lived here. Costumed performers play the role of palace attendants, happy to chat with you about medieval life as you explore. You'll begin in the King's Inner Hall, where he received guests. Notice the 60 colorfully painted oak medallions on the ceiling. The medallions are carved with the faces of Scottish and European royalty. These are copies, painstakingly reconstructed after expert research. You'll soon see the originals up close (and upstairs) in the Stirling Heads Gallery.

Continue (left of the fireplace) into the other rooms: the King's Bedchamber, with a four-poster bed supporting a less-than-luxurious rope mattress; and then the Queen's Bedchamber, the Inner Hall, and the Outer Hall, offering a more vivid example of what these rich spaces would have looked like.

• *From the queen's apartments, you'll exit into the top corner of the Inner Close. Directly ahead and to your left, up the stairs, is the...*

Stirling Heads Gallery: This is, for me, the castle's highlight—a chance to see the originals of the elaborately carved and painted portrait medallions that decorated the ceiling of the king's presence chamber. Each one is thoughtfully displayed and lovingly explained. Don't miss the video at the end of the hall.

• *If you were to leave this gallery through the intended exit, you'd wind up back down in the Queen Anne Garden. Instead, backtrack and exit the way you came in to return to the Inner Close, and visit the two remaining sights.*

The Chapel Royal: One of the first Protestant churches built in Scotland, the Chapel Royal was constructed in 1594 by James VI for the baptism of his first son, Prince Henry. The faint painted frieze high up survives from Charles I's coronation visit to Scotland in 1633. Clearly the holiness of the chapel ended in the 1800s when the army moved in.

Regimental Museum: At the top of the Inner Close, in the King's Old Building, is the excellent **Argyll and Sutherland Highlanders Museum** (www.argylls.co.uk). Another highlight of the castle, it's barely mentioned in castle promotional material because it's run by a different organization. With lots of tartans, tassels, and swords, it shows how the fighting spirit of Scotland was absorbed by Britain. The two regiments, established in the 1790s to defend Britain in the Napoleonic age and combined in the 1880s, have served with distinction in British military campaigns for more than two centuries. Their pride shows here in the building that has served as their headquarters since 1881. Look for exhibits on World War I, with accounts from the battlefield, and on World War II and conflicts in the Middle East to the present day.

• *When you're ready to move on, consider the following scenic route back to the castle exit.*

Rampart Walk to the Kitchen: The skinny lane between church and museum leads to the secluded Douglas Garden at the rock's highest point. Belly up to the ramparts for a commanding view, including the Wallace Monument. From here you can walk the ramparts downhill to the Grand Battery, with its cannon rampart back at the Outer Close. The Outer Close was the service zone, with a well and the kitchen (below the cannon rampart). The great banquets of James VI didn't happen all by themselves, as you'll appreciate when you explore the fine medieval kitchen exhibit (where mannequin cooks oversee medieval recipes); to find it, head down the ramp and look for the *Great Kitchens* sign. Also off the Outer Close are the **Palace Vaults**, with kid-themed exhibits where younger visitors can learn more about life as a musician, artist, or jester in the castle.

• *Your castle visit ends here. For a scenic route down into town, consider a detour through an old churchyard cemetery (described next).*

MORE SIGHTS IN STIRLING
Old Kirkyard Stroll

Stirling has a particularly evocative old cemetery in the kirkyard (churchyard) just below the castle. For a soulful stroll, sneak

down the stairs where the castle meets the esplanade parking lot (near the statue of the Scotsman fighting in the South African War). From here, you can wander through the tombstones—Celtic crosses, Victorian statues, and faded headstones—
from centuries gone by. The rocky crag in the middle of the graveyard is a fine viewpoint. Work your way over to the Church of the Holy Rude (well worth a visit, daily May-Sept 11:00-16:00), where you can re-enter the town. From here, Argyll's Lodging and the castle parking lot are to the left, and the Old Town Jail (also housing the TI) is just to the right.

Argyll's Lodging

Just below the castle esplanade is this 17th-century nobleman's fortified mansion. European aristocrats wanted to live near power—making this location, where the Earl of Argyll's family resided for about a century, prime real estate.

Cost and Hours: Although currently closed for renovations, Argyll's Lodging is usually included with your castle ticket. Check locally for details on whether it has reopened (generally daily 12:45-17:30, last entry once hour before closing).

▲Stirling Ghost Walk

David Kinnaird, a local actor/historian, gives haunted "Happy Hangman" walks through the old kirkyard cemetery at night. Meet at the TI (inside the gates of the Old Town Jail) for the 75-minute tour (£7.50, RS%—ask, July-Aug Tue-Sat at 20:30, Sept-June Fri-Sat at 20:00, tel. 01592/874-449, www.stirlingghostwalk.com). Just show up and pay him directly. David also offers historic walks (by request only), which tell the story of Stirling as you wander through town.

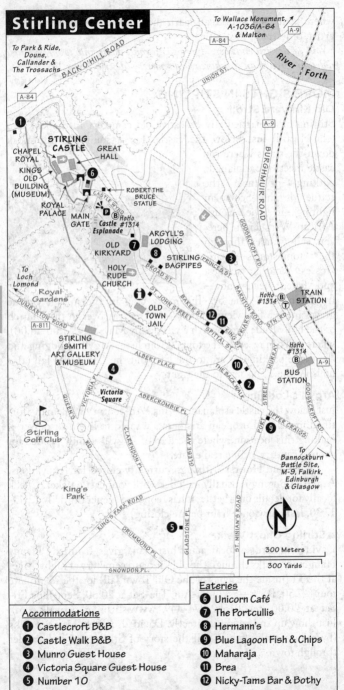

STIRLING & NEARBY

Stirling Center

To Wallace Monument,
A-1036/A-64
& Malton

River Forth

To Park & Ride,
Doune,
Callander &
The Trossachs

BACK O'HILL ROAD

A-84

UNION ST.

A-9

A-84

BURGHMUIR ROAD

STIRLING CASTLE

CHAPEL ROYAL

GREAT HALL

KINGS OLD BUILDING (MUSEUM)

ROBERT THE BRUCE STATUE

ROYAL PALACE

MAIN GATE

Castle Esplanade

HoHo #1314

ARGYLL'S LODGING

OLD KIRKYARD

STIRLING BAGPIPES

PRINCES ST.

GOOSECROFT RD.

To Loch Lomond

Royal Gardens

DUMBARTON ROAD

A-811

HOLY RUDE CHURCH

BROAD ST.

ST. JOHN STREET

BAKER ST.

BARNTON ROAD

HoHo #1314

TRAIN STATION

STN. RD.

OLD TOWN JAIL

SPITTAL ST.

KING ST.

FRIARS

STIRLING SMITH ART GALLERY & MUSEUM

ALBERT PLACE

THE BACK WALK

MURRAY

PORT STREET

HoHo #1314

A-9

BUS STATION

GOOSECROFT RD.

QUEEN'S RD.

Victoria Square

VICTORIA PL.

ABERCROMBIE PL.

Stirling Golf Club

CLARENDON PL.

GLEBE AVE.

UPPER CRAIGS

To Bannockburn Battle Site, M-9, Falkirk, Edinburgh & Glasgow

King's Park

KING'S PARK ROAD

DRUMMOND PL.

GLADSTONE PL.

ST. NINIAN'S ROAD

N

SNOWDON PL.

300 Meters

300 Yards

Accommodations
❶ Castlecroft B&B
❷ Castle Walk B&B
❸ Munro Guest House
❹ Victoria Square Guest House
❺ Number 10

Eateries
❻ Unicorn Café
❼ The Portcullis
❽ Hermann's
❾ Blue Lagoon Fish & Chips
❿ Maharaja
⓫ Brea
⓬ Nicky-Tams Bar & Bothy

Old Town Jail

Stirling's jail was built during the Victorian Age, when the purpose of imprisonment was shifting from punishment to rehabilitation. While there's little to see today, theatrical 30-minute tours entertain families with a light and funny walk through one section of the jail. You'll end at the top of the tower for a Q&A with a commanding view of the surrounding countryside.

Cost and Hours: £7.50, July-early Sept only, tours every 30 minutes daily 10:15-17:15, last tour at 17:15, St. John Street, http://oldtownjail.co.uk/.

▲Stirling Bagpipes

This fun little shop, just a block below the castle on Broad Street, is worth a visit for those curious about bagpipes. Owner Alan refurbishes and repairs old bagpipes here, but also makes new ones from scratch, in a workshop on the premises. The pleasantly cluttered shop, which is a bit of a neighborhood hangout, is littered with bagpipe components—chanters, drones, bags, covers, and cords. If he's not too busy, Alan can answer your questions. He'll explain how the most expensive parts of the bagpipe are the "sticks"—the chanter and drones, carved from blackwood—while the bag and cover are cheaper and changeable. A serious set costs

£700...beginners can consider a £50 starter kit that includes a practice chanter (like a recorder) with a book of sheet music and a CD. Alan hopes to open a wee museum next door to show off his collection of historic bagpipes.

Cost and Hours: Free, Mon-Tue and Thu-Sat 10:00-18:00, closed Wed and Sun, 8 Broad Street, tel. 01786/448-886, www.stirlingbagpipes.com.

Nearby: On the wide street in front of the shop, look for Stirling's **mercat cross** ("market cross"). A standard feature of any medieval Scottish market town, this was the place where townsfolk would gather for the market, and where royal proclamations were read and executions took place. Today the commercial metabolism of this once-thriving street is at a low ebb. Locals joke that every 100 years, the shopping bustle moves one block farther down the road. These days, it's squeezed into the modern shopping mall between the old town and the river.

STIRLING & NEARBY

Stirling Smith Art Gallery and Museum

Tucked at the edge of the grid-planned, Victorian Age neighborhood just below the castle, this endearing and eclectic museum is a hodgepodge of artifacts from Stirling's past: art gallery (where you can meet historical figures with connections to this proud little town), pewter collection, local history exhibits, a steam-powered carriage, the mutton bone shard removed in the world's first documented tracheotomy (1853), and a 19th-century executioner's cloak and ax. The museum's prized piece is what they claim is the world's oldest surviving soccer ball—a 16th-century stitched-up pig's bladder that restorers found stuck in the rafters of Stirling Castle. The building is surrounded by a garden filled with public art.

Cost and Hours: Free, Tue-Sat 10:30-17:00, Sun from 14:00, closed Mon, Dumbarton Road, tel. 01786/471-917, www.smithartgalleryandmuseum.co.uk.

Sleeping in Stirling

IN AND NEAR THE TOWN CENTER

A variety of spots let you sleep in the shadow of Stirling Castle, in the town center, or a bit farther out. For locations, see the map on page 878.

Just Under the Castle

$$ Castlecroft B&B is well cared for by Laura, who keeps everything immaculate, bakes her own bread, and welcomes guests with tea/coffee and shortbread upon arrival. Just under the castle and overlooking a field with "hairy coos," it's a 10-minute walk down a scenic countryside path to the town center. Two of the five rooms come with their own patios, and anyone can make use of the peaceful living room and deck (Ballengeich Road, tel. 01786/474-933, mobile 0755/334-5497, www.castlecroft-uk.co.uk, castlecroft@gmail.com).

In the Town Center

$$ Castle Walk B&B, built into the old city walls, is a moderately priced option with antique touches in a convenient location. The eight rooms are pleasantly updated, but you'll still feel the authenticity of staying in the castle walls (two rooms with bathroom in hallway, family room, City Walls, Back Walk, tel. 07598/029-732, www.stirlingcastlewalk.co.uk, jackiecameron.uk@gmail.com, Jackie and Adrian).

$ Munro Guest House offers six simple but well-maintained rooms in a homey place in the center of town. One room is a single with private bathroom in the hall (family room, street parking, 14 Princes Street, tel. 01786/472-685, www.munroguesthouse.co.uk, munroguesthouse@gmail.com, Richard).

In the Victorian Town, South of the Castle

When Stirling expanded beyond its old walls during the Victorian Age, a modern, grid-planned town sprouted just to the south. Today, this posh-feeling area holds a few B&Bs that are within a (long) walk of Stirling's old town and castle. These places are in large, spacious homes with easy parking.

$$$$ Victoria Square has 10 plush rooms in a beautiful location facing a big, grassy park. While the prices are high, it's neat as a pin, and Kari and Phil keep things running smoothly. They also have a nice restaurant, The Orangery, in their elegant sunroom. It's about a 10-minute walk to the lower part of town, or 20 minutes up to the castle (no kids under 12, minifridges, 12 Victoria Square, tel. 01786/473-920, www.victoriasquare.scot, info@victoriasquare.scot).

$$ Number 10 rents three nice, traditional rooms in a Scottish-feeling home with tartan carpets blanketing the halls and a lovely garden out back (no kids under 5, 10 Gladstone Place, tel. 01786/472-681, www.cameron-10.co.uk, cameron-10@tinyonline.co.uk, Carol and Donald Cameron).

ALONG AND NEAR CAUSEWAYHEAD ROAD, NORTH OF THE CASTLE

A number of moderately priced B&Bs line Causewayhead Road, a busy thoroughfare that connects Stirling to the Wallace Monument. From here, it's a long walk into town (or the Wallace Monument), but the location is handy for drivers (each place has free parking). While this modern residential area lacks charm, it's convenient. For locations see the map on page 871.

$$ The Old Tramhouse is the frilliest of the bunch, with five rooms elegantly decorated with a delicate charm (family room, 42 Causewayhead Road, tel. 01786/449-774, mobile 0759-054-0604, www.theoldtramhouse.com, enquiries@theoldtramhouse.com, Alison Cowie). They also have two apartments for up to five people.

$$ Craigard B&B has four small, modern, tidy, and proper rooms that offer good value and a shared breakfast table (40 Causewayhead Road, mobile 0778/728-8948, www.craigardstirling.co.uk, enquiries@craigardstirling.co.uk, Dee).

$$ Springfield Lodge sits at the back end of the residential zone that lines up along Causewayhead Road. It's across the street from farm fields, giving it a countryside feeling. The five neat rooms fill a spacious modern house. And owners Kim and Kevin can tell you where to find the local "hairy coos" (family room, no kids under 6, Easter Cornton Road, tel. 01786/474-332, mobile 0798/656-4340, www.springfieldlodgebandb.co.uk, springfieldlodgebandb@gmail.com).

Eating in Stirling

Stirling isn't a place to go looking for high cuisine; eateries here tend to be barely satisfying but functional. All of these are open daily unless otherwise noted. For locations, see the map on page 878.

UP NEAR THE CASTLE

$$ Unicorn Café, tucked under the casemates inside the castle, is a decent cafeteria for lunch if touring the grounds (same hours as castle).

$$ The Portcullis, just below the castle esplanade, is a pub that aches with history, from its dark, wood-grained bar area to its stony courtyard. The food, like the setting, is old-school. If the restaurant is full, you can eat at the bar (daily 11:30-15:00 & 17:30-20:30, tel. 01786/472-290).

$$$$ Hermann's, a block below the castle esplanade, is simple, spacious, and homey with a sunny conservatory out back. It serves a mix of Scottish and Austrian food—perfect when you've got a hankering for haggis, but your travel partner wants Wiener schnitzel (daily 12:00-14:30 & 18:00-late, top of Broad Street, tel. 01786/450-632, www.hermanns-restaurant.co.uk).

LOWER DOWN IN THE TOWN

Dumbarton Road, at the bottom of town, has a line of cheap eateries (Indian, Asian, cheap buffets) including **Blue Lagoon Fish & Chips** (11:00-23:00, at Port Street). Among a group of chain pubs and ethnic eateries (Thai and Italian), these three are within about a block of Stirling's clock tower near King Street in the old town center:

$$ Maharaja is popular for its "authentic Indian cuisine" served in a dressy dining room (Mon-Sat 12:00-14:30 & 17:00-22:30, Sun 13:00-15:00 & 17:00-22:00, 39 King Street, tel. 01786/470-728).

$$$ Brea, which means "love" in Gaelic, has a nice Scottish theme, from the menu to the decor to the pop music playing. It's unpretentious and popular for its modern and tasty dishes. Consider treating first courses like tapas and eating family-style (Tue-Thu 12:00-21:00, Fri-Mon until 21:30, 5 Baker Street, tel. 01786/446-277).

$$ Nicky-Tams Bar and Bothy is a fun little hangout with a somewhat gritty Irish-pub ambience, providing a great place to chat up a local and enjoy some good, basic pub grub. They serve meals from 12:00 to 20:00, then make way for drinking and, often, live music (29 Baker Street, tel. 01786/472-194).

Stirling Connections

From Stirling by Train to: Edinburgh (2/hour, 45 minutes), **Glasgow** (3/hour, 45 minutes), **Inverness** (7/day direct, 3 hours, more with transfer in Perth). Train info: Tel. 0345-748-4950, www.nationalrail.co.uk.

By Bus to: Glasgow (hourly on #M8, 45 minutes), **Edinburgh** (every 2 hours on #909, 1.5 hours). Citylink: tel. 0871-266-3333, CityLink.co.uk.

Near Stirling

The Wallace Monument and the Battle of Bannockburn Visitors Centre are just outside of town. Sights within side-trip distance include The Kelpies horse-head sculptures, the Falkirk Wheel boat "elevator," the stuck-in-time village of Culross, and Doune Castle.

JUST OUTSIDE STIRLING
▲Wallace Monument
Commemorating the Scottish hero better known to Americans as "Braveheart," this sandstone tower—built during a wave of Scottish nationalism in the mid-19th century—marks the Abbey Craig hill on the outskirts of Stirling. This is where, in 1297, William Wallace gathered forces and secured his victory against England's King Edward I at the Battle of Stirling Bridge. The victory was a huge boost to the Scottish cause, but England came back to beat the Scots the next year. (For more on Wallace, see page 748.)

Cost and Hours: £10.50; daily July-Aug 9:30-18:00, April-June and Sept-Oct until 17:00; Nov-Feb 10:00-16:00, March until 17:00; last entry 45 minutes before closing, café at visitors center, tel. 01786/472-140, www.nationalwallacemonument.com.

Getting There: The monument is two miles northeast of Stirling on the A-9, signposted from the city center. Bus #52 goes from the Stirling bus station to the roundabout below the monument, near the Co-op supermarket (£2.80, change given, 15-minute ride). From there, it's about a 15-minute hike up to the visitors center.

From July through mid-September, you can take the hop-on, hop-off bus #1314 (see "Orientation to Stirling," earlier) straight to the visitors center parking lot (£4.90, departs every 40 minutes, 15-30-minute ride depending on where you hop on).

Taxis cost about £8 one-way from Stirling. From the visitors center parking lot, you'll need to hike (a steep 15 minutes) or hop on the shuttle bus up the hill to the monument itself (free, departs every 10 minutes).

Visiting the Monument: Buy your ticket either at the visitors center below or the monument above. Then hike or ride the shuttle bus up to the monument's base.

Gazing up, think about how this fanciful 19th-century structure, like so many around Europe in that age, was created and designed to evoke (and romanticize) earlier architectural styles—in this case, medieval Scottish castles. The crown-shaped top—reminiscent of St. Giles' Cathedral on the Royal Mile in Edinburgh—and the dynamic sculpture of William Wallace are patriotic to the max.

Climb the tight, stone spiral staircases (not for the claustrophobic) a total of 246 steps, stopping at each of the three levels to see museum displays. The first level, the Hall of Arms, tells the story of William Wallace and the Battle of Stirling Bridge and gives you the chance to ogle Wallace's five-foot-long broadsword. Second is the Hall of Heroes, adorned with busts of great Scots—suggesting the debt this nation owes to Wallace. But it's not all just hero worship: A thoughtful video presentation on the first level considers the role of Wallace in both Scottish and English history, and raises the point that one person's freedom fighter is another person's terrorist. The third level's exhibits are about the monument itself: why and how it was built.

Finally, you reach the top, with stunning views over Stirling, its castle, the winding River Forth, and Stirling Bridge—a 500-year-old stone version that replaced the original wooden one. Looking out from the same vantage point as Wallace, imagine how the famous battle played out. But if you find yourself picturing the scene in the 1995 movie *Braveheart*—with berserker Scots, their faces painted blue, running across a field to take on the English cavalry—you have the wrong idea. While that portrayal was cinematically powerful, in reality the battle took place on a bridge in a narrow valley.

Battle of Bannockburn Visitors Centre and Monument

Just south of Stirling, this site commemorates what many Scots view as their nation's most significant military victory over the invading English: the Battle of Bannockburn, won by a Scottish army led by Robert the Bruce against England's King Edward II in 1314. The battle memorial is free and always open. The visitors center "Battle Game" is an interactive techy experience, with 3-D screens and a re-creation that basically reduces the battle to a video game.

Cost and Hours: Memorial—free, always open; Visitors Centre and "Battle Game"—£11.50, daily 9:30-18:00, Oct-Feb 10:00-17:00, March until 17:30; 3-D experience lasts 75 minutes and runs every 45 minutes 10:00-16:00, off-season until 15:15 (these are last tour times); café, tel. 01786/812-664, www.battleofbannockburn.com. In summertime, the 3-D experience can sell out, so call or book online 2-3 days in advance.

Getting There: Bannockburn is two miles south of Stirling on the A-872, off the M-80/M-9.

For nondrivers, it's an easy bus ride from the Stirling bus station (bus #X36 or #51, 2/hour, 15 minutes, stop: Whins of Milton/Glasgow Road). You'll get off at the car-rental stop on Glasgow Road, a two-minute walk from the Bannockburn visitors center. To get here from the Wallace Monument, take bus #51 from the roundabout below the monument (£2.80, direction: Cowie, 2/hour, 25 minutes). Or take bus #52 from the roundabout (hourly, 20 minutes), stop at the Stirling bus station, and switch to bus #X36.

Background: In simple terms, Robert the Bruce—who was first and foremost a politician—found himself out of political options after years of failed diplomatic attempts to make peace with the strong-arming English. William Wallace's execution left a vacuum in military leadership, and eventually Robert stepped in, waging a successful guerrilla campaign that came to a head as young Edward's army marched to Stirling. Although the Scots were greatly outnumbered, their strategy and use of terrain at Bannockburn—with its impossibly twisty stream presenting a natural barrier for the invading army—

allowed them to soundly beat the English and drive Edward out of Scotland...for the time being. (For more about Robert the Bruce, see page 752.)

The Battle Experience: Other than a small exhibit and weaponry room (free), there are no historic artifacts here—just the 3-D experience. First, you'll spend 30 minutes learning about the emerging battle from the perspective of both sides, and getting familiar with the characters and weaponry. Then, when your time arrives, you enter the "battle room," (the group gets divided into two sides—English and Scots) around a large, interactive 3-D map of the battleground. On screen, the "Battle Master" leads the

STIRLING & NEARBY

group, but you get to move the troops and lead attacks. At the end, participants learn how the battle actually unfolded in 1314.

Monument and Statue of Robert the Bruce: Leaving the center, hike out into the field behind, where you can see a monument to those lost in the fight. Beyond that, on a plinth, stands an equestrian statue of Robert the Bruce.

FALKIRK

Two engaging landmarks sit just outside the town of Falkirk, 12 miles south of Stirling. Taken together, The Kelpies and the Falkirk Wheel offer a welcome change of pace from Scottish countryside kitsch. These flank Falkirk's otherwise unexciting town center, about a 5-mile, 20-minute drive apart. Driving between the two is a riddle of roundabouts. Think of it as fun: Carefully follow the brown signs and you'll eventually get there. (Ask for a flier illustrating directions between them at either site.)

▲The Kelpies

Unveiled in 2014 and standing over a hundred feet tall, these two giant steel horse heads quickly became a symbol of this town and region. They may seem whimsical, but they're rooted in a mix of mythology and real history: Kelpies are magical, waterborne, shape-shifting sprites of Scottish lore, who often take the form of a horse. And historically, horses—the ancestors of today's Budweiser Clydesdales—were used as

beasts of burden to power Scotland's industrial output. These statues stand over old canals where hardworking horses towed heavily laden barges. But if you prefer, you can just forget all that and ogle the dramatic, energy-charged statues (particularly thrilling to Denver Broncos fans) that make for an entertaining photo op. A café nearby sells drinks and light meals, and a free visitors center shows how the heads were built. A 30-minute guided tour through the inside of one of the great beasts shows how they're supported by a sleek steel skeleton: 300 tons of steel apiece, sitting upon a foundation of 1,200 tons of steel-reinforced concrete, and gleaming with 990 steel panels.

Cost and Hours: Always open and free to view (£3 to park, £4 in July-Aug); visitors center open daily 9:30-17:00. Tours-£7.50, daily every half hour 11:00-16:00 (but no 12:00 or 12:30 tours), fewer tours Oct-March, tel. 01324/590-600, www.thehelix.co.uk.

Getting There: The Kelpies are in a park called The Helix, just off the M-9 motorway—you'll spot them looming high over the motorway as if inviting you to exit. For a closer look, exit the M-9 for the A-905 (Falkirk/Grangemouth), then follow *Falkirk/A-904* and brown *Helix Park & Kelpies* signs.

▲▲Falkirk Wheel

At the opposite end of Falkirk stands this remarkable modern incarnation of Scottish technical know-how. You can watch the beautiful, slow-motion contraption as it spins—like a nautical Ferris wheel— to efficiently shuttle ships between two canals separated by 80 vertical feet.

Cost and Hours: Wheel is free to view, visitors center open daily 10:00-17:30, park open until 20:00, shorter hours Nov-mid-March; cruises run about hourly and cost £13.50, call or go online to check schedule and book your seat, tel. 0870-050-0208, www. thefalkirkwheel.co.uk.

Getting There: Drivers can exit the M-876 motorway for *A-883/ Falkirk/Denny,* then follow brown *Falkirk Wheel* signs. Parking is free and a short walk from the wheel.

Without a car, the journey takes about 45-60 minutes from Stirling. It's a quick train ride from Stirling to Camelon or Falkirk Grahamston station, where you can take a cab (about £7) or ask locally for the best bus option.

Background: Scotland was a big player in the Industrial Revolution, thanks partly to its network of shipping canals (including the famous Caledonian Canal—see page 999). Using dozens of locks to lift barges up across Scotland's hilly spine, these canals were effective...but slow.

The 115-foot-tall Falkirk Wheel, opened in 2002, is a modern take on this classic engineering challenge: linking the Forth and Clyde Canal below with the aqueduct of the Union Canal, 80 feet above. Rather than using rising and lowering water through several locks, the wheel simply picks boats up and—ever so slowly—takes them where they need to go, like a giant waterborne elevator. In the 1930s, it took half a day to ascend or descend through 11 locks; now it takes only five minutes.

The Falkirk Wheel is the critical connection in the Millennium Link project, an ambitious £78 million initiative to restore the long-neglected Forth and Clyde and Union canals connecting Edinburgh and Glasgow. Today this 70-mile-long aquatic connection between Scotland's leading cities is a leisurely traffic jam of pleasure craft, and canalside communities have been rejuvenated.

STIRLING & NEARBY

Visiting the Wheel: Twice an hour, the wheel springs (silently) to life: Gates rise up to seal off each of the water-filled gondolas, and then the entire structure slowly rotates a half-turn to swap the positions of the lower and upper boats—each of which stays comfortably upright. The towering structure is not only functional, but beautiful: The wheel's elegantly sweeping shape—with graceful cogs and pointed tips that slice into the water as they spin. It's strangely exciting to witness this.

The **visitors center** has a cafeteria (with a fine view of the wheel) and a shop, but no information about the wheel. The Falkirk **TI** is just steps away. The park around the canal is cluttered with trampolines, laser tag, and other family amusements.

Riding the Wheel: Each hour, a barge takes 96 people (listening to a recorded narration explaining everything) into the Falkirk Wheel for the slow and graceful ride. Once at the top, the barge cruises a bit of the canal. The slow-motion experience lasts about an hour.

CULROSS

This time warp of a village, sitting across the Firth of Forth from Edinburgh (about a 30-minute drive from Stirling), is a perfectly preserved artifact from the 17th and 18th centuries and worth ▲. If you're looking to let your pulse slow, stroll through a steep and sleepy village, and tour a creaky old manor house, Culross is your place. Filmmakers often use Culross to evoke Scottish villages of yore (most recently in *Outlander*). While not worth a  long detour, it's a workable stop for drivers connecting Edinburgh to either the Stirling area or St. Andrews (free parking lots flank the town center—an easy, 5-minute waterfront stroll away).

The story of Culross (which locals pronounce KOO-russ) is the story of Sir George Bruce, who, in the late 16th century, figured out a way to build coal mines beneath the waters of the Firth of Forth. The hardworking town flourished, Bruce built a fine mansion, and the town was granted coveted "royal burgh" status by the king. But several decades later, with Bruce's death and the flooding of the mines, the town's fortunes tumbled—halting its development and trapping it as if in amber for centuries. Rescued and rehabilitated by the National Trust for Scotland, today the entire village feels like one big open-air folk museum.

The main sightseeing attraction here is the misnamed **Culross "Palace,"** the big but creaky, half-timbered home of George Bruce

STIRLING & NEARBY

(£10.50, April-Sept daily 10:00-17:00, Oct until 16:00, closed Nov-March, tel. 01383/880-359, www. nts.org.uk/culross). Buy your ticket at the office under the Town Hall's clock tower, pick up the included audioguide, then head a few doors down to the ochre-colored palace. Following a 10-minute orientation film, you'll walk through several creaky floors to see how a small town's big shots lived four centuries ago. Docents in each room are happy to answer questions. You'll see the great hall, the "principal stranger's bedchamber" (guest room for VIPs), George Bruce's bedroom and stone strong room (where he stored precious—and flammable—financial documents), and the highlight, the painted chamber. The wood slats of its barrel-arched ceiling are painted with whimsical scenes illustrating Scottish virtues and pitfalls. You can also poke around the densely planted, lovingly tended garden out back.

A 45-minute **guided town walk** takes place for a small fee (April-Oct usually Mon-Sat at 14:00; check "Planning Your Visit" on palace website for current schedule).

The only other real sight, a steep hike up the cobbled lanes to the top of town, is the partially ruined **abbey.** While there are far more evocative ruins in Scotland, it's fun to poke into the stony, mysterious-feeling interior of this church. But the stroll up the town's cobbled streets past pastel houses, with their carefully tended flower boxes, is even better than the church itself.

DOUNE

The village of Doune (pronounced "doon") is just a 15-minute drive north of Stirling. While there's not much to see in town, on its outskirts is a pair of attractions: a castle and a distillery. In the village of Doune itself, notice the town seal: a pair of crossed pistols. Aside from its castle and whisky, the town is known for its historic pistol factory. Locals speculate that the first shot of the American Revolution was fired with a Doune pistol.

Getting There: Bus #59 runs from Stirling to Doune and the distillery (just outside Doune). Drivers head to Doune, then follow castle signs on pretty back roads from there.

Doune Castle

Doune Castle is worth considering for its pop-culture connections: Most recently, Doune stands in for Castle Leoch in the TV series

Outlander. But well before that, parts of *Monty Python and the Holy Grail* were filmed here. And, while the castle may underwhelm *Outlander* fans (only some exterior scenes were shot here), Python fans—and anyone who appreciates British comedy—will be tickled by the included audioguide, narrated by

Python troupe member Terry Jones (featuring sound clips from the film). The audioguide also has a few stops featuring Sam Heughan of *Outlander*. (If you're not into Python or *Outlander*, Scotland has better castles to visit.)

Cost and Hours: £9, daily April-Sept 9:30-17:30, Oct-March 10:00-16:00, tel. 01786/841-742.

Visiting the Castle: Buy your ticket and pick up the 45-minute audioguide, which explains that the castle's most important resident was not Claire Randall or the Knights Who Say Ni, but Robert Stewart, the Duke of Albany (1340-1420)—a man so influential he was called the "uncrowned king of Scotland." You'll see the cellars, ogle the empty-feeling courtyard, and then scramble through the two tall towers and the great hall that connects them. The castle rooms are almost entirely empty, but they're brought to life by the audioguide. You'll walk into the kitchen's ox-sized fireplace to peer up the gigantic chimney, and visit the guest room's privy to peer down the medieval toilet. You'll finish your visit at the top of the main tower, with 360-degree views that allow you to fart in just about anyone's general direction.

Deanston Distillery

This big, attractive red-brick industrial complex (formerly a cotton mill) sits facing the river just outside of Doune. While Deanston has long been respected for its fruity, slightly spicy Highland single-malt whisky, the 2012 movie *The Angels' Share*, filmed partly at this distillery, helped put it on the map. The complex boasts a slick visitors center that's open for tours. On the 50-minute visit, you'll see the equipment used to make the whisky and enjoy a sample. (For more on whisky and the distillation process, see page 755.) A bit more corporate-feeling than some of my favorite Scottish distilleries, Deanston has the advantage of being handy to Stirling.

Cost and Hours: £9-35 depending on number of tastings, tours depart at the top of each hour daily 10:00-16:00 (last tour), best to call ahead to reserve, tel. 01786/843-010, www.deanstonmalt.com.

ST. ANDREWS

St. Andrews may be synonymous with golf, but there's much more to this charming town than its famous links. Dramatically situated at the edge of a sandy bay, St. Andrews is the home of Scotland's most important university—think of it as the Scottish Cambridge. And centuries ago, the town was the religious capital of the country.

In its long history, St. Andrews has seen two boom periods. First, in the early Middle Ages, the relics of St. Andrew made the town cathedral one of the most important pilgrimage sites in Christendom. The faithful flocked here from all over Europe, leaving the town with a medieval all-roads-lead-to-the-cathedral street plan that survives today. But after the Scottish Reformation, the cathedral rotted away and the town became a forgotten backwater. A new wave of visitors arrived in the mid-19th century, when a visionary mayor (with the on-the-nose surname Playfair) began to promote the town's connection with the newly in-vogue game of golf. Most buildings in town date from this Victorian era.

Today St. Andrews remains a popular spot for students, golf devotees (from amateurs to professional golfers to celebrities), and occasionally royal couple Will and Kate (college sweethearts, U. of St. A. class of '05). With vast sandy beaches, golfing opportunities for pros and novices alike, playgrounds of castle and cathedral ruins, and a fun-loving student vibe, St. Andrews is an appealing place to take a vacation from your busy vacation.

PLANNING YOUR TIME

St. Andrews, hugging the east coast of Scotland, is a bit off the main tourist track. But it's well connected by train to Edinburgh

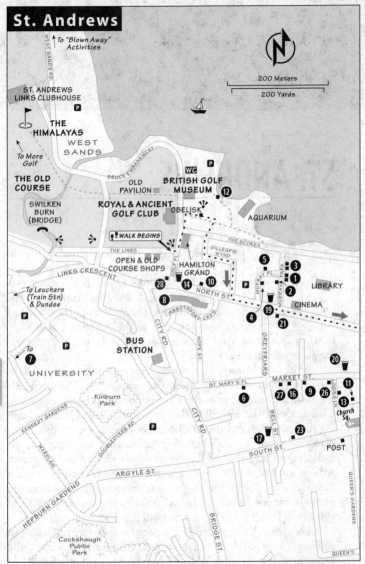

St. Andrews

To "Blown Away" Activities

WEST SANDS RD.

ST. ANDREWS LINKS CLUBHOUSE

THE HIMALAYAS

WEST SANDS

To More Golf

THE OLD COURSE

SWILKEN BURN (BRIDGE)

BRUCE EMBANKMENT

OLD PAVILION

ROYAL & ANCIENT GOLF CLUB

WC

BRITISH GOLF MUSEUM

OBELISK

AQUARIUM

THE LINKS

WALK BEGINS

OPEN & OLD COURSE SHOPS

LINKS CRESCENT

THE SCORES

GILLESPIE WYND

GOLF PL.

HAMILTON GRAND

NORTH ST.

MURRAY PL.

MURRAY PARK

LIBRARY

CINEMA

ABBOTSFORD CRES.

To Leuchars (Train Stn) & Dundee

CITY RD.

HOPE ST.

BUS STATION

UNIVERSITY

Kinburn Park

KENNEDY GARDENS

WARDLAW

DOUBLEDYKES RD.

ST. MARY'S PL.

GREYFRIARS

MARKET ST.

BELL ST.

LOGIE'S LN.

Church Sq.

SOUTH ST.

POST

ARGYLE ST.

HEPBURN GARDENS

CITY RD.

BRIDGE ST.

QUEEN'S GARDENS

Cockshaugh Public Park

QUEEN'S

ST. ANDREWS

200 Meters

200 Yards

Map markers: 1, 2, 3, 4, 5, 6, 7, 8, 9, 10, 11, 12, 13, 14, 16, 17, 19, 20, 21, 23, 26, 27, 28

(via bus from nearby Leuchars), making it a worthwhile day trip from the capital. Better yet, spend a night (or more, if you're a golfer) to enjoy this university town after dark.

If you're not here to golf, this is a good way to spend a day: Follow my self-guided walk, which connects the golf course, the university quad, the castle, and the cathedral. Dip into the Golf Museum, watch the golfers on the Old Course, and play a round

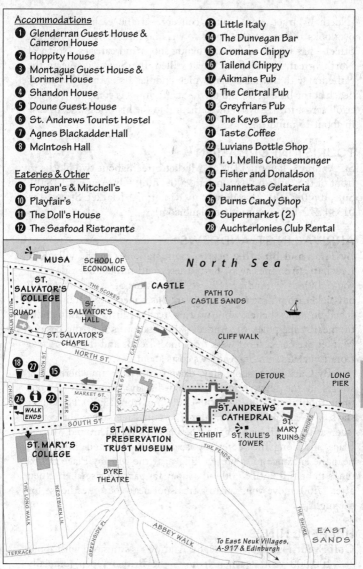

Accommodations

1. Glenderran Guest House & Cameron House
2. Hoppity House
3. Montague Guest House & Lorimer House
4. Shandon House
5. Doune Guest House
6. St. Andrews Tourist Hostel
7. Agnes Blackadder Hall
8. McIntosh Hall

Eateries & Other

9. Forgan's & Mitchell's
10. Playfair's
11. The Doll's House
12. The Seafood Ristorante
13. Little Italy
14. The Dunvegan Bar
15. Cromars Chippy
16. Tailend Chippy
17. Aikmans Pub
18. The Central Pub
19. Greyfriars Pub
20. The Keys Bar
21. Taste Coffee
22. Luvians Bottle Shop
23. I. J. Mellis Cheesemonger
24. Fisher and Donaldson
25. Jannettas Gelateria
26. Burns Candy Shop
27. Supermarket (2)
28. Auchterlonies Club Rental

at "the Himalayas" putting green, or walk along the West Sands beach.

Orientation to St. Andrews

St. Andrews (pop. 16,000, plus several thousand more students during term) is situated at the tip of a peninsula next to a broad bay. The town retains its old medieval street plan: Three main streets

(North, Market, and South) converge at the cathedral, which overlooks the sea at the tip of town. The middle street—Market Street—has the TI and many handy shops and eateries. North of North Street, the seafront street called The Scores connects the cathedral with the golf scene, which huddles along the West Sands beach at the base of the old town. St. Andrews is compact: You can stroll across town—from the cathedral to the historic golf course—in about 15 minutes.

TOURIST INFORMATION

St. Andrews' helpful TI is on Market Street, about two blocks in front of the cathedral (Mon-Sat 9:00-17:00, July-Aug until 18:00, Sun 10:00-17:00, closed Sun in winter; 70 Market Street, tel. 01334/472-021, www.visitscotland.com).

ARRIVAL IN ST. ANDREWS

By Train and Bus: The nearest train station is in the village of Leuchars, five miles away. From there, a 10-minute bus ride takes you right into St. Andrews (bus #99, direction: St. Andrews, £3.30, buy ticket from driver, change given; buses meet most trains—see schedule at bus shelter; while waiting, read the historical info under the nearby flagpole). St. Andrews' bus station is near the base of Market Street—a short walk from most B&Bs and the TI. A taxi from Leuchars into St. Andrews costs about £14.

By Car: For a short stay, drivers can park anywhere along streets in the town center (pay-and-display, coins only, 2-hour limit, monitored Mon-Sat 9:00-17:00, Sun from 13:00). For longer stays, you can park for free along certain streets near the center (such as the small lot near the B&B neighborhood around Murray Place, and along The Scores), or use one of the pay-and-display lots near the entrance to town. Parking near the Murray Place B&Bs tends to be full until 17:00—if so, pay for parking elsewhere, then after 17:00, move your car to a free spot near your guesthouse for the night.

HELPFUL HINTS

Golf Events: Every five years, St. Andrews is swamped with about 100,000 visitors when it hosts the British Open (officially called "The Open Championship"; the next one is the 150th in 2021). The town also fills up every year in early October for the Alfred Dunhill Links Championship. Unless you're a golf pilgrim, avoid the town at these times (as room rates skyrocket).

School Term: The University of St. Andrews has two terms: spring semester ("Candlemas"), from mid-February through May; and fall semester ("Martinmas"), from mid-August until December. St. Andrews has a totally different vibe in the summer, when most students leave and are replaced by upper-crust golfers and tourists.

Sand Surfing and Adventure Activities: Nongolfers who want to stay busy while their travel partners play the Old Course may enjoy some of the adventure activities offered by **Blown Away**—including "land yachting" (zipping across the beach in wind-powered go-carts), kayaking, and paddle boarding. Brothers Guy and Jamie McKenzie set up shop at the northern tip of the West Sands beach (sporadic hours—call first, mobile 07784-121-125, www.blownaway.co.uk, ahoy@blownaway.co.uk).

Baggage Storage: The bus station has pay lockers.

Theater: The **Byre Theatre** regularly hosts concerts, shows, dance, and opera. Check their website or stop in to see what's on (tickets about £10-25, Abbey Street, tel. 01334/475-000, www.byretheatre.com).

Walking Tours: Richard Falconer, who has researched and written books on the history of the area—and its paranormal activity—gives 1.5-hour tours on golf, history, and ghosts (£12, tours at 17:30, 19:30, and 21:00, must book ahead, text 0746-296-3163 or visit https://standrewsghosttours.com).

St. Andrews Walk

This walk links all of St. Andrews' must-see sights and takes you down hidden medieval streets. Allow a couple of hours, or more if you detour for the sights along the way.

• *Start across from the Hamilton Grand (at the corner of Golf Place and The Links), overlooking the famous golf course.*

▲The Old Course

You're looking at the mecca of golf. The 18th hole of the world's first golf course is a few yards away, on your left.

The gray Neoclassical building to the right of the 18th hole is the clubhouse of the **Royal and Ancient Golf Club**—"R&A" for short. R&A is a private club with membership by invitation only; it was men-only until 2014, but now—finally!—women are also allowed to join. (In Scotland, men-only clubs lose tax benefits, which is quite costly, but they generally don't care about expenses because their membership is wealthy.) The **Old Course**

Shop (to your left, across the street from the 18th hole, next to The Open—the oldest golf shop in the world) is a great spot to buy a souvenir for the golf lover back home. Even if you're not golfing, watch the action for a while. (Serious fans can walk around to the low-profile stone bridge across the creek called the Swilken Burn, with golf's single most iconic view: back over the 18th hole and the R&A Clubhouse.)

Overlooking the course at the base of the seaside street called The Scores is the big red-sandstone **Hamilton Grand,** an old hotel. The hotel was turned into university dorms and then swanky apartments (rumor has it Samuel L. Jackson owns one). According to town legend, the Hamilton Grand was originally built to upstage the R&A Clubhouse by an American upset over being declined membership to the exclusive club.

Between Hamilton Grand and the beach is the low-profile but thoughtfully presented **British Golf Museum** (described later, under "Golfing in St. Andrews").

• *Now turn your back to the golf course and walk through the park toward the obelisk (along The Scores). Stop at the top of the bluff.*

Beach Viewpoint

The broad, two-mile-long sandy beach that stretches below the golf course to your left is the **West Sands.** It's a wonderful place for a relaxing and/or invigorating walk (beware the aggressive seagulls). Or do a slo-mo jog, humming the theme to *Chariots of Fire*—this is the beach on which the characters run in the movie's famous opening scene.

From the bluff, look at the **cliffs** on your right. The sea below was once called "Witches' Lake" because of all the women and men pushed off the cliff on suspicion of witchcraft.

The big obelisk is a **martyrs' monument,** commemorating all those who died for their Protestant beliefs during the Scottish Reformation. (We'll learn more about that chapter of St. Andrews history farther along this walk.)

The Victorian bandstand **gazebo** (between here and the Old Course) recalls the town's genteel heyday as a seaside resort, when the train line ran all the way to town.

• *Just opposite the obelisk, across The Scores and next to Alexander's Restaurant, walk down the tiny alley called...*

Gillespie Wynd

This winds through the back gardens of the city's stone houses. Notice how the medieval platting gave each landowner a little bit of street front and a long back garden. St. Andrews' street plan typifies that of a medieval pilgrimage town: All main roads lead to the cathedral; only tiny lanes, hidden alleys, and twisting "wynds" (rhymes with "minds") such as this one connect the main east-west streets.

• *The wynd pops you out onto North Street. Head left, past the cinema toward the church tower with the red clock face on the corner of North Street and Butts Wynd. For some reason, this street sign often goes missing.*

St. Salvator's College

The tower with the red clock marks the entrance to St. Salvator's College. If you're a student, be careful not to stand on the **initials PH** in the reddish cobbles in front of the gate. These mark the spot where St. Andrews alum and professor Patrick Hamilton—the Scottish Reformation's most famous martyr—was burned at the stake. According to student legend, as he suffered in the flames, Hamilton threatened that any students who stood on this spot would fail their exams.

Now enter the grounds by walking through the arch under the tower. (If the entrance is closed, you can go halfway down Butts Wynd and enter, or at least look, through the gate to the green square.) This grassy square, known to students as **Sally's Quad,** is the heart of the university. As most of the university's classrooms, offices, and libraries are spread out across  the medieval town, this quad is the one focal point for student gatherings. It's where graduation is held every July, where the free-for-all food fight of Raisin Monday takes place in November (see sidebar on page 900), and where almost the entire student body gathered on the wedding day of their famous alumni couple Prince William and Kate Middleton for a celebration complete with military flybys.

On the outside wall of St. Salvator's Chapel, under the arcade, are **display cases** holding notices and university information; if you're here in spring, you might see students nervously clustered here, looking to see if they've passed their exams.

Go through the simple wooden door and into the **chapel.** Dating from 1450, this is the town's most beautiful medieval church. It's a Gothic gem, with a wooden ceiling, 19th-century stained glass, a glorious organ, and what's supposedly the pulpit of reformer John Knox.

Stroll around Sally's Quad counterclockwise. On the east (far) side, stop to check out the crazy faces on the heads above the second-floor windows. Find the **university's shield** over the door

The Scottish Reformation

It's easy to forget that during the 16th-century English Reformation—when King Henry VIII split with the Vatican and formed the Anglican Church (so he could get an officially recognized divorce)—Scotland was still its own independent nation. Like much of northern Europe, Scotland eventually chose a Protestant path, but it was more gradual and grassroots than Henry VIII's top-down, destroy-the-abbeys approach. While the English Reformation resulted in the Church of England (a.k.a. the Anglican Church, called "Episcopal" outside of England), with the monarch at its head, the Scottish Reformation created the Church of Scotland, which had groups of elected leaders (called "presbyteries" in church jargon).

One of the leaders of the Scottish Reformation was John Knox (1514-1572), who studied under the great Swiss reformer John Calvin. Returning to Scotland, Knox hopped from pulpit to pulpit, and his feverish sermons incited riots of "born-again" iconoclasts who dismantled or destroyed Catholic churches and abbeys (including St. Andrew's Cathedral). Knox's newly minted Church of Scotland gradually spread from the Lowlands to the Highlands. The southern and eastern part of Scotland, around St. Andrews—just across the North Sea from the Protestant countries of northern Europe—embraced the Church of Scotland long before the more remote and Catholic-oriented part of the country to the north and west. Today about 40 percent of Scots claim affiliation with the Church of Scotland, compared with 20 percent who are Catholic (still mostly in the western Highlands). Glasgow and western Scotland are more Catholic partly because of the Irish immigrants who settled there after fleeing the potato famine in the 1840s.

marked *School 6*. The diamonds are from the coat of arms of the bishop who issued the first university charter in 1411; the crescent moon is a shout-out to Pope Benedict XIII, who gave the OK in 1413 to found the university (his given name was Peter de Luna); the lion is from the Scottish coat of arms; and the X-shaped cross is a stylized version of the Scottish flag (a.k.a. St. Andrew's Cross). On the next building to the left, facing the chapel, is St. Andrew himself (above the door of the building labeled *Lower & Upper College Halls*).

• *Exit the square and make your way back to Butts Wynd. Walk to the end; you're back at The Scores. Across the street and a few steps to the right is the...*

Museum of the University of St. Andrews (MUSA)

This free museum is worth a stop if it's open (as planned) following a major renovation. The new exhibit will be much bigger and the collection rearranged—pick up a map for the latest layout. Among the collection's highlights are medieval artifacts and a copy of the earliest-known map of the town, made in 1580—back when the town walls led directly to the countryside and the cathedral was intact. Notice that the street plan within the town walls has remained the same—but no golf course. Exhibits on student life explain the "silver arrow competition" (which determined the best archer on campus from year to year) and several of the traditions explained in the "Student Life in St. Andrews" sidebar. The museum also hosts scientific equipment, great books tied to the school, and an exhibit on the Scottish Reformation. For a great view of the West Sands, climb to the rooftop terrace.

Cost and Hours: Free; Mon-Sat 10:00-17:00, Sun 12:00-16:00, shorter hours and closed Mon-Wed in winter; 7 The Scores, tel. 01334/461-660, www.st-andrews.ac.uk/museums.

• *Leaving the museum, walk left toward the castle. The turreted stone buildings along here (including one fine example next door to the museum) are built in the Neo-Gothic Scottish Baronial style, and most are academic departments. About 100 yards farther along, the grand building on the right is St. Salvator's Hall, the most prestigious of the university residences and former dorm of Prince William.*

Just past St. Salvator's Hall on the left are the remains of...

St. Andrews Castle

Overlooking the sea, the castle is an evocative empty shell—another casualty of the Scottish Reformation. With a small museum and good descriptions, it offers a quick king-of-the-castle experience in a striking setting.

Cost and Hours: £9, includes audioguide; £12 combo-ticket includes cathedral exhibit; daily April-Sept 9:30-17:30, Oct-March 10:00-16:00, tel. 01334/477-196, www.historicenvironment.scot.

Visiting the Castle: Your visit starts with a colorful, kid-friendly exhibit about the history of the castle. Built by a bishop to entertain visiting diplomats in the late 12th century, the castle was home to the powerful bishops, archbishops, and cardinals of St. Andrews. In 1546, the cardinal burned a Protestant preacher at the stake in front of the castle. In retribution, Protestant reformers took the castle and killed the cardinal. In 1547, the French came to attack the castle on behalf of their Catholic ally, Mary, Queen of Scots. During the ensuing siege, a young Protestant refugee named

Student Life in St. Andrews

St. Andrews is first and foremost a university town. Scotland's most prestigious university, founded in 1411, is the third-oldest in the English-speaking world after Oxford and Cambridge. While U. of St. A. is sometimes called "England's northernmost university" due to the high concentration of English students—as numerous as the Scottish ones—a quarter of the 6,000 undergrads and 1,000 grad students hail from overseas.

Some Scots resent the preponderance of upper-crust English students (disparagingly dubbed "Yahs" for the snooty way they say "yes"). However, these southerners pay the bills—they are on the hook for tuition, unlike Scots and most EU citizens. And no one seems to mind that the school's most famous graduates, Prince William and Kate Middleton (class of '05), are the definition of upper class. Soon after "Wills" started studying art history here, the number of female art history majors skyrocketed. (He later switched to geography.)

As with any venerable university, St. Andrews has its share of quirky customs. Most students own traditional red academic "gowns" (woolen robes) to wear on special occasions, such as graduation. In medieval times, however, they were the daily uniform—supposedly so students could be easily identified in brothels and pubs. (In a leap of faith, divinity students—apparently beyond temptation—wear black.) The way the robe is worn indicates the student's status: First-year students (called "bejants") wear them normally, on the shoulders; second-years ("semi-bejants") wear them slightly off the shoulders; third-years ("tertians") wear them off one shoulder (right for "scientists," left for "artists"); and fourth-years ("magistrands") wear them off both shoulders.

The best time to see these robes is during the Pier Walk on Sundays during the university term. After church services (around noon), gown-clad students parade out to the end of the lonesome pier beyond the cathedral ruins. The tradition dates so far back that no one's sure how it started (probably to bid farewell to a visiting dignitary). Today, students just enjoy being a part of the visual spectacle of a long line of red robes flapping in the North Sea wind.

Another age-old custom is a social-mentoring system in which underclass students choose an "academic family." On Raisin Monday, in mid-November, students give their upperclass "parents" treats—traditionally raisins, but these days more often indulgences like wine and lingerie. Then the "parents" dress up their "children" in outrageous costumes and parade them through town. The underclass students are obliged to carry around "receipts" for their gifts—written on unlikely or unwieldy objects like plastic dinosaurs, microwave ovens, or even refrigerators—and to sing the school song in Latin on demand. This oddball scenario invariably degenerates into a free-for-all food fight on Sally's Quad.

John Knox was captured and sent to France to row on a galley ship. Eventually he traveled to Switzerland and met the Swiss Protestant ringleader, John Calvin. Knox brought Calvin's ideas back home and became Scotland's greatest reformer.

Next, head outside to explore. The audioguide explains the story of the castle and the siege, as told by several of the castle's historical figures. The most interesting parts are underground: the "bottle dungeon," where prisoners were sent, never to return (peer down into it in the Sea Tower—at the far left end of the complex facing the water); and the tight "mine" and even tighter "counter-mine" tunnels (follow the signs; crawling is required to reach it all—go in as far as your claustrophobia allows). This shows how the besieging pro-Catholic Scottish government of the day dug a mine to take (or "undermine") the castle—but were followed at every turn by the Protestant counter-miners.

Nearby: Just below the castle is a small beach called the **Castle Sands,** where university students take a traditional and chilly morning dip on May 1. Supposedly, doing this May Day swim is the only way to reverse the curse of having stepped on Patrick Hamilton's initials (explained earlier).

• *Leaving the castle, turn left and continue along the bluff on The Scores, which soon becomes a pedestrian lane leading directly to the gate to the cathedral graveyard. For a quick detour, continue along the cliffside path, passing the ruins of St. Mary on the Rock, downhill to the pier where university students parade in their robes (see the "Student Life in St. Andrews" sidebar). In nice weather, you'll enjoy views of the little harbor and (behind you) the cathedral and castle ruins. Otherwise, enter the graveyard to stand amid the tombstone-strewn ruins of...*

▲St. Andrews Cathedral

Between the Great Schism and the Reformation (roughly the 14th-16th centuries), St. Andrews was the ecclesiastical capital of Scotland—and this was its showpiece church. Today the site features the remains of the cathedral and cloister (with walls and spires pecked away by centuries of scavengers), a graveyard, and a small exhibit and climbable tower.

Cost and Hours: Cathedral ruins—free, exhibit and tower—£6, £12 combo-ticket includes castle; daily April-Sept 9:30-17:30, Oct-March 10:00-16:00; tel. 01334/472-563, www.historicenvironment.scot.

Background: It was the relics of the Apostle Andrew that first put this town on the map and gave it its name. There are numerous legends associated with the relics. According to one version, in the fourth century, St. Rule was directed in a dream to bring the relics northward from Constantinople. When the ship wrecked offshore from here, it was clear that this was a sacred place. Andrew's bones (an upper arm, a kneecap, some fingers, and a tooth) were kept on this site, and starting in 1160, the cathedral was built and pilgrims began to arrive. Since St. Andrew had a direct connection to Jesus, his relics were believed to possess special properties, making them worthy of pilgrimages on par with St. James' relics in Santiago de Compostela, Spain (of Camino de Santiago fame). St. Andrew became Scotland's patron saint; in fact, the white "X" on the blue Scottish flag evokes the diagonal cross on which St. Andrew was crucified (he chose this type of cross because he felt unworthy to die as Jesus had).

Visiting the Cathedral: You can stroll around the cathedral **ruins**—the best part of the complex—for free. First, walk between

the two ruined but still-towering ends of the church, which used to be the apse (at the sea end, where you entered) and the main entry (at the town end). Visually trace the gigantic footprint of the former church in the ground, including the bases of columns—like giant sawed-off tree trunks. Plaques identify where elements of the church once stood.

Looking at the one wall that's still standing, you can see the architectural changes that were made over the 150 years the cathedral was built—from the rounded, Romanesque windows at the front to the more highly decorated, pointed Gothic arches near the back. Try to imagine this church in its former majesty, when it played host to pilgrims from all over Europe.

The church wasn't destroyed all at once, like all those ruined abbeys in England (demolished in a huff by Henry VIII when he broke with the pope). Instead, because the Scottish Reformation was more gradual, this church was slowly picked apart over time. First just the decorations were removed from inside the cathedral. Then the roof was pulled down to make use of its lead. Without a roof, the cathedral fell further and further into disrepair, and was quarried by locals for its handy precut stones (which you'll still find in the walls of many old St. Andrews homes). The elements—a big storm in the 1270s and a fire in 1378—also contributed to the cathedral's demise.

The surrounding **graveyard,** dating from the post-Reformation Protestant era, is much more recent than the cathedral. In this golf-obsessed town, the game even infiltrates the cemeteries: Many notable golfers from St.

Andrews are buried here, including four-time British Open winner Young Tom "Tommy" Morris.

Go through the surviving wall into the former **cloister,** marked by a gigantic grassy square in the center. You can still see the cleats up on the wall, which once supported beams. Imagine the cloister back in its heyday, its passages filled with strolling monks.

At the end of the cloister is a small **exhibit** (entry fee required), with a relatively dull collection of old tombs and other carved-stone relics that have been unearthed on this site. Your ticket also includes entry to the surviving **tower of St. Rule's Church** (the rectangular tower beyond the cathedral ruins that was built to hold the precious relics of St. Andrew about a thousand years ago). If you feel like hiking up the 157 very claustrophobic steps for the view over St. Andrews' rooftops, it's worth the price. Up top, you can also look out to sea to find the pier where students traditionally parade in their robes (see the "Student Life in St. Andrews" sidebar).

• *Leave the cathedral grounds on the town side of the cathedral. Angling right, head down North Street. Just ahead, on the left, is the adorable...*

▲St. Andrews Preservation Trust Museum and Garden

Filling a 17th-century fishing family's house that was protected from developers, this charming little museum is a time capsule of an earlier, simpler era. The house itself seems built for Smurfs, but it once housed 20 family members. The ground floor features replicas of a grocer's shop and a "chemist's" (pharmacy), using original fittings from actual stores. Upstairs are temporary exhibits. Out back is a tranquil garden (dedicated to the memory of a beloved professor) with "great-grandma's washhouse," featuring an exhibit about the history of soap and washing. Lovingly presented, this quaint, humble house provides a nice contrast to the big-money scene around the golf course at the other end of town.

Cost and Hours: Free but donation requested, generally open June-Sept daily 10:00-17:00 but depends on volunteer presence, closed off-season, 12 North Street, tel. 01334/477-629, https://standrewspreservationtrust.com.

• *From the museum, hang a left around the next corner to South Castle Street. Soon you'll reach...*

Market Street

As you approach the top of Market Street—one of the most atmospheric old streets in town—look left for the tiny white house with the cute curved staircase. What's that chase scene on the roof?

Now turn right down Market Street (which leads directly to the town's center, but we'll take a curvier route). Notice how the streets and even the buildings are smaller at this oldest end of town, as if the whole city were shrinking as the streets close in on the cathedral. Homeowners along Market Street are particularly proud of their address, and pooled their money to spiff up the cobbles and sidewalks.

Passing an antique bookstore on your right, take a left onto Baker Lane, a.k.a. Baxter Wynd. You'll pass a tiny and inviting public garden on your right before landing on South Street.

• *Turn right and head down South Street. After 50 yards, cross the street and enter a gate marked by a cute gray facade and a university insignia.*

St. Mary's College

This is the home of the university's School of Divinity (theology). If the gate's open, find the peaceful quad, with its gnarled tree that was purportedly planted by Mary, Queen of Scots. To get a feel of student life from centuries past, try poking your nose into one of the old classrooms.

• *Back on South Street, continue to your left. Some of the plainest build-ings on this stretch of the street have the most interesting history—several of them were built to fund the Crusades. Turn right on Church Street. You can end this walk at charming Church Square—perhaps while en-joying a decadent pastry from the recommended Fisher and Donaldson bakery. Or if you continue a few more yards down Church Street, you'll spill onto Market Street and the heart of town.*

Golfing in St. Andrews

St. Andrews is the Cooperstown of golf. While St. Andrews lays claim to founding the sport (the first record of golf being played here was in 1553), nobody knows exactly where and when people first hit a ball with a stick for fun. In the Middle Ages, St. Andrews traded with the Dutch; some historians believe they picked up a golf-like Dutch game played on ice and translated it to the bonnie rolling hills of Scotland's east

coast. Since the grassy beachfront strip just outside St. Andrews was too poor to support crops, it was used for playing the game—and, centuries later, it still is. Why do golf courses have 18 holes? Because that's how many fit at the Old Course—golf's single most famous site.

The Home of Golf

For golfers, Scotland is first and foremost the birthplace of the sport. Over 400 golf courses dot the landscape, from the Borders region in the south to John O'Groats in the north, offering pleasure and challenges for experts and duffers alike.

The Old Course at St. Andrews dates to 1553, but golf's Golden Age didn't take shape until the 19th century, when many courses were established and the sport was introduced to the US...by two Scotsmen. The first British Open (officially The Open Championship) was held in Prestwick, Scotland, in 1860 and winner Willie Park was awarded the red leather Challenge Belt, worth £25 (the 2019 winner took home almost $2 million).

Besides St. Andrews—which for golf aficionados is the course of a lifetime—Scotland's other prestigious courses include Carnoustie (on Scotland's east coast), Royal Troon (near Glasgow), and Gleneagles (near Edinburgh). Famous venues are often pricey and crowded, so it's worth seeking out less-renowned courses where you're more likely to rub elbows with locals.

Popular courses require reservations well in advance—especially from May through September. The majority of Scottish courses are private, but most welcome nonmembers on a limited basis. Costs for a round start at £20 at a public course and soar to nearly £200 at the Old Course in St. Andrew's. (Use the excellent FergusonGolf.com website to do some homework).

Most Scottish courses are links courses, meaning they lie amidst treeless coastal dunes. Lining up a putt while being buffeted by rain and sea spray in a howling gale is part of the experience. Good raingear is a must. But weather does change—often rapidly—and minutes after a downpour you may find yourself gazing at blue skies and wonderful views. Rain or shine, that 19th-hole meal and wee dram in the clubhouse are a welcome reward.

ST. ANDREWS

The Old Course

The Old Course hosts the British Open every five years (next in 2021). At other times it's open to the public for golfing. The famous Royal and Ancient Golf Club (R&A) doesn't actually own the course, which is public and managed by the St. Andrews Links Trust. Drop by the St. Andrews Links Clubhouse, overlooking the beach near the Old Course (open long hours daily). They have a well-stocked shop, a restaurant, and a rooftop garden with nice views over the Old Course.

Old Course Tours: 75-minute guided tours visit the 1st, 17th, and 18th holes (£12.50, daily April-Sept at 11:00 and 14:00, mid-June-July also Sun at 15:30, March and Oct daily at 11:00, leaves from the St. Andrews Links Clubhouse, tel. 01334/466-666, www. standrews.com).

Teeing Off at the Old Course: Playing at golf's pinnacle course is pricey (£195/person, less off-season), but open to the public—subject to lottery drawings for tee times and reserved spots by club members. You can play the Old Course only if you have a handicap of 24 (men) or 36 (women and juniors) or better; bring along your certificate or card. If you don't know your handicap—or don't know what "handicap" means—you're not good enough to play here (they want to keep the game moving). If you play, you'll do nine holes out, then nine more back in—however, all but four share the same greens.

Reserving a Tee Time: To ensure a specific tee time at the Old Course, reserve a year ahead during a brief window between late August and early September (fill out form at www.standrews. com). Otherwise, some tee times are determined each day by a lottery called the "daily ballot." Enter your name on their website, in person, or by calling 01334/466-666—by 14:00 two days before (2 players minimum, 4 players max). Lottery results are posted online the same afternoon. Note that no advance reservations are taken on Saturdays or in September, and the courses are closed on Sundays—which is traditionally the day reserved for townspeople to stroll.

Singleton Strategies: Single golfers aren't eligible to reserve or ballot. If you're golfing solo, you could try to team up with someone (ask your B&B for tips). Otherwise, each day, a few single golfers fill out a two- or three-golfer group by showing up in person at the Old Pavilion (in front of the R&A Clubhouse). It's first-come, first-served, and a very long shot, so get there early. The starter generally arrives at 6:00, but die-hard golfers start lining up several hours before or even camp out overnight (especially in peak season). Swing by the day before, when they should have a sense of how likely a spot is to open up and can recommend just how early to arrive.

Other Courses: Two of the seven St. Andrews Links courses are right next to the Old Course—the New Course and the Jubilee Course. And the modern cliff-top Castle Course is just outside the city. These are cheaper, and it's much easier to get a tee time (£85 for New and Jubilee, £120 for Castle Course, much less for others). It's usually possible to get a tee time for the same day or next day (if you want a guaranteed reservation, make it at least 2 weeks in advance). The Castle Course has great views overlooking the town, but even more wind to blow your ball around.

Club Rental: You can rent decent-quality clubs around town for about £35. The **Auchterlonies** shop has a good reputation (on Golf Place—a few doors down from the R&A Clubhouse, tel.

01334/473-253, www.auchterlonies.com); you can also rent clubs from the St. Andrews Links Clubhouse for a few pounds more.

▲The Himalayas

The St. Andrews Ladies' Putting Club, better known as "The Himalayas" (for its dramatically hilly terrain), is basically a very classy (but still relaxed) game of minigolf. The course presents the perfect opportunity for nongolfers (female or male) to say they've played the links at St. Andrews—for about the cost of a Coke. It's remarkable how this cute little patch of undulating  grass can present even more challenging obstacles than the tunnels, gates, and distractions of a miniature golf course back home. Flat shoes are required. You'll see it on the left as you walk toward the St. Andrews Links Clubhouse from the R&A Clubhouse.

Cost and Hours: £3 for 18 holes. The putting green is open to nonmembers (tourists like you) April-Sept Mon and Wed-Fri 10:30-18:30, Tue until 16:30, Sat until 18:00, Sun 12:00-18:30, closed in winter, tel. 01334/466-666, www.standrewsputtingclub.com.

British Golf Museum

This exhibit, which started as a small collection in the R&A Clubhouse across the street, is the best place in Britain to learn about the Scots' favorite sport. It's fascinating for golf lovers and an interesting overview for the casual tourist. The museum will close at the end of 2020 for a few months for a major renovation, and the layout is expected to change. During the renovation, the gift shop and upstairs café will stay open.

Cost and Hours: £8.50, Mon-Sat 9:30-17:00, Sun from 10:00; Nov-March daily 10:00-16:00; last entry 45 minutes before closing; café upstairs; Bruce Embankment—in the blocky modern building squatting behind the R&A Clubhouse by the Old Course, tel. 01334/460-046, www.britishgolfmuseum.co.uk.

Visiting the Museum: The compact, one-way exhibit takes about 45 minutes to explore and reverently presents a meticulous survey of the game's history. Start with the short film, then follow the counterclockwise route to learn about the evolution of golf—from the monarchs who loved and hated golf (including the king who outlawed it because it was distracting men from church and archery practice), to Tom Morris and Bobby Jones, all the way up to the "Golden Bear" and a randy Tiger. Along the way, you'll see plenty of old clubs, balls, medals, and trophies, and learn about how the earliest "feathery" balls and wooden clubs were made. Touchscreens invite you to learn more, and you'll also see a "hall of fame" with items donated by today's biggest golfers. Finally, you'll have a chance to dress up in some old-school golfing duds and try out some of that antique equipment for yourself.

Sleeping in St. Andrews

Owing partly to the high-roller golf tourists flowing through the town, St. Andrews' accommodations are quite expensive. During graduation week in June, hotels often require a four-night stay and book up quickly. All of the guesthouses I've listed are on the streets called Murray Park and Murray Place, between North Street and The Scores in the old town. If you need to find a room on the fly, look around in this same neighborhood, which has far more options than just the ones I've listed below.

$$$ Glenderran Guest House offers five plush rooms (including two true singles) and a few nice breakfast extras (no kids under 12, pay same-day laundry, 9 Murray Park, tel. 01334/477-951, www.glenderran.com, info@glenderran.com, Ray and Maggie).

$$ Hoppity House is a bright and contemporary place, with attention to detail and fun hosts Heather and Valerie, who are helpful and generous with travel tips. There's a lounge and kitchen for guest use and a storage closet for golf equipment. You may find a stuffed namesake bunny or two hiding out among its four impeccable rooms (fridges in rooms, 4 Murray Park, mobile 07967/044-801, www.hoppityhouse.co.uk, enquiries@hoppityhouse.co.uk).

$$ Cameron House has five clean and simple rooms around a beautiful stained-glass atrium. Its common area feels like a refurbished Victorian lounge (two-night minimum in summer, 11 Murray Park, tel. 01334/472-306, www.cameronhouse-sta.co.uk, info@cameronhouse-sta.co.uk, Donna).

$$ Montague Guest House has richly furnished public spaces—with a dark, cozy, leather-couch-filled lounge/breakfast room—and eight decently sized rooms with tartan accents (21 Murray Park, tel. 01334/479-287, www.montaguehouse.com, info@montaguehouse.com, Raj and Judith).

$$ Lorimer House has six comfortable, tastefully decorated rooms, including one on the ground floor. Some doubles are cheaper and more compact than others (two-night minimum preferred, no kids under 12, 19 Murray Park, tel. 01334/476-599, www.lorimerhouse.com, info@lorimerhouse.com, Scott and Ashley).

$$ Shandon House is a refreshing and breezy seaside retreat with six bright and comfortable rooms. Two rooms have private bathrooms across the hall (2-night minimum preferred, 10 Murray Place, tel. 1334/472-412, www.shandonhouse.co.uk, info@shandonhouse.co.uk, Liz and Stuart).

$$ Doune Guest House's seven rooms provide a more impersonal but fine place to stay in St. Andrews (breakfast extra, two-night minimum preferred in summer, single with private bath, 5 Murray Place, tel. 01334/475-195, www.dounehouse.com, info@dounehouse.com, Ilya).

¢ St. Andrews Tourist Hostel has 44 beds in colorful 5- to 8-bed rooms about a block from the base of Market Street. The high-ceilinged lounge is a comfy place for a break, and the friendly staff is happy to recommend their favorite pubs (kitchen, St. Mary's Place, tel. 01334/479-911, www.hostelsscotlandltd.com, info@hostelsstandrews.com).

UNIVERSITY ACCOMMODATIONS

In the summer (early June-Aug), some of the University of St. Andrews' student-housing buildings are tidied up and rented out to tourists. I've listed the most convenient options below (website for both: https://ace.st-andrews.ac.uk; pay when reserving). Both of these include breakfast and Wi-Fi. Because true single rooms are rare in St. Andrews' B&Bs, these dorms are a good option for solo travelers.

$ Agnes Blackadder Hall has double beds and private bathrooms; it's more comfortable, but also more expensive and less central (family rooms, North Haugh, tel. 01334/467-000, agnes.blackadder@st-andrews.ac.uk).

$ McIntosh Hall is cheaper and more central, but it only has twin beds and shared bathrooms (Abbotsford Crescent, tel. 01334/467-035, mchall@st-andrews.ac.uk).

Eating in St. Andrews

RESTAURANTS

$$$ Forgan's, occupying a former golf club factory, is tempting and popular. It's done up country-kitschy, with high ceilings, cool lanterns, a fun energy, and a little taxidermy. It serves up refined Scottish dishes and offers a tempting steak selection (Mon-Fri 11:00-late—kitchen open 12:00-22:00, Sat-Sun 10:00-late—kitchen open 10:00-22:00, reservations strongly recommended, 110 Market Street, tel. 01334/466-973, www.forgans.co.uk). On Friday and Saturday nights after 22:30, they have live *ceilidh* (traditional Scottish) music, and everyone joins in the dancing; consider reserving a booth for a late dinner, then stick around for the show. They also have live acoustic music on Thursday evenings.

$$ Mitchell's, with a casual and rustic dining room, is a simpler alternative to the upscale restaurants in town. The menu features hearty salads, creative sandwiches, burgers, and "sharing boards," and you'll enjoy live music every Friday and Saturday night from 20:30. The attached deli serves up locally made meats, cheeses, and other organic products for takeaway (Mon-Thu 8:00-22:00, Fri-Sat 8:00-late, Sun 9:00-22:00, 110 Market Street, tel. 01334/466-970).

$$$ Playfair's, a restaurant and steakhouse downstairs in the Ardgowan Hotel between the B&B neighborhood and the Old Course, has a cozy/classy interior and outdoor seating at rustic tables set just below the busy street. Their bar next door (Pilmour) serves a similar menu (daily 12:00-late, off-season weekdays open for dinner only, 2 Playfair Terrace on North Street, tel. 01334/472-970).

$$$ The Doll's House serves dressed-up Scottish cuisine in a stone-and-wood interior or at tables on the square in front (daily 9:00-22:00, across from Holy Trinity Church at 3 Church Square, tel. 01334/477-422).

$$$$ The Seafood Ristorante, in a modern glassy building overlooking the beach near the Old Course, is like dining in an aquarium. They serve high-end Italian with a focus on seafood in a formal space with floor-to-ceiling windows providing unhindered views (minimum £20/person food order at dinner, daily 12:00-14:30 & 18:00-21:30, reservations a must on weekends and in summer, The Scores, tel. 01334/479-475, www.theseafoodrestaurant.com, dine@theseafoodristorante.com).

$$ Little Italy is a crowded Italian joint with all the clichés—red-and-white checkered tablecloths, replica Roman busts, a bit of freneticism, and even a moped in the wall. But the food is authentically good and the menu is massive. It's the town favorite—make reservations (daily 12:30-22:30, 2 Logies Lane, tel. 01334/479-299, www.littleitaly.cc).

$$$ The Dunvegan Bar, part of the hotel of the same name and just around the corner from the Old Course, is on the 19th hole of St. Andrews. It serves overpriced, unexciting pub grub, but you're coming for the energetic atmosphere—and the walls (and ceiling) covered with golf photos and memorabilia (daily 11:30-22:00, off-season until 21:00, 7 Pilmour Place, tel. 1334/473-105). Their simple **$$** restaurant, Claret Jug, is in the back, with a calmer ambience.

Fish-and-Chips: Two places battle for the "best chippy in town" crown. **$ Cromars** is a local favorite for takeaway fish-and-chips (and burgers). At the counter, you can order yours to go, or—in good weather—enjoy it at the sidewalk tables; farther in is a small **$$** sit-down restaurant with more choices (both open daily 11:00-22:00, at the corner of Union and Market, tel. 01334/475-

555). **Tailend** also has a **$** takeaway counter up front (fish-and-chips) and a **$$** restaurant with a bigger selection in the back (daily 11:30-22:00, 130 Market Street, tel. 01334/474-070).

BEER, COFFEE, AND WHISKY

Pubs: There's no shortage in this college town. These aren't "gastropubs," but they all serve straightforward pub fare (all open long hours daily).

Aikmans, run by Barbara and Malcolm (two graduates from the university who couldn't bring themselves to leave), features a cozy wood-table ambience, a focus on ales, live music (usually Fri-Sat), and simple soups, sandwiches, and snacks (32 Bell Street, tel. 01334/477-425). **The Central,** right along Market Street, is a St. Andrews standby, with old lamps and lots of brass (77 Market Street, tel. 01334/478-296). **Greyfriars,** with forgettable food, is in a classy, modern hotel steps away from my recommended Murray Park B&Bs (129 North Street, tel. 01334/474-906). **The Keys Bar** is a lively pub in the middle of Market Street. It's a good time any night of the week (87 Market Street, tel. 0133/447-2414).

Coffee: $ Taste, a little café just across the street from the B&B neighborhood, has the best coffee in town and a laid-back, borderline-funky ambience that feels like a big-city coffeehouse back home. It also serves cakes and light food (daily 7:00-18:00 in summer, open later when students are back, 148 North Street, tel. 01334/477-959).

Whisky: Luvians Bottle Shop—run by three brothers (Luigi, Vincenzo, and Antonio)—is a friendly place to talk, taste, and purchase whisky. Distilleries bottle unique single-cask vintages exclusively for this shop to celebrate the British Open every five years (ask about the 21-year-old Springbank they received in 2015 to commemorate the tournament). With nearly 50 bottles open for tastings, a map of Scotland's whisky regions, and helpful team members, this is a handy spot to learn about whisky. They also sell fine wines and a wide range of microbrews (Mon-Sat 10:00-22:00, Sun from 12:30, 66 Market Street, tel. 01334/477-752).

PICNIC FOOD AND SWEETS

Cheese: I.J. Mellis Cheesemonger, the excellent Edinburgh cheese shop with a delectable array of Scottish, English, and international cheeses, has a St. Andrews branch. On Friday and Saturday nights, the shop stays open late as a wine bar (Mon-Thu 9:00-19:00, Fri-Sat until 22:00, Sun 10:00-17:00, 149 South Street, tel. 01334/471-410).

Pastries: Fisher and Donaldson is beloved for its rich, affordable pastries and chocolates. Listen as the straw-hatted bakers chat with their regular customers, then try their Coffee Tower—like a giant cream puff filled with lightly coffee-flavored cream—or their number-one seller, the fudge doughnut (Mon-Sat 6:00-17:00, closed Sun, just around the corner from the TI at 13 Church Street, tel. 01334/472-201).

Gelato: You'll see many people walking around licking cones from **Jannettas Gelateria,** which has been around for more than a century. While waiting in line in the cute pastel parlor, ponder what you want from their range of 50-plus gelato flavors (daily 9:00-22:30, café, 31 South Street, tel. 01334/473-285). If you don't have time to wait in line, the less crowded **Burns** candy shop on Market Street scoops about a dozen flavors of Jannettas gelato (96 Market Street).

Supermarkets: You can stock up for a picnic at **Tesco** or **Sainsbury's Local** on Market Street.

St. Andrews Connections

Trains don't go into St. Andrews—instead, use the Leuchars station (5 miles from St. Andrews, connected by buses coordinated to meet most trains, 2-4/hour, see "Arrival in St. Andrews" at the beginning of this chapter). To head back to the train station, take any #99 bus (several variations of #99—A, B, D, etc.—work for this route; direction: Dundee), but confirm with the driver that it's going straight to Leuchars. Some routes make stops through town first (extending your travel time by 20-30 minutes).

From Leuchars by Train to: Edinburgh (1-2/hour, 1 hour), **Glasgow** (2/hour, 2 hours, transfer in Haymarket or Edinburgh Waverley), **Inverness** (roughly hourly, 3.5 hours, 2 changes). Trains run less frequently on Sundays. Train info: Tel. 0345-748-4950, www.nationalrail.co.uk.

OBAN & THE INNER HEBRIDES

Oban • Mull, Iona & Staffa • Glasgow to Oban Drive

For a taste of Scotland's west coast, head to Oban, a port town that's equal parts endearing and functional. This busy little ferry and train terminus has no important sights, but makes up the difference in character, in scenery (with its low-impact panorama of overlapping islets and bobbing boats), and with one of Scotland's best distillery tours. But Oban is also convenient: It's midway between the Lowland cities (Glasgow and Edinburgh) and the Highland riches of the north. And it's the "gateway to the isles," with handy ferry service to the Hebrides Islands.

If time is tight and serious island-hopping is beyond the scope of your itinerary, Oban is ideally situated for a busy and memorable full-day side trip to three of the most worthwhile Inner Hebrides: big, rugged Mull; pristine little Iona, where buoyant clouds float over its historic abbey; and Staffa, a remote, grassy islet inhabited only by sea birds.

This chapter also outlines the most scenic route between Glasgow and Oban (along the banks of Loch Lomond and through the town of Inveraray, with its fine castle), with a detour through Kilmartin Glen, the prehistoric homeland of the Scottish people.

PLANNING YOUR TIME

If you're on a speedy blitz tour of Scotland, Oban is a strategic and pleasant place to spend the night. But you'll need two nights to enjoy Oban's main attraction: the side-trip to Mull, Iona, and Staffa. There are few actual sights in Oban itself, beyond the distillery tour, but—thanks to its manageable size, scenic waterfront setting, and great restaurants—the town is an enjoyable place to linger.

Getting Around the Highlands

By Car: The Highlands are made for joyriding. There are a lot of miles, but they're scenic, the roads are good, and the traffic is light. The farther north you go, the more away-from-it-all you'll feel. Even on a sunny weekend, you can go miles without seeing another car. Don't wait too long to gas up—village gas stations are few and far between. Stay alert on single-lane roads, and slow down on blind corners. If you do encounter an oncoming vehicle, the driver closest to a pullout is expected to use it—even if they have to back up.

By Public Transportation: Glasgow is the gateway to this region (so you'll most likely transfer there if coming from Edinburgh). **Trains** zip from Glasgow to Fort William and Oban in the west; and up to Stirling and Inverness in the east. For more remote destinations (such as Glencoe), the bus is better.

Most **buses** are operated by Scottish Citylink. In peak season—when these buses fill up—it's smart to buy tickets at least a day in advance: Book at Citylink.co.uk, call 0871-216-3333, or stop by a bus station or TI. Otherwise, you can pay the driver in cash when you board.

Glasgow's Buchanan Station is the main Lowlands hub for reaching Highlands destinations. From Edinburgh, it's best to transfer in Glasgow (fastest by train, also possible by bus)—though there are direct buses from Edinburgh to Inverness, where you can connect to Highlands buses. Once in the Highlands, Inverness and Fort William serve as the main bus hubs.

Note that bus frequency can be substantially reduced on Sundays and in the off-season (Oct-mid-May). Unless otherwise noted, I've listed bus information for summer weekdays. Always confirm schedules locally.

These buses are particularly useful:

Buses **#976** and **#977** connect Glasgow with Oban (5/day, 3 hours).

Buses **#914/#915/#916** go from Glasgow to Fort William, stopping at Glencoe (7-8/day, 2.5 hours to Glencoe, 3 hours total to Fort William).

Bus **#918** goes from Oban to Fort William, stopping en route at Ballachulish near Glencoe (2/day, 1 hour to Ballachulish, 1.5 hours total to Fort William).

Bus **#N44** (operated by Shiel Bus) is a cheaper alternative for connecting Glencoe to Fort William (about 8/day, fewer Sat-Sun, www.shielbuses.co.uk).

Buses **#919** and **#920** connect Fort William with Inverness (6/day, 2 hours, fewer on Sun).

Buses **#M90** and **#G90** run from Edinburgh to Inverness (express #G90, 2/day, 3.5 hours; slower #M90, 6/day, 4 hours).

Bus **#G10** is an express connecting Inverness and Glasgow (5/day, 3 hours). National Express **#588** also goes direct (1/day, 4 hours, www.nationalexpress.com).

Oban

Oban (pronounced OH-bin) is a low-key resort. Its winding promenade is lined by gravel beaches, ice-cream stands, fish-and-chips joints, a tourable distillery, and a good choice of restaurants. Everything in Oban is close together, and the town seems eager to please its many visitors: Wool and tweed are perpetually on sale, and posters announce a variety of day tours to Scotland's wild and wildlife-strewn western islands. When the rain clears, sun-starved Scots sit on benches along the Esplanade, leaning back to catch some rays. Wind, boats, gulls, layers of islands, and the promise of a wide-open Atlantic beyond give Oban a rugged charm.

Orientation to Oban

Oban, with about 10,000 people, is where the train system of Scotland meets the ferry system serving the Hebrides Islands. As "gateway to the isles," its center is not a square or market, but its harbor. Oban's business action, just a couple of streets deep, stretches along the harbor and its promenade.

TOURIST INFORMATION

Oban's TI, located at the North Pier, sells bus and ferry tickets and can help you sort through your island-hopping day-trip options (generally daily July-Aug 9:00-19:00, April-June until 17:30, Sept-March 10:00-17:00, 3 North Pier, tel. 01631/563-122, www.oban.org.uk).

HELPFUL HINTS

Bookstore: Overlooking the harborfront, Waterstones offers maps and a fine collection of books on Scotland (Mon-Sat 9:00-17:30, Sun 11:00-17:00, longer hours July-Aug, 12 George Street, tel. 0843/290-8529).

Baggage Storage: The train station has pay luggage lockers, but is open limited hours (Mon-Sat 5:00-20:30, Sun 10:45-18:00)—confirm the closing time before committing.

Laundry: You'll find **Oban Quality Laundry** tucked a block behind the main drag just off Stevenson Street (same-day

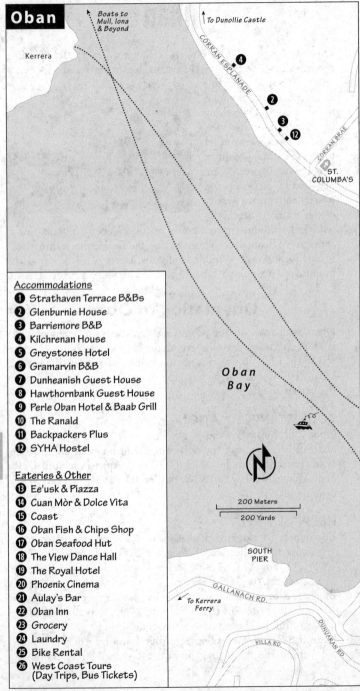

OBAN & INNER HEBRIDES

Oban

Kerrera

Boats to
Mull, Iona
& Beyond

To Dunollie Castle

CORRAN ESPLANADE

4

2

3

12

CORRAN BRAE

ST. COLUMBA'S

Oban Bay

N

200 Meters
200 Yards

SOUTH PIER

GALLANACH RD.

To Kerrera Ferry

VILLA RD.

DUNUARAN RD.

Accommodations
1 Strathaven Terrace B&Bs
2 Glenburnie House
3 Barriemore B&B
4 Kilchrenan House
5 Greystones Hotel
6 Gramarvin B&B
7 Dunheanish Guest House
8 Hawthornbank Guest House
9 Perle Oban Hotel & Baab Grill
10 The Ranald
11 Backpackers Plus
12 SYHA Hostel

Eateries & Other
13 Ee'usk & Piazza
14 Cuan Mòr & Dolce Vita
15 Coast
16 Oban Fish & Chips Shop
17 Oban Seafood Hut
18 The View Dance Hall
19 The Royal Hotel
20 Phoenix Cinema
21 Aulay's Bar
22 Oban Inn
23 Grocery
24 Laundry
25 Bike Rental
26 West Coast Tours
    (Day Trips, Bus Tickets)

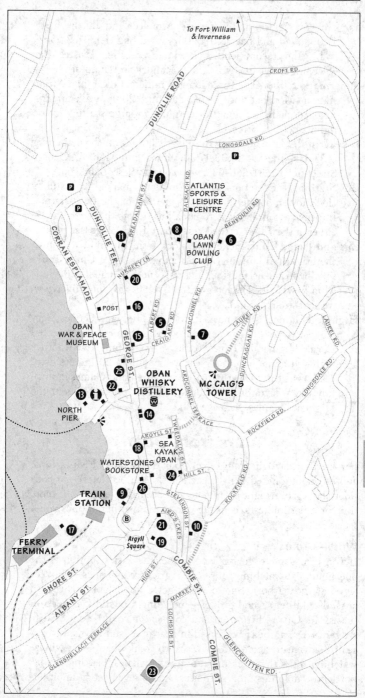

drop-off service, no self-service, Mon-Tue and Thu-Fri 9:00-17:00, Wed and Sat 9:00-13:00, closed Sun, tel. 01631/563-554). The recommended **Backpackers Plus Hostel** (see "Sleeping in Oban") will also do laundry for nonguests.

Supermarket: The giant **Tesco** is a five-minute walk from the train station (Mon-Sat until 24:00, Sun until 20:00, walk through Argyll Square and look for entrance to large parking lot on right, Lochside Street).

Bike Rental: Get wheels at **Oban Cycles,** right on the main drag (£25/day, Tue-Sat 10:00-17:00, closed Sun-Mon, 87 George Street, tel. 01631/566-033, www.obancyclesscotland.com).

Bus Station: The "station" is just a pullout, marked by a stubby clock tower, at the roundabout in front of the train station. In peak season, it's wise to book bus tickets the day before—either at the TI, or at the West Coast Tours office (see next).

Bus and Island Tour Tickets: A block from the train station in the bright-red building along the harbor, **West Coast Tours** sells bus- and island-tour tickets (Tue-Sat 6:30-17:30, Sun-Mon from 8:30, 17 George Street, tel. 01631/566-809, www.westcoasttours.co.uk).

Highland Games: Oban hosts its touristy Highland Games every August (www.obangames.com), and the more local-oriented Lorne Highland Games some years in June (www.lorne-highland-games.org.uk). Nearby Taynuilt, a 20-minute drive east, hosts their sweetly small-town Highland Games in mid-July (www.taynuilthighlandgames.com). For more about the Highland Games, see page 930.

Tours from Oban

For the best day trip from Oban, tour the islands of Mull, Iona, and/or Staffa (offered daily Easter-Oct, described later)—or consider staying overnight on remote and beautiful Iona. With more time or other interests, consider one of many other options you'll see advertised.

Wildlife Tours

If you just want to go for a boat ride, the easiest option is the one-hour seal-watching tour (£10, various companies—look for signs at the harbor). But to really get a good look at Scottish coastal wildlife, several groups—including **Coastal Connection** (based in Oban, https://coastal-connection.co.uk) and **Sealife Adventures** and **SeaFari** (based in nearby coastal towns, https://sealife-adventures.com and www.seafari.co.uk/oban)—run whale-watching tours that seek out rare minke whales, basking sharks, bottlenose dolphins, and porpoises. For an even more ambitious itinerary, the holy grail is Treshnish Island (out past Staffa), which brims with puffins, seals, and other sea critters. For multi-day cruising trips around the islands, try **St. Hilda Sea Adventures,** with their own small fleet of boats (www.sthildaseaadventures.co.uk).

Sea Kayak Tours

If the weather is good and you'd like to get out on the water under your own power, **Sea Kayak Oban** rents gear and offers classes and guided tours for novice and experienced kayakers. A full-day tour costs £90 including equipment (office at 6 Argyll Street, tel. 01631/565-310, www.seakayakoban.com).

Sights in Oban

▲The Burned-Out Sightseer's Visual Tour from the Pier

If the west-coast weather permits, get oriented to the town while taking a break: Head out to the North Pier, just past the TI, and find the benches that face back toward town (in front of the recommended Piazza restaurant). Take a seat and get to know Oban.

Scan the harborfront from left to right, surveying the mix of grand Victorian sandstone buildings and humbler modern storefronts. At the far-right end of town is the **ferry terminal** and—very likely—a huge ferry loading or unloading. Oban has always been on the way to somewhere, and today is no different. (A recent tourism slogan: Oban...it's closer than you think.) The townscape seems dominated by Caledonian-MacBrayne, Scotland's biggest ferry company. CalMac's 30 ships serve 24 destinations and transport over 4 million passengers a year. The town's port has long been a lifeline to the islands.

Hiding near the ferry terminal is the **train station.** With the arrival of the train in 1880, Oban became the unofficial capital of Scotland's west coast and a destination for tourists. Close by is the former Caledonian Hotel, the original terminus hotel (now the Perle Oban Hotel) that once served those train travelers.

Tourism aside, herring was the first big industry. A dozen boats still fish commercially—you'll see them tucked around the ferry terminal. The tourist board, in an attempt to entice tourists to linger longer, is trying to rebrand Oban as a "seafood capital" rather than just the "gateway to the isles." As the ocean's supply has become depleted, most local fish is farmed. There's still plenty of shellfish.

After fishing, big industries here historically included tobacco (imported from the American colonies), then whisky. At the left end of the embankment, find the building marked *The Oban Distillery*. It's rare to find a distillery in the middle of a town, but Oban grew up around this one. With the success of its whisky, the town enjoyed an invigorating confidence, optimism, and, in 1811, a royal charter. Touring Oban's distillery is the best activity in Oban.

Above the distillery, you can't miss the odd mini-Colosseum. This is **McCaig's Tower,** an employ-the-workers-and-build-me-a-fine-memorial project undertaken by an Oban tycoon in 1900. McCaig died before completing the structure, so his complete vision for it remains a mystery. This is an example of a "folly"—that uniquely British notion of an idiosyncratic structure erected by a colorful aristocrat. Building a folly was an in-your-face kind of extravagance many extremely wealthy people enjoyed even when surrounded by struggling working-class people (an urge that survives among some of the upper crust to this day). While the building itself is nothing to see up close, a 10-minute hike through a Victorian residential neighborhood leads you to a peaceful garden and a commanding view (nice at sunset).

Now turn and look out to sea, and imagine this: At the height of the Cold War, Oban played a critical role when the world's first two-way transatlantic telephone cable was laid from Gallanach Bay to Newfoundland in 1956—a milestone in global communication. This technology later provided the White House and the Kremlin with the "hotline" that was created after the Cuban Missile Crisis to avoid a nuclear conflagration.

▲▲Oban Whisky Distillery Tours

Founded in 1794, Oban Whisky Distillery produces more than 25,000 liters a week, and exports much of that to the US. Their exhibition (upstairs, free to all) gives a quick, whisky-centric history of Oban and Scotland.

The distillery offers serious and fragrant one-hour tours explaining the process from start to finish, with two smooth samples of their signature product: Oban whisky is moderately smoky ("peaty") and characterized by notes of sea salt, citrus, and honey. You'll also receive a whisky glass and a discount coupon for the shop. This is the handiest whisky tour you'll encounter—just a block off the harbor—and one of the best. Come 10 minutes before your tour starts to check out the exhibition upstairs. Then your guide will walk you through each step of the process: malting, mashing, fermentation, distillation, and maturation. Photos are not allowed inside. For more on whisky, including tasting tips, see page 755.

Cost and Hours: Tours cost £12, are limited to 16 people and depart every 20 to 30 minutes. Tours fill up, so for the greatest choice of times, book in advance by phone or online. Or drop by in person—unless it's really a busy day, you should be able pay for a tour leaving in the next hour or so, then easily pass time in the town center. Generally open July-Sept Mon-Fri 9:30-19:30, Sat-Sun until 17:00; March-June and Oct-Nov daily 9:30-17:00; Dec-Feb daily 12:00-16:30; last tour 1.25 hours before closing, Stafford Street, tel. 01631/572-004, www.obanwhisky.com.

Serious Tasting: Connoisseurs can ask about their "exclusive tour," which adds a visit to the warehouse and four premium tastings in the manager's office (£75, 2 hours, likely July-Sept Mon-Fri at 16:00 only, reservation required).

Oban War & Peace Museum

Opened in 1995 on the 50th anniversary of Victory in Europe Day, this charming little museum focuses on Oban's experience during World War II. But it covers more than just war and peace. Photos show Oban through the years, and a 15-minute looped video gives a simple tour around the town and region. Volunteer staffers love to chat about the exhibit—or anything else on your mind (free; May-Oct Mon-Thu 10:00-18:00, Fri-Sun and off-season until 16:00; next to Regent Hotel on the promenade, tel. 01631/570-007, www.obanmuseum.org.uk).

Dunollie Castle and Museum

In a park just a mile up the coast, a ruined castle and an old house hold an intimate collection of clan family treasures. This spartan, stocky castle with 10-foot walls offers a commanding, windy view of the harbor—a strategic spot back in the days when transport was mainly by water. For more than a thousand years, clan chiefs ruled this region from this ancestral home of Clan MacDougall, but the castle was abandoned in 1746. The adjacent house, which dates from 1745, shows off the MacDougall clan's heritage with a handful of rooms filled with a humble yet fascinating trove of treasures. While the exhibit won't dazzle you, the family and clan pride in the display, their "willow garden," and the lovely walk from Oban make the visit fun.

To get there, head out of town along the harborfront promenade. At the war memorial (with inviting seaview benches), cross the street. A gate leads to a little lane, lined with historic and nature boards along the way to the castle.

Cost and Hours: £6, Mon-Sat 10:00-17:00, Sun from 13:00; free tours given most days at 10:30 and 14:30, Sun 12:30 only; closed Nov-March, tel. 01631/570-550, www.dunollie.org.

ACTIVITIES IN OBAN
Atlantis Leisure Centre

This industrial-type sports center has a rock-climbing wall, tennis courts, indoor "soft play centre" (for kids under 5), and an indoor swimming pool with a big water slide. The outdoor playground is free and open all the time (pool only-£4.50, no rental towels or suits, fees for other activities; open Mon-Fri 6:30-21:00, Sat-Sun 9:00-18:00; on the north end of Dalriach Road, tel. 01631/566-800, www.atlantisleisure.co.uk).

Oban Lawn Bowling Club

The club has welcomed visitors since 1869. This elegant green is the scene of a wonderfully British spectacle of old men tiptoeing wishfully after their balls. It's fun to watch, and—if there's no match scheduled and the weather's dry—anyone can rent shoes and balls and actually play (£5/person; generally daily 10:00-12:00 & 14:00-16:00 or "however long the weather lasts"; just south of sports center on Dalriach Road, tel. 01631/570-808).

ISLANDS NEAR OBAN

The isles of Mull, Iona, and Staffa are farther out, require a full day to visit, and are described later in this chapter. For a quicker glimpse at the Inner Hebrides, consider these two options.

Isle of Kerrera

Functioning like a giant breakwater, the Isle of Kerrera (KEH-reh-rah) makes Oban possible. Just offshore from Oban, this stark but very green island offers a quick, easy opportunity to get that romantic island experience. While it has no proper roads, it offers nice hikes, a ruined castle, and a few sheep farms. It's also a fine place to bike (ask for advice at Oban Cycles; see "Helpful Hints," earlier). You may see the Kerrera ferry filled with sheep heading for Oban's livestock market.

Getting There: You have two options for reaching the island. A boat operated by the Oban Marina goes from **Oban's North Pier** to the Kerrera Marina in the northern part of the island (£5 round-trip, roughly every hour, book ahead at tel. 01631/565-333, www.obanmarina.com).

A ferry departs from **Gallanach** (two miles south of Oban) and goes to the middle of the island. This is the best option if you want to hike to Kerrera's castle (passengers only, £4.80 round-trip, bikes free, runs 10:30-12:30 & 14:00-18:00, none off-season, 5-minute ride, tel. 01475/650-397, www.calmac.co.uk). To reach Gallanach, drive south, following the coast road past the ferry terminal (parking available).

Eating and Sleeping on Kerrera: With a laidback patio,

$$ Waypoint Bar & Grill has a simple menu of steak, burgers, and seafood; on a nice day the open-air waterside setting is unbeatable (late May-Sept Thu-Sun lunch 12:00-14:30, Tue-Sun dinner 17:30-21:00, bar opens at 17:00, closed Mon and in winter, reservations highly recommended, tel. 01631/565-333, www.obanmarina.com). For lodging, your only option is the **$ Kerrera Bunkhouse,** a refurbished 18th-century stable that can sleep up to seven people in a small, cozy space (1 double and 5 single bunks, 2-night minimum, includes bedding but not towels, open Easter-Oct but must book ahead, kitchen, tel. 01631/566-367, www.kerrerabunkhouse.co.uk, info@kerrerabunkhouse.co.uk, Martin and Aideen). They also run a tea garden that serves meals (daily 10:30-16:30, closed Oct-Easter).

Isle of Seil

Enjoy a drive, a walk, some solitude, and the sea. Drive 12 miles south of Oban on the A-816 to the B-844 to the Isle of Seil (pronounced "seal"), connected to the mainland by a bridge (which, locals like to brag, "crosses the Atlantic"...well, maybe a small part of it).

Just over the bridge on the Isle of Seil is a pub called **Tigh-an-Truish** ("House of Trousers"). After the Jacobite rebellions, a new law forbade the wearing of kilts on the mainland. Highlanders on the island used this pub to change from kilts to trousers before they made the crossing. The pub serves great meals and good seafood dishes to those in either kilts or pants (pub generally open daily—call ahead, tel. 01852/300-242).

Seven miles across the island, on a tiny second island and facing the open Atlantic, is **Easdale,** a historic, touristy, windblown little slate-mining town with a small folk museum (shuttle ferry goes the 300 yards). Wildlife/nature tours plus tours to Iona and Staffa also run from Easdale (www.seafari.co.uk).

Nightlife in Oban

Little Oban has a few options for entertaining its many visitors; check ObanWhatsOn.co.uk. Fun low-key activities may include open-mic, disco, or quiz theme nights in pubs; occasional Scottish folk shows; coffee meetings; and—if you're lucky—duck races. On Wednesday nights, the Oban Pipe Band plays in the square by the train station. Here are a few other ways to entertain yourself while in town.

Music and Group Dancing: On many summer nights, you can climb the stairs to **The View,** a sprawling venue on the main drag for music and dancing. There's *ceilidh* (KAY-lee) dancing a couple of times per week, where you can learn some group dances

OBAN & INNER HEBRIDES

to music performed by a folk band (including, usually, a piper). These group dances are a lot of fun—wallflowers and bad dancers are warmly welcomed, and the staff is happy to give you pointers (£9, May-Sept Mon & Thu at 21:00, sometimes also Sat). They also host concerts by folk and traditional bands (check website for schedule, 34 George Street, tel. 01631/569-599, www.obanview.com).

Traditional Music: Various pubs and hotels in town have live traditional music in the summer; the TI compiles these into its Oban Music Trail map—ask your B&B host or at the TI for the latest. **The Royal Hotel,** just above the train station on Argyll Square, is one popular venue.

Cinema: True to its name, **The Phoenix Cinema** closed down but then was saved by the community. It's now volunteer-run and booming (140 George Street, tel. 01631/562-905, www.obanphoenix.com).

Characteristic Pubs: With decor that shows off Oban's maritime heritage, **Aulay's Bar** has two sides, each with a different personality (I like the right-hand side). Having a drink here invariably comes with a good "blether" (conversation), and the gang is mostly local (daily 11:00-24:00, 8 Airds Crescent, just around the corner from the train station and ferry terminal). The **Oban Inn,** right on the harborfront, is also a fun and memorable place for a pint and possibly live music.

Sleeping in Oban

Oban's B&Bs offer a much better value than its hotels.

ON STRATHAVEN TERRACE

The following B&Bs line up on a quiet, flowery street that's nicely located two blocks off the harbor, three blocks from the center, and a 10-minute walk from the train station. Rooms here are compact and don't have views, but the location can't be beat.

By car, as you enter town from the north, turn left immediately after King's Knoll Hotel, and take your first right onto Breadalbane Street. ("Strathaven Terrace" is actually just the name for this row of houses on Breadalbane Street.) The alley behind the buildings has tight, free parking for all of these places.

$$ Rose Villa Guest House has five crisp and cheery rooms (at #5, tel. 01631/566-874, www.rosevillaoban.co.uk, info@rosevillaoban.co.uk, Stuart and Jacqueline).

$ Raniven Guest House has five simple, tastefully decorated rooms and gracious, fun-loving hosts Moyra and Stuart (cash only, 2-night minimum in summer, continental breakfast, at #1, tel. 01631/562-713, www.ranivenoban.com, bookings@ranivenoban.com).

$ Sandvilla B&B rents five pleasant, polished rooms (2-night minimum in summer, at #4, tel. 01631/564-483, www.holidayoban.co.uk, sandvilla@holidayoban.co.uk, Josephine and Robert).

ALONG THE ESPLANADE

These are along the Corran Esplanade, which stretches north of town above a cobble beach; they are a 10-minute walk from the center. Rooms here are generally spacious and many have beautiful bay views. Walking from town, you'll reach them in this order: Kilchrenan, Glenburnie, and Barriemore.

$$$ Glenburnie House, a stately Victorian home, has an elegant breakfast room overlooking the bay. Its 12 spacious, comfortable, classy rooms feel like plush living rooms. There's a nice lounge and a tiny sunroom with a stuffed "hairy coo" head (closed mid-Nov-March, tel. 01631/562-089, www.glenburnie.co.uk, stay@glenburnie.co.uk, Graeme).

$$$ Barriemore B&B, at the very end of Oban's grand waterfront Esplanade, is a welcome refuge after a day of exploration. Its 14 well-appointed rooms come with robes, sherry, etc. It has a nice front patio, spacious breakfast room, and glassed-in sun porch with a view of the water (family suite, closed Nov-March, tel. 01631/566-356, www.barriemore.co.uk, info@barriemore.co.uk, Jan and Mark).

$$ Kilchrenan House, the turreted former retreat of a textile magnate, has 15 large rooms, most with bay views. The stunning rooms #5, #9, and #15 are worth the few extra pounds, while the "standard" rooms in the newer annex are a good value (2-night minimum for some rooms, welcome drink of whisky or sherry, different "breakfast special" every day, family rooms, closed Oct-March, tel. 01631/562-663, www.kilchrenanhouse.co.uk, info@kilchrenanhouse.co.uk, Colin and Frances).

ABOVE THE TOWN CENTER

These places perch on the hill above the main waterfront zone—a short (but uphill) walk from all of the action. Many rooms come with views, and are priced accordingly.

$$$$ Greystones is an enticing splurge. It fills a big, stately, turreted mansion at the top of town with five spacious rooms that mix Victorian charm and sleek gray-and-white minimalism. Built as the private home for the director of Kimberley Diamond Mine, it later became a maternity hospital, and today Cathy and John run it as a stylish and restful retreat. The lounge and breakfast room offer stunning views over Oban and the offshore isles (closed Nov-mid-Feb, 1-3 Dalriach Road, tel. 01631/562-423, www.greystonesoban. co.uk, stay@greystonesoban.co.uk).

$$ Gramarvin B&B feels a little more homey and personal, with just two rooms and warm host Mary. Window seats in each room provide a lovely view over Oban, but be warned—the climb up from town and then up their stairs is steep (simple breakfast, cash only, 2-night minimum in summer preferred, on-street parking, Benvoulin Road, tel. 01631/564-622, www.gramarvin.co.uk, mary@gramarvin.co.uk, Mary and Joe).

$$ Dunheanish Guest House offers six pleasant rooms (two on the ground floor) and wide-open views from its perch above town, which you can enjoy from the front stone patio, breakfast room, and several guest rooms (lots of stairs, parking, Ardconnel Road, tel. 01631/566-556, www.dunheanish.com, info@ dunheanish.com, William and Linda).

$$ Hawthornbank Guest House fills a big Victorian sandstone house with seven traditional-feeling rooms. Half of the rooms face bay views, and the other half overlook the town's lawn-bowling green (2-night minimum in summer, Dalriach Road, tel. 01631/562-041, www.hawthornbank.co.uk, info@hawthornbank. co.uk).

IN THE TOWN CENTER

A number of hotels are in the center of town along or near the main drag—but you'll pay for the convenience.

$$$$ Perle Oban Hotel is your luxury boutique splurge. Right across from the harbor, it has 59 super-sleek rooms with calming sea-color walls, decorative bath-tile floors, and rain showers (suites, fancy restaurant, bar with light bites, pay parking nearby, Station Square, tel. 01631/700-301, www.perleoban.co.uk, stay@perleoban.co.uk).

$$$ The Ranald is a modern change of pace from the B&B scene. This narrow, 17-room, three-floor hotel has a budget-boutique vibe; they also rent eight studio apartments on the same street (family rooms, bar, no elevator, street parking, a block behind the Royal Hotel at 41 Stevenson Street, tel. 01631/562-887, https:// theranaldhotel.com, info@theranaldhotel.com).

HOSTELS

¢ **Backpackers Plus** is central, laid-back, and fun. It fills part of a renovated old church with a sprawling public living room and a staff generous with travel tips. Check out the walls as you go up to the reception desk—they're covered with graffiti messages from guests (10-minute walk from station, on Breadalbane

Street, tel. 01631/567-189, www.backpackersplus.com, info@
backpackersplus.com, Peter). They have two other locations nearby
with private rooms.

¢ The official **SYHA hostel** is institutional but occupies a
grand building on the waterfront Esplanade with smashing views
of the harbor and islands from the lounges and dining rooms (all
rooms en suite, private rooms available, also has family rooms and
8-bed apartment with kitchen, bike storage, tel. 01631/562-025,
www.hostellingscotland.org.uk, oban@hostellingscotland.org.uk).

Eating in Oban

Oban brags that it is the "seafood capital of Scotland," and indeed
its sit-down restaurants are surprisingly high quality for such a
small town. For something more casual, consider a fish-and-chips
joint.

SIT-DOWN RESTAURANTS
These fill up in summer, especially on weekends. To ensure getting
a table, you'll want to book ahead. The first five are generally open
daily from 12:00-15:00 and 17:30-21:00.

$$$ Ee'usk (Scottish Gaelic for "fish") is a popular, stylish
seafood place on the waterfront. It has a casual-chic, yacht-clubby
atmosphere, with a bright and glassy interior and sweeping views
on three sides—fun for watching the ferries come and go. They
sometimes offer an early-bird special until 18:45, and their seafood
platters are a hit. Reservations are recommended (no kids under
age 12 at dinner, North Pier, tel. 01631/565-666, www.eeusk.com,
MacLeod family).

$$$ Cuan Mòr is a popular, casual restaurant that combines
traditional Scottish food with modern flair—both in its crowd-
pleasing cuisine and in its furnishings, made of wood, stone, and
metal scavenged from the beaches of Scotland's west coast (brewery in back, 60 George Street, tel. 01631/565-078, www.cuanmor.
co.uk). Its harborside tables on the sidewalk are popular when it's
warm.

$$$ Coast proudly serves fresh local fish, meat, and veggies in
a mod pine-and-candlelight atmosphere. As everything is cooked
to order and presented with care by husband-and-wife team Rich-
ard and Nicola—who try to combine traditional Scottish elements
in innovative new ways—this is no place to dine and dash (two-
and three-course specials, closed Sun for lunch, 104 George Street,
tel. 01631/569-900, www.coastoban.co.uk).

$$ Baab Grill brings a refreshing taste of the Eastern Mediterranean to Western Scotland. Besides the usual standbys (baba
ghanoush, tabbouleh, moussaka) the menu includes some "fu-

Scottish Highland Games

Throughout the summer, Highland communities host traditional festivals of local sport and culture. These Highland Games (sometimes called Highland Gatherings) combine the best elements of a track meet and a county fair. They range from huge and glitzy (such as Braemar's world-famous games, which the Queen attends, or the Cowal Highland Gathering, Scotland's biggest) to humble and small-town. Some of the more modern games come with loud pop music and corporate sponsorship, but still manage to celebrate the Highland spirit.

Most Highland Games take place between mid-June and late August (usually on Saturdays, but occasionally on weekdays). The games are typically a one-day affair, kicking off around noon and winding down in the late afternoon. At smaller games, you'll pay a nominal admission fee (typically around £5-7). Events are rain or shine (so bring layers) and take place in a big park ringed by a running track, with the heavy events and Highland dancing stage at opposite ends of the infield. Surrounding the whole scene are junk-food stands, a few test-your-skill carnival games, and local charities raising funds by selling hamburgers, fried sausage sandwiches, baked goods, and bottles of beer and Irn-Bru. The emcee's running commentary is a delightful opportunity to just sit back and enjoy a lilting Scottish accent.

The day's events typically kick off with a **pipe band** parading through town—often led by the local clan chieftain—and ending with a lap around the field. Then the sporting events begin.

In the **heavy events**—or feats of Highland strength—brawny, kilted athletes test their ability to hurl various objects of awkward shapes and sizes as far as possible. In the weight throw, competitors spin like ballerinas before releasing a 28- or 56-pound ball on a chain. The hammer throw involves a similar technique with a 26-pound ball on a long stick, and the stone put (with a 20- to 25-pound ball) has been adopted in American sports as the shot put. In the "weight over the bar" event, Highlanders swing a 56-pound weight over a horizontal bar that begins at 10 feet high and ends at closer to 15 feet. (That's like tossing a 5-year-old child over a double-decker bus.) And, of course, there's the caber toss: Pick up a giant log (the caber), get a running start, and release it end-over-end with enough force to (ideally) make the caber flip all the way over and land at the 12 o'clock position. (Most competitors wind up closer to 6.)

Meanwhile, the **track events** run circles around the muscle: the 90-meter dash, the 1,600-meter, and so on. The hill race adds a Scottish spin: Combine a several-mile footrace with the ascent of a nearby summit. The hill racers begin with a lap in the stadium before disappearing for about an hour. Keep an eye on nearby hillsides to pick out their colorful jerseys bobbing up and down a distant peak. This custom supposedly began when an 11th-century king staged a competition to select his personal letter carrier. After about an hour—when you've forgotten all about them—the hill racers start trickling back into the stadium to cross the finish line.

The **Highland dancing** is a highlight. Accompanied by a lone piper, the dancers (in groups of two to four) toe their routines

with intense concentration. Dancers remain always on the balls of their feet, requiring excellent balance and stamina. While some men participate, most competitors are female—from wee lassies barely out of nappies, all the way to poised professionals. Common steps are the Highland fling (in which the goal is to keep the feet as close as possible to one spot), sword dances (in which the dancers step gingerly over crossed swords on the stage), and a variety of national dances.

Other events further enliven the festivities. The pipe band periodically assembles to play a few tunes, often while marching around the track (giving the runners a break). Larger games may have a massing of multiple pipe bands, or bagpipe and drumming competitions. You may also see re-enactments of medieval battles, herd-dog demonstrations, or dog shows (grooming and obedience). Haggis hurling—in which participants stand on a whisky barrel and attempt to throw a cooked haggis as far as possible—has caught on recently. And many small-town events end with the grand finale of a town-wide tug-of-war, during which everybody gets bruised, muddy, and hysterical.

If you're traveling to Scotland in the summer, check online schedules to see if you'll be near any Highland Games before locking in your itinerary. Rather than target the big, famous gatherings, I make a point of visiting the smaller clan games. A helpful website—listing dates for most but not all of the games around Scotland—is www.shga.co.uk. For many travelers to Scotland, attending a Highland Games can be a trip-capping highlight. And, of course, many communities in the US and Canada also host their own Highland Games.

OBAN & INNER HEBRIDES

sion" dishes such as Scottish salmon in a tahini sauce (attached to the Perle Oban Hotel, no midday closure, Station Road, tel. 01631/707-130, www.baabgrill.co.uk).

$$ Piazza, next door to Ee'usk, is a casual, family-friendly place serving basic Italian dishes with a great harborfront location. They have some outdoor seats and big windows facing the sea (smart to reserve ahead July-Aug, tel. 01631/563-628, www.piazzaoban.com).

$$ Oban Fish and Chips Shop—run by Lewis, Sammy, and their family—serves praiseworthy haddock and mussels among other tasty options in a cheery cabana-like dining room. Consider venturing away from basic fish-and-chips into a world of more creative seafood dishes—like their tiny squat lobster. You can bring your own wine for no charge (daily, sit-down restaurant closes at 21:00, takeaway available later, 116 George Street, tel. 01631/569-828).

LUNCH

$ Oban Seafood Hut, in a green shack facing the ferry dock, is a finger-licking festival of cheap and fresh seafood. John and Marion regularly get fresh deliveries from local fishermen—this is the best spot to pick up a seafood sandwich or a snack. They sell smaller bites (such as cold sandwiches), as well as some bigger cold platters and a few hot dishes (outdoor seating only, daily from 10:00 until the boat unloads from Mull around 18:00).

$ Dolce Vita has a prime location on the main drag to sit outside when the sun shines. It does nice soups, sandwiches, and panini (daily 8:00-18:00, 62 George Street, tel. 01631/571-221).

Oban Connections

By Train: Trains link Oban to the nearest transportation hub in **Glasgow** (6/day, fewer on Sun, 3 hours); to get to **Edinburgh,** you'll transfer in Glasgow (roughly 6/day, 4.5 hours). To reach **Fort William** (a transit hub for the Highlands), you'll take the same Glasgow-bound train, but transfer in Crianlarich (3/day, 4 hours)—the direct bus is easier (see next). Oban's small train station has a ticket window and lockers (both open Mon-Sat 5:00-20:30, Sun 10:45-18:00, train info tel. 0845-748-4950, www.nationalrail.co.uk).

By Bus: Bus #918 passes through Ballachulish—a half-mile from **Glencoe**—on its way to **Fort William** (2/day, 1 hour to Ballachulish, 1.5 hours total to Fort William). Take this bus to Fort William, then transfer to reach **Inverness** (4 hours). A different bus (#976 or #977) connects Oban with **Glasgow** (5/day, 3 hours), from where you can easily connect by bus or train to **Edinburgh**

(figure 4.5 hours). Buses arrive and depart from a roundabout, marked by a stubby clock tower, just before the entrance to the train station (tel. 0871-266-3333, www.citylink.co.uk). You can buy bus tickets at the West Coast shop near the bus stop, or at the TI across the harbor. Book in advance during peak times.

By Boat: Ferries fan out from Oban to the **southern Hebrides** (see information on the islands of Iona and Mull, later). Caledonian MacBrayne Ferry info: Tel. 0800-066-5000, www.calmac.co.uk.

ROUTE TIPS FOR DRIVERS

From Glasgow to Oban via Loch Lomond and Inveraray: For details on this photogenic route from Glasgow to the coast, see the "Glasgow to Oban Scenic Drive" at the end of this chapter.

From Oban to Glencoe and Fort William: It's an easy one-hour drive from Oban to Glencoe. From Oban, follow the coastal A-828 toward Fort William. After about 20 miles—as you leave the village of Appin—you'll see the photogenic **Castle Stalker** marooned on a lonely island (you can pull over at the Castle Stalker View Café for a good photo from just below its parking lot). At North Ballachulish, you'll reach a bridge spanning Loch Leven; rather than crossing the bridge, turn off and follow the A-82 into the Glencoe Valley for about 15 minutes. (For tips on the best views and hikes in Glencoe, see the next chapter.) After exploring the dramatic valley, make a U-turn and return through Glencoe village. To continue on to Fort William, backtrack to the bridge at North Ballachulish (great view from bridge) and cross it, following the A-82 north.

For a scenic shortcut directly back to Glasgow or Edinburgh, continue south on the A-82 after Glencoe via Rannoch Moor and Tyndrum. Crianlarich is where the road splits, and you'll either continue on the A-82 toward Loch Lomond and Glasgow or pick up the A-85 and follow signs for Stirling, then Edinburgh.

OBAN & INNER HEBRIDES

Isles of Mull, Iona, and Staffa

For the easiest one-day look at a good sample of the dramatic and historic Inner Hebrides (HEB-rid-eez) islands, take a tour from Oban to Mull, Iona, and Staffa. Though this trip is spectacular when it's sunny, it's worthwhile in any weather (but if rain or rough seas are expected, I'd skip the Staffa option).

GETTING AROUND THE ISLANDS
Visiting Mull and Iona

To visit Mull and ultimately Iona, you'll take a huge ferry run by Caledonian MacBrayne (CalMac) from Oban to the town of Craignure on Mull (45 minutes). From there, you'll ride a bus or drive across Mull to its westernmost ferry terminal, called Fionnphort (1.25 hours), where you can catch the ferry to Iona (10 minutes) for several hours of free time. It's a long journey, but it's all incredibly scenic.

By Tour (Easiest): If you book a tour with **West Coast Tours**, all of the transportation is taken care of. The CalMac ferry leaves from the Oban pier daily at 9:50 (as schedule can change from year to year, confirm times locally; board at least 20 minutes before departure). You can buy tickets online at www. westcoasttours.co.uk, from the West Coast Tours office, or from the Tour Shop Oban at the ferry building (tel. 01631/562-244, tourshop@calmac.co.uk). Book as far in advance as possible for July and August (tickets can sell out). When you book, you'll receive a strip of tickets—one for each leg; if you book online, you must go to the West Coast Tours office and collect tickets in person (£39; April-Oct only, no tours Nov-March).

Tour Tips: The best inside seats on the **Oban-Mull ferry**—with the biggest windows—are in the sofa lounge on the "observation deck" (level 4) at the back end of the boat. (Follow signs for the toilets, and look for the big staircase to the top floor). The ferry has a fine cafeteria with hot meals and packaged sandwiches, a small snack bar on the top floor (hot drinks and basic sandwiches), and a bookshop. If it's a clear day, ask a local or a crew member to point out Ben Nevis, the tallest mountain in Britain. Five minutes before landing on Mull, you'll see the striking 13th-century Duart Castle on the left.

Walk-on passengers disembark from deck 3, across from the bookshop (port side). Upon arrival in Mull, find your **bus** for the entertaining and informative ride across the Isle of Mull. The right (driver's) side offers better sea views during the second half of the

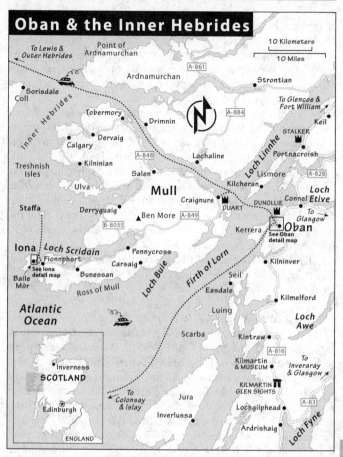

Oban & the Inner Hebrides

journey to Fionnphort, while the left side has fine views of Mull's rolling wilderness. The driver spends the entire ride chattering away about life on Mull, slowing to point out wildlife, and sharing adages like, "If there's no flowers on the gorse, snogging's gone out of fashion." These hardworking locals make historical trivia fascinating—or at least fun. At Fionnphort, you'll board a small, rocking **ferry to Iona.** You'll have about two hours to roam freely around the island before returning to Oban (arrives around 18:00).

By Public Transit: For an early start, fewer crowds, and more time on Iona (including spending the night—see "Sleeping and Eating on Iona"), or if don't get a space on the tour described earlier, you can take the early ferry and public bus across Mull, paying individually per leg (Tue-Sat only; approximate round-trip prices: £7.40 for Oban-Mull ferry, £15 for public bus across Mull, £3.50 for Mull-Iona ferry). Take the first boat of the day (departs about 7:30, buy ticket at Oban ferry terminal), then connect at Mull to bus #96 or #496 to Fionnphort (departs 8:25, 80 minutes, buy ticket from driver, no tour narration, no guarantee you'll get to sit), then hop on the Iona ferry (roughly every 30 minutes, buy ticket from small trailer ferry office; if closed, purchase ticket from ferry worker at the dock; cash or credit/debit cards accepted; leaving Iona, do the same, as there's no ferry office). You'll have about four hours on Iona and will need to return to Fionnphort in time for the bus back (15:15). It's important to confirm all of these times in Oban (just pop in to the West Coast Tours office or the ferry terminal Tour Shop).

By Car: You can do this trip on your own by driving your car onto the ferry to Mull. Space is limited so book way in advance. Keep in mind that because of tight ferry timings, you'll wind up basically following the tour buses anyway, but you'll miss all of the commentary. Note that no visitor cars are allowed on Iona (£27.50 round-trip for the car, plus passengers, www.calmac.co.uk).

By Taxi: Alan from **Mull Taxi** can get you around his home island, and also offers day trips (tel. 07760/426-351, www.mulltaxi.co.uk).

Visiting Staffa

With two extra hours, you can add a Staffa side trip to your Mull/Iona visit. You'll ferry from Oban to Mull, take a bus across Mull to Fionnphort, then board a **Staffa Tours** boat (35-minute trip, about an hour of free time on Staffa). From Staffa you'll head to Iona for about two hours before returning to Mull for the bus then ferry back to Oban. You can either depart Oban on the 9:50 ferry, arriving back to Oban around 20:05; or do the "early bird" tour, departing at 7:30 and returning at 18:00 (£35 for the Staffa portion, daily; book through West Coast Tours or Staffa Tours—mobile 07831-885-985, www.staffatours.com).

For a more relaxed schedule, **Staffa Trips** offers a guided tour with the same route described above, but with more time on Staffa and Iona (£35, daily, depart Fionnphort at 10:30, tel. 01681/700-358, www.staffatrips.co.uk).

Turus Mara offers nature/wildlife tours to just Staffa or Staffa and the small island of Ulva, departing from Oban (book at Tour Shop at Oban ferry terminal or contact Turus Mara—tel. 01688/400-242, www.turusmara.com).

Mull

The Isle of Mull, the second-largest of the Inner Hebrides (after Skye), has nearly 300 scenic miles of coastline and castles and a 3,169-foot-high mountain, one of Scotland's Munros. Called Ben More ("Big Mountain" in Gaelic), it was once much bigger. At 10,000 feet tall,

it made up the entire island of Mull—until a volcano erupted. Things are calmer now, and, similarly, Mull has a noticeably laid-back population. My bus driver reported that there are no deaths from stress, and only a few from boredom.

With steep, fog-covered hillsides topped by cairns (piles of stones, sometimes indicating graves) and ancient stone circles, Mull has a gloomy, otherworldly charm. Bring plenty of rain protection and wear layers in case the sun peeks through the clouds. As my driver said, Mull is a place of cold, wet, windy winters and mild, wet, windy summers.

On the far side of Mull, the caravan of tour buses unloads at Fionnphort, a tiny ferry town. The ferry to the island of Iona takes about 200 walk-on passengers. Confirm the return time with your bus driver, then hustle to the dock to make the first trip over (otherwise, it's a 30-minute wait; on very busy days, those who dillydally may not fit on the first ferry). At the dock, there's a small ferry-passenger building with a meager snack bar and a pay WC; a more enticing seafood bar is across the street. After the 10-minute ride, you wash ashore on sleepy Iona (free WC on this side), and the ferry mobs that crowded you on the boat seem to disappear up the main road and into Iona's back lanes.

Iona

The tiny island of Iona, just 3 miles by 1.5 miles, is famous as the birthplace of Christianity in Scotland. If you're on the West Coast

Tours bus trip from Oban outlined earlier, you'll have about two hours here on your own before you retrace your steps (your bus driver will tell you which return ferry to take back to Mull).

A pristine quality of light and a thoughtful peace pervades the stark, (nearly) car-free island and its tiny community. With buoyant clouds bouncing playfully off distant bluffs, sparkling-white crescents of sand, and lone tourists camped thoughtfully atop huge rocks just looking out to sea, Iona is a place that's perfect for meditation. To experience Iona, it's important to get out and take a little hike; you can follow some or all of my self-guided walk outlined later.

And you can easily climb a peak—nothing's higher than 300 feet above the sea.

Orientation to Iona

The ferry arrives at the island's only real village, Baile Mòr, with shops, a restaurant/pub, a few accommodations, and no bank (get cash back with a purchase at the grocery store). The only taxi based on Iona is **Iona Taxi** (mobile 07810-325-990, www.ionataxi.co.uk). Up the road from the ferry dock is a little **Spar** grocery with free island maps. Iona's official website (www.isle-of-iona.net) has good information about the island.

Iona Walk

Here's a basic self-guided route for exploring Iona on foot (since no private cars are permitted unless you're a resident or have a permit). With the standard two hours on Iona that a day trip allows, you will have time for a visit to the abbey (with a guided tour and/or audioguide) and then a light stroll; or do the entire walk described below, but skip the abbey (unless you have time for a quick visit on your way back).

Nunnery Ruins: From the ferry dock, head directly up the single paved road that passes through the village and up a small hill to visit one of Britain's best-preserved medieval nunneries (free).

Immediately after the nunnery, turn right on North Road. You'll curve up through the fields—passing the parish church.

Heritage Center: This little museum, tucked behind the church (watch for signs), is small but well done, with displays on local and natural history and a tiny tearoom (free but donation requested, closed Sun and in off-season, tel. 01681/700-576, www.ionaheritage.co.uk).

St. Oran's Chapel and Iona Abbey: Continue on North Road. After the road swings right, you'll soon see **St. Oran's Chapel,** in the graveyard of the Iona Abbey. This chapel is the oldest church building on the island. Inside you'll find a few grave slabs carved in the distinctive Iona School style, which was developed by local stone-carvers in the 14th century. On these tall, skinny headstones, look for the depictions of medieval warrior aristocrats with huge swords. Many more of these carvings have

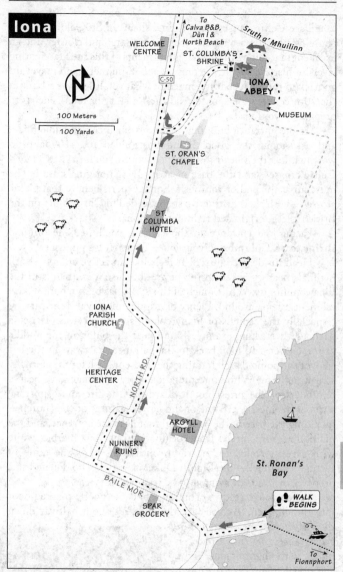

been moved to the abbey, where you can see them in its cloister and museum.

It's free to see the graveyard and chapel; the ▲ **Iona Abbey** itself has an admission fee, but it's worth the cost just to sit in the stillness of its lovely, peaceful interior courtyard (£9, tel. 01681/700-512, www.historicenvironment.scot—search for "Iona Abbey").

The abbey marks the site of Christianity's arrival in Scotland.

You'll see Celtic crosses, the original shrine of St. Columba, a big church slathered with medieval carvings, a tranquil cloister, and an excellent museum with surviving fragments of this site's fascinating layers of history. While the present abbey, nunnery, and graveyard go back to the 13th century, much of what you'll see was rebuilt in the 20th century. Be sure to read the "History of Iona" sidebar to prepare for your visit.

At the entrance building, pick up your included audioguide, and ask about the good 30-minute guided tours (4/day and worthwhile). Then head toward the church. You'll pass two faded **Celtic crosses** (and the base of a third); the originals are in the museum at the end of your visit. Some experts believe that Celtic crosses—with their distinctive shape so tied to Christianity on the British Isles—originated right here on Iona.

Facing the entrance to the church, you'll see the original **shrine to St. Columba** on your left—a magnet for pilgrims.

Head inside the **church.** It feels like an active church—with hymnals neatly stacked in the pews—because it is, thanks to the Iona community. While much of this space has been rebuilt, take a moment to look around. Plenty of original medieval stone carving (especially the capitals of many columns) still survives. To see a particularly striking example, stand near the pulpit in the middle of the church and look back to the entrance. Partway up the left span of the pointed arch framing the transept, look for the eternally screaming face. While interpretations vary, this may have been a reminder for the priest not to leave out the fire-and-brimstone parts of his message. Some of the newer features of the church— including the base of the baptismal font near the entrance, and the main altar—are carved from locally quarried Iona marble: white with green streaks. In the right/south transept is the tomb of George Campbell—the Eighth Duke of Argyll, who donated this property in 1900, allowing it to be restored.

When you're ready to continue, find the poorly marked door into the **cloister.** (As you face the altar, it's about halfway down the nave on the left, before the transept.) This space is filled with harmonious light, additional finely carved capitals (these are modern re-creations), and—displayed along the walls—several more of the tall, narrow tombstones like the ones displayed in St. Oran's Chapel. On these, look for a couple of favorite motifs: the long, intimidating sword (indicating a warrior

History of Iona

St. Columba (521-597), an Irish scholar, soldier, priest, and founder of monasteries, got into a small war over the posses-

sion of an illegally copied psalm book. Victorious but sickened by the bloodshed, Columba left Ireland, vowing never to return. According to legend, the first bit of land out of sight of his homeland was Iona. He stopped here in 563 and established an abbey.

Columba's monastic community flourished, and Iona became the center of Celtic Christianity. Missionaries from Iona spread the gospel throughout Scotland and northern England, while scholarly monks established Iona as a center of art and learning. The Book of Kells—perhaps the finest piece of manuscript art from early medieval Europe—was probably made on Iona in the eighth century. The island was so important that it was the legendary burial place for ancient Scottish clan chieftains and kings (including Macbeth, of Shakespeare fame) and even some Scandinavian monarchs.

Slowly, the importance of Iona ebbed. Vikings massacred 68 monks in 806. Fearing more raids, the monks evacuated most of Iona's treasures to Ireland (including the Book of Kells, which is now in Dublin). Much later, with the Reformation, the abbey was abandoned, and most of its finely carved crosses were destroyed. In the 17th century, locals used the abbey only as a handy quarry for other building projects.

Iona's population peaked at about 500 in the 1830s. In the 1840s, a potato famine hit, and in the 1850s, a third of the islanders emigrated to Canada or Australia. By 1900, the population was down to 210, and today it's only around 200.

But in our generation, a new religious community has given the abbey fresh life. The Iona Community is an ecumenical gathering of men and women who seek new ways of living the Gospel in today's world, with a focus on worship, peace and justice issues, and reconciliation (http://iona.org.uk).

OBAN & INNER HEBRIDES

of the Highland clans) and the ship with billowing sails (a powerful symbol of this seafaring culture).

Around the far side of the cloister is the shop. But before leaving, don't overlook the easy-to-miss **museum.** (To find it, head outside and walk around the left side of the abbey complex, toward the sea.) This modern, well-presented space exhibits a remarkable collection of original stonework from the abbey—including what's left of the three Celtic crosses out front—all eloquently described.

Iona Community's Welcome Centre: Just beyond and across the road from the abbey is the Iona Community's Welcome Centre (free WCs), which runs the abbey with Historic Scotland and hosts modern-day pilgrims who come here to experience the birthplace of Scottish Christianity. (If you're staying longer, you could attend a worship service at the abbey—check the schedule here; tel. 01681/700-404, www.iona.org.uk.) Its gift shop is packed with books on the island's important role in Christian history.

Views: A 10-minute walk on North Road past the welcome center brings you to the footpath for **Dùn Ì**, a steep but short climb with good views of the abbey looking back toward Mull.

North Beach: Returning to the main road, walk another 20-25 minutes to the end of the paved road, where you'll arrive at a gate leading through a sheep- and cow-strewn pasture to Iona's pristine white-sand beach. Dip your toes in the Atlantic and ponder what this Caribbean-like alcove is doing in Scotland. Be sure to allow at least 40 minutes to return to the ferry dock.

Sleeping and Eating on Iona

For a chance to really experience peaceful, idyllic Iona, spend a night or two (Scots bring their kids and stay on this tiny island for a week). To do so, you'll have to buy each leg of the ferry-bus-ferry (and return) trip separately (see "By Public Transit," earlier). These accommodations are listed roughly in the order you'll reach them as you climb the main road from the ferry dock. The first two hotels listed have **$$$** restaurants that are open to the public for lunch, tea, and dinner and closed in winter. For more accommodation options, see Isle-of-Iona.net/accommodation.

$$$ Argyll Hotel, built in 1867, proudly overlooks the waterfront, with 17 cottage-like rooms and pleasingly creaky hallways lined with bookshelves. Of the two hotels, this one feels classier (reserve far in advance for summer, comfortable lounge and sunroom, tel. 01681/700-334, www.argyllhoteliona.co.uk, reception@argyllhoteliona.co.uk).

$$$ St. Columba Hotel, a bit higher up in town and situated in the middle of a peaceful garden with picnic tables, has 27 institutional rooms and spacious lodge-like common spaces—such as a big, cushy seaview lounge (closed Nov-March, next door to abbey on road up from dock, tel. 01681/700-304, www.stcolumba-hotel.co.uk, info@stcolumba-hotel.co.uk).

$$ Calva B&B, a five-minute walk past the abbey, has three spacious rooms (second house on left past the abbey, look for sign in window and gnomes on porch, tel. 01681/700-340; friendly Janetta and Ken).

Staffa

Those more interested in nature than in church history will enjoy the trip to the wildly scenic Isle of Staffa. Completely uninhabited (except for seabirds), Staffa is a knob of rock draped with a vibrant green carpet of turf. Remote and quiet, it feels like a Hebrides nature preserve.

Most day trips give you an hour on Staffa—barely enough time to see its two claims to fame: The basalt columns of Fingal's Cave, and (in summer) a colony of puffins. To squeeze in both, be ready to hop off the boat and climb the staircase. Partway up to the left, you can walk around to the cave (about 7 minutes). Or continue up to the top, then turn right and walk across the spine of the grassy island (about 10-15 minutes) to the cove where the puffins gather. Be sure to get clear instructions from your captain on how and where to best watch the puffins. It's worth doing right.

▲▲Fingal's Cave

Staffa's shore is covered with bizarre, mostly hexagonal basalt columns that stick up at various heights. It's as if the earth were offering God his choice of thousands of six-sided cigarettes. (The island's name likely came from the Old Norse word for "stave"— the building timbers these columns resemble.) This is the other end of Northern Ireland's popular Giant's Causeway. You'll walk along the uneven surface of these columns, curling around the far side of the island, until you can actually step inside the gaping mouth of a cave—where floor-to-ceiling columns and crashing waves combine to create a powerful experience. Listening to the water and air flowing through this otherworldly space inspired Felix Mendelssohn to compose his overture, *The Hebrides*.

While you're ogling the cave, consider this: Geologists claim these unique formations were created by volcanic eruptions more than 60 million years ago. As the surface of the lava flow quick-

Puffins

The Atlantic puffin (Fratercula arctica) is an adorably stout, tuxedo-clad seabird with a too-big orange beak and beady black eyes. Puffins live most of their lives on the open Atlantic, coming to land only to breed. They fly north to Scotland between mid-May and early June, raise their brood, then take off again in August. Puffins mate for life and typically lay just one egg each year, which the male and female take turns caring for. A baby puffin is called—wait for it—a puffling.

To feed their pufflings, puffins plunge as deep as 200 feet below the sea's surface to catch sand eels, herring, and other small fish. Their compact bodies, stubby wings, oil-sealed plumage, and webbed feet are ideal for navigating underwater. Famously, puffins can stuff several small fish into their beaks at once, thanks to their agile tongues and uniquely hinged beaks. This evolutionary trick lets puffins stock up before returning to the nest.

Squat, tiny-winged puffins have a distinctive way of flying. To take off, they either beat their wings like crazy (on sea) or essentially hurl themselves off a cliff (on land). Once aloft, they beat their wings furiously—up to 400 times per minute—to stay airborne. Coming in for a smooth landing on a rocky cliff is a challenge (and highly entertaining to watch): They choose a spot, swoop in at top speed on prevailing currents, then flutter their wings madly to brake as they try to touch down. At the moment of truth, the puffin decides whether to attempt to stick the landing; more often than not, he bails out and does another big circle on the currents...and tries again... and again...and again.

ly cooled, it contracted and crystallized into columns (resembling the caked mud at the bottom of a dried-up lakebed, but with deeper cracks). As the rock later settled and eroded, the columns broke off into the many stair-like steps that now honeycomb Staffa.

Of course, in actuality, these formations resulted from a heated rivalry between a Scottish giant named Fingal, who lived on Staffa, and an Ulster warrior named Finn MacCool, who lived across the sea on Ireland's Antrim Coast. Knowing that the giant was coming to spy on him, Finn had his wife dress him as a sleeping infant. The giant, shocked at the infant's size, fled back to Scotland in terror of whomever had sired this giant baby. Breathing a sigh of relief, Finn tore off the baby clothes and prudently knocked down the bridge.

▲▲Puffin Watching

A large colony of Atlantic puffins settles on Staffa each spring and summer during mating season (generally early May through early August). The puffins tend to scatter when the boat arrives. But after the boat pulls out and its passengers hike across the island, the very tame puffins' curiosity gets the better of them. First you'll see them flutter up from the offshore rocks, with their distinctive, bobbing flight. They'll zip and whirl around, and finally they'll start to land on the lip of the cove. Sit quietly, move slowly, and be patient, and soon they'll get close. (If any seagulls are nearby, shoo them away—puffins are undaunted by humans, who do them no harm, but they're terrified of predator seagulls.)

In the waters around Staffa—on your way to and from the other islands—also keep an eye out for a variety of **marine life**, including seals, dolphins, porpoises, and the occasional minke whale, fin whale, or basking shark (a gigantic fish that hinges open its enormous jaw to drift-net plankton).

Glasgow to Oban Drive

The following drive outlines the best route from Glasgow to Oban, including the appealing town of Inveraray, with an optional stop at one of Scotland's most important prehistoric sites, Kilmartin Glen.

GLASGOW TO OBAN VIA INVERARAY

The drive from Glasgow (or Edinburgh) to Oban via Inveraray provides dreamy vistas and your first look at the dramatic landscapes of the Highlands, as well as historic sites and ample opportunity to stop for a picnic.

• *Leaving Glasgow on the A-82, you'll soon be driving along the west bank of...*

OBAN & INNER HEBRIDES

Loch Lomond

The first picnic turnout has the best views of this famous lake, benches, a park, and a playground.

Twenty-four miles long and speckled with islands, Loch Lomond is Great Britain's biggest lake by surface area, and second in volume only to Loch Ness. Thanks largely to its easy proximity to Glasgow (about 15 miles away), this scenic lake is a favorite retreat for Scots as well as foreign tourists. The southernmost of the Munros, Ben Lomond (3,196 feet), looms over the eastern bank.

Loch Lomond's biggest claim to fame is its role in a beloved folk song: "Ye'll take the high road, and I'll take the low road, and I'll be in Scotland afore ye... For me and my true love will never meet again, on the bonnie, bonnie banks of Loch Lomond." As you'll now be humming that all day (you're welcome), here's one interpretation of the song's poignant meaning: Celtic culture believes that fairies return the souls of the deceased to their homeland through the soil. After the disastrous Scottish loss at the Battle of Culloden, Jacobite ringleaders were arrested and taken for trial in faraway London. In some cases, accused pairs were given a choice: One of you will die, and the other will live. The song is a bittersweet reassurance, sung from the condemned to the survivor, that the soon-to-be-deceased will take the spiritual "low road" back to his Scottish homeland—where his soul will be reunited with the living, who will return on the physical "high road" (over land).

You're driving over an isthmus between Loch Lomond and a sea inlet. Halfway up the loch, you'll find the town of Tarbet—the Viking word for isthmus, a common name on Scottish maps. Imagine, a thousand years ago, Vikings dragging their ships across this narrow stretch of land to reach Loch Lomond.

• At Tarbet, the road forks. The signs for Oban keep you on the direct route along A-82. For the scenic option that takes you past Loch Fyne to Inveraray (about 30 minutes longer to drive), keep left for the A-83 (toward Campbeltown).

Highland Boundary Fault

You'll pass the village of **Arrochar,** then drive along the banks of Loch Long. The scenery crescendos as you pull away from the loch and twist up over the mountains and through a pine forest, getting your first glimpse of bald Highlands mountains—it's clear that you've just crossed the **Highland Boundary Fault.** Enjoy the waterfalls, and notice that the road signs are now in English as well as Gaelic. As you climb into more rugged territory—up the valley called Glen Croe—be mindful that the roads connecting the Lowlands with the Highlands (like the one down in the glen below) were originally a military project designed to facilitate government quelling of the Highland clans.

• *At the summit, watch for the large parking lot with picnic tables on your left (signed for Argyll Forest Park). Stretch your legs at what's aptly named...*

Rest-and-Be-Thankful Pass

The colorful name comes from the 19th century, when just reaching this summit was exhausting. At the top of the military road, just past the last picnic table, there's actually a stone dated 1814 put there by the military with that phrase.

As you drive on, enjoy the dramatic green hills. You may see little bits of hillside highlighted by sunbeams. Each of these is known as a "soot" (Sun's Out Over There). Look for soots as you drive farther north into the Highlands.

• *Continue twisting down the far side of the pass. You'll drive through Glen Kinglas and soon reach...*

Loch Fyne

This saltwater "sea loch" is famous for its shellfish (keep an eye out for oyster farms and seafood restaurants). In fact, Loch Fyne is the namesake of a popular UK restaurant chain with locations across the UK. **$$$$ Loch Fyne Oyster Bar and Deli,** in the big white building at the end of the loch, is the original. It's a famous stop for locals—an elegant seafood restaurant and oyster bar worth traveling for. If the restaurant is full, order from the bar menu (about the same as the restaurant) and grab more casual seating (open daily from 9:00, last order at 17:45, no reservations, tel. 01499/600-482, www. lochfyne.com). Even if you're not eating, it's fun to peruse their salty deli (tasty treats to go, picnic tables outside, good coffee).

• *Looping around Loch Fyne, you approach Inveraray. As you get close, keep an eye on the right (when crossing the bridge, have your camera ready) for the dramatic...*

▲Inveraray Castle

This residence of the Duke of Argyll comes with a dramatic, turreted exterior (one of Scotland's most striking) and an interior that feels spacious, neatly tended, and lived in. Historically a stronghold of one of the more notorious branches of the Campbell clan, this castle is most appealing to those with Campbell connections or fans of *Downton Abbey.*

OBAN & INNER HEBRIDES

The Irish Connection

The Romans called the people living in what is now Ireland the "Scoti" (meaning pirates). When the Scoti crossed the narrow Irish Sea and invaded the land of the Picts 1,500 years ago, that region became known as Scoti-land. Ireland and Scotland were never fully conquered by the Romans, and they retained similar clannish Celtic traits. Both share the same Gaelic branch of the linguistic tree.

On clear summer days, you can actually see Ireland—just 17 miles away—from the Scottish coastline. The closest bit to Scotland is the boomerang-shaped Rathlin Island, part of Northern Ireland. Rathlin is where Scottish leader Robert the Bruce retreated in 1307 after defeat at the hands of the English. Legend has it that he hid in a cave on the island, where he observed a spider patiently rebuilding its web each time a breeze knocked it down. Inspired by the spider's perseverance, Bruce gathered his Scottish forces once more and finally defeated the English at the decisive battle of Bannockburn (see page 752).

Flush with confidence from his victory, Robert the Bruce decided to open a second front against the English...in Ireland. In 1315, he sent his brother Edward over to enlist their Celtic Irish cousins in an effort to thwart the English. After securing Ireland, Edward hoped to move on and enlist the Welsh, thus cornering England with their pan-Celtic nation. But Edward's timing was bad: Ireland was in the midst of famine. His Scottish troops had to live off the land and began to take food and supplies from the starving Irish. Some of Ireland's crops may have been intentionally destroyed to keep it from being used as a colonial "breadbasket" to feed English troops. The Scots quickly wore out their welcome, and Edward the Bruce was eventually killed in battle near Dundalk in 1318.

It's interesting to imagine how things might be different today if Scotland and Ireland had been permanently welded together as a nation 700 years ago. You'll notice the strong Scottish influence in Northern Ireland when you ask a local a question and he answers, "Aye, a wee bit." And in Glasgow—near Scotland's west coast,

closest to Ireland—an Ireland-like division between royalist Protestants and republican Catholics survives today in the form of soccer team allegiances. In big Scottish cities (like Glasgow and Edinburgh), you'll even see "orange parades" of protesters marching in solidarity with their Protestant Northern Irish cousins. The Irish—always quick to defuse tension with humor—joke that the Scots are just Irish people who couldn't swim home.

Cost and Hours: £12.50, daily 10:00-17:45, closed Nov-March, last entry 45 minutes before closing, nice basement café, buy tickets at the car park booth, tel. 01499/302-551, www.inveraray-castle.com).

Visiting the Castle: Roam from room to room, reading the laminated descriptions and asking questions of the gregarious

docents. The highlight is the Armory Hall that fills the main atrium, where swords and rifles are painstakingly arrayed in starburst patterns. The rifles were actually used when the Campbells fought with the British at the Battle of Culloden in 1746.

Upstairs is a room with reminders of *Downton Abbey*. Public-television fans may recognize this as "Duneagle Castle" (a.k.a. Uncle Shrimpy's pad) from one of the *Downton Abbey* Christmas specials—big photos of the Grantham and MacClare clans decorate the genteel rooms.

As with many such castles, the aristocratic clan still lives here (*private* signs mark rooms where the family resides). Another upstairs room is like an Argyll family scrapbook; for example, see photos of the duke playing elephant polo—the ultimate aristocratic sport. The kids attend school in England, but spend a few months here each year; in the winter, the castle is closed to the public and they have the run of the place. After touring the interior, do a loop through the finely manicured gardens

• *After visiting the castle, spend some time exploring...*

▲Inveraray Town

Nearly everybody stops at this lovely, seemingly made-for-tourists town on Loch Fyne. Browse the main street—lined with touristy shops and cafés all the way to the church at its top. As this is the geological and demographic border between the Highlands and the Lowlands, traditionally church services here were held in both Scots and Gaelic. Just before the church is Loch Fyne Whiskies with historic bottles on its ceiling.

There's free parking on the main street and plenty of pay-and-display parking near the pier (TI open daily, on Front Street, tel. 01499/302-063; public WCs at end of nearby pier).

The **Inveraray Jail** is the main site in town—an overpriced, corny, but mildly educational former jail converted into a museum. This "living 19th-century prison" includes a courtroom where mannequins argue the fate of the accused. Then you'll head outside and explore the various cells of the outer courtyard. The

OBAN & INNER HEBRIDES

playful guards may lock you up for a photo op while they explain how Scotland reformed its prison system in 1839—you'll see both "before" and "after" cells in this complex (£12.25, includes 75-minute audioguide, open daily, tel. 01499/302-381, www.inveraryjail.co.uk).

• *To continue directly to Oban from Inveraray (about an hour), leave town through the gate at the woolen mill and get on the A-819, which takes you through Glen Aray and along the aptly named Loch Awe. A left turn on the A-85 takes you into Oban.*

But if you have a healthy interest in prehistoric sites, you can go to Oban by way of Kilmartin Glen (adds about 45 minutes of driving). To get there from Inveraray, head straight up Inveraray's main street and get on the waterfront A-83 (marked for Campbeltown); after a half-hour, in Lochgilphead, turn right onto the A-816, which takes you through Kilmartin Glen and all the way up to Oban. (To avoid backtracking, be ready to stop at the prehistoric sites lining the A-816 between Lochgilphead and Kilmartin village.)

Kilmartin Glen

Except for the Orkney Islands, Scotland isn't as rich with prehistoric sites as South England is, but the ones in Kilmartin Glen, while faint, are some of Scotland's most accessible—and most important. This wide valley, clearly imbued with spiritual and/or strategic power, contains reminders of several millennia's worth of inhabitants. Today it's a playground for those who enjoy tromping through grassy fields while daydreaming about who moved these giant stones here so many centuries ago. This isn't worth a long detour, unless you're fascinated by prehistoric sites.

Four to five thousand years ago, Kilmartin Glen was inhabited by Neolithic people who left behind fragments of their giant, stony monuments. And 1,500 years ago, this was the seat of the kings of the Scoti, who migrated here from Ireland around AD 500, giving rise to Scotland's own branch of Celtic culture. From this grassy valley, the Scoti kings ruled their empire, called Dalriada (also sometimes written Dál Riata), which encompassed much of Scotland's west coast, the Inner Hebrides, and the northern part of Ireland. The Scoti spoke Gaelic and were Christian; as they overtook the rest of the Highlands—

eventually absorbing their rival Picts—theirs became a dominant culture, which is still evident in pockets of present-day Scotland.

Today, Kilmartin Glen is scattered with burial cairns, standing stones, and a hill called Dunadd—the fortress of the Scoti kings.

Visiting Kilmartin Glen: Sites are scattered throughout the valley, including some key locations along or just off the A-816 south of Kilmartin village. If you're coming from Inveraray, you'll pass these *before* you reach the village and museum itself. Each one is explained by good informational signs.

Dunadd: This bulbous hill sits just west of the A-816, about four miles north of Lochgilphead and four miles south of Kilmartin village (watch for blue, low-profile *Dunadd Fort* signs). A fort had stood here since the time of Christ, but it was the Scoti kings—who made it their primary castle from the sixth to ninth centuries—that put Dunadd on the map. Park in the big lot at its base and hike through the faint outlines of terraces to the top, where you can enjoy sweeping views over all of Kilmartin Glen; this southern stretch is a marshland called "The Great Moss" (Moine Mhor). Look for carvings in the rock: early Celtic writing, the image of a boar, and a footprint (carved into a stone crisscrossed with fissures). This "footprint of fealty" (a replica) recalls the inauguration ceremony in which the king would place his foot into the footprint, symbolizing the marriage between the ruler and the land.

Dunchraigaig Cairn: About two miles farther north on the A-816, brown *Dunchraigaig* signs mark a parking lot where you can cross the road to the 4,000-year-old, 100-foot-in-diameter Dunchraigaig Cairn—the burial place for 10 Neolithic VIPs. Circle around to find the opening, where you can still crawl into a small recess. This is one of at least five such cairns that together created a mile-and-a-half-long "linear cemetery" up the middle of Kilmartin Glen.

From this cairn, you can walk five minutes to several more prehistoric structures: Follow signs through the gate, and walk to a farm field with **Ballymeanoch**—an avenue of two stone rows (with six surviving stones), a disheveled old cairn, and a stone circle.

Sites near Kilmartin Burn: About one more mile north on the A-816, just off the intersection with the B-8025 (toward *Tayvallich*), is the small Kilmartin Burn parking lot. From here, cross the stream to a field where the five **Nether Largie Standing Stones** have stood in a neat north-south line for 3,200 years. Were these stones designed as an astronomical observatory? Burial rituals or other religious ceremonies? Sporting events? Or just a handy place for sheep to scratch themselves? From here, you can hike the rest of the way through the field (about 10 minutes) to the **Nether Largie South Cairn** and the **Temple Wood Stone Circles** (which don't have their own parking). The larger, older of these circles dates to more than 5,000 years ago, and both were added onto and modified over the millennia.

Kilmartin Museum: To get the big picture, head for the Kilmartin Museum, in the center of Kilmartin village. The cute stone house has a ticket desk, bookshop, and café; the museum—with exhibits explaining this area's powerful history—fills the basement of the adjacent building (though a new home for the exhibit is in the works). The modest but modern museum features handy explanations, a few original artifacts, and lots of re-creations (£7, daily, closed Christmas-Feb, tel. 01546/510-278, www.kilmartin.org).

From the museum, you can look out across the fields to see **Glebe Cairn,** one of the five cairns of the "linear cemetery." Another one, the **Nether Largie North Cairn,** was reconstructed in the 1970s and can actually be entered (a half-mile south of the museum; ask for directions at museum).

Many more prehistoric sites fill Kilmartin Glen (more than 800 within a six-mile radius); the museum sells in-depth guidebooks for the curious, and can point you in the right direction for what you're interested in.

GLENCOE & FORT WILLIAM

Scotland is a land of great natural wonders. And some of the most spectacular—and most accessible—are in the valley called Glencoe, just an hour north of Oban and on the way to Fort William, Loch Ness, or Inverness. The evocative "Weeping Glen" of Glencoe aches with both history and natural beauty. Beyond that, Fort William anchors the southern end of the Caledonian Canal, offering a springboard to more Highlands scenery. This is where Britain's highest peak, Ben Nevis, keeps its head in the clouds.

PLANNING YOUR TIME

On a quick visit, this area warrants just a few hours between Oban and Inverness: Wander through Glencoe village, tour its modest museum, then drive up Glencoe valley for views before continuing north. But if you have only a day or two to linger in the Highlands, Glencoe is an ideal place to do it. Settle in for a night (or more) to make time for a more leisurely drive and to squeeze in a hike or two.

Beyond Glencoe, Fort William—a touristy and overrated transportation hub—is skippable, but can be a handy lunch stop.

Glencoe

This valley is the essence of the wild, powerful, and stark beauty of the Highlands. Along with its scenery, Glencoe offers a good dose of bloody clan history: In 1692, government Redcoats (led by a local Campbell commander) came to the valley, and were sheltered and fed for 12 days by the MacDonalds—whose leader had

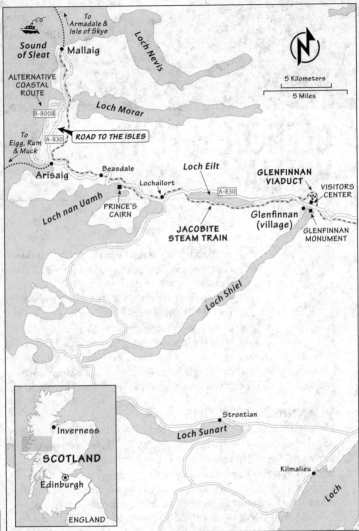

been late in swearing an oath to the British monarch. Then, on the morning of February 13, the soldiers were ordered to rise up early and kill their sleeping hosts, violating the rules of Highland hospitality and earning the valley the nickname "The Weeping Glen." Thirty-eight men were killed outright; hundreds more fled through a blizzard, and some 40 additional villagers (mostly women and children) died from exposure. It's fitting that such an epic, dramatic incident—dubbed the Glencoe Massacre—should be set in this equally epic, dramatic valley, where the cliffsides seem to weep (with running streams) when it rains.

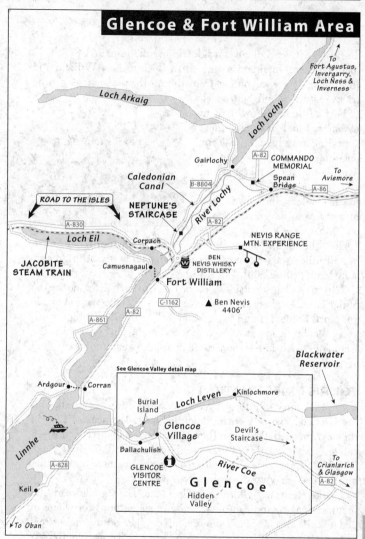

Glencoe & Fort William Area

To Fort Agustus, Invergarry, Loch Ness & Inverness

Loch Arkaig

Loch Lochy

Gairlochy

COMMANDO MEMORIAL

A-82

Caledonian Canal

B-8804

Spean Bridge

To Aviemore

A-86

River Lochy

ROAD TO THE ISLES

A-830

NEPTUNE'S STAIRCASE

A-82

Loch Eil

Corpach

NEVIS RANGE MTN. EXPERIENCE

JACOBITE STEAM TRAIN

Camusnagaul

BEN NEVIS WHISKY DISTILLERY

Fort William

A-861

A-82

C-1162

▲ Ben Nevis 4406'

Blackwater Reservoir

See Glencoe Valley detail map

Ardgour · · · · Corran

Burial Island

Loch Leven

Kinlochmore

Glencoe Village

Devil's Staircase

Linnhe

A-828

Ballachulish

GLENCOE VISITOR CENTRE

River Coe

G l e n c o e

To Crianlarich & Glasgow

A-82

Keil

Hidden Valley

To Oban

GLENCOE & FORT WILLIAM

Aside from its tragic history, this place has captured the imaginations of both hikers and artists. Movies filmed here include everything from *Monty Python and the Holy Grail* to *Harry Potter and the Prisoner of Azkaban* and the James Bond film *Skyfall*, and Glencoe appears in the opening credits of the TV series *Outlander*. When filmmakers want a stunning, rugged backdrop; when hikers want a scenic challenge; and when Scots want to remember their hard-fought past...they all think of Glencoe.

Orientation to Glencoe

The valley of Glencoe is an easy side trip just off the main A-828/A-82 road between Oban and points north (such as Fort William and Inverness). If you're coming from the north, the signage can be tricky—at the roundabout south of Fort William, follow signs to *Crianlarich* and *A-82*. The most appealing town here is the sleepy one-street village of Glencoe, worth a stop for its folk museum and its status as the gateway to the valley. The town's hub of activity is its grocery store, which has an ATM (daily 8:00-19:30). The slightly larger and more modern town of Ballachulish (a half-mile away) has more services, including a Co-op grocery store (daily 7:00-22:00).

In the loch just outside Glencoe (near Ballachulish), notice the burial island—where the souls of those who "take the low road" are piped home. (For an explanation of "Ye'll take the high road, and I'll take the low road," see page 944.) The next island was the Island of Discussion—where those in dispute went until they found agreement.

TOURIST INFORMATION

Your best source of information (especially for walks and hikes) is the **Glencoe Visitor Centre**, described later. The nearest **TI** is in the next town, Ballachulish (buried inside The Quarry Centre—a café/gift shop, daily 9:00-17:00, Nov-Easter 10:00-16:00, tel. 01855/811-866, www.glencoetourism.co.uk). For more information on the area, see www.discoverglencoe.com.

Bike Rental: At **Crank It Up Gear,** Davy rents road and mountain bikes, and can offer plenty of suggestions for where to pedal in the area (£15/half-day, £25/all day, just off the main street to the left near the start of town, 20 Lorn Drive, mobile 07746-860-023, www.glencoebikehire.com, book ahead).

Sights in Glencoe

Glencoe Village

Glencoe village is just a line of houses sitting beneath the brooding mountains. The only real sight in town is the folk museum (described later). But walking the main street gives a good glimpse of village Scotland. From the free parking lot at the entrance to town, go for a stroll. You'll pass a few little B&Bs

renting two or three rooms, the stony Episcopal church, the folk museum, the town's grocery store, and the village hall.

At the far end of the village, on the left just before the bridge, a Celtic cross **WWI** memorial stands on a little hill. Even this wee village lost 11 souls during that war—a reminder of Scotland's disproportionate contribution to Britain's war effort. You'll see memorials like this (usually either a Celtic cross or a soldier with bowed head) in virtually every town in Scotland.

If you were to cross the little bridge, you'd head up into Glencoe's wooded parklands, with some easy hikes (described later). But for one more landmark, turn right just before the bridge and walk about five minutes. Standing on a craggy bluff on your right is another memorial—this one to the **Glencoe Massacre,** which still haunts the memories of people here and throughout Scotland.

Glencoe Folk Museum

This gathering of thatched-roof, early-18th-century croft houses is a volunteer-run community effort. It's jammed with local history, creating a huggable museum filled with humble exhibits gleaned from the town's old closets and attics. When one house was being rethatched, its owner found a cache of 200-year-old swords and pistols hidden there from the government Redcoats after the

disastrous Battle of Culloden. You'll also see antique toys, boxes from old food products, sports paraphernalia, a cabinet of curiosities, evocative old black-and-white photos, and plenty of information on the MacDonald clan. Be sure to look for the museum's little door that leads out back, where additional, smaller buildings are filled with everyday items (furniture, farm tools, and so on) and exhibits on the Glencoe Massacre and a beloved Highland doctor (£3, Mon-Sat 10:00-16:30, closed Sun and Nov-March, tel. 01855/811-664, www.glencoemuseum.com). You can listen to an interview with the late Arthur Smith, a local historian, about the valley and its story in the "Scottish Highlands" program available on my Rick Steves Audio Europe app—for details, see page 30.

Glencoe Visitor Centre

This modern facility, a mile past Glencoe village up the A-82 into the dramatic valley, is designed to resemble a *clachan*, or traditional Highland settlement. The information desk inside the gift shop is your single best resource for advice (and maps or guidebooks) about local walks and hikes (several of which are outlined later in this chapter). At the back of the complex you'll find a viewpoint with a handy 3-D model of the hills for orientation; an easy woodland walk starts from here. There's also a small, rotating exhibit, generally covering the nature and mountaineering of the area, as well as a short film (topic changes yearly). Though worth a quick stop, the whole place can feel like an afterthought to its gift shop, through which you must enter and exit (free, parking-£4; daily 9:00-18:00, Nov-March 10:00-16:00; café, tel. 01855/811-307, http://www.nts.org.uk—search for "Glencoe").

Glencoe Valley Drive

If you have a car, spend an hour or so following the A-82 through the valley, past the Glencoe Visitor Centre, up into the desolate moor beyond, and back again. You'll enjoy grand views, dramatic craggy hills, and, if you're lucky, a chance to hear a bagpiper in the wind: Roadside Highland buskers often set up here on good-weather summer weekends. (If you play the recorder—and the piper's not swarmed with other tourists—ask to finger a tune while he does the hard work.)

Here's a brief explanation of the route. Along the way, I've pointed out sometimes easy-to-miss trailheads, in case you're up for a hike (hikes described in the next section).

From Glencoe Village to the End of the Valley: Leaving Glencoe village on the A-82, it's just a mile to the **Glencoe Visitor Centre** (on the right, described earlier). Soon after, the road pulls out of the forested hills and gives you unobstructed views of the U-shaped valley.

About a mile after the visitor center, on the left, is a parking lot for **Signal Rock and An Torr,** a popular place for low-impact forested hikes. Just beyond, also on the left, is a one-lane road leading to the recommended **Clachaig Inn,** a classic hikers' pub.

Continuing along the A-82, you'll hit a straight stretch,

passing a lake (Loch Achtriochtan), and then a small farm, both on the right. After the farm, the valley narrows a bit as you cut through Glencoe Pass. On the right, you'll pass two small parking lots. Pull into the second one for perhaps the best viewpoint of the entire valley, with point-blank views (directly ahead) of the steep ridge-like mountains known as the **Three Sisters.** Hike about 100 feet away from the pullout to your own private bluff to enjoy the

view alone—it makes a big difference. This is also the starting point for the challenging **Hidden Valley hike,** which leads between the first and second sisters.

As you continue, you'll pass a raging waterfall in a canyon— the Tears of the MacDonalds—on the right. After another mile or so—through more glorious waterfall scenery—watch on the left for the **Coffin Cairn,** which looks like a stone igloo (parking is just across the road if you want a photo op). Just after the cairn, look on the left for pullout parking for the **hike to The Study,** a viewpoint overlooking the road you just drove down.

After this pullout, you'll hit a straightaway for about a mile, followed by an S-curve. At the end of the curve, look for the pullout parking on the left, just before the stand of pine trees. This is the trailhead for the **Devil's Staircase** hike, high into the hills.

Continuing past here, you're nearing the end of the valley. The intimidating peak called the Great Shepherd of Etive (Stob Dearg, on the right) looms like a dour watchman, guarding the far end of the valley. Soon you'll pass the turnoff (on the right) for **Glen Etive,** an even more remote-feeling valley. (This was the setting for the final scenes of *Skyfall*. Yes, this is where James Bond grew up.) Continuing past that, the last sign of civilization (on the right) is the Glencoe Ski Centre. And from here, the terrain flattens out as you enter the vast **Rannoch Moor**—50 bleak square miles of heather, boulders, and barely enough decent land to graze a sheep. Robert Louis Stevenson called it the "Highland Desert."

You could keep driving as far as you like—but the moor looks pretty much the same from here on out. Turn around and head back through Glencoe...it's scenery you'll hardly mind seeing twice.

GLENCOE & FORT WILLIAM

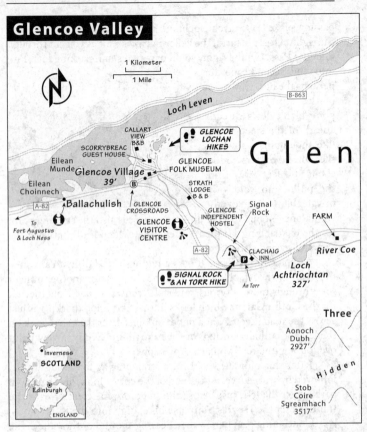

Glencoe Valley

1 Kilometer

1 Mile

Loch Leven

B-863

CALLART VIEW B&B

GLENCOE LOCHAN HIKES

SCORRYBREAC GUEST HOUSE

Eilean Munde

Glencoe Village 39'

GLENCOE FOLK MUSEUM

Eilean Choinnech

STRATH LODGE B&B

A-82

Ballachulish

GLENCOE CROSSROADS

GLENCOE VISITOR CENTRE

GLENCOE INDEPENDENT HOSTEL

Signal Rock

FARM

To Fort Augustus & Loch Ness

A-82

CLACHAIG INN

River Coe

SIGNAL ROCK & AN TORR HIKE

An Torr

Loch Achtriochtan 327'

G l e n

Three

Aonoch Dubh 2927'

Hidden

Stob Coire Sgreamhach 3517'

SCOTLAND

Inverness

Edinburgh

ENGLAND

Hiking in Glencoe

Glencoe is made for hiking. Many routes are not particularly well marked, so it's essential to get very specific instructions (from the rangers at the Glencoe Visitor Centre, or other knowledgeable locals) and equip yourself with a good map (the Ordnance Survey Explorer Map #384, sold at the center). I've suggested a few of the most enticing walks and hikes. These vary from easy, level strolls to challenging climbs. Either way, wear proper footwear (even the easy trails can get swamped in wet weather) and carry rain gear—you never know when a storm will blow in.

I've listed these roughly in order of how close they are to Glencoe village, and given a

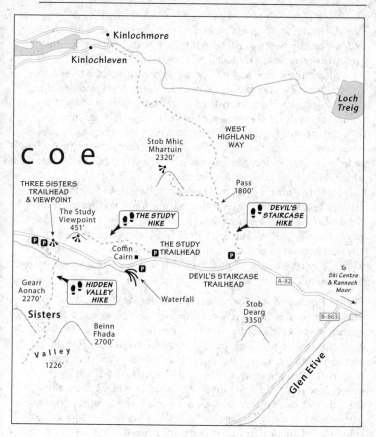

rough sense of difficulty for each. Some of them (including the first two) are more forested, but the ones out in the open—which really let you feel immersed in the wonders of Glencoe—are even better.

While you can walk to the first two areas from Glencoe village, the rest are best for drivers. Some of these trailheads are tricky to find, which is why I've designed the driving commentary in the previous section to help you locate the hikes off the A-82.

Glencoe Lochan (Easy)

Perched on the forested hill above Glencoe village is an improbable slice of the Canadian Rockies. A century ago, this was the personal playground of Lord Strathcona, a local boy done good when he moved to Canada and eventually became a big Canadian Pacific Railway magnate. In 1894, he returned home with his Canadian wife and built the Glencoe House (which is now an exclusive, top-of-the-top hotel). His wife was homesick for the Rockies, so he had the grounds landscaped to represent the lakes, trees, and mountains of her home country. They even carved out a man-made lake (Glencoe Lochan), which looks like a piece of Canada tucked under a craggy Scottish backdrop. (She was still homesick—they eventually returned to Canada.)

Today, the house and immediate surroundings are closed to visitors, but the rest of the area is open for exploration. Head to the end of Glencoe village, cross the bridge, and continue straight up (following signs for *Glencoe Lochan*)—it's a 20-minute uphill walk, or 5-minute drive, from the village center. Once there, a helpful orientation panel in the parking lot suggests three different, color-coded, one-mile walking loops—mostly around that beautiful lake, which reflects the hillsides of Glencoe.

From this area, a good trail network called the **Orbital Recreational Track** follows the river through the forest up the valley, all the way to the Clachaig Inn (about 45 minutes one-way). This links you to the Signal Rock and An Torr areas (described next). Eventually they hope to extend this trail system across the valley and back to the Glencoe Visitor Centre, which would allow a handy loop hike around the valley floor.

Signal Rock and An Torr (Easy to Moderate)

This forested area has nicely tended trails and gives you a better chance of spotting wildlife than the more desolate hikes described later. To explore this area, park at the well-marked lot just off of the A-82 and go for a walk. A well-described panel at the trailhead narrates three options: easy yellow route to the Clachaig Inn; longer blue route to Signal Rock; and strenuous black route along the hillsides of An Torr. The Signal Rock route brings you to a panoramic point overlooking the valley—so named because a fire could be lit here to alert others in case of danger.

Hidden Valley (Challenging)

Three miles east of Glencoe village, this aptly named glen is tucked between two of the dramatic Three Sisters mountains. Also called the Lost Valley (Coire Gabhail in Gaelic), this was supposedly where the MacDonalds hid stolen cattle from their rivals, the Campbells (who later massacred them). This is the most challenging of the hikes I describe—it's strenuous and has stretches with uneven footing. Expect to scramble a bit over rocks, and to cross a river on stepping stones (which may be underwater after a heavy rain). As the rocks can be slippery when wet, skip this hike in bad weather. Figure about two-and-a-half to three hours round-trip (with an ascent of more than 1,000 feet).

Begin at the second parking lot at Glencoe Pass (on the right when coming from Glencoe), with views of the Three Sisters. You're aiming to head between the first and second Sisters (counting from the left). Hike down into the valley between the road and the mountains. Bear left, head down a metal staircase, and cross the bridge over the river. (Don't cross the bridge to the right of the parking lots—a common mistake.) Once across, you'll start the treacherous ascent up a narrow gorge. Some scrambling is required, and at one point a railing helps you find your way. The next tricky part is where you cross the river. You're looking for a pebbly beach and a large boulder; stepping stones lead across the river, and you'll see the path resume on the other side. But if the water level is high, the stones may be covered—though still passable with good shoes and steady footing. (Don't attempt to scramble over the treacherous slopes on the side of the river with the loose rocks called scree.) Once across the stepping stones, keep on the trail, hiking further up into the valley.

Much Easier Alternative: If you'd simply enjoy the feeling of walking deep in Glencoe valley—with peaks and waterfalls overhead—you can start down from the parking lot toward the Hidden Valley trail, and then simply stroll the old road along the valley floor as far as you want in either direction.

The Study (Easy to Moderate)

For a relatively easy, mostly level hike through the valley with a nice viewpoint at the end, consider walking to the flat rock called "The Study" and back. It takes about 45-60 minutes round-trip. The walk essentially parallels the main highway, but on the old road a bit higher up. You'll park just beyond the Three Sisters and the Coffin Cairn. From there, cut through the field of

stone and marshy turf to the old road—basically two gravel tire ruts—and follow them to your left. You'll hike above the modern road, passing several modest waterfalls, until you reach a big, flat rock with stunning views of the Three Sisters and the valley beyond. (Fellow hikers have marked the spot with a pile of stones.)

The Devil's Staircase (Strenuous but Straightforward)

About eight miles east of Glencoe village, near the end of the valley, you can hike this brief stretch of the West Highland Way. It was built by General Wade, the British strategist who came to Scotland after the 1715 Jacobite rebellion to help secure government rule here. Designed to connect Glencoe valley to the lochside town of Kinlochmore to the north, it's named for its challenging switchbacks. Most hikers simply ascend to the pass at the top (an 800-foot gain), then come back down to Glencoe.

It's challenging, but easier to follow and with more comfortable footing than the Hidden Valley hike. Figure about 45-60 minutes up, and 30 minutes back down (add 45-60 minutes for the optional ascent to the summit of 2,320-foot Stob Mhic Mhartuin).

From the parking lot, a green sign points the way. It's a steep but straightforward hike up, on switchback trails, until you reach the pass—marked by a cairn (pile of stones). From here, you can return back down into the valley. Or, if you have stamina left, consider continuing higher—head up to the peak on the left, called **Stob Mhic Mhartuin.** The 30-40-minute hike to the top (an additional gain of 500 feet) earns you even grander views over the entire valley.

For an even longer hike, it's possible to carry on down the other side of the staircase to **Kinlochmore** (about 2-hour descent)—but your car will still be in Glencoe village. Consider this plan: Leave your car in Glencoe. Take a taxi to the trailhead. Hike across to Kinlochmore. From there you can take the #N44 bus back to Glencoe and your car, though be aware that the bus only runs a few times midday (see "Glencoe Connections," later).

Sleeping in Glencoe

Glencoe is an extremely low-key place to spend the night between Oban or Glasgow and the northern destinations. You'll join two kinds of guests: one-nighters just passing through and outdoorsy types settling in for several days of hiking.

B&BS IN GLENCOE VILLAGE

The following B&Bs are along or just off the main road through the middle of the village.

$$ Beechwood Cottage B&B is a shoes-off, slippers-on, whisky-honor-bar kind of place where Jackie rents three lovely rooms and Iain pursues his rock-garden dreams in the yard (look for the sign at the church on Main Street, tel. 01855/811-062, www.beechwoodcottage.scot, stay@beechwoodcottage.scot).

$$ Heatherlea B&B is at the far end of the village, with a relaxed atmosphere, hotel-meets-country-home rooms, and a serene grassy garden with berry bushes (harvested for homemade jam). Host Helen is a fun, outdoorsy type who opened a guesthouse because she "wanted to get out of the rat race" (3 rooms, sack lunches available, tel. 01855/811-519, mobile 07884/367-354, www.heatherleaglencoe.com, info@heatherleaglencoe.com).

OUTSIDE TOWN

These options are a bit outside town, with good proximity to both the village and the valley. Strath Lodge, Glencoe Independent

Hostel, and Clachaig Inn are on the back road that runs through the forest parallel to the A-82 (best-suited for drivers). Scorrybreac is on a hill above the village, and Callart View is along the flat road that winds past Loch Leven.

$$$ Strath Lodge, energetically run by Ann and Dan (who are generous with hiking tips and maps), brings a fresh perspective to Glencoe's sometimes-stodgy accommodations scene. Their four rooms, in a modern, light-filled, lodge-like home, are partway down the road to the Clachaig Inn (2-3 nights preferred, no kids under 16, tel. 01855/811-337, www.strathlodgeglencoe.com, stay@strathlodgeglencoe.com). Take the road up through the middle of Glencoe village, cross the bridge, and keep right following the river for a few minutes; it's on the right.

$$$ Clachaig Inn, which runs two popular pubs on site, also rents 23 rooms, all with private bath. It's a family-friendly place surrounded by a dramatic setting that works well for hikers seeking a comfy mountain inn (recommended pub, tel. 01855/811-252, 3 miles from Glencoe, www.clachaig.com, frontdesk@clachaig.com). Follow the directions for the Strath Lodge, and drive another three miles past the campgrounds and hostels—the Clachaig Inn is on the right.

$$ Glencoe Independent Hostel offers a few snazzy, self-contained "eco-cabins" with kitchenettes and cheap, basic dorm beds in a rehabbed crofter farm building. It's a good choice if you're looking for either a bargain-basement sleep or a private, self-catering option (2-night minimum for cabins, tel. 01855/811-906, www.glencoehostel.co.uk, info@glencoehostel.co.uk, energetic Keith). It's a few minutes farther up the road beyond Strath Lodge.

$$ Scorrybreac Guest House enjoys a secluded forest setting and privileged position next to the restored Glencoe House (now a luxury hotel). From here, walks around the Glencoe Lochan wooded lake park are easy, and it's about a 10-minute walk down into the village. Emma and Graham rent five homey rooms and serve a daily breakfast special that goes beyond the usual offerings (2-3 nights preferred in peak season, tel. 01855/811-354, www.scorrybreacglencoe.com, stay@scorrybreacglencoe.com). After crossing the bridge at the end of the village, head left up the hill and follow signs.

$ Callart View B&B offers four rooms, quilted-home comfort, and a peaceful spot overlooking Loch Leven, less than a mile outside the village and close to the wooded trails of Glencoe Lochan. You'll be spoiled by Lynn's homemade shortbread (family room, self-catering cottages, sack lunches available, tel. 01855/811-259, www.callart-view.co.uk, callartview@hotmail.com, Lynn and Geoff). Turn off from the main road for Glencoe village but instead of turning right into the village, keep left and drive less than a mile along the loch.

IN BALACHULISH

$ St. Munda's Manse sounds rather grand—that's because Colin and Mary renovated a lovely old stone house that once belonged to the church down the road. Now they offer two bright rooms that manage to feel both modern and classic, in a quiet location above Ballachulish village (cash only, tel. 01855/811-966, www.bedandbreakfastglencoe.com, hello@stmundasmanse.com). See their website for driving directions.

$ Strathassynt Guest House sits in the center of Ballachulish, across from the recommended Laroch Bar & Bistro. Katya will make you pancakes for breakfast, and the six bedrooms are a good value (family rooms, closed Nov-Feb, tel. 01855/811-261, www.strathassynt.com, info@strathassynt.com, Neil and Katya).

Eating in Glencoe

Choices around Glencoe are slim—this isn't the place for fine dining. But the following options offer decent food a short walk or drive away. For evening fun, take a walk or ask your B&B host where to find music and dancing.

In Glencoe: The only real restaurant is **$$$ The Glencoe Gathering,** with a busy dining area and a large outdoor deck. The menu has a variety of seafood, burgers, and pasta. While the food is nothing special, it will fill you up after a day in the mountains (daily 8:30-22:00, at junction of A-82 and Glencoe village, tel. 01855/811-265).

The **$ Glencoe Café,** also in the village, is just right for soups and sandwiches, and Deirdre's homemade baked goods—especially the carrot loaf—are irresistible (soup-and-panini lunch combo, daily 10:00-17:00, last order at 16:15, Alan).

Near Glencoe: Set in a stunning valley a few miles from Glencoe village, **$$ Clachaig Inn** serves solid pub grub all day long to a clientele that's half locals and half tourists. This unpretentious and very popular social hub features billiards, live music, and a wide range of whiskies and hand-pulled ales. There are two areas, sharing the same menu: The Bidean Lounge feels a bit like an upscale ski lodge while the Boots Bar has a spit-and-sawdust, pub-around-an-open-fire atmosphere (open daily for lunch and dinner, music Sat from 21:00, Sun open-mike folk music, see hotel listing earlier for driving directions, tel. 01855/811-252, no reservations).

In Ballachulish: Aiming to bring some sophistication to this rugged corner of Scotland, **$$$ The Laroch Bar & Bistro** has both a low-key pub section and a proper restaurant sharing the same menu (Tue-Sat 12:00-15:00 & 18:00-21:00, closed Sun-Mon, tel. 01855/811-940, www.thelarochrestaurantandbar.co.uk). Drive three minutes from Glencoe into Ballachulish village, and you'll see it on the left. There's also a simple **$ fish-and-chips** joint next door (Fri-Sat 16:30-21:30, closed Sun-Thu).

Glencoe Connections

Buses don't actually drive down the main road through Glencoe village, but they stop nearby at a place called **"Glencoe Crossroads"** (a short walk into the village center). They also stop in the town of **Ballachulish,** which is just a half-mile away (or a £3 taxi ride). Tell the bus driver where you're going ("Glencoe village") and ask to be let off as close as possible.

Citylink buses #914/#915/#916 stop at Glencoe Crossroads and Ballachulish, heading north to **Fort William** (7-8/day, 30 minutes) or south to **Glasgow** (3 hours). Another option is Shiel bus #N44, which runs from either Glencoe Crossroads or Ballachulish to **Fort William** (about 8/day, less Sat-Sun). From Ballachulish, you can take Citylink bus #918 to **Oban** (2/day, 1 hour).

To reach **Inverness,** transfer in Fort William. To reach **Edinburgh,** transfer in Glasgow.

Bus info: Citylink tel. 0871-266-3333, Citylink.co.uk; Shiel Buses tel. 01967/431-272, ShielBuses.co.uk.

Fort William

Fort William—after Inverness, the second-biggest town in the Highlands (pop. 10,000)—is Glencoe's opposite. While Glencoe is a humble one-street village, appealing to hikers and nature-lovers, Fort William's glammed-up car-free main drag feels like one big Scottish shopping mall (with souvenir stands and outdoor stores touting perpetual "70 percent off" sales). The town is clogged  with a United Nations of tourists trying to get out of the rain. Big bus tours drive through Glencoe...but they sleep in Fort William.

While Glencoe touches the Scottish soul of the Highlands, Fort William was a steely and intimidating headquarters of the

British counter-insurgency movement—in many ways designed to crush that same Highland spirit. After the English Civil War (early 1650s), Oliver Cromwell built a fort here to control his rebellious Scottish subjects. This was beefed up (and named for King William III) in 1690. And following the Jacobite uprising in 1715, King George I dispatched General George Wade to coordinate and fortify the crown's Highland defenses against further Jacobite dissenters. Fort William was the first of a chain of intimidating bastions (along with Fort Augustus on Loch Ness, and Fort George near Inverness) stretching the length of the Great Glen. But Fort William's namesake fortress is long gone, leaving precious little tangible evidence (except a tiny bit of rampart in a park near the train station) to help today's visitors imagine its militaristic past.

With the opening of the Caledonian Canal in 1822, the first curious tourists arrived. Many more followed with the arrival of the train in 1894, and grand hotels were built. Today, sitting at the foot of Ben Nevis, the tallest peak in Britain, Fort William is considered the outdoors capital of the United Kingdom.

Orientation to Fort William

Given its strategic position—between Glencoe and Oban in the south and Inverness in the east—you're likely to pass through Fort William at some point during your Highlands explorations. And, while "just passing through" is the perfect plan here, Fort William can provide a good opportunity to stock up on whatever you need (last supermarket before Inverness), grab lunch, and get any questions answered at the TI.

Arrival in Fort William: You'll find pay parking lots flanking the main pedestrian zone, High Street. The train and bus stations sit side by side just north of the old town center, where you'll find a handy pay parking lot.

Tourist Information: The TI is on the car-free main drag (daily July-Aug 9:30-18:30, Sept-June 9:00-18:00; 15 High Street, tel. 01397/701-801, FortWilliamTIC@visitscotland.com). Free public WCs are up the street, next to the parking lot.

Sights in Fort William

Fort William's High Street

Enjoy an hour-long stroll up and down the length of Fort William's main street for lots of Scottish clichés, great people watching, and a shop at #125 (near the south end) called Aye2Aye, which favors a new referendum on Scottish independence.

▲West Highland Museum

Fort William's only real sight is its humble but well-presented museum. It's a fine opportunity to escape the elements, and—if you take the time to linger over the many interesting exhibits—genuinely insightful about local history and Highland life.

Cost and Hours: Free, £3 suggested donation, Mon-Sat 10:00-17:00, and maybe Sun in high season; Nov-April until 16:00; closed Jan-Feb; midway down the main street on Cameron Square, tel. 01397/702-169, www.westhighlandmuseum.org.uk.

Visiting the Museum: Follow the suggested one-way route through exhibits on two floors. You'll begin by learning about the WWII green-beret commandos, who were trained in secrecy near here (see "Commando Memorial" listing, later). Then you'll see the historic Governor's Room, decorated with the original paneling from the room in which the order for the Glencoe Massacre was signed. The ground floor also holds exhibits on natural history (lots of stuffed birds and other critters), mountaineering (old equipment), and archaeology (stone and metal tools).

Upstairs, you'll see a selection of old tartans and a salacious exhibit about Queen Victoria and John Brown (her Scottish servant... and, possibly, suitor). The Jacobite exhibit gives a concise timeline of that complicated history, from Charles I to Bonnie Prince Charlie, and displays a selection of items emblazoned with the prince's bonnie face—including a clandestine portrait that you can only see by looking in a cylindrical mirror. Finally, the Highland Life exhibit collects a hodgepodge of tools, musical instruments (some fine old harps that were later replaced by the much louder bagpipes as the battlefield instrument of choice), and other bric-a-brac.

NEAR FORT WILLIAM

Ben Nevis

From Fort William, take a peek at Britain's highest peak, Ben Nevis (4,406 feet). Thousands walk to its summit each year. On a clear day, you can admire it from a distance. Scotland's only mountain cable cars—at the **Nevis Range Mountain Experience**—can take you to a not-very-lofty 2,150-foot perch on the slopes of Aonach Mòr for a closer look (£19.50, 15-minute ride, generally open daily but closed in high winds and winter—call ahead, signposted on the A-82 north of Fort William, café at bottom and restaurant at top, tel. 01397/705-825, www.nevisrange.co.uk). The cable car also provides access to trails particularly popular with mountain bikers.

▲Commando Memorial

This powerful bronze ensemble of three stoic WWII commandos, standing in an evocative mountain setting, is one of Britain's most beloved war memorials. During World War II, Winston Churchill decided that Britain needed an elite military corps. He created the British Commandos, famous for wearing green berets (an accessory—and name—later borrowed by elite fighting forces in the US and other countries). The British Commandos trained in the Lochaber region near Fort William, in the windy shadow of Ben Nevis. Many later died in combat, and this memorial—built in 1952—remembers those fallen British heroes.

Nearby is the Garden of Remembrance, honoring British Commandos who died in more recent conflicts, from the Falkland Islands to Afghanistan. It's also a popular place to spread Scottish military ashes. Taken together, these sights are a touching reminder that the US is not alone in its distant wars. Every nation has its share of honored heroes willing to sacrifice for what they believe to be the greater good.

Getting There: The memorial is about nine miles outside of Fort William, on the way to Inverness (just outside Spean Bridge); see "Route Tips for Drivers" later in this section.

Sleeping and Eating in Fort William

Sleeping: The Hobbit-cute **$ Gowan Brae B&B** ("Hill of the Big Daisy") has an antique-filled dining room and three rooms with loch or garden views (one room has private bath down the hall, cash only, 2-night minimum July-Aug, on Union Road—a 5-minute walk up the hill above High Street, tel. 01397/704-399, www.gowanbrae.co.uk, gowan_brae@btinternet.com, Jim and Ann Clark).

Eating: These places are on traffic-free High Street, near the start of town. For lunch and picnics, try **$ Deli Craft,** with good, made-to-order deli sandwiches and other prepared foods (61 High Street, tel. 01397/698-100), or **$ Hot Roast Company,** which sells beef, turkey, ham, or pork sandwiches topped with some tasty extras, along with soup, salad, and coleslaw (127 High Street, tel. 01397/700-606).

For lunch or dinner, **$$ The Grog & Gruel** serves real ales, good pub grub, and Tex-Mex and Cajun dishes, with some unusual choices such as burgers made from boar and haggis or Highland venison. There's also a variety of "grog dogs" (66 High Street, tel. 01397/705-078).

Fort William Connections

Fort William is a major transit hub for the Highlands, so you'll likely change buses here at some point during your trip.

From Fort William by Bus to: Glencoe or **Ballachulish** (all Glasgow-bound buses—#914, #915, and #916; 8/day, 30 minutes; also Shiel bus #N44, hourly, fewer on Sun), **Oban** (bus #918, 2/day, 1.5 hours), **Inverness** (bus #919, 6/day, 2 hours, fewer on Sun), **Glasgow** (#914/#915/#916, 7-8/day direct, 3 hours). To reach **Edinburgh,** take the bus to Glasgow, then transfer to a train or bus (figure 5 hours total). Citylink: tel. 0871-266-3333, Citylink.co.uk; Shiel Bus: tel. 01397/700-700, www.ShielBuses.co.uk.

ROUTE TIPS FOR DRIVERS

From Fort William to Loch Ness and Inverness: Head north out of Fort William on the A-82. After about eight miles, in the village of Spean Bridge, take the left fork (staying on the A-82). About a mile later, on the left, keep an eye out for the **Commando Memorial** (described earlier and worth a quick stop). From here, the A-82 sweeps north and follows the Caledonian Canal, passing through **Fort Augustus** (a good lunch stop, with its worthwhile Caledonian Canal Centre), and then follows the north side of Loch Ness on its way to Inverness. Along the way, the A-82 passes **Urquhart Castle** and two **Loch Ness Monster exhibits** in Drumnadrochit (described in the Inverness & Loch Ness chapter).

From Oban to Fort William via Glencoe: See page 930 in the Oban chapter.

INVERNESS & LOCH NESS

Inverness • Culloden Battlefield • Clava Cairns • Cawdor Castle • Loch Ness • Urquhart Castle

Inverness, the Highlands' de facto capital, is an almost-unavoidable stop on the Scottish tourist circuit. It's a pleasant town and an ideal springboard for some of the country's most famous sights. Hear the music of the Highlands in Inverness and the echo of muskets at Culloden, where government troops drove Bonnie Prince Charlie into exile and conquered his Jacobite supporters. Ponder the mysteries of Scotland's murky prehistoric past at Clava Cairns, and enjoy a peek at Highland aristocratic life at Cawdor Castle. Just to the southwest of Inverness, explore the locks and lochs of the Caledonian Canal while playing hide-and-seek with the Loch Ness monster.

PLANNING YOUR TIME

Though it has little in the way of sights, Inverness does have a workaday charm and is a handy spot to spend a night or two between other Highland destinations. With two nights, you can find a full day's worth of sightseeing nearby.

With a car, the day trips around Inverness are easy. Without a car, you can get to Inverness by train (better from Edinburgh, Stirling, or Glasgow) or by bus (better from Oban and Glencoe), then side-trip to Loch Ness, Culloden, and other nearby sights by public bus or with a package tour.

Note that Loch Ness is between Inverness and Oban or Glencoe. If you're heading to or from one of those places, it makes sense to see Loch Ness en route, rather than as a side trip from Inverness.

Inverness

Inverness is situated on the River Ness at the base of a castle (now used as a courthouse, but with a public viewpoint). Inverness' charm is its normalcy—it's a nice, midsize Scottish city that gives you a palatable taste of the "urban" Highlands and a contrast to cutesy tourist towns. It has a disheveled, ruddy-cheeked grittiness and is well located for enjoying the surrounding countryside  sights. Check out the bustling, pedestrianized downtown, or meander the picnic-friendly riverside paths and islands—best at sunset, when the light hits the castle and couples hold hands while strolling along the water and over its footbridges.

Orientation to Inverness

Inverness, with about 70,000 people, is one of the fastest-growing cities in Scotland. Marked by its castle, Inverness clusters along the  River Ness. The TI is on High Street, an appealing pedestrian shopping zone a few blocks away from the river; nearby are the train and bus stations. Most of my recommended B&Bs huddle atop a gentle hill behind the castle (a 10-minute uphill walk from the city center).

TOURIST INFORMATION

At the TI, you can pick up the self-guided *City Centre Trail* walking-tour leaflet and the *What's On* weekly events sheet (June-Sept Mon-Sat 9:00-19:00, shorter hours on Sun and off-season, 36 High Street, tel. 01463/252-401, www.visitscotland.com and www.visitinvernesslochness.com).

HELPFUL HINTS

Charity Shops: Inverness is home to several pop-up charity shops. Occupying vacant rental spaces, these are staffed by volunteers who are happy to talk about their philanthropy. You can pick up a memorable knickknack, adjust your wardrobe for the weather, and learn about local causes.

Festivals and Events: The summer is busy with special events; book far ahead during these times: Etape Loch Ness bike race (early June), Highland Games (late July), Belladrum Tartan Heart Festival (music, early Aug), Black Isle farm show (early Aug), and Loch Ness Marathon (late Sept).

In summer (June-Sept), the TI can let you know whether a *ceilidh* (traditional dance and music) is scheduled at City Hall.

For a real Highland treat, catch a **shinty match** (a combination of field hockey, hurling, and American football—but without pads). Inverness Shinty Club plays at Bught Park, along Ness Walk. The TI or your B&B can tell you if there are any matches on, or check www.invernessshinty.com.

Bookstore: Located in a converted church built in 1649, **Leakey's Bookshop** is the place to browse through teetering towers of old books and vintage maps (Mon-Sat 10:00-17:30, closed Sun, Church Street, tel. 01463/239-947, Charles Leakey).

Baggage Storage: The train station has lockers (Mon-Sat 6:40-20:30, Sun from 10:40), or you can leave your bag at the bus station's ticket desk (small fee, daily until 17:30).

Laundry: Head to the west end of the Ness Bridge to find **New City Launderette** (self-service or same-day full-service, Mon-Fri 8:00-20:00, Sat until 18:00, Sun 10:00-16:00, last load one hour before closing, 17 Young Street, tel. 01463/242-507). **Thirty Degrees Laundry** on Church Street is another option (full-service only, drop off before 10:00 for same-day service, Mon-Sat 8:30-17:30, closed Sun, a few blocks beyond Victorian Market at 84 Church Street, tel. 01463/710-380).

Tours in Inverness

IN TOWN

Skip the City Sightseeing hop-on, hop-off bus tour (this format doesn't work in Inverness).

Walking Tours

Walk Inverness offers 1.5-hour walking tours departing from the TI several nights a week in summer at 18:00 and some Saturdays at 11:00. You'll learn about the history of Inverness, its castle, Victorian Market, and Old High Church, with a few *Outlander* landmarks thrown in for good measure (£10, www.walkinverness.com/tours, Cath Findlay). They also organize private tours—see website for details.

Inverness Bike Tours

Hardworking Alison leads small groups on two-hour bike tours. Her six-mile route is nearly all on traffic-free paths along canals and lochs outside of the city and comes with light guiding along the way. You'll pedal through Ness Island, stop at the Botanical Gardens, ride along the Caledonian Canal with its system of locks (you may even catch a boat passing through the locks), and cycle through a nature preserve (£21, generally no kids under 14, 10-person max; daily in season at 10:00, 13:00, and 15:45; best to book a spot in advance online, goes even in light rain, meet at the Prime Restaurant, near the west end of Ness Bridge at 5 Ness Walk, call or text mobile 07443-866-619, www.invernessbiketours.co.uk). Arrive a bit early to size up your bike and helmet.

EXCURSIONS FROM INVERNESS

Inverness is a great home base for day trips. A variety of tour companies offer excursions to other Highlands destinations, including many not covered by this book—details and tickets are available at the TI. While the big sellers are the many Loch Ness tours (because the monster is on every bucket list), I far prefer an all-day trip to the Isle of Skye—which gives you a good look at Loch Ness and Urquhart Castle along the way. For Isle of Skye and Orkney Island tours in summer, it's a good idea to book about a week in advance.

Loch Ness

The famous lake is just a 20-minute drive from Inverness. Tours often include a short boat ride, a visit to Urquhart Castle, and a stop at the Loch Ness monster exhibits. The lake is not particularly scenic, the castle is just a shell, and the monster is mostly a promotional gimmick. Still, if you have no car, this can be the most efficient way to check this off your list. **Jacobite Tours** focuses on trips that include Loch Ness, from a one-hour basic boat ride to a seven-hour extravaganza. Their four-hour "Sensation" tour includes a guided bus tour with live narration, a half-hour Loch Ness cruise, and visits to Urquhart Castle and the Loch Ness exhibits (£35, for more options see www.jacobite.co.uk, tel. 01463/233-999).

Isle of Skye

Several companies do good day tours to the Isle of Skye. They travel 110 miles (a 2.5-hour drive) to the heart of Skye (Portree). With about six hours of driving, and one hour for lunch in Portree, that leaves two or three hours for a handful of quick and scenic photo stops. All travel along Loch Ness so you can see Urquhart Castle and try for a monster sighting. And all stop for a view of

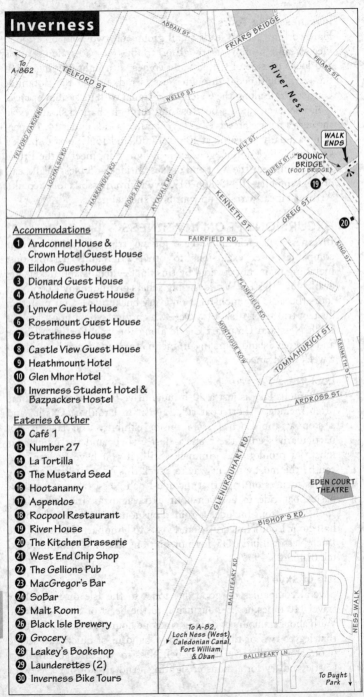

Inverness

Accommodations

1. Ardconnel House & Crown Hotel Guest House
2. Eildon Guesthouse
3. Dionard Guest House
4. Atholdene Guest House
5. Lynver Guest House
6. Rossmount Guest House
7. Strathness House
8. Castle View Guest House
9. Heathmount Hotel
10. Glen Mhor Hotel
11. Inverness Student Hotel & Bazpackers Hostel

Eateries & Other

12. Café 1
13. Number 27
14. La Tortilla
15. The Mustard Seed
16. Hootananny
17. Aspendos
18. Rocpool Restaurant
19. River House
20. The Kitchen Brasserie
21. West End Chip Shop
22. The Gellions Pub
23. MacGregor's Bar
24. SoBar
25. Malt Room
26. Black Isle Brewery
27. Grocery
28. Leakey's Bookshop
29. Launderettes (2)
30. Inverness Bike Tours

INVERNESS & LOCH NESS

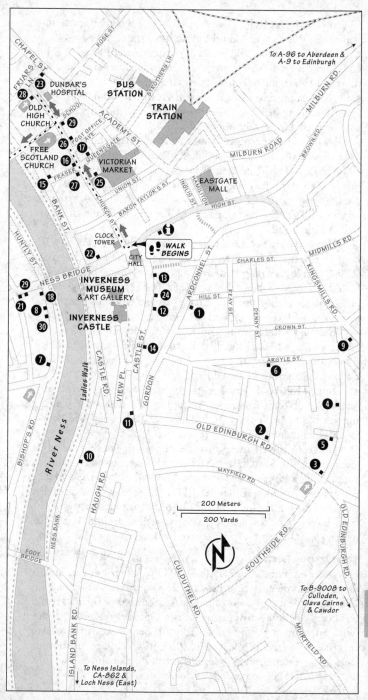

Eilean Donan Castle. The longer rides loop around the Trotternish Peninsula. Websites explain the exact itineraries.

Wow Scotland's ambitious 12-hour itinerary goes in a big bus. They depart at 8:30 from the Inverness bus station and include short but smart and adequate stops all along the way (£79, nearly daily June-Aug, fewer departures in April-May and Sept, none Oct-March, tel. 01808/511-773, www.wowscotlandtours.com). I'd pay the extra for the £99 front row.

Highland Experience Tours runs another, shorter Isle of Skye itinerary in 24-seat buses (daily April-Oct, fewer off-season, 10 hours) but doesn't make it as far north as the Trotternish Peninsula (£55, tel. 0131-285-3314, www.highlandexperience.com). They offer a variety of other daylong tours, including to the far north with John O'Groats, or a trip to Royal Deeside and the Speyside Whisky Trail.

Happy Tours Scotland organizes daily minibus tours on a 10-hour joy ride (getting all the way to Quiraing) with top-notch guides (£80, 8 people per minibus, daily at 8:20, leaves from 7 Ness Walk at Columba Hotel, mobile 07828-154-683, book at www.happy-tours.biz, Cameron). They also offer Loch Ness and *Outlander* itineraries, a Speyside whisky tour, and private minibus tours.

Rabbie's Small Group Tours does 12-hour trips to Skye in its 16-seater buses for £22 nearly daily from Inverness (www.rabbies.com). Their busy list of other tours cover Culloden and Clava Cairns, Cairngorms National Park, and Speyside.

Iona Highland Tours takes eight people on several different Isle of Skye itineraries, including one that allows hiking time at the Fairy Pools (£70, 9 hours, tel. 01463/250-457, www.ionahighlandtours.com).

By Train Then Tour: To avoid a long bus ride or skip the sights along the way to Skye, take the train from Inverness to Kyle of Lochalsh, where a Skye-based tour company will pick you up and take you around. Try **Skye Tours** (tel. 01471/822-716, www.skye-tours.co.uk) or **Tour Skye** (tel. 01478/613-514, www.tourskye.com). The train leaves Inverness before 9:00 and arrives around 11:30; the return train is around 17:15 (covered by BritRail Pass).

The Orkney Islands

For a very ambitious itinerary, John O'Groats Ferries offers an all-day tour that departs Inverness at 7:15 and drives you up to John O'Groats to catch the 40-minute passenger ferry. Then a second bus takes you on a whistle-stop tour of Orkney's main attractions (with an hour in the town of Kirkwall) before returning you to Inverness by 21:00. While it's a long day, it's an efficient use of your time if you're determined to see Orkney (£76, daily June-Aug only, tel. 01955/611-353, www.jogferry.co.uk).

Inverness Walk

Although humble Inverness is best as a jumping-off point for exploring the countryside, spare an hour or two for the town's fun history and quirky charm with this short self-guided walk (walk route shown on map earlier in this chapter).

• *Start at the clock tower.*

Clock Tower: Notice the **Gaelic language** on directional and street signs all around you. While nobody speaks Gaelic as a first language (and only about 60,000 Scottish people speak it fluently), this old Celtic language symbolizes the strength of Scottish Highland culture.

The clock tower looming 130 feet above you is all that remains of a tollbooth building erected in 1791. This is the highest spire in town, and for generations was a collection point for local taxes. Here, four streets—Church, Castle, Bridge, and High—come together, integrating God, defense, and trade—everything necessary for a fine city.

About 800 years ago, a castle was built on the bluff overhead and the town of Inverness coalesced right about here. For centuries, this backwater town's economy was based on cottage industries. Artisans who made things also sold them. In 1854, the train arrived, injecting energy and money from Edinburgh and Glasgow, and the Victorian boom hit. With the Industrial Age came wholesalers, distributors, mass production, and affluence. Much of the city was built during this era, in Neo-Gothic style—over-the-top and fanciful, like the City Hall (from 1882, kitty-corner to the clock tower). With the Victorian Age also came tourism.

Look for the **Bible quotes** chiseled into the facade of the building across the street from the City Hall. A civic leader, tired of his council members being drunkards, edited these Bible verses for maximum impact, especially the bottom two.

Hiding just up the hill (behind the eyesore concrete home of the Inverness Museum and Art Gallery) is **Inverness Castle,** where there is a small exhibition (with plans for a bigger museum) and a chance to climb to the top of the tower (£5). It's worth hiking up to the castle at some point during your visit to enjoy some of the best views of Inverness and its river. The castle has served as a courthouse in modern times, but it doesn't see a lot of action. In the last few decades, there have been only two murders to prosecute. As locals like to say, "no guns, no problems." While hunters can own a gun, gun ownership in Scotland is complicated and tightly regulated.

• Walk a few steps away from the river (toward McDonald's)...

Mercat Cross and Old Town Center: Standing in front of the City Hall (known here as the "Town House") is a well-worn mercat cross, which designated the market in centuries past. This is where the townspeople gathered to hear important proclamations, share news, watch hangings, gossip, and so on. The scant remains of a prehistoric stone at the base of the cross are what's left of Inverness' "Stone of Destiny." According to tradition, whenever someone moved away from Inverness, they'd take a tiny bit of home with them in the form of a chip of this stone—so it's been chipped and pecked almost to oblivion.

The yellow **Caledonian** building faces McDonald's at the base of High Street. (Caledonia was the ancient Roman name for Scotland.) It was built in 1847, complete with Corinthian columns and a Greek-style pediment, as the leading bank in town, back when banks were designed to hold the money of the rich and powerful... and intimidate working blokes. Notice how nicely pedestrianized High Street welcomes people and seagulls...but not cars.

• Next we'll head up Church Street, which begins between the clock tower and The Caledonian.

Church Street: The street art you'll trip over at the start of Church Street is called *Earthquake*—a reminder of the quake that hit Inverness in 1816. As the slabs explain, the town's motto is "Open Heartedness, Insight, and Perseverance."

Stroll down Church Street. Look up above the modern storefronts to see centuries-old facades, more interesting than the town's regrettable post-WWII architecture. **Union Street** (the second corner on the right)—stately, symmetrical, and Neoclassical—was the fanciest street in the Highlands when it was built in the 19th century. Its buildings had indoor toilets. That was big news.

Midway down the next block of Church Street (on the right), an alley marked by an ugly white canopy leads to the **Victorian Market.** Venturing down the alley, you'll pass **The Malt Room** (a small and friendly whisky bar eager to teach you to appreciate Scotland's national tipple; see "Nightlife in Inverness") and

The Old Market Bar (a dive bar worth a peek). Stepping into the Victorian Market, you'll find a gallery of shops under an iron-and-glass domed roof dating from 1876. The first section seems abandoned, but delve deeper to find some

more active areas, where local shops mix with tacky "tartan tat" souvenir stands. If you're seriously into bagpipes, look for **Cabar Fèidh,** where American expat Brian sells CDs and sheet music, and repairs and maintains the precious instruments of local musicians.

Go back out of the market the way you came in and continue down Church Street. At the next corner you come to **Hootananny,** famous locally for its live music (pop in to see what's on tonight). Just past that is **Abertarff House,** the oldest house in Inverness. It was the talk of the town in 1593 for its "turnpike" (spiral staircase) connecting the floors.

Continue about a block farther along Church Street. The lane on the left leads to the **"Bouncy Bridge"** (where we'll finish this walk). Opposite that lane (on the right) is **Dunbar's Hospital,** with four-foot-thick walls. In 1668, Alexander Dunbar was a wealthy landowner who built this as a poor-folks' home. Try reading the auld script in his coat-of-arms above the door.

A few steps farther up Church Street, walk through the iron gate on the left and into the churchyard (we're focusing on the shorter church on the right—ignore the bigger one on the left). Looking at the WWI and WWII memorials on the church's wall, it's clear which war hit Scotland harder. While no one famous is buried here, many tombstones go back to the 1700s. Dodging rabbits, head for the bluff overlooking the river and turn around to see...

Old High Church: There are a lot of churches in Inverness (46 Protestant, 2 Catholic, 2 Gaelic-language, and one offering a Mass in Polish), but these days, most are used for other purposes. This one, dating from the 11th century, is the most historic (but is generally closed). It was built on what was likely the site of a pagan holy ground. Early Christians

called upon St. Michael to take the fire out of pagan spirits, so it only made sense that the first Christians would build their church here and dedicate the spot as St. Michael's Mount.

In the sixth century, the Irish evangelist monk St. Columba brought Christianity to northern England, the Scottish islands (at Iona), and the Scottish Highlands (in Inverness). He stood here amongst the pagans and preached to King Brude and the Picts.

Study the bell tower from the 1600s. The small door to no-where (one floor up) indicates that back before the castle offered protection, this tower was the place of last refuge for townsfolk under attack. They'd gather inside and pull up the ladder. Every night at 20:00, the bell in the tower rings 100 times. It has rung like this since 1730 to remind townsfolk that it's dangerous to be out after dinner.

This church became a prison for Jacobites after the Battle of Culloden; many of the prisoners were executed in the churchyard. (Look for marks where bullets hit the tower wall).

• *From here, you can circle back to the lane leading to the "Bouncy Bridge" and then hike out onto the pedestrian bridge. Or you can just survey the countryside from this bluff.*

The River Ness: Emptying out of Loch Ness and flowing seven miles to the sea (a mile from here), this is one of the short-est rivers in the country. While it's shallow (you can almost walk across it), there are plenty of fish in it. A 64-pound salmon was once pulled out of the river right here. In the 19th century, Inverness was smaller, with open fields across the river. Then, with the Victorian boom, the suspension footbridge (a.k.a. "Bouncy Bridge") was built in 1881 to connect new construction across the river with the town.

• *Your tour is over. Inverness is yours to explore.*

Sights in Inverness

Inverness Museum and Art Gallery

This free, likable town museum is worth poking around on a rainy day to get a taste of Inverness and the Highlands. The ground-floor exhibits on geology and archaeology peel back the layers of Highland history: Bronze and Iron ages, Picts (including some carved stones), Scots, Vikings, and Normans. Upstairs you'll find the "social history" exhibit (everything from Scottish nationalism to hunting and fishing) and temporary art exhibits.

Cost and Hours: Free, April-Oct Tue-Sat 10:00-17:00,

shorter hours off-season, closed Sun-Mon year-round, cheap café, in the ugly modern building on the way up to the castle, tel. 01349/781-730, more info under the visitor attractions tab at www. highlifehighland.com.

Inverness Castle

Aside from nice views from the front lawn, a small exhibition, and a tower climb with a commanding city vista (£5), most of this Inverness landmark is not open to the public. A wooden fortress that stood on this spot was replaced by a stone structure in the 15th century. In 1715, that castle was named Fort George to assert English control over the area. In 1745, it was destroyed by Bonnie Prince Charlie's Jacobite army and remained a ruin until the 1830s, when the present castle was built. Now town leaders are discussing plans to build a new museum here, linking the two castle towers with a large exhibit space, but no timetable has been set. The statue outside (from 1899) depicts Flora MacDonald, who helped Bonnie Prince Charlie escape from the English (see page 988).

River Walks

As with most European cities, where there's a river, there's a walk. Inverness, with both the River Ness and the Caledonian Canal, does not disappoint. Consider an early-morning stroll along the Ness Bank to capture the castle at sunrise, or a post-dinner jaunt to Bught Park for a local shinty match. The path is lit at night. The forested islands in the middle of the River Ness—about a 10-minute walk south of the center—are a popular escape from the otherwise busy city.

Here's a good plan for your Inverness riverside constitutional: From the Ness Bridge, head along the riverbank under the castle (along the path called "Ladies Walk"). As you work your way up the river, you'll see the architecturally bold Eden Court Theatre (across the river), pass a white pedestrian bridge, see a WWI memorial, and peek into the gardens of several fine old Victorian sandstone riverfront homes. Nearing the tree-covered islands, watch for fly-fishers in hip waders on the pebbly banks. Reaching the first, skinny little island, take the bridge with the wavy, wrought-iron railing and head down the path along the middle of the island. Notice that this is part of the Great Glen Way, a footpath that stretches from here all the way to Fort William (79 miles). Enjoy this little nature break, with gurgling rapids—and, possibly, a few midges. Reaching the bigger bridge, cross it and enjoy strolling through tall forests. Continue upriver. After two more green-railinged bridges, traverse yet another island, and find one last white-iron bridge that takes you across to the opposite bank. You'll pop out at the corner of Bught Park, the site of shinty practices and games—are any going on today?

From here, you can simply head back into town on this bank. If you'd like to explore more, near Bught Park you'll find minigolf, a skate park, the Highland Archive building, the free Botanic Gardens (daily 10:00-17:00, until 16:00 Nov-March), and the huge Active Inverness leisure center, loaded with amusements including a swimming pool with adventure slides, a climbing wall, a sauna and steam area, and a gym (www.invernessleisure.co.uk).

Continuing west from these leisure areas, you'll soon hit the Caledonian Canal; to the south, this parallels the River Ness, and to the north it empties into Beauly Firth, then Moray Firth and the North Sea. From the Tomnahurich Bridge, paths on either bank allow you to walk along the Great Glen Way until you're ready to turn around. It takes about an hour to circle around from the center of Inverness all the way to Clachnaharry, where the river meets Beauly Firth.

Nightlife in Inverness

Scottish Folk Music

While you can find traditional folk-music sessions in pubs and hotel bars anywhere in town, two places are well established as *the* music pubs. Neither charges a cover for the music, unless a bigger-name band is playing.

The Gellions has live folk and Scottish music nightly (from 21:30 or sometimes earlier). Very local and a bit rough, it has local ales on tap and brags it's the oldest bar in town (14 Bridge Street, tel. 01463/233-648, www.gellions.co.uk).

Hootananny is an energetic place with several floors of live rock, blues, or folk music, and drinking fun nightly. It's rock (upstairs) and reel (ground floor). Music in the main bar (ground floor) usually begins about 21:30 (traditional music sessions Sun-Wed, trad bands on weekends; also a daytime session on Sat afternoon at 14:30). On Friday and Saturday nights only, upstairs is the Mad Hatter's nightclub, complete with a cocktail bar (67 Church Street, tel. 01463/233-651, www.hootannanyinverness.co.uk).

MacGregor's Bar is run by Bruce MacGregor, a founding member of the Scottish group Blazin' Fiddles, and his wife Jo. Their passion for local music (with several music evenings each week) is matched by good food, good local beers on tap, and a fun local crowd. From spring through fall, they also offer a twice-weekly whisky tasting (£35, Mon and Thu at 19:00) along with traditional Scottish music and stories (a few blocks past the pedestrian bridge at 113 Academy Street, tel. 01463/719-629, www.macgregorsbars.com).

Billiards and Darts

SoBar is a sprawling pub with dart boards (free), pool tables (£7.50 per hour), a museum's worth of sports memorabilia, and the biggest TV screens in town (popular on big game nights). It's a fine place to hang out and meet locals if you'd rather not have live music (just across from the castle at 55 Castle Street, tel. 01463/572-542).

Whisky Tastings and Brew Pubs

For a whisky education, or just a fine cocktail, drop in to the intimate **Malt Room,** with 250 different whiskies ranging from £4 to £115. The whisky-plus-chocolate flight makes for a fun nightcap (just off Church Street in the alley leading to the Victorian Market, 34 Church Street, tel. 01463/221-888, Matt).

At the **Black Isle Brewery,** you can sample their local organic beers and ciders. Choose from 26 beers on tap (including some non-Black Isle brews), all listed on the TV screens over the bar (wood-fired pizzas, 68 Church Street, tel. 01463/229-920).

MacGregor's Bar (listed earlier) also offers whisky tastings and beer flights.

Sleeping in Inverness

B&BS NEAR THE TOWN CENTER

These B&Bs are popular; book ahead for June through August (and during the peak times listed in "Helpful Hints," earlier), and be aware that some require a two-night minimum during busy times. The places I list are a 10-15-minute walk from the train station and town center. To get to the B&Bs, either catch a taxi (£5) or walk: From the train and bus stations, go left on Academy Street. At the first stoplight (the second if you're coming from the bus station), veer right onto Inglis Street in the pedestrian zone. Go up the Market Brae steps. At the top, turn right onto Ardconnel Street.

On or near Ardconnel Street

Find these two above Castle Street (with several recommended restaurants).

$$ Ardconnel House is a classic, traditional place offering a nice, large guest lounge, along with six spacious and comfortable rooms (family room, two-night minimum preferred in summer, no children under 10, 21 Ardconnel Street, tel.

01463/418-242, www.ardconnel-inverness.co.uk, ardconnel@gmail.com, Graeme and Audrey).

$$ Crown Hotel Guest House isn't quite as cute and homey as some, and it has a few dated elements, but its seven rooms (five en suite, two with separate but private bathrooms) are pleasant and a solid value (family room, 19 Ardconnel Street, tel. 01463/231-135, www.crownhotel-inverness.co.uk, crownhotelguesthouse@gmail.com, Munawar and Asia).

Around Old Edinburgh Road and Southside Road

These places are just a couple of minutes farther out from Castle Street and the places on Ardconnel.

$$ Eildon Guesthouse offers five tranquil rooms with spacious baths. The cute-as-a-button 1890s brick home is centrally located yet exudes countryside warmth and serenity from the moment you open the gate (family rooms, 2-night minimum in summer, no kids under 10, in-room fridges, parking, 29 Old Edinburgh Road, tel. 01463/231-969, www.eildonguesthouse.co.uk, eildonguesthouse@yahoo.co.uk, Jacqueline).

$$ Dionard Guest House, wrapped in a fine hedged-in garden, has cheerful common spaces, six lovely rooms, some fun stag art, and lively hosts Gail and Anne—best friends turned business partners (family suite, in-room fridges, they'll do guest laundry for free, parking, 39 Old Edinburgh Road, tel. 01463/233-557, www.dionardguesthouse.co.uk, enquiries@dionardguesthouse.co.uk).

$$ Atholdene Guest House, run by amiable Gillian and Andrew, welcomes many return visitors—maybe they come back for the homemade scones? Most of its nine rooms are on the smaller side but comfortable, and classical music in the morning makes for a civilized breakfast (2-night minimum in summer, guests must be 18 or older, parking, 20 Southside Road, tel. 01463/233-565, www.atholdene.com, info@atholdene.com).

$$ Lynver Guest House will make you feel spoiled, with two large, boutique-y rooms (all with sitting areas), a backyard stone patio that catches the sun, and veggie and fish options at breakfast (2-night minimum preferred in summer, no kids under 10, in-room fridges, 30 Southside Road, tel. 01463/242-906, www.lynver.co.uk, info@lynver.co.uk, Michelle and Brian).

$$ Rossmount Guest House feels like home, with its curl-up-on-the-couch lounge space, unfussy rooms (five in all), and friendly hosts (2-night minimum in summer, Argyle Street, tel. 01463/229-749, www.rossmount.co.uk, mail@rossmount.co.uk, Ruth and Robert).

B&Bs ACROSS THE RIVER

$$$ Strathness House has a prime spot on the river a block from Ness Bridge. Formerly a hotel, it's a bigger place, with 12 rooms and a large ground-floor lounge, but comes with the same intimate touches of a guesthouse. They cater to all diets at breakfast, including vegan, gluten-free, halal, and kosher (family room for 3, no kids under 5, street or off-site parking, 4 Ardross Terrace, tel. 01463/232-765, www.strathnesshouse.co.uk, info@strathnesshouse.com, Joan and Javed).

$$ Castle View Guest House sits right along the River Ness at the Ness Bridge—and, true to its name, it owns smashing views of the castle. Its five big and comfy rooms (some with views) are colorfully furnished, and the delightful place is lovingly run by Eleanor (2A Ness Walk, tel. 01463/241-443, www.castleviewguesthouseinverness.com, enquiries@castleviewguesthouseinverness.com).

HOTELS

Inverness has a number of big chain hotels. These tend to charge a lot when Inverness is busy but are worth a look if the B&Bs are full or if it's outside the main tourist season. Options include the Inverness Palace Hotel & Spa (a Best Western fancy splurge right on the river with a pool and gym), Premier Inn (River Ness location), and Mercure. Or try these more local options.

$$$$ Heathmount Hotel's understated facade hides a chic retreat for comfort-seeking travelers. Its eight elegant rooms come with unique decoration, parking, and fancy extras (family room, no elevator, restaurant, Kingsmill Road, tel. 01463/235-877, www.heathmounthotel.com, info@heathounthotel.com).

$$$ Glen Mhor Hotel, with 122 rooms, sprawls across several buildings right along the river. The location can't be beat, even if the staff and rooms lack a personal touch (restaurant, Ness Bank, tel. 01463/234-308, www.glen-mhor.com, enquiries@glen-mhor.com).

HOSTELS

For funky and cheap dorm beds near the center and the recommended Castle Street restaurants, consider these friendly side-by-side hostels, geared toward younger travelers. They're about a 12-minute walk from the train station.

¢ Bazpackers Hostel, a stone's throw from the castle, has a quieter, more private feel for a hostel with dorm beds arranged in pods (private rooms with shared bath available, reception open 7:30-23:00, pay laundry service, 4 Culduthel Road, tel. 01463/717-663, www.bazpackershostel.co.uk, info@bazpackershostel.co.uk). They also rent a small apartment nearby (sleeps up to 4).

¢ **Inverness Student Hotel** has brightly colored rooms and a laid-back lounge with a bay window overlooking the River Ness. The knowledgeable, friendly staff welcomes any traveler over 18. Dorms are a bit grungy, but each bunk has its own playful name (breakfast extra, free tea and coffee, pay laundry service, kitchen, 8 Culduthel Road, tel. 01463/236-556, www.invernessstudenthotel. com, inverness@scotlandstophostels.com).

Eating in Inverness

In high season, Inverness' top restaurants (including many of those recommended below) can fill up quickly—reservations are wise.

BY THE CASTLE

The first three eateries line Castle Street, facing the back of the castle.

$$$ **Café 1** serves up high-quality modern Scottish and international cuisine with trendy, chic bistro flair. Fresh meat from their farm adds to an appealing menu (lunch and early-bird dinner specials until 18:30, open Mon-Fri 12:00-14:30 & 17:00-21:30, Sat from 12:30 and 17:30, closed Sun, 75 Castle Street, tel. 01463/226-200, www.cafe1.net).

$$ **Number 27** has a straightforward, crowd-pleasing menu that offers something for everyone—burgers, pastas, and more. The food is surprisingly elegant for this price range (daily 12:00-21:00, generous portions, local ales on tap, 27 Castle Street, tel. 01463/241-999).

$$ **La Tortilla** has Spanish tapas, including spicy king prawns (the house specialty), plus a vegan menu. It's an appealing, colorfully tiled, and vivacious dining option that feels like Spain. With the tapas format, three family-style dishes make about one meal (daily 12:00-22:00, 99 Castle Street, tel. 01463/709-809).

IN THE TOWN CENTER

$$$$ **The Mustard Seed** serves Scottish food with a modern twist in an old church with a river view. It's a lively place with nice outdoor tables over the river when sunny (early specials before 19:00, daily 12:00-15:00 & 17:30-22:00, reservations smart, on the corner of Bank and Fraser Streets, 16 Fraser Street, tel. 01463/220-220, www.mustardseedrestaurant.co.uk).

$$ **Hootananny** is a spacious pub with a hardwood-and-candlelight vibe and a fun menu with Scottish pub grub (food served Mon-Sat 12:00-15:00 & 17:00-20:30, dinner-only on Sun). The kitchen closes early to make way for the live music scene that takes over each night after 21:30 (see "Nightlife in Inverness," earlier).

$$ **Aspendos** serves up freshly prepared, delicious Turkish

dishes in a spacious, dressy, and exuberantly decorated dining room (daily 12:00-22:00, 26 Queensgate, tel. 01463/711-950).

Picnic: There's a **Co-op** market with plenty of cheap picnic grub at 59 Church Street (daily until 22:00).

ACROSS THE RIVER

$$$$ Rocpool Restaurant is a hit with locals, good for a splurge, and perhaps the best place in town. Owner/chef Steven Devlin serves creative modern European food to a smart clientele in a sleek, contemporary dining room (early-bird weekday special until 18:45, open Mon-Sat 12:00-14:30 & 17:45-22:00, closed Sun, reservations essential; across Ness Bridge at 1 Ness Walk, tel. 01463/717-274, www.rocpoolrestaurant.com).

$$$$ River House, a classy, sophisticated, but unstuffy place, is the brainchild of Cornishman Alfie—who prides himself on melding the seafood know-how of both Cornwall and Scotland with Venetian-style *cicchetti* small plates (Mon-Sat 15:00-21:30, closed Mon off-season and Sun year-round, reservations smart, 1 Greig Street, tel. 01463/222-033, www.riverhouseinverness.co.uk).

$$$ The Kitchen Brasserie is a modern building overlooking the river, popular for their homemade comfort food—pizza, pasta, and burgers (early-bird special until 19:00, daily 12:00-15:00 & 17:00-22:00, 15 Huntly Street, tel. 01463/259-119, www.kitchenrestaurant.co.uk).

Fish-and-Chips: Consider the **$ West End** chippy for a nicely presented sit-down meal or to go (daily 12:00-14:00 & 16:30-22:00, closed Sun at lunch, a block over Ness Bridge on Young Street, tel. 01463/232-884).

Inverness Connections

From Inverness by Train to: Edinburgh (nearly hourly, 3.5 hours, some with change in Perth), **Glasgow** (4/day direct, 3 hours, more with change in Perth). The Caledonian Sleeper provides overnight service to **London** (www.sleeper.scot). Train info: tel. 0345-748-4950, NationalRail.co.uk.

By Bus: For destinations in western Scotland, you'll first head for **Fort William** (buses #919 or #920, 6/day, 2 hours, fewer on Sun). For connections onward to **Oban** (figure 4 hours total) or **Glencoe** (3 hours total), see "Fort William Connections" on page 969. Inverness is also connected by direct bus to **Edinburgh** (express bus #G90, 2/day, 4 hours or #M90, 2/day, 4 hours, more with transfer) and **Glasgow** (express bus #G10, 5/day, 3 hours; 6/day direct on Megabus, 3.5 hours). Bus info: CityLink.co.uk.

Tickets are sold in advance online, by phone at tel. 0871-266-3333, or in person at the Inverness bus station (daily 7:45-18:15, baggage storage, 2 blocks from train station on Margaret Street, tel. 01463/233-371).

ROUTE TIPS FOR DRIVERS

Inverness to Edinburgh (160 miles, 3.25 hours minimum): Leaving Inverness, follow signs to the A-9 (south, toward Perth). If you haven't seen Culloden Battlefield yet, it's an easy detour: Just as you leave Inverness, head four miles east off the A-9 on the B-9006. Back on the A-9, it's a wonderfully speedy, scenic drive (A-9, M-90, A-90) all the way to Edinburgh.

Inverness to Fort William (65 miles, 1.5 hours): This city, southwest of Inverness via the A-82, is a good gateway to Oban and Glencoe (see page 969).

Near Inverness

Inverness puts you in the heart of the Highlands, within easy striking distance of several famous and worthwhile sights: Commune with the Scottish soul at historic Culloden Battlefield, where British history reached a turning point. Wonder at three mysterious Neolithic cairns, which remind visitors that Scotland's story goes back thousands of years. And enjoy a homey country castle at Cawdor. Loch Ness—with its elusive monster—is another popular and easy day trip.

CULLODEN BATTLEFIELD

Jacobite troops under Bonnie Prince Charlie were defeated at Culloden by supporters of the Hanover dynasty (King George II's family) in 1746. Sort of the "Scottish Alamo," this last major land battle fought on British soil spelled the end of Jacobite resistance and the beginning of the clan chiefs' fall from power. Wandering the desolate, solemn battlefield at Culloden (kuh-LAW-dehn), you sense that something terrible occurred here. Locals still bring white roses and speak of "The '45" (as Bonnie Prince Charlie's entire campaign is called) as if it just happened. Engaging even if you're not interested in military history, the battlefield at Culloden and its high-tech visitors center together are worth ▲▲▲.

Orientation to Culloden

Cost and Hours: £11, £5 guidebook; daily 9:00-18:00, June-Aug until 19:00, Nov-Feb 10:00-16:00; café, tel. 01463/796-090, www.nts.org.uk/culloden.

Tours: The included audioguide leads you through both the exhibition and the battlefield. There are several free tours daily along with costumed events (see schedule posted at entry).

Getting There: It's a 15-minute drive east of Inverness. Follow signs to *Aberdeen*, then *Culloden Moor*—the B-9006 takes you right there (well-signed on the right-hand side). Parking is £2 (pay with coins outside or with your admission inside). Public buses leave from Inverness' Queensgate Street and drop you off in front of the entrance (£5 round-trip, bus #5, roughly hourly, 40 minutes, ask at TI for route/schedule updates). A taxi costs around £15 one-way.

Length of This Tour: Allow 2 hours.

Background

The Battle of Culloden (April 16, 1746) marks the steep decline of the Scottish Highland clans and the start of years of cruel repression of Highland culture by the British. It was the culmination of a year's worth of battles, and at the center of it all was the charismatic, enigmatic Bonnie Prince Charlie (1720-1788).

Though usually depicted as a battle of the Scottish versus the English, in truth Culloden was a civil war between two opposing dynasties: Stuart (Charlie) and Hanover (George). However, as the history has faded into lore, the battle has come to be remembered as a Scottish-versus-English standoff—or, in the parlance of the Scots, the Highlanders versus the Strangers.

Charles Edward Stuart, from his first breath, was raised with a single purpose—to restore his family to the British throne. His grandfather was King James II (VII of Scotland), deposed in 1688 by the English Parliament for his tyranny and pro-Catholic bias. The Stuarts remained in exile in France and Italy until 1745, when young Charlie crossed the Channel from France to retake the throne in the name of his father. He landed on the west coast of Scotland and rallied support for the Jacobite cause. Though Charles was not Scottish-born, he was the rightful heir directly down the line from Mary, Queen of Scots—and why so many Scots joined the rebellion out of resentment at being ruled by a "foreign" king (King George II, who was born in Germany, couldn't even speak English).

Bagpipes droned, and "Bonnie" (handsome) Charlie led an army of 2,000 tartan-wearing, Gaelic-speaking Highlanders across Scotland, seizing Edinburgh. They picked up other supporters of the Stuarts from the Lowlands and from England. Now 6,000 strong, they marched south toward London—quickly advancing as far as Derby, just 125 miles from the capital—and King George II made plans to flee the country. But anticipated support for the Jacobites failed to materialize in the numbers they were hoping for (both in England and from France). The Jacobites had so far been victorious in their battles against the Hanoverian government forces, but the odds now turned against them. Charles retreated to the Scottish Highlands, where many of his men knew the terrain and might gain an advantage when outnumbered. The English government troops followed closely on his heels.

Against the advice of his best military strategist, Charles' army faced the Hanoverian forces at Culloden Moor on flat, barren terrain that was unsuited to the Highlanders' guerrilla tactics. The Jacobites—many of them brandishing only broadswords, targes (wooden shields covered in leather and studs), and dirks (long daggers)—were mowed down by King George's cannons and horsemen. In less than an hour, the government  forces routed the Jacobite army, but that was just the start. They spent the next weeks methodically hunting down ringleaders and sympathizers (and many others in the Highlands who had nothing to do with the battle), ruthlessly killing, imprisoning, and banishing thousands.

Charles fled with a £30,000 price on his head (an equivalent of millions of today's pounds). He escaped to the Isle of Skye, hidden by a woman named Flora MacDonald (her grave is on the Isle of Skye, and her statue is outside Inverness Castle). Flora dressed Charles in women's clothes and passed him off as her maid. Later, Flora was arrested and thrown in the Tower of London before being released and treated like a celebrity.

Charles escaped to France. He spent the rest of his life wandering Europe trying to drum up support to retake the throne. He drifted through short-lived romantic affairs and alcohol, and died in obscurity, without an heir, in Rome.

The Battle of Culloden was the end of 60 years of Jacobite rebellions, the last major battle fought on British soil, and the final stand of the Highlanders. From then on, clan chiefs were deposed; kilts, tartans, and bagpipes were outlawed; and farmers were cleared off their ancestral land, replaced by more-profitable sheep. Scottish culture would never fully recover from the events of the campaign called "The '45."

◗ Self-Guided Tour

Your tour takes you through two sections: the exhibit and the actual battlefield.

The Exhibit

As you pass the ticket desk, note the **family tree:** Bonnie Prince Charlie ("Charles Edward Stuart") and George II were distant cousins. Then the exhibit's shadowy-figure **touchscreens** connect you with historical figures who give you details from both the Hanoverian and Jacobite perspectives. A **map** shows the other power struggles happening in and around Europe, putting this fight for political control of Britain in a wider context. This battle was no small regional skirmish, but rather a key part of a larger struggle between Britain and its neighbors, primarily France, for control over trade and colonial power. In the display case are **medals** from the early 1700s, made by both sides as propaganda.

From here, your path through this building is cleverly designed to echo the course of the Jacobite army. Your short march (with lots of historic artifacts) gets under way as Charlie sails from France to Scotland, then finagles the support of Highland clan chiefs. As he heads south with his army to take London, you, too, are walking south. Along the way, maps show the movement of troops, and wall panels cover the buildup to the attack, as seen from both sides. Note the clever division of information: To the left and in red is the story of the "government" (a.k.a. Hanoverians/Whigs/English, led by the Duke of Cumberland); to the right, in blue, is the Jacobites' perspective (Prince Charlie and his Highlander/French supporters).

But you, like Charlie, don't make it to London—in the dark room at the end, you can hear Jacobite commanders arguing over whether to retreat back to Scotland. Pessimistic about their chances of receiving more French support, they decide to U-turn, and so do you. Heading back up north, you'll get some insight into some of the strategizing that went on behind the scenes.

By the time you reach the end of the hall, it's the night before the battle. Round another bend into a dark passage, and listen to the voices of the anxious troops. While the English slept soundly in their tents (recovering from celebrating the Duke's 25th birthday), the scrappy and exhausted Jacobite Highlanders struggled through the night to reach the battlefield (abandoning their plan of a surprise night attack at Nairn and instead retreating back toward Inverness).

At last the two sides meet. As you wait outside the theater for the next showing, study the chart depicting how the forces were

arranged on the battlefield. Once inside the theater, you'll soon be surrounded by the views and sounds of a windswept moor. An impressive four-minute **360° movie** projects the re-enacted battle with you right in the center of the action. The movie drives home just how outmatched the Jacobites were.

The last room has **period weapons,** including ammunition and artifacts found on the battlefield, as well as **historical depictions** of the battle. You'll also find a section describing the detective work required to piece together the story from historical evidence. Be sure to tour the **aftermath corridor,** which talks about the nearly genocidal years following the battle and the cultural wake of this event to this day. Be sure to examine the **huge map,** with narration explaining the combat you've just experienced while giving you a bird's-eye view of the field through which you're about to roam.

The Battlefield

Leaving the visitors center, survey the battlefield (which you'll tour with the help of your audioguide). In the foreground is a cottage used as a makeshift hospital during the conflict. Red flags show the front line of the government army (8,000 troops). This is where most of the hand-to-hand fighting took place. The blue flags in the distance are where the Jacobite army (5,500 troops) lined up.

As you explore the battlefield, notice how uneven and boggy the ground is in parts, and imagine trying to run across this hummocky terrain with all your gear, toward almost-certain death.

The old stone memorial cairn, erected in 1881, commemorates the roughly 1,500 Jacobites buried in this field. It's known as the Graves of the Clans. As you wander the battlefield, following the audioguide, you'll pass by other **mass graves,** marked by small headstones, and ponder how entire clans fought, died, and were buried here. *Outlander* fans often leave flowers at the Fraser clan headstone.

Near the visitor center, the restored stone-and-turf **Leanach Cottage** predates Culloden and may have been used as a field hospital during the battle. A small exhibit inside explains plans to preserve Culloden for future generations.

Heading back to the parking lot, notice the wall of **protruding bricks.** Each represents a soldier who died. The handful of Hanoverian casualties is on the left (about 50); the rest of the long wall's raised bricks represent the multitude of dead Jacobites.

CLAVA CAIRNS

Scotland is littered with reminders of prehistoric peoples—especially in Orkney and along the coast of the Moray Firth—but

the Clava Cairns, worth ▲ for a quick visit, are among the best-preserved, most interesting, and easiest to reach. You'll find them nestled in the countryside just beyond Culloden Battlefield.

Cost and Hours: Free, always open; just after passing Culloden Battlefield on the B-9006 coming from Inverness, signs on the right point to *Clava Cairns*. Follow this twisty road a couple of miles, over the "weak bridge" and to the free parking lot by the stones. Skip the cairns if you don't have a car.

Visiting the Cairns: These "Balnauran of Clava" are Neolithic burial chambers dating from 3,000 to 4,000 years ago. Although they appear to be just some giant piles of rocks in a sparsely forested clearing, a closer look will help you appreciate the prehistoric logic behind them. (The site is explained by a few information plaques.) There are three structures: a central "ring cairn" with an open space in the center but no access to it, flanked by two "passage cairns," which were once buried under turf-covered mounds. The entrance shaft in each passage cairn lines up with the setting sun at the winter solstice. A stone circle surrounds each cairn, and the entire ensemble is framed by evocative trees—injecting this site with even more mystery.

Enjoy the site's many enigmas: Were the stone circles part of a celestial calendar system? Or did they symbolize guardians?

Why were the clamshell-sized hollows carved into the stones facing the chambers? Was the soul of the deceased transported into the next life by the ray of sunlight on that brief moment that it filled the inner chamber? How many *Outlander* fans have taken selfies in front of the split standing stone (which inspired a similar stone in the novel)? No one knows.

CAWDOR CASTLE

Atmospheric, intimate, and worth ▲, this castle is still the residence of the Dowager (read: widow) Countess of Cawdor, a local aristocratic branch of the Camp-

bell family. While many associate the castle with Shakespeare's *Macbeth* (because "Cawdor" is mentioned more than a dozen times in the play), there is no actual connection with Shakespeare. *Macbeth* is set 300 years before the castle was even built. The castle is worth a visit simply because it's historic and beautiful in its own right—and because the woman who owns it flies a Buddhist flag from its tower. She is from Eastern Europe and was the Earl's second wife.

Cost and Hours: £12.50, includes audioguide, May-Sept daily 10:00-17:30, closed Oct-April, tel. 01667/404-401, www.cawdorcastle.com. The good £5.50 guidebook provides more detail on the family and the rooms. Storage is available for larger bags, which cannot be brought into the castle.

Getting There: It's on the B-9090, just off the A-96, about 15 miles east of Inverness (6 miles beyond Culloden and Clava Cairns). Public transportation to the castle is scant, but check at the TI for current options.

Visiting the Castle: You'll follow a one-way circuit around the castle with each room well described with posted explanations written by the countess' late husband, the sixth Earl of Cawdor. His witty notes bring the castle to life and make you wish you'd known the old chap. Cawdor feels very lived-in because it is. While the Dowager Countess moves out during the tourist season, for the rest of the year this is her home. You can imagine her stretching out in front of the fireplace with a good book. Notice her geraniums in every room.

The drawing room (for "with-drawing" after dinner) is lined

with a family tree of portraits looking down. In the Tapestry Bedroom you'll see the actual marriage bed of Sir Hugh Campbell from 1662 and 17th-century tapestries warming the walls. In the Yellow Room, a flat-screen TV hides inside an 18th-century cabinet (ask a docent to show you). In the Tartan Passage, lined with modern paintings, find today's dowager—Lady Angelika—in a beautiful 1970 pastel portrait, staring at her late husband's predecessors. Notice how their eyes follow you creepily down the hall—but hers do not.

A spiral stone staircase near the end of the tour leads down to the castle's proud symbol: a holly tree dating from 1372. According to the beloved legend, a donkey leaned against this tree to mark the spot where the castle was to be built...and it was, around the tree.

The **gardens,** included with the castle ticket, are worth exploring, with some 18th-century lin-den trees and several surprising species (including sequoia and redwood). The hedge maze, crowned by a minotaur and surrounded by a laburnum arbor (dripping with yellow blossoms in spring), is not open to the public.

The nine-hole **golf course** on the castle grounds provides a quick and affordable way to have a Scottish golfing experience. The course is bigger than pitch-and-putt and fun even for non-golfers (£18.50/person with clubs). You're welcome to try the putting green for £4.

Nearby: The close but remote-feeling **village of Cawdor**—with a few houses, a village shop, and a tavern—is also worth a look if you've got time to kill.

Loch Ness

I'll admit it: I had my zoom lens out and my eyes on the water. The local tourist industry thrives on the legend of the Loch Ness monster. It's a thrilling thought, and there have been several seemingly reliable "sightings" (by monks, police officers, and sonar imaging). But even if you ignore the monster stories, the loch is impressive: 23 miles long, less than a mile wide, 754 feet deep, and containing more water than all of the freshwater bodies of England and Wales combined. It's essentially the vast chasm of a fault line, filled with water.

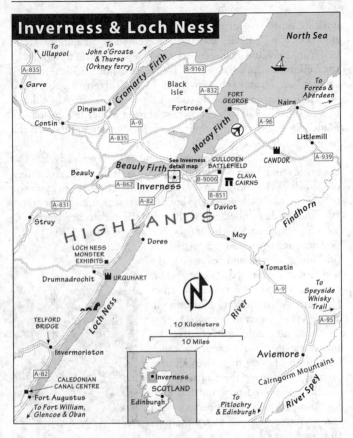

Inverness & Loch Ness

Getting There: The Loch Ness sights are a 20-minute drive southwest of Inverness. To drive the full length of Loch Ness takes about 45 minutes. Fort William-bound buses #919 and #920 make stops at Urquhart Castle and Drumnadrochit (8/day, 40 minutes).

Sights on Loch Ness

In July 1933, a couple swore they saw a giant sea monster shimmy across the road in front of their car by Loch Ness. Within days, ancient legends about giant monsters in the lake (dating as far back as the sixth century) were revived—and suddenly everyone was spotting "Nessie" poke its head above the waters of Loch Ness. Further sightings and photographic "evidence" have bolstered the claim that there's something mysterious living in this unthinkably deep and murky lake. (Most sightings take place in the deepest part of the loch, near Urquhart Castle.) Most witnesses describe a water-bound dinosaur resembling the real, but extinct, plesiosaur. Others cling to the slightly more plausible theory of a gigantic eel. And skeptics figure the sightings can be explained by a combination of reflections, boat wakes, and mass hysteria. The most

famous photo of the beast (dubbed the "Surgeon's Photo") was later discredited—the "monster's" head was actually attached to a toy submarine. But that hasn't stopped various cryptozoologists from seeking photographic, sonar, and other proof.

And that suits the thriving local tourist industry just fine. The Nessie commercialization is so tacky that there are two different monster exhibits within 100 yards of each other, both in the town of Drumnadrochit. Of the two competing sites, Nessieland is pretty cheesy while the Loch Ness Centre and Exhibition (described next) is surprisingly thoughtful. Each has a tour-bus parking lot and more square footage devoted to their kitschy shops than to the exhibits. While Nessieland is a tourist trap, the Loch Ness Centre may appease that small part of you that knows the *real* reason you wanted to see Loch Ness.

▲Loch Ness Centre & Exhibition

This attraction is better and more methodical than you might expect, and is worth visiting if you want to understand the geological and historical environment that bred the monster story. It's spearheaded by Adrian Shine, a naturalist fond of saying "I like mud," who has spent many years researching lake ecology and scientific phenomena. The exhibit has two parts: First you go through a series of rooms with videos and special effects, and then you enter a section on the history of the Great Glen and Loch Ness. The videos detail the various searches that have been conducted; refreshingly, they retain an air of healthy skepticism instead of breathless monster-chasing. You'll also see some artifacts related to the search, such as a hippo-foot ashtray used to fake monster footprints and the *Viperfish*—a harpoon-equipped submarine used in a 1969 Nessie expedition. And you'll learn how in 1952 record-seeker John Cobb died going 200 mph in his speedboat on the loch.

Cost and Hours: £8.45, RS%—ask, daily Easter-Oct 9:30-17:45, July-Aug until 18:45, Nov-Easter 10:00-16:15, last entry 45 minutes before closing, in the big stone mansion right on the main road to Inverness, tel. 01456/450-573, www.lochness.com.

▲Urquhart Castle

The ruins at Urquhart (UR-kurt), just up the loch from the Nessie exhibits, are gloriously situated with a view of virtually the entire lake but create a traffic jam of tourism on busy days.

The visitors center has a tiny exhibit with interesting castle artifacts and an eight-minute film taking you on a sweep through a thousand years of tumultuous history—from St. Columba's visit to the castle's final destruction in 1689. The castle itself, while dramatically situated and fun to climb through, is an empty shell. After its owners (who supported the crown) blew it up to keep the Jacobites from taking it, the largest medieval castle in Scotland (and the most important in the Highlands) wasn't considered worth rebuilding or defending, and was abandoned. Well-placed, descriptive signs help you piece together this once-mighty fortress. As you walk toward the ruins, take a close look at the trebuchet (a working replica of one of the most destructive weapons of English King Edward I), and ponder how this giant catapult helped Edward grab almost every castle in the country away from the native Scots.

Cost and Hours: £12, guidebook-£5, daily April-May and Sept 9:30-18:00, June-Aug until 20:00, Oct until 17:00, shorter hours off-season, last entry 45 minutes before closing, café, tel. 01456/450-551, www.historicenvironment.scot. The parking lot can fill up in summer—either wait in the queue for a space, or park in the overflow lot. It's a 20-minute walk away, back toward Inverness.

Loch Ness Cruises

Cruises on Loch Ness are as popular as they are pointless. The lake is far from Scotland's prettiest—and the time-consuming boat trips show you little more than what you'll see from the road. As it seems that Loch Ness cruises are a mandatory part of every "Highlands Highlights" day tour, there are several options, leaving from the top, bottom, and middle of the loch. The basic one-hour loop costs around £15 and includes views of Urquhart Castle and lots of legends and romantic history (Jacobite is the dominant outfit of the many cruise companies, www.jacobite.co.uk). I'd rather spend my time and money at Fort Augustus or Urquhart Castle.

▲Fort Augustus

Perhaps the most idyllic stop along the Caledonian Canal is the little lochside town of Fort Augustus. It was founded in the 1700s—

The Caledonian Canal

Two hundred million years ago, two tectonic plates collided, creating the landmass we know as Scotland and leaving a crevice of thin lakes slashing diagonally across the country. This Great Glen Fault, from Inverness to Oban, is easily visible on any map.

Scottish engineer Thomas Telford connected the lakes 200 years ago with a series of canals so ships could avoid the  long trip around the north of the country. The Caledonian Canal runs 62 miles from Scotland's east to west coasts; 22 miles of it is man-made. Telford's great feat of engineering took 19 years to complete, opening in 1822 at a cost of one million pounds. But bad timing made the canal a disaster commercially. Napoleon's defeat in 1815 meant that ships could sail the open seas more freely. And by the time the canal opened, commercial ships were too big for its 15-foot depth. Just a couple of decades after the Caledonian Canal opened, trains made the canal almost useless...except for Romantic Age tourism. Since the time of Queen Victoria (who cruised the canal in 1873), the canal has been a popular tourist attraction. To this day the canal is a hit with vacationers, recreational boaters, and lock-keepers who compete for the best-kept lock.

The scenic drive from Inverness along the canal is entertaining, with Drumnadrochit (Nessie centers), Urquhart Castle, Fort Augustus (five locks), and Fort William (under Ben Nevis, with the eight-lock "Neptune's Staircase"). As you cross Scotland, you'll follow Telford's work—22 miles of canals and locks between three lochs, raising ships from sea level to 51 feet (Ness), 93 feet (Lochy), and 106 feet (Oich).

While Neptune's Staircase, a series of eight locks near Fort William, has been cleverly named to sound intriguing, the best lock stop is midway, at Fort Augustus, where the canal hits the south end of Loch Ness. In Fort Augustus, the **Caledonian Canal Centre,** overlooking the canal just off the main road, gives a good rundown on Telford's work (see "Fort Augustus" at the end of this chapter). Stroll past several shops and eateries to the top for a fine view.

Seven miles north, in the town of **Invermoriston,** is another Telford structure: a stone bridge, dating from 1805, that spans the Morriston Falls as part of the original road. Look for a small parking lot just before the junction at A-82 and A-887, on your right as you drive from Fort Augustus. Cross the A-82 and walk three minutes back the way you came. The bridge, which took eight years to build and is still in use, is on your right.

before there was a canal here—as part of a series of garrisons and military roads built by the English to quell the Highland clansmen, even as the Jacobites kept trying to take the throne in London. Before then, there were no developed roads in the Highlands—and without roads, it's hard to keep indigenous people down.

From 1725 to 1733, the English built 250 miles of hard roads and 40 bridges to open up the region; Fort Augustus was a central Highlands garrison at the southern tip of Loch Ness, designed to awe clansmen. It was named for William Augustus, Duke of Cumberland—notorious for his role in destroying the clan way of life in the Highlands. (When there's no media or photographs to get in the way, ethnic cleansing has little effect on one's reputation.)

Fort Augustus makes for a delightful stop if you're driving through the area. Parking is easy. There are plenty of B&Bs, charming eateries, and an inviting park along the town's five locks. You can still see the capstans, surviving from the days when the locks were cranked open by hand.

The fine little **Caledonian Canal Centre** tells the story of the canal's construction (free, daily, tel. 01320/725-581). Also consider the pleasant little canalside stroll out to the head of the loch.

Eating in Fort Augustus: You can eat reasonably at a string of $ eateries lining the same side of the canal. Consider **The Nourish Ness Community Café,** a good choice serving filled rolls and homemade soups; **The Lock Inn,** cozy and pub-like with great canalside tables, ideal if it's sunny; **The Bothy,** another pub with decent food; and the **Canalside Chip Shop** offering fish-and-chips to go (no seating, but plenty of nice spots on the canal). A small grocery store is at the gas station, next to the TI, which is a few steps from the canal just after crossing the River Oich (also housing the post office, a WC, and an ATM).

BRITAIN:
PAST & PRESENT

To fully appreciate the many fascinating sights you'll encounter in your travels, learn the basics of the sweeping story of this land and its people. (Generally speaking, the fascinating stories you'll hear from tour guides are not true...and the boring ones are.)

Regardless of the revolution we had more than 240 years ago, many American travelers feel that they "go home" to Britain. This most popular tourist destination has a strange influence and power over us. The more you know of Britain's roots, the better you'll get in touch with your own.

This chapter starts with a once-over of Britain's illustrious history. It's speckled throughout with more in-depth information about current issues and this great country's future.

British History

ORIGINS (2000 BC-AD 500)

When Julius Caesar landed on the misty and mysterious isle of Britain in 55 BC, England entered the history books. He was met by primitive Celtic tribes whose druid priests made human sacrifices and worshipped trees. (Those Celts were themselves immigrants, who had earlier conquered the even more mysterious people who built Stonehenge.) The Romans eventually settled in England (AD 43) and set about building towns and roads and establishing their capital at Londinium (today's London).

PAST & PRESENT

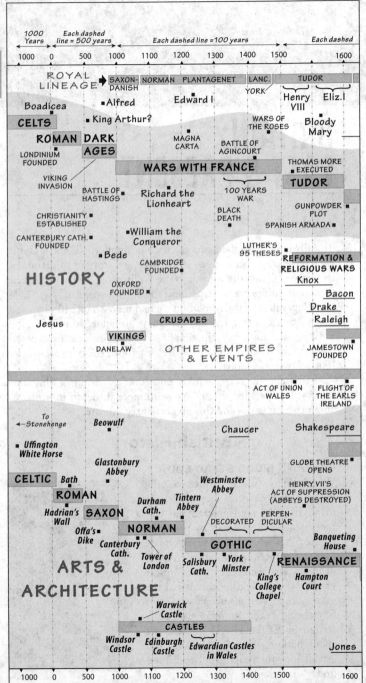

British History & Art Timeline

line = 50 years   Each dashed line = 25 years

1700   1800   1900   1950   2000

STUART

COMMON-WEALTH & PROTECTORATE

HANOVER   George III   Victoria   SAXE-COBURG   WINDSOR   Elizabeth II

Cromwell

EDWARD VIII ABDICATES

Diana R.I.P.

GREAT PLAGUE & GREAT FIRE

WATERLOO

CRIMEAN WAR.

Churchill

KING VS/ PARL.

BATTLE OF TRAFALGAR

TRENCH WARFARE

BLITZ

LONDON OLYMPICS

CIVIL WAR

COLONIAL EXPANSION

BOER WARS

WWI WWII

CHUNNEL

VICTORIAN

MARSHALL PLAN

GLOBAL RECESSION

JACOBITES

WORLD WARS & RECOVERY

Jack the Ripper

Darwin

1ST BBC BROADCAST

JOINS EC

EU

TODAY

PEACE OF WESTPHALIA

Napoleon

GERMAN UNIFICATION

Newton

FRENCH REV.

Gandhi

BREXIT

MAY-FLOWER

FRENCH & INDIAN WARS

AMERICAN REV.

AUSTRALIA INDEP.

CANADA INDEP.

INDIA INDEP.

HONG KONG INDEP.

EXPLORATION & COLONIALISM

BATTLE OF THE BOYNE

INDUSTRIAL REV.

EASTER UPRISING

IRISH FREE STATE

SCOTTISH AUTONOMY

CELTIC TIGER

SCOTLAND, WALES & IRELAND

ACT OF UNION SCOTLAND

ACT OF UNION IRELAND

POTATO FAMINE

N. IRE. FORMED

"TROUBLES"

GOOD FRI. ACCORDS

Picasso

Steves

Hogarth

Woolf

Handel   Austen   Dickens   Orwell   Rowling

LITERATURE

Wordsworth

Tolkein

Byron   Blake

Lewis

ROMANTICISM

Kipling

Monty Python

Turner

Beatles

Gainsborough

Moore

Stones

Constable

Freud

Reynolds

PRE-RAPHAELITE

Bacon

CONTEMP.

Blenheim Palace

Houses of Parliament

CUBISM

POST-WAR

BAROQUE

GEORGIAN

MOD.ART

New St. Paul's

Royal Crescent

REVIVALS

Shard

Wren

Iron Bridge

ART NOUVEAU

MODERNISM

Millennium Bridge

IND. AGE ARCH.

Glasgow School of Art

POSTMOD.

Brown

Crystal Palace

Blackpool Tower

Foster

CONTEMP.

1700   1800   1900   1950   2000

But the Celtic natives—consisting of Gaels, Picts, and Scots—were not easily subdued. Around AD 60, Boadicea, a queen of the Isle's indigenous people, defied the Romans and burned Londinium before the revolt was squelched. Some decades later, the Romans built Hadrian's Wall near the Scottish border as protection against their troublesome northern neighbors. Even today, the Celtic language and influence are strongest in these far reaches of Britain.

Londinium became a bustling Roman river-and-sea trading port. The Romans built the original London Bridge and a city wall, encompassing one square mile, which set the city boundaries for 1,500 years. By AD 200, London was a thriving, Latin-speaking capital of Roman-dominated England.

DARK AGES (500-1000)

As Rome fell, so fell Roman Britain—a victim of invaders and internal troubles. Barbarian tribes from Germany, Denmark, and northern Holland, called Angles, Saxons, and Jutes, swept through the southern part of the island, establishing Angle-land. These were the days of the real King Arthur, possibly a Christianized Roman general who fought valiantly—but in vain—against invading barbarians.

In 793, England was hit with the first of two centuries of savage invasions by barbarians from Norway, called the Vikings, or Norsemen. King Alfred the Great (849-899) liberated London from Danish Vikings, reunited England, reestablished Christianity, and fostered learning. Nevertheless, for most of this 500-year period, the island was plunged into a dark age—wars, plagues, and poverty—lit only by the dim candle of a few learned Christian monks and missionaries trying to convert the barbarians. Today, visitors see little from this Anglo-Saxon period.

WARS WITH FRANCE, WARS OF THE ROSES (1000-1500)

Modern England began with yet another invasion. In 1066, William the Conqueror and his Norman troops crossed the English Channel from France. William crowned himself king in Westminster Abbey (where all subsequent coronations would take place). He began building the Tower of London, as well as Windsor Castle, which would become the residence of many monarchs to come.

Over the succeeding centuries, French-speaking kings would rule England, and English-

Britain Almanac

Official Name: The United Kingdom of Great Britain and Northern Ireland (locals say "the UK" or "Britain").

Size: Britain's 65 million people inhabit one large island and a chunk of another, totaling 95,000 square miles (about the size of Michigan).

Geography: Most of the British Isles consists of low hills and rolling plains, with a moderate climate. The country's highest point is 4,410-foot Ben Nevis in western Scotland. Britain's two longest rivers are the Severn (flowing 220 miles east from Wales and then south) and the Thames (running 215 miles through southern England, including London).

Latitude and Longitude: 54°N and 2°W. The latitude is similar to Alberta, Canada.

Biggest Cities: London is the capital, with 10.3 million people. Industrial Birmingham has about 1 million, Glasgow 621,000, Edinburgh 500,000, and the port of Liverpool 500,000.

People: Britain's population includes a sizable and growing minority of immigrants, largely from Asia and Eastern Europe. Six in ten Brits call themselves Christian (half of those are Anglican), but in any given week, more Brits visit a mosque than an Anglican church.

Economy: The Gross Domestic Product is $2.9 trillion and the GDP per capita is $44,300. Moneymakers include banking, insurance, agriculture, shipping, and trade. Heavy industry—which drove the Industrial Revolution—is in decline.

Government: Queen Elizabeth II officially heads the country, but in practice it's the prime minister, who leads the majority party in Parliament. Conservative leader Boris Johnson became prime minister in 2019 in the wake of the Brexit upheaval triggered by Britain's referendum on exiting the European Union (a process that's been unfolding over years).

In 1999, Scotland, Wales, and Northern Ireland were each granted their own Parliament, a move that provided some autonomy but failed to quash independence movements, particularly in Scotland.

Flag: The "Union Jack" has three crosses on a field of blue: the English cross of St. George, the Irish cross of St. Patrick, and the Scottish cross of St. Andrew.

The Average Brit: Eats 35 pounds of pizza and 25 pounds of chocolate a year, and weighs 12 stone (170 pounds). He or she is 40 years old, has 1.9 children, and will live to age 81.

The average Brit drinks about 8 cups of tea and 2.5 glasses of wine a week. He/she has free health care and gets 28 vacation days a year (versus 13 in the US). He/she sleeps 7.5 hours a night, speaks one language, loves soccer, and enjoys talking about the weather.

speaking kings invaded France as the two budding nations defined their modern borders. Richard the Lionheart (1157-1199) ruled as a French-speaking king who spent most of his energy on distant Crusades. This was the time of the legendary (and possibly real) Robin Hood, a bandit who robbed from the rich and gave to the poor—a populace that felt neglected by its francophone rulers. In 1215, King John (Richard's brother), under pressure from England's barons, was forced to sign the Magna Carta, establishing the principle that even kings must follow the rule of law.

London asserted itself as England's trade center. London Bridge—the famous stone version, topped with houses—was built (1209), and Old St. Paul's Cathedral was finished (1314).

Then followed two centuries of wars, chiefly the Hundred Years' War with France (1337-1443), in which France's Joan of Arc rallied the French to drive English forces back across the Channel. In 1348, the Black Death (bubonic plague) killed half of London's population.

In the 1400s, noble families duked it out for the crown. The York and Lancaster families fought the Wars of the Roses, so called because of the white and red flowers the combatants chose as their symbols. Rife with battles and intrigues, and with kings, nobles, and ladies imprisoned and executed in the Tower, it's a wonder the country survived its rulers.

THE TUDOR RENAISSANCE (1500s)

England was finally united by the "third-party" Tudor family. Henry VIII, a Tudor, was England's Renaissance king. Powerful, charismatic, handsome, athletic, highly sexed, a poet, a scholar, and a musician, Henry VIII thrust England onto the world stage. He was also arrogant, cruel, gluttonous, and paranoid. He went through six wives in 40 years, divorcing, imprisoning, or executing them when they no longer suited his needs. (To keep track of each one's fate, British kids learn this rhyme: "Divorced, beheaded, died; divorced, beheaded, survived.")

When the Pope refused to grant Henry a divorce so he could marry his mistress Anne Boleyn, Henry "divorced" England from the Catholic Church. He established the Protestant Church of England (the Anglican Church), thus setting in motion a century of bitter Protestant/Catholic squabbles. Henry's first daughter, "Bloody" Mary, was a staunch Catholic who presided over the burning of hundreds of prominent Protestants. (For more on Henry VIII, see the sidebar on page 118.)

Mary was followed by her half-sister—Queen Elizabeth I—the daughter of Henry and Anne Boleyn. She reigned for 45 years, making England a great trading and naval power (defeating the Spanish Armada) and treading diplomatically over

the Protestant/Catholic divide. Elizabeth presided over a cultural renaissance known (not surprisingly) as the "Elizabethan Age." Playwright William Shakespeare moved from Stratford-upon-Avon to London, beginning a remarkable career as the earth's greatest playwright. Sir Francis Drake circumnavigated the globe. Sir Walter Raleigh explored the Americas, and Sir Francis Bacon pioneered the scientific method. London's population swelled.

But Elizabeth—the "Virgin Queen"— never married or produced an heir. So the English Parliament invited Scotland's King James (Elizabeth's first cousin twice removed) to inherit the English throne. The two nations have been tied together ever since, however fitfully.

KINGS VS. PARLIAMENT (1600s)

The enduring quarrel between England's kings and Parliament's nobles finally erupted into the Civil War (1642). The war pitted (roughly speaking) the Protestant Puritan Parliament against the Catholic aristocracy. Parliament forces under Oliver Cromwell defeated— and beheaded—King Charles I. After Cromwell died, Parliament invited Charles' son to take the throne— the "restoration of the monarchy." To emphasize the point, Cromwell's corpse was subsequently exhumed and posthumously beheaded.

This turbulent era was followed by back-to-back disasters—the Great Plague of 1665 (which killed 100,000) and the Great Fire of 1666 (which incinerated London). London was completely rebuilt in stone, centered around New St. Paul's Cathedral, which was built by Christopher Wren. With a population over 200,000, London was now Europe's largest city. At home, Isaac Newton watched an apple fall from a tree, leading him to explain the mysterious force of gravity.

In the war between kings and Parliament, Parliament finally got the last word when it deposed Catholic James II and imported the Dutch monarchs William and Mary in 1688, guaranteeing a Protestant succession.

PAST & PRESENT

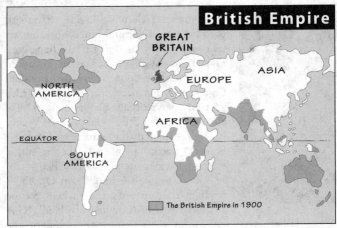

British Empire

GREAT BRITAIN

NORTH AMERICA

EUROPE

ASIA

AFRICA

EQUATOR

SOUTH AMERICA

The British Empire in 1900

COLONIAL EXPANSION (1700s)

Britain grew as a naval superpower, colonizing and trading with all parts of the globe. Eventually, Britannia ruled the waves, exploiting the wealth of India, Africa, and Australia. (And America...at least until they lost their most important colony when those ungrateful Yanks revolted in 1776 in the "American War.") Throughout the century, the country was ruled by the German Hanover family, including four kings named George.

The "Georgian Era" was one of great wealth. London's population was now half a million, and one in seven Brits lived in London. The nation's first daily newspapers hit the streets. The cultural scene was refined: painters (like William Hogarth, Joshua Reynolds, and Thomas Gainsborough), theater (with actors like David Garrick), music (Handel's *Messiah*), and literature (Samuel Johnson's dictionary). Scientist James Watt's steam engines laid the groundwork for a coming Industrial Revolution.

In 1789, the French Revolution erupted, sparking decades of war between France and Britain. Britain finally prevailed in the early 1800s, when Admiral Horatio Nelson defeated Napoleon's fleet at the Battle of Trafalgar and the Duke of Wellington stomped Napoleon at Waterloo. (Nelson and Wellington are memorialized with many arches, columns, and squares throughout England.)

By war's end, Britain had emerged as Europe's top power.

VICTORIAN GENTILITY AND
THE INDUSTRIAL REVOLUTION (1800s)

Britain reigned supreme, steaming into the Industrial Age with her mills, factories, coal mines, gas lights, and trains. By century's end, there was electricity, telephones, and the first Underground.

In 1837, eighteen-year-old Victoria became queen. She ruled for 64 years, presiding over an era of unprecedented wealth, peace, and middle-class ("Victorian") values. Britain was at its zenith of power, with a colonial empire that covered one-fifth of the world (for more on Victoria and her Age, see the sidebar on page 1010).

Meanwhile, there was another side to Britain's era of superiority and industrial might. A generation of Romantic poets (William Wordsworth, John Keats, Percy Shelley, and Lord Byron) longed for the innocence of nature. Jane Austen and the Brontë sisters wrote romantic tales about the landed gentry. Painters like J. M. W. Turner and John Constable immersed themselves in nature to paint moody landscapes.

The gritty modern world was emerging. Popular novelist Charles Dickens brought literature to the masses, educating them about Britain's harsh social and economic realities. Rudyard Kipling critiqued the colonial system. Charles Darwin questioned the very nature of humanity when he articulated the principles of natural selection and evolution. Jack the Ripper, a serial killer of prostitutes, terrorized east London and was never caught. Not even by Sherlock Holmes—a fictional detective living at 221B Baker Street who solved fictional crimes that the real Scotland Yard couldn't.

WORLD WARS AND RECOVERY (20th Century)

The 20th century was not kind to Britain. Two world wars and economic struggles whittled Britain down from a world empire to an island chain struggling to compete in a global economy.

In World War I, Britain joined France and other allies to battle Germany in trench warfare. A million British men died. Meanwhile, after decades of rebellion, Ireland finally gained its independence—except for the Protestant-leaning Northern Ireland, which remained tied to Britain. This division of the Emerald Isle would result in decades of bitter strife, protests, and terrorist attacks known as "The Troubles."

In the 1920s, London was home to a flourishing literary scene, including T. S. Eliot (American-turned-British), Virginia Woolf, and E. M. Forster. In 1936, the country was rocked and scandalized when

Queen Victoria (1819-1901)

Plump, pleasant, and not quite five feet tall, Queen Victoria, with her regal demeanor and 64-year reign, came to symbolize the global dominance of the British Empire during its greatest era.

Born in Kensington Palace, Victoria was the granddaughter of "Mad" King George III, the tyrant who sparked the American Revolution. Her domineering mother raised her in sheltered seclusion, drilling into her the strict morality that would come to be known as "Victorian." At 18, she was crowned queen. Victoria soon fell deeply in love with Prince Albert, a handsome German nobleman. They married and set up house in Buckingham Palace (the first monarchs to do so) and at Windsor Castle. Over the next 17 years, she and Albert had nine children, whom they married off to Europe's crowned heads. Victoria's descendants include Kaiser Wilhelm II of Germany (who started World War I); the current monarchs of Spain, Norway, Sweden, and Denmark; and England's Queen Elizabeth II, who is Victoria's great-great granddaughter.

Victoria and Albert promoted the arts and sciences, organizing a world's fair in Hyde Park (1851) that showed off London as *the* global capital. Just as important, they were role models for an entire nation; this loving couple influenced several generations with their wholesome middle-class values and devoted parenting. Though Victoria is often depicted as dour and stuffy—she supposedly coined the phrase "We are not amused"—in private she was warm, easy to laugh, plainspoken, thrifty, and modest, with a talent for sketching and journal writing.

In 1861, Victoria's happy domestic life ended. Her mother's death was soon followed by the sudden loss of her beloved Albert to typhoid fever. A devastated Victoria dressed in black for the funeral—and for her remaining 40 years. She hunkered down at Windsor with her family. Critics complained she was an absentee monarch. Rumors swirled that her kilt-wearing servant, John Brown, was not only her close friend but also her lover. For two decades, she rarely appeared in public.

King Edward VIII abdicated to marry a divorced American commoner, Wallis Simpson. He was succeeded by his brother, George VI—"Bertie" of *The King's Speech* fame, and father of Queen Elizabeth II.

In World War II, the Nazi Blitz (aerial bombing campaign) reduced much of London to rubble, sending residents into Tube stations for shelter and the government into a fortified bunker (now

Over time, Victoria emerged from mourning to assume her role as one of history's first constitutional monarchs. She had inherited a crown with little real power. But beyond her ribbon-cutting ceremonial duties, Victoria influenced events behind the scenes. She studiously learned politics from powerful mentors (especially Prince Albert and two influential prime ministers) and kept well informed on what Parliament was doing. Thanks to Victoria's personal modesty and honesty, the British public never came to disdain the monarchy, as happened in other countries.

Victoria gracefully oversaw the peaceful transfer of power from the nobles to the people. The secret ballot was introduced during her reign, and ordinary workers acquired voting rights (though this applied only to men—Victoria opposed women's suffrage). The traditional Whigs and Tories morphed into today's Liberal and Conservative parties. Victoria personally promoted progressive charities, and even paid for her own crown.

Most of all, Victoria became the symbol of the British Empire, which she saw as a way to protect and civilize poorer peoples. Britain enjoyed peace at home, while its colonial possessions included India, Australia, Canada, and much of Africa. Because it was always daytime someplace under Victoria's rule, it was often said that "the sun never sets on the British Empire."

The Victorian era saw great changes. The Industrial Revolution was in full swing. When Victoria was born, there were no trains. By 1842, when she took her first train trip (with much fanfare), railroads crisscrossed Europe. The telegraph, telephone, and newspapers further laced the world together. The popular arts flourished—it was the era of Dickens novels, Tennyson poems, Sherlock Holmes stories, Gilbert and Sullivan operettas, and Pre-Raphaelite paintings. Economically, Britain saw the rise of the middle class. Middle-class morality dominated—family, hard work, honor, duty, and sexual modesty.

By the end of her reign, Victoria was wildly popular, both for her personality and as a focus for British patriotism. At her Golden Jubilee (1887), she paraded past adoring throngs to Westminster Abbey. For her Diamond Jubilee (1897), she did the same at St. Paul's Cathedral. Cities, lakes, and military medals were named for her. When she passed away in 1901, it was literally the end of an era.

the Churchill War Rooms). Britain was rallied through its darkest hour by two leaders: Prime Minister Winston Churchill, a remarkable orator, and King George VI, who overcame a persistent stutter. Amid the chaos of war, the colonial empire began to dwindle to almost nothing, and Britain emerged from the war as a shell of its former superpower self.

The postwar recovery began, aided by the United States. Many cheap, concrete (ugly) buildings rose from the rubble.

Culturally, Britain remained world-class. Oxford professor J. R. R. Tolkien wrote *The Lord of the Rings* and his friend C. S. Lewis wrote *The Chronicles of Narnia*. In the 1960s, "Swinging London" became a center for rock music, film, theater, youth culture, and Austin Powers-style joie de vivre. America was conquered by a "British Invasion" of rock bands (The Beatles, The Rolling Stones, and The Who, followed later by Led Zeppelin, Elton John, David Bowie, and others), and James Bond ruled the box office.

Britain joined the European Common Market, an economic precursor to the European Union, in 1973. The decade brought massive unemployment, labor strikes, and recession. A conservative reaction followed in the 1980s and '90s, led by Prime Minister and Eurosceptic Margaret Thatcher—the "Iron Lady." As proponents of traditional Victorian values—community, family, hard work, thrift, and trickle-down economics—the Conservatives took a Reaganesque approach to Britain's serious social and economic problems. They cut government subsidies to old-fashioned heavy industries (closing many factories, earning working-class ire) as they tried to nudge Britain toward a more modern economy.

In 1981, the world was captivated by the spectacle of Prince Charles marrying Lady Diana in St. Paul's Cathedral. Their children, Princes William and Harry, grew up in the media spotlight, and when Diana died in a car crash (1997), the nation—and the world—mourned.

The 1990s saw Britain finally emerging from decades of economic stagnation and social turmoil. An energized nation prepared for the new millennium.

EARLY 2000s

London celebrated the millennium with a new Ferris wheel (the London Eye), the Millennium Bridge, and an exhibition hall dubbed "The O2." Left-of-center Prime Minister Tony Blair ruled Britain until his popularity plummeted when he supported the US invasion of Iraq. On "7/7" in 2005, London was rocked by a terrorist attack—a harbinger of others to come.

Britain suffered mightily in the global recession of 2008. Voters turned to the Conservative Prime Minister David Cameron, who introduced austerity measures, but Britain was slow to recover.

Thankfully, one hot spot—Northern Ireland—was healed. In 2007, ultra-nationalists and ultra-unionists reached an agreement, ending almost 40 years of the Troubles.

In 2011, Prince William married commoner Kate Middleton in a lavish ceremony. And in 2018, William's younger brother Harry married American TV star Meghan Markle. The two cou-

Get It Right

Americans tend to use "England," "Britain," and the "United Kingdom" (or "UK") interchangeably, but they're not quite the same.

- **England** is the country occupying the center and southeast part of the island.
- **Britain** is the name of the island.
- **Great Britain** is the political union of the island's three countries: England, Scotland, and Wales.
- The **United Kingdom** (UK) adds a fourth country, Northern Ireland.
- The **British Isles** (not a political entity) also includes the independent Republic of Ireland.
- The **British Commonwealth** is a loose association of possessions and former colonies (including Canada, Australia, and India) that profess at least symbolic loyalty to the Crown.

You can call the modern nation either the United Kingdom ("the UK"), "Great Britain," or simply "Britain."

ples, along with their children, have stirred renewed enthusiasm for the monarchy (notwithstanding Harry and Meghan's decision to step back from their royal duties).

In 2012, in a one-two punch of festivity, the Brits hosted both the Olympic Games and the Queen's 60th year on the throne. A flurry of renovation turned former urban wastelands into hip, thriving people zones, and the country's future was looking rosy.

Then came Brexit...

Britain Today

Without a doubt, Britain is one of the richest, freest, best-educated, and most culturally powerful nations on earth. But it also has its challenges. To understand the British people today, it's helpful to survey the divided political landscape and global trends that they're dealing with. This includes the most vexing issue Brits have grappled with since World War II—Brexit.

POLITICAL LANDSCAPE

Britain is ruled by the House of Commons, with some guidance from the mostly figurehead Queen and House of Lords. The prime minister is the chief executive but is not elected directly by voters; rather, he or she assumes power as the head of the party that wins a majority in parliamentary elections. Elections are held every five years.

Two parties have traditionally dominated Britain's Parliament: left-leaning Labour (currently led by Jeremy Corbyn) and right-leaning Conservative ("Tories," led by Boris Johnson). The dividing lines between them are familiar: Should government nurture the economy through spending on social programs (Labour's platform), or cut programs and taxes to allow businesses to thrive (as Conservatives say)?

In recent elections, third parties have made gains, including the Scottish National Party (SNP, led by Nicola Sturgeon) and the center-left Liberal Democrats). If no single party wins an outright majority, whoever rules must form a coalition. Because Britain does not have a single "constitution" clearly outlining the system of checks and balances, the British body politic relies more on a tradition of civility and mutual respect to make government work.

CHALLENGES

The biggest challenge facing Britain at the moment is, of course, Brexit—figuring out how to enact the 2016 referendum in which Britain voted to leave the European Union. But Brexit is inextricably tangled up with other issues that have long divided the nation, including the changing economy, immigration, terrorism, the country's place on the world stage, and the role of royalty.

Although prosperous, Britain faces a deepening gap of wealth inequality. The disposable income of the richest households ($85,000) is five times larger than that of the poorest ($16,500). This has ratcheted up the class consciousness that has always divided British society. And it's raised the question of whether the global economy that generates so much wealth has benefitted everyone equally.

Another divisive issue is the impact of immigration. Britain has long been home to immigrants from its former colonies (India, Pakistan, Bangladesh, Africa, the Caribbean), but it's a different story today. The number of people born abroad is now about 14 percent, up from 5 percent two decades ago. And today's newcomers are more likely to be from EU countries, especially Eastern Europe or poorer Mediterranean countries. These transplants can make a lot more money working here than back home. For the most part, Britain has assimilated these immigrants well. But some argue that they're taking British jobs and diluting its culture, all while receiving overgenerous financial aid.

Whenever terrorist attacks occur, the question arises about whether immigration might be to blame. Brits are stunned that many terrorists speak the Queen's English and were born and raised in Britain. It raises larger issues: How well is the nation assimilating its immigrants? Does negativity toward immigrants fuel violence? Whatever the cause, the threat of terrorism has challenged the nation with how to balance security with privacy concerns. You'll see surveillance cameras everywhere.

As Britain ponders whether to remain in the EU, it faces a similar issue in its own backyard. In 2014, Scotland voted to remain a part of the UK, but Scottish nationalists continue to insist that Scotland would be better off free from the shackles of London-based problems.

Finally, Brits are divided on the eternal question of the royals. Is having a monarch (who's politically irrelevant) and a royal family (who fill the tabloids with their scandals) worth it? In decades past, many Brits wanted to toss the whole lot of them. But since the marriages of popular William and Kate, and Harry and Meghan, four out of five Brits now want to let the tradition live on.

BREXIT: BREAKING UP IS HARD TO DO

Since 2016, Brits have hotly debated its most momentous decision in generations: whether or not to exit the EU. Britain has been a member of Europe's customs union since as far back as 1973. But it never fully bought into the European Union, shunning the euro currency and resisting EU regulations and integration. Euroskeptics complained about being "ruled" from Brussels and being "invaded" by immigrants from the EU.

It came to a head in 2016, when Prime Minister David Cameron decided to settle the question once and for all with a nationwide referendum: to stay in the EU and enjoy its trade benefits, or to leave and restore full national sovereignty. Both sides campaigned fiercely. The "Remain" (or anti-Brexit) camp had most of the high-profile supporters—including Cameron himself. The "Leave" (pro-Brexit) side was led by Nigel Farage (a rabble-rousing politician and TV personality with anti-immigration ties) and Boris Johnson (the flamboyant former mayor of London).

The debate was spirited and nasty. Many pro-Brexiteers, with their anti-immigration and rah-rah patriotism, drew charges of racism. The "Remain"-ers were called elitist and privileged.

The pollsters put "Remain" comfortably ahead. But "Leave" shocked the world by winning with 51.9 percent of the vote. It threw Britain (and the EU) into uncharted territory with no clear path forward. The British pound dropped by 10 percent, and David Cameron resigned. His Conservative successor, Theresa May (also a "Remain" supporter), was left with the thankless task of trying to carry out the will of the voters against a hostile EU and a reluctant establishment.

May gave the EU two year's notice that Britain was leaving. But by 2019, there was no agreement in sight, and the deadline was extended. The main debate was: hard or soft? The "Leave" camp lobbied for a clean and decisive break from the EU. This would require renegotiating trade deals, likely resulting in higher tariffs and higher prices all around. Others pushed for a "soft Brexit": keeping in place many of the favored EU trade relationships they enjoy today, without being a full member—similar to what Norway and Switzerland do with the EU. Still others lobby for a whole new referendum that would cancel Brexit altogether.

The issue has split the nation. Business leaders fear a Brexit will hamper London's position as a gateway to European business. Young British people fear losing the world they grew up in, where they can travel freely and live anywhere in Europe. England's industrialized North, which has struggled economically for decades, voted strongly to "Leave" while the "Soft South" of multinational business voted strongly to "Remain." (Think disaffected Rust Belt voters versus latte-sipping Coastal Elites.)

Voters in Scotland voted heavily against Brexit, and now there are murmurs of another Scottish independence vote. The stakes are even higher in Northern Ireland: The fragile peace that ended the Troubles works in part because of the EU's open border between Northern Ireland (part of the UK) and the Republic of Ireland (a separate country and EU member). A hard Brexit would create a hard border, potentially inflaming tensions in these divided communities.

Brexit has even divided the traditional political order. In the past, the Labour Party was always pro-EU while many Conservatives were Eurosceptics. Now both parties have factions on either side of the argument, some favoring close ties with the EU and others wanting a clean break. Prime Minister Boris Johnson was in the unenviable position of trying to negotiate a deal with both a bickering Parliament and with the EU.

The UK officially left the European Union on January 31, 2020, and the countdown clock started ticking on an 11-month transition period toward new arrangements for trade, customs, travel, and regulation. By the time you read this, there will likely be new wrinkles and complications.

NOTABLE BRITS OF TODAY AND TOMORROW

Only history can judge which British names will stand the test of time, but many Brits stand large on the world stage.

There are well-known politicians, like Theresa May, Boris Johnson, and Jeremy Corbyn.

The list of British actors reads like a roll-call of Oscar and Emmy winners: Helen Mirren, Emma Thompson, Daniel Day-Lewis, Gary Oldman, Helena Bonham Carter, Jude Law, Ricky Gervais, James Corden, Daniel Radcliffe, Kate Winslet, Benedict Cumberbatch, John Oliver, Tilda Swinton, Colin Firth, Eddie Redmayne, etc.

Of course, ever since the "British Invasion" of the '60s, Brits have dominated the pop music scene: Adele, Chris Martin of Coldplay, Jessie J, Ellie Goulding, Ed Sheeran, Sam Smith, Florence Welch of Florence and the Machine, etc.

In the literary field, Britain scoops up major awards, including Britain's own Man Booker Prize. Winners include J. K. Rowling, E. L. James, Hilary Mantel, Tom Stoppard, Nick Hornby, Ian McEwan, and Zadie Smith).

There are well-known visual artists (Damien Hirst, Rachel Whiteread, Tracey Emin, Anish Kapoor), athletes (David Beckham, Bradley Wiggins, Andy Murray), and entrepreneurs (Sir Richard Branson, Lord Alan Sugar, James Dyson).

And, of course, there are Britain's biggest tabloid sensations in years, the new generation of royals: William, Kate, Harry, Meghan, and their cute little kids.

BRITISH TV

For many Americans, their first view of the British lifestyle came through British TV programs beamed into American homes. And no wonder: Although it has its share of lowbrow reality programming, much British television is still so good—and so British—that it deserves a mention as a sightseeing treat. After a hard day of castle climbing, watch the telly over tea in your B&B.

For many years there were only five free channels, but now nearly every British television can receive a couple dozen. BBC television is government-regulated and commercial-free. Broadcasting of its eight channels (and of the five BBC radio stations) is funded by a mandatory £154.50-per-year-per-household television and radio license (hmmm, 50 cents per day to escape commercials and public-broadcasting pledge drives...not bad). Channels 3, 4, and 5 are privately owned, are a little more lowbrow, and have commercials—but those "adverts" are often clever and sophisticated, providing a fun look at British life. About 60 percent of households pay for cable or satellite television.

Whereas California "accents" fill US airwaves 24 hours a day, homogenizing the way our country speaks, Britain protects and promotes its regional accents by its choice of TV and radio announcers. See if you can tell where each is from (or ask a local for help).

Commercial-free British TV, while looser than it used to be, is still careful about what it airs and when. But after the 21:00 "watershed" hour, when children are expected to be in bed, some nudity and profanity are allowed, and may cause you to spill your tea.

American programs (such as *Game of Thrones, CSI, Family Guy, Frasier, The Big Bang Theory,* and trash-talk shows) are very popular. But the visiting viewer should be sure to tune the TV to more typically British shows, including a dose of British situational- and

Royal Families: Past and Present

Royal Lineage

802-1066	Saxon and Danish kings
1066-1154	William the Conqueror and Norman kings
1154-1399	Plantagenet (kings with French roots)
1399-1461	Lancaster
1462-1485	York
1485-1603	Tudor (Henry VIII, Elizabeth I)
1603-1649	Stuart (civil war and beheading of Charles I)
1649-1653	Commonwealth, no royal head of state
1653-1659	Protectorate, with Cromwell as Lord Protector
1660-1714	Restoration of Stuart dynasty
1714-1901	Hanover (four Georges, William IV, Victoria)
1901-1910	Saxe-Coburg (Edward VII)
1910-present	Windsor (George V to Elizabeth II)

The Royal Family Today

It seems you can't pick up a British newspaper without some mention of the latest event, scandal, or oddity involving the royal family. Here is the cast of characters:

Queen Elizabeth II wears the traditional crown of her great-great grandmother Victoria, who ruled for 63 years, 7 months, and 2 days. In September 2015, Queen Elizabeth officially over-took Victoria as England's longest-reigning monarch, and in April 2016 she became the first UK sovereign to reach 90 years old. Elizabeth's husband is Prince Philip, who's not considered king.

Their son, Prince Charles (the Prince of Wales), is next in line to become king—and already holds the title as the longest "heir in waiting." For years, Charles' love life was fodder for the British press. There was his fairytale 1981 marriage to Princess Di, then their bitter divorce, Diana's dramatic death in 1997, and the ongo-ing drama with Charles' longtime girlfriend—and now wife—Ca-milla Parker Bowles.

These days it's Prince Charles' sons who generate the tab-loid buzz. The older son, Prince William (b. 1982), is a graduate of Scotland's St. Andrews University and served as a search-and-rescue helicopter pilot with the Royal Air Force. In 2011, when William married Catherine "Kate" Middleton, the TV audi-ence was estimated at one-quarter of the world's population—more than two billion people. Kate—a commoner William met at

political-comedy fun, and the top-notch BBC evening news. Brit-ish comedies have tickled the American funny bone for years, from sketch comedy (*Monty Python's Flying Circus*) to sitcoms (*Fawlty Towers, Blackadder, Red Dwarf, Absolutely Fabulous,* and *The Office*). Quiz shows and reality shows are taken very seriously here (*Ameri-can Idol, America's Got Talent, Dancing with the Stars, Who Wants to Be a Millionaire?,* and *The X Factor* are all based on British shows).

university—is now the Duchess of Cambridge and will eventually become Britain's queen.

Their son, Prince George Alexander Louis, born in 2013—and later voted the most powerful and influential person in London by a poll in the *Evening Standard*—will ultimately succeed William as sovereign. In 2015, the couple welcomed the arrival of their second child, Princess Charlotte Elizabeth Diana, and in 2018, Prince Louis Arthur Charles.

William's brother, redheaded Prince Harry (b. 1984), has shaken his earlier reputation as a bad boy: He's proved his mettle as a career soldier, completing a tour in Afghanistan, doing charity work in Africa, and serving with the Army Air Corps. His marriage to American actress Meghan Markle—and the birth of their son Archie—has added sparkle to the once-musty royals (at least until they stepped back from their royal duties).

Royal Sightseeing

You can see the trappings of royalty at Buckingham Palace (the

Queen's London residence) with its Changing of the Guard; Kensington Palace—with a wing that's home to Will, Kate, and kids; Clarence House, the London home of Prince Charles and Camilla; Althorp Estate (80 miles from London), the childhood home and burial place of Princess Diana; and Windsor Castle, a royal country home near London that includes Frogmore Cottage, the part-time home of Harry and Meghan. Don't forget the crown jewels in the Tower of London.

Your best chances to see the Queen are on three public occasions: State Opening of Parliament (on the first day of a new parliamentary session), Remembrance Sunday (early November, at the Cenotaph), or Trooping the Colour (one Saturday in mid-June, parading down Whitehall and at Buckingham Palace).

Otherwise, check www.royal.uk, where you can search for royal events.

Jonathan Ross is the Jimmy Fallon of Britain for sometimes-edgy late-night talk. Other popular late-night "chat show" hosts include Graham Norton and Alan Carr. For a tear-filled, slice-of-life taste of British soaps dealing in all the controversial issues, see the popular and remarkably long-running *Emmerdale, Coronation Street,* or *EastEnders.* The costume drama *Downton Abbey,* the sci-fi serial *Doctor Who,* the small-town dramedy *Doc Martin,* and the modern crime series *Sherlock* have all become hits on both sides of the Atlantic.

WHAT'S SO GREAT ABOUT BRITAIN?

Brexit is the biggest challenge to the British way of life since the days of the Blitz. But it makes Britain no less Great. The Britain you visit today is vibrant and alive. It's smaller, and no longer the superpower it once was, but it's still a cultural and economic powerhouse.

Think of it. At its peak in the mid-1800s, Britain owned one-fifth of the world and accounted for more than half the planet's industrial output. Today, the Empire is down to the Isle of Britain itself and a few token scraps (the Falklands, Gibraltar, Northern Ireland) and a loose association of former colonies (Canada, Australia) called the "British Commonwealth."

Geographically, the Isle of Britain is small—smaller than the state of Oregon—and its highest mountain (Ben Nevis in Scotland at 4,411 feet) is a foothill by US standards. The population is a fifth that of the United States. Despite its size, Britain is the world's fifth-biggest economy, sixth-biggest manufacturer, and largest financial center (London). Twenty-six of the world's 500 largest companies are headquartered here.

The Britain you visit today remains a global superpower of heritage, culture, and tradition. It's a major exporter of actors, movies, and theater; of rock and classical music; and of writers, painters, and sculptors. It's the perfect place for you to visit and make your own history.

Architecture in Britain

From Stonehenge to Big Ben, travelers are storming castle walls, climbing spiral staircases, and snapping the pictures of 5,000 years of architecture. Let's sort it out.

The oldest ruins—mysterious and prehistoric—date from before Roman times back to 3000 BC. The earliest sites, such as Stonehenge and Avebury, were built during the Stone and Bronze ages. The remains from these periods are made of huge stones or mounds of earth, even man-made hills, and were created as celestial calendars and for worship or burial. Britain is crisscrossed with imaginary lines said to connect these mysterious sights (ley lines). Iron Age people (600 BC-AD 50) left desolate stone forts. The Romans thrived in Britain from AD 50 to 400, building cities, walls, and roads. Evidence of Roman greatness can be seen in lavish villas with ornate mosaic floors, temples uncovered beneath great English churches, and Roman stones in medieval city walls. Roman roads sliced across the island in straight lines. Today, unusually straight rural roads are very likely laid directly on these ancient roads.

As Rome crumbled in the fifth century, so did Roman Britain. Little architecture survives from Dark Ages England, the Saxon period from 500 to 1000. Architecturally, the light was switched on with the Norman Conquest in 1066. As William earned his title "the Conqueror," his French architects built churches and castles in the European Romanesque style.

English Romanesque is called Norman (1066-1200). Norman churches had round arches, thick walls, and small windows; Durham Cathedral and the Chapel of St. John in the Tower of London are

Mysterious Ruins

Inverness
CLAVA CAIRNS
SCOTLAND

Major Prehistoric Sites

Keswick • CASTLERIGG

W
A
L
E
S

ENGLAND

AVEBURY
London

Bath•

CERNE
ABBAS
GIANT
STONEHENGE
GLASTONBURY
SCORHILL

prime examples. The Tower of London, with its square keep, small windows, and spiral stone stairways, is a typical Norman castle. You can see plenty of Norman castles around England—all built to secure the conquest of these invaders from Normandy.

Gothic architecture (1200-1600) replaced the heavy Norman style with light, vertical buildings, pointed arches, soaring spires, and bigger windows. English Gothic is divided into three stages. Early English Gothic (1200-1300) features tall, simple spires; beautifully carved capitals; and elaborate chapter houses (such as the Wells Cathedral). Decorated Gothic (1300-1400) gets fancier, with more elaborate tracery, bigger windows, and ornately carved pinnacles, as you see at Westminster Abbey. Finally, the Perpendicular Gothic style (1400-1600, also called "rectilinear") returns to square towers and emphasizes straight, uninterrupted vertical lines from ceiling to floor, with vast windows and exuberant decoration, including fan-vaulted ceilings (King's College Chapel at Cambridge). Through this evolution, the structural ribs (arches meeting at the top of the ceilings) became more and more decorative and fanciful (the most fancy being the star vaulting and fan vaulting of the Perpendicular style).

Typical Church Architecture

History comes to life when you visit a centuries-old church. Even if you wouldn't know your apse from a hole in the ground, learning a few simple terms will enrich your experience. Note that not every church has every feature, and that a "cathedral" isn't a type of church architecture, but rather a designation for a church that's a governing center for a local bishop.

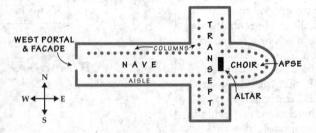

Aisles: The long, generally low-ceilinged arcades that flank the nave.

Altar: The raised area with a ceremonial table (often adorned with candles or a crucifix), where the priest prepares and serves the bread and wine for Communion.

Apse: The space beyond the altar, often bordered with small chapels.

Barrel Vault: A continuous round-arched ceiling that resembles an extended upside-down U.

Choir ("quire" in British English): A cozy area, often screened off, located within the church nave and near the high altar where services are sung in a more intimate setting.

Cloister: Covered hallways bordering a square or rectangular open-air courtyard, traditionally where monks and nuns got fresh air.

Facade: The exterior surface of the church's main (west) entrance, viewable from outside and usually highly decorated.

Groin Vault: An arched ceiling formed where two equal barrel vaults meet at right angles. Less common usage: term for a medieval jock strap.

Narthex: The area (portico or foyer) between the main entry and the nave.

Nave: The long, central section of the church (running west to east, from the entrance to the altar) where the congregation sits or stands through the service.

Transept: In a traditional cross-shaped floor plan, the transept is one of the two parts forming the "arms" of the cross. The transepts run north-south, perpendicularly crossing the east-west nave.

West Portal: The main entry to the church (on the west end, opposite the main altar).

Typical Castle Architecture

Castles were fortified residences for medieval nobles. Castles come in all shapes and sizes, but knowing a few general terms will help you understand them.

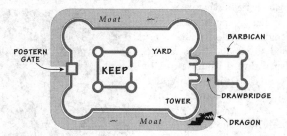

Barbican: A fortified gatehouse, sometimes a stand-alone building located outside the main walls.

Crenellation: A gap-toothed pattern of stones atop the parapet.

Drawbridge: A bridge that could be raised or lowered using counterweights or a chain and winch.

Great Hall: The largest room in the castle, serving as throne room, conference center, and dining hall.

Hoardings (or Gallery or Brattice): Wooden huts built onto the upper parts of the stone walls. They served as watch towers, living quarters, and fighting platforms.

The Keep (or Donjon): A high, strong stone tower in the center of the castle complex; the lord's home and refuge of last resort.

Loopholes (or Embrasures): Narrow wall slits through which soldiers could shoot arrows.

Machicolation: A stone ledge jutting out from the wall, with holes through which soldiers could drop rocks or boiling oil onto wall-scaling enemies below.

Moat: A ditch encircling the wall, often filled with water.

Motte-and-Bailey: A type of early English castle, with a hilltop fort (motte) and an enclosed, fortified yard (bailey).

Parapet: Outer railing of the wall walk.

Portcullis: A heavy iron grille that could be lowered across the entrance.

Postern Gate: A small, unfortified side or rear entrance from which to launch attacks or escape.

Towers: Tall structures with crenellated tops or conical roofs serving as lookouts, chapels, living quarters, or dungeons.

Turret: A small lookout tower rising up from the top of the wall.

Wall Walk (or Allure): A pathway atop the wall where guards could patrol and where soldiers stood to fire at the enemy.

The Yard (or Bailey): An open courtyard inside the castle walls.

As you tour the great medieval churches of Britain, remember that almost everything is symbolic. For instance, on the tombs of knights, if the figure has crossed legs, he was a Crusader. If his feet rest on a dog, he died at home; but if his legs rest on a lion, he died in battle. Local guides and books help us modern pilgrims understand at least a little of what we see.

Wales is particularly rich in English castles, which were needed to subdue the stubborn Welsh. Edward I built a ring of powerful castles in North Wales, including Conwy and Caernarfon.

Gothic houses were a simple mix of woven strips of thin wood, rubble, and plaster called wattle and daub. The famous black-and-white Tudor (or "half-timbered") look came simply from filling in heavy oak frames with wattle and daub.

The Tudor period (1485-1560) was a time of relative peace (the Wars of the Roses were finally over), prosperity, and renaissance. But when Henry VIII broke with the Catholic Church and disbanded its monasteries, scores of Britain's greatest churches were left as gutted shells. These hauntingly beautiful abbey ruins (Glastonbury, Tintern, Whitby, Rievaulx, Battle, St. Augustine's in Canterbury, St. Mary's in York, and lots more), surrounded by lush lawns, are now pleasant city parks.

Although few churches were built during the Tudor period, this was a time of house and mansion construction. Heating a home was becoming popular and affordable, and Tudor buildings featured small square windows and many chimneys. In towns, where land was scarce, many Tudor houses grew up and out, getting wider with each overhanging floor.

The Elizabethan and Jacobean periods (1560-1620) were followed by the English Renaissance style (1620-1720). English architects mixed Gothic and classical styles, then Baroque and classical styles. Although the ornate Baroque never really grabbed Britain, the classical style of the Italian architect Andrea Palladio did. Inigo Jones (1573-1652), Christopher Wren (1632-1723), and those they inspired plastered Britain with enough columns, domes, and symmetry to please a Caesar. The Great Fire of London (1666) cleared the way for an ambitious young Wren to put his mark on London forever with a grand rebuilding scheme, including the great St. Paul's Cathedral and more than 50 other churches.

The celebrants of the Boston Tea Party remember Britain's Georgian period (1720-1840) for its lousy German kings. But in architectural terms, "Georgian" is English for "Neoclassical." Its architecture was rich and showed off by being very classical. Grand ornamental doorways, fine cast-ironwork on balconies and railings, Chippendale furniture, and white-on-blue Wedgwood ceramics graced rich homes everywhere. John Wood Sr. and Jr. led the way, giving the trendsetting city of Bath its crescents and circles of aristocratic Georgian row houses.

The Industrial Revolution shaped the Victorian period (1840-1890) with glass, steel, and iron. Britain had a huge new erector set (so did France's Mr. Eiffel). This was also a Romantic period, reviving the "more Christian" Gothic style. London's Houses of Parliament are Neo-Gothic—they're just 140 years old but look 700, except for the telltale modern precision and craftsmanship. Whereas Gothic was stone or concrete, Neo-Gothic was often red brick. These were Britain's glory days, and there was more building in this period than in all previous ages combined.

The architecture of the mid-20th century obeyed the formula "form follows function"—it worried more about your needs than your eyes. But more recently, the dull "international style" has been nudged aside by a more playful style, thanks to cutting-edge architects such as Lord Norman Foster and Renzo Piano. In the last several years, London has made a point

of adding several creative buildings to its skyline: the City Hall (nicknamed "The Armadillo"), 30 St. Mary Axe ("The Gherkin"), 20 Fenchurch ("The Walkie-Talkie"), and the tallest building in Western Europe, the pointy Shard London Bridge (called simply, "The Shard").

Even as it sets trends for the 21st century, Britain treasures its heritage and takes great pains to build tastefully in historic districts and to preserve its many "listed" (government-protected) buildings. With a booming tourist trade, these quaint reminders of its past—and ours—are becoming a valuable part of the British economy.

For more about British history, consider Europe 101: History and Art for the Traveler *by Rick Steves and Gene Openshaw, available at* www.ricksteves.com.

PRACTICALITIES

Tourist Information 1026
Travel Tips. .1027
Money 1028
Sightseeing. 1034
Sleeping 1039
Eating. 1050
Staying Connected 1060
Transportation 1065
Resources from Rick Steves 1081

This chapter covers the practical skills of European travel: how to get tourist information, pay for things, sightsee efficiently, find good-value accommodations, eat affordably but well, use technology wisely, and get between destinations smoothly. For more information on these topics, see RickSteves.com/travel-tips.

Tourist Information

Before your trip, start with the Visit Britain website, which contains a wealth of knowledge on destinations, activities, accommodations, and transport in Great Britain (www.visitbritain.com). Transportation, sightseeing, and theater tickets can also be purchased (www.visitbritainshop.com/usa).

In Britain, a good first stop is generally the tourist information office (abbreviated **TI** in this book and locally as **TIC,** for "tourist information centre"). In London, the **City of London Information Centre,** near St. Paul's Cathedral, is helpful (see page 42).

TIs are in business to help you enjoy spending money in their town, but even so, I still make a point to swing by to pick up a city map and get information on public transit, walking tours, special events, and nightlife. Anticipating a harried front-line staffer, prepare a list of questions and a proposed plan to double-check. Some TIs have information on the entire country or at least the region, so try to pick up maps and printed information for destinations you'll be visiting later in your trip.

Due to funding constraints, some of Britain's TIs are struggling; village TIs may be staffed by volunteers who need to charge you for maps and informational brochures.

Travel Tips

Emergency and Medical Help: For any emergency service—ambulance, police, or fire—call **112 or 999** from a mobile phone or landline. Operators will deal with your request or route you to the right emergency service. If you get sick, do as the locals do and go to a pharmacy and see a "chemist" (pharmacist) for advice. Or ask at your hotel for help—they'll know of the nearest medical and emergency services.

ETIAS Registration: Beginning in 2021, US and Canadian citizens may be required to register online with the European Travel Information and Authorization System (ETIAS) before entering certain European countries (quick and easy process, $8 fee, valid 3 years). A useful private website with more details is SchengenVisaInfo.com/etias.

Theft or Loss: To replace a passport, you'll need to go in person to an embassy (see next). If your credit and debit cards disappear, cancel and replace them (see "Damage Control for Lost Cards" on page 1032). File a police report, either on the spot or within a day or two; you'll need it to submit an insurance claim for lost or stolen rail passes or electronics, and it can help with replacing your passport or credit and debit cards. For more information, see RickSteves.com/help.

US Consulate and Embassy: Tel. 020/7499-9000 (all services), no walk-in passport services; for emergency two-day passport service, schedule an appointment or fill out the online Emergency Passport Contact Form, 24 Grosvenor Square, London, Tube: Bond Street, http://uk.usembassy.gov.

High Commission of Canada in London: Tel. 020/7004-6000, passport services available Mon-Fri 9:30-12:30, Canada

House, Trafalgar Square, London, Tube: Charing Cross, www.unitedkingdom.gc.ca.

Time Zones: Britain is five/eight hours ahead of the East/West Coasts of the US—and one hour earlier than most of continental Europe. The exceptions are the beginning and end of Daylight Saving Time: Europe "springs forward" the last Sunday in March (two weeks after most of North America), and "falls back" the last Sunday in October (one week before North America). For a handy time converter, use the world clock app on your phone or download one (see www.timeanddate.com/worldclock).

Business Hours: Most stores are open Monday through Saturday (roughly 9:00 or 10:00 to 17:00 or 18:00). In cities, some stores stay open later on Wednesday or Thursday (until 19:00 or 20:00). Some big-city department stores are open later throughout the week (Mon-Sat until about 21:00). Sundays have the same pros and cons as they do for travelers in the US: Sightseeing attractions are generally open, many street markets are lively with shoppers, banks and many shops are closed, public transportation options are fewer (for example, no bus service to or from smaller towns), and there's no rush hour.

Watt's Up? Britain's electrical system is 220 volts, instead of North America's 110 volts. Most electronics (laptops, smartphones, cameras) and newer hair dryers convert automatically, so you won't need a converter, but you will need an adapter plug with three square prongs, sold inexpensively at travel stores in the US. Avoid bringing older appliances that don't automatically convert voltage; instead, buy a cheap replacement in Britain.

Discounts: Discounts (called "concessions" or "concs" in Britain) for sights are generally not listed in this book. However, seniors (age 65 and over), youths under 18, and students and teachers with proper identification cards (obtain from www.isic.org) can get discounts at many sights—always ask. Some discounts are available only for British citizens.

Money

Here's my basic strategy for using money in Europe:

- Upon arrival, head for a cash machine (ATM) at the airport and withdraw some local currency, using a debit card with low international transaction fees.
- In general, pay for bigger expenses with a credit card and use

---

Exchange Rate

1 British pound (£1) = about $1.30

Britain uses the pound sterling. The British pound (£), also called a "quid," is broken into 100 pence (p). Pence means "cents." You'll find coins ranging from 1p to £2 and bills from £5 to £50.

Scotland and Northern Ireland issue their own currency in pounds, worth the same as an English pound. English, Scottish, and Northern Ireland's Ulster pound notes are technically interchangeable in each region, although Scottish and Ulster pounds are considered "undesirable" and sometimes not accepted in England. Banks in any of the three regions will convert your Scottish or Ulster pounds into English pounds for no charge. Don't worry about coins, which are the same throughout the UK.

To convert prices from pounds to dollars, add about 30 percent: £20 = about $26, £50 = about $65. (Check www.oanda.com for the latest exchange rates.)

---

cash for smaller purchases. Use a debit card only for cash withdrawals.

- Keep your cash safe in a money belt.

PLASTIC VERSUS CASH

Although credit cards are widely accepted in Europe, cash is sometimes the only way to pay for cheap food, taxis, tips, and local guides. Some businesses (especially smaller ones, such as B&Bs and mom-and-pop cafés and shops) may charge you extra for using a credit card—or might not accept credit cards at all. Having cash on hand helps you out of a jam if your card randomly doesn't work.

I use my credit card to book and pay for hotel reservations, to buy advance tickets for events or sights, and to cover most other expenses. It can also be smart to use plastic near the end of your trip, to avoid another visit to the ATM.

WHAT TO BRING

I pack the following and keep it all safe in my money belt.

Debit Card: Use this at ATMs to withdraw local cash.

Credit Card: Handy for bigger transactions (at hotels, shops, restaurants, travel agencies, car-rental agencies, and so on), payment machines, and online purchases.

Backup Card: Some travelers carry a third card (debit or credit; ideally from a different bank), in case one gets lost, demagnetized, eaten by a temperamental machine, or simply doesn't work.

Stash of Cash: I carry $100-200 as a cash backup, which

comes in handy in an emergency (such as when banks go on strike or if your ATM card gets eaten by the machine).

What NOT to Bring: Resist the urge to buy pounds before your trip or you'll pay the price in bad stateside exchange rates. Wait until you arrive to withdraw money. I've yet to see a European airport that didn't have plenty of ATMs.

BEFORE YOU GO

Use this pre-trip checklist.

Know your cards. Debit cards from any major US bank will work in any standard European bank's ATM (ideally, use a debit card with a Visa or MasterCard logo). As for credit cards, Visa and MasterCard are universal, American Express is less common, and Discover is unknown in Europe.

Know your PIN. Make sure you know the numeric, four-digit PIN for all of your cards, both debit and credit. Request it if you don't have one, as it may be required for some purchases in Europe (see "Using Credit Cards," later), and allow time to receive the information by mail.

Report your travel dates. Let your bank know that you'll be using your debit and credit cards in Europe, and when and where you're headed.

Adjust your ATM withdrawal limit. Find out how much you can take out daily and ask for a higher daily withdrawal limit if you want to get more cash at once. Note that European ATMs will withdraw funds only from checking accounts; you're unlikely to have access to your savings account.

Ask about fees. For any purchase or withdrawal made with a card, you may be charged a currency conversion fee (1-3 percent) and/or a Visa or MasterCard international transaction fee (less than 1 percent). If you're getting a bad deal, consider getting a new debit or credit card. Reputable no-fee cards include those from Capital One, as well as Charles Schwab debit cards. Most credit unions and some airline loyalty cards have low or no international transaction fees.

IN EUROPE
Using Cash Machines

European cash machines work just like they do at home—except they spit out local currency instead of dollars, calculated at the day's standard bank-to-bank rate.

In most places, ATMs are easy to locate—in Britain ask for a "cashpoint." When possible, withdraw cash from a bank-run ATM located just outside that bank. Ideally, use the machine during the bank's opening hours, so you can go inside for help if your card is munched.

PRACTICALITIES

If your debit card doesn't work, try a lower amount—your request may have exceeded your withdrawal limit or the ATM's limit. If you still have a problem, try a different ATM or come back later—your bank's network may be temporarily down.

Avoid "independent" ATMs, such as Travelex, Euronet, Moneybox, Your Cash, Cardpoint, and Cashzone. These have high fees, can be less secure than a bank ATM, and may try to trick users with "dynamic currency conversion" (see below).

Exchanging Cash

Avoid exchanging money in Europe; it's a big rip-off. In a pinch you can always find exchange desks at major train stations or airports—convenient but with crummy rates. Anything over 5 percent for a transaction is piracy. Banks generally do not exchange money unless you have an account with them.

Using Credit Cards

Despite some differences between European and US cards, there's little to worry about: US credit cards generally work fine in Europe. I've been inconvenienced a few times by self-service payment machines that wouldn't accept my card, but it's never caused me serious trouble (I carry cash just in case).

European cards use chip-and-PIN technology; most chip cards issued in the US instead have a signature option. Some European card readers will accept your card as-is while others may generate a receipt for you to sign or prompt you to enter your PIN (so it's important to know the code for each of your cards). If a cashier is present, you should have no problems.

At self-service payment machines (transit-ticket kiosks, parking, etc.), results are mixed, as US cards may not work in some unattended transactions. If your card won't work, look for a cashier who can process your card manually—or pay in cash.

Drivers Beware: Be aware of potential problems using a US credit card to fill up at an unattended gas station, enter a parking garage, or exit a toll road. Always carry cash as a backup and be prepared to move on to the next gas station if necessary. When approaching a toll plaza, use the "cash" lane.

Dynamic Currency Conversion

If merchants offer to convert your purchase price into dollars (called dynamic currency conversion, or DCC), refuse this "service." You'll pay extra for the expensive convenience of seeing your charge in dollars. If an ATM offers to "lock in" or "guarantee" your conversion rate, choose "proceed without conversion." Other prompts might state, "You can be charged in dollars: Press YES for dollars, NO for pounds." Always choose the local currency.

Security Tips

Even in "Jollie Olde Britain," pickpockets target tourists. Keep your cash, credit cards, and passport secure in your money belt, and carry only a day's spending money in your front pocket or wallet.

Before inserting your card into an ATM, inspect the front. If anything looks crooked, loose, or damaged, it could be a sign of a card-skimming device. When entering your PIN, carefully block other people's view of the keypad.

Don't use a debit card for purchases. Because a debit card pulls funds directly from your bank account, potential charges incurred by a thief will stay on your account while the fraudulent use is investigated by your bank.

To access your accounts online while traveling, be sure to use a secure connection (see the "Tips on Internet Security" sidebar, later).

Damage Control for Lost Cards

If you lose your credit or debit card, report the loss immediately to the respective global customer-assistance centers. With a mobile phone, call these 24-hour US numbers: Visa (tel. +1 303/967-1096), MasterCard (tel. +1 636/722-7111), and American Express (tel. +1 336/393-1111). From a landline, you can call these US numbers collect by going through a local operator. European toll-free numbers can be found at the websites for Visa and MasterCard.

You'll need to provide the primary cardholder's identification-verification details (such as birth date, mother's maiden name, or Social Security number). You can generally receive a temporary card within two or three business days in Europe (see www.ricksteves.com/help for more).

If you report your loss within two days, you typically won't be responsible for unauthorized transactions on your account, although many banks charge a liability fee.

TIPPING

Tipping in Britain isn't as automatic and generous as it is in the US. For special service, tips are appreciated, but not expected. As in the US, the proper amount depends on your resources, tipping philosophy, and the circumstances, but some general guidelines apply.

Restaurants: It's not necessary to tip if a service charge is included in the bill (common in London—usually 12.5 percent). Otherwise, it's appropriate to tip about 10-12 percent for good service. For details on tipping in restaurants, see page 1050.

Taxis: For a typical ride, round up your fare a bit (maximum 10 percent; for instance, if the fare is £7.40, pay £8). If the cabbie hauls your bags and zips you to the airport to help you catch your flight, you might want to toss in a little more. But if you feel like you're being driven in circles or otherwise ripped off, skip the tip.

Services: In general, if someone in the tourism or service industry does a super job for you, a small tip of a pound or two is appropriate...but not required. If you're not sure whether (or how much) to tip, ask a local for advice.

GETTING A VAT REFUND

Wrapped into the purchase price of your British souvenirs is a value-added tax (VAT) of about 20 percent. You're entitled to get most of that tax back if you purchase more than £30 (about $40) worth of goods at a store that participates in the VAT-refund scheme (although individual stores can require that you spend more—Harrods, for example, won't process a refund unless you spend £50). Typically, you must ring up the minimum at a single retailer—you can't add up your purchases from various shops to reach the required amount. (If the store ships the goods to your US home, VAT is not assessed on your purchase.)

Getting your refund is straightforward...and worthwhile if you spend a significant amount on souvenirs.

Get the paperwork. Have the merchant completely fill out the necessary refund document (either an official VAT customs form, or the shop or refund company's own version of it). You'll have to present your passport. Get the paperwork done before you leave the shop to ensure you'll have everything you need (including your original sales receipt).

Get your stamp at the border or airport. Process your VAT document at your last stop in the European Union (such as at the airport) with the customs agent who deals with VAT refunds. Arrive an additional hour before you need to check in to allow time to find the customs office—and wait. Some customs desks are positioned before airport security; confirm the location before going through security.

It's best to keep your purchases in your carry-on. If your item (such as a knife) isn't allowed as carry-on, pack it in your checked bag and alert the check-in agent. You'll be sent (with your tagged bag) to a customs desk outside security; someone will examine your bag, stamp your paperwork, and put your bag on the belt. You're not supposed to use your purchased goods before you leave. If you show up at customs wearing your new Wellingtons, officials might look the other way—or deny you a refund.

Collect your refund. You can claim your VAT refund from refund companies, such as Global Blue or Planet, with offices at major airports, ports, or border crossings (either before or after security, probably strategically located near a duty-free shop). These services (which extract a 4 percent fee) can refund your money in cash immediately or credit your card. Otherwise, mail the stamped refund documents to the address given by the shop where you made your purchase.

CUSTOMS FOR AMERICAN SHOPPERS

You can take home $800 worth of items per person duty-free, once every 31 days. Many processed and packaged foods are allowed, including vacuum-packed cheeses, dried herbs, jams, baked goods, candy, chocolate, oil, vinegar, mustard, and honey. Fresh fruits and vegetables and most meats are not allowed, with exceptions for some canned items. As for alcohol, you can bring in one liter duty-free (it can be packed securely in your checked luggage, along with any other liquid-containing items).

To bring alcohol (or liquid-packed foods) in your carry-on bag on your flight home, buy it at a duty-free shop at the airport. You'll increase your odds of getting it onto a connecting flight if it's packaged in a "STEB"—a secure, tamper-evident bag. But stay away from liquids in opaque, ceramic, or metallic containers, which usually cannot be successfully screened (STEB or no STEB).

For details on allowable goods, customs rules, and duty rates, visit Help.cbp.gov.

Sightseeing

Sightseeing can be hard work. Use these tips to make your visits to Great Britain's finest sights meaningful, fun, efficient, and painless.

MAPS AND NAVIGATION TOOLS

A good map is essential for efficient navigation while sightseeing. The maps in this book are concise and simple, designed to help you locate recommended destinations, sights, and local TIs, where you can pick up more in-depth maps. Maps with even more detail are sold at newsstands and bookstores. The *Rick Steves Britain, Ireland & London City Map* is useful for planning ($9, www.ricksteves.com). For those visiting London, *Bensons London Street Map* is my favorite for efficient sightseeing and might be the best £4 you'll spend. I also like the *Handy London Map and Guide* version, which shows every little lane and all the sights, and comes with a transit map. Many Londoners, along with obsessive-compulsive tourists, rely on the highly detailed *London A-Z* map book (generally £5-7, called "A to Zed" by locals, available at newsstands).

You can also use a mapping app on your mobile device. Be aware that pulling up maps or looking up turn-by-turn walking directions on the fly requires a data connection: To use this feature, it's smart to get an international data plan. With Google Maps or

City Maps 2Go, it's possible to download a map while online, then go offline and navigate without incurring data-roaming charges, though you can't search for an address or get real-time walking directions. A handful of other apps—including Apple Maps and Navmii—also allow you to use maps offline.

PLAN AHEAD

Set up an itinerary that allows you to fit in all your must-see sights. For a one-stop look at opening hours, see this book's "At a Glance" sidebars for London, Bath, the Cotswolds, Liverpool, the Lake District, York, North Wales, South Wales, Glasgow, and Edinburgh. Most sights keep stable hours, but you can easily confirm the latest by checking with the TI or visiting museum websites.

Don't put off visiting a must-see sight—you never know when a place will close unexpectedly for a holiday, strike, or royal audience. Many museums are closed or have reduced hours at least a few days a year, especially on holidays such as Christmas, New Year's, and Bank Holiday Mondays in May and August. A list of holidays is in the appendix; check for possible closures during your trip. In summer, some sights may stay open late. In the off-season, hours may be shorter.

Going at the right time helps avoid crowds. This book offers tips on the best times to see specific sights. Try visiting popular sights very early or very late. Evening visits (when possible) are usually peaceful, with fewer crowds. Late morning is usually the worst time to visit a popular sight.

If you plan to hire a local guide, reserve ahead by email. Popular guides can get booked up.

Study up. To get the most out of the self-guided tours and sight descriptions in this book, read them before you visit. The British Museum rocks if you understand the significance of the Rosetta Stone.

RESERVATIONS AND ADVANCE TICKETS

Given how precious your vacation time is, I recommend getting reservations for any must-see sight that offers them (see page 29).

To deal with lines, many popular sights sell advance tickets that guarantee admission at a certain time of day, or that allow you to skip entry lines. Either way, it's worth giving up some spontaneity to book in advance. While hundreds of tourists sweat in long ticket-buying lines, those who've booked ahead can get in quicker. In some cases, getting a ticket in advance simply means buying your ticket earlier on the same day. But for other sights, you may need to book weeks or even months in advance. As soon as you're ready to commit to a certain date, book it.

The advance-purchase price is often less expensive than what

PRACTICALITIES

Harry Potter Sights

Harry Potter's story is set in a magical, largely fictional Britain, but you can visit many real locations used in the film series. Other settings, like Diagon Alley, exist only at Leavesden Film Studios (north of London; see page 147).

London

Harry first realizes his wizard powers in *The Sorcerer's Stone* (2001) when talking with a snake at the **London Zoo**'s Reptile House. Later, Harry shops for school supplies in the glass-roofed **Leadenhall Market**.

In *The Chamber of Secrets* (2002), Harry catches the train to Hogwarts wizarding school at **King's Cross Station** from the fictional Platform 9¾ (For a fun photo-op, head to King's Cross Station's track 9 to find the *Platform 9¾* sign, the luggage cart that looks like it's disappearing into the wall, a Harry Potter gift shop...and a 30-minute wait in line to snap a photo.)

In *The Prisoner of Azkaban* (2004), a triple-decker bus dumps Harry at the Leaky Cauldron pub, shot on rough-looking Stoney Street at the southeast edge of **Borough Market**.

When the Order takes to the night sky on broomsticks in *The Order of the Phoenix* (2007), they pass over plenty of identifiable landmarks, including the **London Eye, Big Ben,** and **Buckingham Palace.** The **Millennium Bridge** collapses into the Thames in the dramatic finale to *The Half-Blood Prince* (2009). The real govern-

you would pay on-site. And many museums offer convenient mobile ticketing. Simply buy your ticket online and send it to your phone, eliminating the need for a paper ticket.

SIGHTSEEING PASSES

Many sights in Britain are managed by English Heritage, the National Trust, Cadw (a Welsh organization), or Historic Scotland; the sights don't overlap. Each organization has a combo-deal that can save some money for busy sightseers.

Membership in **English Heritage** includes free entry to more than 400 sights in England and discounted or free admission to about 100 more sights in Scotland and Wales. For most travelers, the **Overseas Visitor Pass** is a better choice than the pricier one-year membership (Visitor Pass: £35/9 days, £42/16 days, discounts for couples and families; membership: £56 for one person, £99 for two, discounts for families, seniors, and students, children under ment offices of **Whitehall** serve as exteriors for the Ministry of Magic.

Elsewhere in England

Near Bath: In *The Sorcerer's Stone,* Harry is chosen for Gryffindor's Quidditch team in the halls of the 13th-century **Lacock Abbey.** Harry attends Professor Snape's class in one of the abbey's peeling-plaster rooms.

Oxford: Christ Church College provided the model for Hogwarts' Great Hall. In *The Sorcerer's Stone,* Harry sneaks under a cloak of invisibility into the Hogwarts Library (really Duke Humfrey's Library), and he awakens in the Hogwarts infirmary (the big-windowed Divinity School of the Bodleian Library).

Northeast England: In *The Sorcerer's Stone,* Harry walks with his white owl, Hedwig, through a snowy courtyard in Durham's Cathedral.

Scotland

Glencoe was the main location for outdoor filming in *The Prisoner of Azkaban* and *The Half-Blood Prince,* and many shots of the Hogwarts grounds were filmed in the Fort William and Glencoe areas. The Hogwarts Express that carries Harry, Ron, and Hermione to school runs along the actual **Jacobite Steam Train** line (between Fort William and Mallaig).

In *The Prisoner of Azkaban* and *The Goblet of Fire,* **Loch Shiel, Loch Eilt,** and **Loch Morar** (near Fort William) were stand-ins for the Great Lake. **Steall Falls,** at the base of Ben Nevis, is the locale for the Triwizard Tournament in *The Goblet of Fire.*

19 free, www.english-heritage.org.uk/membership; tel. 0370-333-1181).

Membership in the **National Trust** is best suited for garden-and-estate enthusiasts, ideally those traveling by car. It covers more than 350 historic houses, manors, and gardens throughout Great Britain, including 100 properties in Scotland. From the US, it's easy to join online through the Royal Oak Foundation, the National Trust's American affiliate (one-year membership: single membership-$80, two-person membership-$125, family and student memberships, www.royal-oak.org). For more on National Trust properties, see www.nationaltrust.org.uk.

Cadw's Explorer Pass covers many sights in Wales (3-day pass: £23 for one person, £36 for two, £47 for a family; 7-day pass available; buy at castle ticket desks, www.cadw.wales.gov.uk).

Historic Scotland's Explorer Pass covers its 77 properties, including Edinburgh Castle, Stirling Castle, and several sights on Orkney (5-day pass-£35, 14-day pass-£45, www.historicenvironment.scot). This pass allows you to skip the ticket-buying lines at Edinburgh and Stirling castles.

Factors to Consider: An advantage to these deals is that you'll feel free to dip into lesser sights without considering the cost of admission. But remember that your kids already get in free or cheaply at most places, and people over 60 get discounted prices at many sights. If you're traveling by car and can get to the remote sights, you're more likely to get your money's worth out of a pass or membership, especially during peak season (Easter-Oct), when all the sights are open.

AT SIGHTS

Here's what you can typically expect:

Entering: You may not be allowed to enter if you arrive too close to closing time. And guards start ushering people out well before the actual closing time, so don't save the best for last.

Many sights have a security check. Allow extra time for these lines. Some sights require you to check daypacks and coats. (If you'd rather not check your daypack, try carrying it tucked under your arm like a purse as you enter.)

At ticket desks, you may see references to "Gift Aid"—a tax-deduction scheme that benefits museums—but this only concerns UK taxpayers.

Photography: If the museum's photo policy isn't clearly posted, ask a guard. Generally, taking photos without a flash or tripod is allowed. Some sights ban selfie sticks; others ban photos altogether.

Audioguides and Apps: Many sights rent audioguides with excellent recorded descriptions (about £5). If you bring your own earbuds, you can often enjoy better sound. If you don't mind being tethered to your travel partner, you'll save money by bringing a Y-jack and sharing one audioguide. Museums and sights often offer free apps that you can download to your mobile device (check their websites). And, I've produced free, downloadable audio tours for London's Westminster Walk, the British Museum, the British Library, St. Paul's Cathedral, and Historic London: The City Walk, and for Edinburgh's Royal Mile; look for the 🎧 symbol in this book. For more on my audio tours, see page 30.

Guided tours are most likely to occur during peak season (either for free or a small fee—figure £5-10—and widely ranging in quality). Some sights also run short introductory videos featuring their highlights and history. These are generally well worth your time and a great place to start your visit.

Temporary Exhibits: Museums may show special exhibits in addition to their permanent collection. Some exhibits are included in the entry price, while others come at an extra cost (which you may have to pay even if you don't want to see the exhibit).

Expect Changes: Artwork can be on tour, on loan, out sick, or shifted at the whim of the curator. Pick up a floor plan as you enter, and ask museum staff if you can't find a particular item.

Services: Important sights and cathedrals usually have a reasonably priced on-site café or cafeteria (handy places to rejuvenate during a long visit—try a cheap "cream tea" to pick up your energy in midafternoon, like Brits do). The WCs at sights are free and generally clean.

Before Leaving: At the gift shop, scan the postcard rack or thumb through a guidebook to be sure that you haven't overlooked something that you'd like to see. Every sight or museum offers more than what is covered in this book. Use the information I provide as an introduction—not the final word.

Sleeping

Extensive and opinionated listings of good-value rooms are a major feature of this book's Sleeping sections. Rather than list accommodations scattered throughout a town, I choose places in my favorite neighborhoods that are convenient to your sightseeing.

My recommendations run the gamut, from dorm beds to fancy rooms with all the comforts. I like places that are clean, central, relatively quiet at night, reasonably priced, friendly, small enough to have a hands-on owner or manager, and run with a respect for British traditions. I'm more impressed by a handy location and fun-loving philosophy than flat-screen TVs and a fancy gym. Most of my recommendations fall short of perfection. But if I can find a place with most of these features, it's a keeper.

Book your accommodations as soon as your itinerary is set, especially if you want to stay at one of my top listings or if you'll be traveling during busy times. See the appendix for a list of major holidays and festivals in Great Britain.

Some people make reservations as they travel, calling or emailing ahead a few days to a week before their arrival. If you're trying for a same-day reservation, it's best to call hotels at about 9:00 or 10:00, when the receptionist knows which rooms will be available. Some apps—such as HotelTonight.com—specialize in last-minute rooms, often at boutique or business-class hotels in big cities.

RATES AND DEALS

I've categorized my recommended accommodations based on price, indicated with a dollar-sign rating (see sidebar). The price ranges suggest an estimated cost for a one-night stay in high season in a standard double room with a private toilet and shower, and as-

PRACTICALITIES

Sleep Code

Hotels in this book are categorized according to the average price of a standard double room with breakfast in high season.

$$$$	**Splurge:**	Most rooms over £160
$$$	**Pricier:**	£120-160
$$	**Moderate:**	£80-120
$	**Budget:**	£40-80
¢	**Backpacker:**	Under £40
RS%	**Rick Steves discount**	

Unless otherwise noted, credit cards are accepted and free Wi-Fi is available. Comparison-shop by checking prices at several hotels (on each hotel's own website, on a booking site, or by email). For the best deal, *book directly with the hotel.* Ask for a discount if paying in cash; if the listing includes **RS%**, request a Rick Steves discount.

---

sume you're booking directly with the hotel (not through a booking site, which extracts a commission). Room prices can fluctuate significantly with demand and amenities (size, views, room class, and so on), but relative price categories remain constant. In London, breakfast is often not included in quoted hotel rates; you can opt out of the pricey hotel breakfast and get it on your own for less.

In Britain, small bed-and-breakfast places (B&Bs) generally provide the best value, though I also include some bigger hotels. Great Britain has a rating system for hotels and B&Bs. Its stars are supposed to imply quality, but I find they mean only that the place is paying dues to the tourist board. Rating systems often have little to do with value.

Room rates can be volatile at larger hotels that use "dynamic pricing" to set rates. Prices can skyrocket during festivals and conventions, while business hotels can have deep discounts on weekends when demand plummets. Of the many hotels I recommend, it's difficult to say which will be the best value on a given day—until you do your homework.

Booking Direct: Once your dates are set, compare prices at several hotels. You can do this by checking Hotels.com or Booking.com, and hotel websites. Then book directly with the hotel itself. Contact small family-run hotels directly by phone or email. When you go direct, the owner avoids the commission paid to booking sites, thereby leaving enough wiggle room to offer you a discount, a nicer room, or a free breakfast (if it's not already included). If you prefer to book online or are considering a hotel chain, it's to your advantage to use the hotel's website. When establishing prices, confirm if the charge is per person or per room (if a price is too good to be true, it's probably per person).

Booking directly also increases the chances that the hotelier will be able to accommodate any special needs or requests (such as shifting your reservation). Going through a middleman makes it more difficult for the hotel to adjust your booking.

Getting a Discount: Some hotels extend a discount to those who pay cash or stay longer than three nights. And some accommodations offer a special discount for Rick Steves readers, indicated in this guidebook by the abbreviation **"RS%."** Discounts vary: Ask for details when you reserve. Generally, to qualify for this discount, you must book direct (not through a booking site), mention this book when you reserve, show this book upon arrival, and sometimes pay cash or stay a certain number of nights. In some cases, you may need to enter a discount code (which I've provided in the listing) in the booking form on the hotel's website. Rick Steves discounts apply to readers with either print or digital books. Understandably, discounts do not apply to promotional rates.

Staying in B&Bs and small hotels can save money over sleeping in big hotels. Chain hotels can be even cheaper, but they don't include breakfast. When comparing prices between chain hotels and B&Bs, remember you're getting two breakfasts (about a £25 value) for each double room at a B&B.

TYPES OF ACCOMMODATIONS
Hotels

In cities, you'll find big, Old World-elegant hotels with modern amenities, as well as familiar-feeling business-class and boutique hotels no different from what you might experience at home. But you'll also find hotels that are more uniquely European.

Outside of pricey big cities, you can expect to find good doubles for £80-120, including cooked breakfasts. Bigger cities, swanky B&Bs, and big hotels generally cost significantly more.

A "twin" room has two single beds; a "double" has one double bed. If you'll take either, let the hotel know, or you might be needlessly turned away. Some hotels can add an extra bed (for a small charge) to turn a double into a triple; some offer larger rooms for four or more people (I call these "family rooms" in the listings). If there's space for an extra cot, they'll cram it in for you. In general, a triple room is cheaper than the cost of a double and a single. Three or four people can economize by requesting one big room.

An "en suite" room has a bathroom (toilet and shower/tub) attached to the room; a room with a "private bathroom" can mean that the bathroom is all yours, but it's across the hall. If you want your own bathroom inside the room, request "en suite." If money's tight, ask about a room with a shared bathroom. You'll almost always have a sink in your room, and as more rooms go en suite, the hallway bathroom is shared with fewer guests.

Using Online Services to Your Advantage

From booking services to user reviews, online businesses play a greater role in travelers' planning than ever before. Take advantage of their pluses—and be wise to their downsides.

Booking Sites

Booking websites such as Booking.com and Hotels.com offer one-stop shopping for hotels. While convenient for travelers, they present a real problem for independent, family-run hotels. Without a presence on these sites, small hotels become almost invisible. But to be listed, a hotel must pay a sizeable commission... and promise that its own website won't undercut the price on the booking-service site.

Here's the work-around: Use the big sites to research what's out there, then book directly with the hotel by email or phone, in which case hotel owners are free to give you whatever price they like. Ask for a room without the commission markup (or ask for a free breakfast if not included, or a free upgrade). If you do book online, be sure to use the hotel's website. The price will likely be the same as via a booking site, but your money goes to the hotel, not agency commissions.

As a savvy consumer, remember: When you book with an online booking service, you're adding a middleman who takes roughly 20 percent. To support small, family-run hotels whose world is more difficult than ever, book direct.

Short-Term Rental Sites

Rental juggernaut Airbnb (along with other short-term rental sites) allows travelers to rent rooms and apartments directly from locals, often providing more value than a cookie-cutter hotel. Airbnb fans appreciate feeling part of a real neighborhood and getting into a daily routine as "temporary Europeans." Depending on the host, Airbnb can provide an opportunity to get to know a

Note that to be called a "hotel," a place technically must have certain amenities, including a 24-hour reception (though this rule is loosely applied).

Modern Hotel Chains: Chain hotels—common in bigger cities all over Great Britain—can be a great value (£60-100, depending on location and season; more expensive in London). These hotels are about as cozy as a Motel 6, but they come with private showers/WCs, elevators, good security, and often an attached restaurant. Branches are often located near the train station, on major highways, or outside the city center.

This option is especially worth considering for families, as kids often stay for free. While most of these hotels have 24-hour reception and elevators, breakfast and Wi-Fi generally cost extra, and local person, while keeping the money spent on your accommodations in the community.

Critics view Airbnb as a threat to "traditional Europe," saying it creates unfair, unqualified competition for established guesthouse owners. In some places, the lucrative Airbnb market has forced traditional guesthouses out of business and is driving property values out of range for locals. Some cities have cracked down, requiring owners to occupy rental properties part of the year (and staging disruptive "inspections" that inconvenience guests).

As a lover of Europe, I share the worry of those who see residents nudged aside by tourists. But as an advocate for travelers, I appreciate the value and cultural intimacy Airbnb provides.

User Reviews

User-generated review sites and apps such as Yelp and TripAdvisor can give you a consensus of opinions about everything from hotels and restaurants to sights and nightlife. If you scan reviews of a restaurant or hotel and see several complaints about noise or a rotten location, you've gained insight that can help in your decision-making.

But as a guidebook writer, my sense is that there is a big difference between the uncurated information on a review site and the vetted listings in a guidebook. A user-generated review is based on the limited experience of one person, who stayed at just one hotel in a given city and ate at a few restaurants there. A guidebook is the work of a trained researcher who forms a well-developed basis for comparison by visiting many restaurants and hotels year after year.

Both types of information have their place, and in many ways, they're complementary. If something is well reviewed in a guidebook and also gets good online reviews, it's likely a winner.

the service lacks a personal touch (at some, you'll check in at a self-service kiosk). When comparing your options, keep in mind that for about the same price, you can get a basic room at a B&B that has less predictable comfort but more funkiness and friendliness in a more enjoyable neighborhood.

Room rates change from day to day with volume and vary depending on how far ahead you book. The best deals generally must be prepaid a few weeks ahead and may not be refundable—read the fine print carefully.

The biggest chains are **Premier Inn** (www.premierinn.com) and **Travelodge** (www.travelodge.co.uk). Both have attractive deals for prepaid or advance bookings. Other chains operating in Britain include the Irish **Jurys Inn** (www.jurysinns.com) and the

PRACTICALITIES

Making Hotel Reservations

Reserve your rooms as soon as you've pinned down your travel dates. For busy national holidays, it's wise to reserve far in advance (see the appendix).

Requesting a Reservation: For family-run hotels, it's generally best to book your room directly via email or phone. For business-class and chain hotels, or if you'd rather book online, reserve directly through the hotel's official website (not a booking website). Here's what the hotelier wants to know:

- Type(s) of rooms you want and size of your party
- Number of nights you'll stay
- Your arrival and departure dates, written European-style as day/month/year (for example, 18/06/21 or 18 June 2021)
- Special requests (such as en suite bathroom, cheapest room, twin beds vs. double bed, quiet room)
- Applicable discounts (such as a Rick Steves reader discount, cash discount, or promotional rate)

Confirming a Reservation: Most places will request a credit-card number to hold your room. If you're using an online reservation form, make sure it's secure by looking for the *https* or a lock icon at the top of your browser. If the hotel's website doesn't have a secure form where you can enter the number directly, it's best to share that confidential info via a phone call.

Canceling a Reservation: If you must cancel, it's courteous—and smart—to do so with as much notice as possible, especially for smaller family-run places. Cancellation policies can be strict; read

French-owned **Ibis** (www.ibishotel.com). Couples can consider **Holiday Inn Express,** which generally allows only two people per room. It's like a Holiday Inn lite, with cheaper prices and no restaurant (make sure Express is part of the name or you'll be paying more for a regular Holiday Inn, www.hiexpress.co.uk).

Arrival and Check-In: Hotels and B&Bs are sometimes located on the higher floors of a multipurpose building with a secured door. In that case, look for your hotel's name on the buttons by the main entrance. When you ring the bell, you'll be buzzed in.

Hotel elevators are common, though some older buildings still lack them. You may have to climb a flight of stairs to reach the elevator (if so, you can ask the front desk for help carrying your bags up). Elevators are typically very small—pack light, or you may need to send your bags up without you.

The EU requires that hotels collect your name, nationality, and ID number. When you check in, the receptionist will normally ask for your passport and may keep it for anywhere from a couple of minutes to a couple of hours. If you're not comfortable leaving your passport at the desk for a long time, ask when you can pick it

From:	rick@ricksteves.com
Sent:	Today
To:	info@hotelcentral.com
Subject:	Reservation request for 19-22 July

Dear Hotel Central,

I would like to stay at your hotel. Please let me know if you have a room available and the price for:
- 2 people
- Double bed and en suite bathroom in a quiet room
- Arriving 19 July, departing 22 July (3 nights)

Thank you!
Rick Steves

the fine print before you book. Many discount deals require pre-payment, with no cancellation refunds.

Reconfirming a Reservation: Always call or email to reconfirm your room reservation a few days in advance. For B&Bs or very small hotels, I call again on my day of arrival to tell my host what time to expect me (especially important if arriving late—after 17:00).

Phoning: For tips on calling hotels overseas, see page 1062.

up. Or, if you packed a color photocopy of your passport, you can generally leave that rather than the original.

If you're arriving in the morning, your room probably won't be ready. Check your bag safely at the hotel and dive right into sightseeing.

In Your Room: Most hotel rooms have a TV, telephone, and free Wi-Fi (although in old buildings with thick walls, the Wi-Fi signal might be available only in the lobby). Simpler places rarely have a room phone.

More pillows and blankets are usually in the closet or available on request. Towels and linens aren't always replaced every day.

Air-conditioning isn't a given (I've noted which of my listings have it), but most places have fans.

Electrical outlets may have switches that turn the current on or off; if your appliance isn't working, flip the switch at the outlet.

Breakfast and Meals: Your room cost usually includes a traditional full cooked breakfast (fry-up) or a lighter, healthier continental breakfast.

Checking Out: While it's customary to pay for your room

upon departure, it can be a good idea to settle your bill the day before, when you're not in a hurry and while the manager's in.

Hotelier Help: Hoteliers can be a good source of advice. Most know their city well, and can assist you with everything from public transit and airport connections to finding a good restaurant, the nearest launderette, or a late-night pharmacy.

Hotel Hassles: Even at the best places, mechanical breakdowns occur: Sinks leak, hot water turns cold, toilets may gurgle or smell, the Wi-Fi goes out, or the air-conditioning dies when you need it most. Report your concerns clearly and calmly at the front desk.

If you find that night noise is a problem (if, for instance, your room is over a noisy pub or facing a busy street), ask for a quieter room in the back or on an upper floor. To guard against theft in your room, keep valuables out of sight. Some rooms come with a safe, and other hotels have safes at the front desk. I've never bothered using one and in a lifetime of travel, I've never had anything stolen from my room.

For more complicated problems, don't expect instant results. Above all, keep a positive attitude. Remember, you're on vacation. If your hotel is a disappointment, spend more time out enjoying the place you came to see.

B&Bs and Small Hotels

B&Bs and small hotels are generally family-run places with fewer amenities but more character than a conventional hotel. They range from large inns with 15-20 rooms to small homes renting out a spare bedroom. Places named "guesthouse" or "B&B" typically have eight or fewer rooms. The philosophy of the management determines the character of a place more than its size and amenities. I avoid places run as a business by absentee owners. My top listings are run by people who enjoy welcoming the world to their breakfast table.

Compared to hotels, B&Bs and guesthouses give you double the cultural intimacy for half the price. While you may lose some of the conveniences of a hotel—such as fancy lobbies, in-room phones, and frequent bed-sheet changes—I happily make the trade-off for the personal touches, whether it's joining my hosts for afternoon tea or relaxing by a common fireplace at the end of the day. If you have a reasonable but limited budget, skip hotels and go the B&B way.

B&B proprietors are selective about the guests they invite in for the night. Many do not welcome children. If you'll be staying for more than one night, you are a "desirable." In popular weekend-getaway spots, you're unlikely to find a place to take you for Saturday night only. If my listings are full, ask for guidance. Mentioning this book can help. Owners usually work together and can call up an ally to land you a bed. Many B&B owners are also pet owners. If you're allergic, ask about resident pets when you reserve.

Rules and Etiquette: B&Bs and small hotels come with their own etiquette and quirks. Keep in mind that owners are at the whim of their guests—if you're getting up early, so are they; if you check in late, they'll wait up for you. Most B&Bs have set check-in times (usually in the late afternoon). If arriving outside that time, they will want to know when to expect you (call or email ahead). Most will let you check in earlier if the room is available (or they'll at least let you drop off your bag).

Most B&Bs and guesthouses serve a hearty cooked breakfast of eggs and much more (for details on breakfast, see the "Eating" section, later). Because the owner is often also the cook, breakfast hours are usually abbreviated. Typically the breakfast window lasts for 1-1.5 hours (make sure you know when it is before you turn in for the night). Some B&Bs ask you to fill in your breakfast order the night before. It's an unwritten rule that guests shouldn't show up at the very end of the breakfast period and expect a full cooked breakfast. If you do arrive late (or need to leave before breakfast is served), most establishments are happy to let you help yourself to cereal, fruit, juice, and coffee.

B&Bs and small hotels often come with thin walls and doors, and sometimes creaky floorboards, which can make for a noisy night. If you're a light sleeper, bring earplugs. And please be quiet in the halls and in your rooms at night...those of us getting up early will thank you for it.

Treat these lovingly maintained homes as you would a friend's house. Be careful maneuvering your bag up narrow staircases with fragile walls and banisters. And once in the room, use the luggage rack—putting bags on the bed can damage nice bedding.

In the Room: Most B&Bs offer "tea service" in the room—an electric kettle, cups, tea bags, coffee packets, and a pack of biscuits.

Your bedroom probably won't include a phone, but nearly every B&B has free Wi-Fi. However, the signal may not reach all rooms; you may need to sit in the lounge to access it.

You're likely to encounter unusual bathroom fixtures. The "pump toilet" has a flushing handle or button that doesn't kick in unless you push it just right: too hard or too soft, and it won't go. (Be decisive but not ruthless.) Most B&B baths have an instant water heater. This looks like an electronic box under the showerhead with dials and buttons: One control adjusts the heat, while another turns the flow off and on (let the water run for a bit to moderate the temperature before you hop in). If the hot water doesn't work, you may need to flip a red switch (often located just outside the bathroom). If the shower looks mysterious, ask your B&B host for help...*before* you take off your clothes.

Paying: Many B&Bs take credit cards, but may add the card service fee to your bill (about 3 percent). If you do need to pay cash for your room, plan ahead to have enough on hand when you check out.

Short-Term Rentals

A short-term rental—whether an apartment (or "flat"), house, or room in a local's home—is an increasingly popular alternative, especially if you plan to settle in one location for several nights. For stays longer than a few days, you can usually find a rental that's comparable to—and cheaper than—a hotel room with similar amenities. Plus, you'll get a behind-the-scenes peek into how locals live.

Many places require a minimum stay and have strict cancellation policies. And you're generally on your own: There's no hotel reception desk, breakfast, or daily cleaning service.

Finding Accommodations: Websites such as Airbnb, FlipKey, Booking.com, and the HomeAway family of sites (HomeAway, VRBO, and VacationRentals) let you browse a wide range of properties. Alternatively, rental agencies such as InterhomeUSA.com or RentaVilla.com, which list more carefully selected accommodations that might cost more, can provide more personalized service. For a list of rental agencies for London, see page 174.

Before you commit, be clear on the location. I like to virtually "explore" the neighborhood using the Street View feature on Google Maps. Also consider the proximity to public transportation and how well connected the property is with the rest of the city. Ask about amenities (elevator, air-conditioning, laundry, Wi-Fi, parking, etc.). Reviews from previous guests can help identify trouble spots.

Think about the kind of experience you want: Just a key and an affordable bed...or a chance to get to know a local? There are typically two kinds of hosts: those who want minimal interaction with their guests, and hosts who are friendly and may want to interact with you. Read the promotional text and online reviews to help shape your decision.

Confirming and Paying: Many places require you to pay the entire balance before your trip. It's easiest and safest to pay through the site where you found the listing. Be wary of owners who want to take your transaction offline; this gives you no recourse if things go awry. Never agree to wire money (a key indicator of a fraudulent transaction).

Apartments or Houses: If you're staying in one place for four or more nights, it's worth considering an apartment or rental house (shorter stays aren't worth the hassle of arranging key pickup, buying groceries, etc.). Apartment or house rentals can be especially cost-effective for groups and families. European apartments, like hotel rooms, tend to be small by US standards. But they often come with laundry machines and small, equipped kitchens, making it easier and cheaper to dine in.

Rooms in Private Homes: Renting a room in someone's home is a good option for those traveling alone, as you're more likely to find true single rooms—with just one single bed, and a price to match. These can range from air-mattress-in-living-room basic to plush-B&B-suite posh. Some places allow you to book for a single night; if staying for several nights, you can buy groceries just as you would in a rental house. While you can't expect your host to also be your tour guide—or even to provide you with much info—some may be interested in getting to know the travelers who come through their home.

Other Options: Swapping homes with a local works for people with an appealing place to offer (don't assume where you live is not interesting to Europeans). Good places to start are HomeExchange.com and LoveHomeSwap.com. To sleep for free, Couchsurfing.com is a vagabond's alternative to Airbnb. It lists millions of outgoing members, who host fellow "surfers" in their homes.

Hostels

Britain has hostels of all shapes and sizes. Choose yours selectively. Hostels can be historic castles or depressing tenements, serene and comfy or overrun by noisy school groups.

A hostel provides cheap beds in dorms where you sleep alongside strangers for about £20-30 per night. Travelers of any age are welcome if they don't mind dorm-style accommodations and meeting other travelers. Most hostels offer kitchen facilities, guest computers, Wi-Fi, and a self-service laundry. Hostels almost always provide bedding, but the towel's up to you (though you can usually rent one for a small fee). Family and private rooms are often available.

Independent hostels tend to be easygoing, colorful, and informal (no membership required; www.hostelworld.com). You may pay slightly less by booking directly with the hostel.

Official hostels are part of Hostelling International (HI) and share an online booking site (www.hihostels.com). HI hostels typically require that you be a member or else pay a bit more per night.

In Britain, these official hostels are run by the Youth Hostel Association (YHA, www.yha.org.uk); in Scotland they're run by the Scottish Youth Hostel Association (SYHA, also known as Hostelling Scotland, www.syha.org.uk).

Eating

These days, the stereotype of "bad food in Britain" is woefully dated. Britain has caught up with the foodie revolution—in fact, they're right there, leading the vanguard—and I find it's easy to eat very well here. London, in particular, is one of Europe's best food destinations.

British cooking has embraced international influences and local, seasonal ingredients, making "modern British" food quite delicious. While some dreary pub food still exists, you'll generally find the cuisine scene here innovative and delicious (but expensive). Basic pubs are more likely to dish up homemade, creative dishes than microwaved pies, soggy fries, and mushy peas. Even traditional pub grub has gone upmarket, with gastropubs that serve locally sourced meats and fresh vegetables.

All of Britain is smoke-free. Expect restaurants and pubs to be nonsmoking indoors, with smokers occupying patios and doorways outside. You'll find the Brits eat at about the same time of day as Americans.

For listings in this guidebook, I look for restaurants that are convenient to your hotel and sightseeing. When restaurant-hunting, choose a spot filled with locals, not tourists. Venturing even a block or two off the main drag leads to higher-quality food for a better price.

Tipping: At pubs and places where you order at the counter, you don't have to tip. Regular customers ordering a round sometimes say, "Add one for yourself" as a tip for drinks ordered at the bar—but this isn't expected. At restaurants and fancy pubs with waitstaff, it's not necessary to tip if a service charge is already included in the bill (common in London—usually 12.5 percent). Otherwise, it's appropriate to tip about 10-12 percent; you can add a bit more for finer dining or extra-good service. Tip only what you think the service warrants (if it isn't already added to your bill), and be careful not to tip double.

Restaurant Code

Eateries in this book are categorized according to the average cost of a typical main course. Drinks, desserts, and splurge items can raise the price considerably.

$$$$	**Splurge:** Most main courses over £20
$$$	**Pricier:** £15-20
$$	**Moderate:** £10-15
$	**Budget:** Under £10

In Great Britain, carryout fish-and-chips and other takeout food is **$**; a basic pub or sit-down eatery is **$$**; a gastropub or casual but more upscale restaurant is **$$$**; and a swanky splurge is **$$$$**.

RESTAURANT PRICING

I've categorized my recommended eateries based on the average price of a typical main course, indicated with a dollar-sign rating (see sidebar). Obviously, expensive specialties, fine wine, appetizers, and dessert can significantly increase your final bill.

The categories also indicate the personality of a place: **Budget** eateries include street food, takeaway, order-at-the-counter shops, basic cafeterias, and bakeries selling sandwiches. **Moderate** eateries are nice (but not fancy) sit-down restaurants, ideal for a straightforward, fill-the-tank meal. Most of my listings fall in this category—great for getting a good taste of the local cuisine at a reasonable price.

Pricier eateries are a notch up, with more attention paid to the setting, presentation, and (often inventive) cuisine. **Splurge** eateries are dress-up-for-a-special-occasion-swanky—typically with an elegant setting, polished service, intricate cuisine, and an expansive (and expensive) wine list.

BREAKFAST (FRY-UP)

The traditional fry-up or full English/Scottish/Welsh breakfast—generally included in the cost of your room—is famous as a hearty way to start the day. Also known as a "heart attack on a plate," your standard fry-up is a heated plate with eggs, Canadian-style bacon and/or sausage, a grilled tomato, sautéed mushrooms, baked beans, and sometimes potatoes, kippers (herring), or fried  bread (sizzled in a greasy skillet). Expect regional variations, such as black pudding (a blood sausage; northern England and Scotland) and a dense potato scone or haggis (Scotland). Toast comes in a rack (to cool quickly and crisply) with butter and marmalade. The meal is typically topped off with tea or coffee. At a B&B or hotel, it may start with juice and cereal or porridge. Many progressive B&B owners offer vegetarian, organic, gluten-free, or other creative variations on the traditional breakfast.

As much as the full breakfast fry-up is a traditional way to start the morning, these days most places serve a healthier continental breakfast as well—with a buffet of yogurt, cereal, fruit, and pastries. At some hotels, the buffet may also include hot items, such as eggs and sausage.

LUNCH AND DINNER ON A BUDGET

Even in pricey cities, plenty of inexpensive choices are available: pub grub, daily lunch and early-bird dinner specials, global cuisine, cafeterias, fast food, picnics, greasy-spoon cafés, cheap chain restaurants, and pizza.

I've found that portions are huge, and **sharing plates** is generally just fine. Ordering two drinks, a soup or side salad, and splitting a £10 meat pie can make a good, filling meal. If you're on a limited budget, share a main course in a more expensive place for a nicer eating experience.

Pub grub is the most atmospheric budget option. You'll usually get hearty lunches and dinners priced reasonably at £8-15 under ancient timbers (see "Pubs," later). Gastropubs, with better food, are more expensive.

Classier restaurants have some affordable deals. Lunch is usually cheaper than dinner; a top-end, £30-for-dinner-type restaurant often serves the same quality two-course lunch deals for about half the price.

Many restaurants have **early-bird** or **pre-theater specials** of two or three courses, often for a significant savings. They are usually available only before 18:30 or 19:00 (and sometimes on weekdays only).

Global cuisine adds spice to Britain's food scene. Eating Indian, Bangladeshi, Chinese, or Thai is cheap (even cheaper if you do takeout). Middle Eastern shops sell gyro sandwiches, falafel, and *shawarmas* (grilled meat in pita bread). An Indian samosa (greasy, flaky meat-and-vegetable turnover) costs about £2 and makes a very cheap, if small, meal. (For more, see "Indian Cuisine," later.) You'll find inexpensive, quick Asian options (often Chinese), such as all-you-can-eat buffets and takeaway places serving up standard dishes in to-go boxes.

Fish-and-chips are a heavy, greasy, but tasty British classic. Every town has at least one "chippy" selling takeaway fish-and-chips

in a cardboard box or (more traditionally) wrapped in paper for about £5-7. You can dip your fries in ketchup, American-style, or "go British" and drizzle the whole thing with malt vinegar and fresh lemon.

Most large **museums** (and many historic **churches**) have handy, moderately priced cafeterias with forgettably decent food.

Picnicking saves time and money. Fine park benches and polite pigeons abound in most towns and city neighborhoods. You can easily get prepared food to go. The modern chain eateries on nearly every corner often have simple seating but are designed for takeout. Bakeries serve a wonderful array of fresh sandwiches and pasties (savory meat pastries—sometimes called bridies in Scotland and oggies in Wales). Street markets, generally parked in pedestrian-friendly zones, are fun and colorful places to stock up for a picnic.

Open-air markets and supermarkets sell produce in small quantities. The corner grocery store has fruit, drinks, fresh bread, tasty British cheese, meat, and local specialties. Supermarkets often have good deli sections, even offering Indian dishes, and sometimes salad bars. Decent packaged sandwiches (£3-4) are sold everywhere. Munch a relaxed "meal on wheels" picnic during your open-top bus tour or river cruise to save 30 precious minutes for sightseeing.

PUBS

Pubs are a fundamental part of the British social scene, and whether you're a teetotaler or a beer guzzler, they should be a part of your travel here. "Pub" is short for "public house." It's an extended common room where, if you don't mind the stickiness, you can feel the local pulse. Smart travelers use pubs to eat, drink, get out of the rain, watch sporting events, and make new

friends. Unfortunately, many city pubs have been afflicted with an excess of brass, ferns, and video slot machines. The most traditional atmospheric pubs are in the countryside and in smaller towns.

It's interesting to consider the role pubs filled for Britain's working class in more modest times: For workers with humble domestic quarters and no money for a vacation, a beer at the corner pub was the closest they'd get to a comfortable living room, a place to entertain, and a getaway. And locals could meet people from far away in a pub—today, that's you!

Though hours vary, pubs generally serve beer daily from 11:00 to 23:00, though many are open later, particularly on Friday and Saturday. (Children are served food and soft drinks in pubs, but you must be 18 to order a beer.) As it nears closing time, you'll hear shouts of "last orders." Then comes the 10-minute warning bell. Finally, they'll call "Time!" to pick up your glass, finished or not, when the pub closes.

A cup of darts is free for the asking. People go to a public house to be social. They want to talk. Get vocal with a local. This is easiest at the bar, where people assume you're in the mood to talk (rather than at a table, where you're allowed a bit of privacy). The pub is the next best thing to having relatives in town. Cheers!

Pub Grub: For £8-15, you'll get a basic budget hot lunch or dinner in friendly surroundings. In high-priced London, this is your best indoor eating value. (For something more refined, try a **gastropub,** which serves higher-quality meals for £12-20.) The *Good Pub Guide* is an excellent resource (www.thegoodpubguide.co.uk). Pubs that are attached to restaurants, advertise their food, and are crowded with locals are more likely to have fresh food and a chef—and less likely to sell only lousy microwaved snacks.

Pubs generally serve traditional dishes, such as fish-and-chips, roast beef with Yorkshire pudding (batter-baked in the oven), and assorted meat pies, such as steak-and-kidney pie or shepherd's pie (stewed lamb topped with mashed potatoes) with cooked vegetables. Side dishes include salads, vegetables, and—invariably—"chips" (French fries). "Crisps" are potato chips. A "jacket potato" (baked potato stuffed with fillings of your choice) can almost be a meal in itself. A "ploughman's lunch" is a traditional British meal of bread, cheese, and sweet pickles. These days, you'll likely find more pasta, curried dishes, and quiche on the menu than traditional fare.

Meals are usually served from 12:00 to 14:00 and again from 18:00 to 20:00—with a break in the middle (rather than serving straight through the day). Since they make more money selling beer, many pubs stop food service early in the evening—especially on weekends. There's generally no table service. Order at the bar, and then take a seat. Either they'll bring the food when it's ready or you'll pick it up at the bar. Pay at the bar (sometimes when you order, sometimes after you eat). It's not necessary to tip unless it's a place with full table service. Servings are hearty, and service is quick. A beer, cider, or dram of whisky adds another couple of pounds. Free tap water is always available. For details on ordering beer and other drinks, see the "Beverages" section, later. For a list of recommended historic pubs in London, see page 184.

GOOD CHAIN RESTAURANTS

I know—you're going to Britain to enjoy characteristic little hole-in-the-wall pubs, so mass-produced food is the furthest thing from your mind. But several excellent chains with branches across the UK offer long hours, reasonable prices, reliable quality, and a nice break from pub grub. My favorites are Pret, Wasabi, and Eat. Expect to see these familiar names wherever you go:

$ Pret (a.k.a. Pret à Manger) is perhaps the most pervasive of these modern convenience eateries. Some are takeout only, and others have seating ranging from simple stools to restaurant-quality tables. The service is fast, the price is great, and the food is healthy and fresh. Their slogan: "Made today. Gone today. No 'sell-by' date, no nightlife."

$$ Côte Brasserie is a contemporary French chain serving good-value French cuisine in pleasant settings (early dinner specials).

Two **$** chains have reliably good coffee and pastries: **Paul** (French-style, with croissants, other pastries, and baguette sandwiches) and **Ole & Steen** (Scandinavian, with generous samples of cinnamon rolls). The coffee at either place is typically better than the ubiquitous British chains Costa and Nero.

$$ Le Pain Quotidien is a Belgian chain serving fresh-baked bread and hearty meals in a thoughtfully designed modern-rustic atmosphere.

$$ Byron Hamburgers, an upscale-hamburger chain with hip interiors, is worth seeking out if you need a burger fix. While British burgers tend to be a bit overcooked by American standards, Byron's burgers are your best bet.

$$ Wagamama Noodle Bar, serving pan-Asian cuisine (udon noodles, fried rice, and curry dishes), is a noisy, organic slurpathon. Portions are huge and splittable. There's one in almost every mid-size city in Britain, usually located in sprawling halls filled with long shared tables and busy servers who scrawl your order on the placemat.

$$$ Loch Fyne Restaurant is a Scottish chain that raises its own oysters and mussels. Its branches offer an inviting, lively atmosphere with a fine fishy energy and no pretense (early-bird specials).

$ Marks & Spencer department stores have inviting deli

sections with cheery sit-down eating (along with their popular sandwiches-to-go section). M&S food halls are also handy if you're renting a city flat and want to prepare your own meals.

$$ Busaba Eathai is a hit in several cities for its snappy (sometimes rushed) service, boisterous ambience, and good, inexpensive Thai cuisine.

$$ Thai Square is a dependable Thai option with a nice atmosphere (salads, noodle dishes, curries, meat dishes, and daily lunch box specials). Most branches are in London.

$$ Masala Zone is a London chain providing a good, predictable alternative to the many one-off, hole-in-the-wall Indian joints around town. Try a curry-and-rice dish, a *thali* (platter with several small dishes), or their street food specials. Each branch has its own personality.

$$ Franco Manca is a taverna-inspired pizzeria serving Neapolitan-style pies using organic ingredients and boasting typical Italian charm. If you skip the pricey drinks, you can feast very cheaply here.

$$ Ask and **Pizza Express** serve quality pasta and pizza in a pleasant, sit-down atmosphere that's family-friendly.

$$ Japanese: Three popular chains serve fresh and inexpensive Japanese food. **Itsu** and **Wasabi** are bright and competitive chains that let you assemble your own plate in a fun and efficient way, while **Yo! Sushi** lets you pick your dish off a conveyor belt and pay according to the color of your plate.

Carry-Out Chains: While the following may have some seating, they're best as places to grab prepackaged food on the run.

Major supermarket chains have smaller offshoot branches that specialize in sandwiches, salads, and other prepared foods to go. These can be a picnicker's dream come true. Some shops are stand-alone, while others are located inside a larger store. The most prevalent—and best—is **M&S Simply Food** (an offshoot of Marks & Spencer; there's one in every major train station). **Sainsbury's Local** grocery stores also offer decent prepared food; **Tesco Express** and **Tesco Metro** run a distant third.

Some "cheap and cheery" chains provide office workers with good, healthful sandwiches, salads, and pastries to go. These include **Pod** and **Eat** (with slightly higher-quality food and higher prices).

INDIAN CUISINE

Eating Indian food is "going local" in cosmopolitan, multiethnic Britain. You'll find Indian restaurants in most cities, and even in small towns. Take the opportunity to sample food from Britain's former colony. Indian cuisine is as varied as the country itself. In general, it uses more exotic spices than British or American cuisine—some hot, some sweet. Indian food is very vegetarian-friendly, offering many meatless dishes.

For a simple meal that costs about £10-12, order one dish with rice and naan (Indian flatbread). Generally, one order is plenty for two people to share. Many Indian restaurants offer a fixed-price combination that offers more variety, and is simpler and cheaper than ordering à la carte. For about £20, you can make a mix-and-match platter out of several shareable dishes, including dal (simmered lentils) as a starter, one or two meat or vegetable dishes with sauce (for example, chicken curry, chicken *tikka masala* in a creamy tomato sauce, grilled fish tandoori, or chickpea *chana masala*), *raita* (a cooling yogurt that comes on the side—it helps extinguish your mouth if eating spicy dishes), rice, naan, and an Indian beer (wine and Indian food don't really mix) or spiced chai tea (usually served with milk). An easy way to taste a variety of dishes is to order a *thali*—a sampler plate of various specialties.

AFTERNOON TEA

Once the sole province of genteel ladies in fancy hats, afternoon tea has become more democratic in the 21st century. These days, people of leisure punctuate their day with an afternoon tea at a tearoom. Tearooms, which often serve appealing light meals, are usually open for lunch and close at about 17:00, just before dinner.

The cheapest "tea" on the menu is generally a "cream tea"; the most expensive is the "champagne tea." **Cream tea** is simply a pot of tea and a homemade scone or two with jam and thick clotted cream. (For maximum pinkie-waving taste per calorie, slice your scone thin like a miniature loaf of bread.) **Afternoon tea**—what many Americans would call "high tea"—is a pot of tea, small finger foods (such as sandwiches with the crusts cut off), scones, an assortment of small pastries, jam, and thick clotted cream. **Champagne tea** includes all of the goodies, plus a glass of bubbly. **High tea** to the English generally means a more substantial late afternoon or early evening meal, often served with meat or eggs.

DESSERTS (SWEETS)

To the British, the traditional word for dessert is "pudding," although it's also referred to as "sweets" these days. Sponge cake, cream, fruitcake, and meringue are key players.

Trifle is the best-known British concoction, consisting of sponge cake soaked in brandy or sherry

PRACTICALITIES

British Chocolate

My chocoholic readers are enthusiastic about British chocolates. As with other dairy products, chocolate seems richer and creamier here than it does in the US, so even standbys such as Mars, Kit Kat (which was actually invented in York—see page 540), and Twix have a different taste. Some favorites include Cadbury Gold bars (filled with liquid caramel), Cadbury Crunchie bars, Nestlé's Lion bars (layered wafers covered in caramel and chocolate), Cadbury's Boost bars (a shortcake biscuit with caramel in milk chocolate), Cadbury Flake (crumbly folds of melt-in-your-mouth chocolate), Aero bars (with "aerated" chocolate filling), and Galaxy chocolate bars (especially the ones with hazelnuts). Thornton shops (in larger train stations) sell a box of sweets called the Continental Assortment, which comes with a tasting guide. (The highlight is the mocha white-chocolate truffle.) British M&Ms, called Smarties, are better than American ones. Many Brits feel that the ultimate treat is a box of either Nestlé Quality Street or Cadbury Roses—assortments of filled chocolates in colorful wrappers. (But don't mention the Kraft takeover of Cadbury in 2010—many Brits believe the American company changed the recipe for their beloved Dairy Milk bars, and they're not happy about it). At ice-cream vans, look for the beloved traditional "99p"—a vanilla soft-serve cone with a small Flake bar stuck right into the middle.

(or orange juice for children), then covered with jam and/or fruit and custard cream. Whipped cream can sometimes put the final touch on this "light" treat.

The British version of custard is a smooth, yellow liquid. Cream tops most everything that custard does not. There's single cream for coffee. Double cream is really thick. Clotted cream is the consistency of whipped butter.

Fool is a dessert with sweetened pureed fruit (such as rhubarb, gooseberries, or black currants) mixed with cream or custard and chilled. Elderflower is a popular flavoring for sorbet.

Flapjacks here aren't pancakes, but are dense, sweet oatmeal cakes (a little like a cross between a granola bar and a brownie). They come with toppings such as toffee and chocolate.

Scones are tops, and many inns and restaurants have their secret recipes. Whether made with fruit or topped with clotted cream, scones take the cake.

BEVERAGES

Beer: The British take great pride in their beer. Many locals think that drinking beer cold and carbonated, as Americans do, ruins the taste. Most pubs will have **lagers** (cold, refreshing, American-style beer), **ales** (amber-colored, cellar-temperature beer), **bitters** (hop-flavored ale, perhaps the most typical British beer), and **stouts** (dark and somewhat bitter, like Guinness).

At pubs, long-handled pulls (or taps) are used to draw the traditional, rich-flavored "real ales" up from the cellar. These are the connoisseur's favorites and often come with fun names. Served straight from the brewer's cask at cellar temperature, real ales finish fermenting naturally and are not pasteurized or filtered, so they must be consumed within two or three days after the cask is tapped. Naturally carbonated, real ales have less gassiness and head; they vary from sweet to bitter, often with a hoppy or nutty flavor.

Short-handled pulls mean colder, fizzier, mass-produced, and less interesting keg beers. Mild beers are sweeter, with a creamy malt flavoring. Irish cream ale is a smooth, sweet experience. Try the draft cider (sweet or dry)...carefully.

Order your beer at the bar and pay as you go, with no need to tip. An average beer costs about £4. Part of the experience is standing before a line of hand pulls, and wondering which beer to choose.

As dictated by British law, draft beer and cider are served by the pint (20-ounce imperial size) or the half-pint (9.6 ounces). In 2011, the government sanctioned an in-between serving size—the schooner, or two-thirds pint (it's become a popular size for higher alcohol-content craft beers). A popular summer drink is a **shandy** (half beer and half British "lemonade," similar to 7-Up).

Whisky: While bar-hopping tourists generally think in terms of beer, many pubs are just as enthusiastic about serving whisky (common throughout Britain, but especially popular in Scotland, where much of it is produced). If you are unfamiliar with whisky (what Americans call "Scotch" and the Irish call "whiskey"), it's a great conversation starter. Many pubs list dozens of whiskies and describe their taste profiles (peaty, smoky, woody, and so on).

A glass of basic whisky generally costs around £2.50. Let a local teach you how to drink it "neat," then add a little water. Make a friend, buy a few drams, and learn by drinking. Keep experimenting until you discover the right taste for you.

Consider going beyond single-malt whiskies. Blends can be surprisingly creative—even for someone who thinks they're knowledgeable about whisky—and non-whisky alternatives are pushing boundaries. Like microbrews, small-batch, innovative Scottish spirits are trendy right now. For example, you'll find gin

The British Accent

In the olden days, a British person's accent indicated his or her social standing. Eliza Doolittle had the right idea—elocution could make or break you. Wealthier families would send their kids to fancy private schools to learn proper pronunciation. But these days, in a sort of reverse snobbery that has gripped the nation, accents are back. Politicians, newscasters, and movie stars are favoring deep accents over the Queen's English. While it's hard for American ears to pick out the variations, most Brits can determine where a person is from based on their accent...not just the region, but often the village, and even the part of town.

that's aged in whisky casks, taking off the piney edge and infusing a bit of that distinctive whisky flavor.

Distilleries throughout Scotland offer tours, but you'll often only learn about that one type of whisky. At a good whisky shop, the knowledgeable staff offer guided tastings (for a fee and typically prearranged), explaining four or five whiskies to help you develop your palate. Some shops have several bottles open and will let you try a few wee drams to narrow down your options. If they're providing samples, they're hoping you'll buy a bottle at the end.

But the easiest and perhaps best option for sampling Scotland's national drink is to find a local pub with a passion for whisky that's filled with locals who share that passion.

For much more about whisky, see the "Whisky 101" sidebar on page 755.

Other Alcoholic Drinks: Many pubs also have a good selection of wines by the glass and a fully stocked bar for the gentleman's "G and T" (gin and tonic). **Pimm's** is a refreshing and fruity summer liqueur, traditionally popular during Wimbledon. It's an upper-class drink—a rough bloke might insult a pub by claiming it sells more Pimm's than beer.

Non-Alcoholic Drinks: Teetotalers can order from a wide variety of soft drinks—both the predictable American sodas and other more interesting bottled drinks, such as ginger beer (similar to ginger ale but with more bite), root beers, or other flavors (Fentimans brews some unusual options that are stocked in many pubs).

Staying Connected

One of the most common questions I hear from travelers is, "How can I stay connected in Europe?" The short answer is: more easily and cheaply than you might think.

The simplest solution is to bring your own device—mobile

phone, tablet, or laptop—and use it just as you would at home (following the money-saving tips below, such as getting an international plan or connecting to free Wi-Fi whenever possible). Another option is to buy a European SIM card for your US mobile phone. Or you can use European landlines and computers to connect. Each of these options is described next, and more details are at RickSteves.com/phoning. For a practical one-hour talk covering tech issues for travelers, see RickSteves.com/mobile-travel-skills.

USING A MOBILE PHONE IN EUROPE

Here are some budget tips and options.

Sign up for an international plan. To stay connected at a lower cost, sign up for an international service plan through your carrier. Most providers offer a simple bundle that includes calling, messaging, and data. Your normal plan may already include international coverage (T-Mobile's does).

Before your trip, call your provider or check online to confirm that your phone will work in Europe, and research your provider's international rates. Activate the plan a day or two before you leave, then remember to cancel it when your trip's over.

Use free Wi-Fi whenever possible. Unless you have an unlimited-data plan, you're best off saving most of your online tasks for Wi-Fi. You can access the internet, send texts, and even make voice calls over Wi-Fi.

Most accommodations in Europe offer free Wi-Fi, but some—especially expensive hotels—charge a fee. Many cafés (including Starbucks and McDonald's) have free hotspots for customers; look for signs offering it and ask for the Wi-Fi password when you buy something. You'll also often find Wi-Fi at TIs, city squares, major museums, public-transit hubs, airports, and aboard trains and buses. In Britain, another option is to sign up for Wi-Fi access through a company such as BT (one hour-£4, one day-£10, www.btwifi.co.uk) or The Cloud (free though sometimes slow, www.skywifi.cloud).

Minimize the use of your cellular network. The best way to make sure you're not accidentally burning through data is to put your device in "airplane" mode (which also disables phone calls and texts), turn your Wi-Fi back on, and connect to networks as needed. When you need to get online but can't find Wi-Fi, simply turn on your cellular network (or turn off airplane mode) just long enough for the task at hand.

Even with an international data plan, wait until you're on Wi-Fi to Skype, download apps, stream videos, or do other megabyte-greedy tasks. Using a navigation app such as Google Maps over a cellular network can take lots of data, so do this sparingly or offline.

How to Dial

International Calls

Whether phoning from a US landline or mobile phone, or from a number in another European country, here's how to make an international call. I've used one of my recommended London hotels as an example (tel. 020/7730-8191).

Initial Zero: Drop the initial zero from international phone numbers—except when calling Italy.

Mobile Tip: If using a mobile phone, the "+" sign can replace the international access code (for a "+" sign, press and hold "0").

US/Canada to Europe

Dial 011 (US/Canada international access code), country code (44 for Britain), and phone number.

▶ To call the London hotel from home, dial 011-44-20/7730-8191.

Country to Country Within Europe

Dial 00 (Europe international access code), country code, and phone number.

▶ To call the London hotel from Spain, dial 00-44-20/7730-8191.

Europe to the US/Canada

Dial 00, country code (1 for US/Canada), and phone number.

▶ To call from Europe to my office in Edmonds, Washington, dial 00-1-425-771-8303.

Domestic Calls

To call within Britain (from one British landline or mobile phone to another), simply dial the phone number, including the initial 0 if there is one.

▶ To call the London hotel from Edinburgh, dial 020/7730-8191.

Limit automatic updates. By default, your device constantly checks for a data connection and updates apps. It's smart to disable these features so your apps will only update when you're on Wi-Fi. Also change your device's email settings from "auto-retrieve" to "manual" (or from "push" to "fetch").

Use Wi-Fi calling and messaging apps. Skype, WhatsApp, FaceTime, and Google Hangouts are great for making free or low-cost calls or sending texts over Wi-Fi worldwide. Just log on to a Wi-Fi network, then connect with any of your friends or family members who use the same service. If you buy credit in advance, with some of these services you can call or text anywhere for just pennies.

Some apps, such as Apple's iMessage, will use the cellular

More Dialing Tips

Toll and Toll-Free Numbers: It's generally not possible to dial British toll or toll-free numbers from a US mobile or landline (although you can sometimes get through using Skype). Look for a direct-dial number instead.

More Phoning Help: See HowToCallAbroad.com.

European Country Codes		Ireland & N. Ireland	353 / 44
Austria	43	Italy	39
Belgium	32	Latvia	371
Bosnia-Herzegovina	387	Montenegro	382
Croatia	385	Morocco	212
Czech Republic	420	Netherlands	31
Denmark	45	Norway	47
Estonia	372	Poland	48
Finland	358	Portugal	351
France	33	Russia	7
Germany	49	Slovakia	421
Gibraltar	350	Slovenia	386
Great Britain	44	Spain	34
Greece	30	Sweden	46
Hungary	36	Switzerland	41
Iceland	354	Turkey	90

network for texts if Wi-Fi isn't available: To avoid this possibility, turn off the "Send as SMS" feature.

Buy a European SIM card. If you anticipate making a lot of local calls or need a local phone number, or if your provider's international data rates are expensive, consider buying a SIM card in Europe to replace the one in your (unlocked) US phone or tablet. SIM cards are sold at department-store electronics counters, some newsstands, and vending machines. If you need help setting it up, buy one at a mobile-phone shop (you may need to show your passport).

There are no roaming charges when using a European SIM card in other EU countries, though to be sure you get this "roam-like-at-home" pricing, buy your SIM card at a mobile-phone shop and ask if this feature is included.

Tips on Internet Security

Make sure that your device is running the latest versions of its operating system, security software, and apps. Next, ensure that your device and key programs (like email) are password-protected. On the road, use only secure, password-protected Wi-Fi hotspots. Ask the hotel or café staff for the specific name of their Wi-Fi network, and make sure you log on to that exact one.

If you must access your financial info online, use a banking app rather than accessing your account via a browser. A cellular connection is more secure than Wi-Fi. Avoid logging onto personal finance sites on a public computer.

Never share your credit-card number (or any other sensitive information) online unless you know that the site is secure. A secure site displays a little padlock icon, and the URL begins with *https* (instead of the usual *http*).

WITHOUT A MOBILE PHONE

It's less convenient but possible to travel in Europe without a mobile device. You can make calls from your hotel and check email or get online using public computers.

Most hotels charge a fee for placing calls—ask for rates before you dial. You can use a prepaid international phone card (usually available at newsstands, tobacco shops, and train stations) to call out from your hotel. Dial the toll-free access number, enter the card's PIN code, then dial the number.

If there's no phone in your B&B room, and you have an important, brief call to make, politely ask your hosts if you can use their personal phone. Use a cheap international phone card with a toll-free access number, or offer to pay your host for the call.

Public pay phones are hard to find in Britain, and they're expensive. To use one, you'll pay with a major credit card (minimum charge-£1.20) or coins (minimum charge-£0.60).

Some hotels have **public computers** in their lobbies for guests to use; otherwise you may find them at public libraries (ask your hotelier or the TI for the nearest location). On a European keyboard, use the "Alt Gr" key to the right of the space bar to insert the extra symbol that appears on some keys. If you can't locate a special character (such as @), simply copy and paste it from a web page.

MAIL

You can mail one package per day to yourself worth up to $200 duty-free from Europe to the US (mark it "personal purchases"). If you're sending a gift to someone, mark it "unsolicited gift" (for details, visit www.cbp.gov, select "Travel," and search for "Know Before You Visit"). The British postal service works fine, but for quick transatlantic delivery (in either direction), consider services such as DHL (www.dhl.com). For postcards, get stamps at the neighborhood post office, newsstands within fancy hotels, and some minimarts and card shops.

Transportation

Figuring out how to get around in Europe is one of your biggest trip decisions. **Cars** work well for two or more traveling together (especially families with small kids), those packing heavy, and those delving into the countryside. **Trains** and **buses** are best for solo travelers, blitz tourists, city-to-city travelers, and those who want to leave the driving to others. Smart travelers can use short hop **flights** within Europe to creatively connect the dots on their itineraries. Just be aware of the potential downside of each option: A car is an expensive headache in any major city; with trains and buses you're at the mercy of a timetable; and flying entails a trek to and from a usually distant airport.

If your itinerary mixes cities and countryside, my advice is to connect cities by train (or bus) and to explore rural areas by rental car. Arrange to pick up your car in the last big city you'll visit, then use it to lace together small towns and explore the countryside. For more detailed information on transportation throughout Europe, see RickSteves.com/transportation.

TRAINS

Regular tickets on Britain's great train system (15,000 departures from 2,400 stations daily) are the most expensive per mile in all of Europe. For the greatest savings, book online in advance and leave after rush hour (after 9:30 weekdays).

Since Britain's railways have been privatized, a single train route can be operated by multiple companies. However, one website covers all train lines (www.nationalrail.co.uk), and another covers all bus and train routes (www.traveline.org.uk for information, not ticket sales). Another good resource, which also has schedules for trains throughout Europe, is German Rail's timetable (www.bahn.com).

As with airline tickets, British train tickets can come at many different prices for the same journey. A clerk at any station can figure out the cheapest fare for your trip.

While generally not required, reservations are free and can normally be made well in advance. They are an especially good idea for long journeys or for travel on Sundays or holidays. Make reservations at any train station, by phone, or online when you buy

PRACTICALITIES

Great Britain's Public Transportation

your ticket. With a point-to-point ticket, you can reserve as late as two hours before train time, but rail-pass holders should book seats at least 24 hours in advance (see below for more on rail passes). You must reserve in advance for Caledonian Sleeper overnight trains between London and Scotland (www.sleeper.scot).

For information on the high-speed Eurostar train through the "Chunnel" to Paris, Brussels, or Amsterdam, see page 203.

Rail Passes

Since Britain's pay-as-you-go train tickets are some of the most expensive in Europe, BritRail passes can pay for themselves quickly, especially if you ride a long-distance train (for example, between London and Scotland). A rail pass offers hop-on flexibility and no need to lock in reservations, except for overnight sleeper cars.

The BritRail pass (covering England, Scotland, and Wales) and the BritRail England-only pass come in "consecutive day" and "flexi" versions, with price breaks for youths (under age 26), seniors (60 and up), off-season travelers, and groups of three or more. Most allow one child under 16 to travel free with a paying adult or senior. If you're exploring the backcountry with a BritRail pass, second class is a good choice since many of the smaller train lines don't even offer first-class cars.

Other BritRail options include Scotland-only passes, "London Plus" passes (good for travel in most of southeast England but not in London itself), and South West passes (good for the Cotswolds, Bath, Dorset, Devon, Cornwall, plus part of South Wales).

BritRail passes cannot be purchased locally; buy your pass through an agent before leaving the US. Make sleeper reservations in advance; you can also make optional, free seat reservations (recommended for busy weekends) at staffed train stations.

If your travels are taking you from Britain to the Continent, the Eurail Global Pass covers trains on both sides of the English Channel, and Eurostar trains beneath it (with a paid seat reservation). It's generally cheaper to buy one pass for your whole trip than separate, single-country passes. Global passes also come in "consecutive day" and "flexi" versions, with price breaks for youths (under age 28) and seniors (60 and up). Up to two kids under 12 travel free with you on an adult-rate pass.

For more detailed advice on figuring out the smartest rail-pass options for your train trip, visit RickSteves.com/rail.

PRACTICALITIES

Rail Pass or Point-to-Point Tickets?

Will you be better off buying a rail pass or point-to-point tickets? It pays to know your options and choose what's best for your itinerary.

Rail Passes

A BritRail Pass lets you travel by train in Scotland, England, and Wales for two to eight days within a one-month period, 15 days within two months, or for continuous periods of up to one month. In addition, BritRail sells England-only and other regional passes. Britain is also covered (along with most of Europe) by the classic Eurail Global Pass. Discounted rates are offered for children, youths, and seniors.

Rail passes are best purchased outside Europe (through travel agents or Rick Steves' Europe). For more on rail passes, including current prices, visit RickSteves.com/rail.

Point-to-Point Tickets

If you're taking just a couple of train rides, buying individual point-to-point train tickets may save you money over a pass. Use this map to add up approximate pay-as-you-go fares for your itinerary, and compare that to the price of a rail pass. Keep in mind that significant discounts on point-to-point tickets may be available with advance purchase.

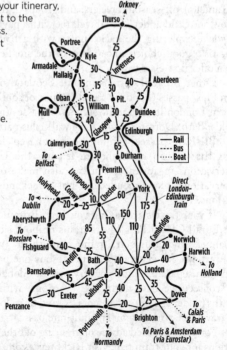

Map shows approximate costs, in US dollars, for one-way, second-class tickets at off-peak rates.

Buying Tickets

In Advance: The best fares go to those who book their trips well in advance of their journey. Savings can be significant. For a London-York round-trip (standard class), the peak "anytime" fare is about £245 (usually paid by business travelers) and up to £106 for "off-peak." However, if you book online at least a week ahead, off-peak and advance-purchase discounts can combine for a rate closer to £50. An "advance" fare for the same ticket booked a couple of months out can cost as little as £30. If traveling longer distances, such as from Scotland to England, expect higher fares but greater advance discounts.

To book ahead, go in person to any station, look online at NationalRail.co.uk, or call 0345-748-4950 (from the US, dial 011-44-20-7278-5240, phone answered 24 hours) to find out the schedule and best fare for your journey; you'll then be referred to the appropriate vendor—depending on the particular rail company—to book your ticket. If you order online, be sure you know what you want; it's tough to reach a person who can change your online reservation. You'll pick up your ticket at the station, or you may be able to print it at home. (BritRail pass holders, however, cannot make online seat reservations.)

A company called **Megabus** (through their subsidiary Megatrain) sells some discounted train tickets well in advance on a few specific routes, though their focus is mainly on selling bus tickets (info tel. 0871-266-3333, www.megatrain.com).

Buying Train Tickets as You Travel: If you'd rather have the flexibility of booking tickets as you go, you can save a few pounds by buying a round-trip ticket, called a "return ticket" (a same-day round-trip, called a "day return," is particularly cheap for short excursions); buying before 18:00 the day before you depart; traveling after the morning rush hour (this usually means after 9:30 Mon-Fri); and going standard class instead of first class. Preview your options at NationalRail.co.uk.

Senior, Youth, Partner, and Family Deals: To get a third off the price of most point-to-point rail tickets, seniors can buy a Senior Railcard (ages 60 and up), younger travelers can buy a 16-25 Railcard (ages 16-25, or full-time students 26 and older), and two people traveling together can buy a Two Together Railcard (ages 16 and over). A Family and Friends Railcard gives adults about 33 percent off for most trips and 60 percent off for their kids age 5 to 15 (maximum 4 adults and 4 kids). Each Railcard costs £30; for non-UK citizens, it's best to purchase the pass at a staffed rail station in England, Scotland, or Wales as you need a UK delivery address to buy it online (pass also sold at some London airports, some passes require passport-type photo, passport needed for proof of age; see www.railcard.co.uk). These cards are valid for a year

Sample Train Journey

Here is a typical example of a personalized train schedule printed out at a British train station (also online at www.nationalrail.co.uk). At the Salisbury station, I told the clerk that I wanted to leave after 16:15 for Moreton-in-Marsh in the Cotswolds. Even though the trip involved two transfers, this schedule allowed me to easily navigate the rails.

Travel by	Leaving	From	Platform	To	Arriving	Platform	Duration
Train	16:21	Salisbury [SAL]	2	Basingstoke [BSK]	16:55	3	0h 34m
		South West Trains service from Exeter St David's to London Waterloo					
Train	17:04	Basingstoke [BSK]	5	Reading [RDG]	17:28	2	0h 24m
		First Great Western service from Basingstoke to Reading					
Train	17:50	Reading [RDG]	9	Moreton-in-Marsh [MIM]	18:54	1	1h 04m
		First Great Western service from London Paddington to Hereford					

Often the conductor on your previous train can tell you which platform your next train will depart from, but it's wise to confirm. Scrolling overhead screens on the platforms often show arrivals, departures, and intermediate stops; some list train departures by their final destination only. If you are traveling to an intermediate stop and aren't sure which platform you need, ask any conductor or at the info desk. For example, after checking with the conductor, I know that I'll need to look for *Oxford* to catch the train for Moreton-in-Marsh.

Britain's train system can experience delays, so don't schedule your connections too tightly if you need to reach your destination at a specific time.

on almost all trains, including special runs such as the Heathrow Express, but are not valid on the Eurostar to Paris, Amsterdam, or Brussels.

BUSES

Although buses are about a third slower than trains, they're also a lot cheaper. And buses go many places that trains don't. Most domestic buses are operated by **National Express** (tel. 0871-781-8181, www.nationalexpress.com); their international departures are called **Eurolines** (www.eurolines.co.uk). Note that Brits distinguish between "buses" (for in-city travel with lots of stops) and "coaches" (long-distance cross-country runs)—though for simplicity in this book, I call both "buses."

A smaller company called **Megabus** undersells National Express with deeply discounted promotional fares—the further ahead you buy, the less you pay (some trips for just £1.50, tel. 0141/352-4444, www.megabus.com). While Megabus can be much cheaper than National Express, they tend to be slower than their competitor and their routes mainly connect cities, not smaller towns. They also sell discounted train tickets on selected routes.

Most long-haul domestic routes in Scotland are operated by **Scottish Citylink.** In peak season, it's worth booking your seat on popular routes at least a few days in advance (at the bus station or TI, online at www.citylink.co.uk, or by calling 0141/352-4444). At slower times, you can just hop on the bus and pay the driver. If you're taking lots of buses, consider Citylink's Explorer pass (£49/3 days in 5-day period, £74/5 days in 10-day period, £99/8 days in 16-day period).

Buy tickets early if you are traveling on Friday or Sunday evening, when weekend travelers are more likely to make buses sell out. The cheapest pre-purchased tickets usually cannot be changed or refunded; other fare types charge a change fee. Check if the ticket is only "amendable" or also "refundable" when you buy. Round-trip bus tickets usually cost less than two one-way fares.

If you want to take a bus from your last destination to the nearest airport, you'll find that National Express often offers **airport buses.** Bus stations are normally at or near train stations (in London, the main bus station is a block southwest of Victoria Station).

TAXIS AND RIDE-BOOKING SERVICES

Most British taxis are reliable and cheap. In many cities, two people can travel short distances by cab for little more than the cost of bus or subway tickets. If you like ride-booking services such as Uber, their apps usually work in Britain just like they do in the US: Request a car on your mobile phone (connected to Wi-Fi or data), and the fare is automatically charged to your credit card. London's Uber is facing a legal challenge; check ahead to confirm it is operating.

RENTING A CAR

It's cheaper to arrange most car rentals from the US, so research and compare rates before you go. Most of the major US rental agencies (including Avis, Budget, Enterprise, Hertz, and Thrifty) have offices throughout Europe. Also consider the two major Europe-based agencies, Europcar and Sixt. Consolidators such as Auto Europe (www.autoeurope.com—or the sometimes cheaper www.autoeurope.eu) compare rates at several companies to get you the best deal.

Wherever you book, always read the fine print. Check for add-on charges—such as one-way drop-off fees, airport surcharges, or

---

British Radio

Local radio broadcasts can be a treat for drivers sightseeing in Britain. Many British radio stations broadcast nationwide; your car radio automatically detects the local frequency a station plays on and displays its name. The most prominent are the five BBC nationwide stations. These government-subsidized stations have no ads.

BBC Radio 1: Pop music, with youthful DJs spinning top 40 hits and interviewing big-name bands.

BBC Radio 2: The highest-rated station nationwide, aimed at a more mature audience, with adult contemporary, retro pop, and other "middle of the road" music.

BBC Radio 3: Mostly classical music, with some jazz and world music.

BBC Radio 4: All talk—current events, entertaining chat shows, special-interest topics such as cooking and gardening, and lots of radio plays.

---

mandatory insurance policies—that aren't included in the "total price."

Rental Costs and Considerations

Figure on paying roughly $250 for a one-week rental for a basic compact car. Allow extra for supplemental insurance, fuel, tolls, and parking.

Manual vs. Automatic: Almost all rental cars in Europe are manual by default—and cars with a stick shift are generally cheaper. If you need an automatic, request one in advance. An automatic makes sense for most American drivers: With a manual transmission in Britain, you'll be sitting on the right side of the car and shifting with your left hand...while driving on the left side of the road. When selecting a car, don't be tempted by a larger model, as it won't be as maneuverable on narrow, winding roads or when squeezing into tight parking lots.

Age Restrictions: Rental companies in Britain require you to be at least 21 years old and to have held your license for one year. Drivers under the age of 25 may incur a young-driver surcharge, and some rental companies will not rent to anyone 75 or older.

Choosing Pick-up/Drop-off Locations: Always check the hours of the locations you choose: Many rental offices close

BBC Radio 5 Live: Sporting events as well as news and sports talk programs.

You'll encounter regional variations of BBC stations, such as BBC London, Radio York, BBC Scotland, and BBC Gaelic. At the top of the hour, many BBC stations broadcast the famous "pips" (indicating Greenwich Mean Time) and a short roundup of the day's news.

Beyond the BBC offerings, several private stations broadcast music and other content with "adverts" (commercials). Some are nationwide, including **XFM** (alternative rock), **Classic FM** (classical), **Absolute Radio** (pop), and **Capital FM** (pop).

Traffic Alerts: Ask your rental-car company about turning on automatic traffic alerts on the car radio (look for the letters *TA* or *TP* on the radio readout). When enabled, traffic reports for the area you are driving in will periodically interrupt programming.

from midday Saturday until Monday morning and, in smaller towns, at lunchtime. When selecting an office, plug the addresses into a mapping website to confirm the location. A downtown site is generally cheaper—and might seem more convenient than the airport. But pedestrianized and one-way streets can make navigation tricky when returning a car at a big-city office or urban train station. Wherever you select, get precise details on the location and allow ample time to find it.

Picking Up Your Car: Before driving off in your rental car, check it thoroughly and make sure any damage is noted on your rental agreement. Rental agencies in Europe tend to charge for even minor damage, so be sure to mark everything. Find out how your car's gearshift, lights, turn signals, wipers, radio, and fuel cap function, and know what kind of fuel the car takes (diesel vs. unleaded). When you return the car, make sure the agent verifies its condition with you. Some drivers take pictures of the returned vehicle as proof of its condition.

Be aware that Brits call it "hiring a car," and directional signs at airports and train stations will read *Car Hire.*

The AA: The services of Britain's Automobile Association are included with most rentals (www.theaa.com), but check for this when booking to be sure you understand its towing and emergency road-service benefits.

Car Insurance Options

When you rent a car in Europe, the price typically includes liability insurance, which covers harm to other cars or motorists—but not the rental car itself. To limit your financial risk in case of damage to the rental, choose one of these three options: Buy a Collision Damage Waiver (CDW) with a low or zero deductible from the car-rental company (roughly 30-40 percent extra), get coverage through your credit card (free, but more complicated), or get collision insurance as part of a larger travel-insurance policy.

Basic **CDW** costs $15-30 a day and typically comes with a $1,000-2,000 deductible, reducing but not eliminating your financial responsibility. When you reserve or pick up the car, you'll be offered the chance to "buy down" the deductible to zero (for an additional $10-30/day; this is sometimes called "super CDW" or "zero-deductible coverage").

If you opt for **credit-card coverage,** you must decline all coverage offered by the car-rental company—which means they can place a hold on your card for up to the full value of the car. In case of damage, it can be time-consuming to resolve the charges. Before relying on this option, quiz your card company about how it works.

If you're already purchasing a **travel-insurance policy** for your trip, adding collision coverage can be an economical option. For example, Travel Guard (www.travelguard.com) sells affordable renter's collision insurance as an add-on to its other policies; it's valid everywhere in Europe except the Republic of Ireland, and some Italian car-rental companies refuse to honor it, as it doesn't cover you in case of theft.

For more on car-rental insurance, see RickSteves.com/cdw.

Navigation Options

If you'll be navigating using your phone or a GPS unit from home, remember to bring a car charger and device mount.

Your Mobile Phone: The mapping app on your phone works fine for navigating Europe's roads, but for real-time turn-by-turn directions and traffic updates, you'll need mobile data access. And driving all day can burn through a lot of very expensive data. The economical work-around is to use map apps that work offline. By downloading in advance from Google Maps, City Maps 2Go, Apple Maps, Here WeGo, or Navmii, you can still have turn-by-turn voice directions and maps that recalibrate even though they're offline.

You must download your maps before you go offline—and it's smart to select large regions. Then turn off your data connection so you're not charged for roaming. Call up the map, enter your destination, and you're on your way. Even if you don't have to pay extra for data roaming, this option is great for navigating in areas with poor connectivity.

GPS Devices: If you want the convenience of a dedicated GPS unit, known as a "satnav" in Britain, consider renting one

Driving in Great Britain

To Durness

To John O' Groats

m = miles
h = hours

Note: Your times may vary based on traffic, sheep, construction & road conditions.

PRACTICALITIES

Ullapool
Portree
Skye
Kyle of Lochalsh
Inverness
Loch Ness (Urquhart Castle)
Aberdeen
Glencoe
Mull
Oban
Fionnphort
Craignure
SCOTLAND
Pitlochry
Stirling
St. Andrews
Glasgow
Edinburgh
Holy Island
Cairnryan
Hadrian's Wall (Housesteads Fort)
Keswick (N. Lake Dist.)
Durham
Windermere (S. Lake Dist.)
Whitby
Blackpool
Preston
York
Liverpool
Holyhead
Conwy
Caernarfon
Ruthin
Betws-y-Coed
ENGLAND
Ironbridge
Coventry
Warwick
WALES
Stratford
Cambridge
Tintern
Cotswolds (Stow)
Cardiff
Oxford
Wells
Bath
Avebury
London
Glastonbury
Salisbury
Canterbury
To Land's End
Dartmoor Nat'l Park
Corfe Castle
Brighton
Dover
Portsmouth

35m · 1h
60m · 2h
120m · 2.5h
70m · 2.25h
85m · 2h
20m · .5h
105m · 2.75h
65m · 1.5h
90m · 1.75h
80m · 2h
9m · .5h
90m · 2.75h
35m · 1h
80m · 1.75h
85m · 1.75h
100m · 2.5h
25m · .5h
40m · 1h
50m · 1.5h
70m · 1.5h
60m · 1.5h
50m · 1h
75m · 2h
135m · 2.5h
90m · 2.25h
130m · 3h
125m · 2.75h
100m · 2.5h
80m · 1.75h
145m · 3h
65m · 1.5h
50m · 1h
85m · 2h
20m · .5h
120m · 3h
75m · 1.5h
50m · 1h
35m · 1h
20m · .5h
100m · 2h
40m · 1h
130m · 3.5h
40m · .75h
60m · 1.25h
140m · 2.5h
160m · 3h
220m · 4h
25m · .5h
15m · .5h
30m · 1h
25m · .75h
30m · 1h
75m · 2h
60m · 1.5h
10m · .25h
150m · 3.5h
70m · 1.5h
70m · 1.5h
10m · .5h
10m · .25h
110m · 2h
170m · 4h
35m · 1.0h
70m · 1.75h
30m
75m
90m · 2h
60m · 1.25h
65m · 1.5h
65m · 1.5h
50m
60m · 1.5h
55m · 1.25h
20m · .75h
30m · 1h
85m · 1.75h
50m · 7.25h
10m · .25h
100m · 2h
55m · 1.75h
60m · 1.25h
75m · 1.5h
100m · 2h
120m · 2.5h
50m · 1.5h
45m · 1h
50m · 1.5h
85m · 3h

with your car ($10-30/day). These units offer real-time turn-by-turn directions and traffic without the data requirements of an app. The unit may come loaded only with maps for its home country; if you need additional maps, ask.

A less-expensive option is to bring a GPS device from home. Be sure to buy and install the maps you'll need before your trip.

Paper Maps and Atlases: Even when navigating primarily with a mobile app or GPS, I always make it a point to have a paper map, ideally a big, detailed regional road map. It's invaluable for getting the big picture, understanding alternate routes, and filling in if my phone runs out of juice. The free maps you get from your car-rental company usually don't have enough detail. It's smart to buy a better map before you go, or pick one up at a local gas station, bookshop, newsstand, or tourist shop.

Several good road atlases cover all of Britain. Ordnance Survey, Collins, AA, and Bartholomew editions are all available at tourist information offices, gas stations, and bookstores. The tourist-oriented Collins Touring maps do a good job of highlighting the many roadside attractions you might otherwise drive right past. Before you buy a map, look at it to be sure it has the level of detail you want.

DRIVING IN BRITAIN

Driving here is basically wonderful—once you remember to stay on the left and after you've mastered the roundabouts. Every year, however, I get a few notes from traveling readers advising me that, for them, trying to drive in Britain was a nerve-racking and regrettable mistake. If you want to get a little slack on the roads, drop by a gas station or auto shop and buy a green *P* (probationary driver with license) sign to put in your car window (don't get the red *L* sign, which means you're a learner driver without a license and thus prohibited from driving on motorways).

Many Yankee drivers find the hardest part isn't driving on the left, but steer-

STOP AND LEARN THESE ROAD SIGNS

Speed Limit (mph) · Yield · No Passing · End of No Passing Zone

One Way · Intersection · Roundabout Ahead · Expressway

Danger · No Entry · Cars Prohibited · All Vehicles Prohibited

No Through Road · Restrictions No Longer Apply · Yield to Oncoming Traffic · No Stopping

Parking · No Parking · Road Narrows · Peace

ing from the right. Your instinct is to put yourself on the left side of your lane, which means you may spend your first day or two drifting into the left shoulder or curb. It helps to remember that the driver always stays close to the center line.

Road Rules: Be aware of Britain's rules of the road. Seat belts are mandatory for all, and kids under age 12 (or less than about 4.5 feet tall) must ride in an appropriate child-safety seat. It's illegal to use a mobile phone while driving—pull over or use a hands-free device. In Britain, you're not allowed to turn left on a red light unless a sign or signal specifically authorizes it, and on motorways it's illegal to pass drivers on the left. Ask your car-rental company about these rules, or check the "International Travel" section of the US State Department website (www.travel.state.gov, search for your country in the "Learn About Your Destination" box, then click "Travel and Transportation").

Speed Limits: Speed limits are in miles per hour: 30 mph in town, 70 mph on the motorways, and 60 or 70 mph elsewhere (though, as back home, many British drivers consider these limits advisory). The national sign for the maximum speed is a white circle with a black slash. Motorways have electronic speed limit signs; posted speeds can change depending on traffic or the weather. Follow them accordingly.

Note that road-surveillance cameras strictly enforce speed limits. Any driver (including foreigners renting cars) photographed speeding will get a nasty bill in the mail. (Cameras—in foreboding gray boxes—flash on rear license plates to respect the privacy of anyone sharing the front seat with someone he or she shouldn't.) Signs (an image of an old-fashioned camera) alert you when you're entering a zone that may be monitored by these "camera cops." Heed them.

Roundabouts: Don't let a roundabout spook you. After all, you routinely merge into much faster traffic on American highways back home. Traffic flows clockwise, and cars already in the roundabout have the right-of-way; entering traffic yields (look to your right as you merge). You'll probably encounter "double-roundabouts"—figure-eights where you'll slingshot from one roundabout directly into another. Just go with the flow and track signs carefully. When approaching an especially complex roundabout, you'll first pass a diagram showing the layout and the various exits. And in many

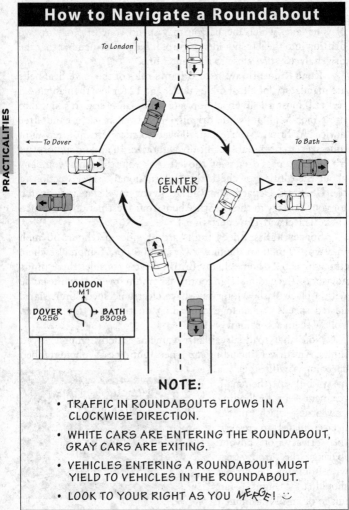

How to Navigate a Roundabout

NOTE:

- TRAFFIC IN ROUNDABOUTS FLOWS IN A CLOCKWISE DIRECTION.
- WHITE CARS ARE ENTERING THE ROUNDABOUT, GRAY CARS ARE EXITING.
- VEHICLES ENTERING A ROUNDABOUT MUST YIELD TO VEHICLES IN THE ROUNDABOUT.
- LOOK TO YOUR RIGHT AS YOU MERGE! ☺

cases, the pavement is painted to indicate the lane you should be in for a particular road or town.

Freeways (Motorways): The shortest distance between any two points is usually the motorway (what we'd call a "freeway"). In Britain, the smaller the number, the bigger the road. For example, the M-4 is a freeway, while the B-4494 is a country road.

Motorway road signs can be confusing, too few, and too late. Miss a motorway exit and you can lose 30 minutes. Study your map before taking off. Know the cities you'll be lacing together, since road numbers are inconsistent. British road signs are never marked with compass directions (e.g., *A-4 West*); instead, you need to know what major town or city you're heading for *(A-4 Bath)*. The driving directions in this book are intended to be used with a good map. Get a road atlas, easily purchased at gas stations in Britain, or download digital maps before your trip (see page 1074).

Unless you're passing, always drive in the "slow" lane on motorways (the lane farthest to the left). The British are very disciplined about this; ignoring this rule could get you a ticket (or into a road-rage incident). Remember to pass on the right, not the left.

Rest areas are called "services" and often have a number of useful amenities, such as restaurants, cafeterias, gas stations, shops, and motels.

Fuel: Gas (petrol) costs about $5.50 per gallon and is self-serve. Pump first and then pay. Diesel costs about the same. Diesel rental cars are common; make sure you know what kind of fuel your car takes before you fill up. Unleaded pumps are usually green. Note that self-service gas pumps and automated tollbooths and parking garages often accept only a chip-and-PIN credit card or cash. It might help if you know the PIN for your US credit and debit cards, but just in case a machine rejects them, be sure to carry sufficient cash. For more on chip and PIN, see page 1031.

Driving in Cities: Whenever possible, avoid driving in cities. Be warned that London assesses a congestion charge (see page 55). Most cities have modern ring roads to skirt the congestion. Follow signs to the parking lots outside the city core—most are a 5- to 10-minute walk to the center—and avoid what can be an unpleasant grid of one-way streets (as in Bath) or roads that are only available to public transportation during the day.

Driving in Rural Areas: Outside the big cities and except for the motorways, British roads tend to be narrow. In towns, you may have to cross over the center line just to get past parked cars. Adjust your perceptions of personal space: It's not "my side of the road" or "your side of the road," it's just "the road"—and it's shared as a cooperative adventure. If the road's wide enough, traffic in both directions can pass parked cars simultaneously, but frequently you'll have to take turns—follow the locals' lead and drive defensively.

Narrow country lanes are often lined with stone walls or woody hedges—and no shoulders. Some are barely wide enough for one car (one-lane roads are often referred to as "single-track" roads). Go slowly, and if you encounter an oncoming car, look for the nearest pullout (or "passing place")—

the driver who's closest to one is expected to use it, even if it means backing up to reach it. If another car pulls over and blinks its headlights, that means, "Go ahead; I'll wait to let you pass." British drivers—arguably some of the most courteous on the planet—are quick to offer a friendly wave to thank you for letting them pass (and they appreciate it if you reciprocate). Pull over frequently—to let faster locals pass and to check the map.

Parking: Pay attention to pavement markings to figure out where to park. One yellow line marked on the pavement means no parking Monday through Saturday during work hours. Double yellow lines mean no parking at any time. Broken yellow lines mean short stops are OK, but you should always look for explicit signs or ask a passerby. White lines mean you're free to park.

In towns, rather than look for street parking, I generally just pull into the most central and handy pay-and-display parking lot I can find. To pay and display, feed change into a machine, receive a timed ticket, and display it on the dashboard or stick it to the driver's-side window. Rates are reasonable by US standards, and locals love to share stickers that have time remaining. If you stand by the machine, someone on their way out with time left on their sticker will probably give it to you. Most machines in larger towns accept credit cards with a chip, but it's smart to keep coins handy for machines that don't.

In some municipalities, drivers will see signs for "disc zone" parking. This is free, time-limited parking. But to use it, you must obtain a clock parking disc from a shop and display it on the dashboard (set the clock to show your time of arrival). Return within the signed time limit to avoid being ticketed.

Some parking garages (a.k.a. car parks) are automated and record your license plate with a camera when you enter. The Brits call a license plate a "number plate" or just "vehicle registration." The payment machine will use these terms when you pay before exiting.

FLIGHTS

To compare flight costs and times, begin with an online travel search engine: Kayak is the top site for flights to and within Europe, easy-to-use Google Flights has price alerts, and Skyscanner includes many inexpensive flights within Europe. To avoid unpleasant surprises, before you book be sure to read the small print about refunds, changes, and the costs for "extras" such as reserving a seat, checking a bag, or printing a boarding pass.

Flights to Europe: Start looking for international flights about four to six months before your trip, especially for peak-season travel. Depending on your itinerary, it can be efficient and no more expensive to fly into one city and out of another. If your flight requires a connection in Europe, see my hints on navigating Europe's top hub airports at RickSteves.com/hub-airports.

Flights Within Europe: Flying between European cities is surprisingly affordable. Before buying a long-distance train or bus ticket, check the cost of a flight on one of Europe's airlines, whether a major carrier or a no-frills outfit like **EasyJet** or **Ryanair.** Other airlines to consider include **CityJet** (based at London City Airport, www.cityjet.com), **TUI Airways** (www.tui.co.uk), **Flybe** (www.flybe.com), and **Brussels Airlines** (with frequent connections from Heathrow to its Brussels hub, www.brusselsairlines.com).

Be aware that flying with a discount airline can have drawbacks, such as minimal customer service and time-consuming treks to secondary airports.

Flying to the US and Canada: Because security is extra tight for flights to the US, be sure to give yourself plenty of time at the airport. Charge your electronic devices before you board in case security checks require you to turn them on (see www.tsa.gov for the latest rules).

Resources from Rick Steves

Begin Your Trip at RickSteves.com

My mobile-friendly **website** is *the* place to explore Europe in preparation for your trip. You'll find thousands of fun articles, videos, and radio interviews; a wealth of money-saving tips for planning your dream trip; travel news dispatches; a video library of my travel talks; my travel blog; my latest guidebook updates (www.ricksteves.com/update); and my free Rick Steves Audio Europe app. You can also follow me on Facebook, Instagram, and Twitter.

Our **Travel Forum** is a well-groomed collection of message boards, where our travel-savvy community answers questions and shares their personal travel experiences—and our well-traveled staff chimes in when they can be helpful (www.ricksteves.com/forums).

Our **online Travel Store** offers bags and accessories that I've designed to help you travel smarter and lighter. These include my popular carry-on bags (which I live out of four months a year), money belts, totes, toiletries kits, adapters, guidebooks, and planning maps (www.ricksteves.com/shop).

Our website can also help you find the perfect **rail pass** for your itinerary and your budget, with easy, one-stop shopping for rail passes, seat reservations, and point-to-point tickets (www.ricksteves.com/rail).

Rick Steves' Tours, Guidebooks, TV Shows, and More

Small Group Tours: Want to travel with greater efficiency and less stress? We offer more than 40 itineraries reaching the best destinations in this book...and beyond. Each year about 30,000 travelers join us on about 1,000 Rick Steves bus tours. You'll enjoy great guides and a fun bunch of travel partners (with small groups of 24 to 28 travelers). You'll find European adventures to fit every vacation length. For all the details, and to get our tour catalog, visit www.ricksteves.com/tours or call us at 425/608-4217.

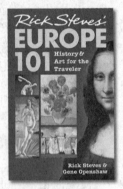

Books: *Rick Steves Great Britain* is just one of many books in my series on European travel, which includes country and city guidebooks, Snapshots (excerpted chapters from bigger guides), Pocket Guides (full-color little books on big cities), "Best Of" guidebooks (condensed, full-color country guides), and my budget-travel skills handbook, *Rick Steves Europe Through the Back Door.* A complete list of my titles—including phrase books; cruising guides; and travelogues on European Art, history, and culture; and more—appears near the end of this book.

TV Shows and Travel Talks: My public television series, *Rick Steves' Europe,* covers Europe from top to bottom with over 100 half-hour episodes—and we're working on new shows every year (watch full episodes at my website for free). My free online video library, Rick Steves Classroom Europe, offers a searchable database of short video clips on European history, culture, and geography (classroom.ricksteves.com). And to raise your travel I.Q., check out the video versions of our popular classes (covering most European countries as well as travel skills, packing smart, cruising, tech for travelers, European art, and travel as a political act—www. ricksteves.com/travel-talks.

Radio: My weekly public radio show, *Travel with Rick Steves,* features interviews with travel experts from around the world. It airs on 400 public radio stations across the US, or you can hear it as a podcast. A complete archive of programs is available at www. ricksteves.com/radio.

Audio Tours on My Free App: I've produced dozens of free, self-guided audio tours of the top sights in Europe. For those tours and other audio content, get my free **Rick Steves Audio Europe app,** an extensive online library organized by destination. For more on my app, see page 30.

APPENDIX

Holidays & Festivals 1083
Books & Films 1085
Conversions & Climate 1094
Packing Checklist 1097
British-Yankee Vocabulary 1098

Holidays and Festivals

This list includes selected festivals and national holidays observed throughout Britain. Many sights and banks close on national holidays—keep this in mind when planning your itinerary. Throughout Britain, hotels get booked up during Easter week; over the Early May, Spring, and Summer Bank Holidays; and during Christmas, Boxing Day, and New Year's Day. On Christmas, virtually everything shuts down, even the Tube in London. Museums also generally close December 24 and 26.

Many British towns have holiday festivals in late November and early December, with markets, music, and entertainment in the Christmas spirit (for instance, Keswick's Victorian Fayre). Throughout the summer, communities small and large across Scotland host their annual Highland Games—a wonderful way to get in touch with local culture and traditions (for more on the games, see page 930).

Before planning a trip around a festival, verify the dates with the festival website, the Visit Britain website (www.visitbritain. com), or my "Upcoming Holidays and Festivals" web page (www. ricksteves.com/europe/festivals).

Jan 1	New Year's Day
Jan 25	Burns Night, Scotland (poetry readings, haggis)
Mid-Feb	London Fashion Week (www.londonfashionweek.co.uk)
Mid-Feb	Jorvik Viking Festival, York (costumed warriors, battles; www.jorvik-viking-festival.co.uk)
April	Easter Sunday-Monday: April 4-5, 2021; April 17-18, 2022
May	Early May Bank Holiday: May 3, 2021; May 2, 2022; Spring Bank Holiday: May 31, 2021; May 30, 2022
Early-mid-May	Jazz Festival, Keswick (www.keswickjazzfestival.co.uk)
Late May	Chelsea Flower Show, London (www.rhs.org.uk/chelsea)
Late May-early June	Bath Festival (www.bathfestivals.org.uk)
Late May-early June	Fringe Festival, Bath (alternative music, dance, and theater; www.bathfringe.co.uk)
Early June	Beer Festival, Keswick (music, shows; www.keswickbeerfestival.co.uk)
Early-mid June	Trooping the Colour, London (military bands and pageantry, Queen's birthday parade; www.qbp.army.mod.uk)
Mid-June	Royal Highland Show, Edinburgh (Scottish-style county fair, www.royalhighlandshow.org)
Late June	Royal Ascot Horse Race, Ascot (near Windsor; www.ascot.co.uk)
Late June-mid-July	Wimbledon Tennis Championship, London (www.wimbledon.org)
July	Edinburgh Jazz and Blues Festival (www.edinburghjazzfestival.com)
Mid-July	Early Music Festival, York (www.ncem.co.uk)
Early Aug	Summer Bank Holiday (Scotland): Aug 3, 2020; Aug 2, 2021; Aug 1, 2022
Aug	Edinburgh Military Tattoo (massing of military bands, www.edintattoo.co.uk)
Aug	Edinburgh Fringe Festival (offbeat theater and comedy, www.edfringe.com)
Aug	Edinburgh International Festival (music, dance, shows; www.eif.co.uk)
Late Aug	Notting Hill Carnival, London (costumes, Caribbean music, www.thelondonnottinghillcarnival.com)

Late Aug	Bank Holiday: Aug 31, 2020; Aug 30, 2021; Aug 29, 2022 (England and Wales)
Mid-Sept	London Fashion Week (www.londonfashionweek.co.uk)
Late Sept	Jane Austen Festival, Bath (www.janeausten.co.uk)
Late Sept	York Food and Drink Festival (www.yorkfoodfestival.com)
Nov 5	Bonfire Night (bonfires, fireworks, effigy burning of 1605 traitor Guy Fawkes)
Nov 30	St. Andrew's Day Bank Holiday (Scotland)
Dec 24-26	Christmas holidays

Books and Films

To learn more about Britain past and present, check out a few of these books and films.

Nonfiction

All Creatures Great and Small (James Herriot, 1972). Herriot's beloved semi-autobiographical tales of life as a Yorkshire veterinarian were made into a long-running BBC series (1978-1990).

The Anglo Files: A Field Guide to the British (Sarah Lyall, 2008). A *New York Times* reporter in London wittily recounts the eccentricities of life in the UK.

Cider with Rosie (Laurie Lee, 1959). This semi-autobiographical boyhood novel set in a Cotswolds village just after World War I has been adapted for TV three times, including once by the BBC in 2015.

Dead Wake (Erik Larson, 2015). Larson gives an evocative account of the doomed 1915 voyage of British luxury liner *Lusitania*, sunk by a German U-boat during World War I.

Edinburgh: Picturesque Notes (Robert Louis Stevenson, 1879). One of the city's most famous residents takes readers on a tour of his hometown.

The Emperor's New Kilt (Jan-Andrew Henderson, 2000). Henderson deconstructs the myths surrounding the tartan-clad Scots.

England: 1000 Things You Need to Know (Nicolas Hobbes, 2009). Hobbes presents a fun peep into the facts, fables, and foibles of English life.

Fever Pitch (Nick Hornby, 1992). Hornby's memoir illuminates the British obsession with soccer.

A History of Britain (Simon Schama, 2000-2002). The respected historian presents a comprehensive, thoroughly readable three-volume collection.

A History of Modern Britain (Andrew Marr, 2007). This searching look at the transformations in British life over the last few decades accompanies a BBC documentary series of the same name.

A History of Wales (John Davies, revised 2007). This insightful history tells the story of Wales from the Ice Age to the present.

How England Made the English: From Hedgerows to Heathrow (Harry Mount, 2012). Mount offers a witty, engaging look at the symbiotic relationship between the English landscape and English culture.

How the Scots Invented the Modern World (Arthur Herman, 2001). The author explains the disproportionately large influence the Scottish Enlightenment had on the rest of Europe.

The Kingdom by the Sea: A Journey Around the Coast of Great Britain (Paul Theroux, 1983). After 11 years as an American expatriate in London, travel writer Theroux takes a witty tour of his adopted homeland.

A Land (Jacquetta Hawkes, 1951). This postwar best seller is a sweeping, poetic natural history of the British landscape and imagination.

The Last Lion (William Manchester, final book completed by Paul Reid; 1983, 1988, and 2012). This superb, three-volume biography recounts the amazing life of Winston Churchill from 1874 to 1965.

Literary Trails (Christina Hardyment, 2000). Hardyment reunites famous authors with the environments that inspired them.

The Matter of Wales (Jan Morris, 1985). The half-English, half-Welsh author reveals the mysteries and joys of life in Wales.

My Love Affair with England (Susan Allen Toth, 1994). Toth brings England vividly to life in a captivating traveler's memoir recalling the country's charms and eccentricities.

Notes from a Small Island (Bill Bryson, 1995). In this irreverent and delightful memoir, US expat Bryson writes about his travels through Britain—his home for two decades.

This Little Britain: How One Small Country Changed the Modern World (Harry Bingham, 2007). Bingham offers an informative, entertaining review of Great Britain's contributions to world history.

A Traveller's History of England (Christopher Daniell, revised 2005). A British archaeologist and historian provides a comprehensive yet succinct overview of English history.

A Traveller's History of Scotland (Andrew Fisher, revised 2009). Fisher probes Scotland's turbulent history, beginning with the Celts.

With Wings Like Eagles (Michael Korda, 2009). An English-born writer gives a historical analysis of Britain's pivotal WWII air battles versus the German Luftwaffe.

Fiction

For the classics of British drama and fiction, read anything—and everything—by William Shakespeare, Charles Dickens, Jane Austen, and the Brontës.

Atonement (Ian McEwan, 2001). This disquieting family saga set in upper-class England at the start of World War II dramatizes the consequences of a childhood lie. The 2007 motion picture starring James McAvoy and Keira Knightley is also excellent.

Behind the Scenes at the Museum (Kate Atkinson, 1995). Starting at her conception, this book's quirky narrator recounts the highs and lows of life in a middle-class English family.

Brideshead Revisited (Evelyn Waugh, 1945). This celebrated novel examines the intense entanglement of a young man with an aristocratic family.

Bridget Jones's Diary (Helen Fielding, 1996). A year in the life of a single 30-something woman in London is humorously chronicled in diary form (also a motion picture, with several sequels).

Complete Poems and Songs of Robert Burns (Robert Burns, 2012, featuring work from 1774–1796). This collection showcases the work of a Scottish icon who wrote in the Scots language, including that New Year's classic "Auld Lang Syne."

The Heart of Midlothian (Sir Walter Scott, 1818). This novel from one of Great Britain's most renowned authors showcases the life-and-death drama of lynchings and criminal justice in 1730s Scotland. Other great reads by Sir Walter include *Waverley* (1814), *Rob Roy* (1818), and *Ivanhoe* (1819).

Here Be Dragons (Sharon Kay Penman, 1985). The author melds history and fiction to bring 13th-century Wales vividly to life (first in a trilogy).

High Fidelity (Nick Hornby, 1995). This humorous novel traces the romantic misadventures and musical musings of a 30-something record-store owner. Another good read is Hornby's 1998 coming-of-age story, *About a Boy*. (Both books were also made into films.)

Knots and Crosses (Ian Rankin, 1987). The Scottish writer's first Inspector Rebus mystery plumbs Edinburgh's seamy underbelly.

Macbeth (William Shakespeare, 1606). Shakespeare's "Scottish Play" depicts a guilt-wracked general who assassinates the king to take the throne.

Mapp and Lucia (E. F. Benson, 1931). A rural village in the 1930s becomes a social battlefield. In *Lucia in London* (1927), the protagonist attempts social climbing in the big city.

A Morbid Taste for Bones (Ellis Peters, 1977). Brother Cadfael, a Benedictine monk-detective, tries to solve a murder in 12th-century Shropshire (first book in a series; also adapted for British TV in 1996).

The Murder at the Vicarage (Agatha Christie, 1930). The prolific mystery writer's inquisitive Miss Marple character is first introduced in this book.

Outlander (Diana Gabaldon, 1991). This genre-defying series kicks off with the heroine time-traveling from the Scotland of 1945 to 1743. Later novels trace the Battle of Culloden, repression of Highland culture, and emigration to the Americas. A popular TV adaptation began airing in 2014.

The Paying Guests (Sarah Waters, 2014). This realistic and suspenseful tale of love, obsession, and murder plays out amid the shifting culture of post-WWII upper-class London.

The Pillars of the Earth (Ken Follett, 1990). This epic set in a fictional town in 12th-century England chronicles the birth of Gothic architecture.

The Prime of Miss Jean Brodie (Muriel Spark, 1961). The story of an unconventional young teacher who plays favorites with her students is a modern classic of Scottish literature. (The film adaptation from 1969 stars Maggie Smith.)

Rebecca (Daphne du Maurier, 1938). This mysterious tale set on the Cornish coast examines upper-class English lives and their secrets.

Restoration (Rose Tremain, 1989). This evocative historical novel takes readers to the heights and depths of 17th-century English society.

SS-GB (Len Deighton, 1979). In a Nazi-occupied Great Britain, a Scotland Yard detective finds there's more to a murder than meets the eye.

The Strange Case of Dr. Jekyll and Mr. Hyde (Robert Louis Stevenson, 1996). This famous Gothic yarn by a Scottish author chronicles a fearful case of transformation in London, exploring Victorian ideas about conflict between good and evil.

A Study in Scarlet (Sir Arthur Conan Doyle, 1888). This mystery novel introduced the world to detective Sherlock Holmes and his trusty sidekick, Dr. Watson.

The Sunne in Splendour (Sharon Kay Penman, 2008). Penman's big entertaining book paints King Richard III as a rather decent chap (one in a series of historical novels).

Sunset Song (Lewis Grassic Gibbon, 1932). Farm girl Chris Guthrie is rudely confronted by adolescence, modernity, and war in this lauded Scottish classic, the first book in the trilogy "A Scots Quair."

The Unlikely Pilgrimage of Harold Fry (Rachel Joyce, 2012). A man impetuously sets off on a walk across Britain to see an old friend—and sees his country as never before.

The Warden (Anthony Trollope, 1855). The first novel in the "Chronicles of Barsetshire" series addresses moral dilemmas in the 19th-century Anglican Church.

Waverley (Sir Walter Scott, 1814). Idealistic young soldier Edward Waverley gets ensnared by the intrigues of the 1745 Jacobite uprising, which aimed to bring back the Stuart dynasty.

White Teeth (Zadie Smith, 2000). The postwar lives of two army buddies, a native Englishman and a Bengali Muslim, are chronicled in this acclaimed debut novel.

Wolf Hall (Hilary Mantel, 2010). At the intrigue-laced Tudor court of Henry VIII, Thomas Cromwell becomes the king's right-hand man. The story continues in *Bring Up the Bodies* (2012) and concludes in *The Mirror and the Light*.

Film and TV

Austin Powers: International Man of Mystery (1997). Mike Myers stars in this loony send-up of midcentury English culture, the first film in a three-part series.

Battle of Britain (1969). An all-star cast and marvelous aerial combat scenes tell the story of Britain's "finest hour" of World War II.

Bend It Like Beckham (2003). A teenage girl of Punjabi descent plays soccer against her traditional parents' wishes in this lighthearted comedy-drama.

Billy Elliot (2000). A young boy pursues his dream to dance ballet amid a coal miners' strike in working-class northern England.

Blackadder (1983-1989). This wickedly funny BBC sitcom starring Rowan Atkinson skewers various periods of English history in the course of four series (also several TV specials).

Braveheart (1995). Mel Gibson stars in this Academy Award-winning adventure about the Scots overthrowing English rule in the 13th century.

Call the Midwife (2012-). London's poor East End comes to gritty, poignant life in this BBC drama tracing the lives of a team of nurse midwives in the late 1950s and early 1960s.

Chariots of Fire (1981). This Academy Award winner traces the lives of two British track stars competing in the 1924 Paris Olympics.

The Crown (2016-). The Netflix biographical drama explores the life of Elizabeth II—England's longest-reigning queen.

Doc Martin (2004-2019). A brilliant but socially inept London surgeon finds new challenges and opportunities when he opens a practice in a seaside village in Cornwall.

Downton Abbey (2010-2015). This popular aristocratic soap opera follows the travails of the Crawley family and their servants in early-20th-century Yorkshire (shot at Highclere Castle, about 70 miles west of London).

Elizabeth (1998). Cate Blanchett portrays Queen Elizabeth I as she learns the royal ropes during the early years of her reign, and reprises her role in the sequel, *Elizabeth: The Golden Age* (2007).

Elizabeth I (2005). In this BBC/HBO miniseries, the inimitable Helen Mirren chronicles the queen's later years with a focus on her court's intrigue and her yearning for love.

The Englishman Who Went up a Hill but Came down a Mountain (1995). Starring Hugh Grant and scored with a Welsh choir, this heartwarming, somewhat-true tale of two cartographers who arrive in a Welsh village in 1917 focuses mainly on what makes the Welsh so different from the English.

Foyle's War (2002-2015). This fine BBC series follows detective Christopher Foyle as he solves crimes in southern England during and shortly after World War II.

Goodbye, Mr. Chips (1939). The headmaster of a boys' boarding school in Victorian-era England recalls his life in this romantic drama.

Gosford Park (2001). This intriguing film is part comedy, part murder mystery, and part critique of England's class stratification in the 1930s.

A Hard Day's Night (1964). The Beatles star in their debut film, a comedy depicting several days in the life of the band.

Highlander (1986). An immortal swordsman remembers his life in 16th-century Scotland while preparing for a pivotal battle in the present day.

A History of Scotland (2010). This BBC series presented by Neil Oliver offers a succinct, lightly dramatized retelling of Scottish history.

Hope and Glory (1987). John Boorman directed this semi-autobiographical story of a boy growing up during World War II's London blitz.

How Green Was My Valley (1941). Director John Ford's Academy Award winner chronicles the lives of a 19th-century Welsh coal-mining family.

Howards End (1992). This Academy Award winner, based on the E. M. Forster novel, captures the stifling societal pressure underneath the gracious manners in turn-of-the-century England.

The Imitation Game (2014). Cryptanalyst Alan Turing (Benedict Cumberbatch) is recruited by British intelligence agency MI6 to help crack the Nazis' Enigma code during World War II.

James Bond films (1962-). These classic films follow a dashing officer in Britain's Secret Intelligence Service, who likes his martinis "shaken, not stirred."

Jane Eyre (2011). Charlotte Brontë's 1847 gothic romance has been made into a movie at least nine times, most recently this one starring Mia Wasikowska and Michael Fassbender.

The King's Speech (2010). Colin Firth stars as the stuttering King George VI on the eve of World War II.

Lark Rise to Candleford (2008-2011). Based on Flora Thompson's memoirs, this evocative series chronicles life in a poor Victorian-era hamlet and its neighboring, more hoity market town.

A Man for All Seasons (1966). Lord Chancellor Sir Thomas More incurs the wrath of Henry VIII when he refuses to help annul the king's marriage to Catherine of Aragon.

Mary, Queen of Scots (2018). Saoirse Ronan stars in this portrayal of Mary upon her return to Scotland (from France) and her complicated relationship with cousin Elizabeth I. (A 1971 movie of the same name stars Vanessa Redgrave and Glenda Jackson.)

Monarch of the Glen (2000). Set on Loch Laggan, this TV series features stunning Highland scenery and the eccentric family of a modern-day laird.

Monty Python and the Holy Grail (1975). This surreal take on Arthurian legend is a classic of British comedy.

Mr. Bean (1990-1995). Rubber-faced comedian Rowan Atkinson's iconic character bumbles through life barely uttering a word in this zany sitcom (that also spawned two motion pictures).

Mrs. Brown (1997). A widowed Queen Victoria (Dame Judy Dench) forges a very close friendship with her Scottish servant, John Brown (Billy Connolly).

Notting Hill (1999). Hugh Grant and Julia Roberts star in this romantic comedy set in the London neighborhood of...you guessed it.

Persuasion (1995). Set in 19th-century England, this Jane Austen tale of status was partially filmed in Bath.

Poldark (2015-). In this hit BBC series, Ross Poldark returns to Cornwall after fighting in the Revolutionary War to find his estate, tin mines, and relationship in ruins.

Pride and Prejudice (1995). Of the many versions of Jane Austen's classic, this BBC miniseries starring Colin Firth is the winner.

The Queen (2006). Helen Mirren expertly channels Elizabeth II at her Scottish Balmoral estate in the days after Princess Diana's death. Its prequel, *The Deal* (2003), probes the relationship between Tony Blair and Gordon Brown.

The Remains of the Day (1993). Anthony Hopkins stars as a butler doggedly loyal to his misguided, politically naive master in 1930s England.

Rob Roy (1995). The Scottish rebel played by Liam Neeson struggles against feudal landlords in 18th-century Scotland.

Sammy and Rosie Get Laid (1987). An unconventional middle-class couple's promiscuous adventures expose racial tensions in multiethnic London.

Sense and Sensibility (1995). Star Emma Thompson wrote the screenplay for this adaptation of Jane Austen's 1811 novel of the Dashwood sisters, who seek financial security through marriage.

Shakespeare in Love (1999). Tudor-era London comes to life in this clever, romantic film set in the original Globe Theatre.

Sherlock (2010-). Holmes (Benedict Cumberbatch) and Watson (Martin Freeman) are excellent in this BBC update of the detective's story, set in present-day London.

Sherlock Holmes (2009). Robert Downey Jr. tackles the role of the world's most famous detective.

Sweeney Todd (2007). Johnny Depp stars as a wrongfully imprisoned barber who seeks revenge in this gritty Victorian-era musical.

Tinker, Tailor, Soldier, Spy (2011). There's a Soviet mole inside Britain's MI6 and retired agent George Smiley is summoned to ferret him out, in this adaptation of John le Carré's 1974 espionage thriller.

To Sir, with Love (1967). Sidney Poitier grapples with social and racial issues in an inner-city school in London's East End.

Trainspotting (1996). Ewan McGregor stars in this award-winning, wild, gritty picture about Edinburgh's drug scene in the 1980s. In *T2 Trainspotting* (2017), McGregor's character returns to Edinburgh 20 years later to reconnect with his buddies.

The Tudors (2007-2010). Showtime's racy, lavish series is a gripping, loosely accurate chronicle of the marriages of Henry VIII.

Upstairs, Downstairs (1971-1975). An aristocratic family and their servants make a new home at 165 Eaton Place in this TV series.

Waterloo Bridge (1940). This Academy Award-nominated romantic drama recalls the lost love between a ballerina (Vivien Leigh) and a WWI army officer.

Wolf Hall (2015). The exploits of Thomas Cromwell, the chief minister to King Henry VIII, are detailed in this excellent BBC historical miniseries.

Victoria (2017-). This PBS Masterpiece Theatre series chronicles the rise and reign of Queen Victoria (Jenna Coleman).

For Kids

B is for Big Ben (Pamela Duncan Edwards, 2008). Explore England from A to Z with rhymes, trivia, and bright illustrations.

A Bear Called Paddington (Michael Bond, 1958). A bear from Peru winds up in a London train station, where he's found and adopted by a human family. The 2014 *Paddington* film is also fun viewing.

Brave (2012). This Disney flick follows an independent young Scottish princess as she fights to take control of her own fate.

The Chronicles of Narnia books (C.S. Lewis, 1950-1956) and movies (2005-2010). Four siblings escape from WWII London into a magical world. The first of the seven novels, *The Lion, the Witch & the Wardrobe,* was also a BBC miniseries (1988).

Harry Potter books (J. K. Rowling, 1997-2007) and films (2001-2011). After discovering he's a wizard, a young boy in England gets whisked off to a magical world of witchcraft and wizardry. There, he finds great friendships as well as grave evils, which he alone can destroy.

An Illustrated Treasury of Scottish Folk and Fairy Tales (Theresa Breslin, 2012). Kelpies, dragons, brownies, and other inhabitants of the Scottish Isles come to life in this lovely volume of traditional lore.

Kidnapped (Robert Louis Stevenson, 1886). This fantastic adventure story is based on events in 18th-century Scotland.

Kids' Travel Guide—United Kingdom (Flying Kids, 2019). In this activity travel guide, kids can explore the UK with a mix of interactive quizzes, tips, and coloring pages.

A Little Princess (1995). In this film adaptation of the classic novel, a young girl's fortunes fall and rise again in a Victorian London boarding school.

Mary Poppins (1964). Though filmed on a set in California, this beloved musical starring Julie Andrews and Dick Van Dyke is set in Edwardian London. In the sequel, *Mary Poppins Returns* (2018), the kids are grown and revisited by Mary (Emily Blunt) and her friend Jack (Lin-Manuel Miranda).

Peter Pan (2003). The latest in a long line of films adapting the classic 1902 novel *Peter and Wendy*, this live-action version flies real English children to Neverland.

Robin Hood and the Golden Arrow (Robert D. San Souci, 2010). This illustrated retelling is a good introduction for youngsters to the legend of Robin Hood and his merry men.

The Secret Garden (Frances Hodgson Burnett, 1911). Orphaned Mary discovers nature and love in a gloomy Yorkshire mansion on the edge of a moor in this beloved classic, which has been adapted for stage and screen.

The Story of Britain from the Norman Conquest to the European Union (Patrick Dillon, 2011). Studious older children will get a healthy dose of history from this elegant, illustrated volume.

This Is Britain (Miroslav Sasek, 1962, updated 2008). Vivid illustrations bring the British Isles to life in this classic picture book.

Wallace & Gromit TV series and films (1990-2012). Absent-minded inventor Wallace and his dog, Gromit, may live in northwest England, but these unique characters are beloved by children around Great Britain and the rest of the world.

Winnie-the-Pooh and *The House at Pooh Corner* (A. A. Milne, 1926-1928). This two-volume classic children's tale, set in England, revolves around a bear and his friends in the Hundred Acre Wood. The success of Milne's books has led to numerous book, film, and TV adaptations.

Young Sherlock Holmes (1985). A young Sherlock and his sidekick, Watson, work to solve the mystery of a series of nonsensical suicides (some scenes may be frightening for younger children).

Conversions and Climate

Numbers and Stumblers

- Some British people write a few of their numbers differently than we do: 1 = 1, 4 = 4, 7 = 7.
- In Europe, dates appear as day/month/year, so Christmas 2021 is 25/12/21.
- What Americans call the second floor of a building is the first floor in Britain.
- On escalators and moving sidewalks, Brits keep the left "lane" open for passing. Keep to the right.
- To avoid the British version of giving someone "the finger," don't hold up the first two fingers of your hand with your palm facing you. (It looks like a reversed victory sign.)

Metric Conversions

Britain uses the metric system for nearly everything. Weight and volume are typically calculated in metric: A kilogram is 2.2 pounds, and one liter is about a quart (almost four to a gallon). Temperatures are given in Celsius, although some newspapers also list them in Fahrenheit.

1 foot = 0.3 meter	1 square yard = 0.8 square meter
1 yard = 0.9 meter	1 square mile = 2.6 square kilometers
1 mile = 1.6 kilometers	1 ounce = 28 grams
1 centimeter = 0.4 inch	1 quart = 0.95 liter
1 meter = 39.4 inches	1 kilogram = 2.2 pounds
1 kilometer = 0.62 mile	32°F = 0°C

Imperial Weights and Measures

Britain hasn't completely gone metric. Driving distances and speed limits are measured in miles. Beer is sold as pints (though milk can be measured in pints or liters), and a person's weight is measured in stone (a 168-pound person weighs 12 stone).

1 stone = 14 pounds

1 British pint = 1.2 US pints

1 imperial gallon = 1.2 US gallons or about 4.5 liters

Clothing Sizes

When shopping for clothing, use these US-to-UK comparisons as general guidelines (but note that no conversion is perfect).

Women: For pants and dresses, add 4 (US 10 = UK 14). For blouses and sweaters, add 2. For shoes, subtract 2½ (US size 8 = UK size 5½).

Men: For clothing, US and UK sizes are the same. For shoes, subtract about ½ (US size 9 = UK size 8½).

Children: Clothing is sized similarly to the US. UK kids' shoe sizes are about one size smaller (US size 6 = UK size 5).

Britain's Climate

First line, average daily high; second line, average low; third line, average days without rain. For more detailed weather statistics for destinations in this book (and elsewhere), check Wunderground.com.

	J	F	M	A	M	J	J	A	S	O	N	D
LONDON												
	43°	44°	50°	56°	62°	69°	71°	71°	65°	58°	50°	45°
	36°	36°	38°	42°	47°	53°	56°	56°	52°	46°	42°	38°
	16	15	20	18	19	19	19	20	17	18	15	16
CARDIFF (SOUTH WALES)												
	45°	45°	50°	56°	61°	68°	69°	69°	64°	58°	51°	46°
	35°	35°	38°	41°	46°	51°	54°	55°	51°	46°	41°	37°
	13	14	18	17	18	17	17	16	14	15	13	13
YORK												
	43°	44°	49°	55°	61°	67°	70°	69°	64°	57°	49°	45°
	33°	34°	36°	40°	44°	50°	54°	53°	50°	44°	39°	36°
	14	13	18	17	18	16	16	17	16	16	13	14
EDINBURGH												
	42°	43°	46°	51°	56°	62°	65°	64°	60°	54°	48°	44°
	34°	34°	36°	39°	43°	49°	52°	52°	49°	44°	39°	36°
	14		13	16	16	17	15	14	15	14	14	13

Fahrenheit and Celsius Conversion

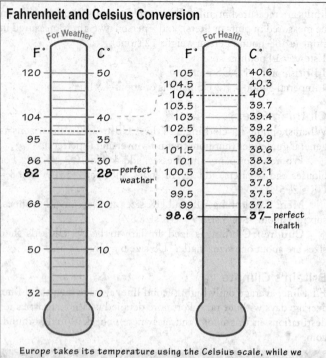

Europe takes its temperature using the Celsius scale, while we opt for Fahrenheit. For a rough conversion from Celsius to Fahrenheit, double the number and add 30. For weather, remember that 28°C is 82°F—perfect. For health, 37°C is just right. At a launderette, 30°C is cold, 40°C is warm (usually the default setting), 60°C is hot, and 95°C is boiling. Your air-conditioner should be set at about 20°C.

APPENDIX

Packing Checklist

Whether you're traveling for five days or five weeks, you won't need more than this. Pack light to enjoy the sweet freedom of true mobility.

Clothing

- ☐ 5 shirts: long- & short-sleeve
- ☐ 2 pairs pants (or skirts/capris)
- ☐ 1 pair shorts
- ☐ 5 pairs underwear & socks
- ☐ 1 pair walking shoes
- ☐ Sweater or warm layer
- ☐ Rainproof jacket with hood
- ☐ Tie, scarf, belt, and/or hat
- ☐ Swimsuit
- ☐ Sleepwear/loungewear

Money

- ☐ Debit card(s)
- ☐ Credit card(s)
- ☐ Hard cash (US $100-200)
- ☐ Money belt

Documents

- ☐ Passport
- ☐ Tickets & confirmations: flights, hotels, trains, rail pass, car rental, sight entries
- ☐ Driver's license
- ☐ Student ID, hostel card, etc.
- ☐ Photocopies of important documents
- ☐ Insurance details
- ☐ Guidebooks & maps

Toiletries Kit

- ☐ Basics: soap, shampoo, toothbrush, toothpaste, floss, deodorant, sunscreen, brush/comb, etc.
- ☐ Medicines & vitamins
- ☐ First-aid kit
- ☐ Glasses/contacts/sunglasses
- ☐ Sewing kit
- ☐ Packet of tissues (for WC)
- ☐ Earplugs

Electronics

- ☐ Mobile phone
- ☐ Camera & related gear
- ☐ Tablet/ebook reader/laptop
- ☐ Headphones/earbuds
- ☐ Chargers & batteries
- ☐ Phone car charger & mount (or GPS device)
- ☐ Plug adapters

Miscellaneous

- ☐ Daypack
- ☐ Sealable plastic baggies
- ☐ Laundry supplies: soap, laundry bag, clothesline, spot remover
- ☐ Small umbrella
- ☐ Travel alarm/watch
- ☐ Notepad & pen
- ☐ Journal

Optional Extras

- ☐ Second pair of shoes (flip-flops, sandals, tennis shoes, boots)
- ☐ Travel hairdryer
- ☐ Picnic supplies
- ☐ Water bottle
- ☐ Fold-up tote bag
- ☐ Small flashlight
- ☐ Mini binoculars
- ☐ Small towel or washcloth
- ☐ Inflatable pillow/neck rest
- ☐ Tiny lock
- ☐ Address list (to mail postcards)
- ☐ Extra passport photos

APPENDIX

British-Yankee Vocabulary

For a longer list, plus a dry-witted primer on British culture, see *The Septic's Companion* (Chris Rae). Note that instead of asking, "Can I help you?" many Brits offer a more casual "You alright?" or "You OK there?"

advert: advertisement

afters: dessert

Antipodean: an Australian or New Zealander

aubergine: eggplant

banger: sausage

bangers and mash: sausage and mashed potatoes

Bank Holiday: legal holiday

bap: small roll, roll sandwich

bespoke: custom-made

biro: ballpoint pen

biscuit: cookie

black pudding: sausage made with onions, pork fat, oatmeal, and pig blood

bloody: damn

blow off: fart

bobby: policeman ("the Bill" is more common)

Bob's your uncle: there you go, there you have it (with a shrug), naturally

boffin: nerd, geek

bollocks: all-purpose expletive (a figurative use of testicles)

bolshy: argumentative, aggressive

bonnet: car hood

boot: car trunk

braces: suspenders

bridle way: path for walkers, bikers, and horse riders

brilliant: cool, awesome

brolly: umbrella

bubble and squeak: cabbage and potatoes fried together

bum: butt

candy floss: cotton candy

caravan: trailer

car-boot sale: temporary flea market, often for charity

car park: parking lot

cashpoint: ATM

casualty, infirmary: emergency room

cat's eyes: road reflectors

ceilidh (KAY-lee): informal evening of song and folk fun (Scottish and Irish)

cheap and cheerful: budget but adequate

cheap and nasty: cheap and bad quality

cheers: good-bye or thanks; also a toast

chemist: pharmacist

Chinese whispers: playing "telephone"

chippy: fish-and-chips shop; carpenter

chips: French fries

chock-a-block: jam-packed

chuffed: pleased

clearway: road where you can't stop

coach: long-distance bus

concession, concs: discounted admission

coronation chicken: curried chicken salad

cos: romaine lettuce

cot: baby crib

cotton buds: Q-tips

courgette: zucchini

craic (pronounced "crack"): fun, good conversation (Irish/Scottish and spreading to England)

crisps: potato chips

cuppa: cup of tea

dear: expensive

dicey: iffy, risky

digestives: round graham cookies

dinner: lunch or dinner

diversion: detour

dogsbody: menial worker, underappreciated staff

donkey's years: ages, long time

draughts: checkers

dual carriageway: divided highway (four lanes)

dummy: pacifier

elevenses: coffee-and-biscuits break before lunch

face flannel: washcloth

faggot: fried sausage meatball

fancy: to like, to be attracted to (a person)

fell: hill or high plain (Lake District)

fiver: £5 bill

fizzy drink: pop or soda

flat: apartment

flutter: a bet

fly tipping: dumping garbage illegally

football, footie: soccer

fortnight: two weeks (shortened from "fourteen nights")

fringe: hair bangs

Frogs: French people

fruit machine: slot machine

full Monty: whole shebang, everything

gallery: balcony

gammon: ham, also an older person with right-wing views

gangway: aisle

ganja: marijuana

gaol: jail (same pronunciation)

gateau (or gateaux): cake

gear lever: stick shift

geezer: "dude"

give way: yield

goods wagon: freight truck

gormless: stupid

goujons: breaded and fried fish or chicken sticks

green fingers: green thumbs

grotty: unpleasant, lousy

half eight: 8:30 (not 7:30)

hard cheese: bad luck

hen night (or **hen do**): bachelorette party

holiday: vacation

homely: homey or cozy

hoover: vacuum cleaner

ice lolly: Popsicle

interval: intermission

ironmonger: hardware store

ish: more or less

jacket potato: baked potato

jelly: Jell-O

jiggery-pokery: nonsense, shenanigans

Joe Bloggs: John Q. Public

jumble (sale): rummage sale

jumper: sweater

just a tick: just a second

kipper: smoked herring

kitchen roll: paper towels

knackered: exhausted (Cockney: cream crackered)

knickers: ladies' panties

knocking shop: brothel

ladybird: ladybug

lady fingers: flat, spongy cookie

lady's finger: okra

lay-by: stopping place on road

left luggage: baggage check

lemonade: lemon-lime pop like 7-Up, fizzy

lemon squash: lemonade, not fizzy

let: rent

licensed: restaurant authorized to sell alcohol

lift: elevator

loo: toilet or bathroom

lorry: truck

mack: mackintosh raincoat
made redundant: laid off
mangetout: snow peas
marrow: summer squash
mate: buddy (boy or girl)
mean: stingy
mental: crazy, wild, memorable
moggie: cat
motorway: freeway
naff: tacky or trashy
nappy: diaper
natter: talk on and on
newsagent: corner store
nought: zero
noughts & crosses: tic-tac-toe
off-licence: liquor store
on the pull: on the prowl
OTT: over the top, excessive
panto, pantomime: silly but fun play performed at Christmas
pants: (noun) underwear, briefs; (adj.) terrible, ridiculous
pear-shaped: messed up, gone wrong
petrol: gas
piccalilli: mustard-pickle relish
pillar box: mailbox
pissed (rude), **paralytic, bevvied, wellied, popped up, merry, trollied, ratted, rat-arsed, pissed as a newt:** drunk
pitch: playing field
plaster: Band-Aid
plonk: cheap, bad wine
plonker: one who drinks bad wine (a mild insult)
prat: idiot
press-on towel: panty liner
public school: private "prep" school (e.g., Eton)
publican: pub owner
pudding: dessert
pukka: first-class

punter: customer, especially in gambling
queue (up): line (up)
quid: pound (£1)
randy: horny
rasher: slice of bacon
read: study, as a college major
return ticket: round trip
revising; doing revisions: studying for exams
ring up: call (telephone)
roundabout: traffic circle
rubber: eraser
rubbish: bad
satnav: satellite navigation, GPS
Scotch egg: hard-boiled egg wrapped in sausage meat and fried
self-catering: accommodation with kitchen
Sellotape: Scotch tape
services: freeway rest area
serviette: napkin
setee: couch
shag: intercourse (cruder than in the US)
shambolic: chaotic
shandy: lager and 7-Up
silencer: car muffler
single ticket: one-way ticket
single track: country lane, often one lane
skip: dumpster
sleeping policeman: speed bumps
smalls: underwear
snap: photo (snapshot)
snogging: kissing, necking, making out
sod: mildly offensive insult
sod it, sod off: screw it, screw off
sod's law: Murphy's law
soda: soda water (not pop)

soldiers: toast sticks for dipping

solicitor: lawyer

spanner: wrench

spend a penny: urinate

spotted dick: raisin cake with custard

stag night (or **stag do**): bachelor party

starkers: buck naked

starters: appetizers

state school: public school

sticking plaster: Band-Aid

sticky tape: Scotch tape

stone: 14 pounds (weight)

stroppy: bad-tempered

subway: underground walkway

surgical spirit: rubbing alcohol

suspenders: garters

suss out: figure out

swede: rutabaga

ta: thank you

take the mickey/take the piss: tease

tatty: worn out or tacky

taxi rank: taxi stand

telly: TV

tenner: £10 bill

theatre: live stage

throw shapes: dance to pop music

tick: check mark

tight as a fish's bum: cheapskate (watertight)

tin: can

tip: public dump

tipper lorry: dump truck

toad in the hole: sausage dipped in batter and fried

top hole: first rate

torch: flashlight

towpath: path along a river

trainers: sneakers

treacle: golden syrup

Tube: subway

twee: quaint, cutesy

twitcher: bird-watcher

Underground: subway

verge: grassy edge of road

verger: church official

wee (verb): urinate

Wellingtons, wellies: rubber boots

whacked: exhausted

whinge (rhymes with hinge): whine

wind up: tease, irritate

witter on: gab and gab

wonky: weird, askew

yob: hooligan

zebra crossing: crosswalk

zed: the letter Z

APPENDIX

INDEX

A

Abbey Road (London): 107

Abbeys: Bath Abbey, 250, 257–258; Glastonbury Abbey, 288–291; Iona Abbey, 937–939; St. Mary's Abbey (York), 521–524; Tintern Abbey, 668, 692–693; Valle Crucis Abbey, 662; Westminster Abbey (London), 64, 68–73

Aberconwy House (Conwy): 620–621

Abertarff House (Inverness): 979

Abraham Darby Furnace (Ironbridge Gorge): 431

Accent, British: 1060

Accommodations: *See* Sleeping; *and specific destinations*

"Actors' Church" (London): 89

Afternoon tea: *See* Tea

Agincourt Square (Monmouth): 694

Aira Force Waterfall: 477, 503

Airbnb: *See* Apartment rentals

Airports: Bristol, 282; Edinburgh, 711, 818; Glasgow, 866–867; Liverpool, 439; London, 43, 195–200, 282. *See also* Gatwick Airport; Heathrow Airport

Air travel: 27, 1080–1081

Albert Dock (Liverpool): 438–439; eating, 469; sights, 444–445, 448–449

Albert Memorial Chapel (Windsor): 216

Alexander Keiller Museum (Avebury): 310

Almanac, Britain: 1005

Ambleside: 508, 510

American Memorial Chapel (London): 112

American Museum and Gardens (Bath): 251, 265

Amusement parks: 216–217, 541–542

Angel of the North: 581

Anglesea Arms (London): 187–188

Anglesey: 636–639, 665

Anglican Church (Church of England): about, 533. *See also* Churches and cathedrals

Anne Hathaway's Cottage (Shottery): 409–410

Antiques (antiquing): Edinburgh, 787; London, 150, 151, 152; York, 547

An Torr: 956, 960

Apartment rentals: 1042–1043, 1048–1049; London, 174–175

Apple cider farms, in Wells: 302

Apps: 30, 1061–1062; baggage storage, 711; hotels, 1039; London, 44; messaging, 1062–1063; navigation, 1034–1035, 1074; sightseeing, 1038; user reviews, 1043

Apsley House (London): 134–135

Archaeological digs: 310; Vindolanda, 596; York, 540

Archaeological museums: 238, 310, 537–539, 541–542, 595–597, 980–981

Archaeological sites: 1020–1021; Cerne Abbas Giant, 335; Clava Cairns, 307, 703, 993–994; Kilmartin Glen, 948–950; map, 1021; Vindolanda, 595–597. *See also* Roman sites; Stone circles

Architecture: overview, 1020–1025. *See also* Castles and palaces; Churches and cathedrals; Country houses

Ardconnel Street (Inverness): 983–984

Arden's (Mary) Farm (Wilmcote): 408–409

Argyle Arcade (Glasgow): 831

Argyle Battery (Edinburgh): 744

Argyle Street (Glasgow): 828–830; eating, 865

Argyll and Sutherland Highlanders Museum (Stirling): 876

Argyll's Lodging (Stirling): 877

Arrochar: 944

Arthur, King: 212, 249, 286, 289–290, 605, 608, 694, 1004

Arthur's Seat (Edinburgh): 766, 781–782

Ascot Racecourse: 159, 219, 1084

Ashness Packhorse Bridge: 493

Ashton Lane (Glasgow): 841, 855; eating, 863

Athenaeum (Glasgow): 833

Atlantis Leisure Centre (Oban): 922

ATMs: 1028–1031. *See also specific destinations*

Audio Europe, Rick Steves: 30, 1082

Austen, Jane: 330, 1009, 1091; Centre (Bath), 251; Festival (Bath), 246, 1085

Avebury: 16, 306–313; eating, 313; itineraries, 304; maps, 305, 308–309; sights, 308–312; tourist information, 306; transportation, 304–305

Avebury Manor and Garden: 310–311

Avebury Ritual Procession Way: 311

Avebury Stone Circle: 306, 307, 310; tours, from Bath, 249–250, 305

Avon River: 258, 259–260, 266–267, 321, 328, 397, 415–417; boating, 416

B

Bagpipes: 751; National Piping Centre (Glasgow), 825, 836, 844–845; Stirling Bagpipes, 879

Baile Mòr: 936

Bakehouse Close (Edinburgh): 763–764

Ballachulish: 954; eating, 964–965; sleeping, 964; transportation, 930–931, 965

Ballymeanoch: 949

Balmoral, the (Edinburgh): 735

Baltic Triangle (Liverpool): 462

Bamburgh Castle: 818

"Banglatown" (London): 121–122, 151, 192

Bank of Scotland (Edinburgh): 727

Banks (banking): alerting to travel, 30. *See also* Money

Bankside Pier (London): 62

Bank Street (Edinburgh): 726–727

Bannockburn Visitors Centre: 884–886

Banqueting House (London): 68, 81

Baptist Hicks Land (Chipping Campden): 354

Barbican Centre (London): 155

Bardon Mill: 588; sleeping, 599

Barley Hall (York): 527, 539

Barrie, J. M.: 361, 763

Bath: 14, 242–283; at a glance, 250–251; eating, 275–281; excursion areas, 284–303; helpful hints, 246–247; itineraries, 242–243; maps, 244–245, 253, 272–273, 276–277; nightlife, 267–269; sights/activities, 250–267; sleeping, 269–275; tourist information, 243; tours, 248–250; transportation, 246, 281–283

Bath Abbey: 250, 257–258

Bath Abbey Churchyard: 250–251

Bathampton: 266–267, 269

Bath at Work, Museum of: 251, 264

Bath Boating Station: 267

Bath Box Office: 246

Bath Chronicle: 267

Bath Festival: 246, 1084

Bath Fringe Festival: 246, 1084

Bath Guildhall Market: 259, 280

Bath Roman Baths: 250, 252–256

Bath Thermae Bath Spa: 251, 265–266

Batsford: 390–391; hiking, 387

Batsford Arboretum and Garden Centre: 391

Battle of Bannockburn: 868, 884–886

Battle of Culloden: 701, 955, 988–993

Bayswater (London): 166; eating, 188; map, 168–169; sleeping, 166–167

BBC: 1072–1073

BBC Drama Village (Cardiff): 681

Beaches: Iona, 940; Llandudno, 627, 628; St. Andrews, 896. *See also* Swimming

Beamish Museum: 582–586

Beatles, the: in Liverpool, 436, 443–447, 453–455, 459–461; guided tours, 439, 442; in London, 105, 107; guided tours, 59

Beatles Museum (Liverpool): 443, 454–455

Beatles Store (London): 107

Beatles Story (Liverpool): 443, 444–445

Beatrix Potter Gallery (Hawkshead): 477, 510

Beaumaris: 637–638

Beaumaris Castle: 625, 637–638

Beaumaris Gaol: 638

Beaumaris Wildlife Cruises: 638

Bed-and-breakfasts (B&Bs): over-view, 1046–1048. *See also specific destinations*

Beddgelert: 642, 643, 649–651

Bede (Venerable Bede): 574

Beefeater Tours (London): 116

Beer: 1059; Tennent's Brewery (Glasgow), 825, 848–849. *See also* Pubs

Belfast: ferries, 470

Belfast, HMS (London): 129

Belgravia (London): 41; eating, 185–186; sleeping, 160–161

Benet Street (Cambridge): 231, 240

Ben More (Mull): 934–935

Ben Nevis: 967

Bethesda: 649

Betws-y-Coed: 633, 636, 646–648

BFI Southbank (London): 158

Bibury: 337, 347, 384–385; sleeping, 384–385

Big Ben (London): 66, 77

Big Bus London Tours: 56, 57–58

Big Pit National Coal Museum (Blaenavon): 690

Biking (bike rentals): Bath, 247; Caernarfon, 640; Cambridge, 224; Conwy, 616; Cotswolds, 342, 358, 380; Edinburgh, 711; Glastonbury, 285; Glencoe, 954; Inverness, 973; Lake District, 478; London, 55–56, 60–61; Oban, 918; Snowdonia National Park, 648, 650; Wells, 285; Windsor, 208, 210; York, 515, 546–547

Bishop's Palace (Wells): 300–301

Bizarre Bath Street Theater: 268

Black Friar, the (London): 184

Blackfriars Pier (London): 62

Blackness Castle: 703

Blaenau Ffestiniog: 654

Blaenavon: 690

Blenheim Palace: 337–338, 347, 391–395

Blists Hill Victorian Town (Iron-bridge Gorge): 428–429

Blockley: 346, 365; hiking, 344, 349

Bloody Tower (London): 120

Boating: Bath, 267; Cambridge, 230–231, 238–239; Derwentwa-ter, 484; Durham, 577; Stratford, 416; Ullswater, 477, 502. *See also* Punting

Boat travel and cruises: Bath, 267; Beaumaris, 638; Caernarfon, 640; Cardiff, 669, 678–679; Conwy, 616; Derwentwater, 478, 484; Durham, 577; Greenwich, 63, 141; Liverpool, 443–444; Llangollen, 660; Loch Ness, 998; London, 49, 61–63, 66; Stratford, 416; Ullswater, 477, 502; Wind-ermere, 505; Windsor, 217; York, 521. *See also* Ferries

Bodnant Garden (Conwy): 613, 633–634

Bodnant Welsh Food Centre: 634

Books, recommended: 1085–1089; for children, 1092–1094

Bootham Bar (York): 513, 525; eat-ing near, 559–560

Borough Market (London): 192, 1036

Borrowdale: sleeping, 498–499

Borrowdale Valley: 492

Bourton Model Railway Exhibi-tion: 380

Bourton-on-the-Hill: 346, 365; eat-ing, 377, 389; hiking, 344, 349

Bourton-on-the-Water: 337, 347, 379–381; biking, 342, 380; hik-ing, 344, 372–373, 381

Bowder Stone: 492–493

Braithwaite: 497

Braveheart (movie): 884, 1089

Breakfast (fry-up): overview, 1051–1052

Brexit: 6, 36, 1015–1016

Briavels Castle: 695

Brick Lane (London): 121–122, 152, 192

Bridge Street (Shottery): 412

Bridgnorth: 432

Bristol Airport: 282

Britain: use of term, 1013

Britannia (Edinburgh): 714–715, 777–779

"British": use of term, 701, 1013

British accent: 1060

British Golf Museum (St. Andrews): 896, 907–908

British Isles: use of term, 1013

British Library (London): 64, 103–106; eating near, 190; map, 104

British Museum (London): 64, 96–102; eating near, 190; map, 97

British Music Experience (Liverpool): 443, 450–451

British Open (St. Andrews): 894, 905

British Parliament (London): 64, 66, 73–77; map, 74

British radio: 1072–1073

British-Yankee vocabulary: 1098–1101

BritRail: *See* Train travel

Broad Campden: 346, 365; hiking, 344, 349

Broadway: 337, 358; biking, 342, 358; hiking, 344–345

Broadway Tower: 358

Broadwell: 378; eating, 376, 378

Brockhole National Park Visitors Centre: 510–511

Browning, Robert: 73

Brush skiing, in Edinburgh: 785

Buchanan Street (Glasgow): 828, 830–831

Buckingham Palace (London): 92–96; Changing of the Guard, 57, 65, 93–96; map, 94

Budgeting: 27. *See also* Money-saving tips

Burns, Robert: 705, 726, 729, 732, 754, 756, 762, 776, 779, 832, 1087; biographical sketch, 758–759

Burns Night: 759, 1084

Burrell Collection (Glasgow): 854

Buses: 1070–1071; London, 43, 51–54, 202–203; to/from airport, 197, 199–200; handy routes, 52–53; ticket, 45–49; tours, 56–58; map, 1066. *See also specific destinations*

Business hours: 1028

Bute Park (Cardiff): 677

Butlers Wharf (London): 121

Buttermere: eating, 500–501; hiking, 476, 490–491; sleeping, 498

Byres Road (Glasgow): 837

Byre Theatre (St. Andrews): 895

C

Cabinet War Rooms (London): 80

Cabs: London, 54–55, 198; tipping, 1032–1033. *See also specific destinations*

Cadenhead's Whisky Shop (Edinburgh): 731, 784, 788–790

Caernarfon: 639–645; map, 641

Caernarfon Castle: 613, 625, 642–643

Caerphilly Castle: 668, 688–689

Caledonian Canal: 966, 982, 998–1000; bike tours, 973

Caledonian Canal Centre (Fort Augustus): 999

Calton Cemetery (Edinburgh): 731, 783

Calton Hill (Edinburgh): 731, 783

Cambridge: 16, 221–241; eating, 240–241; entertainment, 224; itineraries, 222–223; map, 225, 228; self-guided walk, 227–235; sights/activities, 235–240; sleeping, 239–240; tourist information, 223; tours, 227; transportation, 206, 223–224, 241

Cambridge Folk Festival: 224

Cambridge Guildhall: 229

Cambridge University: 221–222; collleges, 226; map, 228; self-guided walk, 227–235; tours, 227

Cambridge University Amateur Dramatic Club: 224

Camden Lock Market (London): 150–151

Camera Obscura (Edinburgh): 715, 723, 753

Cam River: 222, 223, 227, 230–231, 352; punting, 230–231, 238–239

Canary Wharf Pier (London): 62, 141

Candlemaker Row (Edinburgh): 787

Canongate (Edinburgh): 731–733

Canongate Kirk (Edinburgh): 732

Canterbury Tales, The (Chaucer): 105

Cardiff: 667–685; eating, 684–685; helpful hints, 669, 671; history of, 670; map, 672–673; planning tips, 666–667, 668; self-guided walk, 671–675; sights, 675–682; sleeping, 682–683; tourist information, 669; transportation, 669, 685

Cardiff, Museum of: 675

Cardiff Bay: 668, 678–682; map, 679

Cardiff Castle: 668, 676–677

Cardiff Civic Center: 677–678

Cardiff High Street: 671, 673–674

Cardiff Market: 674

Carenza's, Jill, Cotswolds Riding Centre (Stanton): 362
Car insurance: 1073–1074
Carlisle: 589–591; sleeping near, 599–600
Carmel Church (Conwy): 620
Carnaby Street (London): eating, 180
Car navigation: 1074, 1076
Car rentals: 27, 1071–1073. *See also specific destinations*
Carroll, Lewis: 73, 103
Car travel (driving): 1076–1080; best three-week trip, 22–23; budgeting, 27; London, 55; mileage and time, 1075; road signs, 1076; roundabouts, 1077–1078. *See also specific destinations*
Casbah Coffee Club (Liverpool): 447
Castle Arcade (Cardiff): 671–672, 684
Castlehill (Edinburgh): 723
Castlerigg Stone Circle: 307, 476, 485–486
Castles and palaces: architecture, 1023; Beaumaris Castle, 637–638; Bishop's Palace (Wells), 300–301; Caernarfon Castle, 613, 625, 642–643; Caerphilly Castle, 668, 688–689; Cardiff Castle, 668, 676–677; Cawdor Castle, 994–995; Chepstow Castle, 691; Conwy Castle, 613, 623–624; Corfe Castle, 334; Criccieth Castle, 625, 657–658; Doune Castle, 703, 889–890; Dunollie Castle and Museum (Oban), 921; Durham Castle, 570–571, 579; Harlech Castle, 613, 625, 656; Highclere Castle, 218; Inveraray Castle, 945, 947; Inverness Castle, 977–978, 981; Monmouth Castle, 694; Nunney Castle, 302; Palace of Holyroodhouse (Edinburgh), 714, 734, 765–766; St. Andrews Castle, 899, 901; Stirling Castle, 868, 870, 872–877; Urquhart Castle, 998; Windsor Castle, 210–216; York Castle, 520, 543–544. *See also* Buckingham Palace; Edinburgh Castle
Castle Stalker: 931

Castle Welsh Crafts Shop (Cardiff): 669
Catbells High Ridge: 476, 486–490
Cathedral Close (Salisbury): 328–329
Cathedrals: *See* Churches and cathedrals
Catherine, Duchess of Cambridge (Kate Middleton): 71, 87, 136, 149, 221, 897, 900, 1012, 1018–1019
Cavern Club (Liverpool): 447, 453–454, 462
Cavern Quarter (Liverpool): 462, 463
Cawdor Castle: 994–995
Ceilidh: 856, 909, 923–924, 972
Cell phones: 1060–1063. *See also* Apps
Celtic Shop (Glasgow): 829
Cenotaph (London): 66
Central London: 40–41, 68–96; eating, 175–184
Cerne Abbas: 334–335
Cerne Abbas Giant: 335
Chalice Well Gardens (Glastonbury): 291–292
Changing of the Guard: London, 57, 65, 93–96; Windsor, 211
Channel crossing: 203–204
Chapter House (Salisbury): 328, 331, 332
Chapter House (Wells): 298
Chapter House (York): 526, 535
Chapter House Street (York): 526
Charing Cross Road (London): 148
Charing Cross Station (London): 201
Chariots of Fire (movie): 236, 781, 813, 896, 1089
Charlotte Square (Edinburgh): 740, 777
Chastleton House: 347, 389–390
Chaucer, Geoffrey: 73, 105
Cheddar Gorge Cheese Company: 301–302
Chedworth Roman Villa: 383–384
Chedworth Roman Villa (Cheltenham): 383–384
Cheese: 301–302, 792, 911
Chelsea Flower Show (London): 44, 1084
Chepstow: 690–692
Chepstow Castle: 691

Chepstow Museum: 692

Chepstow Riverfront Park: 692

Cherhill: 312

Cherhill White Horse: 312

Childhood, Museum of (Edinburgh): 715, 761

Chinatown (Liverpool): eating, 467–468

Chinatown (London): 88; eating, 180–181

Chipping Campden: 337, 346, 348–357; biking, 342; eating, 356–357; helpful hints, 349; hiking, 344–345, 349; map, 351; self-guided walk, 349–355; sleeping, 355–356; tourist information, 348–349

Chipping Campden High Street: 352–353

Chipping Campden Market Hall: 349–350

Chocolate: 370, 540, 632, 911–912, 1005, 1058

Choirs, in Wales: 607, 628, 642, 661, 663

Christ Church College (Oxford): 1037

Christmas markets: Bath, 246; York, 515

Christ's College (Cambridge): 229

Churches and cathedrals: architecture, 1022; sightseeing tips, 1035; Canongate Kirk (Edinburgh), 732; Carmel Church (Conwy), 620; Durham's Cathedral, 571–576; Glasgow Cathedral, 825, 846–847; Great St. Mary's Church (Cambridge), 232; Hailes Church and Abbey, 360; Holy Trinity Church (Stratford), 406–407; Holy Trinity Church (York), 539; Liverpool Cathedral, 457–459; Metropolitan Cathedral of Christ the King (Liverpool), 443, 455–456; Old High Church (Inverness), 979–980; St. Andrew's and St. George's Church (Edinburgh), 739; St. Andrew's Cathedral, 901–903; St. Edwards Church (Stow), 371–372; St. George's Church (Glasgow), 832–833; St. Giles' Cathedral (Edinburgh), 714, 728, 756–760; St. James Church (Chipping Campden), 354–355; St. John the Baptist Church (Cardiff), 674–675; St. Martin-in-the-Fields (London), 68, 87–88, 157–158, 183; St. Mary's Parish Church (Conwy), 626–627; St. Michael Church (Stanton), 361–362; St. Paul's Cathedral (London), 64, 108–113; Sts. Mary and Nicholas Church (Wilton), 331; Saints Peter and Paul Church (Northleach), 383; St. Thomas's Church (Salisbury), 325; Southwark Cathedral (London), 128–129; Tolbooth Church (Edinburgh), 723; Tron Church (Edinburgh), 730; Wells Cathedral, 296–300; York Minster, 520, 529–537. *See also* Evensong

Churchill, Winston: 393–394, 967–968, 1011; Museum (London), 80; War Rooms (London), 64, 66, 77–80

Churchill War Rooms (London): 64, 66, 77–80

Church of England (Anglican Church): about, 533. *See also* Churches and cathedrals

Church Street (Inverness): 978–979

Church Stretton: 432

Cider farms, in Wells: 302

Circus, the (Bath): 250, 261–262

Cirencester: 347, 385–386

City of London: 41, 108–121; information centre, 42, 1026; maps, 110–111, 176–177, 185; markets, 151; pubs, 184–185; sights, 108–121

Clachaig Inn: 956, 963

Clarinda's Tea Room (Edinburgh): 732, 811

Classroom Europe, Rick Steves: 30, 1082

Clava Cairns: 307, 703, 993–994

Claverton Manor: 265

Clifford's Tower (York): 542–543

Climate: 22–23, 1095

Clothing sizes: 1095

Clyde River: 821, 852–854

Coalbrookdale Museum of Iron (Ironbridge Gorge): 429–431

Coalport China Museum (Ironbridge Gorge): 429

Cockburn Street (Edinburgh): 730

Coffin Cairn: 957
Coln Powell: 383
Coln Rogers: 383
Coln St. Dennis: 383
Coln Valley: 383–384
Columba, Saint: 938, 939, 980, 998
Columbia Road Flower Market (London): 152
Commando Memorial (Fort William): 967–968
Concerts, in London: 78, 88, 157–158
Constantine: 254, 512, 526–527, 537
Consulates: 1027–1028
Conwy: 614–633; eating, 630–632; helpful hints, 615–616; map, 618–619; nightlife, 628; self-guided walk, 616–623; sights/activities, 623–627; sleeping, 628–630; tourist information, 615; transportation, 615, 632–633
Conwy Castle: 613, 623–624
Conwy Culture Centre: 617–618
Conwy Folk Music: 628
Conwy Mountain: 627
Conwy Ramparts: 617
Conwy Suspension Bridge: 622
Conwy Valley Train: 612, 632, 648
Conwy Walls: 614, 617, 618–619, 624–625
Corfe Castle: 334
Corinium Museum (Cirencester): 385
Cornish pasties: 281, 500, 558
Coronation Chair (London): 73
Corpus Christi College (Cambridge): 231
Corpus Clock (Cambridge): 231
Costs of trip: 27
Cotswolds: 16, 336–395; at a glance, 346–347; itineraries, 337–338; map, 340–341; overview, 344–345; tourist information, 338–339; tours, 347–348; from Bath, 249–250; transportation, 339–348. See also specific destinations
Cotswold Falconry Centre (Batsford): 390–391
Cotswold Farm Park: 347, 381
Cotswold Lavender (Snowshill): 363–364
Cotswold Motor Museum (Bourton): 380

Cotswold Olimpicks (Chipping Campden): 349
Cotswolds Discovery Centre (Northleach): 383
Cotswolds Riding Centre (Stanton): 362
Cotswold Way: 343, 349, 350, 355, 360
Counting House, the (London): 185
Country houses: Avebury Manor and Garden, 310–311; Baptist Hicks Land (Chipping Campden), 354; Blenheim Palace, 337–338, 347, 391–395; Bodnant Garden (Conwy), 613, 633–634; Chastleton House, 347, 389–390; Claverton Manor, 265; Crook Hall and Gardens, 577–578; Hidcote Manor Garden, 346, 364–365; Kiftsgate Court Garden, 365; Plas Newydd (Llangollen), 613, 660; Snowshill Manor, 362–363; Stanway House, 346, 359–360; Stourhead House and Gardens, 334; Wilton House and Garden, 330–331
Courtauld Gallery (London): 90–91
Court Barn (Chipping Campden): 354
Covent Garden (London): 41, 65, 89; eating near, 182–183; sleeping near, 170–171
Covent Garden Market (London): 152
Cowbridge Road (Cardiff): 685
Cox's Yard (Stratford): 416–417
Craigmillar Castle: 703
Cream tea: See Tea
Credit cards: 30, 1028–1032
Cresswell Lane (Glasgow): 841, 855
Criccieth Castle: 625, 657–658
Crook Hall and Gardens: 577–578
Crown jewels: 117, 120, 746–749
Crown Square (Edinburgh): 746
Cruises: See Boat travel and cruises
Cuisine: 1051–1055; Scottish, 704–706; Welsh, 603–604. See also Eating
Culloden Battlefield: 988–993
Culross: 703, 888–889
Cunard Building (Liverpool): 450–451
Currency and exchange: 1028–1031; Scotland, 702, 704

Customs regulations: 1034
Cuthbert, Saint: 571, 574, 575–576
Cutty Sark (Greenwich): 141–143
Cwm Idwal: 649

D

Dahl, Roald: 678
Dale End Park (Ironbridge Gorge): 428
Dale House (Ironbridge Gorge): 432
Dalkeith Road (Edinburgh): 709; pubs, 795; sleeping, 803–806
Darby Houses (Ironbridge Gorge): 431–432
Daunts Books (London): 45, 149
Da Vinci Code: 779
Deacon Brodie's Tavern (Edinburgh): 726, 812
Dean, Forest of: 696
Deanston Distillery (Doune): 890
Dean Village: 784
Debit cards: 30, 1028–1032
Dell, the (Stratford): 415
Dennyson Stoddart Gallery (Durham): 571
Department stores: Edinburgh, 737–738, 787; London, 149
Derwent Pencil Museum (Keswick): 485
Derwentwater: 471, 476, 484; boating, 484; cruises, 478, 484; map, 488–489
Desserts (sweets): overview, 1057–1058
Devil's Staircase: 957, 961–962
Dewar, Donald: 833–834
Diana, Princess of Wales: 87, 110, 135–136, 136, 149, 190, 1012, 1018, 1019
Dickens, Charles: 58–59, 73, 105, 182, 833
Digbeth Street (Stow): 370
Dining: *See* Eating; *and specific destinations*
Dinosaurs: 140, 452, 767, 850
Discounts: 1028. *See also* Money-saving tips
Distilleries: *See* Whisky
Docklands (London): 41, 144–145
Dr. Neil's Garden (Edinburgh): 782–783
Doctor Who (TV series): 667, 681, 1019
Dolgarrog: 634–635

Donnington Ale: 375, 378
Dorset: 334–335
Doune: 889–890
Doune Castle: 703, 889–890
Dove Cottage (Grasmere): 477, 505–507
Dover's Hill: 349
Downing Street, #10 (London): 66, 68
Downton Abbey (TV series): 206, 218, 688, 766, 945, 947, 1019, 1089–1090
Doyle, Arthur Conan: 108, 763, 1088
Drinks: 1059–1060. *See also* Whisky
Driving: *See* Car travel; *and specific destinations*
Dublin: ferries, 470, 664–665
Duddingston Village: 782–783
Dunadd: 949
Dunalastair Estate: 703
Dunbar's Hospital (Inverness): 979
Dunchraigaig Cairn: 949
Dunollie Castle and Museum (Oban): 921
Dunvegan Castle: 570–571, 579
Durham: 18, 564–581; eating, 579–581; helpful hints, 565; map, 566–567; planning tips, 563; self-guided walk, 568–571; sights/activities, 571–578; sleeping, 578–579; tourist information, 564–565; tours, 565; transportation, 565, 568, 581
Durham Castle: 570–571, 579
Durham Museum: 577
Durham's Cathedral: 571–576; map, 573; self-guided tour, 572–576
Durham University: 564, 570–571, 579
Durham walls: 569–570
Dutch House (York): 526
Duxford: 239
Dyffryn Ogwen: 648–649
Dynamic currency conversion: 1031
Dynamic Earth (Edinburgh): 767

E

Eagle Pub (Cambridge): 231, 240
Earl's Court (London): sleeping, 164, 166
Early Music Festival (York): 515, 1084
Easdale: 923
East End (London): 41, 121–122;

INDEX

eating, 190–192; maps, 110–111, 122; markets, 151–152

East London: 41, 121–122; eating, 190–192; maps, 110–111, 122

Eating: 1050–1058; budgeting, 27; chain restaurants, 1055–1056; money-saving tips, 28, 1052–1053; tipping, 1032, 1050. *See also* Markets; Pubs; Tea; *and specific destinations*

Ebor Races (York): 515

Economy: 1005, 1015–1016

Edinburgh: 14, 707–818; at a glance, 714–715; arrival in, 709–711; eating, 807–817; festivals, 711–713, 723, 785–786; itineraries, 708; maps, 710, 712–713, 720–721, 736–737, 788–789, 798–799, 801, 804–805, 808–809; nightlife, 792–796; orientation, 708–709; planning tips, 708; self-guided walks, 719–741; shopping, 787–792; sights/activities, 741–786; sleeping, 796–807; tourist information, 709; tours, 716–719; transportation, 709–711, 713, 716, 817–818

Edinburgh, Museum of: 715, 732, 763–764

Edinburgh Airport: 711, 818

Edinburgh Castle: 741–753; general info, 714, 741–743; map, 742–743; self-guided tour, 743–753

Edinburgh Festival: 711, 723, 785–786, 1084

Edinburgh Fringe Festival: 711, 786, 1084

Edinburgh Gin: 784–785

Edinburgh High Street: 726, 729–731

Edinburgh Hub: 723, 786

Edinburgh Literary Pub Tour: 792

Edinburgh Military Tattoo: 711, 722, 785, 786, 1084

Edward I: 605, 614, 700, 748, 749, 752, 883, 1024; castles, 624–625, 1024

Edward IV, tomb of: 215

Edward the Confessor: 71, 120

Egyptian art, in British Museum: 98–100

Electricity: 1028

Electric Mountain (Llanberis): 654

Elgin Marbles: 64, 101–102

Elidir Mountain: 654

Eliot, T. S.: 73, 1009

Eliseg's Pillar: 662

Elizabeth I: 72, 700, 1006–1007

Elizabeth II: 44, 71, 92–93, 120, 702, 1018–1019

Elizabeth The Queen Mother: 120, 215

Elvet Bridge (Durham): 569, 580

Embankment Pier (London): 62

Emergencies: 1027

Emmanuel College (Cambridge): 229–230

Empire Theatre (Liverpool): 452

Enginuity (Ironbridge Gorge): 431

England: 34–600; map, 35; overview, 6, 9–10, 34–36; use of term, 701, 1013; worth-it destinations, 16, 18. *See also specific destinations*

English accent: 1060

English breakfast: overview, 1051–1052

English Heritage: 1036–1037

Entertainment: budgeting, 27. *See also* Evensong; Music; Theater

Epsom Derby: 159

Ernest Wilson Memorial Garden (Chipping Campden): 353–354

ETIAS (European Travel Information and Authorization System): 1027

Eton College (Windsor): 217

Eton High Street (Windsor): 217

Eurostar: 24, 203–204

Euston Station (London): 200, 202

Evensong: Bath, 257; Cambridge, 223, 233; Durham, 572; London, 69, 88, 109, 128–129, 158; Salisbury, 326; Wells, 299–300; Windsor, 211; York, 531

Events: 1083–1085. *See also specific events*

Exchange rate: 1029

Exhibition Square (York): 524–525

F

Fairfax House (York): 520, 542

Falconry: 390–391, 409

Falkirk: 868, 886–888

Falkirk Wheel: 887–888

Falstaff Experience (Stratford): 417–418

Fargo Plantation: 318

Fashion Museum (Bath): 251, 264

Fat Tire Bike Tours (London): 61

Fenchurch, no. 20 (London): 114–115, 1025

Fergusson, Robert: 732

Ferries: Belfast, 470; Dublin, 664–665; Holyhead, 470, 664–665; Iona, 932–934; Kerrera, 922; Liverpool, 443–444, 470; Mull, 932–934; Oban, 932–933

Ferris wheel, in London: *See* London Eye

Festival of Politics (Edinburgh): 786

Festival Pier (London): 62

Festivals: 1083–1085. *See also specific festivals*

Ffestiniog Railway: 612, 643, 645, 648, 655–656

Films, recommended: 1089–1092

Fingal's Cave: 941–943

Finnieston (Glasgow): 821, 843, 855–856, 859–860

Fionnphort (Mull): 932–934, 935

Fish-and-chips: about, 1052–1053. *See also specific destinations*

Fitz Park (Keswick): 485

Fitzrovia (London): 41; eating, 190; sleeping, 170

Fitzwilliam Museum (Cambridge): 237–238

Flag: 1005; English, 36; Scotland, 704; Wales, 605

Flodden Wall (Edinburgh): 731

Floral Street (London): 148

Folk museums: 408–409, 417–418, 428–429, 582–586, 668, 685–688

Folk music: 628, 645, 730, 793, 982. *See also* Scottish folk evenings

Food: *See* Cheese; Chocolate; Cornish pasties; Eating; Haggis; Markets; Mussels; *and specific destinations*

Food tours: Bath, 248; York, 519

Foog's Gate (Edinburgh): 745

Ford: eating, 376–377

Forest of Dean: 696

Fort Augustus: 998, 1000

Fortnum & Mason (London): 149, 193–194

Fort William: 20, 965–969; maps, 952–953; planning tips, 951

Fox Inn (Oddington): 376

Fox Inn Broadwell: 378

Framwellgate Bridge (Durham): 568–569, 577

Frasers (Glasgow): 830–831

Fringe Festivals: Bath, 246, 1084; Edinburgh, 711, 786, 1084; York, 515

Frogmore Cottage (Windsor): 206–207

G

Gaelic language: 704, 977

Gainsborough, Thomas: 86, 87, 131, 238, 261, 773

Galeri Creative Enterprise Centre (Caernarfon): 607, 639, 642

Galilee Chapel (Durham): 574

Gatwick Airport (London): 198–199, 282

Geffrye Museum (London): 122

George, David Lloyd: 639

George III ("Mad King"): 103, 215, 738, 740, 1010

George Square (Glasgow): 832

George Street (Edinburgh): 738–739, 787

Georgian House (Edinburgh): 714, 715, 740, 777

Ghost walks/tours: Bath, 268; Cambridge, 227; Edinburgh, 716–718, 792–793; Salisbury, 321, 324; Stirling, 877; Stratford, 401; York, 518–519, 549

Gillespie Wynd (St. Andrews): 896–897

Gin distillery tours, in Edinburgh: 784–785

Gladstone's Land (Edinburgh): 714, 724–725, 754

Glasgow: 19, 819–867; at a glance, 825; eating, 861–865; helpful hints, 823–824; maps, 822, 826–827, 829, 838–839, 858–859; nightlife, 855–856; orientation, 821; planning tips, 820–821; self-guided walks, 828–843; shopping, 854–855; sights, 844–854; sleeping, 857–861; tourist information, 821–822; tours, 824, 826–828; transportation, 822–823, 824, 865–867

Glasgow Botanic Gardens: 837, 840

Glasgow Cathedral: 825, 846–847

Glasgow Gallery of Modern Art: 831–832, 854

Glasgow International Airport: 866

Glasgow Lighthouse: 831, 835

Glasgow Royal Concert Hall: 833–834

Glasgow School of Art: 834, 835, 862

Glasgow University: 821, 841–843

Glastonbury: 16, 286–293; eating, 293; helpful hints, 287; maps, 285, 288; sights, 287–292; tourist information, 287; tours, from Bath, 249–250; transportation, 284–285, 293

Glastonbury Abbey: 288–291

Glastonbury Festival: 287, 288

Glastonbury Tor: 292

Glebe Cairn: 950

Glen Aray: 948

Glencoe: 20, 951–965; eating, 964–965; maps, 952–953; planning tips, 951; sights/activities, 954–962; sleeping, 962–964; tourist information, 954; transportation, 965

Glencoe Folk Museum: 955–956

Glencoe Lochan: 959–960

Glencoe Massacre: 952, 955, 967

Glencoe Pass: 957

Glencoe Valley: 954, 956–962; hiking, 958–962; map, 958–959

Glencoe Visitor Centre: 954, 956

Glen Croe: 944

Glen Etive: 957

Glenlee (Glasgow): 853–854

Glenridding: 502

Globe Theatre (London): 65, 127–128, 155–156

Golf: 704; Cawdor, 995; Edinburgh, 785; Keswick, 485, 486; St. Andrews, 892–896, 904–908

Golf Museum (St. Andrews): 896, 907–908

Good Spirits Company (Glasgow): 833

Government: 1005, 1013–1015

Gower Memorial (Stratford): 417

Grange: 493

Grasmere: 477, 505–508

Grassmarket (Edinburgh): 772, 787; pubs, 794

Grave of the Unknown Warrior (London): 71

Great Britain: use of term, 1013

Great Glen Way: 981

Great houses: *See* Country houses

Great St. Mary's Church (Cambridge): 232

Great Yorkshire Fringe Festival (York): 515

"Green Dragons" (Chipping Campden): 350, 352

Greenhead: 597

Greenwich: 65, 141–144; cruises, 63, 141; eating, 141; map, 142

Greenwich Market: 141

Grevel, William: 354–355; House (Chipping Campden), 353

Greyfriars Bobby Statue (Edinburgh): 727, 771

Greyfriars Cemetery (Edinburgh): 771–772

Guidebooks, Rick Steves: 1082; updates, 31, 1081

Guided tours: *See* Ghost walks/tours; Tours; Walking tours, guided

Guildhall Art Gallery (London): 114

Guildhall Market (Bath): 259

H

Hadrian's Wall: 587–600; history of, 594; map, 590–591; sights/activities, 592–597; sleeping and eating near, 598–600; tourist information, 588; tours, 590–591; transportation, 589–591, 818

Hadrian's Wall National Trail: 588

Haggis: 704, 705, 1052

Hailes Church and Abbey: 360

Hallin Fell: 502

Hall's Croft (Stratford): 404–406

Haltwhistle: 588; sleeping, 599

Hamilton Grand (St. Andrews): 896

Hampton Court Palace: 65, 146–147; cruises, 63, 146

Hard Day's Night Hotel (Liverpool): 454, 463

Harlech Castle: 613, 625, 656

Harris Tweed: 791

Harrods (London): 149

Harry Potter sights: 529, 576, 771–772, 1036–1037; London, 79, 147–148, 151, 1036–1037; Making of Harry Potter, 147–148

Hart, David: 352

Harvey Nichols (London): 149

Hathaway's (Anne) Cottage (Shottery): 409–410

Hawes End: 484, 486–487

Hawkshead: 510

Hayes, the (Cardiff): 675

Heads, The (Keswick): sleeping, 495–496

Heart of Midlothian (Edinburgh): 728

Heathrow Airport (London): 195–198, 207

Helvellyn: 503

Henry VIII: 71, 72, 77, 105, 116–117, 146–147, 215, 216, 234, 235, 257, 286, 289–290, 330, 360, 390, 417, 512, 522–525, 529, 532, 533, 555, 606, 662, 692, 872, 898, 902, 1006, 1024; biographical sketch, 118–119

Hexham: 589–590; sleeping near, 599

Hidcote Manor Garden: 346, 364–365

Hidden Valley: 957, 960–961

High Brandelhow: 484, 486–487

Highclere Castle: 218

Highland Boundary Fault: 944–945

Highland Folk Museum: 703

Highland Games: 700, 918, 928–929, 972

Highlands: *See* Scottish Highlands

High Lodore Farm Café: 493

Hiking and walking: Bath, 266–267; Buttermere, 476, 490–491; Catbells High Ridge, 476, 486–490; Chepstow, 692; Conwy Mountain, 627; Cotswolds, 342–345, 349, 372–373, 378–379, 381, 386–387; Durham, 577; Edinburgh, 766, 781–784; Forest of Dean, 696; Glastonbury, 292; Glencoe Valley, 958–962; Hadrian's Wall, 588, 592–593; Inverness, 981–982; Keswick, 481, 484, 486–491; Lake District, 478, 481, 484, 486–491; Llandudno, 627; Llangollen, 660; Ruthin, 663; Snowdonia National Park, 648–649, 650; Stirling, 876–877; Stow-on-the-Wold, 344, 372–373; Ullswater, 477, 502; Windsor, 208, 210; York, 525–526, 546–547

Hillary, Edmund: 651

Hillend: 785

Hillhead (Glasgow): 855, 856, 860–861; eating, 863–864

Hillhead Bookclub (Glasgow): 840–841, 864

Hill Top Farm (Near Sawrey): 477, 508–510

Himalayas Course (St. Andrews): 907

History: 1001–1012

HMS *Belfast* (London): 129

Holehird Gardens: 504

Holidays: 1083–1085

Holyhead: ferries, 470, 664–665; sleeping, 665

Holy Island: 818

Holyroodhouse, Palace of (Edinburgh): 714, 734, 765–767

Holyrood Park (Edinburgh): 781–782

Holy Rude Church (Stirling): 877

Holy Trinity Church (Stratford): 406–407

Holy Trinity Church (York): 539

Honister Pass: 490–491, 492

Honister Slate Mine: 476, 492

Hootananny (Inverness): 979, 982

Hope Park (Keswick): 485

Hope Street (Liverpool): 456–457, 466–467

Horse and Groom (Bourton): 377, 389

Horseback riding: 362, 642

Horse Guards (London): 68, 81

Horse racing: 158–159, 515; Ascot, 159, 219, 1084; Windsor, 218–219

Horseshoe Falls: 659, 661–662

Horseshoe Pass: 661

Hostels: London, 174; overview, 1049–1050. *See also specific destinations*

Hotels: modern chains, 1042–1044; overview, 1041–1046; rates and deals, 1039–1041; reservations, 1044–1045. *See also* Sleeping; *and specific destinations*

Houses of Parliament (London): 64, 66, 73–77; map, 74

Housesteads Roman Fort: 593–595

Howtown: 502

Hume, David: 727, 729, 731, 783

Hunterian Gallery (Glasgow): 825, 842, 849–850

Hunterian Museum (Glasgow): 825, 842, 850–851

Hyde Park (London): 135–136

I

Imperial War Museum: Duxford, 239; London, 65, 124–126

Impressionism: 87, 90–91, 131–132, 238

Indian cuisine: overview, 1056–1057. *See also specific destinations*

Industrial Revolution: 336, 416, 512–513, 770, 1009, 1025; Ironbridge Gorge, 423, 425–432

Information: 1026–1027; London, 41–43. *See also specific destinations*

Inner Hebrides: 20, 913–950; map, 933

International Musical Eisteddfod (Llangollen): 658

International Slavery Museum (Liverpool): 443, 445, 448–449

Internet security: 1064

Inveraray: 945, 947–948

Inveraray Castle: 945, 947

Inveraray Jail: 947–948

Invermoriston: 999

Inverness: 20, 971–988; eating, 986–987; helpful hints, 971–972; maps, 974–975, 996; nightlife, 982–983; planning tips, 970; self-guided walk, 977–980; sights, 980–982; sleeping, 983–986; tourist information, 971; tours, 972–973, 976; transportation, 987–988

Inverness Castle: 977–978, 981

Inverness Museum and Art Gallery: 980–981

Inverness Old High Church: 979–980

Iona: 935–940; ferries, 932–934; history of, 939; maps, 933, 937; self-guided walk, 936–940; sleeping and eating, 940; transportation, 933–934

Iona Abbey: 937–939

Iona Community's Welcome Centre: 940

Ireland: ferries, 470, 664–665

Irish Ferries: 664–665

Irish Travellers: 370

Iron Bridge (Ironbridge Gorge): 425–427

Ironbridge Gorge: 18, 423–435; eating, 433–434; itineraries, 423–424; map, 426–427; sights/activities, 425–432; sleeping, 432–433; tourist information, 424; transportation, 424–425, 434–435

Ironbridge Gorge Museums: 428–432

Isle of Anglesey: 636–639, 665

Isle of Iona: 935–940; ferries, 932–934; history of, 939; maps, 933, 937; self-guided walk, 936–940; sleeping and eating, 940; transportation, 933–934

Isle of Kerrera: 922–923

Isle of Mull: 934–935; ferries, 932–934; map, 933; tours, 932–933

Isle of Seil: 923

Isle of Skye: tours, 973, 976

Isle of Staffa: 941–943; tours, 934

Itineraries: designing your own, 21–27; London, 38–40; must-see destinations, 14; worth-it destinations, 16–21

J

Jackfield Tile Museum (Ironbridge Gorge): 429

Jack the Ripper: tours, 58–59

Jamaica Street (Liverpool): 462

Jane Austen Centre (Bath): 251

Jane Austen Festival (Bath): 246, 1085

Jenners Department Store (Edinburgh): 737–738, 787

Jermyn Street (London): 148

Jewel Tower (London): 77

Jill Carenza's Cotswolds Riding Centre (Stanton): 362

John Knox House (Edinburgh): 715, 730–731, 761–762

John Lennon Airport (Liverpool): 439

Johnson, Boris: 533, 1005, 1014, 1015, 1016

Jorvik Viking Centre (York): 520, 541–542

Jorvik Viking Festival (York): 515, 1084

Joseph of Arimathea: 286, 289, 290, 291

Jubilee Hall Market (London): 152

Jubilee Walkway (London): 123, 158

Jugged Hare, the (London): 185, 186–187

K

Kate Middleton: *See* Catherine, Duchess of Cambridge

Kayaking: 502, 895, 919

Keiller (Alexander) Museum (Avebury): 310

Keldas Hill: 477, 502–503

Kelpies, the (Falkirk): 886–887

Kelvin, Lord: 843

Kelvingrove Art Gallery and Museum (Glasgow): 825, 851–852

Kelvingrove Lawn Bowling (Glasgow): 852

Kelvingrove Park (Glasgow): 843

Kendal mint cakes: 480

Kennet and Avon Canal: 266–267

Kensington Palace (London): 136, 194

Kerrera: 922–923

Keswick: 476, 479–501; eating, 499–501; helpful hints, 480; map, 482–483; nightlife, 493–494; sights/activities, 484–493; sleeping, 494–499; tourist information, 479–480; tours, 481; transportation, 501

Keswick Jazz Festival: 1084

Keswick Pitch-and-Putt Golf: 476, 485

Keswick Railway Path: 490

Kew Gardens: 65, 145–146; cruises, 63, 146

Kiftsgate Court Garden: 365

Kilmartin Glen: 948–950

Kilmartin Museum: 950

Kilts: about, 724–725; shopping for, 790–791

Kineton: 379

Kingham: eating, 377

Kings Arms (Stow): 369–370, 373

Kings Arms (York): 549

King's College Chapel (Cambridge): 233–234

King's Cross Station (London): 200, 202, 1036

King's Manor (York): 524–525

Kingsmead Square (Bath): 281

King's Parade (Cambridge): 230 232, 231, 233

King's Square (York): 539–540; eating, 555, 558

Kinlochmore: 962

Kirkstone Pass: 504

Knightsbridge (London): 148, 149

Knight Shop (Conwy): 622–623

Knott Rigg: 492

Knox, John: 728, 729, 756–757, 759–760, 901; House (Edinburgh), 715, 730–731, 761–762

L

Lacock Abbey: 1037

Lady Chapel (London): 72

Lady Chapel (Wells): 298

Lady Stair's House (Edinburgh): 715, 725–726, 754

Lake District: 18, 471–562; at a glance, 476–477; itineraries, 472–473; map, 474–475; planning tips, 472–473; tours, 481; transportation, 473, 476–478. *See also specific destinations*

Lancaster Square (Conwy): 616

Land's End Farm: 302

Language: British-Yankee vocabulary, 1098–1101; Gaelic, 704, 977; Scottish, 704; Welsh, 602–603

Lanty's Tarn: 477, 502–503

Latrigg Peak: 490

Laundress Green (Cambridge): 241

Laundry: *See specific destinations*

Lavender fields, of the Cotswolds: 363–364

Lawn bowling: 415–416, 485, 852, 922

Lawnmarket (Edinburgh): 723–726

Leadenhall Market (London): 151, 1036

Legoland Windsor: 216–217

Leicester Square (London): 68; TKTS booth, 68, 79, 154

Lennon, John: 105, 107, 444–445, 446–447, 452, 453–455; home, in Liverpool, 443, 446, 459–460

Liberty of London: 149

Lindisfarne Gospels: 105, 575

Linlithgow Palace: 703

Lister, Joseph: 843

Liverpool: 18, 436–470; at a glance, 443; eating, 466–469; maps, 440–441, 464–465; nightlife, 461–462; planning tips, 437–438; sights, 444–461; sleeping, 462–466; tourist information, 438; tours, 439, 442–444; transportation, 438–439, 469–470

Liverpool, Museum of: 443, 449–450

Liverpool Arms (Conwy): 621
Liverpool Cathedral: 443, 457–459
Liverpool Central Library: 452
Liverpool John Lennon Airport: 439
Liverpool ONE: 451, 469
Liverpool Street Station (London): 200
Livingstone, David: 736, 847
Llanberis: 651–652
Llanberis Lake Railway: 652
Llandudno: 627, 628, 632
Llanfairpwllgwyngyllgogerychwyrndrobwllllantysiliogogogoch: 638–639
Llangollen: 658–661; map, 659
Llangollen Canal: 659–660
Llechwedd Slate Caverns (Blaenau Ffestiniog): 613, 654–655
Loch Awe: 948
Loch Fyne: 945
Loch Lomond: 944
Loch Long: 944
Loch Ness: 20, 995–1000; cruises, 998; map, 996; tours, from Inverness, 973
Loch Ness Centre & Exhibition: 997
Loch Ness Monster: 995, 996–997
Lodore Falls: 493
London: 14, 37–204; at a glance, 64–65; afternoon tea, 193–195; best views, 114–115; eating, 175–195; entertainment, 152–159; excursion trips, 205–241; Harry Potter sights, 79, 147–148, 151, 1036–1037; helpful hints, 43–45; itineraries, 38–40; layout of, 40–41; money-saving tips, 42–43, 44, 48–49, 78–79, 159; neighborhoods, 40–41; orientation, 40–41; planning tips, 38–40; self-guided walk, 66–68; shopping, 148–152; sights, 68–148; sleeping, 159–175; theater, 152–156; tourist information, 41–43; tours, 56–63, 66, 78–79; transportation, 43, 45–56, 195–204. *See also specific neighborhoods*
London, Museum of: 114–115
London Bridge Pier: 62
London City Airport: 200
London City Hall: 130
London Dungeon: 79
London Eye: 66, 79, 114, 123–124; crowd-beating tips, 123–124; cruises, 62, 63; general info, 65, 123–124; at sunset, 158
London Eye Pier: 62, 63, 66
London Fashion Week: 44, 1084, 1085
London Guildhall: 114
London Natural History Museum: 65, 140
London Pass: 42–43
London Science Museum: 140
London Transport Museum: 89–90
London Walks: 59–60, 78, 314
London Zoo: 1036
Long Mynd Gorge: 432
Lower Oddington: eating, 376
Lower Slaughter: 346, 378; hiking, 344, 372–373, 378, 381
Lower Ward (Windsor): 216
Ludlow Castle: 432
Lusitania: 448–449, 850, 854
Luton Airport (London): 199–200
Lutyens Crypt (Liverpool): 456
Luvians Bottle Shop (St. Andrews): 911

M
McCaig's Tower (Oban): 920
McCartney, Paul: 105, 444–445, 446–447, 453–455; home: in Liverpool, 443, 446, 460–461; in London, 107
Mackintosh, Charles Rennie: 770, 820, 825, 828, 831, 851–852; biographical sketch, 834–835; House (Glasgow), 825, 842, 849–850; at the Willow (Glasgow), 835–836, 861
Madame Tussauds Waxworks (London): 79, 106–107
Madeley: 432
MAD Museum (Stratford): 417
Magical Beatles Museum (Liverpool): 443, 454–455
Magistrate's Court (Chipping Campden): 350
Magna Carta: 105, 326, 328, 695, 1006
Mail: 1064–1065. *See also specific destinations*
Making of Harry Potter (London): 147–148
Maltby Street Market (London): 193
Manor houses: *See* Country houses

INDEX

Maritime museums: 144, 443, 445, 448–449

Market Cross (Stow): 366, 368, 369–370

Market Hall (Chipping Campden): 349–350

Market Hill Square (Cambridge): 228–229, 241

Market Place (Durham): 565, 568–569

Market Place (Northleach): 382–383

Markets: 1053; Caernarfon, 640; Cambridge, 228, 241; Cardiff, 674; Chipping Campden, 349–350; Cirencester, 385–386; Durham, 565, 569; Glastonbury, 287; Greenwich, 141; Inverness, 978; Keswick, 479; Liverpool, 462; London, 150–152, 191, 192–193; Monmouth, 694; Moreton, 386; Salisbury, 321, 324, 325; Stratford, 400; York, 528, 558

Market Street (St. Andrews): 894, 903–904, 911

Martyrs' Monument (Edinburgh): 731

Martyrs' Monument (St. Andrews): 896

Marx, Karl: 97

Mary, Queen of Scots: 747, 749, 761, 765, 766, 769, 775, 868, 872, 874, 899, 901, 904, 989; tomb, in London, 72–73

Mary Arden's Farm (Wilmcote): 408–409

Marylebone High Street (London): 148–149

Marylebone Station (London): 202

Mathew Street (Liverpool): 453–454

Maugersbury: 370; sleeping, 374

Mayfield Gardens (Edinburgh): 709; sleeping, 806–807

Medical help: 43, 1027

Menai Suspension Bridge: 636

Mendip Hills: 292

Mendips (Liverpool): 443, 446, 460

Menier Chocolate Factory (London): 155

Mercat cross: Edinburgh, 729; Inverness, 978; Stirling, 879

Merchant Adventurers' Hall (York): 520, 540–541

Merchant City (Glasgow): 831, 855, 857–858

Merchant Marine Memorial (Cardiff): 682

Mermaid Quay (Cardiff): 681

Mersey Ferries (Liverpool): 443–444

Merseyside Maritime Museum (Liverpool): 443, 445, 448–449

Mersey Tunnel (Liverpool): 453

Metric system: 1094–1095

Metropolitan Cathedral of Christ the King (Liverpool): 443, 455–456

Mickleton: 341, 365

Midges: 480, 700

Midlothian Snowsports Centre (Hillend): 785

Military museums: 124–126, 134, 239, 676, 751, 753, 876, 967–968

Military Tattoo (Edinburgh): 711, 722, 785, 786, 1084

Millbank Pier (London): 62

Millennium Bridge (London): 127

Millennium Bridge (York): 546

Millennium Stadium (Cardiff): 667, 674, 683

Mill Pond (Cambridge): 230–231

Milne, A. A.: 237, 1094

Miniature golf: 476, 485

Ministry of Defence (London): 68

Mobile phones: 1060–1063. *See also* Apps

Model Railway Exhibition (Bourton): 380

Model Village (Bourton): 380–381

Moel Famau: 663

Monarch's Way: 372–373

Money: 1028–1033; average daily expenses, 27; budgeting, 27; Scotland, 702, 704

Money-saving tips: 27–28, 1028; eating, 28, 1052–1053; Edinburgh, 709; London, 42–43, 44, 48–49, 78–79, 159; sightseeing, 27–28, 1036–1038; sleeping, 28, 1039–1041; train travel, 1069–1070; York, 514

Monk Bar (York): 526

Monmouth: 694–695

Monmouth Castle: 694

Monnow Bridge: 695

Mons Meg (Edinburgh): 745–746

Moore, Henry: 112, 127

Moreton-in-Marsh: 337, 347, 386–389; eating, 388–389; hiking, 386–387; map, 387; sleeping, 388

Morgan Arcade (Cardiff): 684

Motor Museum (Bourton): 380

Mound, The (Edinburgh): 735, 754

Mount Inn (Stanton): 362, 377

Mount Snowdon: 609, 613, 646, 652

Mount Street (Liverpool): 446–447

Movies, recommended: 1089–1092

Movie theaters: 158, 549, 856

Much Wenlock: 432

Mudgley: 302

Mull: 934–935; ferries, 932–934; map, 933; tours, 932–933

Multangular Tower (York): 524

Mummies: 98, 100

Mungo, Saint: 831–832, 837, 840, 847

Museum of Bath at Work: 251, 264

Museum of Cardiff: 675

Museum of Childhood (Edinburgh): 715, 761

Museum of Classical Archaeology (Cambridge): 238

Museum of Edinburgh: 715, 732, 763–764

Museum of Liverpool: 443, 449–450

Museum of London: 114–115

Museum of the Gorge (Ironbridge Gorge): 427

Museum of the Home (London): 122

Museum of the University of St. Andrews (MUSA): 898–899

Museum on the Mound (Edinburgh): 727, 754

Music: *See* Concerts, in London; Evensong; Folk music; Welsh choirs

Music Experience (Liverpool): 443, 450–451

Music festivals: 287, 288, 349, 515, 615, 658, 785–786, 1084

Mussels: 621, 622, 626–627, 861

N

Nantclwyd y Dre (Ruthin): 663

Nash's House (Stratford): 403–404

National Army Museum (London): 134

National Assembly of Wales (Cardiff): 682

National Beekeeping Centre (Bodnant): 634

National Covenant: 760, 763

National Gallery (London): 64, 68, 83–87; afternoon tea, 194; map, 84–85

National Gallery, Scottish (Edinburgh): 714, 735, 772–774

National Maritime Museum (Greenwich): 144

National Museum (Cardiff): 677–678

National Museum of Scotland (Edinburgh): 714, 727, 767–771

National Piping Centre (Glasgow): 825, 836, 844–845

National Portrait Gallery (London): 64–65, 87, 115

National Portrait Gallery, Scottish (Edinburgh): 715, 738, 774–777

National Railway Museum (York): 520, 544–546

National Slate Museum (Llanberis): 613, 653–654

National Theatre (London): 155

National Trust: 1037

National War Museum Scotland (Edinburgh): 751, 753

Natural History Museum (London): 65, 140

Near Sawrey: 508–510

Necropolis (Glasgow): 825, 845–846, 848

Nelson Mandela Place (Glasgow): 832–833

Nelson Museum (Monmouth): 694

Neptune's Staircase: 999

Ness River: 971, 980, 981–982

Nether Largie North Cairn: 950

Nether Largie South Cairn: 949

Nether Largie Standing Stones: 949

Nevis Range Mountain Experience (Fort William): 967

New Brewery Arts (Cirencester): 385–386

Newlands Pass: 491–492

Newlands Valley: 491, 497; eating, 500–501; map, 488–489; sleeping, 497–498

New Place (Stratford): 403–404

Newton, Isaac: 10, 103, 105, 221, 236, 237, 1007

New Town (Edinburgh): 707–708, 709, 734; eating, 813–815; map, 736–737; museums, 772–777;

pubs, 795; self-guided walk, 734–741; shopping, 787

New Walk (York): 546–547

Nicolson Kiltmakers (Edinburgh): 790–791

Nightlife: budgeting, 27. *See also* Evensong; Music; Pubs; Theater

Nor' Loch: 734–735

Norman Gate (Windsor): 213

North Beach (Iona): 940

Northeast England: 18, 563–600; map, 583. *See also specific destinations*

Northeast Wales: 658–665

North Lake District: 471–472, 479–501; at a glance, 476; itineraries, 472–473; maps, 474–475, 488–489; tours, 481; transportation, 473, 476–478

Northleach: 381–383

North London: 41, 96–108; eating, 190; maps, 98–99, 172–173; sleeping, 170

Northumberland National Park: 588

North Wales: 18–19, 609–665; at a glance, 613; map, 610–611; planning tips, 610–612; tours, 614; transportation, 612, 614, 664–665. *See also specific destinations*

Norwegian Church Art Centre (Cardiff): 680–681

Notting Hill (London): 41, 167; eating, 189; map, 168–169; market, 150; sleeping, 167

Notting Hill Carnival (London): 44, 1084

Nunnery Ruins (Iona): 936

Nunney Castle: 302

O

O2 Express (London): 66

Oban: 20, 915–931; eating, 927, 930; helpful hints, 915, 918; maps, 916–917, 933; nightlife, 923–924; planning tips, 913; sights/activities, 919–923; sleeping, 924–927; tourist information, 915; tours, 918–919; transportation, 930–931

Oban Lawn Bowling Club: 922

Oban War & Peace Museum: 921

Oban Whisky Distillery: 920–921

Oddington: eating, 376

Offa's Dyke Path: 663, 692

Ogleforth (York): 526

Ogwen Valley: 648–649

Old Bailey (London): 113–114

Old Bank of England (London): 184–185

Old Course (St. Andrews): 895–896, 905–907

Old High Church (Inverness): 979–980

Old Library (Cardiff): 675

Old Market Bar (Inverness): 979

Old Mill Museum (Lower Slaughter): 378

Old Operating Theatre Museum and Herb Garret (London): 129

Old Parliament House (Edinburgh): 728–729, 760–761

Old Royal Naval College (Greenwich): 143

Old Sarum: 329–330

Old Station (Tintern): 694

Old Town (Edinburgh): 707, 708–709; eating, 807–813; map, 808–809; pubs, 794–796; shopping, 787; sights, 741–772; sleeping, 796–800

Once Brewed: 588; sleeping and eating, 598–599

One New Change (London): 114

One O'Clock Gun (Edinburgh): 744–745

Òran Mòr (Glasgow): 837, 856, 864

Orbital Recreational Track: 960

Order of the Garter: 211–212, 214–215

Organized tours: *See* Ghost walks/ tours; Tours; Walking tours, guided

Original London Sightseeing Bus: 56, 57

Orkney Islands: tours, 976

Other Place, The (TOP; Stratford): 415

Ouse River: 520, 546–547, 549; cruises, 521

Outlander: 703, 764, 888, 953, 992, 994, 1088; Doune Castle, 703, 889–890; guided tours, 716, 717, 718, 972, 976; locations in Scotland, 703

Oxford Street (London): 148

Oxford University: 1037

Oyster cards (London): 47–48

INDEX

P

Packing tips and checklist: 30, 1097
Paddington Station (London): 200, 201; sleeping, 167, 170
Painted Hall (Greenwich): 143
Palace Green (Durham): 570
Palace Green Library (Durham): 571
Palace of Holyroodhouse (Edinburgh): 714, 734, 765–767
Palace of Westminster (London): 64, 73–77
Palaces: *See* Castles and palaces
Palmer's Farm (Wilmcote): 409
Parade Gardens (Bath): 251, 259
Paris: transportation, 203–204
Parliament: *See* Houses of Parliament; Scottish Parliament Building
Parliament Square (London): 66
Parthenon Sculptures: 64, 101–102
Passports: 29, 1027
Patterdale: 502
Pembroke College (Cambridge): 230
Pencil Museum (Keswick): 485
Penny Lane (Liverpool): 447
Pensychnant Conservation Centre (Conwy): 627
Pen-y-Gwryd Hotel (Beddgelert): 651
People's Story Museum (Edinburgh): 715, 731–732
Peter Harrison Planetarium (Greenwich): 144
Petticoat Lane Market (London): 151
Petty Cury Lane (Cambridge): 229
Philharmonic Dining Rooms (Liverpool): 457, 467
Phones: 1060–1064
Piccadilly Circus (London): 68, 88; eating near, 181
Pickering's Gin (Edinburgh): 784
Picnicking: 1053. *See also* Markets
Picts: 946, 948, 980, 1004
Pier Head (Liverpool): 443–444, 449–451
Pierhead Building (Cardiff): 680
Pimlico (London): eating, 186–187; sleeping, 161–163
Pimm's: 1060
Pirate Weekend (Conwy): 615
Pitch-and-Putt Golf (Keswick): 476, 485
Planetariums: 144, 452

Plas Mawr (Conwy): 613, 620, 625–626
Plas Newydd (Llangollen): 613, 660
Plays: *See* Theater
Plough Inn (Ford): 376–377
Pockerley: 582, 584–585
Poets' Corner (London): 73
Politics: 1013–1016; Festival of Politics (Edinburgh), 786
Pollok County Park (Glasgow): 703, 854
Pontcysyllte Aqueduct: 659
Porthmadog: 612, 643, 655–656
Portmeirion: 613, 656–657
Portobello Road Market (London): 150
Post offices: 1064–1065. *See also specific destinations*
Potter, Beatrix: 477, 508–510
Potter, Harry: *See* Harry Potter sights
Pound, British: 30, 702, 704, 1015, 1029
Prestonfield Golf Club (Edinburgh): 785
Prestonfield House (Edinburgh): 793, 817
Prestwick Airport (Glasgow): 866–867
Primrose Hill (London): 115
Prince Bishop: 577
Princess Diana Memorial Fountain (London): 135
Princes Square (Glasgow): 831
Princes Street (Edinburgh): 787, 801
Princes Street Gardens (Edinburgh): 735–736, 741
Princes Street Gardens Dancers (Edinburgh): 793
Prisoner, The (TV series): 657
Provand's Lordship (Glasgow): 845, 847–848
Pubs: 7–8, 1053–1055; eating at, 8, 1054–1055; Avebury, 313; Bath, 269, 278; Bourton-on-the-Hill, 377, 389; Broadwell, 376, 378; Buttermere, 500–501; Caernarfon, 645; Cambridge, 231, 240–241; Cardiff, 685; Chipping Campden, 357, 377; Conwy, 621, 628; Durham, 580; Edinburgh, 730, 794–795, 812, 816; Ford, 376–377; Fort William, 968; Glasgow, 855; Glastonbury, 293;

Greenwich, 141; Inverness, 983; Ironbridge Gorge, 433–434; Keswick, 494, 499–500; Kingham, 377; Liverpool, 461–462; Llangollen, 661; London, 182–190; Moreton, 388–389; Northleach, 382; Oban, 924; Oddington, 376; St. Andrews, 911; Salisbury, 333; Seil, 923; Stanton, 362, 377; Stirling, 882; Stow, 374–375, 376; Stratford, 420; Wells, 303; Windsor, 220–221; York, 548–549

Puffin Island: 638

Puffins: 638, 942–943

Pulteney Bridge (Bath): 251, 259–260

Pulteney Estates (Bath): 260

Pulteney Princess: 267

Pump Room (Bath): 250–251, 256–257, 280

Punting: Bath, 267; Cambridge, 230–231, 238–239; Stratford, 416

Q

Queen Mary's Dolls' House (Windsor): 213–214

Queen of the Sea: 640

Queen's Diamond Jubilee Galleries (London): 73

Queen's Gallery (Edinburgh): 715, 733, 766–767

Queen's Gallery at Buckingham Palace (London): 92–93

Queen Square (Bath): 260–261

R

Radio: 1072–1073

Radisson Blu Hotel (Edinburgh): 730

Rafting: 636, 682

Rail passes: 27, 1067, 1068, 1081

Rail travel: *See* Train travel

Railway museums: 380–381, 544–546

Railway Path (Keswick): 490

Railways: *See* Steam trains

Rannoch Moor: 957

Real Mary King's Close (Edinburgh): 715, 761

Red House Antiques Centre (York): 547

Red Spring (Glastonbury): 292

Regent Street (London): 148

Regimental Museum (Stirling): 876

Rental properties: *See* Apartment rentals

Resources from Rick Steves: 1081–1082

Rest-and-Be-Thankful Pass: 945

Restaurants: *See* Eating; *and specific destinations*

Rhyd-Ddu: 650

Richard III Museum (York): 526, 539

Riddle's Court (Edinburgh): 726

Ritual Procession Way (Avebury): 311

Riverside Museum (Glasgow): 825, 852–853

Roald Dahl Plass (Cardiff): 681

Robert the Bruce: 535, 701, 744, 747, 748, 749, 769, 868, 873, 874, 884–886; biographical sketch, 752

Robin Hood's Tower (York): 526

Rogano (Glasgow): 831, 861–862

Rolls, Charles: 694

Roma (Gypsies): 370

Roman Army Museum (Greenhead): 597

Roman Baths (Bath): 250, 252–256, 269

Roman sites (ancient Romans): 312, 321, 330, 605, 700, 1001, 1004, 1020–1021; Bath, 243, 251–257; Chedworth Roman Villa (Cheltenham), 383–384; Cirencester, 385; Hadrian's Wall, 587, 593–597; London, 114–115, 120; Segontium, 644; York, 512, 521, 524, 526–527, 537, 538

Ropewalk (London): 193

Ropewalks (Liverpool): 461, 468

Roseburn: 784

Rosehill House (Ironbridge Gorge): 431–432

Rose Street (Edinburgh): 740, 795

Rosetta Stone: 98–99

Rosslyn Chapel: 715, 779–780

Rowling, J. K.: 727, 735, 763. *See also* Harry Potter sights

Rowntree Park (York): 547

Royal Air Force Chapel (London): 72

Royal Air Force (RAF) Museum Cosford: 432

Royal and Ancient Golf Club (St. Andrews): 895–896, 905–906

Royal Apartments (Edinburgh): 749

Royal Ascot Races: 159, 219, 1084
Royal Botanic Garden (Edinburgh): 780–781
Royal Botanic Gardens of Kew: 65, 145–146; cruises, 63, 146
Royal Cambrian Academy (Conwy): 620
Royal Commonwealth Pool (Edinburgh): 785
Royal Court Theatre (London): 155
Royal Crescent (Bath): 250, 262–263; sleeping near, 270
Royal Exchange Square (Glasgow): 831–832
Royal families: overview, 1018–1019; sightseeing tips, 1019
Royal Mews (London): 93
Royal Mile (Edinburgh): 707, 708, 714, 719–721; eating, 807–812; guided tours, 716–718; maps, 720–721, 808–809; pubs, 794–795, 812; self-guided walk, 719–741; shopping, 787; sights, 753–767
Royal National Lifeboat Institution: 622
Royal Naval College (Greenwich): 143
Royal Observatory Greenwich: 144
Royal Scottish Academy (Edinburgh): 773
Royal Shakespeare Company: in London, 155; in Stratford, 410–415
Royal Windsor Racecourse: 218–219
Royal Yacht Britannia (Edinburgh): 714–715, 777–779
Rubens, Peter Paul: 68, 81, 214, 234–235, 331, 773
Ruthin: 662–664
Ruthin Craft Center: 663
Ruthin Gaol: 662–663
Rydal Mount and Gardens (Grasmere): 477, 507–508
Ryder & Amies (Cambridge): 232

S
Saddler Street (Durham): 569–570
St. Andrews: 19, 891–912; eating, 909–912; golf, 892–896, 904–908; helpful hints, 894–895; maps, 892–893; planning tips, 891–893; self-guided walk, 895–904; sleeping, 908–909; tourist information, 894; transportation, 894, 912
St. Andrew's and St. George's Church (Edinburgh): 739, 814
St. Andrews Castle: 899, 901
St. Andrew's Cathedral: 901–903
St. Andrews Preservation Trust Museum and Garden: 903
St. Andrew Square (Edinburgh): 738
St. Andrews University: 891, 892, 894–895, 897–899, 904; accommodations, 909; student life, 900
St. Benet's Church (Cambridge): 232
St. Briavels: sleeping, 695
St. Crux Parish Hall (York): 529, 558
St. Edwards Church (Stow): 371–372
St. Edwards Hall (Stow): 369
St. Fagans National History Museum: 668, 685–688
St. George's Chapel (Windsor): 215
St. George's Church (Glasgow): 832–833
St. George's Hall (Liverpool): 452
St. George's Plateau (Liverpool): 452
St. Giles' Cathedral (Edinburgh): 714, 728, 756–760; map, 757
St. James Church (Chipping Campden): 354–355
St. John's Gardens (Liverpool): 452–453
St. John the Baptist Church (Cardiff): 674–675
St. Katharine Dock (London): 121
St. Katharine's Pier (London): 62
St. Margaret's Chapel (Edinburgh): 745
St. Martin-in-the-Fields Church (London): 68, 87–88, 157–158, 183
St. Mary's Abbey (York): 521–524
St. Mary's College (St. Andrews): 904
St. Mary's Parish Church (Conwy): 626–627
St. Michael Church (Stanton): 361–362
St. Mungo Museum of Religious Life and Art (Glasgow): 825, 847
St. Oran's Chapel (Iona): 936
St. Pancras International Station (London): 199, 200

St. Paul's Cathedral (London): 64, 108–113; map, 112

St. Peter's Church (Woolton): 446

St. Salvator's College (St. Andrews): 897–898

Sts. Mary and Nicholas Church (Wilton): 331

Saints Peter and Paul Church (Northleach): 383

St. Thomas's Church (Salisbury): 325

Salisbury: 16, 321–333; eating, 332–333; helpful hints, 324; itineraries, 304; maps, 305, 322–323; sights, 325–331; sleeping, 331–332; tourist information, 321, 324; transportation, 304–305, 324, 333

Salisbury Cathedral: 325–329; map, 327

Salisbury Crags: 781–782

Salisbury International Arts Festival: 324

Salisbury Museum: 329

Sand surfing, in St. Andrews: 895

Sargent, John Singer: 131

Science Museum (London): 140

Scotch whisky: *See* Whisky

Scotch Whisky Experience (Edinburgh): 715, 723, 753–754

Scotland: 698–1000; map, 699; overview, 11–12, 698–706; worth-it destinations, 19–20. *See also specific destinations*

Scotland, National Museum of (Edinburgh): 714, 727, 767–771

Scott, Walter: 725, 736, 744, 747, 754, 762–763, 773–774, 832, 1087; Monument (Edinburgh), 736–737

"Scottish": use of term, 701

Scottish Crown Jewels (Edinburgh): 746–749

Scottish folk evenings: 793, 856, 923–924, 982

Scottish Highland Games: 700, 918, 928–929, 972

Scottish Highlands: 951–1000; map, 699; overview, 698–700; tours: from Edinburgh, 718–719; from Glasgow, 828; from Inverness, 973, 976; from Oban, 918–919; transportation, 914

Scottish National Gallery (Edinburgh): 714, 735, 772–774

Scottish National Gallery of Modern Art (Edinburgh): 781

Scottish National Portrait Gallery (Edinburgh): 715, 738, 774–777

Scottish National War Memorial (Edinburgh): 750

Scottish Parliament Building (Edinburgh): 714, 733, 764–765

Scottish Reformation: overview, 898

Scottish Regimental Store (Edinburgh): 791

"Scousers": 437

Scrumpy Farms: 302

Seasons: 22–23

Secret Garden (Edinburgh): 782–783

Segontium Roman Fort: 644

Seil: 923

Senate House (Cambridge): 232

Senedd (Cardiff): 682

Severn River: 424

Shakespeare, William: 105; biographical sketch, 404–405; Globe (London), 65, 127–128, 155–156; plays, 406–407; in Stratford, 400, 402–415; birthplace, 402–403; gravesite, 406–407; guided tours, 401; schoolroom and guildhall, 407–408. *See also* Royal Shakespeare Company

Shakespeare Festival (Cambridge): 224

Shambles, the (York): 512, 520, 528–529; market, 528, 558

Shard London Bridge: 115, 129, 1025

Sheep Street (Stow): 370–371, 419

Shepherds Crag: 493

Sherlock Holmes Museum (London): 108

Shinty: 972, 981

Shire Hall (Monmouth): 694

Shopping: clothing sizes, 1095; hours, 1028; London, 148–152; VAT refunds, 1033–1034. *See also* Antiques; Markets; *and specific destinations*

Shottery: 409–410

Shrewsbury: 432

Shrieve's House Barn (Stratford): 417

Sightseeing: best royal, 1019; best three-week trips, 22–23, 25; budgeting, 27; general tips, 1035,

1038–1039; maps and navigation tools, 1034–1035; money-saving tips, 27–28, 1036–1038; must-see destinations, 14; passes, 1036–1038; reservations, 29, 1035–1036; worth-it destinations, 16–21. *See also specific sights and destinations*

Signal Rock: 956, 960
Silbury Hill (Avebury): 311–312
Silk Mill (Chipping Campden): 352
Sill National Landscape Discovery Centre: 588
SIM cards: 1063
Sir John Soane's Museum (London): 102–103
Sir Walter Scott Monument (Edinburgh): 736–737
Skeldergate Bridge (York): 546
Skiing: Ironbridge Gorge, 432. *See also* Brush skiing, in Edinburgh
Skye: tours, 973, 976
Skyfall (movie): 957
Slate Memorials (Conwy): 617
Slate Museum (Llanberis): 613, 653–654
Slavery Museum (Liverpool): 443, 445, 448–449
Sleep code: 1040
Sleeping: 1039–1050; budgeting, 27; money-saving tips, 28, 1039–1041; reservations, 28, 29, 1044–1045; types of accommodations, 1041–1050; user reviews, 1043. *See also specific destinations*
Smallest House in Great Britain (Conwy): 621–622
Smartphones: 30, 1060–1063. *See also* Apps
Smith, Adam: 729, 732
"Snickelways" (York): 527–528
Snowdonia National Park: 609–610, 646–656; map, 647
Snowdonia Riding Stables (Caernarfon): 642
Snowdon Mountain Railway (Llanberis): 613, 652–653
Snowshill: 362–364
Snowshill Manor: 362–363
Soane's (Sir John) Museum (London): 102–103
Soccer: 158, 667, 674, 704
Soho (London): 41, 68, 88; eating, 175, 178–180

Sotheby's (London): 194
South Bank (London): 41, 123–130; entertainment, 158; map, 124–125; markets, 192–193
Southend Airport (London): 200
South Kensington (London): 41; eating, 187–188; map, 165; sleeping, 164
South Lake District: 471–472, 504–511; at a glance, 477; itineraries, 472–473; map, 474–475; transportation, 473, 476–478, 504–505. *See also specific destinations*
South Wales: 19, 666–696; at a glance, 668; map, 667; planning tips, 666–667; transportation, 695–696. *See also specific destinations*
Southwark Cathedral (London): 128–129
Speakers' Corner (London): 135–136
Spitalfields Market (London): 151, 191
Staffa: 941–943; tours, 934
Stag Inn (Stow): 368
Stansted Airport (London): 199
Stanton: 346, 361–362; eating, 362, 377; hiking, 344; sleeping, 362
Stanway: 359–360; hiking, 344, 360
Stanway House: 346, 359–360
State Apartments (Windsor): 214–215
State Rooms at Buckingham Palace (London): 92
Steam trains: Conwy Valley Train, 612, 632, 648; Ffestiniog Railway, 612, 643, 645, 648, 655–656; Snowdon Mountain Railway (Llanberis), 613, 652–653; Welsh Highland Railway, 612, 643, 650, 651
Steel Rigg: 592–593
Stena Line: 664–665
Stevenson, Robert Louis: 725, 726, 754, 762, 763, 957, 1085, 1088, 1093
Stirling: 19, 869–883; eating, 882; map, 871, 878; maps, 869; planning tips, 869; sights, 870–880; sleeping, 880–881; tourist information, 870; transportation, 870, 883
Stirling Bagpipes: 879

Stirling Castle: 868, 870, 872–877
Stirling Heads Gallery: 875–876
Stirling Old Kirkyard: 877
Stirling Old Town Jail: 879
Stirling Smith Art Gallery and
    Museum: 880
Stob Dearg: 957
Stob Mhic Mhartuin: 962
Stock Exchange (Glasgow): 833
Stone circles: 949–950, 1020–1021;
    about, 307; map, 1021. *See also
    specific stone circles*
Stonegate (York): 527, 558
Stonehenge: 16, 307, 313–321; itin-
    eraries, 304; maps, 305, 314–315,
    318; orientation, 315–316;
    self-guided tour, 317–321;
    tours, 313–314, 324; from Bath,
    249–250, 305, 314; transporta-
    tion, 304–305, 313–315
Stone of Scone: 749
Stourhead House and Gardens: 334
Stourton: 334
Stow Horse Fair: 370
Stow Lodge: 368, 373, 374–375
Stow-on-the-Wold: 337, 346,
    365–378; eating, 374–378; helpful
    hints, 366; hiking, 344, 372–373;
    map, 367; self-guided walk,
    366–372; sleeping, 373–374; tour-
    ist information, 366
Stratford Big Wheel: 415–416
Stratford-upon-Avon: 18, 396–422;
    eating, 419–421; helpful hints,
    400; map, 398–399; planning
    tips, 396–397; sights/activities,
    402–418; sleeping, 418–419;
    theater, 410–415; tourist informa-
    tion, 397; tours, 401; transporta-
    tion, 397, 400, 421–422
Stratford-upon-Avon Guildhall:
    407–408
Strawberry Field (Liverpool): 446
Study, the (Glencoe): 957, 967
Subway, in London: *See* Tube
Sulis Minerva: 252, 254, 255
Sunken Garden (London): 136
Surf Snowdonia: 634–635, 636
Swallow Falls: 648
Swan Theatre (Stratford): 415
Swimming: Bath, 269; Edinburgh,
    782, 785; Ironbridge Gorge, 432;
    Oban, 922. *See also* Beaches
Swinegate (York): 527–528, 558–559

Sycamore Gap: 592–593

T
Tarbet: 944
Tartan Weaving Mill (Edinburgh):
    723, 791
Tate Boat (London): 63, 66, 126,
    132
Tate Britain (London): 65, 132–134
Tate Gallery (Liverpool): eating, 469
Tate Modern (London): 65, 114,
    126–127
Taxes: VAT refunds, 1033–1034
Taxis: London, 54–55, 198; tipping,
    1032–1033. *See also specific destina-
    tions*
Tea (tearooms): 1057; Bath, 280;
    Cardiff, 684; Chipping Campden,
    357; Conwy, 631; Edinburgh,
    732, 811, 817; Glasgow, 835–836,
    861; Keswick, 499–500; London,
    193–195; Stow, 375; Stratford,
    421; Windsor, 220–221; York,
    561. *See also specific destinations*
Telephones: 1060–1064
Television (TV): 1017–1020,
    1089–1092
Telford Snowboard and Ski Centre
    (Madeley): 432
Temperatures, average monthly:
    1095
Temple Wood Stone Circles: 949
Tenement House (Glasgow): 825,
    836, 844
Tennent's Brewery (Glasgow): 825,
    848–849
Tennis, Wimbledon: 44, 158, 1084
Tennyson, Alfred: 236, 1011
Thames Clippers (London): 63, 141
Thames River: 41, 115; boat cruises,
    49, 61–63, 66, 217; boat piers, in
    London, 62
Theater: Bath, 268; Cambridge, 224;
    Edinburgh, 794; Keswick, 476,
    493–494; London, 79, 152–156;
    tickets, 79, 153–155; St. Andrews,
    895; Stratford, 410–415; York,
    549
Theatre by the Lake (Keswick): 476,
    493–494
Theatre Royal (Bath): 268
Theatre Royal (York): 549
Theft alerts: 31, 1027, 1032; London,
    43

Thermae Bath Spa (Bath): 251, 265–266, 269
Thistle Chapel (Edinburgh): 760
Thistle Street (Edinburgh): 739–740, 787; eating, 814–815
Thompson, Emma: 224
Three Sisters: 957
Threlkeld: 490
Tigh-an-Truish (Seil): 923
Time Out London: 44, 58, 152
Time zones: 1028
Tintern: 693–694
Tintern Abbey: 668, 692–693
Tintern Old Station: 694
Tintern Parva: 693–694
Tipping: 1032–1033
Tipu's Tiger: 139
Titanic: 448
TKTS booth (London): 68, 79, 154
Tolbooth Church (Edinburgh): 723
Tolkien, J. R. R.: 371, 1012
Tomb of the Unknown Warrior (London): 71
Tour guides: tipping, 1033. *See also specific destinations*
Tourist information: 1026–1027; London, 41–43. *See also specific destinations*
Tours: Rick Steves, 1082. *See also* Boat travel and cruises; Ghost walks/tours; Walking tours, guided; *and specific destinations*
Tower Bridge (London): 120–121
Tower of London: 64, 115–120; map, 117
Trafalgar Square (London): 40–41, 64, 68, 81–82; eating near, 183–184; map, 82
Trains, steam: *See* Steam trains
Train stations, in London: 43, 200–201; map, 201
Train travel: 1065–1070; budgeting, 27; Eurostar, 24, 203–204; London, 43, 200–202; map, 1066; sample journey, 1070; tickets, 1069–1070. *See also specific destinations*
Transportation: 1065–1081; best three-week trip, 25; budgeting, 27; London, 45–56, 195–204; map, 1066; pre-booking, 29. *See also* Boat travel and cruises; Buses; Car travel; Ferries; Train travel; *and specific destinations*

Transport Museum (London): 89–90
Travelcards (London): 48
Travel insurance: 29–30, 1074
Travel smarts: 31–32
Travel tips: 1027–1028
Treasurer's House (York): 526
Trefriw Woolen Mills: 635
Tremadog Bay: 656
Trinity College (Cambridge): 235–237
Trinity Gate (Cambridge): 235
Trip costs: 27
Tron Church (Edinburgh): 730
Trooping the Colour (London): 44, 1019, 1084
Trout Farm (Bibury): 384
Truman Markets (London): 151–152
Tube (London): 49–51, 197; etiquette, 50–51; tickets, 45–49
Tudor World at the Falstaff Experience (Stratford): 417–418
Turner, J. M. W.: 83, 134, 329, 693, 1009
TV (television): 1017–1020, 1089–1092
Tweed, shopping for: 791
20 Fenchurch (London): 114–115, 1025
Twice Brewed: 588; sleeping and eating, 598–599

U
Uber: 1071; Edinburgh, 716, 803, 818; Glasgow, 824; London, 55, 198
Ugly House, The: 648
Ullswater Lake: 477, 502–504
Undercroft Museum (York): 531, 534, 536–537
Underground (London): *See* Tube
"United Kingdom": use of term, 1013
Universities: *See* Cambridge University; Durham University; Glasgow University; St. Andrews University
Upper Oddington: eating, 376
Upper Slaughter: 346, 378–379; hiking, 344, 372–373, 378–379, 381
Urquhart Castle: 998

V
Valle Crucis Abbey: 662
VAT refunds: 1033–1034

INDEX

Venerable Bede: 574
Vicars' Close (Wells): 300
Victoria, Queen: 206, 208, 216, 452, 751, 832, 1010–1011
Victoria and Albert Museum (London): 64, 136–140, 195; map, 138–139
Victoria Art Gallery (Bath): 251, 259
Victorian Market (Inverness): 978
Victoria Station (London): 159–160, 200; eating near, 184–188; map, 162–163; sleeping near, 159–163
Victoria Street (Edinburgh): 772, 787, 794
Vikings: 512, 524, 536, 539; festival (York), 515, 1084; Jorvik Viking Centre (York), 520, 541–542
Vindolanda: 595–597
Visitor information: 1026–1027; London, 41–43. *See also specific destinations*

W
Waggonway: 584–585
Waldorf Astoria Edinburgh: 735
Wales: 602–696; map, 604; North, 609–665; overview, 10–11, 602–608; South, 666–696; worth-it destinations, 18–19. *See also specific destinations*
Wales Coastal Trail: 627
Wales Millennium Centre (Cardiff): 670, 681
Walker Art Gallery (Liverpool): 443, 452, 453
Walking tours, guided: Bath, 248, 268; Cambridge, 227; Cardiff, 669, 671; Durham, 565; Edinburgh, 716–718; Glasgow, 826–827; Inverness, 972; Keswick, 481; London, 58–60; St. Andrews, 895; Salisbury, 321, 324; Stow, 366; Stratford, 401; Wells, 294; York, 518–519. *See also* Ghost walks/tours
Walking trails: *See* Hiking and walking
Wallace, William "Braveheart": 700, 752, 769, 776, 868, 873, 885; biographical sketch, 748; Monument (Stirling), 873, 883–884
Wallace Collection (London): 106, 195

Walla Crag: 490
Walltown Visitor Centre: 588
Wardour Street (London): eating, 180–181
Warner Bros. Studio Tour London: 147–148
Watendlath: 493
Waterloo Pier (London): 62
Waterloo Station (London): 200, 202
Water of Leith: 784
Waterstones (London): 45, 115, 194
Watt, James: 729, 768, 770, 776, 832, 843, 1008
Waverley Bridge (Edinburgh): 734
Waverley Station (Edinburgh): 709–710, 817
Wear River: 564, 577; cruises, 577
Weather: 22–23, 1095
"Weeping Glen" of Glencoe: 951, 952
Welch, Robert: 352
Weller Astronomy Galleries (Greenwich): 144
Wellington Barracks (London): 94, 95
Wellington Monument (London): 110–111
Wellington Museum (London): 134–135
Wells: 16, 294–305; eating, 303; helpful hints, 296; maps, 285, 295; sights, 296–302; sleeping, 302–303; tourist information, 294; tours, 296; from Bath, 249–250, 300; transportation, 284–285, 294–296, 303
Wells Carnival: 296
Wells Cathedral: 296–300
Welsh choirs: 607, 628, 642, 661, 663
Welsh Highland Railway: 612, 643, 650, 651
Welsh language: 602–603
Welsh Life, Museum of (St. Fagans): 668, 685–688
Welsh Military Museum (Cardiff): 676
West End (Edinburgh): 709; eating, 815; map, 801; sleeping, 801–802
West End (Glasgow): 821, 836–837; eating, 863–865; map, 838–839; nightlife, 855; self-guided walk,

836–843; shopping, 855; sights, 849–852; sleeping, 859–861

West End (London): 40–41, 88–91; eating, 175–183; maps, 90–91; markets, 152; shopping, 148, 149; sights, 88–91; theater, 153–155

West Highland Museum (Fort William): 967

West Kennet Long Barrow: 312

West London: 41, 130–140; map, 132–133; sleeping, 159–170

Westminster (London): 40, 66–68; map, 67; sights, 68–81

Westminster, Palace of (London): 64, 73–77

Westminster Abbey (London): 64, 66, 68–73; map, 70

Westminster Bridge (London): 66

Westminster Pier (London): 61, 62, 63, 66

West Sands (St. Andrews): 896

Whiski Rooms Shop (Edinburgh): 727, 790

Whisky: 705–706, 755, 784, 788–790, 833, 983, 1059–1060; tasting, 755; Cadenhead's Whisky Shop (Edinburgh), 731, 784, 788–790; Deanston Distillery (Doune), 890; Luvians Bottle Shop (St. Andrews), 911; Oban Whisky Distillery, 920–921; The Pot Still (Glasgow), 855, 862; Scotch Whisky Experience (Edinburgh), 715, 723, 753–754; Whiski Rooms Shop (Edinburgh), 727, 790

Whistler, James McNeill: 131–132, 850

Whitehall (London): 66

White Horse Close (Edinburgh): 732–733

White Spring (Glastonbury): 292

White Tower (London): 116–117

Whitewater rafting: 636, 682

Wilkins Cider Farm: 302

Willow Tea Rooms (Glasgow): 835–836, 861

Wilmcote: 408–409

Wilson Memorial Garden (Chipping Campden): 353–354

Wilton House and Garden: 330–331

Wimbledon Tennis Championship: 44, 158, 1084

Winchcombe: hiking, 344

Windermere Jetty Museum: 511

Windermere Lake: 505, 510–511

Windsor: 16, 205–221; eating, 220–221; helpful hints, 208, 210; map, 209; sights, 210–219; sleeping, 219–220; tourist information, 208; transportation, 206, 207, 208

Windsor and Royal Borough Museum: 217

Windsor Castle: 210–216

Windsor Guildhall: 217

Winson: 383

Wolf Hall (TV series): 390, 1089

Wolfson Gallery (Durham): 571

Woodstock: 392–393

WoodWinters (Edinburgh): 790

Wordsworth, William: 477, 505–508, 627, 660, 692–693, 1009

Wordsworth Grasmere: 477, 505–507

World Museum (Liverpool): 452

World of Beatrix Potter (Hawkshead): 510

World's End (Edinburgh): 731

World's End Pub (Edinburgh): 812

World War I: 125, 350, 371, 379, 544, 547, 750, 955, 981, 1009

World War II: 112, 125–126, 371, 379, 547, 676–677, 682, 750, 921, 1010–1012; Churchill War Rooms (London), 64; Commando Memorial (Fort William): 967–968

Wren Library (Cambridge): 235–237

Writers' Museum (Edinburgh): 715, 725–726, 754

Wye River: 690, 692

Wye Valley: 690–695; sleeping, 695

Y

Ye Olde Cheshire Cheese (London): 184

York: 14, 512–562; at a glance, 520; eating, 555–561; helpful hints, 515, 518; itineraries, 513; layout of, 513–514; maps, 516–517, 522–523, 552–553, 556–557; nightlife, 548–549; planning tips, 513; self-guided walk, 521–529; shopping, 547–548; sights, 529–547; sleeping, 549–554; tourist information, 514; tours, 518–519, 521; transportation, 514–515, 561–562

York Castle Museum: 520, 543–544
York Early Music Festival: 515
York Food and Drink Festival: 515
York Guildhall: 540–541
York Minster: 520, 527, 529–537;
    map, 530; self-guided tour,
    531–537
York National Railway Museum:
    520, 544–546
York Pass: 514
York's Chocolate Story: 540
York Shambles: 512, 520, 528–529
York Shambles Market: 528, 558
Yorkshire Museum (York): 520,
    537–539
York walls: 525–526, 537

Z
Ziplines: 636, 649

MAP INDEX

Color Maps
Great Britain's Top Destinations: 13
Britain's Best Three-Week Trip by
    Car: 23
Great Britain: 1146-1147
West London: 1148-1149
East London: 1150-1151
Bath: 1152-1153
Edinburgh: 1154-1155

England
England: 35

London
Greater London: 39
London's Neighborhoods: 40
London: 46–47
Handy Bus Routes: 52-53
Westminster Walk: 67
Westminster Abbey Tour: 70
Houses of Parliament: 74
Trafalgar Square Area: 82
National Gallery: 84–85
West End & Nearby: 90–91
Buckingham Palace Area: 94
British Museum Overview: 97
North London: 98–99
British Library Tour: 104
The City, The Tower & East Lon-
    don: 110–111
St. Paul's Cathedral: 112
Tower of London: 117
East End: 122
The South Bank: 124–125
West London: 132–133
Victoria & Albert Museum Tour:
    138–139
Greenwich: 142
London's Hotel Neighborhoods: 160
Victoria Station Neighborhood:
    162–163
South Kensington Neighborhood:
    165
Earl's Court, Baywater & Notting
    Hill: 168–169
North London Neighborhood:
    172–173

Central London Restaurants:
    176–177
Historic Pubs: 185
London's Airports: 196
London's Major Train Stations: 201
Public Transportation near London:
    203
Rail Routes: 204

Windsor & Cambridge
London Day Trips: 205
Windsor: 209
Cambridge: 225
Cambridge Town and College Walk:
    228

Bath
Bath: 244–245
Bath Town Center: 253
Bath Accommodations: 272–273
Bath Restaurants: 276–277

Glastonbury & Wells
Glastonbury & Wells Area: 285
Glastonbury: 288
Wells: 295

Avebury, Stonehenge & Salisbury
Avebury, Stonehenge & Salisbury
    Area: 305
Avebury: 308-309
Stonehenge Overview: 314–315
Stonehenge: 318
Salisbury: 322–323
Salisbury Cathedral: 327

The Cotswolds
The Cotswolds: 340–341
Chipping Campden: 351
Stow-on-the-Wold: 367
Moreton-in-Marsh: 387

Stratford-upon-Avon
Stratford-upon-Avon: 398–399

Ironbridge Gorge
Ironbridge Gorge: 426–427

Liverpool
Liverpool: 440–441
Liverpool Hotels & Restaurants:
    464–465

The Lake District
The Lake District: 474–475
Keswick: 482–483
Derwentwater & Newlands Valley:
    488–489

York
York: 516–517
York Walk: 522-523
York Minster: 530
York Accommodations: 552–553
York Restaurants: 556–557

Durham & Northeast England
Durham: 566–567
Durham's Cathedral: 573
Near Durham: 583
Hadrian's Wall: 590–591

Wales
Wales: 604

North Wales
North Wales: 610–611
Conwy: 618–619
Caernarfon: 641
Snowdonia Area: 647
Llangollen: 659

South Wales
South Wales: 667
Cardiff Center: 672–673
Cardiff Bay: 679

Scotland
Scotland: 699

Edinburgh
Greater Edinburgh: 710
Edinburgh: 712–713
Royal Mile Walk: 720–721
New Town Walk: Georgian Edin-
    burgh: 736–737
Edinburgh Castle: 742–743
St. Giles' Cathedral: 757
Edinburgh Shopping: 788–789

Edinburgh City Center Hotels:
    798–799
West End Hotels & Restaurants:
    801
B&Bs & Restaurants South of the
    City Center: 804–805
Edinburgh City Center Eateries:
    808–809

Glasgow
Greater Glasgow: 822
Central Glasgow: 826–827
Glasgow Downtown Walk: 829
Glasgow West End: 838–839
Central Glasgow Hotels & Restau-
    rants: 858–859

Stirling & Nearby
Stirling Area: 869
Stirling: 871
Stirling Center: 878

St. Andrews
St. Andrews: 892–893

Oban & the Inner Hebrides
Oban: 916–917
Oban & the Inner Hebrides: 933
Iona: 937

Glencoe & Fort William
Glencoe & Fort William Area:
    952–953
Glencoe Valley: 958–959

Inverness & Loch Ness
Inverness: 974–975
Inverness & Loch Ness: 996

Britain: Past & Present
British History & Art Timeline:
    1002–1003
British Empire: 1008
Mysterious Ruins: 1021

Practicalities
Great Britain's Public Transporta-
    tion: 1066
Driving in Great Britain: 1075
How to Navigate a Roundabout:
    1078

Our website enhances this book and turns

Explore Europe

At ricksteves.com you can browse through thousands of articles, videos, photos and radio interviews, plus find a wealth of money-saving travel tips for planning your dream trip. And with our mobile-friendly website, you can easily access all this great travel information anywhere you go.

TV Shows

Preview the places you'll visit by watching entire half-hour episodes of *Rick Steves' Europe* (choose from all 100 shows) on-demand, for free.

ricksteves.com

your travel dreams into affordable reality

Radio Interviews

Enjoy ready access to Rick's vast library of radio interviews covering travel tips and cultural insights that relate specifically to your Europe travel plans.

Travel Forums

Learn, ask, share! Our online community of savvy travelers is a great resource for first-time travelers to Europe, as well as seasoned pros.

Travel News

Subscribe to our free Travel News e-newsletter, and get monthly updates from Rick on what's happening in Europe.

Classroom Europe

Check out our free resource for educators with 400+ short video clips from the *Rick Steves' Europe* TV show.

Audio Europe™

Pack Light and Right

Gear up for your next adventure at ricksteves.com

Light Luggage

Pack light and right with Rick Steves' affordable, custom-designed rolling carry-on bags, backpacks, day packs and shoulder bags.

Accessories

From packing cubes to moneybelts and beyond, Rick has personally selected the travel goodies that will help your trip go smoother.

Save time and energy

This guidebook is your independent-travel toolkit. But for all it delivers, it's still up to you to devote the time and energy it takes to manage the preparation and logistics that are essential for a happy trip. If that's a hassle, there's a solution.

Rick Steves Tours

A Rick Steves tour takes you to Europe's most interesting places with great

with minimum stress

guides and small groups of 28 or less. We follow Rick's favorite itineraries, ride in comfy buses, stay in family-run hotels, and bring you intimately

close to the Europe you've traveled so far to see. Most importantly, we take away the logistical headaches so you can focus on the fun.

Join the fun

This year we'll take 33,000 free-spirited travelers—nearly half of them repeat customers—along with us on 50 different itineraries, from Athens to Istanbul. Is a Rick Steves tour the right fit for your travel dreams?

Find out at ricksteves.com, where you can also request Rick's latest tour catalog. Europe is best experienced with happy travel partners. We hope you can join us.

See our itineraries at ricksteves.com

A Guide for Every Trip

BEST OF GUIDES

Full-color guides in an easy-to-scan format. Focused on top sights and experiences in the most popular European destinations

Best of England
Best of Europe
Best of France
Best of Germany
Best of Ireland
Best of Italy
Best of Scotland
Best of Spain

COMPREHENSIVE GUIDES

City, country, and regional guides printed on Bible-thin paper. Packed with detailed coverage for a multi-week trip exploring iconic sights and venturing off the beaten path

Amsterdam & the Netherlands
Barcelona
Belgium: Bruges, Brussels, Antwerp & Ghent
Berlin
Budapest
Croatia & Slovenia
Eastern Europe
England
Florence & Tuscany
France
Germany
Great Britain
Greece: Athens & the Peloponnese
Iceland
Ireland
Istanbul
Italy
London
Paris
Portugal
Prague & the Czech Republic
Provence & the French Riviera
Rome
Scandinavia
Scotland
Sicily
Spain
Switzerland
Venice
Vienna, Salzburg & Tirol

Rick Steves books are available from your favorite bookseller. Many guides are available as ebooks.

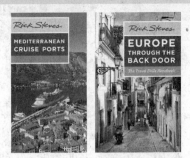

POCKET GUIDES
Compact color guides for shorter trips

Amsterdam
Athens
Barcelona
Florence
Italy's Cinque Terre
London
Munich & Salzburg

Paris
Prague
Rome
Venice
Vienna

SNAPSHOT GUIDES
Focused single-destination coverage

Basque Country: Spain & France
Copenhagen & the Best of Denmark
Dublin
Dubrovnik
Edinburgh
Hill Towns of Central Italy
Krakow, Warsaw & Gdansk
Lisbon
Loire Valley
Madrid & Toledo
Milan & the Italian Lakes District
Naples & the Amalfi Coast
Nice & the French Riviera
Normandy
Northern Ireland
Norway
Reykjavík
Rothenburg & the Rhine
Sevilla, Granada & Southern Spain
St. Petersburg, Helsinki & Tallinn
Stockholm

CRUISE PORTS GUIDES
Reference for cruise ports of call

Mediterranean Cruise Ports
Scandinavian & Northern European
  Cruise Ports

Complete your library with...

TRAVEL SKILLS & CULTURE
Study up on travel skills and gain insight on history and culture

Europe 101
Europe Through the Back Door
Europe's Top 100 Masterpieces
European Christmas
European Easter
European Festivals
For the Love of Europe
Travel as a Political Act

PHRASE BOOKS & DICTIONARIES

French
French, Italian & German
German
Italian
Portuguese
Spanish

PLANNING MAPS

Britain, Ireland & London
Europe
France & Paris
Germany, Austria & Switzerland
Iceland
Ireland
Italy
Spain & Portugal

Credits

RESEARCHERS
To help update this book, Rick relied on...

Ben Curtis

Ben is a native of the Pacific Northwest, but he's lived in the UK, Germany, Spain, Norway, Hungary, and a few other countries besides. He's worked as a professor of history and politics, a tour guide, and an advisor to the British government. These days, home is wherever he can go for a hike, listen to some Beethoven, and write.

Cameron Hewitt

Born in Denver and raised in central Ohio, Cameron settled in Seattle in 2000. Ever since, he has spent three months each year in Europe, contributing to guidebooks, tours, radio and television shows, and other media for Rick Steves' Europe, where he serves as content manager. Cameron married his high school sweetheart (and favorite travel partner), Shawna, and enjoys taking pictures, trying new restaurants, and planning his next trip.

Pål Bjarne Johansen

A tour guide and guidebook researcher for Rick Steves' Europe (covering Scandinavia and Spain), Pål grew up in the Norwegian countryside near Oslo. He discovered his passion for travel and adventure at a young age and has backpacked much of the world. He first visited Spain with his family when he was four and has been back numerous times since, to this land that he considers his second home. When he's not working for Rick Steves, you'll find Pål skiing the Norwegian woods in winter and sailing the seven seas in summer.

Jessica Shaw

Jessica spent four years of her childhood living in Toulouse, France, begrudgingly dragged by her parents through countless museums across Europe. Little did she know, a childhood abroad would ignite her love of travel and inspire her career path. Jessica edits and researches guidebooks at Rick Steves' Europe, packing her free time with art projects and trips near and far with her partner, Felipe.

Carrie Shepherd

After a childhood spent traipsing around New England, Carrie had a college semester in London, spurring her to explore and travel as much as her budget and employers allow. She's spent her career writing and editing arts and entertainment content, and now works as a guidebook editor and researcher for Rick Steves' Europe.

Kevin Williams

Kevin embarked on a European backpacking trip when he was 18, and he's been hooked on Europe ever since. He soon returned to study European history in England and spent his free time exploring the rest of the continent. He is a devoted soccer fan and will catch a match in Europe whenever he can. When he's not on the road, Kevin can be found cheering on the Seattle Sounders or taking in the beauty of Cascadia.

CONTRIBUTOR
Gene Openshaw

Gene has co-authored more than a dozen *Rick Steves* books, specializing in writing walks and tours of Europe's cities, museums, and cultural sights. He also contributes to Rick's public television series, produces audio tours on Europe, and is a regular guest on Rick's public radio show. Outside of the travel world, Gene has co-authored *The Seattle Joke Book*. As a composer, he has written a full-length opera called *Matter,* a violin sonata, and dozens of songs. He lives near Seattle with his daughter, enjoys giving presentations on art and history, and roots for the Mariners in good times and bad.

ACKNOWLEDGMENTS

Thanks to Roy and Jodi Nicholls for their research help, to Melanie Jeschke for the original version of the Oxford chapter, and to friends listed in this book, who put the "Great" in Great Britain.

Avalon Travel
Hachette Book Group
1700 Fourth Street
Berkeley, CA 94710

Text © 2020 by Rick Steves' Europe, Inc. All rights reserved.
Maps © 2020 by Rick Steves' Europe, Inc. All rights reserved.

Printed in Canada by Friesens.
23rd Edition. First printing April 2020.

ISBN 978-1-64171-225-5

For the latest on Rick's talks, guidebooks, tours, public television series, and public radio show, contact Rick Steves' Europe, 130 Fourth Avenue North, Edmonds, WA 98020, 425/771-8303, www.ricksteves.com, rick@ricksteves.com.

Rick Steves' Europe
Managing Editor: Jennifer Madison Davis
Assistant Managing Editor: Cathy Lu
Special Publications Manager: Risa Laib
Editors: Glenn Eriksen, Julie Fanselow, Tom Griffin, Suzanne Kotz, Rosie Leutzinger, Jessica Shaw, Carrie Shepherd
Editorial & Production Assistant: Megan Simms
Editorial Intern: Bridgette Robertson
Contributor: Gene Openshaw
Researchers: Ben Curtis, Cameron Hewitt, Pål Bjarne Johansen, Jessica Shaw, Carrie Shepherd, Kevin Williams
Graphic Content Director: Sandra Hundacker
Maps & Graphics: David C. Hoerlein, Lauren Mills, Mary Rostad
Digital Asset Coordinator: Orin Dubrow

Avalon Travel
Senior Editor and Series Manager: Madhu Prasher
Editors: Jamie Andrade & Sierra Machado
Copy Editor: Maggie Ryan
Proofreader: Kelly Lydick
Indexer: Stephen Callahan
Production & Typesetting: Lisi Baldwin, Rue Flaherty, Jane Musser
Cover Design: Kimberly Glyder Design
Maps & Graphics: Kat Bennett, Mike Morgenfeld

COLOR MAPS

Great Britain • West London • East London
• Bath • Edinburgh

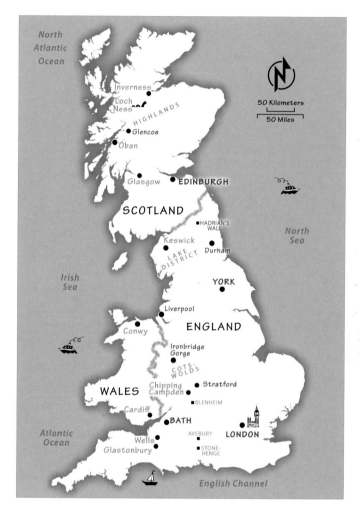

North Atlantic Ocean

Inverness
Loch Ness
HIGHLANDS
Glencoe
Oban
Glasgow
EDINBURGH

SCOTLAND

50 Kilometers
50 Miles

North Sea

HADRIAN'S WALL

Keswick
Durham

LAKE DISTRICT

Irish Sea

YORK

Liverpool

Conwy

ENGLAND

Ironbridge Gorge

COTS-WOLDS

Chipping Campden
Stratford

WALES

BLENHEIM

Cardiff

BATH

Atlantic Ocean

AVEBURY

LONDON

Wells
Glastonbury

STONE-HENGE

English Channel

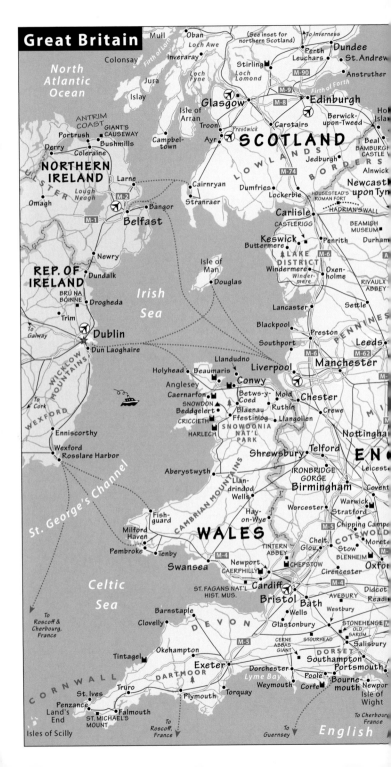

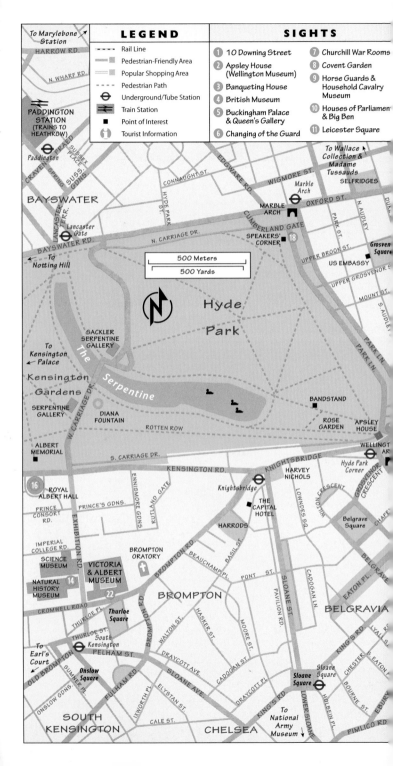

LEGEND		SIGHTS	
---- Rail Line		**1** 10 Downing Street	**7** Churchill War Rooms
▬▬ Pedestrian-Friendly Area		**2** Apsley House (Wellington Museum)	**8** Covent Garden
▬▬ Popular Shopping Area		**3** Banqueting House	**9** Horse Guards & Household Cavalry Museum
---- Pedestrian Path		**4** British Museum	
⊖ Underground/Tube Station		**5** Buckingham Palace & Queen's Gallery	**10** Houses of Parliament & Big Ben
▆ Train Station		**6** Changing of the Guard	**11** Leicester Square
■ Point of Interest			
⋔ Tourist Information			

To Marylebone Station
HARROW RD.
N. WHARF RD.

PADDINGTON STATION (TRAINS TO HEATHROW)

Paddington

SUSSEX PLACE
CRAVEN RD.
SPRING ST.
SUSS. GDNS.
LANCASTER TERR.

BAYSWATER

CONNAUGHT ST.
EDGWARE RD.
WIGMORE ST.

To Wallace Collection & Madame Tussauds
SELFRIDGES

Marble Arch
MARBLE ARCH
OXFORD ST.

Lancaster Gate
BAYSWATER RD.
To Notting Hill

N. CARRIAGE DR.
CUMBERLAND GATE
SPEAKERS' CORNER ■ 18

N. AUDLEY ST.
PARK ST.
DUK.

UPPER BROOK ST.
Grosvenor Square
US EMBASSY
UPPER GROSVENOR ST.

MOUNT ST.
S. AUDLEY

500 Meters
500 Yards

Hyde Park

To Kensington Palace

SACKLER SERPENTINE GALLERY

The Serpentine

Kensington Gardens

SERPENTINE GALLERY

DIANA FOUNTAIN
ROTTEN ROW

BANDSTAND

ROSE GARDEN

APSLEY HOUSE

PARK LN.
PARK LN.

ALBERT MEMORIAL

S. CARRIAGE DR.
W. CARRIAGE DR.

KENSINGTON RD.

WELLINGT AR

Hyde Park Corner

GROSVENOR CRESCENT
CRESCENT

16 ROYAL ALBERT HALL

KNIGHTSBRIDGE
HARVEY NICHOLS

Knightsbridge
THE CAPITAL HOTEL

LOWNDES SQ.
Belgrave Square
CHAPE

PRINCE CONSORT RD.
PRINCE'S GDNS.

EXHIBITION RD.
RUTLAND GATE

HARRODS

BELGRAVE

IMPERIAL COLLEGE RD.
SCIENCE MUSEUM

BROMPTON ORATORY

BROMPTON RD.
BEAUCHAMP PL.

BASIL ST.
PONT ST.

SLOANE ST.
PAVILION RD.
CADOGAN LN.

EATON PL.
BELGRAVIA

NATURAL HISTORY MUSEUM

14

VICTORIA & ALBERT MUSEUM

22

BROMPTON

MOORE ST.

CROMWELL ROAD
THURLOE PL.
Thurloe Square

To Earl's Court

THURLOE ST.
South Kensington
PELHAM ST.

WALTON ST.
HASKER ST.

DRAYCOTT AVE.

CADOGAN LN.

KING'S RD.
LYALL ST.

CHESTER S.
EATON T.

OLD BROMPTON RD.
SUMNER PL.
Onslow Square

FULHAM RD.
SLOANE AVE.

DRAYCOTT PL.
Sloane Square
Sloane Square

BOURNE ST.
EBURY

ONSLOW GDNS.
ONSLOW PL.

IXWORTH PL.
ELYSTAN ST.

KING'S RD.

HOLBEIN PL.

SOUTH KENSINGTON

CALE ST.

CHELSEA

To National Army Museum

PIMLICO RD.

LOWER SLOANE

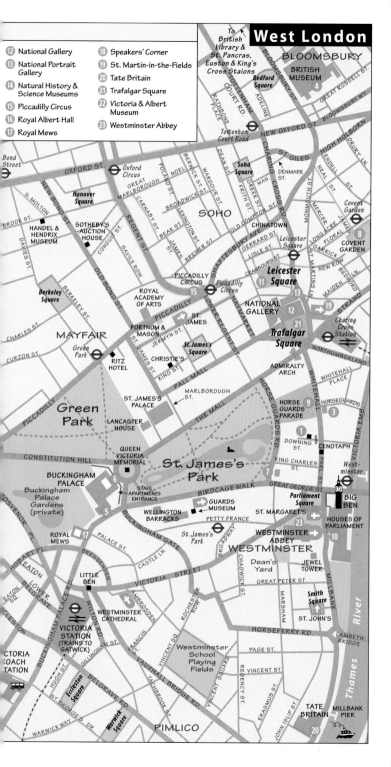

West London

To British Library & St. Pancras, Euston & King's Cross Stations

- 12 National Gallery
- 13 National Portrait Gallery
- 14 Natural History & Science Museums
- 15 Piccadilly Circus
- 16 Royal Albert Hall
- 17 Royal Mews
- 18 Speakers' Corner
- 19 St. Martin-in-the-Fields
- 20 Tate Britain
- 21 Trafalgar Square
- 22 Victoria & Albert Museum
- 23 Westminster Abbey

BLOOMSBURY

BRITISH MUSEUM 4

Bedford Square

Bond Street

Tottenham Court Road

NEW OXFORD ST.

HIGH HOLBORN

OXFORD ST.

Oxford Circus

Hanover Square

SOHO

Soho Square

ST. GILES

DENMARK ST.

Covent Garden

COVENT GARDEN 8

Handel & Hendrix Museum

SOTHEBY'S AUCTION HOUSE

CHINATOWN

Leicester Square

Leicester Square 11

Berkeley Square

PICCADILLY CIRCUS 15

Piccadilly Circus

ROYAL ACADEMY OF ARTS

NATIONAL GALLERY 12

13

STRAND

19

Charing Cross Station

MAYFAIR

ST. JAMES

FORTNUM & MASON

Trafalgar Square 21

Green Park

RITZ HOTEL

CHRISTIE'S

ST. JAMES'S SQUARE

PALL MALL

ADMIRALTY ARCH

NORTHUMBERLAND

WHITEHALL PLACE

ST. JAMES'S PALACE

MARLBOROUGH ST.

THE MALL

HORSE GUARDS PARADE 9

HORSEGUARDS 3

LANCASTER HOUSE

Green Park

QUEEN VICTORIA MEMORIAL

St. James's Park

1 DOWNING ST.

CENOTAPH

Westminster

CONSTITUTION HILL

BUCKINGHAM PALACE

KING CHARLES ST.

7

BUCKINGHAM PALACE

Buckingham Palace Gardens (private)

STATE APARTMENTS ENTRANCE

6

BIRDCAGE WALK

GREAT GEORGE ST.

Parliament Square

BIG BEN

5

GUARDS MUSEUM

ST. MARGARET'S

HOUSES OF PARLIAMENT

ROYAL MEWS 17

WELLINGTON BARRACKS

PETTY FRANCE

St. James's Park

23

WESTMINSTER ABBEY

10

WESTMINSTER

Dean's Yard

JEWEL TOWER

LITTLE BEN

VICTORIA STREET

GREAT PETER ST.

Smith Square

WESTMINSTER CATHEDRAL

ST. JOHN'S

VICTORIA STATION (TRAINS TO GATWICK)

Westminster School Playing Fields

HORSEFERRY RD.

LAMBETH BRIDGE

VICTORIA COACH STATION

PAGE ST.

Thames River

MILLBANK

VAUXHALL BRIDGE RD.

Eccleston Square

Warwick Square

PIMLICO

TATE BRITAIN 20

MILLBANK PIER

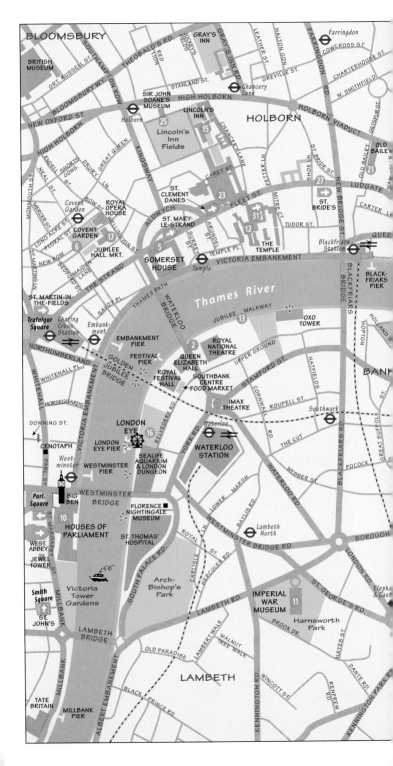

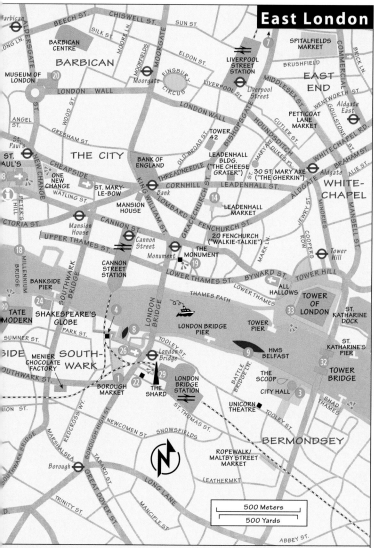

East London

SIGHTS

1. Borough Market
2. BFI Southbank (Cinema)
3. City Hall
4. The Clink Prison Museum
5. Courtauld Gallery
6. Covent Garden
7. To Museum of the Home
8. Golden Hinde Replica
9. HMS Belfast
10. Houses of Parliament & Big Ben
11. Imperial War Museum
12. The Inns of Court
13. Jubilee Walkway
14. Leadenhall Market
15. Lincoln's Inn
16. London Eye
17. London Transport Museum
18. Millennium Bridge
19. The Monument
20. Museum of London
21. Old Bailey
22. Old Operating Theatre Museum & Herb Garret
23. Royal Courts of Justice
24. Shakespeare's Globe
25. Sir John Soane's Museum
26. Southwark Cathedral
27. St. Bride's Church
28. St. Paul's Cathedral
29. The Shard (Observation Decks)
30. Tate Modern
31. Temple Church
32. Tower Bridge
33. Tower of London

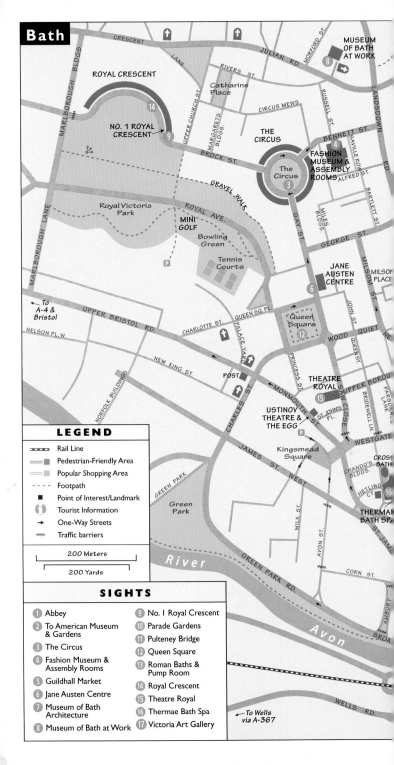

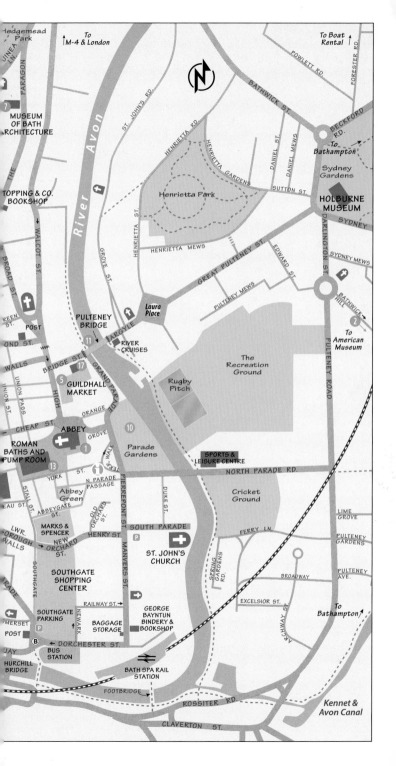

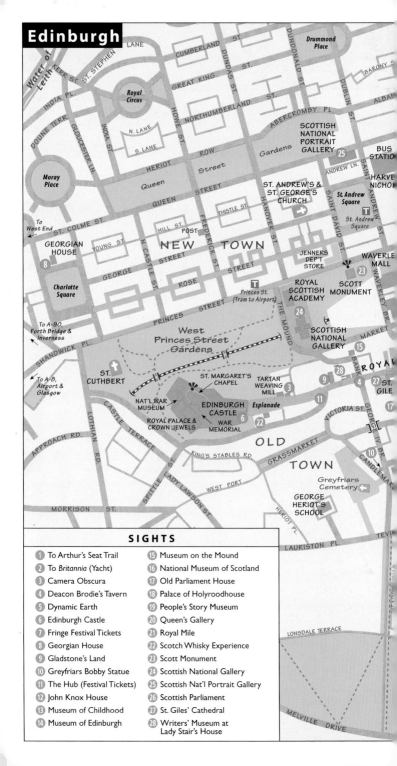

Edinburgh

SIGHTS

1. To Arthur's Seat Trail
2. To *Britannia* (Yacht)
3. Camera Obscura
4. Deacon Brodie's Tavern
5. Dynamic Earth
6. Edinburgh Castle
7. Fringe Festival Tickets
8. Georgian House
9. Gladstone's Land
10. Greyfriars Bobby Statue
11. The Hub (Festival Tickets)
12. John Knox House
13. Museum of Childhood
14. Museum of Edinburgh
15. Museum on the Mound
16. National Museum of Scotland
17. Old Parliament House
18. Palace of Holyroodhouse
19. People's Story Museum
20. Queen's Gallery
21. Royal Mile
22. Scotch Whisky Experience
23. Scott Monument
24. Scottish National Gallery
25. Scottish Nat'l Portrait Gallery
26. Scottish Parliament
27. St. Giles' Cathedral
28. Writers' Museum at Lady Stair's House

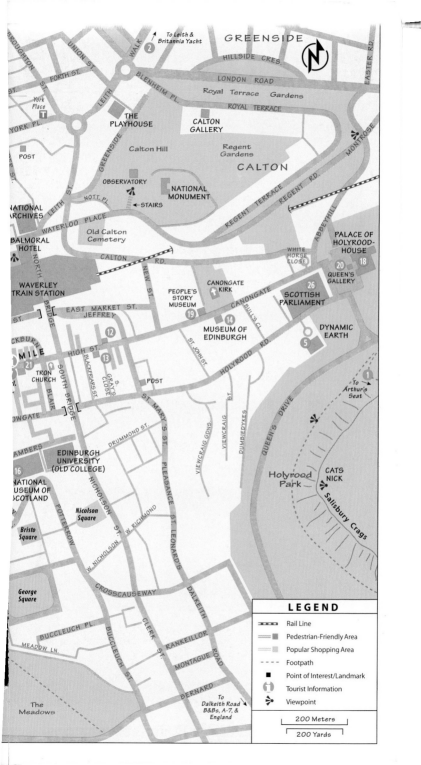

More for your trip!
Maximize the experience with Rick Steves as your guide

Guidebooks
Make side trips smooth and affordable with Rick's London and Ireland guides

Planning Maps
Use Rick's pre-trip planning tool for mapping out your itinerary

Rick's TV Shows
Preview your destinations with a wide variety of shows covering Great Britain

Rick's Audio Europe™ App
Get free self-guided audio tours for London and Edinburgh

Small Group Tours
Take a lively, low-stress Rick Steves tour through England and Scotland

For all the details, visit ricksteves.com